SPEECHES OF THE AMERICAN PRESIDENTS

THIRD EDITION
1789–2018

From the Editors of H.W. Wilson

H.W. Wilson
A Division of EBSCO Information Services, Inc.
Ipswich, Massachusetts
2018

GREY HOUSE PUBLISHING

Publisher's Cataloging-In-Publication Data
(Prepared by The Donohue Group, Inc.)

Names: H.W. Wilson Company, editor.
Title: Speeches of the American presidents / from the editors of H.W. Wilson.
Description: Third edition. | New York : The H.W. Wilson Company, 2018. | Includes index.
Identifiers: ISBN 9781682178829
Subjects: LCSH: Presidents—United States—Messages. | Political oratory—United States. |
　　United States—Politics and government.
Classification: LCC JK587 .S64 2018 | DDC 352.23/8/0973—dc23

Printed in the United States of America

Contents

Publisher's Note

This new edition of *Speeches of the American Presidents* contains more than 220 major speeches by the 45 presidents of the United States, from George Washington, elected in 1788, to Donald Trump, elected in 2016. Twenty-two new speeches have been added, covering the presidencies of George W. Bush, Barack Obama, and Donald Trump, plus new content added to some of the chapters of earlier presidents as well.

Speechmaking is one of the classic devices for communication between the chief executive and the people he represents, one of the methods by which he announces policy, acquires the loyalty of special interest groups, tries to subvert the will of Congress when it suits his purposes, and unifies the nation in time of crisis. *Speeches of the American Presidents* is intended to give readers, especially students, a useful way to study the presidency—its development as an institution and the individual presidents' management of events in their administrations—through the words of the presidents themselves. Although many of the presidents delivered important speeches in their pre- and post-White House years, we have, with a few exceptions, included only speeches made during each president's term in office. Most are reprinted in full from the public record; some very long speeches have been excerpted. Because of the relative scarceness of extant speeches for the earlier presidents, we have included some of their annual messages (now called State of the Union Messages) in the present volume, despite the fact that during the years between Jefferson and Wilson these messages were read to Congress by a clerk rather than by the president himself.

The speeches in this collection were chosen with two main purposes in mind. First, to demonstrate the growth of speechmaking as a political tool throughout the history of the presidency. During the twentieth century, for instance, presidents came to rely on a variety of new media to deliver messages to an increasingly large and diverse audience, ranging from print media at the beginning of the period to television and broadcast media at its end. In the twenty-first century, the development of the Internet and social media changed speechwriting and delivery even further.

Second, these speeches have been chosen to show the ways in which each president revealed his character and the ideals he espoused. A special effort has been made to include speeches from administrations that comment on issues that are important in contemporary America, including intervention in foreign affairs, minority rights, taxation, defense spending, and the eternal argument over the benefits and dangers of a strong federal government. Discussions of questions such as the role of slavery in the early republic hold important lessons for modern readers.

The chapters in this volume are arranged chronologically by president. The speeches are then arranged chronologically within each chapter. Texts for the speeches in this edition were taken from official online sources maintained by the White House (www.whitehouse.gov) and the National Archives and Records Administration (www.nara.gov). This volume closes with a detailed subject index.

Introduction

On the face of it, the duties of the Chief Executive, as conceived by the Founders and described in the Constitution, require certain kinds of expertise—but public speaking is not one of them. The president is in charge of making sure that the decisions of Congress are implemented; of appointing ambassadors, Supreme Court justices, and certain other federal officers, as well as commissioning all federal office holders; of making treaties; of assessing the expert opinion of his cabinet officers; of granting pardons; and of acting as commander in chief of the armed forces. He has to submit occasional reports to Congress concerning the state of the Union and he has to recommend to Congress "such Measures as he shall judge necessary and expedient"; these reports and recommendations are assumed to be in written form. All of these duties could be carried out by a wise administrator who has at heart the best interests of the nation as a whole—which is exactly what the delegates to the Constitutional Convention had in mind. They did not foresee a time when the wise administrator would also have to function as the head of a political party (still unknown in their day), a cheerleader for a political agenda, a symbol of the federal government, a symbol of the entire country, a professor educating the ignorant citizenry about urgent matters, a preacher delivering inspiration and motivation (or warning and remonstrance) in time of crisis, a crusader molding public opinion into a weapon for attacking Congress. Indeed, the prospect of a president standing before the people to exhort and rally them would have struck them as a lapse into the demagoguery they were assiduously trying to avoid.

How strange it appears to us citizens of the 21st century, conditioned from childhood to expect to see presidents solemnly addressing us through our TV screens, when we realize that the great presidents of the early republic, the prescient heroes of our democracy, provided no role modeling whatsoever for their successors in office when it came to communicating with the public. The only oratorical communication from the president to the people was the inaugural address, which was heard directly by a few thousand listeners at best, and which tended to follow certain platitude-ridden conventions. The true presidential audience consisted of the nation's legislators, not its electorate, and the presidents kept their congressional appearances to a minimum. The custom established by George Washington of visiting Congress to deliver his mandated annual message in person was honored by Adams and squelched by Jefferson, to lasting effect—no other president came to the Capitol to address Congress until Woodrow Wilson surprised everyone by doing so in 1913. Even Washington's famous Farewell Address of 1796 was never heard by the congressmen and senators for whom it was intended; it was printed in a newspaper instead.

Jefferson's repudiation of Washington's custom nicely illustrates one reason why the expectations of the Constitution's framers were so quickly confounded, for Jefferson's election in 1800 marked the first time that one political party (the Democratic-Republicans) took the presidency away from another (the Federalists). Although the electors' choice of Washington as president was unanimous in the first two presidential elections, by the third one, in 1796, the two opposing parties were already well in place. In the ensuing decades, the extension of voting rights to greater numbers of adult white males (rather than propertied men only), together with the adoption in most states of the popular vote as a method of choosing presidential electors, inevitably altered the relationship between presidential candidates and the ordinary people who were now empowered to choose them. The result was that American politics lost all hope of becoming what the Founders had intended—a tranquil forum for dispassionate, rational debate—and became instead a battleground for contending factions, each one doing its utmost to grab the attention of the voters.

By the mid-19th century, the ability to entertain large crowds with impressive displays of rhetoric was a recommending qualification for most politicians at the local and state levels. Still, some lingering sense of the dignity of the office of president delayed the entry of presidents and presidential candidates into the tournaments of oration. Whig candidate William Henry Harrison made the first presidential campaign speech on the steps of the National Hotel in Columbus, Ohio, on June 6, 1840, but his efforts were far outclassed by the immense torchlight processions and rallies launched on his behalf in hundreds of locations by Whig operatives. Significantly, none of the great Congressional speechifiers of the golden age of American oratory (1836–1860)—Daniel

Webster, Henry Clay, John C. Calhoun, Thomas Hart Benton, or Stephen A. Douglas—became president, though most tried at least once. The orotund stylings of senatorial and congressional rhetoric were apparently not sufficient to elect a president, nor were they suitable for the communications that the presidents of the era were obliged to undertake. Those politicians who did come to occupy the White House, whether competent or incompetent in other respects, were, with few exceptions, indifferent speakers.

It is with Abraham Lincoln that we find the beginning of true presidential rhetoric, and at a level that has never been bettered until, it might be argued, Barack Obama. He arrived at the White House as a veteran courtroom lawyer, stump speaker, debater, and raconteur, his mind well-seasoned with Shakespeare and the Bible, but no biographer can fully explain the inner development that enabled him to infuse the English language with so much dramatic moral and emotional power. In the Gettysburg Address he succeeded in doing something that would not even have crossed the minds of previous presidents— drawing to the attention of his listeners, and by extension the entire nation, their obligation to confront the ideal of equality embedded in the Declaration of Independence and to collectively set themselves to make it a reality. With Lincoln begins the tradition of the president as an ethical leader modeled after Moses, providing direction to the people during times of physical and spiritual crisis and confronting moral lapses with an appeal to conscience. Alas, many more presidents have aspired to this role than were qualified to fill it. Most attempts to imitate Lincoln, far from evoking his sought-after aura of statesmanship, have appeared as sorry attempts to exploit his legacy.

The current emphasis on speechmaking as an essential part of presidential campaigning and of White House leadership is largely the result of the steady advances, over the course of the 20th century, in the technology of mass communications, coupled with the transformation of the presidential term into a kind of endless beauty contest in which the president has, daily, another chance to win or lose. The now-universal campaigning technique of crisscrossing the nation on speechmaking tours began in the late 19th century with James Baird Weaver and William Jennings Bryan, who bequeathed their method to future contenders, though they lost five races between them. The national conventions of the major political parties, formerly conducted as massive shouting bouts between mobs of delegates, underwent a change of character as first radio (in 1924) and then television (in 1940) opened them up to the rest of the country; by the end of the century, the conventions had devolved into tightly controlled theatrical productions featuring addresses in which even the laughter and applause were prearranged.

Presidents who like to give speeches and relish being in the spotlight have their model in Theodore Roosevelt, who famously took the stage in the 1912 campaign even though he had an assassin's bullet in his chest. Roosevelt and Woodrow Wilson, though very different otherwise, both followed Lincoln in treating the presidency as the nation's source of moral leadership; when they stood at the podium, it was to exhort, to challenge, to teach, even— in Wilson's case—to the point of extreme and nearly fatal self-sacrifice.

Although many people think of Franklin Roosevelt as the first president whose voice became widely familiar through radio talks, he was preceded by the supposedly taciturn Calvin Coolidge, who gave a radio address on the occasion of George Washington's birthday in 1924 and thereafter spoke to the public every few weeks. FDR, of course, was the first president to be heard all over the globe, the first to make a broadcast in a foreign language (in November 1942, to the people of France), and the first to use radio to establish a sense of closeness with his domestic audience; to him also belongs the credit for being the first presidential nominee to deliver an acceptance speech at a convention (in 1932). During Roosevelt's second term he appeared on television, speaking at the opening session of the New York World's Fair, and thus became the first president to have to concern himself with the quality of his television image. His successor, Harry Truman, was the first to deliver a televised speech from the White House, on October 5, 1947.

Over the ensuing half century, the various White House administrations have set themselves the task of making good use of the opportunities offered by televised presidential speechmaking. These include keeping the president and his agenda favorably in the public eye, demonstrating his command of the issues and his physical health and vigor, persuading voters to pressure Congress to enact the president's programs, rallying support in times of trouble, and defining for the American people what their goals are and who their enemies are. Unfortunately for presidents, however, these opportunities come at a high price, since speeches broadcast over television are presented by journalists with agendas of their own. Media hostility has helped bring at least one presidency to the point of collapse and helped prevent several others from achieving second terms. Thus, a president given to frequent speechmaking, as most of the recent ones have been, ends up cycling endlessly between offensive and defensive modes, between building an image of competence through a forceful articulation of policy and countering the subsequent, and potentially devastating, onrush of criticism that it engenders.

Just before the century turned, presidential speechmaking took a step in yet another direction— towards the idea of the president as a kind of super therapist whose job is to listen to the stories of hardship related by ordinary people, publicly acknowledge their pain, take it on as his own, and then craft legislative remedies to be proposed to Congress. Something of this idea was present under Franklin Roosevelt; it was further developed under Jimmy Carter; but it reached full-blown form under Bill Clinton. Clinton's apparent devotion to respecting the needs of others was partly manifested in his mania for delivering speeches to small groups, which he did by the hundreds every year; it also showed up in his attempts to manage the so-called Mideast peace process through a display of what he hoped would be seen as evenhanded attention to the claims on both sides (see "The Oslo Accords," reprinted in this volume). But Clinton's offer to share himself with the electorate proved to have its limits, and many people who were drawn in by his expert rhetorical performances found this out the hard way.

The election of George W. Bush in 2000 perhaps demonstrates that voters have discovered better ways to evaluate their candidates than by mere skill at giving speeches. The campaign leading to the first presidential election of the 21st century was something akin to a contest between two gladiators who have no choice but to enter the arena with rusty swords and chipped armor. Speechmaking became a basic requirement for all candidates for the White House, and it figures prominently in the impressions that voters take with them into the polling booths, most often by way of news clips and political commercials; but in the 2000 presidential race, neither of the two leading candidates was gifted with natural eloquence. The Democratic contender, though plainly intelligent, was wooden and unexciting on the podium. The Republican contender, though hearty and enthusiastic, regularly tripped over his tongue when making remarks. Had one or the other of them been a more competent, more persuasive speaker, the nation might not have ended up with a perfectly divided, and therefore embittered, electorate.

The 2008 presidential election was historic in several ways – Barack Obama not only became the first African American president of the United States, but, with eloquence and literary power, has been described as "orator-in-chief." According to Douglas Brinkley, presidential historian and professor at Rice University, "Barack Obama is one of the great orators in American history. He thinks in constitutional law terms that give him the spine for his speeches, his compass. Obama consistently wanted to feel he was the author."

As the twenty-first century progresses, President Donald Trump has changed the nation's narrative not only politically but poetically. We now have a president who is neither eloquent nor direct, and the Internet and social media continue to change speechwriting and delivery in ways we have never thought possible.

SPEECHES OF THE

AMERICAN PRESIDENTS

George Washington

George Washington

1789–1797

GEORGE WASHINGTON was born to a family of Virginia plantation owners and rose to prominence as a commander of militiamen on the colony's western frontier. In 1774–1775 he was a member of the Virginia delegation to the Continental Congress, where he was asked to lead the Continental army.

During the six years of the Revolutionary War, Washington suffered several crushing defeats at the hands of the British and periodic losses of confidence in his abilities by the Congress. He never lost the loyalty of his men, however, and this, more than any strategic or tactical genius, was the key to his military success. His early victories at Boston, Trenton, and Princeton (in 1776) gave the American cause its initial impetus, and his defeat of General Charles Cornwallis's forces at Yorktown (in 1781) ended the war. In 1787 he was president of the Constitutional Convention; two years later, by unanimous choice of the electors, he was asked to serve as the nation's first president.

Without precedent to guide him, Washington of necessity had to create the office as he went along, and his presidency was in many ways fundamentally different from succeeding ones. Already a revered figure, he was spared the personal politicking that most presidents since have had to undertake. Nor was he a leader of a political party; the first parties were barely established by the end of his second term. In fact, Washington condemned "the baneful effects of the spirit of party" and was disturbed by the growth of party factionalism spurred by the rivalry of his two principal advisers, Secretary of State Thomas Jefferson and Treasury Secretary Alexander Hamilton. In his second term, to which he was elected uncontested, he more openly favored the Federalist principles of Hamilton. The last years of his presidency were occupied with the problem of maintaining neutral relations with the belligerent European powers. He did not seek a third term, although he undoubtedly could have won it, but retired to his Virginia estate, Mount Vernon, where he died in 1799.

By nature scrupulous, reserved, and careful of appearances, Washington always strove to maintain an exalted level of dignity as the nation's "first among equals." In person he could be distant and freezingly proper, appearing to have an exaggerated sense of his own position. The pomp and expense of his formal presidential entertainments, especially toward the end of his presidency, led to accusations that he was attempting to establish an American monarchy. One newspaper characterized Washington, in the overheated invective of the time, as craving "the seclusion of a monk and the supercilious distance of a tyrant." But though he was no tyrant, Washington appreciated the symbolic importance of the executive and probably did allow himself to be idolized. The view of Washington as a Cincinnatus indispensable to the formation and success of the nation began during his lifetime.

Washington was not an accomplished public speaker. Although he always read from a prepared text, he was often tongue-tied. Pennsylvania Senator William Maclay, who listened while Washington delivered his first inaugural address, wrote that Washington the orator was "agitated and embarrassed more than he was ever by the leveled cannon or pointed musket. He trembled, and several times could scarcely make out to read." In Maclay's opinion, Washington's gestures while speaking "left a rather ungainly impression." Yet his natural sincerity and dignity overrode his lack of oratorical skills, and he could deeply affect his listeners. As the French minister, the Comte de Moustier, noted in 1789, Washington had "the soul, look, and figure of a hero united in him."

3

First Inaugural Address

New York City, New York

April 30, 1789

WASHINGTON'S first inauguration, the only one to be held in New York City, took place at Federal Hall, on the corner of Wall and Broad Streets. A huge crowd cheered him as the oath was administered on the portico. Washington then stepped inside to deliver his address to the assembled Congress.

Massachusetts Representative Fisher Ames, a gifted speaker himself, was deeply moved by Washington's earnest oration. "It was a very touching scene and quite of the solemn kind. [His] aspect grave, almost to sadness . . . his voice deep, a little tremulous, and so low as to call for close attention. . . . It seemed to me an allegory in which virtue was personified." This speech exemplifies the first president's style: sober, sincere, and expressed in formal, measured prose.

Among the vicissitudes incident to life no event could have filled me with greater anxieties than that of which the notification was transmitted by your order, and received on the 14th day of the present month. On the one hand, I was summoned by my country, whose voice I can never hear but with veneration and love, from a retreat which I had chosen with the fondest predilection, and, in my flattering hopes with an immutable decision, as the asylum of my declining years—a retreat which was rendered every day more necessary as well as more dear to me by the addition of habit to inclination, and of frequent interruptions in my health to the gradual waste committed on it by time. On the other hand, the magnitude and difficulty of the trust to which the voice of my country called me, being sufficient to awaken in the wisest and most experienced of her citizens a distrustful scrutiny into his qualifications, could not but overwhelm with despondence one who (inheriting inferior endowments from nature and unpracticed in the duties of civil administration) ought to be peculiarly conscious of his own deficiencies. In this conflict of emotions all I dare aver is that it has been my faithful study to collect my duty from a just appreciation of every circumstance by which it might be affected. All I dare hope is that if, in executing this task, I have been too much swayed by a grateful remembrance of former instances, or by an affectionate sensibility to this transcendent proof of the confidence of my fellow citizens, and have thence too little consulted my incapacity as well as disinclination for the weighty and untried cares before me, my error will be palliated by the motives which mislead me, and its consequences be judged by my country with some share of the partiality in which they originated.

Such being the impressions under which I have, in obedience to the public summons, repaired to the present station, it would be peculiarly improper to omit in this first official act my fervent supplications to that Almighty Being who rules over the universe, who presides in the councils of nations, and whose providential aids can supply every human defect, that His benediction may consecrate to the liberties and happiness of the people of the United States a government instituted by themselves for these essential purposes, and may enable every instrument employed in its administration to execute with success the functions allotted to his charge. In tendering this homage to the Great Author of every public and private good, I assure myself that it expresses your sentiments not less than my own, nor those of my fellow citizens at large less than either. No people can be bound to acknowledge and adore the Invisible Hand which conducts the affairs of men more than those of the United States. Every step by which they have advanced to the character of an independent nation seems to have been distinguished by some token of providential agency; and in the important revolution just accomplished in the system of their united government the tranquil deliberations and voluntary consent of so many distinct communities from which the event has resulted can not be compared with the means by which most governments have been established without some return of pious gratitude, along with an humble anticipation of the future blessings which the past seem to presage. These reflections, arising out of the present crisis, have forced themselves too strongly on my mind to be suppressed. You will join with me, I trust, in thinking that there are none under the influence of which the proceedings of a new and free government can more auspiciously commence.

By the article establishing the executive department it is made the duty of the president "to recommend to your consideration such measures as he shall judge necessary and expedient." The circumstances under which I now meet you will acquit me from entering into that subject further than to refer to the great constitutional charter under which you are assembled, and which, in defining your powers, designates the objects to which your attention is to be given. It will be more consistent with those circumstances, and far more congenial with the feelings which actuate me, to substitute, in place of a recommendation of particular measures, the tribute that is due to the talents, the rectitude, and the patriotism which adorn the characters selected to devise and adopt them. In these honorable qualifications I behold the surest pledges that as on one side no local prejudices or attachments, no separate views nor party animosities, will misdirect the comprehensive and equal eye which ought to watch over this great assemblage of communities and interests, so, on another, that the foundation of our national policy will be laid in the pure and immutable principles of private morality, and the preeminence of free government be exemplified by all the attributes which can win the affections of its citizens and command the respect of the world. I dwell on this prospect with every satisfaction which an ardent love for my country can inspire, since there is no truth more thoroughly established than that there exists in the economy and course of nature an indissoluble union between virtue and happiness; between duty and advantage; between the genuine maxims of an honest and magnanimous policy and the solid rewards of public prosperity and felicity; since we ought to be no less persuaded that the propitious smiles of Heaven can never be expected on a nation that disregards the eternal rules of order and right which Heaven itself has ordained; and since the preservation of the sacred fire of liberty and the destiny of the republican model of government are justly considered, perhaps, as deeply, as finally, staked on the experiment intrusted to the hands of the American people.

Besides the ordinary objects submitted to your care, it will remain with your judgment to decide how far an exercise of the occasional power delegated by the fifth article of the Constitution is rendered expedient at the present juncture by the nature of objections which have been urged against the system, or by the degree of inquietude which has given birth to them. Instead of undertaking particular recommendations on this subject, in which I could be guided by no lights derived from official opportunities, I shall again give way to my entire confidence in your discernment and pursuit of the public good; for I assure myself that whilst you carefully avoid every alteration which might endanger the benefits of an united and effective government, or which ought to await the future lessons of experience, a reverence for the characteristic rights of freemen and a regard for the public harmony will sufficiently influence your deliberations on the question how far the former can be impregnably fortified or the latter be safely and advantageously promoted.

To the foregoing observations I have one to add, which will be most properly addressed to the House of Representatives. It concerns myself, and will therefore be as brief as possible. When I was first honored with a call into the service of my country, then on the eve of an arduous struggle for its liberties, the light in which I contemplated my duty required that I should renounce every pecuniary compensation. From this resolution I have in no instance departed; and being still under the impressions which produced it, I must decline as inapplicable to myself any share in the personal emoluments which may be indispensably included in a permanent provision for the executive department, and must accordingly pray that the pecuniary estimates for the station in which I am placed may during my continuance in it be limited to such actual expenditures as the public good may be thought to require.

Having thus imparted to you my sentiments as they have been awakened by the occasion which brings us together, I shall take my present leave; but not without resorting once more to the benign Parent of the Human Race in humble supplication that, since He has been pleased to favor the American people with opportunities for deliberating in perfect tranquillity, and dispositions for deciding with unparalleled unanimity on a form of government for the security of their Union and the advancement of their happiness, so His divine blessing may be equally conspicuous in the enlarged views, the temperate consultations, and the wise measures on which the success of this government must depend.

First Annual Message to Congress

New York City, New York

January 8, 1790

RATHER THAN a vigorous statement of policies and plans, Washington's first address to Congress was a brief series of cautious recommendations. Washington did not see it as his constitutional duty to develop the details of policy (except in the broadest sense of setting an example of official conduct); that task he left to his cabinet, especially to Hamilton and Jefferson.

I embrace with great satisfaction the opportunity which now presents itself of congratulating you on the present favorable prospects of our public affairs. The recent accession of the important state of North Carolina to the Constitution of the United States (of which official information has been received), the rising credit and respectability of our country, the general and increasing good will toward the government of the Union, and the concord, peace, and plenty with which we are blessed are circumstances auspicious in an eminent degree to our national prosperity.

In resuming your consultations for the general good you can not but derive encouragement from the reflection that the measures of the last session have been as satisfactory to your constituents as the novelty and difficulty of the work allowed you to hope. Still further to realize their expectations and to secure the blessings which a gracious Providence has placed within our reach will in the course of the present important session call for the cool and deliberate exertion of your patriotism, firmness, and wisdom.

Among the many interesting objects which will engage your attention, that of providing for the common defense will merit particular regard. To be prepared for war is one of the most effectual means of preserving peace.

A free people ought not only to be armed, but disciplined; to which end a uniform and well-digested plan is requisite; and their safety and interest require that they should promote such manufactories as tend to render them independent of others for essential, particularly military, supplies.

The proper establishment of the troops which may be deemed indispensable will be entitled to mature consideration. In the arrangements which may be made respecting it it will be of importance to conciliate the comfortable support of the officers and soldiers with a due regard to economy.

There was reason to hope that the pacific measures adopted with regard to certain hostile tribes of Indians would have relieved the inhabitants of our southern and western frontiers from their depredations, but you will perceive from the information contained in the papers which I shall direct to be laid before you (comprehending a communication from the Commonwealth of Virginia) that we ought to be prepared to afford protection to those parts of the Union, and, if necessary, to punish aggressors.

The interests of the United States require that our intercourse with other nations should be facilitated by such provisions as will enable me to fulfill my duty in that respect in the manner which circumstances may render most conducive to the public good, and to this end that the compensations to be made to the persons who may be employed should, according to the nature of their appointments, be defined by law, and a competent fund designated for defraying the expenses incident to the conduct of our foreign affairs.

Various considerations also render it expedient that the terms on which foreigners may be admitted to the rights of citizens should be speedily ascertained by a uniform rule of naturalization.

Uniformity in the currency, weights, and measures of the United States is an object of great importance, and will, I am persuaded, be duly attended to.

The advancement of agriculture, commerce, and manufactures by all proper means will not, I trust, need recommendation; but I can not forbear intimating to you the expediency of giving effectual encouragement as well to the introduction of new and useful inventions from abroad as to the exertions of skill and genius in producing them at home, and of facilitating the intercourse between the distant parts of our country by a due attention to the post-office and post-roads.

Nor am I less persuaded that you will agree with me in opinion that there is nothing which can better deserve your patronage than the promotion of science and literature. Knowledge is in every country the surest basis of public happiness. In one in which the measures of government receive their impressions so immediately from the sense of the community as in ours it is proportionably essential. To the security of a free constitution it contributes in various ways—by convincing those who are intrusted with the public administration that every valuable end of government is best answered by the enlightened confidence of the people, and by teaching the people themselves to know and to value their own rights; to discern and provide against invasions of them; to distinguish between oppression and the necessary exercise of lawful authority; between burthens proceeding from a disregard to their convenience and those resulting from the inevitable exigencies of society; to discriminate the spirit of liberty from that of licentiousness—cherishing the first, avoiding the last—and uniting a speedy but temperate vigilance against encroachments, with an inviolable respect to the laws.

Whether this desirable object will be best promoted by affording aids to seminaries of learning already established, by the institution of a national university, or by any other expedients will be well worthy of a place in the deliberations of the legislature.

Gentlemen of the House of Representatives:

I saw with peculiar pleasure at the close of the last session the resolution entered into by you expressive of your opinion that an adequate provision for the support of the public credit is a matter of high importance to the national honor and prosperity. In this sentiment I entirely concur; and to a perfect confidence in your best endeavors to devise such a provision as will be truly consistent with the end I add an equal reliance on the cheerful cooperation of the other branch of the legislature. It would be superfluous to specify inducements to a measure in which the character and permanent interests of the United States are so obviously and so deeply concerned, and which has received so explicit a sanction from your declaration.

Gentlemen of the Senate and House of Representatives:

I have directed the proper officers to lay before you, respectively, such papers and estimates as regard the affairs particularly recommended to your consideration, and necessary to convey to you that information of the state of the Union which it is my duty to afford.

The welfare of our country is the great object to which our cares and efforts ought to be directed, and I shall derive great satisfaction from a cooperation with you in the pleasing though arduous task of insuring to our fellow citizens the blessings which they have a right to expect from a free, efficient, and equal government.

Pacification of the Indians

From the Third Annual Message to Congress
Philadelphia, Pennsylvania
October 25, 1791

THE ESTABLISHMENT of peaceful relations with the Indians was a pressing problem for the new nation. England, France, and Spain were supplying several of the more warlike tribes with weapons, and as a result the western frontiers, notably the Ohio valley, were rarely secure. Less than two weeks after Washington delivered his third annual message, from which this is excerpted, one of the "offensive operations" to which he refers, a major military expedition led by Maj. Gen. Arthur St. Clair, was ambushed and routed by the Miami Indians.

Washington always urged that the Indians be treated fairly. "In vain may we expect peace with the Indians on our frontiers," he wrote, "so long as a lawless set of unprincipled wretches can violate the rights of hospitality, or infringe the most solemn treaties, without receiving the punishment they so justly merit."

. . . In the interval of your recess due attention has been paid to the execution of the different objects which were specially provided for by the laws and resolutions of the last session.

Among the most important of these is the defense and security of the western frontiers. To accomplish it on the most humane principles was a primary wish.

Accordingly, at the same time that treaties have been provisionally concluded and other proper means used to attach the wavering and to confirm in their friendship the well-disposed tribes of Indians, effectual measures have been adopted to make those of a hostile description sensible that a pacification was desired upon terms of moderation and justice.

Those measures having proved unsuccessful, it became necessary to convince the refractory of the power of the United States to punish their depredations. Offensive operations have therefore been directed, to be conducted, however, as consistently as possible with the dictates of humanity. Some of these have been crowned with full success and others are yet depending. The expeditions which have been completed were carried on under the authority and at the expense of the United States by the militia of Kentucky, whose enterprise, intrepidity, and good conduct are entitled of peculiar commendation.

Overtures of peace are still continued to the deluded tribes, and considerable numbers of individuals belonging to them have lately renounced all further opposition, removed from their former situations, and placed themselves under the immediate protection of the United States.

It is sincerely to be desired that all need of coercion in future may cease and that an intimate intercourse may succeed, calculated to advance the happiness of the Indians and to attach them firmly to the United States.

In order to do this it seems necessary—

That they should experience the benefits of an impartial dispensation of justice.

That the mode of alienating their lands, the main source of discontent and war, should be so defined and regulated as to obviate imposition and as far as may be practicable controversy concerning the reality and extent of the alienations which are made.

That commerce with them should be promoted under regulations tending to secure an equitable deportment toward them, and that such rational experiments should be made for imparting to them the blessings of civilization as may from time to time suit their condition.

That the executive of the United States should be enabled to employ the means to which the Indians have been long accustomed for uniting their immediate interests with the preservation of peace.

And that efficacious provision should be made for inflicting adequate penalties upon all those who, by violating their rights, shall infringe the treaties and endanger the peace of the Union.

A system corresponding with the mild principles of religion and philanthropy toward an unenlightened race of men, whose happiness materially depends on the conduct of the United States, would be as honorable to the national character as conformable to the dictates of sound policy. . . .

Fifth Annual Message to Congress

Philadelphia, Pennsylvania
December 3, 1793

WASHINGTON was reelected to a second term without a contest, even though he never officially announced his candidacy. There was, however, a bitter battle for the vice presidency (won again by John Adams) and feuding between followers of Hamilton and Jefferson.

The president betrayed no anxiety over the brewing party battles in his annual address of 1793. Instead he looked outward, to the increasing belligerence of England, which was attempting to block the growth of American trade in the French West Indies by seizing American ships and impressing American sailors. The United States seemed in danger of being drawn into the conflict between revolutionary France and England. War also seemed likely with the British-supplied Indians over the question of American settlements north of the Ohio River. In preparation Washington urged the fortification of American harbors and the expansion of the militia.

Since the commencement of the term for which I have been again called into office no fit occasion has arisen for expressing to my fellow citizens at large the deep and respectful sense which I feel of the renewed testimony of public approbation. While on the one hand it awakened my gratitude for all those instances of affectionate partiality with which I have been honored by my country, on the other it could not prevent an earnest wish for that retirement from which no private consideration should ever have torn me. But influenced by the belief that my conduct would be estimated according to its real motives, and that the people, and the authorities derived from them, would support exertions having nothing personal for their object, I have obeyed the suffrage which commanded me to resume the executive power; and I humbly implore that Being on whose will the fate of nations depends to crown with success our mutual endeavors for the general happiness.

As soon as the war in Europe had embraced those powers with whom the United States have the most extensive relations there was reason to apprehend that our intercourse with them might be interrupted and our disposition for peace drawn into question by the suspicions too often entertained by belligerent nations. It seemed, therefore, to be my duty to admonish our citizens of the consequences of a contraband trade and of hostile acts to any of the parties, and to obtain by a declaration of the existing legal state of things an easier admission of our right to the immunities belonging to our situation. Under these impressions the proclamation which will be laid before you was issued.

In this posture of affairs, both new and delicate, I resolved to adopt general rules which should conform to the treaties [of 1778] and assert the privileges of the United States. These were reduced into a system, which will be communicated to you. Although I have not thought myself at liberty to forbid the sale of the prizes permitted by our treaty of commerce with France to be brought into our ports, I have not refused to cause them to be restored when they were taken within the protection of our territory, or by vessels commissioned or equipped in a warlike form within the limits of the United States.

It rests with the wisdom of Congress to correct, improve, or enforce this plan of procedure; and it will probably be found expedient to extend the legal code and the jurisdiction of the courts of the United States to many cases which, though dependent on principles already recognized, demand some further provisions.

Where individuals shall, within the United States, array themselves in hostility against any of the powers at war, or enter upon military expeditions or enterprises within the jurisdiction of the United States, or usurp and exercise judicial authority within the United States, or where the penalties on violations of the law of nations may have been indistinctly marked, or are inadequate—these offenses can not receive too early and close an attention, and require prompt and decisive remedies.

Whatsoever those remedies may be, they will be well administered by the judiciary, who possess a long-established course of investigation, effectual process, and officers in the habit of executing it.

In like manner, as several of the courts have doubted, under particular circumstances, their power to liberate the vessels of a nation at peace, and even of a citizen of the United States, although seized under a false color of being hostile property, and have denied their power to liberate certain captures within the protection of our territory, it would seem proper to regulate their jurisdiction in these points. But if the executive is to be the resort in either of the two last-mentioned cases, it is hoped that he will be authorized by law to have facts ascertained by the courts when for his own information he shall request it.

I can not recommend to your notice measures for the fulfillment of our duties to the rest of the world without again pressing upon you the necessity of placing ourselves in a condition of complete defense and of exacting from them the fulfillment of their duties toward us. The United States ought not to indulge a persuasion that, contrary to the order of human events, they will forever keep at a distance those painful appeals to arms with which the history of every other nation abounds. There is a rank due to the United States among nations which will be withheld, if not absolutely lost, by the reputation of weakness. If we desire to avoid insult, we must be able to repel it; if we desire to secure peace, one of the most powerful instruments of our rising prosperity, it must be known that we are at all times ready for war. The documents which will be presented to you will shew the amount and kinds of arms and military stores now in our magazines and arsenals; and yet an addition even to these supplies can not with prudence be neglected, as it would leave nothing to the uncertainty of procuring of warlike apparatus in the moment of public danger.

Nor can such arrangements, with such objects, be exposed to the censure or jealousy of the warmest friends of republican government. They are incapable of abuse in the hands of the militia, who ought to possess a pride in being the depository of the force of the republic, and may be trained to a degree of energy equal to every military exigency of the United States. But it is an inquiry which can not be too solemnly pursued, whether the act "more effectually to provide for the national defense by establishing an uniform militia throughout the United States" has organized them so as to produce their full effect; whether your own experience in the several states has not detected some imperfections in the scheme, and whether a material feature in an improvement of it ought not to be to afford an opportunity for the study of those branches of the military art which can scarcely ever be attained by practice alone.

The connection of the United States with Europe has become extremely interesting. The occurrences which relate to it and have passed under the knowledge of the executive will be exhibited to Congress in a subsequent communication.

When we contemplate the war on our frontiers, it may be truly affirmed that every reasonable effort has been made to adjust the causes of dissension with the Indians north of the Ohio. The instructions given to the commissioners evince a moderation and equity proceeding from a sincere love of peace, and a liberality having no restriction but the essential interests and dignity of the United States. The attempt, however, of an amicable negotiation having been frustrated, the troops have marched to act offensively. Although the proposed treaty did not arrest the progress of military preparation, it is doubtful how far the advance of the season, before good faith justified active movements, may retard them during the remainder of the year. From the papers and intelligence which relate to this important subject you will determine whether the deficiency in the number of troops granted by law shall be compensated by succors of militia, or additional encouragements shall be proposed to recruits.

An anxiety has been also demonstrated by the executive for peace with the Creeks and the Cherokees. The former have been relieved with corn and with clothing, and offensive measures against them prohibited during the recess of Congress. To satisfy the complaints of the latter, prosecutions have been instituted for the violences committed upon them. But the papers which will be delivered to you disclose the critical footing on which we stand in regard to both those tribes, and it is with Congress to pronounce what shall be done.

After they shall have provided for the present emergency, it will merit their most serious labors to render tranquillity with the savages permanent by creating ties of interest. Next to a rigorous execution of justice on the violators of peace, the establishment of commerce with the Indian nations in behalf of the United States is most likely to conciliate their attachment. But it ought to be conducted without fraud, without extortion, with constant and plentiful supplies, with a ready market for the commodities of the Indians and a stated price for what they give in payment and receive in exchange. Individuals will not pursue such a traffic unless they be allured by the hope of profit; but it will be enough for the United States to be reimbursed only. Should this recommendation accord with the opinion of Congress, they will recollect that it can not be accomplished by any means yet in the hands of the executive. . . .

Seventh Annual Message to Congress

Philadelphia, Pennsylvania
December 8, 1795

THIS RANKS as Washington's most hopeful address to Congress, reflecting what his biographers J. A. Carroll and M. W. Ashworth called "his own exuberant ambitions for the future of the American republic" expressed in "a well-contrived and confident appeal for national unity in an hour of growing political disparities." Washington had good reason to be pleased: war with England had been avoided, relations with Spain had been normalized, and the end of his own term in office was in view.

I trust I do not deceive myself when I indulge the persuasion that I have never met you at any period when more than at the present the situation of our public affairs has afforded just cause for mutual congratulation, and for inviting you to join with me in profound gratitude to the Author of all Good for the numerous and extraordinary blessings we enjoy.

The termination of the long, expensive, and distressing war in which we have been engaged with certain Indians northwest of the Ohio is placed in the option of the United States by a treaty which the commander of our army has concluded provisionally with the hostile tribes in that region.

In the adjustment of the terms the satisfaction of the Indians was deemed an object worthy no less of the policy than of the liberality of the United States as the necessary basis of durable tranquillity. The object, it is believed, has been fully attained. The articles agreed upon will immediately be laid before the Senate for their consideration.

The Creek and Cherokee Indians, who alone of the southern tribes had annoyed our frontiers, have lately confirmed their preexisting treaties with us, and were giving evidence of a sincere disposition to carry them into effect by the surrender of the prisoners and property they had taken. But we have to lament that the fair prospect in this quarter has been once more clouded by wanton murders, which some citizens of Georgia are represented to have recently perpetrated on hunting parties of the Creeks, which have again subjected that frontier to disquietude and danger, which will be productive of further expense, and may occasion more effusion of blood. Measures are pursuing to prevent or mitigate the usual consequences of such outrages, and with the hope of their succeeding at least to avert general hostility.

A letter from the emperor of Morocco announces to me his recognition of our treaty made with his father, the late emperor, and consequently the continuance of peace with that power. With peculiar satisfaction I add that information has been received from an agent deputed on our part to Algiers importing that the terms of the treaty with the Dey and Regency of that country had been adjusted in such a manner as to authorize the expectation of a speedy peace and the restoration of our unfortunate fellow citizens from a grievous captivity.

The latest advices from our envoy at the Court of Madrid give, moreover, the pleasing information that he had received assurances of a speedy and satisfactory conclusion of his negotiation. While the event depending upon unadjusted particulars can not be regarded as ascertained, it is agreeable to cherish the expectation of an issue which, securing amicably very essential interests of the United States, will at the same time lay the foundation of lasting harmony with a power whose friendship we have uniformly and sincerely desired to cultivate.

Though not before officially disclosed to the House of Representatives, you, gentlemen, are all apprised that a treaty of amity, commerce, and navigation has been negotiated with Great Britain, and that the Senate have advised and consented to its ratification upon a condition which excepts part of one article. Agreeably thereto, and to the best judgment I was able to form of the public interest after full and mature deliberation, I have added my sanction. The result on the part of His Britannic Majesty is unknown. When received, the subject will without delay be placed before Congress.

This interesting summary of our affairs with regard to the foreign powers between whom and the United States controversies have subsisted, and with regard also to those of our Indian neighbors with whom we have been in a state of enmity or misunderstanding, opens a wide field for consoling and gratifying reflections. If by prudence and moderation on every side the extinguishment of all the causes of external discord which have heretofore menaced our tranquillity, on terms compatible with our national rights and honor, shall be the happy result, how firm and how precious a foundation will have been laid for accelerating, maturing, and establishing the prosperity of our country.

Contemplating the internal situation as well as the external relations of the United States, we discover equal cause for contentment and satisfaction. While many of the nations of Europe, with their American dependencies, have been involved in a contest unusually bloody, exhausting, and calamitous, in which the evils of foreign war have been aggravated by domestic convulsion and insurrection; in which many of the arts most useful to society have been exposed to discouragement and decay; in which scarcity of subsistence has imbittered other sufferings; while even the anticipations of a return of the blessings of peace and repose are alloyed by the sense of heavy and accumulating burthens, which press upon all the departments of industry and threaten to clog the future springs of government, our favored country, happy in a striking contrast, has enjoyed general tranquillity—a tranquillity the more satisfactory because maintained at the expense of no duty. Faithful to ourselves, we have violated no obligation to others. Our agriculture, commerce, and manufactures prosper beyond former example, the molestations of our trade (to prevent a continuance of which, however, very pointed remonstrances have been made) being overbalanced by the aggregate benefits which it derives from a neutral position. Our population advances with a celerity which, exceeding the most sanguine calculations, proportionally augments our strength and resources, and guarantees our future security. Every part of the Union displays indications of rapid and various improvement; and with burthens so light as

scarcely to be perceived, with resources fully adequate to our present exigencies, with governments founded on the genuine principles of rational liberty, and with mild and wholesome laws, is it too much to say that our country exhibits a spectacle of national happiness never surpassed, if ever before equaled?

Placed in a situation every way so auspicious, motives of commanding force impel us, with sincere acknowledgment to Heaven and pure love to our country, to unite our efforts to preserve, prolong, and improve our immense advantages. To cooperate with you in this desirable work is a fervent and favorite wish of my heart.

It is a valuable ingredient in the general estimate of our welfare that the part of our country which was lately the scene of disorder and insurrection now enjoys the blessings of quiet and order. The misled have abandoned their errors, and pay the respect of our Constitution and laws which is due from good citizens to the public authorities of the society. These circumstances have induced me to pardon generally the offenders here referred to, and to extend forgiveness to those who had been adjudged to capital punishment. For though I shall always think it a sacred duty to exercise with firmness and energy the constitutional powers with which I am vested, yet it appears to me no less consistent with the public good than it is with my personal feelings to mingle in the operations of government every degree of moderation and tenderness which the national justice, dignity, and safety may permit.

Gentlemen:

Among the objects which will claim your attention in the course of the session, a review of our military establishment is not the least important. It is called for by the events which have changed, and may be expected still further to change, the relative situation of our frontiers. In this review you will doubtless allow due weight to the considerations that the questions between us and certain foreign powers are not yet finally adjusted, that the war in Europe is not yet terminated, and that our western posts, when recovered, will demand provision for garrisoning and securing them. A statement of our present military force will be laid before you by the Department of War.

With the review of our army establishment is naturally connected that of the militia. It will merit inquiry what imperfections in the existing plan further experience may have unfolded. The subject is of so much moment in my estimation as to excite a constant solicitude that the consideration of it may be renewed until the greatest attainable perfection shall be accomplished. Time is wearing away some advantages for forwarding the object, while none better deserves the persevering attention of the public councils.

While we indulge the satisfaction which the actual condition of our western borders so well authorizes, it is necessary that we should not lose sight of an important truth which continually receives new confirmations, namely, that the provisions heretofore made with a view to the protection of the Indians from the violences of the lawless part of our frontier inhabitants are insufficient. It is demonstrated that these violences can now be perpetrated with impunity, and it can need no argument to prove that unless the murdering of Indians can be restrained by bringing the murderers to condign punishment, all the exertions of the government to prevent destructive retaliations by the Indians will prove fruitless and all our present agreeable prospects illusory. The frequent destruction of innocent women and children, who are chiefly the victims of retaliation, must continue to shock humanity, and an enormous expense to drain the Treasury of the Union.

To enforce upon the Indians the observance of justice it is indispensable that there shall be competent means of rendering justice to them. If these means can be devised by the wisdom of Congress, and especially if there can be added an adequate provision for supplying the necessities of the Indians on reasonable terms (a measure the mention of which I the more readily repeat, as in all the conferences with them they urge it with solicitude), I should not hesitate to entertain a strong hope of rendering our tranquillity permanent. I add with pleasure that the probability even of their civilization is not diminished by the experiments which have been thus far made under the auspices of government. The accomplishment of this work, if practicable, will reflect undecaying luster on our national character and administer the most grateful consolations that virtuous minds can know. . . .

Farewell Address

Philadelphia, Pennsylvania
September 17, 1796

As EARLY as 1792, Washington had been contemplating a valedictory address, which he asked James Madison to help him write. The address, he told Madison in a letter, was to express "in plain and modest terms" his "fervent wishes for the prosperity of my country" and to invoke "a continuation of the blessings of Providence upon it—and upon all those who are the supporters of its interests and the promoters of harmony, order, and good government." The material in that letter formed the basis of the final version of the address, with which Washington announced his retirement from public life.

The exact authorship of this influential address is in dispute. Washington, Madison, Hamilton, and John Jay all worked on it at one time or another, but there is little doubt that it expresses Washington's fundamental principles. Although the president never delivered the Farewell Address in person (it was published in David C. Claypoole's paper, the *American Daily Advertiser,* on September 19, 1796), it is still read in Congress every year on Washington's birthday.

The period for a new election of a citizen to administer the executive government of the United States being not far distant, and the time actually arrived when your thoughts must be employed in designating the person who is to be clothed with that important trust, it appears to me proper, especially as it may conduce to a more distinct expression of the public voice, that I should now apprise you of the resolution I have formed to decline being considered among the number of those out of whom a choice is to be made.

I beg you at the same time to do me the justice to be assured that this resolution has not been taken without a strict regard to all the considerations appertaining to the relation which binds a dutiful citizen to his country; and that in withdrawing the tender of service, which silence in my situation might imply, I am influenced by no diminution of zeal for your future interest, no deficiency of grateful respect for your past kindness, but am supported by a full conviction that the step is compatible with both.

The acceptance of and continuance hitherto in the office to which your suffrages have twice called me have been a uniform sacrifice of inclination to the opinion of duty and to a deference for what appeared to be your desire. I constantly hoped that it would have been much earlier in my power, consistently with motives which I was not at liberty to disregard, to return to that retirement from which I had been reluctantly drawn. The strength of my inclination to do this previous to the last election had even led to the preparation of an address to declare it to you; but mature reflection on the then perplexed and critical posture of our affairs with foreign nations and the unanimous advice of persons entitled to my confidence impelled me to abandon the idea. I rejoice that the state of your concerns, external as well as internal, no longer renders the pursuit of inclination incompatible with the sentiment of duty or propriety, and am persuaded, whatever partiality may be retained for my services, that in the present circumstances of our country you will not disapprove my determination to retire.

The impressions with which I first undertook the arduous trust were explained on the proper occasion. In the discharge of this trust I will only say that I have, with good intentions, contributed toward the organization and administration of the government the best exertions of which a very fallible judgment was capable. Not unconscious in the outset of the inferiority of my qualifications, experience in my own eyes, perhaps still more in the eyes of others, has strengthened the motives to diffidence of myself; and every day the increasing weight of years admonishes me more and more that the shade of retirement is as necessary to me as it will be welcome. Satisfied that if any circumstances have given peculiar value to my services they were temporary, I have the consolation to believe that, while choice and prudence invite me to quit the political scene, patriotism does not forbid it.

In looking forward to the moment which is intended to terminate the career of my political life my feelings do not permit me to suspend the deep acknowledgment of that debt of gratitude which I owe to my beloved country for the many honors it has conferred upon me; still more for the steadfast confidence with which it has supported me, and for the opportunities I have thence enjoyed of manifesting my inviolable attachment by services faithful and persevering, though in usefulness unequal to my zeal. If benefits have resulted to our country from these services, let it always be remembered to your praise and as an instructive example in our annals that under circumstances in which the passions, agitated in every direction, were liable to mislead; amidst appearances sometimes dubious; vicissitudes of fortune often discouraging; in situations in which not unfrequently want of success has countenanced the spirit of criticism, the constancy of your support was the essential prop of the efforts and a guaranty of the plans by which they were effected. Profoundly penetrated with this idea, I shall carry it with me to my grave as a strong incitement to unceasing vows that Heaven may continue to you the choicest tokens of its beneficence; that your union and brotherly affection may be perpetual; that the free Constitution which is the work of your hands may be sacredly maintained; that its administration in every department may be stamped with wisdom and virtue; that, in fine, the happiness of the people of these states, under the auspices of liberty, may be made complete by so careful a preservation and so prudent a use of this blessing as will acquire to them the glory of recommending it to the applause, the affection, and adoption of every nation which is yet a stranger to it.

Here, perhaps, I ought to stop. But a solicitude for your welfare which can not end but with my life, and the apprehension of danger natural to that solicitude, urge me on an occasion like the present to offer to your solemn contemplation and to recommend to your frequent review some sentiments which are the result of much reflection, of no inconsiderable observation, and which appear to me all important to the permanency of your felicity as a people. These will be offered to you with the more freedom as you can only see in them the disinterested warnings of a parting friend, who can possibly have no personal motive to bias his counsel. Nor can I forget as an encouragement to it your indulgent reception of my sentiments on a former and not dissimilar occasion.

Interwoven as is the love of liberty with every ligament of your hearts, no recommendation of mine is necessary to fortify or confirm the attachment.

The unity of government which constitutes you one people is also now dear to you. It is justly so, for it is a main pillar in the edifice of your real independence, the support of your tranquillity at home, your peace abroad, of your safety, of your prosperity, of that very liberty which you so highly prize. But as it is easy to foresee that from different causes and from different quarters much pains will be taken, many artifices employed, to weaken in your minds the conviction of this truth, as this is the point in your political fortress against which the batteries of internal and external enemies will be most constantly and actively (though often covertly and insidiously) directed, it is of infinite moment that you should properly estimate the immense value of your national union to your collective and individual happiness; that you should cherish a cordial, habitual, and immovable attachment to it; accustoming yourselves to think and speak of it as of the palladium of your political safety and prosperity; watching for its preservation with jealous anxiety; discountenancing whatever may suggest even a suspicion that it can in any event be abandoned, and indignantly frowning upon the first dawning of every attempt to alienate any portion of our country from the rest or to enfeeble the sacred ties which now link together the various parts.

For this you have every inducement of sympathy and interest. Citizens by birth or choice of a common country, that country has a right to concentrate your affections. The name of American, which belongs to you in your national capacity, must always exalt the just pride of patriotism more than any appellation derived from local discriminations. With slight shades of difference, you have the same religion, manners, habits, and political principles. You have in a common cause fought and triumphed together. The independence and liberty you possess are the work of joint councils and joint efforts, of common dangers, sufferings, and successes.

But these considerations, however powerfully they address themselves to your sensibility, are greatly outweighed by those which apply more immediately to your interest. Here every portion of our country finds the most commanding motives for carefully guarding and preserving the union of the whole.

The North, in an unrestrained intercourse with the South, protected by the equal laws of a common government, finds in the productions of the latter great additional resources of maritime and commercial enterprise and precious materials of manufacturing industry. The South, in the same intercourse, benefiting by the same agency of the North, sees its agriculture grow and its commerce expand. Turning partly into its own channels the seamen of the North, it finds its particular navigation invigorated; and while it contributes in different ways to nourish and increase the general mass of the national navigation, it looks forward to the protection of a maritime strength to which itself is unequally adapted. The East, in a like intercourse with the West, already finds, and in the progressive improvement of interior communications by land and water will more and more find, a valuable vent for the commodities which it brings from abroad or manufactures at home. The West derives from the East supplies requisite to its growth and comfort, and what is perhaps of still greater consequence, it must of necessity owe the secure enjoyment of indispensable outlets for its own productions to the weight, influence, and the future maritime strength of the Atlantic side of the Union, directed by an indissoluble community of interest as one nation. Any other tenure by which the West can hold this essential advantage, whether derived from its own separate strength or from an apostate and unnatural connection with any foreign power, must be intrinsically precarious.

While, then, every part of our country thus feels an immediate and particular interest in union, all the parts combined can not fail to find in the united mass of means and efforts greater strength, greater resource,

proportionably greater security from external danger, a less frequent interruption of their peace by foreign nations, and what is of inestimable value, they must derive from union an exemption from those broils and wars between themselves which so frequently afflict neighboring countries not tied together by the same governments, which their own rivalships alone would be sufficient to produce, but which opposite foreign alliances, attachments, and intrigues would stimulate and imbitter. Hence, likewise, they will avoid the necessity of those overgrown military establishments which, under any form of government, are inauspicious to liberty, and which are to be regarded as particularly hostile to republican liberty. In this sense it is that your union ought to be considered as a main prop of your liberty, and that the love of the one ought to endear to you the preservation of the other.

These considerations speak a persuasive language to every reflecting and virtuous mind, and exhibit the continuance of the Union as a primary object of patriotic desire. Is there a doubt whether a common government can embrace so large a sphere? Let experience solve it. To listen to mere speculation in such a case were criminal. We are authorized to hope that a proper organization of the whole, with the auxiliary agency of governments for the respective subdivisions, will afford a happy issue to the experiment. It is well worth a fair and full experiment. With such powerful and obvious motives to union affecting all parts of our country, while experience shall not have demonstrated its impracticability, there will always be reason to distrust the patriotism of those who in any quarter may endeavor to weaken its bands.

In contemplating the causes which may disturb our Union it occurs as matter of serious concern that any ground should have been furnished for characterizing parties by geographical discriminations—Northern and Southern, Atlantic and Western—whence designing men may endeavor to excite a belief that there is a real difference of local interests and views. One of the expedients of party to acquire influence within particular districts is to misrepresent the opinions and aims of other districts. You cannot shield yourselves too much against the jealousies and heartburnings which spring from these misrepresentations; they tend to render alien to each other those who ought to be bound together by fraternal affection. The inhabitants of our Western country have lately had a useful lesson on this head. They have seen in the negotiation by the executive and in the unanimous ratification by the Senate of the treaty with Spain, and in the universal satisfaction at that event throughout the United States, a decisive proof how unfounded were the suspicions propagated among them of a policy in the general government and in the Atlantic states unfriendly to their interests in regard to the Mississippi. They have been witnesses to the formation of two treaties—that with Great Britain and that with Spain—which secure to them everything they could desire in respect to our foreign relations toward confirming their prosperity. Will it not be their wisdom to rely for the preservation of these advantages on the union by which they were procured? Will they not henceforth be deaf to those advisers, if such there are, who would sever them from their brethren and connect them with aliens?

To the efficacy and permanency of your union a government for the whole is indispensable. No alliances, however strict, between the parts can be an adequate substitute. They must inevitably experience the infractions and interruptions which all alliances in all times have experienced. Sensible of this momentous truth, you have improved upon your first essay by the adoption of a Constitution of government better calculated than your former for an intimate union and for the efficacious management of your common concerns. This government, the offspring of our own choice, uninfluenced and unawed, adopted upon full investigation and mature deliberation, completely free in its principles, in the distribution of its powers, uniting security with energy, and containing within itself a provision for its own amendment, has a just claim to your confidence and your support. Respect for its authority, compliance with its laws, acquiescence in its measures, are duties enjoined by the fundamental maxims of true liberty. The basis of our political systems is the right of the people to make and to alter their constitutions of government. But the constitution which at any time exists till changed by an explicit and authentic act of the whole people is sacredly obligatory upon all. The very idea of the power and the right of the people to establish government presupposes the duty of every individual to obey the established government.

All obstructions to the execution of the laws, all combinations and associations, under whatever plausible character, with the real design to direct, control, counteract, or awe the regular deliberation and action of the constituted authorities, are destructive of this fundamental principle and of fatal tendency. They serve to organize faction; to give it an artificial and extraordinary force; to put in the place of the delegated will of the nation the will of a party, often a small but artful and enterprising minority of the community, and, according to the alternate triumphs of different parties, to make the public administration the mirror of the ill-concerted and incongruous projects of faction rather than the organ of consistent and wholesome plans, digested by common counsels and modified by mutual interests.

However combinations or associations of the above description may now and then answer popular ends, they are likely in the course of time and things to become potent engines by which cunning, ambitious, and unprincipled men will be enabled to subvert the power of the people, and to usurp for themselves the reins of government, destroying afterwards the very engines which have lifted them to unjust dominion.

Toward the preservation of your government and the permanency of your present happy state, it is requisite not only that you steadily discountenance irregular oppositions to its acknowledged authority, but also that you resist with care the spirit of innovation upon its principles, however specious the pretexts. One method of assault may be to effect in the forms of the Constitution alterations which will impair the energy of the system, and thus to undermine what can not be directly overthrown. In all the changes to which you may be invited remember that time and habit are at least as necessary to fix the true character of governments as of other human institutions; that experience is the surest standard by which to test the real tendency of the existing constitution of a country; the facility in changes upon the credit of mere hypothesis and opinion exposes to perpetual change, from the endless variety of hypothesis and opinion; and remember especially that for the efficient management of your common interests in a country so extensive as ours a government of as much vigor as is consistent with the perfect security of liberty is indispensable. Liberty itself will find in such a government, with powers properly distributed and adjusted, its surest guardian. It is, indeed, little else than a name where the government is too feeble to withstand the enterprises of faction, to confine each member of the society within the limits prescribed by the laws, and to maintain all in the secure and tranquil enjoyment of the rights of person and property.

I have already intimated to you the danger of parties in the state, with particular reference to the founding of them on geographical discriminations. Let me now take a more comprehensive view, and warn you in the most solemn manner against the baneful effects of the spirit of party generally.

This spirit, unfortunately, is inseparable from our nature, having its root in the strongest passions of the human mind. It exists under different shapes in all governments, more or less stifled, controlled, or repressed; but in those of the popular form it is seen in its greatest rankness and is truly their worst enemy.

The alternate domination of one faction over another, sharpened by the spirit of revenge natural to party dissension, which in different ages and countries has perpetrated the most horrid enormities, is itself a frightful despotism. But this leads at length to a more formal and permanent despotism. The disorders and miseries which result gradually incline the minds of men to seek security and repose in the absolute power of an individual, and sooner or later the chief of some prevailing faction, more able or more fortunate than his competitors, turns this disposition to the purposes of his own elevation on the ruins of public liberty.

Without looking forward to an extremity of this kind (which nevertheless ought not to be entirely out of sight), the common and continual mischiefs of the spirit of party are sufficient to make it the interest and duty of a wise people to discourage and restrain it.

It serves always to distract the public councils and enfeeble the public administration.

It agitates the community with ill-founded jealousies and false alarms; kindles the animosity of one part against another; foments occasionally riot and insurrection. It opens the door to foreign influence and corruption, which find a facilitated access to the government itself through the channels of party passion. Thus the policy and the will of one country are subjected to the policy and will of another.

There is an opinion that parties in free countries are useful checks upon the administration of the government, and serve to keep alive the spirit of liberty. This within certain limits is probably true; and in governments of a monarchical cast patriotism may look with indulgence, if not with favor, upon the spirit of party. But in those of the popular character, in governments purely elective, it is a spirit not to be encouraged. From their natural tendency it is certain there will always be enough of that spirit for every salutary purpose; and there being constant danger of excess, the effort ought to be by force of public opinion to mitigate and assuage it. A fire not to be quenched, it demands a uniform vigilance to prevent its bursting into a flame, lest, instead of warming, it should consume.

It is important, likewise, that the habits of thinking in a free country should inspire caution in those intrusted with its administration to confine themselves within their respective constitutional spheres, avoiding in the exercise of the powers of one department to encroach upon another. The spirit of encroachment tends to consolidate the powers of all the departments in one, and thus to create, whatever the form of government, a real despotism. A just estimate of that love of power and proneness to abuse it which predominates in the human heart is sufficient to satisfy us of the truth of this position. The necessity of reciprocal checks in the exercise of political power, by dividing and distributing it into different depositories, and constituting each the guardian of the public weal against invasions by the others, has been evinced by experiments ancient and modern, some of them in our country and under our own eyes. To preserve them must be as necessary as to institute them. If in the opinion of the people the distribution or modification of the constitutional powers be in any particular wrong, let it be corrected by an amendment in the way which the Constitution designates. But let there be no change by usurpation; for though this in one instance may be the instrument of good, it is the customary weapon by which free governments are destroyed. The precedent must always greatly overbalance in permanent evil any partial or transient benefit which the use can at any time yield.

Of all the dispositions and habits which lead to political prosperity, religion and morality are indispensable supports. In vain would that man claim the tribute of patriotism who should labor to subvert these great pillars of human happiness—these firmest props of the duties of men and citizens. The mere politician, equally with the pious man, ought to respect and to cherish them. A volume could not trace all their connections with private and public felicity. Let it simply be asked, Where is the security for property, for reputation, for life, if the sense of religious obligation desert the oaths which are the instruments of investigation in courts of justice? And let us with caution indulge the supposition that morality can be maintained without religion. Whatever may be conceded to the influence of refined education on minds of peculiar structure, reason and experience both forbid us to expect that national morality can prevail in exclusion of religious principle.

It is substantially true that virtue or morality is a necessary spring of popular government. The rule indeed extends with more or less force to every species of free government. Who that is a sincere friend to it can look with indifference upon attempts to shake the foundation of the fabric? Promote, then, as an object of primary importance, institutions for the general diffusion of knowledge. In proportion as the structure of a government gives force to public opinion, it is essential that public opinion should be enlightened.

As a very important source of strength and security, cherish public credit. One method of preserving it is to use it as sparingly as possible, avoiding occasions of expense by cultivating peace, but remembering also that timely disbursements to prepare for danger frequently prevent much greater disbursements to repel it; avoiding likewise the accumulation of debt, not only by shunning occasions of expense, but by vigorous exertions in time of peace to discharge the debts which unavoidable wars have occasioned, not ungenerously throwing upon posterity the burthen which we ourselves ought to bear. The execution of these maxims belongs to your representatives; but it is necessary that public opinion should cooperate. To facilitate to them the performance of their duty it is essential that you should practically bear in mind that toward the payment of debts there must be revenue; that to have revenue there must be taxes; that no taxes can be devised which are not more or less inconvenient and unpleasant; that the intrinsic embarrassment inseparable from the selection of the proper objects (which is always a choice of difficulties), ought to be a decisive motive for a candid construction of the conduct of the government in making it, and for a spirit of acquiescence in the measures for obtaining revenue which the public exigencies may at any time dictate.

Observe good faith and justice toward all nations. Cultivate peace and harmony with all. Religion and morality enjoin this conduct. And can it be that good policy does not equally enjoin it? It will be worthy of a free, enlightened, and at no distant period a great nation to give to mankind the magnanimous and too novel example of a people always guided by an exalted justice and benevolence. Who can doubt that in the course of time and things the fruits of such a plan would richly repay any temporary advantages which might be lost by a steady adherence to it? Can it be that Providence has not connected the permanent felicity of a nation with its virtue? The experiment, at least, is recommended by every sentiment which ennobles human nature. Alas! is it rendered impossible by its vices?

In the execution of such a plan nothing is more essential than that permanent, inveterate antipathies against particular nations and passionate attachments for others should be excluded, and that in place of them just and amicable feelings toward all should be cultivated. The nation which indulges toward another an habitual hatred or an habitual fondness is in some degree a slave. It is a slave to its animosity or to its affection, either of which is sufficient to lead it astray from its duty and its interest. Antipathy in one nation against another disposes each more readily to offer insult and injury, to lay hold of slight causes of umbrage, and to be haughty and intractable when accidental or trifling occasions of dispute occur.

Hence frequent collisions, obstinate, envenomed, and bloody contests. The nation prompted by ill will and resentment sometimes impels to war the government contrary to the best calculations of policy. The government sometimes participates in the national propensity, and adopts through passion what reason would reject. At other times it makes the animosity of the nation subservient to projects of hostility, instigated by pride, ambition, and other sinister and pernicious motives. The peace often, sometimes perhaps the liberty, of nations has been the victim.

So, likewise, a passionate attachment of one nation for another produces a variety of evils. Sympathy for the favorite nation, facilitating the illusion of an imaginary common interest in cases where no real common interest exists, and infusing into one the enmities of the other, betrays the former into a participation in the quarrels and wars of the latter without adequate inducement or justification. It leads also to concessions to the favorite nation of privileges denied to others, which is apt doubly to injure the nation making the concessions by unnecessarily parting with what ought to have been retained, and by exciting jealousy, ill will, and a disposition to retaliate in the parties from whom equal privileges are withheld; and it gives to ambitious, corrupted, or deluded citizens (who devote themselves to the favorite nation) facility to betray or sacrifice the interests of their own country without odium, sometimes even with popularity, gilding with the appearances of a virtuous sense of obligation, a commendable deference for public opinion, or a laudable zeal for public good the base or foolish compliances of ambition, corruption, or infatuation.

As avenues to foreign influence in innumerable ways, such attachments are particularly alarming to the truly enlightened and independent patriot. How many opportunities do they afford to tamper with domestic factions, to practice the arts of seduction, to mislead public opinion, to influence or awe the public councils! Such an attachment of a small or weak toward a great and powerful nation dooms the former to be the satellite of the latter. Against the insidious wiles of foreign influence (I conjure you to believe me, fellow citizens) the

jealousy of a free people ought to be constantly awake, since history and experience prove that foreign influence is one of the most baneful foes of republican government. But that jealousy, to be useful, must be impartial, else it becomes the instrument of the very influence to be avoided, instead of a defense against it. Excessive partiality for one foreign nation and excessive dislike of another cause those whom they actuate to see danger only on one side, and serve to veil and even second the arts of influence on the other. Real patriots who may resist the intrigues of the favorite are liable to become suspected and odious, while its tools and dupes usurp the applause and confidence of the people to surrender their interests.

The great rule of conduct for us in regard to foreign nations is, in extending our commercial relations to have with them as little political connection as possible. So far as we have already formed engagements let them be fulfilled with perfect good faith. Here let us stop.

Europe has a set of primary interests which to us have none or a very remote relation. Hence she must be engaged in frequent controversies, the causes of which are essentially foreign to our concerns. Hence, therefore, it must be unwise in us to implicate ourselves by artificial ties in the ordinary vicissitudes of her politics or the ordinary combinations and collisions of her friendships or enmities.

Our detached and distant situation invites and enables us to pursue a different course. If we remain one people, under an efficient government, the period is not far off when we may defy material injury from external annoyance; when we may take such an attitude as will cause the neutrality we may at any time resolve upon to be scrupulously respected; when belligerent nations, under the impossibility of making acquisitions upon us, will not lightly hazard the giving us provocation; when we may choose peace or war, as our interest, guided by justice, shall counsel.

Why forego the advantages of so peculiar a situation? Why quit our own to stand upon foreign ground? Why, by interweaving our destiny with that of any part of Europe, entangle our peace and prosperity in the toils of European ambition, rival-ship, interest, humor, or caprice?

It is our true policy to steer clear of permanent alliances with any portion of the foreign world, so far, I mean, as we are now at liberty to do it; for let me not be understood as capable of patronizing infidelity to existing engagements. I hold the maxim no less applicable to public than to private affairs that honesty is always the best policy. I repeat, therefore, let those engagements be observed in their genuine sense. But in my opinion it is unnecessary and would be unwise to extend them.

Taking care always to keep ourselves by suitable establishments on a respectable defensive posture, we may safely trust to temporary alliances for extraordinary emergencies.

Harmony, liberal intercourse with all nations are recommended by policy, humanity, and interest. But even our commercial policy should hold an equal and impartial hand, neither seeking nor granting exclusive favors or preferences; consulting the natural course of things; diffusing and diversifying by gentle means the streams of commerce, but forcing nothing; establishing with powers so disposed, in order to give trade a stable course, to define the rights of our merchants, and to enable the government to support them, conventional rules of intercourse, the best that present circumstances and mutual opinion will permit, but temporary and liable to be from time to time abandoned or varied as experience and circumstances shall dictate; constantly keeping in view that it is folly in one nation to look for disinterested favors from another; that it must pay with a portion of its independence for whatever it may accept under that character; that by such acceptance it may place itself in the condition of having given equivalents for nominal favors, and yet of being reproached with ingratitude for not giving more. There can be no greater error than to expect or calculate upon real favors from nation to nation. It is an illusion which experience must cure, which a just pride ought to discard.

In offering to you, my countrymen, these counsels of an old and affectionate friend I dare not hope they will make the strong and lasting impression I could wish—that they will control the usual current of the passions or prevent our nation from running the course which has hitherto marked the destiny of nations. But if I may even flatter myself that they may be productive of some partial benefit, some occasional good—that they may now and then recur to moderate the fury of party spirit, to warn against the mischiefs of foreign intrigue, to guard against the impostures of pretended patriotism—this hope will be a full recompense for the solicitude for your welfare by which they have been dictated.

How far in the discharge of my official duties I have been guided by the principles which have been delineated the public records and other evidences of my conduct must witness to you and to the world. To myself, the assurance of my own conscience is that I have at least believed myself to be guided by them.

In relation to the still subsisting war in Europe my proclamation of the 22d of April 1793, is the index to my plan. Sanctioned by your approving voice and by that of your representatives in both houses of Congress, the spirit of that measure has continually governed me, uninfluenced by any attempts to deter or divert me from it.

After deliberate examination, with the aid of the best lights I could obtain, I was well satisfied that our country, under all the circumstances of the case, had a right to take, and was bound in duty and interest to take, a neutral position. Having taken it, I determined as far as should depend upon me to maintain it with moderation, perseverance, and firmness.

The considerations which respect the right to hold this conduct it is not necessary on this occasion to detail. I will only observe that according to my understanding of the matter that right, so far from being denied by any of the belligerent powers, has been virtually admitted by all.

The duty of holding a neutral conduct may be inferred, without anything more, from the obligation which justice and humanity impose on every nation, in cases in which it is free to act, to maintain inviolate the relations of peace and amity toward other nations.

The inducements of interest for observing that conduct will best be referred to your own reflections and experience. With me a predominant motive has been to endeavor to gain time to our country to settle and mature its yet recent institutions, and to progress without interruption to that degree of strength and consistency which is necessary to give it, humanly speaking, the command of its own fortunes.

Though in reviewing the incidents of my administration I am unconscious of intentional error, I am nevertheless too sensible of my defects not to think it probable that I may have committed many errors. Whatever they may be, I fervently beseech the Almighty to avert or mitigate the evils to which they may tend. I shall also carry with me the hope that my country will never cease to view them with indulgence, and that, after 45 years of my life dedicated to its service with an upright zeal, the faults of incompetent abilities will be consigned to oblivion, as myself must soon be to the mansions of rest.

Relying on its kindness in this as in other things, and actuated by that fervent love toward it which is so natural to a man who views in it the native soil of himself and his progenitors for several generations, I anticipate with pleasing expectation that retreat in which I promise myself to realize without alloy the sweet enjoyment of partaking in the midst of my fellow citizens the benign influence of good laws under a free government—the ever-favorite object of my heart, and the happy reward, as I trust, of our mutual cares, labors, and dangers.

John Adams

John Adams

1797–1801

A DESCENDANT of early settlers of Massachusetts, John Adams was born in Braintree (now Quincy), Massachusetts, in 1735. After his graduation from Harvard College in 1755 he became a barrister; in 1770 he won the acquittal of most of the British soldiers involved in the Boston Massacre. From 1774 to 1778 he was a leader in the movement for independence in the Continental Congress. Jefferson called him "our Colossus on the floor" for his success in persuading the wavering delegates to accept the Declaration of Independence. In 1779 he wrote most of the original draft of the Massachusetts Constitution, which became one of the chief models for the federal constitution and in which he set forth the principle of "a government of laws and not of men." For most of the decade between 1778 and 1788 Adams was in Europe on diplomatic missions, including the negotiations for peace with Britain that produced the Treaty of Paris (1783). He served as vice president during Washington's two terms and succeeded him in 1796.

For most of his administration Adams was occupied with strengthening the nation's defenses and avoiding a war with France. In 1801 he turned the presidency over to Jefferson and the Republicans and returned to his farm in Quincy, where he died in 1826, two years after the election to the presidency of his son John Quincy Adams.

During his years with the Continental Congress, Adams was known, in the words of a colleague, as a "most sensible and forceful speaker." Jefferson said of him that he "was not graceful nor eloquent, nor remarkably fluent, but he came out occasionally with a power of thought and expression that moved us from our seats." Short and stout, often moody and irascible, he did not have the physical presence of a great orator; but so attractive was the display of his intellectual powers that when he spoke, according to another colleague, his listeners "fancied an angel was let down from heaven to illumine the Congress." By the time of Adams's election to the presidency, when he was 61, he was afflicted with palsy and had lost most of his teeth, so that he rarely spoke in public. Instead, he spent a good deal of his time replying to hundreds of letters sent to him by individuals and organizations. These letters, known as "addresses," and Adams's lengthy answers, in which he explained his policies and solicited the support of his readers, were widely reprinted in newspapers.

Adams brought to the presidency a deeper understanding of political history than any statesman of his time. To Jefferson's Enlightenment faith in the perfectibility of man he opposed a Puritan distrust of human nature; he favored a system of checks and balances intended to restrain the tendency of those in power to become corrupt, to place self-interest above the public good. Above all he feared the possibility that democracy would degenerate into mob rule, and it was for this reason that he favored a strong and independent executive. "It is not granted to many leaders to carry out in practice what they had conceived in theory," the historian James MacGregor Burns has said of him. "Adams had that privilege—and that misfortune. . . . But intellectually the ultimate victory was his, for he left a bequest of thought and action on which American leaders would long draw."

Inaugural Address

Philadelphia, Pennsylvania

March 4, 1797

THE INAUGURATION of Adams, marking the nation's first change of administration, took place at Philadelphia with little of the fanfare that had accompanied the two inaugurations of Washington. Adams rode to Congress Hall in his own coach with no escort, wearing a simple gray suit and a ceremonial sword. None of Adams's family was present at the ceremony. Writing to his wife, Abigail, afterward, Adams said: "Your dearest friend never had a more trying day than yesterday. A solemn scene it was indeed, and it was made more affecting to me by the presence of the General [Washington], whose countenance was as serene and unclouded as the day. He seemed to me to enjoy a triumph over me. Methought I heard him say, 'Ay! I am fairly out and you fairly in! See which of us will be happiest.'"

When it was first perceived, in early times, that no middle course for America remained between unlimited submission to a foreign legislature and a total independence of its claims, men of reflection were less apprehensive of danger from the formidable power of fleets and armies they must determine to resist than from those contests and dissensions which would certainly arise concerning the forms of government to be instituted over the whole and over the parts of this extensive country. Relying, however, on the purity of their intentions, the justice of their cause, and the integrity and intelligence of the people, under an overruling Providence which had so signally protected this country from the first, the representatives of this nation, then consisting of little more than half its present number, not only broke to pieces the chains which were forging and the rod of iron that was lifted up, but frankly cut asunder the ties which had bound them, and launched into an ocean of uncertainty.

The zeal and ardor of the people during the Revolutionary War, supplying the place of government, commanded a degree of order sufficient at least for the temporary preservation of society. The confederation which was early felt to be necessary was prepared from the models of the Batavian and Helvetic confederacies, the only examples which remain with any detail and precision in history, and certainly the only ones which the people at large had ever considered. But reflecting on the striking difference in so many particulars between this country and those where a courier may go from the seat of government to the frontier in a single day, it was then certainly foreseen by some who assisted in Congress at the formation of it that it could not be durable.

Negligence of its regulations, inattention to its recommendations, if not disobedience to its authority, not only in individuals but in states, soon appeared with their melancholy consequences—universal languor, jealousies and rivalries of states, decline of navigation and commerce, discouragement of necessary manufactures, universal fall in the value of lands and their produce, contempt of public and private faith, loss of consideration and credit with foreign nations, and at length in discontents, animosities, combinations, partial conventions, and insurrection, threatening some great national calamity.

In this dangerous crisis the people of America were not abandoned by their usual good sense, presence of mind, resolution, or integrity. Measures were pursued to concert a plan to form a more perfect union, establish justice, insure domestic tranquillity, provide for the common defense, promote the general welfare, and secure the blessings of liberty. The public disquisitions, discussions, and deliberations issued in the present happy Constitution of government.

Employed in the service of my country abroad during the whole course of these transactions, I first saw the Constitution of the United States in a foreign country. Irritated by no literary altercation, animated by no public debate, heated by no party animosity, I read it with great satisfaction, as the result of good heads prompted by good hearts, as an experiment better adapted to the genius, character, situation, and relations of this nation and country than any which had ever been proposed or suggested. In its general principles and great outlines it was conformable to such a system of government as I had ever most esteemed, and in states, my own native state in particular, had contributed to establish. Claiming a right of suffrage, in common with my fellow citizens, in the adoption or rejection of a constitution which was to rule me and my posterity, as well as them and their, I did not hesitate to express my approbation of it on all occasions, in public and in private. It was not then, nor has been since, any objection to it in my mind that the executive and Senate were not more permanent. Nor have I ever entertained a thought of promoting any alteration in it but such as the people themselves, in the course of their experience, should see and feel to be necessary or expedient, and by their representatives in Congress and the state legislatures, according to the Constitution itself, adopt and ordain.

Returning to the bosom of my country after a painful separation from it for 10 years, I had the honor to be elected to a station under the new order of things, and I have repeatedly laid myself under the most serious obligations to support the Constitution. The operation of it has equaled the most sanguine expectations of its friends, and from an habitual attention to it, satisfaction in its administration, and delight in its effects upon the peace, order, prosperity, and happiness of the nation I have acquired an habitual attachment to it and veneration for it.

What other form of government, indeed, can so well deserve our esteem and love?

There may be little solidity in an ancient idea that congregations of men into cities and nations are the most pleasing objects in the sight of superior intelligences, but this is very certain, that to a benevolent human mind there can be no spectacle presented by any nation more pleasing, more noble, majestic, or august, than an assembly like that which has so often been seen in this and the other chamber of Congress, of a government in which the executive authority, as well as that of all the branches of the legislature, are exercised by citizens selected at regular periods by their neighbors to make and execute laws for the general good. Can anything essential, anything more than mere ornament and decoration, be added to this by robes and diamonds? Can authority be more amiable and respectable when it descends from accidents or institutions established in remote antiquity than when it springs fresh from the hearts and judgments of an honest and enlightened people? For it is the people only that are represented. It is their power and majesty that is reflected, and only for their good, in every legitimate government, under whatever form it may appear. The existence of such a government as ours for any length of time is a full proof of a general dissemination of knowledge and virtue throughout the whole body of the people. And what object or consideration more pleasing than this can be presented to the human mind? If national pride is ever justifiable or excusable it is when it springs, not from power or riches, grandeur or glory, but from conviction of national innocence, information, and benevolence.

In the midst of these pleasing ideas we should be unfaithful to ourselves if we should ever lose sight of the danger to our liberties if anything partial or extraneous should infect the purity of our free, fair, virtuous, and independent elections. If an election is to be determined by a majority of a single vote, and that can be procured by a party though artifice or corruption, the government may be the choice of a party for its own ends not of the nation for the national good. If that solitary suffrage can be obtained by foreign nations by flattery or menaces, by fraud or violence, by terror, intrigue, or venality, the government may not be the choice of the American people, but of foreign nations. It may be foreign nations who govern us, and not we, the people, who govern ourselves; and candid men will acknowledge that in such cases choice would have little advantage to boast of over lot or chance.

Such is the amiable and interesting system of government (and such are some of the abuses to which it may be exposed) which the people of America have exhibited to the admiration and anxiety of the wise and virtuous of all nations for eight years under the administration of a citizen who, by a long course of great actions, regulated by prudence, justice, temperance, and fortitude, conducting a people inspired with the same virtues and animated with the same ardent partriotism and love of liberty to independence and peace, to increasing wealth and unexampled prosperity, has merited the gratitude of his fellow-citizens, commanded the highest praises of foreign nations, and secured immortal glory with posterity.

In that retirement which is his voluntary choice may he long live to enjoy the delicious recollection of his services, the gratitude of mankind, the happy fruits of them to himself and the world, which are daily increasing, and that splendid prospect of the future fortunes of this country which is opening from year to year. His name may be still a rampart, and the knowledge that he lives a bulwark, against all open or secret enemies of his country's peace. This example has been recommended to the imitation of his successors by both Houses of Congress and by the voice of the legislatures and the people throughout the nation.

On this subject it might become me better to be silent or to speak with diffidence; but as something may be expected, the occasion, I hope, will be admitted as an apology if I venture to say that if a preference, upon principle, of a free republican government, formed upon long and serious reflection, after a diligent and impartial inquiry after truth; if an attachment to the Constitution of the United States, and a conscientious determination to support it until it shall be altered by the judgments and wishes of the people, expressed in the mode prescribed in it; if a respectful attention to the constitutions of the individual states and a constant caution and delicacy toward the state governments; if an equal and impartial regard to the rights, interest, honor, and happiness of all the states in the Union, without preference or regard to a northern or southern, an eastern or western, position, their various political opinions on inessential points or their personal attachments; if a love of virtuous men of all parties and denominations; if a love of science and letters and a wish to patronize every rational effort to encourage schools, colleges, universities, academies, and every institution for propagating knowledge, virtue, and religion among all classes of the people, not only for their benign influence on the happiness of life in all its stages and classes, and of society in all its forms, but as the only means of preserving our Constitution from its natural enemies, the spirit of sophistry, the spirit of party, the spirit of intrigue, the profligacy of corruption, and the pestilence of foreign influence, which is the angel of destruction to elective governments; if a love of equal laws, of justice, and humanity in the interior administration; if an inclination to improve agriculture, commerce, and manufactures for necessity, convenience, and defense; if a spirit of equity and humanity toward the aboriginal nations of America, and a disposition to meliorate their condition by inclining them to be more friendly to us, and our citizens to be more friendly to them; if an inflexible determination to maintain peace and inviolable faith with all nations, and that system of neutrality and impartiality among the belligerent powers of Europe which has been adopted by this government and so solemnly sanctioned by both Houses of Congress and applauded by the legislatures of the states and the public opinion, until it shall be otherwise ordained by Congress; if a personal esteem for the French nation, formed in a residence of seven years chiefly among them, and a sincere desire to preserve the friendship which has been so much for the honor and interst of both nations; if, while the conscious honor and integrity of the people of America and the internal sentiment of their own power and energies must be preserved, and earnest endeavor to investigate every just cause and remove every colorable pretense of complaint; if an intention to pursue by amicable negotiation a reparation for the injuries that have been committed on the commerce of our fellow citizens by whatever nation, and if success can not be obtained, to lay the facts before the legislature, that they may consider what further measures the honor and interest of the government and its constituents demand; if a resolution to do justice as far as may depend upon me, at all times and to all nations, and maintain peace, friendship, and benevolence with all the world; if an unshaken confidence in the honor, spirit, and resources of the American people, on which I have so often hazarded my all and never been deceived; if elevated ideas of the high destinies of this country and of my own duties toward it, founded on a knowledge of the moral principles and intellectual improvements of the people deeply engraven on my mind in early life, and not obscured but exalted by experience and age; and, with humble reverence, I feel it to be my duty to add, if a veneration for the religion of a people who profess and call themselves Christians, and a fixed resolution to consider a decent respect for Christianity among the best recommenda-tions for the public service, can enable me in any degree to comply with your wishes, it shall be my strenuous endeavor that this sagacious injunction of the two Houses, shall not be without effect.

With this great example before me, with the sense and spirit, the faith and honor, the duty and interest, of the same American peo-ple pledged to support the Constitution of the United States, I entertain no doubt of its continuance in all its energy, and my mind is prepared without hesitation to lay myself under the most solemn obligations to support it to the utmost of my power.

And may that Being who is supreme over all, the Patron of Order, the Fountain of Jus-tice, and the Protector in all ages of the world of virtuous liberty, continue His blessing upon this nation and its government and give it all possible success and duration consistent with the ends of His providence.

The Quasi War with France

Philadelphia, Pennsylvania

May 16, 1797

FRANCE, WHICH had given assistance to the American Revolution and which had concluded a commercial treaty with the United States in 1788, was infuriated by the ratification in 1795 of Jay's Treaty, which established arbitration procedures and commercial arrangements between the United States and Great Britain, France's chief enemy. American consternation over the seizure of merchant ships by the French was aggravated when France's ruling Directory rejected the credentials of the U.S. ambassador to France. In a special session of Congress in May 1797, Adams made public the suspension of diplomatic ties with France and urged Congress to undertake without delay the construction of a navy and the organization of a provisional army. The Republicans, who had hitherto restrained themselves from criticizing the president, attacked the speech as a "war whoop" designed to fool the public into accepting a standing army with which the Federalists could impose a monarchy. But the following March, when Adams revealed that three agents of the French government had tried to extort a bribe from an American peace commission—the contretemps known as the "XYZ affair"—the country temporarily united behind Adams, while (as Abigail Adams wrote) "the Jacobins [Republicans] in the Senate & House were struck dumb, and opend not their mouths."

The personal inconveniences to the members of the Senate and of the House of Representatives in leaving their families and private affairs at this season of the year are so obvious that I the more regret the extraordinary occasion which has rendered the convention of Congress indispensable.

It would have afforded me the highest satisfaction to have been able to congratulate you on a restoration of peace to the nations of Europe whose animosities have endangered our tranquillity; but we have still abundant cause of gratitude to the Supreme Dispenser of National Blessings for general health and promising seasons, for domestic and social happiness, for the rapid progress and ample acquisitions of industry through extensive territories, for civil, political, and religious liberty. While other states are desolated with foreign war or convulsed with intestine divisions, the United States present the pleasing prospect of a nation governed by mild and equal laws, generally satisfied with the possession of the rights, neither envying the advantages nor fearing the power of other nations, solicitous only for the maintenance of order and justice and the preservation of liberty, increasing daily in their attachment to a system of government in proportion to their experience of its utility, yielding a ready and general obedience to laws flowing from the reason and resting on the only solid foundation—the affections of the people.

It is with extreme regret that I shall be obliged to turn your thoughts to other circumstances, which admonish us that some of these felicities may not be lasting. But if the tide of our prosperity is full and a reflux commencing, a vigilant circumspection becomes us, that we may meet our reverses with fortitude and extricate ourselves from their consequences with all the skill we possess and all the efforts in our power.

In giving to Congress information of the state of the Union and recommending to their consideration such measures as appear to me to be necessary or expedient, according to my constitutional duty, the causes and the objects of the present extraordinary session will be explained.

After the president of the United States received information that the French government had expressed serious discontents at some proceedings of the government of these states said to affect the interests of France, he thought it expedient to send to that country a new minister, fully instructed to enter on such amicable discussions and to give such candid explanations as might happily remove the discontents and suspicions of the French government and vindicate the conduct of the United States. For this purpose he selected from among his fellow citizens a character whose integrity, talents, experience, and services had placed him in the rank of the most esteemed and respected in the nation. The direct object of his mission was expressed in his letter of credence to the French republic, being "to maintain that good understanding which from the commencement of the alliance had subsisted between the two nations, and to efface unfavorable impressions, banish suspicions, and restore that cordiality which was at once the evidence and pledge of a friendly union." And his instructions were to the same effect, "faithfully to represent the disposition of the government and people of the United States (their disposition being one); to remove jealousies and obviate complaints by shewing that they were groundless, to restore that mutual confidence which had been so unfortunately and injuriously impaired, and to explain the relative interests of both countries and the real sentiments of his own."

A minister thus specially commissioned it was expected would have proved the instrument of restoring mutual confidence between the two republics. The first step of the French government corresponded with that expectation. A few days before his arrival at Paris the French minister of foreign relations informed the American minister then resident at Paris of the formalities to be observed by himself in taking leave, and by his successor preparatory to his reception. These formalities they observed, and on the 9th of December presented officially to the minister of foreign relations, the one a copy of his letters of recall, the other a copy of his letters of credence.

These were laid before the Executive Directory. Two days afterwards the minister of foreign relations informed the recalled American minister that the Executive Directory had determined not to receive another minister plenipotentiary from the United States until after the redress of grievances demanded of the American government, and which the French republic had a right to expect from it. The American minister immediately endeavored to ascertain whether by refusing to receive him it was intended that he should retire from the territories of the French republic, and verbal answers were given that such was the intention of the Directory. For his own justification he desired a written answer, but obtained none until toward the last of January,

when, receiving notice in writing to quit the territories of the republic, he proceeded to Amsterdam, where he proposed to wait for instruction from this government. During his residence at Paris cards of hospitality were refused him, and he was threatened with being subjected to the jurisdiction of the minister of police; but with becoming firmness he insisted on the protection of the law of nations due to him as the known minister of a foreign power. You will derive further information from his dispatches, which will be laid before you.

As it is often necessary that nations should treat for the mutual advantage of their affairs, and especially to accommodate and terminate differences, and as they can treat only by ministers, the right of embassy is well known and established by the law and usage of nations. The refusal on the part of France to receive our minister is, then, the denial of a right; but the refusal to receive him until we have acceded to their demands without discussion and without investagion is to treat us neither as allies nor as friends, nor as a sovereign state.

With this conduct of the French government it will be proper to take into view the public audience given to the late minister of the United States on his taking leave of the Executive Directory. The speech of the president discloses sentiments more alarming than the refusal of a minister, because more dangerous to our independence and union, and at the same time studiously marked with indiginities toward the government of the United States. It evinces a disposition to separate the people of the United States from the government, to persuade them that they have different affections, principles, and interests from those of their fellow citizens whom they themselves have chosen to manage their common concerns, and thus to produce divisions fatal to our peace. Such attempts ought to be repelled with a decision which shall convince France and the world that we are not a degraded people, humiliated under a colonial spirit of fear and sense of inferiority, fitted to be the miserable instruments of foreign influence, and regardless of national honor, character, and interest.

I should have been happy to have thrown a veil over these transactions if it had been possible to conceal them; but they have passed on the great theater of the world, in the face of all Europe and America, and with such circumstances of publicity and solemnity that they can not be disguised and will not soon be forgotten. They have inflicted a wound in the American breast. It is my sincere desire, however, that it may be healed.

It is my sincere desire, and in this I presume I concur with you and with our constituents, to preserve peace and friendship with all nations; and believing that neither the honor nor the interest of the United States absolutely forbid the repetition of advances for securing these desirable objects with France, I shall institute a fresh attempt at negotiation, and shall not fail to promote and accelerate an accommodation on terms compatible with the rights, duties, interests, and honor of the nation. If we have committed errors, and these can be demonstrated, we shall be willing to correct them; if we have done injuries, we shall be willing on conviction to redress them; and equal measures of justice we have a right to expect from France and every other nation.

The diplomatic intercourse between the United States and France being at present suspended, the government has no means of obtaining official information from that country. Nevertheless, there is reason to believe that the Executive Directory passed a decree on the 2d of March last contravening in part the treaty of amity and commerce of 1778, injurious to our lawful commerce and endangering the lives of our citizens. A copy of this decree will be laid before you.

While we are endeavoring to adjust all our differences with France by amicable negotiation, the progress of the war in Europe, the depredations on our commerce, the personal injuries to our citizens, and the general complexion of affairs render it my indispensable duty to recommend to your consideration effectual measures of defense.

The commerce of the United States has become an interesting object of attention, whether we consider it in relation to the wealth and finances or the strength and resources of the nation. With a seacoast of near 2,000 miles in extent, opening a wide field for fisheries, navigation, and commerce, a great portion of our citizens naturally apply their industry and enterprise to these objects. Any serious and permanent injury to commerce would not fail to produce the most embarrassing disorders. To prevent it from being undermined and destroyed it is essential that it receive an adequate protection.

The naval establishment must occur to every man who considers the injuries committed on our commerce, the insults offered to our citizens, and the description of vessels by which these abuses have been practiced. As the sufferings of our mercantile and seafaring citizens can not be ascribed to the omission of duties demandable, considering the neutral situation of our country, they are to be attributed to the hope of impunity arising from a supposed inability on our part to afford protection. To resist the consequences of such impressions on the minds of foreign nations and to guard against the degradation and servility which they must finally stamp on the American character is an important duty of government.

A naval power, next to the militia, is the natural defense of the United States. The experience of the last war would be sufficient to shew that a moderate naval force, such as would be easily within the present abilities of the Union, would have been sufficient to have baffled many formidable transportations of troops from one state to another, which were then practiced. Our seacoasts, from their great extent, are more easily annoyed and more easily defended by a naval force than any other. With all the materials our country abounds; in skill our naval architects and navigators are equal to any, and commanders and seamen will not be wanting.

But although the establishment of a permanent system of naval defense appears to be requisite, I am sensible it can not be formed so speedily and extensively as the present crisis demands. Hitherto I have thought proper to prevent the sailing of armed vessels except on voyages to the East Indies, where general usage and the danger from pirates appeared to render the permission proper. Yet the restriction has originated solely from a wish to prevent collisions with the powers at war, contravening the act of Congress of June, 1794, and not from any doubt entertained by me of the policy and propriety of permitting our vessels to employ means of defense while engaged in a lawful foreign commerce. It remains for Congress to prescribe such regulations as will enable our seafaring citizens to defend themselves against violations of the law of nations, and at the same time restrain them from committing acts of hostility against the powers at war. In addition to this voluntary provision for defense by individual citizens, it appears to me necessary to equip the frigates, and provide other vessels of inferior force, to take under convoy such merchant vessels as shall remain unarmed.

The greater part of the cruisers whose depredations have been most injurious have been built and some of them partially equipped in the United States. Although an effectual remedy may be attended with difficulty, yet I have thought it my duty to present the subject generally to your consideration. If a mode can be devised by the wisdom of Congress to prevent the resources of the United States from being converted into the means of annoying our trade, a great evil will be prevented. With the same view, I think it proper to mention that some of our citizens resident abroad have fitted out privateers, and others have voluntarily taken the command, or entered on board of them, and committed spoliations on the commerce of the United States. Such unnatural and iniquitous practices can be restrained only by severe punishments.

But besides a protection of our commerce on the seas, I think it highly necessarty to protect it at home, where it is collected in our most important ports. The distance of the United States from Europe and the well-known promptitude, ardor, and courage of the people in defense of their country happily diminish the probability of invasion. Nevertheless, to guard against sudden and predatory incursions the situation of some of our principal seaports demands your consideration. And as our country is vulnerable in other interests besides those of its commerce, you will seriously deliberate whether the means of general defense ought not to be increased by an addition to the regular artillery and cavalry, and by arrangements for forming a provisional army.

With the same view, and as a measure which, even in a time of universal peace, ought not to be neglected, I recommend to your consideration a revision of the laws for organizing, arming, and disciplining the militia, to render that natural and safe defense of the country efficacious.

Although it is very true that we ought not to involve ourselves in the political system of Europe, but to keep ourselves always distinct and separate from it if we can, yet to effect this separation, early, punctual, and continual information of the current chain of events and of the political projects in contemplation is no less necessary than if we were directly concerned in them. It is necessary, in order to the discovery of the efforts made to draw us into the vortex, in season to make preparations against them. However we may consider ourselves, the maritime and commercial powers of the world will consider the United States of America as forming a weight in that balance of power in Europe which never can be forgotten or neglected. It would not only be against our interst, but it would be doing wrong to one-half of Europe, at least, if we should voluntarily throw ourselves into either scale. It is a natural policy for a nation that studies to be neutral to consult with other nations engaged in the same studies and pursuits. At the same time that measures might be pursued with this view, our treaties with Prussia and Sweden, one of which is expired and the other near expiring, might be renewed.

Gentlemen of the House of Representatives:

It is particularly your province to consider the state of the public finances, and to adopt such measures respecting them as exigencies shall be found to require. The preservation of public credit, the regular extinguishment of the public debt, and a provision of funds to defray any extraordinary expenses will of course call for your serious attention. Although the imposition of new burthens can not be in itself agreeable, yet there is no ground to doubt that the American people will expect from you such measures as their actual engagements, their present security, and future interests demand.

Gentlemen of the Senate and Gentlemen of the House of Representatives:

The present situation of our country imposes an obligation on all the departments of government to adopt an explicit and decided conduct. In my situation an exposition of the principles by which my administration will be governed ought not to be omitted.

It is impossible to conceal ourselves or the world what has been before observed, that endeavors have been employed to foster and establish a division between the government and people of the United States. To investigate the causes which have encouraged this attempt is not necessary; but to repel, by decided and united councils, insinuations so derogatory to the honor and aggressions so dangerous to the Constitution, union, and even independence of the nation is an indispensable duty.

It must not be permitted to be doubted whether the people of the United States will support the government established by their voluntary consent and appointed by their free choice, or whether, by surrendering themselves to the direction of foreign and domestic factions, in opposition to their own government, they will forfeit the honorable station they have hitherto maintained.

For myself, having never been indifferent to what concerned the interests of my country, devoted the best part of my life to obtain and support its independence, and constantly witnessed the patriotism, fidelity, and perseverance of my fellow citizens on the most trying occasions, it is not for me to hesitate or abandon a cause in which my heart has been so long engaged.

Convinced that the conduct of the government has been just and impartial to foreign nations, that those internal regulations which have been established by law for the preservation of peace are in their nature proper, and that they have been fairly executed, nothing will ever be done by me to impair the national engagements, to innovate upon principles which have been so deliberately and uprightly established, or to surrender in any manner the rights of the government. To enable me to maintain this declaration I rely, under God, with entire confidence on the firm and enlightened support of the national legislature and upon the virtue and patriotism of my fellow citizens.

Fourth Annual Message to Congress

Washington, D.C.

November 22, 1800

By 1800 THE SEAT of government had been moved to the District of Columbia, a near-wilderness of swamps, woods, and fields. Congress assembled in November in the unfinished Capitol to hear Adams deliver his fourth annual message, in the preparation of which he had relied on the assistance of his secretary of state, John Marshall, whom Adams was soon to appoint chief justice of the Supreme Court.

Adams took considerable pride in the growth of the navy. At the beginning of his administration, American merchant ships were under constant attack by French privateers and warships, but the nation could provide no defense; its navy consisted of three unfinished frigates. Under Adams's prodding, Congress created the Department of the Navy in 1798 and eventually authorized the construction of 50 war vessels, enabling the United States to maintain its neutrality and protect its trade.

I congratulate the people of the United States on the assembling of Congress at the permanent seat of their government, and I congratulate you, gentlemen, on the prospect of a residence not to be changed. Although there is cause to apprehend that accommodations are not now so complete as might be wished, yet there is great reason to believe that this inconvenience will cease with the present session.

It would be unbecoming the representatives of this nation to assemble for the first time in this solemn temple without looking up to the Supreme Ruler of the Universe and imploring His blessing.

May this territory be the residence of virtue and happiness! In this city may that piety and virtue, and that wisdom and magnanimity, that constancy and self-government, which adorned the great character whose name it bears be forever held in veneration! Here and throughout our country may simple manners, pure morals, and true religion flourish forever!

It is with you, gentlemen, to consider whether the local powers over the District of Columbia vested by the Constitution in the Congress of the United States shall be immediately exercised. If in your opinion this important trust ought now to be executed, you can not fail while performing it to take into view the future probable situation of the territory for the happiness of which you are about to provide. You will consider it as the capital of a great nation advancing with unexampled rapidity in arts, in commerce, in wealth, and in population, and possessing within itself those energies and resources which, if not thrown away or lamentably misdirected, will secure to it a long course of prosperity and self-government.

In compliance with a law of the last session of Congress, the officers and soldiers of the temporary army have been discharged. It affords real pleasure to recollect the honorable testimony they gave of the patriotic motives which brought them into the service of their country, by the readiness and regularity with which they returned to the station of private citizens.

It is in every point of view of such primary importance to carry the laws into prompt and faithful execution, and to render that part of the administration of justice which the Constitution and laws devolve on the federal courts as convenient to the people as may consist with their present circumstances, that I can not omit once more to recommend to your serious consideration the judiciary system of the United States. No subject is more interesting than this to the public happiness, and to none can those improvements which may have been suggested by experience be more beneficially applied....

The envoys extraordinary and ministers plenipotentiary from the United States to France were received by the First Consul with the respect due to their character, and three persons with equal powers were appointed to treat with them. Although at the date of the last official intelligence the negotiation had not terminated, yet it is to be hoped that our efforts to effect an accommodation will at length meet with a success proportioned to the sincerity with which they have been so often repeated.

While our best endeavors for the preservation of harmony with all nations will continue to be used, the experience of the world and our own experience admonish us of the insecurity of trusting too confidently to their success. We can not, without committing a dangerous imprudence, abandon those measures of self-protection which are adapted to our situation and to which, notwithstanding our pacific policy, the violence and injustice of others may again compel us to resort. While our vast extent of seacoast, the commercial and agricultural habits of our people, the great capital they will continue to trust on the ocean, suggest the system of defense which will be most beneficial to ourselves, our distance from Europe and our resources for maritime strength will enable us to employ it with effect. Seasonable and systematic arrangements, so far as our resources will justify, for a navy adapted to defensive war, and which may in case of necessity be quickly brought into use, seem to be as much recommended by a wise and true economy as by a just regard for our future tranquility, for the safety of our shores, and for the protection of our property committed to the ocean.

The present navy of the United States, called suddenly into existence by a great national exigency, has raised us in our own esteem, and by the protection afforded to our commerce has effected to the extent of our expectations the objects for which it was created.

In connection with a navy ought to be contemplated the fortification of some of our principal seaports and harbors. A variety of considerations, which will readily suggest themselves, urge an attention to this measure of precaution. To give security to our principal ports considerable sums have already been expended, but the works remain incomplete. It is for Congress to determine whether additional appropriations shall be made in order to render competent to the intended purposes the fortifications which have been commenced.

The manufacture of arms within the United States still invites the attention of the national legislature. At a considerable expense to the public this manufacture has been brought to such a state of maturity as, with continued encouragement, will supersede the necessity of future importations from foreign countries.

Gentlemen of the House of Representatives:

I shall direct the estimates of the appropriations necessary for the ensuing year, together with an account of the public revenue and expenditure to a late period, to be laid before you. I observe with much satisfaction that the product of the revenue during the present year has been more considerable than during any former equal period. This result affords conclusive evidence of the great resources of this country and of the wisdom and efficiency of the measures which have been adopted by Congress for the protection of commerce and preservation of public credit.

Gentlemen of the Senate and Gentlemen of the House of Representatives:

As one of the grand community of nations, our attention is irresistibly drawn to the important scenes which surround us. If they have exhibited an uncommon portion of calamity, it is the province of humanity to deplore and of wisdom to avoid the causes which may have produced it. If, turning our eyes homeward, we find reason to rejoice at the prospect which presents itself; if we perceive the interior of our country prosperous, free, and happy; if all enjoy in safety, under the protection of laws emanating only from the general will, the fruits of their own labor, we ought to fortify and cling to those institutions which have been the source of such real felicity and resist with unabating perseverance the progress of those dangerous innovations which may diminish their influence.

To your patriotism, gentlemen, has been confided the honorable duty of guarding the public interests; and while the past is to your country a sure pledge that it will be faithfully discharged, permit me to assure you that your labors to promote the general happiness will receive from me the most zealous cooperation.

Courtesy of Library of Congress

Thomas Jefferson

Thomas Jefferson

1801–1809

THE POLYMATH and political philosopher Thomas Jefferson was born in 1743 into a prosperous Virginia family. He was given a classical education, studied law, and by 1769 had been elected to the House of Burgesses. As a delegate in 1775–1776 to the Second Continental Congress, already renowned at the age of 33 for his power of literary expression and for his dedication to the ideals of the Enlightenment, he was asked to draft the Declaration of Independence, a statement of the principles on which the delegates based the legal and moral legitimacy of their rebellion.

In George Washington's first administration, Jefferson served as secretary of state. His disagreements with Secretary of the Treasury Alexander Hamilton over matters of fundamental political principle—above all, over the threat to republicanism posed by Hamilton's promotion of a strong, financially dominant central government—eventually resulted in the development of the two-party system that has dominated American politics ever since. In the election of 1800 he polled the same number of electoral votes as Aaron Burr and was chosen over him by the House of Representatives. Four years later, Jefferson was reelected by a landslide.

Jefferson's dedication to peace and reason was felt throughout his presidency. Not happy to see the division of the citizenry into parties, he sought reconciliation with the more moderate Federalists. In his relations with his cabinet and with Congress he avoided overt conflict, relying on consultation and persuasion, often inviting politicans to dinners at the White House where, in homespun and old slippers, he dazzled them with brilliant table talk. His reform of the economy in accordance with Republican ideology and his purchase of the immense Louisiana Territory in 1803 contributed to his popularity. Jefferson's plans for the development of the nation were nearly wrecked, however, by the devastating results of his embargo of American commerce with Europe, in effect during the last year of his second administration. "I have the consolation," he told a correspondent, "to reflect that during the period of my administration not a drop of blood of a single fellow citizen was shed by the sword of war or of the law." In retirement he lived at Monticello, his Virginia estate, where he died in 1826.

The historian Saul K. Padover noted the paradoxical nature of his achievement: "The most wide-ranging intellect of his day, he was at the same time the champion of democratic rights. A landed gentleman, he was the leader of the common people. The most successful political figure of his generation, he never made a political speech. A party leader of matchless adroitness, he had practically no personal contact with the mass of his followers. He was at once a subtle political theorist and a wily politician, a philosopher and a strategist. Soft-spoken in manner, he was uncompromising in principle. . . . Jefferson was the master formulator of the ideas and ideals of democracy on the philosophical basis of inalienable natural rights and an inherent system of moral values."

As a writer, Jefferson was master of a lively, muscular prose style; he was, according to Padover, "a writer of matchless skill and beguiling felicity." He once observed that "the most valuable of all talents is that of never using two words where one will do." Yet he was a poor orator. His predecessors' custom of going to Congress in person to read the annual presidential message was abandoned by Jefferson, partly because of the inconvenience to the legislators of assembling at the White House to reply, and partly to avoid the discomfort of having to make a speech. Instead, he appointed an aide to deliver the message, a practice that was followed by subsequent presidents until Woodrow Wilson reversed it.

First Inaugural Address

Washington, D.C.

March 4, 1801

THE ELECTION of 1800, which brought the Republicans to power for the first time, was considered by Jefferson a peaceful revolution—a restoration of the ideals of the original Revolution and a vindication of his insistence that it was possible for citizens to change their governors through a contest of ideas rather than of arms. On the day of the inauguration he walked from his boarding house to the unfinished Capitol building and was greeted at the door with an artillery salute. In the Senate chamber, where he took the oath of office, he delivered his inaugural address in a voice so quiet that few of his hundreds of listeners could hear him.

The address was published in the *National Intelligencer* on the same day. Subsequent editors have altered the text, so that, for example, the terms republicans and federalists, used by Jefferson in a general sense, became a specific reference to Republicans and Federalists.

Called upon to undertake the duties of the first executive office of our country, I avail myself of the presence of that portion of my fellow citizens which is here assembled to express my grateful thanks for the favor with which they have been pleased to look toward me, to declare a sincere consciousness that the task is above my talents, and that I approach it with those anxious and awful presentiments which the greatness of the charge and the weakness of my powers so justly inspire. A rising nation, spread over a wide and fruitful land, traversing all the seas with the rich productions of their industry, engaged in commerce with nations who feel power and forget right, advancing rapidly to destinies beyond the reach of mortal eye—when I contemplate these transcendent objects, and see the honor, the happiness, and the hopes of this beloved country committed to the issue and the auspices of this day, I shrink from the contemplation, and humble myself before the magnitude of the undertaking. Utterly, indeed, should I despair did not the presence of many whom I here see remind me that in the other high authorities provided by our Constitution I shall find resources of wisdom, of virtue, and of zeal on which to rely under all difficulties. To you, then, gentlemen, who are charged with the sovereign functions of legislation, and to those associated with you, I look with encouragement for that guidance and support which may enable us to steer with safety the vessel in which we are all embarked amidst the conflicting elements of a troubled world.

During the contest of opinion through which we have passed the animation of discussions and of exertions has sometimes worn an aspect which might impose on strangers unused to think freely and to speak and to write what they think; but this being now decided by the voice of the nation, announced according to the rules of the Constitution, all will, of course, arrange themselves under the will of the law, and unite in common efforts for the common good. All, too, will bear in mind this sacred principle, that though the will of the majority is in all cases to prevail, that will to be rightful must be reasonable; that the minority possess their equal rights, which equal law must protect, and to violate would be oppression. Let us, then, fellow citizens, unite with one heart and one mind. Let us restore to social intercourse that harmony and affection without which liberty and even life itself are but dreary things. And let us reflect that, having banished from our land that religious intolerance under which mankind so long bled and suffered, we have yet gained little if we countenance a political intolerance as despotic, as wicked, and capable of as bitter and bloody persecutions. During the throes and convulsions of the ancient world, during the agonizing spasms of infuriated man, seeking through blood and slaughter his long-lost liberty, it was not wonderful that the agitaiton of the billows should reach even this distant and peaceful shore; and this should be more felt and feared by some and less by others, and should divide opinions as to measures of safety. But every difference of opinion is not a difference of principle. We have called by different names brethren of the same principle. We are all republicans, we are all federalists. If there be any among us who would wish to dissolve this Union or to change its republican form, let them stand undisturbed as monuments of the safety with which error of opinion may be tolerated where reason is left free to combat it. I know, indeed, that some honest men fear that a republican government can not be strong, that this government is not strong enough; but would the honest patriot, in the full tide of successful experiment, abandon a government which has so far kept us free and firm on the theoretic and visionary fear that this government, the world's best hope, may by possibility want energy to preserve itself? I trust not. I believe this, on the contrary, the strongest government on earth. I believe it the only one where every man, at the call of the law, would fly to the standard of the law, and would meet invasions of the public order as his own personal concern. Sometimes it is said that man can not be trusted with the government of himself. Can he, then, be trusted with the government of others? Or have we found angels in the forms of kings to govern him? Let history answer this question.

Let us, then, with courage and confidence pursue our own federal and republican principles, our attachment to union and representative government. Kindly separated by nature and a wide ocean from the exterminating havoc of one quarter of the globe; too high-minded to endure the degradations of the others; possessing a chosen country, with room enough for our descendants to the thousandth and thousandth generation; entertaining a due sense of our equal right to the use of our own faculties, to the acquisitions of our own industry, to honor and confidence from our fellow citizens, resulting not from birth, but from our actions and their sense of them; enlightened by a benign religion, professed, indeed, and practiced in various forms, yet all of them inculcating honesty, truth, temperance, gratitude, and the love of man; acknowledging and adoring an overruling Providence, which by all its dispensations proves that it delights in the happiness of man here and his greater happiness hereafter—with all these blessings, what more is necessary to make us a happy and a prosperous people? Still one thing more, fellow citizens—a wise and frugal government, which shall restrain men from injuring one another, shall leave them otherwise free to regulate their own pursuits of industry and improvement, and shall not take from the mouth of labor the bread it has earned. This is the sum of good government, and this is necessary to close the circle of our felicities.

About to enter, fellow citizens, on the exercise of duties which comprehend everything dear and valuable to you, it is proper you should understand what I deem the essential principles of our government, and consequently those which ought to shape its administration. I will compress them within the narrowest compass they will bear, stating the general principle, but not all its limitations. Equal and exact justice to all men, of whatever state or persuasion, religious or political; peace, commerce, and honest friendship with all nations, entangling alliances with none; the support of the state governments in all their rights, as the most competent administrations for our domestic concerns and the surest bulwarks against antirepublican tendencies; the preservation of the general government in its whole constitutional vigor, as the sheet anchor of our peace at home and safety abroad; a jealous care of the right of election by the people—a mild and safe corrective of abuses which are lopped by the sword of revolution where peaceable remedies are unprovided; absolute acquiescence in the decisions of the majority, the vital principle of republics, from which is no appeal but to force, the vital principle and immediate parent of despotism; a well-disciplined militia, our best reliance in peace and for the first moments of war, till regulars may relieve them; the supremacy of the civil over the military authority; economy in the public expense, that labor may be lightly burthened; the honest payment of our debts and sacred preservation of the public faith; encouragement of agriculture, and of commerce as its handmaid; the diffusion of information and arraignment of all abuses at the bar of the public reason; freedom of religion; freedom of the press, and freedom of person under the protection of the habeas corpus, and trial by juries impartially selected. These principles form the bright constellation which has gone before us and guided our steps through an age of revolution and reformation. The wisdom of our sages and blood of our heroes have been devoted to their attainment. They should be the creed of our political faith, the text of civic instruction, the touchstone by which to try the services of those we trust; and should we wander from them in moments of error or of alarm, let us hasten to retrace our steps and to regain the road which alone leads to peace, liberty, and safety.

I repair, then, fellow citizens, to the post you have assigned me. With experience enough in subordinate offices to have seen the difficulties of this the greatest of all, I have learnt to expect that it will rarely fall to the lot of imperfect man to retire from this station with the reputation and the favor which bring him into it. Without pretensions to that high confidence you reposed in our first and greatest revolutionary character, whose preeminent services had entitled him to the first place in his country's love and destined for him the fairest page in the volume of faithful history, I ask so much confidence only as may give firmness and effect to the legal administration of your affairs. I shall often go wrong through defect of judgment. When right, I shall often be thought wrong by those whose positions will not command a view of the whole ground. I ask your indulgence for my own errors, which will never be intentional, and your support against the errors of others who may condemn what they would not if seen in all its parts. The approbation implied by your suffrage is a great consolation to me for the past, and my future solicitude will be to retain the good opinion of those who have bestowed it in advance, to conciliate that of others by doing them all the good in my power, and to be instrumental to the happiness and freedom of all.

Relying, then, on the patronage of your good will, I advance with obedience to the work, ready to retire from it whenever you become sensible how much better choice it is in your power to make. And may that Infinite Power which rules the destinies of the universe lead our councils to what is best, and give them a favorable issue for your peace and prosperity.

Message to Congress about the Lewis and Clark Expedition

Washington, D.C.
January 18, 1803

AT THE BEGINNING of 1803, President Thomas Jefferson sent a message to both houses of Congress requesting special funding for an expedition through the newly acquired lands of the Louisiana Purchase. Given the political and international situations, at a time when the Napoleonic wars were starting up again, the president thought that the subject of an expedition into the American West had to be brought up with care. As a result, he framed his funding request in terms of economic growth rather than scientific knowledge.

Jefferson begins by discussing unrest among Native Americans about the sale of their lands. He then advocates an increase in the number of trading posts on Native American lands to persuade Indians to follow his plan of assimilation. Jefferson next proposes that Meriwether Lewis and a small party of volunteers be sent to explore the west, perhaps as far as the Pacific Ocean. Their tasks would include contacting Native Americans to discuss commerce and sites for potential trading posts. He notes that other countries undertook trips to explore new areas and that the U.S. government has the right and responsibility to do likewise. He hints at the scientific goal of the expedition only at the end of the message.

As the continuance of the act for establishing trading houses with the Indian tribes will be under the consideration of the Legislature at its present session, I think it my duty to communicate the views which have guided me in the execution of that act, in order that you may decide on the policy of continuing it in the present or any other form, or discontinue it altogether if that shall, on the whole, seem most for the public good.

The Indian tribes residing within the limits of the United States have for a considerable time been growing more and more uneasy at the constant diminution of the territory they occupy, although effected by their own voluntary sales, and the policy has long been gaining strength with them of refusing absolutely all further sale on any conditions, insomuch that at this time it hazards their friendship and excites dangerous jealousies and perturbations in their minds to make any overture for the purchase of the smallest portions of their land. A very few tribes only are not yet obstinately in these dispositions. In order peaceably to counteract this policy of theirs and to provide an extension of territory which the rapid increase of our numbers will call for, two measures are deemed expedient. First. To encourage them to abandon hunting, to apply to the raising stock, to agriculture, and domestic manufacture, and thereby prove to themselves that less land and labor will maintain them in this better than in their former mode of living. The extensive forests necessary in the hunting life will then become useless, and they will see advantage in exchanging them for the means of improving their farms and of increasing their domestic comforts. Secondly. To multiply trading houses among them, and place within their reach those things which will contribute more to their domestic comfort than the possession of extensive but uncultivated wilds. Experience and reflection will develop to them the wisdom of exchanging what they can spare and we want for what we can spare and they want. In leading them thus to agriculture, to factures, and civilization; in bringing together their and our sentiments, and in preparing them ultimately to participate in the benefits of our Government, I trust and believe we are acting for their greatest good. At these trading houses we have pursued the principles of the act of Congress which directs that the commerce shall be carried on liberally, and requires only that the capital stock shall not be diminished. We consequently undersell private traders, foreign and domestic, drive them from the competition, and thus, with the good will of the Indians, rid ourselves of a description of men who are constantly endeavoring to excite in the Indian mind suspicions, fears, and irritations toward us. A letter now enclosed shows the effect of our competition on the operations of the traders, while the Indians, perceiving the advantage of purchasing from us, are soliciting generally our establishment of trading houses among them. In one quarter this is particularly interesting. The Legislature, reflecting on the late occurrences on the Mississippi, must be sensible how desirable it is to possess a respectable breadth of country on that river, from our southern limit to the Illinois, at least, so that we may present as firm a front on that as on our eastern border. We possess what is below the Yazoo, and can probably acquire a certain breadth from the Illinois and Wabash to the Ohio; but between the Ohio and Yazoo the country all belongs to the Chickasaws, the most friendly tribe within our limits, but the most decided against the alienation of lands. The portion of their country most important for us is exactly that which they do not inhabit. Their settlements are not on the Mississippi, but in the interior country. They have lately shown a desire to become agricultural, and this leads to the desire of buying implements and comforts. In the strengthening and gratifying of these wants I see the only prospect of planting on the Mississippi itself the means of its own safety. Duty has required me to submit these views to the judgment of the Legislature, but as their disclosure might embarrass and defeat their effect, they are committed to the special confidence of the two Houses.

While the extension of the public commerce among the Indian tribes may deprive of that source of profit such of our citizens as are engaged in it, it might be worthy the attention of Congress in their care of individual as well as of the general interest to point in another direction the enterprise of these citizens, as profitably for themselves and more usefully for the public. The river Missouri and the Indians inhabiting it are not as well known as is rendered desirable by their connection with the Mississippi, and consequently with us. It is, however, understood that the country on that river is inhabited by numerous tribes, who furnish great supplies of furs and peltry to the trade of another nation, carried on in a high latitude through an infinite number of portages and lakes shut up by ice through a long season. The commerce on that line could bear no competition with that of the Missouri, traversing a moderate climate, offering, according to the best accounts, a continued navigation from its source, and possibly with a single portage from the Western Ocean, and finding to the Atlantic a choice of channels through the Illinois or Wabash, the Lakes and Hudson, through the Ohio and Susquehanna, or Potomac or James rivers, and through the Tennessee and Savannah rivers. An intelligent officer, with ten or twelve chosen men, fit for the enterprise and willing to undertake it, taken from our posts where they may be spared without inconvenience, might explore the whole line, even to the Western Ocean, have conferences with the natives on the subject of commercial intercourse, get admission among them for our traders as others are admitted, agree on convenient deposits for an interchange of articles, and return with the information acquired in the course of two summers. Their arms and accouterments, some instruments of observation, and light and cheap presents for the Indians would be all the apparatus they could carry, and with an expectation of a soldier's portion of land on their return would constitute the whole expense. Their pay would be going on whether here or there. While other civilized nations have encountered great expense to enlarge the boundaries of knowledge by undertaking voyages of discovery, and for other literary purposes, in various parts and directions, our nation seems to owe to the same object, as well as to its own interests, to explore this the only line of easy communication across the continent, and so directly traversing our own part of it. The interests of commerce place the principal object within the constitutional powers and care of Congress, and that it should incidentally advance the geographical knowledge of our own continent can not but be an additional gratification. The nation claiming the territory, regarding this as a literary pursuit, which it is in the habit of permitting within its dominions, would not be disposed to view it with jealousy, even if the expiring state of its interests there did not render it a matter of indifference. The appropriation of $2,500 for "the purpose of extending the external commerce of the United States," while understood and considered by the Executive as giving the legislative sanction, would cover the undertaking from notice and prevent the obstructions which interested individuals might otherwise previously prepare in its way.

Second Inaugural Address

Washington, D.C.

March 4, 1805

THE GREATER PART of Jefferson's speech was devoted to a summary of his performance during his first term. His remarks on the Indians, as he related in his notes to the draft of the address, were intended as an indirect attack on the reactionary mentality that seeks to hinder progress: "This is a proper topic not only to promote the work of humanizing our citizens towards these people, but to conciliate to us the good opinion of Europe on the subject of the Indians. This, however, might have been done in half the compass it here occupies. But every respector of science, every friend to political reformation must have observed with indignation the hue & cry raised against philosophy & the rights of man; and it really seems as if they would be overborne & barbarism, bigotry & despotism would recover the ground they have lost by the advance of the public understanding. I have thought the occasion justified some discountenance of these anti-social doctrines, some testimony against them, but not to commit myself in direct warfare on them, I have thought it best to say what is directly applied to the Indians only, but admits by inference a more general extension."

Proceeding, fellow citizens, to that qualification which the Constitution requires before my entrance on the charge again conferred on me, it is my duty to express the deep sense I entertain of this new proof of confidence from my fellow citizens at large, and the zeal with which it inspires me so to conduct myself as may best satisfy their just expectations.

On taking this station on a former occasion I declared the principles on which I believed it my duty to administer the affairs of our commonwealth. My conscience tells me I have on every occasion acted up to that declaration according to its obvious import and to the understanding of every candid mind.

In the transaction of your foreign affairs we have endeavored to cultivate the friendship of all nations, and especially of those with which we have the most important relations. We have done them justice on all occasions, favored where favor was lawful, and cherished mutual interests and intercourse on fair and equal terms. We are firmly convinced, and we act on that conviction, that with nations as with individuals our interests soundly calculated will ever be found inseparable from our moral duties, and history bears witness to the fact that a just nation is trusted on its word when recourse is had to armaments and wars to bridle others.

At home, fellow citizens, you best know whether we have done well or ill. The suppression of unnecessary offices, of useless establishments and expenses, enabled us to discontinue our internal taxes. These, covering our land with officers and opening our doors to their intrusions, had already begun that process of domiciliary vexation which once entered is scarcely to be restrained from reaching successively every article of property and produce. If among these taxes some minor ones fell which had not been inconvenient, it was because their amount would not have paid the officers who collected them, and because, if they had any merit, the state authorities might adopt them instead of others less approved.

The remaining revenue on the consumption of foreign articles is paid chiefly by those who can afford to add foreign luxuries to domestic comforts, being collected on our seaboard and frontiers only, and, incorporated with the transactions of our mercantile citizens, it may be the pleasure and the pride of an American to ask, What farmer, what mechanic, what laborer ever sees a taxgatherer of the United States? These contributions enable us to support the current expenses of the government, to fulfill contracts with foreign nations, to extinguish the native right of soil within our limits, to extend those limits, and to apply such a surplus to our public debts as places at a short day their final redemption, and that redemption once effected the revenue thereby liberated may, by a just repartition of it among the states and a corresponding amendment of the Constitution, be applied *in time of peace* to rivers, canals, roads, arts, manufactures, education, and other great objects within each state. *In time of war,* if injustice by ourselves or others must sometimes produce war, increased as the same revenue will be by increased population and consumption, and aided by other resources reserved for that crisis, it may meet within the year all the expenses of the year without encroaching on the rights of future generations by burthening them with the debts of the past. War will then be but a suspension of useful works, and a return to a state of peace a return to the progress of improvement.

I have said, fellow citizens, that the income reserved had enabled us to extend our limits, but that extension may possibly pay for itself before we are called on, and in the meantime may keep down the accruing interest; in all events, it will replace the advances we shall have made. I know that the acquisition of Louisiana has been disapproved by some from a candid apprehension that the enlargement of our territory would endanger its union. But who can limit the extent to which the federative principle may operate effectively? The larger our association the less will it be shaken by local passions; and in any view is it not better that the opposite bank of the Mississippi should be settled by our own brethren and children than by strangers of another family? With which should we be most likely to live in harmony and friendly intercourse?

In matters of religion I have considered that its free exercise is placed by the Constitution independent of the powers of the general government. I have therefore undertaken on no occasion to prescribe the religious exercises suited to it, but have left them, as the Constitution found them, under the direction and discipline of the church or state authorities acknowledged by the several religious societies.

The aboriginal inhabitants of these countries I have regarded with the commiseration their history inspires. Endowed with the faculties and the rights of men, breathing an ardent love of liberty and independence, and occupying a country which left them no desire but to be undisturbed, the stream of overflowing population from other regions directed itself on these shores; without power to divert or habits to contend against it, they have been overwhelmed by the current or driven before it; now reduced within limits too narrow for the hunter's state, humanity enjoins us to teach them agriculture and the domestic arts; to encourage them to that industry which alone can enable them to maintain their place in existence and to prepare them in time for that state of society which to bodily comforts adds the improvement of the mind and morals. We have therefore liberally furnished them with the implements of husbandry and household use; we have placed among them instructors in the arts of first necessity, and they are covered with the aegis of the law against aggressors from among ourselves.

But the endeavors to enlighten them on the fate which awaits their present course of life, to induce them to exercise their reason, follow its dictates, and change their pursuits with the change of circumstances have powerful obstacles to encounter; they are combated by the habits of their bodies, prejudices of their minds, ignorance, pride, and the influence of interested and crafty individuals among them who feel themselves something in the present order of things and fear to become nothing in any other. These persons inculcate a sanctimonious reverence for the customs of their ancestors; that whatsoever they did must be done through all time; that reason is a false guide, and to advance under its counsel in their physical, moral, or political condition is perilous innovation; that their duty is to remain as their Creator made them, ignorance being safety and knowledge full of danger; in short, my friends, among them also is seen the action and counteraction of good sense and of bigotry; they too have their antiphilosophists who find an interest in keeping things in their present state, who dread reformation, and exert all their faculties to maintain the ascendency of habit over the duty of improving our reason and obeying its mandates.

In giving these outlines I do not mean, fellow citizens, to arrogate to myself the merit of the measures. That is due, in the first place, to the reflecting character of our citizens at large, who, by the weight of public opinion, influence and strengthen the public measures. It is due to the sound discretion with which they select from among themselves those to whom they confide the legislative duties. It is due to the zeal and wisdom of the characters thus selected, who lay the foundations of public happiness in wholesome laws, the execution of which alone remains for others, and it is due to the able and faithful auxiliaries, whose patriotism has associated them with me in the executive functions.

During this course of administration, and in order to disturb it, the artillery of the press has been leveled against us, charged with whatsoever its licentiousness could devise or dare. These abuses of an institution so important to freedom and science are deeply to be regretted, inasmuch as they tend to lessen its usefulness and to sap its safety. They might, indeed, have been corrected by the wholesome punishments reserved to and provided by the laws of the several states against falsehood and defamation, but public duties more urgent press on the time of public servants, and the offenders have therefore been left to find their punishment in the public indignation.

Nor was it uninteresting to the world that an experiment should be fairly and fully made, whether freedom of discussion, unaided by power, is not sufficient for the propagation and protection of truth—whether a government conducting itself in the true spirit of its constitution, with zeal and purity, and doing no act which it would be unwilling the whole world should witness, can be written down by falsehood and defamation. The experiment has been tried; you have witnessed the scene; our fellow citizens looked on, cool and collected; they saw the latent source from which these outrages proceeded; they gathered around their public functionaries, and when the Constitution called them to the decision by suffrage, they pronounced their verdict, honorable to those who had served them and consolatory to the friend of man who believes that he may be trusted with the control of his own affairs.

No inference is here intended that the laws provided by the states against false and defamatory publications should not be enforced; he who has time renders a service to public morals and public tranquillity in reforming these abuses by the salutary coercions of the law; but the experiment is noted to prove that, since truth and reason have maintained their ground against false opinions in league with false facts, the press, confined to truth, needs no other legal restraint; the public judgment will correct false reasonings and opinions on a full hearing of all parties; and no other definite line can be drawn between the inestimable liberty of the press and its demoralizing licentiousness. If there be still improprieties which this rule would not restrain, its supplement must be sought in the censorship of public opinion.

Contemplating the union of sentiment now manifested so generally as auguring harmony and happiness to our future course, I offer to our country sincere congratulations. With those, too, not yet rallied to the same point the disposition to do so is gaining strength; facts are piercing through the veil drawn over them, and our doubting brethren will at length see that the mass of their fellow citizens with whom they can not yet resolve to act as to principles and measures, think as they think and desire what they desire; that our wish as well as theirs is that the public efforts may be directed honestly to the public good, that peace be cultivated, civil and religious liberty unassailed, law and order preserved equality of rights maintained, and that state of property, equal or unequal, which results to every man from his own industry or that of his father's. When satisfied of these views it is not in human nature that they should not approve and support them. In the meantime let us cherish them with patient affection, let us do them justice, and more than justice, in all competitions of interest, and we need not doubt that truth, reason, and their own interests will at length prevail, will gather them into the fold of their country, and will complete that entire union of opinion which gives to a nation the blessing of harmony and the benefit of all its strength.

I shall now enter on the duties to which my fellow citizens have again called me, and shall proceed in the spirit of those principles which they have approved. I fear not that any motives of interest may lead me astray; I am sensible of no passion which could seduce me knowingly from the path of justice, but the weaknesses of human nature and the limits of my own understanding will produce errors of judgment sometimes injurious to your interests. I shall need, therefore, all the indulgence which I have heretofore experienced from my constituents; the want of it will certainly not lessen with increasing years. I shall need, too, the favor of that Being in whose hands we are, who led our fathers, as Israel of old, from their native land and planted them in a country flowing with all the necessaries and comforts of life; who has covered our infancy with His providence and our riper years with His wisdom and power, and to whose goodness I ask you to join in supplications with me that He will so enlighten the minds of your servants, guide their councils, and prosper their measures that whatsoever they do shall result in your good, and shall secure to you the peace, friendship, and approbation of all nations.

Address to the Wolf and People of the Mandan Nation

Washington, D.C.

December 30, 1806

DESPITE HIS DISTASTE for speechmaking, Jefferson delivered formal welcoming addresses to numerous delegations of Plains Indians who came to meet him in Washington. Many of these groups, the Mandan among them, were invited to Washington by Meriwether Lewis and William Clark in the course of their exploration of the Louisiana Territory and the Oregon Country in 1804–1806. Jefferson was eager to secure the Indians' loyalty and friendship, as well as their land, and hoped eventually to see them assimilated into the new American society as farmers. During his two terms, the federal government concluded fifteen treaties with Indian tribes and acquired from them almost one hundred million acres of land.

I take you by the hand of friendship and give you a hearty welcome to the seat of the government of the United States. The journey which you have taken to visit your fathers on this side of our island is a long one, and your having undertaken it is a proof that you desired to become acquainted with us. I thank the Great Spirit that he has protected you through the journey and brought you safely to the residence of your friends, and I hope He will have you constantly in his safe keeping, and restore you in good health to your nations and families.

My friends and children, we are descended from the old nations which live beyond the great water, but we and our forefathers have been so long here that we seem like you to have grown out of this land. We consider ourselves no longer of the old nations beyond the great water, but as united in one family with our red brethren here. The French, the English, the Spaniards, have now agreed with us to retire from all the country which you and we hold between Canada and Mexico, and never more to return to it. And remember the words I now speak to you, my children, they are never to return again. We are now your fathers; and you shall not lose by the change. As soon as Spain had agreed to withdraw from all the waters of the Missouri and Mississippi, I felt the desire of becoming acquainted with all my red children beyond the Mississippi, and of uniting them with us as we have those on this side of that river, in the bonds of peace and friendship. I wished to learn what we could do to benefit them by furnishing them the necessaries they want in exchange for their furs and peltries. I therefore sent our beloved man, Captain Lewis, one of my own family, to go up the Missouri River to get acquainted with all the Indian nations in its neighborhood, to take them by the hand, deliver my talks to them, and to inform us in what way we could be useful to them. Your nation received him kindly; you have taken him by the hand and been friendly to him. My children, I thank you for the services you rendered him, and for your attention to his words. He will now tell us where we should establish trading houses to be convenient to you all, and what we must send to them.

My friends and children, I have now an important advice to give you. I have already told you that you and all the red men are my children, and I wish you to live in peace and friendship with one another as brethren of the same family ought to do. How much better is it for neighbors to help than to hurt one another; how much happier must it make them. If you will cease to make war on one another, if you live in friendship with all mankind, you can employ all your time in providing food and clothing for yourselves and your families. Your men will not be destroyed in war, and your women and children will lie down to sleep in their cabins without fear of being surprised by their enemies and killed or carried away. Your numbers will be increased instead of diminishing, and you will live in plenty and in quiet. My children, I have given this advice to all your red brethren on this side of the Mississippi; they are following it, they are increasing in their numbers, are learning to clothe and provide for their families as we do. Remember then my advice, my children, carry it home to your people, and tell them that from the day that they have became all of the same family, from the day that we became father to them all, we wish, as a true father should do, that we may all live together as one household, and that before they strike one another, they should go to their father and let him endeavor to make up the quarrel.

My children, you are come from the other side of our great island, from where the sun sets, to see your new friends at the sun rising. You have now arrived where the waters are constantly rising and falling every day, but you are still distant from the sea. I very much desire that you should not stop here, but go and see your brethren as far as the edge of the great water. I am persuaded you have so far seen that every man by the way has received you as his brothers, and has been ready to do you all the kindness in his power. You will see the same thing quite to the sea shore; and I wish you, therefore, to go and visit our great cities in that quarter, and see how many friends and brothers you have here. You will then have travelled a long line from west to east, and if you had time to go from north to south, from Canada to Florida, you would find it as long in that direction, and all the people as sincerely your friends. I wish you, my children, to see all you can, and to tell your people all you see; because I am sure the more they know of us, the more they will be our hearty friends. I invite you, therefore, to pay a visit to Baltimore, Philadelphia, New York, and the cities still beyond that, if you are willing to go further. We will provide carriages to convey you and a person to go with you to see that you want for nothing. By the time you come back the snows will be melted on the mountains, the ice in the rivers broken up, and you will be wishing to set out on your return home.

My children, I have long desired to see you; I have now opened my heart to you, let my words sink into your hearts and never be forgotten. If ever lying people or bad spirits should raise up clouds between us, call to mind what I have said, and what you have seen yourselves. Be sure there are some lying spirits between us; let us come together as friends and explain to each other what is misrepresented or misunderstood, the clouds will fly away like morning fog, and the sun of friendship appear and shine forever bright and clear between us.

My children, it may happen that while you are here occasion may arise to talk about many things which I do not now particularly mention. The secretary at war will always be ready to talk with you, and you are to consider whatever he says as said by myself. He will also take care of you and see that you are furnished with all comforts here.

The Failure of the Embargo

From the Eighth Annual Message to Congress
Washington, D.C.
November 8, 1808

JEFFERSON'S EIGHTH and last annual message to Congress was given to the legislature after the election of James Madison, Jefferson's protégé and secretary of state. Like most of his annual messages, it was drafted with the assistance of Madison and of Secretary of the Treasury Albert Gallatin. Its main subject was the failure of the embargo against overseas trade. France and Britain had remained unmoved by Jefferson's experiment in "peaceful coercion" and had continued the abuse of American shipping that had prompted it. Many Americans, especially in Federalist strongholds such as New England, were engaged in active resistance to it. The embargo was repealed by Congress in February 1809, just before Jefferson left office.

It would have been a source, fellow citizens, of much gratification if our last communications from Europe had enabled me to inform you that the belligerent nations, whose disregard of neutral rights has been so destructive to our commerce, had become awakened to the duty and true policy of revoking their unrighteous edicts. That no means might be omitted to produce this salutary effect, I lost no time in availing myself of the act authorizing a suspension, in whole or in part, of the several embargo laws. Our ministers at London and Paris were instructed to explain to the respective governments there our disposition to exercise the authority in such manner as would withdraw the pretext on which the aggressions were originally founded and open the way for a renewal of that commercial intercourse which it was alleged on all sides had been reluctantly obstructed. As each of those governments had pledged its readiness to concur in renouncing a measure which reached its adversary through the incontestable rights of neutrals only, and as the measure had been assumed by each as a retaliation for an asserted acquiescence in the aggressions of the other, it was reasonably expected that the occasion would have been seized by both for evincing the sincerity of their professions, and for restoring to the commerce of the United States its legitimate freedom. The instructions to our ministers with respect to the different belligerents were necessarily modified with a reference to their different circumstances, and to the condition annexed by law to the executive power of suspension, requiring a decree of security to our commerce which would not result from a repeal of the decrees of France. Instead of a pledge, therefore, of a suspension of the embargo as to her in case of such a repeal, it was presumed that a sufficient inducement might be found in other considerations, and particularly in the change produced by a compliance with our just demands by one belligerent and a refusal by the other in the relations between the other and the United States. To Great Britain, whose power on the ocean is so ascendant, it was deemed not inconsistent with that condition to state explicitly that on her rescinding her orders in relation to the United States their trade would be opened with her, and remain shut to her enemy in case of his failure to rescind his decrees also. From France no answer has been received, nor any indication that the requisite change in her decrees is contemplated. The favorable reception of the proposition to Great Britain was the less to be doubted, as her orders of council had not only been referred for their vindication to an acquiescence on the part of the United States no longer to be pretended, but as the arrangement proposed, whilst it resisted the illegal decrees of France, involved, moreover, substantially the precise advantages professedly aimed at by the British orders. The arrangement has nevertheless been rejected.

This candid and liberal experiment having thus failed, and no other event having occurred on which a suspension of the embargo by the executive was authorized, it necessarily remains in the extent originally given to it. We have the satisfaction, however, to reflect that in return for the privations imposed by the measure, and which our fellow citizens in general have borne with patriotism, it has had the important effects of saving our mariners and our vast mercantile property, as well as of affording time for prosecuting the defensive and provisional measures called for by the occasion. It has demonstrated to foreign nations the moderation and firmness which govern our councils, and to our citizens the necessity of uniting in support of the laws and the rights of their country, and has thus long frustrated those usurpations and spoliations which, if resisted, involved war; if submitted to, sacrificed a vital principle of our national independence.

Under a continuance of the belligerent measures which, in defiance of laws which consecrate the rights of neutrals, overspread the ocean with danger, it will rest with the wisdom of Congress to decide on the course best adapted to such a state of things; and bringing with them, as they do, from every part of the Union the sentiments of our constituents, my confidence is strengthened that in forming this decision they will, with an unerring regard to the essential rights and interests of the nation, weigh and compare the painful alternatives out of which a choice is to be made. Nor should I do justice to the virtues which on other occasions have marked the character of our fellow citizens if I did not cherish an equal confidence that the alternative chosen, whatever it may be, will be maintained with all the fortitude and patriotism which the crisis ought to inspire. . . .

Considering the extraordinary character of the times in which we live, our attention should unremittingly be fixed on the safety of our country. For a people who are free, and who mean to remain so, a well organized and armed militia is their best security. It is therefore incumbent on us at every meeting to revise the condition of the militia, and to ask ourselves if it is prepared to repel a powerful enemy at every point of our territories exposed to invasion. Some of the states have paid a laudable attention to this object, but every degree of neglect is to be found among others. Congress alone having the power to produce an uniform state of preparation in this great organ of defense, the interest which they so deeply feel in their own and their country's security will present this as among the most important objects of their deliberation.

Under the acts of March 11 and April 23 respecting arms, the difficulty of procuring them from abroad during the present situation and dispositions of Europe induced us to direct our whole efforts to the means of internal supply. The public factories have therefore been enlarged, additional machineries erected, and, in proportion as artificers can be found or formed, their effect, already more than doubled, may be increased so as to keep pace with the yearly increase of the militia. The annual sums appropriated by the latter act have been directed to the encouragement of private factories of arms, and contracts have been entered into with individual undertakers to nearly the amount of the first year's appropriation.

The suspension of our foreign commerce, produced by the injustice of the belligerent powers, and the consequent losses and sacrifices of our citizens are subjects of just concern. The situation into which we have thus been forced has impelled us to apply a portion of our industry and capital to internal manufactures and improvements. The extent of this conversion is daily increasing, and little doubt remains that the establishments formed and forming will, under the auspices of cheaper materials and subsistence, the freedom of labor from taxation with us, and of protecting duties and prohibitions, become permanent. The commerce with the Indians, too, within our own boundaries is likely to receive abundant aliment from the same internal source, and will secure to them peace and the progress of civilization, undisturbed by practices hostile to both.

The accounts of the receipts and expenditures during the year ending the 30th of September last being not yet made up, a correct statement will hereafter be transmitted from the Treasury. In the meantime it is ascertained that the receipts have amounted to near $18,000,000, which, with the eight millions and a half in the Treasury at the beginning of the year, have enabled us, after meeting the current demands and interest incurred, to pay $2,300,000 of the principal of our funded debt, and left us in the Treasury on that day near $14,000,000. Of these, $5,350,000 will be necessary to pay what will be due on the 1st day of January next, which will complete the reimbursement of the 8 percent stock. These payments, with those made in the six years and a half preceding, will have extinguished $33,580,000 of the principal of the funded debt, being the whole which could be paid or purchased within the limits of the law and of our contracts, and the amount of principal thus discharged will have liberated the revenue from about $2,000,000 of interest and added that sum annually to the disposable surplus. The probable accumulation of the surpluses of revenue beyond what can be applied to the payment of the public debt whenever the freedom and safety of our commerce shall be restored merits the consideration of Congress. Shall it lie unproductive in the public vaults? Shall the revenue be reduced? Or shall it not rather be appropriated to the improvements of roads, canals, rivers, education, and other great foundations of prosperity and union under the powers which Congress may already possess or such amendment of the Constitution as may be approved by the states? While uncertain of the course of things, the time may be advantageously employed in obtaining the powers necessary for a system of improvement, should that be thought best.

Availing myself of this the last occasion which will occur of addressing the two houses of the legislature at their meeting, I can not omit the expression of my sincere gratitude for the repeated proofs of confidence manifested to me by themselves and their predecessors since my call to the administration and the many indulgences experienced at their hands. The same grateful acknowledgments are due to my fellow citizens generally, whose support has been my great encouragement under all embarrassments. In the transaction of their business I can not have escaped error. It is incident to our imperfect nature. But I may say with truth my errors have been of the understanding, not of intention, and that the advancement of their rights and interests has been the constant motive for every measure. On these considerations I solicit their indulgence. Looking forward with anxiety to their future destinies, I trust that in their steady character, unshaken by difficulties, in their love of liberty, obedience to law, and support of the public authorities I see a sure guaranty of the permanence of our republic; and, retiring from the charge of their affairs, I carry with me the consolation of a firm persuasion that Heaven has in store for our beloved country long ages to come of prosperity and happiness.

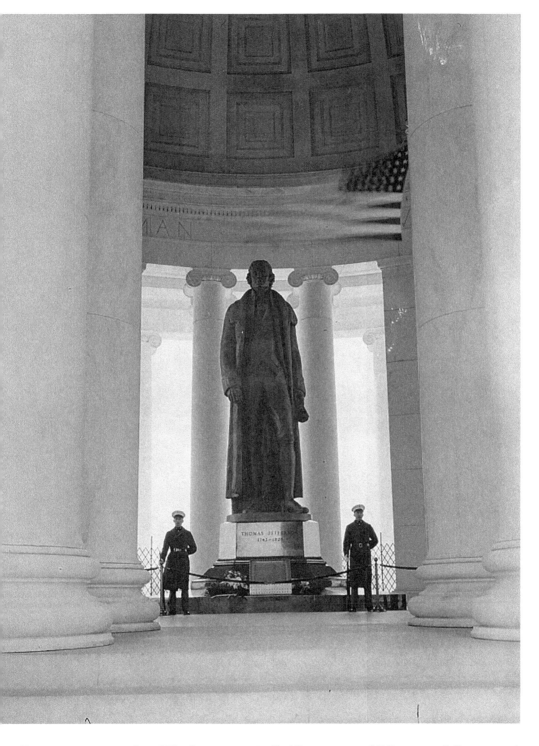

Jefferson Memorial in Washington, D.C. (Courtesy of Library of Congress)

Courtesy of James Madison's Montpelier

James Madison

James Madison

1809–1817

JAMES MADISON, principal architect of the U.S. Constitution, was born in Virginia in 1751 to a well-to-do family of planters. From childhood his health was delicate; he may have suffered from a functional ailment similar to epilepsy. A graduate of the College of New Jersey (now Princeton), he was selected in 1776 to be a delegate to the Virginia Convention, where he took part in the drafting of a new framework of government for the Old Dominion.

Though cautious and slow to take a stand, when Madison thought matters through to his satisfaction he was tenacious in his opinions. Once he entered a debate, he usually prevailed through close reasoning, erudition, and thorough knowledge of the topic at issue. He is acknowledged to have dominated much of the discussion in the second half of the Continental Congress. As a delegate to the Constitutional Convention of 1787 he drafted the basic tenets of the Constitution, and as representative to Congress from Virginia (1789–1797) he sponsored the Bill of Rights. The unifying principle of Madison's Republicanism, reflected in the language of the Constitution, was the establishment and strengthening of a Union of the states.

Appointed secretary of state by his mentor Jefferson in 1801, Madison exerted a decisive influence on foreign policy. With Jefferson's blessing, Madison campaigned for the presidency in 1809 and was elected by a comfortable margin. He was not well suited by experience or temperament to be a wartime president, but when he finally accepted that England's attacks on American shipping would not be altered by diplomacy or embargo, he led the country into the War of 1812. After the inauguration of James Monroe, Madison retired to Montpelier, where he died in 1836, the last surviving signer of the Constitution.

Comparing Madison's prose style to that of Jefferson, Hugh Blair Grigsby, who knew Madison, wrote: "Force and point and rapid analysis are the characteristics of the style of Jefferson; full, clear, and deliberate disquisition, carefully wrought out, as if the author regarded himself rather as the representative of truth than the exponent of the doctrines of a party or even of a nation, is the praise of Madison." But Madison was not a gifted speaker. His small stature, weak voice, and abstract manner made a poor impression on listeners, and he was ill-at-ease in public. But he made up in intellect and ideological determination what he lacked in stage presence. John Quincy Adams, in his eulogy for Madison, noted "the all but irresistible power of his eloquence" that had stirred the delegates to the Continental Congress and the Constitutional Convention. Jefferson himself wrote that Madison inevitably earned the admiration of his audiences, "never wandering from his subject into vain declamation, but pursuing it closely, in language pure, classical, and copious, soothing always to the feelings of his adversaries by civilities and softness and expression."

First Inaugural Address

Washington, D.C.

March 4, 1809

JEFFERSON ARRIVED at the Capitol shortly before Madison and sat beside his friend as the incoming president delivered a short inaugural address. Always a quiet speaker, Madison was hesitant at first, but then his voice gained confidence. The address was a cautious and sober expression of Republican principles: primacy of the Constitution, preservation of the Union, adherence to strict neutrality with respect to the English and French. It is plain, however, that Madison already contemplated the possibility of war, acknowledging that "scrupulous impartiality" had not so far availed against "the injustice and violence of the belligerent powers" toward the United States.

At the inaugural festivities, Jefferson, vastly relieved and even exuberant at handing over executive responsibility, was heard to remark that he "was much happier at this moment than my friend." Madison, on the other hand, was wearied by the crowds that pressed in upon him and was by evening exhausted. Washington Irving, who attended the inaugural ball, later wrote of the pale president, "As to Jemmy Madison, ah! poor Jemmy! he is but a withered little Apple-John."

Unwilling to depart from examples of the most revered authority, I avail myself of the occasion now presented to express the profound impression made on me by the call of my country to the station to the duties of which I am about to pledge myself by the most solemn of sanctions. So distinguished a mark of confidence, proceeding from the deliberate and tranquil suffrage of a free and virtuous nation, would under any circumstances have commanded my gratitude and devotion, as well as filled me with an awful sense of the trust to be assumed. Under the various circumstances which give peculiar solemnity to the existing period, I feel that both the honor and the responsibility allotted to me are inexpressibly enhanced.

The present situation of the world is indeed without a parallel, and that of our own country full of difficulties. The pressure of these, too, is the more severely felt because they have fallen upon us at a moment when the national prosperity being at a height not before attained, the contrast resulting from the change has been rendered the more striking. Under the benign influence of our republican institutions, and the maintenance of peace with all nations whilst so many of them were engaged in bloody and wasteful wars, the fruits of a just policy were enjoyed in an unrivaled growth of our faculties and resources. Proofs of this were seen in the improvements of agriculture, in the successful enterprises of commerce, in the progress of manufactures and useful arts, in the increase of the public revenue and the use made of it in reducing the public debt, and in the valuable works and establishments everywhere multiplying over the face of our land.

It is a precious reflection that the transition from this prosperous condition of our country to the scene which has for some time been distressing us is not chargeable on any unwarrantable views, nor, as I trust, on any involuntary errors in the public councils. Indulging no passions which trespass on the rights or the repose of other nations, it has been the true glory of the United States to cultivate peace by observing justice, and to entitle themselves to the respect of the nations at war by fulfilling their neutral obligations with the most scrupulous impartiality. If there be candor in the world, the truth of these assertions will not be questioned; posterity at least will do justice to them.

This unexceptionable course could not avail against the injustice and violence of the belligerent powers. In their rage against each other, or impelled by more direct motives, principles of retaliation have been introduced equally contrary to universal reason and acknowledged law. How long their arbitrary edicts will be continued in spite of the demonstrations that not even a pretext for them has been given by the United States, and of the fair and liberal attempt to induce a revocation of them, can not be anticipated. Assuring myself that under every vicissitude the determined spirit and united councils of the nation will be safeguards to its honor and its essential interests, I repair to the post assigned me with no other discouragement than what springs from my own inadequacy to its high duties. If I do not sink under the weight of this deep conviction it is because I find some support in a consciousness of the purposes and a confidence in the principles which I bring with me into this arduous service.

To cherish peace and friendly intercourse with all nations having correspondent dispositions; to maintain sincere neutrality toward belligerent nations; to prefer in all cases amicable discussion and reasonable accommodation of differences to a decision of them by an appeal to arms; to exclude foreign intrigues and foreign partialities, so degrading to all countries and so baneful to free ones; to foster a spirit of independence too just to invade the rights of others, too proud to surrender our own, too liberal to indulge unworthy prejudices ourselves and too elevated not to look down upon them in others; to hold the Union of the states as the basis of their peace and happiness; to support the Constitution, which is the cement of the Union, as well in its limitations as in its authorities; to respect the rights and authorities reserved to the states and to the people as equally incorporated with and essential to the success of the general system; to avoid the slightest interference with the rights of conscience or the functions of religion, so wisely exempted from civil jurisdiction; to preserve in their full energy the other salutary provisions in behalf of private and personal rights, and of the freedom of the press; to observe economy in public expenditures; to liberate the public resources by an honorable discharge of the public debts; to keep within the requisite limits a standing military force, always remembering that an armed and trained militia is the firmest bulwark of republics—that without standing armies their liberty can never be in danger, nor with large ones safe; to promote by

authorized means improvements friendly to agriculture, to manufactures, and to external as well as internal commerce; to favor in like manner the advancement of science and the diffusion of information as the best aliment to true liberty; to carry on the benevolent plans which have been so meritoriously applied to the conversion of our aboriginal neighbors from the degradation and wretchedness of savage life to a participation of the improvements of which the human mind and manners are susceptible in a civilized state—as far as sentiments and intentions such as these can aid the fulfillment of my duty, they will be a resource which can not fail me.

It is my good fortune, moreover, to have the path in which I am to tread lighted by examples of illustrious services successfully rendered in the most trying difficulties by those who have marched before me. Of those of my immediate predecessor it might least become me here to speak. I may, however, be pardoned for not suppressing the sympathy with which my heart is full in the rich reward he enjoys in the benedictions of a beloved country, gratefully bestowed for exalted talents zealously devoted through a long career to the advancement of its highest interest and happiness.

But the source to which I look for the aids which alone can supply my deficiencies is in the well-tried intelligence and virtue of my fellow citizens, and in the counsels of those representing them in the other departments associated in the care of the national interests. In these my confidence will under every difficulty be best placed, next to that which we have all been encouraged to feel in the guardianship and guidance of that Almighty Being whose power regulates the destiny of nations, whose blessings have been so conspicuously dispensed to this rising republic, and to whom we are bound to address our devout gratitude for the past, as well as our fervent supplications and best hopes for the future.

The Course of the War

From the Fourth Annual Message to Congress
Washington, D.C.
November 4, 1812

MADISON EXERTED every effort to protect American neutrality and avoid war with Britain and France, even to the point of appearing weak and indecisive. Despite this, England refused to rescind or modify its notorious Orders in Council, which encouraged British seizure of American ships (many bound for trade with France) and impressment of American sailors, without humiliating American concessions. Meanwhile France was burning American grain ships en route to Wellington's armies on the Iberian Peninsula. On June 1, 1812, Madison reluctantly asked for war with England, which he had always considered the greater threat. His war message was read by a clerk before a closed session of Congress. On June 4, the House voted for war; on June 17, the Senate. Ironically, England suspended the Orders in Council in June and repealed them on June 23, but the course of war was already set.

Secretary of the Treasury Albert Gallatin and Secretary of State James Monroe helped Madison write the first annual message to be delivered in wartime. Madison's original draft was more strident, especially toward General William Hull, an aging Revolutionary War veteran who had lost Detroit to the enemy through incompetence and cowardice. The final draft, however, was toned down, probably on the advice of Gallatin, and left out any explicit judgment of Hull. Madison instead emphasized the few early American victories won by the nation's minuscule navy.

On our present meeting it is my first duty to invite your attention to the providential favors which our country has experienced in the unusual degree of health dispensed to its inhabitants, and in the rich abundance with which the earth has rewarded the labors bestowed on it. In the successful cultivation of other branches of industry, and in the progress of general improvement favorable to the national prosperity, there is just occasion also for our mutual congratulations and thankfulness.

With these blessings are necessarily mingled the pressures and vicissitudes incident to the state of war into which the United States have been forced by the perseverance of a foreign power in its system of injustice and aggression.

Previous to its declaration it was deemed proper, as a measure of precaution and forecast, that a considerable force should be placed in the Michigan Territory with a general view to its security, and, in the event of war, to such operations in the uppermost Canada as would intercept the hostile influence of Great Britain over the savages, obtain the command of the lake on which that part of Canada borders, and maintain cooperating relations with such forces as might be most conveniently employed against other parts. Brigadier-General Hull was charged with this provisional service, having under his command a body of troops composed of regulars and of volunteers from the state of Ohio. Having reached his destination after his knowledge of the war, and possessing discretionary authority to act offensively, he passed into the neighboring territory of the enemy with a prospect of easy and victorious progress. The expedition, nevertheless, terminated unfortunately, not only in a retreat to the town and fort of Detroit, but in the surrender of both and of the gallant corps commanded by that officer. The causes of this painful reverse will be investigated by a military tribunal.

A distinguishing feature in the operations which preceded and followed this adverse event is the use made by the enemy of the merciless savages under their influence. Whilst the benevolent policy of the United States invariably recommended peace and promoted civilization among that wretched portion of the human race, and was making exertions to dissuade them from taking either side in the war, the enemy has not scrupled to call to his aid their ruthless ferocity, armed with the horrors of those instruments of carnage and torture which are known to spare neither age nor sex. In this outrage against the laws of honorable war and against the feelings sacred to humanity the British commanders can not resort to a plea of retaliation, for it is committed in the face of our example. They can not mitigate it by calling it a self-defense against men in arms, for it embraces the most shocking butcheries of defenseless families. Nor can it be pretended that they are not answerable for the atrocities perpetrated, since the savages are employed with a knowledge, and even with menaces, that their fury could not be controlled. Such is the spectacle which the deputed authorities of a nation boasting its religion and morality have not been restrained from presenting to an enlightened age.

The misfortune at Detroit was not, however, without a consoling effect. It was followed by signal proofs that the national spirit rises according to the pressure on it. The loss of an important post and of the brave men surrendered with it inspired everywhere new ardor and determination. In the states and districts least remote it was no sooner known than every citizen was ready to fly with his arms at once to protect his brethren against the bloodthirsty savages let loose by the enemy on an extensive frontier, and to convert a partial calamity into a source of invigorated efforts. This patriotic zeal, which it was necessary rather to limit than excite, has embodied an ample force from the states of Kentucky and Ohio and from parts of Pennsylvania and Virginia. It is placed, with the addition of a few regulars, under the command of Brigadier-General Harrison, who possesses the entire confidence of his fellow soldiers, among whom are citizens, some of them volunteers in the ranks, not less distinguished by their political stations than by their personal merits. The greater portion of this force is proceeding on its destination toward the Michigan Territory, having succeeded in relieving an important frontier post, and in several incidental operations against hostile tribes of savages, rendered indispensable by the subserviency into which they had been seduced by the enemy—a seduction the more cruel as it could not fail to impose a necessity of precautionary severities against those who yielded to it.

At a recent date an attack was made on a post of the enemy near Niagara by a detachment of the regular and other forces under the command of Major-General Van Rensselaer, of the militia of the state of New York. The attack, it appears, was ordered in compliance with the ardor of the troops, who executed it with distinguished gallantry, and were for a time victorious; but not receiving the expected support, they were compelled to yield to reenforcements of British regulars and savages. Our loss has been considerable, and is deeply to be lamented. That of the enemy, less ascertained, will be the more felt, as it includes among the killed the commanding general, who was also the governor of the province, and was sustained by veteran troops from unexperienced soldiers, who must daily improve in the duties of the field.

Our expectation of gaining the command of the lakes by the invasion of Canada from Detroit having been disappointed, measures were instantly taken to provide on them a naval force superior to that of the enemy. From the talents and activity of the officer charged with this object everything that can be done may be expected. Should the present season not admit of complete success, the progress made will insure for the next a naval ascendency where it is essential to our permanent peace with and control over the savages.

Among the incidents to the measures of the war I am constrained to advert to the refusal of the governors of Massachusetts and Connecticut to furnish the required detachments of militia toward the defense of the maritime frontier. The refusal was founded on a novel and unfortunate exposition of the provisions of the Constitution relating to the militia. The correspondences which will be laid before you contain the requisite information on the subject. It is obvious that if the authority of the United States to call into service and command the militia for the public defense can be thus frustrated, even in a state of declared war and of course under apprehensions of invasion preceding war, they are not one nation for the purpose most of all requiring it, and that the public safety may have no other resource than in those large and permanent military establishments which are forbidden by the principles of our free government, and against the necessity of which the militia were meant to be a constitutional bulwark.

On the coasts and on the ocean the war has been as successful as circumstances inseparable from its early stages could promise. Our public ships and private cruisers, by their activity, and, where there was occasion, by their intrepidity, have made the enemy sensible of the difference between a reciprocity of captures and the long confinement of them to their side. Our trade, with little exception, has safely reached our ports, having been much favored in it by the course pursued by a squadron of our frigates under the command of Commodore Rodgers, and in the instance in which skill and bravery were more particularly tried with those of the enemy the American flag had an auspicious triumph. The frigate *Constitution,* commanded by Captain Hull, after a close and short engagement completely disabled and captured a British frigate, gaining for that officer and all on board a praise which can not be too liberally bestowed, not merely for the victory actually achieved, but for that prompt and cool exertion of commanding talents which, giving to courage its highest character, and to the force applied its full effect, proved that more could have been done in a contest requiring more. . . .

Second Inaugural Address

Washington, D.C.

March 4, 1813

IN THE 1812 ELECTION Madison was opposed by DeWitt Clinton, the nephew of Madison's vice president, George Clinton, and a New York Republican with strong Federalist backing. Clinton's campaign was hampered by his own duplicitous politicking: He supported the war when appealing to hawkish Republicans and called for peace when addressing Federalists and Republican doves. Clinton carried much of Federalist New England, but Madison carried the South and West by a large margin.

This address was meant to reinforce the president's image as a determined prosecutor of the war, while showing his continued readiness to make an honorable peace.

About to add the solemnity of an oath to the obligations imposed by a second call to the station in which my country heretofore placed me, I find in the presence of this respectable assembly an opportunity of publicly repeating my profound sense of so distinguished a confidence and of the responsibility united with it. The impressions on me are strengthened by such an evidence that my faithful endeavors to discharge my arduous duties have been favorably estimated, and by a consideration of the momentous period at which the trust has been renewed. From the weight and magnitude now belonging to it I should be compelled to shrink if I had less reliance on the support of an enlightened and generous people, and felt less deeply a conviction that the war with a powerful nation, which forms so prominent a feature in our situation, is stamped with that justice which invites the smiles of Heaven on the means of conducting it to a successful termination.

May we not cherish this sentiment without presumption when we reflect on the characters by which this war is distinguished?

It was not declared on the part of the United States until it had been long made on them, in reality though not in name; until arguments and expostulations had been exhausted; until a positive declaration had been received that the wrongs provoking it would not be discontinued; nor until this last appeal could no longer be delayed without breaking down the spirit of the nation, destroying all confidence in itself and in its political institutions, and either perpetuating a state of disgraceful suffering or regaining by more costly sacrifices and more severe struggles our lost rank and respect among independent powers.

On the issue of the war are staked our national sovereignty on the high seas and the security of an important class of citizens, whose occupations give the proper value to those of every other class. Not to contend for such a stake is to surrender our equality with other powers on the element common to all and to violate the sacred title which every member of the society has to its protection. I need not call into view the unlawfulness of the practice by which our mariners are forced at the will of every cruising officer from their own vessels into foreign ones, nor paint the outrages inseparable from it. The proofs are in the records of each successive administration of our government, and the cruel sufferings of that portion of the American people have found their way to every bosom not dead to the sympathies of human nature.

As the war was just in its origin and necessary and noble in its objects, we can reflect with a proud satisfaction that in carrying it on no principle of justice or honor, no usage of civilized nations, no precept of courtesy or humanity, have been infringed. The war has been waged on our part with scrupulous regard to all these obligations, and in a spirit of liberality which was never surpassed.

How little has been the effect of this example on the conduct of the enemy!

They have retained as prisoners of war citizens of the United States not liable to be so considered under the usages of war.

They have refused to consider as prisoners of war, and threatened to punish as traitors and deserters, persons emigrating without restraint to the United States, incorporated by naturalization into our political family, and fighting under the authority of their adopted country in open and honorable war for the maintenance of its rights and safety. Such is the avowed purpose of a government which is in the practice of naturalizing by thousands citizens of other countries, and not only of permitting but compelling them to fight its battles against their native country.

They have not, it is true, taken into their own hands the hatchet and the knife, devoted to indiscriminate massacre, but they have let loose the savages armed with these cruel instruments; have allured them into their service, and carried them to battle by their sides, eager to glut their savage thirst with blood of the vanquished and to finish the work of torture and death on maimed and defenseless captives. And, what was never before seen, British commanders have extorted victory over the unconquerable valor of our troops by presenting to the sympathy of their chief captives awaiting massacre from their savage associates. And now we find them, in further contempt of the modes of honorable warfare, supplying the place of a conquering force by attempts to disorganize our political society, to dismember our confederated republic. Happily, like others these will recoil on the author; but they mark the degenerate counsels from which they emanate, and if they did not belong to a series of unexampled inconsistencies might excite the greater wonder as proceeding from a government which founded the very war in which it has been so long engaged on a charge against the disorganizing and insurrectional policy of its adversary.

To render the justice of the war on our part the more conspicuous, the reluctance to commence it was followed by the earliest and strongest manifestations of a disposition to arrest its progress. The sword was scarcely out of the scabbard before the enemy was apprised of the reasonable terms on which it would be resheathed. Still more precise advances were repeated, and have been received in a spirit forbidding every reliance not placed on the military resources of the nation.

These resources are amply sufficient to bring the war to an honorable issue. Our nation is in number more than half that of the British Isles. It is composed of a brave, a free, a virtuous, and an intelligent people. Our country abounds in the necessaries, the arts, and the comforts of life. A general prosperity is visible in the public countenance. The means employed by the British cabinet to undermine it have recoiled on themselves; have given to our national faculties a more rapid development, and, draining or diverting the precious metals from British circulation and British vaults, have poured them into those of the United States. It is a propitious consideration that an unavoidable war should have found this seasonable facility for the contributions required to support it. When the public voice called for war, all knew, and still know, that without them it could not be carried on through the period which it might last, and the patriotism, the good sense, and the manly spirit of our fellow citizens are pledges for the cheerfulness with which they will bear each his share of the common burden. To render the war short and its success sure, animated and systematic exertions alone are necessary, and the success of our arms now may long preserve our country from the necessity of another resort to them. Already have the gallant exploits of our naval heroes proved to the world our inherent capacity to maintain our rights on one element. If the reputation of our arms has been thrown under clouds on the other, presaging flashes of heroic enterprise assure us that nothing is wanting to correspondent triumphs there also but the discipline and habits which are in daily progress.

Farewell Address

From the Eighth Annual Message to Congress
Washington, D.C.
December 3, 1816

TWO YEARS AFTER the end of the war, the nation was again prosperous and expanding, with a surplus in the Treasury and the Republican succession to James Monroe assured. Madison, who left office in high public esteem, closed his last message to Congress with this farewell.

. . . The period of my retiring from the public service being at little distance, I shall find no occasion more proper than the present for expressing to my fellow citizens my deep sense of the continued confidence and kind support which I have received from them. My grateful recollection of these distinguished marks of their favorable regard can never cease, and with the consciousness that, if I have not served my country with greater ability, I have served it with a sincere devotion will accompany me as a source of unfailing gratification.

Happily, I shall carry with me from the public theater other sources, which those who love their country most will best appreciate. I shall behold it blessed with tranquility and prosperity at home and with peace and respect abroad. I can indulge the proud reflection that the American people have reached in safety and success their 40th year as an independent nation; that for nearly an entire generation they have had experience of their present Constitution, the offspring of their undisturbed deliberations and of their free choice; that they have found it to bear the trials of adverse as well as prosperous circumstances; to contain in its combination of the federate and elective principles a reconcilement of public strength with individual liberty, of national power for the defense of national rights with a security against wars of injustice, of ambition, and of vainglory in the fundamental provision which subjects all questions of war to the will of the nation itself, which is to pay its costs and feel its calamities. Nor is it less a peculiar felicity of this Constitution, so dear to us all, that it is found to be capable, without losing its vital energies, of expanding itself over a spacious territory with the increase and expansion of the community for whose benefit it was established.

And may I not be allowed to add to this gratifying spectacle that I shall read in the character of the American people, in their devotion to true liberty and to the Constitution which is its palladium, sure presages that the destined career of my country will exhibit a government pursuing the public good as its sole object, and regulating its means by the great principles consecrated in its charter and by those moral principles to which they are so well allied; a government which watches over the purity of elections, the freedom of speech and of the press, the trial by jury, and the equal interdict against encroachments and compacts between religion and the state; which maintains inviolably the maxims of public faith, the security of persons and property, and encourages in every authorized mode that general diffusion of knowledge which guarantees to public liberty its permanency and to those who possess the blessing the true enjoyment of it; a government which avoids intrusions on the internal repose of other nations, and repels them from its own; which does justice to all nations with a readiness equal to the firmness with which it requires justice from them; and which, whilst it refines its domestic code from every ingredient not congenial with the precepts of an enlightened age and the sentiments of a virtuous people, seeks by appeals to reason and by its liberal examples to infuse into the law which governs the civilized world a spirit which may diminish the frequency or circumscribe the calamities of war, and meliorate the social and beneficent relations of peace; a government, in a word, whose conduct within and without may bespeak the most noble of all ambitions—that of promoting peace on earth and good will to man.

These contemplations, sweetening the remnant of my days, will animate my prayers for the happiness of my beloved country, and a perpetuity of the institutions under which it is enjoyed.

Courtesy of Library of Congress

James Monroe

James Monroe

1817–1825

THE LAST MEMBER of the "Virginia dynasty," James Monroe was born in 1758. From the age of 16 he was assisted and advised by his paternal uncle, a wealthy and influential judge who was active in Virginia revolutionary politics. He studied law under Thomas Jefferson, then governor of Virginia, and entered politics with his support at the age of 24.

As a senator (1790–1794) he joined with James Madison in opposing the fiscal policies of Alexander Hamilton, Washington's secretary of the Treasury. Nevertheless, Washington appointed him ambassador to France. But Monroe made an unruly and even disloyal diplomat. When he refused to support Jay's Treaty or even to defend it to the suspicious French, he was recalled by Washington, who called him "a mere tool in the hands of the French government." Monroe also served as minister to Great Britain during Jefferson's first administration and as secretary of state under Madison.

The Federalists, virtually destroyed as a party after the war, were unable to field a viable candidate in 1816, and Monroe easily captured the presidency. Compared to his two predecessors, Monroe was a relatively undistinguished president, but he also presided over less tempestuous times—the so-called "era of good feelings." The two significant events of his terms in office were the Missouri Compromise of 1820 (which ended a bitter political debate in Congress by allowing the admission of Missouri as a slave state while prohibiting slavery elsewhere north of 36° 30' north latitude) and the declaration of the Monroe Doctrine.

Like his predecessors, Monroe did not consider public addresses an important form of presidential communication. This was just as well, for he was stiff and soft-spoken on the podium and apparently was unable to craft a well-turned phrase for public occasions. In person, however, Monroe was one of the most likable of presidents, tall and robust, dignified and imposing. His habit of wearing the fashions of the Revolutionary era and his reputation for bravery during the War of Independence and the War of 1812 reinforced in his audiences the impression of seeing a hero from a past age. His biographer Henry Ammon wrote: "In spite of his rather formal manners, Monroe had a rare ability of putting men at ease by his courtesy, his lack of condescension, his frankness and by what his contemporaries looked upon as his essential goodness and kindness of heart." Jefferson, who knew he was not a man of outstanding intellect, wrote of him: "Turn his soul wrong side outwards and there is not a speck on it."

First Inaugural Address

Washington, D.C.

March 4, 1817

MORE THAN eight thousand people attended Monroe's inauguration, a vast crowd by the standards of the time. It was held outdoors on a wooden platform erected in front of the temporary Capitol, a brick building just to the southwest of the first Capitol, which had been burned by the British. Monroe was dressed in the outdated style also favored by Jefferson and Madison—black coat, knee breeches with black hose, and brass knee and shoe buckles. After taking the oath of office, Monroe outlined the goals of his adminstration in simple and uninspiring language. It is likely that his audience responded less to his actual speech, which was inaudible to most of the crowd, than to his personification of sober, stable government and republican virtues.

I should be destitute of feeling if I was not deeply affected by the strong proof which my fellow citizens have given me of their confidence in calling me to the high office whose functions I am about to assume. As the expression of their good opinion of my conduct in the public service, I derive from it a gratification which those who are conscious of having done all that they could to merit it can alone feel. My sensibility is increased by a just estimate of the importance of the trust and of the nature and extent of its duties, with the proper discharge of which the highest interests of a great and free people are intimately connected. Conscious of my own deficiency, I can not enter on these duties without great anxiety for the result. From a just responsibility I will never shrink, calculating with confidence that in my best efforts to promote the public welfare my motives will always be duly appreciated and my conduct be viewed with that candor and indulgence which I have experienced in other stations.

In commencing the duties of the chief executive office it has been the practice of the distinguished men who have gone before me to explain the principles which would govern them in their respective administrations. In following their venerated example my attention is naturally drawn to the great causes which have contributed in a principal degree to produce the present happy condition of the United States. They will best explain the nature of our duties and shed much light on the policy which ought to be pursued in future.

From the commencement of our Revolution to the present day almost 40 years have elapsed, and from the establishment of this Constitution 28. Through this whole term the government has been what may emphatically be called self-government. And what has been the effect? To whatever object we turn our attention, whether it relates to our foreign or domestic concerns, we find abundant cause to felicitate ourselves in the excellence of our institutions. During a period fraught with difficulties and marked by very extraordinary events the United States have flourished beyond example. Their citizens individually have been happy and the nation prosperous.

Under this Constitution our commerce has been wisely regulated with foreign nations and between the states; new states have been admitted into our Union; our territory has been enlarged by fair and honorable treaty, and with great advantage to the original states; the states, respectively protected by the national government under a mild, parental system against foreign dangers, and enjoying within their separate spheres, by a wise partition of power, a just proportion of the sovereignty, have improved their police, extended their settlements, and attained a strength and maturity which are the best proofs of wholesome laws well administered. And if we look to the condition of individuals what a proud spectacle does it exhibit! On whom has oppression fallen in any quarter of our Union? Who has been deprived of any right of person or property? Who restrained from offering his vows in the mode which he prefers to the Divine Author of his being? It is well known that all these blessings have been enjoyed in their fullest extent; and I add with peculiar satisfaction that there has been no example of a capital punishment being inflicted on anyone for the crime of high treason.

Some who might admit the competency of our government to these beneficent duties might doubt it in trials which put to the test its strength and efficiency as a member of the great community of nations. Here too experience has afforded us the most satisfactory proof in its favor. Just as this Constitution was put into action several of the principal states of Europe had become much agitated and some of them seriously convulsed. Destructive wars ensued, which have of late only been terminated. In the course of these conflicts the United States received great injury from several of the parties. It was their interest to stand aloof from the contest, to demand justice from the party committing the injury, and to cultivate by a fair and honorable conduct the friendship of all. War became at length inevitable, and the result has shown that our government is equal to that, the greatest of trials, under the most unfavorable circumstances. Of the virtue of the people and of the heroic exploits of the army, the navy, and the militia I need not speak.

Such, then, is the happy government under which we live—a government adequate to every purpose for which the social compact is formed; a government elective in all its branches, under which every citizen may by his merit obtain the highest trust recognized by the Constitution; which contains within it no cause of discord, none to put at variance one portion of the community with another; a government which protects every citizen in the full enjoyment of his rights, and is able to protect the nation against injustice from foreign powers.

Other considerations of the highest importance admonish us to cherish our Union and to cling to the government which supports it. Fortunate as we are in our political institutions, we have not been less so in other circumstances on which our prosperity and happiness essentially depend. Situated within the temperate zone, and extending through many degrees of latitude along the Atlantic, the United States enjoy all the varieties of climate, and every production incident to that portion of the globe. Penetrating internally to the Great Lakes and beyond the sources of the great rivers which communicate through our whole interior, no country was ever happier with respect to its domain. Blessed, too, with a fertile soil, our produce has always been very abundant, leaving, even in years the least favorable, a surplus for the wants of our fellow men in other countries. Such is our peculiar felicity that there is not a part of our Union that is not particularly interested in preserving it. The great agricultural interest of the nation prospers under its protection. Local interests are not less fostered by it. Our fellow citizens of the North engaged in navigation find great encouragement in being made the favored carriers of the vast productions of the other portions of the United States, while the inhabitants of these are amply recompensed, in their turn, by the nursery for seamen and naval force thus formed and reared up for the support of our common rights. Our manufactures find a generous encouragement by the policy which patronizes domestic industry, and the surplus of our produce a steady and profitable market by local wants in less-favored parts at home.

Such, then, being the highly favored condition of our country, it is the interest of every citizen to maintain it. What are the dangers which menace us? If any exist they ought to be ascertained and guarded against.

In explaining my sentiments on this subject it may be asked, What raised us to the present happy state? How did we accomplish the Revolution? How remedy the defects of the first instrument of our Union, by infusing into the national government sufficient power for national purposes, without impairing the just rights of the states or affecting those of individuals? How sustain and pass with glory through the late war? The government has been in the hands of the people. To the people, therefore, and to the faithful and able depositaries of their trust is the credit due. Had the people of the United States been educated in different principles, had they been less intelligent, less independent, or less virtuous, can it be believed that we should have maintained the same steady and consistent career or been blessed with the same success? While, then, the constituent body retains its present sound and healthful state everything will be safe. They will choose competent and faithful representatives for every department. It is only when the people become ignorant and corrupt, when they degenerate into a populace, that they are incapable of exercising the sovereignty. Usurpation is then an easy attainment, and an usurper soon found. The people themselves become the willing instruments of their own debasement and ruin. Let us, then, look to the great cause, and endeavor to preserve it in full force. Let us by all wise and constitutional measures promote intelligence among the people as the best means of preserving our liberties.

Dangers from abroad are not less deserving of attention. Experiencing the fortune of other nations, the United States may be again involved in war, and it may in that event be the object of the adverse party to overset our government, to break our Union, and demolish us as a nation. Our distance from Europe and the just, moderate, and pacific policy of our government may form some security against these dangers, but they ought to be anticipated and guarded against. Many of our citizens are engaged in commerce and navigation, and all of them are in a certain degree dependent on their prosperous state. Many are engaged in the fisheries. These interests are exposed to invasion in the wars between other powers, and we should disregard the faithful admonition of experience if we did not expect it. We must support our rights or lose our character, and with it, perhaps, our liberties. A people who fail to do it can scarcely be said to hold a place among independent nations. National honor is national property of the highest value. The sentiment in the mind of every citizen is national strength. It ought therefore to be cherished.

To secure us against these dangers our coast and inland frontiers should be fortified, our army and navy, regulated upon just principles as to the force of each, be kept in perfect order, and our militia be placed on the best practicable footing. To put our extensive coast in such a state of defense as to secure our cities and interior from invasion will be attended with expense, but the work when finished will be permanent, and it is fair to presume that a single campaign of invasion by a naval force superior to our own, aided by a few thousand land troops, would expose us to greater expense, without taking into the estimate the loss of property and distress of our citizens, than would be sufficient for this great work.

Our land and naval forces should be moderate, but adequate to the necessary purposes—the former to garrison and preserve our fortifications and to meet the first invasions of a foreign foe, and, while constituting the elements of a greater force, to preserve the science as well as all the necessary implements of war in a state to be brought into activity in the event of war; the latter, retained within the limits proper in a state of peace, might aid in maintaining the neutrality of the United States with dignity in the wars of other powers and in saving the property of their citizens from spoliation. In time of war, with the enlargement of which the great naval resources of the country render it susceptible, and which should be duly fostered in time of peace, it would contribute essentially, both as an auxiliary of defense and as a powerful engine of annoyance, to diminish the calamities of war and to bring the war to a speedy and honorable termination.

But it ought always to be held prominently in view that the safety of these states and of everything dear to a free people must depend in an eminent degree on the militia. Invasions may be made too formidable to be resisted by any land and naval force which it would comport either with the principles of our government or the circumstances of the United States to maintain. In such cases recourse must be had to the great body of the people, and in a manner to produce the best effect. It is of the highest importance, therefore, that they be so organized and trained as to be prepared for any emergency. The arrangement should be such as to put at the command of the government the ardent patriotism and youthful vigor of the country. If formed on equal and just principles, it can not be oppressive. It is the crisis which makes the pressure, and the laws which provide a remedy for it. This arrangement should be formed, too, in time of peace, to be the better prepared for war. With such an organization of such a people the United States have nothing to dread from foreign invasion. At its approach an overwhelming force of gallant men might always be put in motion.

Other interests of high importance will claim attention, among which the improvement of our country by roads and canals, proceeding always with a constitutional sanction, holds a distinguished place. By thus facilitating the intercourse between the states we shall add much to the convenience and comfort of our fellow citizens, much to the ornament of the country, and, what is of greater importance, we shall shorten distances, and, by making each part more accessible to and dependent on the other, we shall bind the Union more closely together. Nature has done so much for us by intersecting the country with so many great rivers, bays, and lakes, approaching from distant points so near to each other, that the inducement to complete the work seems to be peculiarly strong. A more interesting spectacle was perhaps never seen than is exhibited within the limits of the United States—a territory so vast and advantageously situated, containing objects so grand, so useful, so happily connected in all their parts!

Our manufactures will likewise require the systematic and fostering care of the government. Possessing as we do all the raw materials, the fruit of our own soil and industry, we ought not to depend in the degree we have done on supplies from other countries. While we are thus dependent the sudden event of war, unsought and unexpected, can not fail to plunge us into the most serious difficulties. It is important, too, that the capital which nourishes our manufactures should be domestic, as its influence in that case instead of exhausting, as it may do in foreign hands, would be felt advantageously on agriculture and every other branch of industry. Equally important is it to provide at home a market for our raw materials, as by extending the competition it will enhance the price and protect the cultivator against the casualties incident to foreign markets.

With the Indian tribes it is our duty to cultivate friendly relations and to act with kindness and liberality in all our transactions. Equally proper is it to persevere in our efforts to extend to them the advantages of civilization.

The great amount of our revenue and the flourishing state of the Treasury are a full proof of the competency of the national resources for any emergency, as they are of the willingness of our fellow citizens to bear the burdens which the public necessities require. The vast amount of vacant lands, the value of which daily augments, forms an additional resource of great extent and duration. These resources, besides accomplishing every other necessary purpose, put it completely in the power of the United States to discharge the national debt at an early period. Peace is the best time for the improvement and preparation of every kind; it is in peace that our commerce flourishes most, that taxes are most easily paid, and that the revenue is most productive.

The executive is charged officially in the departments under it with the disbursement of the public money, and is responsible for the faithful application of it to the purposes for which it is raised. The legislature is the watchful guardian over the public purse. It is its duty to see that the disbursement has been honestly made. To meet the requisite responsibility every facility should be afforded to the executive to enable it to bring the public agents intrusted with the public money strictly and promptly to account. Nothing should be presumed against them; but if, with the requisite facilities, the public money is suffered to lie long and uselessly in their hands, they will not be the only defaulters, nor will the demoralizing effect be confined to them. It will evince a relaxation and want of tone in the administration which will be felt by the whole community. I shall do all I can to secure economy and fidelity in this important branch of the administration, and I doubt not that the legislature will perform its duty with equal zeal. A thorough examination should be regularly made, and I will promote it.

It is particularly gratifying to me to enter on the discharge of these duties at a time when the United States are blessed with peace. It is a state most consistent with their prosperity and happiness. It will be my sincere desire to preserve it, so far as depends on the executive, on just principles with all nations, claiming nothing unreasonable of any and rendering to each what is its due.

Second Inaugural Address

Washington, D.C.

March 5, 1821

THIS INAUGURAL SPEECH was the longest yet delivered by a president. Monroe had hesitated to deliver a speech at all; had he heeded the objections of some Virginia politicians that an inaugural address was neither republican nor constitutional, the custom might have died with him. However, his cabinet convinced him to speak, at the same time advising Monroe to eliminate controversial statements on government finances and protective tariffs. What resulted was a blandly optimistic address that reviewed the administration's past accomplishments and made very general recommendations for the future.

I shall not attempt to describe the grateful emotions which the new and very distinguished proof of the confidence of my fellow citizens, evinced by my reelection to this high trust, has excited in my bosom. The approbation which it announces of my conduct in the preceding term affords me a consolation which I shall profoundly feel through life. The general accord with which it has been expressed adds to the great and never-ceasing obligations which it imposes. To merit the continuance of this good opinion, and to carry it with me into my retirement as the solace of advancing years, will be the object of my most zealous and unceasing efforts.

Having no pretensions to the high and commanding claims of my predecessors, whose names are so much more conspicuously identified with our Revolution, and who contributed so preeminently to promote its success, I consider myself rather as the instrument than the cause of the union which has prevailed in the late election. In surmounting, in favor of my humble pretensions, the difficulties which so often produce division in like occurrences, it is obvious that other powerful causes, indicating the great strength and stability of our Union, have essentially contributed to draw you together. That these powerful causes exist, and that they are permanent, is my fixed opinion; that they may produce a like accord in all questions touching, however remotely, the liberty, prosperity, and happiness of our country will always be the object of my most fervent prayers to the Supreme Author of All Good.

In a government which is founded by the people, who possess exclusively the sovereignty, it seems proper that the person who may be placed by their suffrages in this high trust should declare on commencing its duties the principles on which he intends to conduct the administration. If the person thus elected has served the preceding term, an opportunity is afforded him to review its principal occurrences and to give such further explanation respecting them as in his judgment may be useful to his constituents. The events of one year have influence on those of another, and, in like manner, of a preceding on the succeeding administration. The movements of a great nation are connected in all their parts. If errors have been committed they ought to be corrected; if the policy is sound it ought to be supported. It is by a thorough knowledge of the whole subject that our fellow citizens are enabled to judge correctly of the past and to give a proper direction to the future.

Just before the commencement of the last term the United States had concluded a war with a very powerful nation on conditions equal and honorable to both parties. The events of that war are too recent and too deeply impressed on the memory of all to require a development from me. Our commerce had been in a great measure driven from the sea; our Atlantic and inland frontiers were invaded in almost every part; the waste of life along our coast and on some parts of our inland frontiers, to the defense of which our gallant and patriotic citizens were called, was immense, in addition to which not less than $120,000,000 were added at its end to the public debt.

As soon as the war had terminated, the nation, admonished by its events, resolved to place itself in a situation which should be better calculated to prevent the recurrence of a like evil, and, in case it should recur, to mitigate its calamities. With this view, after reducing our land force to the basis of a peace establishment, which has been further modified since, provision was made for the construction of fortifications at proper points through the whole extent of our coast and such an augmentation of our naval force as should be well adapted to both purposes. The laws making this provision were passed in 1815 and 1816, and it has been since the constant effort of the executive to carry them into effect.

The advantage of these fortifications and of an augmented naval force in the extent contemplated, in a point of economy, has been fully illustrated by a report of the Board of Engineers and Naval Commissioners lately communicated to Congress, by which it appears that in an invasion by 20,000 men, with a correspondent naval force, in a campaign of six months only, the whole expense of the construction of the works would be defrayed by the difference in the sum necessary to maintain the force which would be adequate to our defense with the aid of those works and that which would be incurred without them. The reason of this difference is obvious. If fortifications are judiciously placed on our great inlets, as distant from our cities as circumstances will permit, they will form the only points of attack, and the enemy will be detained there by a small regular force a sufficient time to enable our militia to collect and repair to that on which the attack is made. A force adequate to the enemy, collected at that single point, with suitable preparation for such others as might be menaced, is all that would be requisite. But if there were no fortifications, then the enemy might go where he pleased; and, changing his position and sailing from place to place, our force must be called out and spread in vast numbers along the whole coast and on both sides of every bay and river as high up in each as it might be navigable for ships of war. By these fortifications, supported by our navy, to which they would afford like support, we should present to other powers an armed front from St. Croix to the Sabine, which would protect in the event of war our whole coast and interior from invasion; and even in the wars of other powers, in which we were neutral, they would be found eminently useful, as, by keeping their public ships at a distance from our cities, peace and order in them would be preserved and the government be protected from insult.

It need scarcely be remarked that these measures have not been resorted to in a spirit of hostility to other powers. Such a disposition does not exist toward any power. Peace and good will have been, and will hereafter be, cultivated with all, and by the most faithful regard to justice. They have been dictated by a love of peace, of economy, and an earnest desire to save the lives of our fellow citizens from that destruction and our country from that devastation which are inseparable from war when it finds us unprepared for it. It is believed, and experience has shown, that such a preparation is the best expedient that can be resorted to to prevent war. I add with much pleasure that considerable progress has already been made in these measures of defense, and that they will be completed in a few years, considering the great extent and importance of the object, if the plan be zealously and steadily persevered in.

The conduct of the government in what relates to foreign powers is always an object of the highest importance to the nation. Its agriculture, commerce, manufactures, fisheries, revenue, in short, its peace, may all be affected by it. Attention is therefore due to this subject.

At the period adverted to the powers of Europe, after having been engaged in long and destructive wars with each other, had concluded a peace, which happily still exists. Our peace with the power with whom we had been engaged had also been concluded. The war between Spain and the colonies in South America, which had commenced many years before, was then the only conflict that remained unsettled. This being a contest between different parts of the same community, in which other powers had not interfered, was not affected by their accommodations.

This contest was considered at an early stage by my predecessor a civil war in which the parties were entitled to equal rights in our ports. This decision, the first made by any power, being formed on great consideration of the comparative strength and resources of the parties, the length of time, and successful opposition made by the colonies, and of all other circumstances on which it ought to depend, was in strict accord with the law of nations. Congress has invariably acted on this princple, having made no change in our relations with either party. Our attitude has therefore been that of neutrality between them, which has been maintained by the government with the strictest impartiality. No aid has been afforded to either, nor has any privilege been enjoyed by the one which has not been equally open to the other party, and every exertion has been made in its power to enforce the execution of the laws prohibiting illegal equipments with equal rigor against both.

By this equality between the parties their public vessels have been received in our ports on the same footing; they have enjoyed an equal right to purchase and export arms, munitions of war, and every other supply, the exportation of all articles whatever being permitted under laws which were passed long before the commencement of the contest; our citizens have traded equally with both, and their commerce with each has been alike protected by the government.

Respecting the attitude which it may be proper for the United States to maintain hereafter between the parties, I have no hesitation in stating it as my opinion that the neutrality heretofore observed should still be adhered to. From the change in the government of Spain and the negotiation now depending, invited by the Cortes and accepted by the colonies, it may be presumed that their differences will be settled on the terms proposed by the colonies. Should the war be continued, the United States, regarding its occurrences, will always have it in their power to adopt such measures respecting it as their honor and interest may require.

Shortly after the general peace a band of adventurers took advantage of this conflict and of the facility which it afforded to establish a system of buccaneering in the neighboring seas, to the great annoyance of the commerce of the United States, and, as was represented, of that of other powers. Of this spirit and of its injurious bearing on the United States strong proofs were afforded by the establishment at Amelia Island, and the purposes to which it was made instrumental by this band in 1817, and by the occurrences which took place in other parts of Florida in 1818, the details of which in both instances are too well known to require to be now recited. I am satisfied had a less decisive course been adopted that the worst consequences would have resulted from it. We have seen that these checks, decisive as they were, were not sufficient to crush that piratical spirit. Many culprits brought within our limits have been condemned to suffer death, the punishment due to that atrocious crime. The decisions of upright and enlightened tribunals fall equally on all whose crimes subject them, by a fair interpretation of the law, to its censure. It belongs to the executive not to suffer the executions under these decisions to transcend the great purpose for which punishment is necessary. The full benefit of example being secured, policy as well as humanity equally forbids that they should be carried further. I have acted on this principle, pardoning those who appear to have been led astray by ignorance of the criminality of the acts they had committed, and suffering the law to take effect on those only in whose favor no extenuating circumstances could be urged.

Great confidence is entertained that the late treaty with Spain, which has been ratified by both the parties, and the ratifications whereof have been exchanged, has placed the relations of the two countries on a basis of permanent friendship. The provision made by it for such of our citizens as have claims on Spain of the character described will, it is presumed, be very satisfactory to them, and the boundary which is established between the territories of the parties westward of the Mississippi, heretofore in dispute, has, it is thought, been settled on conditions just and advantageous to both. But to the acquisition of Florida too much importance can not be attached. It secures to the United States a territory important in itself, and whose importance is much increased by its bearing on many of the highest interest of the Union. It opens to several of the neighboring states a free passage to the ocean, through the province ceded, by several rivers, having their sources high up within their limits. It secures us against all future annoyance from powerful Indian tribes. It gives us several excellent harbors in the Gulf of Mexico for ships of war of the largest size. It covers by its position in the Gulf the Mississippi and other great waters within our extended limits, and thereby enables the United States to afford complete protection to the vast and very valuable productions of our whole western country, which find a market through those streams.

By a treaty with the British government, bearing date on the 20th of October, 1818, the convention regulating the commerce between the United States and Great Britain, concluded on the 3d of July, 1815, which was about expiring, was revived and continued for the term of 10 years from the time of its expiration. By that treaty, also, the differences which had arisen under the treaty of Ghent respecting the right claimed by the United States for their citizens to take and cure fish on the coast of His Britannic Majesty's dominions in America, with other differences on important interests, were adjusted to the satisfaction of both parties. No agreement has yet been entered into respecting the commerce between the United States and the British dominions in the West Indies and on this continent. The restraints imposed on that commerce by Great Britain, and reciprocated by the United States on a principle of defense, continue still in force.

The negotiation with France for the regulation of the commercial relations between the two countries, which in the course of the last summer had been commenced at Paris, has since been transferred to this city, and will be pursued on the part of the United States in the spirit of conciliation, and with an earnest desire that it may terminate in an arrangement satisfactory to both parties.

Our relations with the Barbary Powers are preserved in the same state and by the same means that were employed when I came into this office. As early as 1801 it was found necessary to send a squadron into the Mediterranean for the protection of our commerce, and no period has intervened, a short term excepted, when it was thought advisable to withdraw it. The great interests which the United States have in the Pacific, in commerce and in the fisheries, have also made it necessary to maintain a naval force there. In disposing of this force in both instances the most effectual measures in our power have been taken, without interfering with its other duties, for the suppression of the slave trade and of piracy in the neighboring seas.

The situation of the United States in regard to their resources, the extent of their revenue, and the facility with which it is raised affords a most gratifying spectacle. The payment of nearly $67,000,000 of the public debt, with the great progress made in measures of defense and in other improvements of various kinds since the late war, are conclusive proofs of this extraordinary prosperity, especially when it is recollected that these expenditures have been defrayed without a burthen on the people, the direct tax and excise having been repealed soon after the conclusion of the late war, and the revenue applied to these great objects having been raised in a manner not to be felt. Our great resources therefore remain untouched for any purpose which may affect the vital interests of the nation. For all such purposes they are inexhaustible. They are more especially to be found in the virtue, patriotism, and intelligence of our fellow citizens, and in the devotion with which they would yield up by any just measure of taxation all their property in support of the rights and honor of their country.

Under the present depression of prices, affecting all the productions of the country and every branch of industry, proceeding from causes explained on a former occasion, the revenue has considerably diminshed, the effect of which has been to compel Congress either to abandon these great measures of defense or to resort to loans or internal taxes to supply the deficiency. On the presumption that this depression and the deficiency in the revenue arising from it would be temporary, loans were authorized for the demands of the last and present year. Anxious to relieve my fellow citizens in 1817 from every burthen which could be dispensed with, and the state of the Treasury permitting it, I recommended the repeal of the internal taxes, knowing that such relief was then peculiarly necessary in consequence of the great exertions made in the late war. I made that recommendation under a pledge that should the public exigencies require a recurrence to them at any time while I remained in this trust, I would with equal promptitude perform the duty which would then be alike incumbent on me. By the experiment now making it will be seen by the next session of Congress whether the revenue shall have been so augmented as to be adequate to all these necessary purposes. Should the deficiency still continue, and especially should it be probable that it would be permanent, the course to be pursued appears to me to be obvious. I am satisfied that under certain circumstances loans may be resorted to with great advantage. I am equally well satisfied, as a general rule, that the demands of the current year, especially in time of peace, should be provided for by the revenue of that year.

I have never dreaded, nor have I ever shunned, in any situation in which I have been placed making appeals to the virtue and patriotism of my fellow citizens, well knowing that they could never be made in vain, especially in times of great emergency or for purposes of high national importance. Independently of the exigency of the case, many considerations of great weight urge a policy having in view a provision of revenue to meet to a certain extent the demands of the nation, without relying altogether on the precarious resource of foreign commerce. I am satisfied that internal duties and excises, with corresponding imposts on foreign articles of the same kind, would, without imposing any serious burdens on the people, enhance the price of produce, promote our manufactures, and augment the revenue, at the same time that they made it more secure and permanent.

The care of the Indian tribes within our limits has long been an essential part of our system, but, unfortunately, it has not been executed in a manner to accomplish all the objects intended by it. We have treated them as independent nations, without their having any substantial pretensions to that rank. The distinction has flattered their pride, retarded their improvement, and in many instances paved the way to their destruction. The progress of our settlements westward, supported as they are by a dense population, has constantly driven them back, with almost the total sacrifice of the lands which they have been compelled to abandon. They have claims on the magnanimity and, I may add, on the justice of this nation which we must all feel. We should become their real benefactors; we should perform the office of their Great Father, the endearing title which they emphatically give to the chief magistrate of our Union. Their sovereignty over vast territories should cease, in lieu of which the right of soil should be secured to each individual and his posterity in competent portions; and for the territory thus ceded by each tribe some reasonable equivalent should be granted, to be vested in permanent funds for the support of civil government over them and for the education of their children, for their instruction in the arts of husbandry, and to provide sustenance for them until they could provide it for themselves. My earnest hope is that Congress will digest some plan, founded on these principles, with such improvements as their wisdom may suggest, and carry it into effect as soon as it may be practicable.

Europe is again unsettled and the prospect of war increasing. Should the flame light up in any quarter, how far it may extend it is impossible to foresee. It is our peculiar felicity to be altogether unconnected with the causes which produce this menacing aspect elsewhere. With every power we are in perfect amity, and it is our interest to remain so if it be practicable on just conditions. I see no reasonable cause to apprehend variance with any power, unless it proceed from a violation of our maritime rights. In these contests, should they occur, and to whatever extent they may be carried, we shall be neutral; but as a neutral power we have rights which it is our duty to maintain. For like injuries it will be incumbent on us to seek redress in a spirit of amity, in full confidence that, injuring none, none would knowingly injure us. For more imminent dangers we should be prepared, and it should always be recollected that such preparation adapted to the circumstances and sanctioned by the judgment and wishes of our constituents can not fail to have a good effect in averting dangers of every kind. We should recollect also that the season of peace is best adapted to these preparations.

If we turn our attention, fellow citizens, more immediately to the internal concerns of our country, and more especially to those on which its future welfare depends, we have every reason to anticipate the happiest results. It is now rather more than 44 years since we declared our independence, and 37 since it was acknowledged. The talents and virtues which were displayed in that great struggle were a sure presage of all that has since followed. A people who were able to surmount in their infant state such great perils would be more competent as they rose into manhood to repel any which they might meet in their progress. Their physical strength would be more adequate to foreign danger, and the practice of self-government, aided by the light of experience, could not fail to produce an effect equally salutary on all those questions connected with the internal organization. These favorable anticipations have been realized.

In our whole system, national and state, we have shunned all the defects which unceasingly preyed on the vitals and destroyed the ancient republics. In them there were distinct orders, a nobility and a people, or the people governed in one assembly. Thus, in the one instance there was a perpetual conflict between the orders in society for the ascendency, in which the victory of either terminated in the overthrow of the government and the ruin of the state; in the other, in which the people governed in a body, and whose dominions seldom exceeded the dimensions of a country in one of our states, a tumultuous and disorderly movement permitted only a transitory existence. In this great nation there is but one order, that of the people, whose power, by a peculiarly happy improvement of the representative principle, is transferred from them, without impairing in the slightest degree their sovereignty, to bodies of their own creation, and to persons elected by themselves, in the full extent necessary for all the purposes of free, enlightened, and efficient government. The whole system is elective, the complete sovereignty being in the people, and every officer in every department deriving his authority from and being responsible to them for his conduct.

Our career has corresponded with this great outline. Perfection in our organization could not have been expected at the outset either in the national or state governments or in tracing the line between their respective powers. But no serious conflict has arisen, nor any contest but such as are managed by argument and by a fair appeal to the good sense of the people, and many of the defects which experience had clearly demonstrated in both governments have been remedied. By steadily pursuing this course in this spirit there is every reason to believe that our system will soon attain the highest degree of perfection of which human institutions are capable, and that the movement in all its branches will exhibit such a degree of order and harmony as to command the admiration and respect of the civilized world.

Our physical attainments have not been less eminent. Twenty-five years ago the river Mississippi was shut up and our Western brethren had no outlet for their commerce. What has been the progress since that time? The river has not only become the property of the United States from its source to the ocean, with all its tributary streams (with the exception of the upper part of the Red River only), but Louisiana, with a fair and liberal boundary on the western side and the Floridas on the eastern, have been ceded to us. The United States now enjoy the complete and uninterrupted sovereignity over the whole territory from St. Croix to the Sabine. New states, settled from among ourselves in this and in other parts, have been admitted into our Union in equal participation in the national sovereignty with the original states. Our population has augmented in an astonishing degree and extended in every direction. We now, fellow citizens, comprise within our limits the dimensions and faculties of a great power under a government possessing all the energies of any government ever known to the Old World, with an utter incapacity to oppress the people.

Entering with these views the office which I have just solemnly sworn to execute with fidelity and to the utmost of my ability, I derive great satisfaction from a knowledge that I shall be assisted in the several departments by the very enlightened and upright citizens from whom I have received so much aid in the preceding term. With full confidence in the continuance of that candor and generous indulgence from my fellow citizens at large which I have heretofore experienced, and with a firm reliance on the protection of Almighty God, I shall forthwith commence the duties of the high trust to which you have called me.

The Monroe Doctrine

From the Seventh Annual Message to Congress
Washington, D.C.
December 2, 1823

THE MONROE DOCTRINE (reprinted below in part), drafted by Secretary of State John Quincy Adams and by Monroe himself, has had a profound effect on U.S. foreign policy, especially as it has been reinterpreted—sometimes radically—by later presidents. Monroe's statement was prompted by the efforts of several Latin American colonies to gain their independence from Spain. In 1822 the United States became the first nation to recognize Argentina, Chile, Peru, Colombia, and Mexico as independent states, but Monroe and others feared that Spain, possibly with the support of France, would attempt to regain control of its former colonies by force. These fears intensified when Britain proposed to issue a joint declaration with the United States opposing European intervention in the Americas; Monroe and his cabinet reasoned that the British must believe a Spanish-French expedition imminent to make such a suggestion to their own former colony. The Russians, who already claimed Alaska, also appeared to be eyeing the Oregon Territory.

Although both Jefferson and Madison urged Monroe to accept the British proposal, the president demurred. Joint action with Britain seemed to him and Adams both unnecessary and politically unwise. Instead, Monroe decided to announce the U.S. position in his annual message of 1823. The United States, Monroe stated, would not interfere in the internal affairs of any European power; in turn, however, the United States would not stand by passively and allow any European nation to intervene militarily in the Western Hemisphere or establish new colonies in the Americas. Many historians consider the Monroe Doctrine a reflection of America's achievement of an independent national identity. (See the chapters on Polk, Theodore Roosevelt, Franklin Roosevelt, Truman, Eisenhower, and Carter for reformulations of the doctrine.)

. . . In the wars of the European powers in matters relating to themselves we have never taken any part, nor does it comport with our policy so to do. It is only when our rights are invaded or seriously menaced that we resent injuries or make preparation for our defense. With the movements in this hemisphere we are of necessity more immediately connected, and by causes which must be obvious to all enlightened and impartial observers. The political system of the allied powers is essentially different in this respect from that of America. This difference proceeds from that which exists in their respective governments; and to the defense of our own, which has been achieved by the loss of so much blood and treasure, and matured by the wisdom of their most enlightened citizens, and under which we have enjoyed unexampled felicity, this whole nation is devoted. We owe it, therefore, to candor and to the amicable relations existing between the United States and those powers to declare that we should consider any attempt on their part to extend their system to any portion of this hemisphere as dangerous to our peace and safety. With the existing colonies or dependencies of any European power we have not interfered and shall not interfere. But with the governments who have declared their independence and maintained it, and whose independence we have, on great consideration and on just principles, acknowledged, we could not view any interposition for the purpose of oppressing them, or controlling in any other manner their destiny, by any European power in any other light than as the manifestation of an unfriendly disposition toward the United States. In the war between those new governments and Spain we declared our neutrality at the time of their recognition, and to this we have adhered, and shall continue to adhere, provided no change shall occur which, in the judgment of the competent authorities of this government, shall make a corresponding change on the part of the United States indispensable to their security.

The late events in Spain and Portugal shew that Europe is still unsettled. Of this important fact no stronger proof can be adduced than that the allied powers should have thought it proper, on any principle satisfactory to themselves, to have interposed by force in the internal concerns of Spain. To what extent such interposition may be carried, on the same principle, is a question in which all independent powers whose governments differ from theirs are interested, even those most remote, and surely none more so than the United States. Our policy in regard to Europe, which was adopted at an early stage of the wars which have so long agitated that quarter of the globe, nevertheless remains the same, which is, not to interfere in the internal concerns of any of its powers; to consider the government *de facto* as the legitimate government for us; to cultivate friendly relations with it, and to preserve those relations by a frank, firm, and manly policy, meeting in all instances the just claims of every power, submitting to injuries from none. But in regard to those continents, circumstances are eminently and conspicuously different. It is impossible that the allied powers should extend their political system to any portion of either continent without endangering our peace and happiness; nor can anyone believe that our southern brethren, if left to themselves, would adopt it of their own accord. It is equally impossible, therefore, that we should behold such interposition in any form with indifference. If we look to the comparative strength and resources of Spain and those new governments, and their distance from each other, it must be obvious that she can never subdue them. It is still the true policy of the United States to leave the parties to themselves in the hope that other powers will pursue the same course.

Special Message to the Senate on the Slave Trade Convention with Great Britain

Washington, D.C.

May 21, 1824

SLAVERY WAS the nation's foremost social issue and one with which every early American president had to deal. Although he was a slave owner, James Monroe had severe views on slavery: if he could end slavery in the United States, he would. But his best hope of ending slavery—having the government buy slaves from their owners—was too expensive. Instead, he hoped that slave owning would lose its centers of support in the slave states, become diffuse, and die out because of lack of interest. As president, Monroe could take decisive action through foreign diplomacy. The goal was not to end slavery but to outlaw trading in slaves, which would allow slavery to die a natural death.

Monroe begins his message by rejecting the methods of European nations that had already outlawed the slave trade. Instead, he proposes that the slave trade be regarded as piracy and therefore a violation of law—a proposal he had already made to Great Britain. Monroe is also pleased to report that the British parliament has already declared the slave trade an act of piracy, and he expresses hope that Great Britain will press a similar proposal on the other nations of Europe. Monroe concludes that "the crime will then be universally proscribed as piracy, and the traffic be suppressed forever."

Apprehending from the delay in the decision that some difficulty exists with the Senate respecting the ratification of the convention lately concluded with the British Government for the suppression of the slave trade by making it piratical, I deem it proper to communicate for your consideration such views as appear to me to merit attention. Charged as the Executive is, and as I have long been, with maintaining the political relations between the United States and other nations, I consider it my duty, in submitting for your advice and consent as to the ratification any treaty or convention which has been agreed on with another power, to explain, when the occasion requires it, all the reasons which induced the measure. It is by such full and frank explanation only that the Senate can be enabled to discharge the high trust reposed in them with advantage to their country. Having the instrument before them, with the views which guided the Executive in forming it, the Senate will possess all the light necessary to a sound decision.

By an act of Congress of 15th May, 1820, the slave trade, as described by that act, was made piratical, and all such of our citizens as might be found engaged in that trade were subjected, on conviction thereof by the circuit courts of the United States, to capital punishment. To communicate more distinctly the import of that act, I refer to its fourth and fifth sections, which are in the following words:

SEC. 4. And be it further enacted, That if any citizen of the United States, being of the crew or ship's company of any foreign ship or vessel engaged in the slave trade, or any person whatever, being of the crew or ship's company of any ship or vessel owned in the whole or part or navigated for or in behalf of any citizen or citizens of the United States, shall land from any such ship or vessel, and on any foreign shore seize any negro or mulatto not held to service or labor by the laws of either of the States or Territories of the United States, with intent to make such negro or mulatto a slave, or shall decoy or forcibly bring or carry, or shall receive, such negro or mulatto on board any such ship or vessel, with intent as aforesaid, such citizen or person shall be adjudged a pirate, and on conviction thereof before the circuit court of the United States for the district wherein he may be brought or found shall suffer death.

SEC. 5. And be it further enacted, That if any citizen of the United States, being of the crew or ship's company of any foreign ship or vessel engaged in the slave trade or any person whatever, being of the crew or ship's company of any ship or vessel owned wholly or in part, or navigated for or in behalf of, any citizen or citizens of the United States, shall forcibly confine or detain, or aid and abet in forcibly confining or detaining, on board such ship or vessel any negro or mulatto not held to service by the laws of either of the States or Territories of the United States, with intent to make such negro or mulatto a slave, or shall on board any such ship or vessel offer or attempt to sell as a slave any negro or mulatto not held to service as aforesaid, or shall on the high seas or anywhere on tide water transfer or deliver over to any other ship or vessel any negro or mulatto not held to service as aforesaid, with intent to make such negro or mulatto a slave, or shall land or deliver on shore from on board any such ship or vessel any such negro or mulatto, with intent to make sale of, or having previously sold such negro or mulatto as a slave, such citizen or person shall be adjudged a pirate, and on conviction thereof before the circuit court of the United States for the district wherein he may be brought or found shall suffer death.

And on the 28th February, 1823, the House of Representatives, by a majority of 131 to 9, passed a resolution to the following effect:

Resolved, That the President of the United States be requested to enter upon and prosecute from time to time such negotiations with the several maritime powers of Europe and America as he may deem expedient for the effectual abolition of the African slave trade and its ultimate denunciation as piracy under the law of nations, by the consent of the civilized world.

By the act of Congress above referred to, whereby the most effectual means that could be devised were adopted for the extirpation of the slave trade, the wish of the United States was explicitly declared, that all nations might concur in a similar policy. It could only be by such concurrence that the great object could be accomplished, and it was by negotiation and treaty alone that such concurrence could be obtained, commencing with one power and extending it to others. The course, therefore, which the Executive, who had concurred in the act, had to pursue was distinctly marked out for it. Had there, however, been any doubt respecting it, the resolution of the House of

Representatives, the branch which might with strict propriety express its opinion, could not fail to have removed it.

By the tenth article of the treaty of peace between the United States and Great Britain, concluded at Ghent, it was stipulated that both parties should use their best endeavors to accomplish the abolition of the African slave trade. This object has been accordingly pursued by both Governments with great earnestness, by separate acts of legislation, and by negotiation almost uninterrupted, with the purpose of establishing a concert between them in some measure which might secure its accomplishment.

Great Britain in her negotiations with other powers had concluded treaties with Spain, Portugal, and the Netherlands, in which, without constituting the crime as piracy or classing it with crimes of that denomination, the parties had conceded to the naval officers of each other the right of search and capture of the vessels of either that might be engaged in the slave trade, and had instituted courts consisting of judges, subjects of both parties, for the trial of the vessels so captured.

In the negotiations with the United States Great Britain had earnestly and repeatedly pressed on them the adoption of similar provisions. They had been resisted by the Executive on two grounds: One, that the constitution of mixed tribunals was incompatible with their Constitution; and the other, that the concession of the right of search in time of peace for an offense not piratical would be repugnant to the feelings of the nation and of dangerous tendency. The right of search is the right of war of the belligerent toward the neutral. To extend it in time of peace to any object whatever might establish a precedent which might lead to others with some powers, and which, even if confined to the instance specified, might be subject to great abuse.

Animated by an ardent desire to suppress this trade, the United States took stronger ground by making it, by the act above referred to, piratical, a measure more adequate to the end and free from many of the objections applicable to the plan which had been proposed to them. It is this alternative which the Executive, under the sanction and injunctions above stated, offered to the British Government, and which that Government has accepted.

By making the crime piracy the right of search attaches to the crime, and which when adopted by all nations will be common to all; and that it will be so adopted may fairly be presumed if steadily persevered in by the parties to the present convention. In the meantime, and with a view to a fair experiment, the obvious course seems to be to carry into effect with every power such treaty as may be made with each in succession.

In presenting this alternative to the British Government it was made an indispensable condition that the trade should be made piratical by act of Parliament, as it had been by an act of Congress. This was provided for in the convention, and has since been complied with. In this respect, therefore, the nations rest on the same ground. Suitable provisions have also been adopted to protect each party from the abuse of the power granted to the public ships of the other. Instead of subjecting the persons detected in the slave trade to trial by the courts of the captors, as would be the case if such trade was piracy by the laws of nations, it is stipulated that until that event they shall be tried by the courts of their own country only. Hence there could be no motive for an abuse of the right of search, since such abuse could not fail to terminate to the injury of the captor.

Should this convention be adopted, there is every reason to believe that it will be the commencement of a system destined to accomplish the entire abolition of the slave trade. Great Britain, by making it her own, confessedly adopted at the suggestion of the United States, and being pledged to propose and urge its adoption by other nations in concert with the United States, will find it for her interest to abandon the less-effective system of her previous treaties with Spain, Portugal, and the Netherlands, and to urge on those and other powers their accession to this. The crime will then be universally proscribed as piracy, and the traffic be suppressed forever.

Other considerations of high importance urge the adoption of this convention. We have at this moment pending with Great Britain sundry other negotiations intimately connected with the welfare and even the peace of our Union. In one of them nearly a third part of the territory of the State of Maine is in contestation. In another the navigation of the St. Lawrence, the admission of consuls into the British islands, and a system of commercial intercourse between the United States and all the British possessions in this hemisphere are subjects of discussion. In a third our territorial and other rights upon the northwest coast are to be adjusted, while a negotiation on the same interest is opened with Russia. In a fourth all the most important controvertible points of maritime law in time of war are brought under consideration, and in the fifth the whole system of South American concerns, connected with a general recognition of South American independence, may again from hour to hour become, as it has already been, an object of concerted operations of the highest interest to both nations and to the peace of the world.

It can not be disguised that the rejection of this convention can not fail to have a very injurious influence on the good understanding between the two Governments on all these points. That it would place the Executive Administration under embarrassment, and subject it, the Congress, and the nation to the charge of insincerity respecting the great result of the final suppression of the slave trade, and that its first and indispensable consequence will be to constrain the Executive to suspend all further negotiation with every European and American power to which overtures have been made in compliance with the resolution of the House of Representatives of 28th February, 1823, must be obvious. To invite all nations, with the statute of piracy in our hands, to adopt its principles as the law of nations and yet to deny to all the common right of search for the pirate, whom it would be impossible to detect without entering and searching the vessel, would expose us not simply to the charge of inconsistency.

It must be obvious that the restriction of search for pirates to the African coast is incompatible with the idea of such a crime. It is not doubted also if the convention is adopted that no example of the commission of that crime by the citizens or subjects of either power will ever occur again. It is believed, therefore, that this right as applicable to piracy would not only extirpate the trade, but prove altogether innocent in its operation.

In further illustration of the views of Congress on this subject, I transmit to the Senate extracts from two resolutions of the House of Representatives, one of the 9th February, 1821, the other of 12th April, 1822. I transmit also a letter from the charge' d'affaires of the British Government, which shows the deep interest which that Government takes in the ratification of the treaty.

The United States and the World

From the Eighth Annual Message to Congress
Washington, D.C.
December 7, 1824

THESE EXCERPTS from the closing paragraphs of Monroe's last annual message reveal how much more of an international orientation the United States had acquired since the time of Washington's Farewell Address. While Washington warned against involvement in "foreign alliances, attachments, and intrigues," Monroe firmly believed that to the world, and especially to the new republics of Hispanic America, the United States now had "duties to perform with respect to all to which we must be faithful."

. . . It is manifest that the situation of the United States is in the highest degree prosperous and happy. There is no object which as a people we can desire which we do not possess or which is not within our reach. Blessed with governments the happiest which the world ever knew, with no distinct orders in society or divided interests in any portion of the vast territory over which their dominion extends, we have every motive to cling together which can animate a virtuous and enlightened people. The great object is to preserve these blessings, and to hand them down to the latest posterity. Our experience ought to satisfy us that our progress under the most correct and provident policy will not be exempt from danger. Our institutions form an important epoch in the history of the civilized world. On their preservation and in their utmost purity everything will depend. Extending as our interests do to every part of the inhabited globe and to every sea to which our citizens are carried by their industry and enterprise, to which they are invited by the wants of others, and have a right to go, we must either protect them in the enjoyment of their rights or abandon them in certain events to waste and desolation. Our attitude is highly interesting as relates to other powers, and particularly to our southern neighbors. We have duties to perform with respect to all to which we must be faithful. To every kind of danger we should pay the most vigilant and unceasing attention, remove the cause where it may be practicable, and be prepared to meet it when inevitable.

Against foreign danger the policy of the government seems to be already settled. The events of the late war admonished us to make our maritime frontier impregnable by a well-digested chain of fortifications, and to give efficient protection to our commerce by augmenting our navy to a certain extent, which has been steadily pursued, and which it is incumbent upon us to complete as soon as circumstances will permit. In the event of war it is on the maritime frontier that we shall be assailed. It is in that quarter, therefore, that we should be prepared to meet the attack. It is there that our whole force will be called into action to prevent the destruction of our towns and the desolation and pillage of the interior. To give full effect to this policy great improvements will be indispensable. Access to those works by every practicable communication should be made easy and in every direction. The intercourse between every part of our Union should also be promoted and facilitated by the exercise of those powers which may comport with a faithful regard to the great principles of our Constitution. With respect to internal causes, those great principles point out with equal certainty the policy to be pursued. Resting on the people as our governments do, state and national, with well-defined powers, it is of the highest importance that they severally keep within the limits prescribed to them. Fulfilling that sacred duty, it is of equal importance that the movement between them be harmonious, and in case of any disagreement, should any such occur, a calm appeal be made to the people, and that their voice be heard and promptly obeyed. Both governments being instituted for the common good, we can not fail to prosper while those who made them are attentive to the conduct of their representatives and control their measures. In the pursuit of these great objects let a generous spirit and national views and feelings be indulged, and let every part recollect that by cherishing that spirit and improving the condition of the others in what relates to their welfare the general interest will not only be promoted, but the local advantage be reciprocated by all.

I can not conclude this communication, the last of the kind which I shall have to make, without recollecting with great sensibility and heartfelt gratitude the many instances of the public confidence and the generous support which I have received from my fellow citizens in the various trusts with which I have been honored. Having commenced my service in early youth, and continued it since with few and short intervals, I have witnessed the great difficulties to which our Union has been exposed, and admired the virtue and intelligence with which they have been surmounted. From the present prosperous and happy state I derive a gratification which I can not express. That these blessings may be preserved and perpetuated will be the object of my fervent and unceasing prayers to the Supreme Ruler of the Universe.

Courtesy of Library of Congress

John Quincy Adams

John Quincy Adams

1825–1829

JOHN QUINCY ADAMS was the first president whose father also held the office; and like John Adams he was unable to hold power for more than a single term. His claim to greatness lies not with his presidency but with the two careers that preceded and followed it—as diplomat and secretary of state, and as the voice of the antislavery movement in the House of Representatives.

Adams was born in the family homestead in Braintree (now Quincy), Massachusetts, in 1767. Going with his father to Europe before his 12th birthday, he absorbed a practical education in diplomacy and within a few years was secretary to the American envoy in St. Petersburg. After his graduation from Harvard and his admission to the bar, he became one of the nation's most experienced diplomats, leading the commission that negotiated the Treaty of Ghent with Britain in 1814. As secretary of state under James Monroe, he negotiated the Transcontinental Treaty with Spain and was chiefly responsible for the development of the principles set forth in the Monroe Doctrine. According to his biographer, Samuel Flagg Bemis, "Adams more than any single man helped lay the classic foundations of American foreign policy. If the United States has produced a greater diplomatist it would be difficult to name him."

Adams ran second to Andrew Jackson in the presidential election of 1824, but since neither candidate received a majority of the vote, the decision went to the House of Representatives. Adams's election was assured after another candidate, Henry Clay, directed his supporters in the House to vote for Adams. Clay's subsequent appointment to the office of secretary of state enraged Jackson's followers, who accused the high-minded Adams of making a "corrupt bargain" to steal the presidency from the actual winner. The Jacksonians united in a deadly opposition that prevented the president from exercising executive leadership. Nor could he successfully organize support in his own behalf. A Federalist turned Republican, but with more allegiance to his own judgment than to any party, he saw himself as the "Man of the Whole Nation," a custodian of the future rather than a political manipulator.

He was defeated by Jackson in the election of 1828 and returned to Quincy, but within two years he had accepted the nomination of his district to the House of Representatives, where he served for the last 17 years of his life. Most of his energy was spent in the fight against the "gag rule," which had been established by Southern representatives to block all discussion of slavery. Despite death threats and a trial for censure, Adams, displaying enormous endurance and parliamentary skill, successfully pushed to have the rule rescinded and to restore the First Amendment right to petition Congress. One of his chief antagonists, Henry A. Wise of Virginia, called him the "acutest, the astutest, the archest enemy of Southern slavery that ever existed." "I subject myself to so much toil and enmity with so very little apparent fruit," Adams wrote, "that I sometimes ask myself whether I do not mistake my own motives. The best actions of my life make me nothing but Enemies. . . . In such cases, a man can be sustained only by an overruling consciousness of rectitude. To withstand multitudes is the only unerring test of decisive character."

Adams's reputation as an orator dates from these congressional debates, when he overcame the palsy and rheumatism of his old age to batter the Southern bloc again and again. After one impassioned speech on the House floor he was given the name "Old Man Eloquent." To his pro-slavery opponents he was also known as the Massachusetts Madman, the "hell-hound of abolition" (though he was not in the abolitionist camp). In 1841 he spoke before the Supreme Court in defense of 36 Africans, kidnapped by Spanish slavers, who had freed themselves through mutiny. In his biography of Adams, Bemis describes the scene thus: "As the old man spoke, his years seemed to drop away. Infirmities fell from him as always they did in combat. His aged voice took on the spirit of youth. His watery eyes grew strong with a blaze of righteous scorn. He was bitter in his sarcasm at those who would make slaves out of resolute free men, damning in his strictures on an executive power that would deliver them over to the vengeance of foreign slaveholders— expanding his arguments to general principles of human morality. From the bench the Justices fixed their eyes on him hour after hour." The Africans were freed by a vote of six to one.

Internal Improvement

From the First Annual Message to Congress
Washington, D.C.
December 5, 1825

DESPITE HIS WITHDRAWAL from the Federalist Party, Adams remained sympathetic to the Federalist philosophy outlined by Washington in his Farewell Address. He envisioned the United States of the future as a true union of peoples, with a single culture and a national agenda that would transcend regional and sectarian differences. In his first annual message to Congress he outlined a plan to accelerate the process of unification by constructing a nationwide transportation system and by establishing scientific and educational institutions, the whole scheme to be financed through the sale of the public lands in the West.

Most of the members of Adams's cabinet warned him against including the details of this plan in the message, and their fears were justified. Adams was ridiculed as a would-be tyrant who was willing to sacrifice the prospects of poorer settlers in favor of industrial and financial interests. His enemies in Congress made the most of it, and from this point on they continued to gain momentum. It was, according to George Dangerfield, "an extraordinary, perhaps a unique, example of the art of suicide by manifesto."

Upon this first occasion of addressing the legislature of the Union, with which I have been honored, in presenting to their view the execution so far as it has been effected of the measures sanctioned by them for promoting the internal improvement of our country, I can not close the communication without recommending to their calm and persevering consideration the general principle in a more enlarged extent. The great object of the institution of civil government is the improvement of the condition of those who are parties to the social compact, and no government, in whatever form constituted, can accomplish the lawful ends of its institution but in proportion as it improves the condition of those over whom it is established. Roads and canals, by multiplying and facilitating the communications and intercourse between distant regions and multitudes of men, are among the most important means of improvement. But moral, political, intellectual improvement are duties assigned by the Author of Our Existence to social no less than to individual man. For the fulfillment of those duties governments are invested with power, and to the attainment of the end—the progressive improvement of the condition of the governed—the exercise of delegated powers is a duty as sacred and indispensable as the usurpation of powers not granted is criminal and odious. Among the first, perhaps the very first, instrument for the improvement of the condition of men is knowledge, and to the acquisition of much of the knowledge adapted to the wants, the comforts, and enjoyments of human life public institutions and seminaries of learning are essential. So convinced of this was the first of my predecessors in this office, now first in the memory, as, living, he was first in the hearts, of our countrymen, that once and again in his addresses to the Congresses with whom he cooperated in the public service he earnestly recommended the establishment of seminaries of learning, to prepare for all the emergencies of peace and war—a national university and a military academy. With respect to the latter, had he lived to the present day, in turning his eyes to the institution at West Point he would have enjoyed the gratification of his most earnest wishes; but in surveying the city which has been honored with his name he would have seen the spot of earth which he had destined and bequeathed to the use and benefit of his country as the site for an university still bare and barren.

In assuming her station among the civilized nations of the earth it would seem that our country had contracted the engagement to contribute her share of mind, of labor, and of expense to the improvement of those parts of knowledge which lie beyond the reach of individual acquisition, and particularly to geographical and astronomical science. Looking back to the history only of the half century since the declaration of our independence, and observing the generous emulation with which the governments of France, Great Britain, and Russia have devoted the genius, the intelligence, the treasures of their respective nations to the common improvement of the species in these branches of science, is it not incumbent upon us to inquire whether we are not bound by obligations of a high and honorable character to contribute our portion of energy and exertion to the common stock? The voyages of discovery prosecuted in the course of that time at the expense of those nations have not only redounded to their glory, but to the improvement of human knowledge. We have been partakers of that improvement and owe for it a sacred debt, not only of gratitude, but of equal or proportional exertion in the same common cause. Of the cost of these undertakings, if the mere expenditures of outfit, equipment, and completion of the expeditions were to be considered the only charges, it would be unworthy of a great and generous nation to take a second thought. One hundred expeditions of circumnavigation like those of Cook and La Pérouse would not burden the exchequer of the nation fitting them out so much as the ways and means of defraying a single campaign in war. But if we take into the account the lives of those benefactors of mankind of which their services in the cause of their species were the purchase, how shall the cost of those heroic enterprises be estimated, and what compensation can be made to them or to their countries for them? Is it not by bearing them in affectionate remembrance? Is it not still more by imitating their example—by enabling countrymen of our own to pursue the same career and to hazard their lives in the same cause?

In inviting the attention of Congress to the subject of internal improvements upon a view thus enlarged it is not my design to recommend the equipment of an expedition for circumnavigating the globe for purposes of scientific research and inquiry. We have objects of useful investigation nearer home, and to which our cares may be more beneficially applied. The interior of our own territories has yet been very imperfectly explored. Our coasts along many degrees of latitude upon the shores of the Pacific Ocean, though much frequented by our spirited commercial

navigators, have been barely visited by our public ships. The River of the West, first fully discovered and navigated by a countryman of our own, still bears the name of the ship in which he ascended its waters, and claims the protection of our armed national flag at its mouth. With the establishment of a military post there or at some other point of that coast, recommended by my predecessor and already matured in the deliberations of the last Congress, I would suggest the expediency of connecting the equipment of a public ship for the exploration of the whole northwest coast of this continent.

The establishment of an uniform standard of weights and measures was one of the specific objects contemplated in the formation of our Constitution, and to fix that standard was one of the powers delegated by express terms in that instrument to Congress. The governments of Great Britain and France have scarcely ceased to be occupied with inquiries and speculations on the same subject since the existence of our Constitution, and with them it has expanded into profound, laborious, and expensive researches into the figure of the earth and the comparative length of the pendulum vibrating seconds in various latitudes from the equator to the pole. These researches have resulted in the composition and publication of several works highly interesting to the cause of science. The experiments are yet in the process of performance. Some of them have recently been made on our own shores, within the walls of one of our own colleges, and partly by one of our own fellow citizens. It would be honorable to our country if the sequel of the same experiments should be countenanced by the patronage of our government, as they have hitherto been by those of France and Britain.

Connected with the establishment of an university, or separate from it, might be undertaken the erection of an astronomical observatory, with provision for the support of an astronomer, to be in constant attendance of observation upon the phenomena of the heavens, and for the periodical publication of his observations. It is with no feeling of pride as an American that the remark may be made that on the comparatively small territorial surface of Europe there are existing upward of 130 of these light-houses of the skies, while throughout the whole American hemisphere there is not one. If we reflect a moment upon the discoveries which in the last four centuries have been made in the physical constitution of the universe by the means of these buildings and of observers stationed in them, shall we doubt of their usefulness to every nation? And while scarcely a year passes over our heads without bringing some new astronomical discovery to light, which we must fain receive at second hand from Europe, are we not cutting ourselves off from the means of returning light for light while we have neither observatory nor observer upon our half of the globe and the earth revolves in perpetual darkness to our unsearching eyes? . . .

The Constitution under which you are assembled is a charter of limited powers. After full and solemn deliberation upon all or any of the objects which, urged by an irresistible sense of my own duty, I have recommended to your attention should you come to the conclusion that, however desirable in themselves, the enactment of laws for effecting them would transcend the powers committed to you by that venerable instrument which we are all bound to support, let no consideration induce you to assume the exercise of powers not granted to you by the people. But if the power to exercise exclusive legislation in all cases whatsoever over the District of Columbia; if the power to lay and collect taxes, duties, imposts, and excises, to pay the debts and provide for the common defense and general welfare of the United States; if the power to regulate commerce with foreign nations and among the several states and with the Indian tribes, to fix the standard of weights and measures, to establish post-offices and post-roads, to declare war, to raise and support armies, to provide and maintain a navy, to dispose of and make all needful rules and regulations respecting the territory or other property belonging to the United States, and to make all laws which shall be necessary and proper for carrying these powers into execution—if these powers and others enumerated in the Constitution may be effectually brought into action by laws promoting the improvement of agriculture, commerce, and manufactures, the cultivation and encouragement of the mechanic and of the elegant arts, the advancement of literature, and the progress of the sciences, ornamental and profound, to refrain from exercising them for the benefit of the people themselves would be to hide in the earth the talent committed to our charge—would be treachery to the most sacred of trusts.

The spirit of improvement is abroad upon the earth. It stimulates the hearts and sharpens the faculties not of our fellow citizens alone, but of the nations of Europe and of their rulers. While dwelling with pleasing satisfaction upon the superior excellence of our political institutions, let us not be unmindful that liberty is power; that the nation blessed with the largest portion of liberty must in proportion to its numbers be the most powerful nation upon earth, and that the tenure of power by man is, in the moral purposes of his Creator, upon condition that is shall be exercised to ends of beneficence, to improve the condition of himself and his fellow men. While foreign nations less blessed with that freedom which is power than ourselves are advancing with gigantic strides in the career of public improvement, were we to slumber in indolence or fold up our arms and proclaim to the world that we are palsied by the will of our constituents, would it not be to cast away the bounties of Providence and doom ourselves to perpetual inferiority? In the course of the year now drawing to its close we have beheld, under the auspices and at the expense of one state of this Union, a new university unfolding its portals to the sons of science and holding up the torch of human improvement to eyes that seek the light. We have seen under the persevering and enlightened enterprise of another state the waters of our western lakes mingle with those of the ocean. If undertakings like these have been accomplished in the compass of a few years by the authority of single members of our confederation, can we, the representative authorities of the whole Union, fall behind our fellow servants in the exercise of the trust committed to us for the benefit of our common sovereign by the accomplishment of works important to the whole and to which neither the authority nor the resources of any one state can be adequate?

Finally, fellow citizens, I shall await with cheering hope and faithful cooperation the result of your deliberations, assured that, without encroaching upon the powers reserved to the authorities of the respective states or to the people, you will, with a due sense of your obligations to your country and of the high responsibilities weighing upon yourselves, give efficacy to the means committed to you for the common good. And may He who searches the hearts of the children of men prosper your exertions to secure the blessings of peace and promote the highest welfare of our country.

The Right of Petition

Washington, D.C.

June 16, 1838

THE ATTEMPT BY Southern congressmen to have the republic of Texas admitted to the Union as a slave state opened the way for Representative Adams to attack the gag rule and to introduce into House debates the forbidden subject of slavery. The following excerpt illustrates the perseverance and shrewdness with which he pressed his case and fended off the maneuvers of the opposition. The members of the committee on foreign affairs had refused to read a batch of petitions against annexation signed by more than 100,000 citizens and had recommended that the petitions be tabled in order to avoid all discussion of the subject; Adams's scathing remarks on their behavior showed to what absurd lengths the proannexation, proslavery congressmen were prepared to go.

Long before his election to Congress, Adams was convinced that the Union was threatened with destruction because of the refusal of the South to reconcile its way of life with the demands of justice. In 1820 he wrote: "If slavery be the destined sword in the hand of the destroying angel which is to sever the ties of this Union, the same sword will cut in sunder the bonds of slavery itself. A dissolution of the Union for the cause of slavery would be followed by a servile war in the slave-holding states, combined with a war between the two severed portions of the Union. It seems to me that its result must be the extirpation of slavery from this whole continent; and, calamitous and desolating as this course of events in its progress must be, so glorious would be its final issue, that, as God shall judge me, I dare not say that it is not to be desired."

MR. ADAMS ROSE AND SAID: I do not wish, in the present stage of the debate, to introduce the general question of the annexation of Texas to the Union. I particularly desire the House so to understand me. The proposition of my colleague is this:

That the report and accompanying papers be recommitted to the same committee, with instructions to make report thereon in full as to the merits of the questions presented by the resolutions of the legislatures of the several states of Tennessee, Alabama, Michigan, Ohio, and Massachusetts, and of the various petitions before the House on the subject of Texas.

His desire is, that the subject be recommitted, in order to have a deliberate report on the merits of the several resolutions of state legislatures, and of the numerous private memorials, petitions, and remonstrances which had, at different periods of the session, been referred to the committee. That, also, is my desire. The resolution he offered does not involve the general question: it seeks only the recommitment of the subject, and of the various documents relating thereto, which have been sent to that committee, but which the committee have not taken into consideration.

I take it for granted, when the general question comes up (unless we are again to have the previous question called upon us, and debate smothered, as happened when it was up before), the question will be divided, and taken first on the recommitment, and then on the different propositions of instruction, in their order. I now state that my only object, at present, is to recommit the subject to get a report upon it. It was in this view that I found it necessary to take issue with the gentleman from Virginia [George C.] Dromgoole on the question of *the rights of this House, of the rights of members of this House, and of the rights and duties of the committees of this House.*

When the subject first came up, I rose in my place and inquired of the speaker, not of the gentleman from Virginia, whether the committee had given as much as five minutes' consideration to the several resolutions of the legislatures of sovereign states of this Union, and the very memorials and petitions of individual citizens which had been, by order of this House, referred to their consideration? When I put that question to the chair, the gentleman from Virginia rose, and denied my right to do so, and declared that he would not be catechised by me. I said, at the time, that the reluctance of the committee to answer that question was, of itself, sufficient for me, and that I trusted it would be sufficient for this House and for the American people. It was a concession that the committee never had taken these papers into consideration at all. That, I trust, will be the deliberate conviction of the people of the United States.

But this interference is not enough. The gentleman from Virginia assumed a general principle as to the rights of this House, the rights of members of this House, and the rights and duties of committees of this House. My question was not personal to the gentleman from Virginia. I did not ask what consideration *he* had given to these documents; I asked whether the *committee* had considered the memorials of the thousands and hundreds of thousands of American citizens, and the solemn resolutions of the legislators of not a few of the states of this Union, which had been sent to them that they might be considered. The only answer is that of an individual, that *"he* will not be catechised." This is not the answer to which I was entitled; and I demand an answer yet. Until I get it, my inference will be that those documents never were considered by the committee.

When this question was up during the morning hour, yesterday, I had *only* time, as the hour was about expiring, to give notice to the House that I took an issue with the gentleman from Virginia on the great and important principle laid down by him touching the rights of this House, the rights of members of this House, and the rights and duties of the committees of this House. I was arrested by the expiration of the hour. I had time only to inquire of the chairman of the committee [Benjamin C. Howard] whether he endorsed the principle laid down by his colleague on the Committee on Foreign Affairs. And I understood him to say that he went the full length of the ground taken by that gentleman. I then asked if there was any other of the members of that committee who took the same position. But before any response was given, the orders of the day were named by the chair, and the subject was for the time cut off.

It was, at that time, my intention to ask each member of that committee; in order, whether he endorsed the doctrine of the gentleman from Virginia; but, on further consideration, I have concluded not to do so; and for this reason: that some of those gentlemen might probably find themselves in the situation of the honorable chairman—between a great principle of duty on the one hand, and, on the other, of party obligation to a personal and political friend; for to this moment I cannot believe that the chairman of that committee does, in his heart, assent to the soundness of any such principle as that to which he has committed himself. . . .

[Hugh S.] Legare said that, for one, he was prepared to answer the gentleman's question, though he protested against his right to catechise the committee; and as soon as he could obtain the floor he should give the reasons why the committee declined being more explicit in their report, or entering on the merits of the general question. They were under no obligation to do so; and that for the reason stated in their report. He was fully aware of the importance and novelty of the general principle to which the gentleman was now speaking, and would give his views of it as soon as an opportunity should be allowed him to get the floor.

Mr. Adams. I did not distinctly hear the gentleman. I now understand him to decline answering my question.

Mr. Legare. *What I said related to the committee. For myself, I have no hesitation in admitting that I have not read the papers, or looked into them, nor was I bound to do so.*

Mr. Adams. I understand the gentleman from South Carolina now formally to admit that he has never looked into the documents referred to the committee on the subject of Texas at all.

Mr. Legare. *Not one of them.*

Mr. Adams. *Into not one of them?*

Mr. Legare. *Not one.*

Mr. Adams. I beg leave, now, to read the 76th standing rule of this House:

It shall be the duty of the Committee on Foreign Affairs to take into consideration all matters which concern the relations of the United States with foreign nations, and which shall be referred to them by the House, and to report their opinion on the same.

There is the letter of the law. [Mr. A. here read the rule, very slowly, a second time.] The gentleman from South Carolina says that he is aware the question is one of immense importance.

MR. LEGARE said he had done nothing incompatible with that rule. He had fully *considered the subject* on which the committee reported, as far as the report went. It was by no means necessary to look into the arguments for or against admitting Texas, when the committee concluded that no question as to the admission of Texas had yet arisen in the House, and did not choose themselves to become the authors of any proposition, without the express order of the House.

MR. ADAMS. The gentleman has taken into consideration the resolutions of sovereign states and of a vast body of memorials and petitions, and has never looked into one of them. [A laugh.] Sir, the time has been when I despaired to speak to this House on a great principle, when I despaired to speak to the people of this country on a great principle. I will not say that the time has passed when I despair to appeal to this House on a great national principle. I remember the report of the Committee of Elections in the Mississippi case. I remember the report of the Duelling Committee. I do not know but that it is desperate to make an appeal to this House when party crosses its path, but I do not despair to appeal to the people. To them I call to mark the principles assumed in this House by members of one of the most important committees of the House—a committee to whom of destiny of this nation is committed in a greater degree than to any other. I call them to note what is now passing here. The resolutions of the legislatures of six or seven states of this Union, standing on the principles they respectively maintain, together with memorials, and petitions, and remonstrances, from thousands and hundreds of thousands of American citizens, have been referred to that committee to consider and report thereon. When a question is put, a member of that committee rises in his place and denies the right of the House, or of any member, to ask whether the committee ever did consider those resolutions and memorials. And another member of that same committee answers that he is willing to report on these papers without looking into any one of them. Now, I beg leave to say, in the face of the country, that I denounce both as utterly incorrect, and I hope the people of the United States will do themselves justice in this case, as the people of Mississippi have nobly done themselves justice in regard to another report

to this House. Sir, we are in a process in which I hope we shall persevere until such principles shall be forever swept away. Would to God they could be swept from the records of this House, as they will be from the practice of all future Congresses. I assert, as a great general principle, that when resolutions from the legislatures of states, and the petitions of a vast multitude of our fellow citizens on a subject of deep and vital importance to the country, are referred to a committee of this House, if that committee make up an opinion without looking into such resolutions and memorials, the committee betray their duty to their constituents and to this House. I give this out to the nation. I ask this nation to reflect on the proceedings of the committee and of the House on such principles. When the meanest petition of the lowest and poorest individual in the country (I will not say slave) is presented in this House and referred, I hold it the duty of the committee, to the House, to the country, and to the petitioners, to look into the petition before they make up their opinion. Here is a broad principle; if I am wrong, let the country put me down. It is affirmed that the report of a committee is to be made without even looking into the resolutions of legislatures and the petitions of citizens referred to that committee for consideration.

Why do you refer any paper to a committee, if their mind is previously so made up that they will not look into one of those papers? What is it but a waste of time to refer documents to a committee who have thus prejudged the subject? I say it is contrary to the very vital existence of this House, and of the committees of this House; and I say that if the avowal of such a principle was made in respect to the memorial of a single individual, it would not be tolerated. Supposing it were a petition of a soldier of the Revolution, or the case of Mrs. Heileman, which we had but yesterday before us, a case not provided for by law, and the committee should take such ground, what would this House say? I ask the gentleman from South Carolina himself to tell me what would this House say? A committee comes in and reports against the petition of Mrs. Heileman. They are asked whether they looked at her petition, and one of the committee rises and says, no; I had made up my mind before; I did not care what was in the petition; I had considered *the subject,* and I thought the provisions of existing laws to be sufficient. What would this House say to such an answer as that? And if it would not be tolerated in the case of one poor widow, what shall be said when the question referred to the committee is the fate and fortune of this Union—the existence of this Union—the existence of freedom among the race of man?

The Nature of Federal Government

New York City, New York

April 30, 1839

DURING ADAMS'S YEARS in the House, the integrity of the Union was threatened by the doctrine of nullification—the claim, put forth by many Southerners, that the sovereignty of the individual states supersedes the powers of the federal government. According to this claim, any state had the right within its borders to void any federal law of which it disapproved. Adams was at pains to refute the theory behind this doctine, which he recognized as the ultimate refuge of the slaveholders. "Democracy is self-government of the community by the conjoint will of the majority of members," he wrote to his constituents. "What communion, what affinity, can there be between that principle and nullification, which is the despotism of a corporation—unlimited, unrestrained, sovereign power? . . . Slavery stands aghast at the prospective promotion of the general welfare, and flies to nullification for defence against the energies of freedom, and the inalienable rights of man."

The address from which this excerpt was taken was delivered before the New York Historical Society at a ceremony commemorating the 50th anniversary of Washington's inauguration.

The motive for the Declaration of Independence was on its face avowed to be "a decent respect for the opinions of mankind"; its *purpose* to declare the *causes* which impelled the people of the English colonies on the continent of North America to separate themselves from the political community of the British nation. They declare *only* the *causes* of their separation, but they announce at the same time their assumption of the separate and equal station to which the laws of nature and of nature's God entitle them among the powers of the earth. Thus their first movement is to recognize and appeal to the laws of nature and to nature's God for their *right* to assume the attributes of sovereign power as an independent nation. . . .

It is not immaterial to remark that the signers of the Declaration, though qualifying themselves as the representatives of the United States of America, in general Congress assembled, yet issue the Declaration *in the name and by the authority of the good people of the colonies;* and that they declare, *not* each of the separate colonies but the *united colonies*, free and independent states. The whole people declared the colonies in *their united condition* of *right,* free, and independent states. The dissolution of allegiance to the British Crown, the severance of the colonies from the British Empire, and their actual existence as independent states, thus declared of *right,* were definitely established *in fact* by war and peace. The independence of each separate state had

never been delcared of *right*. It never existed *in fact*. Upon the principles of the Declaration of Independence, the dissolution of the ties of allegiance, the assumption of sovereign power, and the institution of civil government are all acts of transcendent authority which the people *alone* are competent to perform; and, accordingly, it is in the name and by the authority of the people that two of these acts—the dissolution of allegiance, with the severance from the British Empire, and the declaration of the united colonies as free and independent states—were performed by that instrument.

But there still remained the last and crowning act, which the *people* of the Union alone were competent to perform—the institution of civil government for that compound nation, the United States of America.

At this day it cannot but strike us as extraordinary that it does not appear to have occurred to any one member of that assembly, which had laid down in terms so clear, so explicit, so unequivocal the foundation of all just government, in the imprescriptible rights of man, and the transcendent sovereignty of the people, and who, in those principles, had set forth their only personal vindication from the charges of rebellion against their king and of treason to their country, that their last crowning act was still to be performed upon the same principles—that is, the institution by the *people* of the United States, of a civil government, to guard and protect and defend them all. On the contrary, that same assembly which issued the Declaration of Independence, instead of continuing to act in the name and by the authority of the good people of the United States, had immediately after the appointment of the committee to prepare the Declaration, appointed another committee of one member from each colony to prepare and digest the form of confederation to be entered into between the colonies.

That committee reported on the 12th of July, eight days after the Declaration of Independence had been issued, a draft of Articles of Confederation between the colonies. This draft was prepared by John Dickinson, then a delegate from Pennsylvania, who voted against the Declaration of Independence and never signed it—having been superseded by a new election of delegates from that state eight days after his draft was reported.

There was thus no congeniality of principle between the Declaration of Independence and the Articles of Confederation. The foundation of the former were a superintending Providence—the rights of man and the constituent revolutionary power of the people. That of the latter was the sovereignty of organized power and the independence of the separate or disunited states. The fabric of the Declaration and that of the Confederation were each consistent with its own foundation, but they could not form one consistent, symmetrical edifice. They were the productions of different minds and of adverse passions—one, ascending for the foundation of human government to the laws of nature and of God, written upon the heart of man; the other, resting upon the basis of human institutions, and prescriptive law and colonial charters. The cornerstone of the one was *right;* that of the other was *power.*

The work of the founders of our independence was thus but half done. Absorbed in that more than herculean task of maintaining that independence and its principles, by one of the most cruel wars that ever glutted the furies with human woe, they marched undaunted and steadfast though that fiery ordeal, and consistent in their principles to the end, concluded, as an acknowledged sovereignty of the United States, proclaimed by their people in 1776, a peace with that same monarch whose sovereignty over them they had abjured in obedience to the laws of nature and of nature's God.

But for these United States, they had formed no constitution. Instead of resorting to the source of all constituted power, they had wasted their time, their talents, and their persevering, untiring toils in erecting and roofing buttressing a frail and temporary shed to shelter the nation from the storm, or rather a mere baseless scaffolding on which to stand, when they should raise the marble palace of the people to stand the test of time.

Five years were consumed by Congress and the state legislatures in debating and altercating and adjusting these Articles of Confederation. The first of which was:

"Each state *retains* its sovereignty, freedom, and independence, and every power, jurisdiction, and right which is not by this Confederation expressly delegated to the United States, in Congress assembled."

Observe the departure from the language, and the consequent contrast of principles, with those of the Declaration of Independence. Each state *retains* its sovereignty, etc. Where did each state get the sovereignty which it *retains?*

In the Declaration of Independence, the delegates of the colonies, in Congress assembled, *in the name and by the authority of the good people of the colonies,* declare, not each colony but the *united* colonies, in fact and of right, not *sovereign* but free and independent states. And why did they make this declaration in the name and by the authority of the one people of all the colonies? Because, by the principles before laid down in the Declaration, the people, and the people alone, as the rightful source of all legitimate government, were competent to dissolve the bands of subjection of all the colonies to the nation of Great Britain, and to constitute them free and independent states.

Now the people of the colonies, speaking by their delegates in Congress, had not declared *each* colony a sovereign, free, and independent state; nor had the people of each colony so declared the colony itself, nor could they so declare it, because each was already bound in union with all the rest—a union formed *de facto* by the spontaneous revolutionary movement of the whole people, and organized by the meeting of the first Congress, in 1774, a year and 10 months before the Declaration of Independence.

Where, then, did *each* state get the sovereignty, freedom, and independence which the

Articles of Confederation declare it *retains?* Not from the whole people of the whole Union; not from the Declaration of Independence; not from the people of the state itself. It was assumed by agreement between the legislatures of the several states and their delegates in Congress, without authority from or consultation of the people at all. . . .

Washington, though in retirement, was brooding over the cruel injustice suffered by his associates in arms, the warriors of the Revolution; over the prostration of the public credit and the faith of the nation in the neglect to provide for the payment even of the interest upon the public debt; over the disappointed hopes of the friends of freedom; in the language of the address from Congress to the states of the 18th of April, 1783—"the pride and boast of America, that the rights for which she contended were the rights of human nature."

At his residence of Mount Vernon, in March 1785, the first idea was started of a revisal of the Articles of Confederation by an organization of means differing from that of a compact between the state legislatures and their own delegates in Congress. A . . . convention of delegates [met] at Philadelphia, in May 1787, from all the states. . . .

The Constitution of the United States was the work of this convention. But in its construction the convention immediately perceived that they must retrace their steps and fall back from a league of friendship between sovereign states to the constituent sovereignty of the *people;* from *power* to *right;* from the irresponsible despotism of state sovereignty to the self-evident truths of the Declaration of Independence. In that instrument, the right to institute and to alter governments among men was ascribed exclusively to the *people;* the ends of government were declared to be to *secure* the natural rights of man; and that *when* the government degenerates from the promotion to the destruction of that end, the right and the duty accrues to the people to dissolve this degenerate government and to institute another.

The signers of the Declaration further averred that the one people of the *united colonies* were then precisely in that situation—with a government degenerated into tyranny and called upon by the laws of nature and of nature's God to dissolve that government and

to institute another. Then, in the name and by the authority of the good people of the colonies, they pronounced the dissolution of their allegiance to the king and their eternal separation from the nation of Great Britain, and declared the united colonies independent states. And here, as the representatives of the one people, they had stopped. They did not require the confirmation of this act, for the power to make the Declaration had already been conferred upon them by the people; delegating the power, indeed, separately in the separate colonies, not by colonial authority but by the spontaneous revolutionary movement of the people in them all.

From the day of that Declaration, the constituent power of the people had never been called into action. A confederacy had been substituted in the place of a government; and state sovereignty had usurped the constituent sovereignty of the people.

The convention assembled at Philadelphia had themselves no direct authority from the people. Their authority was all derived from the state legislatures. But they had the Articles of Confederation before them, and they saw and felt the wretched condition into which they had brought the whole people, and that the Union itself was in the agonies of death. They soon perceived that the indispensably needed powers were such as no state government, no combination of them was, by the principles of the Declaration of Independence, competent to bestow. They could emanate only from the people. A highly respectable portion of the assembly, still clinging to the confederacy of states, proposed as a substitute for the Constitution a mere revival of the Articles of Confederation, with a grant of additional powers to the Congress. Their plan was respectfully and thoroughly discussed, but the want of a government and of the sanction of the people to the delegation of power happily prevailed.

A constitution for the people and the distribution of legislative, executive, and judicial powers was prepared. It announced itself as the work of the people themselves and as this was unquestionably a power assumed by the convention not delegated to them by the people, they religiously confined it to a simple power to propose, and carefully provided that it should be no more than a proposal until sanctioned by the confederation Congress, by the state legislatures, in conventions specially assembled by authority of their legislatures for the single purpose of examining and passing upon it.

And thus was consummated the work commenced by the Declaration of Independence—a work in which the people of the North American Union, acting under the deepest sense of responsibility to the Supreme Ruler of the universe, had achieved the most transcendent act of power that social man in his mortal condition can perform. Even that of dissolving the ties of allegiance which he is bound to his country, of renouncing that country itself, of demolishing its government, of instituting another government, and of making for himself another country in its stead.

And on that day, of which you now commemorate the 50th anniversary—on that 30th day of April, 1789—was this mighty revolution, not only in the affairs of our own country but in the principles of government over civilized man, accomplished.

The Revolution itself was a work of 13 years—and had never been completed until that day. The Declaration of Independence and the Constitution of the United States are parts of one consistent whole, founded upon one and the same theory of government, then, new, not as a theory, for it had been working itself into the mind of man for many ages, and been especially expounded in the writings of Locke, but had never before been adopted by a great nation in practice.

There are yet, even at this day, many speculative objections to this theory. Even in our own country there are still philosophers who deny the principles asserted in the Declaration as self-evident truths; who deny the natural equality and inalienable rights of man; who deny that the people are the only legitimate source of power; who deny that all just powers of government are derived from the consent of the governed. Neither your time, nor perhaps the cheerful nature of this occasion, permit me here to enter upon the examination of this antirevolutionary theory which arrays state sovereignty against the constituent sovereignty of the people, and distorts the Constitution of the United States into a league of friendship between confederate corporations.

I speak to matters of fact. There is the Declaration of Independence and there is the Constitution of the United States—let them speak for themselves. The grossly immoral and dishonest doctrine of despotic state sovereignty, the exclusive judge of its own obligations, and responsible to no power on earth or in Heaven, for the violation of them, is not there. . . .

The signers of the Declaration of Independence themselves were the persons who had first fallen into the error of believing that a confederacy of independent states would serve as a substitute for the repudiated government of Great Britain. Experience had demonstrated their mistake, and the condition of the country was a shriek of terror at its awful magnitude. They did retrace their steps, not to extinguish the federative feature in which their Union had been formed—nothing could be wider from their intention—but to restore the order of things conformably to the principles of the Declaration of Independence and as they had been arranged in the first plans for a confederation—to make the people of the Union the constituent body and the reservation of the rights of the states subordinate to the Constitution. Hence the delegation of powers was not from each state retaining its sovereignty, and all rights not expressly delegated by the states, but from the people of each and of all the states to the United States, in Congress assembled, representing at once the whole people and all the states of the Union.

They retained the federative feature preeminently in the constitution of the Senate, and in the complication of its great powers—legislative, executive, and judicial—making that body a participant in all the great departments of constituent power of the people in the mode of electing the president of the United States, whether by the electoral colleges or by the House of Representatives voting by states. They preserved it even in the constitution of the House, the popular branch of the legislature, by giving separate delegations to the people of each state. But they expressly made the Constitution and constitutional laws of the United States paramount not only to the laws but to the constitutions of the separate states inconsistent with them. . . .

Every change of a president of the United States has exhibited some variety of policy from that of his predecessor. In more than one case, the change has extended to political and even to moral principle; but the policy of the country has been fashioned far more by the influences of public opinion and the prevailing humors in the two houses of Congress than by the judgment, the will, or the principles of the president of the United States. The president himself is no more than a representative of public opinion at the time of his election; and as public opinion is subject to great and frequent fluctuations, he *must* accommodate his policy to them; or the people will speedily give him a successor; or either House of Congress will effectually control his power.

It is thus, and in no other sense, that the Constitution of the United States is democratic; for the government of our country, instead of a democracy the most simple, is the most complicated government on the face of the globe. From the immense extent of our territory, the difference of manners, habits, opinions, and above all, the clashing interests of the North, South, East, and West, public opinion formed by the combination of numerous aggregates becomes itself a problem of compound arithmetic, which nothing but the result of the popular elections can solve.

It has been my purpose, fellow citizens, in this discourse to show:

1. That this Union was formed by spontaneous movement of the *people of 13 English colonies, all subjects of the King of Great Britain, bound to him in allegiance and to the British Empire as their country; that the first object of this Union was united resistance against oppression, and to obtain from the government of their country redress of their wrongs.*

2. That failing in this object, their petitions having been spurned and the oppressions of which they complained aggravated beyond endurance, their delegates in Congress, *in their name and by their authority* issued the Declaration of Independence—proclaiming them to the world as *one people,* absolving them from their ties and oaths of allegiance to their king and country, renouncing that country; declaring the *united* colonies, independent states, and announcing that this *one people* of 13 united, independent states, by that act, assumed among the powers of the earth that separate and equal station to which the laws of nature and of nature's God entitled them.

3. That in justification of themselves for this act of transcendent power, they proclaimed the principles upon which they held all lawful government upon earth to be founded; which principles were the natural, unalienable, imprescriptible rights of man, specifying among them, life, liberty, and the pursuit of happiness; that the institution of government is to *secure* to men in society the possession of those rights; that the institution, dissolution, and reinstitution of government belong exclusively to *the people* under a moral responsibility to the Supreme Ruler of the universe; and that all *the just* powers of government are derived from the *consent* of the governed.

4. That under this proclamation of principles, the dissolution of allegiance to the British king, and the compatriot connection with the people of the British Empire, were accomplished; and the *one people* of the United States of America became one separate, sovereign, independent power, assuming an equal station among the nations of the earth.

5. That this one people did not immediately institute a government for themselves. But instead of it, their delegates in Congress, by authority from their separate state legislatures, without voice or consultation of the people, instituted a mere confederacy.

6. That this confederacy totally departed from the principles of the Declaration of Independence, and substituted, instead of the constituent power of the people, an assumed sovereignty of each separate state as the source of all its authority.

7. That as a primitive source of power, this separate state sovereignty was not only a departure from the principles of the Declaration of Independence but directly contrary to and utterly incompatible with them.

8. That the tree was made known by its fruits; that after five years wasted in its preparation, the confederacy dragged out a miserable existence of eight years more, and expired like a candle in the socket, having brought the Union itself to the verge of dissolution.

9. That the Constitution of the United States was a *return* to the principles of the Declaration of Independence, and the exclusive constituent power of the people; that it was the work of the *one people* of the United States; and that those United States, though doubled in the numbers, still constitute as a nation but *one people.*

10. That this Constitution, making due allowance for the imperfections and errors incident to all human affairs, has under all the vicissitudes and changes of war and peace been administered upon those same principles during a career of 50 years.

11. That its fruits have been, still making allowance for human imperfection, a more perfect Union, established justice, domestic tranquillity, provision for the common defense, promotion of the general welfare, and the enjoyment of the blessings of liberty by the constituent *people* and their posterity to the present day.

And now the future is all before us, and Providence our guide.

Courtesy of The Hermitage

Andrew Jackson

Andrew Jackson

1829–1837

ANDREW JACKSON, more than most presidents, was the symbol of his age—a self-made man for a self-made nation. The son of poor South Carolina settlers, orphaned and wounded during the Revolution, he made his fortune through toughness, shrewdness, and audacity. His reputation as a military hero was made in the War of 1812, when, as a major general in the United States army, he trounced the British at New Orleans; a few years later, acting without authorization, he invaded and occupied Spanish-held Florida. By 1824 these exploits had won him so much admiration that despite his minimal political experience (a few years in the House and Senate) he came in first among four contenders to succeed James Monroe, though John Quincy Adams was chosen over him in the House of Representatives. Four years later he defeated Adams with the help of the first mass political organization in the United States, the Democratic Party.

Jackson was in every way a commander—of his administration, on which he kept a firm grip; of his constituents, who regarded him with a degree of affection rarely accorded presidents; and above all of himself. Tall and cadaverously thin, bearing a saber scar on his face and two bullets in his body, he suffered constantly from a hemorrhaging lung abscess and wracking headaches, forcing himself to keep going through sheer willpower. Senator Thomas Hart Benton of Missouri said of him: "The character of his mind was that of judgment, with a rapid and almost intuitive perception, followed by an instant and decisive action." Although as a young man he was known, in the words of one witness, as a "roaring, rollicking, game-cocking, horse-racing, card-playing, mischievous" frontiersman who was always ready for a fight, as president he was the embodiment of dignity. "Virtually all the direct testimony agrees in describing the Jackson of these late years as a man of great urbanity," said historian Arthur M. Schlesinger Jr. "On foot, with firm military step, compressed lips and resolute expression, or on horseback, where his seat was excellent, his hand light and his carriage easy, he had a natural grandeur which few could resist."

The widespread adoration of Jackson had some unexpected consequences. After his inaugural speech in 1828 an ecstatic mob burst into the White House to congratulate him, and his friends had to shield him with their bodies to prevent him from being suffocated, while the crowd wrecked the White House furnishings. His successful reelection campaign of 1832 was the first to make use of such publicity gimmicks as local clubs, torchlight parades, rallies, and souvenirs (hickory canes for "Old Hickory"). Jackson was also the first president to seek direct contact with crowds, including handshaking and baby-kissing. He made few speeches, however, preferring to communicate his views to the public through an administration-controlled newspaper, the *Globe*. When the occasion demanded a speech—at his inaugural ceremonies, for example—he could barely be heard. When Harvard University conferred an honorary degree on him in 1833, a ritual that usually called for a Latin oration by the recipient, Jackson managed a brief reply in English (though one apocryphal account says that his oration consisted of the words *"ex post facto; e pluribus unum; sic semper tyrannis; quid pro quo")*. Yet on the occasion of the Jefferson Day Dinner in 1830 he silenced a convention of states'-righters and nullifiers with a single toast—"Our Union: It must be preserved!"—delivered with utmost sternness.

For the composition of his state papers Jackson relied on good literary stylists in his cabinet, who worked from his notes. His decisive Proclamation Against Nullification, drafted by Secretary of State Edward Livingston and issued on December 10, 1832, was studied by Abraham Lincoln, then a young lawyer, who used it 28 years later as a model for his first inaugural address. "Thus in his 24th year," wrote Lincoln's biographer Albert J. Beveridge, "Lincoln was given a supreme example of the force of calm but strong methods in public discussion, even on the gravest of subjects and in the most perilous of crises."

The Removal of the Indians

From the Second Annual Message to Congress
Washington, D.C.
December 6, 1830

THE SUCCESSFUL SPREAD of Jacksonian democracy was accomplished only through the sacrifice of the Indians. Jackson gave them the choice of complete assimilation or removal to a western region where they would retain autonomy; no independent nations within the borders of the United States would be tolerated. In May 1830 Jackson's supporters in Congress passed legislation that in effect brought about forced removal of Indians westward. The process of removal was far more brutal than Jackson had anticipated, and the tribes did not receive the promised autonomy, but Jackson did not hesitate to put down with violence any attempts by the Indians to resist. Chief Justice John Marshall's ruling, in *Worcester v. Georgia,* that "the Cherokee nation . . . is a distinct community, occupying its own territory, . . . in which the laws of Georgia can have no force" was said to have been rebuffed by Jackson with the words: "John Marshall has made his opinion, now let him enforce it."

. . . It gives me pleasure to announce to Congress that the benevolent policy of the government, steadily pursued for nearly 30 years, in relation to the removal of the Indians beyond the white settlements is approaching to a happy consummation. Two important tribes have accepted the provision made for their removal at the last session of Congress, and it is believed that their example will induce the remaining tribes also to seek the same obvious advantages.

The consequences of a speedy removal will be important to the United States, to individual states, and to the Indians themselves. The pecuniary advantages which it promises to the government are the least of its recommendations. It puts an end to all possible danger of collision between the authorities of the general and state governments on account of the Indians. It will place a dense and civilized population in large tracts of country now occupied by a few savage hunters. By opening the whole territory between Tennessee on the north and Louisiana on the south to the settlement of the whites it will incalculably strengthen the southwestern frontier and render the adjacent states strong enough to repel future invasions without remote aid. It will relieve the whole state of Mississippi and the western part of Alabama of Indian occupancy, and enable those states to advance rapidly in population, wealth, and power. It will separate the Indians from immediate contact with settlements of whites; free them from the power

of the states; enable them to pursue happiness in their own way and under their own rude institutions; will retard the progress of decay, which is lessening their numbers, and perhaps cause them gradually, under the protection of the government and through the influence of good counsels, to cast off their savage habits and become an interesting, civilized, and Christian community. These consequences, some of them so certain and the rest so probable, make the complete execution of the plan sanctioned by Congress at their last session an object of much solicitude.

Toward the aborigines of the country no one can indulge a more friendly feeling than myself, or would go further in attempting to reclaim them from their wandering habits and make them a happy, prosperous people. I have endeavored to impress upon them my own solemn convictions of the duties and powers of the general government in relation to the state authorities. For the justice of the laws passed by the states within the scope of their reserved powers they are not responsible to this government. As individuals we may entertain and express our opinions of their acts, but as a government we have as little right to control them as we have to prescribe laws for other nations.

With a full understanding of the subject, the Choctaw and the Chickasaw tribes have with great unanimity determined to avail themselves of the liberal offers presented by the act of Congress, and have agreed to remove beyond the Mississippi River. Treaties have been made with them, which in due season will be submitted for consideration. In negotiating these treaties they were made to understand their true condition, and they have preferred maintaining their independence in the western forests to submitting to the laws of the states in which they now reside. These treaties, being probably the last which will ever be made with them, are characterized by great liberality on the part of the government. They give the Indians a liberal sum in consideration of their removal, and comfortable subsistence on their arrival at their new homes. If it be their real interest to maintain a separate existence, they will there be at liberty to do so without the inconveniences and vexations to which they would unavoidably have been subject in Alabama and Mississippi.

Humanity has often wept over the fate of the aborigines of this country, and philanthropy has been long busily employed in devising means to avert it, but its progress has never for a moment been arrested, and one by one have many powerful tribes disappeared from the earth. To follow to the the tomb the last of his race and to tread on the graves of extinct nations excite melancholy reflections. But true philanthropy reconciles the mind to these vicissitudes as it does to the extinction of one generation to make room for another. In the monuments and fortresses of an unknown people, spread over the extensive regions of the West, we behold the memorials of a once powerful race, which was exterminated or has disappeared to make room for the existing savage tribes. Nor is there anything in this which, upon a comprehensive view of the general interests of the human race, is to be regretted. Philanthropy could not wish to see this continent restored to the condition in which it was found by our forefathers. What good man would prefer a country covered with forests and ranged by a few thousand savages to our extensive republic, studded with cities, towns, and prosperous farms, embellished with all the improvements which art can devise or industry execute, occupied by more than 12,000,000 happy people, and filled with all the blessings of liberty, civilization, and religion?

The present policy of the government is but a continuation of the same progressive change by a milder process. The tribes which occupied the countries now constituting the eastern states were annihilated or have melted away to make room for the whites. The waves of population and civilization are rolling to the westward, and we now propose to acquire the countries occupied by the red men of the South and West by a fair exchange, and, at the expense of the United States, to send them to a land where their existence may be prolonged and perhaps made perpetual. Doubtless it will be painful to leave the graves of their fathers; but what do they more than our ancestors did or than our children are now doing? To better their condition in an unknown land our forefathers left all that was dear in earthly objects. Our children by thousands yearly leave the land of their birth to seek new homes in distant regions. Does humanity weep at these painful separations from everything, animated and inanimate, with which the young heart has become entwined? Far from it. It is rather a source of joy that our country affords scope where our young population may range unconstrained in body or in mind, developing the power and faculties of man in their highest perfection. These remove hundreds and almost thousands of miles at their own expense, purchase the lands they occupy, and support themselves at their new homes from the moment of their arrival. Can it be cruel in this government when, by events which it cannot control, the Indian is made discontented in his ancient home to purchase his lands, to give him a new and extensive territory, to pay the expense of his removal, and support him a year in his new abode? How many thousands of our own people would gladly embrace the opportunity of removing to the West on such conditions! If the offers made to the Indians were extended to them, they would be hailed with gratitude and joy.

And is it supposed that the wandering savage has a stronger attachment to his home than the settled, civilized Christian? Is it more afflicting to him to leave the graves of his fathers than it is to our brothers and children? Rightly considered, the policy of the general government toward the red man is not only liberal, but generous. He is unwilling to submit to the laws of the states and mingle with their population. To save him from this alternative, or perhaps utter annihilation, the general government kindly offers him a new home, and proposes to pay the whole expense of his removal and settlement.

In the consummation of a policy originating at an early period, and steadily pursued by every administration within the present century—so just to the states and so generous to the Indians—the executive feels it has a right to expect the cooperation of Congress and of all good and disinterested men. The states, moreover, have a right to demand it. It was substantially a part of the compact which made them members of our confederacy. With Georgia there is an express contract; with the new states an implied one of equal obligation. Why, in authorizing Ohio, Indiana, Illinois, Missouri, Mississippi, and Alabama to form constitutions and become separate states, did Congress include within their limits extensive tracts of Indian lands, and, in some instances, powerful Indian tribes? Was it not understood by both parties that the power of the states was to be coextensive with their limits, and that with all convenient dispatch the general government should extinguish the Indian title and remove every obstruction to the complete jurisdiction of the state governments over the soil? Probably not one of those states would have accepted a separate existence—certainly it would never have been granted by Congress—had it been understood that they were to be confined forever to those small portions of their nominal territory the Indian title to which had at the time been extinguished.

It is, therefore, a duty which this government owes to the new states to extinguish as soon as possible the Indian title to all lands which Congress themselves have included within their limits. When this is done the duties of the general government in relation to the states and the Indians within their limits are at an end. The Indians may leave the state or not, as they choose. The purchase of their lands does not alter in the least their personal relations with the state government. No act of the general government has ever been deemed necessary to give the states jurisdiction over the persons of the Indians. That they possess by virtue of their sovereign power within their own limits in as full a manner before as after the purchase of the Indian lands; nor can this government add to or diminish it.

May we not hope, therefore, that all good citizens, and none more zealously than those who think the Indians oppressed by subjection to the laws of the states, will unite in attempting to open the eyes of those children of the forest to their true condition and by a speedy removal to relieve them from all the evils, real or imaginary, present or prospective, with which they may be supposed to be threatened. . . .

Second Inaugural Address

Washington, D.C.

March 4, 1833

BY THE TIME of Jackson's second inauguration, it was plain to all that the Union was in danger of collapse over the issue of states' rights. The South Carolinians, led by Vice President John Calhoun, had advanced the doctrine of nullification to protect the state from federal tariff laws and threatened to secede entirely if the federal government attempted to force on them unwanted economic or social changes, including, of course, any interference with slavery. Jackson replaced Calhoun with Martin Van Buren and announced that he would send an army against any state that rebelled. As a slaveowning Tennessee planter, however, he placed the ultimate blame for the Union's troubles on the abolitionists.

The will of the American people, expressed through their unsolicited suffrages, calls me before you to pass through the solemnities preparatory to taking upon myself the duties of president of the United States for another term. For their approbation of my public conduct through a period which has not been without its difficulties, and for this renewed expression of their confidence in my good intentions, I am at a loss for terms adequate to the expression of my gratitude. It shall be displayed to the extent of my humble abilities in continued efforts so to administer the government as to preserve their liberty and promote their happiness.

So many events have occurred within the last four years which have necessarily called forth—sometimes under circumstances the most delicate and painful—my views of the principles and policy which ought to be pursued by the general government that I need on this occasion but allude to a few leading considerations connected with some of them.

The foreign policy adopted by our government soon after the formation of our present Constitution, and very generally pursued by successive administrations, has been crowned with almost complete success, and has elevated our character among the nations of the earth. To do justice to all and to submit to wrong from none has been during my administration its governing maxim, and so happy have been its results that we are not only at peace with all the world, but have few causes of controversy, and those of minor importance, remaining unadjusted.

In the domestic policy of this government there are two objects which especially deserve the attention of the people and their representatives, and which have been and will continue to be the subjects of my increasing solicitude. They are the preservation of the rights of the several states and the integrity of the Union.

These great objects are necessarily connected, and can only be attained by an enlightened exercise of the powers of each within its appropriate sphere in conformity with the public will constitutionally expressed. To this end it becomes the duty of all to yield a ready and patriotic submission to the laws constitutionally enacted, and thereby promote and strengthen a proper confidence in those institutions of the several states and of the United States which the people themselves have ordained for their own government.

My experience in public concerns and the observation of a life somewhat advanced confirm the opinions long since imbibed by me, that the destruction of our state governments or the annihilation of their control over the local concerns of the people would lead directly to revolution and anarchy, and finally to despotism and military domination. In proportion, therefore, as the general government encroaches upon the rights of the states, in the same proportion does it impair its own power and detract from its ability to fulfill the purposes of its creation. Solemnly impressed with these considerations, my countrymen will never find me ready to exercise my constitutional powers in arresting measures which may directly or indirectly encroach upon the rights of the states or tend to consolidate all political power in the general government. But of equal, and, indeed, of incalculable, importance is the union of these states, and the sacred duty of all to contribute to its preservation by a liberal support of the general government in the exercise of its just powers. . . . Without union our independence and liberty would never have been achieved; without union they never can be maintained. Divided into 24, or even a smaller number, of separate communities, we shall see our internal trade burdened with numberless restraints and exactions; communication between distant points and sections obstructed or cut off; our sons made soldiers to deluge with blood the fields they now till in peace; the mass of our people borne down and impoverished by taxes to support armies and navies, and military leaders at the head of their victorious legions becoming our lawgivers and judges. The loss of liberty, of all good government, of peace, plenty, and happiness, must inevitably follow a dissolution of the Union. In supporting it, therefore, we support all that is dear to the freeman and the philanthropist.

The time at which I stand before you is full of interest. The eyes of all nations are fixed on our republic. The event of the existing crisis will be decisive in the opinion of mankind of the practicability of our federal system of government. Great is the stake placed in our hands; great is the responsibility which must rest upon the people of the United States. Let us realize the importance of the attitude in which we stand before the world. Let us exercise forbearance and firmness. Let us extricate our country from the dangers which surround it and learn wisdom from the lessons they inculcate.

Deeply impressed with the truth of these observations, and under the obligation of that solemn oath which I am about to take, I shall continue to exert all my faculties to maintain the just powers of the Constitution and to transmit unimpaired to posterity the blessings of our federal Union. At the same time, it will be my aim to inculcate by my official acts the necessity of exercising by the general government those powers only that are clearly designated; to encourage simplicity and economy in the expenditures of the government; to raise no more money from the people than may be requisite for these objects, and in a manner that will best promote the interest of all classes of the community and of all portions of the Union. Constantly bearing in mind that in entering into society "individuals must give up a share of liberty to preserve the rest," it will be my desire so to discharge my duties as to foster with our brethren in all parts of the country a spirit of liberal concession and compromise, and by reconciling our fellow-citizens to those partial sacrifices which they must unavoidably make for the preservation of a greater good, to recommend our invaluable government and Union to the confidence and affections of the American people.

Finally, it is my most fervent prayer to that Almighty Being before whom I now stand, and who has kept us in His hands from the infancy of our republic to the present day, that He will so overrule all my intentions and actions and inspire the hearts of my fellow citizens that we may be preserved from dangers of all kinds and continue forever a united and happy people.

The Heroes of Bunker Hill

Charlestown, Massachusetts
July 2, 1833

IN THE SPRING of 1833 Jackson made a triumphal tour of New England to celebrate the end of the nullification crisis. Although New Englanders had long been suspicious of him, at every town Jackson was greeted with banners, banquets, artillery salutes, and parades. Frequently the banners bore a quote from his first annual message to Congress: "Ask nothing not right—submit to nothing wrong." Jackson, mastering his exhaustion and constant pain, endured endless ceremonies and shook hands with innumerable constituents. At Charlestown, Massachusetts, where a monument to the Battle of Bunker Hill was under construction, Jackson gave a brief speech about patriotism that was received with enormous enthusiasm.

. . . It is one of the most gratifying incidents of my life to meet my fellow citizens upon Bunker Hill, at the base of that monument which their patriotism is erecting, and upon the sacred spot hallowed by so many interesting recollections: a spot rich in the various national objects which it presents to view, and richer still in the associations, moral and historical, which belong to it.

The earlier incidents of the revolution—the high-toned patriotic declarations; the stern determination to meet the coming events, and the vigorous preparations to resist them successfully; the great battle which opened the revolutionary contest whose full results upon human institutions are yet to be disclosed, and in which, if your sacred mount was lost and if your devoted town was consumed, imperishable glory was acquired; the services, the sacrifices, and the sufferings of this generous and enlightened state, and the memory of the renowned men she has furnished for the field and the cabinet—all these recollections crowd upon the mind, and render this one of the high places where the American citizen will ever repair to contemplate the past and indulge in the anticipation of the future.

And when to all these are added your moral, social, literary and religious institutions—your happy equality of condition—your charitable establishments—your foundations for education—the general diffusion of knowledge—your industry and enterprise—and when we reflect that most of this is common to the New England states, you may well be proud of your native land, and our country may well be proud of New England. . . .

Defense of the Specie Circular

From the Eighth Annual Message to Congress
Washington, D.C.
December 5, 1836

AFTER A PROLONGED BATTLE against the rechartering of the Bank of the United States, during which Jackson ordered the removal from the bank of all federal funds and their deposit in "pet banks" around the country, Jackson began a general reform of the banking system. One of his goals was the elimination of paper currency in favor of hard money. In July 1836 he issued his Specie Circular, which required purchasers of public lands to pay the Treasury in gold or silver.

Jackson's opposition to the banking system was rooted in his concern for the laborers and farmers, whom he described as "the bone and sinew of the country. . . . The mischief springs from the power which the moneyed interest derives from a paper currency which they are about to control; from the multitude of corporations with exclusive privileges which they have succeeded in obtaining in the different states and which are employed altogether for their benefit; and unless you become more watchful in your states and check this spirit of monopoly and thirst for exclusive privileges, you will, in the end, find that the most important powers of government have been given or bartered away, and the control over your dearest interests has passed into the hands of these corporations."

. . . It is apparent from the whole context of the Constitution, as well as the history of the times which gave birth to it, that it was the purpose of the convention to establish a currency consisting of the precious metals. These, from their peculiar properties which rendered them the standard of value in all other countries, were adopted in this as well to establish its commercial standard in reference to foreign countries by a permanent rule as to exclude the use of a mutable medium of exchange, such as of certain agricultural commodities recognized by the statutes of some states as a tender for debts, or the still more pernicious expedient of a paper currency. The last, from the experience of the evils of the issues of paper during the Revolution, had become so justly obnoxious as not only to suggest the clause in the Constitution forbidding the emission of bills of credit by the states, but also to produce that vote in the convention which negatived the proposition to grant power to Congress to charter corporations—a proposition well understood at the time as intended to authorize the establishment of a national bank, which was to issue a currency of bank notes on a capital to be created to some extent out of government stocks. Although this proposition was refused by a direct vote of the convention, the object was afterwards in effect obtained by its ingenious advocates through a strained construction of the Constitution. The debts of the Revolution were funded at prices which formed no equivalent compared with the nominal amount of the stock, and under circumstances which exposed the motives of some of those who participated in the passage of the act to distrust.

The facts that the value of the stock was greatly enhanced by the creation of the bank, that it was well understood that such would be the case, and that some of the advocates of the measure were largely benefited by it belong to the history of the times, and are well calculated to diminish the respect which might otherwise have been due to the action of the Congress which created the institution.

On the establishment of a national bank it became the interest of its creditors that gold should be superseded by the paper of the bank as a general currency. A value was soon attached to the gold coins which made their exportation to foreign countries as a mercantile commodity more profitable than their retention and use at home as money. It followed as a matter course, if not designed by those who established the bank, that the bank became in effect a substitute for the Mint of the United States.

Such was the origin of a national-bank currency, and such the beginning of those difficulties which now appear in the excessive issues of the banks incorporated by the various states.

Although it may not be possible by any legislative means within our power to change at once the system which has thus been introduced, and has received the acquiescence of all portions of the country, it is certainly our duty to do all that is consistent with our constitutional obligations in preventing the mischiefs which are threatened by its undue extension. That the efforts of the fathers of our government to guard against it by a constitutional provision were founded on an intimate knowledge of the subject has been frequently attested by the bitter experience of the country. The same causes which led them to refuse their sanction to a power authorizing the establishment of incorporations for banking purposes now exist in a much stronger degree to urge us to exert the utmost vigilance in calling into action the means necessary to correct the evils resulting from the unfortunate exercise of the power, and it is to be hoped that the opportunity for effecting this great good will be improved before the country witnesses new scenes of embarrassment and distress.

Variableness must ever be the characteristic of a currency of which the precious metals are not the chief ingredient, or which can be expanded or contracted without regard to the principles that regulate the value of those metals as a standard in the general trade of the world. With us bank issues constitute such a currency, and must ever do so until they are made dependent on those just proportions of gold and silver as a circulating medium which experience has proved to be necessary not only in this but in all other commercial countries. Where those proportions are not infused into the circulation and do not control it, it is manifest that prices must vary according to the tide of bank issues, and the value of stability of property must stand exposed to all the uncertainty which attends the administration of institutions that are constantly liable to the temptation of an interest distinct from that of the community in which they are established.

The progress of an expansion, or rather a depreciation, of the currency by excessive bank issues is always attended by a loss to the laboring classes. This portion of the community have neither time nor opportunity to watch the ebbs and flows of the money market. Engaged from day to day in their useful toils, they do not perceive that although their wages are nominally the same, or even somewhat higher, they are greatly reduced in fact by the rapid increase of a spurious currency, which, as it appears to make money abound, they are at first inclined to consider a blessing. It is not so with the speculator, by whom this operation is better understood, and is made to contribute to his advantage. It is not until the prices of the necessaries of life become so dear that the laboring classes cannot supply their wants out of their wages that the wages rise and gradually reach a justly proportioned rate to that of the products of their labor. When thus, by the depreciation in consequence of the quantity of paper in circulation, wages as well as prices become exorbitant, it is soon found that the whole effect of the adulteration is a tariff on our home industry for the benefit of the countries where gold and silver circulate and maintain uniformity and moderation in prices. It is then perceived that the enhancement of the price of land and labor produces a corresponding increase in the price of products until these products do not sustain a competition with similar ones in other countries, and thus both manufactured and agricultural productions cease to bear exportation from the country of the spurious currency, because they cannot be sold for cost. This is the process by which specie is banished by the paper of the banks. Their vaults are soon exhausted to pay for foreign commodities. The next step is a stoppage of specie payment—a total degradation of paper as a currency—unusual depression of prices, the ruin of debtors, and the accumulation of property in the hands of creditors and cautious capitalists.

It was in view of these evils, together with the dangerous power wielded by the Bank of the United States and its repugnance to our Constitution, that I was induced to exert the power conferred upon me by the American people to prevent the continuance of that institution. But although various dangers to our republican institutions have been obviated by the failure of that bank to extort from the government a renewal of its charter, it is obvious that little has been accomplished except a salutary change of public opinion toward restoring to the country the sound currency provided for in the Constitution. In the acts of several of the states prohibiting the circulation of small notes, and the auxiliary enactments of

Congress at the last session forbidding their reception or payment on public account, the true policy of the country has been advanced and a larger portion of the precious metals infused into our circulating medium. These measures will probably be followed up in due time by the enactment of state laws banishing from circulation bank notes of still higher denominations, and the object may be materially promoted by further acts of Congress forbidding the employment as fiscal agents of such banks as continue to issue notes of low denominations and throw impediments in the way of the circulation of gold and silver.

The effects of an extension of bank credits and overissues of bank paper have been strikingly illustrated in the sales of the public lands. From the returns made by the various registers and receivers in the early part of last summer it was perceived that the receipts arising from the sales of the public lands were increasing to an unprecedented amount. In effect, however, these receipts amounted to nothing more than credits in the bank. The banks lent out their notes to speculators. They were paid to the receivers and immediately returned to the banks, to be lent out again and again, being mere instruments to transfer to speculators the most valuable public land and pay the government by a credit on the books of the banks. Those credits on the books of some of the western banks, usually called deposits, were already greatly beyond their immediate means of payment, and were rapidly increasing. Indeed, each speculation furnished means for another; for no sooner had one individual or company paid in the notes than they were immediately lent to another for a like purpose, and the banks were extending their business and their issues so largely as to alarm considerate men and render it doubtful whether these bank credits if permitted to accumulate would ultimately be the least value to the government. The spirit of expansion and speculation was not confined to the deposit banks, but pervaded the whole multitude of banks throughout the Union and was giving rise to new institutions to aggravate the evil.

The safety of the public funds and the interest of the people generally required that these operations should be checked; and it became the duty of every branch of the general and state governments to adopt all legitimate and proper means to produce that salutary effect. Under this view of my duty I directed the issuing of the order which will be laid before you by the secretary of the Treasury, requiring payment for the public lands sold to be made in specie, with an exception until the 15th of the present month in favor of actual settlers. This measure has produced many salutary consequences. It checked the career of the western banks and gave them additional strength in anticipation of the pressure which has since pervaded our eastern as well as the European commercial cities. By preventing the extension of the credit system it measurably cut off the means of speculation and retarded its progress in monopolizing the most valuable of the public lands. It has tended to save the new states from a nonresident proprietorship, one of the greatest obstacles to the advancement of a new country and the prosperity of an old one. It has tended to keep open the public lands for entry by emigrants at government prices instead of their being compelled to purchase of speculators at double or triple prices. And it is conveying into the interior large sums of silver and gold, there to enter permanently into the currency of the country and place it on a firmer foundation. It is confidently believed that the country will find in the motives which induced that order and the happy consequences which will have ensued much to commend and nothing to condemn.

It remains for Congress if they approve the policy which dictated this order to follow it up in its various bearings. Much good, in my judgment, would be produced by prohibiting sales of the public lands except to actual settlers at a reasonable reduction of price, and to limit the quantity which shall be sold to them. Although it is believed the general government never ought to receive anything but the constitutional currency in exchange for the public lands, that point would be of less importance if the lands were sold for immediate settlement and cultivation. Indeed, there is scarcely a mischief arising out of our present land system, including the accumulating surplus of revenues, which would not be remedied at once by a restriction on land sales to actual settlers; and it promises other advantages to the country in general and to the new states in particular which cannot fail to receive the most profound consideration of Congress. . . .

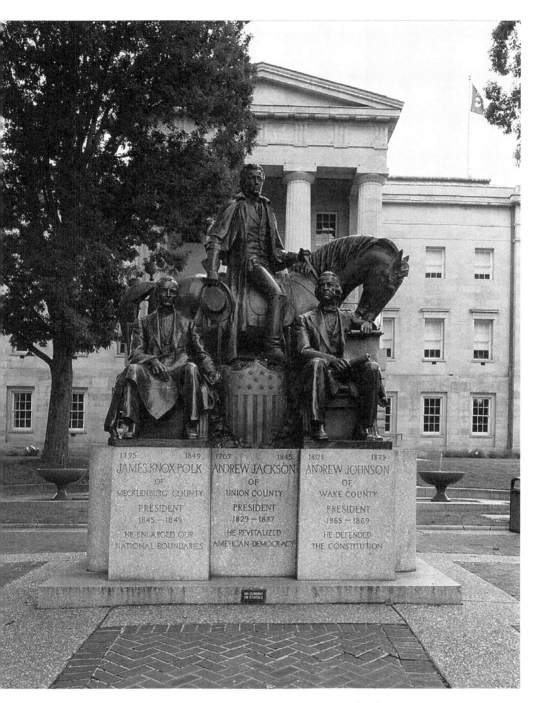

Charles Keck's statue honoring three North Carolina-born
U.S. presidents: James K. Polk, Andrew Jackson, and Andrew Johnson,
outside the state capitol in Raleigh, North Carolina.
(Courtesy of Library of Congress)

Courtesy of Library of Congress

Martin Van Buren

Martin Van Buren

1837–1841

MARTIN VAN BUREN was the first professional politician among the presidents. His entire career was spent in organizing and party-building, first in New York State and then on the national level. The son of a farmer and tavern keeper, he was born in Kinderhook, New York, in 1782, passed his adolescence as a student and office boy in a law firm, opened his own successful law practice, and was soon rising through the ranks of the Democratic-Republicans as state senator and attorney general. As U.S. senator and leader of the New York political machine that he had helped to form, he was instrumental in arranging the political coalition that brought Andrew Jackson to the presidency in 1828. He was secretary of state during Jackson's first term, vice president and heir apparent during his second; in 1836 he was elected to succeed Jackson and was immediately engulfed in the long financial crisis produced partly by Jackson's hard-money policies. After his loss to William Harrison in 1840 he made two more bids for the presidency and finally retired to his farm, where he died in 1862.

In many ways Van Buren was the antithesis of Jackson, who once declared that he loved his protégé like a son. Where Jackson was all iron and grit, as befitted a veteran of the battlefield, the short, portly Van Buren had the amiable personality and smooth manners of the conciliatory politician. Said the Tennessee frontiersman Davy Crockett, "Van Buren is as opposite to General Jackson as dung is to a diamond."

So adept was Van Buren at the art of making friends that he often adopted an elaborate and ingenious style of waffling to avoid declaring his position on a controversial issue. In his autobiography he recounts the story of a speech he gave in 1827 on the subject of the tariff. "That was a very able speech!" one listener exclaimed. "On what side of the tariff question was it?" Van Buren's reluctance to make plain his intentions sometimes led to confusion during his administration and gave the language an adjective, vanburenish, that has since passed out of common usage.

Van Buren got his first taste of public speaking in the courtroom and plenty of experience on the stump and in political meetings. He spoke quickly and softly, but with animation. In the middle of his maiden speech in Congress he suddenly had to stop, but this loss of concentration was rare for him; he had an agile mind, and according to Senator John Randolph he knew less than anyone else at the beginning of a debate and more than anyone else at the end of it.

Van Buren's real skill, however, was not in oratory but in political maneuvering. As Arthur M. Schlesinger Jr. has written, Van Buren "was the first national leader really to take advantage of the growing demand of the people for more active participation in the decisions of government. . . . The great party leader was no longer the eloquent parliamentary orator, whose fine periods could sweep his colleagues into supporting his measures, but the popular hero, capable of bidding directly for the confidence of the masses." Making alliances, controlling appointments, organizing support through committees and mass rallies, building good relations with the press, delivering legislative votes, working to influence public opinion, and using every opportunity events offered—this was the new style of political leadership that Van Buren fostered, and the great declamatory orators of Congress found that they could make little headway against it. In his memoirs, Thomas Hart Benton remembered one occasion when Vice President Van Buren, presiding over the Senate, punctured with a single gesture the oratorical sails of Henry Clay. Clay had delivered a tirade against Jackson's banking policies, at the end of which he demanded that Van Buren plead with Jackson to change his course. While the senators held their breath, Van Buren left the rostrum, walked over to Clay's desk, courteously asked him for a pinch of snuff, and strolled away, leaving Clay and the Senate completely nonplussed.

Inaugural Address

Washington, D.C.

March 4, 1837

THE CROWDS AT Van Buren's inauguration treated the incoming president with respect, but saved their adulation for Jackson. The two men rode to the Capitol together in a carriage, escorted by a military honor guard. When Van Buren, speaking in a calm, clear voice, had delivered his speech and taken the oath of office, the presidential party returned to the carriage, and the crowd, catching sight of Jackson, broke into an ovation that made the streets roar.

In his address, Van Buren showed that he more than anyone was aware that he was standing in Jackson's shadow. With the departure of Jackson, the generation of the Revolution was finally passing away. Van Buren, the first president born an American citizen, saw himself in the role of a manager whose job was to consolidate and strengthen the institutions founded by the Revolutionary statesmen. In only one respect did he break new ground: his inaugural address was the first to mention the word slavery, in the context of a promise to sign no legislation on slavery that did not have the approval of the South. In Van Buren's view, like Jackson's, the abolitionists' desire to impose a new moral order on the South constituted a threat to the stability of the entire nation.

The practice of all my predecessors imposes on me an obligation I cheerfully fultill—to accompany the first and solemn act of my public trust an avowal of the principles that will guide me in performing it and an expression of my feelings on assuming a charge so responsible and vast. In imitating their example I tread in the footsteps of illustrious men, whose superiors it is our happiness to believe are not found on the executive calendar of any country. Among them we recognize the earliest and firmest pillars of the republic—those by whom our national independence was first declared, him who above all others contributed to establish it on the field of battle, and those whose expanded intellect and patriotism constructed, improved, and pefected the inestimable institutions under which we live. If such men in the position I now occupy felt themselves overwhelmed by a sense of gratitude for this the highest of all marks of their country's confidence, and by a consciousness of their inability adequately to discharge the duties of an office so difficult and exalted, how much more must these considerations affect one who can rely on no such claims for favor or forbearance! Unlike all who have preceded me, the Revolution that gave us existence as one people was achieved at the period of my birth; and whilst I contemplate with grateful reverence that memorable event, I feel that I belong to a later age and that I may not expect my countrymen to weigh my actions with the same kind and partial hand.

So sensibly, fellow citizens, do these circumstances press themselves upon me that I should not dare to enter upon my path of duty did I not look for the generous aid of those who will be associated with me in the various and coordinate branches of the government; did I not repose with unwavering reliance on the patriotism, the intelligence, and the kindness of a people who never yet deserted a public servant honestly laboring in their cause; and, above all, did I not permit myself humbly to hope for the sustaining support of an ever-watchful and beneficent Providence.

To the confidence and consolation derived from these sources it would be ungrateful not to add those which spring from our present fortunate condition. Though not altogether exempt from embarrassments that disturb our tranquillity at home and threaten it abroad, yet in all the attributes of a great, happy, and flourishing people we stand without a parallel in the world. Abroad we enjoy the respect and, with scarcely an exception, the friendship of every nation; at home, while our government quietly but efficiently performs the sole legitimate end of political institutions—in doing the greatest good to the greatest number—we present an aggregate of human prosperity surely not elsewhere to be found.

How imperious, then, is the obligation imposed upon every citizen, in his own sphere of action, whether limited or extended, to exert himself in perpetuating a condition of things so singularly happy! All the lessons of history and experience must be lost upon us if we are content to trust alone to the peculiar advantages we happen to possess. Position and climate and the bounteous resources that nature has scattered with so liberal a hand—even the diffused intelligence and elevated character of our people—will avail us nothing if we fail sacredly to uphold those political institutions that were wisely and deliberately formed with reference to every circumstance that could preserve or might endanger the blessings we enjoy. The thoughtful framers of our Constitution legislated for our country as they found it. Looking upon it with the eyes of statesmen and patriots, they saw all the sources of rapid and wonderful prosperity; but they saw also that various habits, opinions, and institutions peculiar to the various portions of so vast a region were deeply fixed. Distinct sovereignties were in actual existence, whose cordial union was essential to the welfare and happiness of all. Between many of them there was, at least to some extent, a real diversity of interests, liable to be exaggerated through sinister designs; they differed in size, in population, in wealth, and in actual and prospective resources and power; they varied in the character of their industry and staple productions, and [in some] existed domestic institutions which, unwisely disturbed, might endanger the harmony of the whole. Most carefully were all these circumstances weighed, and the foundations of the new government laid upon principles of reciprocal concession and equitable compromise. The jealousies which the smaller states might entertain of the power of the rest were allayed by a rule of representation confessedly unequal at the time, and designed forever to remain so. A natural fear that the broad scope of general legislation might bear upon and unwisely control particular interests was counteracted by limits strictly drawn around the action of the federal authority, and to the people and the states was left unimpaired their sovereign power over the innumerable subjects embraced in the internal government of a just republic, excepting such only as necessarily appertain to the concerns of the whole confederacy or its intercourse as a united community with the other nations of the world.

This provident forecast has been verified by time. Half a century, teeming with extraordinary events, and elsewhere producing astonishing results, has passed along, but on our institutions it has left no injurious mark. From a small community we have risen to a people powerful in numbers and in strength; but with our increase has gone hand in hand the progress of just principles. The privileges, civil and religious, of the humblest individual are still sacredly protected at home, and while the valor and fortitude of our people have removed far from us the slightest apprehension of foreign power, they have not yet induced us in a single instance to forget what is right. Our commerce has been extended to the remotest nations; the value and even nature of our production have been greatly changed; a wide difference has arisen in the relative wealth and resources of every portion of our country; yet the spirit of mutual regard and of faithful adherence to existing compacts has continued to prevail in our councils and never long been absent from our conduct. We have learned by experience a fruitful lesson—that an implicit and undeviating adherence to the principles on which we set out can carry us prosperously onward through all the conflicts of circumstances and vicissitudes inseparable from the lapse of years.

The success that has thus attended our great experiment is in itself a sufficient cause for gratitude, on account of the happiness it has actually conferred and the example it has unanswerably given. But to me, my fellow citizens, looking forward to the far-distant future with ardent prayers and confiding hopes, this retrospect presents a ground for still deeper delight. It impresses on my mind a firm belief that the perpetuity of our institutions depends upon ourselves; that if we maintain the principles on which they were established they are destined to confer their benefits on countless generations yet to come, and that America will present to every friend of mankind the cheering proof that a popular government, wisely formed, is wanting in no element of endurance or strength. Fifty years ago its rapid failure was boldly predicted. Latent and uncontrollable causes of dissolution were supposed to exist even by the wise and good, and not only did unfriendly or speculative theorists anticipate for us the fate of past republics, but the fears of many an honest patriot overbalanced his sanguine hopes. Look back on these forebodings, not hastily but reluctantly made, and see how in every instance they have completely failed.

An imperfect experience during the struggles of the Revolution was supposed to warrant the belief that the people would not bear the taxation requisite to discharge an immense public debt already incurred and to pay the necessary expenses of the government. The cost of two wars has been paid, not only without a murmur, but with unequaled alacrity. No one is now left to doubt that every burden will be cheerfully borne that may be necessary to sustain our civil institutions or guard our honor or welfare. Indeed, all experience has shown that the willingness of the people to contribute to these ends in cases of emergency has uniformly outrun the confidence of their representatives.

In the early stages of the new government, when all felt the imposing influence as they recognized the unequaled services of the first president, it was a common sentiment that the great weight of his character could alone bind the discordant materials of our government together and save us from the violence of contending factions. Since his death nearly 40 years are gone. Party exasperation has been often carried to its highest point; the virtue and fortitude of the people have sometimes been greatly tried; yet our system, purified and enhanced in value by all it has encountered, still preserves its spirit of free and fearless discussion, blended with unimpaired fraternal feeling.

The capacity of the people for self-government, and their willingess, from a high sense of duty and without those exhibitions of coercive power so generally employed in other countries, to submit to all needful restraints and exactions of municipal law, have also been favorably exemplified in the history of the American states. Occasionally, it is true, the ardor of public sentiment, outrunning the regular progress of the judicial tribunals or seeking to reach cases not denounced as criminal by the existing law, has displayed itself in a manner calculated to give pain to the friends of free government and to encourage the hopes of those who wish for its overthrow. These occurrences, however, have been far less frequent in our country than in any other of equal population on the globe, and with the diffusion it may well be hoped that they will constantly diminish in frequency and violence. The generous patriotism and sound common sense of the great mass of our fellow citizens will assuredly in time produce this result; for as every assumption of illegal power not only wounds the majesty of the law, but furnishes a pretext for abridging the liberties of the people, the latter have the most direct and permanent interest in preserving the landmarks of social order and maintaining on all occasions the inviolability of those constitutional and legal provisions which they themselves have made.

In a supposed unfitness of our institutions for those hostile emergencies which no country can always avoid their friends found a fruitful source of apprehension, their enemies of hope. While they foresaw less promptness of action than in governments differently formed, they overlooked the far more important consideration that with us war could never be the result of individual or irresponsible will, but must be a measure of redress for injuries sustained, voluntarily resorted to by those who were to bear the necessary sacrifice, who would consequently feel an individual interest in the contest, and whose energy would be commensurate with the difficulties to be encountered. Actual events have proved their error; the last war, far from impairing, gave new confidence to our government, and amid recent apprehensions of a similar conflict we saw that the energies of our country would not be wanting in ample season to vindicate its rights. We may not possess, as we should not desire to possess, the extended and ever-ready military organization of other nations; we may occasionally suffer in the outset for the want of it; but among ourselves all doubt upon this great point has ceased, while a salutary experience will prevent a contrary opinion from inviting aggression from abroad.

Certain danger was foretold from the extension of our territory, the multiplication of states, and the increase of population. Our system was supposed to be adapted only to boundaries comparatively narrow. These have been widened beyond conjecture; the members of our confederacy are already doubled, and the numbers of our people are incredibly augmented. The alleged causes of danger have long surpassed anticipation, but none of the consequences have followed. The power and influence of the republic have risen to a height obvious to all mankind; respect for its authority was not more apparent at its ancient than it is at its present limits; new and inexhaustible sources of general prosperity have been opened; the effects of distance have been averted by the inventive genius of our people, developed and fostered by the spirit of our institutions; and the enlarged variety and amount of interests, productions, and pursuits have strengthened the chain of mutual dependence and formed a circle of mutual benefits too apparent ever to be overlooked.

In justly balancing the powers of the federal and state authorities difficulties nearly insurmountable arose at the outset, and subsequent collisions were deemed inevitable. Amid these it was scarcely believed possible that a scheme of government so complex in construction could remain uninjured. From time to time embarrassments have certainly occurred; but how just is the confidence of future safety imparted by the knowledge that each in succession has been happily removed! Overlooking partial and temporary evils as inseparable from the practical operation of all human institutions, and looking only to the general result, every patriot has reason to be satisfied. While the federal government has successfully performed its appropriate functions in relation to foreign affairs and concerns evidently national, that of every state has remarkably improved in protecting and developing local interests and individual welfare; and if the vibrations of authority have occasionally tended too much toward one or the other, it is unquestionably certain that the ultimate operation of the entire system has been to strengthen all the existing institutions and to elevate our whole country in prosperity and renown.

The last, perhaps the greatest, of the prominent sources of discord and disaster supposed to lurk in our political condition was the institution of domestic slavery. Our forefathers were deeply impressed with the delicacy of this subject, and they treated it with a forbearance so evidently wise that in spite of every sinister foreboding it never until the present period disturbed the tranquillity of our common country. Such a result is sufficient evidence of the justice and the patriotism of their course; it is evidence not to be mistaken that an adherence to it can prevent all embarrassment from this as well as from every other anticipated cause of difficulty or danger. Have not recent events made it obvious to the slightest reflection that the least deviation from this spirit of forbearance is injurious to every interest, that of humanity included? Amidst the violence of excited passions this generous and fraternal feeling has been sometimes disregarded; and standing as I now do before my countrymen, in this high place of honor and of trust, I cannot refrain from anxiously involving my fellow citizens never to be deaf to its dictates. Perceiving before my election the deep interest this subject was beginning to excite, I believed it a solemn duty fully to make known my sentiments in regard to it, and now, when every motive for misrepresentation has passed away, I trust that they will be candidly weighed and understood. At least they will be my standard of conduct in the path before me. I then declared that if the desire of those of my countrymen who were favorable to my election was gratified "I must go into the presidential chair the inflexible and uncompromising opponent of every attempt on the part of Congress to abolish slavery in the District of Columbia against the wishes of the slaveholding states, and also with a determination equally decided to resist the slightest interference with it in the states where it exists." I submitted also to my fellow citizens, with fullness and frankness, the reasons which led me to this determination. The result authorizes me to believe that they have been approved and are confided in by a majority of the people of the United States, including those whom they most immediately affect. It now only remains to add that no bill conflicting with these views can ever receive my constitutional sanction. These opinions have been adopted in the firm belief that they are in accordance with the spirit that actuated the venerated fathers of the republic, and that succeeding experience has proved them to be humane, patriotic, expedient, honorable, and just. If the agitation of this subject was intended to reach stability or our institutions, enough has occurred to show that it has signally failed, and that in this as in every other instance the apprehensions of the timid and the hopes of the wicked for the destruction of our government are again destined to be disappointed. Here and there, indeed, scenes of dangerous excitement have occurred, terrifying instances of local violence have been witnessed, and a reckless disregard of the consequences of their conduct has exposed individuals to popular indignation; but neither masses of the people nor sections of the country have been swerved from their devotion to the bond of union and the principles it has made sacred. It will be ever thus. Such attempts at dangerous agitation may periodically return, but with each the object will be better understood. That predominating affection for our political system which prevails throughout our territorial limits, that calm and enlightened judgment which ultimately governs our people as one vast body, will always be at hand to resist and control every effort, foreign or domestic, which aims or would lead to overthrow our institutions.

What can be more gratifying than such a retrospect as this? We look back on obstacles avoided and dangers overcome, on expectations more than realized and prosperity perfectly secured. To the hopes of the hostile, the fear of the timid, and the doubts of the anxious actual experience has given the conclusive reply. We have seen time gradually dispel every unfavorable foreboding and our Constitution surmount every adverse circumstance dreaded at the outset as beyond control. Present excitement will at all times magnify present dangers, but true philosophy must teach us that none more threatening than the past can remain to be overcome; and we ought (for we have just reason) to entertain an abiding confidence in the stability of our institutions and an entire conviction that if administered in the true form, character, and spirit in which they were established they are abundantly adequate to preserve to us and our children the rich blessings already derived from them, to make our beloved land for a thousand generations that chosen spot where happiness springs from a perfect equality of political rights.

For myself, therefore, I desire to declare that the principle that will govern me in the high duty to which my country calls me is a strict adherence to the letter and spirit of the Constitution as it was designed by those who framed it. Looking back to it as a sacred instrument carefully and not easily framed; remembering that it was throughout a work of concession and compromise; viewing it as limited to national objects; regarding it as leaving to the people and the states all power not explicitly parted with, I shall endeavor to preserve, protect, and defend it by anxiously referring to its provision for direction in every action. To matters of domestic concernment which it has intrusted to the federal government and to such as relate to our intercourse with foreign nations I shall zealously devote myself; beyond those limits I shall never pass.

To enter on this occasion into a further or more minute exposition of my views on the various questions of domestic policy would be as obtrusive as it is probably unexpected. Before the suffrages of my countrymen were conferred upon me I submitted to them, with great precision, my opinions on all the most prominent of these subjects. Those opinions I shall endeavor to carry out with my utmost ability.

Our course of foreign policy has been so uniform and intelligible as to constitute a rule of executive conduct which leaves little to my discretion, unless, indeed, I were willing to run counter to the lights of experience and the known opinions of my constituents. We sedulously cultivate the friendship of all nations as the condition most compatible with our welfare and the principles of our government. We decline alliances as adverse to our peace. We desire commercial relations on equal terms, being ever willing to give a fair equivalent for advantages received. We endeavor to conduct our intercourse with openness and sincerity, promptly avowing our subjects and seeking to establish that mutual frankness which is as beneficial in the dealings of nations as of men. We have no disposition and we disclaim all right to meddle in disputes, whether internal or foreign, that may molest other countries, regarding them in their actual state as social communities, and preserving a strict neutrality in all their controversies. Well knowing the tried valor of our people and our exhaustless resources, we neither anticipated nor fear any designed aggression; and in the consciousness of our own just conduct we feel a security that we shall never be called upon to exert our determination never to permit an invasion of our rights without punishment or redress.

In approaching, then, in the presence of my assembled countrymen, to make the solemn promise that yet remains, and to pledge myself that I will faithfully execute the office I am about to fill, I bring with me a settled purpose to maintain the institutions of my country, which I trust will atone for the errors I commit.

In receiving from the people the sacred trust twice confided to my illustrious predecessor, and which he has discharged so faithfully and so well, I know that I cannot expect to perform the arduous task with equal ability and success; But united as I have been in his counsels, a daily witness of his exclusive and unsurpassed devotion to his country's welfare, agreeing with him in sentiments which his countrymen have warmly supported, and permitted to partake largely of his confidence, I may hope that somewhat of the same cheering approbation will be found to attend upon my path. For him I but express with my own the wishes of all, that he may yet long live to enjoy the brilliant evening of his well-spent life; and for myself, conscious of but one desire, faithfully to serve my country, I throw myself without fear on its justice and its kindness. Beyond that I only look to the gracious protection of the Divine Being whose strengthening support I humbly solicit, and whom I fervently pray to look down upon us all. May it be among the dispensations of His providence to bless our beloved country with honors and with length of days. May her ways be ways of pleasantness and all her paths be peace!

The Path of Financial Recovery

From the Fourth Annual Message to Congress
Washington, D.C.
December 5, 1840

MUCH OF VAN BUREN'S fourth annual message to Congress was given over to a discussion of the accomplishments of his administration, especially its handling of the Panic of 1837. The financial crisis had diverted public attention from Van Buren's able management of border disputes with England and Mexico. Within two months of his inauguration, banks were failing by the score, and government funds on deposit were in danger. Van Buren, in a special session of Congress, proposed the creation of an independent treasury, the so-called subtreasury. This proposal ran counter to orthodox Democratic ideas and provoked a split in the party that helped prevent Van Buren's reelection, though he eventually marshalled enough congressional support to win its enactment. In his last message to Congress he reminded the legislators of his success in following the Jeffersonian principles on which the Democrats' fiscal policy was based: no tax increases, no federal debt, and no national bank. It was, according to one supporter, a proper definition of the "true political creed of the Republican Party."

. . . I have deemed this brief summary of our fiscal affairs necessary to the due performance of a duty specially enjoined upon me by the Constitution. It will serve also to illustrate more fully the principles by which I have been guided in reference to two contested points in our public policy which were earliest in their development and have been more important in their consequences than any that have arisen under our complicated and difficult, yet admirable, system of government. I allude to a national debt and a national bank. It was in these that the political contests by which the country has been agitated ever since the adoption of the Constitution in a great measure originated, and there is too much reason to apprehend that the conflicting interests and opposing principles thus marshaled will continue as heretofore to produce similar if not aggravated consequences.

Coming into office the declared enemy of both, I have earnestly endeavored to prevent a resort to either.

The consideration that a large public debt affords an apology, and produces in some degree a necessity also, for resorting to a system and extent of taxation which is not only oppressive throughout, but is likewise so apt to lead in the end to the commission of that most odious of all offenses against the principles of republican government, the prostitution of political power, conferred for the general benefit, to the aggrandizement of particular classes and the gratification of individual cupidity, is alone sufficient, independently of the weighty objections which have already been urged, to render its creation and existence the sources of bitter and unappeasable discord. If we add to this its inevitable tendency to produce and foster extravagant expenditures of the public moneys, by which is necessity created for new loans and new burdens on the people, and, finally, refer to the examples of every government which has existed for proof, how seldom it is that the system, when once adopted and implanted in the policy of a country, has failed to expand itself until public credit was exhausted and the people were not longer able to endure its increasing weight, it seems impossible to resist the conclusion that no benefits resulting from its career, no extend of conquest, no accession of wealth to particular classes, nor any nor all its combined advantages, can counterbalance its ultimate but certain results—a splendid government and an impoverished people.

If a national bank was, as is undeniable, repudiated by the framers of the Constitution as incompatible with the rights of the states and the liberties of the people; if from the beginning it has been regarded by large portions of our citizens as coming in direct collision with that great and vital amendment of the Constitution which declares that all powers not conferred by that instrument on the general government are reserved to the states and to the people; if it has been viewed by them as the first great step in the march of latitudinous construction, which unchecked would render that sacred instrument of as little value as an unwritten constitution, dependent, as it would alone be, for its meaning on the interested interpretation of a dominant party, and affording no security to the rights of the minority—if such is undeniably the case, what rational grounds could have been conceived for anticipating aught but determined opposition to such an institution at the present day.

Could a different result have been expected when the consequences which have flowed from its creation, and particularly from its struggles to perpetuate its existence, had confirmed in so striking a manner the apprehensions of its earliest opponents; when it had been so clearly demonstrated that a concentrated money power, wielding so vast a capital and combining such incalculable means of influence, may in those peculiar conjunctures to which this government it unavoidably exposed prove an overmatch for the political power of the people themselves; when the true character of its capacity to regulate according to its will and its interests and the interests of its favorites the value and production of the labor and property of every man in this extended country had been so fully and fearfully developed; when it was notorious that all classes of this great community had, by means of the power and influence it thus possesses, been infected to madness with a spirit of heedless speculation; when it had been seen that, secure in the support of the combination of influences by which it was surrounded, it could violate its charter and set the laws at defiance with impunity; and when, too, it had become most apparent that to believe that such an accumulation of powers can ever be granted without the certainty of being abused was to indulge in a fatal delusion?

To avoid the necessity of a permanent debt and its inevitable consequences I have advocated and endeavored to carry into effect the policy of confining the appropriations for the public service to such objects only as are clearly within the constitutional authority of the federal government; of excluding from its expenses those improvident and unauthorized grants of public money for works of internal improvement which were so wisely

arrested by the constitutional interposition of my predecessor, and which, if they had not been so checked, would long before this time have involved the finances of the general government in embarrassments far greater than those which are now experienced by any of the states; of limiting all our expenditures to that simple, unostentatious, and economical administration of public affairs which is alone consistent with the character of our institutions; of collecting annually from the customs, and the sales of public lands a revenue fully adequate to defray all the expenses thus incurred; but under no pretense whatsoever to impose taxes upon the people to a greater amount than was actually necessary to the public service conducted upon the principles I have stated.

In lieu of a national bank or a dependence upon banks of any description for the management of our fiscal affairs, I recommended the adoption of the system which is now in successful operation. That system affords every requisite facility for the transaction of the pecuniary concerns of the government; will, it is confidently anticipated, produce in other respects many of the benefits which have been from time to time expected from the creation of a national bank, but which have never been realized; avoid the manifold evils inseparable from such an institution; diminish to a greater extent than could be accomplished by any other measure of reform the patronage of the federal government—a wise policy in all governments, but more especially so in one like ours, which works well only in proportion as it is made to rely for its support upon the unbiased and unadulterated opinions of its constituents; do away forever all dependence on corporate bodies either in the raising, collecting, safekeeping, or disbursing the public revenues, and place the government equally above the temptation of fostering a dangerous and unconstitutional institution at home or the necessity of adapting its policy to the views and interests of a still more formidable money power abroad.

It is by adopting and carrying out these principles under circumstances the most arduous and discouraging that the attempt has been made, thus far successfully, to demonstrate to the people of the United States that a national bank at all times, and a national debt except it be incurred at a period when the honor and safety of the nation demand the temporary sacrifice of a policy which should only be abandoned in such exigencies, are not merely unnecessary, but in direct and deadly hostility to the principles of their government and to their own permanent welfare.

The progress made in the development of these positions appears in the preceding sketch of the past history and present state of the financial concerns of the federal government. The facts there stated fully authorize the assertion that all the purposes for which this government was instituted have been accomplished during four years of greater pecuniary embarrassment than were ever before experienced in time of peace, and in the face of opposition as formidable as any that was ever before arrayed against the policy of an administration', that this has been done when the ordinary revenues of the government were generally decreasing as well from the operation of the laws as the condition of the country, without the creation of a permanent public debt or incurring any liability other than such as the ordinary resources of the government will speedily discharge, and without the agency of a national bank.

If this view of the proceedings of the government for the period it embraces be warranted by the facts as they are known to exist; if the army and navy have been sustained to the full extent authorized by law, and which Congress deemed sufficient for the defense of the country and the protection of its rights and its honor; if its civil and diplomatic service has been equally sustained; if ample provision has been made for that administration of justice and the execution of the laws; if the claims upon public gratitude in behalf of the soldiers of the Revolution have been promptly met and faithfully discharged; if there have been no failures in defraying the very large expenditures growing out of the long-continued and salutary policy of peacefully removing the Indians to regions of conparative safety and prosperity; if the public faith has at all times and everywhere been most scrupulously maintained by a prompt discharge of the numerous, extended, and diversified claims on the Treasury—if all these great and permanent objects, with many others that might be stated, have for a series of years, marked by peculiar obstacles and difficulties, been successfully accomplished without a resort of a

permanent debt or the aid of a national bank, have we not a right to expect that a policy the object of which has been to sustain the public service independently of either of these fruitful sources of discord will receive the final sanction of a people whose unbiased and fairly elicited judgment upon public affairs is never ultimately wrong?

That embarrassments in the pecuniary concerns of individuals of unexampled extent and duration have recently existed in this as in other commerical nations is undoubtedly true. To suppose it necessary now to trace these reverses to their sources would be a reflection on the intelligence of my fellow citizens. Whatever may have been the obscurity in which the subject was involved during the earlier stages of the revulsion, there cannot now be many by whom the whole question is not fully understood.

Not deeming it within the constitutional power of the general government to repair private losses sustained by reverses in business having no connection with the public service, either by direct appropriations from the Treasury or by special legislation designed to secure exclusive privileges and immunities to individuals or classes in preference to or at the expense of the great majority necessarily debarred from any participation in them, no attempt to do so has been either made, recommended, or encouraged by the present executive.

It is believed, however, that the great purposes for the attainment of which the federal government was instituted have not been lost sight of. Intrusted only with certain limited powers, cautiously enumerated, distinctly specified, and defined with a precision and clearness which would seem to defy misconstruction, it has been my constant aim to confine myself within the limits so clearly marked out and so carefully guarded. Having always been of opinion that the best preservative of the union of the states is to be found in a total abstinence from the exercise of all doubtful powers on the part of the federal government rather than in attempts to assume them by a loose construction of the Constitution or an ingenious perversion of its words, I have endeavored to avoid recommending any measure which I had reason to apprehend would, in the opinion even of a considerable minority of my fellow citizens, be regarded as trenching on the rights of the states or the provisions of the hallowed instrument of our Union. Viewing the aggregate powers of the federal government as a voluntary concession of the states, it seemed to me that such only should be exercised as were at the time intended to be given.

I have been strengthened, too, in the propriety of this course by the conviction that all efforts to go beyond this tend only to produce dissatisfaction and distrust, to excite jealousies, and to provoke resistance. Instead of adding strength to the federal government, even when successful they must ever prove a source of incurable weakness by alienating a portion of those whose adhesion is indispensable to the great aggregate of united strength and whose voluntary attachment is in my estimation far more essential to the efficiency of a government strong in the best of all possible strength—the confidence and attachment of all those who make up its constituent elements.

Thus believing, it has been my purpose to secure to the whole people and to every member of the confederacy, by general, salutary, and equal laws alone, the benefit of those republican institutions which it was the end and aim of the Constitution to establish, and the impartial influence of which is in my judgment indispensable to their preservation. I cannot bring myself to believe that the lasting happiness of the people, the prosperity of the states, or the permanency of their union can be maintained by giving preference or priority to any class of citizens in the distribution of benefits or privileges, or by the adoption of measures which enrich one portion of the Union at the expense of another; nor can I see in the interference of the federal government with the local legislation and reserved rights of the states a remedy for present or a security against future dangers.

The first, and assuredly not the least, important step toward relieving the country from the condition into which it has been plunged by excesses in trade, banking, and credits of all kinds was to place the business transactions of the government itself on a solid basis, giving and receiving in all cases value for value, and neither countenancing nor encouraging in others that delusive system of credits from which it has been found so difficult to escape, and which has left nothing behind it but the wrecks that mark its fatal career.

That the financial affairs of the government are now and have been during the whole period of these wide-spreading difficulties conducted with a strict and invariable regard to this great fundamental principle and that by the assumption and maintenance of the stand thus taken on the very threshold of the approaching crisis more than by any other cause or causes whatever the community at large has been shielded from the incalculable evils of a general and indefinite suspension of specie payments, and a consequent annihilation for the whole period it might have lasted of a just and invariable standard of value, will, it is believed, at this period scarcely be questioned.

A steady adherence on the part of the government to the policy which has produced such salutary results, aided by judicious state legislation and, what is not less important, by the industry, enterprise, perseverance, and economy of the American people, cannot fail to raise the whole country at an early period to a state of solid and enduring prosperity, not subject to be again overthrown by the suspension of banks or the explosion of a bloated credit system. It is for the people and their representatives to decide whether or not the permanent welfare of the country (which all good citizens equally desire, however, widely they may differ as to the means of its accomplishment) shall be in this way secured, or whether the management of the pecuniary concerns of the government, and by consequence to a great extent those of individuals also, shall be carried back to a condition of things which fostered those contractions and expansions of the currency and those reckless abuses of credit from the baleful effects of which the country has so deeply suffered—a return that can promise in the end no better results than to reproduce the embarrassments the government has experienced, and to remove from the shoulders of the present to those of fresh victims the bitter fruits of that spirit of speculative enterprise to which our countrymen are so liable and upon which the lessons of experience are so unavailing. The choice is an important one, and I sincerely hope that it may be wisely made. . . .

Courtesy of Library of Congress

William Henry Harrison

William Henry Harrison

1841–1841

WILLIAM HENRY HARRISON was the first "media-created" president. The son of a wealthy Virginia planter, Harrison became an Ohio farmer and professional soldier, serving in the Northwest Indian Wars and the War of 1812. He entered politics as a Whig, winning the party's presidential nomination in 1836 and again in 1840, despite his uncertain ability as a party leader.

The 1840 contest has been called "the most exuberent, exciting, and nonsensical campaign in American presidential history." Using many of the devices of modern political campaigns—mass rallies, direct mailings, campaign songs and slogans, manufactured news stories, even slide-shows—the Whigs created an image of Harrison as the poor man's candidate, a simple farmer who lived in a log cabin and drank nothing stronger than hard cider. (Harrison, one of the wealthiest men in Ohio, did nothing to contradict this.) Under the watchful eye of Whig leaders, Harrison became the first candidate to campaign on his own behalf, giving what is considered the first presidential campaign speech on the steps of the National Hotel in Columbus, Ohio, on June 6, 1840. He rarely spoke on issues of substance—the Whigs had not even drafted a party platform—but his audiences did not seem to mind.

The Whig strategy worked brilliantly. The incumbent, Martin Van Buren, lost the election essentially by default. Disdaining to challenge Harrison on the hustings, he fell prey to Whig propaganda that portrayed him as "Little Van" and "King Mat," a profligate near-tyrant who was responsible for the nationwide economic depression.

Noted mainly for his genial and unassuming manners and his ability to avoid serious error on the battlefield, Harrison lived only a month after taking office; Ralph Waldo Emerson quipped that the old general had "died of the presidency."

Inaugural Address

Washington, D.C.

March 4, 1841

AT ONE HOUR and 45 minutes, this remains the longest of inaugural addresses, and is Harrison's only significant presidential speech. It was edited and partly written by his secretary of state, Daniel Webster, and is excerpted here.

Flushed with his election victory, the 68-year-old general rode to his inauguration on a white charger, as had Jackson before him. Despite the biting March wind, Harrison stood outside the Capitol building without hat, coat, or gloves to read a florid, rambling address that, according to historian James MacGregor Burns, "promised presidential impotence and left policy up to Congress." Soon after, Harrison caught a cold that led to a fatal case of pneumonia.

Called from a retirement which I had supposed was to continue for the residue of my life to fill the chief executive office of this great and free nation, I appear before you, fellow citizens, to take the oaths which the Constitution prescribes as a necessary qualification for the performance of its duties; and in obedience to a custom coeval with our government and what I believe to be your expectations I proceed to present to you a summary of the principles which will govern me in the discharge of the duties which I shall be called upon to perform.

It was the remark of a Roman consul in an early period of that celebrated republic that a most striking contrast was observable in the conduct of candidates for offices of power and trust before and after obtaining them, they seldom carrying out in the latter case the pledges and promises made in the former. However much the world may have improved in many respects in the lapse of upward of two thousand years since the remark was made by the virtuous and indignant Roman, I fear that a strict examination of the annals of some of the modern elective governments would develop similar instances of violated confidence.

Although the fiat of the people has gone forth proclaiming me the chief magistrate of this glorious Union, nothing upon their part remaining to be done, it may be thought that a motive may exist to keep up the delusion under which they may be supposed to have acted in relation to my principles and opinions; and perhaps there may be some in this assembly who have come here either prepared to condemn those I shall now deliver, or, approving them, to doubt the sincerity with which they are now uttered. But the lapse of a few months will confirm or dispel their fears. The outline of principles to govern and measures to be adopted by an administration not yet begun will soon be exchanged for immutable history, and I shall stand either exonerated by my countrymen or classed with the mass of those who promised that they might deceive and flattered with the intention to betray. However strong may be my present purpose to realize the expectations of a magnanimous and confiding people, I too well understand the dangerous temptations to which I shall be exposed from the magnitude of the power which it has been the pleasure of the people to commit to my hands not to place my chief confidence upon the aid of that Almighty Power which has hitherto protected me and enabled me to bring to favorable issues other important but still greatly inferior trusts heretofore confided to me by my country.

The broad foundation upon which our Constitution rests being the people—a breath of theirs having made, as a breath can unmake, change, or modify it—it can be assigned to none of the great divisions of government but to that of democracy. If such is its theory, those who are called upon to administer it must recognize as its leading principle the duty of shaping their measures so as to produce the greatest good to the greatest number. But with these broad admissions, if we would compare the sovereignty acknowledged to exist in the mass of our people with the power claimed by other sovereignties, even by those which have been considered most purely democratic, we shall find a most essential difference. All others lay claim to power limited only by their own will. The majority of our citizens, on the contrary, possess a sovereignty with an amount of power precisely equal to that which has been granted to them by the parties to the national compact, and nothing beyond. We admit of no government by divine right, believing that so far as power is concerned the Beneficent Creator has made no distinction amongst men that all are upon an equality, and that the only legitimate right to govern is an express grant of power from the governed. The Constitution of the United States is the instrument containing this grant of power to the several departments composing the government. On an examination of that instrument it will be found to contain declarations of power granted and of power withheld. The latter is also susceptible of division into power which the majority had the right to grant, but which they did not think proper to intrust to their agents, and that which they could not have granted, not being possessed by themselves. In other words, there are certain rights possessed by each individual American citizen which in his compact with the others he had never surrendered. Some of them, indeed, he is unable to surrender, being, in the language of our system, unalienable. The boasted privilege of a Roman citizen was to him a shield only against a petty provincial ruler, whilst the proud democrat of Athens would console himself under a sentence of death for a supposed violation of the national faith—which no one understood and which at times was the subject of the mockery of all—or the banishment from his home, his family, and his country with or without an alleged cause, that it was the act not of a single tyrant or hated aristocracy, but of his assembled countrymen. Far different is the power of our sovereignty. It can interfere with no one's faith, prescribe forms of worship for no one's observance, inflict no punishment but after well-ascertained guilt, the result of investigation under rules prescribed by the Constitution itself. These precious privileges, and those scarcely less important of giving expression to his thoughts and opinions, either by writing or speaking, unrestrained but by the liability for injury to others, and that of a full participation in all the advantages which flow from the government, the acknowledged property of all, the American citizen derives from no charter granted by his fellow man. He claims them because he is himself a man, fashioned by the same Almighty hand as the rest of his species and entitled to a full share of the blessings with which He has endowed them. Notwithstanding the limited sovereignty possessed by the people of the United States and the restricted grant of power of the government which they have adopted, enough has been given to accomplish all the objects for which it was created. It has been found powerful in war, and hitherto justice has been administered, an intimate union effected, domestic tranquillity preserved, and personal liberty secured to the citizen. As was to be expected, however, from the defect of language and the necessarily sententious manner in which the Constitution is written, disputes have arisen as to the amount of power which it has actually granted or was intended to grant.

This is more particularly the case in relation to that part of the instrument which treats of the legislative branch, and not only as regards the exercise of powers claimed under a general clause giving that body the authority to pass laws necessary to carry into effect the specified powers, but in relation to the latter also. It is, however, consolatory to reflect that *most* of the instances of alleged departure from the letter or spirit of the Constitution have ultimately received the sanction of a majority of the people. And the fact that many of our statesmen most distinguished for talent and patriotism have been at one time or other of their political career on both sides of each of the most warmly disputed questions forces upon us the inference that the errors, if errors there were, are attributable to the intrinsic difficulty in many instances of ascertaining the intentions of the framers of the Constitution rather than the influence of any sinister or unpatriotic motive. But the great danger to our institutions does not appear to me to be in a usurpation by the government of power not granted by the people, but by the accumulation in one of the departments of that which was assigned to others. Limited as are the powers which have been granted, still enough have been granted to constitute a despostism if concentrated in one of the departments. This danger is greatly heightened, as it has been always observable that men are less jealous of encroachments of one department upon another than upon their own reserved rights. When the Constitution of the United States first came from the hands of the convention which formed it, many of the sternest republicans of the day were alarmed at the extent of the power which had been granted to the federal government, and more particularly of that portion which had been assigned to the executive branch. There were in it features which appeared not to be in harmony with their ideas of a simple representative democracy or republic, and knowing the tendency of power to increase itself, particularly when exercised by a single individual, predictions were made that at no very remote period the government would terminate in virtual monarchy. It would not become me to say that the fears of these patriots have been already realized; but as I sincerely believe that the tendency of measures and of men's opinions for some years past has been in that direction, it is, I conceive, strictly proper that I should take this occasion to repeat the assurances I have heretofore given of my determination to arrest the progress of that tendency if it really exists and restore the government to its pristine health and vigor, as far as this can be effected by any legitimate exercise of the power placed in my hands.

Upon another occasion I have given my opinion at some length upon the impropriety of executive interference in the legislation of Congress—that the article in the Constitution making it the duty of the president to communicate information and authorizing him to recommend measures was not intended to make him the source in legislation, and, in particular, that he should never be looked to for schemes of finance. It would be very strange, indeed, that the Constitution should have strictly forbidden one branch of the legislature from interfering in the origination of such bills and that it should be considered proper that an altogether different department of the government should be permitted to do so. Some of our best political maxims and opinions have been drawn from our parent isle. There are others, however, which cannot be introduced in our system without singular incongruity and the production of much mischief, and this I conceive to be one. No matter in which of the houses of Parliament a bill may originate nor by whom introduced—a minister or a member of the opposition—by the fiction of law, or rather of constitutional principle, the sovereign is supposed to have prepared it agreeably to his will and then submitted it to Parliament for their advice and consent. Now the very reverse is the case here, not only with regard to the principle, but the forms prescribed by the Constitution. The principle certainly assigns to the only body constituted by the Constitution (the legislative body) the power to make laws, and the forms even direct that the enactment should be ascribed to them. The Senate, in relation to revenue bills, have the right to propose amendments, and so has the executive by the power given him to return them to the House of Representatives with his objections. It is in his power also to propose amendments in the existing revenue laws, suggested by his observations upon their defective or injurious operation. But the delicate duty of devising schemes of revenue should be left where the Constitution has placed it—with the immediate representatives of the people. For similar reasons the mode of keeping the public treasure should be prescribed by them, and the further removed it may be from the control of the executive the more wholesome the arrangement and the more in accordance with republican principle. . . .

Before concluding, fellow citizens, I must say something to you on the subject of the parties at this time existing in our country. To me it appears perfectly clear that the interest of that country requires that the violence of the spirit by which those parties are at this time governed must be greatly mitigated, if not entirely extinguished, or consequences will ensue which are appalling to be thought of.

If parties in a republic are necessary to secure a degree of vigilance sufficient to keep the public functionaries within the bounds of law and duty, at that point their usefulness ends. Beyond that they become destructive of public virtue, the parent of a spirit antagonist to that of liberty, and eventually its inevitable conqueror. We have examples of republics where the love of country and of liberty at one time were the dominant passions of the whole mass of citizens, and yet, with the continuance of the name and forms of free government, not a vestige of these qualities remaining in the bosoms of any one of its citizens. It was the beautiful remark of a distinguished English writer that "in the Roman senate Octavius had a party and Anthony a party, but the Commonwealth had none." Yet the senate continued to meet in the temple of liberty to talk of the sacredness and beauty of the commonwealth and gaze at the statues of the elder Brutus and of the Curtii and Decii, and the people assembled in the forum, not, as in the days of Camillus and the Scipios, to cast their free votes for annual magistrates or pass upon the acts of the senate, but to receive from the hands of the leaders of the respective parties their share of the spoils and to shout for one or the other, as those collected in Gaul or Egypt and the lesser Asia would furnish the larger dividend. The spirit of liberty had fled, and, avoiding the abodes of civilized man, had sought protection in the wilds of Scythia or Scandinavia; and so under the operation of the same causes and influences it will fly from our Capitol and our forums. A calamity so awful, not only to our country, but to the world, must be deprecated by every patriot and every tendency to a state of things likely to produce it immediately checked. Such a tendency has existed—does exist. Always the friend of my countrymen, never their flatterer, it becomes my duty to say to them from this high place to which their partiality has exalted me that there exists in the land a spirit hostile to their best interests—hostile to liberty itself. It is a spirit contracted in its views, selfish in its objects. It looks to the aggrandizement of a few even to the destruction of the interests of the whole. The entire remedy is with the people. Something, however, may be effected by the means which they have placed in my hands. It is union that we want, not of a party for the sake of that party, but a union of the whole country for the sake of the whole country, for the defense of its interests and its honor against foreign aggression, for the defense of those principles for which our ancestors so gloriously contended. As far as it depends upon me it shall be accomplished. All the influence that I possess shall be exerted to prevent the formation at least of an executive party in the halls of the legislative body. I wish for the support of no member of that body to any measure of mine that does not satisfy his judgment and his sense of duty to those from whom he hold his appointment, nor any confidence in advance from the people but that asked for by Mr. Jefferson, "to give firmness and effect to the legal administration of their affairs."

I deem the present occasion sufficiently important and solemn to justify me in expressing to my fellow citizens a profound reverence for the Christian religion and a thorough conviction that sound morals, religious liberty, and a just sense of religious responsibility are essentially connected with all true and lasting happiness; and to that good Being who has blessed us by the gifts of civil and religious freedom, who watched over and prospered the labors of our fathers and has hitherto preserved to us institutions far exceeding in excellence those of any other people, let us unite in fervently commending every interest of our beloved country in all future time.

Fellow citizens, being fully invested with that high office to which the partiality of my countrymen has called me, I now take an affectionate leave of you. You will bear with you to your homes the remembrance of the pledge I have this day given to discharge all the high duties of my exalted station according to the best of my ability, and I shall enter upon their performance with entire confidence in the support of a just and generous people.

Courtesy of Sherwood Forest Plantation

John Tyler

John Tyler

1841–1845

WILLIAM HENRY HARRISON'S vice president, John Tyler, a well-to-do Virginian, was the first man to come to the presidency through the death of the elected officeholder. As governor of Virginia, congressman, and senator, he was a strict constructionist and a diehard states' righter. The Whigs added him to their ticket in 1840 to attract Southern support, but within a month of the inauguration Harrison was dead and Tyler was in the White House, where he quickly asserted his independence of the Whigs. For the rest of his single term he administered the government without party support.

Tall and lean, with an air of patrician dignity, Tyler during his congressional years was a fiery orator in the mode of Clay and Calhoun. Jefferson Davis called him the most felicitous extemporaneous speaker he had ever heard. He learned his oratory in the courtroom, where as a young criminal lawyer he more than once salvaged an apparently hopeless case with a histrionic appeal to the jurors. The most famous speech of his congressional career was his denunciation from the Senate floor of the Force Bill, which empowered President Jackson to use military force to prevent the secession of South Carolina over the nullification issue. (Tyler was the only senator to vote against the bill; the other Southerners abstained.) During his administration he refrained from speechmaking, but in retirement, still a powerful figure in Virginia politics, he made several orations in which he sought to vindicate his presidential decisions and to ease the pressures of sectionalism. Eventually he was persuaded that secession alone could help the South escape "the despotism which now holds its gloomy reign over the North." He died in 1861, shortly after his election to the Congress of the Confederate States.

The Annexation of Texas

From the Fourth Annual Message to Congress
Washington, D.C.
December 3, 1844

TYLER'S DEVOTION to the principle of strict construction in the interpretation of the Constitution twice gave way under the pressure of events: first when he took office, claiming for himself the title and privileges of an elected president, and then when he suggested to Congress, in his fourth annual message, that the annexation of Texas could be accomplished by a joint resolution of Congress rather than by a treaty approved by two-thirds of the Senate. The Senate had already rejected just such a treaty; its opponents charged that annexation was a plot to extend the domain of slavery and would lead to war with Mexico. But the public was in favor of it, and once James K. Polk was elected president on a proannexation platform, Congress passed the joint resolution Tyler had proposed. Tyler offered Texas statehood just before he left office.

... In my last message I felt it to be my duty to make known to Congress, in terms both plain and emphatic, my opinion in regard to the war which has so long existed between Mexico and Texas, which since the battle of San Jacinto has consisted altogether of predatory incursions, attended by circumstances revolting to humanity. I repeat now what I then said, that after eight years of feeble and ineffectual efforts to reconquer Texas it was time that the war should have ceased. The United States have a direct interest in the question. The contiguity of the two nations to our territory was but too well calculated to involve our peace. Unjust suspicions were engendered in the mind of one or the other of the belligerents against us, and as a necessary consequence American interests were made to suffer and our peace became daily endangered; in addition to which it must have been obvious to all that the exhaustion produced by the war subjected both Mexico and Texas to the interference of other powers, which, without the interposition of this government, might eventuate in the most serious injury to the United States. This government from time to time exerted its friendly offices to bring about a termination of hostilities upon terms honorable alike to both the belligerents. Its efforts in this behalf proved unavailing. Mexico seemed almost without an object to persevere in the war, and no other alternative was left the executive but to take advantage of the well known dispositions of Texas and to invite her to enter into a treaty for annexing her territory to that of the United States.

Since your last session Mexico has threatened to renew the war, and has either made or proposes to make formidable preparations for invading Texas. She has issued decrees and proclamations, preparatory to the commencement of hostilities, full of threats revolting to humanity, and which if carried into effect would arouse the attention of all Christendom. This new demonstration of feeling, there is too much reason to believe, has been produced in consequences of the negotiation of the late treaty of annexation with Texas. The executive, therefore, could not be indifferent to such proceedings, and it felt it to be due as well to itself as to the honor of the country that a strong representation should be made to the Mexican government upon the subject. This was accordingly done, as will be seen by the copy of the accompanying dispatch from the secretary of state to the United States envoy at Mexico. Mexico has no right to jeopard the peace of the world by urging any longer a useless and fruitless contest. Such a condition of things would not be tolerated on the European continent. Why should it be on this? A war of desolation, such as is now threatened by Mexico, cannot be waged without involving our peace and tranquillity. It is idle to believe that such a war could be looked upon with indifference by our own citizens inhabiting adjoining states; and our neutrality would be violated in despite of all efforts on the part of the government to prevent it. The country is settled by emigrants from the United States under invitations held out to them by Spain and Mexico. Those emigrants have left behind them friends and relatives, who would not fail to sympathize with them in their difficulties, and who would be led by those sympathies to participate in their struggles, however energetic the action of the government to prevent it. Nor would the numerous and formidable bands of Indians—the most warlike to be found in any land—which occupy the extensive regions contiguous to the states of Arkansas and Missouri, and who are in possession of large tracts of country within the limits of Texas, be likely to remain passive. The inclinations of those numerous tribes lead them invariably to war whenever pretexts exist.

Mexico had no just ground of displeasure against this government or people for negotiating the treaty. What interest of hers was affected by the treaty? She was despoiled of nothing, since Texas was forever lost to her. The independence of Texas was recognized by several of the leading powers of the earth. She was free to treat, free to adopt her own line of policy, free to take the course which she believed was best calculated to secure her happiness.

Her government and people decided on annexation to the United States, and the executive saw in the acquisition of such a territory the means of advancing their permanent happiness and glory. What principle of good faith, then, was violated? What rule of political morals trampled under foot? So far as Mexico herself was concerned, the measure should have been regarded by her as highly beneficial. Her inability to reconquer Texas had been exhibited, I repeat, by eight (now nine) years of fruitless and ruinous contest. In the meantime Texas has been growing in population and resources. Emigration has flowed into her territory from all parts of the world in a current which continues to increase in strength. Mexico requires a permanent boundary between that young republic and herself. Texas at no distant day, if she continues separate and detached from the United States, will inevitably seek to consolidate her strength by adding to her domain the contiguous provinces of Mexico. The spirit of revolt from the control of the central government has heretofore manifested itself in some of those provinces, and it is fair to infer that they would be inclined to take the first favorable opportunity to proclaim their independence and to form close alliances with Texas. The war would thus be endless, or if cessations of hostilities should occur they would only endure for a season. The interests of Mexico, therefore, could in nothing be better consulted than in a peace with her neighbors which would result in the establishment of a permanent boundary. Upon the ratification of the treaty the executive was prepared to treat with her on the most liberal basis. Hence the boundaries of Texas were left undefined by the treaty. The executive proposed to settle these upon terms that all the world should have pronounced just and reasonable. No negotiation upon that point could have been undertaken between the United States and Mexico in advance of the ratification of the treaty. We should have had no right, no power, no authority, to have conducted such a negotiation, and to have undertaken it would have been an assumption equally revolting to the pride of Mexico and Texas and subjecting us to the charge of arrogance, while to have proposed in advance of annexation to satisfy Mexico for any contingent interest she might have in Texas would have been to have treated Texas not as an independent power, but as a mere dependency of Mexico. This assumption could not have been acted on by the executive without setting at defiance your own solemn declaration that that republic was an independent state. Mexico had, it is true, threatened war against the United States in the event the treaty of annexation was ratified. The executive could not permit itself to be influenced by this threat. It represented in this the spirit of our people, who are ready to sacrifice much for peace, but nothing to intimidation. A war under any circumstances is greatly to be deplored, and the United States is the last nation to desire it; but if, as the condition of peace, it be required of us to forego the unquestionable right of treating with an independent power of our own continent upon matters highly interesting to both, and that upon a naked and unsustained pretension of claim by a third power to control the free will of the power with whom we treat, devoted as we may be to peace and anxious to cultivate friendly relations with the whole world, the executive does not hesitate to say that the people of the United States would be ready to brave all consequences sooner than submit to such condition. But no apprehension of war was entertained by the executive, and I must express frankly the opinion that had the treaty been ratified by the Senate it would have been followed by a prompt settlement, to the entire satisfaction of Mexico, of every matter in difference between the two countries. Seeing, then, that new preparations for hostile invasion of Texas were about to be adopted by Mexico, and that these were brought about because Texas had adopted the suggestions of the executive upon the subject of annexation, it could not passively have folded its arms and permitted a war, threatened to be accompanied by every act that could mark a barbarous age, to be waged against her because she had done so.

Other considerations of a controlling character influenced the course of the executive. The treaty which had thus been negotiated had failed to receive the ratification of the Senate. One of the chief objections which was urged against it was found to consist in the fact that the question of annexation had not been submitted to the ordeal of public opinion in the United States. However untenable such an objection was esteemed to be, in view of the unquestionable power of the executive to negotiate the treaty and the great and lasting interests involved in the question, I felt it to be my duty to submit the whole subject to Congress as the best expounders of popular sentiment. No definitive action having been taken on the subject by Congress, the question referred itself directly to the decision of the states and people. The great popular election which has just terminated afforded the best opportunity of ascertaining the will of the states and the people upon it. Pending that issue it became the imperative duty of the executive to inform Mexico that the question of annexation was still before the American people, and that until their decision was pronounced any serious invasion of Texas would be regarded as an attempt to forestall their judgment and could not be looked upon with indifference. I am most happy to inform you that no such invasion has taken place; and I trust that whatever your action may be upon it Mexico will see the importance of deciding the matter by a resort to peaceful expedients in preference to those of arms. The decision of the people and the states on this great and interesting subject has been decisively

manifested. The question of annexation has been presented nakedly to their consideration. By the treaty itself all collateral and incidental issues which were calculated to divide and distract the public councils were carefully avoided. These were left to the wisdom of the future to determine. It presented, I repeat, the isolated question of annexation, and in that form it has been submitted to the ordeal of public sentiment. A controlling majority of the people and a large majority of the states have declared in favor of immediate annexation. Instructions have thus come up to both branches of Congress from their respective constituents in terms the most emphatic. It is the will of both the people and the states that Texas shall be annexed to the Union promptly and immediately. It may be hoped that in carrying into execution the public will thus declared all collateral issues may be avoided. Future legislatures can best decide as to the number of states which should be formed out of the territory when the time has arrived for deciding that question. So with all others. By the treaty the United States assumed the payment of the debts of Texas to an amount not exceeding $10,000,000, to be paid, with the exception of a sum falling short of $400,000, exclusively out of the proceeds of the sales of her public lands. We could not with honor take the lands without assuming the full payment of all incumbrances upon them.

Nothing has occurred since your last session to induce a doubt that the dispositions of Texas remain unaltered. No intimation of an altered determination on the part of her government and people has been furnished to the executive. She still desires to throw herself under the protection of our laws and to partake of the blessings of our federative system, while every American interest would seem to require it. The extension of our coastwise and foreign trade to an amount almost incalculable, the enlargement of the market for our manufactures, a constantly growing market for our agricultural production, safety to our frontiers, and additional strenth and stability to the Union—these are the results which would rapidly develop themselves upon the consummation of the measure of annexation. In such even I will not doubt but that Mexico would find her true interest to consist in meeting the advances of this government in a spirit of amity. Nor do I apprehend any serious complaint from any other quarter; no sufficient ground exists for such complaint. We should interfere in no respect with the rights of any other nation. There cannot be gathered from the act any design on our part to do so with their possessions on this continent. We have interposed no impediments in the way of such acquisitions of territory, large and extensive as many of them are, as the leading powers of Europe have made from time to time in every part of the world. We seek no conquest made by war. No intrigue will have been resorted to or acts of diplomacy essayed to accomplish the annexation of Texas. Free and independent herself, she asks to be received into our Union. It is a question for our own decision whether she shall be received or not.

The two governments having already agreed through their respective organs on the terms of annexation, I would recommend their adoption by Congress in the form of a joint resolution or act to be perfected and made binding on the two countries when adopted in like manner by the government of Texas. . . .

The Secession of Virginia

From an Address to the Virginia State Convention
Richmond, Virginia
March 13–14, 1861

IN EARLY 1861, after the election of Abraham Lincoln and the secession of seven Southern states, ex-President Tyler represented Virginia at the Peace Convention in Washington, D.C., where an attempt was made to arrange a settlement. He returned to Virginia convinced that the South could escape invasion only by setting up a confederacy of slave and border states whose combined military power would deter any coercive moves by Lincoln. Two weeks later, in a speech to the president and delegates of the Virginia State Convention, he denounced the various compromises that had been suggested and demanded Virginia's immediate withdrawal from the Union. Tyler's biographer, Robert Seager II, called the speaker "the oratorical Tyler of old,"—with a voice "filled with equal measures of indignation, pathos, morality, derision, and bitter sarcasm." But it was not until April 17, after South Carolina's attack on the federal garrison at Fort Sumter, that the convention voted to secede.

I am about to make, Mr. President, a very bold and daring adventure. The condition of my health might very well justify me to this convention in withholding from it any remarks upon the interesting subjects which were discussed yesterday. But, sir, I am acting under an impulse of duty—an impulse which I always obey, and which I shall attempt to carry out on the present occasion.

Mr. President, an aged man who had retired from the pursuits of busy life, surrounded by those comforts which should most properly surround one whose life had been spent in the public service—with prattlers at his knee and a light illuminating his household forever beaming around him—was startled from his quietude and repose by a voice which came from his legislative halls of his native state, admonishing him of danger to the country, and making a requisition for all of energy that still remained with him, either physically or mentally, in the effort to rescue that country from the imminent peril that threatened it. It was the voice of Virginia, appealing, sir, to a son, who, from the early morning of manhood, she had nurtured and petted, even as a fond mother does her firstborn infant. At the age of 21, having scarcely put on the *toga virilis,* he entered the public service of the state, cheered on his way by the approving smiles of those who had elected him a member of the legislature; and his presence there was greeted by his brother members with an almost affectionate

cordiality. The pathway of his life was lighted up by gracious smiles which he was continually receiving. Without anything of the spirit of boastfulness, which would ill-become me, I might say that that aged man had sounded, in the language of Cardinal Wolsey, "all the shoals and depths of honor." The highest public stations which the state of Virginia held in her gift she had conferred upon him.

When I left the government, 16 years ago, sir, it had not entered into my contemplation that I should ever afterwards appear in a public assembly. I left that government prosperous and happy. The voice which startled me in my retirement told me of feud, and discontent, and discord; of a tearing in twain of that beautiful flag which had floated so trimphantly over us in the days that had gone by, which I had never looked upon but my heart had throbbed with an emotion it is impossible for me to give utterance to. The Father of his Country had left behind an admonition to his children to avoid sectional feuds, but those feuds had arisen and had progressed until they had culminated into disunion. I had seen their beginning, sir, 30 years before, when the dark cloud which now overspreads the hemisphere just rose above the horizon, no bigger than a man's hand. It was the cloud of abolitionism. Washington, looking to the probable contingency that has now arisen, warned us against sectionalism and sectional parties. With the tongue and the pen of an inspired prophet, he foretold what has befallen us. From the school-room where the youthful mind was impressed with doctrines in one section inimical to those of another; from the pulpit where traduction and abuse have been levelled at the very memories of the great dead who assisted to build up what was but yesterday a glorious government, desecrating the very altar itself, and pronouncing against us anathema and violent vituperation, bidding us "go forth from the communion table; you are miserable slaveholders, and we cannot partake with you in the feast of peace and religion." Such the anathema. And when all is made ready—the masses excited and stirred up with an undefinable love of human liberty—the politician, regardless of his country, and intent only upon his own elevation, steps forth upon the stage to control those masses and lead them to the disastrous point of sectionalism and separation.

Where is that Union now which we once so much loved? Where its beautiful flag, which waved over a land of wealth, of grandeur, and of beauty? Wrong, abuse, contumely, unconstitutional acts, looking to a higher law than the Constitution, thus setting men free from their obligations to society, have cut the ship of state loose from her moorings; and here she is, drifting without helm or compass amid rocks and whirlpools, her fragments floating in every direction—one part has gone South, while other parts, moored for this moment, will probably at the next break loose from his insecure anchorage. I grieve over this state of things by day and by night. When I think of the manner in which all this has been brought about by a race of hungry, artful Catalines, who have misled the Northern mind solely for their own aggrandizement, my blood becomes so heated in my veins as to scald and burn them in its rapid flow.

I was told that in this hour of the country's danger, my services were needed, and under the resolutions of the legislature of Virginia, which I will very briefly advert to as containing my letter of instructions, I resolved, at peril to myself and at every possible personal inconvenience, to venture upon the task which my native state had imposed upon me. I have not felt myself at liberty to wander or depart from those instructions. One of them I will read:

"Whereas, it is the deliberate opinion of the General Assembly of Virginia that unless the unhappy controversy which now divides the states of this confederacy shall be satisfactorily adjusted, a permanent dissolution of the Union is inevitable, and the General Assembly, representing the wishes of the people of the commonwealth, is desirous of employing every reasonable means to avert so dire a calamity, and determined to make a final effort to restore the Union and the Constitution in the spirit in which they were established by the fathers of the republic."

An effort was to be made to restore the Union: not to enter into a sort of bargain, embracing only the border states; not merely to enter into a covenant with those who have brought about this state of things through misleading the public mind of the North; nor yet to consult the interests of Virginia exclusively in any arrangement which might be made to restore the Constitution and the Union of the states; but to bring back, if possible, the cotton states, thereby to restore the Union to what it was; to have the glorious old flag floating over one and all; to make the name of an American citizen, which had won respect in every part of the world, again a word of passport and of honor, as it had been before.

What could have carried me to Washington but the debt of gratitude which I felt I owed my state and my fellow-countrymen, and the deep solicitude which I experienced in this hour of the nation's peril? I confess to an additional motive of a personal character. If ever there lived a man ambitious of winning that true glory which can alone arise from the fulfilment of the whole duty of a patriot— that man now addresses you. I aspired to the glory of aiding to settle this controversy. I had worn the honors of office through each grade to the highest. I had been surrounded by the echoes of applause in the course of my journey through life; but to encircle my brow, Mr. President, with the wreath to be won by the restoration of this Union in all its plenitude, perfect as it was before the severance, would have been to me the proud crowning act of my life. That was the feeling that inspired my heart. You saw my address upon taking the chair of the convention. Mr. President, I can speak of it without vanity and impropriety. You all saw it. Did it please you? Was it of a character to draw around Virginia the sympathies of her co-states? That was my sole object in uttering it.

I had hoped, in the manner of consultation, and from the spirit evinced at the opening of the conference, that we were likely to accomplish the great object that Virginia had in view. Massachusetts came up, and her daughter, Maine, along with her. We had all New England and all the border states, until we reached Michigan. A voice could not be heard on the Pacific coast; it was uttered too late to reach California and Oregon in time—I wish, with all my heart they had been there. New York soon joined us. But I found that many had come with no olive branch in their hands; nay, more, that with them the feeling of fraternity seemed to be gone. They had nothing to give—nothing to yield. The Constitution was enough for them. New York, with her potent voice, would not yield one iota—not an "i" dotted nor a "t" crossed. "The Constitution must be maintained; we have nothing more to grant." Such was, in substance, her language.

Notwithstanding all these discouragements, we went to work, and no man ever had more faithful colleagues than myself. We worked together, and we tried every possible expedient to overrule this state of things. It was soon perfectly obvious that, without a close approach to unanimity on the part of the convention, no measures originated by us would be of any avail. Here you have a measure passed by a minority of that convention—a measure which was defeated by a majority the night before, but which was afterwards passed by a minority, upon a reconsideration the next day, of nine to eight. The majority which passed it being a minority of the states represented in the convention; of what value and consequence, then, is it?. . .

Italy can rise up from the thraldom of centuries, and win the bright coronet of free government. The iron crown of Austria may be removed from the brow of its wearer to do honor to Hungary. But Mr. Lincoln recognizes no such principle as lying at the base of American institutions, as the right of the people of any of these states to seek their happiness under any other government than that inaugurated by himself, of a sectional majority. Hence the Pacific and Mediterranean fleets are, it is said, ordered home, to cluster about our coast! Hence, the whole border, stretching off to California, is to be left exposed to the attacks of the savages, by withdrawing from it the 2,500 regular troops. Rumor speaks of a portion of these troops being stationed at Washington as a strategic point. If it be accurate, I shall regard it as "bearding the lion in his den, the Douglas in his hall." It looks like a strategic operation to coerce Virginia, and keep you under subjection and control. Virginia is the bright star that now fixes the attention of the country. Every eye is turned to her. I fear that the game is to hold Virginia in thraldom, if possible. If it can be done by the practice of chicanery and smiles, she will be kept in her present attitude of inaction. Depend upon it, all means will be resorted to to accomplish this object. Troops may be concentrated in considerable numbers at Fort Washington and Fortress Monroe. In that event what will be the condition of Alexandria and Richmond? Fort Washington upon the Potomac, garrisoned—and not a barrel of flour, not a hogshead of tobacco, no article of commerce, can float by without being under the range of its guns? If Fortress Monroe is to be garrisoned by 5,000 men, as speculation has sometimes intimated, the trade of Richmond—that trade which floats down the James, the York, the Rappahannock, and the other rivers of the commonwealth—is essentially blocked out from the ocean by a ship of war stationed in the bay, to cooperate with the fort. Look at it, I pray you, and let your action here anticipate, and as far as it can avail, guard against the state of things which may soon exist. . . .

Mr. President, my policy stretches still farther than to the slave-states. I want the government of the whole Union, sir; and you can acquire it if you pursue a wise and determined course of policy. New Jersey will not stay an appendage to a Northern confederacy. You cannot fasten her to the North, and what is there to induce Pennsylvania to remain? I have great hope of change in the politics of Pennsylvania. Sir, I heard a voice from New York last night. It was mellifluous, powerful, truthful. I know not whether the gentleman who uttered those sentiments be present in my hearing, the Honorable John Cochrane, of New York, if he is, let me tell him that his own great imperial city of New York cannot stay where she is. The South is her natural ally, and she must come with us.

And now what result may be anticipated? I say to you here, play your part properly; open your eyes and take a full expansive survey of all the circumstances that surround you.

What will you have done if you get three or four of the free states and all the slave states to go with you? What becomes of Mr. Lincoln's general government? Why, you constitute a majority of the whole number of states; and if a majority power means anything, it means that you are entitled to the sceptre and the crown. The government becomes yours most decidedly.

Sir, you cannot do without the cotton states. It is idle to talk of it. You must have the cotton states, if they can on proper terms be brought back. If those states tomorrow were put up at market overt, and you invited to the place of bidding, the nations of the earth—Russia, wrapped up in her furs, would be there. England with argosies freighted with treasure, would be there; France would come with her imperial crown—and what price would be bid for them, it would puzzle arithmetic to determine. What would be the price to be paid down for them? Would you count it by millions? Or would you go up to billions and trillions? Why, look at it. The foundation of all the exchanges of the world, the clothing of the world, the commerce of the world, proceeds chiefly from them.

Go to the exchanges of the world, and you see that they are all regulated by cotton. Go to the North—why, the whole North is covered over with glittering gems through the cotton trade. And yet it is to be thrown away because of your conception that South Carolina has acted badly. The North will not give guaranties which cost nothing to reclaim a great treasure. Why cannot the free states, if they really design you no harm, give the necessary guaranties to secure you? I fear that they desire disunion. Disunion is to them the high road to office; and I fear that many of our politicians would rather "rule in hell than serve in heaven." South Carolina was a glorious star in the firmament, and I want her to shine there again in all her brightness and glory. Who has forgotten her Marion, her Pickens, and her Sumter? Who has forgotten—even the boys at their schools have learned it—who has forgotten King's Mountain and its glory? Sir, I remember an incident connected with King's Mountain. When travelling in the railroad cars, I fell in with Mr. Bancroft, the historian.

"I am just from King's Mountain," he said, "they have had a great celebration there, and I have been delighted beyond measure. I went over with William C. Preston; I accompanied him in his carriage upon that occasion. Stricken down as he was in the flower of his life, there was enough of intellect still to coruscate into jewels everything around him, magnificent in its splendor, brilliant in everything that related to him. There he was. They called upon him for a speech; and even there, amidst that decrepitude, broken down as he was by paralysis, a stranger at his home by the severance of his domestic ties, which he lamented and mourned over 'like a stricken deer,' he found his way to the heart of every human being who heard him." That was what Mr. Bancroft said.

Well, sir, you are going to throw up this. Gems so bright as your cotton interest you are going to discard. Whither are you going? You have to choose your association. Will you find it among the icebergs of the North or the cotton fields of the South? What will you gain by going North? Will you jeopardize for an association with the North your great interest arising under your domestic institutions? That interest is worth $300,000,000. Decide upon association with the North, and you reduce it to two-thirds in value. Nor is that all—a still more evil day will befall you. Brennus may not yet be in the capital, but he will soon be there, and the sword will be thrown into the scale to weigh against our liberties, and there will be no Camillus to expel him.

Sir, I am done. I know that I have presented my views to you most feebly. I have presented them, however, with all the frankness with which one Virginian should talk to another upon this great occasion. You have much more wisdom than I possess. I look with fear and trembling, to some extent, at the condition of my country. But I do want to see Virginia united; I wish to see her carrying her head as she carried it in former times. The time was when she did not fear. I have entire confidence that her proud crest will you be seen waving in that great procession of states that go up to the temple to make their vows to maintain their liberties, "peaceably if they can, forcibly if they must." Sir, I am done.

Courtesy of James K. Polk Memorial Associated

James Knox Polk

James Knox Polk

1845–1849

THE ONLY PRESIDENT between Jackson and Lincoln considered to have been a strong executive is James K. Polk, a Jacksonian Democrat from Tennessee who came to the White House with 14 years' experience in the House of Representatives, the last four as Speaker of the House. A deadlock at the 1844 convention brought him to the ticket as a compromise candidate, and he was elected largely on the strength of campaign promises to annex Texas and Oregon. In his single term in office—he had agreed before his nomination not to run for reelection—he succeeded, through a combination of war, bluff, and diplomacy, in acquiring the entire western third of the continental United States, as well as in reorganizing the nation's fiscal system and lowering the tariff.

Though Polk was a tremendously hard worker and a conscientious administrator, he was a humorless, secretive man with none of the appeal of his mentor Jackson. John Quincy Adams wrote in his memoirs: "He has no wit, no literature, no point of argument, no gracefulness of delivery, no elegance of language, no philosophy, no pathos, no felicitous impromptus; nothing that can constitute an orator, but confidence, fluency, and labor." He rarely appeared in public and relied on the *Union,* his administration newspaper, to announce his views to the people. Eventually Polk's diligence brought him to the point of exhaustion; he died three months after leaving office.

Texas and Oregon

From the Inaugural Address
Washington, D.C.
March 4, 1845

JAMES K. Polk was a master at coining phrases that would stick in the memory of his audience, and his presidential inaugural address of March 4, 1845, represented the pinnacle of his abilities. It became a classic American document by combining unabashed patriotism with a pragmatic statement of principles. He promises that he will not interfere with states' rights while at the same time urging the states not to claim powers that the Constitution does not grant them. He pushes for the admission of Texas as a state rather than a territory, which would have the added benefit of warding off foreign powers if Mexico were to declare war on the United States. Polk goes on to assert the U.S. interest in the Oregon territory (which was also claimed by Great Britain), restating and reviving the Monroe Doctrine, and calls for the creation of overland mail routes from east to west to help bind the country together. He also calls for reducing tariffs (taxes on imported goods) to improve the standard of living of ordinary Americans and to encourage fiscal responsibility in government, which relied on tariffs for income. Overall, Polk accomplished in his inaugural address something that few other presidents succeeded in doing: laying out a clear, specific agenda.

Without solicitation on my part, I have been chosen by the free and voluntary suffrages of my countrymen to the most honorable and most responsible office on earth. I am deeply impressed with gratitude for the confidence reposed in me. Honored with this distinguished consideration at an earlier period of life than any of my predecessors, I can not disguise the diffidence with which I am about to enter on the discharge of my official duties.

If the more aged and experienced men who have filled the office of President of the United States even in the infancy of the Republic distrusted their ability to discharge the duties of that exalted station, what ought not to be the apprehensions of one so much younger and less endowed now that our domain extends from ocean to ocean, that our people have so greatly increased in numbers, and at a time when so great diversity of opinion prevails in regard to the principles and policy which should characterize the administration of our Government? Well may the boldest fear and the wisest tremble when incurring responsibilities on which may depend our country's peace and prosperity, and in some degree the hopes and happiness of the whole human family.

In assuming responsibilities so vast I fervently invoke the aid of that Almighty Ruler of the Universe in whose hands are the destinies of nations and of men to guard this Heaven-favored land against the mischiefs which without His guidance might arise from an unwise public policy. With a firm reliance upon the wisdom of Omnipotence to sustain and direct me in the path of duty which I am appointed to pursue, I stand in the presence of this assembled multitude of my countrymen to take upon myself the solemn obligation "to the best of my ability to preserve, protect, and defend the Constitution of the United States."

A concise enumeration of the principles which will guide me in the administrative policy of the Government is not only in accordance with the examples set me by all my predecessors, but is eminently befitting the occasion.

The Constitution itself, plainly written as it is, the safeguard of our federative compact, the offspring of concession and compromise, binding together in the bonds of peace and union this great and increasing family of free and independent States, will be the chart by which I shall be directed.

It will be my first care to administer the Government in the true spirit of that instrument, and to assume no powers not expressly granted or clearly implied in its terms. The Government of the United States is one of delegated and limited powers, and it is by a strict adherence to the clearly granted powers and by abstaining from the exercise of doubtful or unauthorized implied powers that we have the only sure guaranty against the recurrence of those unfortunate collisions between the Federal and State authorities which have occasionally so much disturbed the harmony of our system and even threatened the perpetuity of our glorious Union.

"To the States, respectively, or to the people" have been reserved "the powers not delegated to the United States by the Constitution nor prohibited by it to the States." Each State is a complete sovereignty within the sphere of its reserved powers. The Government of the Union, acting within the sphere of its delegated authority, is also a complete sovereignty. While the General Government should abstain from the exercise of authority not clearly delegated to it, the States should be equally careful that in the maintenance of their rights they do not overstep the limits of powers reserved to them. One of the most distinguished of my predecessors attached deserved importance to "the support of the State governments in all their rights, as the most competent administration for our domestic concerns and the surest bulwark against anti-republican tendencies," and to the "preservation of the General Government in its whole constitutional vigor, as the sheet anchor of our peace at home and safety abroad."

To the Government of the United States has been entrusted the exclusive management of our foreign affairs. Beyond that it wields a few general enumerated powers. It does not force reform on the States. It leaves individuals, over whom it casts its protecting influence, entirely free to improve their own condition by the legitimate exercise of all their mental and physical powers. It is a common protector of each and all the States; of every man who lives upon our soil, whether of native or foreign birth; of every religious sect, in their worship of the Almighty according to the dictates of their own conscience; of every shade of opinion, and the most free inquiry; of every art, trade, and occupation consistent with the laws of the States. And we rejoice in the general happiness, prosperity, and advancement of our country, which have been the offspring of freedom, and not of power.

This most admirable and wisest system of well-regulated self-government among men ever devised by human minds has been tested by its successful operation for more than half a century, and if preserved from the usurpations of the Federal Government on the one hand and the exercise by the States of powers not reserved to them on the other, will, I fervently hope and believe, endure for ages to come and dispense the blessings of civil and religious liberty to distant generations. To effect objects so dear to every patriot I shall devote myself with anxious solicitude. It will be my desire to guard against that most fruitful source of danger to the harmonious action of our system which consists in substituting the mere discretion and caprice of the Executive or of majorities in the legislative department of the Government for powers which have been withheld from the Federal Government by the Constitution. By the theory of our Government majorities rule, but this right is not an arbitrary or unlimited one. It is a right to be exercised in subordination to the Constitution and in conformity to it. One great object of the Constitution was to restrain majorities from oppressing minorities or encroaching upon their just rights. Minorities have a right to appeal to the Constitution as a shield against such oppression.

That the blessings of liberty which our Constitution secures may be enjoyed alike by minorities and majorities, the Executive has been wisely invested with a qualified veto upon the acts of the Legislature. It is a negative power, and is conservative in its character. It arrests for the time hasty, inconsiderate, or unconstitutional legislation, invites reconsideration, and transfers questions at issue between the legislative and executive departments to the tribunal of the people. Like all other powers, it is subject to be abused. When judiciously and properly exercised, the Constitution itself may be saved from infraction and the rights of all preserved and protected.

The inestimable value of our Federal Union is felt and acknowledged by all. By this system of united and confederated States our people are permitted collectively and individually to seek their own happiness in their own way, and the consequences have been most auspicious. Since the Union was formed the number of the States has increased from thirteen to twenty-eight; two of these have taken their position as members of the Confederacy within the last week. Our population has increased from three to twenty millions.

New communities and States are seeking protection under its aegis, and multitudes from the Old World are flocking to our shores to participate in its blessings. Beneath its benign sway peace and prosperity prevail. Freed from the burdens and miseries of war, our trade and intercourse have extended throughout the world. Mind, no longer tasked in devising means to accomplish or resist schemes of ambition, usurpation, or conquest, is devoting itself to man's true interests in developing his faculties and powers and the capacity of nature to minister to his enjoyments. Genius is free to announce its inventions and discoveries, and the hand is free to accomplish whatever the head conceives not incompatible with the rights of a fellow-being. All distinctions of birth or of rank have been abolished. All citizens, whether native or adopted, are placed upon terms of precise equality. All are entitled to equal rights and equal protection. No union exists between church and state, and perfect freedom of opinion is guaranteed to all sects and creeds.

These are some of the blessings secured to our happy land by our Federal Union. To perpetuate them it is our sacred duty to preserve it. Who shall assign limits to the achievements of free minds and free hands under the protection of this glorious Union? No treason to mankind since the organization of society would be equal in atrocity to that of him who would lift his hand to destroy it. He would overthrow the noblest structure of human wisdom, which protects himself and his fellow-man. He would stop the progress of free government and involve his country either in anarchy or despotism. He would extinguish the fire of liberty, which warms and animates the hearts of happy millions and invites all the nations of the earth to imitate our example. If he say that error and wrong are committed in the administration of the Government, let him remember that nothing human can be perfect, and that under no other system of government revealed by Heaven or devised by man has reason been allowed so free and broad a scope to combat error. Has the sword of despots proved to be a safer or surer instrument of reform in government than enlightened reason? Does he expect to find among the ruins of this Union a happier abode for our swarming millions than they now have under it? Every lover of his country must shudder at the thought of the possibility of its dissolution, and will be ready to adopt the patriotic sentiment, "Our Federal Union—it must be preserved." To preserve it the compromises which alone enabled our fathers to form a common constitution for the government and protection of so many States and distinct communities, of such diversified habits, interests, and domestic institutions, must be sacredly and religiously observed. Any attempt to disturb or destroy these compromises, being terms of the compact of union, can lead to none other than the most ruinous and disastrous consequences.

It is a source of deep regret that in some sections of our country misguided persons have occasionally indulged in schemes and agitations whose object is the destruction of domestic institutions existing in other sections—institutions which existed at the adoption of the Constitution and were recognized and protected by it. All must see that if it were possible for them to be successful in attaining their object the dissolution of the Union and the consequent destruction of our happy form of government must speedily follow.

I am happy to believe that at every period of our existence as a nation there has existed, and continues to exist, among the great mass of our people a devotion to the Union of the States which will shield and protect it against the moral treason of any who would seriously contemplate its destruction. To secure a continuance of that devotion the compromises of the Constitution must not only be preserved, but sectional jealousies and heart burnings must be discountenanced, and all should remember that they are members of the same political family, having a common destiny. To increase the attachment of our people to the Union, our laws should be just. Any policy which shall tend to favor monopolies or the peculiar interests of sections or classes must operate to the prejudice of the interest of their fellow-citizens, and should be avoided. If the compromises of the Constitution be preserved, if sectional jealousies and heart burnings be discountenanced, if our laws be just and the Government be practically administered strictly within the limits of power prescribed to it, we may discard all apprehensions for the safety of the Union.

With these views of the nature, character, and objects of the Government and the value of the Union, I shall steadily oppose the creation of those institutions and systems which in their nature tend to pervert it from its legitimate purposes and make it the instrument of sections, classes, and individuals. We need no national banks or other extraneous institutions planted around the Government to control or strengthen it in opposition to the will of its authors. Experience has taught us how unnecessary they are as auxiliaries of the public authorities–how impotent for good and how powerful for mischief.

Ours was intended to be a plain and frugal government, and I shall regard it to be my duty to recommend to Congress and, as far as the Executive is concerned, to enforce by all the means within my power the strictest economy in the expenditure of the public money which may be compatible with the public interests.

A national debt has become almost an institution of European monarchies. It is viewed in some of them as an essential prop to existing governments. Melancholy is the condition of that people whose government can be sustained only by a system which periodically transfers large amounts from the labor of the many to the coffers of the few. Such a system is incompatible with the ends for which our republican Government was instituted. Under a wise policy the debts contracted in our Revolution and during the War of 1812 have been happily extinguished. By a judicious application of the revenues not required for other necessary purposes, it is not doubted that the debt which has grown out of the circumstances of the last few years may be speedily paid off.

I congratulate my fellow-citizens on the entire restoration of the credit of the General Government of the Union and that of many of the States. Happy would it be for the indebted States if they were freed from their liabilities, many of which were incautiously contracted. Although the Government of the Union is neither in a legal nor a moral sense bound for the debts of the States, and it would be a violation of our compact of union to assume them, yet we can not but feel a deep interest in seeing all the States meet their public liabilities and pay off their just debts at the earliest practicable period. That they will do so as soon as it can be done without imposing too heavy burdens on their citizens there is no reason to doubt. The sound moral and honorable feeling of the people of the indebted States can not

be questioned, and we are happy to perceive a settled disposition on their part, as their acility returns after a season of unexampled pecuniary embarrassment, to pay off all just demands and to acquiesce in any reasonable measures to accomplish that object.

One of the difficulties which we have had to encounter in the practical administration of the Government consists in the adjustment of our revenue laws and the levy of the taxes necessary for the support of Government. In the general proposition that no more money shall be collected than the necessities of an economical administration shall require all parties seem to acquiesce. Nor does there seem to be any material difference of opinion as to the absence of right in the Government to tax one section of country, or one class of citizens, or one occupation, for the mere profit of another. "Justice and sound policy forbid the Federal Government to foster one branch of industry to the detriment of another, or to cherish the interests of one portion to the injury of another portion of our common country." I have heretofore declared to my fellow-citizens that "in my judgment it is the duty of the Government to extend, as far as it may be practicable to do so, by its revenue laws and all other means within its power, fair and just protection to all of the great interests of the whole Union, embracing agriculture, manufactures, the mechanic arts, commerce, and navigation." I have also declared my opinion to be "in favor of a tariff for revenue," and that "in adjusting the details of such a tariff I have sanctioned such moderate discriminating duties as would produce the amount of revenue needed and at the same time afford reasonable incidental protection to our home industry," and that I was "opposed to a tariff for protection merely, and not for revenue."

The power "to lay and collect taxes, duties, imposts, and excises" was an indispensable one to be conferred on the Federal Government, which without it would possess no means of providing for its own support. In executing this power by levying a tariff of duties for the support of Government, the raising of 'revenue' should be the 'object' and 'protection' the 'incident'. To reverse this principle and make 'protection' the 'object' and 'revenue' the 'incident' would be to inflict manifest injustice upon all other than the protected interests. In levying duties for revenue it is doubtless proper to make such discriminations within the 'revenue principle' as will afford incidental protection to our home interests. Within the revenue limit there is a discretion to discriminate; beyond that limit the rightful exercise of the power is not conceded. The incidental protection afforded to our home interests by discriminations within the revenue range it is believed will be ample. In making discriminations all our home interests should as far as practicable be equally protected. The largest portion of our people are agriculturists. Others are employed in manufactures, commerce, navigation, and the mechanic arts. They are all engaged in their respective pursuits and their joint labors constitute the national or home industry. To tax one branch of this home industry for the benefit of another would be unjust. No one of these interests can rightfully claim an advantage over the others, or to be enriched by impoverishing the others. All are equally entitled to the fostering care and protection of the Government. In exercising a sound discretion in levying discriminating duties within the limit prescribed, care should be taken that it be done in a manner not to benefit the wealthy few at the expense of the toiling millions by taxing 'lowest' the luxuries of life, or articles of superior quality and high price, which can only be consumed by the wealthy, and 'highest' the necessaries of life, or articles of coarse quality and low price, which the poor and great mass of our people must consume. The burdens of government should as far as practicable be distributed justly and equally among all classes of our population. These general views, long entertained on this subject, I have deemed it proper to reiterate. It is a subject upon which conflicting interests of sections and occupations are supposed to exist, and a spirit of mutual concession and compromise in adjusting its details should be cherished by every part of our widespread country as the only means of preserving harmony and a cheerful acquiescence of all in the operation of our revenue laws. Our patriotic citizens in every part of the Union will readily submit to the payment of such taxes as shall be needed for the support of their Government, whether in peace or in war, if they are so levied as to distribute the burdens as equally as possible among them.

The Republic of Texas has made known her desire to come into our Union, to form a part of our Confederacy and enjoy with us the blessings of liberty secured and guaranteed by our Constitution. Texas was once a part of our country—was unwisely ceded away to a foreign power—is now independent, and possesses an undoubted right to dispose of a part or the whole of her territory and to merge her sovereignty as a separate and independent state in ours. I congratulate my country that by an act of the late Congress of the United States the assent of this Government has been given to the reunion, and it only remains for the two countries to agree upon the terms to consummate an object so important to both.

I regard the question of annexation as belonging exclusively to the United States and Texas. They are independent powers competent to contract, and foreign nations have no right to interfere with them or to take exceptions to their reunion. Foreign powers do not seem to appreciate the true character of our Government. Our Union is a confederation of independent States, whose policy is peace with each other and all the world. To enlarge its limits is to extend the dominions of peace over additional territories and increasing millions. The world has nothing to fear from military ambition in our Government. While the Chief Magistrate and the popular branch of Congress are elected for short terms by the suffrages of those millions who must in their own persons bear all the burdens and miseries of war, our Government can not be otherwise than pacific. Foreign powers should therefore look on the annexation of Texas to the United States not as the conquest of a nation seeking to extend her dominions by arms and violence, but as the peaceful acquisition of a territory once her own, by adding another member to our confederation, with the consent of that member, thereby diminishing the chances of war and opening to them new and ever-increasing markets for their products.

To Texas the reunion is important, because the strong protecting arm of our Government would be extended over her, and the vast resources of her fertile soil and genial climate would be speedily developed, while the safety of New Orleans and of our whole southwestern frontier against hostile aggression, as well as the interests of the whole Union, would be promoted by it.

In the earlier stages of our national existence the opinion prevailed with some that our system of confederated States could not operate successfully over an extended territory, and serious objections have at different times been made to the enlargement of our boundaries. These objections were earnestly urged when we acquired Louisiana. Experience has shown that they were not well founded. The title of numerous Indian tribes to vast tracts of country has been extinguished; new States have been admitted into the Union; new Territories have been created and our jurisdiction and laws extended over them. As our population has expanded, the Union has been cemented and strengthened. As our boundaries have been enlarged and our agricultural population has been spread over a large surface, our federative system has acquired additional strength and security. It may well be doubted whether it would not be in greater danger of overthrow if our present population were confined to the comparatively narrow limits of the original thirteen States than it is now that they are sparsely settled over a more expanded territory. It is confidently believed that our system may be safely extended to the utmost bounds of our territorial limits, and that as it shall be extended the bonds of our Union, so far from being weakened, will become stronger.

None can fail to see the danger to our safety and future peace if Texas remains an independent state or becomes an ally or dependency of some foreign nation more powerful than herself. Is there one among our citizens who would not prefer perpetual peace with Texas to occasional wars, which so often occur between bordering independent nations? Is there one who would not prefer free intercourse with her to high duties on all our products and manufactures which enter her ports or cross her frontiers? Is there one who would not prefer an unrestricted communication with her citizens to the frontier obstructions which must occur if she remains out of the Union? Whatever is good or evil in the local institutions of Texas will remain her own whether annexed to the United States or not. None of the present States will be responsible for them any more than they are for the local institutions of each other. They have confederated together for certain specified objects. Upon the same principle that they would refuse to form a perpetual union with Texas because of her local institutions our forefathers would have been prevented from forming our present Union. Perceiving no valid objection to the measure and many reasons for its adoption vitally affecting the peace, the safety, and the prosperity of both countries, I shall on the broad principle which formed the basis and produced the adoption of our Constitution, and not in any narrow spirit of sectional policy, endeavor by all constitutional, honorable, and appropriate means to consummate the expressed will of the people and Government of the United States by the reannexation of Texas to our Union at the earliest practicable period.

Nor will it become in a less degree my duty to assert and maintain by all constitutional means the right of the United States to that portion of our territory which lies beyond the Rocky Mountains. Our title to the country of the Oregon is "clear and unquestionable," and already are our people preparing to perfect that title by occupying it with their wives and children. But eighty years ago our population was confined on the west by the ridge of the Alleghanies. Within that period—within the lifetime, I might say, of some of my hearers—our people, increasing to many millions, have filled the eastern valley of the Mississippi, adventurously ascended the Missouri to its headsprings, and are already engaged in establishing the blessings of self-government in valleys of which the rivers flow to the Pacific. The world beholds the peaceful triumphs of the industry of our emigrants. To us belongs the duty of protecting them adequately wherever they may be upon our soil. The jurisdiction of our laws and the benefits of our republican institutions should be extended over them in the distant regions which they have selected for their homes. The increasing facilities of intercourse will easily bring the States, of which the formation in that part of our territory can not be long delayed, within the sphere of our federative Union. In the meantime every obligation imposed by treaty or conventional stipulations should be sacredly respected.

In the management of our foreign relations it will be my aim to observe a careful respect for the rights of other nations, while our own will be the subject of constant watchfulness. Equal and exact justice should characterize all our intercourse with foreign countries. All alliances having a tendency to jeopard the welfare and honor of our country or sacrifice any one of the national interests will be studiously avoided, and yet no opportunity will be lost to cultivate a favorable understanding with foreign governments by which our navigation and commerce may be extended and the ample products of our fertile soil, as well as the manufactures of our skillful artisans, find a ready market and remunerating prices in foreign countries.

In taking "care that the laws be faithfully executed," a strict performance of duty will be exacted from all public officers. From those officers, especially, who are charged with the collection and disbursement of the public revenue will prompt and rigid accountability be required. Any culpable failure or delay on their part to account for the moneys entrusted to them at the times and in the manner required by law will in every instance terminate the official connection of such defaulting officer with the Government.

Although in our country the Chief Magistrate must almost of necessity be chosen by a party and stand pledged to its principles and measures, yet in his official action he should not be the President of a part only, but of the whole people of the United States. While he executes the laws with an impartial hand, shrinks from no proper responsibility, and faithfully carries out in the executive department of the Government the principles and policy of those who have chosen him, he should not be unmindful that our fellow-citizens who have differed with him in opinion are entitled to the full and free exercise of their opinions and judgments, and that the rights of all are entitled to respect and regard.

Confidently relying upon the aid and assistance of the coordinate departments of the Government in conducting our public affairs, I enter upon the discharge of the high duties which have been assigned me by the people, again humbly supplicating that Divine Being who has watched over and protected our beloved country from its infancy to the present hour to continue His gracious benedictions upon us, that we may continue to be a prosperous and happy people.

Restatement of the Monroe Doctrine

From the First Annual Message to Congress
Washington, D.C.
December 2, 1845

POLK, LIKE MANY AMERICANS, subscribed to the doctrine of Manifest Destiny—the romantic idea that a benevolent Providence had preordained the expansion of the American nation across the continent. In his first annual message to Congress, written while France and Britain were attempting to persuade Texas to remain independent, Polk reaffirmed the Monroe Doctrine of 1823. To Monroe's assertion that Europe had no further colonial rights in the Western Hemisphere, Polk added the warning that the United States would resist European attempts to interfere with its plans for continental expansion. The message was enthusiastically received; in Philadelphia, where it was read aloud at the post office, listeners cried, "Hurrah! Jackson is alive again."

It is submitted to the wisdom of Congress to determine whether at their present session, and until after the expiration of the year's notice, any other measures may be adopted consistently with the convention of 1827 for the security of our rights and the government and protection of our citizens in Oregon. That it will ultimately be wise and proper to make liberal grants of land to the patriotic pioneers who amidst privations and dangers lead the way through savage tribes inhabiting the vast wilderness intervening between our frontier settlements and Oregon, and who cultivate and are ever ready to defend the soil, I am fully satisfied. To doubt whether they will obtain such grants as soon as the convention between the United States and Great Britain shall have ceased to exist would be to doubt the justice of Congress; but, pending the year's notice, it is worthy of consideration whether a stipulation to this effect may be made consistently with the spirit of that convention.

The recommendations which I have made as to the best manner of securing our rights in Oregon are submitted to Congress with great deference. Should they in their wisdom devise any other mode better calculated to accomplish the same object, it shall meet with my hearty concurrence.

At the end of the year's notice, should Congress think it proper to make provision for giving that notice, we shall have reached a period when the national rights in Oregon must either be abandoned or firmly maintained. That they cannot be abandoned without a sacrifice of both national honor and interest is too clear to admit of doubt.

Oregon is a part of the North American continent, to which, it is confidently affirmed, the title of the United States is the best now in existence. For the grounds on which that title rests I refer you to the correspondence of the late and present secretary of state with the British plenipotentiary during the negotiation. The British proposition of compromise, which would make the Columbia the line south of 49×, with a trifling addition of detached territory to the United States north of that river, and would leave on the British side two-thirds of the whole Oregon Territory, including the free navigation of the Columbia and all the valuable harbors on the Pacific, can never for a moment be entertained by the United States without an abandonment of their just and clear territorial rights, their own self-respect, and the national honor. . . .

The rapid extension of our settlements over our territories heretofore unoccupied, the addition of new states to our confederacy, the expansion of free principles, and our rising greatness as a nation are attracting the attention of the powers of Europe, and lately the doctrine has been broached in some of them of a "balance of power" on this continent to check our advancement. The United States, sincerely desirous of preserving relations of good understanding with all nations, cannot in silence permit any European interference on the North American continent, and should any such interference be attempted will be ready to resist it at any and all hazards.

It is well known to the American people and to all nations that this government has never interfered with the relations subsisting between other governments. We have never made ourselves parties to their wars or their alliances; we have not sought their territories by conquest: we have not mingled with parties in their domestic struggles; and believing our own form of government to be the best, we have never attempted to propagate it by intrigues, by diplomacy, or by force. We may claim on this continent a like exemption from European interference. The nations of America are equally sovereign and independent with those of Europe. They possess the same rights, independent of all foreign interposition, to make war, to conclude peace, and to regulate their internal affairs. The people of the United States cannot, therefore, view with indifference attempts of European powers to interfere with the independent action of the nations on this continent. The American system of government is entirely different from that of Europe. Jealousy among the different sovereigns of Europe, lest any one of them might become too powerful for the rest, has caused them anxiously to desire the establishment of what they term the "balance of power." It cannot be permitted to have any application on the North American continent, and especially to the United States. We must ever maintain the principle that the people of this continent alone have the right to decide their own destiny. Should any portion of them, constituting an independent state, propose to unite themselves with our confederacy, this will be a question for them and us to determine without any foreign interposition. We can never consent that European powers shall interfere to prevent such a union because it might disturb the "balance of power" which they may desire to maintain upon this continent. Near a quarter of a century ago the principle was distinctly announced to the world, in the annual message of one of my predecessors, that the American continents, by the free and independent condition which they have assumed and maintain, are henceforth not to be considered as subjects for future colonization by any European powers.

This principle will apply with greatly increased force should any European power attempt to establish any new colony in North America. In the existing circumstances of the world the present is deemed a proper occasion to reiterate and reaffirm the principle avowed by Mr. Monroe and to state my cordial concurrence in its wisdom and sound policy. The reassertion of this principle, especially in reference to North America, is at this day but the promulgation of a policy which no European power should cherish the disposition to resist. Existing rights of every European nation should be respected, but it is due alike to our safety and our interests that the efficient protection of our laws should be extended over our whole territorial limits, and that it should be distinctly announced to the world as our settled policy that no future European colony or dominion shall with our consent be planted or established on any part of the North American continent. . . .

The War with Mexico

From the Third Annual Message to Congress
Washington, D.C.
December 7, 1847

IN HIS EAGERNESS to defend Texas's border claims and to acquire territory from Mexico, Polk found it convenient to adopt a provocative posture that eventually resulted in war. By the end of 1847 American troops had occupied Mexico's capital and ports, but neither military action nor diplomacy could break the impasse with the disorganized Mexican government. Polk was now caught between opponents of the war who demanded withdrawal from Mexico and ultraexpansionists who demanded its wholesale annexation. In his hotly debated third message to Congress Polk outlined his version of events, asked for more money to continue the war, and insisted that bankrupt Mexico be forced to pay an indemnity in the form of land. In February of the following year Mexico agree to to cede New Mexico and the Californias, but Polk refused to pay the American diplomat who negotiated the treaty because he had acted without authorization.

. . In the enjoyment of the bounties of Providence at home such as have rarely fallen to the lot of any people, it is cause of congratulation that our intercourse with all the powers of the earth except Mexico continues to be of an amicable character.

It has ever been our cherished policy to cultivate peace and goodwill with all nations, and this policy has been steadily pursued by me.

No change has taken place in our relations with Mexico since the adjournment of the last Congress. The war in which the United States were forced to engage with the government of that country still continues. . . .

It is sufficient on the present occasion to say that the wanton violation of the rights of person and property of our citizens committed by Mexico, her repeated acts of bad faith through a long series of years, and her disregard of solemn treaties stipulating for indemnity to our injured citizens not only constituted ample cause of war on our part, but were of such an aggravated character as would have justified us before the whole world in resorting to this extreme remedy. With an anxious desire to avoid a rupture between the two countries we forbore for years to assert our clear rights by force, and continued to seek redress for the wrongs we had suffered by amicable negotiation in the hope that Mexico might yield to pacific counsels and the demands of justice. In this hope we were disappointed. Our minister of peace sent to Mexico was insultingly rejected. The Mexican government refused even to hear the terms of adjustment which he was authorized to propose, and finally, under wholly unjustifiable pretexts, involved the two countries in war by invading the territory of the state of Texas, striking the first blow, and shedding the blood of our citizens on our own soil.

Though the United States were the aggrieved nation, Mexico commenenced the war, and we were compelled in self-defense to repel the invader and to vindicate the national honor and interests by prosecuting it with vigor until we could obtain a just and honorable peace. . . .

It is well known that the only indemnity which it is in the power of Mexico to make in satisfaction of the just and long-deferred claims of our citizens against her and the only means by which she can reimburse the United States for the expenses of the war is a cession to the United States of a portion of her territory. Mexico has no money to pay, and no other means of making the required indemnity. If we refuse this, we can obtain nothing else. To reject indemnity by refusing to accept a cession of territory would be to abandon all our just demands, and to wage the war, bearing all its expenses, without a purpose or definite object.

A state of war abrogates treaties previously existing between the belligerents and a treaty of peace puts an end to all claims for indemnity for tortious acts committed under the authority of one government against the citizens or subjects of another unless they are provided for in its stipulations. A treaty of peace which would terminate the existing war witout providing for indemnity would enable Mexico, the acknowledged debtor and herself the aggressor in the war, to relieve herself from her just liabilities. By such a treaty our citizens who hold just demands against her would have no remedy either against Mexico or their own government. Our duty to these citizens must forever prevent such a peace, and no treaty which does not provide ample means of discharging these demands can receive my sanction.

A treaty of peace should settle all existing differences between the two countries. If an adequate cession of territory should be made by such a treaty, the United States should release Mexico from all her liabilities and assume their payment to our own citizens. If instead of this the United States were to consent to a treaty by which Mexico should again engage to pay the heavy amount of indebtedness which a just indemnity to our government and our citizens would impose on her, it is notorious that she does not possess the means to meet such an undertaking. From such a treaty no result could be anticipated but the same irritating disappointments which have heretofore attended the violations of similar treaty stipulations on the part of Mexico. Such a treaty would be but a temporary cessation of hostilities, without the restoration of the friendship and good understanding which should characterize the future intercourse between the two countries. . . .

The doctrine of no territory is the doctrine of no indemnity, and if sanctioned would be a public acknowledgment that our country was wrong and that the war declared by Congress with extraordinary unanimity was unjust and should be abandoned—an admission unfounded in fact and degrading to the national character. . .

The cession to the United States by Mexico of the provinces of New Mexico and the Californias, as proposed by the commissioner of the United States, it was believed would be more in accordance with the convenience and interests of both nations than any other cession of territory which it was probable Mexico could be induced to make.

It is manifest to all who have observed the actual condition of the Mexican government for some years past and at present that if these provinces should be retained by her she could not long continue to hold and govern them. Mexico is too feeble a power to govern these provinces, lying as they do at a distance of more than 1,000 miles from her capital, and if attempted to be retained by her they would constitute but for a short time even nominally a part of her dominions. This would be especially the case with Upper California.

The sagacity of powerful European nations has long since directed their attention to the commercial importance of that province, and there can be little doubt that the moment the United States shall relinquish their present occupation of it and their claim to it as indemnity an effort would be made by some foreign power to possess it, either by conquest or by purchase. If not foreign government should acquire it in either of these modes, an independent revolutionary government would probably be established by the inhabitants and such foreigners as may remain in or remove to the country as soon as it shall be known that the United States have abandoned it. Such a government would be too feeble long to maintain its separate independent existence, and would finally become annexed to or be a dependent colony of some more powerful state.

Should any foreign government attempt to possess it as a colony, or otherwise to incorporate it with itself, the principle avowed by President Monroe in 1824, and reaffirmed in my first annual message, that no foreign power shall with our consent be permitted to plant or establish any new colony or dominion on any part of the North American continent must be maintained. In maintaining this principle and in resisting its invasion by any foreign power we might be involved in other wars more expensive and more difficult than that in which we are now engaged.

The provinces of New Mexico and the Californias are contiguous to the territories of the United States, and if brought under the government of our laws their resources-mineral, agricultural, manufacturing, and commerical-would soon be developed.

Upper California is bound on the north by our Oregon possessions, and if held by the United States would soon be settled by a hardy, enterprising, and intelligent portion of our population. The bay of San Francisco and other harbors along the Californian coast would afford shelter for our navy, for our numerous whale ships, and other merchant vessels employed in the Pacific Ocean, and would in a short period become the marts of an extensive and profitable commerce with China and other countries of the East.

These advantages, in which the whole commercial world would participate, would at once be secured to the United States by the cession of this territory; while it is certain that as long as it remains a part of the Mexican dominions they can be enjoyed neither by Mexico herself nor by any other nation.

New Mexico is a frontier province, and has never been of any considerable value to Mexico. From its locality it is naturally connected with our western settlements. The territorial limits of the state of Texas, too, as defined by her laws before her admission into our Union, embrace all that portion of New Mexico lying east of the Rio Grande, while Mexico still claims to hold this territory as a part of her dominions. The adjustment of this question of boundary is important.

There is another consideration which induced the belief that the Mexican government might even desire to place this province under the protection of the government of the United States. Numerous bands of fierce and warlike savages wander over it and upon its borders. Mexico has been and must continue to be too feeble to restrain them from committing depredations, robberies, and murders, not only upon the inhabitants of New Mexico itself, but upon those of the other northern states of Mexico. It would be a blessing to all these northern states to have their citizens protected against them by the power of the United States. At this moment many Mexicans, principally females and children, are in captivity among them. If New Mexico were held and governed by the United States, we could effectually prevent these tribes from committing such outrages, and compel them to release these captives and restore them to their families and friends.

In proposing to acquire New Mexico and the Californias, it was known that but an inconsiderable portion of the Mexican people would be transferred with them, the country embraced within these provinces being chiefly an uninhabited region. . . .

Our arms having been everywhere victorious, having subjected to our military occupation a large portion of the enemy's country, including his capital, and negotiations for peace having failed, the important questions arise, in what manner the war ought to be prosecuted and what should be our future policy. I cannot doubt that we should secure and render available the conquests which we have already made, and that with this view we should hold and occupy by our naval and military forces all the ports, towns, cities, and provinces now in our occupation or which may hereafter fall into our possession; that we should press forward our military operations and levy such military contributions on the enemy as may, as far as practicable, defray the future expenses of the war.

Had the government of Mexico acceded to the equitable and liberal terms proposed, that mode of adjustment would have been preferred. Mexico having declined to do this and failed to offer any other terms which could be accepted by the United States, the national honor, no less than the public interests, requires that the war should be prosecuted with increased energy and power until a just and satisfactory peace can be obtained. In the meantime, as Mexico refuses all indemnity, we should adopt measures to indemnify ourselves by appropriating permanently a portion of her territory. Early after the commencement of the war New Mexico and the Californias were taken possession of by our forces. Our military and naval commanders were ordered to conquer and hold them, subject to be disposed of by a treaty of peace.

These provinces are now in our undisputed occupation, and have been so for many months, all resistance on the part of Mexico having ceased within their limits. I am satisfied that they should never be surrendered to Mexico. Should Congress concur with me in this opinion, and that they should be retained by the United States as indemnity, I can perceive no good reason why the civil jurisdiction and laws of the United States should not at once be extended over them. To wait for a treaty of peace such as we are willing to make, by which our relations toward them would not be changed, cannot be good policy; whilst our own interest and that of the people inhabiting them require that a stable, responsible, and free government under our authority should as soon as possible be established over them. Should Congress, therefore, determine to hold these provinces permanently, and that they shall hereafter be considered as constituent parts of our country, the early establishment of territorial governments over them will be important for the more perfect protection of persons and property; and I recommend that such territorial governments be established. It will promote peace and tranquillity among the inhabitants, by allaying all apprehension that they may still entertain of being again subjected to the jurisdiction of Mexico. I invite the early and favorable consideration of Congress to this important subject.

Rear view of the "Presidents North Carolina Gave to the Nation" statue on the grounds of the North Carolina state capitol in Raleigh, North Carolina. (Courtesy of Library of Congress)

Zachary Taylor

Zachary Taylor

1849–1850

ZACHARY TAYLOR was a Virginia-born, Kentucky-bred career soldier and planter who had no political experience whatever when he was boosted to the White House by the Whigs in 1848. A backwoodsman with only the barest education, he had risen to command the army in Mexico, where he defeated a much larger Mexican force at Buena Vista. The Whigs, who nominated him in order to attract the Southern vote, were correct in thinking that he would be a popular candidate, but Taylor was a lukewarm Whig at best, and once in office he refused to support the party's proposed solution to the national dispute over the extension of slavery into newly acquired territories. The program was enacted as the Compromise of 1850 after the death of Taylor 16 months into his term.

Taylor, whose nickname was "Old Rough and Ready," was well liked for his cordial, unassuming manners, his boldness and calmness in a crisis, and his willingness to undergo the same hardships as his men. During his years as a general he wore tattered clothes and an oilskin hat and was often mistaken for a farmer. In his public appearances as president he was received with admiration, but his few attempts at speechmaking elicited the ridicule of the Democrats. At his inaugural address—one of the briefest ever delivered—he read "in a very low voice and very badly as to his pronunciation and manner," according to President Polk. Holman Hamilton, Taylor's biographer, explained that "the modesty of Taylor's nature and his inexperience on the hustings made him at least as inadequate an orator as Andrew Jackson had been."

The President's Plan

From the First Annual Message to Congress
Washington, D.C.

December 24, 1849

DURING TAYLOR'S ADMINISTRATION Congress was preoccupied with the impossible task of finding a way to defuse regional antagonism over the extension of slavery beyond its traditional borders. The number of free and slave states were equal; a policy of admitting only free states would soon have given the abolitionists a majority in Congress. Southern agitation for the admission of new slave states was blocked by the Wilmot Proviso, voted by the House, which prevented the extension of slavery into any part of the vast new territories acquired from Mexico. In his annual message to Congress, Taylor, though himself a slaveowner, recommended that California be admitted to statehood under the no-slavery constitution that it had already adopted and lectured the congressmen on the necessity of preserving national unity. Most of the message was drafted by Secretary of State John M. Clayton.

... No civil government having been provided by Congress for California, the people of that territory, impelled by the necessities of their political condition, recently met in convention for the purpose of forming a constitution and state government, which the latest advices give me reason to suppose has been accomplished; and it is believed they will shortly apply for the admission of California into the Union as a sovereign state. Should such be the case, and should their constitution be conformable to the requisitions of the Constitution of the United States, I recommend their application to the favorable consideration of Congress. The people of New Mexico will also, it is believed, at no very distant period present themselves for admission into the Union. Preparatory to the admission of California and New Mexico the people of each will have instituted for themselves a republican form of government, "laying its foundation in such principles and organizing its powers in such form as to them shall seem most likely to effect their safety and happiness." By awaiting their action all causes of uneasiness may be avoided and confidence and kind feeling preserved. With a view of maintaining the harmony and tranquillity so dear to all, we should abstain from the introduction of those exciting topics of a sectional character which have hitherto produced painful apprehensions in the public mind; and I repeat the solemn warning of the first and most illustrious of my predecessors against

furnishing "any ground for characterizing parties by geographical discriminations."

...

Our government is one of limited powers, and its successful administration eminently depends on the confinement of each of its coordinate branches within its own appropriate sphere. The first section of the constitution ordains that—

> All legislative powers herein granted shall be vested in a Congress of the United States, which shall consist of a Senate and House of Representatives.

The executive has authority to recommend (not to dictate) measures to Congress. Having performed that duty, the executive department of the government cannot rightfully control the decision of Congress on any subject of legislation until that decision shall have been officially submitted to the president for approval. The check provided by the Constitution in the clause conferring the qualified veto will never be exercised by me except in the cases contemplated by the fathers of the republic. I view it as an extreme measure, to be resorted to only in extraordinary cases, as where it may become necessary to defend the executive against the encroachments of the legislative power or to prevent hasty and inconsiderate or unconstitutional legislation. By cautiously confining this remedy within the sphere prescribed to it in the contemporaneous expositions of the framers of the

Constitution, the will of the people, legitimately expressed on all subjects of legislation through their constitutional organs, the senators and Representatives of the United States, will have its full effect. As indispensable to the preservation of our system of self-government, the independence of the representatives of the states and the people is guaranteed by the Constitution, and they owe no responsibility to any human power but their constituents. By holding the representative responsible only to the people, and exempting him from all other influences, we elevate the character of the constituent and quicken his sense of responsibility to his country. It is under these circumstances only that the elector can feel that in the choice of the lawmaker he is himself truly a component part of the sovereign power of the nation. With equal care we should study to defend the rights of the executive and judicial departments. Our government can only be preserved in its purity by the suppression and entire elimination of every claim or tendency of one coordinate branch to encroachment upon another. With the strict observance of this rule and the other injunctions of the Constitution, with a sedulous inculcation of that respect and love for the Union of the states which our fathers cherished and enjoined upon their children, and with the aid of that overruling Providence which has so long and so kindly guarded our liberties and institutions, we may reasonably expect to transmit them, with their innumerable blessings, to the remotest posterity.

But attachment to the Union of the states should be habitually fostered in every American heart. For more than half a century, during which kingdoms and empires have fallen, this Union has stood unshaken. The patriots who formed it have long since descended to the grave; yet still it remains, the proudest monument to their memory and the object of affection and admiration with everyone worthy to bear the American name. In my judgment its dissolution would be the greatest of calamities, and to avert that should be the study of every American. Upon its preservation must depend our own happiness and that of countless generations to come. Whatever dangers may threaten it, I shall stand by it and maintain it in its integrity to the full extent of the obligations imposed and the powers conferred upon me by the Constitution.

Millard Fillmore

Millard Fillmore

1850–1853

ZACHARY TAYLOR'S vice president was Millard Fillmore of Buffalo, New York, a longtime Whig politician. Fillmore, from a poor farm family, had worked his way up from apprentice cloth dresser to successful lawyer and had served three terms in the House of Representatives, where he had won the chairmanship of the Ways and Means Committee. After his succession to the White House in 1850 he quickly removed the previous administration's obstacles to passage of the Whigs' elaborate program for the resolution of the slavery issue. This package of bills, known as the Compromise of 1850, provided for the admission of California as a free state; the organization of New Mexico under the principle of popular sovereignty, which entitled the territorial legislature to decide on the legality of slavery; and the abolition of the slave trade in Washington, D.C. It also included the Fugitive Slave Act, which required federal agencies to assist in the capture of runaway slaves, punished anyone who collaborated in an escape, denied accused runaways the right to a jury trial and the right to testify in their own defense, and made it possible for free blacks to be kidnapped and enslaved. The refusal of many Northerners to accept this law eventually destroyed the Compromise and resulted in the dissolution of the Whig Party.

Denied renomination in 1852 and easily defeated in his bid for election in 1856 as the American Party's nominee, Fillmore returned to Buffalo, where he spent a long retirement as a fund-raiser and officer of educational and charitable institutions.

Fillmore was a portly man with an affable demeanor and a friendly gaze. Though he made scores of speeches in the course of his congressional service, election campaigns, presidential tours, and years as Buffalo's leading citizen, his biographer, Robert J. Rayback, admitted that "no one ever credited him with great oratorical ability." According to Rayback, he was a competent parliamentarian but "lacked the elegant language and the turgid figures of speech which the 19th century usually associated with masterful orators. In situations where accepted elocution required impassioned utterances that fused thought and feeling, he resorted to logic, simple exposition, and called for reasonableness. . . . He was not a showman, but rather a citizen-in-office, and about him was always an aura of dignity."

On Neutrality in Foreign Affairs and the Compromise of 1850

From the First Annual Message to Congress

Washington, D.C.

December 2, 1850

FILLMORE BEGAN his first annual message with a belated inaugural address. His declaration of America's refusal to aid struggling nationalist movements—coupled with an affirmation of America's respect for the rights of all peoples to self-determination—was prompted by Hungary's recent attempt to break away from Austria. Later he invoked the same reasoning to block efforts by American expansionists to assist in the overthrow of the Spanish regime in Cuba.

At the end of his message, Fillmore counseled the nation to practice patience and tolerance while the Compromise of 1850 took effect. Fillmore himself did not approve of slavery but could find no constitutional grounds for its abolition by Congress. He was convinced that the presence of blacks in the United States, whether slave or free, would eventually lead to a race war similar to the 1791 slave uprising in Haiti. To avoid it, he proposed that all blacks be emancipated and resettled in Africa or the West Indies. He intended to publish this plan in his third annual message to Congress but omitted it on the advice of cabinet members.

Being suddenly called in the midst of the last session of Congress by a painful dispensation of Divine Providence to the responsible station which I now hold, I contented myself with such communications to the legislature as the exigency of the moment seemed to require. The country was shrouded in mourning for the loss of its venerable chief magistrate and all hearts were penetrated with grief. Neither the time nor the occasion appeared to require or to justify on my part any general expression of political opinions or any announcement of the principles which would govern me in the discharge of the duties to the performance of which I had been so unexpectedly called. I trust, therefore, that it may not be deemed inappropriate if I avail myself of this opportunity of the reassembling of Congress to make known my sentiments in a general manner in regard to the policy which ought to be pursued by the government both in its intercourse with foreign nations and its management and administration of internal affairs.

Nations, like individuals in a state of nature, are equal and independent, possessing certain rights and owing certain duties to each other, arising from their necessary and unavoidable relations; which rights and duties there is no common human authority to protect and enforce. Still, they are rights and duties, binding in morals, in conscience, and in honor, although there is no tribunal to which an injured party can appeal but the disinterested judgment of mankind, and ultimately the arbitrament of the sword.

Among the acknowledged rights of nations is that which each possesses of establishing that form of government which it may deem most conducive to the happiness and prosperity of its own citizens, of changing that form as circumstances may require, and of managing its internal affairs according to its own will. The people of the United States claim this right for themselves, and they readily concede it to others. Hence it becomes an imperative duty not to interfere in the government or internal policy of other nations; and although we may sympathize with the unfortunate or the oppressed everywhere in their struggles for freedom, our principles forbid us from taking any part in such foreign contests. We make no wars to promote or to prevent successions to thrones, to maintain any theory of a balance of power, or to suppress the actual government which any country chooses to establish for itself. We instigate no revolutions, nor suffer any hostile military expeditions to be fitted out in the United States to invade the territory or provinces of a friendly nation. The great law of morality ought to have a national as well as a personal and individual application. We should act toward other nations as we wish them to act toward us, and justice and conscience should form the rule of conduct between governments, instead of mere power, self-interest, or the desire of aggrandizement. To maintain a strict neutrality in foreign wars, to cultivate friendly relations, to reciprocate every noble and generous act, and to perform punctually and scrupulously every treaty obligation—these are the duties which we owe to other states, and by the performance of which we best entitle ourselves to like treatment from them; or, if that, in any case, be refused, we can enforce our own rights with justice and a clear conscience.

In our domestic policy the Constitution will be my guide, and in questions of doubt I shall look for its interpretation to the judicial decisions of that tribunal which was established to expound it and to the usage of the government, sanctioned by the acquiescence of the country. I regard all its provisions as equally binding. In all its parts it is the will of the people expressed in the most solemn form, and the constituted authorities are but agents to carry that will into effect. Every power which it has granted is to be exercised for the public good; but no pretense of utility, no honest conviction, even, of what might be expedient, can justify the assumption of any power not granted. The powers conferred upon the government and their distribution to the several departments are as clearly expressed in that sacred instrument as the imperfection of human language will allow, and I deem it my first duty not to question its wisdom, add to its provisions, evade its requirements, or nullify its commands.

Upon you, fellow citizens, as the representatives of the states and the people, is wisely devolved the legislative power. I shall comply with my duty in laying before you from time to time any information calculated to enable you to discharge your high and responsible trust for the benefit of our common constituents.

My opinions will be frankly expressed upon the leading of legislation; and if—which I do not anticipate—any act should pass the two Houses of Congress which should appear to me unconstitutional, or an encroachment on the just powers of other departments, or with provisions hastily adopted and likely to produce consequences injurious and unforeseen, I should not shrink from the duty of returning it to you, with my reasons, for your further consideration. Beyond the due performance of these constitutional obligations, both my respect for the legislature and my sense of propriety will restrain me from any attempt to control or influence your proceedings. With you is the power, the honor, and the responsibility of the legislation of the country.

The government of the United States is a limited government. It is confined to the exercise of powers expressly granted and such others as may be necessary for carrying those powers into effect; and it is at all times an especial duty to guard against any infringement on the just rights of the states. Over the objects and subjects intrusted to Congress its legislative authority is supreme. But here that authority ceases, and every citizen who truly loves the Constitution and desires the continuance of its existence and its blessings will resolutely and firmly resist any interference in those domestic affairs which the Constitution has clearly and unequivocally left to the exclusive authority of the states. And every such citizen will also deprecate useless irritation among the several members of the Union and all reproach and recrimination tending to alienate one portion of the country from another. The beauty of our system of government consists, and its safety and durability must consist, in avoiding mutual collisions and encroachments and in the regular separate action of all, which each is revolving in its own distinct orbit.

The Constitution has made it the duty of the president to take care that the laws be faithfully executed. In a government like ours, in which all laws are passed by a majority of the representatives of the people, and these representatives are chosen for such short periods that any injurious or obnoxious law can very soon be repealed, it would appear unlikely that any great numbers should be found ready to resist the execution of the laws. But it must be borne in mind that the country is extensive; that there may be local interests or prejudices rendering a law odious in one part which is not so in another, and that the thoughtless and inconsiderate, misled by their passions or their imaginations, may be induced madly to resist such laws as they disapprove. Such persons should recollect that without law there can be no real practical liberty; that when law is trampled under foot tyranny rules, whether it appears in the form of a military despotism or of popular violence. The law is the only sure protection of the weak and the only efficient restraint upon the strong. When impartially and faithfully administered, none is beneath its protection and none above its control. You, gentlemen, and the country may be assured that to the utmost of my ability and to the extent of the power vested in me I shall at all times and in all places take care that the laws be faithfully executed. In the discharge of this duty, solemnly imposed upon me by the Constitution and by my oath of office, I shall shrink from no responsibility, and shall endeavor to meet events as they may arise with firmness, as well as with prudence and discretion. . . .

It was hardly to have been expected that the series of measures passed at your last session with the view of healing the sectional differences which has sprung from the slavery and territorial questions should at once have realized their beneficent purpose. All mutual concession in the nature of a compromise must necessarily be unwelcome to men of extreme opinions. And though without such concessions our Constitution could not have been formed, and cannot be permanently sustained, yet we have seen them made the subject of bitter controversy in both sections of the republic. It required many months of discussion and deliberation to secure the concurrence of a majority of Congress in their favor. It would be strange if they had been received with immediate approbation by people and states prejudiced and heated by the exciting controversies of their representatives. I believe those measures to have been required by the circumstances and condition of the country. I believe they were necessary to allay asperities and animosities that were rapidly alienating one section of the country from another and destroying those fraternal sentiments which are the strongest supports of the Constitution. They were adopted in the spirit of conciliation and for the purpose of conciliation. I believe that a great majority of our fellow citizens sympathize in that spirit and that purpose, and in the main approve and are prepared in all respect to sustain these enactments. I cannot doubt that the American people, bound together by kindred blood and common traditions, still cherish a paramount regard for the Union of their fathers, and that they are ready to rebuke any attempt to violate its integrity, to disturb the compromises on which it is based, or to resist the laws which have been enacted under its authority.

The series of measures to which I have alluded are regarded by me as a settlement in principle and substance—a final settlement of the dangerous and exciting subjects which they embraced. Most of these subjects, indeed, are beyond your reach, as the legislation which disposed of them was in its character final and irrevocable. It may be presumed from the opposition which they all encountered that none of those measures was free from imperfections, but in their mutual dependence and connection they formed a system of compromise the most conciliatory and best for the entire country that could be obtained from conflicting sectional interests and opinions.

For this reason I recommend your adherence to the adjustment established by those measures until time and experience shall demonstrate the necessity of further legislation to guard against evasion or abuse.

By that adjustment we have been rescued from the wide and boundless agitation that surrounded us, and have a firm, distinct, and legal ground to rest upon. And the occasion, I trust, will justify me in exhorting my countrymen to rally upon and maintain that ground as the best, if not the only, means of restoring peace and quiet to the country and maintaining inviolate the integrity of the Union. . . .

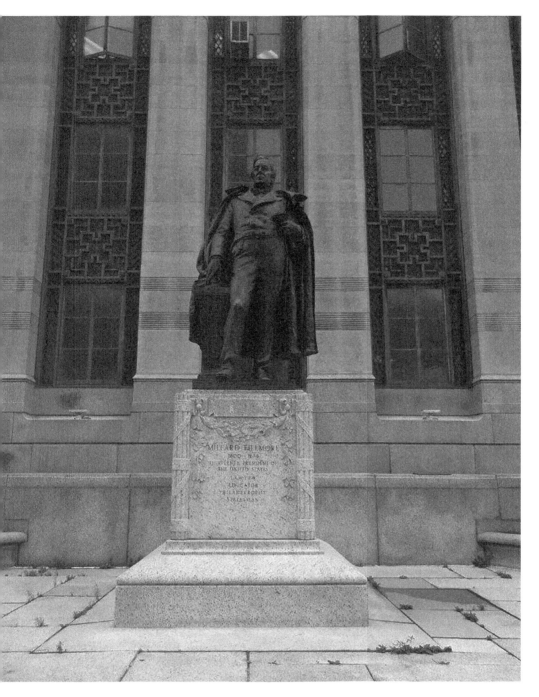

Millard Fillmore statue in Buffalo, New York.
(Courtesy of PresidentsUSA.net)

Franklin Pierce

Franklin Pierce

1853–1857

THE SON OF A REVOLUTIONARY WAR hero from backwoods New Hampshire, Franklin Pierce was a loyal Democrat with 10 years' experience in the House and Senate when the divided party nominated him in 1852 as a compromise candidate of last resort. Historian Allan Nevins described him as "gay, loquacious, bubbling over with kindness and beguilingly demonstrative," a "charming, pliable, vacillating executive" who yielded to "men of stronger intellect and greater determination."

As a Northerner with proslavery sympathies, Pierce was expected to unite moderates on both sides of the slavery question, but his concessions to Southern demands eventually alienated the North. The Democrats' Kansas-Nebraska Act of 1853, which repealed the Missouri Compromise and gave settlers in those territories the right to choose or reject slavery, produced rival governments and a civil war in Kansas. Pierce's inept administration ended after one term; denied renomination in 1856, he returned to New Hampshire and obscurity, dying an alcoholic.

Pierce's biographer, Roy Franklin Nichols, describing the class of politician to which Pierce belonged, wrote: "They were artists and made themselves practised in oratory that they might sway human emotions by the voice and personality. Flowery, fiery, rhetorical, flowing, flamboyant, their speech drew a pleasure-starved people out of themselves, stimulated their imaginations and roused their feelings. To address the audiences of the shire towns and villages was to play the keys and stops of their emotions by means of the cadence of the voice, the commanding gesture and flashing eye." Pierce, trained in oration at Bowdoin College, knew how to command attention on the podium; his ability to charm jurors made him one of New Hampshire's richest trial lawyers. During the Civil War he made a number of speeches in defense of the Confederacy. In his last speech, made on July 4, 1863, he denounced the Emancipation Proclamation, while through the crowd spread the news of the Union victory at Gettysburg.

Inaugural Address

Washington, D.C.

March 4, 1853

WHEN HE TOOK the oath of office, Pierce was in mourning for his 11-year-old son, his last surviving child, who had been killed in a train wreck two months before. Snow fell while he delivered his inaugural address from memory, the first president ever to do so. During the course of his administration he never deviated from the proslavery views he announced in the address, nor could he imagine the United States with a free black population. In his 1855 annual message to Congress, Pierce said: "If the passionate rage of fanaticism and partisan spirit did not force the fact upon our attention, it would be difficult to believe that any considerable portion of the people of this enlightened country could have so surrendered themselves to a fanatical devotion to the supposed interests of the relatively few Africans in the United States as totally to abandon and disregard the interests of the 25 million Americans; to trample under foot the injunctions of moral and constitutional obligation, and to engage in plans of vindictive hostility against those who are associated with them in the enjoyment of the common heritage of our national institutions."

It is a relief to feel that no heart but my own can know the personal regret and bitter sorrow over which I have been borne to a position so suitable for others rather than desirable for myself.

The circumstances under which I have been called for a limited period to preside over the destinies of the republic fill me with a profound sense of responsibility, but with nothing like shrinking apprehension. I repair to the post assigned me not as to one sought, but in obedience to the unsolicited expression of your will, answerable only for a fearless, faithful, and diligent exercise of my best powers. I ought to be, and am, truly grateful for the rare manifestation of the nation's confidence; but this, so far from lightening my obligations, only adds to their weight. You have summoned me in my weakness; you must sustain me by your strength. When looking for the fulfillment of reasonable requirements, you will not be unmindful of the great changes which have occurred, even within the last quarter of a century, and the consequent augmentation and complexity of duties imposed in the administration both of your home and foreign affairs.

Whether the elements of inherent force in the republic have kept pace with its unparalleled progression in territory, population, and wealth has been the subject of earnest thought and discussion on both sides of the ocean. Less than 64 years ago the Father of his Country made "the" then "recent accession of the important state of North Carolina to the Constitution of the United States" one of the subjects of his special congratulation. At that moment, however, when the agitation consequent upon the Revolutionary struggle had hardly subsided, when we were just emerging from the weakness and embarrassments of the confederation, there was an evident consciousness of vigor equal to the great mission so wisely and bravely fulfilled by our fathers. It was not a presumptuous assurance, but a calm faith, springing from a clear view of the sources of power in a government constituted like ours. It is no paradox to say that although comparatively weak the new-born nation was intrinsically strong. Inconsiderable in population and apparent resources, it was upheld by a broad and intelligent comprehension of rights and an all-pervading purpose to maintain them, stronger than armaments. It came from the furnace of the Revolution, tempered to the necessities of the times. The thoughts of the men of that day were as practical as their sentiments were patriotic. They wasted no portion of their energies upon idle and delusive speculations, but with a firm and fearless step advanced beyond the governmental landmarks which had hitherto circumscribed the limits of human freedom and planted their standard, where it has stood against dangers which have threatened from abroad, and internal agitation, which has at times fearfully menaced at home. They proved themselves equal to the solution of the great problem, to understand which their minds had been illuminated by the dawning lights of the Revolution. The object sought was not a thing dreamed of; it was a thing realized. They had exhibited not only the power to achieve, but, what all history affirms to be so much more unusual, the capacity to maintain. The oppressed throughout the world from that day to the present have turned their eyes hitherward, not to find those lights extinguished or to fear lest they should wane, but to be constantly cheered by their steady and increasing radiance.

In this our country has, in my judgment, thus far fulfilled its highest duty to suffering humanity. It has spoken and will continue to speak, not only by its words, but by its acts, the language of sympathy, encouragement, and hope to those who earnestly listen to tones which pronounce for the largest rational liberty. But after all, the most animating encouragement and potent appeal for freedom will be its own history—its trials and its triumphs. Preeminently, the power of our advocacy reposes in our example; but no example, be it remembered, can be powerful for lasting good, whatever apparent advantages may be gained, which is not based upon eternal principles of right and justice. Our fathers decided for themselves, both upon the hour to declare and the hour to strike. They were their own judges of the circumstances under which it became them to pledge to each other "their lives, their fortunes, and their sacred honor" for the acquisition of the priceless inheritance transmitted to us. The energy with which that great conflict was opened and, under the guidance of manifest and beneficent Providence, the uncomplaining endurance which it was prosecuted to its consummation were only surpassed by the wisdom and patriotic spirit of concession which characterized all the counsels of the early fathers.

One of the most impressive evidences of that wisdom is to be found in the fact that the actual working of our system has dispelled a degree of solicitude which at the outset disturbed bold hearts and far-reaching intellects. The apprehension of dangers from extended territory, multiplied states, accumulated wealth, and augmented population has proved to be unfounded. The stars upon your banner have become nearly threefold their original number; your densely populated possessions skirt the shores of the two great oceans; and yet this vast increase of people and territory has not only shown itself compatible with the harmonious action of the states and federal government in their respective constitutional spheres, but has afforded an additional guaranty of the strength and integrity of both.

With an experience thus suggestive and cheering, the policy of my administration will not be controlled by any timid forebodings of evil from expansion. Indeed, it is not to be disguised that our attitude as a nation and our position on the globe render the acquisition of certain possessions not within our jurisdiction eminently important for our protection, if not in the future essential for the preservation of the rights of commerce and the peace of the world. Should they be obtained, it will be through no grasping spirit, but with a view to obvious national interest and security, and in a manner entirely consistent with the strictest observance of national faith. We have nothing in our history or position to invite aggression; we have everything to beckon us to the cultivation of relations of peace and amity with all nations. Purposes, therefore, at once just and pacific will be significantly marked in the conduct of our foreign affairs. I intend that my administration shall leave no blot upon our fair record, and trust I may safely give the assurance that no act within the legitimate scope of my constitutional control will be tolerated on the part of any portion of our citizens which cannot challenge a ready justification before the tribunal of the civilized world. An administration would be unworthy of confidence at home or respect abroad should it cease to be influenced by the conviction that no apparent advantage can be purchased at a price so dear as that of national wrong or dishonor. It is not your privilege as a nation to speak of a distant past. The striking incidents of your history, replete with instruction and furnishing abundant grounds for hopeful confidence, are comprised in a period comparatively brief. But if your past is limited, your future is boundless. Its obligations throng the unexplored pathway of advancement, and will be limitless as duration. Hence a sound and comprehensive policy should embrace not less the distant future than the urgent present.

The great objects of our pursuit as a people are best to be attained by peace, and are entirely consistent with the tranquillity and interests of the rest of mankind. With the neighboring nations upon our continent we should cultivate kindly and fraternal relations. We can desire nothing in regard to them so much as to see them consolidate their strength and pursue the paths of prosperity and happiness. If in the course of their growth we should open new channels of trade and create additional facilities for friendly intercourse, the benefits realized will be equal and mutual. Of the complicated European systems of national polity we have heretofore been independent. From their wars, their tumults, and anxieties we have been, happily, almost entirely exempt. Whilst these are confined to the nations which gave them existence, and within their legitimate jurisdiction, they cannot affect us except as they appeal to our sympathies in the cause of human freedom and universal advancement. But the vast interests of commerce are common to all mankind, and the advantages of trade and international intercourse must always present a noble field for the moral influence of a great people.

With these views firmly and honestly carried out, we have a right to expect, and shall under all circumstances require, prompt reciprocity. The rights which belong to us as a nation are not alone to be regarded, but those which pertain to every citizen in his individual capacity, at home and abroad, must be sacredly maintained. So long as he can discern every star in its place upon that ensign, without wealth to purchase for him preferment or title to secure for him place, it will be his privilege, and must be his acknowledged right, to stand unabashed even in the presence of princes, with a proud consciousness that he is himself one of a nation of sovereigns and that he cannot in legitimate pursuit wander so far from home that the agent whom he shall leave behind the place which I now occupy will not see that no rude hand of power or tyrannical passion is laid upon him with impunity. He must realize that upon every sea and on every soil where our enterprise may rightfully seek the protection of our flag American citizenship is an inviolable panoply for the security of American rights. And in this connection it can hardly be necessary to reaffirm a principle which should now be regarded as fundamental. The rights, security, and repose of this confederacy reject the idea of interference or colonization on this side of the ocean by any

foreign power beyond present jurisdiction as utterly inadmissible.

The opportunities of observation furnished by my brief experience as a soldier confirmed in my own mind the opinion, entertained and acted upon by others from the formation of the government, that the maintenance of large standing armies in our country would be not only dangerous, but unnecessary. They also illustrated the importance—I might well say the absolute necessity—of the military science and practical skill furnished in such an eminent degree by the institution which has made your army what it is, under the discipline and instruction of officers not more distinguished for their solid attainments, gallantry, and devotion to the public service than for unobtrusive bearing and high moral tone. The army as organized must be the nucleus around which in every time of need the strength of your military power, the sure bulwark of your defense—a national militia—may be readily formed into a well-disciplined and efficient organization. And the skill and self-devotion of the navy assure you that you may take the performance of the past as a pledge for the future, and may confidently expect that the flag which has waved its untarnished folds over every sea will still float in undiminished honor. But these, like many other subjects, will be appropriately brought at a future time to the attention of the coordinate branches of the government, to which I shall always look with profound respect and with trustful confidence that they will accord to me the aid and support which I shall so much need and which their experience and wisdom will readily suggest.

In the administration of domestic affairs you expect a devoted integrity in the public service and an observance of rigid economy in all departments, so marked as never justly to be questioned. If this reasonable expectation be not realized, I frankly confess that one of your leading hopes is doomed to disappointment, and that my efforts in a very important particular must result in a humiliating failure. Offices can be properly regarded only in the light of aids for the accomplishment of these objects, and as occupancy can confer no prerogative nor importunate desire for preferment any claim, the public interest imperatively demands that they be considered with sole reference to the duties to be performed. Good citizens may well claim the protection of good laws and the benign influence of good government, but a claim for office is what the people of a republic should never recognize. No reasonable man of any party will expect the administration to be so regardless of its responsibility and of the obvious elements of success as to retain persons known to be under the influence of political hostility and partisan prejudice in positions which will require not only severe labor, but cordial cooperation. Having no implied engagements to ratify, no rewards to bestow, no resentments to remember, and no personal wishes to consult in selections for official station, I shall fulfill this difficult and delicate trust, admitting no motive as worthy either of my character or position which does not contemplate an efficient discharge of duty and the best interests of my country. I acknowledge my obligations to the masses of my countrymen, and to them alone. Higher objects than personal aggrandizement gave direction and energy to their exertions in the late canvass, and they shall not be disappointed. They require at my hands diligence, integrity, and capacity wherever there are duties to be performed. Without these qualities in their public servants, more stringent laws for the prevention or punishment of fraud, negligence, and peculation will be vain. With them they will be unnecessary.

But these are not the only points to which you look for vigilant watchfulness. The dangers of a concentration of all power in the general government of a confederacy so vast as ours are too obvious to be disregarded. You have a right, therefore, to expect your agents in every department to regard strictly the limits imposed upon them by the Constitution of the United States. The great scheme of our constitutional liberty rests upon a proper distribution of power between the state and federal authorities, and experience has shown that the harmony and happiness of our people must depend upon a just discrimination between the separate rights and responsibilities of the states and your common rights and obligations under the general government; and here, in my opinion, are the considerations which should form the true basis of future concord in regard to the questions which have most seriously disturbed public tranquillity. If the federal government will confine itself to the exercise of powers clearly granted by the Constitution, it can hardly happen that its action upon any question should endanger the institutions of the states or interfere with their right to manage matters strictly domestic according to the will of their own people.

In expressing briefly my views upon an important subject which has recently agitated the nation to almost a fearful degree, I am moved by no other impulse than a most earnest desire for the perpetuation of that Union which has made us what we are, showering upon us blessings and conferring a power and influence which our fathers could hardly have anticipated, even with their most sanguine hopes directed to a far-off future. The sentiments I now announce were not unknown before the expression of the voice which called me here. My own position upon this subject was clear and unequivocal, upon the record of my words and my acts, and it is only recurred to at this time because silence might perhaps be misconstrued. With the Union my best and dearest earthly hopes are entwined. Without it what are we individually or collectively? What becomes of the noblest field ever opened for the advancement of our race in religion, in government, in the arts, and in all that dignifies and adorns mankind? From that radiant constellation which both illumines our own way and points out to struggling nations their course, let but a single star be lost, and, if there be not utter darkness, the luster of the whole is dimmed. Do my countrymen need any assurance that such a catastrophe is not to overtake them while I possess the power to stay it? It is with me an earnest and vital belief that as the Union has been the source, under Providence, of our prosperity to this time, so it is the surest pledge of a continuance of the blessings we have enjoyed, and which we are sacredly bound to transmit undiminished to our children. The field of calm and free discussion in our country is open, and will always be so, but never has been and never can be traversed for good in a spirit of sectionalism and uncharitableness. The founders of the republic dealt with things as they were presented to them, in a spirit of self-sacrificing patriotism, and, as time has proved, with a comprehensive wisdom which it will always be safe for us to consult. Every measure tending to strengthen the fraternal feelings of all the members of our Union has had my heartfelt approbation. To every theory of society or government, whether the offspring of feverish ambition or of morbid enthusiasm, calculated to dissolve the bonds of law and affection which unite us, I shall interpose a ready and stern resistance. I believe that involuntary servitude, as it exists in different states of this confederacy, is recognized by the Constitution. I believe that it stands like any other admitted right, and that the states where it exists are entitled to efficient remedies to enforce the constitutional provisions. I hold that the laws of 1850, commonly called the "compromise measures," are strictly constitutional and to be unhesitatingly carried into effect. I believe that the constituted authorities of this republic are bound to regard the rights of the South in this respect as they would view any other legal and constitutional right, and that the laws to enforce them should be respected and obeyed, not with reluctance encouraged by abstract opinions as to their propriety in a different state of society, but cheerfully and according to the decisions of the tribunal to which their exposition belongs. Such have been, and are, my convictions, and upon them I shall act. I fervently hope that the question is at rest, and that no sectional or ambitious or fanatical excitement may again threaten the durability of our institutions or obscure the light of our prosperity.

But let not the foundation of our hope rest upon man's wisdom. It will not be sufficient that sectional prejudices find no place in the public deliberations. It will not be sufficent that the rash counsels of human passion are rejected. It must be felt that there is no national security but in the nation's humble, acknowledged dependence upon God and His overruling providence.

We have been carried in safety through a perilous crisis. Wise counsels, like those which gave us the Constitution, prevailed to uphold it. Let the period be remembered as an admonition, and not as an encouragement, in any section of the Union, to make experiments where experiments are fraught with such fearful hazard. Let it be impressed upon all hearts that, beautiful as our fabric is, no earthly power or wisdom could ever reunite its broken fragments. Standing, as I do, almost within view of the green slopes of Monticello, and, as it were, within reach of the tomb of Washington, with all the cherished memories of the past gathering around me like so many eloquent voices of exhortation from heaven, I can express no better hope for my country than that the kind Providence which smiled upon our fathers may enable their children to preserve the blessings they have inherited.

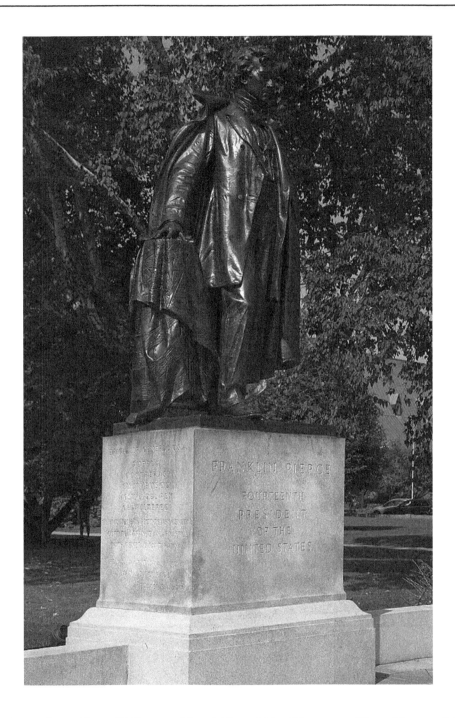

Statue of onetime U.S. president Franklin Pierce, a New Hampshire native, on the state capitol grounds in Concord, New Hampshire. (Courtesy of Library of Congress)

James Buchanan

James Buchanan

1857–1861

JAMES BUCHANAN, the last president to hold office before the outbreak of the Civil War, was a Pennsylvania Democrat who had served under Polk as secretary of state and under Pierce as minister to Britain. Like Pierce, he was a Northerner who sympathized with the South, believed slavery to be protected by the Constitution, and refused to acknowledge any degree of validity in Northern views. Once out of office, he was denounced by Southerners as a Unionist and by Northerners as a traitor.

From the beginning of his career in the Pennsylvania legislature, Buchanan, the son of an immigrant grocer, worked hard to impress constituents with his fine clothes and dignified bearing. As a lawyer he made up in diligence what he lacked in imagination. Said his biographer, Philip S. Klein: "His arguments before court and addresses to juries were anything but brilliant or spell-binding, but they achieved their object by sheer mass of data tightly knit by logic. . . . This habit was to affect his political speeches, from which it is extremely difficult to extract any sentence without materially damaging his train of thought." This reputation followed him to Congress. Shortly after his arrival he was asked to speak in defense of the Southern leader John C. Calhoun, then secretary of war, who had overspent his departmental budget. His speech on this occasion, according to Klein, exemplified his style of oratory. After engaging the sympathies of his listeners, "Buchanan launched into the details of his problem, examining every possible meaning and ramification, and tracing all to the stage of *reductio ad absurdam* except the one he supported, which at length stood out like a beacon of sanity and good judgment by contrast. . . . In a reasoned debate, Buchanan could so exhaust a subject that any reply was bound to be a reiteration. Against wit or ridicule he was helpless, but in serious debate he was formidable."

The Equality of the States

Washington, D.C.

July 9, 1860

BUCHANAN HAD PLEDGED to serve only one term, but he was determined to see the Democrats nominate a Southerner to succeed him. The differences between the various factions of the party led to the nomination of three candidates who split the vote and thus helped ensure Lincoln's election. Rather than work to unite the party under the official candidate, Stephen A. Douglas, the president gave his support to the Southerners' candidate, John C. Breckinridge of Kentucky, his own vice president, who ran on a platform requiring the federal government to protect slavery in the territories. Buchanan endorsed the platform at a rally on the White House lawn.

. . . I am in favor of Mr. Breckinridge, because he sanctions and sustains the perfect equality of all the states within their common territories, and the opinion of the Supreme Court of the United States, establishing this equality. The sovereign states of this Union are one vast partnership. The territories were acquired by the common blood and common treasure of them all. Each state, and each citizen of each state, has the same right in the territories as any other state and the citizens of any other state possess. Now what is sought for at present is, that a portion of these states should turn around to their sister states and say, "We are holier than you are, and while we will take our property to the territories and have it protected there, you shall not place your property in the same position." That is precisely what is contended for. What the Democratic Party maintain, and what is the true principle of Democracy is, that all shall enjoy the same rights, and that all shall be subject to the same duties. Property—this government was framed for the protection of life, liberty, and property. They are the objects for the protection of which all enlightened governments were established. But it is sought now to place the property of the citizen, under what is called the principle of squatter sovereignty, in the power of the territorial legislature to confiscate it at their will and pleasure. That is the principle sought to be established at present; and there seems to be an entire mistake and misunderstanding among a portion of the public upon this subject. When was property ever submitted to the will of the majority? If you hold property as an individual, you hold it independent of Congress or of the state legislature, or of the territorial legislature—it is

yours, and your Constitution was made to protect your private property against the assaults of legislative power. Well, now, any set of principles which will deprive you of your property, is against the very essence of republican government, and to that extent makes you a slave; for the man who has power over your property to confiscate it, has power over your means of subsistence; and yet it is contended, that although the Constitution of the United States confers no such power—although no state legislature has any such power, yet a territorial legislature, in the remote extremities of the country, can confiscate your property!

There is but one mode, and one alone, to abolish slavery in the territories. That mode is pointed out in the Cincinnati platform, which has been as much misrepresented as anything I have ever known. That platform declares that a majority of the actual residents in a territory, whenever their number is sufficient to entitle them to admission as a state, possess the power to "form a constitution with or without domestic slavery, to be admitted into the Union upon terms of perfect equality with the other states." If there be squatter sovereignty in this resolution, I have never been able to perceive it. If there be any reference in it to a territorial legislature, it has entirely escaped my notice. It presents the clear principle that, at the time the people form their constitution, they shall then decide whether they will have slavery or not. And yet it has been stated over and over again that, in accepting the nomination under that platform, I endorsed the doctrine of squatter sovereignty. I suppose you have all heard this repeated a thousand times.

How beautifully this plain principle of constitutional law corresponds with the best interests of the people! Under it, emigrants from the North and the South, from the East and the West proceed to the territories. They carry with them that property which they suppose will best promote their material interests; they lie together in peace and harmony. The question of slavery will become a foregone conclusion before they have inhabitants enough to enter the Union as a state. There will then be no "bleeding Kansas" in the territories; they will all live together in peace and harmony, promoting the prosperity of the territory and their own prosperity, until the time shall arrive when it becomes necessary to frame a constitution. Then the whole question will be decided to the general satisfaction. But, upon the opposite principle, what will you find in the territories? Why, there will be strife and contention all the time. One territorial legislature may establish slavery and another territorial legislature may abolish it, and so the struggle will be continued throughout the territorial existence. The people instead of devoting their energies and industry to promote their own prosperity, will be in a state of constant strife and turmoil, just as we have witnessed in Kansas. Therefore, there is no possible principle that can be so injurious to the best interests of a territory as what has been called squatter sovereignty.

Now, let me place the subject before you in another point of view. The people of the Southern states can never abandon this great principle of state equality in the Union without self-degraduation. Never without an acknowledgment that they are inferior in this respect to their sister states. While it is vital to them to preserve their equality, the Northern states surrender nothing by admitting this principle. In doing this they only yield obedience to the Constitution of their country as expounded by the Surpeme Court of the United States. While for the North it is comparatively a mere abstraction, with the South it is a question of co-equal state sovereignty in the Union.

If the decrees of the high tribunal established by the Constitution for the very purposes are to be set at naught and disregarded, it will tend to render all property of every description insecure. What, then, have the North to do? Merely to say that, as good citizens, they will yield obedience to the decision of the Supreme Court, and admit the right of a Southern man to take his property into the territories, and hold it there just as a Northern man may do; and it is to me the most extraordinary thing in the world that this country should now be distracted and divided because certain persons at the North will not agree that their brethren at the South shall have the same rights in the territories which they enjoy. What would I, as a Pennsylvanian, say or do, supposing anybody was to contend that the legislature of any territory could outlaw iron or coal within the territory? The principle is precisely the same. The Supreme Court of the United States have decided—what was known to us all to have been the existing state of affairs for 50 years—that slaves are property. Admit that fact, and you admit everything. Then that property in the territories must be protected precisely in the same manner with any other property. If it be not so protected in the territories, the holders of it are degraded before the world.

We have been told that non-intervention on the part of Congress with slavery in the territories is the true policy. Very well. I must cheerfully admit that Congress has no right to pass any law to establish, impair, or abolish slavery in the territories. Let this principle of non-intervention be extended to the territorial legislatures, and let it be declared that they in like manner have no power to establish, impair or destroy slavery, and then the controversy is in effect ended. This is all that is required at present, and I verily believe all that will ever be required. Hands off by Congress and hands off by the territorial legislature. With the Supreme Court of the United States I hold that neither Congress nor the territorial legislature has any power to establish, impair or abolish slavery in the territories. But if, in the face of this positive prohibition, the territorial legislature should exercise the power of intervening, then this would be a mere transfer of the Wilmot Proviso and the Buffalo platform from Congress, to be carried into execution in the territories to the destruction of all property in slaves.

An attempt of this kind, if made in Congress, would be resisted by able men on the floor of both houses, and probably defeated. Not so in a remote territory. To every new territory there will be a rush of free-soilers from the Northern states. They would elect the first territorial legislature before the people of the South could arrive with their property, and this legislature would probably settle forever the question of slavery according to their own will.

And shall we for the sake of squatter sovereignty, which, from its nature, can only continue during the brief period of territorial existence, incur the risk of dividing the great Democratic Party of the country into two sectional parties, the one North and the other South? Shall this great party which has governed the country in peace and war, which has raised it from humble beginnings to be one of the most prosperous and powerful nations in the world— shall this party be broken up for such a cause? That is the question. The numerous, powerful, pious and respectable Methodist Church has been thus divided. The division was a severe shock to the Union. A similar division of the great Democratic Party, should it continue, would rend asunder one of the most powerful links which bind the Union together.

I entertain no such fearful apprehensions. The present issue is transitory, and will speedily pass away. In the nature of things it cannot continue. There is but one possible contingency which can endanger the Union, and against this all Democrats, whether squatter sovereigns or popular sovereigns, will present a united resistance. Should the time ever arrive when Northern agitation and fanaticism shall proceed so far as to render the domestic firesides of the South insecure, then,

and not till then, will the Union be in danger. A united Northern Democracy will present a wall of fire against such a catastrophe!

There are in our midst numerous persons who predict the dissolution of the great Democratic Party, and others who contend that it has already been dissolved. The wish is father to the thought. It has been heretofore in great peril; but when divided for the moment, it has always closed up its ranks and become more powerful, even from defeat. It will never die whilst the Constitution and the Union survive. It will live to protect and defend both. It has its roots in the very vitals of the Constitution and, like one of the ancient cedars of Lebanon, it will flourish to afford shelter and protection to that sacred instrument, and to shield it against every storm of faction.

Now, friends and fellow citizens, it is probable that this is the last political speech that I shall ever make. It is now nearly 40 years since I first came to Washington as a member of Congress, and I wish to say this night, that during that whole period I have received nothing but kindness and attention from your fathers and from yourselves. Washington was then comparatively a small town; now it has grown to be a great and beautiful city; and the first wish of my heart is that its citizens may enjoy uninterrupted health and prosperity. I thank you for the kind attention you have paid to me, and now bid you all a good-night.

The Federal Government's Helplessness

From the Fourth Annual Message to Congress
Washington, D.C.
December 3, 1860

WHEN BUCHANAN delivered his fourth annual message, the Union was on the verge of collapse. South Carolina had declared its intention to secede if Lincoln were elected. All federal activities there had come to a halt, and the state authorities were demanding that Buchanan turn over control of the federal forts in the Charleston harbor. In his message, Buchanan, though denying the right of secession, argued that the South was entitled to rebel against oppression, by which he meant laws passed by Northern states to obstruct the Fugitive Slave Act. The message weakened Union loyalists in the South and made a peaceful compromise even less likely.

Throughout the year since our last meeting, the country has been eminently prosperous in all its material interests. The general health has been excellent, our harvests have been abundant, and plenty smiles throughout the land. Our commerce and manufactures have been prosecuted with energy and industry, and have yielded fair and ample returns. In short, no nation in the tide of time has ever presented a spectacle of greater material prosperity than we have done, until within a very recent period.

Why is it, then, that discontent now so extensively prevails, and the Union of the states, which is the source of all these blessings is threatened with destruction?

The long continued and intemperate interference of the Northern people with the question of slavery in the Southern states has at length produced its natural effects. The different sections of the Union are now arrayed against each other, and the time has arrived, so much dreaded by the Father of his Country, when hostile geographical parties have been formed.

I have long foreseen, and often forewarned my countrymen of, the now impending danger. This does not proceed solely from the claim on the part of Congress or the territorial legislatures to exclude slavery from the territories, nor from the efforts of different states to defeat the execution of the fugitive slave law. All or any of these evils might have been endured by the South, without danger to the Union (as others have been), in the hope that time and reflection might apply the remedy. The immediate peril arises, not so much from these causes, as from the fact that the incessant and violent agitation of the slavery question throughout the North for the last quarter of a century has at length produced its malign influence on the slaves, and inspired them with vague notions of freedom. Hence a sense of security no longer exists around the family altar. This feeling of peace at home has given place to apprehensions of servile insurrections. Many a matron throughout the South retires at night in dread of what may befall herself and her children before the morning. Should the apprehension of domestic danger, whether real or imaginary, extend, and intensify itself, until it shall pervade the masses of the Southern people, then disunion will become inevitable. Self-preservation is the first law of nature, and has been implanted in the heart of man by his Creator, for the wisest purpose; and no political union, however fraught with blessings and benefits in all other respects, can long continue, if the necessary consequence be to render the homes and the firesides of nearly half the parties to its habitually and hopelessly insecure. Sooner or later the bonds of such a union must be severed. It is my conviction that this fatal period has not yet arrived; and my prayer to God is, that he would preserve the Constitution and the Union throughout all generations.

But let us take warning in time, and remove the cause of danger. It cannot be denied that for five and twenty years the agitation at the North against slavery has been incessant. In 1835, pictorial handbills and inflammatory appeals were circulated extensively throughout the South of a character to excite the passions of the slaves, and, in the language of General Jackson, "to stimulate them to insurrection and produce all the horrors of a servile war." This agitation has ever since been continued by the public press, by the proceedings of state and county conventions, and by abolition sermons and lectures. The time of Congress has been occupied in violent speeches on this never-ending subject; and appeals, in pamphlet and other forms, indorsed by distinguished names have been sent forth from this central point and spread broadcast over the Union.

How easy would it be for the American people to settle the slavery question forever, and to restore peace and harmony to this distracted country! They, and they alone, can do it. All that is necessary to accomplish the object, and all for which the slave states have ever contended, is to be let alone and permitted to manage their domestic institutions in their own way. As sovereign states, they and they alone are responsible before God and the world for the slavery existing among them. For this the people of the North are not more responsible, and have no more right to interfere, than with similar institutions in Russia or in Brazil.

Upon their good sense and patriotic forbearance, I confess, I still greatly rely. Without their aid it is beyond the power of any president, no matter what may be his own political proclivities, to restore peace and harmony among the states. Wisely limited and restrained as is his power under our Constitution and laws, he alone can accomplish but little for good or for evil on such a momentous question.

And this brings me to observe, that the election of any one of our fellow citizens to the office of president does not of itself afford just cause for dissolving the Union. This is more especially true if his election has been effected by a mere plurality and not a majority of the people, and has resulted from transient and temporary causes, which may probably never again occur. In order to justify a resort to revolutionary resistance the federal government must be guilty of "a deliberate, palpable, and dangerous exercise" of powers not granted by the Constitution. The late presidential election, however, has been held in strict conformity with its express provisions. How, then, can the result justify a revolution to destroy this very Constitution? Reason, justice, a regard for the Constitution, all require that we shall wait for some overt and dangerous act on

the part of the president-elect, before resorting to such a remedy. It is said, however, that the antecedents of the president-elect have been sufficient to justify the fears of the South that he will attempt to invade their constitutional rights. But are such apprehensions of contingent danger in the future sufficient to justify the immediate destruction of the noblest system of government ever devised by mortals? From the very nature of his office, and its high responsibilities, he must necessarily be conservative. The stern duty of administering the vast and complicated concerns of this government affords in itself a guarantee that he will not attempt any violation of a clear constitutional right.

After all, he is no more than the chief executive officer of the government. His province is not to make but to execute the laws; and it is a remarkable fact in our history that, notwithstanding the repeated efforts of the antislavery party, no single act has ever passed Congress, unless we may possibly except the Missouri Compromise, impairing in the slighest degree the rights of the South to their property in slaves. And it may also be observed, judging from present indications, that no probability exists of the passage of such an act by a majority of both houses, either in the present or the next Congress. . . .

It is alleged as one cause for immediate secession, that the Southern states are denied equal rights with the other states in the common territories. But by what authority are these denied? Not by Congress, which has never passed, and I believe never will pass, any act to exclude slavery from these territories. And certainly not by the Supreme Court, which has solemnly decided that slaves are property, and like all other property their owners have a right to take them into the common territories and hold them there under the protection of the Constitution. . . .

The most palpable violations of constitutional duty which have yet been committed consist in the acts of different state legislatures to defeat the execution of the fugitive slave law. . . . Let us trust that the state legislatures will repeal their unconstitutional and obnoxious enactments. Unless this shall be done without unnecessary delay, it is impossible for any human power to save the Union.

The Southern states, standing on the basis of the Constitution, have a right to demand this act of justice from the states of the North. Should it be refused, then the Constitution, to which all the states are parties, will have been wilfully violated by one portion of them in a provision essential to the domestic security and happiness of the remainder. In that event, the injured states, after having first used all peaceful and constitutional means to obtain redress, would be justified in revolutionary resistance to the government of the Union.

I have purposely confined my remarks to revolutionary resistance, because it has been claimed within the last few years that any state, whenever this shall be its sovereign will and pleasure, may secede from the Union in accordance with the Constitution, and without any violation of the constitutional rights of the other members of the confederacy [i.e, the Union]. That as each became parties to the Union by the vote of its own people assembled in convention, so any one of them may retire from the Union in a similar manner by the vote of such a convention.

In order to justify secession as a constitutional remedy it must be on the principle that the federal government is a mere voluntary association of states, to be dissolved at pleasure by any one of the contracting parties. If this be so, the confederacy is a rope of sand, to be penetrated and dissolved by the first adverse wave of public opinion in any of the states. In this manner our 33 states may resolve themselves into as many petty, jarring, and hostile republics, each one retiring from the Union without responsibility whenever any sudden excitement might impel them to such a course. By this process a Union might be entirely broken into fragments in a few weeks which cost our forefathers many years of toil, privation, and blood to establish. . . .

It may be asked, then, are the people of the states without redress against the tyranny and oppression of the federal government? By no means. The right of resistance on the part of the governed against the oppression of their governments cannot be denied. It exists independently of all constitutions, and has been exercised at all periods of the world's history. Under it, old governments have been destroyed and new ones have taken their place. It is embodied in strong and express language in our own Declaration of Independence. But the distinction must ever be observed that this is revolution against an established government,

and not a voluntary secession from it by virtue of any inherent constitutional right. In short, let us look the danger fairly in the face: secession is neither more nor less than revolution. It may or it may not be a justifiable revolution; but still it is revolution.

What, in the meantime, is the responsibility and true position of the executive? He is bound by solemn oath, before God and the country, "to take care that the laws be faithfully executed," and from this obligation he cannot be absolved by any human power. But what if the performance of this duty, in whole or in part has been rendered impracticable by events over which he could have exercised no control? Such, at the present moment, is the case throughout the state of South Carolina, so far as the laws of the United States to secure the administration of justice by means of the federal judiciary are concerned. All the federal officers within its limits, through whose agency alone these laws can be carried into execution, have already resigned. We no longer have a district judge, a district attorney, or a marshall in South Carolina. In fact, the whole machinery of the federal government necessary for the distribution of remedial justice among the people has been demolished, and it would be difficult, if not impossible, to replace it. The only acts of Congress on the statute book bearing upon this subject are those of the 28th February, 1795, and 3d March, 1807. These authorize the president, after he shall have ascertained that the marshall, with his *posse comitatus,* is unable to execute civil or criminal process in any particular case, to call forth the militia and employ the army and navy to aid him in performing this service, having first by proclamation commanded the insurgents "to disperse and retire peaceably to their respective abodes within a limited time." This duty cannot by possibility be performed in a state where no judicial authority exists to issue process, and where there is no marshall to execute it, and where, even if there were such an officer, the entire population would constitute one solid combination to resist him.

The bare enumeration of these provisions proves how inadequate they are without further legislation to overcome a united opposition in a single state, not to speak of other states who may place themselves in a similar attitude. Congress alone has power to decide whether the present laws can or cannot be amended so as to carry out more effectually the objects of the Constitution. . . .

Then, in regard to the property of the United States in South Carolina. This has been purchased for a fair equivalent, "by the consent of the legislature of the state," "for the erection of forts, magazines, arsenals," &c., and over these the authority "to exercise exclusive legislation" has been expressly granted by the Constitution to Congress. It is not believed that any attempt will be made to expel the United States from this property by force; but if in this I should prove to be mistaken, the officer in command of the forts has received orders to act strictly on the defensive. In such a contingency the responsibility for consequences would rightfully rest upon the heads of the assailants. . . .

Apart from the execution of the laws, so far as this may be practicable, the executive has no authority to decide what shall be the relations between the federal government and South Carolina. He has been invested with no such discretion. He possess no power to change the relations heretofore existing between them, much less to acknowledge the independence of that state. This would be to invest a mere executive officer with the power of recognizing the dissolution of the confederacy among our 33 sovereign states. It bears no resemblance to the recognition of a foreign *de facto* government, involving no such responsibility. Any attempt to do this would, on his part, be a naked act of usurpation. It is, therefore, my duty to submit to Congress the whole question in all its bearings. The course of events is so rapidly hastening forward that the emergency may soon arise when you may be called upon to decide the momentous question whether you possess the power, by force of arms, to compel a state to remain in the Union. I should feel myself recreant to my duty were I not to express an opinion on this important subject.

The question fairly stated is: Has the Constitution delegated to Congress the power to coerce a state into submission which is attempting to withdraw or has actually withdrawn from the confederacy? If answered in the affirmative, it must be on the principle that the power has been conferred upon Congress to declare and to make war against a state. After much serious reflection, I have arrived at the conclusion that no such power

has been delegated to Congress or to any other department of the federal government. It is manifest, upon an inspection of the Constitution, that this is not among the specific and enumerated powers granted to Congress; and it is equally apparent that its exercise is not "necessary and proper for carrying into execution" any one of these powers. So far from this power having been delegated to Congress, it was expressly refused by the convention which framed the Constitution.

It appears from the proceedings of that body that on the 31st May, 1787, the clause *"authorizing an exertion of the force of the whole against a delinquent state"* came up for consideration. Mr. Madison opposed it in a brief, but powerful speech, from which I shall extract but a single sentence. He observed: "The use of force against a state would look more like a declaration of war than an infliction of punishment, and would probably be considered by the party attacked as a dissolution of all previous compacts by which it might be bound." Upon his motion the clause was unanimously postponed, and was never, I believe, again presented. Soon afterwards, on the 8th June, 1787, when incidentally adverting to the subject, he said: "Any government for the United States, formed on the supposed practicability of using force against the unconstitutional proceedings of the states, would prove as visionary and fallacious as the government of Congress," evidently meaning the then existing Congress of the old confederation.

Without descending to particulars, it may be safely asserted that the power to make war against a state is at variance with the whole spirit and intent of the Constitution. Suppose such a war should result in the conquest of a state: how are we to govern it afterwards? Shall we hold it as a province and govern it by despotic power? In the nature of things, we could not, by physical force, control the will of the people and compel them to elect senators and representatives to Congress, and to perform all the other duties depending upon their own volition and required from the free citizens of a free state as a constituent member of the confederacy.

But, if we possessed this power, would it be wise to exercise it under existing circumstances? The object would doubtless be to preserve the Union. War would not only present the most effectual means of destroying it, but would banish all hope of its peaceable reconstruction. Besides, in the fraternal conflict a vast amount of blood and treasure would be expended, rendering future reconciliation between the states impossible. In the meantime, who can foretell what would be the sufferings and privations of the people during its existence?

The fact is, that our Union rests upon public opinion, and can never be cemented by the blood of its citizens shed in civil war. If it cannot live in the affections of the people it must one day perish. Congress possesses many means of preserving it by conciliation; but the sword was not placed in their hand to preserve it by force. . . .

Congress can contribute much to avert it, by proposing and recommending to the legislatures of the several states the remedy for existing evils which the Constitution has itself provided for its own preservation. This has been tried at different critical periods of our history, and always with eminent success. It is to be found in the fifth article, providing for its own amendment. . . . This is the very course which I earnestly recommend, in order to obtain an "explanatory amendment" of the Constitution on the subject of slavery. This might originate with Congress or the state legislatures, as may be deemed most advisable to attain the object.

The explanatory amendment might be confined to the final settlement of the true construction of the Constitution on three special points:

1. An express recognition of the right of property in slaves in the states where it now exists or may hereafter exist.

2. The duty of protecting this right in all the common territories throughout their territorial existence, and until they shall be admitted as states into the Union, with or without slavery, as their constitutions may prescribe.

3. A like recognition of the right of the master to have his slave, who has escaped from one state to another, restored and "delivered up" to him, and of the validity of the fugitive slave law enacted for this purpose, together with a declaration that all state laws impairing or defeating this right, are violations of the Constitution, and are consequently null and void. It may be objected that this construction of the Constitution has already been settled by the Supreme Court of the United States, and what more ought to be required? The answer is, that a very large proportion of the people of the United States still contest the correctness of this decision, and never will cease from agitation and admit its binding force until clearly established by the people of the several states in their sovereign character. Such an explanatory amendment, would, it is believed, forever terminate the existing dissensions, and restore peace and harmony among the states. . . .

Courtesy of Library of Congress

Abraham Lincoln

Abraham Lincoln

1861–1865

THE DETAILS of Abraham Lincoln's life are more widely known than those of any other president, forming as they do a quintessentially American story. Born in a frontier cabin outside Hodgenville, Kentucky, in 1809, Lincoln was mainly self-educated and spent most of his career as a lawyer in Springfield, Illinois. His political experience before the presidency was minimal: two months in the Illinois General Assembly and two years in the U.S. House of Representatives. It was Lincoln's series of debates with Democrat Stephen A. Douglas in 1858 that brought him to wider public attention: with precise logic and unmatched eloquence Lincoln demolished Douglas's defense of the extension of slavery to the new western territories. The popularity he gained in this contest led to his nomination for the presidency by the Republicans in 1860.

As Lincoln himself noted, upon assuming the presidency in 1861 he faced a task "greater than that which rested upon Washington." The slave states saw Lincoln as an arch abolitionist, although in fact he was a moderate on the slavery issue, and his election as the final break between North and South. Between his election and inauguration the Deep South seceded from the Union; a month after he took office, the Confederacy took Fort Sumter, and the Civil War began. Throughout the war, Lincoln held firm to his primary goal, the costliest in American history—the restoration of the Union and the preservation of democracy. He was assassinated less than a week after the surrender of Robert E. Lee.

Years of stump speaking and courtroom battles made Lincoln feel at home before a crowd—so at home that during his Illinois years he was occasionally criticized in the press for "clowning" on the podium. But his jokes and stories, which were nearly always didactic in intent, rarely alienated his audiences. Stephen Douglas called him "the best stump speaker, with his droll ways and dry jokes, in the West." Like any natural raconteur, Lincoln was able to adapt his delivery to the requirements of his audience and subject. During his years in the White House, he exchanged his country wit for a simple lyricism and nobility of feeling that no other president has matched. His style had its foundation in the classics, especially Aesop's Fables, the King James Bible, and the works of Shakespeare. He made frequent and memorable use of such devices as alliteration, assonance, parallel construction, and prosody. His insistence on exact and simple words, according to his friend and biographer William Herndon, grew out of Lincoln's desire "to be distinctly understood by the common people." "In language seemingly effortless and yet grandly beautiful," wrote Lincoln scholar Roy P. Basler, "he phrased the emotional convictions upon which he believed human political progress to be founded."

Lincoln would, on occasion, accept ideas and even drafts of speeches from others but would always put his own mark on the material. He worked and reworked each sentence, simplifying and polishing. Individual phrases of the Gettysburg Address, for example, were tested and refined in many earlier speeches; and the address itself, which was only two minutes long, went through several drafts before Lincoln was satisfied. The immortal quality of his speeches was recognized even in his own time. Soon after Lincoln's death, his friend Joshua Speed remarked, "While no set speech of his (save the Gettysburg Address) will be considered as entirely artistic and complete, yet when the gems of American literature come to be selected, as many will be culled from Lincoln's speeches as from any American orator."

Address at Cooper Institute

New York City, New York

February 27, 1860

MUCH IN DEMAND as an orator after his successful series of debates with Stephen Douglas, Lincoln was invited to speak before the 1,500 members of the Central Republican Union of New York. Considerable research went into his concise, thorough, and highly polished discussion of the history of American slavery. In the opinion of many historians, it was this address that clinched, in the minds of Republican leaders, Lincoln's fitness as a presidential candidate for the upcoming election.

The facts with which I shall deal this evening are mainly old and familiar; nor is there anything new in the general use I shall make of them. If there shall be any novelty, it will be in the mode of presenting the facts, and the inferences and observations following that presentation.

In his speech last autumn, at Columbus, Ohio, as reported in the *New York Times,* Senator Douglas said:

"Our fathers, when they framed the government under which we live, understood this question just as well, and even better, than we do now."

I fully indorse this, and I adopt it as a text for this discourse. I so adopt it because it furnishes a precise and an agreed starting point for a discussion between Republicans and that wing of the Democracy headed by Senator Douglas. It simply leaves the inquiry: "What was the understanding those fathers had of the question mentioned?"

What is the frame of government under which we live?

The answer must be: "The Constitution of the United States." That Constitution consists of the original, framed in 1787 (and under which the present government first went into operation), and 12 subsequently framed amendments, the first 10 of which were framed in 1789.

Who were our fathers that framed the Constitution? I suppose the "39" who signed the original instrument may be fairly called our fathers who framed that part of the present government. It is almost exactly true to say they framed it, and it is altogether true to say they fairly represented the opinion and sentiment of the whole nation at that time. Their names, being familiar to nearly all, and accessible to quite all, need not now be repeated.

I take these "39," for the present, as being "our fathers who framed the government under which we live."

What is the question which, according to the text, those fathers understood "just as well, and even better than we do now?"

It is this: Does the proper division of local from federal authority, or anything in the Constitution, forbid our federal government to control as to slavery in our federal territories?

Upon this, Senator Douglas holds the affirmative, and Republicans the negative. This affirmation and denial form an issue; and this issue—this question—is precisely what the text declares our fathers understood "better than we."

Let us now inquire whether the "39," or any of them, ever acted upon this question; and if they did, how they acted upon it— how they expressed that better understanding?

In 1784, three years before the Constitution—the United States then owning the Northwestern Territory, and no other, the Congress of the Confederation had before them the question of prohibiting slavery in that territory; and four of the "39" who afterward framed the Constitution, were in that Congress, and voted on that question. Of these, Roger Sherman, Thomas Mifflin, and Hugh Williamson voted for the prohibition, thus showing that, in their understanding, no line dividing local from federal authority, nor anything else, properly forbade the federal government to control as to slavery in federal territory. The other of the four—James McHenry—voted against the prohibition, showing that, for some cause, he thought it improper to vote for it.

In 1787, still before the Constitution, but while the convention was in session framing it, and while the Northwestern Territory still was the only territory owned by the United States, the same question of prohibiting slavery in the territory again came before the Congress of the Confederation; and two more of the "39" who afterward signed the Constitution, were in that Congress, and voted on the question. They were William Blount and William Few; and they both voted for the prohibition— thus showing that, in their understanding, no line dividing local from federal authority, nor anything else, properly forbids the federal government to control as to slavery in federal territory. This time the prohibition became a law, being part of what is now well known as the Ordinance of '87.

The question of federal control of slavery in the territories, seems not to have been directly before the convention which framed the original Constitution; and hence it is not recorded that the "39," or any of them, while engaged on that instrument, expressed any opinion on that precise question.

In 1789, by the first Congress which sat under the Constitution, an act was passed to enforce the Ordinance of '87, including the prohibition of slavery in the Northwestern Territory. The bill for this act was reported by one of the "39," Thomas Fitzsimmons, then a member of the House of Representatives from Pennsylvania. It went through all its stages without a word of opposition, and finally passed both branches without yeas and nays, which is equivalent to an unanimous passage. In this Congress there were 16 of the 39 fathers who framed the original Constitution. They were John Langdon, Nicholas Gilman, William S. Johnson, Roger Sherman, Robert Morris, Thomas Fitzsimmons, William Few, Abraham Baldwin, Rufus King, William Paterson, George Clymer, Richard Bassett, George Read, Pierce Butler, Daniel Carroll, James Madison.

This shows that, in their understanding, no line dividing local from federal authority, nor anything in the Constitution, properly forbade Congress to prohibit slavery in the federal territory; else both their fidelity to correct principle, and their oath to support the Constitution, would have constrained them to oppose the prohibition.

Again, George Washington, another of the "39," was then president of the United States, and, as such, approved and signed the bill; thus completing its validity as a law, and thus showing that, in his understanding, no line dividing local from federal authority, nor anything in the Constitution forbade the federal government to control as to slavery in federal territory.

No great while after the adoption of the original Constitution, North Carolina ceded to the federal government the country now constituting the state of Tennessee; and a few years later Georgia ceded that which now constitutes the states of Mississippi and Alabama. In both deeds of cession it was made a condition by the ceding states that the federal government should not prohibit slavery in the ceded country. Besides this, slavery was then actually in the ceded country. Under these circumstances, Congress, on taking charge of these countries, did not absolutely prohibit slavery within them. But they did interfere with it—take control of it—even there, to a certain extent. In 1798, Congress organized the territory of Mississippi. In the act of organization, they prohibited the bringing of slaves into the territory, from any place without the United States, by fine, and giving freedom to slaves so brought. This act passed both branches of Congress without yeas and nays. In that Congress were three of the "39" who framed the original Constitution. They were John Langdon, George Read and Abraham Baldwin. They all, probably, voted for it. Certainly they would have placed their opposition to it upon record, if, in their understanding, any line dividing local from federal authority, or anything in the Constitution, properly forbade the federal government to control as to slavery in federal territory.

In 1803, the federal government purchased the Louisiana country. Our former territorial acquisitions came from certain of our own states; but this Louisiana country was acquired from a foreign nation. In 1804, Congress gave a territorial organization to that part of it which now constitutes the state of Louisiana. New Orleans, lying within that part, was an old and comparatively large city. There were other considerable towns and settlements, and slavery was extensively and thoroughly intermingled with the people. Congress did not, in the Territorial Act, prohibit slavery; but they did interfere with it—take control of it—in a more marked and extensive way than they did in the case of Mississippi. The substance of the provision therein made, in relation to slaves, was:

First. That no slave should be imported into the territory from foreign parts.

Second. That no slave should be carried into it who had been imported into the United States since the first day of May, 1798.

Third. That no slave should be carried into it, except by the owner, and for his own use as a settler; the penalty in all the cases being a fine upon the violator of the law, and freedom to the slave.

This act also was passed without yeas and nays. In the Congress which passed it, there were two of the "39." They were Abraham Baldwin and Jonathan Dayton. As stated in the case of Mississippi, it is probable they both voted for it. They would not have allowed it to pass without recording their opposition to it, if, in their understanding, it violated either the line properly dividing local from federal authority, or any provision of the Constitution.

In 1819–1820, came and passed the Missouri question. Many votes were taken, by yeas and nays, in both branches of Congress, upon the various phases of the general question. Two of the "39"—Rufus King and Charles Pinckney—were members of that Congress. Mr. King steadily voted for slavery prohibition and against all compromises, while Mr. Pinckney as steadily voted against slavery prohibition and against all compromises. By this, Mr. King showed that, in his understanding, no line dividing local from federal authority, nor anything in the Constitution, was violated by Congress prohibiting slavery in federal territory; while Mr. Pinckney, by his votes, showed that, in his understanding, there was some sufficient reason for opposing such prohibition in that case.

These cases I have mentioned are the only acts of the "39," or of any of them, upon the direct issue, which I have been able to discover.

To enumerate the persons who thus acted, as being four in 1784, two in 1787, 17 in 1789, three in 1798, two in 1804, and two in 1819–1820—there would be 30 of them. But this would be counting John Langdon, Roger Sherman, William Few, Rufus King, and George Read each twice, and Abraham Baldwin, three times. The true number of those of the "39" whom I have shown to have acted upon the question, which, by the text, they understood

better than we, is 23, leaving 16 not shown to have acted upon it in any way.

Here, then, we have 23 out of our 39 fathers "who framed the government under which we live," who have, upon their official responsibility and their corporal oaths, acted upon the very question which the text affirms they "understood just as well, and even better than we do now"; and 21 of them—a clear majority of the whole "39"— so acting upon it as to make them guilty of gross political impropriety and wilful perjury, if, in their understanding, any proper division between local and federal authority, or anything in the Constitution they had made themselves, and sworn to support, forbade the federal government to control as to slavery in the federal territories. Thus the 21 acted; and, as actions speak louder than words, so actions, under such responsibility, speak still louder.

Two of the 23 voted against Congressional prohibition of slavery in the federal territories, in the instances in which they acted upon the question. But for what reasons they so voted is not known. They may have done so because they thought a proper division of local from federal authority, or some provision or principle of the Constitution, stood in the way; or they may, without any such question, have voted against the prohibition, on what appeared to them to be sufficient grounds of expediency. No one who has sworn to support the Constitution can conscientiously vote for what he understands to be an unconstitutional measure, however expedient he may think it; but one may and ought to vote against a measure which he deems constitutional, if, at the same time, he deems it inexpedient. It, therefore, would be unsafe to set down even the two who voted against the prohibition, as having done so because, in their understanding, any proper division of local from federal authority, or anything in the Constitution, forbade the federal government to control as to slavery in federal territory.

The remaining 16 of the "39," so far as I have discovered, have left no record of their understanding upon the direct question of federal control of slavery in the federal territories. But there is much reason to believe that their understanding upon that question would not have appeared different from that of their 23 compeers, had it been manifested at all.

For the purpose of adhering rigidly to the text, I have purposely omitted whatever understanding may have been manifested by any person, however distinguished, other than the 39 fathers who framed the original Constitution; and, for the same reason, I have also omitted whatever understanding may have been manifested by any of the "39" even, on any other phase of the general question of slavery. If we should look into their acts and declarations of those other phases, as the foreign slave trade, and the morality and policy of slavery generally, it would appear to us that on the direct question of federal control of slavery in federal territories, the 16, if they had acted at all, would probably have acted just as the 23 did. Among that 16 were several of the most noted anti-slavery men of those times—as Dr. Franklin, Alexander Hamilton and Gouverneur Morris—while there was not one now known to have been otherwise, unless it may be John Rutledge, of South Carolina.

The sum of the whole is, that of our 39 fathers who framed the original Constitution, 21—a clear majority of the whole— certainly understood that no proper division of local from federal authority, nor any part of the Constitution, forbade the federal government to control slavery in the federal territories; while all the rest probably had the same understanding. Such, unquestionably, was the understanding of our fathers who framed the original Constitution; and the text affirms that they understood the question "better than we."

But, so far, I have been considering the understanding of the question manifested by the framers of the original Constitution. In and by the original instrument, a mode was provided for amending it; and, as I have already stated, the present frame of "the government under which we live" consists of that original, and 12 amendatory articles framed and adopted since. Those who now insist that federal control of slavery in federal territories violates the Constitution, point us to the provisions which they suppose it thus violates; and, as I understand, that all fix upon provisions in these amendatory articles, and not in the original instrument. The Supreme Court, in the Dred Scott case, plant themselves upon the Fifth Amendment, which provides that no person shall be deprived of "life, liberty or property without due process of law"; while Senator Douglas and his peculiar adherents plant themselves upon the Tenth Amendment, providing that "the powers not delegated to the United States by the Constitution" "are reserved to the states respectively, or to the people."

Now, it so happens that these amendments were framed by the first Congress which sat under the Constitution—the identical Congress which passed the act already mentioned, enforcing the prohibition of slavery in the Northwestern Territory. Not only was it the same Congress, but they were the identical, same individual men who, at the same session, and at the same time within the session, had under consideration, and in progress toward maturity, these Constitutional amendments, and this act prohibiting slavery in all the territory the nation then owned. The Constitutional amendments were introduced before, and passed after, the act enforcing the Ordinance of '87; so that, during the whole pendency of the act to enforce the Ordinance, the Constitutional amendments were also pending.

The 76 members of that Congress, including 16 of the framers of the original Constitution, as before stated, were preeminently our fathers who framed that part of "the government under which we live," which is now claimed as forbidding the federal government to control slavery in the federal territories.

Is it not a little presumptuous in any one at this day to affirm that the two things which that Congress deliberately framed, and carried to maturity at the same time, are absolutely inconsistent with each other? And does not such affirmation become impudently absurd when coupled with the other affirmation from the same mouth, that those who did the two things, alleged to be inconsistent, understood whether they really were inconsistent better than we—better than he who affirms that they are inconsistent?

It is surely safe to assume that the 39 framers of the original Constitution, and the 76 members of the Congress which framed the amendments thereto, taken together, do certainly include those who may be fairly called "our fathers who framed the government under which we live." And so assuming, I defy any man to show that any one of them ever, in his whole life, declared that, in his understanding, any proper division of local from federal authority, or any part of the Constitution, forbade the federal government to control as to slavery in the federal territories. I go a step further. I defy any one to show that any living man in the whole world ever did, prior to the beginning of the present century (and I might almost say prior to the beginning of the last half of the present century), declare that, in his understanding, any proper division of local from federal authority, or any part of the Constitution, forbade the federal government to control as to slavery in the federal territories. To those who now so declare, I give, not only "our fathers who framed the government under which we live," but with them all other living men within the century in which it was framed, among whom to search, and they shall not be able to find the evidence of a single man agreeing with them.

Now, and here, let me guard a little against being misunderstood. I do not mean to say we are bound to follow implicitly in whatever our fathers did. To do so, would be to discard all the lights of current experience—to reject all progress—all improvement. What I do say is, that if we would supplant the opinions and policy of our fathers in any case, we should do so upon evidence so conclusive, and argument so clear, that even their great authority, fairly considered and weighed, cannot stand; and most surely not in a case whereof we ourselves declare they understood the question better than we.

If any man at this day sincerely believes that a proper division of local from federal authority, or any part of the Constitution, forbids the federal government to control as to slavery in the federal territories, he is right to say so, and to enforce his position by all truthful evidence and fair argument which he can. But he has no right to mislead others, who have less access to history, and less leisure to study it, into the false belief that "our fathers who framed the government under which we live" were of the same opinion—thus substituting falsehood and deception for truthful evidence and fair argument. If any man at this day sincerely believes "our fathers who framed the government under which we live," used and applied principles, in other cases, which ought to have led them to understand that a proper division of local from federal authority or some part of the Constitution, forbids the federal government to control as to slavery in the federal territories, he is right to say so. But he should, at the same time, brave the responsibility of declaring that, in his opinion,

he understands their principles better than they did themselves; and especially should he not shirk that responsibility by asserting that they "understood the question just as well, and even better, than we do now."

But enough! Let all who believe that "our fathers, who framed the government under which we live, understood this question just as well, and even better, than we do now," speak as they spoke, and act as they acted upon it. This is all Republicans ask—all Republicans desire—in relation to slavery. As those fathers marked it, so let it be again marked, as an evil not to be extended, but to be tolerated and protected only because of and so far as its actual presence among us makes that toleration and protection a necessity. Let all the guaranties those fathers gave it, be, not grudgingly, but fully and fairly, maintained. For this Republicans contend, and with this, so far as I know or believe, they will be content.

And now, if they would listen—as I suppose they will not—I would address a few words to the Southern people.

I would say to them: You consider yourselves a reasonable and a just people; and I consider that in the general qualities of reason and justice you are not inferior to any other people. Still, when you speak of us Republicans, you do so only to denounce us as reptiles, or, at the best, as no better than outlaws. You will grant a hearing to pirates or murderers, but nothing like it to "Black Republicans." In all your contentions with one another, each of you deems an unconditional condemnation of "Black Republicanism" as the first thing to be attended to. Indeed, such condemnation of us seems to be an indispensable prerequisite—license, so to speak—among you to be admitted or permitted to speak at all. Now, can you, or not, be prevailed upon to pause and to consider whether this is quite just to us, or even to yourselves? Bring forward your charges and specifications, and then be patient long enough to hear us deny or justify.

You say we are sectional. We deny it. That makes an issue; and the burden of proof is upon you. You produce your proof; and what is it? Why, that our party has no existence in your section—gets no votes in your section. The fact is substantially true; but does it prove the issue? If it does, then in case we should, without change of principle, begin to get votes in your section, we should thereby cease to be sectional. You cannot escape this conclusion; and yet, are you willing to abide by it? If you are, you will probably soon find that we have ceased to be sectional, for we shall get votes in your section this very year. You will then begin to discover, as the truth plainly is, that your proof does not touch the issue. The fact that we get no votes in your section, is a fact of your making, and not of ours. And if there be fault in that fact, that fault is primarily yours, and remains until you show that we repel you by some wrong principle or practice. If we do repel you by any wrong principle or practice, the fault is ours; but this brings you to where you ought to have started—to a discussion of the right or wrong of our principle. If our principle, put in practice, would wrong your section for the benefit of ours, or for any other object, then our principle, and we with it, are sectional, and are justly opposed and denounced as such. Meet us, then, on the question of whether our principle, put in practice, would wrong your section; and so meet it as if it were possible that something may be said on our side. Do you accept the challenge? No! Then you really believe that the principle which "our fathers who framed the government under which we live" thought so clearly right as to adopt it, and indorse it again and again, upon their official oaths, is in fact so clearly wrong as to demand your condemnation without a moment's consideration.

Some of you delight to flaunt in our faces the warning against sectional parties given by Washington in his Farewell Address. Less than eight years before Washington gave that warning, he had, as president of the United States, approved and signed an act of Congress, enforcing the prohibition of slavery in the Northwestern Territory, which act embodied the policy of the government upon that subject up to and at the very moment he penned that warning; and about one year after he penned it, he wrote LaFayette that he considered that prohibition a wise measure, expressing in the same connection his hope that we should at some time have a confederacy of free states.

Bearing this in mind, and seeing that sectionalism has since arisen upon this same subject, is that warning a weapon in your hands against us, or in our hands against you? Could Washington himself speak, would he cast the blame of that sectionalism upon us, who sustain his policy, or upon you who repudiate it? We respect that warning of Washington, and we commend it to you, together with his example pointing to the right application of it.

But you say you are conservative—eminently conservative—while we are revolutionary, destructive, or something of the sort. What is conservatism? It is not adherence to the old and tried, against the new and untried? We stick to, contend for, the identical old policy on the point in controversy which was adopted by "our fathers who framed the government under which we live"; while you with one accord reject, and scout, and spit upon that old policy, and insist upon substituting something new. True, you disagree among yourselves as to what that substitute shall be. You are divided on new propositions and plans, but you are unanimous in rejecting and denouncing the old policy of the fathers. Some of you are for reviving the foreign slave trade; some for a Congressional slave-code for the territories; some for Congress forbidding the territories to prohibit slavery within their limits; some for maintaining slavery in the territories through the judiciary; some for the "gur-reat purrinciple" that "if one man would enslave another, no third man should object," fantastically called "popular sovereignty"; but never a man among you is in favor of federal prohibition of slavery in federal territories, according to the practice of "our fathers who framed the government under which we live." Not one of all your various plans can show a precedent or an advocate in the century within which our government originated. Consider, then, whether your claim of conservatism for yourselves, and your charge of destructiveness against us, are based on the most clear and stable foundations.

Again, you say we have made the slavery question more prominent than it formerly was. We deny it. We admit that it is more prominent, but we deny that we made it so. It was not we, but you, who discarded the old policy of the fathers. We resisted, and still resist, your innovation; and thence comes the greater prominence of the question. Would you have that question reduced to its former proportions? Go back to that old policy. What has been will be again, under the same conditions. If you would have the peace of the old times, readopt the precepts and policy of the old times.

You charge that we stir up insurrections among your slaves. We deny it; and what is your proof? Harper's Ferry! John Brown!! John Brown was no Republican; and you have failed to implicate a single Republican in his Harper's Ferry enterprise. If any member of our party is guilty in that matter, you know it or you do not know it. If you do know it, you are inexcusable for not designating the man and proving the fact. If you do not know it, you are inexcusable for asserting it, and especially for persisting in the assertion after you have tried and failed to make the proof. You need not be told that persisting in a charge which one does not know to be true, is simply malicious slander.

Some of you admit that no Republican designedly aided or encouraged the Harper's Ferry affair, but still insist that our doctrines and declarations necessarily lead to such results. We do not believe it. We know we hold to no doctrine, and make no declaration, which were not held to and made by "our fathers who framed the government under which we live." You never dealt fairly by us in relation to this affair. When it occurred, some important state elections were near at hand, and you were in evident glee with the belief that, by charging the blame upon us, you could get an advantage of us in those elections. The elections came, and your expectations were not quite fulfilled. Every Republican man knew that, as to himself at least, your charge was a slander, and he was not much inclined by it to cast his vote in your favor. Republican doctrines and declarations are accompanied with a continual protest against any interference whatever with your slaves, or with you about your slaves. Surely, this does not encourage them to revolt. True, we do, in common with "our fathers, who framed the government under which we live," declare our belief that slavery is wrong; but the slaves do not hear us declare even this. For anything we say or do, the slaves would scarcely know there is a Republican Party. I believe they would not, in fact, generally know it but for your misrepresentations of us, in their hearing. In your political contests among yourselves, each faction charges the other with sympathy with Black Republicanism; and then, to give point to the charge, defines Black Republicanism to simply be insurrection, blood and thunder among the slaves.

Slave insurrections are no more common now than they were before the Republican Party was organized. What induced the Southampton insurrection, 28 years ago, in which, at least three times as many lives were lost as at Harper's Ferry? You can scarcely stretch your very elastic fancy to the conclusion that Southampton was "got up by Black Republicanism." In the present state of things in the United States, I do not think a general, or even a very extensive slave insurrection is possible. The indispensable concert of action cannot be attained. The slaves have no means of rapid communication; nor can incendiary freemen, black or white, supply it. The explosive materials are everywhere in parcels; but there neither are, nor can be supplied, the indispensable connecting trains.

Much is said by Southern people about the affection of slaves for their masters and mistresses; and a part of it, at least, is true. A plot for an uprising could scarcely be devised and communicated to 20 individuals before some one of them, to save the life of a favorite master or mistress, would divulge it. This is the rule; and the slave revolution in Hayti was not an exception to it, but a case occurring under peculiar circumstances. The gunpowder plot of British history, though not connected with slaves, was more in point. In that case, only about 20 were admitted to the secret; and yet one of them, in his anxiety to save a friend, betrayed the plot to that friend, and, by consequence, averted the calamity. Occasional poisonings from the kitchen, and open or stealthy assassinations in the field, and local revolts extending to a score or so, will continue to occur as the natural results of slavery; but no general insurrection of slaves, as I think, can happen in this country for a long time. Whoever much fears, or much hopes for such an event, will be alike disappointed.

In the language of Mr. Jefferson, uttered many years ago, "It is still in our power to direct the process of emancipation, and deportation, peaceably, and in such slow degrees, as that the evil will wear off insensibly; and their places be, *pari passu*, filled up by free white laborers. If, on the contrary, it is left to force itself on, human nature must shudder at the prospect held up."

Mr. Jefferson did not mean to say, nor do I, that the power of emancipation is in the federal government. He spoke of Virginia; and, as to the power of emancipation, I speak of the slave-holding states only. The federal government, however, as we insist, has the power of restraining the extension of the institution—the power to insure that a slave insurrection shall never occur on any American soil which is now free from slavery.

John Brown's effort was peculiar. It was not a slave insurrection. It was an attempt by white men to get up a revolt among slaves, in which the slaves refused to participate. In fact, it was so absurd that the slaves, with all their ignorance, saw plainly enough it could not succeed. That affair, in its philosophy, corresponds with the many attempts, related in history, at the assassination of kings and emperors. An enthusiast broods over the oppression of a people till he fancies himself commissioned by Heaven to liberate them. He ventures the attempt, which ends in little else than his own execution. Orsini's attempt on Louis Napoleon, and John Brown's attempt at Harper's Ferry were, in their philosophy, precisely the same. The eagerness to cast blame on old England in the one case, and on New England in the other, does not disprove the sameness of the two things.

And how much would it avail you, if you could, by the use of John Brown, Helper's Book, and the like, break up the Republican organization? Human action can be modified to some extent, but human nature cannot be changed. There is a judgment and a feeling against slavery in this nation, which cast at least a million and a half of votes. You cannot destroy that judgment and feeling—that sentiment—by breaking up the political organization which rallies around it. You can scarcely scatter and disperse an army which has been formed into order in the face of your heaviest fire; but if you could, how much would you gain by forcing the sentiment which created it out of the peaceful channel of the ballot-box, into some other channel? What would that other channel probably be? Would the number of John Browns be lessened or enlarged by the operation?

But you will break up the Union rather than submit to a denial of your Constitutional rights.

That has a somewhat reckless sound; but it would be palliated, if not fully justified, were we proposing, by the mere force of numbers, to deprive you of some right, plainly written down in the Constitution. But we are proposing no such thing.

When you make these declarations, you have a specific and well-understood allusion to an assumed Constitutional right of yours, to take slaves into the federal territories, and to hold them there as property. But no such right is specifically written in the Constitution. That instrument is literally silent about any such right. We, on the contrary, deny that such a right has any existence in the Constitution, even by implication.

Your purpose, then, plainly stated, is that you will destroy the government, unless you be allowed to construe and enforce the Constitution as you please, on all points in dispute between you and us. You will rule or ruin in all events.

This, plainly stated, is your language. Perhaps you will say the Supreme Court has decided the disputed Constitutional question in your favor. Not quite so. But waiving the lawyer's distinction between dictum and decision, the Court have decided the question for you in a sort of way. The Court have substantially said, it is your constitutional right to take slaves into the federal territories, and to hold them there as property. When I say the decision was made in a sort of way, I mean it was made in a divided Court, by a bare majority of the judges, and they not quite agreeing, with one another in the reasons for making it; that it is so made as that its avowed supporters disagree with one another about its meaning, and that it was mainly based upon a mistaken statement of fact—the statement in the opinion that "the right of property in a slave is distinctly and expressly affirmed in the Constitution."

An inspection of the Constitution will show that the right of property in a slave is not "distinctly and expressly affirmed" in it. Bear in mind, the judges do not pledge their judicial opinion that such right is impliedly affirmed in the Constitution; but they pledge their veracity that it is "distinctly and expressly" affirmed there— "distinctly," that is, not mingled with anything else—"expressly," that is, in words meaning just that, without the aid of any inference, and susceptible of no other meaning.

If they had only pledged their judicial opinion that such right is affirmed in the instrument by implication, it would be open to others to show that neither the word slave nor slavery is to be found in the Constitution, nor the word property even, in any connection with language alluding to the things slave, or slavery; and that wherever in that instrument the slave is alluded to, he is called a "person"; and wherever his master's legal right in relation to him is alluded to, it is spoken of as "service or labor which may be due"—as a debt payable in service or labor. Also, it would be open to show, by contemporaneous history, that this mode of alluding to slaves and slavery, instead of speaking of them, was employed on purpose to exclude from the Constitution the idea that there could be property in man.

To show all this, is easy and certain.

When this obvious mistake of the Judges shall be brought to their notice, is it not reasonable to expect that they will withdraw the mistaken statement, and reconsider the conclusion based upon it?

And then it is to be remembered that "our fathers, who framed the government under which we live"—the men who made the Constitution—decided this same Constitutional question in our favor, long ago—decided it without division among themselves, when making the decision; without division among themselves about the meaning of it after it was made, and, so far as any evidence is left, without basing it upon any mistaken statement of facts.

Under all these circumstances, do you really feel yourselves justified to break up this government unless such a court decision as yours is, shall be at once submitted to as a conclusive and final rule of political action? But you will not abide the election of a Republican president! In that supposed event, you say, you will destroy the Union; and then, you say, the great crime of having destroyed it will be upon us! That is cool. A highwayman holds a pistol to my ear, and mutters through his teeth, "Stand and deliver, or I shall kill you, and then you will be a murderer!"

To be sure, what the robber demanded of me—my money—was my own; and I had a clear right to keep it; but it was no more my own than my vote is my own; and the threat of death to me, to extort my money, and the threat of destruction to the Union, to extort my vote, can scarcely be distinguished in principle.

A few words now to Republicans. It is exceedingly desirable that all parts of this great confederacy shall be at peace, and in harmony, one with another. Let us Republicans do our part to have it so. Even though much provoked, let us do nothing through passion and ill temper. Even though the Southern people will not so much as listen to us, let us calmly consider their demands, and yield to them if, in our deliberate view of our duty, we possibly can. Judging by all they say and do, and by the subject and nature of their controversy with us, let us determine, if we can, what will satisfy them.

Will they be satisfied if the territories be unconditionally surrendered to them? We know they will not. In all their present complaints against us, the territories are scarcely mentioned. Invasions and insurrections are the rage now. Will it satisfy them, if, in the future, we have nothing to do with invasions and insurrections? We know it will not. We so know, because we know we never had anything to do with invasions and insurrections; and yet this total abstaining does not exempt us from the charge and the denunciation.

The question recurs, what will satisfy them? Simply this: We must not only let them alone, but we must somehow, convince them that we do let them alone. This, we know by experience, is no easy task. We have been so trying to convince them from the very beginning of our organization, but with no success. In all our platforms and speeches we have constantly protested our purpose to let them alone; but this has had no tendency to convince them. Alike unavailing to convince them, is the fact that they have never detected a man of us in any attempt to disturb them.

These natural, and apparently adequate means all failing, what will convince them? This, and this only: cease to call slavery wrong, and join them in calling it right. And this must be done thoroughly—done in acts as well as in words. Silence will not be tolerated—we must place ourselves avowedly with them. Senator Douglas's new sedition law must be enacted and enforced, suppressing all declarations that slavery is wrong, whether made in politics, in presses, in pulpits, or in private. We must arrest and return their fugitive slaves with greedy pleasure. We must pull down our free state constitutions. The whole atmosphere must be disinfected from all taint of opposition to slavery, before they will cease to believe that all their troubles proceed from us.

I am quite aware they do not state their case precisely in this way. Most of them would probably say to us, "Let us alone, do nothing to us, and say what you please about slavery." But we do let them alone— have never disturbed them—so that, after all, it is what we say, which dissatisfies them. They will continue to accuse us of doing, until we cease saying.

I am also aware they have not, as yet, in terms, demanded the overthrow of our free state constitutions. Yet those constitutions declare the wrong of slavery, with more solemn emphasis, than do all other sayings against it; and when all these other sayings shall have been silenced, the overthrow of these constitutions will be demanded, and nothing be left to resist the demand. It is nothing to the contrary, that they do not demand the whole of this just now. Demanding what they do, and for the reason they do, they can voluntarily stop nowhere short of this consummation. Holding, as they do, that slavery is morally right, and socially elevating, they cannot cease to demand a full national recognition of it, as a legal right, and a social blessing.

Nor can we justifiably withhold this, on any ground save our conviction that slavery is wrong. If slavery is right, all words, acts, laws, and constitutions against it, are themselves wrong, and should be silenced, and swept away. If it is right, we cannot justly object to its nationality—its universality; if it is wrong, they cannot justly insist upon its extension—its enlargement. All they ask, we could readily grant, if we thought slavery right; all we ask, they could as readily grant, if they thought it wrong. Their thinking it right, and our thinking it wrong, is the precise fact upon which depends the whole controversy. Thinking it right, as they do, they are not to blame for desiring its full recognition, as being right; but, thinking it wrong, as we do, can we yield to them? Can we cast our votes with their view, and against our own? In view of our moral, social, and political responsibilities, can we do this?

Wrong as we think slavery is, we can yet afford to let it alone where it is, because that much is due to the necessity arising from its actual presence in the nation; but can we, while our votes will prevent it, allow it to spread into the national territories, and to overrun us here in these free states? If our sense of duty forbids this, then let us stand by our duty, fearlessly and effectively. Let us be diverted by none of those sophistical contrivances wherewith we are so industriously plied and belabored—contrivances such as groping for some middle ground between the right and the wrong, vain as the search for a man who should be neither a living man nor a dead man—such as a policy of "don't care" on a question about which all true men do care— such as Union appeals beseeching true Union men to yield to disunionists, reversing the divine rule, and calling, not the sinners, but the righteous to repentance—such as invocations to Washington, imploring men to unsay what Washington said, and undo what Washington did.

Neither let us be slandered from our duty by false accusations against us, nor frightened from it by menaces of destruction to the government nor of dungeons to ourselves. Let us have faith that right makes might, and in that faith, let us, to the end, dare to do our duty as we understand it.

Farewell Address at Springfield

Springfield, Illinois
February 11, 1861

THOUGH LINCOLN could masterfully carry a theme through many pages, as he did at the Cooper Institute, his short addresses are the most memorable, perhaps because their emotion is undiluted by logical exposition. This speech was delivered to the citizens of Springfield from the rear platform of the train that was taking him to Washington.

No one, not in my situation, can appreciate my feeling of sadness at this parting. To this place, and the kindness of these people, I owe everything. Here I have lived a quarter of a century, and have passed from a young to an old man. Here my children have been born, and one is buried. I now leave, not knowing when or whether ever I may return, with a task before me greater than that which rested upon Washington. Without the assistance of that Divine Being who ever attended him, I cannot succeed. With that assistance, I cannot fail. Trusting in Him who can go with me, and remain with you, and be everywhere for good, let us confidently hope that all will yet be well. To His care commending you, as I hope in your prayers you will commend me, I bid you an affectionate farewell.

First Inaugural Address

Washington, D.C.
March 4, 1861

BY FEBRUARY 23, 1861, little more than a week before Lincoln's inauguration, seven Southern states had seceded from the Union, formed the Confederacy, adopted a separate constitution, and elected Jefferson Davis president. In his first inaugural address, heard by an audience of 50,000 or more, Lincoln attempted a last reconciliation between North and South. "You can have no conflict," he told the seceding states, "without being yourselves the aggressors." But when the Confederacy accepted that role by besieging Fort Sumter in Charleston Harbor, Lincoln did not hesitate to declare war.

The rough draft of the last paragraph of the inaugural was penned by William H. Seward, Lincoln's secretary of state. The final version, however, is indisputably in Lincoln's own style.

In compliance with a custom as old as the government itself, I appear before you to address you briefly, and to take in your presence the oath prescribed by the Constitution of the United States to be taken by the president "before he enters on the execution of his office." . . .

Apprehension seems to exist among the people of the Southern states that by the accession of a Republican administration their property and their peace and personal security are to be endangered. There has never been any reasonable cause for such apprehension. Indeed, the most ample evidence to the contrary has all the while existed and been open to their inspection. It is found in nearly all the published speeches of him who now addresses you. I do but quote from one of those speeches when I declare that "I have no purpose, directly or indirectly, to interfere with the institution of slavery in the states where it exists. I believe I have no lawful right to do so, and I have no inclination to do so." . . .

I now reiterate these sentiments; and, in doing so, I only press upon the public attention the most conclusive evidence of which the case is susceptible, that the property, peace and security of no section are to be in any wise endangered by the now incoming administration. I add, too, that all the protection which, consistently with the Constitution and the laws, can be given, will be cheerfully given to all the states when lawfully demanded, for whatever cause—as cheerfully to one section as to another. . . .

I take the official oath to-day with no mental reservations, and with no purpose to construe the Constitution or laws by any hypercritical rules. And, while I do not choose now to specify particular acts of Congress as proper to be enforced, I do suggest that it will be much safer for all, both in official and private stations, to conform to and abide by all those acts which stand unrepealed, than to violate any of them, trusting to find impunity in having them held to be unconstitutional. . . .

A disruption of the federal Union, heretofore only menaced, is now formidably attempted.

I hold that, in contemplation of universal law and of the Constitution, the Union of these states is perpetual. Perpetuity is implied, if not expressed, in the fundamental law of all national governments. It is safe to assert that no government proper ever had a provision in its organic law for its own termination. Continue to execute all the express provisions of our national Constitution, and the Union will endure forever—it being impossible to destroy it except by some action not provided for in the instrument itself.

Again, if the United States be not a government proper, but an association of states in the nature of contract merely, can it as a contract be peaceably unmade by less than all the parties who made it? One party to a contract may violate it—break it, so to speak; but does it not require all to lawfully rescind it?

Descending from these general principles, we find the proposition that in legal contemplation the Union is perpetually confirmed by the history of the Union itself. The Union is much older than the Constitution. It was formed, in fact, by the Articles of Association in 1774. It was matured and continued by the Declaration of Independence in 1776. It was further matured, and the faith of all the then 13 states expressly plighted and engaged that it should be perpetual, by the Articles of Confederation in 1778. And, finally, in 1787 one of the declared objects for ordaining and establishing the Constitution was "to form a more perfect Union."

But if the destruction of the Union by one or by a part only of the states be lawfully possible, the Union is less perfect than before the Constitution, having lost the vital element of perpetuity.

It follows from these views that no state upon its own mere motion can lawfully get out of the Union; that resolves and ordinances to that effect are legally void; and that acts of violence, within any state or states, against the authority of the United States, are insurrectionary or revolutionary, according to circumstances.

I therefore consider that, in view of the Constitution and the laws, the Union is unbroken; and to the extent of my ability I shall take care, as the Constitution itself expressly enjoins upon me, that the laws of the Union be faithfully executed in all the states. Doing this I deem to be only a simple duty on my part; and I shall perform it so far as practicable, unless my rightful masters, the American people, shall withhold the requisite means, or in some authoritative manner direct the contrary. I trust this will not be regarded as a menace, but only as the declared purpose of the Union that it will constitutionally defend and maintain itself.

In doing this there needs to be no bloodshed or violence; and there shall be none, unless it be forced upon the national authority. The power confided to me will be used to hold, occupy, and possess the property and places belonging to the government, and to collect the duties and imposts; but beyond what may be necessary for these objects, there will be no invasion, no using of force against or among the people anywhere. Where hostility to the United States, in any interior locality, shall be so great and universal as to prevent competent resident citizens from holding the federal offices, there will be no attempt to force obnoxious strangers among the people for that object. While the strict legal right may exist in the government to enforce the exercise of these offices, the attempt to do so would be so irritating, and so nearly impracticable withal, that I deem it better to forego for the time the uses of such offices.

The mails, unless repelled, will continue to be furnished in all parts of the Union. So far as possible, the people everywhere shall have that sense of perfect security which is most favorable to calm thought and reflection. The course here indicated will be followed unless current events and experience shall show a modification or change to be proper, and in every case and exigency my best discretion will be exercised according to circumstances actually existing, and with a view and a hope of a peaceful solution of the national troubles and the restoration of fraternal sympathies and affections.

That there are persons in one section or another who seek to destroy the Union at all events, and are glad of any pretext to do it, I will neither affirm nor deny; but if there be such, I need address no word to them. To those, however, who really love the Union may I not speak?

Before entering upon so grave a matter as the destruction of our national fabric, with all its benefits, its memories, and its hopes, would it not be wise to ascertain precisely why we do it? Will you hazard so desperate a step while there is any possibility that any portion of the ills you fly from have no real existence? Will you, while the certain ills you fly to are greater than all the real ones you fly from—will you risk the commission of so fearful a mistake?

All profess to be content in the Union if all constitutional rights can be maintained. Is it true, then, that any right, plainly written in the Constitution, has been denied? I think not. Happily the human mind is so constituted that no party can reach to the audacity of doing this. Think, if you can, of a single instance in which a plainly written provision of the Constitution has ever been denied. If by the mere force of numbers a majority should deprive a minority of any clearly written constitutional right, it might, in a moral point of view, justify revolution—certainly would if such a right were a vital one. But such is not our case. All the vital rights of minorities and of individuals are so plainly assured to them by affirmations and negations, guaranties and prohibitions, in the Constitution, that controversies never arise concerning them. But no organic law can ever be framed with a provision specifically applicable to every question which may occur in practical administration. No foresight can anticipate, nor any document of reasonable length contain, express provisions for all possible questions. Shall fugitives from labor be surrendered by national or by state authority? The Constitution does not expressly say. May Congress prohibit slavery in the territories? The Constitution does not expressly say. Must Congress protect slavery in the territories? The Constitution does not expressly say.

From questions of this class spring all our constitutional controversies, and we divide upon them into majorities and minorities. If the minority will not acquiesce, the majority must, or the government must cease. There is no other alternative; for continuing the government is acquiescence on one side or the other.

If a minority in such case will secede rather than acquiesce, they make a precedent which in turn will divide and ruin them; for a minority of their own will secede from them whenever a majority refuses to be controlled by such minority. For instance, why may not any portion of a new confederacy a year or two hence arbitrarily secede again, precisely as portions of the present Union now claim to secede from it? All who cherish disunion sentiments are now being educated to the exact temper of doing this.

Is there such perfect identity of interests among the states to compose a new Union as to produce harmony only, and prevent renewed secession?

Plainly, the central idea of secession is the essence of anarchy. A majority held in restraint by constitutional checks and limitations, and always changing easily with deliberate changes of popular opinions and sentiments, is the only true sovereign of a free people. Whoever rejects it does, of necessity, fly to anarchy or to despotism. Unanimity is impossible; the rule of a minority, as a permanent arrangement, is wholly inadmissible; so that, rejecting the majority principle, anarchy or despotism in some form is all that is left.

I do not forget the position assumed by some, that constitutional questions are to be decided by the Supreme Court; nor do I deny that such decisions must be binding, in any case, upon the parties to a suit, as to the object of that suit, while they are also entitled to a very high respect and consideration in all parallel cases by all other departments of the government. And, while it is obviously possible that such decision may be erroneous in any given case, still the evil effect following it, being limited to that particular case, with the chance that it may be overruled and never become a precedent for other cases, can better be borne than could the evils of a different practice. At the same time, the candid citizen must confess that if the policy of the government, upon vital questons affecting the whole people, is to be irrevocably fixed by decisions of the Supreme Court, the instant they are made, in ordinary litigation between parties in personal actions, the people will have ceased to be their own rulers, having to that extent practically resigned the government into the hands of that eminent tribunal. Nor is there in this view any assault upon the court or the judges. It is a duty from which they may not shrink to decide cases properly brought before them, and it is no fault of theirs if others seek to turn their decisions to political purposes.

One section of our country believes slavery is right, and ought to be extended, while the other believes it is wrong, and ought not to be extended. This is the only substantial dispute. The fugitive slave clause of the Constitution and the law for the suppression of the foreign slave trade are each as well enforced, perhaps, as any law can ever be in a community where the moral sense of the people imperfectly supports the law itself. The great body of the people abide by the dry legal obligation in both cases, and a few break over in each. This, I think, cannot be perfectly cured; and it would be worse in both cases after the separation of the sections than before. The foreign slave trade, now imperfectly suppressed, would be ultimately revived, without restriction, in one section, while fugitive slaves, now only partially surrendered, would not be surrendered at all by the other.

Physically speaking, we cannot separate. We cannot remove our respective sections from each other, nor build an impassable wall between them. A husband and wife may be divorced and go out of the presence and beyond the reach of each other; but the different parts of our country cannot do this. They cannot but remain face to face, and intercourse, either amicable or hostile, must continue between them. Is it possible, then, to make that intercourse more advantageous or more satisfactory after separation than before? Can aliens make treaties easier than friends can make law? Can treaties be more faithfully enforced between aliens than laws can among friends? Suppose you go to war, you cannot fight always; and when, after much loss on both sides, and no gain on either, you cease fighting, the identical old questions as to terms of intercourse are again upon you.

This country, with its institutions, belongs to the people who inhabit it. Whenever they shall grow weary of the existing government, they can exercise their constitutional right of amending it, or their revolutionary right to dismember or overthrow it. I cannot be ignorant of the fact that many worthy and patriotic citizens are desirous of having the national Constitution amended. While I make no recommendation of amendments, I fully recognize the rightful authority of the people over the whole subject, to be exercised in either of the modes prescribed in the instrument itself, and I should, under existing circumstances, favor rather than oppose a fair opportunity being afforded the people to act upon it. I will venture to add that to me the convention mode seems preferable, in that it allows amendments to originate with the people themselves, instead of only permitting them to take or reject propositions originated by others not especially chosen for the purpose, and which might not be precisely such as they would wish to either accept or refuse. I understand a proposed amendment to the Constitution— which amendment, however, I have not seen—has passed Congress, to the effect that the federal government shall never interfere with the domestic institutions of the states, including that of persons held to service. To avoid misconstruction of what I have said, I depart from my purpose not to speak of particular amendments so far as to say that, holding such a provision to now be implied constitutional law, I have no objection to its being made express and irrevocable. . . .

Why should there not be a patient confidence in the ultimate justice of the people? Is there any better or equal hope in the world? In our present differences is either party without faith of being in the right? If the Almighty Ruler of nations, with His eternal truth and justice, be on your side of the North, or on yours of the South, that truth and that justice will surely prevail by the judgment of this great tribunal of the American people.

By the frame of the government under which we live, this same people have wisely given their public servants but little power for mischief; and have, with equal wisdom, provided for the return of that little to their own hands at very short intervals. While the people retain their virtue and vigilance, no administration, by any extreme of wickedness or folly, can very seriously injure the government in the short space of four years.

My countrymen, one and all, think calmly and well upon this whole subject. Nothing valuable can be lost by taking time. If there be an object to hurry any of you in hot haste to a step which you would never take deliberately, that object will be frustrated by taking time; but no good object can be frustrated by it. Such of you as are now dissatisfied still have the old Constitution unimpaired, and, on the sensitive point, the laws of your own framing under it; while the new administration will have no immediate power, if it would, to change either. If it were admitted that you who are dissatisfied hold the right side in the dispute, there still is no single good reason for precipitate action. Intelligence, patriotism, Christianity, and a firm reliance on Him who has never yet forsaken this favored land, are still competent to adjust in the best way all our present difficulty.

In your hands, my dissatisfied fellow countrymen, and not in mine, is the momentous issue of civil war. The government will not assail you. You can have no conflict without being yourselves the aggressors. You have no oath registered in Heaven to destroy the government, while I shall have the most solemn one to "preserve, protect, and defend" it.

I am loath to close. We are not enemies, but friends. We must not be enemies. Though passion may have strained, it must not break, our bonds of affection. The mystic chords of memory, stretching from every battlefield and patriot grave to every living heart and hearthstone all over this broad land, will yet swell the chorus of the Union when again touched, as surely they will be, by the better angels of our nature.

Second Annual Message to Congress

Washington, D.C.
December 1, 1862

THIS IS the most eloquent of Lincoln's annual messages. Roy P. Basler held that "no American living at the time save Walt Whitman ever expressed so large a vision of the future of American democracy, the magnitude of its geographic and economic potentialities, and the infinitude of its social destiny in the quest for human liberty. . . . From the opening paragraph to the splendid peroration, the message is charged with an electric feeling for the drama of a crisis in which the citizens of the United States 'shall nobly save, or meanly lose, the last best hope of earth.'"

Since your last annual assembling another year of health and bountiful harvests has passed. And while it has not pleased the Almighty to bless us with a return of peace, we can but press on, guided by the best light He gives us, trusting that in His own good time, and wise way, all will yet be well.

The correspondence touching foreign affairs which has taken place during the last year is herewith submitted, in virtual compliance with a request to that effect, made by the House of Representatives near the close of the last session of Congress.

If the condition of our relations with other nations is less gratifying than it has usually been at former periods, it is certainly more satisfactory than a nation so unhappily distracted as we are might reasonably have apprehended. In the month of June last there were some grounds to expect that the maritime powers which, at the beginning of our domestic difficulties, so unwisely and unnecessarily, as we think, recognized the insurgents as a belligerent, would soon recede from that position, which has proved only less injurious to themselves than to our own country. But the temporary reverses which afterwards befell the national arms, and which were exaggerated by our own disloyal citizens abroad have hitherto delayed that act of simple justice.

The civil war, which has so radically changed for the moment, the occupations and habits of the American people, has necessarily disturbed the social condition, and affected very deeply the prosperity of the nations with which we have carried on a commerce that has been steadily increasing throughout a period of half a century. It has, at the same time, excited political ambitions and apprehensions which have produced a profound agitation throughout the civilized world. In this unusual agitation we have forborne from taking part in any controversy between foreign states, and between parties or factions in such states. We have attempted no propagandism, and acknowledged no revolution. But we have left to every nation the exclusive conduct and management of its own affairs. Our struggle has been, of course, contemplated by foreign nations with reference less to its own merits, than to its supposed, and often exaggerated effects and consequences resulting to those nations themselves. Nevertheless, complaint on the part of this government, even if it were just, would certainly be unwise.

The treaty with Great Britain for the suppression of the slave trade has been put into operation with a good prospect of complete success. It is an occasion of special pleasure to acknowledge that the execution of it, on the part of Her Majesty's government has been marked with a jealous respect for the authority of the United States, and the rights of their moral and loyal citizens.

The convention with Hanover for the abolition of the state dues has been carried into full effect, under the act of Congress for that purpose.

A blockade of 3,000 miles of seacoast could not be established, and vigorously enforced, in a season of great commercial activity like the present, without committing occasional mistakes, and inflicting unintentional injuries upon foreign nations and their subjects.

A civil war occurring in a country where foreigners reside and carry on trade under treaty stipulations, is necessarily fruitful of complaints of the violation of neutral rights. All such collisions tend to excite misapprehensions, and possibly to produce mutual reclamations between nations which have a common interest in preserving peace and friendship. In clear cases of these kinds I have, so far as possible, heard and redressed complaints which have been presented by friendly powers. There is still, however, a large and an augmenting number of doubtful cases upon which the government is unable to agree with the governments whose protection is demanded by the claimants. There are, moreover, many cases in which the United States, or their citizens, suffer wrongs from the naval or military authorities of foreign nations, which the governments of those states are not at once prepared to redress. I have proposed to some of the foreign states, thus interested, mutual conventions to examine and adjust such complaints. This proposition has been made especially to Great Britain, to France, to Spain, and to Prussia. In each case it has been kindly received but has not yet been formally adopted.

I deem it my duty to recommend an appropriation in behalf of the owners of the Norwegian bark Admiral P. Tordenskiold, which vessel was, in May 1861, prevented by the commander of the blockading force off Charleston from leaving that port with cargo, notwithstanding a similar privilege had, shortly before, been granted to an English vessel. I have directed the secretary of state to cause the papers in the case to be communicated to the proper committees.

Applications have been made to me by many free Americans of African descent to favor their emigration, with a view to such colonization as was contemplated in recent acts of Congress. Other parties, at home and abroad—some from interested motives, others upon patriotic considerations, and still others influenced by philanthropic sentiments—have suggested similar measures; while, on the other hand, several of the Spanish-American republics have protested against the sending of such colonies to their respective territories. Under these circumstances, I have declined to move any such colony to any state, without first obtaining the consent of its government, with an agreement on its part to receive and protect such emigrants in all the rights of freemen; and I have, at the same time, offered to the several states situated within the tropics, or having colonies there, to negotiate with them, subject to the advice and consent of the

Senate, to favor the voluntary emigration of persons of that class to their respective territories, upon conditions which shall be equal, just, and humane. Liberia and Hayti are, as yet, the only countries to which colonists of African descent from here, could go with certainty of being received and adopted as citizens; and I regret to say such persons, contemplating colonization do not seem so willing to migrate to those countries as to some others, nor so willing as I think their interest demands. I believe, however, opinion among them, in this respect, is improving; and that, ere long, there will be an augmented, and considerable migration to both these countries, from the United States.

The new commercial treaty between the United States and the sultan of Turkey has been carried into execution.

A commercial and consular treaty has been negotiated, subject to the Senate's consent, with Liberia; and a similar negotiation is now pending with the republic of Hayti. A considerable improvement of our national commerce is expected to result from these measures.

Our relations with Great Britain, France, Spain, Portugal, Russia, Prussia, Denmark, Sweden, Austria, the Netherlands, Italy, Rome, and the other European states, remain undisturbed. Very favorable relations also continue to be maintained with Turkey, Morocco, China, and Japan.

During the last year there has not only been no change of our previous relations with the independent states of our own continent, but, more friendly sentiments than have heretofore existed are believed to be entertained by these neighbors, whose safety and progress are so intimately connected with our own. This statement especially applies to Mexico, Nicaragua, Costa Rica, Honduras, Peru, and Chile.

The commission under the convention with the republic of New Granada closed its session, without having audited and passed upon, all the claims which were submitted to it. A proposition is pending to revive the convention, that it may be able to do more complete justice. The joint commission between the United States and the republic of Costa Rica has completed its labors and submitted its report.

I have favored the project for connecting the United States with Europe by an Atlantic telegraph, and a similar project to extend the telegraph from San Francisco, to connect by a Pacific telegraph with the line which is being extended across the Russian empire.

The territories of the United States, with unimportant exceptions, have remained undisturbed by the civil war, and they are exhibiting such evidence of prosperity as justifies an expectation that some of them will soon be in a condition to be organized as states, and be constitutionally admitted into the federal Union.

The immense mineral resources of some of those territories ought to be developed as rapidly as possible. Every step in that direction would have a tendency to improve the revenues of the government, and diminish the burdens of the people. It is worthy of your serious consideration whether some extraordinary measures to promote that end cannot be adopted. The means which suggests itself as most likely to be effective, is a scientific exploration of the mineral regions in those territories, with a view to the publication of its results at home and in foreign countries— results which cannot fail to be auspicious.

The condition of the finances will claim your most diligent consideration. The vast expenditures incident to the military and naval operations required for the suppression of the rebellion have hitherto been met with a promptitude, and certainty, unusual in similar circumstances, and the public credit has been fully maintained. The continuance of the war, however, and the increased disbursements made necessary by the augmented forces now in the field, demand your best reflections as to the best modes of providing the necessary revenue, without injury to business and with the least possible burdens upon labor.

The suspension of specie payments by the banks, soon after the commencement of your last session, made large issues of United States notes unavoidable. In no other way could the payment of the troops, and the satisfaction of other just demands, be so economically, or so well provided for. The judicious legislation of Congress, securing the receivability of these notes for loans and internal duties, and making them a legal tender for other debts, has made them an universal currency; and has satisfied, partially, at least, and for the time, the long felt want of an uniform circulating medium, saving thereby to the people, immense sums in discounts and exchanges.

A return to specie payments, however, at the earliest period compatible with due regard to all interests concerned, should ever be kept in view. Fluctuations in the value of currency are always injurious, and to reduce these fluctuations to the lowest possible point will always be a leading purpose in wise legislation. Convertibility, prompt and certain convertibility into coin, is generally acknowledged to be the best and surest safeguard against them; and it is extremely doubtful whether a circulation of United States notes, payable in coin, and sufficiently large for the wants of the people, can be permanently, usefully, and safely maintained.

Is there, then, any other mode in which the necessary provision for the public wants can be made, and the great advantages of a safe and uniform currency secured?

I know of none which promises so certain results, and is, at the same time, so unobjectionable, as the organization of banking associations, under a general act of Congress, well guarded in its provisions. To such associations the government might furnish circulating notes, on the security of United States bonds deposited in the Treasury. These notes, prepared under the supervision of proper officers, being uniform in appearance and security, and convertible always into coin, would at once protect labor against the evils of a vicious currency, and facilitate commerce by cheap and safe exchanges.

A moderate reservation from the interest on the bonds would compensate the United States for the preparation and distribution of the notes and a general supervision of the system, and would lighten the burden of that part of the public debt employed as securities. The public credit, moreover, would be greatly improved, and the negotiation of new loans greatly facilitated by the steady market demand for government bonds which the adoption of the proposed system would create.

It is an additional recommendation of the measure, of considerable weight, in my judgment, that it would reconcile, as far as possible, all existing interests, by the opportunity offered to existing institutions to reorganize under the act, substituting only the secured uniform national circulation for the local and various circulation, secured and unsecured, now issued by them.

The receipts into the Treasury from all sources, including loans and balance from the preceding year, for the fiscal year ending on the 30th June, 1862, were $583,885,247.06, of which sum $49,056,397.62 were derived from customs; $1,795,331.73 from the direct tax; from public lands, $152,203.77; from miscellaneous sources, $931,787.64; from loans in all forms, $529,692,460.50. The remainder, $2,257,065.80, was the balance from last year.

The disbursements during the same period were for congressional, executive, and judicial purposes, $5,939,009.29; for foreign intercourse, $1,339,710.35; for miscellaneous expenses, including the mints, loans, post office deficiencies, collection of revenue, and other like charges, $14,129,771.50; for expenses under the Interior Department, $3,102,985.52; under the War Department, $394,368,407.36; under the Navy Department, $42,674,569.69; for interest on public debt, $13,190,324.45; and for payment of public debt, including reimbursement of temporary loan, and redemptions, $96,096,922.09; making an aggregate of $570,841,700.25, and leaving a balance in the Treasury on the first day of July, 1862, of $13,043,546.81.

It should be observed that the sum of $96,096,922.09, expended for reimbursements and redemption of public debt, being included also in the loans made, may be properly deducted, both from receipts and expenditures, leaving the actual receipts for the year $487,788,324.97; and the expenditures, $474,744,778.16.

Other information on the subject of the finances will be found in the report of the secretary of the Treasury, to whose statements and views I invite your most candid and considerate attention.

The reports of the secretaries of war, and of the navy, are herewith transmitted. These reports, though lengthy, are scarcely more than brief abstracts of the very numerous and extensive transactions and operations conducted through those departments. Nor could I give a summary of them here, upon any principle, which would admit of its being much shorter than the reports themselves. I therefore content myself with laying the reports before you, and asking your attention to them.

It gives me pleasure to report a decided improvement in the financial condition of the Post Office Department, as compared with several preceding years. The receipts for the fiscal year 1861 amounted to $8,349,296.40,

which embraced the revenue from all the states of the Union for three quarters of that year. Notwithstanding the cessation of revenue from the so-called seceded states during the last fiscal year, the increase of the correspondence of the loyal states has been sufficient to produce a revenue during the same year of $8,299,820.90, being only $50,000 less than was derived from all the states of the Union during the previous year. The expenditures show a still more favorable result. The amount expended in 1861 was $13,606,759.11. For the last year the amount has been reduced to $11,125,364.13, showing a decrease of about $2,481,000 in the expenditures as compared with the preceding year and about $3,750,000 as compared with the fiscal year 1860. The deficiency in the department for the previous year was $4,551,966.98. For the last fiscal year it was reduced to $2,112,814.57. These favorable results are in part owing to the cessation of mail service in the insurrectionary states, and in part to a careful review of all expenditures in that department in the interest of economy. The efficiency of the postal service, it is believed, has also been much improved. The postmaster general has also opened a correspondence, through the Department of State, with foreign governments, proposing a convention of postal representatives for the purpose of simplifying the rates of foreign postage, and to expedite the foreign mails. This proposition, equally important to our adopted citizens, and to the commercial interests of this country, has been favorably entertained, and agreed to, by all the governments from whom replies have been received.

I ask the attention of Congress to the suggestions of the postmaster general in his report respecting the further legislation required, in his opinion, for the benefit of the postal service.

The secretary of the interior reports as follows in regard to the public lands:

"The public lands have ceased to be a source of revenue. From the 1st July, 1861, to the 30th September, 1862, the entire cash receipts from the sale of lands were $137,476.26—a sum much less than the expenses of our land system during the same period. The homestead law, which will take effect on the 1st of January next, offers such inducements to settlers, that sales for cash cannot be expected, to an extent sufficient to meet the expenses of the General Land Office, and the cost of surveying and bringing the land into market."

The discrepancy between the sum here stated as arising from the sales of the public lands, and the sum derived from the same source as reported from the Treasury Department, arises, as I understand, from the fact that the periods of time, though apparently, were not really, coincident at the beginning point—the Treasury report including a considerable sum now, which had previously been reported from the Interior—sufficiently large to greatly overreach the sum derived from the three months now reported upon the Interior, and not by the Treasury.

The Indian tribes upon our frontiers have, during the past year, manifested a spirit of insubordination, and, at several points, have engaged in open hostilities against the white settlements in their vicinity. The tribes occupying the Indian country south of Kansas renounced their allegiance to the United States and entered into treaties with the insurgents. Those who remained loyal to the United States were driven from the country. The chief of the Cherokees has visited this city for the purpose of restoring the former relations of the tribe with the United States. He alleges that they were constrained, by superior force, to enter into treaties with the insurgents, and that the United States neglected to furnish the protection which their treaty stipulations required.

In the month of August last the Sioux Indians, in Minnesota, attacked the settlements in their vicinity with extreme ferocity, killing, indiscriminately, men, women, and children. This attack was wholly unexpected, and, therefore, no means of defence had been provided. It is estimated that not less than 800 persons were killed by the Indians, and a large amount of property was destroyed. How this outbreak was induced is not definitely known, and suspicions, which may be unjust, need not to be stated. Information was received by the Indian bureau, from different sources, about the time hostilities were commenced, that a simultaneous attack was to be made upon the white settlements by all the tribes between the Mississippi River and the Rocky Mountains. The state of Minnesota has suffered great injury from this Indian war. A large portion of her territory has been depopulated,

and a severe loss has been sustained by the destruction of property. The people of that state manifest much anxiety for the removal of the tribes beyond the limits of the state as a guarantee against future hostilities. The commissioner of Indian Affairs will furnish full details. I submit for your especial consideration whether our Indian system shall not be remodelled. Many wise and good men have impressed me with the belief that this can be profitably done.

I submit a statement of the proceedings of commissioners, which shows the progress that has been made in the enterprise of constructing the Pacific railroad. And this suggests the earliest completion of this road, and also the favorable action of Congress upon the projects now pending before them for enlarging the capacities of the great canals in New York and Illinois, as being of vital and rapidly increasing importance to the whole nation, and especially to the vast interior region hereinafter to be noticed at some greater length. I propose having prepared and laid before you at an early day some interesting and valuable statistical information upon this subject. The military and commercial importance of enlarging the Illinois and Michigan canal, and improving the Illinois River, is presented in the report of Colonel Webster to the secretary of war, and now transmitted to Congress. I respectfully ask attention to it.

To carry out the provisions of the act of Congress of the 15th of May last, I have caused the Department of Agriculture of the United States to be organized.

The commissioner informs me that within the period of a few months this department has established an extensive system of correspondence and exchanges, both at home and abroad, which promises to effect highly beneficial results in the development of a correct knowledge of recent improvements in agriculture, in the introduction of new products, and in the collection of the agricultural statistics of the different states.

Also, that it will soon be prepared to distribute largely seeds, cereals, plants and cuttings, and has already published, and liberally diffused, much valuable information in anticipation of a more elaborate report, which will in due time be furnished, embracing some valuable tests in chemical science now in progress in the laboratory.

The creation of this department was for the more immediate benefit of a large class of our most valuable citizens; and I trust that the liberal basis upon which it has been organized will not only meet your approbation, but that it will realize, at no distant day, all the fondest anticipations of its most sanguine friends, and become the fruitful source of advantage to all our people.

On the twenty-second day of September last a proclamation was issued by the executive, a copy of which is herewith submitted.

In accordance with the purpose expressed in the second paragraph of that paper, I now respectfully recall your attention to what may be called "compensated emancipation."

A nation may be said to consist of its territory, its people, and its laws. The territory is the only part which is of certain durability. "One generation passeth away, and another generation cometh, but the earth abideth forever." It is of the first importance to duly consider, and estimate, this ever-enduring part. That portion of the earth's surface which is owned and inhabited by the people of the United States, is well adapted to be the home of one national family; and it is not well adapted for two, or more. Its vast extent, and its variety of climate and productions, are of advantage, in this age, for one people, whatever they might have been in former ages. Steam, telegraphs, and intelligence have brought these to be an advantageous combination for one united people.

In the inaugural address I briefly pointed out the total inadequacy of disunion as a remedy for the differences between the people of the two sections. I did so in language which I cannot improve, and which, therefore, I beg to repeat:

"One section of our country believes slavery is right, and ought to be extended, while the other believes it is wrong, and ought not to be extended. This is the only substantial dispute. The fugitive slave clause of the Constitution, and the law for the suppression of the foreign slave trade, are each as well enforced, perhaps, as any law can ever be in a community where the moral sense of the people imperfectly supports the law itself. The great body of the people abide by the dry legal obligation in both cases, and a few break over in each. This, I think, cannot be perfectly cured; and it would be worse in both cases after the separation of the sections, than before. The foreign slave trade, now imperfectly suppressed, would be ultimately revived without restriction in one section; while fugitive slaves, now only partially surrendered, would not be surrendered at all by the other.

"Physically speaking, we cannot separate. We cannot remove our respective sections from each other, nor build an impassable wall between them. A husband and wife may be divorced, and go out of the presence, and beyond the reach of each other; but the different parts of our country cannot do this. They cannot but remain face to face; and intercourse, either amicable or hostile, must continue between them. Is it possible, then, to make that intercourse more advantageous, or more satisfactory, after separation than before? Can aliens make treaties, easier than friends can make laws? Can treaties be more faithfully enforced between aliens, than laws can among friends? Suppose you go to war, you cannot fight always; and when, after much loss on both sides, and no gain on either, you cease fighting, the identical old questions, as to terms of intercourse, are again upon you."

There is no line, straight or crooked, suitable for a national boundary, upon which to divide. Trace through, from east to west, upon the line between the free and slave country, and we shall find a little more than one-third of its length are rivers, easy to be crossed, and populated, or soon to be populated, thickly upon both sides; while nearly all its remaining length are merely surveyor's lines, over which people may walk back and forth without any consciousness of their presence. No part of this line can be made any more difficult to pass, by writing it down on paper, or parchment, as a national boundary. The fact of separation, if it comes, gives up, on the part of the seceding section, the fugitive slave clause, along with all other constitutional obligations upon the section seceded from, while I should expect no treaty stipulation would be ever made to take its place.

But there is another difficulty. The great interior region, bounded east by the Alleghenies, north by the British dominions, west by the Rocky Mountains, and south by the line along which the culture of corn and cotton meets, and which includes part of Virginia, part of Tennessee, all of Kentucky, Ohio, Indiana, Michigan, Wisconsin, Illinois, Missouri, Kansas, Iowa, Minnesota, and the territories of Dakota, Nebraska, and part of Colorado, already has above 10 millions of people, and will have 50 millions within 50 years, if not prevented by any political folly or mistake. It contains more than one third of the country owned by the United States—certainly more than one million of square miles. Once half as populous as Massachusetts already is, it would have more than 75 millions of people. A glance at the map shows that, territorially speaking, it is the great body of the republic. The other parts are but marginal borders to it, the magnificent region sloping west from the Rocky Mountains to the Pacific, being the deepest and also the richest in undeveloped resources. In the production of provisions, grains, grasses, and all which proceed from them, this great interior region is naturally one of the most important in the world. Ascertain from the statistics the small proportion of the region which has, as yet, been brought into cultivation, and also the large and rapidly increasing amount of its products, and we shall be overwhelmed with the magnitude of the prospect presented. And yet this region has no seacoast, touches no ocean anywhere. As part of one nation, its people now find, and may forever find, their way to Europe by New York, to South America and Africa by New Orleans, and to Asia by San Francisco. But separate our common country into two nations, as designed by the present rebellion, and every man of this great interior region is thereby cut off from some one or more of these outlets, not, perhaps, by a physical barrier, but by embarrassing and onerous trade regulations.

And this is true, wherever a dividing, or boundary line, may be fixed. Place it between the now free and slave country, or place it south of Kentucky, or north of Ohio, and still the truth remains, that none south of it, can trade to any port or place north of it, and none north of it, can trade to any port or place south of it, except upon terms dictated by a government foreign to them. These outlets, east, west, and south, are indispensable to the well-being of the people inhabiting, and to inhabit, this vast interior region. Which of the three may be the best, is no proper question. All, are better than either, and all, of right, belong to that people, and to their successors forever. True to themselves, they will not ask where a line of separation shall be, but will vow, rather, that there shall be no such line.

Nor are the marginal regions less interested in these communications to, and through them, to the great outside world. They, too, and each of them, must have access to this Egypt of the West, without paying toll at the crossing of any national boundary.

Our national strife springs not from our permanent part; not from the land we inhabit; not from our national homestead. There is no possible severing of this, but would multiply, and not mitigate, evils among us. In all its adaptations and aptitudes, it demands union, and abhors separation. In fact, it would, ere long, force reunion, however much of blood and treasure the separation might have cost.

Our strife pertains to ourselves-to the passing generations of men; and it can, without convulsion, be hushed forever with the passing of one generation.

In this view, I recommend the adoption of the following resolution and articles amendatory to the Constitution of the United States:

"Resolved by the Senate and House of Representatives of the United States of America in Congress assembled (two-thirds of both Houses concurring), that the following articles be proposed to the legislatures (or conventions) of the several states as amendments to the Constitution of the United States, all or any of which articles when ratified by three fourths of the said legislatures (or conventions) to be valid as part or parts of the said Constitution, viz:

Article—.

"Every state, wherein slavery now exists, which shall abolish the same therein, at any time, or times, before the first day of January, in the year of Our Lord 1,900, shall receive compensation from the United States, as follows, to wit:

"The president of the United States shall deliver to every such state, bonds of the United States, bearing interest at the rate of — per cent, per annum, to an amount equal to the aggregate sum of—— for each slave shown to have been therein, by the eighth census of the United States, said bonds to be delivered to such state by instalments, or in one parcel, at the completion of the abolishment, accordingly as the same shall have been gradual, or at one time, within such state; and interest shall begin to run upon any such bond, only from the proper time of its delivery as aforesaid. Any state having received bonds as aforesaid, and afterwards reintroducing or tolerating slavery therein, shall refund to the United States the bonds so received, or the value thereof, and all interest paid thereon.

Article—.

"All slaves who shall have enjoyed actual freedom by the chances of the war, at any time before the end of the rebellion, shall be forever free; but all owners of such, who shall not have been disloyal, shall be compensated for them, at the same rates as is provided for states adopting abolishment of slavery, but in such way, that no slave shall be twice accounted for.

Article—.

"Congress may appropriate money, and otherwise provide, for colonizing free colored persons, with their own consent, at any place or places without the United States."

I beg indulgence to discuss these proposed articles at some length. Without slavery the rebellion could never have existed; without slavery it could not continue.

Among the friends of the Union there is great diversity of sentiment, and of policy, in regard to slavery, and the African race amongst us. Some would perpetuate slavery; some would abolish it suddenly, and without compensation; some would abolish it gradually, and with compensation; some would remove the freed people from us, and some would retain them with us; and there are yet other minor diversities. Because of these diversities, we waste much strength in struggles among ourselves. By mutual concession we should harmonize, and act together. This would be compromise; but it would be compromise among the friends, and not with the enemies of the Union. These articles are intended to embody a plan of such mutual concessions. If the plan shall be adopted, it is assumed that emancipation will follow, at least, in several of the states.

As to the first article, the main points are: first, the emancipation; secondly, the length of time for consummating it—37 years; and thirdly, the compensation.

The emancipation will be unsatisfactory to the advocates of perpetual slavery; but the length of time should greatly mitigate their dissatisfaction. The time spares both races from the evils of sudden derangement—in fact, from the necessity of any derangement—while most of those whose habitual course of thought will be disturbed by the measure will have passed away before its consummation. They will never see it. Another class will hail the prospect of emancipation, but will deprecate the length of time. They will feel that it gives too little to the now living slaves. But it really gives them much. It saves them from the vagrant destitution which must largely attend immediate emancipation in localities where their numbers are very great; and it gives the inspiring assurance that their posterity shall be free forever. The plan leaves to each state, choosing to act under it, to abolish slavery now, or at the end of the century, or at any intermediate time, or by degrees, extending over the whole or any part of the period; and it obliges no two states to proceed alike. It also provides for compensation, and generally the mode of making it. This, it would seem, must further mitigate the dissatisfaction of those who favor perpetual slavery, and especially of those who are to receive the compensation. Doubtless some of those who are to pay, and not to receive will object. Yet the measure is both just and economical. In a certain sense the liberation of slaves is the destruction of property—property acquired by descent, or by purchase, the same as any other property. It is no less true for having been often said, that the people of the South are not more responsible for the original introduction of this property, than are the people of the North; and when it is remembered how unhesitatingly we all use cotton and sugar, and share the profits of dealing in them, it may not be quite safe to say, that the South has been more responsible than the North for its continuance. If then, for a common object, this property is to be sacrificed is it not just that it be done at a common charge?

And if, with less money, or money more easily paid, we can preserve the benefits of the Union by this means, than we can by the war alone, is it not also economical to do it? Let us consider it then. Let us ascertain the sum we have expended in the war since compensated emancipation was proposed last March, and consider whether, if that measure had been promptly accepted, by even some of the slave states, the same sum would not have done more to close the war, than has been otherwise done. If so the measure would save money, and in that view, would be a prudent and economical measure. Certainly it is not so easy to pay something as it is to pay nothing; but it is easier to pay a large sum than it is to pay a larger one. And it is easier to pay any sum when we are able, than it is to pay it before we are able. The war requires large sums, and requires them at once. The aggregate sum necessary for compensated emancipation, of course, would be large. But it would require no ready cash; nor the bonds even, any faster than the emancipation progresses. This might not, and probably would not, close before the end of the 37 years. At that time we shall probably have 100 millions of people to share the burden, instead of 31 millions, as now. And not only so, but the increase of our population may be expected to continue for a long time after that period, as rapidly as before; because our territory will not have become full. I do not state this inconsiderately. At the same ratio of increase which we have maintained, on an average, from our first national census, in 1790, until that of 1860, we should, in 1900, have a population of 103,208,415. And why may we not continue that ratio far beyond that period? Our abundant room—our broad national homestead—is our ample resource. Were our territory as limited as are the British Isles, very certainly our population could not expand as stated. Instead of receiving the foreign born, as now, we should be compelled to send part of the native born away. But such is not our condition. We have 2,963,000 square miles. Europe has 3,800,000, with a population averaging 73 1/3 persons to the square mile. Why may not our country, at some time, average as many? Is it less fertile? Has it more waste surface, by mountains, rivers, lakes, deserts, or other causes? Is it inferior to Europe in any natural advantage? If, then, we are, at some time, to be as populous as Europe, how soon? As to when this may be, we can judge by the past and the present; as to when it will be, if ever, depends much on whether we maintain the Union. Several of our states are already above the average of Europe—73 1/3 to the square mile. Massachusetts has 157; Rhode Island, 133; Connecticut, 99; New York and New Jersey, each, 80; also two other great states, Pennsylvania and Ohio, are not far below, the former having 63, and the latter 59. The states already above the European average, except New York, have increased in as rapid a ratio,

since passing that point, as ever before; while no one of them is equal to some other parts of our country in natural capacity for sustaining a dense population.

Taking the nation in the aggregate, and we find its population and ratio of increase, for the several decennial periods, to be as follows:

1790	3,929,827	
1800	5,305,937	35.02 percent ratio of increase.
1810	7,239,814	36.45 percent ratio of increase.
1820	9,638,131	33.13 percent ratio of increase.
1830	12,866,020	33.49 percent ratio of increase.
1840	17,069,453	32.67 percent ratio of increase.
1850	23,191,876	35.87 percent ratio of increase.
1860	31,443,790	35.58 percent ratio of increase.

This shows an average decennial increase of 34.60 percent in population through the 70 years from our first, to our last census yet taken. It is seen that the ratio of increase, at no one of these seven periods, is either 2 percent below, or 2 percent above, the average; thus showing how inflexible, and, consequently, how reliable, the law of increase, in our case, is. Assuming that it will continue, gives the following results:

1870	42,323,341
1880	56,967,216
1890	76,677,872
1900	103,208,415
1910	138,918,526
1920	186,984,335
1930	251,680,914

These figures show that our country may be as populous as Europe now is, at some point between 1920 and 1930—say about 1925—our territory, at 73 1/3 persons to the square mile, being of capacity to contain 217,186,000.

And we will reach this, too, if we do not ourselves relinquish the chance, by the folly and evils of disunion, or by long, and exhausting war springing from the only great element of national discord among us. While it cannot be foreseen exactly how much one huge example of secession, breeding lesser ones indefinitely, would retard population, civilization, and prosperity, no one can doubt that the extent of it would be very great and injurious.

The proposed emancipation would shorten the war, perpetuate peace, insure this increase of population, and proportionately the wealth of the country. With these, we should pay all the emancipation would cost, together with our other debt, easier than we should pay our other debt, without it. If we had allowed our old national debt to run at 6 percent per annum, simple interest, from the end of our revolutionary struggle until today, without paying anything on either principal or interest, each man of us would owe less upon that debt now, than each owed upon it then; and this because our increase of men, through the whole period, has been greater than 6 percent; has run faster than the interest upon the debt. Thus, time alone relieves a debtor nation, so long as its population increases faster than unpaid interest accumulates on its debt.

This fact would be no excuse for delaying payment of what is justly due; but it shows the great importance of time in this connexion—the great advantage of a policy by which we shall not have to pay until we number 100,000,000, what, by a different policy, we would have to pay now, when we number but 31,000,000. In a word, it shows that a dollar will be much harder to pay for the war, than will be a dollar for emancipation on the proposed plan. And then the latter will cost no blood, no precious life. It will be a saving of both.

As to the second article, I think it would be impracticable to return to bondage the class of persons therein contemplated. Some of them, doubtless, in the property sense, belong to loyal owners; and hence, provision is made in this article for compensating such.

The third article relates to the future of the freed people. It does not oblige, but merely authorizes, Congress to aid in colonizing such as may consent. This ought not to be regarded as objectionable, on the one hand, or on the other, in so much as it comes to nothing, unless by the mutual consent of the people to be deported, and the American voters, through their representatives in Congress.

I cannot make it better known than it already is, that I strongly favor colonization. And yet I wish to say there is an objection urged against free colored persons remaining in the country, which is largely imaginary, if not sometimes malicious.

It is insisted that their presence would injure, and displace white labor and white laborers. If there ever could be a proper time for mere catch arguments, that time surely is not now. In times like the present, men should utter nothing for which they would not willingly be responsible through time and in eternity. Is it true, then, that colored people can displace any more white labor, by being free, than by remaining slaves? If they stay in their old places, they jostle no white laborers; if they leave their old places, they leave them open to white laborers. Logically, there is neither more nor less of it. Emancipation, even without deportation, would probably enhance the wages of white labor, and, very surely, would not reduce them. Thus, the customary amount of labor would still have to be performed; the freed people would surely not do more than their old proportion of it, and very probably, for a time, would do less, leaving an increased part to white laborers, bringing their labor into greater demand, and, consequently, enhancing the wages of it. With deportation, even to a limited extent, enhanced wages to white labor is mathematically certain. Labor is like any other commodity in the market— increase the demand for it, and you increase the price of it. Reduce the supply of black labor, by colonizing the black laborer out of the country, and, by precisely so much, you increase the demand for, and wages of, white labor.

But it is dreaded that the freed people will swarm forth, and cover the whole land? Are they not already in the land? Will liberation make them any more numerous? Equally distributed among the whites of the whole country, and there would be but one colored to seven whites. Could the one, in any way, greatly disturb the seven? There are many communities now, having more than one free colored person, to seven whites; and this, without any apparent consciousness of evil from it. The District of Columbia, and the states of Maryland and Delaware, are all in this condition.

The District has more than one free colored to six whites; and yet, in its frequent petitions to Congress, I believe it has never presented the presence of free colored persons as one of its grievances. But why should emancipation south, send the freed people north? People, of any color, seldom run, unless there be something to run from. Heretofore colored people, to some extent, have fled north from bondage; and now, perhaps, from both bondage and destitution. But if gradual emancipation and deportation be adopted, they will have neither to flee from. Their old masters will given them wages at least until new laborers can be procured; and the freed men, in turn, will gladly give their labor for the wages, till new homes can be found for them, in congenial climes, and with people of their own blood and race. This proposition can be trusted on the mutual interests involved. And, in any event, cannot the North decide for itself, whether to receive them?

Again, as practice proves more than theory, in any case, has there been any irruption of colored people northward, because of the abolishment of slavery in this District last spring?

What I have said of the proportion of free colored persons to the whites, in the District, is from the census of 1860, having no reference to persons called contrabands, nor to those made free by the act of Congress abolishing slavery here.

The plan consisting of these articles is recommended, not but that a restoration of the national authority would be accepted without its adoption.

Nor will the war, nor proceedings under the proclamation of September 22, 1862, be stayed because of the recommendation of this plan. Its timely adoption, I doubt not, would bring restoration and thereby stay both.

And, notwithstanding this plan, the recommendation that Congress provide by law for compensating any state which may adopt emancipation, before this plan shall have been acted upon, is hereby earnestly renewed. Such would be only an advance part of the plan, and the same arguments apply to both.

This plan is recommended as a means, not in exclusion of, but additional to, all others for restoring and preserving the national authority throughout the Union. The subject is presented exclusively in its economical aspect. The plan would, I am confident, secure peace more speedily, and maintain it more permanently, than can be done by force alone; while all it would cost, considering amounts, and manner of payment, and times of payment, would be easier paid than will be the additional cost of the war, if we rely solely upon force. It is much—very much—that it would cost no blood at all.

The plan is proposed as permanent constitutional law. It cannot become such without the concurrence of, first, two-thirds of Congress, and, afterwards, three-fourths of the states. The requisite three-fourths of the states will necessarily include seven of the slave states. Their concurrence, if obtained, will give assurance of their severally adopting emancipation, at no very distant day, upon the new constitutional terms. This assurance would end the struggle now, and save the Union forever.

I do not forget the gravity which should characterize a paper addressed to the Congress of the nation by the chief magistrate of the nation. Nor do I forget that some of you are my seniors, nor that many of you have more experience than I, in the conduct of public affairs. Yet I trust that in view of the great responsibility resting upon me, you will perceive no want of respect yourselves, in any undue earnestness I may seem to display.

Is it doubted, then, that the plan I propose, if adopted, would shorten the war, and thus lessen its expenditure of money and of blood? Is it doubted that it would restore the national authority and national prosperity, and perpetuate both indefinitely? Is it doubted that we here—Congress and executive—can secure its adoption? Will not the good people respond to a united, and earnest appeal from us? Can we, can they, by any other means, so certainly, or so speedily, assure these vital objects? We can succeed only by concert. It is not "can any of us imagine better?" but, "can we all do better?" Object whatsoever is possible, still the question recurs, "can we do better?" The dogmas of the quiet past, are inadequate to the stormy present. The occasion is piled high with difficulty, and we must rise—with the occasion. As our case is new, so we must think anew, and act anew. We must disenthrall ourselves, and then we shall save our country.

Fellow citizens, we cannot escape history. We of this Congress and this administration will be remembered in spite of ourselves. No personal significance, or insignificance, can spare one or another of us. The fiery trial through which we pass will light us down, in honor or dishonor, to the latest generation. We say we are for the Union. The world will not forget that we say this. We know how to save the Union. The world knows we do know how to save it. We—even we here—hold the power, and bear the responsibility. In giving freedom to the slave, we assure freedom to the free—honorable alike in what we give, and what we preserve. We shall nobly save, or meanly lose, the last best hope of earth. Other means may succeed; this could not fail. The way is plain, peaceful, generous, just—a way which, if followed, the world will forever applaud, and God must forever bless.

Gettysburg Address

Gettysburg, Pennsylvania
November 19, 1863

THE PRESIDENT carefully prepared this text several days before delivering it at the consecration of a national cemetery on the field of Gettysburg, where the pivotal battle of the war had been fought the previous July. Some 15,000 people were present. After a lengthy address by the well-known orator Edward Everett, Lincoln rose to give this most famous of American speeches. "The tall form of the president appeared on the stand," recalled one spectator, "and never before have I seen a crowd so vast and restless, after standing so long, so soon stilled and quieted. Hats were removed and all stood motionless to catch the first words he should utter." Later Everett wrote him: "I should be glad, if I could flatter myself that I came as near to the central idea of the occasion, in two hours, as you did in two minutes."

Entire books have been devoted to the gestation of the Gettysburg Address, the culmination of Lincoln's development as a spokesman for the democratic ideal. The forerunners of its measured phrases can be found in Lincoln's speeches as early as 1838. Five manuscript versions of the Gettysburg Address exist, differing mainly in punctuation. This is the version prepared by Lincoln for publication in 1864.

Four score and seven years ago our fathers brought forth on this continent, a new nation, conceived in liberty, and dedicated to the proposition that all men are created equal.

Now we are engaged in a great civil war, testing whether that nation or any nation so conceived and so dedicated, can long endure. We are met on a great battlefield of that war. We have come to dedicate a portion of that field, as a final resting place for those who here gave their lives that that nation might live. It is altogether fitting and proper that we should do this.

But, in a larger sense, we cannot dedicate—we can not consecrate—we cannot hallow—this ground. The brave men, living and dead, who struggled here, have consecrated it, far above our poor power to add or detract. The world will little note, nor long remember what we say here, but it can never forget what they did here. It is for us the living, rather, to be dedicated here to the unfinished work which they who fought here have thus far so nobly advanced. It is rather for us to be here dedicated to the great task remaining before us—that from these honored dead we take increased devotion to that cause for which they gave the last full measure of devotion—that we here highly resolve that these dead shall not have died in vain—that this nation, under God, shall have a new birth of freedom—and that government of the people, by the people, for the people, shall not perish from the earth.

Second Inaugural Address

Washington, D.C.

March 4, 1865

LINCOLN CARRIED the 1864 election easily, mainly because of the change in the fortunes of the Union campaigns. By inauguration day the defeat of the Confederacy was at hand. Noah Brooks, Lincoln's favorite journalist, described the inauguration ceremony. "The crowd . . . became still, and Abraham Lincoln, rising tall and gaunt among the groups about him, stepped forward to read his inaugural address, printed in two broad columns upon a single page of large paper. As he advanced from his seat, a roar of applause shook the air, and again and again repeated, finally died far away on the outer fringe of the throng, like a sweeping wave upon the shore. Just at that moment, the sun, obscured all day, burst forth in its unclouded meridian splendor, and flooded the spectacle with glory and with light. Every heart beat quicker at the unexpected omen."

Lincoln had already turned his thoughts to the aftermath of the war. Just as he had preached conciliation in his first inaugural address, in his second he asked that the defeated states be treated magnanimously, "with malice toward none," despite the calls for vengeance from many in Congress.

At this second appearing to take the oath of the presidential office there is less occasion for an extended address than there was at the first. Then a statement somewhat in detail of a course to be pursued seemed fitting and proper. Now, at the expiration of four years, during which public declarations have been constantly called forth on every point and phase of the great contest which still absorbs the attention and engrosses the energies of the nation, little that is new could be presented. The progress of our arms, upon which all else chiefly depends, is as well known to the public as to myself, and it is, I trust, reasonably satisfactory and encouraging to all. With high hope for the future, no prediction in regard to it is ventured.

On the occasion corresponding to this four years ago all thoughts were anxiously directed to an impending civil war. All dreaded it, all sought to avert it. While the inaugural address was being delivered from this place, devoted altogether to saving the Union without war, insurgent agents were in the city seeking to destroy it without war—seeking to dissolve the Union and divide effects by negotiation. Both parties deprecated war, but one of them would make war rather than let the nation survive, and the other would accept war rather than let it perish, and the war came.

One-eighth of the whole population was colored slaves, not distributed generally over the Union, but localized in the southern part of it. These slaves constituted a peculiar and powerful interest. All knew that this interest was somehow the cause of the war. To strengthen, perpetuate, and extend this interest was the object for which the insurgents would rend the Union even by war, while the government claimed no right to do more than to restrict the territorial enlargement of it. Neither party expected for the war the magnitude or the duration which it has already attained. Neither anticipated that the cause of the conflict might cease with or even before the conflict itself should cease. Each looked for an easier triumph, and a result less fundamental and astounding. Both read the same Bible and pray to the same God, and each invokes His aid against the other. It may seem strange that any men should dare to ask a just God's assistance in wringing their bread from the sweat of other men's faces, but let us judge not, that we be not judged. The prayers of both could not be answered. That of neither has been answered fully. The Almighty has His own purposes. "Woe unto the world because of offenses; for it must needs be that offenses come, but woe to that man by whom the offense cometh." If we shall suppose that American slavery is one of those offenses which, in the providence of God, must needs come, but which, having continued through His appointed time, He now wills to remove, and that He gives to both North and South this terrible war as the woe due to those by whom the offense came, shall we discern therein any departure from those divine attributes which the believers in a living God always ascribe to Him? Fondly do we hope, fervently do we pray, that this mighty scourge of war may speedily pass away. Yet, if God wills that it continue until all the wealth piled by the bondsman's 250 years of unrequited toil shall be sunk, and until every drop of blood drawn with the lash shall be paid by another drawn with the sword, as was said 3,000 years ago, so still it must be said, "The judgments of the Lord are true and righteous altogether."

With malice toward none, with charity for all, with firmness in the right as God gives us to see the right, let us strive on to finish the work we are in, to bind up the nation's wounds, to care for him who shall have borne the battle and for his widow and his orphan, to do all which may achieve and cherish a just and lasting peace among ourselves and with all nations.

Last Public Address

Washington, D.C.
April 11, 1865

THE OFFICIAL news of Lee's surrender on the 10th of April created an uproar in Washington. That night a large crowd gathered at the White House to "serenade" the president; from the balcony he promised them a speech the following evening. The address—his last—was not celebratory, but cautionary. Lincoln understood better than most in his audience the difficulties presented by the task of Reconstruction, a task made much harder by his murder three days later.

We meet this evening, not in sorrow, but in gladness of heart. The evacuation of Petersburg and Richmond, and the surrender of the principal insurgent army, give hope of a righteous and speedy peace whose joyous expression cannot be restrained. In the midst of this, however, He from whom all blessings flow, must not be forgotten. A call for a national thanksgiving is being prepared, and will be duly promulgated. Nor must those whose harder part gives us the cause of rejoicing, be overlooked. Their honors must not be parcelled out with others. I myself was near the front, and had the high pleasure of transmitting much of the good news to you; but no part of the honor, for plan or execution, is mine. To General Grant, his skilful officers, and brave men, all belongs. The gallant navy stood ready, but was not in reach to take active part.

By these recent successes the re-inauguration of the national authority—Reconstruction—which has had a large share of thought from the first, is pressed much more closely upon our attention. It is fraught with great difficulty. Unlike a case of a war between independent nations, there is no authorized organ for us to treat with. No one man has authority to give up the rebellion for any other man. We simply must begin with, and mould from, disorganized and discordant elements. Nor is it a small additional embarrassment that we, the loyal people, differ among ourselves as to the mode, manner, and means of reconstruction.

As a general rule, I abstain from reading the reports of attacks upon myself, wishing not to be provoked by that to which I cannot properly offer an answer. In spite of this precaution, however, it comes to my knowledge that I am much censured for some supposed agency in setting up, and seeking to sustain, the new state government of Louisiana. In this

I have done just so much as, and no more than, the public knows. In the Annual Message of December 1863 and accompanying Proclamation, I presented a plan of re-construction (as the phrase goes) which, I promised, if adopted by any state, should be acceptable to, and sustained by, the executive government of the nation. I distinctly stated that this was not the only plan which might possibly be acceptable; and I also distinctly protested that the executive claimed no right to say when, or whether members should be admitted to seats in Congress from such states. This plan was, in advance, submitted to the then cabinet, and distinctly approved by every member of it. One of them suggested that I should then, and in that connection, apply the Emancipation Proclamation to the theretofore excepted parts of Virginia and Louisiana; that I should drop the suggestion about apprenticeship for freed-people, and that I should omit the protest against my own power, in regard to the admission of members to Congress; but even he approved every part and parcel of the plan which has since been employed or touched by the action of Louisiana. The new constitution of Louisiana, declaring emancipation for the whole state, practically applies the Proclamation to the part previously excepted. It does not adopt apprenticeship for freed-people; and it is silent, as it could not well be otherwise, about the admission of members to Congress. So that, as it applies to Louisiana, every member of the cabinet fully approved the plan. The message went to Congress, and I received many commendations of the plan, written and verbal; and not a single objection to it, from any professed emancipationist, came to my knowledge, until after the news reached Washington that the people of Louisiana had begun to move in accordance with it. From about July 1862, I had corresponded with different persons, supposed to be interested, seeking a reconstruction of a state government for Louisiana. When the message of 1863, with the plan before mentioned, reached New Orleans, General Banks wrote me that he was confident the people, with his military cooperation, would reconstruct, substantially on that plan. I wrote him, and some of them to try it; they tried it, and the result is known. Such only has been my agency in getting up the Louisiana government. As to sustaining it, my promise is out, as before stated. But, as bad promises are better broken than kept, I shall treat this as a bad promise, and break it, whenever I shall be convinced that keeping it is adverse to the public interest. But I have not yet been so convinced.

I have been shown a letter on this subject, supposed to be an able one, in which the writer expresses regret that my mind has not seemed to be definitely fixed on the question whether the seceded states, so called, are in the Union or out of it. It would perhaps, add astonishment to his regret, were he to learn that since I have found professed Union men endeavoring to make that question, I have purposely forborne any public expression upon it. As appears to me that question has not been, nor yet is, a practically material one, and that any discussion of it, while it thus remains practically immaterial, could have no effect other than the mischievous one of dividing our friends. As yet, whatever it may hereafter become, that question is bad, as the basis of a controversy, and good for nothing at all—a merely pernicious abstraction.

We all agree that the seceded states, so called, are out of their proper practical relation with the Union; and that the sole object of the government, civil and military, in regard to those states is to again get them into that proper practical relation. I believe it is not only possible, but in fact, easier to do this, without deciding, or even considering, whether these states have ever been out of the Union, than with it. Finding themselves safely at home, it would be utterly immaterial whether they had ever been abroad. Let us all join in doing the acts necessary to restoring the proper practical relations between these states and the Union; and each forever after, innocently indulge his own opinion whether, in doing the acts, he brought the states from without, into

the Union, or only gave them proper assistance, they never having been out of it.

The amount of constituency, so to speak, on which the new Louisiana government rests, would be more satisfactory to all, if it contained 50, 30, or even 20,000, instead of only about 12,000, as it does. It is also unsatisfactory to some that the elective franchise is not given to the colored man. I would myself prefer that it were now conferred on the very intelligent, and on those who serve our cause as soldiers. Still the question is not whether the Louisiana government, as it stands, is quite all that is desirable. The question is, "Will it be wiser to take it as it is, and help to improve it; or to reject, and disperse it?" "Can Louisiana be brought into proper practical relation with the Union sooner by sustaining, or by discarding her new state government?"

Some 12,000 voters in the heretofore slave-state of Louisiana have sworn allegiance to the Union, assumed to be the rightful political power of the state, held elections, organized a state government, adopted a free-state constitution, giving the benefit of public schools equally to black and white, and empowering the legislature to confer the elective franchise upon the colored man. Their legislature has already voted to ratify the constitutional amendment recently passed by Congress, abolishing slavery throughout the nation. These 12,000 persons are thus fully committed to the Union, and to perpetual freedom in the state—committed to the very things, and nearly all the things the nation wants—and they ask the nation's recognition and its assistance to make good their committal. Now, if we reject, and spurn them, we do our utmost to disorganize and disperse them. We in effect say to the white men "You are worthless, or worse—we will neither help you, nor be helped by you." To the blacks we say "This cup of liberty which these, your old masters, hold to your lips, we will dash from you, and leave you to the chances of gathering the spilled and scattered contents in some vague and undefined when, where, and how." If this course, discouraging and paralyzing both white and black, has any tendency to bring Louisiana into proper practical relations with the Union, I have, so far, been unable to perceive it. If, on the contrary, we recognize, and sustain the new government of Louisiana the converse of all this is made true. We encourage the hearts, and nerve the arms of the 12,000 to adhere to their work, and argue for it, and proselyte for it, and fight for it, and feed it, and grow it, and ripen it to a complete success. The colored man too, in seeing all united for him, is inspired with vigilance, and energy, and daring, to the same end. Grant that he desires the elective franchise, will he not attain it sooner by saving the already advance steps toward it, than by running backward over them? Concede that the new government of Louisiana is only to what it should be as the *egg* is to the fowl, we shall sooner have the fowl by hatching the *egg* than by smashing it? Again, if we reject Louisiana, we also reject one vote in favor of the proposed amendment to the national Constitution. To meet this proposition, it has been argued that no more than three-fourths of those states which have not attempted secession are necessary to validly ratify the amendment. I do not commit myself against this, further than to say that such a ratification would be questionable, and sure to be persistently questioned; while a ratification by three-fourths of all the states would be unquestioned and unquestionable.

I repeat the question. Can Louisiana be brought into proper practical relation with the Union sooner by sustaining or by discarding her new state government?

What has been said of Louisiana will apply generally to other states. And yet so great peculiarities pertain to each state, and such important and sudden changes occur in the same state; and, withal, so new and unprecedented is the whole case, that no exclusive, and inflexible plan can safely be prescribed as to details and colatterals [sic]. Such exclusive, and inflexible plan, would surely become a new entanglement. Important principles may, and must, be inflexible.

In the present "situation" as the phrase goes, it may be my duty to make some new announcement to the people of the South. I am considering, and shall not fail to act, when satisfied that action will be proper.

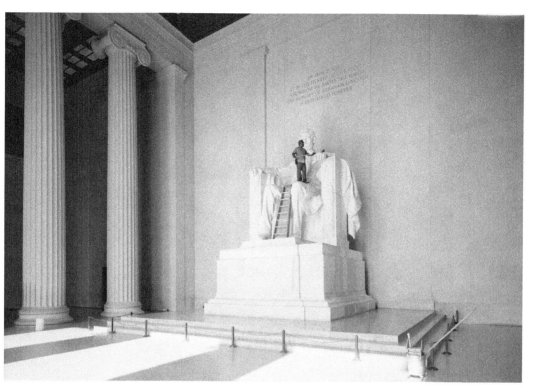

View of the Lincoln Statue being cleaned by James Hudson, who died at the Lincoln Memorial on July 4, 1993. The Lincoln Memorial is located at West Potomac Park, Washington, District of Columbia, DC. (Courtesy of Library of Congress)

Andrew Johnson

Andrew Johnson

1865–1869

THE POLITICAL CAREER of Andrew Johnson rose and fell with his qualities as a speechmaker. It was his blazing attacks on the stump in Tennessee that brought him to the Senate; his defiant pro-Union speeches in the Senate that brought him to the military governorship of his state, from which he moved to the vice presidency and thence, after Lincoln's assassination, to the presidency; and his verbal sparring with hostile crowds that helped bring him to impeachment by Congress.

Though Johnson, through an enormous effort of will, spectacularly transcended poverty and illiteracy to become chief executive, he never managed to transcend the political style of his east Tennessee years. A tailor by trade, the son of a handyman and a washerwoman, he had no schooling at all; he taught himself to read in his teens, and his wife taught him how to write. He organized local workingmen into a political organization that helped elect him first to the town council and then to the state legislature, the House of Representatives, the governorship, and finally the Senate. A politician who heard him speak at a rally in 1840 described him as a muscular man with piercing eyes and an air of energy and intensity that made the crowd roar with excitement. "He knew their names and they knew his voice. He could lead them whithersoever he would."

According to the historian Eric L. McKitrick, "Johnson was not accustomed to thinking of a speech as a statement . . . that a man went 'on record' with. It was rather something mystical that happened between him and the people in front of him." His performance, said McKitrick, was "essentially a spellbinding and conjuring operation" in which Johnson was "possessed of the spirit" to inspire the Democratic faithful. One journalist, impressed with Johnson's boldness on the stump, wrote that his rhetorical attacks on his opponents "tore big wounds and left something behind to fester and be remembered." Before hostile audiences he displayed unusual courage; he lectured crowds of anti-Catholic Know-No things with a loaded pistol on the table in front of him.

In the Senate, Johnson was one of the few Southern Democrats to stand by the Unionist ideals of Andrew Jackson. In December 1860, at the height of the secessionist agitation, he denounced secession in a boiling speech that made him a hero in the North and anathema in the South, where he barely escaped lynching. The Georgia politician Alexander H. Stephens said of it, "I know of no instance in history when one speech effected such results, immediate and remote, as this one did. Characterized by extraordinary fervor and eloquence, it did more to strengthen and arouse the . . . people [in] the North than everything else combined." Of this and similar speeches, Johnson's biographer Lately Thomas wrote: "In this critical juncture, when the forces of secession seemed sweeping on almost unopposed, Andrew Johnson's indomitable Senate speeches kept alive the faith and courage of thousands who clung to the Union in spite of all. . . . Johnson, acting almost alone, had managed to throw up a roadblock in the path of disunion that had prevented the swift consummation of a breakup of the nation." His July 1861 speech in favor of Lincoln's war policies, made just after the Union loss at Bull Run and while Johnson was exiled from Confederate Tennessee, gave the North a boost of idealism and persuaded thousands of men to join the army.

These speeches, and Johnson's service as military governor of Tennessee during the war, encouraged Lincoln to name him as his running mate in the 1864 reelection campaign. At the inaugural ceremonies, Johnson, who had been ill, dosed himself with brandy and made a rambling address that nearly sank his career. A month later came Lincoln's assassination.

Johnson's presidency soon degenerated into a contest of wills with the Radical Republicans in Congress over the goals and methods of Reconstruction. He was accused of demagoguery and treason for his refusal to punish the South. His appeals for support from the public and press were rebuffed, especially after cartoonists and humorists made him the butt of ridicule. By 1868 his enemies succeeded in bringing him to trial in the Senate on 11 articles of impeachment, of which the 10th accused Johnson of attempting "to bring into disgrace, ridicule, hatred, contempt, and reproach the Congress of the United States" by making and delivering "with a loud voice certain intemperate, inflammatory, and scandalous harangues" and uttering "loud threats and bitter menaces" against Congress and its laws. Johnson, who was not allowed by his lawyers to testify in his own defense, was acquitted by a single vote. Six years after he left office he was reelected to the Senate, the only retired president to serve there. He died four months into his term. In his last speeches he attacked his successor in the White House, U.S. Grant, who he believed had connived against him with the Radical Republicans.

The Progress of Reconstruction

From the First Annual Message to Congress
Washington, D.C.
December 5, 1865

EIGHT MONTHS after he took office, Johnson submitted to Congress his first annual message, composed by the historian and diplomat George Bancroft from Johnson's notes. It contained an impressive exposition of Johnson's policy on Reconstruction—a rapid end to military rule of the Confederate states and restoration of their functions as members of the Union as soon as they ratified the Thirteenth Amendment (abolishing slavery). The statesmanlike tone of the message, and Johnson's emphasis on cooperation and harmony, won the approval of most congressmen and increased Johnson's stature abroad. "This is what our *tailors* can do!" exulted one legislator. But some observers noted that the president had left unclear the degree to which he would accept congressional involvement in Reconstruction and that he had suppressed all mention of the South's attempts to intimidate its black population, issues that were shortly to provoke the bitter conflict between the president and the Radical Republicans.

To express gratitude to God in the name of the people for the preservation of the United States is my first duty in addressing you. Our thoughts next revert to the death of the late president by an act of parricidal treason. The grief of the nation is still fresh. It finds some solace in the consideration that he lived to enjoy the highest proof of its confidence by entering on the renewed term of the chief magistracy to which he had been elected; that he brought the Civil War substantially to a close; that his loss was deplored in all parts of the Union, and that foreign nations have rendered justice to his memory. His removal cast upon me a heavier weight of cares than ever devolved upon any one of his predecessors. To fulfill my trust I need the support and confidence of all who are associated with me in the various departments of government and the support and confidence of the people. There is but one way in which I can hope to gain their necessary aid. It is to state with frankness the principles which guide my conduct, and their application to the present state of affairs, well aware that the efficiency of my labors will in a great measure depend on your and their undivided approbation.

The Union of the United States of America was intended by its authors to last as long as the states themselves shall last. "The Union shall be perpetual" are the words of the Confederation. "To form a more perfect Union," by an ordinance of the people of the United States, is the declared purpose of the Constitution. The hand of Divine Providence was never more plainly visible in the affairs of men than in the framing and the adopting of that instrument. It is beyond comparison the greatest event in American history, and, indeed, is it not of all events in modern times the most pregnant with consequences for every people of the earth? The members of the Convention which prepared it brought to their work the experience of the Confederation, of their several states, and of other republican governments, old and new; but they needed and they obtained a wisdom superior to experience. And when for its validity it required the approval of a people that occupied a large part of a continent and acted separately in many distinct conventions, what is more wonderful than that, after earnest contention and long discussion, all feelings and all opinions were ultimately drawn in one way to its support? The Constitution to which life was thus imparted contains within itself ample resources for its own preservation. It has power to enforce the laws, punish treason, and insure domestic tranquillity. In case of the usurpation of the government of a state by one man or an oligarchy, it becomes a duty of the United States to make good the guaranty to that state of a republican form of government, and so to maintain the homogeneousness of all. Does the lapse of time reveal defects? A simple mode of amendment is provided in the Constitution itself, so that its conditions can always be made to conform to the requirements of advancing civilization. No room is allowed even for the thought of a possibility of its coming to an end. And these powers of self-preservation have always been asserted in their complete integrity by every patriotic chief magistrate—by Jefferson and Jackson not less than by Washington and Madison. The parting advice of the Father of his Country, while yet president, to the people of the United States was that the free Constitution, which was the work of their hands, might be sacredly maintained; and the inaugural words of President Jefferson held up "the preservation of the general government in its whole constitutional vigor as the sheet anchor of our peace at home and safety abroad." The Constitution is the work of "the people of the United States," and it should be as indestructible as the people.

It is not strange that the framers of the Constitution, which had no model in the past, should not have fully comprehended the excellence of their own work. Fresh from a struggle against arbitrary power, many patriots suffered from harassing fears of an absorption of the state governments by the general government, and many from a dread that the states would break away from their orbits. But the very greatness of our country should allay the apprehension of encroachments by the general government. The subjects that come unquestionably within its jurisdiction are so numerous that it must ever naturally refuse to be embarrassed by questions that lie beyond it. Were it otherwise the executive would sink beneath the burden, the channels of justice would be choked, legislation would be obstructed by excess, so that there is a greater temptation to exercise some of the functions of the general government through the states than to trespass on their rightful sphere. The "absolute acquiescence in the decisions of the majority" was at the beginning of the century enforced by Jefferson as "the vital principle of republics"; and the events of the last four years have established, we will hope forever, that there lies no appeal to force.

The maintenance of the Union brings with it "the support of the state governments in all their rights," but it is not one of the rights of any state government to renounce its own place in the Union or to nullify the laws of the Union. The largest liberty is to be maintained in the discussion of the acts of the federal government, but there is no appeal from its laws except to the various branches of that government itself, or to the people, who grant to the members of the legislative and of the executive departments no tenure but a limited one, and in that manner always retain the powers of redress. "The sovereignty of the states" is the language of the Confederacy, and not the language of the Constitution. The latter contains the emphatic words—

This Constitution and the laws of the United States which shall be made in pursuance thereof, and all treaties made or which shall be made under the authority of the United States, shall be the supreme law of the land, and the judges in every state shall be bound thereby, anything in the constitution of laws of any state to the contrary notwithstanding.

Certainly the government of the United States is a limited government, and so is every state government a limited government. With us this idea of limitation spreads through every form of administration—general, state, and municipal—and rests on the great distinguishing principle of the recognition of the rights of man. The ancient republics absorbed the individual in the state—prescribed his religion and controlled his activity. The American system rests on the assertion of the equal right of every man to life, liberty, and the pursuit of happiness, to freedom of conscience, to the culture and exercise of all his faculties. As a consequence the state government is limited—as to the general government in the interest of union, as to the individual citizen in the interest of freedom.

States, with proper limitations of power, are essential to the existence of the Constitution of the United States. At the very commencement, when we assumed a place among the powers of the earth, the Declaration of Independence was adopted by states; so also were the Articles of Confederation; and when "the people of the United States" ordained and established the Constitution it was the assent of the states, one by one, which gave it vitality. In the event, too, of any amendment to the Constitution, the proposition of Congress needs the confirmation of states. Without states one great branch of the legislative government would be wanting. And if we look beyond the letter of the Constitution to the character of our country, its capacity for comprehending within its jurisdiction a vast continental empire is due to the system of states. The best security for the perpetual existence of the states is the "supreme authority" of the Constitution of the United States. The perpetuity of the Constitution brings with it the perpetuity of the states; their mutual relation makes us what we are, and in our political system their connection is indissoluble. The whole can not exist without the parts, nor the parts without the whole. So long as the Constitution of the United States endures, the states will endure. The destruction of the one is the destruction of the other; the preservation of the one is the preservation of the other.

I have thus explained my views of the mutual relations of the Constitution and the states, because they unfold the principles on which I have sought to solve the momentous questions and overcome the appalling difficulties that met me at the very commencement of my administration. It has been my steadfast object to escape from the sway of momentary passions and to derive a healing policy from the fundamental and unchanging principles of the Constitution.

I found the states suffering from the effects of a civil war. Resistance to the general government appeared to have exhausted itself. The United States had recovered possession of their forts and arsenals, and their armies were in the occupation of every state which had attempted to secede. Whether the territory, within the limits of those states should be held as conquered territory, under military authority emanating from the president as the head of the army, was the first question that presented itself for decision.

Now military governments, established for an indefinite period, would have offered no security for the early suppression of discontent, would have divided the people into the vanquishers and the vanquished, and would have envenomed hatred rather than have restored affection. Once established, no precise limit to their continuance was conceivable. They would have occasioned an incalculable and exhausting expense. Peaceful emigration to and from that portion of the country is one of the best means that can be thought of for the restoration of harmony, and that emigration would have have been prevented; for what emigrant from abroad, what industrious citizen at home, would place himself willingly under military rule? The chief persons who would have followed in the train of the army would have been dependents on the general government or men who expected profit from the miseries of their erring fellow citizens. The powers of patronage and rule which would have been exercised, under the president, over a vast and populous and naturally wealthy region are greater than, unless under extreme necessity, I should be willing to intrust to any one man. They are such as, for myself, I could never, unless on occasions of great emergency, consent to exercise. The willful use of such powers, if continued through a period of years, would have endangered the purity of the general administration and the liberties of the states which remained loyal.

Besides, the policy of military rule over a conquered territory would have implied that the states whose inhabitants may have taken part in the rebellion had by the act of those inhabitants ceased to exist. But the true theory is that all pretended acts of secession were from the beginning null and void. The states cannot commit treason nor screen the individual who may have committed treason any more than they can make valid treaties or engage in lawful commerce with any foreign power. The states attempting to secede placed themselves in a condition where their vitality was impaired, but not extinguished; their functions suspended, but not destroyed.

But if any state neglects or refuses to perform its offices there is the more need that the general government should maintain all its authority and as soon as practicable resume the exercise of all its functions. On this principle I have acted, and have gradually and quietly, and by almost imperceptible steps, sought to restore the rightful energy of the general government and of the states. To that end provisional governors have been appointed for the states, conventions called, governors elected, legislatures assembled, and senators and representatives chosen to the Congress of the United States. At the same time the courts of the United States, as far as could be done, have been reopened, so that the laws of the United States may be enforced through their agency. The blockade has been removed and the customhouses reestablished in ports of entry, so that the revenue of the United States may be collected. The Post Office Department renews its ceaseless activity, and the general government is thereby enabled to communicate promptly with its officers and agents. The courts bring security to persons and property; the opening of the ports invites the restoration of industry and commerce; the post-office renews the facilities of social intercourse and of business. And is it not happy for us all that the restoration of each one of these functions of the general government brings with it a blessing to the states over which they are extended? Is it not a sure promise of harmony and renewed attachment to the Union that after all that has happened the return of the general government is known only as a beneficence?

I know very well that this policy is attended with some risk; that for its success it requires at least the acquiescence of the states which it concerns; that it implies an invitation to those states, by renewing their allegiance to the United States, to resume their functions as states of the Union. But it is a risk that must be taken. In the choice of difficulties it is the smallest risk; and to diminish and if possible to remove all danger, I have felt it incumbent on me to assert one other power of the general government—the power of pardon. As no state can throw a defense over the crime of treason, the power of pardon is exclusively vested in the executive government of the United States. In exercising that power I have taken every precaution to connect it with the clearest recognition of the binding force of the laws of the United States and an unqualified acknowledgment of the great social change of condition in regard to slavery which has grown out of the war.

The next step which I have taken to restore the constitutional relations of the states has been an invitation to them to participate in the high office of amending the Constitution. Every patriot must wish for a general amnesty at the earliest epoch consistent with public safety. For this great end there is need of a concurrence of all opinions and the spirit of mutual conciliation. All parties in the late terrible conflict must work together in harmony. It is not too much to ask, in the name of the whole people, that on the one side the plan of restoration shall proceed in conformity with a willingness to cast the disorders of the past into oblivion, and that on the other the evidence of sincerity in the future maintenance of the Union shall be put beyond any doubt by the ratification of the proposed amendment to the constitution, which provides for the abolition of slavery forever within the limits of our country. So long as the adoption of this amendment is delayed, so long will doubt and jealousy and uncertainty prevail. This is the measure which will efface the sad memory of the past: this is the measure which will most certainly call population and capital and security to those parts of the Union that need them most. Indeed, it is not too much to ask of the states which are now resuming their places in the family of the Union to give this pledge of perpetual loyalty and peace. Until it is done, the past, however much we may desire it, will not be forgotten. The adoption of the amendment reunites us beyond all power of disruption; it heals the wound that is still imperfectly closed; it removes slavery, the element which has so long perplexed and divided the country; it makes of us once more a united people, renewed and strengthened, bound more than ever to mutual affection and support.

The amendment to the Constitution being adopted, it would remain for the states whose powers have been so long in abeyance to resume their places in the two branches of the national legislature, and thereby complete the work of restoration. Here it is for you, fellow citizens of the Senate, and for you, fellow citizens of the House of Representatives, to judge, each of you for yourselves, of the elections, returns, and qualifications of your own members.

The full assertion of the powers of the general government requires the holding of circuit courts of the United States within the districts where their authority has been interrupted. In the present posture of our public affairs strong objections have been urged to holding those courts in any of the states where the rebellion has existed; and it was ascertained by inquiry that the circuit court of the United States would not be held within the district of Virginia during the autumn or early winter, nor until Congress should have "an opportunity to consider and act on the whole subject." To your deliberations the restoration of this branch of the civil authority of the United States is therefore necessarily referred, with the hope that early provision will be made for the resumption of all its functions. It is manifest that treason, most flagrant in character, has been committed. Persons who are charged with its commission should have fair and impartial trials in the highest civil tribunals of the country, in order that the Constitution and the laws may be fully vindicated, the truth clearly established and affirmed that treason is a crime, that traitors should be punished and the offense made infamous, and, at the same time, that the question may be judicially settled, finally and forever, that no state of its own will has the right to renounce its place in the Union.

The relations of the general government toward the 4,000,000 inhabitants whom the war has called into freedom have engaged my most serious consideration. On the propriety of attempting to make the freedmen electors by the proclamation of the executive I took for my counsel the Constitution itself, the interpretations of that instrument by its authors and their contemporaries, and recent legislation by Congress. When, at the first movement toward independence, the Congress of the United States instructed the several states to institute governments of their own, they left each state to decide for itself the conditions for the enjoyment of the elective franchise. During the period of the Confederacy there continued to exist a very great diversity in the qualifications of electors in the several states, and even within a state a distinction of qualifications prevailed with regard to the officers who were to be chosen. The Constitution of the United States recognizes these diversities when it enjoins that in the choice of members of the House of Representatives of the United States "the electors in each state shall have the qualifications requisite for electors of the most numerous branch of the state legislature." After the formation of the Constitution it remained, as before, the uniform usage for each state to enlarge the body of its electors according to its own judgment, and under this system one state after another has proceeded to increase the number of its electors, until now universal suffrage, or something very near it, is the general rule. So fixed was this reservation of power in the habits of the people and so unquestioned has been the interpretation of the Constitution that during the Civil War the late president never harbored the purpose—certainly never avowed the purpose—of disregarding it; and in the acts of Congress during that period nothing can be

found which, during the continuance of hostilities, much less after their close, would have sanctioned any departure by the executive from a policy which has so uniformly obtained. Moreover, a concession of the elective franchise to the freedmen by act of the president of the United States must have been extended to all colored men, wherever found, and so must have established a change of suffrage in the northern, middle, and western states, not less than in the southern and southwestern. Such an act would have created a new class of voters, and would have been an assumption of power by the president which nothing in the Constitution or laws of the United States would have warranted.

On the other hand, every danger of conflict is avoided when the settlement of the question is referred to the several states. They can, each for itself, decide on the measure, and whether it is to be adopted at once and absolutely or introduced gradually and with conditions. In my judgment the freedmen, if they show patience and manly virtues, will sooner obtain a participation in the elective franchise through the states than through the general government, even if it had power to intervene. When the tumult of emotions that have been raised by the suddenness of the social change shall have subsided, it may prove that they will receive the kindest usage from some of those on whom they have heretofore most closely depended.

But while I have no doubt that now, after the close of the war, it is not competent for the general government to extend the elective franchise in the several states, it is equally clear that good faith requires the security of the freedmen in their liberty and their property, their right to labor, and their right to claim the just return of their labor. I cannot too strongly urge a dispassionate treatment of this subject, which should be carefully kept aloof from all party strife. We must equally avoid hasty assumptions of any natural impossibility for the two races to live side by side in a state of mutual benefit and good will. The experiment involves us in no inconsistency; let us, then, go on and make that experiment in good faith, and not be too easily disheartened. The country is in need of labor, and the freedmen are in need of employment, culture, and protection. While their right of voluntary migration and expatriation is not to be questioned,

I would not advise their forced removal and colonization. Let us rather encourage them to honorable and useful industry, where it may be beneficial to themselves and to the country; and, instead of hasty anticipations of the certainty of failure, let there be nothing wanting to the fair trial of the experiment. The change in their condition is the substitution of labor by contract for the status of slavery. The freedman cannot fairly be accused of unwillingness to work so long as a doubt remains about his freedom of choice in his pursuits and the certainty of his recovering his stipulated wages. In this the interests of the employer and the employed coincide. The employer desires in his workmen spirit and alacrity, and these can be permanently secured in no other way. And if the one ought to be able to enforce the contract, so ought the other. The public interest will be best promoted if the several states will provide adequate protection and remedies for the freedmen. Until this is in some way accomplished there is no chance for the advantageous use of their labor, and the blame of ill success will not rest on them.

I know that sincere philanthropy is earnest for the immediate realization of its remotest aims; but time is always an element in reform. It is one of the greatest acts on record to have brought 4,000,000 people into freedom. The career of free industry must be fairly opened to them, and then their future prosperity and condition must, after all, rest mainly on themselves. If they fail, and so perish away, let us be careful that the failure shall not be attributable to any denial of justice. In all that relates to the destiny of the freedmen we need not be too anxious to read the future; many incidents which, from a speculative point of view, might raise alarm will quietly settle themselves. Now that slavery is at an end, or near its end, the greatness of its evil in the point of view of public economy becomes more and more apparent. Slavery was essentially a monopoly of labor, and as such locked the states where it prevailed against the incoming of free industry. Where labor was the property of the capitalist, the white man was excluded from employment, or had but the second best chance of finding it; and the foreign emigrant turned away from the region where his condition would be so precarious. With the destruction of the monopoly free labor will hasten from all parts of the civilized world to assist in developing various and immeasurable resources which have hitherto lain dormant. The eight or nine states nearest the Gulf of Mexico have a soil of exuberant fertility, a climate friendly to long life, and can sustain a denser population than is found as yet in any part of our country. And the future influx of population to them will be mainly from the North or from the most cultivated nations in Europe. From the sufferings that have attended them during our late struggle let us look away to the future, which is sure to be laden for them with greater prosperity than has ever before been known. The removal of the monopoly of slave labor is a pledge that those regions will be peopled by a numerous and enterprising population, which will vie with any in the Union in compactness, inventive genius, wealth, and industry.

Our government springs from and was made for the people—not the people for the government. To them it owes allegiance; from them it must derive its courage, strength, and wisdom. But while the government is thus bound to defer to the people, from whom it derives its existence, it should, from the very consideration of its origin, be strong in its power of resistance to the establishment of inequalities. Monopolies, perpetuities, and class legislation are contrary to the genius of free government, and ought not to be allowed. Here there is no room for favored classes or monopolies; the principle of our government is that of equal laws and freedom of industry. Wherever monopoly attains a foothold, it is sure to be a source of danger, discord, and trouble. We shall but fulfill our duties as legislators by according "equal and exact justice to all men," special privileges to none. The government is subordinate to the people; but, as the agent and representative of the people, it must be held superior to monopolies, which in themselves ought never to be granted, and which, where they exist, must be subordinate and yield to the government. . . .

Washington's Birthday Speech

Washington, D.C.

February 22, 1866

THE FREEDMAN'S BUREAU BILL, passed by Congress in February 1866, was intended to protect freed slaves from the retaliatory and oppressive codes enacted by Southern legislatures. Johnson vetoed it on the ground that Congress "has no right to pass any bill affecting the interests of the late Confederate states while they are not represented in Congress," nor could he and Congress agree on the criteria by which those states would be judged fit to reenter the government. A few days later, while chatting with a crowd of sympathizers on the White House lawn, the president, forgetting the warnings of his advisers, broke into an impromptu defense of his program. Egged on by the crowd, he denounced his enemies by name and accused them of conspiring to assassinate him. The tirade lasted for more than an hour.

The public reaction was mainly one of shock; Northerners not used to Tennessee-style stump oratory suspected Johnson of being drunk (it was his first major public appearance since his disastrous inauguration ceremony). More damaging yet was his open declaration of the split between himself and Congress. As Eric L. McKitrick points out, "the president, by the act of saying a word, could make certain things true that were not true before he spoke." The chances of repairing the breach and of making rapid progress in the restoration of normal relations among the states all but disappeared with this speech.

... I am free to say to you on this occasion that it is extremely gratifying to me to know that so large a portion of our fellow citizens endorse the policy which has been adopted and which is intended to be carried out.

This policy has been one which was intended to restore the glorious Union—to bring those great states, now the subject of controversy, to their original relations to the government of the United States. And this seems to be a day peculiarly appropriate for such a manifestation as this—the day that gave birth to him who founded the government—that gave birth to the Father of our Country—that gave birth to him who stood at the portal when all these states entered into this glorious confederacy. I say that the day is peculiarly appropriate to the endorsement of measures for the restoration of the Union that was founded by the Father of his Country. Washington, whose name this city bears, is embalmed in the hearts of all who love their government. Washington, in the language of his eulogists, was first in peace, first in war, and first in the hearts of his countrymen. No people can claim him—no nation can appropriate him. His eminence is acknowledged throughout the civilized world by all those who love free government. I have had the pleasure of a visit from the association which has been directing its efforts towards the completion of a monument erected to his name. I was prepared to meet them and give them my humble influence and countenance in aid of the work. Let the monument be erected to him who founded the government, and that almost within the throw of a stone from the spot from which I now address you. Let it be completed. Let the pledges which all these states and corporations and associations have put in that monument be preserved as an earnest of our faith in and love of this Union, and let the monument be completed. And in connection with Washington, in speaking of the pledges that have been placed in that mounment, let me refer to one from my own state— God bless her!—which has struggled for the preservation of this Union in the field and in the councils of the nation. Let me repeat, that she is now struggling in consequence of an innovation that has taken place in regard to her relation with the federal government growing out of the rebellion—she is now struggling to renew her relations with this government and take the stand which she has occupied since 1796. Let me repeat the sentiment which that state inscribed upon her stone that is deposited within the monument of freedom and in commemoration of Washington; she is struggling to stand by the sentiment inscribed on that stone, and she is now willing to maintain that sentiment. And what is the sentiment? It is the sentiment which was enunciated by the immortal and the illustrious Jackson—"The federal Union, it must be preserved."

Were it possible for that old man, who in statue is before me and in portrait behind me, to be called forth—were it possible to communicate with the illustrious dead, and he could be informed of the progress in the work of faction, and rebellion, and treason—that old man would turn over in his coffin, he would rise, shake off the habiliments of the tomb, and again extend that long arm and finger and reiterate the sentiment before enunciated, "the federal Union, it must be preserved." But we witness what has transpired since his day. We remember what he said in 1833. When treason and treachery and infidelity to the government and the Constitution of the United States stalked forth, it was his power and influence that went forth and crushed it in its incipiency. It was then stopped. But it was only stopped for a time, and the spirit continued. There were men disaffected towards the government in both the North and South. There were peculiar institutions in the country to which some were adverse and others attached. We find that one portion of our countrymen advocated an institution in the South which others opposed in the North. This resulted in two extremes. That in the South reached a point at which the people there were disposed to dissolve the government of the United States, and they sought to preserve their peculiar institutions. (What I say on this occasion I want to be understood.) There was a portion of our countrymen opposed to this, and they went to that extreme that they were willing to break up the government to destroy this peculiar institution of the South.

I assume nothing here to-day but the citizen—one of you—who has been pleading for his country and the preservation of the Constitution. These two parties have been arrayed against each other, and I stand before you as I did in the Senate of the United States in 1860. I denounced there those who wanted to disrupt the government, and I portrayed their true character. I told them that those who were engaged in the effort to break up the government were traitors. I have not ceased to repeat that, and, as far as endeavor could accomplish it, to carry out the sentiment. I

remarked, though, that there were two parties. One would destroy the government to preserve slavery; the other would break up the government to destroy slavery. The objects to be accomplished were different, it is true, so far as slavery was concerned; but they agreed in one thing—the destruction of the government, precisely what I was always opposed to; and whether the disunionists came from the South or from the North, I stand now where I did then, vindicating the Union of these states and the Constitution of our country. The rebellion manifested itself in the South. I stood by the government. I said I was for the Union with slavery. I said I was for the Union without slavery. In either alternative I was for the government and the Constitution. The government has stretched forth its strong arm, and with its physical power it has put down treason in the field. That is, the section of country that arrayed itself against the government has been conquered by the force of the government itself. Now, what had we said to those people? We said: "No compromise; we can settle this question with the South in eight and forty hours."

I have said it again and again, and I repeat it now, "disband your armies, acknowledge the supremacy of the Constitution of the United States, give obedience to the law, and the whole question is settled."

What has been done since? Their armies have been disbanded. They come now to meet us in a spirit of magnanimity and say, "We were mistaken; we made the effort to carry out the doctrine of secession and dissolve this Union, and having traced this thing to its logical and physical results, we now acknowledge the flag of our country, and promise obedience to the Constitution and the supremacy of the law."

I say, then, when you comply with the Constitution, when you yield to the law, when you acknowledge allegiance to the government—I say let the door of the Union be opened, and the relation be restored to those that had erred and had strayed from the fold of our fathers.

Who has suffered more than I have? I ask the question. I shall not recount the wrongs and the sufferings inflicted upon me. It is not the course to deal with a whole people in a spirit of revenge. I know there has been a great deal said about the exercise of the pardon power, as regards the executive; and there is no one who has labored harder than I to have the principals, the intelligent and conscious offenders, brought to justice and have the principle vindicated that "treason is a crime."

But, while conscious and intelligent traitors are to be punished, should whole communities and states be made to submit to the penalty of death? I have quite as much asperity, and perhaps as much resentment, as a man ought to have; but we must reason regarding man as he is, and must conform our action and our conduct to the example of Him who founded our holy religion.

I came into power under the Constitution of the country, and with the approbation of the people, and what did I find? I found eight millons of people who were convicted, condemned under the law, and the penalty was death; and, through revenge and resentment, were they all to be annihilated? Oh! may I not exclaim, how different would this be from the example set by the Founder of our holy religion, whose divine arch rests its extremities on the horizon while its span embraces the universe! Yes, He that founded this great scheme came into the world and saw men condemned under the law, and the sentence was death. What was his example? Instead of putting the world or a nation to death, He went forth on the cross and testified with His wounds that He would die and let the world live. Let them repent; let them acknowledge their rashness; let them become loyal, and let them be supporters of our glorious stripes and stars, and the constitution of our country. I say let the leaders, the conscious, intelligent traitors, meet the penalities of the law. But as for the great mass, who have been forced into the rebellion—misled in other instances— let there be clemency and kindness, and a trust and a confidence in them. But, my countrymen, after having passed through this rebellion, and having given as much evidence of enmity to it as some who croak a great deal about the matter— when I look back over the battlefield and see many of those brave men in whose company I was, in localities of the rebellion where the contest was most difficult and doubtful, and who yet were patient; when I look back over these fields, and where the smoke has scarcely passed away; where the blood that has been shed has scarcely been absorbed—before their bodies have passed through the stages of decomposition—what do I find? The rebellion

is put down by the strong arm of the government in the field. But is this the only way in which we can have rebellions? This was a struggle against a change and a revolution of the government, and before we fully get from the battlefields—when our brave men have scarcely returned to their homes and renewed the ties of affection and love to their wives and their children—we are now almost inaugurated into another rebellion.

One rebellion was the effort of states to secede, and the war on the part of the government was to prevent them from accomplishing that, and thereby changing the character of our government and weakening its power. When the government has succeeded, there is an attempt now to concentrate all power in the hands of a few at the federal head, and thereby bring about a consolidation of the republic, which is equally objectionable with its dissolution. We find a power assumed and attempted to be exercised of a most extraordinary character. We see now that governments can be revolutionized without going into the battlefield; and sometimes the revolutions most distressing to a people are effected without the shedding of blood. That is, the substance of your government may be taken away, while there is held out to you the form and the shadow. And now, what are the attempts, and what is being proposed? We find that by an irresponsible central directory nearly all the powers of Congress are assumed, without even consulting the legislative and executive departments of the government. By a resolution reported by a committee, upon whom and in whom the legislative power of the government has been lodged, that great principle in the constitution which authorizes and empowers the legislative department, the Senate and House of Representatives, to be the judges of elections, returns, and qualifications of its own members, has been virtually taken away from the two respective branches of the national legislature, and conferred upon a committee, who must report before the body can act on the question of the admission of members to their seats. By this rule they assume a state is out of the Union, and to have its practical relations restored by that rule, before the House can judge of the qualifications of its own members. What position is that? You have been struggling for four years to put down a rebellion. You contended at the beginning of that struggle that a state had not a right to go out. You said it had neither the right nor the power, and it has been settled that the states had neither the right nor the power to go out of the Union. And when you determine by the executive, by the military, and by the public judgment, that these states cannot have any right to go out, this committee turns around and assumes that they are out, and that they shall not come in.

I am free to say to you, as your executive, that I am not prepared to take any such position. I said in the Senate, in the very inception of this rebellion, that the states had no right to secede. That question has been settled. Thus determined, I cannot turn round and give the lie direct to all that I profess to have done during the last four years. I say that when the states that attempted to secede comply with the Constitution, and give sufficient evidence of loyalty, I shall extend to them the right hand of fellowship, and let peace and union be restored. I am opposed to the Davises, the Toombses, the Slidells, and the long list of such. But when I perceive, on the other hand, men—I care not by what name you call them—still opposed to the Union, I am free to say to you that I am still with the people. I am still for the preservation of these states, for the preservation of this Union, and in favor of this great government accomplishing its destiny.

[Here the president was called upon to give the names of three of the members of Congress to whom he had alluded as being opposed to the Union.]

The gentleman calls for three names. I am talking to my friends and fellow citizens here. Suppose I should name to you those whom I look upon as being opposed to the fundamental principles of this government, and as now laboring to destroy them. I say [Radical Republicans] Thaddeus Stevens, of Pennsylvania; I say Charles Sumner, of Massachusetts; I say Wendell Phillips, of Massachusetts. [A voice, "Forney!" (newspaper editor).]

I do not waste my fire on dead ducks. I stand for the country, and though my enemies may traduce, slander, and vituperate, I may say, that has no force.

In addition to this, I do not intend to be governed by real or pretended friends, nor do I intend to be bullied by my enemies. An honest conviction is my sustenance, the Constitution my guide. I know, my countrymen, that it has

been insinuated—nay, said directly, in high places—that if such a usurpation of power had been exercised 200 years ago, in particular reigns, it would have cost an individual his head. What usurpation has Andrew Johnson been guilty of? My only usurpation has been committed by standing between the people and the encroachments of power. And because I dared say in a conversation with a fellow citizen and a senator too, that I thought amendments to the constitution ought not to be so frequent, lest the instrument lose all its sanctity and dignity, and be wholly lost sight of in a short time, and because I happened to say in conversation that I thought that such and such an amendment was all that ought to be adopted it was said that I had suggested such a usurpation of power as would have cost a king his head in a certain period! In connection with this subject, one has exclaimed that we are in the "midst of earthquakes and he trembled." Yes, there is an earthquake approaching, there is a grounds well coming, of popular judgment and indignation. The American people will speak, and by their instinct, if in no other way, know who are their friends, when and where and in whatever position I stand—and I have occupied many positions in the government, going through both branches of the legislature. Some gentleman here behind me says, "And was a tailor." Now, that don't affect me in the least. When I was a tailor I always made a close fit, and was always punctual to my customers, and did good work.

[A voice. No patchwork.]

THE PRESIDENT. No, I did not want any patchwork. But we pass by this digression. Intimations have been thrown out—and when principles are involved and the existence of my country imperiled, I will, as on former occasions, speak what I think. Yes! Cost him his head! Usurpation! When and where have I been guilty of this? Where is the man in all the positions I have occupied, from that of alderman to the vice presidency, who can say that Andrew Johnson ever made a pledge that he did not redeem, or ever made a promise that he violated, or that he acted with falsity to the people!

They may talk about beheading; but when I am beheaded I want the American people to be the witness. I do not want by innuendoes of an indirect character in high places to have one say to a man who has assassination broiling in his heart, "there is a fit subject," and also exclaim that the "presidential obstacle" must be got out of the way, when possibly the intention was to institute assassination. Are those who want to destroy our institutions and change the character of the government not satisfied with the blood that has been shed? Are they not satisfied with one martyr? Does not the blood of Lincoln appease the vengeance and wrath of the opponents of this government? Is their thirst still unslaked? Do they want more blood? Have they not honor and courage enough to effect the removal of the presidential obstacle otherwise than through the hands of the assassin? I am not afraid of assassins; but if it must be, I would wish to be encountered where one brave man can oppose another. I hold him in dread only who strikes cowardly. But if they have courage enough to strike like men, (I know they are willing to wound, but they are afraid to strike); if my blood is to be shed because I vindicate the Union and the preservation of this government in its original purity and character, let it be so; but when it is done, let an altar of the Union be erected, and then, if necessary, lay me upon it, and the blood that now warms and animates my frame shall be poured out in a last libation as a tribute to the Union; and let the opponents of this government remember that when it is poured out the blood of the martyr will be the seed of the church. The Union will grow. It will continue to increase in strength and power, though it may be cemented and cleansed with blood.

I have talked longer, my countrymen, than I intended. With many acknowledgments for the honor you have done me, I will say one word in reference to the amendments to the Constitution of the United States. Shortly after I reached Washington, for the purpose of being inaugurated vice president, I had a conversation with Mr. Lincoln. We were talking about the condition of affairs, and in reference to matters in my own state. I said we had called a convention and demanded a constitution abolishing slavery in the state, which provision was not contained in the president's proclamation. This met with his approbation, and he gave me encouragement. In talking upon the subject of amendments to the Constitution, he said, "when the amendment to the Constitution now proposed is adopted by three-fourths of the states, I shall

be pretty nearly or quite done as regards forming amendments to the Constitution if there should be one other adopted." I asked what that other amendment suggested was, and he replied, "I have labored to preserve this Union. I have toiled four years. I have been subjected to calumny and misrepresentation, and my great and sole desire has been to preserve these states intact under the Constitution, as they were before; and there should be an amendment to the Constitution which would *compel* the states to send their senators and representatives to the Congress of the United States." He saw, as part of the doctrine of secession, that the states could, if they were prepared, withdraw their senators and representatives; and he wished to remedy this evil by the adoption of the amendment suggested. Even that portion of the Constitution which differs from other organic law says that no state shall be deprived of its representation. We now find the position taken that states shall not be recognized; that we will impose taxation; and where taxes are to be imposed the representatives-elect from thence are met at the door, and told: "No; you must pay taxes, but you cannot participate in a government which is to affect you for all time." Is this just?

We see, then, where we are going. I repeat, that I am for the Union. I am for preserving all the states. They may have erred, but let us admit those into the counsels of the nation who are unmistakably loyal. Let the man who acknowledges allegiance to the government, and swears to support the Constitution (he cannot do this in good faith unless he is loyal; no amplification of the oath can make any difference; it is mere detail, which I care nothing about); let him be unquestionably loyal to the Constitution of the United States and its government, and willing to support it in its peril, and I am willing to trust him. I know that some do not attach so much importance to the principle as I do. One principle that carried us through the revolution was, that there should be no taxation without representation. I hold that that principle, which was laid down by our fathers for the country's good then, is important to its good now. If it was worth battling for then, it is worth battling for now. It is fundamental, and should be preserved so long as our government lasts. I know it was said by some during the rebellion that the Constitution had been rolled up as a piece of parchment, and should be put away, and that in time of rebellion there was no constitution. But it is now unfolding; it must now be read and adjusted and understood by the American people.

I come here today to vindicate, in so far as I can in these remarks, the Constitution; to save it, as I believe; for it does seem that encroachment after encroachment is to be pressed; and as I resist encroachments on the government, I stand today prepared to resist encroachments on the Constitution, and thereby preserve the government. It is now peace, and let us have peace. Let us enforce the Constitution. Let us live under and by its provisions. Let it be published in blazoned characters, as though it were in the heavens, so that all may read and all may understand it. Let us consult that instrument, and, understanding its principles, let us apply them. I tell the opponents of this government, and I care not from what quarter they come—East or West, North or South—"you that are engaged in the work of breaking up this government are mistaken. The Constitution and the principles of free government are deeply rooted in the American heart." All the powers combined, I care not of what character they are, cannot destroy the image of freedom. They may succeed for a time, but their attempts will be futile. They may as well attempt to lock up the winds or chain the waves. Yes, they may as well attempt to repeal it (as it would seem the Constitution can be), by a concurrent resolution; but when it is submitted to the popular judgment, they will find it just as well to introduce a resolution repealing the law of gravitation; and the idea of preventing the restoration of the Union is as about as feasible as resistance to the great law of gravity which binds all to a common centre. This great law of gravitation will bring back those states to harmony and their relations to the federal government, and all machinations North and South cannot prevent it. All that is wanting is time, until the American people can understand what is going on, and be ready to accept the view just as it appears to me. I would to God that the whole American people could be assembled here to-day as you are. I could wish to have an amphitheatre large enough to contain the whole 30 millions, that they could be here and witness the great struggle to preserve the Constitution of our fathers. They could at once see what it is, and how it is, and what kind of

spirit is manifested in the attempt to destroy the great principles of free government; and they could understand who is for them and who is against them, and who was for ameliorating their condition. Their opposers could be placed before them, and there might be a regular contest, and in the first tilt the enemies of the country would be crushed. I have detained you longer than I intended; but in this struggle I am your instrument. Where is the man or woman, in private or public life, that has not always received my attention and my time? Sometimes it is said, "that man Johnson is a lucky man." I will tell you what constitutes good fortune. Doing right and being for the people. The people in some particular or other, notwithstanding their sagacity and judgment, are frequently underrated or underestimated; but somehow or other the great mass of the people will find out who is for them and who is against them. You must indulge me in this allusion, when I say I can lay my hand on my bosom and say that in all the positions in which I have been placed— many of them as trying as any in which mortal man could be put—so far, thank God, I have not deserted the people, nor do I believe they will desert me. What sentiment have I swerved from? Can my calumniators put their finger on it? Can they dare indicate a discrepancy or a deviation from principle?

Have you heard them at any time quote my predecessor, who fell a martyr to his course, as coming in controversy with anything I advocated? An inscrutable Providence saw proper to remove him to, I trust, a better world than this, and I came into power. Where is there one principle in reference to this restoration that I have departed from? Then the war is not simply upon me, but it is upon my predecessor. I have tried to do my duty. I know some are jealous in view of the White House, and I say all that flummery has as little influence on me as it had heretofore. The conscious satisfaction of having performed my duty to my country, my children, and my God, is all the reward which I shall ask.

In conclusion of what I have to say, let me ask this vast concourse, this sea of upturned faces, to go with me—or I will go with you—and stand around the Constitution of our country; it is again unfolded, and the people are invited to read and understand it, and to maintain its provisions. Let us stand by the principles of our fathers, though the heavens fall; and then, though factions array their transient forces to give vituperation after vituperation in the most virulent manner, I intend to stand by the Constitution as the chief ark of our safety, as the palladium of our civil and religious liberty. Yes, let us cling to it as the mariner clings to the last plank when the night and the tempest close around him.

Accept my thanks, gentlemen, for the indulgence you have given me in my extemporaneous remarks. Let us go on, forgetting the past and looking only upon the future, and trusting in Him that can control all that is on high and here below, and hoping that hereafter our Union will be restored, and that we will have peace on earth and good will towards man.

Forgiving the South

New York City, New York

August 29, 1867

TO PROMOTE his national unity campaign and to help boost the chances of moderate Republicans in the upcoming congressional elections, Johnson embarked on a whistle-stop trip between Washington and Chicago, accompanied by an entourage of generals and cabinet secretaries. The tour, known as the "swing around the circle," took 19 days, during which Johnson gave more than 100 speeches. Although it started out well, it proved to be a debacle for the president and a boon to the Radical Republicans. Johnson's knack for developing infinite variations on the same basic speech—a necessity for a politician stumping the isolated towns of rural Tennessee—made him appear boringly repetitious to city dwellers who read daily accounts of his speeches in newspapers, and the fervor of his appeal seemed a mere parody of the intensity with which he had stirred the imaginations of his followers at home. Audiences in the Midwest were so hostile that Johnson was reduced to trading insults with hecklers; in some cities the noise of catcalls prevented him from speaking at all. The crowds were especially incensed at his refusal to condemn the recent massacre of black demonstrators by police officers in New Orleans. In the fall, the Radical Republicans won a majority in Congress, giving them the power to enforce their own program for Reconstruction by overturning Johnson's vetoes and to organize the president's impeachment.

The speech reprinted here was given in New York at the beginning of the "swing around the circle," before the public became contemptuous of the president. A procession of dignitaries escorted Johnson to Delmonico's restaurant on Fifth Avenue, where he delivered this address to a cheering crowd. Newspaper accounts of Johnson's speeches differ according to the publisher's ideological views (some versions were entire fictions); this text is reprinted from the *Political Manual for 1867,* compiled by Edward McPherson, clerk of the House of Representatives.

The toast which has just been drunk, and the kind sentiments which preceded in the remarks of your distinguished representative, the mayor of this city, are peculiarly, under existing circumstances, gratifying to me; and in saying they are gratifying to me I wish not to indulge in any vanity. If I were to say less I should not speak the truth, and it is always best to speak the truth and to give utterance to our sincere emotions. In being so kindly attended to, and being received as I have been received on this occasion—here tonight, and in your city today by such a demonstration—I am free to confess that this overwhelms me. But the mind would be exceedingly dull and the heart almost without an impulse that could not give utterance to something responsive to what has been said and been done. And believe me on this occasion, warm is the heart that feels and willing is the tongue that speaks, and I would to God it were in my power to reduce to sentences and to language the feelings and emotions that this day and this night have produced.

I shall not attempt, in reference to what has been said and the manifestations that have been made, to go into any speech, or to make any argument before you on this occasion, but merely to give utterance to the sincere sentiments of my heart. I would that I could utter what I do feel in response to this outpouring of the popular heart which has gone forth on this occasion, and which will as a legion spread itself and communicate with every heart throughout the confederacy. All that is wanting in the great struggle in which we are engaged is simply to develop the popular heart of the nation. It is like latent fire. All that is necessary is a sufficient amount of friction to develop the popular sentiment of the popular feeling of the American people.

I know, as you know, that we have just passed through a bloody, perilous conflict; that we have gentlemen who are associated with us on this occasion, who have shared their part and participated in these struggles for the preservation of the Union. Here is the army [pointing to the right, where sat General Grant] and here the navy [pointing to the left in the direction of Admiral Farragut]. They have performed their part in restoring the government to its present condition of safety and security; and will it be considered improper in me, on this occasion, to say that the secretary of state has done his part? As for the humble individual who now stands before you, and to whom you have so kindly and pleasantly alluded, as to what part he has performed in this great drama, in this struggle for the restoration of the government and the suppression of rebellion, I will say that I feel, though I may be included in this summing up, that the government has done its duty.

But though the government has done its duty, the work is not yet complete. Though we have passed through fields of battle, and at times have almost been constrained and forced to the conclusion that we should be compelled to witness the Goddess of Liberty, as it were, go scourged through fields of carnage and of blood, and make her exit, and that our government would be a failure, yet we are brought to a period and to a time in which the government has been successful. While the enemy have been put down in the field there is still a greater and more important task for you and others to perform. I must be permitted—and I shall not trespass upon you a moment—I must be permitted to remark in this connection, that the government commenced the suppression of this rebellion for the express purpose of preserving the Union of these states. That was the declaration that it made, and under that declaration we went into the war and continued in it until we suppressed the rebellion. The rebellion has been suppressed, and in the suppression of the rebellion it has declared and announced and established the great fact that these states had not the power, and it denied their right, by forcible or by peaceable means, to separate themselves from the Union. That having been determined and settled by the government of the United States in the field and in one of the departments of government—the executive department of the government—there is an open issue; there is another department of your government which has declared by its official acts, and by the position of the government, notwithstanding the rebellion was suppressed, for the purpose of preserving the Union of the states and establishing the doctrine that the states could not secede, yet they have practically assumed and declared, and carried up to the present point, that the

government was dissolved and the states were out of the Union. We who contend for the opposite doctrine years ago contended that even the states had not the right to peaceably secede; and one of the means and modes of possible secession was that the states of the Union might withdraw their representatives from the Congress of the United States, and that would be practical dissolution. We denied that they had any such right.

And now, when the doctrine is established that they have no right to withdraw, and the rebellion is at an end, and the states again assume their position and renew their relations, as far as in them lies, with the federal government, we find that when they present representatives to the Congress of the United States, in violation of the sacred charter of liberty, which declares that you cannot, even by amendment of the Constitution of the United States, deprive any one of them of their representation—we find that in violation of the constitution, in express terms, as well as in spirit, that these states of the Union have been and still are denied their representation in the Senate and in the House of Representatives. Will we then, in the struggle which is now before us, submit, will the American people submit, to this practical dissolution, a doctrine that we have repudiated, a doctrine that we have declared as having no justice or right? The issue is before you and before the country. Will these states be permitted to continue and remain as they are in practical dissolution and destruction, so far as representation is concerned? It is giving the lie direct—it is subverting every single argument and position we have made and taken since the rebellion commenced. Are we prepared now, after having passed through this rebellion; are we prepared, after the immense amount of blood that has been shed; are we prepared after having accumulated a debt of over 3,000 millions of dollars; are we prepared, after all the injury that has been inflicted upon the people, North and South, of this confederacy, now to continue this disrupted condition of the country? Let me ask this intelligent audience here tonight, in the spirit of Christianity and of sound philosophy, are we prepared to renew the scenes through which we have passed? Are we prepared again to see one portion of this government arrayed in deadly conflict against another portion? Are we prepared to see the

North arrayed against the South, and the South against the North? Are we prepared, in this fair and happy government of freedom and of liberty, to see man again set upon man, and in the name of God lift his hand against the throat of his fellow? Are we again prepared to see these fair fields of ours, this land that gave a brother birth, again drenched in a brother's blood? Are we not rather prepared to bring from Gilead the balm that has relief in its character and pour it into the wound? Have not we seen enough to talk practically of this matter? Has not this array of the intelligence, the integrity, the patriotism, and the wealth a right to talk practically?

Let us talk about this thing. We have known of feuds among families of the most respectable character, which would separate, and the contest would be angry and severe, yet when the parties would come together and talk it all over, and the differences were understood, they let their quarrel pass to oblivion; and we have seen them approach each other with affection and kindness, and felt gratified that the feud had existed, because they could feel better afterwards. They are our brethren. They are part of ourselves. They are bone of our bone and flesh of our flesh. They have lived with us and been part of us from the establishment of the government to the commencement of the rebellion. They are identified with its history, with all its prosperity, in every sense of the word. We have had a hiatus, as it were, but that has passed by and we have come together again; and now, after having understood what the feud was, and the great apple of discord removed; having lived under the Constitution of the United States in the past, they ask to live under it in the future.

May I be permitted to indulge in a single thought here? I will not detain you a moment. What is now said, gentlemen, after the Philadelphia Convention has met to pronounce upon the condition of the country? What is now said? Why, that these men who met in that convention were insincere; that their utterances were worthless; that it is all pretense, and they are not to be believed. When you talk about it, and talk about red-handed rebels, and all that, who has fought these traitors and rebels with more constancy and determination than the individual now before you? Who has sacrificed and suffered more? But because my sacrifices and sufferings

have been great, and as an incident growing out of a great civil war, should I become dead or insensible to truth or principle? But these men, notwithstanding they may profess new loyalty and devotion to the Union of the states, are said to be pretenders, not to be believed. What better evidence can you have of devotion to the government than profession and action? Who dare, at this day of religious and political freedom, to set up an inquisition, and come into the human bosom to inquire what are the sentiments there? How many men have lived in this government from its origin to the present time that have been loyal, that have obeyed all its laws, that have paid its taxes, and sustained the government in the hour of peril, yet in sentiment would have preferred a change, or would have preferred to live under some other form of government? But the best evidence you can have is their practical loyalty, their professions, and their actions. Then, if these gentlemen in convention, from the North and South, come forward and profess devotion to the Union and the Constitution of these states, when their actions and professions are for loyalty, who dare assume the contrary? If we have reached that point in our country's history, all confidence is lost in man. If we have reached that point that we are not to trust each other, and our confidence is gone, I tell you your government is not as strong as a rope of sand. It has no weight; it will crumble to pieces. This government has no tie, this government has no binding and adhesive power, beyond the confidence and trust in the people.

But these men who sit in convention, who sit in a city whose professions have been, in times gone by, that they were a peace-loving and war-hating people—they said there, and their professions should not be doubted, that they have reached a point at which they say peace must be made; they have come to a point at which they want peace on earth and goodwill to men. And now, what is the argument in excuse? We won't believe you, and therefore this dissolution, this practical dissolution, must be continued to exist. Your attention to a single point. Why is a Southern man not to be believed? And I do not speak here tonight because I am a Southern man, and because my infant view first saw the light of Heaven in a Southern state. Thank God, though I say it myself, I feel that I have attained opinions and notions that are coextensive with all these states, with all the people of them. While I am a Southern man, I am a Northern man; that is to say, I am a citizen of the United States, and I am willing to concede to all other citizens what I claim for myself. But I was going to bring to your attention, as I am up, and you must not encourage me too much, for some of those men who have been engaged in this thing, and pretty well broken down, require sometimes a little effort to get them warmed. I was going to call your attention to a point. The Southern states or their leaders proposed a separation. Now, what was the reason that they offered for that separation?

Your attention. The time has come to think; the time has come to consult our brain, and not the impulses and passions of the heart. The time has come when reason should bear sway, and feeling and impulse should be subdued. What was the reason, or one of the reasons at least, that the South gave for separation? It was that the Constitution was encroached upon, and that they were not secured in their rights under it. That was one of the reasons; whether it was true or false, that was the reason assumed. We will separate from this government, they said, because we cannot have the Constitution executed; and, therefore, we will separate and set up the same Constitution, and enforce it under a government of our own. But it was separation. I fought then against those who proposed this. I took my position in the Senate of the United States, and assumed then, as I have since, that this Union was perpetual, that it was a great magic circle never to be broken. But the reason the South gave was that the Constitution could not be enforced in the present condition of the country, and hence they would separate. They attempted to separate, but they failed. But while the question was pending, they established a form of government; and what form of government was it? What kind of Constitution did they adopt? Was it not the same, with a few variations, as the Constitution of the United States, under which they had lived from the origin of the government up to the time of their attempt at separation? They made the experiment of an attempted separation under the plea that they desired to live under that Constitution in a government where it would be enforced. We said "You shall not separate, you shall remain with us, and the Constitution shall be preserved and enforced." The rebellion has ceased. And when their arms were put down by the army and navy of the United States, they accepted the terms of the government. We said to them, before the termination of the rebellion, "Disband your armies, return to your original position in the government, and we will receive you with open arms." The time came when their armies were disbanded under the leadership of my distinguished friend on the right. The army and the navy dispersed their forces. What were the terms of capitulation? They accepted the proposition of the government, and said, "We have been mistaken; we selected the arbitrament of the sword, and that arbiter has decided against us; and that being so, as honorable and manly men, we accept the terms you offer us." The query comes up, will they be accepted? Do we want to humiliate them and degrade them, and tread them in the dust? I say this, and I repeat it here to-night, I do not want them to come back into this Union a degraded and debased people. They are not fit to be a part of this great American family if they are degraded and treated with ignominy and contempt. I want them when they come back to become a part of this great country, an honored portion of the American people. I want them to come back with all their manhood; then they are fit, and not without that, to be a part of these United States.

I have not, however, approached the point that I intended to mention, and I know I am talking too long. Why should we distrust the Southern people and say they are not to be believed? I have just called your attention to the Constitution under which they were desirious to live, and that was the Constitution of their fathers, yet they wanted it in a separate condition. Having been defeated in bringing about that separation, and having lost the institution of slavery, the great apple of discord, they now, in returning, take up that Constitution, under which they always lived, and which they established for themselves, even in a separate government. Where, then, is the cause for distrust? Where, then, is the cause for the want of confidence? Is there any? I do not come here tonight to apologize for persons who have tried to destroy this government; and if every act of my life, either in speeches or in practice, does not disprove the charge that I want to apologize for them, then there is no use in a man's having a public record. But I am one of those who take the Southern people, with all their heresies and errors, admitting that in rebellion they did wrong. The leaders coerced thousands and thousands of honest men into the rebellion who saw the old flag flap in the breeze for the last time with unfeigned sorrow, and welcomed it again with joy and thanksgiving. The leaders betrayed and led the Southern people astray upon this great doctrine of secession. We have in the West a game called hammer and anvil, and anvil and hammer, and while Davis and others were talking about separation in the South, there was another class, Phillips, Garrison, and men of that kind, who were talking about dissolution in the North; and of these extremes one was the hammer and the other was the anvil; and when the rebellion broke out one extreme was carrying it out, and now that it is suppressed the other class are still trying to give it life and effect. I fought those in the South who commenced the rebellion, and now I oppose those in the North who are trying to break up the Union. I am for the Union. I am against all those who are opposed to the Union. I am for the Union, the whole Union, and nothing but the Union. I have helped my distinguished friend on my right, General Grant, to fight the rebels South, and I must not forget a peculiar phrase, that he was going to fight it out on that line. I was with him, and I did all that I could; and when we whipped them at one end of the line, I want to say to you that I am for whipping them at the other end of the line. I thank God that if He is not in the field, militarily speaking, thank God! He is civilly in the field on the other side.

This is a contest and struggle for the Union, for the Union of these states. The North can't get along without the South, and the South can't get along without the North. I have heard an idea advanced, that if we let the Southern members of Congress in they will control the government. Do you want to be governed by rebels? We want to let loyal men in, and none but loyal men. But, I ask here tonight, in the face of this intelligent audience, upon what does the face of the observation rest, that men coming in from the South will control the country to its destruction? Taking the entire delegation of the South, 58 members, what is it compared with the 242 members of the rest of the Union? Is it complimentary to the North to say we are afraid of them? Would the free states let in 58 members from the South that we doubt, that we distrust, that we have no confidence in? If we bring them into the government, these 58 representatives, are they to control the 242? There is no argument that the influence and talent and the principles they can bring to bear against us, placing them in the worst possible light can be a cause for alarm. We are represented as afraid of these 58 men, afraid that they will repudiate our public debt; that they can go into the Congress of the United States under the most favorable conditions they could require, the most offensive conditions to us, and could overwhelm a majority of 150 to 180—that these men are going to take charge of the country. Why, it is croaking; it is to excite your fears, to appeal to your prejudice. Consider the immense sums of money that have been expended, the great number of lives that have been lost, and the blood that has been shed; that our bleeding arteries have been stayed and tied up; that commerce, and mechanical industry, and agriculture, and all the pursuits of peace restored, and we are represented as cowards enough to clamor that if these 58 men are admitted as the representatives of the South the government is lost. We are told that our people are afraid of the people of the South; that we are cowards. Did they control you before the rebellion commenced? Have they any more power now than they had then?

Let me say to this intelligent audience here to-night, I am no prophet, but I predicted at different times, in the beginning of the late rebellion, what has been literally fulfilled. I told the Southern people years ago, that whenever they attempted to break up this Union, that whenever they attempted to do that, even if they succeeded, that the institution of slavery would be gone. Yes, sir [turning to Secretary of State William H. Seward] you know that I made that argument to Jeff Davis. You will bear witness to the position I then occupied.

MR. SEWARD. I guess so.

MR. JOHNSON. Yes, and you were among the few that gave me encouragement. I told them then that the institution of slavery could not survive an attempt to break up this Union. They thought differently. They put up a stake: what was it? It was four millions of slaves, in which they had invested their capital. Their investment in the institution of slavery amounted to $3,000,000,000. This they put up at stake, and said they could maintain it by separating these states. That was the experiment; what are the facts of the result? The Constitution still exists. The Union is still preserved. They have not succeeded in going out, and the institution of slavery is gone. Since it has been gone they have come up manfully and acknowledged the fact in their state conventions and organizations, and they ratify its fall now and forever.

I have got one other idea to put right alongside of this. You have got a debt of about $3,000,000,000. How are you going to preserve the credit of that? Will you tell me. How are you to preserve the credit of this $3,000,000,000? Yes, perhaps when the account is made up your debt will be found $3,000,000,000 or $4,000,000,000. Will you tell me how you are to secure it, how the ultimate payment of the principal and interest of this sum is to be secured? Is it by having this government disrupted? Is it by the division of these states? Is it by separating this Union into petty states? Let me tell you here tonight, my New York friends, I tell you that there is no way by which these bonds can be ultimately paid, by which the interest can be paid, by which the national debt can be sustained, but by the continuity and perpetuity and by the complete Union of these states. Let me tell you who fall into this fallacy, and into this great heresy, you will reap a more bitter reward than the Southern brethren have reaped in putting their capital into slavery. . . .

You who play a false part, now the great issue is past, you who play into the hands of those who wish to dissolve the government, to continue the disreputable conditions to impair and destroy the public credit, let us unite the government and you will have more credit than you need. Let the South come back with its great mineral resources; give them a chance to come back and bear a part, and I say they will increase the national resources and the national capacity for meeting these national obligations. I am proud to say on this occasion, not by way of flattery, to the people of New York, but I am proud to find a liberal and comprehensive and patriotic view of this whole question on the part of the people of New York. I am proud to find, too, that here you don't believe that your existence depends upon aggression and destruction; that while

you are willing to live, you are willing to let others live. You don't desire to live by the destruction of others. Some have grown fat, some have grown rich by the aggression and destruction of others. It is for you to make the application, and not me. These men talk about this thing, and ask what is before you? What is before you? New York, this great state, this great commercial emporium—I was asking your mayor to-day the amount of your taxation, and he informs me it is $18,000,000! Where did your government start from but the other day? Do you remember that when General Washington was inaugurated president, that your annual bill was $2,500,000 for the entire general government. Yet today I am told that my distinguished friend on my left controls the destinies of a city whose taxes amount to $18,000,000, and whose population numbers four millions—double what the entire nation had at the time when it commenced its existence. . . . Thus may we advance, entertaining the principles which are coextensive with the states of this Union, feeling, like you, that our system of government comprehends the whole people, not merely a part.

New York has a great work to perform in the restoration of this great Union. As I have told you, they who talk about destroying the great elements that bind this government together deny the power, the inherent power, of the government, which will, when its capacities are put to the test, reestablish and readjust its position, and the government be restored. I tell you that we shall be sustained in this effort to preserve the Union. It would be just about as futile to attempt the resistance of the ocean wave, or to check the wind, as to prevent the result I predict. You might as well attempt to turn the Mississippi back upon its source as to resist this great law of gravitation that is bringing these states back and be united with us as strong as ever. I have been called a demagogue, and would to God that there were more demagogues in the land to save it! The demonstration here today is the result of some of these demagogical ideas; that the great mass of the people, when called to take care of the people, will do right.

I tell you, you have commenced the grand process now. I tell those present who are croaking and talking about individual aggrandizement and perpetuation of party, I tell them that they had better stand from under, they had better get out of the way; the government is coming together, and they cannot resist it. Sometimes, when my confidence gives out, when my reason fails me, my faith comes to my rescue, and tells me that this government will be perpetuated and this Union preserved. I tell you here tonight, and I have not turned philanthropist and fanatic, that men sometimes err, and can again do right; that sometimes the fact that men have erred in the cause of making them better men. I am not for destroying all men, or condemning to total destruction all men who have erred once in their lives. I believe in the memorable example of Him who came with peace and healing on His wings; and when He descended and found men condemned unto the law, instead of executing it, instead of shedding the blood of the world, He placed himself upon the cross, and died, that man might be saved. If I have pardoned many, I trust in God that I have erred on the right side. If I have pardoned many, I believe it is all for the best interests of the country; and so believing, and convinced that our Southern brethren were giving evidence by their practice and profession that they were repentant, in imitation of Him of old who died for the preservation of men, I exercised that mercy which I believed to be my duty.

I have never made a prepared speech in my life, and only treat these topics as they occur to me. The country, gentlemen, is in your hands. The issue is before you. I stand here to-night, not in the first sense in the character of the chief magistrate of the nation, but as a citizen, defending the restoration of the Union and the perpetuation of the Constitution of my country. Since becoming the chief magistrate I have tried to fulfill my duty—to bring about reconciliation and harmony; my record is before you. You know how politicians will talk; and if you people will get right, don't trouble yourselves about the politicians, for when the people get right the politicians are very accommodating. But let me ask this audience here to-night, What am I to gain by taking the course I am taking if it was not patriotic and for my country? Pardon me; I talk to you in plain parlance. I have filled every office in this government. You may talk to me as you will, and slander—that foul whelp of sin—may subsidize, a mercenary press may traduce and vilify, mendacious and unprincipled writers may write and talk, but all of them cannot drive me from my purpose. What have I to gain? I repeat. From the position of the lowest alderman in your city to president of the United States, I have filled every office to the country. Who can do more? Ought not men of reasonable ambition to be satisfied with this? And ought not I to be willing to quit right here, so far as I am concerned?

I tell this audience here tonight, that the cup of my ambition has been filled to overflowing, with the exception of one thing. Will you hear what that is? At this particular crisis and period of our country's history I find the Union of these states in peril. If I can now be instrumental in keeping the possession of it in your hands, in the hands of the people; in restoring prosperity and advancement in all that makes a nation great, I will be willing to exclaim, as Simeon did of old, of Him who had been born in a manger, that I have seen the glory of thy salvation, let thy servant depart in peace. That being done, my ambition is complete. I would rather live in history, in the affections of my countrymen, as having consummated this great end, than to be president of the United States 40 times.

In conclusion, gentlemen, let me tender to you my sincere thanks on this occasion. So long as reason continues to occupy her empire, so long as my heart shall beat with one kind emotion, so long as my memory shall contain or be capable of recurring to one event, so long will I remember the kindnesses, so long will I feel the good that has been done on this occasion, and so long will I cherish in my heart the kindness which has been manifested towards me by the citizens of New York.

Statue of Andrew Johnson in Nashville, Tennessee.
(Courtesy of PresidentsUSA.net)

Courtesy of Library of Congress

Ulysses Simpson Grant

Ulysses Simpson Grant

1869–1877

FOUR DAYS AFTER President Andrew Johnson's narrow escape from conviction of "high crimes and misdemeanors" in the Senate, the Republicans chose General Ulysses S. Grant, commander of the Union army, as their nominee for president in 1868. The general's popularity carried him to victory in this and the next election with barely a word of public speaking on his part. "I am no speaker," he told a Republican Party leader, "and I don't want to be beaten."

Stolid, colorless, reticent even with close friends, Grant at the time of his nomination had no experience in politics. A tanner's son, a graduate of West Point, and a veteran of the Mexican War, he had failed at farming and in business and had been rescued from a life as a leather-goods clerk by the Civil War. He was a well-intentioned president and made progress toward the completion of Reconstruction, but his inexperience and secretiveness helped make his administration the most corrupt so far. He died nine years after leaving office, impoverished by the collapse of a business venture at the hands of yet another swindler. "Only a person as devoid of dramatic characteristics, of dynamic force, and of any definite direction could emerge so calmly from years of adversity and as inertly proceed to years of success," wrote his biographer William B. Hesseltine. "Essentially, Grant's was a submerged personality—an unimaginative albeit sensitive soul which shrank from contacts with the world, and hid its sensitiveness under an impervious and taciturn shell."

Grant's natural reserve gave him an air of sincerity and dignity that endeared him to a worshipful public. It served him on the battlefield as well. Hamlin Garland, his hagiographer, described him in the act of taking command of a regiment as looking "like a grave and thoughtful country doctor, who had been weatherbeaten in storms and saddened by scenes of human suffering, and was entirely lacking in martial bearing." His voice, continued Garland, was "not loud, but clear and calm, and with a peculiar quality and inflection which surprised and impressed every officer." After his victory at Appomattox he was mobbed by crowds of admirers as he crossed the country. His standard address was two sentences long: "I rise only to say I do not intend to say anything. I thank you for your kind words and your hearty welcome." "From head to foot, from limb to limb," wrote a *New York Times* reporter of such an occasion, "the entranced and bewildered multitude trembled with extraordinary delight. . . with the foregoing 'speech.'"

It was not until Grant left the White House and embarked on a two-year world tour that he finally developed some polish as a speaker, although he still thought it was "a terrible trial." Back in America, and interested in the Republican nomination for a third term in 1880, he made a cross-country trip to reintroduce himself to the voters, and when the Republicans chose James Garfield instead, Grant spoke in his behalf. "When I was in Europe, I had to speak," Grant explained, "and having done so, it seemed to me it would be very uncivil to refuse the folks at home. It is very embarrassing. I think I am improving, for my knees don't knock together as they did at first; but I don't like it, and I am sorry I yielded in the first place."

First Inaugural Address

Washington, D.C.

March 4, 1869

TO THE SURPRISE of the crowd, Grant, when he appeared on the platform on the east portico of the Capitol, was wearing a black suit with yellow kid gloves instead of his army uniform. He read his brief inaugural address in a murmur, with his young daughter sitting near him. Congressional Republicans, who were not consulted either in the preparation of the address or the selection of the cabinet, were somewhat reassured to hear Grant promise that he would be a dutiful executive and a monetary conservative. According to Grant's biographer William S. McFeely, the speech "was pure Grant prose. The word usage was slightly wrong, the effect compellingly right."

Your suffrages having elected me to the office of president of the United States, I have, in conformity to the Constitution of our country, taken the oath of office prescribed therein. I have taken this oath without mental reservation and with the determination to do to the best of my ability all that is required of me. The responsibilities of the position I feel, but accept them without fear. The office has come to me unsought; I commence its duties untrammeled. I bring to it a conscious desire and determination to fill it to the best of my ability to the satisfaction of the people.

On all leading questions agitating the public mind I will always express my views to Congress and urge them according to my judgment, and when I think it advisable will exercise the constitutional privilege of interposing a veto to defeat measures which I oppose; but all laws will be faithfully executed, whether they meet my approval or not.

I shall on all subjects have a policy to recommend, but none to enforce against the will of the people. Laws are to govern all alike—those opposed as well as those who favor them. I know no method to secure the repeal of bad or obnoxious laws so effective as their stringent execution.

The country having just emerged from a great rebellion, many questions will come before it for settlement in the next four years which preceding administrations have never had to deal with. In meeting these it is desirable that they should be approached calmly, without prejudice, hate, or sectional pride, remembering that the greatest good to the greatest number is the object to be attained.

This requires security of person, property, and free religious and political opinion in every part of our common country, without regard to local prejudice. All laws to secure these ends will receive my best efforts for their enforcement.

A great debt has been contracted in securing to us and our posterity the Union. The payment of this, principal and interest, as well as the return to a specie basis as soon as it can be accomplished without material detriment to the debtor class or to the country at large, must be provided for. To protect the national honor, every dollar of government indebtedness should be paid in gold, unless otherwise expressly stipulated in the contract. Let it be understood that no repudiator of one farthing of our public debt will be trusted in public place, and it will go far toward strengthening a credit which ought to be the best in the world, and will ultimately enable us to replace the debt with bonds bearing less interest than we now pay. To this should be added a faithful collection of the revenue, a strict accountability to the Treasury for every dollar collected, and the greatest practicable retrenchment in expenditure in every department of government.

When we compare the paying capacity of the country now, with the 10 states in poverty from the effects of war, but soon to emerge, I trust, into greater prosperity than ever before, with its paying capacity 25 years ago, and calculate what it probably will be 25 years hence, who can doubt the feasibility of paying every dollar then with more ease than we now pay for useless luxuries? Why, it looks as though Providence had bestowed upon us a strong box in the precious metals locked up in the sterile mountains of the far west, and which we are now forging the key to unlock, to meet the very contingency that is now upon us.

Ultimately it may be necessary to insure the facilities to reach these riches, and it may be necessary also that the general government should give its aid to secure this access; but that should only be when a dollar of obligation to pay secures precisely the same sort of dollar to use now, and not before. Whilst the question of specie payments is in abeyance the prudent business man is careful about contracting debts payable in the distant future. The nation should follow the same rule. A prostrate commerce is to be rebuilt and all industries encouraged.

The young men of the country—those who from their age must be its rulers 25 years hence—have a peculiar interest in maintaining the national honor. A moment's reflections as to what will be our commanding influence among the nations of the earth in their day, if they are only true to themselves, should inspire them with national pride. All divisions—geographical, political, and religious—can join in this common sentiment. How the public debt is to be paid or specie payments resumed is not so important as that a plan should be adopted and acquiesced in. A united determination to do is worth more than divided counsels upon the method of doing. Legislation upon this subject may not be necessary now, nor even advisable, but it will be when the civil law is more fully restored in all parts of the country and trade resumes its wonted channels.

It will be my endeavor to execute all laws in good faith, to collect all revenues assessed, and to have them properly accounted for and economically disbursed. I will to the best of my ability appoint to office those only who will carry out this design.

In regard to foreign policy, I would deal with nations as equitable law requires individuals to deal with each other, and I would protect the law-abiding citizen, whether of native or foreign birth, wherever his rights are jeopardized or the flag of our country floats. I would respect the rights of all nations, demanding equal respect for our own. If others depart from this rule in their dealings with us, we may be compelled to follow their precedent.

The proper treatment of the original occupants of this land—the Indians—is one deserving of careful study. I will favor any course toward them which tends to their civilization and ultimate citizenship.

The question of suffrage is one which is likely to agitate the public so long as a portion of the citizens of the nation are excluded from its privileges in any state. It seems to me very desirable that this question should be settled now, and I entertain the hope and express the desire that it may be by the ratification of the Fifteenth Article of Amendment to the Constitution.

In conclusion I ask patient forbearance one toward another throughout the land, and a determined effort on the part of every citizen to do his share toward cementing a happy Union; and I ask the prayers of the nation to Almighty God in behalf of this consummation.

Special Message to Congress Announcing Ratification of the Fifteenth Amendment

Washington, D.C

March 30, 1870

As BOTH GENERAL AND PRESIDENT, Ulysses S. Grant played a major role in preserving the Union, destroying slavery, and battling for equal rights for blacks in the face of white supremacist terrorism. After the Civil War, it was not clear what the United States would look like, especially because approximately four million African Americans, formerly slaves, were now free people. The black vote secured Grant the presidency in 1868, and the Republicans began to look to amending the Constitution as the best way to secure suffrage for black men in all states of the Union. The Fifteenth Amendment was ratified in 1870, and Grant marked the occasion with a special message to Congress.

Grant states that the enfranchisement of African Americans by constitutional amendment finally fulfills the promises of the American Revolution. In an effort to secure the benefits of this fundamental revolution in the composition of the electorate, Grant also calls for measures to promote public education. Many white Americans, especially in the South, did not heed the president's plea for fairness, and within the year, Grant advocated measures that would allow him to suspend the writ of habeas corpus, declare martial law, and employ federal troops to quash white supremacist terrorists.

It is unusual to notify the two Houses of Congress by message of the promulgation, by proclamation of the Secretary of State, of the ratification of a constitutional amendment. In view, however, of the vast importance of the fifteenth amendment to the Constitution, this day declared a part of that revered instrument, I deem a departure from the usual custom justifiable. A measure which makes at once 4,000,000 people voters who were heretofore declared by the highest tribunal in the land not citizens of the United States, nor eligible to become so (with the assertion that "at the time of the Declaration of Independence the opinion was fixed and universal in the civilized portion of the white race, regarded as an axiom in morals as well as in politics, that black men had no rights which the white man was bound to respect"), is indeed a measure of grander importance than any other one act of the kind from the foundation of our free Government to the present day.

Institutions like ours, in which all power is derived directly from the people, must depend mainly upon their intelligence, patriotism, and industry. I call the attention, therefore, of the newly enfranchised race to the importance of their striving in every honorable manner to make themselves worthy of their new privilege. To the race more favored heretofore by our laws I would say, withhold no legal privilege of advancement to the new citizen. The framers of our Constitution firmly believed that a republican government could not endure without intelligence and education generally diffused among the people. The Father of his Country, in his Farewell Address, uses this language:

Promote, then, as an object of primary importance, institutions for the general diffusion of knowledge. In proportion as the structure of a government gives force to public opinion, it is essential that public opinion should be enlightened.

In his first annual message to Congress the same views are forcibly presented, and are again urged in his eighth message.

I repeat that the adoption of the fifteenth amendment to the Constitution completes the greatest civil change and constitutes the most important event that has occurred since the nation came into life. The change will be beneficial in proportion to the heed that is given to the urgent recommendations of Washington. If these recommendations were important then, with a population of but a few millions, how much more important now, with a population of 40,000,000, and increasing in a rapid ratio. I would therefore call upon Congress to take all the means within their constitutional powers to promote and encourage popular education throughout the country, and upon the people everywhere to see to it that all who possess and exercise political rights shall have the opportunity to acquire the knowledge which will make their share in the Government a blessing and not a danger. By such means only can the benefits contemplated by this amendment to the Constitution be secured.

Confession of Failure

From the Eighth Annual Message to Congress
Washington, D.C.
December 5, 1876

IN HIS LAST ANNUAL MESSAGE to Congress, delivered in the midst of the congressional wrangling over the disputed 1876 election, Grant went to the unusual length of apologizing for the scandals in his administration and offering excuses for his failure to do better. The message also contained a summary of his activities in support of Reconstruction, a condemnation of gold miners who had illegally invaded Indian lands in the Dakotas, and a restatement of his desire to annex the island of Santo Domingo as a haven for American blacks and an investor's paradise. The *New York Tribune* called it "the message . . . of a man who is weary of public life and tired of political strife."

In submitting my eighth and last annual message to Congress it seems proper that I should refer to and in some degree recapitulate the events and official acts of the past eight years.

It was my fortune, or misfortune, to be called to the office of chief executive without any previous political training. From the age of 17 I had never even witnessed the excitement attending a presidential campaign but twice antecedent to my own candidacy, and at but one of them was I eligible as a voter.

Under such circumstances it is but reasonable to suppose that errors of judgment must have occurred. Even had they not, differences of opinion between the executive, bound by an oath to the strict performance of his duties, and writers and debaters must have arisen. It is not necessarily evidence of blunder on the part of the executive because there are these differences of views. Mistakes have been made, as all can see and I admit, but it seems to me oftener in the selections made of the assistants appointed to aid in carrying out the various duties of administering the government—in nearly every case selected without a personal acquaintance with the appointee, but upon recommendations of the representatives chosen directly by the people. It is impossible, where so many trusts are to be allotted, that the right parties should be chosen in every instance. History shows that no administration from the time of Washington to the present has been free from these mistakes. But I leave comparisons to history, claiming only that I have acted in every instance from a conscientious desire to do what was right, constitutional, within the law, and for the very best interests of the whole people. Failures have been errors of judgment, not of intent. . . .

A policy has been adopted toward the Indian tribes inhabiting a large portion of the territory of the United States which has been humane and has substantially ended Indian hostilities in the whole land except in a portion of Nebraska, and Dakota, Wyoming, and Montana Territories—the Black Hills region and approaches thereto. Hostilities there have grown out of the avarice of the white man, who has violated our treaty stipulations in his search for gold. The question might be asked why the government has not enforced obedience to the terms of the treaty prohibiting the occupation of the Black Hills region by whites. The answer is simple: The first immigrants to the Black Hills were removed by troops, but rumors of rich discoveries of gold took into that region increased numbers. Gold has actually been found in paying quantity, and an effort to remove the miners would only result in the desertion of the bulk of the troops that might be sent there to remove them. All difficulty in this matter has, however, been removed—subject to the approval of Congress—by a treaty ceding the Black Hills and approaches to settlement by citizens. . . .

The attention of Congress cannot be too earnestly called to the necessity of throwing some greater safeguard over the method of choosing and declaring the election of a president. Under the present system there seems to be no provided remedy for contesting the election in any one state. The remedy is partially, no doubt, in the enlightenment of electors.

The compulsory support of the free school and the disfranchisement of all who cannot read and write the English language, after a fixed probation, would meet my hearty approval. I would not make this apply, however, to those already voters, but I would to all becoming so after the expiration of the probation fixed upon. Foreigners coming to this country to become citizens, who are educated in their own language, should acquire the requisite knowledge of ours during the necessary residence to obtain naturalization. If they did not take interest enough in our language to acquire sufficient knowledge of it to enable them to study the institutions and laws of the country intelligently, I would not confer upon them the right to make such laws nor to select those who do.

I append to this message, for convenient reference, a synopsis of administrative events and of all recommendations to Congress made by me during the last seven years. Time may show some of these recommendations not to have been wisely conceived, but I believe the larger part will do no discredit to the administration. One of these recommendations met with the united opposition of one political party in the Senate and with a strong opposition from the other, namely, the treaty for the annexation of Santo Domingo to the United States, to which I will specially refer, maintaining, as I do, that if my views had been concurred in the country would be in a more prosperous condition today, both politically and financially.

Santo Domingo is fertile, and upon its soil may be grown just those tropical products of which the United States use so much, and which are produced or prepared for market now by slave labor almost exclusively, namely, sugar, coffee, dyewoods, mahogany, tropical fruits, tobacco, etc. About 75 percent of the exports of Cuba are consumed in the United States. A large percentage of the exports of Brazil also find the same market. These are paid for almost exclusively in coin, legislation, particularly in Cuba, being unfavorable to a mutual exchange of the products of each country. Flour shipped from the Mississippi River to Havana can pass by the very entrance to the city on its way to a port in Spain, there pay a duty fixed upon articles to be reexported, transferred to a Spanish vessel and brought back almost to the point of starting, paying a second duty, and still leave a profit over what would be received by direct shipment. All that is produced in Cuba could be produced in Santo Domingo. Being a part of the United States, commerce between the island and mainland would be free. There would be no export duties on her shipments nor import duties on those coming here. There would be no import duties upon the supplies, machinery, etc., going from the states. The effect that would have been produced upon Cuban commerce, with these advantages to a rival, is observable at a glance. The Cuban question would have been settled long ago in favor of "free Cuba." Hundreds of American vessels would now be advantageously used in transporting the valuable woods and other products of the soil of the island to a market and in carrying supplies and emigrants to it. The island is but sparsely settled, while it has an area sufficient for the profitable employment of several millions of people. The soil would have soon fallen into the hands of United States capitalists. The products are so valuable in commerce that emigration there would have been encouraged; the emancipated race of the South would have found there a congenial home, where their civil rights would not be disputed and where their labor would be so much sought after that the poorest among them could have found the means to go. Thus in cases of great oppression and cruelty, such as has been practiced upon them in many places within the last 11 years, whole communities would have sought refuge in Santo Domingo. I do not suppose the whole race would have gone, nor is it desirable that they should go. Their labor is desirable—indispensable almost—where they now are. But the possession of this territory would have left the Negro "master of the situation," by enabling him to demand his rights at home on pain of finding them elsewhere.

I do not present these views now as a recommendation for a renewal of the subject of annexation, but I do refer to it to vindicate my previous action in regard to it.

With the present term of Congress my official life terminates. It is not probable that public affairs will ever again receive attention from me further than as a citizen of the republic, always taking a deep interest in the honor, integrity, and prosperity of the whole land.

Rutherford Birchard Hayes

Rutherford Birchard Hayes

1877–1881

IN 1876, with the bad odor of the Grant administration still lingering, the Republicans nominated the irreproachably honest Rutherford B. Hayes, graduate of Harvard Law School, successful criminal lawyer, brevet major-general in the Civil War, congressman, and three-time governor of Ohio. The election results remained in doubt for four months while a special commission investigated double sets of returns from three Southern states.

As a speaker, Hayes was good at gently inspiring his listeners to take the virtuous course. He was a champion debater at Kenyon College, and his valedictorian address, on "College Life," was said by one observer to be "chaste, beautiful, and sublime, pure in diction, and lofty in sentiment." During his years as a lawyer and party worker in Cincinnati he practiced his oratory at political meetings and settled on a style based, according to his own account, on "energy, brevity, and sound positions; clearness in argument and control of temper." Most of his innumerable campaign and civic speeches were extemporaneous; those composed in advance, said Hayes's early biographer, Charles Richard Williams, "while never notable for rhetorical grace, were characterized by . . . a wholesome manliness of expression" that lifted them "far above the commonplace." Hayes noted in his diary that "I have not in such work been careful as to style, except to have my papers state principles in a way to satisfy men of ability that the statement is sound, and to so phrase and put my propositions that the plain people can readily understand them."

Williams described Hayes's political speeches as appeals to reason over prejudice. "His controlling purpose was not to stir men's hearts, but by the calm presentation of facts, by the lucid exposition of principles, and by the orderly array of conclusions that he believed flowed necessarily from these premises, to convince their minds and bring them to his way of thinking. However vigorously he assailed the position and programme of the opposite party or criticized the political record and principles of the opposing candidate, he carefully avoided personalities or the aspersion of motives and purposes." Hayes was a diligent campaigner, both for himself and for fellow Republicans; his speeches in support of Ulysses S. Grant's candidacy in 1872 won him the offer of the post of assistant U.S. treasurer, which he declined. His code of honor did not allow him to campaign for the presidency, however, nor did he comment publicly on the situation while the election remained in dispute.

As president, Hayes made a specialty of traveling through the country to address the people, usually to invite them to set aside the old sectional rivalries and rebuild the nation in a spirit of conciliation, or to expound on the beneficial effects of his financial policies. In the first year of his term he toured New England, Ohio, and the South; the following year he journeyed to North Dakota by way of Illinois, Minnesota, and Wisconsin. In 1880 Hayes made the first visit of any president to the Pacific Coast, covering 10,000 miles in two months, mostly by rail but also by steamer, stagecoach, yacht, ferry, and by army field ambulance across the desert. On all these trips Hayes made a point of avoiding speechmaking on Sundays. According to a correspondent for the Baltimore *American,* his speeches were "not the studied efforts of the politician, eager to impress his hearers with an idea of his own importance; but the frank expressions of a well-informed man desirous of fostering sound views of national questions among the masses, and of cultivating a feeling of hearty good-will between different sections of the country." Historian Kenneth E. Davison wrote that "by using presidential tours to manifest the power of the presidency and to develop loyalty for the central government, he revived an important method of maintaining executive authority practiced earlier by Washington and Monroe."

After his departure from the White House, Hayes retired to his Ohio estate and became an enthusiastic education and prison reformer; he spent much of his retirement addressing charitable organizations and presiding over reunions of his Civil War unit, the 23d Regiment.

The Reconstructed South

Atlanta, Georgia
September 24, 1877

WELL-READ AND WELL-MANNERED, Hayes was in all things a gentleman. The reformer George William Curtis, writing in *Harper's Weekly,* called him "a true representative of the good old cause; pure, honorable, sagacious, and self-restrained." Concerned to do the right thing in matters of fairness and tolerance, he was slow to recognize intolerance in others. In fulfillment of a promise made to the Democrats during the settlement of the election dispute, he withdrew the last federal troops from the South, trusting the revived Democratic governments to protect the rights of the black population. On his tour of the South in 1877 he made many speeches like this one, in which he encouraged both sides to forget the past and even joked about his own war wounds. The following year, the Democrats swept the South in the congressional elections and took control of both houses of Congress—exactly the situation the Radical Republicans had warned against. In his diary for November 12, 1878, Hayes recorded his belated realization that "by state legislation, by frauds, by intimidation, and by violence of the most atrocious character, colored citizens have been deprived of the right of suffrage—a right guaranteed by the Constitution, and to the protection of which the people of those states have been solemnly pledged."

. . . I suppose that here, as everywhere else, I am in the presence of men of both great political parties. I am speaking, also, in the presence of citizens of both races. I am quite sure that there are before me very many of the brave men who fought in the Confederate army: some, doubtless, of the men who fought in the Union army. And here we are, Republicans, Democrats, colored people, white people, Confederate soldiers, and Union soldiers, all of one mind and one heart today! And why should we not be? What is there to separate us longer? Without any fault of yours or any fault of mine, or of any one of this great audience, slavery existed in this country. It was in the Constitution of the country. The colored man was here, not by his voluntary action. It was the misfortune of his fathers that he was here. I think it is safe to say that it was by the crime of our fathers that he was here. He was here, however, and we of the two sections differed about what should be done with him. As Mr. Lincoln told us in the war, there were prayers on both sides for him. Both sides found in the Bible confirmation of their opinions, and both sides finally undertook to settle the question by that last final means of arbitration— force of arms. You here mainly joined the Confederate side, and fought bravely, risked your lives heroically in behalf of your convictions; and can I, can any true man anywhere, fail to respect the man who risks his life for

his convictions? And as I accord that respect to you, and believe you to be equally liberal and generous and just, I feel that, as I stand before you as one who fought in the Union army for his convictions, I am entitled to your respect. Now that conflict is over, my friends.

Governor Hampton repeated to you last night the way in which I have been in the habit of putting it since I came to the South. There was a larger proportion of trained soldiers in your army at first than in ours; in a much larger proportion you were good marksmen and good horsemen—and that is two-thirds of a good soldier. But gradually we learned to ride, too; and, as some of you know, gradually we learned to shoot. I happen to know how well you shoot. Well, having learned how to ride and shoot, then it was a case of fight between Greek and Greek; and when Greek meets Greek you know what the conflict is; and more than that, you know exactly how it will terminate. That party in that fight will always conquer that has the most Greeks. So, with no discredit to you and no special credit to us, the war turned out as it did.

Now, shall we quit fighting? I have been in the habit of telling an anecdote of General Scott and a statesman at Washington, in which the statesman said that as soon as the war was over and the combatants laid down their arms, we should have complete peace. "No," said General Scott, "it will take several years in which all the powers of the general government will be employed in keeping peace between the belligerent non-combatants!" Now, I think, we have got through with that and having peace between the soldiers and the non-combatants, that is an end of the war. Is there any reason, then, why we should not be at peace forevermore? We are embarked upon the same voyage, upon the same ship, under the same old flag. Good fortune or ill fortune affects you and your children as well as my people and my children.

Every interest you possess is to be promoted by peace. Here is this great city of Atlanta, gathering to itself from all parts of the country its wealth and business by its railroads; and I say to you that every description of industry and legitimate business needs peace. That is what capital wants. Discord, discontent, and dissatisfaction are the enemies of these enterprises. Then, all our interests are for peace. Are we not agreed about that? What do we want for the future? I believe it is the duty of the general government to regard equally and alike the interests and rights of all sections of this country. I am glad that you agree with me about that. I believe, further, that it is the duty of the government to regard alike and equally the rights and interests of all classes of citizens. That covers the whole matter. That wipes out in the future in our politics the section line forever. Let us wipe out in our politics the color line forever.

And let me say a word upon what has been done. I do not undertake to discuss or defend particular measures. I leave the people with their knowledge of the facts to examine, discuss, and decide for themselves as to them. I speak of general considerations and notions. What troubles our people at the North, what has troubled them, was that they feared that these colored people, who had been made freemen by the war, would not be safe in their rights and interests in the South unless it was by the interference of the general government. Many good people had that idea. I had given that matter some consideration, and now, my colored friends, who have thought, or who have been told, that I was turning my back upon the men whom I fought for, now, listen! After thinking over it, I believed that your right and interests would be safer if this great mass of intelligent white men were let alone by the general government. And now, my colored friends, let me say another thing. We have been trying it for these six months, and, in my opinion in no six months since the war have there been so few outrages and invasions of your rights, nor you so secure in your rights, persons, and homes, as in the last six months.

Then, my friends, we are all together upon one proposition. We believe, and in this all those who are here agree, in the Union of our fathers, in the old flag of our fathers, the Constitution as it is with all its amendments, and are prepared to see it fully and fairly obeyed and enforced. Now, my friends, I see it stated occasionally that President Hayes has taken the course he has because he was compelled to it. Now, I was compelled to it. I was compelled to it by my sense of duty under my oath of office. What was done by us was done, not merely by force of special circumstances, but because it was just and right to do it.

Now let us come together. Let each man make up his mind to be a patriot in his own home and place. You may quarrel about the tariff, get up a sharp contest about the currency, about the removal of state capitals and where they shall go to, but upon the great question of the Union of the states and the rights of all the citizens, we shall agree forevermore.

Civilizing the Indians

From the First Annual Message to Congress
Washington, D.C.
December 3, 1877

THE LONG HISTORY of confrontations between white settlers and Indians culminated during Hayes's term in the massacre of George Armstrong Custer's regiment at the Battle of the Little Big Horn; the Nez Percé War; and the forced relocation of the Ponca tribe, with the usual devastating results. Carl Schurz, Hayes's secretary of the interior, made the first efforts at reforming the corrupt Indian Bureau and turning public opinion of the Indians toward tolerance rather than hostility.

. . . The present condition of the Indian tribes in the territory of the United States and our relations with them are fully set forth in the reports of the secretary of the interior and the commissioner of Indian Affairs. After a series of most deplorable conflicts—the successful termination of which, while reflecting honor upon the brave soldiers who accomplished it, cannot lessen our regret at their occurrence—we are now at peace with all the Indian tribes within our borders. To preserve that peace by a just and humane policy will be the object of my earnest endeavors. Whatever may be said of their character and savage propensities, of the difficulties of introducing among them the habits of civilized life, and of the obstacles they have offered to the progress of settlement and enterprise in certain parts of the country, the Indians are certainly entitled to our sympathy and to a conscientious respect on our part for their claims upon our sense of justice. They were the aboriginal occupants of the land we now possess. They have been driven from place to place. The purchase money paid to them in some cases for what they called their own has still left them poor. In many instances, when they had settled down upon land assigned to them by compact and begun to support themselves by their own labor, they were rudely jostled off and thrust into the wilderness again. Many, if not most, of our Indian wars have had their origin in broken promises and acts of injustice upon our part, and the advance of the Indians in civilization has been slow because the treatment they received did not permit it to be faster and more general. We cannot expect them to improve and to follow our guidance unless we keep faith with them in respecting the rights they possess, and unless, instead of depriving them of their opportunities, we lend them a helping hand.

I cordially approve the policy regarding the management of Indian affairs outlined in the reports of the secretary of the interior and of the commissioner of Indian Affairs. The faithful performance of our promises is the first condition of a good understanding with the Indians. I cannot too urgently recommend to Congress that prompt and liberal provision be made for the conscientious fulfillment of all engagements entered into by the government with the Indian tribes. To withhold the means necessary for the performance of a promise is always false economy, and is apt to prove disastrous in its consequences. Especial care is recommended to provide for Indians settled on their reservations cattle and agricultural implements, to aid them in whatever efforts they may make to support themselves, and by the establishment and maintenance of schools to bring them under the control of civilized influences. I see no reason why Indians who can give satisfactory proof of having by their own labor supported their families for a number of years, and who are willing to detach themselves from their tribal relations, should not be admitted to the benefit of the Homestead Act and the privileges of citizenship, and I recommend the passage of a law to that effect. It will be an act of justice as well as a measure of encouragement. Earnest efforts are being made to purify the Indian service, so that every dollar appropriated by Congress shall redound to the benefit of the Indians, as intended. Those efforts will have my firm support. With an improved service and every possible encouragement held out to the Indians to better their condition and to elevate themselves in the scale of civilization, we may hope to accomplish at the same time a good work for them and for ourselves. . . .

Sound Currency

Madison, Wisconsin
September 10, 1878

THE HAYES ADMINISTRATION was preoccupied with combating an economic depression, refunding the nation's war debt at a lower rate of interest, and adjusting the currency system through the resumption of government payments in specie (coin) rather than in legaltender notes ("greenbacks"). Hayes's Northwest trip of 1878, conducted just prior to the midterm elections, was intended to convince the voters that the Republicans had the situation under control, and most of his speeches mentioned what he called "honest money"—money whose value was unimpaired by inflation.

. . . May I talk a little of my own convictions as to remedies that are proposed for these hard times? I do not like to mingle in mere partisan discussions and I do not propose to; but I have some friends who tell me, and very good friends, too—as I heard at my home—that, after all, our trouble is that our currency is not cheap enough and that it will not stay at home. It goes abroad, and therefore they tell me that they want a currency that is so cheap that it is better for us than that costly currency, gold and silver, and of such quality that it will not go away. Now, I say that that is a very desirable quality in currency. You have all found it so. If you can keep it, it is a good thing. Let us talk about that a little. First, the cheapness of the currency. They tell me what they wish is this: The United States ought to say [the speaker holding up a piece of paper the size of a dollar bill], "This is one dollar anywhere in the United States, by act of Congress"—a piece of paper about the size of that, probably. "Of course, we do not want it counterfeited." I am afraid it would not be a great while after it was issued that nobody would want to counterfeit it. But, in order that it should be as good as possible, we would print it on good paper like a national bank note, or a greenback—good type, good-looking pictures on it, good engraving. And now what does it cost? They say they want a cheap currency. What does that "dollar" cost? If we have a good dollar, or a silver dollar, we know what it costs: it costs, take the world over, about a day's work or about a bushel of wheat; that is what each dollar costs. But what does the new currency cost, each dollar? Well, it costs rather less than a cent! That piece of paper, all pictured off nicely, ready for currency, cost

about a cent. Now, that is a good operation. To make a dollar out of gold or silver will cost us a bushel of wheat. That is a good operation. "We will do that; we will do that." But stop! Is that best? Let us see. Why, it won't cost any more to make that "two dollars" than "one."

Then, were we not a little hasty only to make it "one"? We will make it "two," and it still costs only a cent. Now, my friends, don't you see that we made only 99 cents? But if we would undertake to make two dollars out of gold and silver, it would take two days' work or two bushels of wheat. But it is just as cheap to make that "10 dollars and 99 cents in the operation. Instead of paying for it 10 days' work or 10 bushels of wheat, we will give just exactly the onehundredth part of a day's work for our 10-dollar bill. We are doing well, but not wisely for we might just as well make it a 100—it will cost no more; or a 1,000—it will cost no more; and now we will pay off our whole national debt wth it, and that is what we want, they tell us. Why stop at that? Why not pay all the expenses of our government with it and not tax the people at all? Now, my friends, doesn't it begin to dawn upon the simplest mind that there is some mistake about this? That that is inflation, and that inflation is nonsense? The real thing is what we want—no sham.

But the friends say: "It will stay at home; it won't go abroad; good here, good nowhere else; therefore, it will stay here." Is that good? Let us see about that. Let us have the United States act upon that principle; none of our money will be taken abroad—and so we will keep it. If that is good for the United States, would it not be well for Wisconsin? Wisconsin sends her money to New York and to New England and the big cities East. Why not keep it at home? Let Wisconsin make her own money in the same way, then; and if that is good for Wisconsin, why is it not good for Madison—not be sending off to Milwaukee and Chicago, and so on? Let Madison make her own money! If it is good for Madison, why isn't it good for John Smith, the grocer? Let him make his own money: "This is One Dollar. John Smith." He will never spend it; he can keep it; it will stay at home.

No, no, my fellow citizens, the men who made the constitution of the United States said: "Congress shall have power to coin money." Gold and silver are the money of the world and have been ever since the days of Abraham, and you cannot change it by legislation. Either that, or paper that will command that, is a sound constitutional currency.

Let us remember that with every day more and more our products of the soil and our products of the shop are going to Europe connecting us with the commerce of the world. We should conduct our financial system, then, on principles and instrumentalities such as the experience of the world and the general judgment of the commericial world sanction, and we know what these are. We know how the commerce of the world is bound together. Anything seriously affecting any great nation soon affects all the others. This panic that has afflicted us has afflicted others also, clear around the globe.

Now, my friends, let me say: The true need is, when we are marching steadily on to the threshold of times, "Be wise enough to let well enough alone." What we want is a restoration of confidence. A restoration of confidence comes only with stability in legislation and in conduct. Let us, then, try no new experiments, but march in the path marked out by the fathers. Let us say our restored financial prosperity shall rest upon a national credit unimpaired, without taint or stain, and upon a currency solid and constitutional—that defrauds no one. Let it be a currency such that honest capital—for there is honest capital and plenty of it; that honest business enterprise— for there is honest business enterprise; that honest labor—for there is honest labor, shall we have, also, honest money.

Federal Aid to Education

Canton, Ohio

September 1, 1880

IN HIS FIRST annual message to Congress, Hayes reminded Congress that one-seventh of the country's voters were illiterate and added: "It is vain to hope for the success of a free government without the means of insuring the intelligence of those who are the source of power." Many of his speeches, during and after his presidency, concerned the importance of instituting federal aid to nonsectarian elementary schools as a way of countering the threat to democracy posed by the inability of some states, particularly in the impoverished South, to provide basic education for their citizens. One such address was made at a reunion of the 23d Regiment at the beginning of Hayes's transcontinental journey.

. . . The means at the command of the local and state authorities are in many cases wholly inadequate to deal with the question [of providing education]. The magnitude of the evil to be eradicated is not, I apprehend, generally and fully understood. Consider these facts:

1. By the latest available statistics it appears that in 1878 the total school population, white and colored, in the late slaveholding states, was 5,187,584, and that only 2,710,096 were during that year enrolled in any school. This leaves 2,477,488—almost two and a half millions—of the young who are growing up without the means of education. Citizenship and the right to vote were conferred upon the colored people by the government and people of the United States. It is, therefore, the sacred duty, as it is the highest interest, of the United States to see that these new citizens and voters are fitted by education for the grave responsibility which has been cast upon them.

2. In the territories of the United States it is estimated that there are over 200,000 Indians, almost all of whom are uncivilized. . . . The solution of the Indian question will speedily be either the extinction of the Indians or their absorption into American citizenship by means of the civilizing influences of education. With the disappearance of game there can no longer remain Indian hunters or warriors. . . .

3. The people of the Territory of New Mexico have never been provided with the means of education. The number of people in that territory in 1870, 10 years old and upwards, who could not read and write was 52,220.

This is largely more than half the population. The school population is now over 30,000, of whom only about one-sixth are enrolled in schools. It will not be questioned that the power of the general government to make all needful rules and regulations respecting the territory belonging to the United States is sufficient to authorize it to provide for the education of the increasing mass of illiterate citizens growing up in New Mexico and in the other territories of the United States.

4. The number of immigrants arriving in the United States is greater than ever before. It is not improbable, from present indications, that, from this source alone, there will be added, during the current decade, to the population of our country five millions of people. . . . It may reasonably be estimated that at least from 20 to 25 percent of the immigrants are illiterate. In the current decade we shall probably receive from abroad more than a million of people of school age and upwards who are unable to read and write any language; and of these, about a quarter of a million, in a few years, will share with us equally, man for man, the duties and responsiblities of the citizen and the voter.

Jefferson, with his almost marvellous sagacity and foresight, declared nearly a hundred years ago, that free schools were an essential part—one of the columns, as he expressed it—of the republican edifice, and that, "without instruction free to all, the sacred flame of liberty could not be kept burning in the hearts of Americans."

Madison said, almost 60 years ago: "A popular government, without popular information or the means of acquiring it, is but a prologue to a farce or a tragedy, or perhaps both."

Already, in too many instances, elections have become the farce which Madison predicted; and the tremendous tragedy which we saw when we were soldiers of the Union, and in which we bore a part, could never have occurred if in all sections of our country there had been universal suffrage based upon universal education. In our county, as everywhere else, it will be found that, in the long run, ignorant voters are powder and ball for the demagogues. The failure to support free schools in any part of our country tends to cheapen and degrade the right of suffrage, and will ultimately destroy its value in every other part of the republic.

The unvarying testimony of history is, that the nations which win the most renowned victories in peace and war are those which provide ample means for popular education. Without free schools, there is no such thing

as affording to "every man an unfettered start and a fair chance in the race of life." In the present condition of our country, universal education requires the aid of the general government. The authority to grant such aid is established by a line of precedents, beginning with the origin of the republic and running down through almost every administration to the present time. Let this aid be granted wherever it is essential to the enjoyment of free popular instruction.

In the language of Mr. Webster: "The census of these states shows how great a proportion of the whole population occupies the classes between infancy and manhood. These are the wide fields, and here is the deep and quick soil for the seeds of knowledge and virtue; and this is the favored season—the very spring-time for sowing them. Let them be disseminated without stint. Let them be scattered with a bountiful hand broadcast. Whatever the government can fairly do toward these objects, in my opinion, ought to be done." . . .

Civil Service Reform

From the Fourth Annual Message to Congress
Washington, D.C.
December 6, 1880

THE SCANDALS of the Grant years prompted both parties in the 1876 elections to pledge reforms in the civil service system (or "snivel service," as one Republican leader called it). In his inaugural address Hayes asked for a "thorough, radical, and complete . . . return to the principles and practices of the founders of our government," who "neither expected nor desired from public officers any partisan service," adding: "He serves his party best who serves his country best." Hayes succeeded in taking away from his own party's spoilsmen their lucrative control over the New York Customhouse, but most of his reforms had little effect.

. . . In my former annual messages I have asked the attention of Congress to the urgent necessity of a reformation of the civil service system of the government. My views concerning the dangers of patronage, or appointments for personal or partisan considerations, have been strengthened by my observation and experience in the executive office, and I believe these dangers threaten the stability of the government. Abuses so serious in their nature cannot be permanently tolerated. They tend to become more alarming with the enlargement of administrative service, as the growth of the country in population increases the number of officers and placement employed.

The reasons are imperative for the adoption of fixed rules for the regulation of appointments, promotions, and removals, establishing a uniform method having exclusively in view in every instance the attainment of the best qualifications for the position in question. Such a method alone is consistent with the equal rights of all citizens and the most economical and efficient administration of the public business.

Competitive examinations in aid of impartial appointments and promotions have been conducted for some years past in several of the executive departments, and by my direction this system has been adopted in the custom-houses and post-offices of the larger cities of the country. In the city of New York over 2,000 positions in the civil service have been subject in their appointments and tenure of place to the operation of published rules for this purpose during the past two years. The results of these practical trials have been very satisfactory, and have confirmed my opinion in favor of this system of selection. All are subjected to the same tests, and the result is free from prejudice by personal favor or partisan influence. It secures for the position applied for the best qualifications attainable among the competing applicants. It is an effectual protection from the pressure of importunity, which under any other course pursued largely exacts the time and attention of appointing officers, to their great detriment in the discharge of other official duties, preventing the abuse of the service for the mere furtherance of private or party purposes, and leaving the employee of the government, freed from the obligations imposed by patronage, to depend solely upon merit for retention and advancement, and with this constant incentive to exertion and improvement.

These invaluable results have been attained in a high degree in the offices where the rules for appointment by competitive examination have been applied.

A method which has so approved itself by experimental tests at points where such tests may be fairly considered conclusive should be extended to all subordinate positions under the government. I believe that a strong and growing public sentiment demands immediate measures for securing and enforcing the highest possible efficiency in the civil service and its protection from recognized abuses, and that the experience referred to has demonstrated the feasibility of such measures.

The examinations in the custom-houses and post-offices have been held under many embarrassments and without provision for compensation for the extra labor performed by the officers who have conducted them, and whose commendable interest in the improvement of the public service has induced this devotion of time and labor without pecuniary reward. A continuance of these labors gratuitously ought not to be expected, and without an appropriation by Congress for compensation it is not practicable to extend the system of examinations generally throughout the civil service. It is also highly important that all such examinations should be conducted upon a uniform system and under general supervision. Section 1753 of the Revised Statutes authorizes the president to prescribe the regulations for admission to the civil service of the United States, and for this purpose to employ suitable persons to conduct the requisite inquiries with reference to "the fitness of each candidate, in respect to age, health, character, knowledge, and ability for the branch of service into which he seeks to enter"; but the law is practically inoperative for want of the requisite appropriation.

I therefore recommend an appropriation of $25,000 per annum to meet the expenses of a commission, to be appointed by the president in accordance with the terms of this section, whose duty it shall be to devise a just, uniform, and efficient system of competitive examinations and to supervise the application of the same throughout the entire civil service of the government. I am persuaded that the facilities which such a commission will afford for testing the fitness of those who apply for office will not only be as welcome a relief to members of Congress as it will be to the president and heads of departments, but that it will also greatly tend to remove the causes of embarrassment which now inevitably and constantly attend the conflicting claims of patronage between the legislative and executive departments. The most effectual check upon the pernicious competition of influence and official favoritism in the bestowal of office will be the substitution of an open competition of merit between the applicants, in which everyone can make his own record with the assurance that his success will depend upon this alone.

I also recommend such legislation as, while leaving every officer as free as any other citizen to express his political opinions and to use his means for their advancement, shall also enable him to feel as safe as any private citizen in refusing all demands upon his salary for political purposes. A law which should thus guarantee true liberty and justice to all who are engaged in the public service, and likewise contain stringent provisions against the use of official authority to coerce the political action of private citizens or of official subordinates, is greatly to be desired.

The most serious obstacle, however, to an improvement of the civil service, and especially to a reform in the method of appointment and removal, has been found to be the practice, under what is known as the spoils system, by which the appointing power has been so largely encroached upon by members of Congress. The first step in the reform of the civil service must be a complete divorce between Congress and the executive in the matter of appointments. The corrupting doctrine that "to the victors belong the spoils" is inseparable from Congressional patronage as the established rule and practice of parties in power. It comes to be understood by applicants for office and by the people generally that Representatives and senators are entitled to disburse the patronage of their respective districts and states. It is not necessary to recite at length the evils resulting from this invasion of the executive functions. The true principles of government on the subject of appointments to office, as stated in the national conventions of the leading parties of the country, have again and again been approved by the American people, and have not been called in question in any quarter. These authentic expressions of public opinion upon this all-important subject are the statement of principles that belong to the constitutional structure of the government. . . .

Believing that to reform the system and method of civil service in our county is one of the highest and most imperative duties of statesmanship, and that it can be permanently done only by the cooperation of the legislative and executive departments of the government, I again commend the whole subject to your considerate attention. . . .

Courtesy of Library of Congress

James Abram Garfield

James Abram Garfield

1881–1881

JAMES A. GARFIELD was "the best stump and platform speaker the Republican Party had," wrote the journalist E. V. Smalley in 1881. "He had a strong, far-reaching voice, pitched in the middle key, a dignified, manly presence, and an abundance of the quality which . . . we call personal magnetism. His manner in his speech was first engaging by reason of its frankness and moderation, and afterward impressive by its earnestness and vigor. At the climax of a speech he gathered up all the forces of statement and logic he had been marshaling, and hurled them upon his listeners with tremendous force."

A good part of Garfield's life was spent in public speaking—first in the pulpit and the classroom, then from the podium. He was born in the Western Reserve (now Ohio) to an impoverished farm family who had recently joined the Disciples of Christ. As a student at the sect's academy, he co-founded a debating society, where he developed a combative style, declaring in his diary: "I love agitation and investigation and glory in defending unpopular truth against popular error." During his years as a teacher and principal at the school, he traveled to two or three churches every Sunday to preach. One of his classmates at Williams College remembered how Garfield's "massive figure, commanding, self-confident manner, and magnificent bursts of fiery eloquence, won and held the attention of his audience from the moment he opened his lips."

Garfield caught the interest of local Republican leaders when he engaged in a week-long debate with a freethinker over the validity of the biblical account of creation. Elected to the Ohio Senate in 1860, he quickly became the party's leading campaigner, making some 50 speeches on behalf of Lincoln's presidential bid. According to Margaret Leech, his biographer, "The families of rural America, flocking in thousands to hear speechmaking of every description, were looking for drama as well as guidance, hoping to find in the licensed emotionalism of the orator some release from lives that were always hard and often starved and barren. Good-looking young 'Gaffield,' with his throbbing voice and impassioned rhetoric, repaid his hearers for the hardships of a long outing."

In 1863, after two years' service as an officer in the Union army, General Garfield entered the House of Representatives, where he spent the next 17 years as a leader of the Republicans. Here he abandoned his grandiloquent, heavily mannered speaking style in favor of a plain, logical, direct style modeled on Lincoln's. James G. Blaine, his colleague in the House and later Garfield's secretary of state, observed in his eulogy for Garfield: "He was a pre-eminently fair and candid man in debate, took no petty advantage, stooped to no unworthy methods, avoided personal allusions, rarely appealed to prejudice, did not seek to inflame passion. . . . When the history of this period shall be impartially written, when war legislation, measures of reconstruction, protection of human rights, amendments to the Constitution, maintenance of public credit, steps toward specie resumption, true theories of revenue, may be reviewed . . . the speeches of Garfield will be estimated at their true value, and will be found to comprise a vast magazine of fact and argument, of clear analysis and sound conclusion." Laborious preparation and constant study contributed to Garfield's success in both parliamentary oratory and constitutional arguments before the Supreme Court. He also delivered addresses to all kinds of civic groups and private societies (although he refused an invitation by Elizabeth Cady Stanton to address a women's suffrage convention).

The best-known incident in Garfield's oratorical career is probably apocryphal. When the news of Lincoln's assassination broke, Garfield was on Wall Street in New York, where an angry crowd threatened to wreck the offices of a newspaper that had been sympathetic to the South. Garfield is said to have raised his arm and pacified the crowd with this call: "Fellow citizens! Clouds and darkness are round about Him! His pavilion is dark waters and thick clouds of the skies! Justice and judgment are the establishment of His throne! Mercy and truth shall go before His face! Fellow citizens! God reigns, and the government at Washington still lives!"

By the middle of Hayes's administration, Garfield's speeches, especially on monetary policy, had brought him enough national attention to suggest that he might make a viable presidential candiate in 1880. He made one of his finest off-the-cuff speeches at the Republican convention, where he stood on a table to appeal for party unity. On the 36th ballot the badly divided party finally chose Garfield over Ulysses S. Grant. During the campaign Garfield made numerous speeches but not on political subjects, though it was his opinion that "if it were the custom, it would insure better nominations." In the four months that he occupied the White House, he spent most of his time in a fight with the Stalwart wing of the Republicans over control of cabinet and civil service posts. He was shot in July by a deranged Stalwart sympathizer and died two months later, leaving Chester Alan Arthur in the presidency.

Revolution in Congress

Washington, D.C.
March 29, 1879

THE SPEECH that made Garfield a contender for the Republican nomination, excerpted below, was delivered during a debate in the House over an army appropriations bill to which the Democrats had attached a rider barring the use of federal troops to supervise Southern elections. Garfield put on an unusually emotional display of shouting and fistbrandishing as he charged the Democrats with attempting to hold the government hostage to their demands. The Republicans, divided by infighting, were temporarily united by Garfield's attack, and half a million copies of the speech were printed and distributed to enthusiastic Northern voters.

Mr. Chairman, I have no hope of being able to convey to the members of this House my own conviction of the very great gravity and solemnity of the crisis which this decision of the chair [overruling a point of order that objected to the rider] and of the Committee of the Whole has brought upon this country. I wish I could be proved a false prophet in reference to the result of this action. I wish I could be overwhelmed with the proof that I am utterly mistaken in my views. But no view I have ever taken has entered more deeply and more seriously into my conviction than this, that the House has to-day resolved to enter upon a revolution against the Constitution and government of the United States. I do not know that this intention exists in the minds of half the representatives who occupy the other side of this hall; I hope it does not; I am ready to believe it does not exist to any great extent; but I affirm that the consequence of the programme just adopted, if persisted in, will be nothing less than the total subversion of this government. Let me in the outset state, as carefully as I may, the precise situation.

At the last session, all our ordinary legislative work was done in accordance with the usages of the House of Senate, except the passage of two bills. Two of the 12 great appropriation bills for the support of the government were agreed to in both houses as to every matter of detail concerning the appropriations proper. We were assured by the committees of conference in both bodies that there would be no difficulty in adjusting all differences in reference to the amounts of money to be appropriated and the objects of their appropriation. But the House of Representatives proposed three measures of distinctly independent legislation; one upon the army appropriation bill, and two upon the legislative appropriation bill. The three grouped together are briefly these: first, the substantial modification of certain sections of the law relating to the use of the army; second, the repeal of the jurors' test oath; and third, the repeal of the laws regulating elections of members of Congress. These three propositions of legislation were insisted upon by the House, but the Senate refused to adopt them. So far it was an ordinary proceeding, one which occurs frequently in all legislative bodies. The Senate said to us through their conferees, "We are ready to pass the appropriation bills; but we are unwilling to pass as riders the three legislative measures you ask us to pass." Thereupon the House, through its conference committee, made the following declaration,—and in order that I may do exact justice, I read from the speech of the distinguished senator from Kentucky, on the report of the second conference committee on the Legislative, Executive, and Judicial Appropriation Bill:—"The Democratic conferees on the part of the House seemed determined that unless those rights were secured to the people"—alluding to the three points I have named—"in the bills sent to the Senate, they would refuse, under their constitutional right, to make appropriations to carry on the government, if the dominant majority in the Senate insisted upon the maintenance of these laws and *refused to consent* to their repeal."

Then, after stating that, if the position they had taken compelled an extra session, the new Congress would offer the repealing bills separately, and forecasting what would happen when the new House should be under no necessity of coercing the Senate, he said:—

> If, however, the president of the United States, in the exercise of the power vested in him, should see fit to veto the bills thus presented to him, . . . then I have no doubt those same amendments will be again made part of the appropriation bills, and it will be for the president to determine whether he will block the wheels of government and refuse to accept necessary appropriations rather than allow the representatives of the people to repeal odious laws which they regard as subversive of their rights and privileges. . . . Whether that course is right or wrong, it will be adopted, and I have no doubt adhered to, no matter what happens with the appropriation bills.

That was the proposition made by the Democracy in Congress at the close of the Congress now dead.

Another distinguished senator, Mr. Thurman, of Ohio—and I may properly refer to senators of a Congress not now in existence—reviewing the situation, declared in still more succinct terms: "We claim the right, which the House of Commons in England established after two centuries of contest, to say that we will not grant the money of the people unless there is a redress of grievances."

These propositions were repeated with various degrees of vehemence by the majority in the House. The majority in the Senate and the minority on this floor expressed the deepest anxiety to avoid an extra session and to avert the catastrophe thus threatened,—the stoppage of the government. They pointed out the danger to the country and its business interests of an extra session of Congress, and expressed their willingness to consent to any compromise consistent with their views of duty which should be offered,—not in the way of coercion, but in the way of fair adjustment,—and asked to be met in a spirit of just accommodation on the other side. Unfortunately no spirit of adjustment was manifested in reply to their advances. In consequence the new Congress is assembled, and, after 10 days of caucus deliberation, the House of Representatives has resolved, substantially,

to reaffirm the positions of its predecessors, except that the suggestion of Senator Beck to offer the independent legislation in a separate bill has been abandoned. By a construction of the rules of the House far more violent than any heretofore given, a part of this independent legislation is placed on the pending bill for the support of the army; and this House has determined to begin its career by the extremest form of coercive legislation. In my remarks to-day I shall confine myself almost exclusively to the one phase of the controversy presented in this bill. . . .

The question, Mr. Chairman, may be asked, Why make any special resistance to certain repealing clauses in this bill, which a good many gentlemen on this side declared at the last session that they cared but little about, and regarded as of very little practical importance, because for years there had been no actual use for any part of the laws proposed to be repealed, and they had no expectation there would be any? It may be asked, Why make any controversy on either side? So far as we are concerned, Mr. Chairman, I desire to say this. We recognize the other side as accomplished parliamentarians and strategists, who have adopted with skill and adroitness their plan of assault. You have placed in the front one of the least objectionable of your measures; but your whole programme has been announced, and we reply to your whole order of battle. The logic of your position compels us to meet you as promptly on the skirmish line as afterward when our intrenchments are assailed; and therefore, at the outset, we plant our case upon the general ground where we have chosen to defend it.

And here, sir, I wish to make a brief digression, which I hope no gentleman will consider as controversial or personal. I had occasion at a late hour of the last Congress to say something on what may be called the voluntary element in our institutions. I spoke of the distribution of the powers of government: first, to the nation; second, to the states; and, third, the reservation of powers to the people themselves. I called attention to the fact, that under our form of government the most precious rights that men can possess on this earth are not delegated to the nation nor to the states, but are reserved to the third estate, the people themselves. I called attention to the interesting fact that lately the chancellor of the

German Empire had made the declaration that it was the chief object of the existence of the German government to defend and maintain the religion of Jesus Christ—an object in reference to which our Congress is absolutely forbidden by the Constitution to legislate at all. Congress can establish no religion,—indeed, can make no law respecting it, because in the view of our fathers, the founders of our government, religion was too precious a right to be intrusted by delegation to any government. Its maintenance was left to the voluntary action of the people themselves. In continuation of that thought, I wish now to speak of the voluntary element inside our government,—a topic that I have not heard discussed, but one which appears to me of vital importance in any comprehensive view of our institutions.

Mr. Chairman, viewed from the standpoint of a foreigner, our government may be said to be the feeblest on the earth; from our standpoint, and with our experience, it is the mightiest. But why would a foreigner call it the feeblest? He can point out a half-dozen ways in which it can be destroyed without violence. Of course, all governments may be overturned by the sword; but there are several ways in which ours may be annihilated without the firing of a gun. For example, if the people of the United States should say we will elect no House of Representatives—of course this is a violent supposition—but suppose they do not, is there any remedy? Does our Constitution provide any remedy whatever? In two years there would be no House of Representatives; of course no support of the government, and no government. Suppose, again, the states should say, through their legislatures, we will elect no senators. Such abstention alone would absolutely destroy this government; and our system provides no process of compulsion to prevent it.

Again, suppose the two houses were assembled in their usual order, and a majority of one in this body, or in the Senate, should firmly band themselves together and say they would vote to adjourn the moment the hour of meeting arrives, and continue so to vote at every session during our two years of existence, the government would perish, and there is no provision of the Constitution to prevent it. Or, again, if a majority of one in either body should declare that they would vote down, and should vote down, every bill to support the government by appropriations, can you find in the whole range of our judicial or our executive authority any remedy whatever? A senator or a representative is free, and may vote "no" on every proposition. Nothing but his oath and his honor restrains him. Not so with executive and judicial officers. They have no power to destroy this government. Let them travel an inch beyond the line of the law, and they fall within the power of impeachment. But against the people who create representatives, against the legislatures who create senators, against senators and representatives in these halls, there is no power of impeachment; there is no remedy, if by abstention or by adverse votes they refuse to support the government.

At a first view, it would seem strange that a body of men so wise as our fathers were should have left one whole side of their fabric open to these deadly assaults; but on a closer view of the case their wisdom will appear. What was their reliance? This: the sovereign of this nation, the Godcrowned and Heaven-anointed sovereign, in whom resides "the state's collected will," and to whom we all owe allegiance, is the people themselves. Inspired by love of country, and by a deep sense of obligation to perform every public duty—being themselves the creators of all the agencies and forces to execute their own will, and choosing from themselves their representatives to express that will in the forms of law—it would have been like a suggestion of suicide to assume that any of these great voluntary powers would be turned against the life of the government. Public opinion was trusted as a power amply able, and always willing, to guard all the approaches on that side of the Constitution against any assault on the life of the nation.

Up to this hour our sovereign has never failed us. There had never been such a refusal to exercise those primary functions of sovereignty as either to endanger or cripple the government; nor have the majority of the representatives of that sovereign, in either house of Congress, ever before announced their purpose to use their voluntary powers for its destruction. And now, for the first time in our history—and I will add, for the first time for at least two centuries in the history of any English-speaking nation—it is suggested and threatened that these voluntary powers of Congress shall be used for the destruction of the government. I want it distinctly understood that the proposition which I read at the beginning of my remarks, and which is the programme announced to the American people to-day, is this: that if this House cannot have its own way in certain matters not connected with appropriations, it will so use or refrain from using its voluntary powers as to destroy the government.

Now, Mr. Chairman, it has been said on the other side, that, when a demand for the redress of grievances is made, the authority that runs the risk of stopping and destroying the government is the one that resists the redress. Not so. If gentlemen will do me the honor to follow my thought for a moment more, I trust I shall make this denial good.

Our theory of law is free consent. That is the granite foundation of our whole superstructure. Nothing in this republic can be law without consent—the free consent of the House, the free consent of the Senate, the free consent of the executive, or, if he refuse it, the free consent of two-thirds of these bodies. Will any man deny that? Will any man challenge a letter of the statement that free consent is the foundation of all our institutions? And yet the programme announced two weeks ago was, that, if the Senate refused to consent to the demand of the House, the government should stop. And the proposition was then, and the proposition is now, that, although there is not a Senate to be coerced, there is still a third independent branch of the legislative power of the government whose consent is to be coerced at the peril of the destruction of this government; that is, if the president, in the discharge of his duty, shall exercise his plain constitutional right to refuse his consent to this proposed legislation, the Congress will so use its voluntary powers as to destroy the government. This is the proposition which we confront; and we denounced it as revolution.

It makes no difference, Mr. Chairman, what the issue is. If it were the simplest and most inoffensive proposition in the world, yet if you demand, as a measure of coercion, that it shall be adopted against the free consent prescribed in the Constitution, every fair-minded man in America is bound to resist you as much as though his own life depended upon his resistance. Let it be understood that I am not arguing the merits of any one of the three amendments. I am discussing the proposed method of legislation; and I declare that it is against the Constitution of our country. It is revolutionary to the core, and is destructive of the fundamental principle of American liberty, the free consent of all the powers that unite to make laws. In opening this debate, I challenge all comers to show a single instance in our history where this consent has been thus coerced. This is the great, the paramount issue, which dwarfs all others into insignificance.

I now turn aside from the line of my argument, for a moment, to say that it is not a little surprising that our friends on the other side should have gone into this great contest on so weak a cause as the one embraced in the pending amendment to this bill. Victor Hugo said, in his description of the battle of Waterloo, that the struggle of the two armies was like the wrestling of two giants, when a chip under the heel of either might determine the victory. It may be that this amendment is the chip under your heel, or it may be that it is the chip on our shoulder; as a chip, it is of small account to you or to us; but when it represents the integrity of the Constitution, and is assailed by revolution, we fight for it as for a Kohinoor of purest water.

The distinguished and venerable gentleman from Georgia spoke of the law which is sought to be repealed as "odious and dangerous." It has been denounced as a piece of partisan war legislation, to enable the army to control elections. Do gentlemen know its history? Do they know whereof they affirm? Who made this law which is denounced as so great an offence as to justify the destruction of the government rather than let it remain on the statute-book? Its first draft was introduced into the Senate by a prominent Democrat from the state of Kentucky, Mr. Powell, who made an able speech in its favor. It was reported against by a Republican committee of that body, whose printed report I hold in my hand. It encountered weeks of debate, was amended and passed, and then came into the House. Every Democrat present in the Senate voted for it on its final passage. Every senator who voted against it was a Republican. No Democrat voted against it. . . . The bill then came to the House of Representatives, and was put upon its passage here. How did the vote stand in this body? Every Democrat present at the time in the House of Representatives of the 38th Congress voted for it. The total vote in its favor in the House was 113, and of these 58 were Democrats. And who were they? The magnates of the party. . . . Every Democrat of conspicuous name and fame in that House voted for the bill, and not one against it. There were but few Republicans who voted against it. I was one of the few. Thaddeus Stevens and Judge Kelley were others.

But what was the controversy? What was the object of the bill? It was alleged by Democrats that in those days of war there were interferences with the proper freedom of elections in the border states. We denied the charge; but lest there might be some infraction of the freedom of elections, many Republicans, unwilling that there should be even the semblance of interference with that freedom, voted for it. This law is an expression of their purpose that the army should not be used at any election except for the purpose of keeping the peace. Those Republicans who voted against it did so on the ground that there was no cause for such legislation; that it was a slander upon the government and the army to say that they were interfering with the proper freedom of elections. I was among that number. . . . The proposition now is, that after 14 years have passed, and not one petition from one American citizen has come to us asking that this law be repealed, while not one memorial has found its way to our desks complaining of the law, so far as I have heard, the Democratic Representatives declare that, if they are not permitted to force upon the other house and upon the executive, against their consent, the repeal of a law that Democrats made, this refusal will be considered a sufficient ground for starving this government to death. That is the proposition which we denounced as revolution. . . .

MR. FERNANDO WOOD. *I desire to submit another question to my friend. It is whether, in 1865, at the time of the passage of this law, when the war had not really subsided,—whether there was not in a portion of this country a condition of things rendering it almsot impossible to exercise the elective franchise unless there was some degree of military interference. And further, whether, after the experience of 14 years since the war has subsided, that gentleman is yet prepared to continue a war measure in a time of profound peace in this country.*

No doubt the patriotic gentleman from New York took all these things into consideration when he voted for this law; and I may have been unpatriotic in voting against it at that time; but he and I must stand by our records, as they were made. Let it be understood that I am not discussing the merits of this law. I have merely turned aside from the line of my argument to show the inconsistency of the other side in proposing to stop the government if they cannot force the repeal of a law which they themselves helped to make. I am discussing a method of revolution against the Constitution now proposed by this House, and to that issue I hold gentlemen in this debate, and challenge them to reply.

And now, Mr. Chairman, I ask the forbearance of gentlemen on the other side while I offer a suggestion, which I make with reluctance. They will bear me witness that I have, in many ways, shown my desire that the wounds of the war should be healed; that the grass which has grown green over the graves of the dead of both armies might symbolize the returning spring of friendship and peace between citizens who were lately in arms against each other. But I am compelled by the conduct of the other side to refer to a chapter of our recent history.

The last act of Democratic domination in this Capitol, 18 years ago, was striking and dramatic, perhaps heroic. Then the Democratic Party said to the Republicans, "If you elect the man of your choice president of the United States, we will shoot your government to death"; but the people of this country, refusing to be coerced by threats or violence, voted as they pleased, and lawfully elected Abraham Lincoln president. Then your leaders, though holding a majority in the other branch of Congress, were heroic enough to withdraw from their seats and fling down the gage of mortal battle. We called it rebellion; but we recognized it as courageous and manly to avow your purpose, take all the risks, and fight it out in the open field. Notwithstanding your utmost efforts to destroy it, the government was saved. Year by year, since the war ended, those who resisted you have come to believe that you have finally renounced your purpose to destroy, and are willing to maintain the government. In that belief you have been permitted to return to power in the two houses. Today, after 18 years of defeat, the book of your domination is again opened, and your first act awakens every unhappy memory, and threatens to destroy the confidence which your professions of patriotism inspired. You turned down a leaf of the history that recorded your last act of power in 1861, and you have now signalized your return to power by beginning a second chapter at the same page; not this time by an heroic act that declares war on the battlefield; but you say, if all the legislative powers of the government do not consent to let you tear certain laws out of the statute-book, put there by the will of the people, if you cannot coerce an independent branch of this government, not that you will shoot our government to death, as you tried to do before, but that you will starve the government to death. Between death on the field and death by starvation, I do not know that the American people will see any great difference. The end, if successfully reached, will be death in either case. Gentlemen, you have it in your power to kill this government; you have it in your power, by withholding these two bills, to smite the nerve-centres of our Constitution with the paralysis of death; and you have declared your purpose to do this, if you cannot break down that fundamental principle of free consent which, up to this hour, has always ruled in the legislation of this government.

MR. JOSEPH J. DAVIS. *Do I understand the gentleman to say that the refusal to permit the army at the polls will be the death of this government? That is the logic of the gentleman's argument, if it means anything. But we say that it will be the preservation of this government to keep the military power from destroying liberty at the polls.*

I have too much respect for the intellect of the gentleman from North Carolina to believe that he thinks that is my argument. He does not say he thinks so. On the contrary, I am sure that every clearminded man on this floor knows that such is not my argument. The position on the other side is simply this: that unless some independent branch of the legislative power of his government is forced against its will to vote for or to approve what it does not freely consent to, you will use the voluntary power in your hands to starve the government to death.

MR. DAVIS. *Will the gentleman permit me to ask him another question? Do I understand him to assume that we are forcing some branch of the government to do what it does not wish to do? How do we know that, or how does the*

gentleman know it? Does the gentleman, when he speaks of "the government," mean to say that it is not the government of the majority, or does he assume that the majority is on his side?

I am perfectly protected against the suggestion of the gentleman. I read in the outset declarations of leading members of his party, in both branches of Congress, asserting this programme, and declaring the intention of carrying it through to the end, in spite of the Senate and in spite of an executive veto, which they anticipate. The method here proposed invites, possibly compels, a veto. . . .

In leaving this topic, let me ask, What would you have said if, in 1861, the Democratic members of the Senate, being then a majority of that body, instead of taking the heroic course and going out to battle, had simply said, "We will put on an appropriation bill an amendment declaring the right of any state to secede from the Union at pleasure, and forbidding the president or any officer of the army or navy of the United States from interfering with any state in its work of secession"? Suppose they had said to the president, "Unless you consent to the incorporation of this provision in an appropriation bill, we will refuse supplies to the government." Perhaps they could then have killed the government by starvation; but even in the madness of that hour the leaders of rebellion did not think it worthy of their manhood to put their fight on that dishonorable ground. They planted themselves on the higher plane of battle, and fought it out to defeat. Now, by a method which the wildest secessionist scorned to adopt, it is proposed to make this new assault upon the life of the republic.

Gentlemen, we have calmly surveyed this new field of conflict; we have tried to count the cost of the struggle, as we did that of 1861 before we took up your gage of battle. Though no human foresight could forecast the awful loss of blood and treasure, yet in the name of liberty and union we accepted the issue and fought it out to the end. We made the appeal to our august sovereign, to the omnipotent public opinion of America, to determine whether the Union should perish at your hands. You know the result. And now lawfully, in the exercise of our right as representatives, we take up the gage you have this day thrown down, and appeal again to our common sovereign to determine whether you shall be permitted to destroy the principle of free consent in legislation under the threat of starving the government to death.

We are ready to pass these bills for the support of the government at any hour when you will offer them in the ordinary way, by the methods prescribed by the Constitution. If you offer your other propositions as separate measures, we will meet you in the fraternal spirit of fair debate and will discuss their merits. Some of your measures many of us will vote for in separate bills. But you shall not coerce any independent branch of this government, even by the threat of starvation, to surrender its lawful powers until the question has been appealed to the sovereign and decided in your favor. On this ground we plant ourselves, and here we will stand to the end.

Let it be remembered that the avowed object of this new revolution is to destroy all the defences which the nation has placed around its ballot-box to guard the fountain of its own life. You say that the United States shall not employ even its civil power to keep peace at the polls. You say that the marshals shall have no power to arrest either rioters or criminals who seek to destroy the freedom and purity of the ballot-box. I remind you that you have not always shown this great zeal in keeping the civil officers of the general government out of the states. Only six years before the war, your law authorized marshals of the United States to enter all our hamlets

and households to hunt for fugitive slaves. Not only that, it empowered the marshals to summon the *posse comitatus,* to command all bystanders to join in the chase and aid in remanding the fleeing slave to eternal bondage. And your Democratic attorney-general, in an opinion published in 1854, declared that the marshal of the United States might summon to his aid the whole able-bodied force of his precinct, all bystanders, including not only the citizens generally, "but any and all organized armed forces, whether militia of the state, or officers, soldiers, sailors, and marines of the United States," to join in the chase and hunt down the fugitive. Now, gentleman, if, for the purpose of making eternal slavery the lot of an American, you could send your marshals, summon your posse, and use the armed force of the United States, with what face or grace can you tell us that this government cannot lawfully employ the same marshals, with their armed posse of citizens, to maintain the purity of our own elections and keep the peace at our own polls?

You have made the issue, and we have accepted it. In the name of the Constitution, and on behalf of good government and public justice, we make the appeal to our common sovereign. For the present, I refrain from discussing the merits of the election laws. I have sought only to state the first fundamental ground of our opposition to this revolutionary method of legislation by coercion.

Inaugural Address

Washington, D.C.

March 4, 1881

DESPITE GARFIELD'S experience as a preacher and speaker, the prospect of writing a formal composition daunted him, and the thought of writing an inaugural address gave him blinding headaches. It was not finished until 2:30 A.M. on the morning of the inauguration, and Garfield's personal secretary stayed up for the rest of the night copying it over. Uncharacteristically dry and platitudinous (except for some vigorous remarks on black suffrage and education), this was Garfield's only speech as president.

. . . We stand to-day upon an eminence which overlooks a hundred years of national life—a century crowded with perils, but crowned with the triumphs of liberty and law. Before continuing the onward march, let us pause on this height, for a moment, to strengthen our faith and to renew our hope by a glance at the pathway along which our people have travelled.

It is now three days more than a hundred years since the adoption of the first written Constitution of the United States—the Articles of Confederation and Perpetual Union. The new republic was then beset with dangers on every hand. It had not conquered a place in the family of nations. The decisive battle of the war for independence, whose centennial anniversary will soon be gratefully celebrated at Yorktown, had not yet been fought. The colonists were struggling, not only against the armies of a great nation, but against the settled opinions of mankind; for the world did not then believe that the supreme authority of government could be safely intrusted to the guardianship of the people themselves.

We cannot overestimate the fervent love of liberty, the intelligent courage, and the saving common-sense with which our fathers made the great experiment of self-government. When they found, after a short trial, that the confederacy of states was too weak to meet the necessities of a vigorous and expanding republic, they boldly set it aside, and in its stead established a national Union, founded directly upon the will of the people, and endowed with full power of self-preservation and with ample authority for the accomplishment of its great objects.

Under this Constitution the boundaries of freedom have been enlarged, the foundations of order and peace have been strengthened, and the growth of our people in all the better elements of national life has vindicated the wisdom of the founders and given new hope to their descendants. Under this Constitution our people long ago made themselves safe against danger from without, and secured for their mariners and flag equality of rights on all the seas. Under this Constitution, 25 states have been added to the Union, with constitutions and laws, framed and enforced by their own citizens, to secure the manifold blessings of local self-government. The jurisdiction of this Constitution now covers an area 50 times greater than that of the original 13 states, and a population 20 times greater than that of 1780.

The supreme trial of the Constitution came at last under the tremendous pressure of civil war. We ourselves are witnesses that the Union emerged from the blood and fire of that conflict purified and made stronger for all the beneficent purposes of good government.

And now, at the close of this first century of growth, with the inspirations of its history in their hearts, our people have lately reviewed the condition of the nation, passed judgment upon the conduct and opinions of political parties, and registered their will concerning the future administration of the government. To interpret and to execute that will, in accordance with the Constitution, is the paramount duty of the executive.

Even from this brief review it is manifest that the nation is resolutely facing to the front, resolved to employ its best energies in developing the great possibilities of the future. Sacredly preserving whatever has been gained to liberty and good government during the century, our people are determined to leave behind them all those bitter controversies concerning things which have been irrevocably settled, and the further discussion of which can only stir up strife and delay the onward march.

The supremacy of the nation and its laws should be no longer a subject of debate. That discussion which for half a century threatened the existence of the Union was closed at last in the high court of war by a decree from which there is no appeal, that the Constitution and the laws made in pursuance thereof are, and shall continue to be, the supreme law of the land, binding alike upon the states and upon the people. This decree does not disturb the autonomy of the states, nor interfere with any of their necessary rights of local self-government, but it does fix and establish the permanent supremacy of the Union.

The will of the nation, speaking with the voice of battle and through the amended Constitution, has fulfilled the great promise of 1776, by proclaiming "liberty throughout the land to all the inhabitants thereof."

The elevation of the Negro race from slavery to the full rights of citizenship is the most important political change we have known since the adoption of the Constitution of 1787. No thoughtful man can fail to appreciate its beneficent effects upon our institutions and people. It has freed us from the perpetual danger of war and dissolution. It has added immensely to the moral and industrial forces of our people. It has liberated the master, as well as the slave, from a relation which wronged and enfeebled both. It has surrendered to their own guardianship the manhood of more than five millions of people, and has opened to each one of them a career of freedom and usefullness. It has given new inspiration to the power of self-help in both races, by making labor more honorable to the one and more necessary to the other. The influence of this force will grow greater and bear richer fruit with the coming years.

No doubt this great change has caused serious disturbance to our Southern communities. This is to be deplored, though it was perhaps unavoidable. But those who resisted the change should remember that, under our institutions, there was no middle ground for the Negro race between slavery and equal citizenship. There can be no permanent disfranchised peasantry in the United States. Freedom can never yield its fulness of blessings so long as the law or its administration places the smallest obstacle in the pathway of any virtuous citizen.

The emancipated race has already made remarkable progress. With unquestioning devotion to the Union, with a patience and gentleness not born of fear, they have "followed the light as God gave them to see the light." They are rapidly laying the material foundation of self-support, widening their circle of intelligence, and beginning to enjoy the blessings that gather around the homes of the industrious poor. They deserve the generous encouragement of all good men. So far as my authority lawfully extends, they shall enjoy the full and equal protection of the Constitution and the laws.

The free enjoyment of equal suffrage is still in question, and a frank statement of the issue may aid its solution. It is alleged that in many communities Negro citizens are practically denied the freedom of the ballot. In so far as the truth of this allegation is admitted, it is answered that in many places honest local government is impossible if the mass of uneducated Negroes are allowed to vote. These are grave allegations. So far as the latter is true, it is the only palliation that can be offered for opposing the freedom of the ballot. Bad local government is certainly a great evil, which ought to be prevented; but to violate the freedom and sanctity of the suffrage is more than an evil—it is a crime which, if persisted in, will destroy the government itself. Suicide is not a remedy. If in other lands it be high-treason to compass the death of the king, it shall be counted no less a crime here to strangle our sovereign power and stifle its voice.

It has been said that unsettled questions have no pity for the repose of nations. It should be said with the utmost emphasis, that this question of the suffrage will never give repose or safety to the state or to the nation until each within its own jurisdiction makes and keeps the ballot free and pure by the strong sanctions of the law.

But the danger which arises from ignorance in the voter cannot be denied. It covers a field far wider than that of Negro suffrage and the present condition of the race. It is a danger that lurks and hides in the sources and fountains of power in every state. We have no standard by which to measure the disaster that may be brought upon us by ignorance and vice in the citizen, when joined to corruption and fraud in the suffrage.

The voters of the Union, who make and unmake constitutions, and upon whose will hang the destinies of our governments, can transmit their supreme authority to no successors save the coming generation of voters, who are the sole heirs of sovereign power. If that generation comes to its inheritance blinded by ignorance and corrupted by vice, the fall of the republic will be certain and remediless. The census has already sounded the alarm in the appalling figures which mark how dangerously high the tide of illiteracy has risen among our voters and their children. To the South this question is of supreme importance. But the responsibility for the existence of slavery did not rest upon the South alone. The nation itself is responsible for the extension of the suffrage, and is under special obligations to aid in removing the illiteracy which it has added to the voting population. For the North and South alike there is but one remedy. All the constitutional power of the nation and of the states, and all the volunteer forces of the people, should be summoned to meet this danger by the saving influence of universal education.

It is the high privilege and sacred duty of those now living to educate their successors, and fit them, by intelligence and virtue, for the inheritance which awaits them. In this beneficent work sections and races should be forgotten, and partisanship should be unknown. Let our people find a new meaning in the divine oracle which declares that "a little child shall lead them"; for our own little children will soon control the destinies of the republic.

My countrymen, we do not now differ in our judgment concerning the controversies of past generations, and 50 years hence our children will not be divided in their opinions concerning our controversies. They will surely bless their fathers and their fathers' God that the Union was preserved, that slavery was overthrown, and that both races made equal before the law. We may hasten or we may retard, but we cannot prevent, the final reconciliation. Is it not possible for us now to make a truce with time by anticipating and accepting its inevitable verdict?

Enterprises of the highest importance to our moral and material well-being invite us, and offer ample employment for our best powers. Let all our people, leaving behind them the battlefields of dead issues, move forward, and, in the strength of liberty and the restored Union, win the grander victories of peace. The prosperity which now prevails is without a parallel in our history. Fruitful seasons have done much to secure it, but they have not done all. The preservation of the public credit and the resumption of specie payments so successfully attained by the administration of my predecessors have enabled our people to secure the blessings which the seasons brought.

By the experience of commercial nations in all ages, it has been found that gold and silver afford the only safe foundation for a monetary system. Confusion has recently been created by variations in the relative value of the two metals. But I confidently believe that arrangements can be made between the leading commercial nations which will secure the general use of both metals. Congress should provide that the compulsory coinage of silver now required by law may not disturb our monetary system, and that neither metal shall be driven out of circulation. If possible, such an adjustment should be made that the purchasing power of every coined dollar will be exactly equal to its debt-paying in all the markets of the world.

The chief duty of the national government, in connection with the currency of the country, is to coin money and to declare its value. Grave doubts have been entertained whether Congress is authorized by the Constitution to make any form of paper money a legal tender. The present issue of United States notes has been sustained by the necessities of war; but such paper should depend for its value and currency upon its convenience in use and its prompt redemption in coin at the will of the holder, and not upon its compulsory circulation. These notes are not money, but promises to pay money. If the holders demand it, the promise should be kept.

The refunding of the national debt at a lower rate of interest should be accomplished without compelling the withdrawal of the national bank notes, and thus disturbing the business of the country.

I venture to refer to the position I have occupied on financial questions during a long service in Congress, and to say that time and experience have strengthened the opinions I have so often expressed on these subjects. The finances of the government shall suffer no detriment which it may be possible for my administration to prevent.

The interests of agriculture deserve more attention from the government than they have yet received. The farms of the United States afford homes and employment for more than one half our people, and furnish much the larger part of all our exports. As the government lights our coasts for the protection of mariners and for the benefit of commerce, so it should give to the tillers of the soil the best lights of practical science and experience.

Our manufactures are rapidly making us industrially independent, and are opening to capital and labor new and profitable fields of employment. Their steady and healthy growth should still be maintained. Our facilities for transportation should be promoted by the continued improvement of our harbors and great interior waterways, and by the increase of our tonnage on the ocean.

The development of the world's commerce has led to an urgent demand for shortening the great sea voyage around Cape Horn by constructing ship-canals or railways across the isthmus which unites the continents. Various plans to this end have been suggested, and will need consideration; but none of them has been sufficiently matured to warrant the United States in extending pecuniary aid. The subject, however, is one which will immediatly engage the attention of the government, with a view to a thorough protection of American interests. We shall urge no narrow policy, nor seek peculiar or exclusive privileges in any commercial route; but, in the language of my predecessor, I believe it to be "the right and duty of the United States to assert and maintain such supervision and authority over any inter-oceanic canal across the isthmus that connects North and South America as will protect our national interests."

The Constitution guarantees absolute religious freedom. Congress is prohibited from making any law respecting an establishment of religion, or prohibiting the free exercise thereof. The territories of the United States are subject to the direct legislative authority of Congress; and hence the general government is responsible for the violation of the Constitution in any of them. It is therefore a reproach to the government, that, in the most populous of the territories, the constitutional guarantee is not enjoyed by the people, and the authority of Congress is set at naught. The Mormon Church not only offends the moral sense of mankind by sanctioning polygamy, but prevents the administration of justice through the ordinary instrumentalities of law.

In my judgment, it is the duty of Congress, while respecting to the uttermost the conscientious convictions and religious scruples of every citizen, to prohibit within its jurisdiction all criminal practices, especially of the class which destroy the family relations and endanger social order. Nor can any ecclesiastical organization be safely permitted to usurp in the smallest degree the functions and powers of the national government.

The civil service can never be placed on a satisfactory basis until it is regulated by law. For the good of the service itself, for the protection of those who are intrusted with the appointing power against the waste of time and obstruction to the public business caused by the inordinate pressure for place, and for the protection of incumbents against intrigue and wrong, I shall, at the proper time, ask Congress to fix the tenure of the minor offices of the several executive departments, and to prescribe the grounds upon which removals shall be made during the terms for which incumbents have been appointed.

Finally, acting always within the authority and limitations of the Constitution, invading neither the rights of the states nor the reserved rights of the people, it shall be the purpose of my administration to maintain the authority of the nation in all places within its jurisdiction; to enforce obedience to all the laws of the Union in the interests of all the people; to demand rigid economy in all expenditures of the government; and to require the honest and faithful service of all executive officers, remembering that the offices were created, not for the benefit of incumbents or their supporters, but for the service of the government.

And now, fellow citizens, I am about to assume the great trust which you have committed to my hands. I appeal to you for that earnest and thoughtful support which makes this government in fact, as it is in law, a government of the people.

I shall greatly rely upon the wisdom and patriotism of Congress, and of those who may share with me the responsibilities and duties of administration. And, above all, upon our efforts to promote the welfare of this great people and their government, I reverently invoke the support and blessings of Almighty God.

Courtesy of Library of Congress

Chester Alan Arthur

Chester Alan Arthur

1881–1885

CHESTER A. ARTHUR's entrance into the White House after the death of James A. Garfield replaced a highly visible president with a very private one. Where Garfield had been a great orator and campaigner and a veteran congressman, Arthur was a professional politician who worked behind the scenes as the ally of more prominent men; he never ran for elective office. When he became president, he was best known as one of the Republicans' ablest spoilsmen, a loyal functionary whose career had been built on the exploitation of patronage.

Arthur was the son of a Vermont Baptist minister. His involvement with the Republican Party dates from the early 1850s, when he was a young lawyer sympathetic to abolition. During the Civil War he served as quartermaster-general of New York State. He became head of the state Republican committee and the chief lieutenant of Senator Roscoe Conkling, leader of the party's Stalwart wing. In 1871, as a reward for his services to Ulysses S. Grant's reelection campaign, Arthur was appointed collector of the Customhouse of the port of New York City, a job that put him in control of $840 million in customs receipts each year. He was fired in 1878 by President Hayes on charges of corruption, but this scandal did not prevent his being added to the Garfield ticket in 1880 to pay off the Conkling forces for their support. To the surprise of his former colleagues, Arthur, once he was sworn in to the presidency in September 1881, had an attack of conscience and became an advocate of civil service reform.

During his career as a Republican power broker, Arthur naturally preferred not to attract publicity. He made an exception on February 11, 1880, when, as vice president–elect, he attended a Republican banquet in New York City and made a comical speech that alluded to the party's purchase of votes in the key state of Indiana. Reformers and editorialists registered their outrage, and Arthur was careful to make no more indiscreet remarks.

Even as president the patrician Arthur kept his distance from the press and the public, giving few interviews or speeches. "When I have anything to say to the country," he told reporters, "I shall probably say it in black and white." The activist minister Henry Ward Beecher remarked that Arthur had "proved himself to be a safe man in the administration of government, prudent in counsel, felicitous in all that he has written, wise in the selection of men for office, with remarkable capacity for silence, and yet frank when he speaks." The president had an additional reason to avoid public appearances after 1882, when he was diagnosed as having Bright's disease, a debilitating kidney ailment that he succeeded in keeping secret. A single day of ceremonies for the opening of the Brooklyn Bridge in 1883 cost him a week in recovery. Despite his exhaustion, however, Arthur presided over a full schedule of state banquets, balls, receptions, and parties in the White House and partly because he enjoyed them and partly to maintain public confidence in his health. He died two years after leaving office.

Dedication of the Washington National Monument

Washington, D.C.

December 6, 1884

THE WASHINGTON MONUMENT obelisk, begun in 1848, stood half-finished for more than 20 years while the capital struggled with secession, war, and Reconstruction. Congress appropriated funds for its completion in 1876, and the capstone was finally set in 1884. Arthur gave one of his rare speeches at the ceremony.

Before the dawn of the century whose eventful years will soon have faded into the past—when death had but lately robbed this republic of its most beloved and illustrious citizen—the Congress of the United States pledged the faith of the nation that in this city, bearing his honored name and then as now the seat of the general government, a monument should be erected "to commemorate the great events of his military and political life." The stately column that stretches heavenward from the plain whereon we stand bears witness to all who behold it that the covenant which our fathers made their children have fulfilled.

In the completion of this great work of patriotic endeavor there is abundant cause for national rejoicing, for while this structure shall endure it shall be to all mankind a steadfast token of the affectionate and reverent regard in which this people continue to hold the memory of Washington. Well may he ever keep the foremost place in the hearts of his countrymen. The faith that never faltered; the wisdom that was broader and deeper than any learning taught in schools; the courage that shrank from no peril and was dismayed by no defeat; the loyalty that kept all selfish purpose subordinate to the demands of patriotism and honor; the sagacity that displayed itself in camp and cabinet alike, and above all that harmonious union of moral and intellectual qualities which has never found its parallel among men—these are the attributes of character which the intelligent thought of this century ascribes to the grandest figure of the last. But other and more eloquent lips than mine will today rehearse to you the story of his noble life and its glorious achievements. To myself has been assigned a simpler and moral formal duty, in fulfilment of which I do now, as president of the United States and in behalf of the people, receive this monument from the hands of its builder and declare it dedicated from this time forth to the immortal name and memory of George Washington.

Statue of Chester A. Arthur in New York City.
(Courtesy of PresidentsUSA.net)

Courtesy of Library of Congress

Grover Cleveland

Grover Cleveland

1885–1889

1893–1897

THE 1884 PRESIDENTIAL race produced the first Democratic administration since that of James Buchanan more than two decades earlier. The winner, Grover Cleveland, was that rare thing in politics, a thoroughly honest man who refused to compromise principles in exchange for votes, sometimes to the detriment of his own future or that of his party. His opposition to protective tariffs on foreign goods cost him reelection in 1888, when he won the popular but lost the electoral vote. Warned that his views on sound money might cost him the Democratic nomination in 1892, he answered: "Damn the nomination. I will say what I think is right." He was renominated anyway and was returned to the White House, only to find himself blamed by both parties for the country's economic depression.

The son of a Presbyterian minister, Cleveland was a lawyer in Buffalo, New York, until 1881, when he became the city's reform mayor. His success in cleaning up corruption brought him the governorship of New York in 1883 and the Democratic nomination the following year—a remarkably rapid rise to national attention.

Stolid and unimaginative, Cleveland was scrupulous about carrying out the duties of the executive in conformance with his limited view of it. Public speaking was one of those duties, although it was repugnant to him. He once told a friend, "I have never made a speech or written a letter except in compliance with importunities which I could not resist from those engaged in some good work, or from those entitled to claim my consideration on party grounds. . . . I often have a pretty blue time of it, and confess to frequent spells of resentment, but I shall get on in a fashion." After his final departure from the White House he continued to receive frequent invitations to speak to civic, philanthropic, and professional associations and was appointed the first Stafford Little Lecturer in Public Affairs at Princeton University, delivering one or two lectures a year.

In speechmaking as in everything else, Cleveland was ploddingly diligent, studying his subject at length and revising by hand, then testing out the final project on his advisers. One of these, George F. Parker, quotes him as admitting that "in no respect can I be said to have a style which either so stands out that I can be recognized by it—and this one of the tests—or that has in it any of the elements of eloquence and polish, also a necessary quality. . . . I simply say what is in my mind and seems to be necessary at the time, and say it in my blundering way and that is all there is to it." But if he did not have an elegant style, he did have one unusual oratorical skill—the ability to deliver hour-long speeches entirely from memory. Reporters listening to his speeches with preprinted copies in their hands were surprised to find that he could negotiate them without a single slip. He had the equally useful capacity for forgetting the speeches immediately afterward.

Cleveland did little of his own campaigning, leaving that to the regular party orators. According to Parker, "he had the quality now somewhat unfashionable: reticence." The slogan of his first presidential race, "The Public Office Is a Public Trust," was coined by William C. Hudson, a reporter commissioned to write a campaign biography, who condensed the phrase from sentiments expressed by Cleveland in previous speeches. But Cleveland, as his biographer Robert McElroy noted, "continued to express this, his most cherished conviction, not in the words of Hudson's brilliant slogan, but in ponderous phrases of his own which he persisted in considering better because longer."

Against Bimetallism

From the First Annual Message to Congress
Washington, D.C.
December 8, 1885

CLEVELAND'S FIRST annual message to Congress contained a plea for the repeal of the Bland-Allison Act of 1878, which directed the government to purchase and coin silver as well as gold in order to increase the supply of money in circulation—a goal eagerly sought by the debt-ridden farmers of the West and South. Cleveland, along with many bankers and businessmen, was convinced that adoption of a dual standard would cause inflation and produce a disastrous loss of confidence in American currency. By 1895, in his second term, so much gold had been lost from the Treasury through the exchange of silver certificates that he made an unpopular deal to buy $65 million in gold from a group of private financiers headed by J. Pierpont Morgan. The economic depression that gripped the nation when Cleveland returned for his second term was not alleviated by the repeal of additional silver purchase legislation, and when, at the 1892 presidential convention, the Democrats adopted a prosilver platform, Cleveland backed a splinter group in the hope that it would split the party and ensure the election of the monometallist Republican William McKinley.

. . . Nothing more important than the present condition of our currency and coinage can claim your attention.

Since February 1878, the government has, under the compulsory provisions of law, purchased silver bullion and coined the same at the rate of more than $2,000,000 every month. By this process up to the present date 215,759,431 silver dollars have been coined.

A reasonable appreciation of a delegation of power to the general government would limit its exercise, without express restrictive words, to the people's needs and the requirements of the public welfare.

Upon this theory the authority to "coin money" given to Congress by the Constitution, if it permits the purchase by the government of bullion for coinage in any event, does not justify such purchase and coinage to an extent beyond the amount needed for a sufficient circulating medium.

The desire to utilize the silver product of the country should not lead to a misuse or the perversion of this power.

The necessity for such an addition to the silver currency of the nation as is compelled by the silver-coinage act is negatived by the fact that up to the present time only about 50,000,000 of the silver dollars so coined have actually found their way into circulation, leaving more than 165,000,000 in the possession of the government, the custody of which has entailed a considerable expense for the construction of vaults for its deposit. Against this latter amount there are outstanding silver certificates amounting to about $93,000,000.

Every month two millions of gold in the public Treasury are paid out for two millions or more of silver dollars, to be added to the idle mass already accumulated.

If continued long enough, this operation will result in the substitution of silver for all the gold the government owns applicable to its general purposes. . . . The proportion of silver and its certificates received by the government will probably increase as time goes on, for the reason that the nearer the period approaches when it will be obliged to offer silver in payment of its obligations the greater inducement there will be to hoard gold against depreciation in the value of silver or for the purpose of speculating.

This hoarding of gold has already begun.

When the time comes that gold has been withdrawn from circulation, then will be apparent the difference between the real value of the silver dollar and a dollar in gold, and the two coins will part company. Gold, still the standard of value and necessary in our dealings with other countries, will be at a premium over silver; banks which have substituted gold for the deposits of their customers may pay them with silver bought with such gold, thus making a handsome profit;

rich speculators will sell their hoarded gold to their neighbors who need it to liquidate their foreign debts, at a ruinous premium over silver, and the laboring men and women of the land, most defenseless of all, will find that the dollar received for the wage of their toil has sadly shrunk in its purchasing power. It may be said that the latter result will be but temporary, and that ultimately the price of labor will be adjusted to the change; but even if this takes place the wage-worker cannot possibly gain, but must inevitably lose, since the price he is compelled to pay for his living will not only be measured in a coin heavily depreciated and fluctuating and uncertain in its value, but this uncertainty in the value of the purchasing medium will be made the pretext for an advance in prices beyond that justified by actual depreciation.

The words uttered in 1834 by Daniel Webster in the Senate of the United States are true today:

> The very man of all others who has the deepest interest in a sound currency, and who suffers most by mischievous legislation in money matters, is the man who earns his daily bread by his daily toil.

The most distinguished advocate of bimetallism, discussing our silver coinage, has lately written:

> No American citizen's hand has yet felt the sensation of cheapness, either in receiving or expending the silver-act dollars.

And those who live by labor or legitimate trade never will feel that sensation of cheapness. However plenty silver dollars may become, they will not be distributed as gifts among the people; and if the laboring man should receive four depreciated dollars where he now receives but two, he will pay in the depreciated coin more than double the price he now pays for all the necessaries and comforts of life.

Those who do not fear any disastrous consequences arising from the continued compulsory coinage of silver as now directed by law, and who suppose that the addition to the currency of the country intended as its result will be a public benefit, are reminded that history demonstrates that the point is easily reached in the attempt to float at the same time two sorts of money of different excellence when the better will cease to be in general circulation. The hoarding of gold which has already taken place indicates that we shall not escape the usual experience in such cases. So if this silver coinage be continued we may reasonably expect that gold and its equivalent will abandon the field of circulation to silver alone. This of course must produce a severe contraction of our circulating medium, instead of adding to it.

It will not be disputed that any attempt on the part of the government to cause the circulation of silver dollars worth 80 cents side by side with gold dollars worth 100 cents, even within the limit that legislation does not run counter to the laws of trade, to be successful must be seconded by the confidence of the people that both coins will retain the same purchasing power and be interchangeable at will. A special effort has been made by the secretary of the Treasury to increase the amount of our silver coin in circulation; but the fact that a large share of the limited amount thus put out has soon returned to the public Treasury in payment of duties leads to the belief that the people do not now desire to keep it in hand, and this, with the evident disposition to hoard gold, gives rise to the suspicion that there already exists a lack of confidence among the people touching our financial processes. There is certainly not enough silver now in circulation to cause uneasiness, and the whole amount coined and now on hand might after a time be absorbed by the people without apprehension; but it is the ceaseless stream that threatens to overflow the land which causes fear and uncertainty. . . .

The so-called debtor class, for whose benefit the continued compulsory coinage of silver is insisted upon, are not dishonest because they are in debt, and they should not be suspected of a desire to jeopardize the financial safety of the country in order that they may cancel their present debts by paying the same in depreciated dollars. Nor should it be forgotten that it is not the rich nor the money lender alone that must submit to such a readjustment, enforced by the government and their debtors. The pittance of the widow and the orphan and the incomes of helpless beneficiaries of all kinds would be disastrously reduced. The depositors in savings banks and in other institutions which hold in trust the savings of the poor, when their little accumulations are scaled down to meet the new order of things, would in their distress painfully realize the delusion of the promise made to them that plentiful money would improve their condition.

We have now on hand all the silver dollars necessary to supply the present needs of the people and to satisfy those who from sentiment wish to see them in circulation, and if their coinage is suspended they can be readily obtained by all who desire them. If the need of more is at any time apparent, their coinage may be renewed.

That disaster has not already overtaken us furnishes no proof that danger does not wait upon a continuation of the present silver coinage. We have been saved by the most careful management and unusual expedients, by a combination of fortunate conditions, and by a confident expectation that the course of the government in regard to silver coinage would be speedily changed by the action of Congress.

Prosperity hesitates upon our threshold because of the dangers and uncertainties surrounding this question. Capital timidly shrinks from trade, and investors are unwilling to take the chance of the questionable shape in which their money will be returned to them, while enterprise halts at a risk against which care and sagacious management do not protect.

As a necessary consequence, labor lacks employment and suffering and distress are visited upon a portion of our fellow citizens especially entitled to the careful consideration of those charged with the duties of legislation. No interest appeals to us so strongly for a safe and stable currency as the vast army of the unemployed.

I recommend the suspension of the compulsory coinage of silver dollars, directed by the law passed in February, 1878. . . .

The Centennial of the Constitution

Philadelphia, Pennsylvania
September 17, 1887

CLEVELAND TRAVELED to Philadelphia in September 1887 to participate in the centennial celebrations for the Constitution and took advantage of the occasion to make three speeches in one day. His remarks at the official ceremony, reprinted below, quoted extensively from Benjamin Franklin and looked forward to the bicentennial year of 1987 in the hope that 200 years of interpretation and amendment would leave intact the liberties guaranteed by the Constitution.

I deem it a very great honor and pleasure to participate in these impressive exercises.

Every American citizen should on this centennial day rejoice in his citizenship.

He will not find the cause of his rejoicing in the antiquity of his country, for among the nations of the earth his stands with the youngest. He will not find it in the glitter and the pomp that bedeck a monarch and dazzle abject and servile subjects, for in his country the people themselves are rulers. He will not find it in the story of bloody foreign conquests, for his government has been content to care for its own domain and people.

He should rejoice because the work of framing our Constitution was completed 100 years ago today, and also because, when completed, it established a free government. He should rejoice because this Constitution and government have survived so long, and also because they have survived so many blessings and have demonstrated so fully the strength and value of popular rule. He should rejoice in the wondrous growth and achievements of the past 100 years, and also in the glorious promise of the Constitution through centuries to come.

We shall fail to be duly thankful for all that was done for us 100 years ago, unless we realize the difficulties of the work then in hand, and the dangers avoided in the task of forming "a more perfect Union" between disjointed and inharmonious states, with interests and opinions radically diverse and stubbornly maintained.

The perplexities of the convention which undertook the labor of preparing our Constitution are apparent in these earnest words of one of the most illustrious of its members:

The small progress we have made after four or five weeks of close attendance and continued reasonings with each other, our different sentiments on almost every question—several of the last producing as many noes as yeas— is, methinks, a melancholy proof of the imperfection of the human understanding. We, indeed, seem to feel our own want of political wisdom, since we have been running about in search of it. We have gone back to ancient history for models of government, and examined the different forms of those republics which, having been formed with the seeds of their own dissolution, now no longer exist. In this situation of this assembly, groping as it were in the dark to find political truth, and scarce able to distinguish it when presented to us, how has it happened, sir, that we have not heretofore once thought of humbly applying to the Father of Light to illuminate our understandings?

And this wise man, proposing to his fellows that the aid and blessing of God should be invoked in their extremity, declared:

I have lived, sir, a long time, and the longer I live the more convincing proofs I see of the truth that God governs in the affairs of men. And if a sparrow cannot fall to the ground without his notice, is it probable that an empire can rise without his aid? We have been assured, sir, in the sacred writings that "except the Lord build the house, they labor in vain that build it." I firmly believe this; and I also believe that without his concurring aid we shall succeed in this political building no better than the builders of Babel. We shall be divided by our little partial, local interests, our projects will be confounded, and we ourselves shall become a reproach and a byword down to future ages; and, what is worse, mankind may hereafter, from this unfortunate instance, despair of establishing governments by human wisdom, and leave it to chance, war, and conquest.

In the face of all discouragements, the fathers of the republic labored on for four long, weary months, in alternate hope and fear, but always with rugged resolve, never faltering in a sturdy endeavor sanctified by a prophetic sense of the value to posterity of their success, and always with unflinching faith in the principles which make the foundation of a government by the people.

At last their task was done. It is related that upon the back of the chair occupied by Washington as the president of the convention a sun was painted, and that as the delegates were signing the completed Constitution one of them said: "I have often and often, in the course of the session, and in the solicitude of my hopes and fears as to its issue, looked at that sun behind the president without being able to tell whether it was rising or setting. But now at length I know that it is a rising and not a setting sun."

We stand today on the spot where this rising sun emerged from political night and darkness; and in its own bright meridian light we mark its glorious way. Clouds have sometimes obscured its rays, and dreadful storms have made us fear; but God has held it in its course, and through its life-giving warmth has performed his latest miracle in the creation of this wonderous land and people.

As we look down the past century to the origin of our Constitution, as we contemplate its trials and its triumphs, as we realize how completely the principles upon which it is based have met every national peril and every national need, how devoutly should we confess, with Franklin, "God governs in the affairs of men"; and how solemn should be the reflection that to our hands is committed this ark of the people's covenant, and that ours is the duty to shield it from impious hands. We receive it sealed with the tests of a century. It has been found sufficient in the past; and in all the future years it will be found sufficient, if the American people are true to their sacred trust.

Another centennial day will come, and millions yet unborn will inquire concerning our stewardship and the safety of their Constitution. God grant that they may find it unimpaired; and as we rejoice in the patriotism and devotion of those who lived a hundred years ago, so may others who follow us rejoice in our fidelity and in our jealous love for constitutional liberty.

The Tariff Message

From the Third Annual Message to Congress
Washington, D.C.
December 6, 1887

OF ALL CLEVELAND'S reform interests, he came to be most adamant on the issue of the tariff. Congress's unwillingness to reduce protective tariffs on many goods, including war tariffs dating from the Civil War, had produced a yearly $100 million surplus in the Treasury. The result was a restriction of circulating money that hurt the economy, as well as artifically high prices that hurt the public. To focus attention on the problem, Cleveland broke precedent by giving over his annual message of 1887 to the single subject of tariff reform. By so doing, said his biographer, Allan Nevins, "Cleveland displayed again the hard practical sense which served him so much better than brilliancy or profundity." Reprinted in newspapers throughout the country, the message, said Nevins, "was read as no presidential messages since Lincoln's had been." The reform magazine *The Nation* called it "the most courageous document that has been sent from the Executive Mansion since the close of the Civil War." But Cleveland failed to follow up on his initiative, and tariff revisions enacted during his second term were gutted by protectionist amendments.

You are confronted at the threshold of your legislative duties with a condition of the national finances which imperatively demands immediate and careful consideration.

The amount of money annually exacted, through the operation of present laws, from the industries and necessities of the people largely exceeds the sum necessary to meet the expenses of the government.

When we consider that the theory of our institutions guarantees to every citizen the full enjoyment of all the fruits of his industry and enterprise, with only such deduction as may be his share toward the careful and economical maintenance of the government which protects him, it is plain that the exaction of more than this is indefensible extortion and a culpable betrayal of American fairness and justice. This wrong inflicted upon those who bear the burden of national taxation, like other wrongs, multiplies a brood of evil consequences. The public Treasury, which should only exist as a conduit conveying the people's tribute to its legitimate objects of expenditure, becomes a hoarding place for money needlessly withdrawn from trade and the people's use, thus crippling our national energies, suspending our country's development, preventing investment in productive enterprise, threatening financial disturbance, and inviting schemes of public plunder.

This condition of our Treasury is not altogether new, and it has more than once of late been submitted to the people's representatives in the Congress, who alone can apply a remedy. And yet the situation still continues, with aggravated incidents, more than ever presaging financial convulsion and widespread disaster.

It will not do to neglect this situation because its dangers are not now palpably imminent and apparent. They exist none the less certainly and await the unforeseen and unexpected occasion when suddenly they will be precipitated upon us. . . .

In the present state of legislation the only pretense of any existing executive power to restore at this time any part of our surplus revenues to the people by its expenditure consists in the supposition that the secretary of the Treasury may enter the market and purchase the bonds of the government not yet due, at a rate of premium to be agreed upon. . . .

In considering the question of purchasing bonds as a means of restoring to circulation the surplus money accumulating in the Treasury, it should be borne in mind that premiums must of course be paid upon such purchase, that there may be a large part of these bonds held as investments which cannot be purchased at any price, and that combinations among holders who are willing to sell may unreasonably enhance the cost of such bonds to the government. . . .

The proposition to deposit the money held by the government in banks throughout the country for use by the people is, it seems to me, exceedingly objectionable in principle, as establishing too close a relationship between the operations of the government Treasury and the business of the country and too extensive a commingling of their money, thus fostering an unnatural reliance in private business upon public funds. If this scheme should be adopted, it should only be done as a temporary expedient to meet an urgent necessity. Legislative and executive effort should generally be in the opposite direction, and should have a tendency to divorce, as much and as fast as can be safely done, the Treasury Department from private enterprise.

Of course it is not expected that unnecessary and extravagant appropriations will be made for the purpose of avoiding the accumulation of an excess of revenue. Such expenditure, besides the demoralization of all just conceptions of public duty which it entails, stimulates a habit of reckless improvidence not in the least consistent with the mission of our people or the high and beneficent purposes of our government.

I have deemed it my duty to thus bring to the knowledge of my countrymen, as well as to the attention of their representatives charged with the responsibility of legislative relief, the gravity of our financial situation. The failure of the Congress heretofore to provide against the dangers which it was quite evident the very nature of the difficulty must necessarily produce caused a condition of financial distress and apprehension since your last adjournment which taxed to the utmost all the authority and expedients within executive control; and these appear now to be exhausted. If disaster results from the continued inaction of Congress, the responsibility must rest where it belongs.

Though the situation thus far considered is fraught with danger which should be fully realized, and though it presents features of wrong to the people as well as peril to the country, it is but a result growing out of a perfectly palpable and apparent cause, constantly reproducing the same alarming circumstances—a congested national Treasury and a depleted monetary condition in the business of the country. It need hardly be stated that while the present situation demands a remedy, we can only be saved from a like predicament in the future by the removal of its cause.

Our scheme of taxation, by means of which this needless surplus is taken from the people and put into the public Treasury, consists of a tariff or duty levied upon importations from abroad and internal— revenue taxes levied upon the consumption of tobacco and spirituous and malt liquors. It must be conceded that none of the things subjected to internal—revenue taxation are, strictly speaking, necessaries. There appears to be no just complaint of this taxation by the consumers of these articles, and there seems to be nothing so well able to bear the burden without hardship to any portion of the people.

But our present tariff laws, the vicious, inequitable, and illogical source of unnecessary taxation, ought to be at once revised and amended. These laws, as their primary and plain effect, raise the price to consumers of all articles imported and subject to duty by precisely the sum paid for such duties. Thus the amount of the duty measures the tax paid by those who purchase for use these imported articles. Many of these things, however, are raised or manufactured in our own country, and the duties now levied upon foreign goods and products are called protection to these home manufactures, because they render it possible for those of our people who are manufacturers to make these taxed articles and sell them for a price equal to that demanded for the imported goods that have paid customs duty. So it happens that while comparatively a few use the imported articles, millions of our people, who never used and never saw any of the foreign products, purchase and use things of the same kind made in this country, and pay therefore nearly or quite the same enhanced price which the duty adds to the imported articles. Those who buy imports pay the duty charged thereon into the public Treasury, but the great majority of our citizens, who buy domestic articles of the same class, pay a sum at least approximately equal to this duty to the home manufacturer. This reference to the operation of our tariff laws is not made by way of instruction, but in order that we may be constantly reminded of the manner in which they impose a burden upon those who consume domestic products as well as those who consume imported articles, and thus create a tax upon all our people.

It is not proposed to entirely relieve the country of this taxation. It must be extensively continued as the source of the government's income; and in a readjustment of our tariff the interests of American labor engaged in manufacture should be carefully considered, as well as the preservation of our manufacturers. It may be called protection or by any other name, out relief from the hardships and dangers of our present tariff laws should be devised with especial precaution against imperiling the existence of our manufacturing interests. But this existence should not mean a condition which, without regard to the public welfare or a national exigency, must always insure the realization of immense profits instead of moderately profitable returns. As the volume and diversity of our national activities increase, new recruits are added to those who desire a continuation of the advantages which they conceive the present system of tariff taxation directly affords them. So stubbornly have all efforts to reform the present condition been resisted by those of our fellow citizens thus engaged that they can hardly complain of the suspicion, entertained to a certain extent, that there exists an organized combination all along the line to maintain their advantage.

We are in the midst of centennial celebrations, and with becoming pride we rejoice in American skill and ingenuity, in American energy and enterprise, and in the wonderful natural advantages and resources developed by a century's national growth. Yet when an attempt is made to justify a scheme which permits a tax to be laid upon every consumer in the land for the benefit of our manufacturers, quite beyond a reasonable demand for governmental regard, it suits the purposes of advocacy to call our manufactures infant industries still needing the highest and greatest degree of favor and fostering care that can be wrung from federal legislation.

It is also said that the increase in the price of domestic manufactures resulting from the present tariff is necessary in order that higher wages may be paid to our workingmen employed in manufactories than are paid for what is called the pauper labor of Europe. All will acknowledge the force of an argument which involves the welfare and liberal compensation of our laboring people. Our labor is honorable in the eyes of every American citizen; and as it lies at the foundation of our development and progress, it is entitled, without affectation or hypocrisy, to the utmost

regard. The standard of our laborers' life should not be measured by that of any other country less favored, and they are entitled to their full share of all our advantages.

By the last census it is made to appear that of the 17,392,099 of our population engaged in all kinds of industries 7,670,493 are employed in agriculture, 4,074,238 in professional and personal service (2,934,876 of whom are domestic servants and laborers), while 1,810,256 are employed in trade and transportation and 3,837,112 are classed as employed in manufacturing and mining.

For present purposes, however, the last number given should be considerably reduced. Without attempting to enumerate all, it will be conceded that there should be deducted from those which it includes 375,143 carpenters and joiners, 285,401 milliners, dressmakers, and seamstresses, 172,726 blacksmiths, 133,756 tailors and tailoresses, 102,473 masons, 76,241 butchers, 41,309 bakers, 22,083 plasterers, and 4,891 engaged in manufacturing agricultural implements, amounting in the aggregate to 1,214,023, leaving 2,623,089 persons employed in such manufacturing industries as are claimed to be benefited by a high tariff.

To these the appeal is made to save their employment and maintain their wages by resisting a change. There should be no disposition to answer such suggestions by the allegations that they are in a minority among those who labor, and therefore should forego an advantage in the interest of low prices for the majority. Their compensation, as it may be affected by the operation of tariff laws, should at all times be scrupulously kept in view; and yet with slight reflection they will not overlook the fact that they are consumers with the rest; that they too have their own wants and those of their families to supply from their earnings, and that the price of the necessaries of life, as well as the amount of their wages, will regulate the measure of their welfare and comfort.

But the reduction of taxation demanded should be so measured as not to necessitate or justify either the loss of employment by the working man or the lessening of his wages; and the profits still remaining to the manufacturer after a necessary readjustment should furnish no excuse for the sacrifice of the interests of his employees, either in their opportunity to work or in the diminution of their compensation. Nor can the worker in manufactures fail to understand that while a high tariff is claimed to be necessary to allow the payment of remunerative wages, it certainly results in a very large increase in the price of nearly all sorts of manufactures, which, in almost countless forms, he needs for the use of himself and his family. He receives at the desk of his employer his wages, and perhaps before he reaches his home is obliged, in a purchase for family use of an article which embraces his own labor, to return in the payment of the increase in price which the tariff permits the hardearned compensation of many days of toil.

The farmer and the agriculturist, who manufacture nothing, but who pay the increased price which the tariff imposes upon every agricultural implement, upon all he wears, and upon all he uses and owns, except the increase of his flocks and herds and such things as his husbandry produces from the soil, is invited to aid in maintaining the present situation; and he is told that a high duty on imported wool is necessary for the benefit of those who have sheep to shear, in order that the price of their wool may be increased. They, of course, are not reminded that the farmer who has no sheep is by this scheme obliged, in his purchases of clothing and woolen goods, to pay a tribute to his fellow farmer as well as to the manufacturer and merchant, nor is any mention made of the fact that the sheep owners themselves and their households must wear clothing and use other articles manufactured from the wool they sell at tariff prices, and thus as consumers must return their share of this increased price to the tradesman. . . . When it must be conceded that the increase of the cost of living caused by such tariff becomes a burden upon those with moderate means and the poor, the employed and unemployed, the sick and well, and the young and old, and that it constitutes a tax which with relentless grasp is fastened upon the clothing of every man, woman, and child in the land, reasons are suggested why the removal or reduction of this duty should be included in a revision of our tariff laws.

In speaking of the increased cost to the consumer of our home manufactures resulting from a duty laid upon imported articles of the same description, the fact is not overlooked that competition among our domestic producers sometimes has the effect of keeping the price of their products below the highest limit allowed by such duty. But it is notorious that this competition is too often strangled by combinations quite prevalent at this time, and frequently called trusts, which have for their object the regulation of the supply and price of commodities made and sold by members of the combination. The people can hardly hope for any consideration in the operation of these selfish schemes.

If, however, in the absence of such combination, a healthy and free competition reduces the price of any particular dutiable article of home production below the limit which it might otherwise reach under our tariff laws, and if with such reduced price its manufacture continues to thrive, it is entirely evident that one thing has been discovered which should be carefully scrutinized in an effort to reduce taxation.

The necessity of combination to maintain the price of any commodity to the tariff point furnishes proof that someone is willing to accept lower prices for such commodity and that such prices are remunerative; and lower prices produced by competition prove the same thing. Thus where either of these conditions exist a case would seem to be presented for an easy reduction of taxation.

The considerations which have been presented touching our tariff laws are intended only to enforce an earnest recommendation that the surplus revenues of the government be prevented by the reduction of our customs duties, and at the same time to emphasize a suggestion that in accomplishing this purpose we may discharge a double duty to our people by granting to them a measure of relief from tariff taxation in quarters where it is most needed and from sources where it can be most fairly and justly accorded.

Nor can the presentation made of such considerations be with any degree of fairness regarded as evidence of unfriendliness toward our manufacturing interests or of any lack of appreciation of their value and importance.

These interests constitute a leading and most substantial element of our national greatness and furnish the proud proof of our country's progress. But if in the emergency that presses upon us our manufacturers are asked to surrender something for the public good and to avert disaster, their patriotism, as well as a grateful recognition of advantages already afforded, should lead them to willing cooperation. No demand is made that they shall forego all the benefits of governmental regard; but they cannot fail to be admonished of their duty, as well as their enlightened self-interest and safety, when they are reminded of the fact that financial panic and collapse, to which the present condition tends, afford no greater shelter or protection to our manufacturers than to other important enterprises. Opportunity for safe, careful, and deliberate reform is now offered; and none of us should be unmindful of a time when an abused and irritated people, heedless of those who have resisted timely and reasonable relief, may insist upon a radical and sweeping rectification of their wrongs.

The difficulty attending a wise and fair revision of our tariff laws is not underestimated. It will require on the part of the Congress great labor and care, and especially a broad and national contemplation of the subject and a patriotic disregard of such local and selfish claims as are unreasonable and reckless of the welfare of the entire country.

Under our present laws more than 4,000 articles are subject to duty. Many of these do not in any way compete with our own manufactures, and many are hardly worth attention as subjects of revenue. A considerable reduction can be made in the aggregate by adding them to the free list. The taxation of luxuries presents no features of hardship; but the necessaries of life used and consumed by all the people, the duty upon which adds to the cost of living in every home, should be greatly cheapened.

The radical reduction of the duties imposed upon raw material used in manufactures, or its free importation, is of course an important factor in any effort to reduce the price of these necessaries. It would not only relieve them from the increased cost caused by the tariff on such material, but the manufactured product being thus cheapened that part of the tariff now laid upon such product, as a compensation to our manufacturers for the present price of raw material, could be accordingly modified. Such reduction or free importation would serve besides to largely reduce the revenue. It is not apparent how such a change can have any injurious effect upon our manufacturers. On the contrary, it would appear to give them a better chance in foreign markets with the manufacturers of other countries, who cheapen their wares by free material. Thus our people might have the opportunity of extending their sales beyond the limits of home consumption, saving them from the depression, interruption in business, and loss caused by a glutted domestic market and affording their employees more certain and steady labor, with its resulting quiet and contentment.

The question thus imperatively presented for solution should be approached in a spirit higher than partisanship and considered in the light of that regard for patriotic duty which should characterize the action of those intrusted with the weal of a confiding people. But the obligation to declared party policy and principle is not wanting to urge prompt and effective action. Both of the great political parties now represented in the government have by repeated and authoritative declarations condemned the condition of our laws which permit the collection from the people of unnecessary revenue, and have in the most solemn manner promised its correction; and neither as citizens nor partisans are our country-men in a mood to condone the deliberate violation of these pledges.

Our progress toward a wise conclusion will not be improved by dwelling upon the theories of protection and free trade. This savors too much of bandying epithets. It is a condition which confronts us, not a theory. Relief from this condition may involve a slight reduction of the advantages which we award our home productions, but the entire withdrawal of such advantages should not be contemplated. The question of free trade is absolutely irrelevant, and the persistent claim made in certain quarters that all the efforts to relieve the people from unjust and unnecessary taxation are schemes of so-called free traders is mischievous and far removed from any consideration for the public good.

The simple and plain duty which we owe the people is to reduce taxation to the necessary expenses of an economical operation of the government and to restore to the business of the country the money which we hold in the Treasury through the perversion of governmental powers. These things can and should be done with safety to all our industries, without danger to the opportunity for remunerative labor which our workingmen need, and with benefit to them and all our people by cheapening their means of subsistence and increasing the measure of their comforts. . . .

The Principles of Democracy

Philadelphia, Pennsylvania
January 8, 1891

DESPITE CLEVELAND'S protestations during Benjamin Harrison's term that he did not wish to run again for the presidency, he made frequent speeches denouncing the McKinley Tariff of 1890 and the extravagant expenditures of what came to be known as the Billion Dollar Congress. On Jackson Day 1891—the anniversary of the Battle of New Orleans—he spoke to the Young Men's Democratic Association of Philadelphia on the meaning of democracy and the proper role of government and political parties in preserving it. Robert McElroy wrote that the speech "was one of his ablest addresses . . . calculated . . . to rally [the Democrats] to the defense of the great reforms for which his name stood. . . . The speech represents near-eloquence and in some passages, weeded of the usual Clevelandesque verbiage, we catch the gleam of real eloquence."

As I rise to respond to the sentiment which has been assigned to me, I cannot avoid the impression made upon my mind by the announcement of the words true democracy. I believe them to mean a sober conviction or conclusion touching political topics, which, formulated into a political belief or creed, inspires a patriotic performance of the duties of citizenship. I am satisfied that the principles of this belief or creed are such as underlie our free institutions, and that they may be urged upon our fellow countrymen, because, in their purity and integrity, they accord with the attachment of our people for their government and their country. A creed based upon such principles is by no means discredited because illusions and perversions temporarily prevent their popular acceptance, any more than it can be irretrievably shipwrecked by mistakes made in its name or by its prostitution to ignoble purposes. When illusions are dispelled, when misconceptions are rectified, and when those who guide are consecrated to truth and duty, the ark of the people's safety will still be discerned in the keeping of those who hold fast to the principles of true democracy.

These principles are not uncertain nor doubtful. The illustrious founder of our party has plainly announced them. They have been reasserted and followed by a long line of great political leaders, and they are quite familiar. They comprise: Equal and exact justice to all men; peace, commerce, and honest friendship with all nations—entangling alliance with none; the support of the state governments in all their rights; the preservation of the general government in its whole constitutional vigor; a jealous care of the right of election by the people; absolute acquiescence in the decisions of the majority; the supremacy of the civil over the military authority; economy in the public expenses; the honest payment of our debts and sacred preservation of the public faith; the encouragement of agriculture, and commerce as its handmaid, and freedom of religion, freedom of the press, and freedom of the person.

The great president and intrepid Democratic leader whom we especially honor tonight, who never relaxed his strict adherence to the democratic faith nor faltered in his defense of the rights of the people against all comers, found his inspiration and guidance in these principles. On entering upon the presidency he declared his loyalty to them; in his long and useful incumbency of that great office he gloriously illustrated their value and sufficiency; and his obedience to the doctrines of true democracy, at all times during his public career, permitted him on his retirement to find satisfaction in the declaration; "At the moment when I surrender my last public trust, I leave this great people prosperous and happy and in the full enjoyment of liberty and peace, and honored and respected by every nation of the world."

Parties have come and parties have gone. Even now the leaders of the party which faces in opposition the Democratic host, listen for the footsteps of that death which destroys parties false to their trust.

Touched by thine
The extortioner's hard hand foregoes the
    gold

Wrung from the o'erworn poor.
. . . . .
Thou, too, dost purge from earth its
    horrible
And old idolatries; from the proud fanes,
Each to his grave, their priests go out, till
    none
Is left to teach their worship.

But there has never been a time, from Jefferson's day to the present hour, when our party did not exist, active and aggressive and prepared for heroic conflict. Not all who have followed the banner have been able by a long train of close reasoning to demonstrate, as an abstraction, why democratic principles are best suited to their wants and the country's good; but they have known and felt that as their government was established for the people, the principles and the men nearest to the people and standing for them could be the safest trusted. Jackson has been in their eyes the incarnation of the things which Jefferson declared. If they did not understand all that Jefferson declared, if they did not understand all that Jefferson wrote, they saw and knew what Jackson did. Those who insisted upon voting for Jackson after his death felt sure that, whether their candidate was alive or dead, they were voting the ticket of true democracy. The devoted political adherent of Jackson who, after his death, became involved in a dispute as to whether his hero had gone to heaven or not, was prompted by democratic instinct when he disposed of the question by declaring, "I tell you, sir, that if Andrew Jackson has made up his mind to go to heaven you may depend upon it he's there." The single Democratic voter in more than one town who, year after year, deposited his single Democratic ballot undismayed by the number of his misguided opponents, thus discharged his political duty with the utmost pride and satisfaction in his Jacksonian Democracy.

Democratic steadfastness and enthusiasm, and the satisfaction arising from our party history and traditions, certainly ought not to be discouraged. But it is hardly safe for us because we profess the true faith, and can boast of distinguished political ancestry, to rely upon these things as guarantees of our present usefulness as a party organization, or to regard their glorification as surely making the way easy to the accomplishment of our

political mission. The Democratic Party, by an intelligent study of existing conditions, should be prepared to meet all the wants of the people as they arise, and to furnish a remedy for every threatening evil. We may well be proud of our party membership; but we cannot escape the duty which such membership imposes upon us, to urge constantly upon our fellow citizens of this day and generation the sufficiency of the principles of true democracy for the protection of their rights and the promotion of their welfare and happiness, in all their present diverse conditions and surroundings.

There should, of course, be no suggestion that a departure from the time-honored principles of our party is necessary to the attainment of these objects. On the contrary, we should constantly congratulate ourselves that our party creed is broad enough to meet any emergency that can arise in the life of a free nation.

Thus, when we see the functions of government used to enrich a favored few at the expense of the many, and see also its inevitable result in the pinching privation of the poor and the profuse extravagance of the rich; and when we see in operation an unjust tariff which banishes from many humble homes the comforts of life, in order that, in the palaces of wealth, luxury may more abound, we turn to our creed and find that it enjoins "equal and exact justice to all men." Then, if we are well grounded in our political faith, we will not be deceived, nor will we permit others to be deceived, by any plausible pretext or smooth sophistry excusing the situation. For our answer to them all, we will point to the words which condemn such inequality and injustice, as we prepare for the encounter with wrong, armed with the weapons of true democracy.

When we see our farmers in distress, and know that they are not paying the penalty of slothfulness and mismanagement, when we see their long hours of toil so pooly requited that the money-lender eats out their substance, while for everything they need they pay a tribute to the favorites of governmental care, we know that all this is far removed from the "encouragement of agriculture" which our creed commands. We will not violate our political duty by forgetting how well entitled our farmers are to our best efforts for their restoration to the independence of a former time and to the rewards of better days.

When we see the extravagance of public expenditure fast reaching the point of reckless waste, and the undeserved distribution of public money debauching its recipients, and by pernicious example threatening the destruction of the love of frugality among our people, we will remember that "economy in the public expense" is an important article in the true democratic faith.

When we see our political adversaries bent upon the passage of a federal law, with the scarcely denied purpose of perpetuating partisan supremacy, which invades the states with election machinery designed to promote federal interference with the rights of the people in the localities concerned, discrediting their honesty and fairness, and justly arousing their jealousy of centralized power, we will stubbornly resist such a dangerous and revolutionary scheme, in obedience to our pledge for "the support of the state governments in all their rights."

Under anti-democratic encouragement we have seen a constantly increasing selfishness attach to our political affairs. A departure from the sound and safe theory that the people should support the government for the sake of the benefits resulting to all, has bred a sentiment manifesting itself with astounding boldness, that the government may be enlisted in the furtherance and advantage of private interests, through their willing agents in public place. Such an abandonment of the idea of patriotic political action on the part of these interests, has naturally led to an estimate of the people's franchise so degrading that it has been openly and palpably debauched for the promotion of selfish schemes. Money is invested in the purchase of votes with the deliberate calculation that it will yield a profitable return in results advantageous to the investor. Another crime akin to this in motive and design is the intimidation by employers of the voters dependent upon them for work and bread.

Nothing could be more hateful to true and genuine democracy than such offenses against our free institutions. In several of the states the honest sentiment of the party has asserted itself, in the support of every plan proposed for the rectification of this terrible wrong. To fail in such support would be to violate that principle in the creed of true democracy which commands "a jealous care of the right of election by the people," for certainly no one can claim that suffrages purchased or cast under the stress of threat or intimidation represent the right of election by the people.

Since a free and unpolluted ballot must be conceded as absolutely essential to the maintenance of our free institutions, I may perhaps be permitted to express the hope that the state of Pennsylvania will not long remain behind her sister states in adopting an effective plan to protect her people's suffrage. In any event the democracy of the state can find no justification in party principle, nor in party traditions, nor in a just apprehension of democratic duty, for a failure earnestly to support and advocate ballot reform.

I have thus far attempted to state some of the principles of true democracy, and their application to present conditions. Their enduring character and their constant influence upon those who profess our faith have also been suggested. If I were now asked why they have so endured and why they have been invincible, I should reply in the words of the sentiment to which I respond: "They are enduring because they are right, and invincible because they are just."

I believe that among our people the ideas which endure, and which inspire warm attachment and devotion, are those having some elements which appeal to the moral sense. When men are satisfied that a principle is morally right, they become its adherents for all time. There is sometimes a discouraging distance between what our fellow countrymen believe and what they do, in such a case; but their action in accordance with their belief may always be confidently expected in good time. A government for the people and by the people is everlastingly right. As surely as this is true so surely is it true that party principles which advocate the absolute equality of American manhood, and an equal participation by all the people in the management of their government, and in the benefit and protection which it affords, are also right. Here is common ground where the best educated thought and reason may meet the most impulsive and instinctive Americanism. It is right that every man should enjoy the result of his labor to the fullest extent consistent with his membership in a civilized community. It is right that our government should be but the instrument of the people's will, and that its cost should be limited within the lines of strict economy. It is right that the influence of the government should be known in every humble home as the guardian of frugal comfort and content, and a defense against unjust exactions, and the unearned tribute persistently coveted by the selfish and designing. It is right that efficiency and honesty in public service should not be sacrificed to partisan greed; and it is right that the suffrage of our people should be pure and free.

The belief in these propositions, as moral truths, is nearly universal among our countrymen. We are mistaken if we suppose the time is distant when the clouds of selfishness and perversion will be dispelled and their conscientious belief will become the chief motive force in the political action of the people.

I understand all these truths to be included in the principles of true democracy. If we have not all times trusted as implicitly as we ought to the love our people have for the right, in political action, or if we have not always relied sufficiently upon the sturdy advocacy of the best things which belong to our party faith, these have been temporary aberrations which have furnished their inevitable warning.

We are permitted to contemplate tonight the latest demonstration of the people's appreciation of the right, and of the acceptance they accord to democratic doctrine when honestly presented. In the campaign which has just closed with such glorious results, while party managers were anticipating the issue in the light of the continued illusion of the people, the people themselves and for themselves were considering the question of right and justice. They have spoken, and the democracy of the land rejoice.

In the signs of the times and in the result of their late state campaign, the democracy of Pennsylvania must find hope and inspiration. Nowhere has the sensitiveness of the people, on questions involving right and wrong, been better illustrated than here. At the head of your state government there will soon stand a disciple of true democracy, elected by voters who would have the right and not the wrong when their consciences were touched. Though there have existed here conditions and influences not altogether favorable to an unselfish apprehension of the moral attributes of political doctrine, I believe that if these features of the principles of true democracy are persistently advocated, the time will speedily come when, as in a day, the patriotic hearts of the people of your great commonwealth will be stirred to the support of our cause.

It remains to say that, in the midst of our rejoicing and in the time of party hope and expectation, we should remember that the way of right and justice should be followed as a matter of duty and regardless of immediate success. Above all things let us not for a moment forget that grave responsibilities await the party which the people trust; and let us look for guidance to the principles of true democracy, which "are enduring because they are right, and invincible because they are just."

Second Inaugural Address

Washington, D.C.

March 4, 1893

As THE COUNTRY's first Democratic president to take office in a nation free of slavery, Cleveland in his first inaugural address sought to reassure the country that "this is still the government of all the people, and it should be none the less an object of their affectionate solicitude." His second inaugural address expanded on his favorite theme: the need for efficient and ethical government. It was received with particular interest in Europe (extracts were distributed to the public schools in France). In practice, Cleveland's conception of the limited role of the executive hobbled his ability to make progress on reform issues, especially since the Senate was dominated by hostile members of his own party who refused to cooperate.

In obedience to the mandate of my countrymen I am about to dedicate myself to their service under the sanction of a solemn oath. Deeply moved by the expression of confidence and personal attachment which has called me to this service, I am sure my gratitude can make no better return than the pledge I now give before God and these witnesses of unreserved and complete devotion to the interests and welfare of those who have honored me.

I deem it fitting on this occasion, while indicating the opinions I hold concerning public questions of present importance, to also briefly refer to the existence of certain conditions and tendencies among our people which seem to menace the integrity and usefulness of their government.

While every American citizen must contemplate with the utmost pride and enthusiasm the growth and expansion of our country, the sufficiency of our institutions to stand against the rudest shocks of violence, the wonderful thrift and enterprise of our people, and the demonstrated superiority of our free government, it behooves us to constantly watch for every symptom of insidious infirmity that threatens our national vigor.

The strong man who in the confidence of sturdy health courts the sternest activities of life and rejoices in the hardihood of constant labor may still have lurking near his vitals the unheeded disease that dooms him to sudden collapse.

It cannot be doubted that our stupendous achievement as a people and our country's robust strength have given rise to heedlessness of those laws governing our national health which we can no more evade than human life can escape the laws of God and nature.

Manifestly nothing is more vital to our supremacy as a nation and to the beneficent purposes of our government than a sound and stable currency. Its exposure to degradation should at once arouse to activity the most enlightened statesmanship, and the danger of depreciation in the purchasing power of the wages paid to toil should furnish the strongest incentive to prompt and conservative precaution.

In dealing with our present embarrassing situation as related to this subject we will be wise if we temper our confidence and faith in our national strength and resources with the frank concession that even these will not permit us to defy with impunity the inexorable laws of finance and trade. At the same time, in our efforts to adjust differences of opinion we should be free from intolerance or passion, and our judgments should be unmoved by alluring phrases and unvexed by selfish interests.

I am confident that such an approach to the subject will result in prudent and effective remedial legislation. In the meantime, so far as the executive branch of the government can intervene, none of the powers with which it is invested will be withheld when their exercise is deemed necessary to maintain our national credit or avert financial disaster.

Closely related to the exaggerated confidence in our country's greatness which tends to a disregard of the rules of national safety, another danger confronts us not less serious. I refer to the prevalence of a popular disposition to expect from the operation of the government especial and direct individual advantages.

The verdict of our voters which condemned the injustice of maintaining protection for protection's sake enjoins upon the people's servants the duty of exposing and destroying the brood of kindred evils which are the unwholesome progeny of paternalism. This is the bane of republican institutions and the constant peril of our government by the people. It degrades to the purposes of wily craft the plan of rule our fathers established and bequeathed to us as an object of our love and veneration. It perverts the patriotic sentiments of our countrymen and tempts them to pitiful calculation of the sordid gain to be derived from their government's maintenance. It undermines the self-reliance of our people and substitutes in its place dependence upon governmental favoritism. It stifles the spirit of true Americanism and stupefies every ennobling trait of American citizenship.

The lessons of paternalism ought to be unlearned and the better lesson taught that while the people should patriotically and cheerfully support their government its functions do not include the support of the people.

The acceptance of this principle leads to a refusal of bounties and subsidies, which burden the labor and thrift of a portion of our citizens to aid ill-advised or languishing enterprises in which they have no concern. It leads also to a challenge of wild and reckless pension expenditure, which overleaps the bounds of grateful recognition of patriotic service and prostitutes to vicious uses the people's prompt and generous impulse to aid those disabled in their country's defense.

Every thoughtful American must realize the importance of checking at its beginning any tendency in public or private station to regard frugality and economy as virtues which we may safely outgrow. The toleration of this idea results in the waste of the people's money by their chosen servants and encourages prodigality and extravagance in the home life of our countrymen.

Under our scheme of government the waste of public money is a crime against the citizen, and the contempt of our people for economy and frugality in their personal affairs deplorably saps the strength and sturdiness of our national character.

It is a plain dictate of honesty and good government that public expenditures should be limited by public necessity, and that this should be measured by the rules of strict economy; and it is equally clear that frugality among the people is the best guaranty of a contented and strong support of free institutions.

One mode of the misappropriation of public funds is avoided when appointments to office, instead of being the rewards of partisan activity, are awarded to those whose efficiency promises a fair return of work for the compensation paid to them. To secure the fitness and competency of appointees to office and remove from political action the demoralizing madness for spoils, civil service reform has found a place in our public policy and laws. The benefits already gained through this instrumentality and the further usefulness it promises entitled it to the hearty support and encouragement of all who desire to see our public service well performed or who hope for the elevation of political sentiment and the purification of political methods.

The existence of immense aggregations of kindred enterprises and combinations of business interests formed for the purpose of limiting production and fixing prices is inconsistent with the fair field which ought to be open to every independent activity. Legitimate strife in business should not be superseded by an enforced concession to the demands of combinations that have the power to destroy, nor should the people to be served lose the benefit of cheapness which usually results from wholesome competition. These aggregations and combinations frequently constitute conspiracies against the interests of the people, and in all their phases they are unnatural and opposed to our American sense of fairness. To the extent that they can be reached and restrained by federal power the general government should relieve our citizens from their interference and exactions.

Loyalty to the principles upon which our government rests positively demands that the equality before the law which it guarantees to every citizen should be justly and in good faith conceded in all parts of the land. The enjoyment of this right follows the badge of citizenship wherever found, and, unimpaired by race or color, it appeals for recognition to American manliness and fairness.

Our relations with the Indians located within our border impose upon us responsibilities we cannot escape. Humanity and consistency require us to treat them with forbearance and in our dealings with them to honestly and considerately regard their rights and interests. Every effort should be made to lead them, through the paths of civilization and education, to self-supporting and independent citizenship. In the meantime, as the nation's wards, they should be promptly defended against the cupidity of designing men and shielded from every influence or temptation that retards their advancement.

The people of the United States have decreed that on this day the control of their government in its legislative and executive branches shall be given to a political party pledged in the most positive terms to the accomplishment of tariff reform. They have thus determined in favor of a more just and equitable system of federal taxation. The agents they have chosen to carry out their purposes are bound by their promises not less than by the command of their masters to devote themselves unremittingly to this service.

While there should be no surrender of principle, our task must be undertaken wisely and without heedless vindictiveness. Our mission is not punishment, but the rectification of wrong. If in lifting burdens from the daily life of our people we reduce inordinate and unequal advantages too long enjoyed, this is but a necessary incident of our return to right and justice. If we exact from unwilling minds acquiescence in the theory of an honest distribution of the fund of the governmental beneficence treasured up for all, we but insist upon a principle which underlies our free institutions. When we tear aside the delusions and misconceptions which have blinded our countrymen to their condition under vicious tariff laws, we but show them how far they have been led away from the paths of contentment and prosperity. When we proclaim that the necessity for revenue to support the government furnishes the only justification for taxing the people, we announce a truth so plain that its denial would seem to indicate the extent to which judgment may be influenced by familiarity with perversions of the taxing power. And when we seek to reinstate the self-confidence and business enterprise of our citizens by discrediting an abject dependence upon governmental favor, we strive to stimulate those elements of American character which support the hope of American achievement.

Anxiety for the redemption of the pledges which my party has made and solicitude for the complete justification of the trust the people have reposed in us constrain me to remind those with whom I am to cooperate that we can succeed in doing the work which has been especially set before us only by the most sincere, harmonious, and disinterested effort. Even if insuperable obstacles and opposition prevent the consummation of our task, we shall hardly be excused; and if failure can be traced to our fault or neglect we may be sure the people will hold us to a swift and exacting accountability.

The oath I now take to preserve, protect, and defend the Constitution of the United States not only impressively defines the great responsibility I assume, but suggests obedience to constitutional commands as the rule by which my official conduct must be guided. I shall to the best of my ability and within my sphere of duty preserve the Constitution by loyally protecting every grant of federal power it contains, by defending all its restraints when attacked by impatience and restlessness, and by enforcing its limitations and reservations in favor of the states and the people.

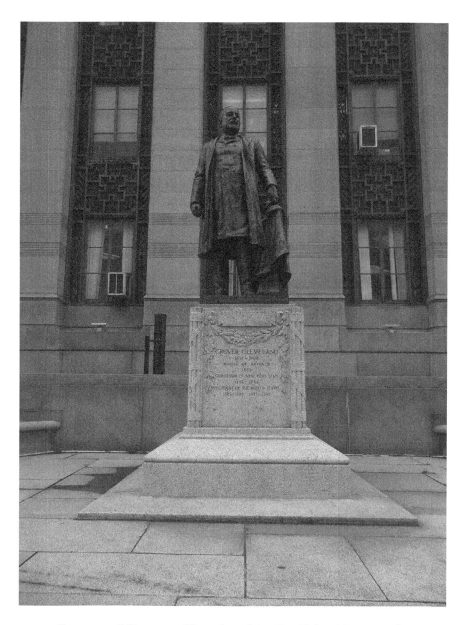

Statue of Grover Cleveland in Buffalo, New York.
(Courtesy of PresidentsUSA.net)

Benjamin Harrison

Benjamin Harrison

1889–1893

BENJAMIN HARRISON, who defeated incumbent Grover Cleveland in the 1888 election and was then unseated by him in 1892, came from a family that had been prominent in politics since the colonial era. As a young lawyer in Indianapolis, he joined the Republicans. His forceful delivery, clear expression, and quick thinking in debate soon made him one of Indiana's most impressive stump speakers in the era when oratory was still a major form of entertainment and persuasion. Said one local politician who was present at an impromptu contest between Harrison and a Democrat: "I have heard a good many political debates in my day, but I never heard a man skin an opponent as quickly as Benjamin Harrison did Hendricks that day."

Coming back from a distinguished Civil War career with the rank of general, Harrison went back on the campaign trail for the Republicans and by 1881 had won a seat in the Senate himself. A fellow campaigner observed that the short but sturdy Harrison "dominated his audiences through the nobility of his character and the strength and integrity of his intellect," though on occasion—when denouncing Democratic malfeasance in administering prisons and asylums, for example—he had his listeners shouting "Glory to God" and weeping.

For his presidential race against Cleveland in 1888, Harrison conducted a "front porch" campaign at his Indiana home, speaking to nearly 300,000 visitors in less than four months until, he said, "I am quite tired of hearing my own voice, and if there was a party pledged to the prohibition of public speaking I would join it." The main issue was the protective tariff, which Harrison defended skillfully.

Unfortunately for Harrison, the coolness and control that made him an effective speaker brought him the distrust of his fellow Republicans as well as Democrats. According to historian R. Hal Williams, "Addressing small crowds, he was at his best, informal, expansive, moving, with a sure touch for the right word and the stirring phrase. In individual conversation, on the other hand, he was brusque and cold. . . . Collectively he swayed audiences; individually he made enemies." Before and after the 1890 midterm elections he toured large areas of the country by rail, speechmaking all the way; on his 1891 journey through Texas and the West he made more than 140 speeches in a single month. But his administration's attempts to handle the problems of industrial growth—including the currency and tariff disputes, militancy among farmers and workers, the proliferation of trusts and monopolies, and unregulated speculation—were insufficient.

The illness and death of his wife kept Harrison from campaigning during his second race against Cleveland, and after his defeat he retired to Indianapolis to take up again his lucrative law practice and to deliver law lectures at Stanford University. Still interested in recapturing the presidency, he continued to make political speeches until 1896, when he took the stump on behalf of McKinley. He died in 1901.

Inaugural Address

Washington, D.C.

March 4, 1889

HARRISON TOOK office in the centennial year of the presidency. His inaugural address reflected the nation's efforts to come to grips with the social, economic, and technological changes of the past half century. As R. Hal Williams notes, "An onlooker only 50 years old at Harrison's inaugural had witnessed the advent for practical purposes of steel, oil, electricity, the electronic light, telephones, telegraphs, and phonographs, iron-clad warships, the use of steam in ocean travel, the vast railroad network integrating the country, and a good deal more. The automobile and the airplane were only a few years away." Harrison's message was one of faith in progress.

Harrison delivered his speech from the Capitol terrace in a pouring rain, clad in a suit of leather beneath his broadcloth suit to preserve him from the fate of his grandfather, William Henry Harrison, who caught pneumonia at his own inauguration. The parade that followed included Buffalo Bill riding a Turkish stallion, and the evening's Inaugural Ball was the occasion for the premiere of John Philip Sousa's "Presidential Polonaise."

There is no constitutional or legal requirement that the president shall take the oath of office in the presence of the people. But there is so manifest an appropriateness in the public induction to office of the chief executive officer of the nation that from the beginning of the government the people, to whose service the official oath consecrates the officer, have been called to witness the solemn ceremonial. The oath taken in the presence of the people becomes a mutual covenant; the officer covenant; to serve the whole body of the people by a faithful execution of the laws, so that they may be the unfailing defence and security of those who respect and observe them, and that neither wealth and station nor the power of combinations shall be able to evade their just penalties or to wrest them from a beneficent public purpose to serve the ends of cruelty or selfishness. My promise is spoken; yours unspoken, but not the less real and solemn. The people of every state have here their representatives. Surely I do not misinterpret the spirit of the occasion when I assume that the whole body of the people covenant with me and wish each other today to support and defend the Constitution and the Union of the states, to yield willing obedience to all the laws and each to every other citizen his equal civil and political rights. Entering thus solemnly in covenant with each other, we may reverently invoke and confidently expect the favor and help of Almighty God, that He will give to me wisdom, strength, and fidelity, and to our people a spirit of fraternity and a love of righteousness and peace.

This occasion derives peculiar interest from the fact that the presidential term which begins this day is the 26 under our Constitution. The first inauguration of President Washington took place in New York, where Congress was then sitting, on April 30, 1789, having been deferred by reason of delays attending the organization of the Congress and the canvass of the electoral vote. Our people have already worthily observed the centennials of the Declaration of Independence, of the battle of Yorktown, and of the adoption of the Constitution, and will shortly celebrate in New York the institution of the second great department of our constitutional scheme of government. When the centennial of the institution of the judicial department by the organization of the Supreme Court shall have been suitably observed, as I trust it will be, our nation will have fully entered its second century.

I will not attempt to note the marvellous and, in great part, happy contrasts between our country as it steps over the threshold into its second century of organized existence under the Constitution, and that weak but wisely ordered young nation that looked undauntedly down the first century, when all its years stretched out before it.

Our people will not fail at this time to recall the incidents which accompanied the institution of government under the Constitution, or to find inspiration and guidance in the teachings and example of Washington and his great associates, and hope and courage in the contrast which 38 populous and prosperous states offer to the 13 states, weak in everything except courage and the love of liberty, that then fringed our Atlantic seaboard.

The Territory of Dakota has now a population greater than any of the original states—except Virginia—and greater than the aggregate of five of the smaller states in 1790. The centre of population when our national capital was located was east of Baltimore, and it was arugued by many well-informed persons that it would move eastward rather than westward. Yet in 1880 it was found to be near Cincinnati, and the new census, about to be taken, will show another stride to the westward. That which was the body has come to be only the rich fringe of the nation's robe. But our growth has not been limited to territory, population, and aggregate wealth, marvellous as it has been in each of those directions. The masses of our people are better fed, clothed, and housed than their fathers were. The facilities for popular education have been vastly enlarged and more generally diffused. The virtues of courage and patriotism have given recent proof of their continued presence and increasing power in the hearts and over the lives of our people. The influences of religion have been multiplied and strengthened. The sweet offices of charity have greatly increased. The virtue of temperance is held in higher estimation. We have not attained an ideal condition. Not all of our people are happy and prosperous; not all of them are virtuous and law abiding. But, on the whole, the opportunities offered to the individual to secure the comforts of life are better than are found elsewhere, and largely better than they were here 100 years ago.

The surrender of a large measure of sovereignty to the general government, effected by the adoption of the Constitution, was not accomplished until the suggestions of reason were strongly reenforced by the more imperative voice of experience. The divergent interests of peace speedily demanded a "more perfect Union." The merchant, the ship-master, and the manufacturer discovered and disclosed to our statesmen and to the people that commercial emancipation must be added to the political freedom which had been so bravely won. The commercial policy of the mother country had not relaxed any of its hard and oppressive features. To hold in check the development of our commercial marine, to prevent or retard the establishment and growth of manufactures in the states, and so to secure the American market for their shops and the carrying trade for their ships, was the policy of European statesmen, and was pursued with the most selfish vigor. Petitions poured in upon Congress urging the imposition of discriminating duties that should encourage the production of needed things at home. The patriotism of the people, which no longer found a field of exercise in war, was energetically directed to the duty of equipping the young republic for the defense of its independence by making its people self-dependent. Societies for the promotion of home manufactures and for encouraging the use of domestics in the dress of the people were organized in many of the states. The revival at the end of the century of the same patriotic interest in the preservation and development of domestic industries and the defence of our working people against injurious foreign competition is an incident worthy of attention.

It is not a departure, but a return, that we have witnessed. The protective policy had then its opponents. The argument was made, as now, that its benefits inured to particular classes or sections. If the question became in any sense, or at any time, sectional, it was only because slavery existed in some of the states. But for this there was no reason why the cotton-producing states should not have led or walked abreast with the New England states in the production of cotton fabrics. There was this reason only why the states that divide with Pennsylvania the mineral treasures of the great southeastern and central mountain ranges should have been so tardy in bringing to the smelting furnace and the mill the coal and iron from their near opposing hillsides. Mill-fires were lighted at the funeral pile of slavery. The emancipation proclamation was heard in the depths of the earth as well as in the sky—men were made free and material things became our better servants.

The sectional element has happily been eliminated from the tariff discussion. We have no longer states that are necessarily only planting states. None are excluded from achieving that diversification of pursuit among the people which brings wealth and contentment.

The cotton plantation will not be less valuable when the product is spun in the country town by operatives whose necessities call for diversified crops and create a home demand for garden and agricultural products. Every new mine, furnace, and factory is an extension of the productive capacity of the state more real and valuable than added territory.

Shall the prejudices and paralysis of slavery continue to hang upon the skirts of progress? How long will those who rejoice that slavery no longer exists cherish or tolerate the incapacities it puts upon their communities? I look hopefully to the continuance of our protective system and to the consequent development of manufacturing and mining enterprises in the states hitherto wholly given to agriculture as a potent influence in the perfect unification of our people. The men who have invested their capital in these enterprises, the farmers who have felt the benefit of their neighborhood, and the men who work in shop or field will not fail to find and to defend a community of interest. Is it not quite possible that the farmers and the promoters of the great mining and manufacturing enterprises which have recently been established in the South may yet find that the free ballot of the working-man, without distinction of race, is needed for their defence as well as for his own? I do not doubt that if these men in the South who now accept the tariff views of Clay and the constitutional expositions of Webster would courageously avow and defend their real convictions they would not find it difficult, by friendly instruction and co-operation, to make the black man their efficient and safe ally, not only in establishing correct principles in our national administration, but in preserving for their local communities the benefits of social order and economical and honest government. At least until the good offices of kindness and educaton have been fairly tried to contrary conclusion cannot be plausibly urged.

I have altogether rejected the suggestion of a special executive policy for any section of our country. It is the duty of the executive to administer and enforce in the methods and by the instrumentalities pointed out and provided by the Constitution all the laws enacted by Congress. These laws are general, and their administration should be uniform and equal. As a citizen may not elect what laws he will obey, neither may the executive elect which he will enforce. The duty to obey and execute embraces the Constitution in its entirety and the whole code of laws enacted under it. The evil example of permitting individuals, corporations, or communities to nullify the laws because they cross some selfish or local interests or prejudices is full of danger, not only to the nation at large, but much more to those who use this pernicious expedient to escape their just obligatons or to obtain an unjust advantage over others. They will presently themselves be compelled to appeal to the law for protection, and those who would use the law as a defence must not deny that use of it to others.

If our great corporations would more scrupulously observe their legal obligations and duties they would have less cause to complain of the unlawful limitations of their rights or of violent interference with their operations. The community that by concert, open or secret, among its citizens denies to a portion of its members their plain rights under the law has severed the only safe bond of social order and prosperity. The evil works, from a bad centre, both ways. It demoralizes those who practise it, and destroys the faith of those who suffer by it in the efficiency of the law as a safe protector. The man in whose breast that faith has been darkened is naturally the subject of dangerous and uncanny suggestions. Those who use unlawful methods, if moved by no higher motive than the selfishness that prompts them, may well stop and inquire what is to be the end of this. An unlawful expedient cannot become a permanent condition of government. If the educated and influential classes in a community either practise or connive at the systematic violation of laws that seem to them to cross their convenience, what can they expect when the lesson that convenience or a supposed class interest is a sufficient cause for lawlessness has been well learned by the ignorant classes? A community where law is the rule of conduct, and where courts, not mobs, execute its penalties, is the only attractive field for business investments and honest labor.

Our naturalization laws should be so amended as to make the inquiry into the character and good disposition of persons applying for citizenship more careful and searching. Our existing laws have been in their administration an unimpressive and often an unintelligible form. We accept the man as a citizen without any knowledge of his fitness, and he assumes the duties of citizenship without any knowledge as to what they are. The privileges of American citizenship are so great and its duties so grave that we may well insist upon a good knowledge of every person applying for citizenship and a good knowledge by him of our institutions. We should not cease to be hospitable to immigration, but we should cease to be careless as to the character of it. There are men of all races, even the best, whose coming is necessarily a burden upon our public revenues or a threat to social order. These should be identified and excluded.

We have happily maintained a policy of avoiding all interference with European affairs. We have been only interested spectators of their contentions in diplomacy and in war, ready to use our friendly offices to promote peace, but never obtruding our advice and never attempting unfairly to coin the distresses of other powers into commercial advantage to ourselves. We have a just right to expect that our European policy will be the American policy of European courts.

It is so mainfestly incompatible with those precautions for our peace and safety, which all the great powers habitually observe and enforce in matters affecting them, that a shorter waterway between our eastern and western seaboards should be dominated by any European government, that we may confidently expect that such a purpose will not be entertained by any friendly power. We shall in the future, as in the past, use every endeavor to maintain and enlarge our friendly relations with all the great powers, but they will not expect us to look kindly upon any project that would leave us subject to the dangers of a hostile observation or environment.

We have not sought to dominate or to absorb any of our weaker neighbors, but rather to aid and encourage them to establish free and stable governments, resting upon the consent of their own people. We have a clear right to expect, therefore, that no European government will seek to establish colonial dependencies upon the territory of these independent American states. That which a sense of justice restrains us from seeking they may be reasonably expected willingly to forego.

It must not be assumed, however, that our interests are so exclusively American that our entire inattention to any events that may transpire elsewhere can be taken for granted. Our citizens domiciled for purposes of trade in all countries and in many of the islands of the sea demand and will have our adequate care in their personal and commercial rights. The necessities of our navy require convenient coaling stations and dock and harbor privileges. These and other trading privileges we will feel free to obtain only by means that do not in any degree partake of coercion, however feeble the government from which we ask such concessions. But having fairly obtained them by methods and for purposes entirely consistent with the most friendly disposition toward all other powers, our consent will be necessary to any modification or impairment of the concession.

We shall neither fail to respect the flag of any friendly nation or the just rights of its citizens, nor to exact the like treatment for our own. Calmness, justice, and consideration should characterize our diplomacy. The office of an intelligent diplomacy or of friendly arbitration, in proper cases, should be adequate to the peaceful adjustment of all international difficulties. By such methods we will make our contribution to the world's peace, which no nation values more highly, and avoid the opprobrium which must fall upon the nation that ruthlessly breaks it.

The duty devolved by law upon the president to nominate and, by and with the advice and consent of the Senate, to appoint all public officers whose appointment is not otherwise provided for in the Constitution or by act of Congress has become very burdensome, and its wise and efficient discharge full of difficulty. The civil list is so large that a personal knowledge of any large number of the applicants is impossible. The president must rely upon the representations of others, and these are often made inconsiderately and without any just sense of responsibility.

I have a right, I think, to insist that those who volunteer or are invited to give advice as to appointments shall exercise consideration and fidelity. A high sense of duty and an ambition to improve the service should characterize all public officers. There are many ways in which the convenience and comfort of those who have business with our public officers may be promoted by a thoughtful and obliging officer, and I shall expect those whom I may appoint to justify their selection by a conspicuous efficiency in the discharge of their duties. Honorable party service will certainly not be esteemed by me a disqualification for public office; but it will in no case be allowed to serve as a shield for official negligence, incompetency, or delinquency. It is entirely creditable to seek public office by proper methods and with proper motives; and all applications will be treated with consideration; but I shall need, and the heads of departments will need, time for inquiry and deliberaton. Persistent importunity will not, therefore, be best support of an application for office.

Heads of departments, bureaus, and all other public officers having any duty connected therewith, will be expected to enforce the Civil Service law fully and without evasion. Beyond this obvious duty I hope to do something more to advance the reform of the civil service. The ideal, or even my own ideal, I shall probably not attain. Retrospect will be a safer basis of judgment than promises. We shall not, however, I am sure, be able to put our civil service upon a nonpartisan basis until we have secured an incumbency that fairminded men of the opposition will approve for impartiality and integrity. As the number of such in the civil list is increased removals from office will diminish.

While a Treasury surplus is not the greatest evil, it is a serious evil. Our revenue should be ample to meet the ordinary annual demands upon our Treasury, with a sufficient margin for those extraordinary but scarcely less imperative demands which arise now and then. Expenditure should always be made with economy, and only upon public necessity. Wastefulness, profligacy, or favoritism in public expenditures is criminal, but there is nothing in the condition of our country or of our people to suggest that anything present necessary to the public prosperity, security, or honor should be unduly postponed. It will be the duty of Congress wisely to forecast and estimate these extraordinary demands, and, having added them to our ordinary expenditures, to so adjust our revenue laws that no considerable annual surplus will remain. We will fortunately be able to apply to the redemption of the public debt any small and unforeseen excess of revenue. This is better than to reduce our income below our necessary expenditures with the resulting choice between another change of our revenue laws and an increase of the public debt. It is quite possible, I am sure, to effect the necessary reduction in our revenues without breaking down our protective tariff or seriously injuring any domestic industry.

The construction of a sufficient number of modern war ships and of their necessary armament should progress as rapidly as is consistent with care and perfection in plans and workmanship. The spirit, courage, and skill of our naval officers and seamen have many times in our history given to weak ships and inefficient guns a rating greatly beyond that of the naval list. That they will again do so upon occasion I do not doubt; but they ought not, by premeditation or neglect, to be left to the risks and exigencies of an unequal combat.

We should encourage the establishment of American steamship lines. The exchanges of commerce demand stated, reliable, and rapid means of communication, and until these are provided the development of our trade with the states lying south of us is impossible.

Our pension law should give more adequate and discriminating relief to the Union soldiers and sailors and to their widows and orphans. Such occasions as this should remind us that we owe everything to their valor and sacrifice.

It is a subject of congratulation that there is a near prospect of the admission into the Union of the Dakotas and Montana and Washington Territories. This act of justice has been unreasonably delayed in the case of some of them. The people who have settled those territories are intelligent, enterprising, and patriotic, and the accession of these new states will add strength to the nation. It is due to the settlers in the territories who have availed themselves of the invitations of our land laws to make homes upon the public domain that their titles should be speedily adjusted and their honest entries confirmed by patent.

It is very gratifying to observe the general interest now being manifested in the reform of our election laws. Those who have been for years calling attention to the pressing necessity of throwing about the ballot-box and about the elector further safeguards, in order that our elections might not only be free and pure, but might clearly appear to be so, will welcome the accession of any who did not so soon discover the need of reform. The national Congress has not as yet taken control of elections in that case over which the Constitution gives it jurisdiction, but has accepted and adopted the election laws of the several states, provided penalties for their violation and a methods of supervision. Only the inefficiency of the state laws or an unfair partisan administration of them could suggest a departure from this policy. It was clearly, however, in the contemplation of the framers of the Constitution that such an exigency might arise, and provision was widely made for it. No power vested in Congress or in the executive to secure or perpetuate it should remain unused upon occasion.

The people of all the Congressional districts have an equal interest that the election in each shall truly express the views and wishes of a majority of the qualified electors residing within it. The results of such elections are not local, and the insistence of electors residing in other districts that they shall be pure and free does not savor at all of impertinence. If in any of the states the public security is thought to be threatened by ignorance among the electors, the obvious remedy is education. The sympathy and help of our people will not be withheld for any community struggling with special embarrassments or difficulties connected with the suffrage, if the remedies proposed proceed upon lawful lines and are promoted by just and honorable methods. How shall those who practise election frauds recover that respect for the sanctity of the ballot which is the first condition and obligation of good citizenship? The man who has come to regard the ballot-box as a juggler's hat has renounced his allegiance.

Let us exalt patriotism and moderate our party contentions. Let those who would die for the flag on the field of battle give a better proof of their patriotism and a higher glory to their country by promoting fraternity and justice. A party success that is achieved by unfair methods or by practices that partake of revolution is hurtful and evanescent, even from a party standpoint. We should hold our differing opinions in mutual respect, and, having submitted them to the arbitrament of the ballot, should accept an adverse judgment with the same respect that we would have demanded of our opponents if the decision had been in our favor.

No other people have a government more worthy of their respect and love, or a land so magnificent in extent, so pleasant to look upon, and so full of generous suggestion to enterprise and labor. God has placed upon our head a diadem, and has laid at our feet power and wealth beyond definition or calculation. But we must not forget that we take these gifts upon the condition that justice and mercy shall hold the reins of power, and that the upward avenues of hope shall be free to all the people.

I do not mistrust the future. Dangers have been in frequent ambush along our path, but we have uncovered and vanquished them all. Passion has swept some of our communities, but only to give us a new demonstration that the great body of our people are stable, patriotic, and lawabiding. No political party can long pursue advantage at the expense of public honor or by rude and indecent methods, without protest and fatal disaffection in its own body. The peaceful agencies of commerce are more fully revealing the necessary unity of all our communities, and the increasing intercourse of our people is promoting mutual respect. We shall find unalloyed pleasure in the revelation which our next census will make of the swift development of the great resources of some of the states. Each state will bring its generous contribution to the great aggregate of the nation's increase. And when the harvest from the fields, the cattle from the hills, and the ores of the earth shall have been weighted, counted, and valued, we will turn from them all to crown with the highest honor the state that has most promoted education, virtue, justice, and patriotism among the people.

The American Worker

Alliance, Ohio

October 13, 1890

HARRISON'S 1890 tour of the Midwest, a 3,000-mile trip, was made just after he signed the McKinley Tariff into law and just as Populism and militant unionism were gathering strength. At some of his stops, such as this one in Ohio, he presented a hopeful vision of American workers. But his sympathy did not extend to active resistance against wage cuts or dangerous working conditions. In 1892, during the presidential race, he ordered federal troops to put down an insurrection at an Idaho silver mine. "If the injustice of his employer tempts the workman to strike back," he warned, "he should be very sure that his blow does not fall upon his own head or upon his wife and children."

There is nothing in which the American people are harder upon their public servants than in the insatiable demand they make for public speech. I began talking before breakfast this morning, and have been kept almost continuously at it through the day, with scarcely time for lunch; and yet, as long as the smallest residuum of strength or voice is left I cannot fail to recognize these hearty greetings and to say some appreciative word in return. I do very much thank you, and I do very deeply feel the cordial enthusiasm with which you have recieved me. It is very pleasant to know that as American citizens we love our government and its institutions, and are all ready to pay appropriate respect to any public officer who endeavors in such light as he has to do his public duty. This homage is not withheld by one's political opponents, and it is pleasant to know that in all things that affect the integrity and honor and perpetuity of our government we rise above party ties and considerations. The interests of this government are lodged with you.

There is not much that a president can do to shape its policy. He is charged under the Constitution with the duty of making suggestions to Congress, but, after all, legislation originates with the Congress of the United States, and the policy of our laws is directed by it. The president may veto, but he cannot frame a bill. Therefore it is of great interest to you, and to all our people, that you should choose such men to represent you in the Congress of the United States as will faithfully promote those policies to which you have given your intelligent adhesion. This country of ours is secure, and social order is maintained, because the great masses of our people live in contentment and some good measure of comfort. God forbid that we should ever reach the condition which has been reached by some other countries, where all that is before many of their population is the question of bare subsistence, where it is simply "how shall I find bread for today?" No hopes of accumulation; no hope of comfort; no hope of education, or higher things for the children that are to come after them. God be blessed that that is not our condition in America! Here is a chance to every man; here fair wages for fair work, with education for the masses, with no classes or distinctions to keep down the ambitious young. We have a happy lot. Let us not grumble if now and then things are not prosperous as they might be. Let us think of the average, and if this year's crop is not as full as we could wish, we have already in these green fields the promise of a better one to come. Let us not doubt that we are now—as I have seen the evidence of it in a very extended trip through the West—entering upon an upgrade in all departments of business.

Everywhere I went, in the great city of St. Louis and the smaller manufacturing towns through which we passed, there was one story to tell—and I have no doubt it is true in your midst—every wheel is running and every hand is busy. I believe the future is bright before us for increasingly better times for all, and as it comes I hope it may be so generally diffused that its kindly touch may be felt by every one who hears me, and that its beneficent help may come into every home.

Remarks on the Tariff and on Voting Rights

From the Second Annual Message to Congress
Washington, D.C.
December 1, 1890

HARRISON'S 1890 message to Congress was a general defense of his administration's policies. A large portion of it was given over to the newly established McKinley Tariff, which Harrison believed would protect American industry and jobs from foreign competition. He expected the Sherman Anti-Trust Law, also signed that year, to encourage domestic competition, thus alleviating the high prices resulting from a high tariff.

Another section of the message dealt with election fraud, a serious problem in late-19th-century America. Harrison's own success in 1888 was partly due to purchased votes, although he was too idealistic to recognize it. But as the head of Lincoln's party he did recognize that the voting rights of blacks were regularly being violated. During his presidential campaign he told a journalist: "I have never failed in any campaign . . . to insist that the settlement of that question preceded all others in natural order. There would be no tariff question now, if the labor vote of the South had not been suppressed." But a bill he supported to place southern elections under federal supervision was killed by the alignment of western Republicans and southern Democrats in the Senate.

. . . The general tariff act has only partially gone into operation, some of its important provisions being limited to take effect at dates yet in the future. The general provisions of the law have been in force less than 60 days. Its permanent effects upon trade and prices still largely stand in conjecture. It is curious to note that the advance in the prices of articles wholly unaffected by the tariff act was by many hastily ascribed to that act. Notice was not taken of the fact that the general tendency of the markets was upward, from influences wholly apart from the recent tariff legislation. The enlargement of our currency by the silver bill undoubtedly gave an upward tendency to trade and had a marked effect on prices; but this natural and desired effect to the silver legislation was by many erroneously attributed to the tariff act.

There is neither wisdom nor justice in the suggestion that the subject of tariff revision shall be again opened before this law has had a fair trial. It is quite true that every tariff schedule is subject to objections. No bill was ever framed, I suppose, that in all of its rates and classificatons had the full approval even of a party caucus. Such legislation is always and necessarily the product of compromise as to details, and the present law is no exception. But in its general scope and effect I think it will justify the support of those who believe that American legislation should conserve and defend American trade and the wages of American workmen.

The misinformation as to the terms of the act which has been so widely disseminated at home and abroad will be corrected by experience, and the evil auguries as to its results confounded by the market reports, the savings bank, international trade balances, and the general prosperity of our people. Already we begin to hear from abroad and from our customhouses that the prohibitory effect upon importations imputed to the act is not justified. The imports at the port of New York for the first three weeks of November were nearly 8 percent greater than for the same period in 1889 and 29 percent greater than in the same period of 1888. And so far from being an act to limit exports, I confidently believe that under it we shall secure a larger and more profitable participation in foreign trade than we have ever enjoyed, and that we shall recover a proportionate participation in the ocean carrying trade of the world.

The criticisms of the bill that have come to us from foreign sources may well be rejected for repugnancy. If these critics really believe that the adoption by us of a free-trade policy, or of tariff rates having reference solely to revenue, would diminish the participation of their own countries in the commerce of the world, their advocacy and promotion, by speech and other forms of organized effort, of this movement among our people is a rare exhibition of unselfishness in trade. And, on the other hand, if they sincerely believe that the adoption of a protective tariff policy by this country inures to their profit and our hurt, it is noticeably strange that they should lead the outcry against the authors of a policy so helpful to their countrymen and crown with their favor those who would snatch from them a substantial share of a trade with other hands already inadequate to their necessities.

There is no disposition among any of our people to promote prohibitory or retaliatory legislation. Our policies are adopted not to the hurt of others, but to secure for ourselves those advantages that fairly grow out of our favored position as a nation. Our form of government, with its incident of universal suffrage, makes it imperative that we shall save our working people from the agitations and distresses which scant work and wages that have no margin for comfort always beget. But after all this is done it will be found that our markets are open to friendly commercial exchanges of enormous value to the other great powers.

From the time of my induction into office the duty of using every power and influence given by law to the executive department for the development of larger markets for our products, especially our farm products, has been kept constantly in mind, and no effort has been or will be spared to promote that end. We are under no disadvantage in any foreign market, except that we pay our workmen and workwomen better wages than are paid elsewhere—better abstractly, better relatively to the cost of the necessaries of life. I do not doubt that a very largely increased foreign trade is accessible to us without bartering for it either our home market for such products of the farm and shop as our own people can supply or the wages of our working people.

In many of the products of wood and iron and in meats and breadstuffs we have advantages that only need better facilities of intercourse and transportation to secure for them large foreign markets. The reciprocity clause of the tariff act wisely and effectively opens the way to secure a large reciprocal trade in exchange for the free admission to our ports of certain products. The right of independent nations to make special reciprocal trade concessions is well established, and does not impair either the comity due to other powers or what is known as the "favored-nation clause," so generally found in commercial treaties. What is given to one for an adequate agreed consideration cannot be claimed by another freely. The state of the revenues was such that we could dispense with any import duties upon coffee, tea, hides and the lower grades of sugar and molasses. That the large advantage resulting to the countries producing and exporting these articles by placing them on the free list entitled us to expect a fair return in the way of customs concessions upon articles exported by us to them was so obvious that to have gratuitously abandoned this opportunity to enlarge our trade would have been an unpardonable error.

There were but two methods of maintaining control of this question open to Congress—to place all of these articles upon the dutiable list, subject to such treaty agreements as could be secured, or to place them all presently upon the free list but subject to the reimposition of specified duties if the countries from which we received them should refuse to give to us suitable reciprocal benefits. This latter method, I think, possesses great advantages. It expresses in advance the consent of Congress to reciprocity arrangements affecting these products, which must otherwise have been delayed and unascertained until each treaty was ratified by the Senate and the necessary legislation enacted by Congress. Experience has shown that some treaties looking to reciprocal trade have failed to secure a two-thirds vote in the Senate for ratification, and others having passed that stage have for years awaited the concurrence of the House and Senate in such modifications of our revenue laws as were necessary to give effect to their provisions. We now have the concurrence of both houses in advance in a distinct and definite offer of free entry to our ports of specific articles. The executive is not required to deal in conjecture as to what Congress will accept. Indeed, this reciprocity provision is more than an offer. Our part of the bargain is complete; delivery has been made; and when the countries from which we receive sugar, coffee, tea, and hides have placed on their free lists such of our products as shall be agreed upon as an equivalent for our concession, a proclamation of that fact completes the transaction; and in the meantime our own people have free sugar, tea, coffee, and hides.

The indications thus far given are very hopeful of early and favorable action by the countries from which we receive our large imports of coffee and sugar, and it is confidently believed that if steam communication with these countries can be promptly and enlarged the next year will show a most gratifying increase in our exports of breadstuffs and provisions, as well as of some important lines of manufactured goods. . . .

If any intelligent and loyal company of American citizens were required to catalgoue the essential human conditions of national life, I do not doubt that with absolute unanimity they would begin with "free and honest elections." And it is gratifying to know that generally there is a growing and nonpartisan demand for better election laws; but against this sign of hope and progress must be set the depressing and undeniable fact that election laws and methods are sometimes cunningly contrived to secure minority control, while violence completes the shortcomings of fraud.

In my last message I suggested that the development of the existing law providing a federal supervision of congressional elections offered an effective method of reforming these abuses. The need of such a law has manifested itself in many parts of the country, and its wholesome restraints and penalties will be useful in all. The constitutionality of such legislation has been affirmed by the Supreme Court. Its probable effectiveness is evidenced by the character of the opposition that is made to it. It has been denounced as if it were a new exercise of federal power and an invasion of the rights of states. Nothing could be further from the truth. Congress has already fixed the time for the election of members of Congress. It has declared that votes for members of Congress must be by written or printed ballot; it has provided for the appointment by the circuit courts in certain cases, and upon the petition of a certain number of citizens, of election supervisors, and made it their duty to supervise the registration of voters conducted by the state officers; to challenge persons offering to register; to personality inspect and scrutinize the registry lists, and to affix their names to the lists for the purpose of identification and the prevention of frauds; to attend at elections and remain with the boxes till they are all cast and counted; to attach to the registry lists and election returns any statement touching the accuracy and fairness of the registry and election, and to take and transmit to the clerk of the House of Representatives any evidence of fraudulent practices which may be presented to them. The same law provides for the appointment of deputy United States marshals to attend at the polls, support the supervisors in the discharge of their duties, and to arrest persons violating the election laws. The provisions of this familiar title of the Revised Statutes have been put into exercise by both the great political parties, and in the North as well as in the South, by the filing with the court of the petitions required by the law.

It is not, therefore, a question whether we shall have a federal election law, for we now have one and have had for nearly 20 years, but whether we shall have an effective law. The present law stops just short of effectiveness, for it surrenders to the local authorities all control over the certification which establishes the *prima facie* right to a seat in the House of Representatives. This defect should be cured. Equality of representation and the parity of the electors must be maintained or everything that is valuable in our system of government is lost. The qualifications of an elector must be sought in the law, not in the opinions, prejudices, or fears of any class, however powerful. The path of the elector to the ballot box must be free from the ambush of fear and the enticements of fraud; the count so true and open that none shall gainsay it. Such a law should be absolutely nonpartisan and impartial. It should give the advantage to honesty and the control to majorities. Surely there is nothing sectional about this creed, and if it shall happen that the penalties of laws intended to enforce these rights fall here and not there it is not because the law is sectional, but because, happily, crime is local and not universal. Nor should it be forgotten that every law, whether relating to elections or to any other subject, whether enacted by the state or by the nation, has force behind it; the courts, the marshal or constable, the *posse comitatus,* the prison, are all and always behind the law.

One cannot be justly charged with unfriendliness to any section or class who seeks only to restrain violations of law and of personal right. No community will find lawlessness profitable. No community can afford to have it known that the officers who are charged with the preservation of the public peace and the restraint of the criminal classes are themselves the product of fraud or violence. The magistrate is then without respect and the law without sanction. The floods of lawlessness cannot be leveed and made to run in one channel. The killing of a United States marshal carrying a writ of arrest for an election offense is full of prompting and suggestion to men who are pursued by a city marshal for a crime against life or property.

But it is said that this legislation will revive race animosities, and some have been suggested that when the peaceful methods of fraud are made impossible they may be supplanted by intimidation and violence. If the proposed law gives to any qualified elector by a hair's weight more than his equal influence or detracts by so much from any other qualified elector, it is fatally impeached. But if the law is equal and the animosities it is to evoke grow out of the fact that some electors have been accustomed to exercise the franchise for others as well as for themselves, then these animosities ought not to be confessed without shame, and cannot be given any weight in the discussion without dishonor. No choice is left to me but to enforce with vigor all laws intended to secure to the citizen his constitutional rights and to recommend that the inadequacies of such laws be promptly remedied. If to promote with zeal and ready interest every project for the development of its material interests, its rivers, harbors, mines, and factories, and the intelligence, peace, and security under the law of its communities and its homes is not accepted as sufficient evidence of friendliness to any state or section, I cannot add connivance at election practices that not only disturb local results, but rob the electors of other states and sections of their most priceless political rights. . . .

Statue of Benjamin Harrison in Indianapolis, Indiana.
(Courtesy of PresidentsUSA.net)

Courtesy of McKinley Memorial Library

William McKinley

William McKinley

1897–1901

HISTORIANS ARE undecided as to whether William McKinley represents the last of the weak 19th-century presidents or the first of the forceful 20th-century ones. He made some efforts to extend the reach of presidential power, and had he not been assassinated early in his second term he might have attained real stature. As it was, McKinley was the most popular president since Grant and one of the most personable and charming ever to hold the office.

Born in Niles, Ohio, the son of a pig-iron manufacturer, McKinley loved to make speeches even as a boy and founded a debating society at his grammar school. He served with distinction in the Civil War, then turned to law and Republican politics. During two terms in the House of Representatives he gained national attention as the party's foremost advocate of protective tariffs. From the governorship of Ohio (then the stepping-stone to the presidency), McKinley won the 1896 Republican nomination.

In one of the nation's most exciting presidential campaigns, McKinley defeated the dark-horse Democratic candidate, William Jennings Bryan, whose immensely powerful oratory and extensive touring could not overcome the efficient Republican political machine. McKinley defeated Bryan a second time in 1900. In the first race he stayed home in Canton, Ohio, while hundreds of surrogate speechmakers campaigned for him. The railroads lowered their rates so that the people—750,000 or more—could visit McKinley and hear him make brief speeches from his front porch. He would make as many as 19 carefully prepared speeches in one day "without anxiety or strain," wrote his secretary of state, John Hay, and "with nerves as quiet and free from care as if [he] had been spending a holiday at the seaside." In 1900 his chief speechmaker was the vice-presidential candidate, Theodore Roosevelt, who tirelessly toured the country to advertise the Republican slogan, "Four More Years of the Full Dinner Pail."

Neither a political hack nor a figurehead for the Cleveland industrialist and kingmaker Mark Hanna, as has sometimes been claimed, McKinley nonetheless was a passive leader who ruled his Republican coalition largely by diplomacy. His serene confidence in the status quo was expressed in his speeches, which he wrote himself, by the fluent use of hackneyed phrases and political platitudes. But Hay, among others, believed that McKinley carefully maintained a mask that was impossible for even his closest associates to penetrate, and that underneath the smooth, dignified, and gracious surface was a skillful, sometimes ruthless politician. McKinley "shook hands with exactly the amount of cordiality and with precisely the lack of intimacy that deceived men into thinking well of him, too well of him," wrote William Allen White. His speeches were equally studied—earnest, plain, and lacking originality in language or thought, a marked contrast to the elaborate rhetorical figures of his opponent Bryan or the barely controlled energy of Roosevelt.

Handsome and always impeccably dressed, McKinley was at his best when making speeches. He projected grandeur, nobility, and generosity—a triumph of image over substance—and in return received genuine though not lasting affection from his audiences. Robert La Follette called him "a magnetic speaker" with "a clear, bell-like quality of voice." When he spoke, La Follette wrote, "the pupils of his eyes would dilate until they were almost black, and his face, naturally without much color, would become almost like marble—a strong face and a noble head." A journalist commented that McKinley's features revealed "dominant will and energy rather than subtlety of mind or emotion."

Inaugural Address

Washington, D.C.

March 4, 1897

"WHAT AN IMPRESSIVE thing it is to assume tremendous responsibilities," McKinley remarked to Grover Cleveland as they rode together to the inauguration. In his first address as president he steered a tactful middle course among the issues, recommending several noncontroversial revisions to labor, trust, currency, and tariff laws and condemning territorial aggression by the United States, an indication of his desire to avoid war with Spain over its colonial maltreatment of Cuba. "The new administration was pledged to stimulate business and fill the dinner pail, uphold American honor, and keep the nation at peace," wrote historian Margaret Leech. "McKinley had voiced the aspirations of the vast majority of his countrymen."

In obedience to the will of the people, and in their presence, by the authority vested in me by this oath, I assume the arduous and responsible duties of president of the United States, relying upon the support of my countrymen and invoking the guidance of Almighty God. Our faith teaches that there is no safer reliance than upon the God of our fathers, who has so singularly favored the American people in every national trial, and who will not foresake us so long as we obey His commandments and walk humbly in His footsteps.

The responsibilities of the high trust to which I have been called—always of grave importance—are augmented by the prevailing business conditions, entailing idleness upon willing labor and loss to useful enterprises. The country is suffering from industrial disturbances from which speedy relief must be had. Our financial system needs some revision; our money is all good now, but its value must not further be threatened. It should all be put upon an enduring basis, not subject to easy attack, nor its stability to doubt or dispute. Our currency should continue under the supervision of the government. The several forms of our paper money offer, in my judgment, a constant embarrassment to the government and a safe balance in the Treasury. Therefore I believe it necessary to devise a system which, without diminishing the circulating medium or offering a premium for its contraction, will present a remedy for those arrangements which, temporary in their nature, might well in the years of our prosperity have been displaced by wiser provisions. With adequate revenue secured, but not until then, we can enter upon such changes in our fiscal laws as will, while insuring safety and volume to our money, no longer impose upon the government the necessity of maintaining so large a gold reserve, with its attendant and inevitable temptations to speculation. Most of our financial laws are the outgrowth of experience and trial, and should not be amended without investigation and demonstration of the wisdom of the proposed changes. We must be both "sure we are right" and "make haste slowly." If, therefore, Congress, in its wisdom, shall deem it expedient to create a commission to take under early consideration the revision of our coinage, banking and currency laws, and give them that exhaustive, careful and dispassionate examination that their importance demands, I shall cordially concur in such action. If such power is vested in the president, it is my purpose to appoint a commission of prominent, wellinformed citizens of different parties, who will command public confidence, both on account of their ability and special fitness for the work. Business experience and public training may thus be combined, and the patriotic zeal of the friends of the country be so directed that such a report will be made as to receive the support of all parties, and our finances cease to be the subject of mere partisan contention. The experiment is, at all events, worth a trial, and, in my opinion, it can but prove beneficial to the entire country.

The question of international bimetallism will have early and earnest attention. It will be my constant endeavor to secure it by co-operation with the other great commercial powers of the world. Until that condition is realized when the parity between our gold and silver money springs from and is supported by the relative value of the two metals, the value of the silver already coined and of that which may hereafter be coined, must be kept constantly at par with gold by every resource at our command. The credit of the government, the integrity of its currency, and the inviolability of its obligations must be preserved. This was the commanding verdict of the people, and it will not be unheeded.

Economy is demanded in every branch of the government at all times, but especially in periods, like the present, of depression in business and distress among the people. The severest economy must be observed in all public expenditures, and extravagance stopped wherever it is found, and prevented wherever in the future it may be developed. If the reveneus are to remain as now, the only relief that can come must be from decreased expenditures. But the present must not become the permanent condition of the government. It has been our uniform practice to retire, not increase our outstanding obligations, and this policy must again be resumed and vigorously enforced. Our revenues should always be large enough to meet with ease and promptness not only our current needs and the principal and interest of the public debt, but to make proper and liberal provision for that most deserving body of public creditors, the soldiers and sailors and the widows and orphans, who are the pensioners of the United States.

The government should not be permitted to run behind or increase its debt in times like the present. Suitably to provide against this is the mandate of duty—the certain and easy remedy for most of our financial difficulties. A deficiency is inevitable so long as the expenditures of the government exceed its receipts. It can only be met by loans or increased revenue. While a large annual surplus of revenue may invite waste and extravagance, inadequate revenue creates distrust and undermines public and private credit. Neither should be encouraged. Between more loans and more revenue there ought to be but one opinion. We should have more revenue, and that without delay, hindrance or postponement. A surplus in the Treasury created by loans is not a permanent or safe reliance. It will suffice while it lasts, but it cannot last long while the outlays of the government are greater than its receipts, as has been the case during the past two years. Nor must it be forgotten that however

much such loans may temporarily relieve the situation, the government is still indebted for the amount of the surplus thus accrued, which it must ultimately pay, while its ability to pay is not strengthened, but weakened by a continued deficit. Loans are imperative in great emergencies to preserve the government or its credit, but a failure to supply needed revenue in time of peace for the maintenance of either has no justification.

The best way for the government to maintain its credit is to pay as it goes—not by resorting to loans, but by keeping out of debt—through an adequate income secured by a system of taxation, external or internal, or both. It is the settled policy of the government, pursued from the beginning and practised by all parties and administrations, to raise the bulk of our revenue from taxes upon foreign productions entering the United States for sale and consumption, and avoiding, for the most part, every form of direct taxation, except in time of war. The country is clearly opposed to any needless additions to the subject of internal taxation, and is committed by its latest popular utterance to the system of tariff taxation. There can be no misunderstanding, either, about the principle upon which this tariff taxation shall be levied. Nothing has ever been made plainer at a general election than that the controlling principle in the raising of revenue from duties on imports is zealous care for American interests and American labor. The people have declared that such legislation should be had as will give ample protection and encouragement to the industries and the development of our country. It is, therefore, earnestly hoped and expected that Congress will, at the earliest practicable moment, enact revenue legislation that shall be fair, reasonable, conservative, and just, and which, while supplying sufficient revenue for public purposes, will still be signally beneficial and helpful to every section and every enterprise of the people. To this policy we are all, of whatever party, firmly bound by the voice of the people—a power vastly more potential than the expression of any political platform. The paramount duty of Congress is to stop deficiencies by the restoration of that protective legislation which has always been the firmest prop of the Treasury. The passage of such a law or laws would strengthen the credit of the government both at home and abroad, and go far toward stopping the drain upon the gold reserve held for the redemption of our currency, which has been heavy and wellnigh constant for several years.

In the revision of the tariff especial attention should be given to the re-enactment and extension of the reciprocity principle of the law of 1890, under which so great a stimulus was given to our foreign trade in new and advantageous markets for our surplus agricultural and manufactured products. The brief trial given this legislation amply justifies a further experiment and additional discretionary power in the making of commercial treaties, the end in view always to be the opening up of new markets for the products of our country, by granting concessions to the products of other lands that we need and cannot produce ourselves, and which do not involve any loss of labor to our own people, but tend to increase their employment.

The depression of the past four years has fallen with especial severity upon the great body of toilers of the country, and upon none more than the holders of small farms. Agriculture has languished and labor suffered. The revival of manufacturing will be a relief to both. No portion of our population is more devoted to the institution of free government nor more loyal in their support, while none bears more cheerfully or fully its proper share in the maintenance of the government or is better entitled to its wise and liberal care and protection. Legislation helpful to producers is beneficial to all. The depressed condition of industry on the farm and in the mine and factory has lessened the ability of the people to meet the demands upon them, and they rightfully expect that only a system of revenue shall be established that will secure the largest income with the least burden, but that every means will be taken to decrease, rather than increase, our public expenditures. Business conditions are not the most promising. It will take time to restore the prosperity of former years. If we cannot promptly attain it, we can resolutely turn our faces in that direction and aid its return by friendly legislation. However troublesome the situation may appear, Congress will not, I am sure, be found lacking in disposition or ability to relieve it as far as legislation can do so. The restoration of confidence and the revival of business, which men of all parties so much desire, depend more largely upon the prompt, energetic, and intelligent action of Congress than upon any other single agency affecting the situation.

It is inspiring, too, to remember that no great emergency in the 108 years of our eventful national life has ever arisen that has not been met with wisdom and courage by the American people, with fidelity to their best interests and highest destiny, and to the honor of the American name. These years of glorious history have exalted mankind and advanced the cause of freedom throughout the world, and immeasurably strengthened the precious free institutions which we enjoy. The people love and will sustain these institutions. The great essential to our happiness and prosperity is that we adhere to the principles upon which the government was established and insist upon their faithful observance. Equality of rights must prevail, and our laws be always and everywhere respected and obeyed. We may have failed in the discharge of our full duty as citizens of the great republic, but it is consoling and encouraging to realize that free speech, a free press, free thought, free schools, the free and unmolested right of religious liberty and worship, and free and fair elections are dearer and more universally enjoyed to-day than ever before. These guaranties must be sacredly preserved and wisely strengthened. The constituted authorities must be cheerfully and vigorously upheld. Lynchings must not be tolerated in a great and civilized country like the United States; courts, not mobs, must execute the penalties of the law. The preservation of public order, the right of discussion, the integrity of courts, and the orderly administration of justice must continue forever the rock of safety upon which our government securely rests.

One of the lessons taught by the late election, which all can rejoice in, is that the citizens of the United States are both law-respecting and law-abiding people, not easily swerved from the path of patriotism and honor. This is in entire accord with the genius of our institutions, and but emphasizes the advantages of inculcating even a greater love for law and order in the future. Immunity should be granted to none who violate the laws, whether individuals, corporations, or communities; and as the Constitution imposes upon the president the duty of both its own execution, and of the statutes enacted in pursuance of its provisions, I shall endeavor carefully to carry them into effect. The declaration of the party now restored to power has been in the past that of "opposition to all combinations of capital organized in trusts, or otherwise, to control arbitrarily the condition of trade among our citizens," and it has supported "such legislation as will prevent the execution of all schemes to oppress the people by undue charges on their supplies, or by unjust rates for the transportation of their products to the market." This purpose will be steadily pursued, both by the enforcement of the laws now in existence and the recommendation and support of such new statutes as may be necessary to carry it into effect.

Our naturalization and immigration laws should be further improved to the constant promotion of a safer, a better, and a higher citizenship. A grave peril to the republic would be a citizenship too ignorant to understand or too vicious to appreciate the great value and beneficence of our institutions and laws, and against all who come here to make war upon them our gates must be promptly and tightly closed. Nor must we be unmindful of the need of improvement among our own citizens, but with the zeal of our forefathers encourage the spread of knowledge and free education. Illiteracy must be banished from the land if we shall attain that high destiny as the foremost of the enlightened nations of the world which, under Providence, we ought to achieve.

Reforms in the civil service must go on; but the changes should be real and genuine, not perfunctory, or prompted by a zeal in behalf of any party simply because it happens to be in power. As a member of Congress I voted and spoke in favor of the present law, and I shall attempt its enforcement in the spirit in which it was enacted. The purpose in view was to secure the most efficient service of the best men who would accept appointment under the government, retaining faithful and devoted public servants in office, but shielding none, under the authority of any rule or custom, who are inefficient, incompetent, or unworthy. The best interests of the country demand this, and the people heartily approve the law wherever and whenever it has been thus administered.

Congress should give prompt attention to the restoration of our American merchant marine, once the pride of the seas in all the great ocean highways of commerce. To my mind, few more important subjects so imperatively demand its intelligent consideration. The United States has progressed with marvelous rapidity in every field of enterprise and endeavor until we have become foremost in nearly all the great lines of inland trade, commerce, and industry. Yet, while this is true, our American merchant marine has been steadily declining until it is now lower, both in the percentage of tonnage and the number of vessels employed, than it was prior to the Civil War. Commendable progress has been made of late years in the upbuilding of the American navy, but we must suppplement these efforts by providing as a proper consort for it a merchant marine amply sufficient for our own carrying trade to foreign countries. The question is one that appeals both to our business necessities and the patriotic aspirations of a great people.

It has been the policy of the United States since the foundation of the government to cultivate relations of peace and amity with all the nations of the world, and this accords with my conception of our duty now. We have cherished the policy of noninterference with the affairs of foreign governments wisely inaugurated by Washington, keeping ourselves free from entanglement, either as allies or foes, content to leave undisturbed with them the settlement of their own domestic concerns. It will be our aim to pursue a firm and dignified foreign policy, which shall be just, impartial, ever watchful of our national honor, and always insisting upon the enforcement of the lawful rights of American citizens everywhere. Our diplomacy should seek nothing more and accept nothing less than is due us. We want no wars of conquest; we must avoid the temptation of territorial aggression. War should never be entered upon until every agency of peace has failed; peace is preferable to war in almost every contingency. Arbitration is the true method of settlement of international as well as local or individual differences. It was recognized as the best means of adjustment of differences between employers and employees by the 49th Congress, in 1886, and its application was extended to our diplomatic relations by the unanimous concurrence of the Senate and House of the 51st Congress in 1890. The latter resolution was accepted as the basis of negotiations with us by the British House of Commons in 1893, and upon our invitation a treaty of arbitration between the United States and

Great Britain was signed at Washington and transmitted to the Senate for its ratification in January last. Since this treaty is clearly the result of our own initiative; since it has been recognized as the leading feature of our foreign policy throughout our entire national history—the adjustment of difficulties by judicial methods rather than force of arms—and since it presents to the world the glorious example of reason and peace, not passion and war, controlling the relations between two of the greatest nations in the world, an example certain to be followed by others, I respectfully urge the early action of the Senate thereon, not merely as a matter of policy, but as a duty to mankind. The importance and moral influence of the ratification of such a treaty can hardly be overestimated in the cause of advancing civilization. It may well engage the best thought of the statesmen and people of every country, and I cannot but consider it fortunate that it was reserved to the United States to have the leadership in so grand a work.

It has been the uniform practice of each president to avoid, as far as possible, the convening of Congress in extraordinary session. It is an example which, under ordinary circumstances and in the absence of a public necessity, is to be commended. But a failure to convene the representatives of the people in Congress in extra session when it involves neglect of a public duty places the responsibility of such neglect upon the executive himself. The condition of the public Treasury, as has been indicated, demands the immediate consideration of Congress. It alone has the power to provide revenues for the government. Not to convene it under such circumstances I can view in no other sense than the neglect of a plain duty. I do not sympathize with the sentiment that Congress in session is dangerous to our general business interests. Its members are the agents of the people, and their presence at the seat of government in the execution of the sovereign will should not operate as an injury, but a benefit. There could be no better time to put the government upon a sound financial and economic basis than now. The people have only recently voted that this should be done, and nothing is more binding upon the agents of their will than the obligation of immediate action. It has always seemed to me that the postponement of the meeting of Congress until more than a year after it has been chosen deprived Congress too often of the inspiration of the popular will and the country of the corresponding benefits. It is evident, therefore, that to postpone action in the presence of so great a necessity would be unwise on the part of the executive because unjust to the interests of the people. Our action now will be freer from mere partisan consideration than if the question of tariff revision was postponed until the regular session of Congress. We are nearly two years from a Congressional election, and politics cannot so greatly distract us as if such contest was immediately pending. We can approach the problem calmly and patriotically, without fearing its effect upon an early election.

Our fellow citizens who may disagree with us upon the character of this legislation prefer to have the question settled now, even against their preconceived views, and perhaps settled so reasonably, as I trust and believe it will be, as to insure great permanence, than to have further uncertainty menacing the vast and varied business interests of the United States. Again, whatever action Congress may take will be given a fair opportunity for trial before the people are called to pass judgment upon it, and this I consider a great essential to the rightful and lasting settlement of the question. In view of these considerations, I shall deem it my duty as president to convene Congress in extraordinary session on Monday, the 15th day of March, 1897.

In conclusion, I congratulate the country upon the fraternal spirit of the people and the manifestations of good will everywhere so apparent. The recent election not only most fortunately demonstrated the obliteration of sectional or geographical lines, but to some extent also the prejudices which for years have distracted our councils and marred our true greatness as a nation. The triumph of the people, whose verdict is carried into effect to-day, is not the triumph of one section, nor wholly of one party, but of all sections and all the people. The North and the South no longer divide on the old lines, but upon principles and policies; and in this fact surely every lover of the country can find cause for true felicitation. Let us rejoice in and cultivate this spirit; it is ennobling and will be both a gain and a blessing to our beloved country. It will be my constant aim to do nothing, and permit nothing to be done, that will arrest or disturb this growing sentiment of unity and co-operation, this revival of esteem and affiliation which now animates so many thousands in both the old antagonistic sections, but I shall cheerfully do everything possible to promote and increase it.

Let me again repeat the words of the oath administered by the chief justice which, in their respective spheres, so far as applicable, I would have all my countrymen observe: "I will faithfully execute the office of president of the United States, and will, to the best of my ability, preserve, protect, and defend the Constitution of the United States."

This is the obligation I have reverently taken before the Lord Most High. To keep it will be my single purpose, my constant prayer; and I shall confidently rely upon the forebearance, and assistance of all the people in the discharge of my solemn responsibilities.

War with Spain

From the Second Annual Message to Congress
Washington, D.C.
December 5, 1898

FOR YEARS, Cuban rebels had been fighting for the island's independence from Spain. American sympathies, fanned by lurid tales of Spanish atrocities published in William Randolph Hearst's New York *Journal* and Joseph Pulitzer's New York *World,* lay mainly with the rebels. As the clamor for U.S. intervention increased, McKinley calmly pursued negotiations with Spain to end the conflict and, if possible, to gain possession of the islands. The sinking in February 1898 of the American battleship *Maine* in Havana harbor, widely attributed in the government and the press to Spanish agents, ended reasonable discussion. In April 1898 McKinley signed a resolution authorizing American intervention to help Cuba achieve independence. Spain broke relations with the United States, and the Senate then voted for war.

In this excerpt from his second annual message to Congress, McKinley outlines the course of the conflict, which lasted a mere three months but which left the United States a major maritime power and the possessor of a Pacific empire.

Notwithstanding the added burdens rendered necessary by the war, our people rejoice in a very satisfactory and steadily increasing degree of prosperity, evidenced by the largest volume of business ever recorded. Manufacture has been productive, agricultural pursuits have yielded abundant returns, labor in all fields of industry is better rewarded, revenue legislation passed by the present Congress has increased the Treasury's receipts to the amount estimated by its authors, the finances of the government have been successfully administered and its credit advanced to the first tank, while its currency has been maintained at the world's highest standard. Military service under a common flag and for a righteous cause has strengthened the national spirit and served to cement more closely than ever the fraternal bonds between every section of the country.

A review of the relation of the United States to other powers, always appropriate, is this year of primary importance in view of the momentous issues which have arisen, demanding in one instance the ultimate determination by arms and involving far-reaching consequences which will require the earnest attention of the Congress.

In my last annual message very full consideration was given to the question of the duty of the government of the United States toward Spain and and the Cuban insurrection as being by far the most important problem with which we were then called upon to deal. The considerations then advanced and the exposition of the views therein expressed disclosed my sense of the extreme gravity of the situation. Setting aside as logically unfounded or practically inadmissible the recognition of the Cuban insurgents as belligerents, the recognition of the independence of Cuba, neutral intervention to end the war by imposing a rational compromise between the contestants, intervention in favor of one or the other party, and forcible annexation of the island, I concluded it was honestly due to our friendly relations with Spain that she should be given a resonable chance to realize her expectations of reform to which she had become irrevocably committed. Within a few weeks previously she had announced comprehensive plans which it was confidently asserted would be efficacious to remedy the evils so deeply affecting our own country, so injurious to the true interests of the mother country as well as to those of Cuba, and so repugnant to the universal sentiment of humanity.

The ensuing month brought little sign of real progress toward the pacification of Cuba. The autonomous administrations set up in the capital and some of the principal cities appeared not to gain the favor of the inhabitants nor to be able to extend their influence to the large extent of territory held by the insurgents, while the military arm, obviously unable to cope with the still active rebellion, continued many of the most objectionable and offensive policies of the government that had preceded it. No tangible relief was afforded the vast numbers of unhappy reconcentrados, despite the reiterated professions made in that regard and the amount appropriated by Spain to that end. The proffered expedient of zones of cultivation proved illusory. Indeed no less practical nor more delusive promises of succor could well have been tendered to the exhausted and destitute people, stripped of all that made life and home dear and herded in a strange region among unsympathetic strangers hardly less necessitous than themselves.

By the end of December the mortality among them had frightfully increased. Conservative estimates from Spanish sources placed the deaths among these distressed people at over 40 percent from the time General Weyler's decree of reconcentration was enforced. With the acquiescence of the Spanish authorities, a scheme was adopted for relief by charitable contributions raised in this country and distributed, under the direction of the consul-general and the several consuls, by noble and earnest individual effort through the organized agencies of the American Red Cross. Thousands of lives were thus saved, but many thousands more were inaccessible to such forms of aid.

The war continued on the old footing, without comprehensive plan, developing only the same spasmodic encounters, barren of strategic result, that had marked the course of the earlier 10 years' rebellion as well as the present insurrection from its start. No alternative save physical exhaustion of either combatant, and therewithal the practical ruin of the island, lay in sight, but how far distant no one could venture to conjecture.

At this juncture, on the 15th of February last, occurred the destruction of the battleship *Maine* while rightfully lying in the harbor of Havana on a mission of international courtesy and good will—a catastrophe the suspicious nature and horror of which stirred the nation's heart profoundly. It is a striking evidence of the poise and sturdy good sense distinguishing our national character that this shocking blow, falling upon a generous people already deeply touched by preceding events in Cuba, did not move them to an instant desperate resolve to tolerate no longer the existence of a condition of danger and disorder at our doors that made possible such a deed, by whomsoever wrought. Yet the instinct of justice prevailed, and the nation anxiously awaited the result of the searching investigation at once set on foot. The finding of the naval board of inquiry established that the origin of the explosion was external, by a submarine mine, and only halted through lack of positive testimony to fix the responsibility of its authorship.

All these things carried conviction to the most thoughtful, even before the finding of the naval court, that a crisis in our relations with Spain and toward Cuba was at hand. So strong was this belief that it needed but a brief executive suggestion to the Congress to receive immediate answer to the duty of making instant provision for the possible and perhaps speedily probable emergency of war, and the remarkable, almost unique, spectacle was presented of a unanimous vote of both houses, on the 9th of March appropriating $50,000,000 "for the national defense and for each and every purpose connected therewith, to be expended at the discretion of the president." That this act of prevision came none too soon was disclosed when the application of the fund was undertaken. Our coasts were practically undefended. Our navy needed large provision for increased ammunition and supplies, and even numbers to cope with any sudden attack from the navy of Spain, which comprised modern vessels of the highest type of continental perfection. Our army also required enlargement of men and munitions. The details of the hurried preparation for the dreaded contingency are told in the reports of the secretaries of war and of the navy, and need not be repeated here. It is sufficient to say that the outbreak of war when it did come found our nation not unprepared to meet the conflict.

Nor was the apprehension of coming strife confined to our own country. It was felt by the continental powers, which on April 6, through their ambassadors and envoys, addressed to the executive an expression of hope that humanity and moderation might mark the course of this government and people, and that further negotiations would lead to an agreement which, while securing the maintenance of peace, would afford all necessary guaranties for the reestablishment of order in Cuba. In responding to that representation I said I shared the hope the envoys had expressed that peace might be preserved in a manner to terminate the chronic condition of disturbance in Cuba, so injurious and menacing to our interests and tranquillity, as well as shocking to our sentiments of humanity; and while appreciating the humanitarian and disinterested character of the communication they had made on behalf of the powers, I stated the confidence of this government, for its part, that equal appreciation would be shown for its own earnest and unselfish endeavors to fulfill a duty to humanity by ending a situation the indefinite prolongation of which had become insufferable.

Still animated by the hope of a peaceful solution and obeying the dictates of duty, no effort was relaxed to bring about a speedy ending of the Cuban struggle. Negotiations to this object continued actively with the government of Spain, looking to the immediate conclusion of a six months' armistice in Cuba, with a view to effect the recognition of her people's right to independence. Besides this, the instant revocation of the order of reconcentration was asked, so that the sufferers, returning to their homes and aided by united America and Spanish effort, might be put in a way to support themselves and, by orderly resumption of the well-nigh destroyed productive energies of the island, contribute to the restoration of its tranquillity and well-being. Negotiations continued for some little time at Madrid, resulting in offers by the Spanish government which could not but be regarded as inadequate. It was proposed to confide the preparation of peace to the insular parliament, yet to be convened under the autonomous decrees of November 1897, but without impairment in any wise of the constitutional powers of the Madrid government, which to that end would grant an armistice, if solicited by the insurgents, for such time as the general in chief might see fit to fix. How and with what scope of discretionary powers the insular parliament was expected to set about the "preparation" of peace did not appear. If it were to be by negotiation with the insurgents, the issue seemed to rest on the one side with a body chosen by a fraction of the electors in the districts under Spanish control, and on the other with the insurgent population holding the interior country, unrepresented in the so-called parliament and defiant at the suggestion of suing for peace.

Grieved and disappointed at this barren outcome of my sincere endeavors to reach a practicable solution, I felt it my duty to remit the whole question to the Congress. In the message of April 11, 1898, I announced that with this last overture in the direction of immediate peace in Cuba and its disappointing reception by Spain the effort of the executive was brought to an end. I again reviewed the alternative courses of action which had been proposed, concluding that the only one consonant with international policy and compatible with our firm-set historical traditions was intervention as a neutral to stop the war and check the hopeless sacrifice of life, even though that resort involved "hostile constraint upon both the parties to the contest, as well to enforce a truce as to guide the eventual settlement." The grounds justifying that step were the interests of humanity, the duty to protect the life and property of our citizens in Cuba, the right to check injury to our commerce and people through the devastation of the island, and, most important, the need of removing at once and forever the constant menace and the burdens entailed upon our government by the uncertainties and perils of the situation caused by the unendurable disturbance in Cuba. I said:

> The long trial has proved that the object for which Spain has waged the war can not be attained. The fire of insurrection may flame or may smolder with varying seasons, but it has not been and it is plain that it can not be extinguished by present methods. The only hope of relief and repose from a condition which can no longer be endured is the enforced pacification of Cuba. In the name of humanity, in the name of civilization, in behalf of endangered American interests which give us the right and the duty to speak and to act, the war in Cuba must stop.

In view of all this the Congress was asked to authorize and empower the president to take measures to secure a full and final termination of hostilities between Spain and the people of Cuba and to secure in the island the establishment of a stable government, capable of maintaining order and observing its international obligations, insuring peace and tranquillity and the security of its citizens as well as our own, and for the accomplishment of those ends to use the military and naval forces of the United States as might be necessary, with added authority to continue generous relief to the starving people of Cuba.

The response of the Congress, after nine days of earnest deliberation, during which the almost unanimous sentiment of your body was developed on every point save as to the expediency of coupling the proposed action with a formal recognition of the republic of Cuba as the true and lawful government of that island—a proposition which failed of adoption—the Congress, after conference, on the 19th of April, by a vote of 42 to 35 in the Senate and 311 to 6 in the House of Representatives, passed the memorable joint resolution declaring—

First. That the people of the island of Cuba are, and of right ought to be, free and independent.

Second. That it is the duty of the United States to demand, and the government of the United States does hereby demand, that the government of Spain at once relinquish its authority and government in the island of Cuba and withdraw its land and naval forces from Cuba and Cuban waters.

Third. That the president of the United States be, and he hereby is, directed and empowered to use the entire land and naval forces of the United States and to call into the actual service of the United States the militia of the several states to such extent as may be necessary to carry these resolutions into effect.

Fourth. That the United States hereby disclaims any disposition or intention to exercise sovereignty, jurisdiction, or control over said island except for the pacification thereof, and asserts its determination when that is accomplished to leave the government and control of the island to its people.

This resolution was approved by the executive on the next day, April 20. A copy was at once communicated to the Spanish minister at this capital, who forthwith announced that his continuance in Washington had thereby become impossible, and asked for his passports, which were given him. He thereupon withdrew from Washington, leaving the protection of Spanish interests in the United States to the French ambassador and the Austro-Hungarian minister. Simultaneously with its communication to the Spanish minister here, General Woodford, the American minister at Madrid, was telegraphed confirmation of the text of the joint resolution and directed to communicate it to the government of Spain with the formal demand that it at once relinquish its authority and government in the island of Cuba and withdraw its forces therefrom, coupling this demand with announcement of the intentions of this government as to the future of the island, in conformity with the fourth clause of the resolution, and giving Spain until noon of April 23 to reply.

That demand, although, as above shown, officially made known to the Spanish envoy here, was not delivered at Madrid. After the instruction reached General Woodford on the morning of April 21, but before he could present it, the Spanish minister of state notified him that upon the president's approval of the joint resolution the Madrid government, regarding the act as "equivalent to an evident declaration of war," had ordered its minister in Washington to withdraw, thereby breaking off diplomatic relations between the two countries and ceasing all official communication between their respective representatives. General Woodford thereupon demanded his passports and quitted Madrid the same day.

Spain having thus denied the demand of the United States and initiated that complete form of rupture of relations which attends a state of war, the executive powers authorized by the resolution were at once used by me to meet the enlarged contingency of actual war between sovereign states. On April 22 I proclaimed a blockade of the north coast of Cuba, including ports on said coast between Cardenas and Bahia Honda, and the port of Cienfuegos, on the south coast of Cuba, and on the 23d I called for volunteers to execute the purpose of the resolution. By my message of April 25 the Congress was informed of the situation, and I recommended formal declaration of the existence of a state of war between the United States and Spain. The Congress accordingly voted on the same day the act approved April 25, 1898, declaring the existence of such war from and including the 21st day of April, and reenacted the provision of the resolution of April 20 directing the president to use all the armed forces of the nation to carry that act into effect. . . .

It is not within the province of this message to narrate the history of the extraordinary war that followed the Spanish declaration of April 21, but a brief recital of its more salient features is appropriate.

The first encounter of the war in point of date took place April 27, when a detachment of the blockading squadron made a reconnaissance in force at Matanzas, shelled the harbor forts, and demolished several new works in construction.

The next engagement was destined to mark a memorable epoch in maritime warfare. The Pacific fleet, under Commodore George Dewey, had lain for some weeks at Hong Kong. Upon the colonial proclamation of neutrality being issued and the customary 24 hours' notice being given, it repaired to Mirs Bay, near Hong Kong, whence it proceeded to the Philippine Islands under telegraphed orders to capture or destroy the formidable Spanish fleet then assembled at Manila. At daybreak on the 1st of May the American force entered Manila Bay, and after a few hours' engagement effected the total destruction of the Spanish fleet, consisting of 10 war ships and a transport, besides capturing the naval station and forts at Cavite, thus annihilating the Spanish naval power in the Pacific Ocean and completely controlling the bay of Manila, with the ability to take the city at will. Not a life was lost on our ships, the wounded only numbering seven, while not a vessel was materially injured. For this gallant achievement the Congress, upon my recommendation, fitly bestowed upon the actors preferment and substantial reward.

The effect of this remarkable victory upon the spirit of our people and upon the fortunes of the war was instant. A prestige of invincibility thereby attached to our arms which continued throughout the struggle. Reinforcements were hurried to Manila under the command of Major-General Merritt and firmly established within sight of the capital, which lay helpless before our guns.

On the 7th day of May the government was advised officially of the victory at Manila, and at once inquired of the commander of our fleet what troops would be required. The information was received on the 15th day of May, and the first army expedition sailed May 25 and arrived off Manila June 30. Other expeditions soon followed, the total force consisting of 641 officers and 15,058 enlisted men.

Only reluctance to cause needless loss of life and property prevented the early storming and capture of the city, and therewith the absolute military occupancy of the whole group. The insurgents meanwhile had resumed the active hostilities suspended by the uncompleted truce of December 1897. Their forces invested Manila from the northern and eastern sides, but were constrained by Admiral Dewey and General Merritt from attempting assault. It was fitting that whatever was to be done in the way of decisive operations in that quarter should be accomplished by the strong arm of the United States alone. Obeying the stern precept of war which enjoins the overcoming of the adversary and the extinction of his power wherever assailable as the speedy and sure means to win a peace, divided victory was not permissible, for no partition of the rights and responsibilities attending the enforcement of a just and advantageous peace could be thought of.

Following the comprehensive scheme of general attack, powerful forces were assembled at various points on our coast to invade Cuba and Puerto Rico. Meanwhile naval demonstrations were made at several exposed points. On May 11 the cruiser *Wilmington* and torpedo boat *Winslow* were unsuccessful in an attempt to silence the batteries at Cardenas, a gallant ensign, Worth Bagley, and four seamen falling. These grievous fatalities were, strangely enough, among the very few which occurred during our naval operations in this extraordinary conflict.

Meanwhile the Spanish naval preparations had been pushed with great vigor. A powerful squadron under Admiral Cervera, which had assembled at the Cape Verde Islands before the outbreak of hostilities, had crossed the ocean, and by its erratic movements in the Caribbean Sea delayed our military plans while baffling the pursuit of our fleets. For a time fears were felt lest the *Oregon* and *Marietta*, then nearing home after their long voyage from San Francisco of over 15,000 miles, might be surprised by Admiral Cervera's fleet, but their fortunate arrival dispelled these apprehensions and lent much-needed reenforcement. Not until Admiral Cervera took refuge in the harbor of Santiago de Cuba, about May 19, was it practicable to plan a systematic naval and military attack upon the Antillean possessions of Spain.

Several demonstrations occurred on the coasts of Cuba and Puerto Rico in preparation for the larger event. On May 13 the North Atlantic Squadron shelled San Juan de Puerto Rico. On May 30 Commodore Schley's squadron bombarded the forts guarding the mouth of Santiago Harbor. Neither attack had any material result. It was evident that well-ordered land operations were indispensable to achieve a decisive advantage.

The next act in the war thrilled not alone the hearts of our countrymen but the world by its exceptional heroism. On the night of June 3 Lieutenant Hobson, aided by seven devoted volunteers, blocked the narrow outlet from Santiago Harbor by sinking the collier *Merrimac* in the channel, under a fierce fire from the shore batteries, escaping with their lives as by a miracle, but falling into the hands of the Spaniards. It is a most gratifying incident of the war that the bravery of this little band of heroes was cordially appreciated by the Spanish admiral, who sent a flag of truce to notify Admiral Sampson of their safety and to compliment them on their daring act. They were subsequently exchanged July 7.

By June 7 the cutting of the last Cuban cable isolated the island. Thereafter the invasion was vigorously prosecuted. On June 10, under a heavy protecting fire, a landing of 600 marines from the *Oregon, Marblehead,* and *Yankee* was effected in Guantanamo Bay, where it had been determined to establish a naval station.

This important and essential port was taken from the enemy, after severe fighting, by the marines, who were the first organized force of the United States to land in Cuba.

The position so won was held despite desperate attempts to dislodge our forces. By June 16 additional forces were landed and strongly intrenched. On June 22 the advance of the invading army under Major-General Shafter landed at Daiquiri, about 15 miles east of Santiago. This was accomplished under great difficulties, but with marvelous dispatch. On June 23 the movement against Santiago was begun. On the 24th the first serious engagement took place, in which the First and 10th Cavalry and the First United States Volunteer Cavalry, General Young's brigade of General Wheeler's division, participated, losing heavily. By nightfall, however, ground within five miles of Santiago was won. The advantage was steadily increased. On July 1 a severe battle took place, our forces gaining the outworks of Santiago; on the 2d El Caney and San Juan were taken after a desperate charge, and the investment of the city was completed. The navy cooperated by shelling the town and the coast forts.

On the day following this brilliant achievement of our land forces, the 3d of July, occurred the decisive naval combat of the war. The Spanish fleet, attempting to leave the harbor, was met by the American squadron under command of Commodore Sampson. In less than three hours all the Spanish ships were destroyed, the two torpedo boats being sunk and the *Maria Teresa, Almirante Oquendo, Vizcaya,* and *Cristobal Colon* driven ashore. The Spanish admiral and over 1,300 men were taken prisoners. While the enemy's loss of life was deplorably large, some 600 perishing, on our side but one man was killed, on the *Brooklyn,* and one man seriously wounded. Although our ships were repeatedly struck, not one was seriously injured. Where all so conspicuously distinguished themselves, from the commanders to the gunners and the unnamed heroes in the boiler rooms, each and all contributing toward the achievement of this astounding victory, for which neither ancient nor modern history affords a parallel in the completeness of the event and the marvelous disproportion of casualties, it would be invidious to single out any for especial honor. Deserved promotion has rewarded the more conspicuous actors. The nation's profoundest gratitude is due to all of these brave men who by their skill and devotion in a few short hours crushed the sea power of Spain and wrought a triumph whose decisiveness and far-reaching consequences can scarcely be measured. Nor can we be unmindful of the achievements of our builders, mechanics, and artisans for their skill in the construction of our war ships.

With the catastrophe of Santiago Spain's effort upon the ocean virtually ceased. A spasmodic effort toward the end of June to send her Mediterranean fleet, under Admiral Camara, to relieve Manila was abandoned, the expedition being recalled after it had passed through the Suez Canal.

The capitulation of Santiago followed. The city was closely besieged by land, while the entrance of our ships into the harbor cut off all relief on that side. After a truce to allow of the removal of noncombatants protracted negotiations continued from July 3 until July 15, when, under menace of immediate assault, the preliminaries of surrender were agreed upon. On the 17th General Shafter occupied the city. The capitulation embraced the entire eastern end of Cuba. The number of Spanish soldiers surrendering was 22,000, all of whom were subsequently conveyed to Spain at the charge of the United States. The story of this successful campaign is told in the report of the secretary of war, which will be laid before you. The individual valor of officers and soldiers was never more strikingly shown than in the several engagements leading to the surrender of Santiago, while the prompt movements and successive victories won instant and universal applause. To those who gained this complete triumph, which established the ascendency of the United States upon land as the fight off Santiago had fixed our supremacy on the seas, the earnest and lasting gratitude of the nation is unsparingly due. Nor should we alone remember the gallantry of the living; the dead claim our tears, and our losses by battle and disease must cloud any exultation at the result and teach us to weigh the awful cost of war, however rightful the cause or signal the victory.

With the fall of Santiago the occupation of Puerto Rico became the next strategic necessity. General Miles had previously been assigned to organize an expedition for that purpose. Fortunately he was already at Santiago, where he had arrived on the 11th of July with reenforcements for General Shafter's army.

With these troops, consisting of 3,415 infantry and artillery, two companies of engineers, and one company of the Signal Corps, General Miles left Guantanamo on July 21, having nine transports convoyed by the fleet under Captain Higginson with the *Massachusetts* (flagship), *Dixie, Gloucester, Columbia,* and *Yale,* the two latter carrying troops. The expedition landed at Guanica July 25, which port was entered with little opposition. Here the fleet was joined by the *Annapolis* and the *Wasp,* while the *Puritan* and *Amphitrite* went to San Juan and joined the *New Orleans,* which was engaged in blockading that port. The major-general commanding was subsequently reenforced by General Schwan's brigade of the Third Army Corps, by General Wilson with a part of his division, and also by General Brooke with a part of his corps, numbering in all 16,973 officers and men.

On July 27 he entered Ponce, one of the most important ports in the island, from which he thereafter directed operations for the capture of the island.

With the exception of encounters with the enemy at Guayama, Hormigueros, Coamo, and Yauco and an attack on a force landed at Cape San Juan, there was no serious resistance. The campaign was prosecuted with great vigor, and by the 12th of August much of the island was in our possession and the acquisition of the remainder was only a matter of a short time. At most of the points in the island our troops were enthusiastically welcomed. Protestations of loyalty to the flag and gratitude for delivery from Spanish rule met our commanders at every stage. As a potent influence toward peace the outcome of the Puerto Rican expedition was of great consequence, and generous commendation is due to those who participated in it.

The last scene of the war was enacted at Manila, its starting place. On August 15, after a brief assault upon the works by the land forces, in which the squadron assisted, the capital surrendered unconditionally. The casualties were comparatively few. By this the conquest of the Philippine Islands, virtually accomplished when the Spanish capacity for resistance was destroyed by Admiral Dewey's victory of the 1st of May, was formally sealed. To General Merritt, his officers and men, for their uncomplaining and devoted service and for their gallantry in action, the nation is sincerely grateful. Their long voyage was made with singular success, and the soldierly conduct of the men, most of whom were without previous experience in the military service, deserves unmeasured praise.

The total casualties in killed and wounded in the army during the war with Spain were: Officers killed, 23; enlisted men killed, 257; total, 280; officers wounded, 113; enlisted men wounded, 1,464; total, 1,577. Of the navy: Killed, 17; wounded, 67; died as result of wounds, 1; invalided from service, 6; total, 91.

It will be observed that while our navy was engaged in two great battles and in numerous perilous undertakings in blockade and bombardment, and more than 50,000 of our troops were transported to distant lands and were engaged in assault and siege and battle and many skirmishes in unfamiliar territory, we lost in both arms of the service a total of 1,668 killed and wounded; and in the entire campaign by land and sea we did not lose a gun or a flag or a transport or a ship, and, with the exception of the crew of the *Merrimac,* not a soldier or sailor was taken prisoner.

On August 7 forty-six days from the date of the landing of General Shafter's army in Cuba and 21 days from the surrender of Santiago, the United States troops commenced embarkation for home, and our entire force was returned to the United States as early as August 24. They were absent from the United States only two months. . . .

On Imperialism

New York City, New York

March 3, 1900

IN FEBRUARY 1900 McKinley appointed William Howard Taft, then a U.S. circuit court judge in Cleveland, to head the commission charged with establishing a civil government in the Philippines, newly acquired from Spain during the war. Taft was on record as opposing American imperialism; his appointment was in part engineered by McKinley to ease the fears of the many Americans who felt the way Taft did. McKinley followed up this move a month later with a well-received speech on imperialism before the Ohio Society of New York. Among its ringing platitudes can be found a clear denunciation of imperialism mixed with an equally clear call in favor of it, in the guise of bringing American civilization to the inhabitants of "our distant acquisitions." Overall, McKinley encouraged economic expansion, especially in the Far East, while disavowing the kind of ideological commitment professed by Theodore Roosevelt and other believers in America's manifest imperial destiny.

The statement which has so often been made is not far from the truth, "Once an Ohioan, always an Ohioan." It has been some years since I was your guest. Much has happened in the meantime. We have our blessings and our burdens, and still have both. We will soon have legislative assurance of the continuance of the gold standard, with which we measure our exchanges, and we have the open door in the Far East through which to market our products. We are neither in alliance nor antagonism for entanglement with any foreign power, but on terms of amity and cordiality with all. We buy from them all and sell to them all, and our sales exceeded our purchases in the past two years by over one billion dollars.

Markets have been increased and mortgages have been reduced. Interest has fallen and wages have advanced. The public debt is decreasing. The country is well-to-do. Its people for the most part are happy and contented. They have good times and are on good terms with the nations of the world. There are unfortunately those among us, few in number I am sure, who seem to thrive best under hard times, and who, when good times overtake them in the United States, feel constrained to put us on bad terms with the rest of mankind. With them I can have no sympathy. I would rather give expression to what I believe to be the nobler and almost universal sentiment of our countrymen in the wish, not only for our peace and prosperity, but for the peace and prosperity of all the nations and people of the earth.

After 33 years of unbroken peace came an unavoidable war. Happily, the conclusion was quickly reached without a suspicion of unworthy motive, or practice, or purpose on our part and with fadeless honor on our arms. I cannot forget the quick response of the people to the country's need, and the quarter of a million men who freely offered their lives to the country's service. It was an impressive spectacle of national strength. It demonstrated our mighty reserve power and taught us that large standing armies are unnecessary as a "Minute Man" ready to join the ranks for national defense.

Out of these recent events have come to the United States grave trials and responsibilities. As it was the nation's war, so are its results the nation's problem. Its solution rests upon us all. It is too serious to stifle. It is too earnest for response. No phrase or catchword can conceal the sacred obligation it involves. No use of epithets, no aspersion of motive of those who differ, will contribute to that sober judgment so essential to right conclusions. No political outcry can abrogate our treaty of peace with Spain, or absolve us from its solemn engagements. It is the people's question, and will be until its determination is written out in their enlightened verdict. We must choose between manly doing and base desertion. It will never be the latter. It must be soberly settled in justice and good conscience, and it will be. Righteousness which exalteth a nation must control in its solution.

No great emergency has arisen in this nation's history and progress which has not been met by the sovereigns with high capacity, with ample strength, and with unflinching fidelity to every honorable obligation. Partisanship can hold few of us against solemn public duty. We have seen this so often demonstrated in the past as to mark unerringly what it will be in the future. The national sentiment and the national conscience were never stronger or higher than now.

There has been a reunion of the people around the holy altar consecrated to country newly sanctified by common sacrifices. The followers of Grant and Lee have fought under the same flag, and fallen for the same fate. Party lines have loosened and ties of Union have been strengthened. Sectionalism has disappeared, and fraternity has been rooted in the hearts of the American people. Political passion has altogether expired, and patriotism glows with unextinguishable fervor in every home of the land. The flag has been sustained on distant seas and islands by the men of all parties and sections and creeds and races and nationalities, and its stars are only those of radiant hope to the remote people over whom it floats.

There can be no imperialism. Those who fear it are against it. Those who have faith in the republic are against it. So that there is universal abhorrence for it and unanimous opposition to it. Our only difference is that those who do not agree with us have no confidence in the virtue or capacity or high purpose or good faith of this free people as a civilizing agency: while we believe that the century of free government which the American people has enjoyed has not rendered them irresolute and faithless, but has fitted them for the great task of lifting up and assisting to better conditions and larger liberty those distant people who have through the issue of battle become our wards.

Let us fear not. There is no occasion for faint hearts, no excuse for regrets. Nations do not grow in strength and the cause of liberty and law by the doing of easy things. The harder the task the greater will be the result, the benefit, and the honor. To doubt our power to accomplish it is to lose our faith in the soundness and strengths of our popular institutions.

The liberators will never become the oppressors. A self-governed people will never permit despotism in any government which they foster and defend.

Gentlemen, we have the new care and cannot shift it. And, breaking up the camp of ease and isolation, let us bravely and hopefully and soberly continue the march of faithful service and falter not until the work is done. It is not possible that 75 million American freemen are unable to establish liberty and justice and good government in our new possessions. The burden is our opportunity. The opportunity is greater than the burden. May God give us strength to bear the one and wisdom so to embrace the other as to carry to our distant acquisitions the guarantees of "life, liberty, and the pursuit of happiness."

Trade Reciprocity

Buffalo, New York
September 5, 1901

ON PRESIDENTS' DAY, a triumphant reception greeted McKinley as he rose to speak before the festive crowds at the annual Pan-American Exposition. This was the last stop of a national speaking tour, and McKinley's address on trade reciprocity was the most important of the trip. The president, a devout protectionist, had helped create and maintain the high tariffs that kept domestic industry strong but that would later cause much trouble for his party. Despite his long advocacy of high tariffs—the Dingley Tariff, passed within months of his first inauguration, was the highest ever—McKinley understood the need for reciprocal commercial agreements between trading partners, treaties that would allow each partner to lower trade restrictions in concert with the other, thus expanding international trade while protecting domestic manufacturers. McKinley now believed that a "universal brotherhood of man" could be attained through the careful and fair structuring of international commerce. But in this he had moved beyond the reactionaries of his own party; attempts to ratify reasonable trade agreements with U.S. allies led to constant battles in Congress between protectionists and tariff reformers.

McKinley, at the height of his power, might have been able to push such a program through a reluctant Congress. But the day after he gave this speech McKinley was shot by an anarchist, Leon Czolgosz, while he stood shaking hands with a crowd of well-wishers. He died eight days later. The goal of trade reciprocity eluded his Republican successors, Roosevelt and Taft; it was left to a Democrat, Woodrow Wilson, to effect major trade and tariff reforms.

. . . Expositions are the timekeepers of progress. They record the world's advancement. They stimulate the energy, enterprise, and intellect of the people and quicken human genius. They go into the home. They broaden and brighten the daily life of the people. They open mighty storehouse of information to the student. Every exposition, great or small, has helped to some onward step. Comparison of ideas is always educational, and as such instruct the brain and hand of man. Friendly rivalry follows, which is the spur to industrial improvement, the inspiration to useful invention and to high endeavor in all departments of human activity. It exacts a study of the wants, comforts, and even the whims of the people and recognizes the efficiency of high quality and new pieces to win their favor. The quest for trade is an incentive to men of business to devise, invent, improve, and economize in the cost of production.

Business life, whether among ourselves or with other people, is ever a sharp struggle for success. It will be none the less so in the future. Without competition we would be clinging to the clumsy antiquated processes of farming and manufacture and the methods of business of long ago, and the 20th would be no further advanced than the 18th century. But though commercial competitors we are, commercial enemies we must not be.

The Pan-American Exposition has done its work thoroughly, presenting in its exhibits evidences of the highest skill and illustrating the progress of the human family in the Western Hemisphere. This portion of the earth has no cause for humiliation for the part it has performed in the march of civilization. It has not accomplished everything from it. It has simply done its best, and without vanity or boastfulness, and recognizing the manifold achievements of others, it invites the friendly rivalry of all the powers in the peaceful pursuits of trade and commerce and will co-operate with all in advancing the highest and best interests of humanity.

The wisdom and energy of all the nations are none too great for the world's work. The success of art, science, industry, and invention is an international asset and a common glory.

After all, how near one to the other is every part of the world. Modern inventions have brought into close relation widely separated peoples and made them better acquainted. Geographic and political divisions will continue to exist, but distances have been effaced.

Swift ships and swift trains are becoming cosmopolitan. They invade fields which a few years ago were impenetrable. The world's products are exchanged as never before, and with increasing transportation facilities come increasing knowledge and larger trade. Prices are fixed with mathematical precision by supply and demand. The world's selling prices are regulated by market and crop reports.

We travel greater distances in a shorter space of time and with more ease than was ever dreamed of by the fathers. Isolation is no longer possible or desirable. The same important news is read, though in different languages, the same day in all Christendom. The telegraph keeps us advised of what is occurring everywhere, and the press foreshadows, with more or less accuracy, the plans and purposes of the nations.

Market prices of products and of securities are hourly known in every commercial mart, and the investments of the people extend beyond their own national boundaries into the remotest parts of the earth. Vast transactions are conducted and international exchanges are made by the tick of the cable. Every event of interest is immediately bulletined. The quick gathering and transmission of news, like rapid transit, are of recent origin and are only made possible by the genius of the inventor and the courage of the investor. It took a special messenger of the government, with every facility known at the time for rapid travel 19 days to go from the city of Washington to New Orleans with a message to General Jackson that the war with England had ceased and a treaty of peace had been signed. How different now!

We reached General Miles in Puerto Rico by cable, and he was able, through the military telegraph, to stop his army on the firing line with the message that the United States and Spain had signed a protocol suspending hostilities. We knew almost instantly of the first shots fired at Santiago, and the subsequent surrender of the Spanish forces was known at Washington within less than an hour of its consummation. The first ship of Cervera's fleet had hardly emerged from that historic harbor when the fact was flashed to our capital, and the swift destruction that followed was announced immediately through the wonderful medium of telegraphy.

So accustomed are we to safe and easy communication with distant lands that its temporary interruption, even in ordinary times, results in loss and inconvenience. We shall never forget the days of anxious waiting and awful suspense when no information was permitted to be sent from Peking, and the diplomatic representatives of the nations in China, cut off from all communication, inside and outside of the walled capital, were surrounded by an angry and misguided mob that threatened their lives; nor the joy that filled the world when a single message from the government of the United States brought through our minister the first news of the safety of the besieged diplomats.

At the beginning of the 19th century there was not a mile of steam railroad on the globe. Now there are enough miles to make its circuit many times. Then there was not a line of electric telegraph; now we have a vast mileage traversing all lands and seas. God and man have linked the nations together. No nation can longer be indifferent to any other. And as we are brought more and more in touch with each other the less occasion there is for misunderstandings and the stronger the disposition, when we have differences, to adjust them in the court of arbitration, which is the noblest forum for the settlement of international disputes.

My fellow citizens, trade statistics indicate that this country is in a state of unexampled prosperity. The figures are almost appalling. They show that we are utilizing our fields and forests and mines and that we are furnishing profitable employment to the millions of workingmen throughout the United States, bringing comfort and happiness to their homes and making it possible to lay by savings for old age and disability. That all the people are participating in this great prosperity is seen in every American community, and shown by the enormous and unprecedented deposits in our savings banks. Our duty is the care and security of these deposits, and their safe investment demands the highest integrity and the best business capacity of those in charge of these depositories of the people's earnings.

We have a vast and intricate business, built up through years of toil and struggle, in which every part of the country has its stake, and will not permit of either neglect or of undue selfishness. No narrow, sordid policy will subserve it. The greatest skill and wisdom on the part of the manufacturers and producers will be required to hold and increase it. Our industrial enterprises which have grown to such great proportions affect the homes and occupations of the people and the welfare of the country. Our capacity to produce has developed so enormously and our products have so multiplied that the problem of more markets requires our urgent and immediate attention. Only a broad and enlightened policy will keep what we have. No other policy will get more. In these times of marvelous business energy and gain we ought to be looking to the future, strengthening the weak places in our industrial and commercial system, that we may be ready for any storm or strain.

By sensible trade arrangements which will not interrupt our home production we shall extend the outlets for our increasing surplus. A system which provides a mutual exchange of commodities, a mutual exchange is manifestly essential to the continued and healthful growth of our export trade. We must not repose in fancied security that we can forever sell everything and buy little or nothing. If such a thing were possible, it would not be best for us or for those with whom we deal. We should take from our customers such of their products as we can use without harm to our industries and labor. Reciprocity is the natural outgrowth of our wonderful industrial development under the domestic policy now firmly established. What we produce beyond our domestic consumption must have a vent abroad. The excess must be relieved through a foreign outlet and we should sell everywhere we can, and buy wherever the buying will enlarge our sales and productions, and thereby make a greater demand for home labor.

The period of exclusiveness is past. The expansion of our trade and commerce is the pressing problem. Commercial wars are unprofitable. A policy of goodwill and friendly trade relations will prevent reprisals. Reciprocity treaties are in harmony with the spirit of the times, measures of retaliation are not. If perchance some of our tariffs are no longer needed, for revenue or to encourage and protect our industries at home, why should they not be employed to extend and promote our markets abroad? Then, too, we have inadequate steamship service. New lines of steamers have already been put in commission between the Pacific coast ports of the United States and those on the western coasts of Mexico and Central and South America. These should be followed up with direct steamship lines between the eastern coast of the United States and South American ports. One of the needs of the times is to direct commercial lines from our vast fields of production to the fields of consumption that we have but barely touched. Next in advantage to having the thing to sell is to have the convenience to carry it to the buyer. We must encourage our merchant marine. We must have more ships. They must be under the American flag, built and manned and owned by Americans. These will not only be profitable in a commercial sense; they will be messengers of peace and amity wherever they go. We must build the Isthmian canal, which will unite the two oceans and give a straight line of water communication with the western coasts of Central and South America and Mexico. The construction of a Pacific cable cannot be longer postponed.

In the fathering of these objects of national interest and concern you are performing an important part. This exposition would have touched the heart of that American statesman whose mind was ever alert and thought ever constant for a larger commerce and a truer fraternity of the republics of the new world. His broad American spirit is felt and manifested here. He needs no identification to an assemblage of Americans anywhere, for the name of Blaine is inseparably associated with the Pan-American movement, which finds this practical and substantial expression, and which we all hope will be firmly advanced by the Pan-American congress that assembles this autumn in the capital of Mexico. The good work will go on. It cannot be stopped. These buildings will disappear; this creation of art and beauty and industry will perish from sight, but their influence will remain to

> Make it live beyond its too short living
> With praises and thanksgiving.

Who can tell the new thoughts that have been awakened, the ambitions fired and the high achievements that will be wrought through this exposition? Gentlemen, let us ever remember that our interest is in concord, not conflict, and that our real eminence rests in the victories of peace, not those of war. We hope that all who are represented here may be moved to higher and nobler effort for their own and the world's good, and that out of this city may come, not only greater commerce and trade, but more essential than these, relations of mutual respect, confidence and friendship which will deepen and endure.

Our earnest prayer is that God will graciously vouchsafe prosperity, happiness and peace to all our neighbors, and like blessings to all the peoples and powers of earth.

Courtesy of Library of Congress

Theodore Roosevelt

Theodore Roosevelt

1901–1909

THEODORE ROOSEVELT, scion of a wealthy and prominent New York family, entered New York Republican politics soon after his graduation from Harvard College in 1880. He first appeared on the national political scene as McKinley's assistant secretary of the navy, a post he gleefully resigned a year later to fight in Cuba during the Spanish-American War. Leading his company of volunteer cavalry, the Rough Riders, in the San Juan charge was, he often claimed, the high point of his life. A national hero on his return, he won the New York governorship in 1898, but the Republican Party bosses, suspicious of his reformist tendencies, convinced him to accept the nomination for the relatively powerless post of vice president in the 1900 election. McKinley's assassination six months after taking office brought Roosevelt to the presidency. He was elected in his own right by a vast majority in 1904.

During his two terms, Roosevelt rejuvenated the office, which for decades had been in eclipse. His immense popularity stemmed not so much from his policies as from the ebullience of his personality and his activist perception of the role of the chief executive as "a steward of the people bound actively and affirmatively to do all he could for the people." The essence of his social program, known as the Square Deal, was equal treatment of all groups involved in a dispute, a balancing of interests that was previously unknown in the federal government. A skillful manipulator of Congress, his party, and the press, Roosevelt succeeded in introducing a series of moderate social reforms and extended the power of the presidency into entirely new areas, as when he used his influence to settle the coal strike of 1902, the first time a federal official had sought to mediate a labor dispute to protect the public welfare.

In world affairs, Roosevelt was a rampant nationalist who consolidated America's role as a world power. He built up the navy and in 1907 sent a fleet of battleships on a tour of the globe to demonstrate the country's military readiness. But despite his belligerence over such matters as the Panama Canal—he threatened to send troops to seize the area when Colombia refused to grant use of the land to the United States—Roosevelt anticipated and feared the possibility of world war and attempted to arrange a peaceful balance of power in Europe and Asia.

Roosevelt's annual messages to Congress show his gradual development from a conciliatory reformer to a full-fledged progressive with near-radical views on such issues as the need for a graduated income tax, the rights of farmers and workers, and the regulation of commerce and industry. He handed the presidency over to his Republican successor, William Howard Taft, in 1909 but formed a separate Progressive Party in 1912 when the Republicans refused him the nomination. After the failure of this campaign, he wrote, went on scientific and hunting expeditions, and promoted the Allied cause during World War I. He died in 1919.

Roosevelt belongs to that small group of presidents, among them Jefferson, Lincoln, and Wilson, who had a natural literary gift. He sometimes described himself as a professional man of letters, and his total output of words, which numbers in the tens of millions, dwarfs that of any other president. Prodigiously erudite, he was the author of more than 30 books, on subjects ranging from American and British history to politics, nature, and biography. His style was energetic, direct, and sometimes genuinely stirring. Usually he wrote his own speeches, often dictating them in outline form; he showed major speeches and congressional messages to confidants such as Henry Cabot Lodge before casting them in final form. Advance copies and follow-up interviews were always provided to reporters.

Many of his contemporaries remarked on the self-consciously moralistic tone of his speeches, which is even more evident when we read them today. To Roosevelt, who was once a Sunday-school teacher, the presidential podium was a "bully pulpit." In his speeches he inevitably adopts the rhetoric of a Protestant preacher, exhorting his audience toward the path of righteousness and virtue, which, he felt, could be attained only through constant struggle. By unremitting effort he had transformed himself from a weak and asthmatic child into an athlete who preferred action to deliberation; often he seemed to be asking the nation to attain greatness through an analogous process of "hard and dangerous endeavor." His biographer, Henry Pringle, called this his "gospel of strenuosity."

While delivering a speech, Roosevelt would pace back and forth, brandishing his manuscript at the audience; his high-pitched voice would occasionally rise to a falsetto at crucial points in the text. According to William Roscoe Thayer, his listeners were fascinated by "his gestures, the way in which his pent-up thoughts seemed almost to strangle him before he could utter them, his smile showing the white rows of teeth, his fist clenched to strike an invisible adversary." He took pleasure in oratory, and few things could deter him from speaking to any crowd that was available. During his unsuccessful presidential campaign of 1912, he was shot in the chest by a deranged saloonkeeper in Milwaukee but refused to go to the hospital until he had gone to the auditorium and delivered the speech that he had prepared.

Speechmaking for Roosevelt was a way both to educate the public and to inspire it. The progressive politician Robert La Follette, a rival and critic of Roosevelt's, thought the president "the keenest, ablest living interpreter of what I call the superficial public sentiment of a given time, and he is spontaneous in his response to it." His friend Henry Cabot Lodge attributed Roosevelt's power over his listeners to the "force of conviction" with which he preached his vision of the just society: "If he speaks at all he must perforce say what he thinks, and thus it comes to pass that men may know him as he is." In his presidential years, before his progressivism became too extreme for the electorate, the American people understood him to be the epitome of the age, a leader whose enthusiasms and faults exactly coincided with those of his times.

The Strenuous Life

Chicago, Illinois
April 10, 1899

ROOSEVELT, then governor of New York and still fresh from his triumph in Cuba with the Rough Riders, addressed Chicago's conservative leadership at the Hamilton Club in an effort to raise support for a future presidential candidacy. But speeches such as this one in praise of "strenuous endeavor" and "bodily vigor"—concepts central to his own philosophy—only served to frighten the national party bosses. Senator Mark Hanna of Ohio, one of the party's kingmakers, called Roosevelt "that damned cowboy," while to Charles C. Platt, the Republican boss of New York, Roosevelt was "the perfect bull in a china shop." In 1900 the party leaders attempted to neutralize Roosevelt politically, while still capitalizing on his popularity, by levering him out of state politics and into the vice presidency (a job he had earlier vowed he would never accept) under the more pliable William McKinley.

In speaking to you, men of the greatest city of the West, men of the state which gave to the country Lincoln and Grant, men who preeminently and distinctly embody all that is most American in the American character, I wish to preach not the doctrine of ignoble ease but the doctrine of the strenuous life; the life of toil and effort; of labor and strife, to preach that highest form of success which comes not to the man who desires mere easy peace but to the man who does not shrink from danger, from hardship, or from bitter toil, and who out of these wins the splendid ultimate triumph.

The timid man, the lazy man, the man who distrusts his country, the overcivilized man, who has lost the great fighting, masterful virtues, the ignorant man and the man of dull mind, whose soul is incapable of feeling the mighty lift that thrills "stern men with empires in their brains"—all these, of course, shrink from seeing the nation undertake its new duties; shrink from seeing us build a navy and army adequate to our needs; shrink from seeing us do our share of the world's work by bringing order out of chaos in the great, fair tropic islands from which the valor of our soldiers and sailors has driven the Spanish flag.

These are the men who fear the strenuous life, who fear the only national life which is really worth leading. They believe in that cloistered life which saps the hardy virtues in a nation, as it saps them in the individual; or else they are wedded to that base spirit of gain and greed which recognizes in commercialism the be-all and end-all of national life, instead of realizing that, though an indispensable element, it is after all but one of the many elements that go to make up true national greatness. No country can long endure if its foundations are not laid deep in the material prosperity which comes from thrift, from business energy and enterprise, from hard unsparing effort in the fields of industrial activity; but neither was any nation ever yet truly great if it relied upon material prosperity alone.

All honor must be paid to the architects of our material prosperity; to the great captains of industry who have built our factories and our railroads; to the strong men who toil for wealth with brain or hand; for great is the debt of the nation to these and their kind. But our debt is yet greater to the men whose highest type is to be found in a statesmen like Lincoln, a soldier like Grant. They showed by their lives that they recognized the law of work; the law of strife; they toiled to win a competence for themselves and those dependent upon them; but they recognized that there were yet other and even loftier duties—duties to the nation and duties to the race.

I preach to you, then, my countrymen, that our country calls not for the life of ease, but for the life of strenuous endeavor. The 20th century looms before us big with the fate of many nations. If we stand idly by, if we seek merely swollen, slothful ease, and ignoble peace, if we shrink from the hard contests where men must win at hazard of their lives and at the risk of all they hold dear, then the bolder and stronger peoples will pass us by and will win for themselves the domination of the world. Let us therefore boldly face the life of strife, resolute to do our duty well and manfully; resolute to uphold righteousness by deed and by word; resolute to be both honest and brave, to serve high ideals, yet to use practical methods. Above all, let us shrink from no strife, moral or physical, within or without the nation, provided we are certain that the strife is justified; for it is only through strife, through hard and dangerous endeavor, that we shall ultimately win the goal of true national greatness.

Trusts

Cincinnati, Ohio
September 20, 1902

AT THE TURN of the century, there were few controls on the operations of large corporations, then known as trusts. Industrial magnates such as J. Pierpont Morgan, John D. Rockefeller, and Henry Clay Frick devoured smaller competitors, manipulated the stock market at will, and bought the government's silence about—or acquiescence to—their abuses.

The popular image of Roosevelt is that he was a "trust buster" who demanded fair play from businessmen. In his battles with the Northern Securities Company and other monopolies and trusts, he was the first president to assert the power of his office in behalf of the common people and against the entrenched commercial interests that threatened them. But, as this excerpt from a speech at Cincinnati's Music Hall shows, he also believed firmly in the nation's need for corporations, as long as they were legally and morally run, and he cautioned his audiences to avoid lumping good big business with bad. His primary aim was not the dissolution of the trusts, but their regulation by the federal government.

I shall ask your attention to what I say tonight, because I intend to make a perfectly serious argument to you, and I shall be obliged if you will remain as still as possible; and I ask that those at the very back will remember that if they talk or make a noise it interferes with the hearing of the rest. I intend to speak to you on a serious subject and to make an argument as the chief executive of a nation, who is the president of all the people, without regard to party, without regard to section. I intend to make to you an argument from the standpoint simply of one American talking to his fellow Americans upon one of the great subjects of interest to all alike; and the subject is what are commonly known as trusts. The word is used very loosely and almost always with technical inaccuracy. The average man, however, when he speaks of the trusts means rather vaguely all of the very big corporations, the growth of which has been so signal a feature of our modern civilization, and especially those big corporations which, though organized in one state, do business in several states, and often have a tendency to monopoly.

The whole subject of the trusts is of vital concern to us, because it presents one, and perhaps the most conspicuous, of the many problems forced upon our attention by the tremendous industrial development which has taken place during the last century, a development which is occurring in all civilized countries, notably in our own. There have been many factors responsbile for bringing about

these changed conditions. Of these, steam and electricity are the chief. The extraordinary changes in the methods of transporation of merchandise and of transmission of news have rendered not only possible, but inevitable, the immense increase in the rate of growth of our great industrial centers—that is, of our great cities. I want you to bring home to yourselves that fact. When Cincinnati was founded news could be transmitted and merchandise carried exactly as has been the case in the days of the Roman Empire. You had here on your river the flat-boat, you had on the ocean the sailing-ship, you had the pack-train, you had the wagon, and every one of the four was known when Babylon fell. The change in the last 100 years has been greater by far than the changes in all the preceding 3,000. Those are the facts. Because of them have resulted the specialization of industries, and the unexampled opportunities offered for the employment of huge amounts of capital, and therefore for the rise in the business world of those master-minds through whom alone it is possible for such vast amounts of capital to be employed with profit. It matters very little whether we like these new conditions or whether we dislike them; whether we like the creation of these new opportunities or not. Many admirable qualities which were developed in the older, simpler, less progressive life have tended to atrophy under our rather feverish, high-pressure, complex life of today. But our likes and dislikes have nothing to do with the matter.

The new conditions are here. You can't bring back the old days of the canalboat and stagecoach if you wish. The steamboat and the railroad are here. The new forces have produced both good and evil. We cannot get rid of them—even it if were not undesirable to get rid of them; and our instant duty is to try to accommodate our social, economic and legislative life to them, and to frame a system of law and conduct under which we shall get out of them the utmost possible benefit and the least possible amount of harm. It is foolish to pride ourselves upon our progress and prosperity, upon our commanding position in the international industrial world, and at the same time have nothing but denunciation for the men to whose commanding position we in part owe this very progress and prosperity, this commanding position.

Whenever great social or industrial changes take place, no matter how much good there may be to them, there is sure to be some evil; and it usually takes mankind a number of years and a good deal of experimenting before they find the right ways in which so far as possible to control the new evil without at the same time nullifying the new good. I am stating facts so obvious that if each one of you will think them over you will think them trite, but if you read or listen to some of the arguments advanced, you will come to the conclusion that there is need of learning these trite truths. In these circumstances the effort to bring the new tendencies to a standstill is always futile and generally mischievous; but it is possible somewhat to develop them aright. Law can to a degree guide, protect and control industrial development, but it can never cause it, or play more than a subordinate part in its healthy development—unfortunately it is easy enough by bad laws to bring it to an almost complete stop.

In dealing with the big corporations which we call trusts, we must resolutely purpose to proceed by evolution and not revolution. We wish to face the facts, declining to have our vision blinded either by the folly of those who say there are no evils, or by the more dangerous folly of those who either see, or make believe that they see, nothing but evil in all the existing system, and who if given their way would destroy the evil by the simple process of bringing ruin and disaster to the entire country. The evils attendant upon overcapitalization alone are, in my judgment, sufficient to warrant a far closer supervision and control than now exists over the great corporations. Wherever a substantial monopoly can be shown to exist we should certainly try our utmost to devise an expedient by which it can be controlled. Doubtless some of the evils existing in or because of the great corporations can not be cured by any legislation which has yet been proposed, and doubtless others, which have really been incident to the sudden development in the formation of corporations of all kinds, will in the end cure themselves. But there will remain a certain number which can be cured if we decide that by the power of the government they are to be cured. The surest way to prevent the possibility of curing any of them is to approach the subject in a spirit of violent rancor complicated with total ignorance of business interests and fundamental incapacity or unwillingness to understand the limitations upon all lawmaking bodies. No problem, and least of all so difficult a problem as this, can be solved if the qualities brought to its solution are panic, fear, envy, hatred, and ignorance. There can exist in a free republic no man more wicked, no man more dangerous to the people, than he who would arouse these feelings in the hope that they would redound to his own political advantage. Corporations that are handled honestly and fairly, so far from being an evil, are a natural business evolution and make for the general prosperity of our land. We do not wish to destroy corporations, but we do wish to make them subserve the public good. All individuals, rich or poor, private or corporate, must be subject to the law of the land, and the government will hold them to a rigid obedience thereof. The biggest corporation, like the humblest private citizen, must be held to strict compliance with the will of the people as expressed in the fundamental law. The rich man who does not see that this is in his interest is indeed short-sighted. When we make him obey the law we ensure for him the absolute protection of the law.

The savings banks show what can be done in the way of genuinely beneficent work by large corporations when intelligently administered and supervised. They now hold over 2,600 millions of the people's money and pay annually about 100 millions of interest or profit to their depositors. There is no talk of danger from these corporations; yet they possess great power, holding over three times the amount of our present national debt, more than all the currency, gold, silver, greenbacks, etc., in circulation in the United States. The chief reason for there being no talk of danger from them is that they are on the whole faithfully administered for the benefit of all, under wise laws which require frequent and full publication of their condition, and which prescribe certain needful regulations with which they have to comply, while at the same time giving full scope for the business enterprise of their managers within these limits.

Now of course savings banks are as highly specialized a class of corporations as railroads, and we can not force too far the analogy with other corporations; but there are certain conditions which I think we can lay down as indispensable to the proper treatment of all corporations which from their size have become important factors in the social development of the community.

Before speaking, however, of what can be done by way of remedy let me say a word or two as to certain proposed remedies which, in my judgment, would be ineffective or mischievous. The first thing to remember is that if we are to accomplish any good at all it must be by resolutely keeping in mind the intention to do away with any evils in the conduct of big corporations, while steadfastly refusing to assent to indiscriminate assault upon all forms of corporate capital as such. The line of demarcation we draw must always be on conduct, not upon wealth; our objection of any given corporation must be, not that it is big, but that it behaves badly. Perfectly simple again, my friends, but not always heeded by some of those who would strive to teach us how to act toward big corporations. Treat the head of the corporation as you would treat all other men. If he does well stand by him. You will occasionally find the head of a big corporation who objects to that treatment; very good, apply it all the more carefully. Remember, after all, that he who objects because he is the head of a big corporation to being treated like anyone else is only guilty of the same sin as the man who wishes him treated worse than anyone else because he is the head of a big corporation. Demagogic denunciation of wealth is never wholesome and is generally dangerous, and not a few of the proposed methods of curbing the trusts are dangerous chiefly because all insincere

advocacy of the impossible is dangerous. It is an unhealthy thing for a community when the appeal is made to follow a course which those who make the appeal either do know, or ought to know, cannot be followed; and which, if followed, would result in disaster to everybody. Loose talk about destroying monopoly out of hand without a hint as to how the monopoly should even be defined offers a case in point.

Nor can we afford to tolerate any proposal which will strike at the so-called trusts only by striking at the general wellbeing. We are now enjoying a period of great prosperity. The prosperity is generally diffused through all sections and through all classes. Doubtless there are some individuals who do not get enough of it, and there are others who get too much. That is simply another way of saying that the wisdom of mankind is finite; and that even the best human system does not work perfectly. You don't have to take my word for that. Look back just nine years. In 1893 nobody was concerned in downing the trusts. Everybody was concerned in trying to get up himself. The men who propose to get rid of the evils of the trusts by measures which would do away with the general well-being, advocate a policy which would not only be a damage to the community as a whole, but which would defeat its own professed object. If we are forced to the alternative of choosing either a system under which most of us prosper somewhat, though a few of us prosper too much, or else a system under which no one prospers enough, of course we will choose the former. If the policy advocated is so revolutionary and destructive as to involve the whole community in the crash of common disaster, it is as certain as anything can be that when the disaster has occurred all efforts to regulate the trusts will cease, and that the one aim will be to restore prosperity. . . .

You must face the fact that only harm will come from a proposition to attack the so-called trusts in a vindictive spirit by measures conceived solely with a desire of hurting them, without regard as to whether or not discrimination should be made between the good and evil in them, and without even any regard as to whether a necessary sequence of the action would be the hurting of other interests. The adoption of such a policy would mean temporary damage to the trusts, because it would mean temporary damage to all of our business interests; but the effect would be only temporary, for exactly as the damage affected all alike, good and bad, so the reaction would affect all alike, good and bad. The necessary supervision and control, in which I firmly believe as the only methods of eliminating the real evils of the trusts, must come through wisely and cautiously framed legislation, which shall aim in the first place to give definite control to some sovereign over the great corporations, and which shall be followed, when once this power has been conferred, by a system giving to the government the full knowledge which is the essential for satisfactory action. Then when this knowledge—one of the essential features of which is proper publicity—has been gained, what further steps of any kind are necessary can be taken with the confidence born of the possession of power to deal with the subject and of a thorough knowledge of what should and can be done in the matter.

We need additional power; and we need knowledge. Our Constitution was framed when the economic conditions were so different that each state could wisely be left to handle the corporations within its limits as it saw fit. Nowadays all the corporations which I am considering do what is really an interstate business, and as the states have proceeded on very different lines in regulating them, at present a corporation will be organized in one state, not because it intends to do business in that state, but because it does not, and therefore that state can give it better privileges, and then it will do business in some other states, and will claim not to be under the control of the states in which it does business; and of course it is not the object of the state creating it to exercise any control over it, as it does not do any business in that state. Such a system cannot obtain. There must be some sovereign. It might be better if all the states could agree along the same lines in dealing with these corporations, but I see not the slightest prospect of such an agreement. Therefore, I personally feel that ultimately the nation will have to assume the responsibility of regulating these very large corporations which do an interstate business. The states must combine to meet the way in which capital has combined; and the way in which the states can combine is through the national government. But I firmly believe that all these obstacles can be met if only we face them, both with the determination to overcome them, and with the further determination to overcome them in ways which shall not do damage to the country as a whole; which on the contrary shall further our industrial development, and shall help instead of hindering all corporations which work out their success by means that are just and fair toward all men.

Without the adoption of a constitutional amendment, my belief is that a good deal can be done by law. It is difficult to say exactly how much, because experience has taught us that in dealing with these subjects, where the lines dividing the rights and duties of the states and of the nation are in doubt, it has sometimes been difficult for Congress to forecast the action of the courts upon its legislation. Such legislation (whether obtainable now, or obtainable only after a constitutional amendment) should provide for a reasonable supervision, the most prominent feature of which at first should be publicity; that is, the making public, both to the governmental authorities and to the people at large, the essential facts in which the public is concerned. This would give us exact knowledge of many points which are now not only in doubt, but the subject of fierce controversy. Moreover, the mere fact of the publication would cure some very grave evils, for the light of day is a deterrent to wrong-doing. It would doubtless disclose other evils with which, for the time being, we could devise no way to grapple. Finally, it would disclose others which could be grappled with and cured by further legislative action.

Remember, I advocate the action which the president can only advise, and which he has no power himself to take. Under our present legislative and constitutional limitations the national execution can work only between narrow lines in the field of action concerning great corporations. Between these lines, I assure you that exact and even-handed justice will be dealt, and is being dealt, to all men, without regard to persons.

I wish to repeat with all emphasis that desirable though it is that the nation should have the power I suggest, it is equally desirable that it should be used with wisdom and self-restraint. The mechanism of modern business is tremendous in its size and complexity, and ignorant intermeddling with it would be disastrous. We should not be made timid or daunted by the size of the problem; we should not feat to undertake it; but we should undertake it with ever present in our minds dread of the sinister spirits of rancor, ignorance, and vanity. We need to keep steadily in mind the fact that besides the tangible property in each corporation there lies behind the spirit which brings it success, and in the case of each very successful corporation this is usually the spirit of some one man or set of men. Under exactly similar conditions one corporation will make a stupendous success where another makes a stupendous failure, simply because one is well managed and the other is not. While making it clear that we do not intend to allow wrong-doing by one of the captains of industry any more than by the humblest private in the industrial ranks, we must also in the interests of all of us avoid cramping a strength which, if beneficently used, will be for the good of all of us. The marvelous prosperity we have been enjoying for the past few years has been due primarily to the high average of honesty, thrift, and business capacity among our people as a whole; but some of it has also been due to the ability of the men who are the industrial leaders of the nation. In securing just and fair dealing by these men let us remember to do them justice in return, and this not only because it is our duty, but because it is our interest; not only for their sakes, but for ours. We are neither the friend of the rich man as such, nor the friend of the poor man as such; we are the friend of the honest man, rich or poor, and we intend that all men, rich and poor alike, shall obey the law alike and receive its protection alike.

Westward Expansion

St. Louis, Missouri

April 30, 1903

THOUGH AN Easterner by birth, the author *of Hunting Trips of a Ranchman* and *The Winning of the West* was often identified with the western frontier. Roosevelt had spent two years (1884 to 1886) in the Dakota Territory as a cattle rancher and retained a romanticized view of the West. Even his serious historical writing on the subject is marked by his belief in the manifest destiny of white settlers to take possession of and bring civilization to the Western lands. Throughout history, he claimed, all successful peoples have rightfully sought territorial expansion, but none with as great a prospect for success as the people of the United States, who possessed, in his view, both a vigorous spirit and a perfectable form of government.

Roosevelt's speeches on this subject often took on the character of historical sermons, as in this address at the dedication ceremonies for the Louisiana Purchase Centennial Exposition, in which he lectured his audience on the need to convert the original pioneer qualities into the kind of self-discipline that would help build an industrial society imbued with a sense of justice.

At the outset of my address let me recall to the minds of my hearers that the soil upon which we stand, before it was ours, was successively the possession of two mighty empires, Spain and France, whose sons made a deathless record of heroism in the early annals of the New World. No history of the western country can be written without paying heed to the wonderful part played therein in the early days by the soldiers, missionaries, explorers, and traders, who did their work for the honor of the proud banners of France and Castile. While the settlers of English-speaking stock, and those of Dutch, German, and Scandinavian origin who were associated with them, were still clinging close to the eastern seaboard, the pioneers of Spain and of France had penetrated deep into hitherto unknown wilderness of the West, had wandered far and wide within the boundaries of what is now our mighty country. The very cities themselves—St. Louis, New Orleans, Santa Fe—bear witness by their titles to the nationalities of their founders. It was not until the Revolution had begun that the English-speaking settlers pushed west across the Alleghenies, and not until a century ago that they entered in to possess the land upon which we now stand.

We have met here today to commemorate the hundredth anniversary of the event which more than any other, after the foundation of the government and always excepting its preservation, determined the character of our national life—determined that we should be a great expanding nation instead of relatively a small and stationary one.

Of course it was not with the Louisiana Purchase that our career of expansion began. In the middle of the Revolutionary War the Illinois Region, including the present states of Illinois and Indiana, was added to our domain by force of arms, as a sequel to the adventurous expedition of George Rogers Clark and his frontier riflemen. Later the treaties of Jay and Pinckney materially extended our real boundaries to the West. But none of these events was of so striking a character as to fix the popular imagination. The old 13 colonies had always claimed that their rights stretched westward to the Mississippi, and vague and unreal though these claims were until made good by conquest, settlement, and diplomacy, they still served to give the impression that the earliest westward movements of our people were little more than the filling-in of already existing national boundaries.

But there could be no illusion about the acquisition of the vast territory beyond the Mississippi stretching westward to the Pacific, which in that day was known as Louisiana. This immense region was admittedly the territory of a foreign power, of a European kingdom. None of our people had ever laid claim to a foot of it. Its acquisition could in no sense be treated as rounding out any existing claims. When we acquired it we made evident once for all that consciously and of set purpose we had embarked on a career of expansion, that we had taken our place among those daring and hardy nations who risk much with the hope and desire of winning high position among the great powers of the earth. As is so often the case in nature, the law of development of a living organism showed itself in its actual workings to be wiser than the wisdom of the wisest.

This work of expansion was by far the greatest work of our people during the years that intervened between the adoption of the Constitution and the outbreak of the Civil War. There were other questions of real moment and importance, and there were many which at the time seemed such to those engaged in answering them; but the greatest feat of our forefathers of those generations was the deed of the men who, with pack train or wagon train, on horseback, on foot, or by boat, pushed the frontier ever westward across the continent.

Never before had the world seen the kind of national expansion which gave our people all that part of the American continent lying west of the 13 original states; the greatest landmark in which was the Louisiana Purchase. Our triumph in this process of expansion was indissolubly bound up with the success of our peculiar kind of federal government; and this success has been so complete that because of its very completeness we now sometimes fail to appreciate not only the all-importance but the tremendous difficulty of the problem with which our nation was originally faced.

When our forefathers joined to call into being this nation, they undertook a task for which there was but little encouraging precedent. The development of civilization from the earliest period seemed to show the truth of two propositions: In the first place, it has always proved exceedingly difficult to secure both freedom and strength in any government; and in the second place it had always proved well nigh impossible for a nation to expand without either breaking up or becoming a centralized tyranny. With the success of our effort to combine a strong and efficient national Union, able to put down disorder at home and to maintain our honor and interest abroad, I have not now to deal. This success was signal and all important, but it was by no means unprecedented in the same sense that our type of expansion was unprecedented. The history of Rome and of Greece illustrates very well the two types of expansion which had taken place in ancient time and which had

been universally accepted as the only possible types up to the period when as a nation we ourselves began to take possession of this continent. The Grecian states performed remarkable feats of colonization, but each colony as soon as created became entirely independent of the mother state, and in after years was almost as apt to prove its enemy as its friend. Local self-government, local independence, was secured, but only by the absolute sacrifice of anything resembling national unity. In consequnce, the Greek world, for all its wonderful brilliancy and the extraordinary artistic, literary, and philosophical development which has made all mankind its debtors for the ages, was yet wholly unable to withstand a formidable foreign foe, save spasmodically. As soon as powerful, permanent empires arose on its outskirts, the Greek states in the neighborhood of such empires fell under their sway. National power and greatness were completely sacrificed to local liberty.

With Rome the exact opposite occurred. The imperial city rose to absolute dominion over all the peoples of Italy and then expanded her rule over the entire civilized world by a process which kept the nation strong and united, but gave no room whatever for local liberty and self-government. All other cities and countries were subject to Rome. In consequence this great and masterful race of warriors, rulers, roadbuilders, and administrators stamped their indelible impress upon all the after life of our race, and yet let an over-centralization eat out the vitals of their empire until it became an empty shell; so that when the barbarians came they destroyed only what had already become worthless to the world.

The underlying viciousness of each type of expansion was plain enough and the remedy now seems simple enough. But when the fathers of the republic first formulated the Constitution under which we live this remedy was untried and no one could foretell how it would work. They themselves began the experiment almost immediately by adding new states to the original 13. Excellent people in the east viewed this initial expansion of the country with great alarm. Exactly as during the colonial period many good people in the mother-country thought it highly important that settlers should be kept out of the Ohio Valley in the interest of the fur companies, so after we had become a nation many good people on the Atlantic Coast felt grave apprehension lest they might somehow be hurt by the westward growth of the nation. These good people shook their heads over the formation of states in the fertile Ohio Valley which now forms part of the heart of our nation; and they declared that the destruction of the republic had been accomplished when through the Louisiana Purchase we acquired nearly half of what is now that same republic's present territory. Nor was their feeling unnatural. Only the adventurous and the far-seeing can be expected heartily to welcome the process of expansion, for the nation that expands is a nation which is entering upon a great career, and with greatness there must of necessity come perils which daunt all save the most stouthearted.

We expanded by carving the wilderness into territories and out of these territories building new states when once they had received as permanent settlers a sufficient number of our own people. Being a practical nation we have never tried to force on any section of our new territory an unsuitable form of government merely because it was suitable for another under different conditions. Of the territory covered by the Louisiana Purchase a portion was given statehood within a few years. Another portion has not been admitted to statehood, although a century has elapsed—although doubtless it soon will be. In each case we showed the practical government genius of our race by devising methods suitable to meet the actual existing needs; not by insisting upon the application of some abstract shibboleth to all our new possessions alike, no matter how incongruous this applicaton might sometimes be.

Over by far the major part of the territory, however, our people spread in such numbers during the course of the 19th century that we were able to build up state after state, each with exactly the same complete local independence in all matters affecting purely its own domestic interests as in any of the original 13 states—each owing the same absolute fealty to the Union of all the states which each of the original 13 states also owes—and finally each having the same proportional right to its share in shaping and directing the common policy of the Union which is possessed by any other state, whether of the original 13 or not.

This process now seems to us part of the natural order of things, but it was wholly unknown until our own people devised it. It seems to us a mere matter of course, a matter of elementary right and justice, that in the deliberations of the national representative bodies the representatives of a state which came into the Union but yesterday stand on a footing of exact and entire equality with those of the commonwealths whose sons once signed the Declaration of Independence. But this way of looking at the matter is purely modern, and in its origin purely American. When Washington during his presidency saw new states come into the Union on a footing of complete equality with the old, every European nation which had colonies still administered them as dependencies, and every other mother-country treated the colonist not as a self-governing equal but as a subject.

The process which we began has since been followed by all the great peoples who were capable both of expansion and of self-government, and now the world accepts it as the natural process, as the rule; but a century and a quarter ago it was not merely exceptional; it was unknown.

This, then, is the great historic significance of the movement of continental in which the Louisiana Purchase was the most striking single achievement. It stands out in marked relief even among the feats of a nation of pioneers, a nation whose people have from the beginning been picked out by a process of natural selection from among the most enterprising individuals of the nations of western Europe. The acquisition of the territory is a credit to the broad and far-sighted statesmanship of the great statesmen to whom it was immediately due, and above all to the aggressive and masterful character of the hardy pioneer folk to whose restless energy these statesmen gave expression and direction, whom they followed rather than led. The history of the land comprised within the limits of the Purchase is an epitome of the entire history of our people. Within these limits we have gradually built up state after state until now they many times surpass in wealth, in population, and in manysided development, the original 13 states as they were when their delegates met in the Continental Congress. The people of these states have shown themselves mighty in war with their fellow man, and mighty in strength to tame the rugged wilderness. They could not thus have conquered the forest and the prairie, the mountain and the desert, had they not possessed the great fighting virtues, the qualities which enable a people to overcome the forces of hostile men and hostile nature. On the other hand, they could not have used aright their conquest had they not in addition possessed the qualities of self-mastery and self-restraint, the power of acting in combination with their fellows, the power of yielding obedience to the law and of building up an orderly civilization. Courage and hardihood are indispensable virtues in a people; but the people which possesses no others can never rise high in the scale either of power or of culture. Great peoples must have in addition the governmental capacity which comes only when individuals fully recognize their duties to one another and to the whole body politic, and are able to join together in feats of constructive statesmanship and of honest and effective administration.

The old pioneer days are gone, with their roughness and their hardship, their incredible toil and their wild half-savage romance. But the need for the pioneer virtues remains the same as ever. The peculiar conditions have vanished; but the manliness and stalwart hardihood of the frontiersmen can be given even freer scope under the conditions surrounding the complex industrialism of the present day. In this great region acquired for our people under the presidency of Jefferson this region stretching from the Gulf to the Canadian border, from the Mississippi to the Rockies, the material and social progress has been so vast that alike for weal and for woe its people now share the opportunities and bear the burdens common to the entire civilized world. The problems before us are fundamentally the same east and west of the Mississippi, in the new states and in the old, and exactly the same qualities are required for their successful solution.

We meet here today to commemorate a great event, an event which marks an era in statesmanship no less than in pioneering. It is fitting that we should pay homage in words; but we must in honor make our words good by deeds. We have every right to take a just pride in the great deeds of our forefathers; but we show ourselves unworthy to be their descendants if we make what they did an excuse for our lying supine instead of an incentive to the effort to show ourselves by our acts worthy of them. In the administration of city, state, and nation, in the management of our home life and the conduct of our business and social relations, we are bound to show certain high and fine qualities of character under penalty of seeing the whole heart of our civilization eaten out while the body still lives.

We justly pride ourselves on our marvelous material prosperity, and such prosperity must exist in order to establish a foundation upon which a higher life can be built; but unless we do in very fact build this higher life thereon, the material prosperity itself will go for but very little. Now, in 1903, in the altered conditions, we must meet the changed and changing problems with the spirit shown by the men who in 1803 and in the subsequent years gained, explored, conquered, and settled this vast territory, then a desert, now filled with thriving and populous states.

The old days were great because the men who lived in them had mighty qualities; and we must make the new days great by showing these same qualities. We must insist upon courage and resolution, upon hardihood, tenacity, and fertility in resource; we must insist upon the strong, virile virtues; and we must insist no less upon the virtues of self-restraint, self-mastery, regard for the rights of others; we must show our abhorrence of cruelty, brutality, and corruption, in public and in private life alike. If we come short in any of these qualities we shall measurably fail; and if, as I believe we surely shall, we develop these qualities in the future to an even greater degree than in the past, then in the century now beginning we shall make of this republic the freest and most orderly, the most just and most mighty, nation which has ever come forth from the womb of time.

The Roosevelt Corollary to the Monroe Doctrine

From the Fourth Annual Message to Congress
Washington, D.C.
December 6, 1904

THE MONROE DOCTRINE, formulated by James Monroe in 1823, states that the United States is resolved to resist European intervention and colonization in the New World, and in return promises that it will not interfere in the affairs of Europe. To Roosevelt, the Monroe Doctrine provided the cornerstone of American military policy in the Western Hemisphere, but the original document did not go far enough for him. Roosevelt the imperialist believed that it was the mission of the United States to bring Anglo-American civilization to "savage" races and nations, including several of the Latin American countries, for whom he felt the contempt of the strong for the weak. To satisfy his impulses and beliefs, he added his own corollary to the Monroe Doctrine, claiming that the United States possesses the right in unusual cases to intervene in the internal affairs of other American nations for their own good and for the peace of the hemisphere.

Although many commentators in the American press and in Europe dismissed Roosevelt's policy as flagrant jingoism, its impact has endured. Subsequent presidents from Coolidge to Reagan have used his extension of the Monroe Doctrine to justify military interventions in Nicaragua, the Dominican Republic, Cuba, and Grenada.

In treating of our foreign policy and of the attitude that this great nation should assume in the world at large, it is absolutely necessary to consider the army and the navy, and the Congress, through which the thought of the nation finds its expression, should keep ever vividly in mind the fundamental fact that it is impossible to treat our foreign policy, whether this policy takes shape in the effort to secure justice for others or justice for ourselves, save as conditioned upon the attitude we are willing to take toward our army, and especially toward our navy. It is not merely unwise, it is contemptible, for a nation, as for an individual, to use high-sounding language to proclaim its purposes, or to take positions which are ridiculous if unsupported by potential force, and then to refuse to provide this force. If there is no intention of providing and of keeping the force necessary to back up a strong attitude, then it is far better not to assume such an attitude.

The steady aim of this nation, as of all enlightened nations, should be to strive to bring ever nearer the day when there shall prevail throughout the world the peace of justice. There are kinds of peace which are highly undesirable, which are in the long run as destructive as any war. Tyrants and oppressors have many times made a wilderness and called it peace. Many times peoples who were slothful or timid or shortsighted, who had been enervated by ease or by luxury, or misled by false teachings, have shrunk in unmanly fashion from doing duty that was stern and that needed self-sacrifice, and have sought to hide from their own minds their shortcomings, their ignoble motives by calling them love of peace. The peace of tyrannous terror, the peace of craven weakness, the peace of injustice, all these should be shunned as we shun unrighteous war. The goal to set before us as a nation, the goal which should be set before all mankind, is the attainment of the peace of justice, of the peace which comes when each nation is not merely safeguarded in its own rights, but scrupulously recognizes and performs its duty toward others. Generally peace tells for righteousness; but if there is conflict between the two, then our fealty is due first to the cause of righteousness. Unrighteous wars are common, and unrighteous peace is rare; but both should be shunned. The right to freedom and the responsibility for the exercise of that right cannot be divorced. One of our great poets has well and finely said that freedom is not a gift that tarries long in the hands of cowards. Neither does it tarry long in the hands of those too slothful, too dishonest, or too unintelligent to exercise it. The eternal vigilance which is the price of liberty must be exercised, sometimes to guard against outside foes; although of course far more often to guard against our own selfish or thoughtless shortcomings.

If these self-evident truths are kept before us, and only if they are so kept before us, we shall have a clear idea of what our foreign policy in its larger aspects should be. It is our duty to remember that a nation has no more right to do injustice to another nation, strong or weak, than an individual has to do injustice to another individual; that the same moral law applies in one case as in the other. But we must also remember that it is as much the duty of the nation to guard its own rights and its own interests as it is the duty of the individual so to do. Within the nation the individual has now delegated this right to the state, that is, to the representative of all the individuals, and it is a maxim of the law that for every wrong there is remedy. But in international law we have not advanced by any means as far as we have advanced in municipal law. There is as yet no judicial way of enforcing a right in international law. When one nation wrongs another or wrongs many others, there is no tribunal before which the wrongdoer can be brought. Either it is necessary supinely to acquiesce in the wrong, and thus put a premium upon brutality and aggression, or else it is necessary for the aggrieved nation valiantly to stand up for its rights. Until some method is devised by which there shall be a degree of international control over offending nations, it would be a wicked thing for the most civilized powers, for those with most sense of international obligations and with keenest and most generous appreciation of the difference between right and wrong, to disarm. If the great civilized nations of the present day should completely disarm, the result would mean an immediate recrudescence of barbarism in one form or another. Under any circumstances, a sufficient armament would have to be kept up to serve the purposes of international police; and until international cohesion and the sense of international duties and rights are far more advanced than at present, a nation desirous both of securing respect for itself and of doing good to others must have a force adequate for the work which it feels is allotted to it as its part of the general world duty.

Therefore it follows that a self-respecting, just, and far-seeing nation should on the one hand endeavor by every means to aid in the development of the various movements which tend to provide substitutes for war, which tend to render nations in their actions toward one another, and indeed toward their own peoples, more responsive to the general sentiment of humane and civilized mankind; and on the other hand that it should keep prepared, while scrupulously avoiding wrongdoing itself, to repel any wrong, and in exceptional cases to take action which in a more advanced stage of international relations would come under the head of the exercise of the international police. A great free people owes it to itself and to all mankind not to sink into helplessness before the powers of evil.

We are in every way endeavoring to help on, with cordial goodwill, every movement which will tend to bring us into more friendly relations with the rest of mankind. In pursuance of this policy I shall shortly lay before the Senate treaties of arbitration with all powers which are willing to enter into these treaties with us. It is not possible at this period of the world's development to agree to arbitrate all matters, but there are many matters of possible difference between us and other nations which can be thus arbitrated. Furthermore, at the request of the Interparliamentary Union, an eminent body composed of practical statesmen from all countries, I have asked the powers to join with this government in a second Hague conference, at which it is hoped that the work already so happily begun at The Hague may be carried some steps further toward completion. This carries out the desire expressed by the first Hague conference itself.

It is not true that the United States feels any land hunger or entertains any projects as regards the other nations of the Western Hemisphere save such as are for their welfare. All that this country desires is to see the neighboring countires stable, orderly, and prosperous. Any country whose people conduct themselves well can count upon our hearty friendship. If a nation shows that it knows how to act with reasonable efficiency and decency in social and political matters, if it keeps order and pays its obligations, it need fear no interference from the United States. Chronic wrongdoing, or an impotence which results in a general loosening of the ties of civilized society, may in America, as elsewhere, ultimately require intervention by some civilized nation, and in the Western Hemisphere the adherence of the United States to the Monroe Doctrine may force the United States, however reluctantly, in flagrant cases of such wrongdoing or impotence, to the exercise of an international police power. If every country washed by the Caribbean Sea would show the progress in stable and just civilization which with the aid of the Platt amendment Cuba has shown since our troops left the island, and which so many of the republics in both Americas are constantly and brilliantly showing, all question of interference by this nation with their affairs would be at an end. Our interests and those of our southern neighbors are in reality identical. They have great natural riches, and if within their borders the reign of law and justice obtains, prosperity is sure to come to them. While they thus obey the primary laws of civilized society they may rest assured that they will be treated by us in a spirit of cordial and helpful sympathy. We would interfere with them only in the last resort, and then only if it became evident that their inability or unwillingness to do justice at home and abroad had violated the rights of the United States or had invited foreign aggression to the detriment of the entire body of American nations. It is a mere truism to say that every nation, whether in America or anywhere else, which desires to maintain its freedom, its independence, must ultimately realize that the right of such independence cannot be separated from the responsibility of making good use of it.

In asserting the Monroe Doctrine, in taking such steps as we have taken in regard to Cuba, Venezuela, and Panama, and in endeavoring to circumscribe the theater of war in the Far East, and to secure the open door in China, we have acted in our own interest as well as in the interest of humanity at large.

Second Inaugural Address

Washington, D.C.

March 4, 1905

THE DAY before the inauguration, Roosevelt is reported to have said: "Tomorrow I shall come into my office in my own right. Then watch out for me!" The relative caution he displayed in his first term was succeeded in his second by an eagerness to do battle with entrenched interests. Having received the largest popular majority then recorded in an election, Roosevelt was now in a position to carry out such controversial programs as federal regulation of the railroads, the enactment of consumer protection laws, and the preservation of vast tracts of wilderness.

Inauguration Day was windy but clear. Roosevelt was accompanied to the ceremony by Rough Riders, who had been carousing in the capital all week. The president wore a ring containing a lock of Lincoln's hair; it had been given to him by his secretary of state, John Hay, who had been Lincoln's personal secretary. Roosevelt's measured and dignified address, which Henry Cabot Lodge helped him write, ends with a reference to Lincoln, the president Roosevelt most admired.

My fellow citizens, no people on earth have more cause to be thankful than ours, and this is said reverently, in no spirit of boastfulness in our own strength, but with gratitude to the Giver of Good who has blessed us with the conditions which have enabled us to achieve so large a measure of wellbeing and of happiness. To us as a people it has been granted to lay the foundations of our national life in a new continent. We are the heirs of the ages, and yet we have had to pay few of the penalties which in old countries are exacted by the dead hand of a bygone civilization. We have not been obliged to fight for our existence against any alien race; and yet our life has called for the vigor and effort without which the manlier and hardier virtues wither away. Under such conditions it would be our own fault if we failed; and the success which we have had in the past, the success which we confidently believe the future will bring, should cause in us no feeling of vainglory, but rather a deep and abiding realization of all which life has offered us; a full acknowledgment of the responsibility which is ours; and a fixed determination to show that under a free government a mighty people can thrive best, alike as regards the things of the body and the things of the soul.

Much has been given by us, and much will rightfully be expected from us. We have duties to others and duties to ourselves; and we can shirk neither. We have become a great nation, forced by the fact of its greatness into relations with the other nations of the earth, and we must behave as beseems a people with such responsibilities. Toward all other nations, large and small, our attitude must be one of cordial and sincere friendship. We must show not only in our words, but in our deeds, that we are earnestly desirous of securing their goodwill by acting toward them in a spirit of just and generous recognition of all their rights. But justice and generosity in a nation, as in an individual, count most when shown not by the weak but by the strong. While ever careful to refrain from wrongdoing others, we must be no less insistent that we are not wronged ouselves. We wish peace, but we wish the peace of justice, the peace of righteousness. We wish it because we think it is right and not because we are afraid. No weak nation that acts manfully and justly should ever have cause to fear us, and no strong power should ever be able to single us out as a subject for insolent aggression.

Our relations with the other powers of the world are important; but still more important are our relations among ourselves. Such growth in wealth, in population, and in power as this nation has seen during the century and a quarter of its national life is inevitably accompanied by a like growth in the problems which are ever before every nation that rises to greatness. Power invariably means both responsibility and danger. Our forefathers faced certain perils which we have outgrown. We now face other perils, the very existence of which it was impossible that they should foresee. Modern life is both complex and intense, and the tremendous changes wrought by the extraordinary industrial development of the last half century are felt in every fiber of our social and political being. Never before have men tried so vast and formidable an experiment as that of administering the affairs of a continent under the forms of a democratic republic. The conditions which have told for our marvelous material well-being, which have developed to a very high degree our energy, self-reliance, and individual initiative, have also brought the care and anxiety inseparable from the accumulation of great wealth in industrial centers. Upon the success of our experiment much depends, not only as regards our own welfare, but as regards the welfare of mankind. If we fail, the cause of free self-government throughout the world will rock to its foundations, and therefore our responsibility is heavy, to ourselves, to the world as it is today and to the generations yet unborn. There is no good reason why we should fear the future, but there is every reason why we should face it seriously, neither hiding from ourselves the gravity of the problems before us nor fearing to approach these problems with the unbending, unflinching purpose to solve them aright.

Yet, after all, though the problems are new, though the tasks before us differ from the tasks set before our fathers who founded and preserved this republic, the spirit in which these tasks must be undertaken and these problems faced, if our duty is to be well done, remains essentially unchanged. We know that self-government is difficult. We know that no people needs such high traits of character as that people which seeks to govern its affairs aright through the freely expressed will of the freemen who compose it. But we have faith that we shall not prove false to the memories of the men of the mighty past. They did their work, they left us the splendid heritage we now enjoy. We in our turn have an assured confidence that we shall be able to leave this heritage unwasted and enlarged to our children and our children's children. To do so we must show, not merely in great crises, but in the everyday affairs of life, the qualities of practical intelligence, of courage, of hardihood, and endurance, and above all the power of devotion to a lofty ideal, which made great the men who founded this republic in the days of Washington, which made great the men who preserved this republic in the days of Abraham Lincoln.

The Man with the Muckrake

Washington, D.C.

April 14, 1906

DESPITE ROOSEVELT'S formidable achievements as a reformer, he was no friend to reformers generally. His career as president was dedicated to building up and preserving the social order—a matter that required compromise and good faith on all sides. He had no patience with businessmen, such as the coal operators in the strike of 1902, who refused to cooperate in finding solutions to economic problems. (In that instance, he was prepared to send troops to seize and run the mines, a move that was rendered unnecessary by the intervention of J. P. Morgan.) By the same token, he was distrustful of journalists and activists who exposed corruption in government and industry, although their work formed the basis for many of his own reforms. The passage in 1906 of the Pure Food and Drug Act and the meat inspection bill, for which Roosevelt had fought, was due in large measure to the public outrage stirred up by Upton Sinclair's novel *The Jungle,* which dramatized filthy conditions in the meatpacking industry; yet Roosevelt, though mindful of Sinclair's role in this success, still thought him "hysterical, unbalanced, and untruthful."

"The Man with the Muckrake," an elaboration of remarks made a month earlier at Washington's Gridiron Club, was delivered at the ceremony for the laying of the cornerstone of the Congressional Office Building. Roosevelt's use of the term muckrakers to describe crusading journalists has passed into the language in a somewhat less derogatory sense.

Over a century ago Washington laid the cornerstone of the Capitol in what was then little more than a tract of wooden wilderness here beside the Potomac. We now find it necessary to provide by great additional buildings for the business of the government.

This growth in the need for the housing of the government is but a proof and example of the way in which the nation has grown and the sphere of action of the national government has grown. We now administer the affairs of a nation in which the extraordinary growth of population has been outstripped by the growth of wealth in complex interests. The material problems that face us today are not such as they were in Washington's time, but the underlying facts of human nature are the same now as they were then. Under altered external form we war with the same tendencies toward evil that were evident in Washington's time, and are helped by the same tendencies for good. It is about some of these that I wish to say a word today.

In Bunyan's *Pilgrim's Progress* you may recall the description of the Man with the Muckrake, the man who could look no way but downward, with the muckrake in his hand; who was offered a celestial crown for his muckrake, but who would neither look up nor regard the crown he was offered; but continued to rake to himself the filth of the floor.

In *Pilgrim's Progress* the Man with the Muckrake is set forth as the example of him whose vision is fixed on carnal instead of spiritual things. Yet he also typifies the man who in this life consistently refuses to see aught that is lofty, and fixes his eyes with solemn intentness only on that which is vile and debasing.

Now, it is very necessary that we should not flinch from seeing what is vile and debasing. There is filth on the floor, and it must be scraped up with the muckrake; and there are times and places where this service is the most needed of all the services that can be performed. But the man who never does anything else, who never thinks or speaks or writes, save of his feats with the muckrake, speedily becomes, not a help but one of the most potent forces for evil.

There are in the body politic, economic and social, many and grave evils, and there is urgent necessity for the sternest war upon them. There should be relentless exposure of and attack upon every evil man, whether politician or business man, every evil practice, whether in politics, business, or social life. I hail as a benefactor every writer or speaker, every man who, on the platform or in a book, magazine, or newspaper, with merciless severity makes such attack, provided always that he in his turn remembers that the attack is of use only if it is absolutely truthful.

The liar is no whit better than the thief, and if his mendacity takes the form of slander he may be worse than most thieves. It puts a premium upon knavery untruthfully to attack an honest man, or even with hysterical exaggeration to assail a bad man with untruth.

An epidemic of indiscriminate assault upon character does no good, but very great harm. The soul of every scoundrel is gladdened whenever an honest man is assailed, or even when a scoundrel is untruthfully assailed.

Now, it is easy to twist out of shape what I have just said, easy to affect to misunderstand it, and if it is slurred over in repetition not difficult really to misunderstand it. Some persons are sincerely incapable of understanding that to denounce mud slinging does not mean the endorsement of whitewashing; and both the interested individuals who need whitewashing and those other who practice mud slinging like to encourage such confusion of ideas.

One of the chief counts against those who make indiscriminate assault upon men in business or men in public life is that they invite a reaction which is sure to tell powerfully in favor of the unscrupulous scoundrel who really ought to be attacked, who ought to be exposed, who ought, if possible, to be put in the penitentiary. If Aristides is praised overmuch as just, people get tired of hearing it; and overcensure of the unjust finally and from similar reasons results in their favor.

Any excess is almost sure to invite a reaction; and, unfortunately, the reaction, instead of taking the form of punishment of those guilty of the excess, is apt to take the form either of punishment of the unoffending or of giving immunity, and even strength, to offenders. The effort to make financial or political profit out of the destruction of character can only result in public calamity. Gross and reckless assaults on character, whether on the stump or in newspaper, magazine, or book, create a morbid and vicious public sentiment, and at the same time act as a profound deterrent to able men of normal sensitiveness and tend to prevent them from entering the public service at any price.

As an instance in point, I may mention that one serious difficulty encountered in getting the right type of men to dig the Panama Canal is the certainty that they will be exposed, both without, and, I am sorry to say, sometimes within, Congress, to utterly rekcless assaults on their character and capacity.

At the risk of repetition let me say again that my plea is not for immunity to, but for the most unsparing exposure of, the politician who betrays his trust, of the big business man who makes or spends his fortune in illegitimate or corrupt ways. There should be a resolute effort to hunt every such man out of the position he has disgraced. Expose the crime, and hunt down the criminal; but remember that even in the case of crime, if it is attacked in sensational, lurid, and untruthful fashion, the attack may do more damage to the public mind than the crime itself.

It is because I feel that there should be no rest in the endless war against the forces of evil that I ask the war be conducted with sanity as well as with resolution.

The men with the muckrakes are often indispensable to the well being of society; but only if they know when to stop raking the muck, and to look upward to the celestial crown above them, to the crown of worthy endeavor. There are beautiful things above and round about them; and if they gradually grow to feel that the whole world is nothing but muck, their power of usefulness is gone.

If the whole picture is painted black there remains no hue whereby to single out the rascals for distinction from their fellows. Such painting finally induces a kind of moral color blindness; and people affected by it come to the conclusion that no man is really black, and no man really white, but they are all gray.

In other words, they neither believe in the truth of the attack, nor in the honesty of the man who is attacked; they grow as suspicious of the accusation as of the offense; it becomes well nigh hopeless to stir them either to wrath against wrongdoing or to enthusiasm for what is right; and such a mental attitude in the public gives hope to every knave, and is the despair of honest men.

To assail the great and admitted evils of our political and industrial life with such crude and sweeping generalizations as to include decent men in the general condemnation means the searing of the public conscience. There results a general attitude either of cynical belief in and indifference to public corruption or else of a distrustful inability to discriminate between the good and the bad. Either attitude is fraught with untold damage to the country as a whole.

The fool who has not sense to discriminate between what is good and what is bad is well nigh as dangerous as the man who does discriminate and yet chooses the bad. There is nothing more distressing to every good patriot, to every good American, than the hard, scoffing spirit which treats the allegation of dishonesty in a public man as a cause for laughter. Such laughter is worse than the crackling of thorns under a pot, for it denotes not merely the vacant mind, but the heart in which high emotions have been choked before they could grow to fruition.

There is any amount of good in the world, and there never was a time when loftier and more disinterested work for the betterment of mankind was being done than now. The forces that tend for evil are great and terrible, but the forces of truth and love and courage and honesty and generosity and sympathy are also stronger than ever before. It is a foolish and timid, no less than a wicked thing, to blink the fact that the forces of evil are strong, but it is even worse to fail to take into account the strength of the forces that tell for good.

Hysterical sensationalism is the poorest weapon wherewith to fight for lasting righteousness. The men who with stern sobriety and truth assail the many evils of our time, whether in the public press, or in magazines, or in books, are the leaders and allies of all engaged in the work for social and political betterment. But if they give good reason for distrust of what they say, if they chill the ardor of those who demand truth as a primary virtue, they thereby betray the good cause and play into the hands of the very men against whom they are nominally at war.

In his Ecclesiastical Polity that fine old Elizabethan divine, Bishop Hooker, wrote:

He that goeth about to persuade a multitude that they are not so well governed as they ought to be shall never want attentive and favorable hearers, because they know the manifold defects whereunto every kind of regimen is subject, but the secret lets and difficulties, which in public proceedings are innumerable and inevitable, they have not ordinarily the judgment to consider.

This truth should be kept constantly in mind by every free people desiring to preserve the sanity and poise indispensable to the permanent success of self-government. Yet, on the other hand, it is vital not to permit this spirit of sanity and self-command to degenerate into mere mental stagnation. Bad though a state of hysterical excitement is, and evil though the results are which come from the violent oscillations such excitement invariably produces, yet a sodden acquiescence in evil is even worse.

At this moment we are passing through a period of great unrest—social, political, and industrial unrest. It is of the utmost importance for our future that this should prove to be not the unrest of mere rebelliousness against life, of mere dissatisfaction with the inevitable inequality of conditions, but the unrest of a resolute and eager ambition to secure the betterment of the individual and the nation.

So far as this movement of agitation throughout the country takes the form of a fierce discontent with evil, of a determination to punish the authors of evil, whether in industry or politics, the feeling is to be heartily welcomed as a sign of healthy life.

If, on the other hand, it turns into a mere crusade of appetite against appetite, of a contest between the brutal greed of the "have nots" and the brutal greed of the "haves," then it has no significance for good, but only for evil. If it seeks to establish a line of cleavage, not along the line which divides good men from bad, but along that other line, running at right angles thereto, which divides those who are well off from those who are less well off, then it will be fraught with immeasurable harm to the body politic.

We can no more and no less afford to condone evil in the man of capital than evil in the man of no capital. The wealthy man who exults because there is a failure of justice in the effort to bring some trust magnate to account for his misdeeds is as bad as, and no worse than, the so-called labor leader who clamorously strives to excite a foul class feeling on behalf of some other labor leader who is implicated in murder. One attitude is as bad as the other, and no worse; in each case the accused is entitled to exact justice; and in neither case is there need of action by others which can be construed into an expression of sympathy for crime.

It is a prime necessity that if the present unrest is to result in permanent good the emotion shall be translated into action, and that the action shall be marked by honesty, sanity, and self-restraint. There is mighty little good in a mere spasm of reform. The reform that counts is that which comes through steady, continuous growth; violent emotionalism leads to exhaustion.

It is important to this people to grapple with the problems connected with the amassing of enormous fortunes, and the use of those fortunes, both corporate and individual, in business. We should discriminate in the sharpest way between fortunes well won and fortunes ill won; between those gained as an incident to performing great services to the community as a whole and those gained in evil fashion by keeping just within the limits of mere law honesty. Of course, no amount of charity in spending such fortunes in any way compensates for misconduct in making them.

As a matter of personal conviction, and without pretending to discuss the details or formulate the system, I feel that we shall ultimately have to consider the adoption of some such scheme as that of a progressive tax on all fortunes, beyond a certain amount, either given in life or devised or bequeathed upon death to any individual—a tax so framed as to put it out of the power of the owner of one of these enormous fortunes to hand on more than a certain amount to any one individual; the tax, of course, to be imposed by the national and not the state government. Such taxation should, of course, be aimed merely at the inheritance or transmission in their entirety of those fortunes swollen beyond all healthy limits.

Again, the national government must in some form exercise supervision over corporations engaged in interstate business—and all large corporations engaged in interstate business—whether by license or otherwise, so as to permit us to deal with the far reaching evils of overcapitalization.

This year we are making a beginning in the direction of serious effort to settle some of these economic problems by the railway rate legislation. Such legislation, if so framed, as I am sure it will be, as to secure definite and tangible results, will amount of something of itself; and it will amount to a great deal more in so far as it is taken as a first step in the direction of a policy of superintendence and control over corporate wealth engaged in interstate commerce; this superintendence and control not to be exercised in a spirit of malevolence toward the men who have created the wealth, but with the firm purpose both to do justice to them and to see that they in their turn do justice to the public at large.

The first requisite in the public servants who are to deal in this shape with corporations, whether as legislators or as executives, is honesty. This honesty can be no respecter of persons. There can be no such thing as unilateral honesty. The danger is not really from corrupt corporations; it springs from the corruption itself, whether exercised for or against corporations.

The eighth commandment reads. "Thou shalt not steal." It does not read, "Thou shalt not steal from the rich man." It does not read, "Thou shalt not steal from the poor man." It reads simply and plainly, "Thou shalt not steal."

No good whatever will come from that warped and mock morality which denounces the misdeeds of men of wealth and forgets the misdeeds practiced at their expense; which denounces bribery, but blinds itself to blackmail; which foams with rage if a corporation secures favors by improper methods, and merely leers with hideous mirth if the corporation is itself wronged.

The only public servant who can be trusted honestly to protect the rights of the public against the misdeeds of a corporation is that public man who will just as surely protect the corporation itself from wrongful aggression.

If a public man is willing to yield to popular clamor and do wrong to the men of wealth or to rich corporations, it may be set down as certain that if the opportunity comes he will secretly and furtively do wrong to the public in the interest of a corporation.

But in addition to honesty, we need sanity. No honesty will make a public man useful if that man is timid or foolish, if he is a hot-headed zealot or an impracticable visionary. As we strive for reform we find that it is not at all merely the case of a long uphill pull. On the contrary, there is almost as much of breeching work as of collar work. To depend only on traces means that there will soon be a runaway and an upset.

The men of wealth who today are trying to prevent the regulation and control of their business in the interest of the public by the proper government authorities will not succeed, in my judgment, in checking the progress of the movement. But if they did succeed they would find that they had sown the wind and would surely reap the whirlwind, for they would ultimately provoke the violent excess which accompany a reform coming by convulsion instead of by steady and natural growth.

On the other hand, the wild preachers of unrest and discontent, the wild agitators against the entire existing order, the men who act crookedly, whether because of sinister design or from mere puzzle-headedness, the men who preach destruction without proposing any substitute for what they intend to destroy, or who propose a substitute which would be far worse than the existing evils—all these men are the most dangerous opponents of real reform. If they get their way they will lead the people into a deeper pit than any into which they could fall under the present system. If they fail to get their way they will still do incalculable harm by provoking the kind of reaction which in its revolt against the senseless evil of their teaching would enthrone more securely than ever the evils which their misguided followers believe thay are attacking.

More important than aught else is the development of the broadest sympathy of man for man. The welfare of the wage worker, the welfare of the tiller of the soil, upon these depend the welfare of the entire country; their good is not to be sought in pulling down others; but their good must be the prime object of all our statesmanship.

Materially we must strive to secure a broader economic opportunity for all men, so that each shall have a better chance to show the stuff of which he is made. Spiritually and ethically we must strive to bring about clean living and right thinking. We appreciate that the things of the body are important; but we appreciate also that the things of the soul are immeasurably more important.

The foundation stone of national life is, and ever must be, the high individual character of the average citizen.

Forests

From the Seventh Annual Message to Congress
Washington, D.C.
December 3, 1907

ROOSEVELT APPEARS at his most modern in the role of conservationist. No president before or since has had the genuine love of nature that he possessed. All of his annual messages, and many of his speeches and writings, discuss forest, water, and mineral conservation with the detailed knowledge and unsullied enthusiasm of the amateur naturalist.

When Roosevelt took office, the natural resources of the nation, left unprotected by Congress, were undergoing dangerous exploitation by business interests—including power companies, livestock ranchers, and timber and mining companies—who profited from the use of these resources without recompense to the public. Roosevelt was the first president to take the position, now commonly accepted, that the federal government has an obligation to preserve and control these resources for the benefit of the nation as a whole. During his administration he established programs to reclaim arid land and protect forest reserves; created four volunteer commissions to oversee the regulation of inland waterways and other resources; and added 194 million acres to the lands under federal protection, five times the combined amount set aside by Benjamin Harrison, Grover Cleveland, and William McKinley.

The conservation of our natural resources and their proper use constitute the fundamental problem which underlies almost every other problem of our national life. We must maintain for our civilization the adequate material basis without which that civilization cannot exist. We must show foresight, we must look ahead. As a nation we not only enjoy a wonderful measure of present prosperity but if this prosperity is used aright it is an earnest of future success such as no other nation will have. The reward of foresight for this nation is great and easily foretold. But there must be the look ahead, there must be a realization of the fact that to waste, to destroy, our natural resources, to skin and exhaust the land instead of using it so as to increase its usefulness, will result in undermining in the days of our children the very prosperity which we ought to right to hand down to them amplified and developed. For the last few years, through several agencies, the government has been endeavoring to get our people to look ahead and to substitute a planned and orderly development of our resources in place of a haphazard striving for immediate profit. Our great river systems should be developed as national water highways, the Mississippi, with its tributaries, standing first in importance, and the Columbia second, although there are many others of importance on the Pacific, the Atlantic and the Gulf slopes. The national government should undertake this work, and I hope a beginning will be made in the present Congress; and the greatest of all our rivers, the Mississippi, should receive especial attention. From the Great Lakes to the mouth of the Mississippi there should be a deep waterway, with deep waterways leading from it to the East and the West. Such a waterway would practically mean the extension of our coastline into the very heart of our country. It would be of incalculable benefit to our people. If begun at once it can be carried through in time appreciably to relieve the congestion of our great freight-carrying lines of railroads. The work should be systematically and continuously carried forward in accordance with some well-conceived plan. The main streams should be improved to the highest point of efficiency before the improvement of the branches is attempted; and the work should be kept free from every taint of recklessness or jobbery. The inland waterways which lie just back of the whole eastern and southern coasts should likewise be developed. Moreover, the developement of our waterways involves many other important water problems, all of which should be considered as part of the same general scheme. The government dams should be used to produce hundreds of thousands of horsepower as an incident to improving navigation; for the annual value of the unused water-power of the United States perhaps exceeds the annual value of the products of all our mines. As an incident to creating the deep waterways down the Mississippi, the government should build along its whole lower length levees which taken together with the control of the headwaters, will at once and forever put a complete stop to all threat of floods in the immensely fertile Delta region. The territory lying adjacent to the Mississippi along its lower course will thereby become one of the most prosperous and populous, as it already is one of the most fertile, farming regions in all the world. I have appointed an Inland Waterways Commission to study and outline a comprehensive scheme of development along all the lines indicated. Later I shall lay its report before the Congress.

Irrigation should be far more extensively developed than at present, not only in the states of the Great Plains and the Rocky Mountains, but in many others, as, for instance, in large portions of the South Atlantic and Gulf states, where it should go hand in hand with the reclamation of swamp land. The federal government should seriously devote itself to this task, realizing that utilization of waterways and water-power, forestry, irrigation, and the reclamation of lands threatened with overflow, are all interdependent parts of the same problem. The work of the Reclamation Service in developing the larger opportunities of the western half of our country for irrigation is more important than almost any other movement. The constant purpose of the government in connection with the Reclamation Service has been to use the water resources of the public lands for the ultimate greatest good of the greatest number; in other words, to put upon the land permanent home-makers, to use and develop it for themselves and for their children and children's children. There has been, of course, opposition to this work; opposition from some interested men who desire to exhaust the land for their own immediate profit without regard to the welfare of the next generation, and opposition from honest and well-meaning men who did not fully understand the subject or who did not look far enough ahead. This opposition is, I think, dying away, and our people are understanding that it would be utterly wrong to allow a few individuals to exhaust for their own temporary personal profit the resources which ought to be developed through use so as to be conserved for the permanent common advantage of the people as a whole.

The effort of the government to deal with the public land has been based upon the same principle as that of the Reclamation Service. The land law system which was designed to meet the needs of the fertile and well-watered regions of the Middle West has largely broken down when applied to the dryer regions of the Great Plains, the mountains, and much of the Pacific slope, where a farm of 160 acres is inadequate for self-support. In these regions the system lent itself to fraud, and much land passed out of the hands of the government without passing into the hands of the home-maker. The Department of the Interior and the Department of Justice joined in prosecuting the offenders against the law; and they have accomplished much, while where the administration of the law has been defective it has been changed. But the laws themselves are defective. Three years ago a public lands commission was appointed to scrutinize the law, and defects, and recommend a remedy. Their examination specifically showed the existence of great fraud upon the public domain, and their recommendations for changes in the law made with the design of conserving the natural resources of every part of the public lands by putting it to its best use. Especial attention was called to the prevention of settlement by the passage of great areas of public land into the hands of a few men, and to the enormous waste caused by unrestricted grazing upon the open range. The recommendations of the Public Lands Commission are sound, for they are especially in the interest of the actual home-maker; and where the small home-maker cannot at present utilize the land they provide that the government shall keep control of it so that it may not be monopolized by a few men. The Congress has not yet acted upon these recommendations; but they are so just and proper, so essential to our national welfare, that I feel confident, if the Congress will take time to consider them, that they will ultimately be adopted. Some such legislation as that proposed is essential in order to preserve the great stretches of public grazing land which are unfit for cultivation under present methods and are valuable only for the forage which they supply. These stretches amount in all to some 300,000,000 acres, and are open to the free grazing of cattle, sheep, horses and goats, without restriction. Such a system, or lack of system, means that the range is not so much used as wasted by abuse. As the West settles the range becomes more and more overgrazed. Much of it cannot be used to advantage unless it is fenced, for fencing is the only way by which to keep in check the owners of nomad flocks which roam hither and thither, utterly destroying the pastures and leaving a waste behind so that their presence is incompatible with the presence of home-makers. The existing fences are all illegal. Some of them represent the improper exclusion of actual settlers, actual home-makers, from territory which is usurped by great cattle companies. Some of them represent what is in itself a proper effort to use the range for those upon the land, and to prevent its use by nomadic outsiders. All these fences, those that are hurtful and those that are beneficial, are alike illegal and must come down. But it is an outrage that the law should necessitate such action on the part of the administration. The unlawful fencing of public lands for private grazing must be stopped, but the necessity which occasioned it must be provided for. The federal government should have control of the range, whether by permit or lease, as local necessities may determine. Such control could secure the great benefit of legitimate fencing, while at the same time securing and promoting the settlement of the country. In some places it may be that the tracts of range adjacent to the homesteads of actual settlers should be allotted to them severally or in common for the summer grazing of their stock. Elsewhere it may be that a lease system would serve the purpose; the leases to be temporary and subject to the rights of settlement, and the amount charged being large enough merely to permit the efficient and beneficial control of the range by the government, and of the payment to the county of the equivalent of what it would otherwise receive in taxes. The destruction of the public range will continue until some such laws as these are enacted. Fully to prevent the fraud in the public lands which, through the joint action of the Interior Department and the Department of Justice, we have been endeavoring to prevent, there must be further legislation, and especially a sufficient appropriation to permit the Department of the Interior to examine certain classes of entries

on the ground before they pass into private ownership. The government should part with its title only to the actual home-maker, not to the profit-maker who does not care to make a home. Our prime object is to secure the rights and guard the interests of the small ranchman, the man who plows and pitches hay for himself. It is this small ranchman, this actual settler and homemaker, who in the long run is most hurt by permitting thefts of the public land in whatever form.

Optimism is a good characteristic, but if carried to an excess it becomes foolishness. We are prone to speak of the resources of this country as inexhaustible; this is not so. The mineral wealth of the country, the coal, iron, oil, gas, and the like, does not reproduce itself, and therefore is certain to be exhausted ultimately; and wastefulness in dealing with it to-day means that our descendants will feel the exhaustion a generation or two before they otherwise would. But there are certain other forms of waste which could be entirely stopped—the waste of soil by washing, for instance, which is among the most dangerous of all wastes now in progress in the United States, is easily preventable, so that this present enormous loss of fertility is entirely unnecessary. The preservation or replacement of the forests is one of the most important means of preventing this loss. We have made a beginning in forest preservation, but it is only a beginning. At present lumbering is the fourth-greatest industry in the United States; and yet, so rapid has been the rate of exhaustion of timber in the United States in the past, and so rapidly is the remainder being exhausted, that the country is unquestionably on the verge of a timber famine which will be felt in every household in the land. There has already been a rise in the price of lumber, but there is certain to be a more rapid and heavier rise in the future. The present annual consumption of lumber is certainly three times as great as the annual growth; and if the consumption and growth continue unchanged, practically all our lumber will be exhausted in another generation, while long before the limit to complete exhaustion is reached the growing scarcity will make itself felt in many blighting ways upon our national welfare. About 20 percent of our forested territory is now reserved in national forests; but these do not include the most valuable timber lands, and in any event the proportion is too small to expect that the reserves can accomplish more than a mitigation of the trouble which is ahead for the nation. Far more drastic action is needed. Forests can be lumbered so as to give to the public the full use of their mercantile timber without the slightest detriment to the forest, any more than it is a detriment to a farm to furnish a harvest; so that there is no parallel between forests and mines, which can only be completely used by exhaustion. But forests, if used as all our forests have been used in the past and as most of them are still used, will be either wholly destroyed, or so damaged that many decades have to pass before effective use can be made of them again.

All these facts are so obvious that it is extraordinary that it should be necessary to repeat them. Every business man in the land, every writer in the newspapers, every man or woman of an ordinary school education, ought to be able to see that immense quantities of timber are used in the country, that the forests which supply this timber are rapidly being exhausted, and that, if no change takes place, exhaustion will come comparatively soon, and that the effects of it will be felt severely in the everyday life of our people. Surely, when these facts are so obvious, there should be no delay in taking preventive measures. Yet we seem as a nation to be "willing to proceed in this matter with happy-go-lucky indifference even to the immediate future. It is this attitude which permits the self-interest of a very few persons to weigh for more than the ultimate interest of all our people.

There are persons who find it to their immense pecuniary benefit to destroy the forests by lumbering. They are to be blamed for thus sacrificing the future of the nation as a whole to their own self-interest of the moment; but heavier blame attaches to the people at large for permitting such action, whether in the White Mountains, in the southern Alleghenies, or in the Rockies and Sierras. A big lumbering company, impatient for immediate returns and not caring to look far enough ahead, will often deliberately destroy all the good timber in a region, hoping afterwards to move on to some new country. The shiftless man of small means, who does not care to become an actual homemaker but would like immediate profit, will find it to his advantage to take up timber land simply to turn it over to such a big company, and leave it valueless for future settlers. A big mine owner, anxious only to develop his mine at the moment, will care only to cut all the timber that he wishes without regard to the future—probably not looking ahead to the condition of the country when the forests are exhausted, any more than he does to the condition when the mine is worked out. I do not blame these men nearly as much as I blame the supine public opinion, the indifferent public opinion, which permits their action to go unchecked. Of course to check the waste of timber means that there must be on the part of the public the acceptance of a temporary restriction in the lavish use of the timber, in order to prevent the total loss of this use in the future. There are plenty of men in public and private life who actually advocate the continuance of the present system of unchecked and wasteful extravangance, using as an argument the fact that to check it will of course mean interference with the ease and comfort of certain people who now get lumber at less cost than they ought to pay, at the expense of the future generations. Some of these persons actually demand that the present forest reserves be thrown open to destruction, because, forsooth, they think that thereby the price of lumber could be put down again for two or three or more years. Their attitude is precisely like that of an agitator protesting against the outlay of money by farmers on manure and in taking care of their farms generally. Undoubtedly, if the average farmer were content absolutely to ruin his farm, he could for two or three years avoid spending any money on it, and yet make a good deal of money out of it. But only a savage would, in his private affairs, show such reckless disregard of the future; yet it is precisely this reckless disregard of the future which the opponents of the forestry system are now endeavoring to get the people of the United States to show. The only trouble with the movement for the preservation of our forests is that it has not gone nearly far enough, and was not begun soon enough. It is a most fortunate thing, however, that we began it when we did. We should acquire in the Appalachian and White Mountain regions all the forest lands that it is possible to acquire for the use of the nation. These lands, because they form a national asset, are as emphatically national as the rivers which they feed, and which flow through so many states before they reach the ocean.

The New Nationalism

Osawatomie, Kansas

August 31, 1910

ROOSEVELT IS the president most strongly identified with early-20th-century progressivism, although he was not the only chief executive to be influenced by its ideas. Progressivism was a mass movement, born of agrarian populism but also including urban reformers, that sought to rectify the widespread social and economic abuses growing out of unchecked industrialization, weak federal regulation, and corrupt local government. With the restoration of social justice, the progressives believed, would come a resurgence of true civic morality such as had existed in the early days of the republic. Roosevelt, who had pursued a wide range of domestic reforms during his presidency, remained the movement's champion even after he left office in 1909.

In the summer of 1910, the progressive wing of the Republican Party asked Roosevelt to campaign for their cause on a railway tour of the West. At the dedication of a state park on the site of the abolitionist John Brown's battle with Missouri slave raiders in 1856, before a crowd of cheering admirers, he outlined a vision of the future that electrified the progressives. Roosevelt called for a new national spirit, one in which all individuals and groups would willingly subordinate their interests to those of the community. Inspiring and shaping the "new nationalism" would be a strong central government and a vigorous president who would lead the way in instituting reforms and educating the people in their civic responsibilities. The Republican progressives rallied behind Roosevelt's new nationalism and later advanced him as their candidate for the presidency in 1912.

We come here today to commemorate one of the epoch-making events of the long struggle for the rights of man—the long struggle for the uplift of humanity. Our country—this great republic—means nothing unless is means the triumph of a real democracy, the triumph of popular government, and, in the long run, of an economic system under which each man shall be guaranteed the opportunity to show the best that there is in him. That is why the history of America is now the central feature of the history of the world; for the world has set its face hopefully toward our democracy; and, O my fellow citizens, each one of you carries on your shoulders not only the burden of doing well for the sake of your own country, but the burden of doing well and of seeing that this nation does well for the sake of mankind.

There have been two great crises in our country's history: first, when it was formed, and then, again, when it was perpetuated; and, in the second of these great crises—in the time of stress and strain which culminated in the Civil War, on the outcome of which depended the justification of what had been done earlier, you men of the Grand Army, you men who fought through the Civil War, not only did you justify your generation, not only did you render life worth living for our generation, but you justified the wisdom of Washington and Washington's colleagues. If this republic had been founded by them only to be split asunder into fragments when the strain came, then the judgment of the world would have been that Washington's work was not worth doing. It was you who crowned Washington's work, as you carried to achievement the high purpose of Abraham Lincoln.

Now, with this second period of our history the name of John Brown will be forever associated; and Kansas was the theater upon which the first act of the second of our great national life dramas was played. It was the result of the struggle in Kansas which determined that our country should be in deed as well as in name devoted to both union and freedom; that the great experiment of democratic government on a national scale should succeed and not fail. In name we had the Declaration of Independence in 1776; but we gave the lie by our acts to the words of the Declaration of Independence until 1865; and words count for nothing except insofar as they represent acts. This is true everywhere; but, O my friends, it should be truest of all in political life. A broken promise is bad enough in private life. It is worse in the field of politics. No man is worth his salt in public life who makes on the stump a pledge which he does not keep after election; and, if he makes such a pledge and does not keep it, hunt him out of public life. I care for the great deeds of the past chiefly as spurs to drive us onward in the present. I speak of the men of the past partly that they may be honored by our praise of them, but more that they may serve as examples for the future.

It was a heroic struggle; and, as is inevitable with all such struggles, it had also a dark and terrible side. Very much was done of good, and much also of evil; and, as was inevitable in such a period of revolution, often the same man did both good and evil. For our great good fortune as a nation, we, the people of the United States as a whole, can now afford to forget the evil, or, at least, to remember it without bitterness, and to fix our eyes with pride only on the good that was accomplished. Even in ordinary times there are very few of us who do not see the problems of life as through a glass, darkly; and when the glass is clouded by the murk of furious popular passion, the vision of the best and the bravest is dimmed. Looking back, we are all of us now able to do justice to the valor and the disinterestedness and the love of the right, as to each it was given to see the right, shown both by the men of the North and the men of the South in that contest which was finally decided by the attitude of the West. We can admire the heroic valor, the sincerity, the self-devotion shown alike by the men who wore the blue and the men who wore the gray; and our sadness that such men should have had to fight one another is tempered by the glad knowledge that ever hereafter their descendants shall be found fighting side by side, struggling in peace as well as in war for the uplift of their common country, all alike resolute to raise to the highest pitch of honor and usefulness the nation to which they all belong. As for the veterans of the Grand Army of the Republic, they deserve honor and recognition such as is paid to no other citizens of the republic; for to them the republic owes its all; for to them it owes its very existence. It is because of what you and your comrades did in the dark years that we of today walk, each of us, head erect, and proud that we belong, not to one of a dozen little squabbling contemptible commonwealths, but to the mightiest nation upon which the sun shines.

I do not speak of this struggle of the past merely from the historic standpoint. Our interest is primarily in the application today of the lessons taught by the contest of half a century ago. It is of little use for us to pay lip loyalty to the mighty men of the past unless we sincerely endeavor to apply to the problems of the present precisely the qualities which in other crises enabled the men of that day to meet those crises. It is half melancholy and half amusing to see the way in which well-meaning people gather to do honor to the men who, in company with John Brown, and under the lead of Abraham Lincoln, faced and solved the great problems of the 19th century, while, at the same time, these same good people nervously shrink from, or frantically denounce, those who are trying to meet the problems of the 20th century in the spirit which was accountable for the successful solution of the problems of Lincoln's time.

Of that generation of men to whom we owe so much, the man to whom we owe most is, of course, Lincoln. Part of our debt to him is because he forecast our present struggle and saw the way out. He said:

I hold that while man exists it is his duty to improve not only his own condition, but to assist in ameliorating mankind.

And again:—

Labor is prior to, and independent of, capital. Capital is only the fruit of labor, and could never have existed if labor had not first existed. Labor is the superior of capital, and deserves much the higher consideration.

If that remark was original with me, I should be even more strongly denounced as a communist agitator than I shall be anyhow. It is Lincoln's. I am only quoting it; and that is one side; that is the side the capitalist should hear. Now, let the workingman hear his side.

Capital has its rights, which are as worthy of protection as any other rights. . . . Nor should this lead to a war upon the owners of property. Property is the fruit of labor; . . . property is desirable; is a positive good in the world.

And then comes a thoroughly Lincolnlike sentence:

> Let not him who is houseless pull down the house of another, but let him work diligently and build one for himself, thus by example assuring that his own shall be safe from violence when built.

It seems to me that, in these words, Lincoln took substantially the attitude that we ought to take; he showed the proper sense of proportion in his relative estimates of capital and labor, of human rights and property rights. Above all, in his speech, as in many others, he taught a lesson in wise kindliness and charity; an indispensable lesson to us of to-day. But this wise kindliness and charity never weakened his arm or numbed his heart. We cannot afford weakly to blind ourselves to the actual conflict which faces us today. The issue is joined, and we must fight or fail. . . .

Practical equality of opportunity for all citizens, when we achieve it, will have two great results. First, every man will have a fair chance to make of himself all that in him lies; to reach the highest point to which his capacities, unassisted by special privilege of his own and unhampered by the special privilege of others, can carry him, and to get for himself and his family substantially what he has earned. Second, equality of opportunity means that the commonwealth will get from every citizen the highest service of which he is capable. No man who carries the burden of the special privileges of another can give to the commonwealth that service to which it is fairly entitled.

I stand for the square deal. But when I say that I am for the square deal, I mean not merely that I stand for fair play under the present rules of the game, but that I stand for having those rules changed so as to work for a more substantial equality of opportunity and of reward for equally good service. One word of warning, which, I think, is hardly necessary in Kansas. When I say I want a square deal for the poor man, I do not mean that I want a square deal for the man who remains poor because he has not the energy to work for himself. If a man who has had a chance will not make good, then he has got to quit. And you men of the Grand Army, you want justice for the brave man who fought, and punishment for the coward who shirked his work. Is not that so?

Now, this means that our government, national and state, must be freed from the sinister influence or control of special interests. . . .

The true friend of property, the true conservative, is he who insists that property shall be the servant and not the master of the commonwealth; who insists that the creature of man's making shall be the servant and not the master of the man who made it. The citizens of the United States must effectively control the mighty commercial forces which they have themselves called into being. . . .

Nothing is more true than that excess of every kind is followed by reaction; a fact which should be pondered by reformer and reactionary alike. We are face to face with new conceptions of the relations of property to human welfare, chiefly because certain advocates of the rights of property as against the rights of men have been pushing their claims too far. The man who wrongly holds that every human right is secondary to his profit must now give way to the advocate of human welfare, who rightly maintains that every man holds his property subject to the general right of the community to regulate its use to whatever degree the public welfare may require it.

But I think we may go still further. The right to regulate the use of wealth in the public interest is universally admitted. Let us admit also the right to regulate the terms and conditions of labor, which is the chief element of wealth, directly in the interest of the common good. The fundamental thing to do for every man is to give him a chance to reach a place in which he will make the greatest possible contribution to the public welfare. Understand what I say there. Give him a chance, not push him up if he will not be pushed. Help any man who stumbles; if he lies down, it is a poor job to try to carry him; but if he is a worthy man, try your best to see that he gets a chance to show the worth that is in him. No man can be a good citizen unless he has a wage more than sufficient to cover the bare cost of living, and hours of labor short enough so that after his day's work is done he will have time and energy to bear his share in the management of the community, to help in carrying the general load. We keep countless men from being good citizens by the conditions of life with which we surround them. We need comprehensive workmen's compensation acts, both state and national laws to regulate child labor and work for women, and, especially, we need in our common schools not merely education in book learning, but also practical training for daily life and work. We need to enforce better sanitary conditions for our workers and to extend the use of safety applicances for our workers in industry and commerce, both within and between the states. Also, friends, in the interest of the workingman himself we need to set our faces like flint against mob violence just as against corporate greed; against violence and injustice and lawlessness by wage workers just as much as against lawless cunning and greed and selfish arrogance of employers. If I could ask one thing of my fellow countrymen, my request would be that, whenever they go in for reform, they remember the two sides, and that they always exact justice from one side as much as from the other. I have small use for the public servant who can always see and denounce the corruption of the capitalist, but who cannot persuade himself, especially before election, to say a word about lawless mob violence. And I have equally small use for a man, be he a judge on the bench, or editor of a great paper, or wealthy and influential private citizen, who can see clearly enough and denounce the lawlessness of mob violence, but whose eyes are closed so that he is blind when the question is one of corruption in business on a gigantic scale. Also remember what I said about excess in reformer and reactionary alike. If the reactionary man, who thinks of nothing but the rights of property, could have his way, he would bring about a revolution; and one of my chief fears in connection with progress comes because I do not want to see our people, for lack of proper leadership, compelled to follow men whose intentions are excellent, but whose eyes are a little too wild to make it really safe to trust them. Here in Kansas there is one paper which habitually denounces me as the tool of Wall Street, and at the same time frantically repudiates the statement that I am a Socialist on the ground that that is an unwarranted slander of the Socialists.

National efficiency has many factors. It is a necessary result of the principle of conservation widely applied. In the end it will determine our failure or success as a nation. National efficiency has to do, not only with natural resources and with men, but it is equally concerned with institutions. The state must be made efficient for the work which concerns only the people of the state; and the nation for that which concerns all the people. There must remain no neutral ground to serve as a refuge for lawbreakers, and especially for lawbreakers of great wealth, who can hire the vulpine legal cunning which will teach them how to avoid both jurisdictions. It is a misfortune when the national legislature fails to do its duty in providing a national remedy, so that the only national activity is the purely negative activity of the judiciary in forbidding the state to exercise power in the premises.

I do not ask for overcentralization; but I do ask that we work in a spirit of broad and far-reaching nationalism when we work for what concerns our people as a whole. We are all Americans. Our common interests are as broad as the continent. I speak to you here in Kansas exactly as I would speak in New York or Georgia, for the most vital problems are those which affect us all alike. The national government belongs to the whole American people, and where the whole American people are interested, that interest can be guarded effectively only by the national government. The betterment which we seek must be accomplished, I believe, mainly through the national government.

The American people are right in demanding the New Nationalism, without which we cannot hope to deal with new problems. The New Nationalism puts the national need before sectional or personal advantage. It is impatient of the utter confusion that results from local legislatures attempting to treat national issues as local issues. It is still more impatient of the impotence which springs from overdivision of governmental powers, the impotence which makes it possible for local selfishness or for legal cunning, hired by wealthy special interests, to bring national activities to a deadlock. This New Nationalism regards the executive power as the steward of the public welfare. It demands of the judiciary that it shall be interested primarily in human welfare rather than in property, just as it demands that the representative body shall represent all the people rather than any one class or section of the people.

I believe in shaping the ends of government to protect property as well as human welfare.

Normally, and in the long run, the ends are the same; but whenever the alternative must be faced, I am for men and not for property, as you were in the Civil War. I am far from underestimating the importance of dividends; but I rank dividends below human character. Again, I do not have any sympathy with the reformer who says he does not care for dividends. Of course, economic welfare is necessary, for a man must pull his own weight and be able to support his family. I know well that the reformers must not bring upon the people economic ruin, or the reforms themselves will go down in the ruin. But we must be ready to face temporary disaster, whether or not brought on by those who will war against us to the knife. Those who oppose all reform will do well to remember that ruin in its worst form is inevitable if our national life brings us nothing better than swollen fortunes for the few and the triumph in both politics and business of a sordid and selfish materialism.

If our political institutions were perfect, they would absolutely prevent the political domination of money in any part of our affairs. We need to make our political representatives more quickly and sensitively responsive to the people whose servants they are. More direct action by the people in their own affairs under proper safeguards is vitally necessary. The direct primary is a step in this direction, if it is associated with a corrupt practices act effective to prevent the advantage of the man willing recklessly and unscrupulously to spend money over his more honest competitor. It is particularly important that all moneys received or expended for campaign purposes should be publicly accounted for, not only after election, but before election as well. Political action must be made simpler, easier, and freer from confusion for every citizen. I believe that the prompt removal of unfaithful or incompetent public servants should be made easy and sure in whatever way experience shall show to be most expedient in any given class of cases.

One of the fundamental necessities in a representative government such as ours is to make certain that the men to whom the people delegate their power shall serve the people by whom they are elected, and not the special interests. I believe that every national officer, elected or appointed, should be forbidden to perform any service or receive any compensation,

directly or indirectly, from interstate corporations; and a similar provision could not fail to be useful within the states.

The object of government is the welfare of the people. The material progress and prosperity of a nation are desirable chiefly so far as they lead to the moral and material welfare of all good citizens. Just in proportion as the average man and woman are honest, capable of sound judgment and high ideals, active in public affairs,—but, first of all, sound in their home life, and the father and mother of healthy children whom they bring up well,—just so far, and no farther, we may count our civilization a success. We must have—I believe we have already—a genuine and permanent moral awakening, without which no wisdom of legislation or administration really means anything; and, on the other hand, we must try to secure the social and economic legislation without which any improvement due to purely moral agitation is necessarily evanescent. Le me again illustrate by a reference to the Grand Army. You could not have won simply as a disorderly and disorganized mob. You needed generals; you needed careful administration of the most advanced type; and a good commissary—the cracker line. You well remember that success was necessary in many different lines in order to bring about general success. You had to have the administration at Washington good, just as you had to have the administration in the field; and you had to have the work of the generals good. You could not have triumphed without that administration and leadership; but it would all have been worthless if the average soldier had not had the right stuff in him. He had to have the right stuff in him, or you could not get it out of him. In the last analysis, therefore, vitally necessary though it was to have the right kind of organization and the right kind of generalship, it was even more vitally necessary that the average soldier should have the fighting edge, the right character. So it is in our civil life. No matter how honest and decent we are in our private lives, if we do not have the right kind of law and the right kind of administration of the law, we cannot go forward as a nation. That is imperative; but it must be an addition to, and not a substitution for, the qualities that make us good citizens. In the last analysis, the most important elements in any man's career must be the sum of those qualities which, in the aggregate, we speak of as character. If he has not got it, then no law that the wit of man can devise, no administration of the law by the boldest and strongest executive, will avail to help him. We must have the right kind of character—character that makes a man, first of all, a good man in the home, a good father, a good husband—that makes a man a good neighbor. You must have that, and, then, in addition, you must have the kind of law and the kind of administration of the law which will give to those qualities in the private citizen the best possible chance for development. The prime problem of our nation is to get the right type of good citizenship, and, to get it, we must have progress, and our public men must be genuinely progressive.

A Confession of Faith

Chicago, Illinois

August 6, 1912

THE INSURGENT progressive faction of the Republican Party wanted Roosevelt as its candidate for president in 1912. He did well in the primaries, but President Taft, who controlled the Republican National Committee, was assured of sufficient delegates to clinch the nomination at the party convention. In disgust, the progressives, with Roosevelt at their head, withdrew from the convention and formed their own Progressive Party, nicknamed the Bull Moose Party for the qualities of native American strength and fearlessness supposedly embodied by Roosevelt himself.

At the Progressive convention, described by one participant as "a great revival meeting," Roosevelt spoke with near-religious fervor before 10,000 hastily assembled delegates. The written version of his address was far too long to be read outright and had to be cut by half for the podium. He proposed a reform program so ambitious that it would have been difficult to enact in its entirety. But the chance did not come: In November, the Democrat, Woodrow Wilson, won easily over Roosevelt, who came in second, and Taft, who took third.

To you, men and women who have come here to this great city of this great state formally to launch a new party, a party of the people of the whole Union, the National Progressive Party, I extend my hearty greeting. You are taking a bold and a greatly needed step for the service of our beloved country. The old parties are husks, with no real soul within either, divided on artificial lines, boss-ridden and privilege-controlled, each a jumble of incongruous elements, and neither daring to speak out wisely and fearlessly what should be said on the vital issues of the day. This new movement is a movement of truth, sincerity, and wisdom, a movement which proposes to put at the service of all our people the collective power of the people, through their governmental agencies, alike in the nation and in the several states. We propose boldly to face the real and great questions of the day, and not skillfully to evade them as do the old parties. We propose to raise aloft a standard to which all honest men can repair, and under which all can fight, no matter what their past political differences, if they are content to face the future and no longer to dwell among the dead issues of the past. We propose to put forth a platform which shall not be a platform of the ordinary and insincere kind, but shall be a contract with the people; and, if the people accept this contract by putting us in power, we shall hold ourselves under honorable obligation to fulfil every promise it contains as loyally as if it were actually enforceable under the penalties of the law.

The prime need today is to face the fact that we are now the midst of a great economic evolution. There is urgent necessity of applying both common sense and the highest ethical standard to this movement for better economic conditions among the mass of our people if we are to make it one of healthy evolution and not one of revolution. It is, from the standpoint of our country, wicked as well as foolish longer to refuse to face the real issues of the day. Only by so facing them can we go forward; and to do this we must break up the old party organizations and obliterate the old cleavage lines on the dead issues inherited from 50 years ago. . . .

Neither the Republican nor the Democratic platform contains the slightest promise of approaching the great problems of today either with understanding or good faith; and yet never was there greater need in this nation than now of understanding and of action taken in good faith, on the part of the men and the organizations shaping our governmental policy. Moreover, our needs are such that there should be coherent action among those responsible for the conduct of national affairs and those responsbile for the conduct of state affairs; because our aim should be the same in both state and nation; that is, to use the government as an efficient agency for the practical betterment of social and economic conditions throughout this land. There are other important things to be done, but this is the most important thing. It is preposterous to leave such a movement in the hands of men who have broken their promises as have the present heads of the Republican organization (not of the Republican voters, for they in no shape represent the rank and file of the Republican voters). These men by their deed give the lie to their words. There is no health in them, and they cannot be trusted. But the Democratic Party is just as little to be trusted. . . .

The Democratic platform not only shows an utter failure to understand either present conditons or the means of making these conditions better but also a reckless willingness to try to attract various sections of the electorate by making mutually incompatible promises which there is not the slightest intention of redeeming, and which, if redeemed, would result in sheer ruin. Far-seeing patriots should turn scornfully from men who seek power on a platform which with exquisite nicety combines silly inability to understand the national needs and dishonest insincerity in promising conflicting and impossible remedies.

If this country is really to go forward along the path of social and economic justice, there must be a new party of nationwide and nonsectional principles, a party where the titular national chiefs and the real state leaders shall be in genuine accord, a party in whose counsels the people shall be supreme, a party that shall represent in the nation and the several states alike the same cause, the cause of human rights and of governmental efficiency. At present both the old parties are controlled by professional politicians in the interests of the privileged classes, and apparently each has set up as its ideal of business and political development a government by financial despotism tempered by make-believe political assassination. Democrat and Republican alike, they represent government of the needy many of professional politicians in the interests of the rich few. This is class government, and class government of a peculiarly unwholesome kind.

It seems to me, therefore, that the time is ripe, and overripe, for a genuine Progressive movement, nation-wide and justice-loving, sprung from and responsbile to the people themselves, and sundered by a great gulf from both of the old party organizations, while representing all that is best in the hopes, beliefs, and aspirations of the plain people who make up the immense majority of the rank and file of both the old parties.

The first essential in the Progressive programme is the right of the people to rule. But a few months ago our opponents were assuring us with insincere clamor that it was absurd for us to talk desiring that the people should rule, because, as a matter of fact, the people actually do rule. Since that time the actions of the Chicago Convention, and to an only less degree of the Baltimore Convention, have shown in striking fashion how little the people do rule under our present conditions.

We should provide by national law for presidential primaries. We should provide for the election of United States senators by popular vote. We should provide for a short ballot; nothing makes it harder for the people to control their public servants than to force them to vote for so many officials that they cannot really keep track of any one of them, so that each becomes indistinguishable in the crowd around him. There must be stringent and efficient corrupt-practices acts, applying to the primaries as well as the elections; and there should be publicity of campaign contributions during the campaign.

We should provide throughout this Union for giving the people in every state the real right to rule themselves, and really and not nominally to control their public servants and their agencies for doing the public business; an incident of this being giving the people the right themselves to do this public business if they find it impossible to get what they desire through the existing agencies. I do not attempt to dogmatize as to the machinery by which this end should be achieved. In each community it must be shaped so as to correspond not merely with the needs but with the customs and ways of thought of that community, and no community has a right to dictate to any other in this matter. But wherever representative government has in actual fact become nonrepresentative there the people should secure to themselves the initiative, the referendum, and the recall, doing it in such fashion as to make it evident that they do not intend to use these instrumentalities wantonly or frequently, but to hold them ready for use in order to correct the misdeeds or failures of the public servants when it has become evident that these misdeeds and failures cannot be corrected in ordinary and normal fashion.

The administrative officer should be given full power, for otherwise he cannot do well the people's work; and the people should be given full power over him. . . .

The American people, and not the courts, are to determine their own fundamental policies. The people should have power to deal with the effect of the acts of all their governmental agencies. This must be extended to include the effects of judicial acts as well as the acts of the executive and legislative representatives of the people. Where the judge merely does justice as between man and man, not dealing with constitutional questions, then the interest of the public is only to see that he is a wise and upright judge. Means should be devised for making it easier than at present to get rid of an incompetent judge; means should be devised by the bar and the bench acitng in conjunction with the various legislative bodies to make justice far more expeditious and more certain than at present. The stick-in-the-bark legalism, the legalism that subordinates equity to technicalities, should be recognized as a potent enemy of justice. But this is not the matter of most concern at the moment. Our prime concern is that in dealing with the fundamental law of the land, in assuming finally to interpret it, and therefore finally to make it, the acts of the courts should be subject to and not above the final control of the people as a whole. I deny that the American people have surrendered to any set of men, no matter what their position or their character, the final right to determine those fundamental questions upon which free self-government ultimately depends. The people themselves must be the ultimate makers of their own Constitution, and where their agents differ in their interpretations of the Constitution the people themselves should be given the chance, after full and deliberate judgment, authoritatively to settle what interpretation it is that their representatives shall thereafter adopt as binding. . . .

I am well aware that every upholder of privilege, every hired agent or beneficiary of the special interests, including many well-meaning parlor reformers, will denounce all this as "Socialism" or "anarchy"—the same terms they used in the past in denouncing the movements to control the railways and to control public utilities. As a matter of fact, the propositions I make constitute neither anarchy nor Socialism, but, on the contrary, a corrective to Socialism and an antidote to anarchy.

I especially challenge the attention of the people to the need of dealing in farreaching fashion with our human resources, and therefore our labor power. In a century and a quarter as a nation the American people have subdued and settled the vast reaches of a continent; ahead lies the greater task of building up on this foundation, by themselves, for themselves, and with themselves, an American commonwealth which in its social and economic structure shall be four square with democracy. . . .

In the last 20 years an increasing percentage of our people have come to depend on industry for their livelihood, so that today the wage-workers in industry rank in importance side by side with the tillers of the soil. As a people we cannot afford to let any group of citizens or any individual citizen live or labor under conditions which are injurious to the common welfare. Industry, therefore, must submit to such public regulation as will make it a means of life and health, not of death or inefficiency. We must protect the crushable elements at the base of our present industrial structure.

The first charge on the industrial statesmanship of the day is to prevent human waste. The dead weight of orphanage and depleted craftsmanship, of crippled workers and workers suffering from trade diseases, of casual labor, of insecure old age, and of household depletion due to industrial conditions are, like our depleted soils, our gashed mountainsides, and flooded river-bottoms, so many strains upon the national structure, draining the reserve strength of all industries and showing beyond all peradventure the public element and public concern in industrial health. . . .

We pledge the federal government to an investigation of industries along the lines pursued by the Bureau of Mines with the view to establishing standards of sanitation and safety; we call for the standardization of mine and factory inspection by interstate or the establishment of a federal standard. We stand for the passage of legislation in the nation and in all states providing standards of compensation for industrial accidents and death, and for diseases clearly due to the nature of conditions of industry, and we stand for the adoption by law of a fair standard of compensation for casualties resulting fatally which shall clearly fix the minimum compensation in all cases.

In the third place, certain industrial conditions fall clearly below the levels which the public today sanction.

We stand for a living wage. Wages are subnormal if they fail to provide a living for those who devote their time and energy to industrial occupations. The monetary equivalent of a living wage varies according to local conditions, but must include enough to secure the elements of a normal standard of living—a standard high enough to make morality possible, to provide for education and recreation, to care for immature members of the family, to maintain the family during periods of sickness, and to permit of reasonable saving for old age.

Hours are excessive if they fail to afford the worker sufficient time to recuperate and return to his work thoroughly refreshed. We hold that the night labor of women and children is abnormal and should be prohibited; we hold that the employment of women over 48 hours per week is abnormal and should be prohibited. We hold that the seven-day working week is abnormal, and we hold that one day of rest in seven should be provided by law. We hold that the continuous industries, operating 24 hours out of 24, are abnormal, and where, because of public necessity or of technical reasons (such as molten metal), the 24 hours muxt be divided into two shifts of 12 hours or three shifts of eight, they should by law be divided into three of eight.

Safety conditions are abnormal when, through unguarded machinery, poisons, electrical voltage, or otherwise, the workers are subjected to unnecessary hazards of life and limb; and all such occupations should come under governmental regulation and control.

Home life is abnormal when tenement manufacture is carried on in the household. It is a serious menace to health, education, and childhood, and should therefore be entirely prohibited. Temporary construction camps are abnormal homes and should be subjected to governmental sanitary regulation.

The premature employment of children is abnormal and should be prohibited; so also the employment of women in manufacturing, commerce, or other trades where work compels standing constantly; and also any employment of women in such trades for a period of at least eight weeks at time of childbirth.

Our aim should be to secure conditions which will tend everywhere toward regular industry, and will do away with the necessity for rush periods, followed by out-of-work seasons, which put so severe a strain on wage-workers.

It is abnormal for any industry to throw back upon the community the human wreckage due to its wear and tear, and the hazards of sickness, accident, invalidism, involuntary unemployment, and old age should be provided for through insurance. This should be made a charge in whole or in part upon the industries, the employer, the employee, and perhaps the people at large to contribute severally in some degree. . . .

What is needed is the application to all industrial concerns and all cooperating interests engaged in interstate commerce in which there is either monopoly or control of the market of the principles on which we have gone in regulating transportation concerns engaged in such commerce. The antitrust law should be kept on the statute-books and strengthened so as to make it genuinely and thoroughly effective against every big concern tending to monopoly or guilty of antisocial practices. At the same time, a national industrial commission should be created which should have complete power to regulate and control all the great industrial concerns engaged in interstate business—which practically means all of them in this country. This commission should exercise over these industrial concerns like powers to those exercised over the railways by the Interstate Commerce Commission, and over the national banks by the comptroller of the currency, and additional powers if found necessary.

The establishment of such a commission would enable us to punish the individual rather than merely the corporation, just as we now do with banks, where the aim of the government is, not to close the bank, but to bring to justice personally any bank official who has gone wrong.

This commission should deal with all the abuses of the trusts—all the abuses such as those developed by the government suit against the Standard Oil and Tobacco Trusts—as the Interstate Commerce Commission now deals with rebates. It should have complete power to make the capitalization absolutely honest and put a stop to all stock watering.

Such supervision over the issuance of corporate securities would put a stop to exploitation of the people by dishonest capitalists desiring to declare dividends on watered securities, and would open this kind of industrial property to ownership by the people at large. It should have free access to the books of each corporation and power to find out exactly how it treats its employees, its rivals, and the general public. It should have power to compel the unsparing publicity of all the acts of any corporation which goes wrong. The regulation should be primarily under the administrative branch of the government, and not by lawsuit. It should prohibit and effectively punish monopoly achieved through wrong, and also actual wrongs done by industrial corporations which are not monopolies, such as the artificial raising of prices, the artificial restriction on productivity, the elimination of competition by unfair or predatory practices, and the like; leaving industrial organizations free within the limits of fair and honest dealing to promote through the inherent efficiency of organization the power of the United States as a competitive nation among nations, and the greater abundance at home that will come to our people from that power wisely exercised. . . .

In international affairs this country should behave toward other nations exactly as an honorable private citizen behaves toward other private citizens. We should do no wrong to any nation, weak or strong, and we should submit to no wrong. Above all, we should never in any treaty make any promise which we do not intend in good faith to fulfil. I believe it essential that our small army should be kept at a high pitch of perfection, and in no way can it be so damaged as by permitting it to become the playing of men in Congress who wish to gratify either spite or favoritism, or to secure to localities advantages to which those localities are not entitled. The navy should be steadily built up; and the process of upbuilding must not be stopped until—and not before—it proves possible to secure by international agreement a general reduction of armaments. . . .

Now, friends, this is my confession of faith. I have made it rather long because I wish you to know what my deepest convictions are on the great questions of today, so that if you choose to make me your standard-bearer in the fight you shall make your choice understanding exactly how I feel—and if, after hearing me, you think you ought to choose some one else, I shall loyally abide by your choice. The convictions to which I have come have not been arrived at as the result of study in the closet or the library, but from the knowledge I have gained through hard experience during the many years in which, under many and varied conditions, I have striven and toiled with men. I believe in a larger use of the governmental power to help remedy industrial wrongs, because it has been borne in on me by actual experience that without exercise of such power many of the wrongs will go unremedied. I believe in a larger opportunity for the people themselves directly to participate in government and to control their governmental agents, because long experience has taught me that without such control many of their agents will represent them badly. By actual experience in office I have found that, as a rule, I could secure the triumph of the causes in which I most believe, not from the politicians and the men who claim an exceptional right to speak in business and government, but by going over their heads, and appealing directly to the people themselves. I am not under the slightest delusion as to any power that during my political career I have at any time possessed. Whatever of power I at any time had, I obtained from the people. I could exercise it only so long as, and to the extent that, the people not merely believed in me, but heartily backed me up. Whatever I did as president I was able to do only because I had the backing of the people. When on any point I did not have that backing, when on any point I differed from the people, it mattered not whether I was right or whether I was wrong, my power vanished. I tried my best to lead the people, to advise them, to tell them what I thought was right; if necessary, I never hesitated to tell them what I thought they ought to hear, even though I thought it would be unpleasant for them to hear it; but I recognized that my task was to try to lead them and not to drive them, to take them into my confidence, to try to show them that I was right, and then loyally and in good faith to accept their decision. I will do anything for the people except what my conscience tells me is wrong, and that I can do for no man and no set of men; I hold that a man cannot serve the people well unless he serves his conscience; but I hold also that where his conscience bids him refuse to do what the people desire, he should not try to continue in office against their will. Our government system should be so shaped that the public servant, when he cannot conscientiously carry out the wishes of the people, shall at their desire leave his office and not misrepresent them in office; and I hold that the public servant can by so doing, better than in any other way, serve both them and his conscience.

Surely there never was a fight better worth making than the one in which we are engaged. It little matters what befalls any one of us who for the time being stands in the forefront of the battle. I hope we shall win, and I believe that if we can wake the people to what the fight really means we shall win. But, win or lose, we shall not falter. Whatever fate may at the moment overtake any of us, the movement itself will not stop. Our cause is based on the eternal principle of righteousness; and even though we who now lead may for the time fail, in the end the cause itself shall triumph. Six weeks ago, here in Chicago, I spoke to the honest representatives of a convention which was not dominated by honest men; a convention wherein sat, alas!, a majority of men who, with sneering indifference to every principle of right, so acted as to bring to a shameful end a party which had been founded over a half-century ago by men in whose souls burned the fire of lofty endeavor. Now to you men, who, in your turn, have come together to spend and be spent in the endless crusade against wrong, to you who face the future resolute and confident, to you who strive in a spirit of brotherhood for the betterment of our nation, to you who gird yourselves for this great new fight in the never-ending warfare for the good of humankind, I say in closing what in that speech, I said in closing: We stand at Armageddon, and we battle for the Lord.

Courtesy of Library of Congress

William Howard Taft

William Howard Taft

1909–1913

WILLIAM HOWARD TAFT, Theodore Roosevelt's handpicked successor, was nearly the exact opposite of his mentor. Of a juridical rather than political bent, Taft had been a successful lawyer, law professor, and judge in his native Ohio before entering politics. His oft-stated goal was a seat on the Supreme Court. In 1900 William McKinley appointed him commissioner and then governor-general of the Philippines, with the task of restoring civil government to the islands. After his election, Roosevelt brought Taft into his cabinet as secretary of war, though it was Roosevelt who actually ran the military, of course, while Taft oversaw a variety of other matters, such as work on the Panama Canal and administration of the Philippines.

At the repeated urging of Roosevelt and his own family, Taft accepted the Republican nomination in 1908, and with TR's active support easily defeated the Democratic candidate, William Jennings Bryan. By all accounts honest, selfless, and well-intentioned, an effective organizer and administrator, Taft proved an inept chief executive who hated the political maneuvering that goes with the office. "Politics," he told his wife, "when I am in it, makes me sick." He lacked the common touch and the ability to arrange a compromise between opposing political forces, and, worst of all, appeared dull, colorless, and lazy in comparison with his energetic predecessor.

Although he had pledged to continue and extend Roosevelt's progressive policies, Taft's natural conservatism soon came to the fore. Because his conception of the scope of the presidency was far more limited than Roosevelt's, he denied himself the power to lead his party and the nation in a progressive direction; instead, powerful Republican conservatives in Congress led him. He quickly alienated the Republican left wing over issues such as tariff reform and conservation. Ultimately the party fractured, with the progressives splitting off to support Roosevelt in the 1912 election, while party regulars backed Taft. Taft and Roosevelt, formerly good friends, fought bitterly in the campaign. With the Republicans so divided, the Democrats, who had been out of power for 16 years, swept into office with Wilson. Rather relieved at the result, Taft returned to the law. In 1921 he finally received the long-coveted chief justiceship from Warren G. Harding. He died in 1930.

Before his presidency and after, Taft, the practiced lawyer and professor, made hundreds of speeches, which he wrote himself. But during his term he spoke with the greatest reluctance, dreading, he said, "the necessity for speaking every day on some subject or other to a listening multitude. . . . It becomes a brain-racking performance." He procrastinated on speechwriting whenever possible and never showed drafts to his advisers. Thus he was often careless in thinking through the implications of what he was about to say, sometimes with disastrous results. His frequent blunders, both oratorical and political, earned him the nickname of "Mr. Malaprop" and ultimately cost him the support of much of his party. "At least one unfortunate phrase,"—wrote his biographer Henry Pringle, "seems to have been inevitable in every campaign conducted by Taft."

Taft's great personal charm and good humor were not evident in his speaking style, which was ponderous and undemonstrative. As an orator he was no match for his opponents, Bryan, Roosevelt, and Wilson, the greatest speakers of their time. Taft's speeches themselves sound like verbose, overprecise court statements, complete with tables of figures and detailed legal references. They lacked drama and political canniness, as did the man himself.

The Achievements of the Republican Party

Kansas City, Missouri

February 10, 1908

AT THE BEGINNING of this speech to the Young Men's Republican Club of Missouri, Secretary of War Taft called Lincoln "a party man." Taft was a party man as well, but another kind: a team player, who, in politics at least, was most comfortable as a follower rather than a leader. Though about to embark on a campaign for the highest office himself, Taft exhibits in this speech all the best qualities of a loyal subordinate, including unquestioning adherence to the policies of party leader Roosevelt. This gap between Taft's own inclinations and the leadership requirements of a successful presidency were at the root of his, and the party's, defeat in 1912.

We meet today to celebrate the memory of Abraham Lincoln. One of the bases for the everlasting gratitude which the country owes him is the part he took in the successful establishment in national political control of the Republican Party. Lincoln was a party man, as all men must be who expect to leave their individual impress upon the political character of the nation.

A modern government of a people of 80,000,000 is complicated under any system. The difficulties of its management are not lessened when we commit its control to all males over the age of 21, and call it a republic. How is it possible to reduce the varying views of the entire population to one resultant executive force which shall carry on this machine of government in the public interest and for the public weal? The problem has been solved by the institution of parties. A party cannot be useful unless those who are members of it yield their views on some issues and unite with respect to the main policies to be pursued. The resultant solidarity is necessary to secure efficacy. The sense of responsibility for the continued successful operation of the government must furnish cohesive power. The party is the more efficient, in which the members are more nearly united on the great principles of governmental action. Though a party has its platform, and on the faith of it has been elected to power, many issues may unexpectedly arise in the course of an administration not controlled by the party's declared principles. The disposition of such issues must depend on the ability and courage of the party leaders. A party may divide on a new issue until by a process of education the sounder view prevails, and the party becomes united

again in the enforcement of the new principle. As a party shows itself homogeneous, able to grasp the truth with respect to new issues, able to discard unimportant differences of opinion, sensitive with respect to the successful maintenance of government, and highly charged with the responsibility of its obligation to the people at large, it establishes its claim to the confidence of the public and to its continuance in political power. We are apt to deny to parties characteristics and traits like those of a person, but I venture to think that a history of political parties in which the description is clothed with life and truth must always treat them as having some personal attributes.

The course of the Republican Party since its organization in 1856, and its real assumption of control in 1861, down to the present day, is remarkable for the foresight and ability of its leaders, for the discipline and solidarity of its members, for its efficiency and deep sense of responsibility, for the preservation and successful maintenance of the government, and for the greatest resourcefulness in meeting the various trying and difficult issues which a history of now a full half century has presented for solution. It was born of a desire to maintain inviolate the Union of the states. Its essence was that of nationalism, and its spirit was that of sacrifice, no matter how great, to maintain the integrity of our whole country. The federalism of Washington, Marshall, and Hamilton was the guide of its constitutional construction, and it did not hesitate, when the issue was presented, to submit its view of the great fundamental instrument of our government to the arbitrament of a long and bloody war. The leader of the Republican Party during the Civil War was Abraham Lincoln.

In all the varieties of controversy with which it has since had to deal, it has never lost the inspiration of his leadership.

When the Republican Party entered upon the war in 1861, the only issue it was willing to fight out was that of the preservation of the Union. It did not then assume the burden of the complete abolition of slavery. There were many in its ranks who pressed for such a declaration, but the time had not come. The course of war made abolition inevitable, and Mr. Lincoln, who was the greatest politician of his age, led his party a long way by the Emancipation Proclamation. Even as he did this, he created a division in his party. It was one of the first instances in which the party showed its own power of self-preservation by gradually convincing the minority of the righteousness of the new issue.

After the martyrdom of Lincoln came the period of reconstruction and the adoption of the so-called War Amendments. The Thirteenth Amendment gave to the Negro the boon of freedom, but it left as children in the world four or five millions of people, not 5 percent of whom could read or write, and all of whom had been dependent upon others for what they ate and wore and did. Their emancipation was, of course, the first great step in their elevation as a race, but it involved at first great hardship and suffering and discouragement, as all great changes in existing conditions must. Still the Thirteenth Amendment has accomplished its purpose.

The Fourteenth Amendment secured to the Negro the equal protection of the laws of the state in which he lived. This is the amendment which, second to his emancipation, has become the most important in his development. Living in the same community in which he had been a chattel, the great danger was that legislation would be enacted which might prevent him from enjoying the same benefit from the guaranties of life, liberty, and property that were extended to his white fellow citizens. It was of the highest importance to him to be assured of those economic rights in the enjoyment and pursuit of which lay the hope of his future progress.

The opportunity of the Southern Negro lay, first, in education; second, in the skill of his hands as a laborer and in his industry as a tiller of the soil; and, third, in his capacity to save from his earnings sufficient to enable him to accumulate capital to buy land and establish his economic independence. Thus could he make himself useful to the community in which he lived and secure the respect which would certainly come to one showing himself indispensable to the growth and prosperity of the South. Thus would flow all the incidents of power and influence to which he aspired. When we regard the history of the 40 years through which the colored man of this country has been obliged to struggle, the progress which he has made, material and educational, is wonderful.

The third great War Amendment—the Fifteenth—forbade any state to deprive the Negro of his vote on account of his color or previous condition of servitude. The operation of this amendment has not been as successful as that of the Thirteenth and Fourteenth. Nor is this surprising. Consider the condition of things immediately after the war. Here was a masterful people, who had been used to a social condition in which the Negro occupied a servile status, brought by law to face the prospect of sharing political control with the poor, ignorant and bewildered masses, who but the day before had been their property. Declarations of equality and popular rights and universal suffrage offer but a feather's weight against the inevitable impulses of human nature. It was impossible that with the elements I have stated, there should not have been developed fraud and violence and illegality. It was impossible that that which was written on the tables of the fundamental law or in the statute book should be immediately carried into effective execution. After a long struggle, the history of which I shall not recall, the Negro's vote in the Southern states was made to count for nothing. Then the leaders of the South in many states came to realize the dreadful demoralization of all society if law was to be flouted and fraud was to constitute the basis of government. So they cast about to make the law square with the existing condition by property and educational qualifications which should exclude most of the Negro vote.

This very desire to avoid the violent methods which were wont to overcome the colored vote in the South itself indicates a turn for the better. It is said, however, and with truth, that these election laws are intended to be enforced by means of the discretion vested in election officers, so as to exclude the ineligible colored men with rigor and to allow the ineligible whites, who ought also to be excluded, to enjoy the franchise. Deplorable as this is, still the situation is by no means a hopeless one for the Southern Negro and the political power that he may in the future exercise. In the first place, if he continues to increase in intelligence by the acceptance of his educational opportunities, and if industrially he becomes a power, and thus gradually increases the number of his race who are eligible to vote in accordance with law, he will introduce into the electorate a body of individuals well qualified to act with common sense and judgment, and who, by their very position in the community, will give weight to the vote they cast. Their position and influence as a growing representation of their race, qualified to exercise the right of suffrage, will become stronger and stronger. Such a gradual acquisition of political power will secure them real influence and an opportunity to help their race to further progress. The greatest friend the Southern Negro is likely to have is the broad-minded Southern white man who sympathizes with the colored man and knows his value to the South. Nor is it unreasonable to hope that the men who have already sought to come within the law, and avoid violence, will ultimately see the wisdom and righteousness of the equal enforcement of the law of eligibility against white and black. While I fully recognize the fact that the Fifteenth Amendment has not accomplished all that it was intended to accomplish, and that for a time it seemed to be a dead letter, I am confident that in the end it will prove to be a bulwark equally beneficial with that of the Thirteenth and Fourteenth Amendments to an unfortunate, down-trodden, struggling race, to whom, in view of the circumstances under which they were brought to this country and the conditions of bondage in which they were continued for more than two centuries, we owe every obligation of care and protection. That which has been done for the benefit of the Negro race is the work of the Republican Party. It is one of those great issues presented by the exigencies of the war which the party has had the firmness and courage to meet. The party has not yet been entirely successful in fully working out the problem, but nearly all that has been done at its instance or with its aid.

Another issue which the Republican Party found itself pursued by as an outgrowth of the war was the question of money, and on that the party showed a marked capacity for reaching a unanimous and sound conclusion after much controversy within its ranks. In order to maintain the government during the dark days of the war, we departed from the gold and silver monetary medium and issued as currency paper promises of the government to pay. The students of finance today are disposed generally to think that the issue of greenbacks was not necessary to sustain the government, and that it might have been possible to conduct the enormous operations of the war and still retain gold and silver coin. However this may be, we found ourselves at the end of the war with a great volume of greenback currency and no means of redeeming it. For a time many members of the Republican Party seemed to think that the wise course to pursue was to reduce the evil by increasing our irredeemable obligations. They imbibed the theory of fiat currency, that the government might create money and pay all its debts by merely printing promises to pay. Gradually the greenback heresy was eliminated. The Republican Party sloughed off its diseased members and took the firm, solid and righteous position that it would redeem every dollar of its bonds and of its other indebtedness in coin of the United States. On the 1st of January, 1878, specie payments were resumed and the paper of the government became as good as gold.

In the decade between 1880 and 1890, the greater production of silver had cheapened the metal in comparison with gold, and quack remedies for financial troubles, in the form of the greater use of silver money, seized a large part of the electorate, both Republicans and Democrats. The silver question was fought out for 12 or 15 years, and in that time many of the Republican leaders supported doctrines which now would seem heretical. Gradually, however, the lines were formed. The democracy under Mr. Bryan advanced the theory that the free coinage of silver, which was in effect repudiation of half of every debt, was the solution of all our difficulties, while the Republican Party, gradually and reluctantly, took its position in favor of the single gold standard and against any depreciation of it to make easier payment of debts. In the great battle of 1896 the Republican Party again stood for the maintenance of the integrity of the nation. The fight was against odds produced by a great industrial depression, and against the most sophistical arguments. The Republican Party maintained a campaign of education among the wage-earners and the farmers, which ultimately led to the complete defeat of this second financial heresy which had threatened the integrity of our business structure.

One of the great policies to which the Republican Party has been pledged from the beginning has been the protective system, by which industries have been diversified and domestic manufactures and farm productions have been enormously developed. The method consists in the imposition of customs duties upon imported products equal to the difference in the cost of producing the article in foreign countries and in this country, allowing for a reasonable profit to the home producer. Our whole business structure rests on the system, and the wage-earners dependent on it are myriad. The system has continued without a break from the time of the Morrill Tariff in 1861 until the present day, except that during the second administration of Mr. Cleveland an attempt was made to pass a revenue tariff, which failed, but resulted in the passage of a tariff which illustrated no theory of taxation at all and only brought disaster. There was put in force by the Republicans a new tariff in 1890, called the McKinley Tariff, which was repealed by the Gorman-Wilson Tariff of 1893, which in turn was repealed by the Dingley Tariff of 1897. In the 10 years which have elapsed since the enactment of the Dingley Tariff, the conditions have so changed as to make a number of the schedules under that tariff too high and some too low. This renders it necessary to reexamine the schedules in order that the tariff shall be placed on a purely protective basis. By that I mean it should properly protect, against foreign competitions, and afford a reasonable profit to all manufacturers, farmers, and business men, but should not be so high as to furnish a temptation to the formation of monopolies to appropriate the undue profit of excessive rates.

In 1898 came the war with Spain. While both parties lent their aid in Congress and there was an outburst of patriotism in all sections, the war, for which we were so little prepared, had to be conducted by the Republican Party. Whatever efficiency was displayed in its maintenance was due to that party, and the ability with which it could meet a new issue. After the Spanish War, comparatively so short and bloodless in its extent, there have developed national questions for settlement of greater importance than any save those of the great Civil War. The Republican Party has marched up to their solution with the same courage, the same skill, and the same persistence that it has shown in respect to all the questions arising in its history. After peace with Spain was signed, Congress left to McKinley to pioneer in respect to the government of Porto Rico, Cuba, and the Philippines, imposing only as to the Cuban policy the condition that there should be an early date for turning over that island to the people of Cuba in accordance with the self-denying ordinance known as the Teller resolution. Congress did not interfere in the Philippines for a full four years, and in that time McKinley had worked out a policy which substantially received the full confirmation of Congress and to which the Republican Party is today pledged. The policy of expansion is what distinguishes the administration of McKinley and adds another to the list of patriotic victories of the Republican Party. By this policy the United States has become a world power. In the course of it we have built up a navy, not large enough as yet, but large enough to be respectable and to make our influence felt for peace and good international morals the world over.

In every one of these policies which I have thus enumerated—in the war of the Union—the building up and protection of the Negro race with the war amendments—in the maintenance of the sacredness of our promises to pay contained in the greenbacks and in the national bonds—in our maintenance of the national integrity by an adherence to the gold standard and a refusal to enter upon the free coinage of silver—in the support of a policy of protection under which our manufactures and our farm productions have found a prosperity never before known in the world—in the policy of expansion and the development of the unfortunate peoples intrusted to our care by Providence—and in our progress toward worldwide influence—we have encountered the official and persistent opposition of the Democratic Party. At times we have been beaten. Only twice, however, in all that remarkable history of 48 years have we lost the confidence of the people of the United States to the point of their turning over the government to a Democratic executive. I venture to say that neither in this nor any other country can be disclosed such a remarkable record of arduous deeds done as in that history of a half a century of the Republican Party.

By reason of circumstances I need not detail, the influence of the Republican Party has been little felt south of Mason and Dixon's line. It is true that in Maryland, West Virginia, Kentucky, and Missouri the Republican Party has been often in the majority, but in the other Southern states a contest has seemed hopeless. The time has come, in my judgment, when it is the duty of our party to make an earnest effort to win to our support the many Southerners who think with us on every living national issue and have only been kept from our ranks by the ghost of the past.

During the present administration the Republican Party has been called again to meet a great national need and to save the country from a growing danger. In the enormous industrial development and the accumulation of capital due to the combination in corporate form of the wealth of the country, there have arisen abuses which have threatened to undermine our whole business fabric. The intense desire for gain, stimulated by the prospect of enormous profits, produced a reckless spirit with reference to the methods of acquisition. Official investigations have disclosed a lack of business integrity on the part of some charged in a fiduciary capacity with the custody and management of great accumulations of capital. Other official investigations showed the eagerness with which certain industrial combinations were willing to use their patronage to induce or compel railroad companies to grant to them unjust and secret discriminations and rebates. The fact that the Interstate Commerce law was violated with perfect impunity became known to the public at large, and a conviction seized the people that there were many engaged in the management of corporate wealth who regarded the statutes of their country as dead letters and themselves as a privileged class. Their corrupting influence in politics and in respect of state and national legislation was naturally becoming greater and greater as their wealth grew and their associations spread. We were passing into a régime of an irresponsible plutocracy. During the last four years there has been a great moral awakening

to this danger among the people and a popular demand that the lawbreakers—no matter how wealthy or high or powerful their position—shall be made to suffer. Under the leadership of Theodore Roosevelt the Republican Party has not faltered in its determination to meet the requirements of this situation and to enact such legislation as may be necessary to bring to a close this period of illegitimate corporate immunity.

At the insistance of the president Congress was called upon to pass an amendment to the Interstate Commerce law known as the Rate Bill. What has been the effect of the Rate Bill? Everyone who knows anything about the management of railroads knows that there has been a revolution in respect to their obedience to the law. No longer are special privileges granted to the few—no longer are secret rebates extended to build up the monopoly of the trusts. The railroads are operating within the law, and the railroad directors and officers and stockholders ought to rise up and call blessed the men who are responsible for the passage of the Rate Bill. It may be that it has not reduced rates where it was expected. It may be that it has not furnished local relief at various points, as was hoped, but it has put the railroad business in this country on an honest basis, has eliminated from the operation of the railroads privilege and discrimination, and has enabled railroad men to look their fellows in the face without a consciousness that they are conducting a business in violation of law. It has put every railroad man in the country on his good behavior, and has created a complete change of attitude on the part of him and of his subordinates in respect to the statutes of his country.

I am not now speaking of what may be accomplished, but what has been accomplished—not what the result of litigation under a new law has been or will be, but I am speaking of the result of the movement which found expression in the passage of the Rate law.

Another policy proposed as a means of regulating railway rates is that of the improvement of our national waterways. Much money has been spent on sea harbors and the mouths of our rivers at the sea, but comparatively little upon the internal waterways which nature has furnished to the country, and which form highways of travel from one border of it to the other. The call from the country for the development of a well-thought-out plan for the improvement of all these waterways is so emphatic that it can not longer be resisted. That which has been done is largely piece work. What is needed now is the consistent development of this method of inter-communication, so that a certain amount a year can be assigned to the execution of the plan. The direct effect in the transportation of merchandise will doubtless be most beneficial, while the indirect effect of regulating and reducing excessive railroad rates will be even of greater benefit.

Other corporate abuses have been made manifest besides discrimination in rates. They consist in suing the corporate form of investment to float bonds and stocks whose par value is far in excess of the real money value invested in the enterprise—a practice which, in addition to deceiving and defrauding the public, involves consequences with reference to reckless corporate management that are most demoralizing. Legislation looking to the restraint in this regard of interstate commerce railways has been recommended to, and doubtless will receive, the careful consideration and approval of the national legislature.

Under the stimulus of the revelations in respect to the illegal combinations of wealth for purposes of monopoly, prosecutions under the Interstate Commerce law and the anti-trust law by the executive have been important and effective, and the whole weight of the Republican administration has been thrown in favor of holding up to a strict compliance with the antitrust law those who in times past had regarded it as of no effect.

In the midst of this reform movement for the elimination from our business methods of illegal monopoly and discrimination, our country has been visited by a severe financial panic. The panic was doubtless chiefly due to the exhausting of the free capital of the world by reason of the over-investment in enterprises that have not been as productive as expected. The enormous industrial expansion had at last tied up nearly all the world's capital which was available and the new investments had to halt. This result was worldwide. In addition to this general condition, the revelations concerning the management of a number of our large corporations affected the confidence of European investors in our whole business fabric. Then our monetary system is not of such an elastic nature as to meet the emergency produced by sudden fright on the part of the holders of money, who withdraw it from business uses and hoard it against disaster. The result has been an industrial depression which we all hope and believe from the conditions prevailing will be of short duration. But those who have been made to feel the lash of public criticism by the moral awakening have been quick to seize upon and hold up the panic as a result of the measures taken or agitated to stamp out corporate abuses and illegality, and they have not been slow most unjustly to attack the Republican administration, and Mr. Roosevelt at its head, as the responsible authors of this industrial depression. There are those who have been members of the Republican Party who differ with Mr. Roosevelt in respect to the proper course to be taken in stamping out these abuses of corporate wealth. The great bulk of the Republican Party, however, stands solidly at his back in the work which he and the representatives of the party in Congress are doing.

His recent message, urging the reenactment of the employers' liability act, which, because of bungling language, was declared unconstitutional, and asking additional power for the interstate commerce commission, has given rise in certain quarters to much criticism. I have read the message with care, and I am bound to say that the measures which he recommends to Congress, and the position he takes with respect to them, are all of a most conservative character. His position in favor of a general employers' liability act, which shall put the burden of the trade risk upon the employer, except where the injury is due solely to the negligence of the employee, is in the line of the best considered modern legislation of Europe and England. It was secure uniformity and reasonableness of compensation for the family of the deceased or injured employee, instead of the inequalities and uncertainties of court trials, which under our present system give excessive damages to some and deny any recovery to others equally meritorious. The president stands forth stoutly for the power of the courts and the efficacy of their orders, but properly calls attention to the abuses to which the reckless issuing of *ex parte* injunctions in labor cases have given rise.

The message contains an answer to the charges made that the administration is responsible for the industrial depression which has followed; and the sharpness and emphasis with which this unfounded attack is met have heartened the great body of the people as by a bugle call to renewed support of the policies of the administration.

From beginning to the end the message shows his earnest desire to protect the honest business man and the honest laborer, and to secure to them the possibility of living under an equal administration of the law. He would not destroy or injure the stock of innocent holders for value though it had its inception in the machinations of unprincipled promoters; but he would make the law to prevent a recurrence of such methods. He takes the utmost pains to point out that railroads should be relieved from the restrictions of the antitrust law, and that that law should be amended so as to give greater freedom for corporate action in combinations that are not hurtful to the public. No man can find within the four corners of the message anything to shake in the slightest the guaranties of life, liberty, and property secured by the constitution. The measures he recommends, and the positions that he takes, are in accord with the conservative position of the Republican Party which has ever looked upon the right of property as only less sacred than the right of liberty, and which has ever made the goal of all its efforts the equal protection of the laws.

Vigorous action and measures to stamp out existing abuses and effect reforms are necessary to vindicate society as at present constituted. Otherwise, we must yield to those who seek to introduce a new order of things on a socialistic basis.

The Republican Party follows the administration upon this social and moral reform—approves its attitude in favor of vested rights, of maintaining the power of the courts, of rendering more equal by legislation the basis of dealing between employer and employee, of strengthening the regulative power over railroads and other interstate corporations, and of prosecuting those lawbreakers who continue to defy public opinion. Roosevelt leads his party as Lincoln led his—as McKinley led his—to meet the new issues presented, to arm our present civilization, and fit it with a bold front to resist the attacks of socialism, and to transmit to the coming generations unharmed the great institutions of civil liberty inherited from our fathers.

Inaugural Address

Washington, D.C.

March 4, 1909

AN UNEXPECTED ice storm forced the inauguration to be held indoors. That morning, Taft was beset by last-minute doubts. Hearing the storm outside, he remarked to Roosevelt, "Even the elements do protest." Replied Roosevelt: "I knew there would be a blizzard when I went out." The solemn Taft delivered his earnest inaugural address in the Senate chamber. Uninspiring though it was, Roosevelt bounced up the moment Taft had finished to shake the president's hand, calling the address "a great state document."

Anyone who has taken the oath I have just taken must feel a heavy weight of responsibility. If not, he has no conception of the powers and duties of the office upon which he is about to enter, or he is lacking in a proper sense of the obligation which the oath imposes.

The office of an inaugural address is to give a summary outline of the main policies of the new administration, so far as they can be anticipated. I have had the honor to be one of the advisers of my distinguished predecessor, and, as such, to hold up his hands in the reforms he has initiated. I should be untrue to myself, to my promises, and to the declarations of the party platform upon which I was elected to office, if I did not make the maintenance of enforcement of those reforms a most important feature of my administration. They were directed to the suppression of the lawlessness and abuses of power of the great combinations of capital invested in railroads and in industrial enterprises carrying on interstate commerce. The steps which my predecessor took and the legislation passed on his recommendation have accomplished much, have caused a general halt in the vicious policies which created popular alarm, and have brought about in the business affected a much higher regard for existing law.

To render the reforms lasting, however, and to secure at the same time freedom from alarm on the part of those pursuing proper and progressive business methods, further legislative and executive action are needed. Relief of the railroads from certain restrictions of the antitrust law have been urged by my predecessor and will be urged by me. On the other hand, the administration is pledged to legislation looking to a proper federal supervision and restriction to prevent excessive issues of bonds and stocks by companies owning and operating interstate-commerce railroads.

Then, too, a reorganization of the Department of Justice, of the Bureau of Corporations in the Department of Commerce and Labor, and of the Interstate Commerce Commission, looking to effective cooperation of these agencies, is needed to secure a more rapid and certain enforcement of the laws affecting interstate railroads and industrial combinations.

I hope to be able to submit at the first regular session of the incoming Congress, in December next, definite suggestions in respect to the needed amendments to the antitrust and the interstate commerce law and the changes required in the executive departments concerned in their enforcement.

It is believed that with the changes to be recommended American business can be assured of that measure of stability and certainty in respect to those things that may be done and those that are prohibited which is essential to the life and growth of all business. Such a plan must include the right of the people to avail themselves of those methods of combining capital and effort deemed necessary to reach the highest degree of economic efficiency, at the same time differentiating between combinations based upon legitimate economic reasons and those formed with the intent of creating monopolies and artificially controlling prices.

The work of formulating into practical shape such changes is creative work of the highest order, and requires all the deliberation possible in the interval. I believe that the amendments to be proposed are just as necessary in the protection of legitimate business as in the clinching of the reforms which properly bear the name of my predecessor.

A matter of most pressing importance is the revision of the tariff. In accordance with the promises of the platform upon which I was elected, I shall call Congress into extra session to meet on the 15th day of March, in order that consideration may be at once given to a bill revising the Dingley Act. This should secure an adequate revenue and adjust the duties in such a manner as to afford to labor and to all industries in this country, whether of the farm, mine, or factory, protection by tariff equal to the difference between the cost of production here, and have a provision which shall put into force, upon executive determination of certain facts, a higher or maximum tariff against those countries whose trade policy toward us equitably requires such discrimination. It is thought that there has been such a change in conditions since the enactment of the Dingley Act, drafted on a similarly protective principle, that the measure of the tariff above stated will permit the reduction of rates in certain schedules and will require the advancement of few, if any.

The proposal to revise the tariff made in such an authoritative way as to lead the business community to count upon it necessarily halts all those branches of business directly affected; and as these are most important, it disturbs the whole business of the country. It is imperatively necessary, therefore, that a tariff bill be drawn in good faith in accordance with promises made before the election by the party in power, as promptly passed as due consideration will permit. It is not that the tariff is more important in the long run that the perfecting of the reforms in respect to antitrust legislation and interstate commerce regulation, but the need for action when the revision of the tariff has been determined upon is more immediate to avoid embarrassment of business. To secure the needed speed in the passage of the tariff bill, it would seem wise to attempt no other legislation at the extra session. I venture this as a suggestion only, for the course to be taken by Congress, upon the call of the executive, is wholly within its discretion.

In the making of a tariff bill the prime motive is taxation and the securing thereby of a revenue. Due largely to the business depression which followed the financial panic of 1907, the revenue from customs and other sources has decreased to such an extent that the expenditures for the current fiscal year will exceed the receipts by $100,000,000. It is imperative that such a deficit shall not continue, and the framers of the tariff bill must, of course, have in mind the total revenues likely to be produced by it and so arrange the duties as to secure an adequate income. Should it be impossible to do so by import duties, new kinds of taxation must be adopted, and among these I recommend a graduated inheritance tax as correct in principle and as certain and easy of collection.

The obligation on the part of those responsible for the expenditures made to carry on the government, to be as economical as possible, and to make the burden of taxation as light as possible, is plain, and should be affirmed in every declaration of government policy. This is especially true when we are face to face with a heavy deficit. But when the desire to win the popular approval leads to the cutting off of expenditures really needed to make the government effective and to enable it to accomplish its proper objects, the result is as much to be condemned as the waste of government funds in unnecessary expenditure. The scope of a modern government in what it can and ought to accomplish for its people has been widened far beyond the principles laid down by the old "laissez faire" school of political writers, and this widening has met popular approval.

In the Department of Agriculture the use of scientific experiments on a large scale and the spread of information derived from them for the improvement of general agriculture must go on.

The importance of supervising business of great railways and industrial combinations and the necessary investigation and prosecution of unlawful business methods are another necessary tax upon government which did not exist half a century ago.

The putting into force of laws which shall secure the conservation of our resources, so far as they may be within the jurisdiction of the federal government, including the most important work of saving and restoring our forests and the great improvement of waterways, are all proper government functions which must involve large expenditure if properly performed. While some of them, like the reclamation of arid lands, are made to pay for themselves, others are of such an indirect benefit that this cannot be expected of them. A permanent improvement, like the Panama

Canal, should be treated as a distinct enterprise, and should be paid for by the proceeds of bonds, the issue of which will distribute its cost between the present and future generations in accordance with the benefits derived. It may well be submitted to the serious consideration of Congress whether the deepening and control of the channel of a great river system, like that of the Ohio or of the Mississippi, when definite and practical plans for the enterprise have been approved and determined upon, should not be provided for in the same way.

Then, too, there are expenditures of government absolutely necessary if our country is to maintain its proper place among the nations of the world, and is to exercise its proper influence in defense of its own trade interests in the maintenance of traditional American policy against the colonization of European monarchies in this hemisphere, and in the promotion of peace and international morality. I refer to the cost of maintaining a proper army, a proper navy, and suitable fortifications upon the mainland of the United States and in its dependencies.

We should have an army so organized and so officered as to be capable in time of emergency, in cooperation with the national militia and under the provisions of a proper national volunteer law, rapidly to expand into a force sufficient to resist all probable invasion from abroad and to furnish a respectable expeditionary force if necessary in the maintenance of our traditional American policy which bears the name of President Monroe.

Our fortifications are yet in a state of only partial completeness, and the number of men to man them is insufficient. In a few years however, the usual annual appropriations for our coast defenses, both on the mainland and in the dependencies, will make them sufficient to resist all direct attack, and by that time we may hope that the men to man them will be provided as a necessary adjunct. The distance of our shores from Europe and Asia of course reduces the necessity for maintaining under arms a great army, but it does not take away the requirement of mere prudence—that we should have an army sufficiently large and so constituted as to form a nucleus out of which a suitable force can quickly grow.

What has been said of the army may be affirmed in even a more emphatic way of the navy. A modern navy can not be improvised. It must be built and in existence when the emergency arises which calls for its use and operation. My distinguished predecessor has in many speeches and messages set out with great force and striking language the necessity for maintaining a strong navy commensurate with the coastline, the governmental resources, and the foreign trade of our nation; and I wish to reiterate all the reasons which he has presented in favor of the policy of maintaining a strong navy as the best conservator of our peace with other nations, and the best means of securing respect for the assertion of our rights, the defense of our interests, and the exercise of our influence in international matters.

Our international policy is always to promote peace. We shall enter into any war with a full consciousness of the awful consequences that it always entails, whether successful or not, and we, of course, shall make every effort consistent with national honor and the highest national interest to avoid a resort to arms. We favor every instrumentality, like that of the Hague Tribunal and arbitration treaties made with a view to its use in all international controversies, in order to maintain peace and to avoid war. But we should be blind to existing conditions and should allow ourselves to become foolish idealists if we did not realize that, with all the nations of the world armed and prepared for war, we must be ourselves in a similar condition, in order to prevent other nations from taking advantage of us and of our inability to defend our interests and assert our rights with a strong hand.

In the international controversies that are likely to arise in the Orient growing out of the question of the open door and other issues the United States can maintain her interests intact and can secure respect for her just demands. She will not be able to do so, however, if it is understood that she never intends to back up her assertion of right and her defense of her interest by anything but mere verbal protest and diplomatic note. For these reasons the expenses of the army and navy and of coast defenses should always be considered as something which the government must pay for, and they should not be cut off through mere consideration of economy. Our government is able to afford a suitable army and a suitable navy. It may maintain them without the slightest danger to the republic or the cause of free institutions, and fear of additional taxation ought not to change a proper policy in this regard.

The policy of the United States in the Spanish war and since has given it a position of influence among the nations that it never had before, and should be constantly exerted to securing to its bona fide citizens, whether native or naturalized, respect for them as such in foreign countries. We should make every effort to prevent humiliating and degrading prohibition against any of our citizens wishing temporarily to sojourn in foreign countries because of race or religion.

The admission of Asiatic immigrants who cannot be amalgamated with our population has been made the subject either of prohibitory clauses in our treaties and statutes or of strict administrative regulation secured by diplomatic negotiation. I sincerely hope that we may continue to minimize the evils likely to arise from such immigration without unnecessary friction and by mutual concessions between self-respecting governments. Meantime we must take every precaution to prevent, or failing that, to punish outbursts of race feeling among our people against foreigners of whatever nationality who have by our grant a treaty right to pursue lawful business here and to be protected against lawless assault or injury.

This leads me to point out a serious defect in the present federal jurisdiction, which ought to be remedied at once. Having assured to other countries by treaty the protection of our laws for such of their subjects or citizens as we permit to come within our jurisdiction, we now leave to a state or a city, not under control of the federal government, the duty of performing our international obligations in this respect. By proper legislation we may, and ought to, place in the hands of the federal executive the means of enforcing the treaty rights of such aliens in the courts of the federal government. It puts our government in a pusillanimous position to make definite engagements to protect aliens and then to excuse the failure to perform those engagements by an explanation that the duty to keep them is in states or cities, not within our control. If we would promise we must put ourselves in a position to perform our promise. We cannot permit the possible failure of justice, due to local prejudice in any state or municipal government, to expose us to the risk of a war which might be avoided if federal jurisdiction was asserted by suitable legislation by Congress and carried out by proper proceedings instituted by the executive in the courts of the national government.

One of the reforms to be carried out during the incoming administration is a change of our monetary and banking laws, so as to secure greater elasticity in the forms of currency available for trade and to prevent the limitations of law from operating to increase the embarrassment of a financial panic. The monetary commission, lately appointed, is giving full consideration to existing conditions and to all proposed remedies, and will doubtless suggest one that will meet the requirements of business and of public interest.

We may hope that the report will embody neither the narrow view of those who believe that the sole purpose of the new system should be to secure a large return on banking capital or of those who would have greater expansion of currency with little regard to provisions for its immediate redemption or ultimate security. There is no subject of economic discussion so intricate and so likely to evoke differing views and dogmatic statements as this one. The commission, in studying the general influence of currency on business and of business on currency, have wisely extended their investigations in European banking monetary methods. The information that they have derived from such experts as they have found abroad will undoubtedly be found helpful in the solution of the difficult problem they have in hand.

The incoming Congress should promptly fulfill the promise of the Republican platform and pass a proper postal savings bank bill. It will not be unwise or excessive paternalism. The promise to repay by the government will furnish an inducement to savings deposits which private enterprise cannot supply and at such a low rate of interest as not to withdraw custom from existing banks. It will substantially increase the funds available for investment as capital in useful enterprises. It will furnish absolute security which makes the proposed scheme of government guaranty of deposits so alluring, without its pernicious results.

I sincerely hope that the incoming Congress will be alive, as it should be to the importance of our foreign trade and of encouraging it in every way feasible. The possibility of increasing this trade in the Orient, in the Philippines, and in South America are known to everyone who has given the matter attention. The direct effect of free trade between this country and the Philippines will be marked upon our sales of cottons, agricultural machinery, and other manufactures. The necessity of the establishment of direct lines of steamers between North and South America has been brought to the attention of Congress by my predecessor and by Mr. Root before and after his noteworthy visit to that continent, and I sincerely hope that Congress may be induced to see the wisdom of a tentative effort to establish such lines by the use of mail subsidies.

The importance of the part which the Departments of Agriculture and of Commerce and Labor may play in ridding the markets of Europe of prohibitions and discriminations against the importation of our products is fully understood, and it is hoped that the use of the maximum and minimum feature of our tariff law to be soon passed will be effective to remove many of those restrictions.

The Panama Canal will have a most important bearing upon the trade between the eastern and far western sections of our country, and will greatly increase the facilities for transportation between the eastern and the western seaboard, and may possibly revolutionize the transcontinental rates with respect to bulky merchandise. It will also have a most beneficial effect to increase the trade between the eastern seaboard of the United States and the western coast of South America, and, indeed, with some of the important ports on the east coast of South America reached by rail from the west coast.

The work on the canal is making most satisfactory progress. The type of the canal as a lock canal was fixed by Congress after a full consideration of the conflicting reports of the majority and minority of the consulting board, and after the recommendation of the War Department and the executive upon those reports. Recent suggestion that something had occurred on the Isthmus to make the lock type of the canal less feasible than it was supposed to be when the reports were made and the policy determined on led to a visit to the Isthmus of a board of competent engineer to examine the Gatun dam and locks, which are the key of the lock type. The report of that board shows nothing has occurred in

the nature of newly revealed evidence which should change the views once formed in the original discussion. The construction will go on under a most effective organization controlled by Colonel Goethals and his fellow army engineers associated with him, and will certainly be completed early in the next administration, if not before.

Some type of canal must be constructed. The lock type has been selected. We are all in favor of having it built as promptly as possible. We must not now, therefore, keep up a fire in the rear of the agents whom we have authorized to do our work on the Isthmus. We must hold up their hands, and speaking for the incoming administration I wish to say that I propose to devote all the energy possible and under my control to pushing of this work on the plans which have been adopted, and to stand behind the men who are doing faithful, hard work to bring about the early completion of this, the greatest constructive enterprise of modern times.

The governments of our dependencies in Porto Rico and the Philippines are progressing as favorably as could be desired. The prosperity of Porto Rico continues unabated. The business conditions in the Philippines are not all that we could wish them to be, but with the passage of the new tariff bill permitting free trade between the United States and the archipelago, with such limitations on sugar and tobacco as shall prevent injury to domestic interests in those products, we can count on an improvement in business conditions in the Philippines and the development of a mutually profitable trade between this country and the islands. Meantime our government in each dependency is upholding the traditions of civil liberty and increasing popular control which might be expected under American auspices. The work which we are doing there redounds to our credit as a nation.

I look forward with hope to increasing the already good feeling between the South and the other sections of the country. My chief purpose is not to effect a change in the electoral vote of the Southern states. That is a secondary consideration. What I look forward to is an increase in the tolerance of political views of all kinds and their advocacy throughout the South, and the existence of a respectable political opposition in every state; even more than this, to an increased feeling on the part of all the people in the South that this government is their government, and that its officers in their states are their officers.

The consideration of this question cannot, however, be complete and full without reference to the Negro race, its progress and its present condition. The Thirteenth Amendment secured them freedom; the Fourteenth Amendment due process of law, protection of property, and the pursuit of happiness; and the Fifteenth Amendment attempted to secure the Negro against any deprivation of the privilege to vote because he was a Negro. The Thirteenth and Fourteenth Amendments have been generally enforced and have secured the objects for which they are intended. While the Fifteenth Amendment has not been generally observed in the past, it ought to be observed, and the tendency of Southern legislation today is toward the enactment of electoral qualifications which shall square with that amendment. Of course, the mere adoption of a constitutional law is only one step in the right direction. It must be fairly and justly enforced as well. In time both will come. Hence it is clear to all that the domination of an ignorant, irresponsible element can be prevented by constitutional laws which shall exclude from voting both Negroes and whites not having education or other qualifications though to be necessary for a proper electorate. The danger of the control of an ignorant electorate has therefore passed. With this change, the interest which many of the Southern white citizens take in the welfare of the Negroes has increased. The colored men must base their hope on the results of their own industry, self-restraint, thrift, and business success, as well as upon the aid and comfort and sympathy which they may receive from their white neighbors of the South.

There was a time when Northerners who sympathized with the Negro in his necessary struggle for better conditions sought to give him the suffrage as a protection to enforce its exercise against the prevailing sentiment of the South. The movement proved to be a failure. What remains is the Fifteenth Amendment to the Constitution and the right to have statutes of states specifying qualifications for electors subjected to the test of compliance with that amendment. This is a great protection to the Negro. It never will be repealed, and it never ought to be repealed. If it had not passed, it might be difficult now to adopt it; but with it in our fundamental law, the policy of Southern legislation must and will tend to obey it, and so long as the statutes of the states meet the test of this amendment and are not otherwise in conflict with the Constitution and laws of the United States, it is not the disposition or within the province of the federal government to interfere with the regulation by Southern states of their domestic affairs. There is in the South a stronger feeling than ever among the intelligent well-to-do, an influential element in favor of the industrial education of the Negro and the encouragement of the race to make themselves useful members of the community. The progress which the Negro has made in the last 50 years, from slavery, when its statistics are reviewed, is marvelous, and it furnishes every reason to hope that in the next 25 years a still greater improvement in his condition as a productive member of society, on the farm, and in the shop, and in other occupations may come.

The Negroes are now Americans. Their ancestors came here years ago against their will, and this is their only country and their only flag. They have shown themselves anxious to live for it and to die for it. Encountering the race feeling against them, subjected at times to cruel injustice growing out of it, they may well have our profound sympathy and aid in the struggle they are making. We are charged with the sacred duty of making their path as smooth and easy as we can. Any recognition of their distinguished men, any appointment to office from among their number, is properly taken as an encouragement and an appreciation of their progress, and this just policy should be pursued when suitable occasion offers.

But it may well admit of doubt whether, in the case of any race, an appointment of one of their number to a local office in a community in which the race feeling is so widespread and acute as to interfere with the ease and facility with which the local government business can be done by the appointee is of sufficient benefit by way of encouragement to the race to outweigh the recurrence and increase of race feeling which such an appointment is likely to engender. Therefore the executive, in recognizing the Negro race by appointments, must exercise a careful discretion not thereby to do it more harm than good. On the other hand, we must be careful not to encourage the mere pretense of race feeling manufactured in the interest of individual political ambition.

Personally, I have not the slightest race prejudice or feeling, and recognition of its existence only awakens in my heart a deeper sympathy for those who have to bear it or suffer from it, and I question the wisdom of a policy which is likely to increase it. Meantime, if nothing is done to prevent it, a better feeling between the Negroes and the whites in the South will continue to grow, and more and more of the white people will come to realize that the future of the South is to be much benefited by the industrial and intellectual progress of the Negro. The exercise of political franchises by those of this race who are intelligent and well to do will be acquiesced in, and the right to vote will be withheld only from the ignorant and irresponsible of both races.

There is one other matter to which I shall refer. It was made the subject of great controversy during the election and calls for at least a passing reference now. My distinguished predecessor has given much attention to the cause of labor, with whose struggle for better things he has shown the sincerest sympathy. At his instance Congress has passed the bill fixing the liability of interstate carriers to their employees for injury sustained in the course of employment, abolishing the rule of fellow-servant and the common-law rule as to contributory negligence, and substituting therefore the so-called rule of "comparative negligence." It has also passed a law fixing the compensation of government employees for injuries sustained in the employ of the government through the negligence of the superior. It has also passed a model child-labor law for the District of Columbia. In previous administrations an arbitration law for interstate commerce railroads and their employees, and laws for the application of safety devices to save the lives and limbs of employees of interstate railroads had been passed. Additional legislation of this kind was passed by the outgoing Congress.

I wish to say that insofar as I can I hope to promote the enactment of further legislation of this character. I am strongly convinced that the government should make itself as responsible to employees injured in its employ as an interstate-railway corporation is made responsible by federal law to its employees; and I shall be glad, whenever any additional reasonable safety device can be invented to reduce the loss of life and limb among railway employees, to urge Congress to require its adoption by interstate railways.

Another labor question has arisen which has awakened the most excited discussion. That is in respect to the power of the federal courts to issue injunctions in industrial disputes. As to that, my convictions are fixed. Take away from the courts, if it could be taken away, the power to issue injunctions in labor disputes, and it would create a privileged class among the labor disputes, and it would create a privileged class among the laborers and save the lawless among their number from a most needful remedy available to all men for the protection of their business against lawless invasion. The proposition that business is not a property or pecuniary right which can be protected by equitable injunction is utterly without foundation in precedent or reason. The proposition is usually linked with one to make the secondary boycott lawful. Such a proposition is at variance with the American instinct, and will find no support, in my judgment, when submitted to the American people. The secondary boycott is an instrument of tyranny, and ought not to be made legitimate.

The issue of a temporary restraining order without notice has in several instances been abused by its inconsiderate exercise, and to remedy this the platform upon which I was elected recommends the formulation in a statute of the conditions under which such a temporary restraining order ought to issue. A statute can and ought to be framed to embody the best modern practice, and can bring the subject so closely to the attention of the court as to make abuses of the process unlikely in the future. The American people, if I understand them, insist that the authority of the courts shall be sustained, and are opposed to any change in the procedure by which the powers of a court may be weakened and the fearless and effective administration of justice be interfered with.

Having thus reviewed the questions likely to recur during my administration, and having expressed in a summary way the position which I expect to take in recommendations to Congress and in my conduct as an executive, I invoke the considerate sympathy and support of my fellow citizens and the aid of the Almighty God in the discharge of my responsible duties.

The Tariff

Winona, Minnesota

September 17, 1909

"SPEECH HASTILY prepared, but I hope it may do some good," Taft cabled his wife the day before he was to defend the controversial Payne-Aldrich tariff bill in the Minnesota village of Winona. In fact, the speech was a disaster.

The lowering of tariffs to encourage foreign trade had been one of Roosevelt's primary goals, but the Rough Rider never achieved any substantial progress in the face of determined opposition from conservative Republicans, who sought to protect domestic industry by maintaining high tariff duties. Though Taft initially attempted to advance Roosevelt's liberalization plan with the backing of party progressives, he really believed in protectionism and quickly came to support a token tariff reform bill sponsored by congressional conservatives Sereno E. Payne and Nelson W. Aldrich. The new law did lower the general tariff rate—the first time Republicans had ever voted to do so—but by only 5 percent, and it raised the rate on some goods.

Taft believed, with some justice, that he needed the support of men like Payne and Aldrich to maintain his own political effectiveness. But he lost the sympathy of progressives in the bargain; they felt he had betrayed their cause. To make matters worse, when he went on a national speaking tour to defend administration policies, including the new tariff, he made no effort to mollify progressives even when speaking in their home states. The tour was a resounding political failure, capped by the Winona speech. The press, which faced a rise in paper costs under the new tariff, ridiculed Taft's statement that "the Payne bill is the best tariff bill that the Republican Party ever passed" and made Taft appear to care little for the people who had to pay the high prices that high tariffs created.

As long ago as August 1906, in the congressional campaign in Maine, I ventured to announce that I was a tariff revisionist and thought that the time had come for a readjustment of the schedules. I pointed out that it had been 10 years prior to that time that the Dingley bill had been passed; that great changes had taken place in the conditions surrounding the productions of the farm, the factory, and the mine, and that under the theory of protection in that time the rates imposed in the Dingley bill in many instances might have become excessive; that is, might have been greater than the difference between the cost of production abroad and the cost of production at home with a sufficient allowance for a reasonable rate of profit to the American producer. I said that the party was divided on the issue, but that in my judgment the opinion of the party was crystallizing and would probably result in the near future in an effort to make such revision. I pointed out the difficulty that there always was in a revision of the tariff, due to the threatened disturbance of industries to be affected and the suspension of business, in a way which made it unwise to have too many revisions. In the summer of 1907 my position on the tariff was challenged, and I then entered into a somewhat fuller discussion of the matter. It was contended by the so-called "standpatters" that rates beyond the necessary measure of protection were not objectionable, because behind the tariff wall competition always reduced the prices, and thus saved the consumer. But I pointed out in that speech what seems to me as true today as it then was, that the danger of excessive rates was in the temptation they created to form monopolies in the protected articles, and thus to take advantage of the excessive rates by increasing the prices, and therefore, and in order to avoid such a danger, it was wise at regular intervals to examine the question of what the effect of the rates had been upon the industries in this country, and whether the conditions with respect to the cost of production here had so changed as to warrant a reduction in the tariff, and to make a lower rate truly protective of the industry.

It will be observed that the object of the revision under such a statement was not to destroy protected industries in this country, but it was to continue to protect them where lower rates offered a sufficient protection to prevent injury by foreign competition. That was the object of the revision as advocated by me, and it was certainly the object of the revision as promised in the Republican platform.

I want to make as clear as I can this proposition, because, in order to determine whether a bill is in compliance with the terms of that platform, it must be understood what the platform means. A free trader is opposed to any protected rate because he thinks that our manufacturers, our farmers, and our miners ought to withstand the competition of foreign manufacturers and miners and farmers, or else go out of business and find something else more profitable to do. Now, certainly the promises of the platform did not contemplate the downward revision of the tariff rates to such a point that any industry theretofore protected should be injured. Hence, those who contend that the promise of the platform was to reduce prices by letting in foreign competition are contending for a free trade, and not for anything that they had the right to infer from the Republican platform.

The Ways and Means Committee of the House, with Mr. Payne at its head, spent a full year in an investigation, assembling evidence in reference to the rates under the tariff, and devoted an immense amount of work in the study of the question where the tariff rates could be reduced and where they ought to be raised with a view to maintaining a reasonably protective rate, under the principles of the platform, for every industry that deserved protection. They found that the determination of the question, what was the actual cost of production and whether an industry in this country could live under a certain rate and withstand threatened competition from abroad, was most difficult. The manufacturers were prone to exaggerate the injury which a reduction in the duty would give and to magnify the amount of duty that was needed; while the importers, on the other hand, who were interested in developing the importation from foreign shores, were quite likely to be equally biased on the other side.

Mr. Payne reported a bill—the Payne tariff bill—which went to the Senate and was amended in the Senate by increasing the duty on some things and decreasing it on others. The difference between the House bill and the Senate bill was very much less than the newspapers represented. It turns out upon examination that the reductions in the Senate were about equal to those in the House, though they differed in character. Now, there is nothing quite so difficult as the discussion of a tariff bill, for the reason that it covers so many different items, and the meaning of the terms and the percentages are very hard to understand. The passage of a new bill, especially where a change in the method of assessing the duties has been followed, presents an opportunity for various modes and calculations of the percentages of increases and decreases that are most misleading and really throw no light at all upon the changes made. . . .

Now, the promise of the Republican platform was not to revise everything downward, and in the speeches which have been taken as interpreting that platform, which I made in the campaign, I did not promise that everything should go downward. What I promised was, that there should be many decreases, and that in some few things increases would be found to be necessary; but that on the whole I conceived that the change of conditions would make the revision necessarily downward—and that, I contend, under the showing which I have made, has been the result of the Payne bill. I did not agree, nor did the Republican Party agree, that we would reduce rates to such a point as to reduce prices by the introduction of foreign competition. That is what the free traders desire. That is what the revenue tariff reformers desire; but that is not what the Republican platform promised, and it is not what the Republican Party wished to bring about. To repeat the statement with which I opened this speech, the proposition of the Republican Party was to reduce rates so as to maintain a difference between the cost of production abroad and the cost of production here, insuring a reasonable profit to the manufacturer on all articles produced in this country; and the proposition to reduce rates and prevent their being excessive was to avoid the opportunity for monopoly and the suppression of competition, so that the excessive rates could be taken advantage of to force prices up.

Now, it is said that there was not a reduction in a number of the schedules where there should have been. It is said that there was no reduction in the cotton schedule. There was not. The House and the Senate took evidence and found from cotton manufacturers and from other sources that the rates upon the lower class of cottons were such as to enable them to make a decent profit—but only a decent profit—and they were contented with it; but that the rates on the higher grades of cotton cloth, by reason of court decisions, had been reduced so that they were considerably below those of the cheaper grades of cotton cloth, and that by undervaluations and otherwise the whole cotton schedule had been made unjust and the various items were disproportionate in respect to the varying cloths. Hence, in the Senate a new system was introduced attempting to make the duties more specific rather than *ad valorem,* in order to prevent by judicial decision or otherwise a disproportionate and unequal operation of the schedule. Under this schedule it was contended that there had been a general rise of all the duties on cotton. This was vigorously denied by the experts of the Treasury Department. At last, the Senate in conference consented to a reduction amounting to about 10 percent on all the lower grades of cotton and thus reduced the lower grades substantially to the same rates as before and increased the higher grades to what they ought to be under the Dingley law and what they were intended to be. Now, I am not going into the question of evidence which Congress passed upon, after they heard the statements of cotton manufacturers and such other evidence as they could avail themselves of. I agree that the method of taking evidence and the determination was made in a general way, and that there ought to be other methods of obtaining evidence and reaching a conclusion more satisfactory.

Criticism has also been made of the crockery schedule and the failure to reduce that. The question whether it ought to have been reduced or not was a question of evidence which both committees of Congress took up, and both concluded that the present rates on crockery were such as were needed to maintain the business in this country. I have been informed that the crockery schedule was not high enough, and mentioned that in one of my campaign speeches as a schedule probably where there ought to be some increases. It turned out that the difficulty was rather in undervaluations than in the character of the schedule itself, and so it was not changed. It is entirely possible to collect evidence to attack almost any of the schedules, but one story is good until another is told, and I have heard no reason for sustaining the contention that the crockery schedule is unduly high. So with respect to numerous details—items of not great importance—in which, upon what they regarded as sufficient evidence, the committee advanced the rates in order to save a business which was likely to be destroyed.

I have never known a subject that will evoke so much contradictory evidence as the question of tariff rates and the question of cost of production at home and abroad. Take the subject of paper. A committee was appointed by Congress a year before the tariff sittings began, to determine what the difference was between the cost of production in Canada of print paper and the cost of production here, and they reported that they thought that a good bill would be one imposing $2 a ton on paper, rather than $6, the Dingley rate, provided that Canada could be induced to take off the export duties and remove the other obstacles to the importation of spruce wood in this country out of which wood pulp is made. An examination of the evidence satisfied Mr. Payne—I believe it satisfied some of the Republican dissenters—that $2, unless some change was made in the Canadian restrictions upon the exports of wood to this country, was much too low, and that $4 was only a fair measure of the difference between the cost of production here and in Canada. In other words, the $2 found by the special committee in the House was rather an invitation to Canada and the Canadian print-paper people to use their influence with their government to remove the wood restrictions by reducing the duty on print paper against Canadian print-paper mills. It was rather a suggestion of a diplomatic nature than a positive statement of the difference in actual cost of production under existing conditions between Canada and the United States.

There are other subjects which I might take up. The tariff on hides was taken off because it was thought that it was not necessary in view of the high price of cattle thus to protect the man who raised them, and that the duty imposed was likely to throw the control of the sale of hides into the hands of the meat packers in Chicago. In order to balance the reduction on hides, however, there was a great reduction in shoes, from 25 to 10 percent; on sole leather, from 20 to 5 percent; on harness, from 45 to 20 percent. So there was a reduction in the duty on coal of 33 1/3 percent. All countervailing duties were removed from oil, naphtha, gasoline, and its refined products. Lumber was reduced from $2.00 to $1.25; and these all on articles of prime necessity. It is said that there might have been more. But there were many business interests in the South, in Maine, along the border, and especially in the far Northwest, which insisted that it would give great advantage to Canadian lumber if the reduction were made more than $0.75 cents. Mr. Pinchot, the chief forester, thought that it would tend to make better lumber in this country if a duty were retained on it. The lumber interests thought that $2.00 was none too much, but the reduction was made and the compromise effected. Personally I was in favor of free lumber, because I did not think that if the tariff was taken off there would be much suffering among the lumber interests. But in the controversy the House and Senate took a middle course, and who can say they were not justified.

With respect to the wool schedule, I agree that it probably represents considerably more than the difference between the cost of production abroad and the cost of production here. The difficulty about the woolen schedule is that there were two contending factions early in the history of Republican tariffs, to wit, woolgrowers and the woolen manufacturers, and that finally, many years ago, they settled on a basis by which wool in the grease should have 11 cents a pound, and by which allowance should be made for the shrinkage of the washed wool in the differential upon woolen manufactures. The percentage of duty was very heavy—quite beyond the difference in the cost of production, which was not then regarded as a necessary or proper limitation upon protective duties.

When it came to the question of reducing the duty at this hearing in the tariff bill on wool, Mr. Payne, in the House, and Mr. Aldrich, in the Senate, although both favored reduction in the schedule, found that in the Republican Party the interests of the woolgrowers of the Far West and the interests of the woolen manufacturers in the East and in other states, reflected through their representatives in Congress, was sufficiently strong to defeat any attempt to change the woolen tariff, and that

had it been attempted it would have beaten the bill reported from either committee. I am sorry this is so, and I could wish that it had been attempted it would have beaten the bill reported from either committee. I am sorry this is so, and I could wish that it had been otherwise. It is the one important defect in the present Payne tariff bill and in the performance of the promise of the platform to reduce rates to a difference in the cost of production, with reasonable profit to the manufacturer. That it will increase the price of woolen cloth or clothes, I very much doubt. There have been increases by the natural product, but this was not due to the tariff, because the tariff was not changed. The increase would, therefore, have taken place whether the tariff would have been changed or not. The cost of woolen cloths behind the tariff wall, through the effect of competition, has been greatly less than the duty, if added to the price, would have made it.

There is a complaint now by the woolen clothiers and by the carded woolen people of this woolen schedule. They have honored me by asking in circulars sent out by them that certain questions be put to me in respect to it, and asking why I did not veto the bill in view of the fact that the woolen schedule was not made in accord with the platform. I ought to say in respect to this point that all of them in previous tariff bills were strictly in favor of maintaining the woolen schedule as it was. The carded woolen people are finding that carded wools are losing their sales because they are going out of style. People prefer worsteds. The clothing people who are doing so much circularizing were contented to let the woolen schedule remain as it was until very late in the tariff discussion, long after the bill had passed the House, and, indeed, they did not grow very urgent until the bill had passed the Senate. This was because they found that the price of woolen cloth was going up, and so they desired to secure reduction in the tariff which would enable them to get cheaper material. They themselves are protected by a large duty; and I can not with deference to them ascribe their intense interest only to a deep sympathy with the ultimate consumers, so-called. But, as I have already said, I am quite willing to admit that allowing the woolen schedule to remain where it is, is not a compliance with the terms of the platform as I interpret it and as it is generally understood.

On the whole, however, I am bound to say that I think the Payne tariff bill is the best tariff bill that the Republican Party ever passed; that in it the party has conceded the necessity for following the changed conditions and reducing tariff rates accordingly. This is a substantial achievement in the direction of lower tariffs and downward revision, and it ought to be accepted as such. Critics of the bill utterly ignore the very tremendous cuts that have been made in the iron schedule, which heretofore has been subject to criticism in all tariff bills. From iron ore, which was cut 75 percent, to all the other items as low as 20 percent, with an average of something like 40 or 50 percent, that schedule has been reduced so that the danger of increasing prices through a monopoly of the business is very much lessened, and that was the chief purpose of revising the tariff downward under Republican protection principles. The severe critics of the bill passed this reduction in the metal schedule with a sneer, and say that the cut did not hurt the iron interests of the country. Well, of course it did not hurt them. It was not expected to hurt them. It was expected only to reduce excessive rates, so that business should still be conducted at a profit, and the very character of the criticism is an indication of the general injustice of the attitude of those who make it, in assuming that it was the promise of the Republican Party to hurt the industries of the country by the reductions which they were to make in the tariff, whereas it expressly indicated as plainly as possible in the platform that all of the industries were to be protected against injury by foreign competition, and the promise only went to the reduction of excessive rates beyond what was necessary to protect them.

The high cost of living, of which 50 percent is consumed in food, 25 percent in clothing, and 25 percent in rent and fuel, has not been produced by the tariff, because the tariff has remained the same while the increases have gone on. It is due to the change of conditions the world over. Living has increased everywhere in cost— in countries where there is free trade and in countries where there is protection— and that increase has been chiefly seen in the cost of food products. In other words, we have had to pay more for the products of the farmer, for meat, for grain, for everything that enters into food. Now, certainly no one will contend that protection has increased the cost of food in this country, when the fact is that we have been the greatest exporters of food products in the world. It is only that the demand has increased beyond the supply, that farm lands have not been opened as rapidly as the population, and the demand has increased. I am not saying that the tariff does not increase prices in clothing and in building and in other items that enter into the necessities of life, but what I wish to emphasize is that the recent increases in the cost of living in this country have not been due to the tariff. We have a much higher standard of living in this country than they have abroad, and this has been made possible by higher income for the workingman, the farmer, and all classes. Higher wages have been made possible by the encouragement of diversified industries, built up and fostered by the tariff.

Now, the revision downward of the tariff that I have favored will not, I hope, destroy the industries of the country. Certainly it is not intended to. All that it is intended to do, and that is what I wish to repeat, is to put the tariff where it will protect industries here from foreign competition, but will not enable those who will wish to monopolize to raise prices by taking advantage of excessive rates beyond the normal difference in the cost of production.

If the country desires free trade, and the country desires a revenue tariff and wishes the manufacturers all over the country to go out of business, and to have cheaper prices at the expense of the sacrifice of many of our manufacturing interests, then it ought to say so and ought to put the Democratic Party in power if it thinks that party can be trusted to carry out any affirmative policy in favor of a revenue tariff. Certainly in the discussions in the Senate there was a great manifestation on the part of our Democratic friends in favor of reducing rates on necessities. They voted to maintian the tariff rates on everything that came from their particular sections. If we are to have free trade, certainly it cannot be had through the maintenance of Republican majorities in the Senate and House and a Republican administration.

And now the question arises, what was the duty of a member of Congress who believed in a downward revision greater than that which has been accomplished, who thought that the wool schedules ought to be reduced, and that perhaps there were other respects in which the bill could be improved? Was it his duty because, in his judgment, it did not fully and completely comply with the promises of the party platform as he interpreted it, and indeed as I had interpreted it, to vote against the bill? I am here to justify those who answer this question in the negative. Mr. Tawney was a downward revisionist like myself. He is a low-tariff man, and has been known to be such in Congress all the time he has been there. He is a prominent Republican, the head of the Appropriations Committee, and when a man votes as I think he ought to vote, and an opportunity such as this presents itself, I am glad to speak in behalf of what he did, not in defense of it, but in support of it.

This is a government by a majority of the people. It is a representative government. People select some 400 members to constitute the lower House and some 92 members to constitute the upper House through their legislatures, and the varying views of a majority of the voters in 80 or 90 millions of people are reduced to one resultant force to take affirmative steps in carrying on a government by a system of parties. Without parties popular government would be absolutely impossible. In a party, those who join it, if they would make it effective, must surrender their personal predilections on matters comparatively of less importance in order to accomplish the good which united action on the most important principles at issue secures.

Now, I am not here to criticize those Republican members and senators whose views on the subject of the tariff were so strong and intense that they believed it their duty to vote against their party on the tariff bill. It is a question for each man to settle for himself. The question is whether he shall help maintain the party solidarity for accomplishing its chief purposes, or whether the departure from principle in the bill as he regards it is so extreme that he must in conscience abandon the party. All I have to say is, in respect to Mr. Tawney's action, and in respect to my own in signing the bill, that I believed that the interests of the country, the interest of the party, required me to sacrifice the accomplishment of certain things in the revision of the tariff which I had hoped for, in order to maintain party solidarity, which I believe to be much more important than the reduction of rates

in one or two schedules of the tariff. Had Mr. Tawney voted against the bill, and there had been others of the House sufficient in number to have defeated the bill, or if I had vetoed the bill because of the absence of a reduction of rates in the wool schedule, when there was a general downward revision, and a substantial one though not a complete one, we should have left the party in a condition of demoralization that would have prevented the accomplishment of purposes and a fulfillment of other promises which we had made just as solemnly as we had entered into that with respect to the tariff. When I could say without hesitation that this is the best tariff bill that the Republican Party has ever passed, and therefore the best tariff bill that has been passed at all, I do not feel that I could have reconciled any other course to my conscience than that of signing the bill, and I think Mr. Tawney feels the same way. Of course, if I had vetoed the bill I would have received the applause of many Republicans who may be called low-tariff Republicans, and who think deeply on that subject, and of all the democracy. Our friends the Democrats would have applauded, and then laughed in their sleeve at the condition in which the party would have been left; but, more than this, and waiving considerations of party, where would the country have been had the bill been vetoed, or been lost by a vote? It would have left the question of the revision of the tariff open for further discussion during the next session. It would have suspended the settlement of all our business down to a known basis upon which prosperity could proceed and investments be made, and it would have held up the coming of prosperity to this country certainly for a year and probably longer. These are the reasons why I signed it. . . .

Now, I think it is utterly useless, as I think it would be greatly distressing to business, to talk of another revision of the tariff during the present Congress. I should think that it would certainly take the rest of this administration to accumulate the data upon which a new and proper revision of the tariff might be had. By that time the whole Republican Party can express itself again in respect to the matter and bring to bear upon its representatives in Congress that sort of public opinion which shall result in solid party action. I am glad to see that a number of those who thought it their duty to vote against the bill insist that they are still Republicans and intend to carry on their battle in favor of lower duties and a lower revision within the lines of the party. That is their right and, in their view of things, is their duty.

It is vastly better that they should seek action of the party than that they should break off from it and seek to organize another party, which would probably not result in accomplishing anything more than merely defeating our party and inviting in the opposing party, which does not believe, or says that it does not believe, in protection. I think that we ought to give the present bill a chance. After it has been operating for two or three years, we can tell much more accurately than we can today its effect upon the industries of the country and the necessity for any amendment in its provisions.

I have tried to state as strongly as I can, but not more strongly than I think the facts justify, the importance of not disturbing the business interests of this country by an attempt in this Congress or the next to make a new revision; but meantime I intend, so far as in me lies, to secure official data upon the operation of the tariff, from which, when a new revision is attempted, exact facts can be secured. . . .

Dollar Diplomacy

From the Fourth Annual Message to Congress
Washington, D.C.
December 3, 1912

TAFT'S ANNUAL messages have been called "the high water mark of the all-encompassing, carefully documented, conscientiously prepared 'state of the Union' reviews." Far too long (and, with their profusion of tables and statistics, too dull) to be read at one time, they were issued in installments, each covering one major area of national affairs. Taft made little attempt to forge his annual messages into political documents; instead, they took the form of impartial administrative reports.

Taft used the phrase "dollar diplomacy" in a 1910 speech in which he said of U.S. foreign policy that it "may well be made to include active intervention to secure for our merchandise and our capitalists opportunity for profitable investment which shall insure to the benefit of both countries concerned." In other words, as he says in this excerpt from the first section of his last address to Congress, he favored a diplomacy "characterized as substituting dollars for bullets." Dollar diplomacy was applied to China and Latin America during Taft's term, with little diplomatic success, and with the benefits going primarily to U.S. financiers and industrialists. Many Latin Americans perceived dollar diplomacy as especially patronizing, an extension by more insidious means of Roosevelt's belligerent imperialism.

The foreign relations of the United States actually and potentially affect the state of the Union to a degree not widely realized and hardly surpassed by any other factor in the welfare of the whole nation. The position of the United States in the moral, intellectual, and material relations of the family of nations should be a matter of vital interest to every patriotic citizen. The national prosperity and power impose upon us duties which we cannot shirk if we are to be true to our ideals. The tremendous growth of the export trade of the United States has already made that trade a very real factor in the industrial and commercial prosperity of the country. With the development of our industries the foreign commerce of the United States must rapidly become a still more essential factor in its economic welfare. Whether we have a farseeing and wise diplomacy and are not recklessly plunged into unnecessary wars, and whether our foreign policies are based upon an intelligent grasp of present-day world conditions and a clear view of the potentialities of the future, or are governed by a temporary and timid expediency or by narrow views befitting an infant nation, are questions in the alternative consideration of which must convince any thoughtful citizen that no department of national polity offers greater opportunity for promoting the interests of the whole people on the one hand, or greater chance on the other of permanent national injury, than that which deals with the foreign relations of the United States.

The fundamental foreign policies of the United States should be raised high above the conflict of partisanship and wholly dissociated from differences as to domestic policy. In its foreign affairs the United States should present to the world a united front. The intellectual, financial, and industrial interest of the country and the publicist, the wage earner, the farmer, and citizen of whatever occupation must cooperate in a spirit of high patriotism to promote that national solidarity which is indispensable to national efficiency and to the attainment of national ideals.

The relations of the United States with all foreign powers remain upon a sound basis of peace, harmony, and friendship. A greater insistence upon justice to American citizens or interests wherever it may have been denied and a stronger emphasis of the need of mutuality in commercial and other relations have only served to strengthen our friendships with foreign countries by placing those friendships upon a firm foundation of realities as well as aspirations. . . .

The diplomacy of the present administration has sought to respond to modern ideas of commercial intercourse. This policy has been characterized as substituting dollars for bullets. It is one that appeals alike to idealistic humanitarian sentiments, to the dictates of sound policy and strategy, and to legitimate commercial aims. It is an effort frankly directed to the increase of American trade upon the axiomatic principle that the government of the United States shall extend all proper support to every legitimate and beneficial American enterprise abroad. How great have been the results of this diplomacy, coupled with the maximum and minimum provision of the tariff law, will be seen by some consideration of the wonderful increase in the export trade of the United States. Because modern diplomacy is commercial, there has been a disposition in some quarters to attribute to it none but materialistic aims. How strikingly erroneous is such an impression may be seen from a study of the results by which the diplomacy of the United States can be judged. . . .

China

In China the policy of encouraging financial investment to enable that country to help itself has had the result of giving new life and practical application to the Open Door policy. The consistent purpose of the present administration has been to encourage the use of American capital in the development of China by the promotion of those essential reforms to which China is pledged by treaties with the United States and other powers. The hypothecation to foreign bankers in connection with certain industrial enterprises, such as the Hukuang railways, of the national revenues upon which these reforms depended, led the Department of State early in the administration to demand for American citizens participation in such enterprises, in order that the United States might have equal rights and an equal voice in all questions pertaining to the disposition of the public revenues concerned. The same policy of promoting international accord among the powers having similar treaty rights as ourselves in the matters of reform, which could not be put into practical effect without the common consent of all, was likewise adopted in the case of the loan desired by China for the reform of its currency. The principle of international cooperation in matters of common interest upon which our policy had already been based in all of the above instances has admittedly been a great factor in that concert of the powers which has been so happily conspicuous during the perilous period of transition through which the great Chinese nation has been passing.

Central America Needs Our Help in Debt Adjustment

In Central America the aim has been to help such countries as Nicaragua and Honduras to help themselves. They are the immediate beneficiaries. The national benefit to the United States is two-fold. First, it is obvious that the Monroe Doctrine is more vital in the neighborhood of the Panama Canal and the zone of the Caribbean than anywhere else. There, too, the maintenance of that doctrine falls most heavily upon the United States. It is therefore essential that the countries within that sphere shall be removed from the jeopardy involved by heavy foreign debt and chaotic national finances and from the ever-present danger of international complication due to disorder at home. Hence the United States has been glad to encourage and support American bankers who were willing to lend a helping hand to the financial rehabilitation of such countries because this financial rehabilitation and the protection of their customhouses from being the prey of would-be dictators would remove at one stroke the menace of foreign creditors and the menace of revolutionary disorder.

The second advantage of the United States is one affecting chiefly all the southern and Gulf ports and the business and industry of the South. The republics of Central America and the Caribbean possess great natural wealth. They need only a measure of stability and the means of financial regeneration to enter upon an era of peace and prosperity, bringing profit and happiness to themselves and at the same time creating conditions sure to lead to a flourishing interchange of trade with this country.

I wish to call your especial attention to the recent occurrences in Nicaragua, for I believe the terrible events recorded there during the revolution of the past summer—the useless loss of life, the devastation of property, the bombardment of defenseless cities, the killing and wounding of women and children, the torturing of noncombatants to exact contributions, and the suffering of thousands of human beings—might have been averted had the Department of State, through approval of the loan convention by the Senate, been permitted to carry out its now well-developed policy of encouraging the extending of financial aid to weak Central American states with the primary objects of avoiding just such revolutions by assisting those republics to rehabilitate their finances, to establish their currency on a stable basis, to remove the customhouses from the danger of revolutions by arranging for their secure administration, and to establish reliable banks.

During this last revolution in Nicaragua, the government of that republic having admitted its inability to protect American life and property against acts of sheer lawlessness on the part of the malcontents, and having requested this government to assume that office, it became necessary to land over 2,000 marines and bluejackets in Nicaragua. Owing to their presence the constituted government of Nicaragua was free to devote its attention wholly to its internal troubles, and was thus enabled to stamp out the rebellion in a short space of time. When the Red Cross supplies sent to Granada had been exhausted, 8,000 persons having been given food in one day upon the arrival of the American forces, our men supplied other unfortunate, needy Nicaraguans from their own haversacks. I wish to congratulate the officers and men of the United States navy and marine corps who took part in reestablishing order in Nicaragua upon their splendid conduct, and to record with sorrow the death of seven American marines and bluejackets. Since the reestablishment of peace and order, elections have been held amid conditions of quiet and tranquility. Nearly all the American marines have now been withdrawn. The country should soon be on the road to recovery. The only apparent danger now threatening Nicaragua arises from the shortage of funds. Although American bankers have already rendered assistance, they may naturally be loath to advance a loan adequate to set the country upon its feet without the support of some such convention as that of June 1911, upon which the Senate has not yet acted.

Our Mexican Policy

For two years revolution and counterrevolution has distraught the neighboring republic of Mexico. Brigandage has involved a great deal of depredation upon foreign interests. There

have constantly recurred questions of extreme delicacy. On several occasions very difficult situations have arisen on our frontier. Throughout this trying period, the policy of the United States has been one of patient nonintervention, steadfast recognition of constituted authority in the neighboring nation, and the exertion of every effort to care for American interests. I profoundly hope that the Mexican nation may soon resume the path of order, prosperity, and progress. To that nation in its sore troubles, the sympathetic friendship of the United States has been demonstrated to a high degree. There were in Mexico at the beginning of the revolution some 30,000 or 40,000 American citizens engaged in enterprises contributing greatly to the prosperity of that republic and also benefiting the important trade between the two countries. The investment of American capital in Mexico has been estimated at $1,000,000,000. The responsibility of endeavoring to safeguard those interests and the dangers inseparable from propinquity to so turbulent a situation have been great, but I am happy to have been able to adhere to the policy above outlined—a policy which I hope may be soon justified by the complete success of the Mexican people in regaining the blessings of peace and good order.

Central America and the Caribbean

During the past summer the revolution against the administration which followed the assassination of President Caceres a year ago last November brought the Dominican Republic to the verge of administrative chaos, without offering any guaranties of eventual stability in the ultimate success of either party. In pursuance of the treaty relations of the United States with the Dominican Republic, which were threatened by the necessity of suspending the operation under American administration of the customhouses on the Haitian frontier, it was found necessary to dispatch special commissioners to the island to reestablish the customhouses and with a guard sufficient to insure needed protection to the customs administration. The efforts which have been made appear to have resulted in the restoration of normal conditions throughout the republic. The good offices which the commissioner were able to exercise were instrumental in bringing the contending parties together and in furnishing a basis of adjustment which it is hoped will result in permanent benefit to the Dominican people.

Mindful of its treaty relations, and owing to the position of the government of the United States as mediator between the Dominican Republic and Haiti in their boundary dispute, and because of the further fact that the revolutionary activities on the Haitian-Dominican frontier had become so active as practically to obliterate the line of demarcation that had been heretofore recognized pending the definitive settlement of the boundary in controversy, it was found necessary to indicate to the two island governments a provisional *de facto* boundary line. This was done without prejudice to the rights or obligations of either country in a final settlement to be reached by arbitration. The tentative line chosen was one which, under the circumstances brought to the knowledge of this government, seemed to conform to the best interests of the disputants. The border patrol which it had been found necessary to reestablish for customs purposes between the two countries was instructed provisionally to observe this line.

The republic of Cuba last May was in the throes of a lawless uprising that for a time threatened the destruction of a great deal of valuable property—much of it owned by Americans and other foreigners—as well as the existence of the government itself. The armed forces of Cuba being inadequate to guard property from attack and at the same time properly to operate against the rebels, a force of American marines was dispatched from our naval station at Guantanamo into the province of Oriente for the protection of American and other foreign life and property. The Cuban government was thus able to use all its forces in putting down the outbreak, which it succeeded in doing in a period of six weeks. The presence of two American warships in the harbor of Havana during the most critical period of this disturbance contributed in great measure to allay the fears of the inhabitants, including a large foreign colony.

There has been under discussion with the government of Cuba for some time the question of the release by this government of its leasehold rights at Bahia Honda, on the northern coast of Cuba, and the enlargement, in exchange therefore, of the naval station which has been established at Guantanamo Bay, on

the south. As the result of the negotiations thus carried on an agreement has been reached between the two governments providing for the suitable enlargement of the Guantanamo Bay station upon terms which are entirely fair and equitable to all parties concerned.

At the request alike of the government and both political parties in Panama, an American commission undertook supervision of the recent presidential election in that republic, where our treaty relations, and, indeed, every geographical consideration, make the maintenance of order and satisfactory conditions of peculiar interest to the government of the United States. The elections passed without disorder, and the new administration has entered upon its functions.

The government of Great Britain has asked the support of the United States for the protection of the interests of British holders of the foreign bonded debt of Guatemala. While this government is hopeful of an arrangement equitable to the British bondholders, it is naturally unable to view the question apart from its relation to the broad subject of financial stability in Central America, in which the policy of the United States does not permit it to escape a vital interest. Through a renewal of negotiations between the government of Guatemala and American bankers, the aim of which is a loan for the rehabilitation of Guatemalan finances, a way appears to be open by which the government of Guatemala could promptly satisfy any equitable and just British claims, and at the same time so improve its whole financial position as to contribute greatly to the increased prosperity of the republic and to redound to the benefit of foreign investments and foreign trade with that country. Failing such an arrangement, it may become impossible for the government of the United States to escape its obligations in connection with such measures as may become necessary to exact justice to legitimate foreign claims.

In the recent revolution in Nicaragua, which, it was generally admitted, might well have resulted in a general Central American conflict but for the intervention of the United States, the government of Honduras was especially menaced; but fortunately peaceful conditions were maintained within the borders of that republic. The financial condition of that country remains unchanged, no means having been found for the final adjustment of pressing outstanding foreign claims. This makes it the more regrettable that the financial convention between the United States and Honduras has thus far failed of ratification. The government of the United States continues to hold itself ready to cooperate with the government of Honduras, which it is believed, cannot much longer delay the meeting of its foreign obligations, and it is hoped at the proper time American bankers will be willing to cooperate for this purpose.

Necessity for Greater Governmental Effort in Retention and Expansion of Our Foreign Trade

It is not possible to make the Congress a communication upon the present foreign relations of the United States so detailed as to convey an adequate impression of the enormous increase in the importance and activities of those relations. If this government is really to preserve to the American people that free opportunity in foreign markets which will soon be indispensable to our prosperity, ever greater efforts must be made. Otherwise the American merchant, manufacturer, and exporter will find many a field in which American trade should logically predominate preempted through the more energetic efforts of other governments and other commercial nations.

There are many ways in which through hearty cooperation the legislative and executive branches of this government can do much. The absolute essential is the spirit of united effort and singleness of purpose. I will allude only to a very few specific examples of action which ought then to result. America cannot take its proper place in the most important fields for its commercial activity and enterprise unless we have a merchant marine. American commerce and enterprise cannot be effectively fostered in those fields unless we have good American banks in the countries refered to. We need American newspapers in those countries and proper means for public information about them. We need to assure the permanency of a trained foreign service. We need legislation enabling the members of the foreign service to be systematically brought in direct contact with the industrial, manufacturing, and exporting interests of this country in order that American businessmen may enter the foreign field with a clear perception of the exact conditions to be dealt with and the officers themselves may prosecute their work with a clear idea of what American industrial and manufacturing interest require.

Conclusion

Congress should fully realize the conditions which obtain in the world as we find ourselves at the threshold of our middle age as a nation. We have emerged full grown as a peer in the great concourse of nations. We have passed through various formative periods. We have been self-centered in the struggle to develop our domestic resources and deal with our domestic questions. The nation is now too matured to continue in its foreign relations those temporary expedients natural to a people to whom domestic affairs are the sole concern. In the past our diplomacy has often consisted, in normal times, in a mere assertion of the right to international existence. We are now in a larger relation with broader rights of our own and obligations to others than ourselves. A number of great guiding principles were laid down early in the history of this government. The recent task of our diplomacy has been to adjust those principles to the conditions of to-day, to develop their corollaries, to find practical applications of the old principles expanded to meet new situations. Thus are being evolved bases upon which can rest the superstructure of policies which must grow with the destined progress of this nation. The successful conduct of our foreign relations demands a broad and a modern view. We cannot meet new questions nor build for the future if we confine ourselves to outworn dogmas of the past and to the perspective appropriate at our emergence from colonial times and conditions. The opening of the Panama Canal will mark a new era in our international life and create new and worldwide conditions which, with their vast correlations and consequences, will obtain for hundreds of years to come. We must not wait for events to overtake us unawares. With continuity of purpose we must deal with the problems of our external relations by a diplomacy modern, resourceful, magnanimous, and fittingly expressive of the high ideals of a great nation.

Courtesy of Library of Congress

Woodrow Wilson

Woodrow Wilson

1913–1921

WILSON, one of the two most gifted orators among 20th-century presidents (the other was Franklin Roosevelt), was a native of Virginia. He was slow to learn to read and write—he may have been dyslexic—but overcame this handicap to earn a Ph.D. in political science from Johns Hopkins University in 1886. After a long career as a professor of political science, culminating in the presidency of Princeton University, he was elected governor of New Jersey in 1911 and was nominated for president as a longshot candidate by the Democrats in the election of 1912. The other two candidates—Taft, the incumbent, and rebel Progressive Theodore Roosevelt—split the Republican vote, enabling Wilson to carry the election with only 42 percent of the tally.

During his two terms, Wilson continued the progressive reforms begun by Roosevelt, assisted by his talent for public administration, his strong Presbyterian faith, his equally fervent faith in the spiritual superiority of democracy as a system of government, and his powerful oratory. He was an effective party leader and drafter of progressive legislation. But his domestic reforms, which included revision of protectionist tariffs, the passage of antitrust measures, and the establishment of the Federal Reserve and the Federal Trade Commission, were overshadowed by the international conflicts that led to the First World War. No sooner had the United States entered the war than Wilson, with characteristic idealism, began planning for the establishment of a lasting postwar peace. But he lacked the flexibility and experience in international politics to convince the Allies of his plan; nor could he sell it at home to a Republican-dominated Congress and an apathetic public. Weakened by several strokes and a serious bout of influenza, Wilson died in 1924.

Wilson regarded oratory as the principal means of influencing, even controlling, public opinion. He yearned, he said, "to make great truths attractive in the telling and of inspiring with great purposes by sheer force of eloquence or by gentle stress of persuasion." As president he reinstated the chief executive's old custom, in abeyance since the days of John Adams, of visiting the Capitol to address Congress in person. It was through his speeches advocating neutrality that Wilson convinced America to stay out of the European war, and through his most famous speech—his war message to Congress on April 2, 1917—that he brought America into the war. For his part Wilson felt that "whatever strength I have and whatever authority I possess are mine only so long and so far as I express the spirit and purpose of the American people."

Most of Wilson's speeches he wrote himself, often on a typewriter. The higher the ideals he expounded, the more elegant his expression of them. "He found phrases that were exalted in rhythm and connotation," wrote historian Louis Filler, "while seeming not to lose their earthbound substance. No one else but Winston Churchill of his generation infused the democratic ideal with equal drama." When some his supporters expressed the fear that his elevated phrases were going over the heads of the public, Wilson replied, "I think that is all right because you see the people have gotten used by this time to having a highbrow president." In his striving toward loftiness of expression he sometimes resorted, especially in his later speeches, to stock phrases and academic locutions that gave his remarks a curiously impersonal flavor. One contemporary critic of his writings, William Bayard Hall, noted that Wilson "does not concur, he entirely concurs; he is seldom gratified, he is usually profoundly gratified; he does not feel pleasure, he experiences unaffected pleasure; he seldom says anything, but he is always privileged to say." Despite these stylistic excesses, Wilson as a crafter of mighty phrases had few peers—his "the world must be made safe for democracy" (from the War Message) has the same stirring ring today that it had more than 80 years ago.

The cool intellectuality that Wilson projected in public had been polished during his teaching years (at Princeton he was voted best lecturer on the faculty), and he was extraordinarily skillful at impromptu speechmaking. Except on important occasions of state, when he would prepare his remarks beforehand, Wilson usually spoke without notes. Awkward in dealing with individuals, he was masterful on the podium, which for him as for Roosevelt was a kind of pulpit. Observers frequently compared him to a Calvinist preacher—he was, in fact, a lay preacher during his years at Princeton, as well as the son of a minister—and he relished the role of spiritual educator of the public. But he also possessed the rare ability to create a sense of intimacy with his audiences, who accepted the sincerity of his idealism. Much as he desired it, the masses did not love him as Lincoln or Roosevelt had been loved, but they respected him.

First Inaugural Address

Washington, D.C.

March 4, 1913

THIS INAUGURAL has been described by Henry Steele Commager as "one of the most notable expressions of democratic faith in our political literature." Wilson was giving notice of his intention to establish a progressive administration. "I am going to appoint forward-looking men," he said, "and I am going to satisfy myself that they are honest and capable." The antitrust, tariff, and labor legislation that he proposes in this speech formed the basis of his "New Freedom"—program, a rapid-fire series of reforms that historian John Milton Cooper called "a spectacular, possibly unmatched record of legislative and party leadership."

There has been a change of government. It began two years ago, when the House of Representatives became Democratic by a decisive majority. It has now been completed. The Senate about to assemble will also be Democratic. The offices of president and vice president have been put into the hands of Democrats. What does the change mean? That is the question that is uppermost in our minds today. That is the question I am going to try to answer, in order, if I may, to interpret the occasion.

It means much more than the mere success of a party. The success of a party means little except when the nation is using that party for a large and definite purpose. No one can mistake the purpose for which the nation now seeks to use the Democratic Party. It seeks to use it to interpret a change in its own plans and point of view. Some old things with which we had grown familiar, and which had begun to creep into the very habit of our thought and of our lives, have altered their aspect as we have latterly looked critically upon them, with fresh, awakened eyes; have dropped their disguises and shown themselves alien and sinister. Some new things, as we look frankly upon them, willing to comprehend their real character, have come to assume the aspect of things long believed in and familiar, stuff of our own convictions. We have been refreshed by a new insight into our own life.

We see that in many things that life is very great. It is incomparably great in its material aspects, in its body of wealth, in the diversity and sweep of its energy, in the industries which have been conceived and built up by the genius of individual men and the limitless enterprise of groups of men. It is great, also, very great, in its moral force. Nowhere else in the world have noble men and women exhibited in more striking forms the beauty and the energy of sympathy and helpfulness and counsel in their efforts to rectify wrong, alleviate suffering, and set the weak in the way of strength and hope. We have built up, moreover, a great system of government, which has stood through a long age as in many respects a model for those who seek to set liberty upon foundations that will endure against fortuitous change, against storm and accident. Our life contains every great thing, and contains it in rich abundance.

But the evil has come with the good, and much fine gold has been corroded. With riches has come inexcusable waste. We have squandered a great part of what we might have used, and have not stopped to conserve the exceeding bounty of nature, without which our genius for enterprise would have been worthless and impotent, scorning to be careful, shamefully prodigal as well as admirably efficient. We have been proud of our industrial achievements, but we have not hitherto stopped thoughtfully enough to count the human cost, the cost of lives snuffed out, of energies overtaxed and broken, the fearful physical and spiritual cost to the men and women and children upon whom the dead weight and burden of it all has fallen pitilessly the years through. The groans and agony of it all had not yet reached our ears, the solemn, moving undertone of our life, coming up out of the mines and factories and out of every home where the struggle had its intimate and familiar seat. With the great government went many deep secret things which we too long delayed to look into and scrutinize with candid, fearless eyes. The great government we loved has too often been made use of for private and selfish purposes, and those who used it had forgotten the people.

At last a vision has been vouchsafed us of our life as a whole. We see the bad with the good, the debased and decadent with the sound and vital. With this vision we approach new affairs. Our duty is to cleanse, to reconsider, to restore, to correct the evil without impairing the good, to purify and humanize every process of our common life without weakening or sentimentalizing it. There has been something crude and heartless and unfeeling in our haste to succeed and be great. Our thought has been "Let every man look out for himself, let every generation look out for itself," while we reared giant machinery which made it impossible that any but those who stood at the levers of control should have a chance to look out for themselves. We had not forgotten our morals. We remembered well enough that we had set up a policy which was meant to serve the humblest as well as the most powerful, with an eye single to the standards of justice and fair play, and remembered it with pride. But we were very heedless and in a hurry to be great.

We have come now to the sober second thought. The scales of heedlessness have fallen from our eyes. We have made up our minds to square every process of our national life again with the standards we so proudly set up at the beginning and have always carried at our hearts. Our work is a work of restoration.

We have itemized with some degree of particularity the things that ought to be altered and here are some of the chief items: A tariff which cuts us off from our proper part in the commerce of the world, violates the just principles of taxation, and makes the government a facile instrument in the hands of private interests; a banking and currency system based upon the necessity of the government to sell its bonds 50 years ago and perfectly adapted to concentrating cash and restricting credits; an industrial system which, take it on all its sides, financial as well as administrative, holds capital in leading strings, restricts the liberties and limits the opportunities of labor, and exploits without renewing or conserving the natural resources of the country; a body of agricultural activities never yet given the efficiency of great business undertakings or served as it should be through the instrumentality of science taken directly to the farm,

or afforded the facilities of credit best suited to its practical needs; watercourses undeveloped, waste places unreclaimed, forests untended, fast disappearing without plan or prospect of renewal, unregarded waste heaps at every mine. We have studied as perhaps no other nation has the most effective means of production, but we have not studied cost or economy as we should either as organizers of industry, as statesmen, or as individuals.

Nor have we studied and perfected the means by which government may be put at the service of humanity, in safeguarding the health of the nation, the health of its men and its women and its children, as well as their rights in the struggle for existence. This is no sentimental duty. The firm basis of government is justice, not pity. These are matters of justice. There can be no equality or opportunity, the first essential of justice in the body politic, if men and women and children be not shielded in their lives, their very vitality, from the consequences of great industrial and social processes which they can not alter, control, or singly cope with. Society must see to it that it does not itself crush or weaken or damage its own constituent parts. The first duty of law is to keep sound the society it serves. Sanitary laws, pure food laws, and laws determining conditions of labor which individuals are powerless to determine for themselves are intimate parts of the very business of justice and legal efficiency.

These are some of the things we ought to do, and not leave the others undone, the old-fashioned, never-to-be-neglected, fundamental safeguarding of property and of individual right. This is the high enterprise of the new day: To lift everything that concerns our life as a nation to the light that shines from the hearthfire of every man's conscience and vision of the right. It is inconceivable that we should do this as partisans; it is inconceivable we should do it in ignorance of the facts as they are or in blind haste. We shall restore, not destroy. We shall deal without economic system as it is and as it may be modified, not as it might be if we had a clean sheet of paper to write upon; and step by step we shall make it what it should be, in the spirit of those who question their own wisdom and seek counsel and knowledge, not shallow self-satisfaction or the excitement of excursions whither they cannot tell. Justice, and only justice, shall always be our motto.

And yet it will be no cool process of mere science. The nation has been deeply stirred, stirred by a solemn passion, stirred by the knowledge of wrong, of ideals lost, of government too often debauched and made an instrument of evil. The feelings with which we face this new age of right and opportunity sweep across our heartstrings like some air out of God's own presence, where justice and mercy are reconciled and the judge and the brother are one. We know our task to be no mere task of politics but a task which shall search us through and through, whether we be able to understand our time and the need of our people, whether we be indeed their spokesmen and interpreters, whether we have the pure heart to comprehend and the rectified will to choose our high course of action.

This is not a day of triumph; it is a day of dedication. Here muster, not the forces of party, but the forces of humanity. Men's hearts wait upon us; men's lives hang in the balance; men's hopes call upon us to say what we will do. Who shall live up to the great trust? Who dares fail to try? I summon all honest men, all patriotic, all forward-looking men, to my side. God helping me, I will not fail them, if they will but counsel and sustain me!

The Tariff

Washington, D.C.

April 8, 1913

THE FIRST ACT of the new administration was the general relaxation of protectionist tariff duties passed under Taft. Wilson presented his position in a special address to Congress, the first appearance of a president before Congress since Jefferson. This was an opportunity that Wilson had in a sense been anticipating since his days as a student of American government. In the past, he had argued as a lecturer at Columbia, "the presidential messages were [often] utterly without practical significance, perfunctory documents which few persons except the editors of newspapers took the trouble to read." But, he continued, "if the president has personal force and cares to exercise it, there is this tremendous difference between his messages and the views of any other citizen either outside Congress or in it; that the whole country reads them and feels the writer speaks with an authority and responsibility which the people themselves have given him."

I am very glad indeed to have this opportunity to address the two houses directly and to verify for myself the impression that the president of the United States is a person, not a mere department of the government hailing Congress from some isolated island of jealous power, sending messages, not speaking naturally and with his own voice—that he is a human being trying to cooperate with other human beings in a common service. After this pleasant experience I shall feel quite normal in all our dealings with one another.

I have called the Congress together in extraordinary session because a duty was laid upon the party now in power at the recent elections which it ought to perform promptly, in order that the burden carried by the people under existing law may be lightened as soon as possible, and in order, also, that the business interests of the country may not be kept too long in suspense as to what the fiscal changes are to be to which they will be required to adjust themselves. It is clear to the whole country that the tariff duties must be altered. They must be changed to meet the radical alteration in the conditions of our economic life which the country has witnessed within the last generation. While the whole face and method of our industrial and commercial life were being changed beyond recognition the tariff schedules have remained what they were before the change began, or have moved in the direction they were given when no large circumstance of our industrial development was what it is today. Our task is to square them with the actual facts. The sooner that is done the sooner we shall escape from suffering from the facts and the sooner our men of business will be free to thrive by the law of nature—the nature of free business—instead of by the law of legislation and artificial arrangement.

We have seen tariff legislation wander very far afield in our day—very far indeed from the field in which our prosperity might have had a normal growth and stimulation. No one who looks the facts squarely in the face or knows anything that lies beneath the surface of action can fail to perceive the principles upon which recent tariff legislation has been based. We long ago passed beyond the modest notion of "protecting" the industries of the country and moved boldly forward to the idea that they were entitled to the direct patronage of the government. For a long time—a time so long that the men now active in public policy hardly remember the conditions that preceded it—we have sought in our tariff schedules to give each group of manufacturers or producers what they themselves thought that they needed in order to maintain a practically exclusive market as against the rest of the world. Consciously or unconsciously, we have built up a set of privileges and exemptions from competition behind which it was easy by any, even the crudest, forms of combination to organize monopoly; until at last nothing is normal, nothing is obliged to stand the tests of efficiency and economy, in our world of big business, but everything thrives by concerted arrangement. Only new principles of action will save us from a final hard crystallization of monopoly and a complete loss of the influences that quicken enterprise and keep independent energy alive.

It is plain what those principles must be. We must abolish everything that bears even the semblance of privilege or of any kind of artificial advantage, and put our businessmen and producers under the stimulation of a constant necessity to be efficient, economical, and enterprising, masters of competitive supremacy, better workers and merchants than any in the world. Aside from the duties laid upon articles which we do not, and probably cannot, produce, therefore, and the duties laid upon luxuries and merely for the sake of the revenues they yield, the object of the tariff duties henceforth laid must be effective competition, the whetting of American wits by contest with the wits of the rest of the world.

It would be unwise to move toward this end headlong, with reckless haste, or with strokes that cut at the very roots of what has grown up amongst us by long process and at our own invitation. It does not alter a thing to upset it and break it and deprive it of a chance to change. It destroys it. We must make changes in our fiscal laws, in our fiscal system, whose object is development, a more free and wholesome development, not revolution or upset or confusion. We must build up trade, especially foreign trade. We need the outlet and the enlarged field of energy more than we ever did before. We must build up industry as well, and must adopt freedom in the place of artificial stimulation only so far as it will build, not put down. In dealing with the tariff the method by which this may be done will be a matter of judgment exercised item by item. To some not accustomed to the excitements and responsibilities of greater freedom our methods may in some respects and at some points seem heroic but remedies may be heroic and yet be remedies. It is our business to make sure that they are genuine remedies. Our object is clear. If our motive is above just challenge and only an occasional error of judgment is chargeable against us, we shall be fortunate.

We are called upon to render the country a great service in more matters than one. Our responsibility should be met and our methods should be thorough, as thorough as moderate and well considered, based upon the facts as they are, and not worked out as if we were beginners. We are to deal with the facts of our own day, with the facts of no other and to make laws which square with those facts. It is best, indeed it is necessary, to begin with the tariff. I will urge nothing upon you now at the opening of your session which can obscure that first object or divert our energies from that clearly defined duty. At a later time I may take the liberty of calling your attention to reforms which should press close upon the heels of the tariff changes, if not accompany them, of which the chief is the reform of our banking and currency laws; but just now I refrain. For the present, I put these matters on one side and think only of this one thing— of the changes in our fiscal system which may best serve to open once more the free channels of prosperity to a great people whom we would serve to the utmost and throughout both rank and file.

I sincerely thank you for your courtesy.

Latin American Policy

Mobile, Alabama

October 27, 1913

ROOSEVELT'S policy toward Latin America had been arrogant and condescending. Wilson hoped to cultivate a more equable and respectful friendship; he was the first executive to publicly condemn the exploitation of the region by North American business interests. But his diplomatic relations with Latin America were not especially warm, although better than under Roosevelt, and with Mexico they were disastrous. Wilson refused to recognize Mexican president Adolfo de la Huerta, and twice ordered U.S. troops onto Mexican soil to search for the bandit and revolutionary Pancho Villa.

It is with unaffected pleasure that I find myself here today. I once before had the pleasure, in another southern city, of addressing the Southern Commercial Congress. I then spoke of what the future seemed to hold in store for this region, which so many of us love and toward the future of which we all look forward with so much confidence and hope. But another theme directed me here this time. I do not need to speak of the South. She has, perhaps, acquired the gift of speaking for herself. I come because I want to speak of our present and prospective relations with our neighbors to the south. I deemed it a public duty, as well as a personal pleasure, to be here to express for myself and for the government I represent the welcome we all feel to those who represent the Latin American states.

The future, ladies and gentlemen, is going to be very different for this hemisphere from the past. These states lying to the south of us, which have always been our neighbors, will now be drawn closer to us by innumerable ties, and, I hope, chief of all, by the tie of a common understanding of each other. Interest does not tie nations together; it sometimes separates them. But sympathy and understanding does unite them, and I believe that by the new route that is just about to be opened, while we physically cut two continents asunder, we spiritually unite them. It is a spiritual union which we seek.

I wonder if you realize, I wonder if your imaginations have been filled with the significance of the tides of commerce. Your governor alluded in very fit and striking terms to the voyage of Columbus, but Columbus took his voyage under compulsion of circumstances. Constantinople had been captured by the Turks and all the routes of trade with the East had been suddenly closed. If there was not a way across the Atlantic to open those routes again, they were closed forever, and Columbus set out not to discover the eastern shores of Asia. He set sail for Cathay and stumbled upon America. With that change in the outlook of the world, what happened? England, that had been at the back of Europe with an unknown sea behind her, found that all things had turned as if upon a pivot and she was at the front of Europe; and since then all the tides of energy and enterprise that have issued out of Europe have seemed to be turned westward across the Atlantic. But you will notice that they have turned westward chiefly north of the equator and that it is the northern half of the globe that has seemed to be filled with the media of intercourse and of sympathy and of common understanding.

Do you not see now what is about to happen? These great tides which have been running along parallels of latitude will now swing southward athwart parallels of latitude, and that opening gate at the Isthmus of Panama will open the world to a commerce that she has not known before, a commerce of intelligence, of thought and sympathy between North and South. The Latin American states, which, to their disadvantage, have been off the main lines, will now be on the main lines. I feel that these gentlemen honoring us with their presence today will presently find that some part, at any rate, of the center of gravity of the world has shifted. Do you realize that New York, for example, will be nearer the western coast of South America than she is now to the eastern coast of South America? Do you realize that a line drawn northward parallel with the greater part of the western coast of South America will run only about 150 miles west of New York? The great bulk of South America, if you will look at your globes (not at your Mercator's projection), lies eastward of the continent of North America. You will realize that when you realize that the canal will run southeast, not southwest, and that when you get in to the Pacific you will be farther east than you were when you left the Gulf of Mexico. These things are significant, therefore, of this, that we are closing one chapter in the history of the world and are opening another, of great, unimaginable significance.

There is one peculiarity about the history of the Latin American states which I am sure they are keenly aware of. You hear of "concessions" to foreign capitalists in Latin America. You do not hear of concessions to foreign capitalists in the United States. They are not granted concessions. They are invited to make investments. The work is ours, though they are welcome to invest in it. We do not ask them to supply the capital and do the work. It is an invitation, not a privilege; and states that are obliged, because their territory does not lie within the main field of modern enterprise and action, to grant concessions are in this condition, that foreign interests are apt to dominate their domestic affairs, a condition of affairs always dangerous and apt to become intolerable. What these states are going to see, therefore, is an emancipation from the subordination, which has been inevitable, to foreign enterprise and an assertion of the splendid character which, in spite of these difficulties, they have again and again been able to demonstrate. The dignity, the courage, the self-possession, the self-respect of the Latin American states, their achievements in the face of all these adverse circumstances, deserve nothing but the admiration and applause of the world. They have had harder bargains driven with them in the matter of loans than any other peoples in the world. Interest has been exacted of them that was not exacted of anybody else, because the risk was said to be greater; and then securities were taken that destroyed the risk—an admirable arrangement for those who were forcing the terms! I rejoice in nothing so much as in the prospect that they will now be emancipated from these conditions, and we ought to be the first to take part in assisting in that emancipation. I think some of

these gentlemen have already had occasion to bear witness that the Department of State in recent months has tried to serve them in that wise. In the future they will draw closer and closer to us because of circumstances of which I wish to speak with moderation and, I hope, without indiscretion.

We must prove ourselves their friends and champions upon terms of equality and honor. You cannot be friends upon any other terms than upon the terms of equality. You cannot be friends at all except upon the terms of honor. We must show ourselves friends by comprehending their interest whether it squares with our own interest or not. It is a very perilous thing to determine the foreign policy of a nation in the terms of material interest. It not only is unfair to those with whom you are dealing, but it is degrading as regards your own actions.

Comprehension must be the soil in which shall grow all the fruits of friendship, and there is a reason and a compulsion lying behind all this which is dearer than anything else to the thoughtful men of America. I mean the development of constitutional liberty in the world. Human rights, national integrity, and opportunity as against material interests—that, ladies and gentlemen, is the issue which we now have to face. I want to take this occasion to say that the United States will never again seek one additional foot of territory by conquest. She will devote herself to showing that she knows how to make honorable and fruitful use of the territory she has, and she must regard it as one of the duties of friendship to see that from no quarter are material interests made superior to human liberty and national opportunity. I say this, not with a single thought that anyone will gainsay it, but merely to fix in our consciousness what our real relationship with the rest of America is. It is the relationship of a family of mankind devoted to the development of true constitutional liberty. We know that that is the soil out of which the best enterprise springs. We know that this is a cause which we are making in common without our neighbors, because we have had to make it for ourselves.

Reference has been made here today to some of the national problems which confront us as a nation. What is at the heart of all our national problems? It is that we have seen the hand of material interest sometimes about to close upon our dearest rights and possessions. We have seen material interests threaten constitutional freedom in the United States. Therefore we will now know how to sympathize with those in the rest of America who have to contend with such powers, not only within their borders but from outside their borders also.

I know what the response of the thought and heart of America will be to the program I have outlined, because America was created to realize a program like that. This is not America because it is rich. This is not America because it has set up for a great population great opportunities of material prosperity. America is a name which sounds in the ears of men everywhere as a synonym with individual opportunity because a synonym of individual liberty. I would rather belong to a poor nation that was free than to a rich nation that had ceased to be in love with liberty. But we shall not be poor if we love liberty, because the nation that loves liberty truly sets every man free to do his best and be his best, and that means the release of all the splendid energies of a great people who think for themselves. A nation of employees cannot be free any more than a nation of employers can be.

In emphasizing the points which must unite us in sympathy and in spiritual interest with the Latin American peoples we are only emphasizing the points of our own life, and we should prove ourselves untrue to our own traditions if we proved ourselves untrue friends to them.

Do not think, therefore, gentlemen, that the questions of the day are mere questions of policy and diplomacy. They are shot through with the principles of life. We dare not turn from the principle that morality and not expediency is the thing that must guide us and that we will never condone iniquity because it is most convenient to do so. It seems to me that this is a day of infinite hope, of confidence in a future greater than the past has been, for I am fain to believe that in spite of all the things that we wish to correct the 19th century that now lies behind us has brought us a long stage toward the time when, slowly ascending the tedious climb that leads to the final uplands, we shall get our ultimate view of the duties of mankind. We have breasted a considerable part of that climb and shall presently—it may be in a generation or two—come out upon those great heights where there shines unobstructed the light of the justice of God.

Too Proud to Fight

Philadelphia, Pennsylvania
May 10, 1915

THIS ADDRESS was a political blunder for Wilson. He was speaking on American citizenship before a crowd of 7,000 newly naturalized citizens, just three days after the *Lusitania* was sunk by a German submarine with the loss of many American lives. The sentence "There is such a thing as a nation being so right that it does not need to convince others by force that it is right" was widely misinterpreted as evidence of his cowardice. In fact, Wilson had been carried away by his own rhetoric and had not intended any connection between the *Lusitania* affair and his own remarks. "I have a bad habit of thinking out loud," he said later. "That thought occurred to me while I was speaking and I let it out. I should have kept it in, or developed it further." The image of weakness that this speech helped to create cost him many votes in the following year's election.

It warms my heart that you should give me such a reception; but it is not of myself that I wish to think tonight, but of those who have just become citizens of the United States.

This is the only country in the world which experiences this constant and repeated rebirth. Other countries depend upon the multiplication of their own native people. This country is constantly drinking strength out of new sources by the voluntary association with it of great bodies of strong men and forward-looking women out of other lands. And so by the gift of the free will of independent people it is being constantly renewed from generation to generation by the same process by which it was originally created. It is as if humanity had determined to see to it that this great nation, founded for the benefit of humanity, should not lack for the allegiance of the people of the world.

You have just taken an oath of allegiance to the United States. Of allegiance to whom? Of allegiance to no one, unless it be God— certainly not of allegiance to those who temporarily represent this great government. You have taken an oath of allegiance to a great ideal, to a great body of principles, to a great hope of the human race. You have said, "We are going to America not only to earn a living, not only to seek the things which it was more difficult to obtain where we were born, but to help forward the great enterprises of the human spirit—to let men know that everywhere in the world there are men who will cross strange oceans and go where a speech is spoken which is alien to them if they can but satisfy their quest for what their spirits crave; knowing that whatever the speech there is but one longing and utterance of the human heart, and that is for liberty and justice." And while you bring all countries with you, you come with a purpose of leaving all other countries behind you—bringing what is best of their spirit, but not looking over your shoulders and seeking to perpetuate what you intended to leave behind in them. I certainly would not be one even to suggest that a man cease to love the home of his birth and the nation of his origin—these things are very sacred and ought not to be put out of our hearts—but it is one thing to love the place where you were born and it is another thing to dedicate yourself to the place to which you go. You cannot dedicate yourself to America unless you become in every respect and with every purpose of your will thorough Americans. You cannot become thorough Americans if you think of yourselves in groups. America does not consist of groups. A man who thinks of himself as belonging to a particular national group in America has not yet become an American, and the man who goes among you to trade upon your nationality is no worthy son to live under the Stars and Stripes.

My urgent advice to you would be, not only always to think first of America, but always, also, to think first of humanity. You do not love humanity if you seek to divide humanity into jealous camps. Humanity can be welded together only by love, by sympathy, by justice, not by jealousy and hatred. I am sorry for the man who seeks to make personal capital out of the passions of his fellowmen. He has lost the touch and ideal of America, for America was created to unite mankind by those passions which lift and not by the passions which separate and debase. We came to America, either ourselves or in the persons of our ancestors, to better the ideals of men, to make them see finer things than they had seen before, to get rid of the things that divide and to make sure of the things that united. It was but an historical accident no doubt that this great country was called the United States; yet I am very thankful that it has that word United in its title, and the man who seeks to divide man from man, group from group, interest from interest in this great Union is striking at its very heart.

It is a very interesting circumstance to me, in thinking of those of you who have just sworn allegiance to this great government, that you were drawn across the ocean by some beckoning finger of hope, by some belief, by some vision of a new kind of justice, by some expectation of a better kind of life. No doubt you have been disappointed in some of us. Some of us are very disappointing. No doubt what you found here did not seem touched for you, after all, with the complete beauty of the ideal which you had conceived beforehand. But remember this: If we had grown at all poor in the ideal, you brought some of it with you. A man does not go out to seek the thing that is not in him. A man does not hope for the thing that he does not believe in, and if some of us have forgotten what America believed in, you, at any rate, imported in your own hearts a renewal of the belief. That is the reason that I, for one, make you welcome. If I have in any degree forgotten what America was intended for, I will thank God if you will remind me. I was born in America. You dreamed dreams of what America was to be, and I hope you brought the dreams with you. No man that does not see visions will ever realize any high hope or undertake any high enterprise. Just because you brought dreams with you, America is more likely to realize dreams such as you brought. You are enriching us if you came expecting us to be better than we are.

See, my friends, what that means. It means that Americans must have a consciousness different from the consciousness of every other nation in the world. I am not saying this with even the slightest thought of criticism of other nations. You know how it is with a family. A family gets centered on itself if it is not careful and is less interested in the neighbors than it is in its own members. So a nation that is not constantly renewed out of new sources is apt to have the narrowness and prejudice of a family; whereas, America must have this consciousness, that on all sides it touches elbows and touches hearts with all the nations of mankind. The example of America must be a special example. The example of America must be the example not merely of peace because it will not fight, but of peace because peace is the healing and elevating influence of the world and strife is not. There is such a thing as a man being too proud to fight. There is such a thing as a nation being so right that it does not need to convince others by force that it is right.

You have come into this great nation voluntarily seeking something that we have to give, and all that we have to give is this: We cannot exempt you from work. No man is exempt from work anywhere in the world. We cannot exempt you from the strife and the heartbreaking burden of the struggle of the day—that is common to mankind everywhere; we cannot exempt you from the loads that you must carry. We can only make them light by the spirit in which they are carried. That is the spirit of hope, it is the spirit of liberty, it is the spirit of justice.

When I was asked, therefore, by the mayor and the committee that accompanied him to come up from Washington to meet this great company of newly admitted citizens, I could not decline the invitation. I ought not to be away from Washington, and yet I feel that it has renewed my spirit as an American to be here. In Washington men tell you so many things every day that are not so, and I like to come and stand in the presence of a great body of my fellow citizens, whether they have been my fellow citizens a long time or a short time, and drink, as it were, out of the common fountains with them and go back feeling what you have so generously given me—the sense of your support and of the living vitality in your hearts of the great ideals which have made America the hope of the world.

The *Sussex* Affair

Washington, D.C.

April 19, 1916

THE TORPEDOING of the French liner *Sussex* by the Germans on March 24, 1916, ending a nine-month hiatus in submarine warfare and causing the deaths of some 80 persons, prompted this special address to Congress. Several Americans had been wounded, and Wilson was further angered by Germany's suggestion that the ship had been struck by a floating mine. On April 18 an official protest was sent to Berlin; the next day Wilson, speaking slowly and in a low voice, read the note to Congress, which applauded him. Nonetheless the Republican leaders insisted that Wilson wanted war and was using this incident to bring the country into the conflict. The imminent diplomatic rupture between Germany and the United States was temporarily forestalled when, on May 4, Germany promised that it would not sink merchant vessels without warning unless they resisted capture or tried to escape.

A situation has arisen in the foreign relations of the country of which it is my plain duty to inform you very frankly.

It will be recalled that in February 1915, the imperial German government announced its intention to treat the waters surrounding Great Britain and Ireland as embraced within the seat of war and to destroy all merchant ships owned by its enemies that might be found within any part of that portion of the high seas, and that it warned all vessels, of neutral as well as of belligerent ownership, to keep out of the waters it had thus proscribed or else enter them at their peril. The government of the United States earnestly protested. It took the position that such a policy could not be pursued without the practical certainty of gross and palpable violations of the law of nations, particularly if submarine craft were to be employed as its instruments, inasmuch as the rules prescribed by that law, rules founded upon principles of humanity and established for the protection of the lives of noncombatants at sea, could not in the nature of the case be observed by such vessels. It based its protest on the ground that persons of neutral nationality and vessels of neutral ownership would be exposed to extreme and intolerable risks, and that no right to close any part of the high seas against their use or to expose them to such risks could lawfully be asserted by any belligerent government. The law of nations in these matters, upon which the government of the United States based its protest, is not of recent origin or founded upon merely arbitrary principles set up by convention. It is based, on the contrary, upon mainfest and imperative principles of humanity and has long been established with the approval and by the express assent of all civilized nations.

Notwithstanding the earnest protest of our government, the imperial German government at once proceeded to carry out the policy it had announced. It expressed the hope that the dangers involved, at any rate the dangers to neutral vessels, would be reduced to a minimum by the instructions which it had issued to its submarine commanders, and assured the government of the United States that it would take every possible precaution both to respect the rights of neutrals and to safeguard the lives of noncombatants.

What has actually happened in the year which has since elapsed has shown that those hopes were not justified, those assurances insusceptible of being fulfilled. In pursuance of the policy of submarine warfare against the commerce of its adversaries, thus announced and entered upon by the imperial German government in despite of the solemn protest of this government, the commanders of German undersea vessels have attacked merchant ships with greater and greater activity, not only upon the high sea surrounding Great Britain and Ireland but wherever they could encounter them, in a way that has grown more and more ruthless, more and more indiscriminate as the months have gone by, less and less observant of restraints of any kind; and have delivered their attacks without compunction against vessels of every nationality and bound upon every sort of errand. Vessels of neutral ownership, even vessels of neutral ownership bound from neutral port to neutral port, have been destroyed along with vessels of belligerent ownership in constantly increasing numbers. Sometimes the merchantman attacked has been warned and summoned to surrender before being fired on or torpedoed; sometimes passengers or crews have been vouchsafed the poor security of being allowed to take to the ship's boats before she was sent to the bottom. But again and again no warning has been given, no escape even to the ship's boats allowed to those on board. What this government foresaw must happen has happened. Tragedy has followed tragedy on the seas in such fashion, with such attendant circumstances, as to make it grossly evident that warfare of such a sort, if warfare it be, cannot be carried on without the most palpable violation of the dictates alike of right and of humanity. Whatever the disposition and intention of the imperial German government, it has manifestly proved impossible for it to keep such methods of attack upon the commerce of its enemies within the bounds set by either the reason or the heart of mankind.

In February of the present year the imperial German government informed this government and the other neutral governments of the world that it had reason to believe that the government of Great Britain had armed all merchant vessels of British ownership and have given them secret orders to attack any submarine of the enemy they might encounter upon the seas, and that the imperial German government felt justified in the circumstances in treating all armed merchantmen of belligerent ownership as auxiliary vessels of war, which it would have the right to destroy without warning. The law of nations has long recognized the right of merchantmen to carry arms for protection and to use them to repel attack, although to use them, in such circumstances, at their own risk; but the imperial German government claimed the right to set these understanding aside in circumstances which it deemed extraordinary. Even the terms in which it announced its pupose thus still further to relax the restraints it had previously professed its willingness and desire to put upon the operation of its submarines carried the plain implication that at least vessels which were not armed would still be exempt from destruction without warning and that

personal safety would be accorded their passengers and crews; but even that limitation, if it was ever practicable to observe it, has in fact constituted no check at all upon the destruction of ships of every sort.

Again and again the imperial German government has given this government its solemn assurances that at least passenger ships would not be thus dealt with, and yet it has again and again permitted its undersea commanders to disregard those assurances with entire impunity. Great liners like the *Lusitania* and the *Arabic* and mere ferryboats like the *Sussex* have been attacked without a moment's warning, sometimes before they had even become aware that they were in the presence of an armed vessel of the enemy, and the lives of noncombatants, passengers, and crew have been sacrificed wholesale, in a manner which the government of the United States cannot but regard as wanton and without the slightest color of justification. No limit of any kind has in fact been set to the indiscriminate pursuit and destruction of merchantmen of all kinds and nationalities within the waters, constantly extending in area, where these operations have been carried on; and the roll of Americans who have lost their lives on ships thus attacked and destroyed has grown month by month until the ominous toll has mounted into the hundreds.

One of the latest and most shocking instances of this method of warfare was that of the destruction of the French cross channel steamer *Sussex*. It must stand forth, as the sinking of the steamer *Lusitania* did, as so singularly tragical and unjustifiable as to constitute a truly terrible example of the inhumanity of submarine warfare as the commanders of German vessels have for the past twelvemonth been conducting it. If this instance stood alone, some explanation, some disavowal by the German government, some evidence of criminal mistake or wilful disobedience on the part of the commander of the vessel that fired the torpedo might be sought or entertained; but unhappily it does not stand alone. Recent events make the conclusion inevitable that it is only one instance, even though it be one of the most extreme and distressing instances, of the spirit and method of warfare which the imperial German government has mistakenly adopted, and which from the first exposed that government to the reproach of thrusting all neutral rights aside in pursuit of its immediate objects.

The government of the United States has been very patient. At every stage of this distressing experience of tragedy after tragedy in which its own citizens were involved it has sought to be restrained from any extreme course of action or of protest by a thoughtful consideration of the extraordinary circumstances of this unprecedented war, and actuated in all that it said or did by the sentiments of genuine friendship which the people of the United States have always entertained and continue to entertain towards the German nation. It has of course accepted the successive explanations and assurances of the imperial German government as given in entire sincerity and good faith, and has hoped, even against hope, that it would prove to be possible for the German government so to order and control the acts of its naval commanders as to square its policy with the principles of humanity as embodied in the law of nations. It has been willing to wait until the significance of the facts became absolutely unmistakable and susceptible of but one interpretation.

That point has now unhappily been reached. The facts are susceptible of but one interpretation. The imperial German government has been unable to put any limits or restraints upon its warfare against either freight or passenger ships. It has therefore become painfully evident that the position which this government took at the very outset is inevitable, namely, that the use of submarines for the destruction of an enemy's commerce is of necessity, because of the very character of the vessels employed and the very methods of attack which their employment of course involves, incompatible with the principles of humanity, the long established and incontrovertible rights of neutrals, and the sacred immunities of noncombatants.

I have deemed it my duty, therefore, to say to the imperial German goverment that if it is still its purpose to prosecute relentless and indiscriminate warfare against vessels of commerce by the use of submarines, notwithstanding the now demonstrated impossibility of conducting that warfare in accordance with what the government of the United States must consider the sacred and indisputable rules of international law and the universally recognized dictates of humanity, the government of the United States is at last forced to the conclusion that there is but one course it can pursue; and that unless the imperial German government should now immediately declare and effect an abandonment of its present methods of warfare against passenger and freight carrying vessels this government can have no choice but to sever diplomatic relations with the government of the German empire altogether.

This decision I have arrived at with the keenest regret; the possibility of the action contemplated I am sure all thoughtful Americans will look forward to with unaffected reluctance. But we cannot forget that we are in some sort and by the force of circumstances the responsible spokesmen of the rights of humanity, and that we cannot remain silent while those rights seem in process of being swept utterly away in the maelstrom of this terrible war. We owe it to a due regard for our own rights as a nation, to our sense of duty as a representative of the rights of neutrals the world over, and to a just conception of the rights of mankind to take this stand now with the utmost solemnity and firmness.

I have taken it, and taken it in the confidence that it will meet with your approval and support. All soberminded men must unite in hoping that the imperial German government, which has in other circumstances stood as the champion of all that we are now contending for in the interest of humanity, may recognize the justice of our demands and meet them in the spirit in which they are made.

War Message

Washington, D.C.

April 2, 1917

AT THE END of January 1917 Germany unleashed its submarines against U.S. shipping. This action made it impossible, Wilson knew, to maintain even the appearance of American neutrality, and nullified all his delicate negotiations to keep out of the war. On April 2, in the packed chamber of the House of Representatives, he asked for a declaration of war against the Central Powers. Wilson spoke in a cold, deliberate voice, with characteristic self-mastery. A witness, Edwin A. Alderman, described him thus: "The air . . . was tense with emotion. . . . Wilson—the lithe figure, the bony structure of the forehead, the long, lean visage as of a Covenanter, somber with fixed purpose. . . . I was somehow reminded of the unbending lineaments and figure of Andrew Jackson, whom Woodrow Wilson resembled physically." Congress and the crowd in the gallery applauded him again and again, waving flags and cheering. "Think what it was they were applauding," Wilson later said, according to his secretary, Joseph Tumulty. "My message today was a message of death for our young men. How strange it seems to applaud that." Many of his contemporaries remarked that during the address Wilson attained the status of a true national leader.

Congress approved the war resolution on April 6. "The old isolation is finished," wrote Frank I. Cobb, editor of the *New York World*. "For weal or woe, whatever happens now concerns us, and from none of it can be withheld the force of our influence."

I have called the Congress into extraordinary session because there are serious, very serious, choices of policy to be made, and made immediately, which it was neither right nor constitutionally permissible that I should assume the responsibility of making.

On the third of February last I officially laid before you the extraordinary announcement of the imperial German government that on and after the first day of February it was its purpose to put aside all restraints of law or of humanity and use its submarines to sink every vessel that sought to approach either the ports of Great Britain and Ireland or the western coasts of Europe or any of the ports controlled by the enemies of Germany within the Mediterranean. That had seemed to be the object of the German submarine warfare earlier in the war, but since April of last year the imperial government had somewhat restrained the commanders of its undersea craft in conformity with its promise then given to us that passenger boats should not be sunk and that due warning would be given to all other vessels which its submarines might seek to destroy, when no resistance was offered or escape attempted, and care taken that their crews were given at least a fair chance to save their lives in their open boats. The precautions taken were meagre and haphazard

enough, as was proved in distressing instance after instance in the progress of the cruel and unmanly business, but a certain degree of restraint was observed. The new policy has swept every restriction aside. Vessels of every kind, whatever their flag, their character, their cargo, their destination, their errand, have been ruthlessly sent to the bottom without warning and without thought of help or mercy for those on board, the vessels of friendly neturals along with those of belligerents. Even hospital ships and ships carrying relief to the sorely bereaved and stricken people of Belgium, though the latter were provided with safe conduct through the proscribed areas by the German government itself and were distinguished by unmistakable marks of identity, have been sunk with the same reckless lack of compassion or of principle.

I was for a little while unable to believe that such things would in fact be done by any government that had hitherto subscribed to the humane practices of civilized nations. International law had its origin in the attempt to set up some law which would be respected and observed upon the seas, where no nation had right of dominion and where lay the free highways of the world. By painful stage after stage has that law been built up, with meagre enough results, indeed, after all was accomplished that could be accomplished, but always with a clear view, at least, of what the heart and conscience of mankind demanded. This minimum of right the German government has swept aside under the plea of retaliation and necessity and because it had no weapons which it could use at sea except these which it is impossible to employ as it is employing them without throwing to the winds all scruples of humanity or of respect for the understandings that were supposed to underlie the intercourse of the world. I am not now thinking of the loss of property involved, immense and serious as that is, but only of the wanton and wholesale destruction of the lives of noncombatants, men, women, and children, engaged in pursuits which have always, even in the darkest periods of modern history, been deemed innocent and legitimate. Property can be paid for; the lives of peaceful and innocent people cannot be. The present German submarine warfare against commerce is a warfare against mankind.

It is a war against all nations. American ships have been sunk, American lives taken, in ways which it has stirred us very deeply to learn of, but the ships and people of other neutral and friendly nations have been sunk and overwhelmed in the waters in the same way. There has been no discrimination. The challenge is to all mankind. Each nation must decide for itself how it will meet it. The choice we make for ourselves must be made with a moderation of counsel and a temperateness of judgment befitting our character and our motives as a nation. We must put excited feeling away. Our motive will not be revenge or the victorious assertion of the physical might of the nation, but only the vindication of right, of human right, of which we are only a single champion.

When I addressed the Congress on the 26th of February last I thought that it would suffice to assert our neutral rights with arms, our right to use the seas against unlawful violence. But armed neutrality, it now appears, is impracticable. Because submarines are in effect outlaws when used as the German submarines have been used against merchant shipping, it is impossible to defend ships against their attacks as the law of nations has assumed that merchantmen would defend themselves against privateers or cruisers, visible craft giving chase upon the open sea. It is common prudence in such circumstances, grim necessity indeed, to endeavor to destroy them before they have shown their own intention. They must be dealt with upon sight, if dealt with at all. The German government denies the right of neutrals to use arms at all within the areas of the sea which it has proscribed, even in the defense of rights which no modern publicist has ever before questioned their right to defend. The intimation is conveyed that the armed guards which we have placed on our merchant ships will be treated as beyond the pale of law and subject to be dealt with as pirates would be. Armed neutrality is ineffectual enough at best; in such circumstances and in the face of such pretensions it is worse than ineffectual; it is likely only to produce what it was meant to prevent; it is practically certain to draw us into the war without either the rights or the effectiveness of belligerents. There is one choice we cannot make, we are incapable of making: we will not choose the path of submission and suffer the most sacred rights of our nation and our people to be ignored or violated. The wrongs against which we now array ourselves are no common wrongs; they cut to the very roots of human life.

With a profound sense of the solemn and even tragical character of the step I am taking and of the grave responsibilities which it involves, but in unhesitating obedience to what I deem my constitutional duty, I advise that the Congress declare the recent course of the imperial German government to be in fact nothing less than war against the government and people of the United States; that it formally accept the status of belligerent which has thus been thrust upon it; and that it take immediate steps not only to put the country in a more thorough state of defense but also to exert all its power and employ all its resources to bring the government of the German empire to terms and end the war.

What this will involve is clear. It will involve the utmost practicable cooperation in counsel and action with the governments now at war with Germany, and, as incident to that, the extension to those governments of the most liberal financial credits, in order that our resources may so far as possible be added to theirs. It will involve the organization and mobilization of all the material resources of the country to supply the materials of war and serve the incidental needs of the nation in the most abundant and yet the most economical and efficient way possible. It will involve the immediate full equipment of the navy in all respects but particularly in supplying it with the best means of dealing with the enemy's submarines. It will involve the immediate addition to the armed forces of the United States already provided for by law in case of war at least 500,000 men, who should, in my opinion, be chosen upon the principle of universal liability to service, and also the authorization of subsequent additional increments of equal force so soon as they may be needed and can be handled in training. It will involve also, of course, the granting of adequate credits to the government, sustained, I hope, so far as they can equitably be sustained by the present generation, by well conceived taxation.

I say sustained so far as may be equitable by taxation because it seems to me that it would be most unwise to base the credits which will now be necessary entirely on money borrowed. It is our duty, I most respectfully urge, to protect our people so far as we may against the very serious hardships and evils which would be likely to arise out of the inflation which would be produced by vast loans.

In carrying out the measures by which these things are to be accomplished we should keep constantly in mind the wisdom of interfering as little as possible in our own preparation and in the equipment of our own military forces with the duty—for it will be a very practical duty—of supplying the nations already at war with Germany with the materials which they can obtain only from us or by our assistance. They are in the field and we should help them in every way to be effective there.

I shall take the liberty of suggesting, through the several executive departments of the government, for the consideration of your committees, measures for the accomplishment of the several objects I have mentioned. I hope that it will be your pleasure to deal with them as having been framed after very careful thought by the branch of the government upon which the responsibility of conducting the war and safeguarding the nation will most directly fall.

While we do these things, these deeply momentous things, let us be very clear, and make very clear to all the world what our motives and our objects are. My own thought has not been driven from its habitual and normal course by the unhappy events of the last two months, and I do not believe that the thought of the nation has been altered or clouded by them. I have exactly the same things in mind now that I had in mind when I addressed the Senate on the 22nd of January last; the same that I had in mind when I addressed the Congress on the 3rd of February and on the 26th of February. Our object now, as then, is to vindicate the principles of peace and justice in the life of the world as against selfish and autocratic power and to set up amongst the really free and self-governed people of the world such a concert of purpose and of action as will henceforth ensure the observance of those principles. Neutrality is no longer feasible or desirable where the peace of the world is involved and the freedom of its peoples, and the menace to that peace and freedom lies in the existence of autocratic governments backed by organized force which is controlled wholly by their will, not by the will of their people. We have seen the last of neutrality in such circumstance. We are at the beginning of an age in which it will be insisted that the same standards of conduct and of responsibility for wrong done shall be observed among nations and their governments that are observed among the individual citizens of civilized states.

We have no quarrel with the German people. We have no feeling towards them but one of sympathy and friendship. It was not upon their impulse that their government acted in entering this war. It was not with their previous knowledge or approval. It was a war determined upon as wars used to be determined upon in the old, unhappy days when peoples were nowhere consulted by their rulers and wars were provoked and waged in the interest of dynasties or of little groups of ambitious men who were accustomed to use their fellow men as pawns and tools. Self-governed nations do not fill their neighbour states with spies or set the course of intrigue to bring about some critical posture of affairs which will give them an opportunity to strike and make conquest. Such designs can be successfully worked out only under cover and where no one has the right to ask questions. Cunningly contrived plans of deception or aggression, carried, it may be, from generation to generation, can be worked out and kept from the light only within the privacy of courts or behind the carefully guarded confidences of a narrow and privileged class. They are happily impossible where public opinion commands and insists upon full information concerning all the nation's affairs.

A steadfast concert for peace can never be maintained except by a partnership of democratic nations. No autocratic government could be trusted to keep faith within it or observe its covenants. It must be a league of honour, a partnership of opinion. Intrigue would eat its vitals away; the plottings of inner circles who could plan what they would and render account to no one would be a corruption seated at its very heart. Only free peoples can hold their purpose and their honour steady to a common end and prefer the interests of mankind to any narrow interest of their own.

Does not every American feel that assurance has been added to our hope for the future peace of the world by the wonderful and heartening things that have been happening within the last few weeks in Russia? Russia was known by those who knew it best to have been always in fact democratic at heart, in all the vital habits of her thought, in all the intimate relationships of her people that spoke their natural instinct, their habitual attitude towards life. The autocracy that crowned the summit of her political structure, long as it had stood and terrible as was the reality of its power, was not in fact Russian in origin, character, or purpose; and now it has been shaken off and the great, generous Russian people have been added in all their naive majesty and might to the forces that are fighting for freedom in the world, for justice, and for peace. Here is a fit partner for a League of Honor.

One of the things that has served to convince us that the Prussian autocracy was not and could never be our friend is that from the very outset of the present war it has filled our unsuspecting communities and even our offices of government with spies and set criminal intrigues everywhere afoot against our national unity of counsel, our peace within and without, our industries and our commerce. Indeed it is now evident that its spies were here even before the war began; and it is unhappily not a matter of conjecture but a fact proved in our courts of justice that the intrigues which have more than once come perilously near to disturbing the peace and dislocating the industries of the country have been carried on at the instigation, with the support, and even under the personal direction of official agents of the imperial government accredited to the government of the United States. Even in checking these things and trying to extirpate them we have sought to put the most generous interpretation possible upon them because we knew that their source lay, not in any hostile feeling or purpose of the German people towards us (who were, no doubt as ignorant of them as we ourselves were), but only in the selfish designs of a government that did what it pleased and told its people nothing. But they have played their part in serving to convince us at last that that government entertains no real friendship for us and means to act against our peace and security at its convenience. That it means to stir up enemies against us at our very doors the intercepted note to the German minister at Mexico City is eloquent evidence.

We are accepting this challenge of hostile purpose because we know that in such a government, following such methods, we can never have a friend; and that in the presence of its organized power, always lying in wait to accomplish we know not what purpose, there can be no assured security for the democratic governments of the world. We are now about to accept gauge of battle with this natural foe to liberty and shall, if necessary, spend the whole force of the nation to check and nullify its pretensions and its power. We are glad, now that we see the facts with no veil of false pretence about them, to fight thus for the ultimate peace of the world and for the liberation of its peoples, the German peoples included: for the rights of nations great and small and the privilege of men everywhere to choose their way of life and of obedience. The world must be made safe for democracy. Its peace must be planted upon the tested foundations of political liberty. We have no selfish ends to serve. We desire no conquest, no dominion. We seek no indemnities for ourselves, no material compensation for the sacrifices we shall freely make. We are but one of the champions of the rights of mankind. We shall be satisfied when those rights have been made as secure as the faith and freedom of nations can make them.

Just because we fight without rancour and without selfish object, seeking nothing for ourselves but what we shall wish to share with all free peoples, we shall, I feel confident, conduct our operations as belligerents without passion and ourselves observe with proud punctilio the principles of right and of fair play we profess to be fighting for.

I have said nothing of the governments allied with the imperial government of Germany because they have not made war upon us or challenged us to defend our right and our honour. The Austro-Hungarian government has, indeed, avowed its unqualified endorsement and acceptance of the reckless and lawless submarine warfare adopted now without disguise by the imperial German government, and it has therefore not been possible for this government to receive Count Tarnowski, the ambassador recently accredited to this government by the imperial and royal government of Austria-Hungary; but that government has not actually engaged in warfare against citizens of the United States on the seas, and I take the liberty, for the present at least, of postponing a discussion of our relations with the authorities at Vienna. We enter this war only where we are clearly forced into it because there are no other means of defending our rights.

It will be all the easier for us to conduct ourselves as belligerents in a high spirit of right and fairness because we act without animus, not in enmity towards a people or with the desire to bring any injury or disadvantage upon them, but only in armed opposition to an irresponsible government which has thrown aside all considerations of humanity and of right and is running amuck. We are, let me say again, the sincere friends of the German people, and shall desire nothing so much as the early reestablishment of intimate relations of mutual advantage between us—however hard it may be for them, for the time being, to believe that this is spoken from our hearts. We have borne with their present government through all these bitter months because of that friendship—exercising a patience and forbearance which would otherwise have

been impossible. We shall, happily, still have an opportunity to prove that friendship in our daily attitude and actions towards the millions of men and women of German birth and native sympathy who live amongst us and share our life, and we shall be proud to prove it towards all who are in fact loyal to their neighbours and to the government in the hour of test. They are, most of them, as true and loyal Americans as if they had never known any other fealty or allegiance. They will be prompt to stand with us in rebuking and restraining the few who may be of a different mind and purpose. If there should be disloyalty, it will be dealt with a firm hand of stern repression; but, if it lifts its head at all, it will fit it only here and there and without countenance except from a lawless and malignant few.

It is a distressing and oppressive duty, gentlemen of the Congress, which I have performed in thus addressing you. There are, it may be, many months of fiery trial and sacrifice ahead of us. It is a fearful thing to lead this great peaceful people into war, into the most terrible and disastrous of all wars, civilization itself seeming to be in the balance. But the right is more precious than peace, and we shall fight for the things which we have always carried nearest our hearts—for democracy, for the right of those who submit to authority to have a voice in their own governments, for the rights and liberties of small nations, for a universal dominion of right by such a concert of free peoples as shall bring peace and safety to all nations and make the world itself at last free. To such a task we can dedicate our lives and our fortunes, everything that we are and everything that we have, with the pride of those who know that the day has come when America is privileged to spend her blood and her might for the principles that gave her birth and happiness and the peace which she has treasured. God helping her, she can do no other.

The Fourteen Points

Washington, D.C.

January 8, 1918

THE IMMEDIATE IMPETUS for this speech was the recent revelation of secret treaties among several of the Allies by which they agreed to divide up the territories and wealth of the conquered nations. Wilson saw in these revelations the chance to articulate an alternative American position free of nationalism or greed. His plan, two years in the making, articulated 14 war aims, including one advocating "open covenants of peace, openly arrived at."

The text was drafted over the course of a week by Wilson and his confidant and adviser Col. Edward House and was delivered by the president before the combined houses of Congress. It was Wilson's supreme moment as a prophet of peace; Arthur Link, his biographer, called the speech "a bold projection of American philosophy into world affairs." To the Allies, however, the Fourteen Points were simply too utopian to accept. In a famous remark, the premier of France, Georges Clemenceau, noted that God had imposed only 10 commandments.

Once more, as repeatedly before, the spokesmen of the Central Empires have indicated their desire to discuss the objects of the war and the possible bases of a general peace. Parleys have been in progress at Brest-Litovsk between representatives of the Central Powers to which the attention of all the belligerents has been invited for the purpose of ascertaining whether it may be possible to extend these parleys into a general conference with regard to terms of peace and settlement. The Russian representatives presented not only a perfectly definite statement of the principles upon which they would be willing to conclude peace but also an equally definite program of the concrete application of those principles. The representatives of the Central Powers, on their part, presented an outline of settlement which, if much less definite, seemed susceptible of liberal interpretation until their specific program of practical terms was added. That program proposed no concessions at all either to the sovereignty of Russia or to the preferences of the populations with whose fortunes it dealt, but meant, in a word, that the Central Empires were to keep every foot of territory their armed forces had occupied—every province, every city, every point of vantage—as a permanent addition to their territories and their power. It is a reasonable conjecture that the general principles of settlement which they at first suggested originated with the more liberal statesmen of Germany and Austria, the men who have begun to feel the force of their own peoples' thought and purpose, while the concrete terms of actual settlement came from the military leaders who have no thought but to keep what they have got. The negotiations have been broken off. The Russian representatives were sincere and in earnest. They cannot entertain such proposals of conquest and domination.

The whole incident is full of significance. It is also full of perplexity. With whom are the Russian representatives dealing? For whom are the representatives of the Central Empires speaking? Are they speaking for the majorities of their respective parliaments or for the minority parties, that military and imperialistic minority which has so far dominated their whole policy and controlled the affairs of Turkey and of the Balkan States which have felt obliged to become their associates in this war? The Russian representatives have insisted, very justly, very wisely, and in the true spirit of modern democracy, that the conferences they have been holding with the Teutonic and Turkish statesmen should be held within open, not closed, doors, and all the world has been audience, as was desired. To whom have we been listening, then? To those who speak the spirit and intention of the Resolutions of the German Reichstag of the ninth of July last, the spirit and intention of the liberal leaders and parties of Germany, or to those who resist and defy that spirit and intention and insist upon conquest and subjugation? Or are we listening, in fact to both, unreconciled and in open and hopeless contradiction? These are very serious and pregnant questions. Upon the answer to them depends the peace of the world.

But, whatever the results of the parleys at Brest-Litovsk, whatever the confusions of counsel and of purpose in the utterances of the spokesmen of the Central Empires, they have again attempted to acquaint the world with their objects in the war and have again challenged their adversaries to say what their objects are and what sort of settlement they would deem just and satisfactory. There is no good reason why that challenge should not be responded to, and responded to with the utmost candor. We did not wait for it. Not once, but again and again, we have laid our whole thought and purpose before the world, not in general terms only, but each time with sufficient definition to make it clear what sort of definitive terms of settlement must necessarily spring out of them. Within the last week Mr. Lloyd George has spoken with admirable candor and in admirable spirit for the people and government of Great Britain. There is no confusion of counsel among the adversaries of the Central Powers, no uncertainty of principle, no vagueness of detail. The only secrecy of counsel, the only lack of fearless frankness, the only failure to make definite statement of the objects of the war, lies with Germany and her allies. The issues of life and death hang upon these definitions. No statesman who has the least conception of his responsibility ought for a moment to permit himself to continue this tragical and appalling outpouring of blood and treasure unless he is sure beyond a peradventure that the objects of the vital sacrifice are part and parcel of the very life of society and that the people for whom he speaks think them right and imperative as he does.

There is, moreover, a voice calling for these definitions of principle and of purpose which is, it seems to me, more thrilling and more compelling than any of the many moving voices with which the troubled air of the world is filled. It is the voice of the Russian people. They are prostrate and all but helpless, it would seem, before the grim power of Germany, which has hitherto known no relenting and no pity. Their power, apparently, is shattered. And yet their soul is not subservient. They will not yield either in principle or in action. Their conception of what is right, of what it is humane and

honorable for them to accept, has been stated with a frankness, a largeness of view, a generosity of spirit, and a universal human sympathy which must challenge the admiration of every friend of mankind; and they have refused to compound their ideal or desert others that they themselves may be safe. They call to us to say what it is that we desire, in what, if anything, our purpose and our spirit differ from theirs and I believe that the people of the United States would wish me to respond, with utter simplicity and frankness. Whether their present leaders believe it or not it is our heartfelt desire and hope that some way may be opened whereby we may be privileged to assist the people of Russia to attain their utmost hope of liberty and ordered peace.

It will be our wish and purpose that the processes of peace, when they are begun, shall be absolutely open and that they shall involve and permit henceforth no secret understandings of any kind. The day of conquest and aggrandizement is gone by; so is also the day of secret covenants entered into in the interest of particular governments and likely at some unlooked-for moment to upset the peace of the world. It is this happy fact, now clear to the view of every public man whose thoughts do not still linger in an age that is dead and gone, which makes it possible for every nation whose purposes are consistent with justice and the peace of the world to avow now or at any other time the objects it has in view.

We entered this war because violations of right had occurred which touched us to the quick and made the life of our own people impossible unless they were corrected and the world secured once for all against their recurrence. What we demand in this war, therefore, is nothing peculiar to ourselves. It is that the world be made fit and safe to live in; and particularly that it be made safe for every peace-loving nation which, like our own, wishes to live its own life, determine its own institutions, be assured of justice and fair dealing by the other peoples of the world as against force and selfish aggression. All the peoples of the world are in effect partners in this interest, and for our own part we see very clearly that unless justice be done to others it will not be done to us. The program of the world's peace, therefore, is our program;

and that program, the only possible program, as we see it, is this:

I. Open covenants of peace, openly arrived at, after which there shall be no private international understandings of any kind but diplomacy shall proceed always frankly and in the public view.

II. Absolute freedom of navigation upon the seas, outside territorial waters, alike in peace and in war, except as the seas may be closed in whole or in part by international action for the enforcement of international covenants.

III. The removal, so far as possible, of all economic barriers and the establishment of an equality of trade conditions among all the nations consenting to the peace and associating themselves for its maintenance.

IV. IV.Adequate guarantees given and taken that national armaments will be reduced to the lowest point consistent with domestic safety.

V. A free, open-minded, and absolutely impartial adjustment of all colonial claims, based upon a strict observance of the principle that in determining all such questions of sovereignty the interests of the populations concerned must have equal weight with the equitable claims of the government whose title is to be determined.

VI. The evacuation of all Russian territory and such a settlement of all questions affecting Russia as will secure the best and freest cooperation of the other nations of the world in obtaining for her an unhampered and unembarrassed opportunity for the independent determination of her own political development and national policy and assure her of a sincere welcome into the society of free nations under institutions of her own choosing; and, more than a welcome, assistance also of every kind that she may need and may herself desire. The treatment accorded Russia by her sister nations in the months to come will be the acid test of their goodwill, of their comprehension of her need as distinguished from their own interests, and of the intelligent and unselfish sympathy.

VII. Belgium, the whole world will agree, must be evacuated and restored, without any attempt to limit the sovereignty which she enjoys in common with all other free nations. No other single act will serve as this will serve to restore confidence among the nations in the laws which they have themselves set and determined for the government of their relations with one another. Without this healing act the whole structure and validity of international law is forever impaired.

VIII. All French territory should be freed and invaded portions restored, and the wrong done to France by Prussia in 1871 in the matter of Alsace-Lorraine, which has unsettled the peace of the world for nearly 50 years, should be righted, in order that peace may once more be made secure in the interest of all.

IX. A readjustment of the frontiers of Italy should be effected along clearly recognizable lines of nationality.

X. The peoples of Austria-Hungary, whose place among the nations we wish to see safeguarded and assured, should be accorded the freest opportunity of autonomous development.

XI. Rumania, Serbia, and Montenegro should be evacuated; occupied territories restored; Serbia accorded free and secure access to the sea; and the relations of the several Balkan States to one another determined by friendly counsel along historically established lines of allegiance and nationality; and international guarantees of the political and economic independence and territorial integrity of the several Balkan States should be entered into.

XII. The Turkish portions of the present Ottoman Empire should be assured a secure sovereignty, but the other nationalities which are now under Turkish rule should be assured an undoubted security of life and an absolutely unmolested opportunity of autonomous development, and the Dardanelles should be permanently opened as a free passage to the ships and commerce of all nations under international guarantees.

XIII. An independent Polish state should be erected which should include the territories inhabited by indisputably Polish populations, which should be assured a free and secure access to the sea, and whose political and economic independence and territorial integrity should be guaranteed by international covenant.

XIV. A general association of nations must be formed under specific covenants for the purpose of affording mutual guarantees of political independence and territorial integrity to great and small states alike.

In regard to these essential rectifications of wrong and assertions of right we feel ourselves to be intimate partners of all the governments and peoples associated together against the imperialists. We cannot be separated in interest or divided in purpose. We stand together until the end.

For such arrangements and covenants we are willing to fight and to continue to fight until they are achieved; but only because we wish the right to prevail and desire a just and stable peace such as can be secured only by removing the chief provocations to war, which this program does remove. We have no jealousy of German greatness, and there is nothing in this program that impairs it. We grudge her no achievement or distinction of learning or of pacific enterprise such as have made her record very bright and very enviable. We do not wish to injure her or to block in any way her legitimate influence or power. We do not wish to fight her either with arms or with hostile arrangements of trade if she is willing to associate herself with us and the other peace-loving nations of the world in covenants of justice and law and fair dealing. We wish her only to accept a place of equality among the peoples of the world—the new world in which we now live—instead of a place of mastery.

Neither do we presume to suggest to her any alteration or modification of her institutions. But it is necessary, we must frankly say, and necessary as a preliminary to any intelligent dealings with her on our part that we should know whom her spokesmen speak for when they speak to us, whether for the Reichstag majority or for the military party and the men whose creed is imperial domination.

We have spoken now, surely, in terms too concrete to admit of any further doubt or question. An evident principle runs through the whole program I have outlined. It is the principle of justice to all peoples and nationalities, and their right to live on equal terms of liberty and safety with one another, whether they be strong or weak. Unless this principle be made its foundation no part of the structure of international justice can stand. The people of the United States could act upon no other principle; and to the vindication of this principle they are ready to devote their lives, their honor, and everything that they possess. The moral climax of this the culminating and final war for human liberty has come, and they are ready to put their own strength, their own highest purpose, their own integrity and devotion to the test.

Sixth Annual Message

Washington, D.C.
December 2, 1918

MOST OF WILSON'S annual messages focused on a specific plan of action—for example, revision of the tariff in his first message—but this speech was more wide-ranging and speculative. With the war over, Wilson sought to place the great conflict in historical perspective and link it with the domestic problems that the war had left behind. But his ability to take effective executive action had ebbed. The breaches of basic freedoms his administration had allowed for the sake of the war effort alienated many voters and hurt his image. After the election of 1918, despite a public appeal by the president to return a Democratic majority to Congress, the Republicans held control of both houses. The legislative successes of his first few years as president were no longer possible, and Wilson became increasingly occupied with the greater goal of world peace.

This was the last annual message Wilson delivered in person. He suffered a paralyzing stroke in 1919.

The year that has elapsed since I last stood before you to fulfill my constitutional duty to give to the Congress from time to time information on the state of the Union has been so crowded with great events, great processes, and great results that I cannot hope to give you an adequate picture of its transactions or of the far-reaching changes which have been wrought in the life of our nation and of the world. You have yourselves witnessed these things, as I have. It is too soon to assess them; and we who stand in the midst of them and are part of them are less qualified than men of another generation will be to say what they mean, or even what they have been. But some great outstanding facts are unmistakable and constitute, in a sense, part of the public business with which it is our duty to deal. To state them is to set the stage for the legislative and executive action which must grow out of them and which we have yet to shape and determine.

A year ago we had sent 145,918 men overseas. Since then we have sent 1,950,513, an average of 162,542 each month, the number in fact rising, in May last to 245,951, in June to 278,760, in July to 307,182, and continuing to reach similar figures in August and September—in August 289,570 and in September 257,438. No such movement of troops ever took place before, across 3,000 miles of sea, followed by adequate equipment and supplies, and carried safely through extraordinary dangers of attack—dangers which were alike strange and infinitely difficult to guard against. In all this movement only 758 men were lost by enemy attack, 630 of whom were upon a single English transport which was sunk near the Orkney Islands.

I need not tell you what lay back of this great movement of men and material. It is not invidious to say that back of it lay a supporting organization of the industries of the country and of all its productive activities more complete, more thorough in method and effective in result, more spirited and unanimous in purpose and effort than any other great belligerent had been able to effect. We profited greatly by the experience of the nations which had already been engaged for nearly three years in the exigent and exacting business, their every resource and every executive proficiency taxed to the utmost. We were their pupils. But we learned quickly and acted with a promptness and a readiness of cooperation that justify our great pride that we were able to serve the world with unparalleled energy and quick accomplishment.

But it is not the physical scale and executive efficiency of preparation, supply, equipment, and dispatch that I would dwell upon, but the mettle and quality of the officers and men we sent over and of the sailors who kept the seas, and the spirit of the nation that stood behind them. No soldiers or sailors ever proved themselves more quickly ready for the test of battle or acquitted themselves with more splendid courage and achievement when put to the test. Those of us who played some part in directing the great processes by which the war was pushed irresistibly forward to

431

the final triumph may now forget all that and delight our thoughts with the story of what our men did. Their officers understood the grim and exacting task they had undertaken and performed it with an audacity, efficiency, and unhesitating courage that touch the story of convoy and battle with imperishable distinction at every turn, whether the enterprise were great or small—from their great chiefs, Pershing and Sims, down to the youngest lieutenant; and their men were worthy of them— such terrible adventure blithely and with the quick intelligence of those who know just what it is they would accomplish. I am proud to be fellow countryman of men of such stuff and valor. Those of us who stayed at home did our duty; the war could not have been won or the gallant men who fought it given their opportunity to win it otherwise; but for many a long day we shall think ourselves "accurs'd we were not there, and hold our manhoods cheap while any speaks that fought" with these at St. Mihiel or Thierry. The memory of those days of triumphant battle will go with these fortunate men to their graves; and each will have his favorite memory. "Old men forget; yet all shall be forgot, but he'll remember with advantages what feats he did that day!"

What we all thank God for with deepest gratitude is that our men went in force into the line of battle just at the critical moment when the whole fate of the world seemed to hang in the balance and threw their fresh strength into the ranks of freedom in time to turn the whole tide and sweep of the fateful struggle—turn it once for all, so that thenceforth it was back, back, back for their enemies, always back, never again forward! After that it was only a scant four months before the commanders of the Central Empires knew themselves beaten; and now their very empires are in liquidation!

And throughout it all how fine the spirit of the nation was: what unity of purpose, what untiring zeal! What elevation of purpose ran through all its splendid display of strength, its untiring accomplishment. I have said that those of us who stayed at home to do the work of organization and supply will always wish that we had been with the men whom we sustained by our labor; but we can never be ashamed. It has been an inspiring thing to be here in the midst of fine men who had turned aside from every private interest of their own

and devoted the whole of their trained capacity to the tasks that supplied the sinews of the whole great undertaking! The patriotism, the unselfishness, the thoroughgoing devotion and distinguished capacity that marked their toilsome labors, day after day, month after month, have made them fit mates and comrades of the men in the trenches and on the sea. And not the men here in Washington only. They have but directed the vast achievement. Throughout innumerable factories, upon inumerable farms, in the depths of coal mines and iron mines and copper mines, wherever the stuffs of industry were to be obtained and prepared, in the shipyards, on the railways, at the docks, on the sea, in every labor that was needed to sustain the battle lines, men have vied with each other to do their part and do it well. They can look any man-at-arms in the face, and say, We also strove to win and gave the best that was in us to make our fleets and armies sure of their triumph!

And what shall we say of the women—of their instant intelligence, quickening every task that they touched; their capacity for organization and cooperation, which gave their action discipline and enhanced the effectiveness of everything they attempted; their aptitude at tasks to which they had never before set their hands; their utter self-sacrifice alike in what they did and in what they gave? Their contribution to the great result is beyond appraisal. They have added a new luster to the annals of American womanhood.

The least tribute we can pay them is to make them the equals of men in political rights as they have proved themselves their equals in every field of practical work they have entered, whether for themselves or for their country. These great days of completed achievement would be sadly marred were we to omit that act of justice. Besides the immense practical services they have rendered, the women of the country have been the moving spirits in the systematic economies by which our people have voluntarily assisted to supply the suffering peoples of the world and the armies upon every front with food and everything else that we had that might serve the common cause. The details of such a story can never be fully written, but we carry them at our hearts and thank God that we can say that we are the kinsmen of such.

And now we are sure of the great triumph for which every sacrifice was made. It has come, come in its completeness, and with the pride and inspiration of these days of achievement quick within us we turn to the tasks of peace again—a peace secure against the violence of irresponsible monarchs and ambitious military coteries and made ready for a new order, for new foundations of justice and fair dealing.

We are about to give order and organization to this peace not only for ourselves but for the other peoples of the world as well, so far as they will suffer us to serve them. It is international justice that we seek, not domestic safety merely. Our thoughts have dwelt of late upon Europe, upon Asia, upon the Near and the Far East, very little upon the acts of peace and accommodation that wait to be performed at our own doors. While we are adjusting our relations with the rest of the world is it not of capital importance that we should clear away all grounds of misunderstanding with our immediate neighbors and give proof of the friendship we really feel? I hope that the members of the Senate will permit me to speak once more of the unratified treaty of friendship and adjustment with the republic of Colombia. I very earnestly urge upon them an early and favorable action upon that vital matter. I believe that they will feel, with me, that the stage of affairs is now set for such action as will be not only just but generous and in the spirit of the new age upon which we have so happily entered.

So far as our domestic affairs are concerned the problem of our return to peace is a problem of economic and industrial readjustment. That problem is less serious for us than it may turn out to be for the nations which have suffered the disarrangements and the losses of war longer than we. Our people, moreover, do not wait to be coached and led. They know their own business, are quick and resourceful at every readjustment, definite in purpose, and self-reliant in action. Any leading strings we might seek to put them in would speedily become hopelessly tangled because they would pay no attention to them and go their own way. All that we can do as their legislative and executive servants is to mediate the process of change here, there, and elsewhere as we may. I have heard much counsel as to the plans that should be formed and personally

conducted to a happy consummation, but from no quarter have I seen any general scheme of "reconstruction" emerge which I thought it likely we could force our spirited businessmen and self-reliant laborers to accept with due pliancy and obedience.

While the war lasted we set up many agencies by which to direct the industries of the country in the services it was necessary for them to render, by which to make sure of an abundant supply of the materials needed, by which to check undertakings that could for the time be dispensed with and stimulate those that were most serviceable in war, by which to gain for the purchasing departments of the governments a certain control over the prices of essential articles and materials, by which to restrain trade with alien enemies, make the most of the available shipping, and systematize financial transactions, both public and private, so that there would be no unnecessary conflict or confusion—by which, in short, to put every material energy of the country in harness to draw the common load and make of us one team in the accomplishment of a great task. But the moment we knew the armistice to have been signed we took the harness off. Raw materials upon which the government had kept its hand for fear there should not be enough for the industries that supplied the armies have been released and put into the general market again. Great industrial plants whose whole output and machinery had been taken over for the uses of the government have been set free to return to the uses to which they were put before the war. It has not been possible to remove so readily or so quickly the control of foodstuffs and of shipping, because the world has still to be fed from our granaries and the ships are still needed to send supplies to our men overseas and to bring the men back as fast as the disturbed conditions on the other side of the water permit; but even there restraints are being relaxed as much as possible and more and more as the weeks go by.

Never before have there been agencies in existence in this country which knew so much of the field of supply, of labor, and of industry as the War Industries Board, the War Trade Board, the Labor Department, the Food Administration, and the Fuel Administration, have know since their labors became thoroughly systematized; and they have not been isolated agencies; they have been directed by men who represented the permanent departments of the government and so have been the centers of unified and cooperative action. It has been the policy of the executive, therefore, since the armistice was assured (which is in effect a complete submission of the enemy) to put the knowledge of these bodies at the disposal of the business men of the country and to offer their intelligent mediation at every point and in every matter where it was desired. It is surprising how fast the process of return to a peace footing has moved in the three weeks since the fighting stopped. It promises to outrun any inquiry that may be instituted and any aid that may be offered. It will not be easy to direct it any better than it will direct itself. The American businessman is of quick initiative.

The ordinary and normal processes of private initiative will not, however, provide immediate employment for all of the men of our returning armies. Those who are of trained capacity, those who are skilled workmen, those who have acquired familiarity with established businesses, those who are ready and willing to go to the farms, all those whose aptitudes are known or will be sought out by employers will find no difficulty, it is safe to say, in finding place and employment. But there will be others who will be at a loss where to gain a livelihood unless pains are taken to guide them and put them in the way of work. There will be a large floating residuum of labor which should not be left wholly to shift for itself. It seems to me important, therefore, that the development of public works of every sort should be promptly resumed, in order that opportunities should be created for unskilled labor in particular, and that plans should be made for such development of our unused lands and our natural resources as we have hitherto lacked stimulation to undertake.

I particularly direct your attention to the very practical plans which the secretary of the interior has developed in his annual report and before your committees for the reclamation of arid, swamp, and cut-over lands which might, if the states were willing and able to cooperate, redeem some 300 million acres of land for cultivation. There are said to be 15 or 20 million acres of land in the West, at present arid, for whose reclamation water is available, if properly conserved. There are about 230 million acres from which the forests have been cut but which have never yet been cleared for the plow and which lie waste and desolate. These lie scattered all over the Union. And there are nearly 80 million acres of land that lie under swamps or subject to periodical overflow or too wet for anything but grazing which it is perfectly feasible to drain and protect and redeem. The Congress can at once direct thousands of the returning soldiers to the reclamation of the arid lands which it has already undertaken, if it will but enlarge the plans and the appropriations which it has intrusted to the Department of the Interior. It is possible in dealing with our unused land to effect a great rural and agricultural development which will afford the best sort of opportunity to men who want to help themselves; and the secretary of the interior has thought the possible methods out in a way which is worthy of your most friendly attention.

I have spoken of the control which must yet for a while, perhaps for a long while, be exercised over shipping because of the priority of service to which our forces overseas are entitled and which should also be accorded the shipments which are to save recently liberated peoples from starvation and many devasted regions from permanent ruin. May I not say a special word about the needs of Belgium and northern France? No sums of money paid by way of indemnity will serve of themselves to save them from hopeless disadvantage for years to come. Something more must be done than merely find the money. If they had money and raw materials in abundance tomorrow they could not resume their place in the industry of the world tomorrow—the very important place they held before the flame of war swept across them. Many of their factories are razed to the ground. Much of their machinery is destroyed or has been taken away. Their people are scattered and many of their best workmen are dead. Their markets will be taken by others, if they are not in some special way assisted to rebuild their factories and replace their lost instruments of manufacture. They should not be left to the vicissitudes of the sharp competition for materials and for industrial facilities which is now to set in. I hope, therefore, that the Congress will not be unwilling, if it should become necessary, to grant to some such agency as the War Trade Board the right to establish priorities of export and supply for the benefit of these people whom we have been so happy to assist in saving from the German terror and whom we must not now thoughtlessly leave to shift for themselves in a pitiless competitive market.

For the steadying and facilitation of our own domestic business readjustments nothing is more important than the immediate determination of the taxes that are to be levied for 1918, 1919, and 1920. As much of the burden of taxation must be lifted from business as sound methods of financing the government will permit, and those who conduct the great essential industries of the country must be told as exactly as possible what obligations to the government they will be expected to meet in the years immediately ahead of them. It will be of serious consequence to the country to delay removing all uncertainties in this matter a single day longer than the right processes of debate justify. It is idle to talk of successful and confident business reconstruction before those uncertainties are resolved.

If the war had continued it would have been necessary to raise at least 8 billion dollars by taxation payable in the year 1919; but the war has ended and I agree with the secretary of the Treasury that it will be safe to reduce the amount to 6 billions. An immediate rapid decline in the expenses of the government is not to be looked for. Contracts made for war supplies will, indeed, be rapidly canceled and liquidated, but their immediate liquidation will make heavy drains on the Treasury for the months just ahead of us. The maintenance of our forces on the other side of the sea is still necessary. A considerable proportion of those forces must remain in Europe during the period of occupation, and those which are brought home will be transported and demobilized at heavy expense for months to come. The interest on our war debt must of course be paid and provision made for the retirement of the obligations of the government which represent it. But these demands will of course fall much below what a continuation of military operations would have entailed and 6 billions should suffice to supply a sound foundation for their financial operations of the year.

I entirely concur with the secretary of the Treasury in recommending that the 2 billions needed in addition to the 4 billions provided by existing law be obtained from the profits which have accrued and shall accrue from

war contracts and distinctively war business, but that these taxes be confined to the war profits accruing in 1918, or in 1919 from business originating in war contracts. I urge your acceptance of his recommendation that provision be made now, not subsequently, that the taxes to be paid in 1920 should be reduced from 6 to 4 billions. Any arrangements less definite than these would add elements of doubt and confusion to the critical period of industrial readjustment through which the country must now immediately pass, and which no true friend of the nation's essential business interests can afford to be responsible for creating or prolonging. Clearly determined conditions, clearly and simply charted, are indispensable to the economic revival and rapid industrial development which may confidently be expected if we act now and sweep all interrogation points away.

I take it for granted that the Congress will carry out the naval program which was undertaken before we entered the war. The secretary of the navy has submitted to your committees for authorization that part of the program which covers the building plans of the next three years. These plans have been prepared along the lines and in accordance with the policy which the Congress established, not under the exceptional conditions of the war, but with the intention of adhering to a definite method of development for the navy I earnestly recommend the uninterrupted pursuit of that policy. It would clearly be unwise for us to attempt to adjust our programs to a future world policy as yet undetermined.

The question which causes me the greatest concern is the question of the policy to be adopted towards the railroads. I frankly turn to you for counsel upon it. I have no confident judgment of my own. I do not see how any thoughtful man can have who knows anything of the complexity of the problem. It is a problem which must be studied, studied immediately, and studied without bias or prejudice. Nothing can be gained by becoming partisans of any particular plan of settlement.

It was necessary that the administration of the railways should be taken over by the government so long as the war lasted. It would have been impossible otherwise to establish and carry through under a single direction the necessary priorities of shipment. It would have been impossible otherwise to combine maximum production at the factories and mines and farms with the maximum possible car supply to take the products to the ports and markets; impossible to route troop shipments and freight shipments without regard to the advantage or disadvantage of the roads employed; impossible to subordinate, when necessary, all questions of convenience to the public necessity; impossible to give the necessary financial support to the roads from the public Treasury. But all these necessities have now been served, and the question is, what is best for the railroads and for the public in the future.

Exceptional circumstances and exceptional methods of administration were not needed to convince us that the railroads were not equal to the immense tasks of transportation imposed upon them by the rapid and continuous development of the industries of the country. We knew that already. And we knew that they were unequal to it partly because their full cooperation was rendered impossible by law and their competition made obligatory, so that it has been impossible to assign to them severally the traffic which could best be carried by their respective lines in the interests of expedition and national economy.

We may hope, I believe, for the formal conclusion of the war by treaty by the time spring has come. The 21 months to which the present control of the railways is limited after formal proclamation of peace shall have been made will run at the farthest, I take it for granted, only to the January of 1921. The full equipment of the railways which the federal administration had planned could not be completed within any such period. The present law does not afford sufficient authority to undertake improvements upon the scale upon which it would be necessary to undertake them. Every approach to this difficult subject-matter of decision brings us face to face, therefore, with this unanswered question: What is it right that we should do with the railroads, in the interest of the public and in fairness to their owners?

Let me say at once that I have no answer ready. The only thing that is perfectly clear to me is that it is not fair either to the public or to the owners of the railroads to leave the question unanswered and that it will presently become my duty to relinquish control of the roads, even before the expiration of the statutory period, unless there should appear some

clear prospect in the meantime of a legislative solution. Their release would at least produce one element of a solution, namely certainty and a quick stimulation of private initiative.

I believe that it will be serviceable for me to set forth as explicitly as possible the alternative courses that lie open to our choice. We can simply release the roads and go back to the old conditions of private management, unrestricted competition, and multiform regulation by both state and federal authorities; or we can go to the opposite extreme and establish complete government control, accompanied, if necessary, by actual government ownership; or we can adopt an intermediate course of modified private control, under a more unified and affirmative public regulation and under such alterations of the law as will permit wasteful competition to be avoided and a considerable degree of unification of administration to be effected, as, for example, by regional corporations under which the railways of definable areas would be in effect combined in single systems.

The one conclusion that I am ready to state with confidence is that it would be a disservice alike to the country and to the owners of the railroads to return to the old conditions unmodified. Those are conditions of restraint without development. There is nothing affirmative or helpful about them. What the country chiefly needs is that all its means of transportation should be developed, its railways, its waterways, its highways, and its countryside roads. Some new element of policy, therefore, is absolutely necessary—necessary for the service of the public, necessary for the release of credit to those who are administering the railways, necessary for the protection of their security holders. The old policy may be changed much or little, but surely it cannot wisely be left as it was. I hope that the Congress will have a complete and impartial study of the whole problem instituted at once and prosecuted as rapidly as possible. I stand ready and anxious to release the roads from the present control and I must do so at a very early date if by waiting until the statutory limit of time is reached I shall be merely prolonging the period of doubt and uncertainty which is hurtful to every interest concerned.

I welcome this occasion to announce to the Congress my purpose to join in Paris the representatives of the governments with which we have been associated in the war against the Central Empires for the purpose of discussing with them the main features of the treaty of peace. I realize the great inconveniences that will attend my leaving the country, particularly at this time, but the conclusion that it was my paramount duty to go has been forced upon me by considerations which I hope will seem as conclusive to you as they have seemed to me.

The allied governments have accepted the bases of peace which I outlined to the Congress on the eighth of January last, as the Central Empires also have, and very reasonably desire my personal counsel in their interpretation and application, and it is highly desirable that I should give it in order that the sincere desire of our government to contribute without selfish purpose of any kind to settlements that will be of common benefit to all the nations concerned may be made fully manifest. The peace settlements which are now to be agreed upon are of transcendent importance both to us and to the rest of the world, and I know of no business or interest which should take precedence of them. The gallant men of our armed forces on land and sea have consciously fought for the ideals which they knew to be the ideals of their country; I have sought to express those ideals; they have accepted my statements of them as the substance of their own thought and purpose, as the associated governments have accepted them; I owe it to them to see to it, so far as in me lies, that no false or mistaken interpretation is put upon them, and no possible effort omitted to realize them. It is now my duty to play my full part in making good what they offered their life's blood to obtain. I can think of no call to service which could transcend this.

I shall be in close touch with you and with affairs on this side of the water, and you will know all that I do. At my request, the French and English governments have absolutely removed the censorship of cable news which until within a fortnight they had maintained and there is now no censorship whatever exercised at this end except upon attempted trade communications with enemy countries. It has been necessary to keep an open wire constantly available between Paris and the Department of State and another between France and the Department of War. In order that this might be done with the least possible interference with the other uses of the cables, I have temporarily taken over the control of both cables in order that they may be used as a single system. I did so at the advice of the most experienced cable officials, and I hope that the results will justify my hope that the news of the next few months may pass with the utmost freedom and with the least possible delay from each side of the sea to the other.

May I not hope, gentlemen of the Congress, that in the delicate tasks I shall have to perform on the other side of the sea, in my efforts truly and faithfully to interpret the principles and purposes of the country we love, I may have the encouragement and the added strength of your united support? I realize the magnitude and difficulty of the duty I am undertaking; I am poignantly aware of its grave responsibilities. I am the servant of the nation. I can have no private thought or purpose of my own in performing such an errand. I go to give the best that is in me to the common settlements which I must now assist in arriving at in conference with the other working heads of the associated governments. I shall count upon your friendly countenance and encouragement. I shall not be inaccessible. The cables and the wireless will render me available for any counsel or service you may desire of me, and I shall be happy in the thought that I am constantly in touch with the weighty matters of domestic policy with which we shall have to deal. I shall make my absence as brief as possible and shall hope to return with the happy assurance that it has been possible to translate into action the great ideals for which America has striven.

For the League of Nations

Des Moines, Iowa

September 6, 1919

IN PARIS, where he was treated as a world hero, Wilson fought to have his 14-point peace program incorporated into the Versailles Treaty. The last point, the one most dear to him, was the establishment of a League of Nations, a supranational congress that would provide a forum for international discussion and maintain peace through neutral arbitration. By compromising many of his other aims—a task excruciatingly hard for such an idealist—he convinced the Allies to include the League in the treaty. In the process, however, he traded away the "peace without victory" that might have saved Germany from the despair that helped bring Hitler to power.

On his return, Wilson undertook a cross-country speaking tour to win the confidence of the American people in the treaty. On the tour, speaking from the rear platform of his train with an urgency listeners had not heard in his voice before, Wilson went far toward bending public opinion in his direction. The speech that follows is thought to be the most eloquent of the 40 he delivered. But the strain of the trip broke his health, preventing him from consolidating the gains he had made, and his own stubbornness prevented him from reaching a compromise with a hostile, Republican-controlled Congress. The treaty, and with it membership in the League, was never ratified.

You make my heart very warm with your generous welcome, and I want to express my unaffected gratitude to your chairman for having so truly struck the note of an occasion like this. He has used almost the very words that were in my thought, that the world is inflamed and profoundly disturbed, and we are met to discuss the measures by which its spirit can be quieted and its affairs turned to the right courses of human life. My fellow countrymen, the world is desperately in need of the settled conditions of peace, and it cannot wait much longer. It is waiting upon us. That is the thought, that is the burdensome thought, upon my heart tonight, that the world is waiting for the verdict of the nation to which it looked for leadership and which it thought would be the last that would ask the world to wait.

My fellow citizens, the world is not at peace. I suppose that it is difficult for one who has not had some touch of the hot passion of the other side of the sea to realize how all the passions that have been slumbering for ages have been uncovered and released by the tragedy of this war. We speak of the tragedy of this war, but the tragedy that lay back of it was greater than the war itself, because back of it lay long ages in which the legitimate freedom of men was suppressed. Back of it lay long ages of recurrent war in which little groups of men, closeted in capitals, determined whether the sons of the land over which they ruled should go out upon the field and shed their blood. For what? For liberty? No; not for liberty, but for the aggrandizement of those who ruled them. And this had been slumbering in the hearts of men. They had felt the suppression of it. They had felt the mastery of those whom they had not chose as their masters. They had felt the oppression of laws which did not admit them to the equal exercise of human rights. Now, all of this is released and uncovered and men glare at one another and say, "Now we are free and what shall we do with our freedom?"

What happened in Russia was not a sudden and accidental thing. The people of Russia were maddened with the suppression of czarism. When at last the chance came to throw off those chains, they threw them off, at first with hearts full of confidence and hope, and then they found out that they had been again deceived. There was no assembly chosen to frame a constitution for them and it was suppressed and dispersed, and a little group of men just as selfish, just as ruthless, just as pitiless, as the agents of the czar himself, assumed control and exercised their power by terror and not by right. And in other parts of Europe the poison spread—the poison of disorder, the poison of revolt, the poison of chaos. And do you honestly think, my fellow citizens, that none of that poison has got in the veins of this free people? Do you not know that the world is all now one single whispering gallery? Those antennae of the wireless telegraph are the symbols of our age. All the impulses of mankind are thrown out upon the air and reach to the ends of the earth; quietly upon steamships, silently under the cover of the Postal Service, with the tongue of the wireless and the tongue of the telegraph, all the suggestions of disorder are spread through the world. Money coming from nobody knows where is deposited by the millions in capitals like Stockholm, to be used for the progaganda of disorder and discontent and dissolution throughout the world, and men look you calmly in the face in America and say they are for that sort of revolution, when that sort of revolution means government by terror, government by force, not government by vote. It is the negation of everything that is American; but it is spreading, and so long as disorder continues, so long as the world is kept waiting for the answer to the question, What kind of peace are we going to have and what kind of guarantees are there to be behind that peace, that poison will steadily spread more and more rapidly, spread until it may be that even this beloved land of ours will be distracted and distorted by it?

That is what is concerning me, my fellow countrymen. I know the splendid steadiness of the American people, but, my fellow citizens, the whole world needs that steadiness, and the American people are the makeweight in the fortunes of mankind. How long are we going to debate into which scale we will throw that magnificent equipoise that belongs to us? How long shall we be kept waiting for the answer whether the world may trust us or despise us? They have looked to us for leadership. They have looked to us for example. They have built their peace upon the basis of our suggestions. That great volume that contains the treaty of peace is drawn along the specifications laid down by the American government, and now the world stands amazed because an authority in America hesitates whether it will indorse an American document or not.

You know what the necessity of peace is. Political liberty can exist only when there is peace. Social reform can take place only when there is peace. The settlement of every question that concerns our daily life waits for peace. I have been receiving delegations in Washington of men engaged in the service of the government temporarily in the administration of the railways, and I have had to say to them, "My friends, I cannot tell what the railways can earn until commerce is restored to its normal courses. Until I can tell what the railroads can earn I cannot tell what the wages that the railroads can pay will be. I cannot suggest what the increase of freight and passenger rates will be to meet these increases in wages if the rates must be increased. I cannot tell yet whether it will be necessary to increase the rates or not, and I must ask you to wait." But they are not the only people that have come to see me. There are all sorts of adjustments necessary in this country. I have asked representatives of capital and labor to come to Washington next month and confer— confer about the fundamental thing of our life at present; that is to say, the conditions of labor. Do you realize, my fellow citizens, that all through the world the one central question of civilization is, "What shall be the conditions of labor?" The profound unrest in Europe is due to the doubt prevailing as to what shall be the conditions of labor, and I need not tell you that that unrest is spreading to America.

In the midst of the treaty of peace is a Magna Charta, a great guarantee for labor. It provides that labor shall have the counsels of the world devoted to the discussion of its conditions and of its betterment, and labor all over the world is waiting to know whether America is going to take part in those conferences or not. The confidence of the men who sat at Paris was such that they put it in the document that the first meeting of the labor conference under that part of the treaty should take place in Washington upon the invitation of the president of the United States. I am going to issue that invitation, whether we can attend the conference or not. But think of the mortification! Think of standing by in Washington itself and seeing the world take counsel upon the fundamental matter of civilization without us. The thing is inconceivable, but it is true. The world is waiting, waiting to see, not whether we will take part but whether we will serve and lead, for it has expected us to lead. I want to testify that the most touching and thrilling thing that has ever happened to me was what happened almost every day when I was in Paris. Delegations from all over the world came to me to solicit the friendship of

America. They frankly told us that they were not sure they could trust anybody else, but that they did absolutely trust us to do them justice and to see that justice was done them. Why, some of them came from countries which I have, to my shame, to admit that I never heard of before, and I had to ask as privately as possible what language they spoke. Fortunately they always had an interpreter, but I always wanted to know at least what family of languages they were speaking. The touching thing was that from the ends of the earth, from little pocketed valleys, where I did not know that a separate people lived, there came men—men of dignity, men of intellectual parts, men entertaining in their thought and in their memories a great tradition, some of the oldest people of the world—and they came and sat at the feet of the youngest nation of the world and said, "Teach us the way to liberty."

That is the attitude of the world, and reflect, my fellow countrymen, upon the reaction, the reaction of despair, that would come if America said: "We do not want to lead you. You must do without our advice. You must shift without us." Now, are we going to bring about a peace, for which everything waits? We cannot bring it about by doing nothing. I have been very much amazed and very much amused, if I could be amused in such critical circumstances, to see that the statesmanship of some gentlemen consists in the very interesting propositon that we do nothing at all. I had heard of standing pat before, but I never had before heard of standpatism going to the length of saying it is none of our business and we do not care what happens to the rest of the world.

Your chairman made a profoundly true remark just now. The isolation of the United States is at an end, not because we chose to go into the politics of the world, but because by the sheer genius of this people and the growth of our power we have become a determining factor in the history of mankind, and after you have become a determining factor you cannot remain isolated, whether you want to or not. Isolation ended by the processes of history, not by the process of our independent choice, and the process of history merely fulfilled the prediction of the men who founded our republic. Go back and read some of the immortal sentences of the men that assisted to frame this government and see how they set up a standard to which they intended that the nations

of the world should rally. They said to the people of the world, "Come to us; this is the home of liberty; this is the place where mankind can learn how to govern their own affairs and straighten out their own difficulties," and the world did come to us.

Look at your neighbor. Look at the statistics of the people of your state. Look at the statistics of the people of the United States. They have come, their hearts full of hope and confidence, from practically every nation in the world, to constitute a portion of our strength and of our hope and a contribution to our achievement. Sometimes I feel like taking off my hat to some of those immigrants. I was born an American. I could not help it, but they chose to be Americans. They were not born Americans. They saw this star in the west rising over the peoples of the world and they said, "That is the star of hope and the star of salvation. We will set our footsteps towards the west and join that great body of men whom God has blessed with the vision of liberty." I honor those men. I say, "You made a deliberate choice which showed that you saw what the drift and history of mankind was." I am very grateful, I may say in parentheses, that I did not have to make that choice. I am grateful that ever since I can remember I have breathed this blessed air of freedom. I am grateful that every instinct in me, every drop of blood in me remembers and stands up and shouts at the traditions of the United States. But some gentlemen are not shouting now about that. They are saying, "Yes; we made a great promise to mankind, but it will cost too much to redeem it." My fellow citizens, that is not the spirit of America, and you cannot have peace, you cannot have even your legitimate part in the business of the world unless you are partners with the rest. If you are going to say to the world, "We will stand off and see what we can get out of this," the world will see to it that you do not get anything out of it. If it is your deliberate choice that instead of being friends you will be rivals and antagonists, then you will get exactly what rivals and antagonists always get, just as little as can be grudgingly vouchsafed you.

Yet you must keep the world on its feet. Is there any businessman here who would be willing to see the world go bankrupt and the business of the world stop? Is there any man here who does not know that America is the only nation left by the war in a position to see that the world does go on with its business? And is it your idea that if we lend our money, as we must, to men whom we have bitterly disappointed, that money will bring back to us the largess to which we are entitled? I do not like to argue this thing on this basis, but if you want to talk business, I am ready to talk business. If it is a matter of how much you are going to get from your money, I say you will not get half as much as antagonists as you will get as partners. Think that over, if you have none of that thing that is so lightly spoken of, known as altruism. And, believe me, my fellow countrymen, the only people in the world who are going to reap the harvest of the future are the people who can entertain ideals, who can follow ideals to the death.

I was saying to another audience today that one of the most beautiful stories I know is the story that we heard in France about the first effect of the American soldiers when they got over there. The French did not believe at first, the British did not believe, that we could finally get two million men over there. The most that they hoped at first was that a few American soldiers would restore their morale, for let me say that their morale was gone. The beautiful story to which I referred is this, the testimony that all of them rendered that they got their morale back the minute they saw the eyes of those boys. Here were not only soldiers. There was no curtain in front of the retina of those eyes. They were American eyes. They were eyes that had seen visions. They were eyes the possessors of which had brought with them a great ardor for a supreme cause, and the reason those boys never stopped was that their eyes were lifted to the horizon. They saw a city not built with hands. They saw a citadel towards which their steps were bent where dwelt the oracles of God himself. And on the battlefield were found German orders to commanders here and there to see to it that the Americans did not get lodgment in particular places, because if they ever did you never could get them out. They had gone to Europe to go the whole way towards the realization of the teaching which their fathers had handed down to them. There never were crusaders that went to the Holy Land in the old ages that we read about that were more truly devoted to a holy cause than these gallant, incomparable sons of America.

My fellow citizens, you have got to make up your minds, because, after all, it is you who are going to make up the minds of this country. I do not owe a report or the slightest responsibility to anybody but you. I do not mean only you in this hall, though I am free to admit that this is just as good a sample of America as you can find anywhere, and the sample looks mighty good to me. I mean you and the millions besides you, thoughtful, responsible American men and women all over this country. They are my bosses, and I am mighty glad to be their servant. I have come out upon this journey not to fight anybody, but to report to you, and I am free to predict that if you credit the report there will be no fighting. It is not only necessary that we should make peace with Germany and make peace with Austria, and see that a reasonable peace with Turkey and Bulgaria—that is not only not all of it, but it is a very dangerous beginning if you do not add something to it. I said just now that the peace with Germany, and the same is true of the pending peace with Austria, was made upon American specifications not unwillingly. Do not let me leave the impression on your mind that the representatives of America in Paris had to insist and force their principles upon the rest. That is not true. Those principles were accepted before we got over there, and the men I dealt with carried them out in absolute good faith; but they were our principles, and at the heart of them lay this, that there must be a free Poland, for example.

I wonder if you realize what that means. We had to collect the pieces of Poland. For a long time one piece had belonged to Russia, and we cannot get a clear title to that yet. Another part belonged to Austria. We got a title to that. Another part belonged to Germany and we have settled the title to that. But we found Germany also in possession of other pieces of territory occupied predominately or exclusively by patriotic Poles, and we said to Germany, "You will have to give that up, too; that belongs to Poland." Not because it is ground, but because those people there are Poles and want to be parts of Poland, and it is not our business to force any sovereignty upon anybody who does not want to live under it. When we had determined the boundaries of Poland we set it up and recognized it as an independent republic. There is a minister, a diplomatic representative, of the United

States at Warsaw right now in virtue of our formal recognition of the republic of Poland.

But upon Poland center some of the dangers of the future. South of Poland is Bohemia, which we cut away from the Austrian combination. Below Bohemia is Hungary, which can no longer rely upon the assistant strength of Austria, and below her is an enlarged Rumania. Alongside of Rumania is the new Slavic Kingdom, that never could have won its own independence, which had chafed under the chains of Austria-Hungary, but never could throw them off. We have said, "The fundamental wrongs of history center in these regions. These people have the right to govern their own government and control their own fortunes." That is at the heart of the treaty, but, my fellow citizens, this is at the heart of the future.

The businessmen of Germany did not want the war that we have passed through. The bankers and the manufacturers and the merchants knew that it was unspeakable folly. Why? Because Germany by her industrial genius was beginning to dominate the world economically, all she had to do was to wait for about two more generations when her credit, her merchandise, her enterprise, would have covered all the parts of the world that the great fighting nations did not control. The formula of pan-Germanism, you remember, was Bremen to Bagdad—Bremen on the North Sea to Bagdad in Persia. These countries that we have set up as the new home of liberty lie right along that road. If we leave them there without the guarantee that the combined force of the world will assure their independence and their territorial integrity, we have only to wait a short generation when our recent experience will be repeated. We did not let Germany dominate the world this time. Are we then? If Germany had known then that all the other fighting nations of the world would combine to prevent her action, she never would have dreamed of attempting it. If Germany had known—this is the common verdict of every man familiar with the politics of Europe—if Germany had known that England would go in, she never would have started it. If she had known that America would come in, she never would have dreamed of it. And now the only way to make it certain that there never will be another world war like that is that we should assist in guaranteeing the peace and its settlement.

It is a very interesting circumstance, my fellow countrymen, that the League of Nations will contain all the nations of the world, great and small, except Germany, and Germany is merely put on probation. We have practically said to Germany, "If it turns out that you really have had a change of heart and have gotten nonsense out of your system; if it really does turn out that you have substituted a genuine self-governing republic for a kingdom where a few men on Wilhelmstrasse plotted the destiny of the world, then we will let you in as partners, because then you will be respectable." In the meantime, accepting the treaty, Germany's army is reduced to 100,000 men, and she has promised to give up all the war material over and above what is necessary for 100,000 men. For a nation of 60,000,000! She has surrendered to the world. She has said, "Our fate is in your hands. We are ready to do what you tell us to do." The rest of the world is combined, and the interesting circumstance is that the rest of the world, excluding us, will continue combined if we do not go into it. Some gentlemen seem to think they can break up this treaty and prevent this League by not going into it. Not at all.

I can give you an interesting circumstance. There is the settlement, which you have heard so much discussed, about that rich and ancient province of Shantung in China. I do not like that settlement any better than you do, but these were the circumstances: In order to induce Japan to cooperate in the war and clear the Pacific of the German power England, and subsequently France, bound themselves without any qualification to see to it that Japan got anything in China that Germany had, and that Japan would take it away from her, upon the strength of which promise Japan proceeded to take Kiauchau and occupy the portions of Shantung Province, which had been ceded by China for a term of years to Germany. The most that could be got out of it was that, in view of the fact that America had nothing to do with it, the Japanese were ready to promise that they would give up every item of sovereignty which Germany would otherwise have enjoyed in Shantung Province and return it without restriction to China, and that they would retain in the province only the economic concessions such as other nations already had elsewhere in China—though you do not hear anything about that—concessions in the railway and the mines which had become attached to the railway for operative purposes. But suppose that you say that is not enough. Very well, then, stay out of the treaty, and how will that accomplish anything? England and France are bound and cannot escape their obligation. Are you going to institute a war against Japan and France and England to get Shantung back for China? That is an enterprise which does not commend itself to the present generation.

I am putting it in brutal terms, my fellow citizens, but that is the fact. By disagreeing to that provision, we accomplish nothing for China. On the contrary, we stay out of the only combination of the counsels of nations in which we can be of service to China. With China as a member of the League of Nations, and Japan as a member of the League of Nations, and America as a member of the League of Nations, there confronts every one of them that now famous Article X, by which every member of the League agrees to respect and preserve the territorial integrity and existing political independence of all the other member states. Do not let anybody persuade you that you can take that article out and have a peaceful world. That cuts at the root of the German war. That cuts at the root of the outrage against Belgium. That cuts at the root of the outrage against France. That pulls that vile, unwholesome Upas tree of Pan-Germanism up by the roots, and it pulls all other "pans" up, too. Every land-grabbing nation is served notice: "Keep on your own territory. Mind your own business. That territory belongs to those people and they can do with it what they please, provided they do not invade other people's rights by the use they make of it." My fellow citizens, the thing is going to be done whether we are in it or not. If we are in it, then we are going to be the determining factor in the development of civilization. If we are out of it, we ourselves are going to watch every other nation with suspicion, and we will be justified, too; and we are going to be watched with suspicion. Every movement of trade, every relationship of manufacture, every question of raw materials, every matter that affects the intercourse of the world, will be impeded by the consciousness that America wants to hold off and get something which she is not willing to share with the rest of mankind. I am painting the picture for you, because I know that it

is as tolerable to you as it is to me. But do not go away with the impression, I beg you, that I think there is any doubt about the issue. The only thing that can be accomplished is delay. The ultimate outcome will be the triumphant acceptance of the treaty and the League.

Let me pay the tribute which it is only just that I should pay to some of the men who have been, I believe, misunderstood in this business. It is only a handful of men, my fellow citizens, who are trying to defeat the treaty or to prevent the League. The great majority, in official bodies and out, are scrutinizing it, as it is perfectly legitimate that they should scrutinize it, to see if it is necessary that they should qualify it in any way, and my knowledge of their conscience, my knowledge of their public principle, makes me certain that they will sooner or later see that it is safest, since it is all expressed in the plainest English that the English dictionary affords, not to qualify it—to accept it as it is. I have been a student of the English language all my life and I do not see a single obscure sentence in the whole document. Some gentlemen either have not read it or do not understand the English language; but, fortunately, on the right-hand page it is printed in English and on the left-hand page it is printed in French. Now, if they do not understand English, I hope they will get a French dictionary and dig out the meaning on that side. The French is a very precise language, more precise than the English language, I am told. I am not on a speaking acquaintance with it, but I am told that it is the most precise language in Europe, and that any given phrase in French always means the same thing. That cannot be said of English. In order to satisfy themselves, I hope these gentlemen will master the French version and then be reassured that there are no lurking monsters in that document; that there are no sinister purposes; that everything is said in the frankest way.

For example, they have been very much worried at the phrase that nothing in the document shall be taken as impairing in any way the validity of such regional understandings as the Monroe Doctrine. They say: "Why put in 'such regional understandings as'? What other understandings are there? Have you got something up your sleeve? Is there going to be a Monroe Doctrine in Asia? Is there going to be a Monroe Doctrine in China?" Why, my fellow citizens, the phrase was written in perfect innocence. The men that I was associated with said, "It is not wise to put a specific thing that belongs only to one nation in a document like this. We do not know of any other regional understanding like it, we never heard of any other; we never expect to hear of any other, but there might some day be some other, and so we will say 'such regional understandings as the Monroe Doctrine,'" and their phrase was intended to give right of way to the Monroe Doctrine in the Western Hemisphere. I reminded the Committee on Foreign Relations of the Senate the other day that the conference I held with them was not the first conference I had held about the League of Nations. When I came back to this our own dear country in March last I held a conference at the White House with the Senate Committee on Foreign Relations, and they made various suggestions as to how the covenant should be altered in phraseology. I carried those suggestions back to Paris, and every one of them was accepted. I think that is a sufficient guarantee that no mischief was intended. The whole document is of the same plain, practical, explicit sort, and it secures peace, my fellow citizens, in the only way in which peace can be secured.

I remember, if I may illustrate a very great thing with a very trivial thing. I had two acquaintances who were very much addicted to profanity. Their friends were very distress about it. It subordinated a rich vocabulary which they might otherwise have cultivated, and so we induced them to agree that they never would swear inside the corporate limits, that if they wanted to swear they would go out of town. The first time the passion of anger came upon them they rather sheepishly got in a street car and went out of town to swear, and by the time they got out of town they did not want to swear. That very homely illustration illustrates in my mind the value of discussion. Let me remind you that every fighting nation in the world is going to belong to this League, because we are going to belong to it, and they all make this solemn engagem at with each other, that they will not resort to war in the case of any controversy until they have done one or other of two things, until they have either submitted the question at issue to arbitration, in which case they promise to abide by the verdict whatever it may be, or, if they do not want to submit it to arbitration, have submitted it to discussion by the council of the League.

They agree to give the council six months to discuss the matter, to supply the council with all the pertinent facts regarding it, and that, after the opinion of the council is rendered, they will not then go to war if they are dissatisfied with the opinion until three more months have elapsed. They give nine months in which to spread the whole matter before the judgment of mankind, and if they violate this promise, if any one of them violates it, the covenant prescribes that that violation shall in itself constitute an act of war against the other members of the League. It does not provide that there shall be war. On the contrary, it provides for something very much more effective than war. It provides that that nation, that covenant-breaking nation, shall be absolutely cut off from intercourse of every kind with the other nations of the world; that no merchandise shall be shipped out of it or into it; that no postal messages shall go into it or come out of it; that no telegraphic messages shall cross its borders; and that the citizens of the other member states shall not be permitted to have any intercourse or transactions whatever with its citizens or its citizens with them. There is not a single nation in Europe that can stand that boycott for six months. There is not a single nation in Europe that is self-sufficing in its resources of food or anything else that can stand that for six months. And in those circumstances we are told that this covenant is a covenant of war. It is the most drastic covenant of peace that was ever conceived, and its processes are the processes of peace. The nation that does not abide by its covenants is taboo, is put out of the society of covenant-respecting nations.

So that this is a covenant of arbitration and discussion, of compulsory arbitration or discussion, and just so soon as you discuss matters, my fellow citizens, peace looks in at the window. Did you ever really sit down and discuss matters with your neighbor when you had a difference and come away in the same temper that you went in? One of the difficulties in our labor situation is that there are some employers who will not meet their employees face to face and talk with them. I have never known an instance in which such a meeting and discussion took place that both sides did not come away in a softened temper and with an access of respect for the other side. The processes of frank discussion are the processes of peace not only, but the processes of settlement, and those are the processes which are set up for all the powerful nations of the world.

I want to say that this is an unparalleled achievement of thoughtful civilization. To my dying day I shall esteem it the crowning privilege of my life to have permitted to put my name to a document like that; and in my judgment, my fellow citizens, when passion is cooled and men take a sober, second thought, they are all going to feel that the supreme thing that America did was to help bring this about and then put her shoulder to the great chariot of justice and of peace which was going to lead men along in that slow and toilsome march, toilsome and full of the kind of agony that brings bloody sweat, but nevertheless going up a slow incline to those distant heights upon which will shine at the last the serene light of justice, suffusing a whole world in blissful peace.

Courtesy of Library of Congress

Warren Gamaliel Harding

Warren Gamaliel Harding

1921–1923

BY HIS OWN ADMISSION, Warren Harding was more suited to remain editor of a small-town Ohio newspaper (the *Marion Star)* than to serve as president of the United States. The Republican machine that he had faithfully served in the Ohio legislature and the U.S. Senate nominated him for the presidency because he had voter appeal—he "looked like a president"—and because, as a man of weak will and mediocre intellect, he was easy to control. His cabinet secretaries and advisers were mainly old friends and poker cronies who indulged in the worst graft since the days of Ulysses S. Grant. His own role, as he saw it, was to lead the country back to what he called "normalcy" and to let well enough alone.

Part of Harding's appeal was his old-fashioned, crowd-pleasing oratorical style—patriotic cliches delivered in a mellifluous voice, accompanied by dramatic flourishes. Early in his career he appeared at civic ceremonies and political rallies across Ohio, delivering more than 300 speeches in the first six months of 1910 alone. At the 1912 national convention—the one that produced TR's breakaway Bull Moose Party—the mainstream Republicans chose "Harding the Harmonizer" to make the nominating speech for William Howard Taft. Eight years later, after his own nomination, he was instructed by the Republican leaders *not* to orate, in order to keep his inadequacies from becoming better known. "What a treat it will be," wrote David F. Houston, Wilson's secretary of agriculture, "to have to witness Mr. Harding's efforts to think and his efforts to say what he thinks." Once in the White House (by a landslide), Harding tried to function as a ceremonial figurehead, leaving the running of the government to his friends. Most of his minor speeches were drafted by his political adviser Judson Welliver; major speeches were drafted by Harding in longhand.

Harding was a likable man and with his impressive bearing seemed to embody political ideals that he lacked the intellect and the ethical sense to fully comprehend. Senator William G. McAdoo, writing in 1931, remembered him as a "'good fellow' in the ordinary locker room, poker-game sense of the term" but a man with an "adjustable conscience." He repeatedly voted in favor of Prohibition while holding liquor parties at the White House. As a senator he dutifully followed the party line or, if none was evident, waffled as long as possible. This moral and intellectual laxity was mirrored in the notoriously ungrammatical and confused language of his speeches. McAdoo said he had "a big bow-wow style of oratory. He would use rolling words which had no application to the topic in hand, and his speeches left the impression of an army of pompous phrases moving over the landscape in search of an idea."

Harding's sharpest critic was the political journalist H. L. Mencken, who lampooned his idiom as "Gamalielese." "He writes the worst English that I have ever encountered. It reminds me of a string of wet sponges; it reminds me of tattered washing on the line; it reminds me of stale bean-soup, of college yells, of dogs barking idiotically through endless nights. It is so bad that a sort of grandeur creeps into it." Amazingly, the *New York Times* came to Harding's defense in an editorial that proclaimed: "Mr. Harding's official style is excellent. . . . In the first place, it is a style that looks presidential. It contains the long sentences and big words that are expected. . . . In the president's misty language the great majority see a reflection of their own indeterminate thoughts." "In other words," Mencken replied, "bosh is the right medicine for boobs. . . . To argue so much is to argue further that the ideal president would be a complete idiot."

But the *Times* was right when it said that "Mr. Harding is not writing for the superfine weighers of verbs and adjectives, but for the men and women who see in his expressions their own ideas, and are truly happy to meet them." The public eagerly lapped up Harding's verbal puddings. So did the press, with whom the affable Harding enjoyed singularly cordial relations. In his lifetime he never lost the friendship of either. He died 29 months after taking office, just as the corruption scandals in his administration were reaching the headlines.

Inaugural Address

Washington, D.C.

March 4, 1921

HARDING declaimed most of his inaugural address from memory, standing with one hand in his coat pocket in the pose made famous by the great senatorial orator Henry Clay. The speech was a tour de force of high-toned platitudes. On the controversial subject of the League of Nations, Harding managed to voice approval and disapproval at the same time. Mencken called it "sonorous nonsense driven home with gestures. . . . a loud burble of words, a procession of phrases that roar, a series of whoops." It was the first inaugural address to reach the crowd through loudspeakers and the first to be described over the radio.

When one surveys the world about him after the great storm, noting the marks of destruction and yet rejoicing in the ruggedness of the things which withstood it, if he is an American he breathes the clarified atmosphere with a strange mingling of regret and new hope. We have seen a world passion spend its fury, but we contemplate our republic unshaken, and hold our civilization secure. Liberty—liberty within the law—and civilization are inseparable, and though both were threatened we find them now secure; and there comes to Americans the profound assurance that our representative government is the highest expression and surest guaranty of both.

Standing in this presence, mindful of the solemnity of this occasion, feeling the emotions which no one may know until he senses the great weight of responsibility for himself, I must utter my belief in the divine inspiration of the founding fathers. Surely there must have been God's intent in the making of this new-world republic. Ours is an organic law which had but one ambiguity, and we saw that effaced in a baptism of sacrifice and blood, with union maintained, the nation supreme, and its concord inspiring. We have seen the world rivet its hopeful gaze on the great truths on which the founders wrought. We have seen civil, human, and religious liberty verified and glorified. In the beginning the Old World scoffed at our experiment; today our foundations of political and social belief stand unshaken, a precious inheritance to ourselves, an inspiring example of freedom and civilization to all mankind. Let us express renewed and strengthened devotion, in grateful reverence for the immortal beginning, and utter our confidence in the supreme fulfillment.

The recorded progress of our republic, materially and spiritually, in itself proves the wisdom of the inherited policy of non-involvement in Old World affairs. Confident of our ability to work out our own destiny, and jealously guarding our right to do so, we seek no part in directing the destinies of the Old World. We do not mean to be entangled. We will accept no responsibility except as our own conscience and judgment, in each instance, may determine.

Our eyes never will be blind to a developing menace, our ears never deaf to the call of civilization. We recognize the new order in the world, with the closer contacts which progress has wrought. We sense the call of the human heart for fellowship, fraternity, and cooperation. We crave friendship and harbor no hate. But America, our America, the America builded on the foundation laid by the inspired fathers, can be a party to no permanent military alliance. It can enter into no political commitments, nor assume any economic obligations which will subject our decisions to any other than our own authority.

I am sure our own people will not misunderstand, nor will the world misconstrue. We have no thought to impede the paths to closer relationship. We wish to promote understanding. We want to do our part in making offensive warfare so hateful that governments and peoples who resort to it must prove the righteousness of their cause or stand as outlaws before the bar of civilization.

We are ready to associate ourselves with the nations of the world, great and small, for conference, for counsel; to seek the expressed views of world opinion; to recommend a way to approximate disarmament and relieve the crushing burdens of military and naval establishments. We elect to participate in suggesting plans for mediation, conciliation, and arbitration, and would gladly join in that expressed conscience of progress, which seeks to clarify and write the laws of international relationship, and establish a world court for the disposition of such justiciable questions as nations are agreed to submit thereto. In expressing aspirations, in seeking practical plans, in translating humanity's new concept of righteousness and justice and its hatred of war into recommended action we are ready most heartily to unite, but every commitment must be made in the exercise of our national sovereignty. Since freedom impelled, and independence inspired, and nationality exalted, a world super-government is contrary to everything we cherish and can have no sanction by our republic. This is not selfishness, it is sanctity. It is not aloofness, it is security. It is not suspicion of others, it is patriotic adherence to the things which made us what we are.

Today, better than ever before, we know the aspirations of human-kind, and share them. We have come to a new realization of our place in the world and a new appraisal of our nation by the world. The unselfishness of these United States is a thing proven; our devotion to peace for ourselves and for the world is well established; our concern for preserved civilization has had its impassioned and heroic expression. There was no American failure to resist the attempted reversion of civilization; there will be no failure today or tomorrow.

The success of our popular government rests wholly upon the correct interpretation of the deliberate, intelligent, dependable popular will of America. In a deliberate questioning of a suggested change of national policy, where internationally was to supersede nationality, we turned to a referendum, to the American people. There was ample discussion, and there is a public mandate in manifest understanding.

America is ready to encourage, eager to initiate, anxious to participate in any seemly program likely to lessen the probability of war, and promote that brotherhood of mankind which must be God's highest conception of human relationship. Because we cherish ideals of justice and peace, because we appraise international comity and helpful relationship no less highly than any people of the world, we aspire to a high place in the moral leadership

of civilization, and we hold a maintained America, the proven republic, the unshaken temple of representative democracy, to be not only an inspiration and example, but the highest agency of strengthening goodwill and promoting accord on both continents.

Mankind needs a worldwide benediction of understanding. It is needed among individuals, among peoples, among governments, and it will inaugurate an era of good feeling to mark the birth of a new order. In such understanding men will strive confidently for the promotion of their better relationships and nations will promote the comities so essential to peace.

We must understand that ties of trade bind nations in closest intimacy, and none may receive except as he gives. We have not strengthened ours in accordance with our resources or our genius, notably on our own continent, where a galaxy of republics reflects the glory of new-world democracy, but in the new order of finance and trade we mean to promote enlarged activities and seek expanded confidence.

Perhaps we can make no more helpful contribution by example than prove a republic's capacity to emerge from the wreckage of war. While the world's embittered travail did not leave us devastated lands nor desolated cities, left no gaping wounds, no breast with hate, it did involve us in the delirium of expenditure, in expanded currency and credits, in unbalanced industry, in unspeakable waste, and disturbed relationships. While it uncovered our portion of hateful selfishness at home, it also revealed the heart of America as sound and fearless, and beating in confidence unfailing.

Amid it all we have riveted the gaze of all civilization to the unselfishness and the righteousness of representative democracy, where our freedom never has made offensive warfare, never has sought territorial aggrandizement through force, never has turned to the arbitrament of arms until reason has been exhausted. When the governments of the earth shall have established a freedom like our own and shall have sanctioned the pursuit of peace as we have practiced it, I believe the last sorrow and the final sacrifice of international warfare will have been written.

Let me speak to the maimed and wounded soldiers who are present today, and through them convey to their comrades the gratitude of

449

the republic for their sacrifices in its defense. A generous country will never forget the services you rendered, and you may hope for a policy under government that will relieve any maimed successors from taking your places on another such occasion as this.

Our supreme task is the resumption of our onward, normal way. Reconstruction, readjustment, restoration—all these must follow. I would like to hasten them. If it will lighten the spirit and add to the resolution with which we take up the task, let me repeat for our nation, we shall give no people just cause to make war upon us; we hold no national prejudices; we entertain no spirit of revenge; we do not hate; we do not covet; we dream of no conquest, nor boast of armed prowess.

If, despite this attitude, war is again forced upon us, I earnestly hope a way may be found which will unify our individual and collective strength and consecrate all America, materially and spiritually, body and soul, to national defense. I can vision the ideal republic, where every man and woman is called under the flag for assignment to duty for whatever service, military or civic, the individual is best fitted; where we may call to universal service every plant, agency, or facility, all in the sublime sacrifice for country, and not one penny of war profit shall inure to the benefit of private individual, corporation, or combination, but all above the normal shall flow into the defense chest of the nation. There is something inherently wrong, something out of accord with the ideals of representative democracy, when one portion of our citizenship turns its activities to private gain amid defensive war while another is fighting, sacrificing, or dying for national preservation.

Out of such universal service will come a new unity of spirit and purpose, a new confidence and consecration, which would make our defense impregnable, our triumph assured. Then we should have little or no disorganization of our economic, industrial, and commercial systems at home, no staggering war debts, no swollen fortunes to flout the sacrifices of our soldiers, no excuse for sedition, no pitiable slackerism, no outrage of treason. Envy and jealousy would have no soil for their menacing development, and revolution would be without the passion which engenders it.

A regret for the mistakes of yesterday must not, however, blind us to the tasks of today. War never left such an aftermath. There has been staggering loss of life and measureless wastage of materials. Nations are still groping for return to stable ways. Discouraging indebtedness confronts us like all the war-torn nations, and these obligations must be provided for. No civilization can survive repudiation.

We can reduce the abnormal expenditures, and we will. We can strike at war taxation, and we must. We must face the grim necessity, with full knowledge that the task is to be solved, and we must proceed with a full realization that no stature enacted by man can repeal the inexorable laws of nature. Our most dangerous tendency is to expect too much of government, and at the same time do for it too little.

We contemplate the immediate task of putting our public household in order. We need a rigid and yet sane economy, combined with fiscal justice, and it must be attended by individual prudence and thrift, which are so essential to this trying hour and reassuring for the future.

The business world reflects the disturbance of war's reaction. Herein flows the lifeblood of material existence. The economic mechanism is intricate and its parts interdependent, and has suffered the shocks and jars incident to abnormal demands, credit inflations, and price upheavals. The normal balances have been impaired, the channels of distribution have been clogged, the relations of labor and management have been strained. We must seek the readjustment with care and courage. Our people must give and take. Prices must reflect the receding fever of war activities. Perhaps we never shall know the old levels of wages again, because war invariably readjusts compensations, and the necessaries of life will show their inseparable relationship, but we must strive for normalcy to reach stability. All the penalties will not be light, nor evenly distributed. There is no way of making them so. There is no instant step from disorder to order. We must face a condition of grim reality, charge off our losses and start afresh. It is the oldest lesson of civilization. I would like government to do all it can to mitigate; then, in understanding, in mutuality of interest, in concern for the common good, our tasks will be solved. No altered system will work a miracle. Any wild experiment will only add to the confusion. Our best assurance lies in efficient administration of our proven system.

The forward course of the business cycle is unmistakable. People are turning from destruction to production. Industry has sensed the changed order and our own people are turning to resume their normal, onward way. The call is for productive America to go on. I know that Congress and the administration will favor every wise government policy to aid the resumption and encourage continued progress.

I speak for administrative efficiency, for lightened tax burdens, for sound commercial practices, for adequate credit facilities, for sympathetic concern for all agriculture problems, for the omission of unnecessary interference of government with business, for an end to government's experiment in business, and for more efficient business in government administration. With all of this must attend a mindfulness of the human side of all activities, so that social, industrial, and economic justice will be squared with the purposes of a righteous people.

With the nationwide induction of womanhood into our political life, we may count upon her intuitions, her refinements, her intelligence, and her influence to exalt the social order. We count upon her exercise of the full privileges and the performance of the duties of citizenship to speed the attainment of the highest state.

I wish for an America no less alert in guarding against dangers from within than it is watchful against enemies from without. Our fundamental law recognizes no class, no group, no section; there must be none in legislation or administration. The supreme inspiration is the common weal. Humanity hungers for international peace, and we crave it with all mankind. My most reverent prayer for America is for industrial peace, with its rewards, widely and generally distributed, amid the inspirations of equal opportunity. No one justly may deny the equality of opportunity which made us what we are. We have mistaken unpreparedness to embrace it to be a challenge of the reality, and due concern for making all citizens fit for participation will give added strength of citizenship and magnify our achievement.

If revolution insists upon overturning established order, let other peoples make the tragic experiment. There is no place for it in America. When world war threatened civilization we pledged our resources and our lives to its preservation, and when revolution threatens we unfurl the flag of law and order and renew our consecration. Ours is a constitutional freedom where the popular will is the law supreme and minorities are sacredly protected. Our revisions, reformations, and evolutions reflect a deliberate judgment and an orderly progress, and we mean to cure our ills, but never destroy or permit destruction by force.

I had rather submit our industrial controversies to the conference table in advance than to a settlement table after conflict and suffering. The earth is thirsting for the cup of goodwill, understanding is its fountain source. I would like to acclaim an era of good feeling amid dependable prosperity and all the blessings which attend.

It has been proved again and again that we cannot, while throwing our markets open to the world, maintain American standards of living and opportunity, and hold our industrial eminence in such unequal competition. There is a luring fallacy in the story of banished barriers of trade, but preserved American standards require our higher production costs to be reflected in our tariffs on imports. Today, as never before, when peoples are seeking trade restoration and expansion, we must adjust our tariffs to the new order. We seek participation in the world's exchanges, because therein lies our way to widened influence and the triumphs of peace. We know full well we cannot sell where we do not buy, and we cannot sell successfully where we do not carry. Opportunity is calling not alone for the restoration, but for a new era in production, transportation, and trade. We shall answer it best by meeting the demand of a surpassing home market, by promoting self-reliance in production, and by bidding enterprise, genius, and efficiency to carry our cargoes in American bottoms to the marts of the world.

We would not have an America living within and for herself alone, but we would have her self-reliant, independent, and ever nobler, stronger, and richer. Believing in our higher standards, reared through constitutional liberty and maintained opportunity, we invite the world to the same heights. But pride in things wrought is no reflex of a completed task. Common welfare is the goal of our national endeavor. Wealth is not inimical to welfare; it ought to be its friendliest agency. There never can be equality of rewards or possessions so long as the human plan contains varied talents and differing degrees of industry and thrift, but ours ought to be a country free from the great blotches of distressed poverty. We ought to find a way to guard against the perils and penalties of unemployment. We want an America of homes, illumined with hope and happiness, where mothers, freed from the necessity for long hours of toil beyond their own doors, may preside as befits the hearthstone of American citizenship. We want the cradle of American childhood rocked under conditions so wholesome and so hopeful that no blight may touch it in its development, and we want to provide that no selfish interest, no material necessity, no lack of opportunity shall prevent the gaining of that education so essential to best citizenship.

There is no shortcut to the making of these ideals into glad realities. The world has witnessed again and again the futility and the mischief of ill-considered remedies for social and economic disorders. But we are mindful today as never before of the friction of modern industrialism, and we must learn its causes and reduce its evil consequences by sober and tested methods. Where genius has made for great possibilities, justice and happiness must be reflected in a greater common welfare.

Service is the supreme commitment of life. I would rejoice to acclaim the era of the golden rule and crown it with the autocracy of service. I pledge an administration wherein all the agencies of government are called to serve, and ever promote an understanding of government purely as an expression of the popular will.

One cannot stand in this presence and be unmindful of the tremendous responsibility. The world upheaval has added heavily to our tasks. But with the realization comes the surge of high resolve, and there is reassurance in belief in the God-given destiny of our republic. If I felt that there is to be sole responsibility in the executive for the America of tomorrow I should shrink from the burden. But here are a hundred millions, with common concern and shared responsibility, answerable to God and country. The republic summons them to their duty, and I invite cooperation.

I accept my part with single-mindedness of purpose and humility of spirit, and implore the favor and guidance of God in his heaven. With these I am unafraid, and confidently face the future.

I have taken the solemn oath of office on that passage of Holy Writ wherein it is asked: "What doth the Lord require of thee but to do justly, and to love mercy, and to walk humbly with thy God?" This I plight to God and country.

The Rights of Black Citizens

Birmingham, Alabama
October 26, 1921

AT THE FESTIVITIES commemorating the 50th anniversary of the founding of Birmingham, Harding, speaking to a segregated audience of 20,000 whites and 10,000 blacks, surprised his listeners and his party by calling for political, economic, and educational equality between the races. Social equality, he admitted, was more than he could accept. This speech marked the first time since Reconstruction that any president had dared to confront the South with the subject of civil rights for blacks. Harding's main purpose was to hinder attempts by white supremacists to eliminate black voters from the Republican ranks, but he also had vague ideas of social justice; his first annual message to Congress recommended antilynching legislation and the creation of a commission to promote better race relations.

... Politically and economically there need be no occasion for great and permanent differentiation, provided on both sides there shall be recognition of the absolute divergence in things social and racial. I would say let the black man vote when he is fit to vote; prohibit the white man voting when he is unfit to vote. I wish that both the tradition of a solidly Democratic South and the tradition of a solidly Republican black race might be broken up. I would insist upon equal educational opportunity for both.

Men of both races may well stand uncompromisingly against every suggestion of social equality. This is not a question of social equality, but a question of recognizing a fundamental, eternal, inescapable difference.

Racial amalgamation there cannot be. Partnership of the races in developing the highest aims of all humanity there must be if humanity is to achieve the ends which we have set for it. The black man should seek to be, and he should be encouraged to be, the best possible black man and not the best possible imitation of a white man.

The World War brought us to full recognition that the race problem is national rather than merely sectional. There are no authentic statistics, but it is common knowledge that the World War was marked by a great migration of colored people to the North and West. They were attracted by the demand for labor and the higher wages offered. It has brought the question of race closer to North and West, and, I believe, it has served to modify somewhat the views of those sections on this question. It has made the South realize its industrial dependence on the labor of the black man and made the North realize the difficulties of the community in which two greatly differing races are brought to live side by side. I should say that it has been responsible for a larger charity on both sides, a beginning of better understanding; and in the light of that better understanding perhaps we shall be able to consider this problem together as a problem of all sections and of both races, in whose solution the best intelligence of both must be enlisted.

Indeed, we will be wise to recognize it as wider yet. Whoever will take the time to read and ponder Mr. Lothrop Stoddard's book on *The Rising Tide of Color,* or, say, the thoughtful review of some recent literature on this question which Mr. F. D. Lugard presented in a recent Edinburgh Review, must realize that our race problem here in the United States is only a phase of a race issue that the whole world confronts. Surely we shall gain nothing by blinking the facts, by refusing to give thought to them. That is not the American way of approaching such issues.

Mr. Lugard, in his recent essay, after surveying the world's problem of races, concludes thus:

> Here, then, is the true conception of the interrelation of color—complete uniformity in ideals, absolute equality in the paths of knowledge and culture, equal opportunity for those who strive, equal admiration for those who achieve; in matters social and racial a separate path, each pursuing his own inherited

traditions, preserving his own race purity, and race pride; equality in things spiritual; agreed divergence in the physical and material.

Here, it has seemed to me, is suggestion of the true way out. Politically and economically there need be no occasion for great and permanent differentiation, for limitations of the individual's opportunity, provided that on both sides there shall be recognition of the absolute divergence in things social and racial. When I suggest the possibility of economic equality between the races, I mean it in precisely the same way and to the same extent that I would mean it if I spoke of equality of economic opportunity as between members of the same race. In each case I would mean equality proportioned to the honest capacities and deserts of the individual.

Men of both races may well stand uncompromisingly against every suggestion of social equality. Indeed, it would be helpful to have that word equality eliminated from this consideration; to have it accepted on both sides that this is not a question of social equality, but a question of recognizing a fundamental, eternal, and inescapable difference. We shall have made real progress when we develop an attitude in the public and community thought of both races which recognizes this difference.

Take the political aspect. I would say let the black man vote when he is fit to vote: prohibit the white man voting when he is unfit to vote. Especially would I appeal to the self-respect of the colored race. I would inculcate in it the wish to improve itself as a distinct race, with a heredity, a set of traditions, an array of aspirations all its own. Out of such racial ambitions and pride will come natural segregations without narrowing and rights, such as are proceeding in both rural and urban communities now in Southern states satisfying natural inclinations and adding notably to happiness and contentment.

On the other hand I would insist upon equal educational opportunity for both. This does not mean that both would become equally educated within a generation or two generations or ten generations. Even men of the same race do not accomplish such an equality as that. There must be such education among the colored people as will enable them to develop their own leaders capable of understanding and sympathizing with such a differentiation between the races as I have suggested—leaders who will inspire the race with proper ideals of race pride, of national pride, of an honorable destiny; and important participation in the universal effort for advancement of humanity as a whole. Racial amalgamation there cannot be. Partnership of the races in developing the highest aims to all humanity there must be if humanity, not only here but everywhere, is to achieve the ends which we have set for it.

I can say to you people of the South, both white and black, that the time has passed when you are entitled to assume that this problem of races is peculiarly and particularly your problem. More and more it is becoming a problem of the North; more and more it is the problem of Africa, of South America, of the Pacific of the South Seas, of the world. It is the problem of democracy everywhere, if we mean the things we say about democracy as the ideal political state.

The one thing we must sedulously avoid is the development of group and class organizations in this country. There has been time when we heard too much about the labor vote, the business vote, the Irish vote, the Scandinavian vote, the Italian vote, and so on. But the demagogues who would array class against class and group against group have fortunately found little to reward their efforts. That is because, despite the demagogues, the idea of our oneness as Americans has risen superior to every appeal to mere class and group. And so I would with it might be in this matter of our national problem of races. I would accept that a black man cannot be a white man, and that he does not need and should not aspire to be as much like a white man as possible in order to accomplish the best that is possible for him. He should seek to be, and he should be encouraged to be, the best possible black man, and not the best possible imitation of a white man.

It is a matter of the keenest national concern that the South shall not be encouraged to make its colored population a vast reservoir of ignorance, to be drained away by the processes of migration into all other sections. That is what has been going on in recent years at a rate so accentuated that it has caused this question of races to be, as I have already said, no longer one of a particular section. Just as I do not wish the South to be politically entirely one party; just as I believe that is bad for the South, and for the rest of the country as well, so I do not want the colored people to be entirely of one party. I wish that both the tradition of a solidly Democratic South and the tradition of a solidly Republican black race might be broken up. Neither political sectionalism nor any system of rigid groupings of the people will in the long run prosper our country.

With such convictions one must urge the people of the South to take advantage of their superior understanding of this problem and to assume an attitude toward it that will deserve the confidence of the colored people. Likewise, I plead with my own political party to lay aside every program that looks to lining up the black man as a mere political adjunct. Let there be an end of prejudice and of demagogy in this line. Let the South understand the menace which lies in forcing upon the black race an attitude of political solidarity.

Every consideration, it seems to me, brings us back at last to the question of education. When I speak of education as a part of this race question, I do not want the states or the nation to attempt to educate people, whether while or black, into something they are not fitted to be. I have no sympathy with the half-baked altruism that would overstock us with doctors and lawyers, of whatever color, and leave us, in need of people fit and willing to do the manual work of a workaday world. But I would like to see an education that would fit every man not only to do his particular work as well as possible but to rise to a higher plane if he would deserve it. For that sort of

education I have no fears, whether it be given to a black man or a white man. From that sort of education, I believe black man, white man, the whole nation, would draw immeasurable benefit.

It is probable that as a nation we have come to the end of the period of very rapid increase in our population. Restricted immigration will reduce the rate of increase, and force us back upon our older population to find people to do the simpler, physically harder manual tasks. This will require some difficult readjustments.

In anticipation of such a condition the South may well recognize that the North and West are likely to continue their drafts upon its colored population, and that if the South wishes to keep its fields producing and its industry still expanding it will have to compete for the services of the colored man. If it will realize its need for him and deal quite fairly with him, the South will be able to keep him in such numbers as your activities make desirable.

Is it not possible, then, that in the long era of readjustment upon which we are entering, for the nation to lay aside old prejudices and old antagonisms, and in the broad, clear light of nationalism enter upon a constructive policy in dealing with these intricate issues? Just as we shall prove ourselves capable of doing this we shall insure the industrial progress, the agricultural security, the social and political safety of our whole country, regardless of race or sections, and along the lines of ideals superior to every consideration of groups or class, of race or color or section or prejudices. . . .

The Burial of the Unknown Soldier

Arlington, Virginia
November 11, 1921

FOLLOWING THE LEAD of England and other participants in World War I, the United States prepared a tomb for the body of an unidentified soldier who would symbolize all the American war dead. The body was interred in Arlington National Cemetery on Armistice Day, 1921, amid elaborate pageantry. Harding's speech at the gravesite was carried by wire to audiences in Washington, New York City, and San Francisco. Harding's biographer, Francis Russell, wrote: "Never before in history had so many thousands simultaneously heard the sound of a single human voice. Harding spoke resonantly and movingly, in the grave generalities that came so easily to him and that carried conviction when he spoke them in his full-throated voice, even if in cold print they defied exacter meanings." At the close of the speech he led the audience in the Lord's Prayer. The ceremony formed a prelude to the opening of the ambitious Arms Limitations Conference the following day.

We are met today to pay the impersonal tribute. The name of him whose body lies before us took flight with his imperishable soul. We know not whence he came, but only that his death marks him with the everlasting glory of an American dying for his country.

He might have come from any one of millions of American homes. Some mother gave him in her love and tenderness, and, with him, her most cherished hopes. Hundreds of mothers are wondering today, finding a touch of solace in the possibility that the nation bows in grief over the body of one she bore to live and die, if need be, for the republic. If we give rein to fancy, a score of sympathetic chords are touched, for in his body there once glowed the soul of an American, with the aspirations and ambitions of a citizen who cherished life and its opportunities. He may have been a native or an adopted son; that matters little, because they glorified the same loyalty, they sacrificed alike.

We do not know his station in life, because from every station came the patriotic response of the five millions. I recall the days of creating armies and the departing of caravels which braved the murderous seas to reach the battle lines for maintained nationality and preserved civilization. The service flag marked mansion and cottage alike, and riches were common to all homes in the consciousness of service to country.

We do not know the eminence of his birth, but we do know the glory of his death. He died for his country, and greater devotion hath no man than this. He died unquestioning,

uncomplaining, with faith in his heart and hope on his lips, that his country should triumph and its civilization survive. As a typical soldier of this representative democracy, he fought and died, believing in the indisputable justice of his country's cause. Conscious of the world's upheaval, appraising the magnitude of a war the like of which had never horrified humanity before, perhaps he believed his to be a service destined to change the tide of human affairs.

In the death gloom of gas, the bursting of shells and rain of bullets, men face more intimately the great God over all, their souls are aflame, and consciousness expands and hearts are searched. With the din of battle, the glow of conflicts, and the supreme trial of courage, come involuntarily the hurried appraisal of life and the contemplation of death's great mystery. On the threshold of eternity, many a soldier, I can well believe, wondered how his ebbing blood would color the stream of human life, flowing on after his sacrifice. His patriotism was none less if he craved more than triumph of country; rather, it was greater if he hoped for a victory for all human kind. Indeed, I revere that citizen whose confidence in the righteousness of his country inspired belief that its triumph is the victory of humanity.

This American soldier went forth to atone for the losses of heroic dead by making a better republic for the living.

Sleeping in these hallowed grounds are thousands of Americans who have given their blood for the baptism of freedom and its maintenance, armed exponents of the nation's conscience. It is better and nobler for their deeds. Burial here is rather more than a sign of the government's favor, it is a suggestion of a tomb in the heart of the nation, sorrowing for its noble dead.

Today's ceremonies proclaim that the hero unknown is not unhonored. We gather him to the nation's breast, within the shadow of the Capitol, of the towering shaft that honors Washington, the great father, and of the exquisite monument to Lincoln, the martyred savior. Here the inspirations of yesterday and the conscience of today forever unite to make the republic worthy of his death for flag and country.

Ours are lofty resolutions today, as with tribute to the dead we consecrate ourselves to a better order for the living. With all my heart, I wish we might say to the defenders who survive, to mothers who sorrow, to widows and children who mourn, that no such sacrifice shall be asked again.

It was my fortune recently to see a demonstration of modern warfare. It is no longer a conflict in chivalry, no more a test of militant manhood. It is only cruel, deliberate, scientific destruction. There was no contending enemy, only the theoretical defense of a hypothetic objective. But the attack was made with all the relentless methods of modern destruction. There was the rain of ruin from the aircraft, the thunder of artillery, followed by the unspeakable devastation wrought by bursting shells; there were mortars belching their bombs of desolation; machine guns concentrating their leaden storms; there was the infantry, advancing, firing, and falling—like men with souls sacrificing for the decision. The flying missiles were revealed by illuminating tracers, so that we could note their flight and appraise their deadliness. The air was streaked with tiny flames marking the flight of massed destruction; while the effectiveness of the theoretical defense was impressed by the stimulation of dead and wounded among those going forward, undaunted and unheeding. As this panorama of unutterable destruction visualized the horrors of modern conflict, there grew on the sense of the failure of a civilization which can leave its problems to such cruel arbitrament. Surely no one in authority, with human attributes and a full appraisal of the patriotic loyalty of his countrymen, could ask the

manhood of kingdom, empire, or republic to make each sacrifice until all reason had failed, until appeal to justice through understanding had been denied, until every effort of love and consideration for fellow men had been exhausted, until freedom itself and inviolate honor had been brutally threatened.

I speak not as a pacifist fearing war, but as one who loves justice and hates war. I speak as one who believes the highest function of government is to given its citizens security of peace, the opportunity to achieve, and the pursuit of happiness.

The loftiest tribute we can bestow today— the heroically earned tribute—fashioned in deliberate conviction out of unclouded thought, neither shadowed by remorse nor made vain by fancies, is the commitment of this republic to an advancement never made before. If American achievement is a cherished pride at home, if our unselfishness among nations is all we wish it to be, and ours is a helpful example in the world, then let us give of our influence and strength, yea, of our aspiration and convictions, to put mankind on a little higher plane, exulting and exalting, with war's distressing and depressing tragedies barred from the stage of righteous civilization.

There have been a thousand defenses justly and patriotically made; a thousand offenses which reason and righteousness ought to have stayed. Let us beseech all men to join us in seeking the rule under which reason and righteousness shall prevail.

Standing today on hallowed ground, conscious that all America has halted to share in the tribute of heart and mind and soul to this fellow American, and knowing that the world is noting this expression of the republic's mindfulness, it is fitting to say that his sacrifice, and that of the millions dead, shall not be in vain. There must be, there shall be, the commanding voice of a conscious civilization against armed warfare.

As we return this poor clay to its mother soil, garlanded by love and covered with the decorations that only nations can bestow, I can sense the prayers of our people, of all peoples, that this Armistice Day shall mark the beginning of a new and lasting era of peace on earth, goodwill among men. Let me join in that prayer.

Calvin Coolidge

Calvin Coolidge

1923–1929

THE SUDDEN DEATH of Harding in 1923 gave the presidency to Calvin Coolidge, a cautious, conservative, unpretentious Vermonter. Coolidge had spent a long career in Massachusetts Republican politics, ending with two terms as governor; his role in putting down the Boston police strike of 1919 had made him popular enough to be added to the national ticket in 1920. Once in the White House (he was elected in his own right by a landslide in 1924) he placidly oversaw a season of prosperity, ignoring signs of trouble in the economy. Declining to run for reelection, he left office just before the onset of the Depression and died two months before the inauguration of Franklin Delano Roosevelt.

For a man of few words—his name has come to be synonymous with taciturnity—Coolidge was a surprisingly prolific speechmaker. As vice president, with little to do, he accepted dozens of speaking invitations. As president he made more speeches than any previous president except Theodore Roosevelt—28 in 1925 alone, to every kind of group from Boy Scouts to movie magnates. He was expert at tailoring his material to his audience, elaborating on the virtues of independence, patriotism, hard work, and frugality in solemn, dignified tones, with none of the wit that he occasionally displayed in private. Most of his speeches were laboriously drafted in pencil or dictated to a stenographer; he may also have used the services of speechwriters. One speech—on the menace of dishonest insurance agents—resulted in a lawsuit against Coolidge by an insurance salesman; it was settled out of court. Of his six annual messages to Congress, only the first was delivered orally by Coolidge.

Opinions differ as to the quality of Coolidge's literary style. Heywood Broun thought him "the least gifted author the White House has known in many generations." More sympathetic readers credit him with the ability to distill into his plain, unembellished sentences the essence of his philosophy. According to his biographer, Claude M. Fuess, his speeches reveal him to be a man "with a working creed not too rarefied and ethereal for the average citizen to comprehend . . . an optimist, confident that all things do, in the end, work together for good." In a Coolidge speech, wrote Fuess, "the words are simple, the sentence structure is never involved, the thought is never confused."

Coolidge's style was well suited to the radio broadcast, a medium just coming into its own. As the journalist William Allen White noted, "He developed talent as a radio speaker. He spoke slowly, used short sentences, discarded unusual words, was direct, forthright, and unsophisticated. And so, over the radio, he went straight to the popular heart." He campaigned over the airwaves in 1924, and after the successful broadcast of his inaugural address he made radio speeches to the public every few weeks. Coolidge's nasal Yankee drawl was thus the first presidential voice to become familiar to Americans all across the country.

Inaugural Address

Washington, D.C.

March 4, 1925

COOLIDGE'S first swearing-in ceremony, in 1923, took place after midnight in the kitchen of his father's Vermont cabin, by the light of a kerosene lamp and with his father as officiant. His second, in 1925, was an unostentatious affair that included the first radio broadcast of an inaugural address. Coolidge complacently surveyed the nation's economic and social stability and promised to do nothing to disturb it. William Allen White wrote that the last paragraph of the speech is "Coolidge at his zenith. . . . Probably nothing he said or wrote elsewhere represents so perfectly the Coolidge ideal, the Coolidge literary style, which in itself deeply reveals the man; a sentimentally aspiring man, full of goodwill, a man not without an eye to the political main chance, a man always considering the vote-giving group, shrewdly eloquent about accepted beliefs, never raising debatable issues, a good man honestly proclaiming his faith in a moral government of the universe."

No one can contemplate current conditions without finding much that is satisfying and still more that is encouraging. Our own country is leading the world in the general readjustment to the results of the great conflict. Many of its burdens will bear heavily upon us for years, and secondary and indirect effects we must expect to experience for some time. But we are beginning to comprehend more definitely what course should be pursued, what remedies ought to be applied, actions should be taken for our deliverance, and are clearly manifesting a determined will faithfully and conscientiously to adopt these methods of relief. Already we have sufficiently rearranged our domestic affairs so that confidence has returned, business has revived, and we appear to be entering an era of prosperity which is gradually reaching into every part of the nation. Realizing that we cannot live unto ourselves alone, we have contributed of our resources and our counsel to the relief of the suffering and the settlement of the disputes among the European nations. Because of what America is and what America has done, a firmer courage, a higher hope, inspires the heart of all humanity.

These results have not occurred by mere chance. They have been secured by a constant and enlightened effort marked by many sacrifices and extending over many generations. We cannot continue these brilliant successes in the future, unless we continue to learn from the past. It is necessary to keep the former experiences of our country both at home and abroad continually before us, if we are to have any science of government. If we wish to erect new structures, we must have a definite knowledge of the old foundations. We must realize that human nature is about the most constant thing in the universe and that the essentials of human relationship do not change. We must frequently take our bearing from these fixed stars of our political firmament if we expect to hold a true course. If we examine carefully what we have done, we can determine the more accurately what we can do.

We stand at the opening of the 150th year since our national consciousness first asserted itself by unmistakable action with an array of force. The old sentiment of detached and dependent colonies disappeared in the new sentiment of a united and independent nation. Men began to discard the narrow confines of a local charter for the broader opportunities of a national constitution. Under the eternal urge of freedom we became an independent nation. A little less than 50 years later that freedom and independence were reasserted in the face of all the world, and guarded, supported, and secured by the Monroe Doctrine. The narrow fringe of states along the Atlantic seaboard advanced its frontiers across the hills and plains of an intervening continent until it passed down the golden slope to the Pacific. We made freedom a birthright. We extended our domain over distant islands in order to safeguard our own interests and accepted the consequent obligation to bestow justice and liberty upon less favored peoples.

In the defense of our own ideals and in the general cause of liberty we entered the Great War. When victory had been fully secured, we withdrew to our own shores unrecompensed save in the consciousness of duty done.

Throughout all these experiences we have enlarged our freedom, we have strengthened our independence. We have been, and proposed to be, more and more American. We believe that we can best serve our own country and most successfully discharge our obligations to humanity by continuing to be openly and candidly, intensely and scrupulously, American. If we have any heritage, it has been that. If we have any destiny, we have found it in that direction.

But if we wish to continue to be distinctively American, we must continue to make that term comprehensive enough to embrace the legitimate desires of a civilized and enlightened people determined in all their relations to pursue a conscientious and religious life. We can not permit ourselves to be narrowed and dwarfed by slogans and phrases. It is not the adjective, but the substantive, which is of real importance. It is not the name of the action, but the result of the action, which is the chief concern. It will be well not to be too much disturbed by the thought of either isolation or entanglement of pacifists and militarists. The physical configuration of the earth has separated us from all of the Old World, but the common brotherhood of man, the highest law of all our being, has united us by inseparable bonds with all humanity. Our country represents nothing but peaceful intentions toward all the earth, but it ought not to fail to maintain such a military force as comports with the dignity and security of a great people. It ought to be a balanced force, intensely modern, capable of defense by sea and land, beneath the surface and in the air. But it should be so conducted that all the world may see in it, not a menace, but an instrument of security and peace.

This nation believes thoroughly in an honorable peace under which the rights of its citizens are to be everywhere protected. It has never found that the necessary enjoyment of such a peace could be maintained only by a great and threatening array of arms. In common with other nations, it is now more determined than ever to promote peace through friendliness and goodwill, through mutual understanding and mutual forbearance. We have never practiced the policy of competitive armaments. We have recently committed ourselves by covenants with the other great nations to a limitation of our sea power. As one result of this, our navy ranks larger, in comparison, than it ever did before. Removing the burden of expense and jealousy, which must always accrue from a keen rivalry, is one of the most effective methods of diminishing that unreasonable hysteria and misunderstanding which are the most potent means of fomenting war. This policy represents a new departure in the world. It is a thought, an ideal, which has led to an entirely new line of action. It will not be easy to maintain. Some never move from their old position, some are constantly slipping back to the old ways of thought and the old action of seizing a musket and relying on force. America has taken the lead in this new direction, and that lead America must continue to hold. If we expect others to rely on our fairness and justice we must show that we rely on their fairness and justice.

If we are to judge by past experience, there is much to be hoped for in international relations from frequent conferences and consultations. We have before us the beneficial results of the Washington conference and the various consultations recently held upon European affairs, some of which were in response to our suggestions and in some of which we were active participants. Even the failures cannot but be accounted useful and immeasurable advance over threatened or actual warfare. I am strongly in favor of a continuation of this policy, whenever conditions are such that there is even a promise that practical and favorable results might be secured.

In conformity with the principle that a display of reason rather than a threat of force should be the determining factor in the intercourse among nations, we have long advocated the peaceful settlement of disputes by methods of arbitration and have negotiated many treaties to secure that result. The same considerations should lead to our adherence to the Permanent Court of International Justice. Where great principles are involved, where great movements are under way which promise much for the welfare of humanity by reason of the very fact that many other nations have given such movements their actual support, we ought not to withhold our own sanction because of any small

461

and inessential difference, but only upon the ground of the most important and compelling fundamental reasons. We can not barter away our independence or our sovereignty, but we ought to engage in no refinements of logic, no sophistries, and no subterfuges, to argue away the undoubted duty of this country by reason of the might of its numbers, the power of its resources, and its position of leadership in the world, actively and comprehensively to signify its approval and to bear its full share of the responsibility of a candid and disinterested attempt at the establishment of a tribunal for the administration of even-handed justice between nation and nation. The weight of our enormous influence must be cast upon the side of a reign not of force but of law and trial, not by battle but by reason.

We have never any wish to interfere in the political conditions of any other countries. Especially are we determined not to become implicated in the political controversies of the Old World. With a great deal of hesitation, we have responded to appeals for help to maintain order, protect life and property, and establish responsible government in some of the small countries of the Western Hemisphere. Our private citizens have advanced large sums of money to assist in the necessary financing and relief of the Old World. We have not failed, nor shall we fail to respond, whenever necessary to mitigate human suffering and assist in the rehabilitation of distressed nations. These, too, are requirements which must be met by reason of our vast powers and the place we hold in the world.

Some of the best thought of mankind has long been seeking for a formula for permanent peace. Undoubtedly the clarification of the principles of international law would be helpful, and the efforts of scholars to prepare such a work for adoption by the various nations should have our sympathy and support. Much may be hoped for from the earnest studies of those who advocate the outlawing of aggressive war. But all these plans and preparations, these treaties and covenants, will not of themselves be adequate. One of the greatest dangers to peace lies in the economic pressure to which people find themselves subjected. One of the most practical things to be done in the world is to seek arrangements under which such pressure may be removed, so that opportunity may be renewed and hope may be revived. There must be some assurance that effort and endeavor will be followed by success and prosperity. In the making and financing of such adjustments there is not only an opportunity, but a real duty, for America to respond with her counsel and her resources. Conditions must be provided under which people can make a living and work out of their difficulties. But there is another element, more important than all, without which there cannot be the slightest hope of a permanent peace. That element lies in the heart of humanity. Unless the desire for peace be cherished there, unless this fundamental and only natural source of brotherly love be cultivated to its highest degree all artificial efforts will be in vain. Peace will come when there is realization that only under a reign of law, based on righteousness and supported by the religious conviction of the brotherhood of man, can there be any hope of a complete and satisfying life. Parchment will fail, the sword will fail, it is only the spiritual nature of man that can be triumphant.

It seems altogether probable that we can contribute most to these important objects by maintaining our position of political detachment and independence. We are not identified with any Old World interests. This position should be made more and more clear in our relations with all foreign countries. We are at peace with all of them. Our program is never to oppress, but always to assist. But while we do justice to others, we must require that justice be done to us. With us a treaty of peace means peace, and a treaty of amity means amity. We have made great contributions to the settlement of contentious differences in both Europe and Asia. But there is a very definite point beyond which we cannot go. We can only help those who help themselves. Mindful of these limitations, the one great duty that stands out requires us to use our enormous powers to trim the balance of the world.

While we can look with a great deal of pleasure upon what we have done abroad, we must remember that our continued success in that direction depends upon what we do at home. Since its very outset, it has been found necessary to conduct our government by means of political parties. That system would not have survived from generation to generation if it had not been fundamentally sound and provided the best instrumentalities for the most complete expression of the popular will. It is not necessary to claim that it has always worked perfectly. It is enough to know that nothing better has been devised. No one would deny that there should be full and free expression and an opportunity for independence of action within the party. There is no salvation in a narrow and bigoted partisanship. But if there is to be responsible party government, the party label must be something more than a mere device for securing office. Unless those who are elected under the same party designation are willing to assume sufficient responsibility and exhibit sufficient loyalty and coherence, so that they can cooperate with each other in the support of the broad general principles of the party platform, the election is merely a mockery, no decision is made at the polls, and there is no representation of the popular will. Common honesty and good faith with the people who support a party at the polls require that party, when it enters office, to assume the control of that portion of the government to which it has been elected. Any other course is bad faith and a violation of the party pledges.

When the country has bestowed its confidence upon a party by making it a majority in the Congress, it has a right to expect such unity of actions as will make the party majority an effective instrument of government. This administration has come into power with a very clear and definite mandate from the people. The expression of the popular will in favor of maintaining our constitutional guarantees was overwhelming and decisive. There was a manifestation of such faith in the integrity of the courts that we can consider that issue rejected for some time to come. Likewise, the policy of public ownership of railroads and certain electric utilities met with unmistakable defeat. The people declared that they wanted their rights to have not a political but a judicial determination, and their independence and freedom continued and supported by having the ownership and control of their property, not in the government, but in their own hands. As they always do when they have a fair chance, the people demonstrated that they are sound and are determined to have a sound government.

When we turn from what was rejected to inquire what was accepted, the policy that stands out with the greatest clearness is that of economy in public expenditure with reduction and reform of taxation. The principle involved in this effort is that of conservation. The resources of this country are almost beyond computation. No mind can comprehend them. But the cost of our combined governments is likewise almost beyond definition. Not only those who are now making their tax returns, but those who meet the enhanced cost of existence in their monthly bills, know by hard experience what this great burden is and what it does. No matter what others may want, these people want a drastic economy. They are opposed to waste. They know that extravagance lengthens the hours and diminishes the rewards of their labor. I favor the policy of economy, not because I wish to save money, but because I wish to save people. The men and women of this country who toil are the ones who bear the cost of the government. Every dollar that we carelessly waste means that their life will be so much the more meager. Every dollar that we prudently save means that their life will be so much the more abundant. Economy is idealism in its most practical form.

If extravagance were not reflected in taxation, and through taxation both directly and indirectly injuriously affecting the people, it would not be of so much consequence. The wisest and soundest method of solving our tax problem is through economy. Fortunately, of all the great nations this country is best in a position to adopt that simple remedy. We do not any longer need war-time revenues. The collection of any taxes which are not absolutely required, which do not beyond reasonable doubt contribute to the public welfare, is only a species of legalized larceny. Under this republic the rewards of industry belong to those who earn them. The only constitutional tax is the tax which ministers to public necessity. The property of the country belongs to the people of the country. Their title is absolute. They do not support any privileged class; they do not need to maintain great military forces; they ought not to be burdened with a great array of public employees. They are not required to make any contribution to government expenditures except that which they voluntarily assess upon themselves through the action of their own representatives. Whenever taxes become burdensome a remedy can be applied by the people; but if they do not act for themselves, no one can be very successful in acting for them.

The time is arriving when we can have further tax reduction, when, unless we wish to hamper the people in the right to earn a living, we must have tax reform. The method of raising revenue ought not to impede the transaction of business; it ought to encourage it. I am opposed to extremely high rates, because they produce little or no revenue, because they are bad for the country, and, finally, because they are wrong. We can not finance the country, we can not improve social conditions, through any system of injustice, even if we attempt to inflict it upon the rich. Those who suffer the most harm will be the poor. This country believes in prosperity. It is absurd to suppose that it is envious of those who are already prosperous. The wise and correct course to follow in taxation and all other economic legislation is not to destroy those who have already secured success but to create conditions under which every one will have a better chance to be successful. The verdict of the country has been given on this question. That verdict stands. We shall do well to heed it.

These questions involve moral issues. We need not concern ourselves much about the rights of property if we will faithfully observe the rights of persons. Under our institutions their rights are supreme. It is not property but the right to hold property, both great and small, which our Constitution guarantees. All owners of property are charged with a service. These rights and duties have been revealed, through the conscience of society, to have a divine sanction. The very stability of our society rests upon production and conservation. For individuals or for governments to waste and squander their resources is to deny these rights and disregard these obligations. The result of economic dissipation to a nation is always moral decay.

These policies of better international understanding, greater economy, and lower taxes have contributed largely to peaceful and prosperous industrial relations. Under the helpful influences of restrictive immigration and a protective tariff, employment is plentiful, the rate of pay is high, and wage earners are in a state of contentment seldom before seen. Our transportation systems have been gradually recovering and have been able to meet all the requirements of the service. Agriculture has been very slow in reviving, but the price of cereals at last indicates that the day of its deliverance is at hand.

We are not without our problems, but our most important problem is not to secure new advantages but to maintain those which we already possess. Our system of government made up of three separate and independent departments, our divided sovereignty composed of nation and state, the matchless wisdom that is enshrined in our Constitution, all these need constant effort and tireless vigilance for their protection and support.

In a republic the first rule for the guidance of the citizen is obedience to law. Under a despotism the law may be imposed upon the subject. He has no voice in its making, no influence in its administration, it does not represent him. Under a free government the citizen makes his own laws, chooses his own administrators, which do represent him. Those who want their rights respected under the Constitution and the law ought to set the example themselves of observing the Constitution and the law. While there may be those of high intelligence who violate the law at times, the barbarian and the defective always violate it. Those who disregard the rules of society are not exhibiting a superior intelligence, are not promoting freedom and independence, are not following the path of civilization, but are displaying the traits of ignorance, of servitude, of savagery, and treading the way that leads back to the jungle.

The essence of a republic is representative government. Our Congress represents the people and the states. In all legislative affairs it is the natural collaborator with the president. In spite of all the criticism which often falls to its lot, I do not hesitate to say that there is no more independent and effective legislative body in the world. It is, and should be, jealous of its prerogative. I welcome its cooperation, and expect to share with it not only the responsibility, but the credit, for our common effort to secure beneficial legislation.

These are some of the principles which America represents. We have not by any means put them fully into practice, but we have strongly signified our belief in them. The encouraging feature of our country is not that it has reached its destination, but that it has overwhelmingly expressed its determination to proceed in the right direction. It is true that we could, with profit, be less sectional and more national in our thought. It would be well if we could replace much that is only a false and ignorant prejudice with a true and enlightened pride of race. But the last election showed that appeals to class and nationality had little effect. We were all found loyal to a common citizenship. The fundamental precept of liberty is toleration. We cannot permit any inquisition either within or without the law or apply any religious test to the holding of office. The mind of America must be forever free.

It is in such contemplations, my fellow countrymen, which are not exhaustive but only representative, that I find ample warrant for satisfaction and encouragement. We should not let the much that is to do obscure the much which has been done. The past and present show faith and hope and courage fully justified. Here stands our country, an example of tranquillity at home, a patron of tranquillity abroad. Here stands its government, aware of its might but obedient to its conscience. Here it will continue to stand, seeking peace and prosperity, solicitous for the welfare of the wage earner, promoting enterprise, developing waterways and natural resources, attentive to the intuitive counsel of womanhood, encouraging education, desiring the advancement of religion, supporting the cause of justice and honor among the nations. America seeks no earthly empire built on blood and force. No ambition, no temptation, lures her to thought of foreign dominions. The legions which she sends forth are armed, not with the sword, but with the cross. The higher state to which she seeks the allegiance of all mankind is not of human, but of divine origin. She cherishes no purpose save to merit the favor of Almighty God.

Government and Business

New York City, New York

November 19, 1925

THE MOST FREQUENTLY quoted of Coolidge's remarks is his statement that "the chief business of America is business." Coolidge had great confidence in the skill and probity of businessmen and was happy to let the federal regulatory commissions do their work with no contributions from him. His policy was articulated in this speech to the New York State Chamber of Commerce. Donald R. McCoy observed that Coolidge was privately uneasy about the dangerous level of stock-market speculation but thought it his duty to keep the public's trust intact by announcing that all was well. "Coolidge was unable to act for he was stalled on dead center. The influence of his business friends, his distaste for federal intervention, his pride in the Coolidge Prosperity, his hope that things would work themselves out naturally, his lassitude, and perhaps his mounting dividends, outweighed his suspicions that serious economic trouble was in the offing."

This time and place naturally suggest some consideration of commerce in its relation to government and society. We are finishing a year which can justly be said to surpass all others in the overwhelming success of general business. We are met not only in the greatest American metropolis, but in the greatest center of population and business that the world has ever known. If any one wishes to gauge the power which is represented by the genius of the American spirit, let him contemplate the wonders which have been wrought in this region in the short space of 200 years. Not only does it stand unequaled by any other place on earth, but it is impossible to conceive of any other place where it could be equaled.

The foundation of this enormous development rests upon commerce. New York is an imperial city, but it is not a seat of government. The empire over which it rules is not political, but commercial. The great cities of the ancient world were the seats of both government and industrial power. The Middle Ages furnished a few exceptions. The great capitals of former times were not only seats of government but they actually governed. In the modern world government is inclined to be merely a tenant of the city. Political life and industrial life flow on side by side, but practically separated from each other. When we contemplate the enormous power, autocratic and uncontrolled, which would have been created by joining the authority of government with the influence of business, we can better appreciate the wisdom of the fathers in their wise dispensation which made Washington the political center of the country and left New York to develop into its business center. They wrought mightily for freedom.

The great advantages of this arrangement seem to me to be obvious. The only disadvantages which appear lie in the possibility that otherwise business and government might have had a better understanding of each other and been less likely to develop mutual misapprehensions and suspicions. If a contest could be held to determine how much those who are really prominent in our government life know about business, and how much those who are really prominent in our business life know about government, it is my firm conviction that the prize would be awarded to those who are in government life. This is as it ought to be, for those who have the greater authority ought to have the greater knowledge. But it is my even firmer conviction that the general welfare of our country could be very much advanced through a better knowledge by both of those parties of the multifold problems with which each has to deal. While our system gives an opportunity for great benefit by encouraging detachment and breadth of vision which ought not to be sacrificed, it does not have the advantages which could be secured if each had a better conception of their mutual requirements.

While I have spoken of what I believe would be the advantages of a more sympathetic understanding, I should put an even stronger emphasis on the desirability of the largest possible independence between government and business. Each ought to be sovereign in its own sphere. When government comes unduly under the influence of business, the tendency is to develop an administration which closes the door of opportunity; becomes narrow and selfish in its outlook, and results in an oligarchy. When government enters the field of business with its great resources, it has a tendency of extravagance and inefficiency, but, having the power to crush all competitors, likewise closes the door to opportunity and results in monopoly. It is always a problem in a republic to maintain on the one side that efficiency which comes only from trained and skillful management without running into fossilization and autocracy, and to maintain on the other that equality of opportunity which is the result of political and economic liberty without running into dissolution and anarchy. The general results in our country, our freedom and prosperity, warrant the assertion that our system of institutions has been advancing in the right direction in the attempt to solve these problems. We have order, opportunity, wealth, and progress.

While there has been in the past and will be in the future a considerable effort in this country of different business interests to attempt to run the government in such a way as to set up a system on privilege, and while there have been and will be those who are constantly seeking to commit the government to a policy of infringing upon the domain of private business, both of these efforts have been very largely discredited, and with reasonable vigilance on the part of the people to preserve their freedom do not now appear to be dangerous.

When I have been referring to business, I have used the word in its all-inclusive sense to denote alike the employer and employee, the production of agriculture and industry, the distribution of transportaion and commerce, and the service of finance and banking. It is the work of the world. In modern life, with all its intricacies, business has come to hold a very dominant position in the thoughts of all enlightened people. Rightly understood, this is not a criticism, but a compliment. In its great economic organization it does not represent, as some have hastily concluded, a mere desire to minister to selfishness. The New York Chamber of Commerce is not made up of men merely animated with a purpose to get the better of each other. It is something far

more important than a sordid desire for gain. It could not successively succeed on that basis. It is dominated by a more worthy impulse; it rests on a higher law. True business represents the mutual organized effort of society to minister to the economic requirements of civilization. It is an effort by which men provide for the material needs of each other. While it is not an end in itself, it is the important means for the attainment of a supreme end. It rests squarely on the law of service. It has for its main reliance truth and faith and justice. In its larger sense it is one of the greatest contributing forces to the moral and spiritual advancement of the race.

It is the important and righteous position that business holds in relation to life which gives warrant to the great interest which the national government constantly exercises for the promotion of its success. This is not exercised as has been the autocratic practice abroad of directly supporting and financing different business projects, except in case of great emergency; but we have rather held to a democratic policy of cherishing the general structure of business while holding its avenues open to the widest competition, in order that its opportunties and its benefits might be given the broadest possible participation. While it is true that the government ought not to be and is not committed to certain methods of acquisition which, while partaking of the nature of unfair practices, try to masquerade under the guise of business, the government is and ought to be thoroughly committed to every endeavor of production and distribution which is entitled to be designated as true business. Those who are so engaged, instead of regarding the government as their opponent and enemy, ought to regard it as their vigilant supporter and friend.

It is only exceptional instances that this means a change on the part of the national administration so much as it means a change on the part of trade. Except for the requirements of safety, health, and taxation, the law enters very little into the work of production. It is mostly when we come to the problems of distribution that we meet the more rigid exactions of legislation. The main reason why certain practices in this direction have been denounced is because they are a species of unfair competition on the one hand or tend to monopoly and restraint of trade on the other.

The whole policy of the government in its system of opposition to monopoly, and its public regulation of transportation and trade, has been animated by a desire to have business remain business. We are politically free people and must be an economically free people.

It is my belief that the whole material development of our country has been enormously stimulated by reason of the general insistence on the part of the public authorities that economic effort ought not to partake of privilege, and that business should be unhampered and free. This could never have been done under a system of freight-rate discriminations or monopolistic trade associations. These might have enriched a few for a limited period, but they never would have enriched the country, while on the firmer foundation of justice we have achieved even more ample individual fortunes and a perfectly unprecedented era of general prosperity. This has resulted in no small part from the general acceptance on the part of those who own and control the wealth of the nation, that it is to be used not to oppress but to serve. It is that policy, sometimes perhaps imperfectly expressed and clumsily administered, that has animated the national government. In its observance there is unlimited opportunity for progress and prosperity.

It would be difficult, if not impossible, to estimate the contribution which government makes to business. It is notorious that where the government is bad, business is bad. The mere fundamental precepts of the administration of justice, the providing of order and security, are priceless. The prime element in the value of all property is the knowledge that its peaceful enjoyment will be publicly defended. If disorder should break out in your city, if there should be a conviction extending over any length of time that the rights of persons and property could no longer be protected by law, the value of your tall buildings would shrink to about the price of what are now water fronts of old Carthage or what are now corner lots in ancient Babylon. It is really the extension of these fundamental rights that the government is constantly attempting to apply to modern business. It wants its rightful possessors to rest in security, it wants any wrongs that they may suffer to have a legal remedy, and it is all the time striving through administrative machinery to prevent in advance the infliction of injustice.

These undoubtedly represent policies which are wise and sound and necessary. That they have often been misapplied and many times run into excesses, nobody can deny. Regulation has often become restriction, and inspection has too frequently been little less than obstruction. This was the natural result of those times in the past when there were practices in business which warranted severe disapprobation. It was only natural that when these abuses were reformed by an aroused public opinion a great deal of prejudice which ought to have been discriminating and directed only at certain evil practices came to include almost the whole domain of business, especially where it had been gathered into large units. After the abuses had been discontinued the prejudice remained to produced a large amount of legislation, which, however well meant in its application to trade, undoubtedly hampered but did not improve. It is this misconception and misapplication, disturbing and wasteful in their results, which the national government is attempting to avoid. Proper regulation and control are disagreeable and expensive. They represent the suffering that the just must endure because of the injust. They are a part of the price which must be paid to promote the cause of economic justice.

Undoubtedly if public vigilance were relaxed, the generation to come might suffer a relapse. But the present generation of business almost universally throughout its responsible organization and management has shown every disposition to correct its own abuses with as little intervention of the government as possible. This position is recognized by the public, and due to the appreciation of the needs which the country has for great units of production in time of war, and to the better understanding of the service which they perform in time of peace, resulting very largely from the discussion of our tax problems, a new attitude of the public mind is distinctly discernible toward great aggregations of capital. Their prosperity goes very far to insure the prosperity of all the country. The contending elements have each learned a most profitable lesson.

This development has left the government free to advance from the problems of reform and repression to those of economy and construction. A very large progress is being made in these directions. Our country is in a state of unexampled and apparently sound and well distributed prosperity. It did not gain wealth, as some might hastily conclude, as a result of the war. Here and there individuals may have profited greatly, but the country as a whole was a heavy loser. Forty billions of the wealth of the nation was directly exhausted, while the indirect expenditure and depreciation cannot be estimated. The government appreciated that the only method of regeneration lay in economy and production. It has followed a policy of economy in national expenditures. By an enormous reduction in taxation it has released great amounts of capital for use in productive effort. It has sought to stimulate domestic production by a moderate application of the system of protective tariff duties. The results of these efforts are known to all the world.

Another phase of this progress is not so well understood, but upon its continuance depends our future ability to meet the competition of the lower standards of living in foreign countries. During the past five years the Department of Commerce has unceasingly directed attention to the necessity for the elimination of waste. This effort has been directed toward better cooperation to improve efficiency in the use of labor and materials in all branches of business. This has been sought by the necessary cooperative action among individual concerns within groups, and between producers and consumers. This does not imply any diminution of fair competition or any violation of the laws against restraint of trade. In fact, these proposals have been a protection to the smaller units of business and a most valuable asset alike to the producer, wage earner, and consumer.

The result of the realization of these wastes and the large cooperative effort that has been instituted in the community to cure them, whether with the assistance of the government departments or by independent action of the groups, has been the most profound factor in this recovery made in the past five years. There can be no question that great wastes have been eliminated by these activities in the business community through such actions as the abolition of car shortages; by improved equipment and methods of management of our railways; the cooperation with shippers

to save delays; the remarkable advance in electrification of the country with all of its economies in labor and coal; the provision of better economic and statistical information as to production, stocks, and consumption of all commodities in order that producers and consumers may better adjust supply to demand, thereby eliminating speculation and loss; the great progress made in the technology of standardizing quality and dimensions in heavy manufactured products like building materials and commodities generally which do not involve problems of style or individuality; the reduction of seasonal employment in the construction and other industries and of losses through fire and through traffic accidents; advancement of commercial arbitration; development of farmers' cooperatives for the more economical and stable marketing of farm produce; and in general the elimination of waste due to lost motion and material throughout our whole economic fabric.

All this represents a movement as important as that of 20 years ago for the regulation of corporations and conservation of our natural resources. This effort for conservation of use of materials and conservation of energy in which our whole country has engaged during these five years has been in no small part responsible for the rich reward in the increasing comfort and living standards of the people. But in addition to bringing about a condition in which the government debt is being rapidly liquidated while at the same time taxes are greatly reduced, capital has become abundant and prosperity reigns. The most remarkable results of economy and the elimination of waste are shown in the wage and commodity indexes. In 1920 wages were about 100 percent above the pre-war rates and the average wholesale price of commodities was about 120 percent above the pre-war rates. A steady increase in the wage index took place, so that during the last year it was 120 percent above the prewar rate. As the cost of our production is so largely a matter of wages, and as tax returns show that for the last year profits were ample, it would naturally have been expected that the prices of commodities would have increased. Yet during this period the average wholesale price level of commodities declined from 120 percent above the pre-war level that it was in 1920, to only 57 percent above the pre-war level in 1925. Thus, as a result of greater economy and efficiency, and the elimination of waste in the conduct of the national government and of the business of the country, prices went down while wages went up. The wage earner receives more, while the dollar of the consumer will purchase more. The significance and importance of this result cannot be overestimated.

This is real and solid progress. No one can deny that it represents an increase in national efficiency. It must be maintained. Great as the accomplishments have been they are yet but partly completed. We need further improvement in transportation facilities by development of inland waterways; we need railroad consolidations; we need further improvement of our railway terminals for more economical distribution of commodities in the great congested centers; we need reorganization of government departments; we need still larger extension of electrification; in general, we need still further effort against all the various categories of waste which the Department of Commerce has enumerated and so actively attacked, for in this direction lies not only increased economic progress but the maintenance of that progress against foreign competition. There is still plenty of work for business to do.

By these wise policies, pursued with tremendous economic effort, our country has reached its present prosperous condition. The people have been willing to work because they have had something to work for. The per capita production has greatly increased. Out of our surplus savings we have been able to advance great sums for refinancing the Old World and developing the New. While Europe has attracted more public attention, Latin America, Japan, and even Australia, have been very large participators in these loans. If rightly directed, they ought to be of benefit to both lender and borrower. If used to establish industry and support commerce abroad, through adding to the wealth and productive capacity of those countries, they create their own security and increase consuming power to the probable advantage of our trade. But when used in ways that are not productive, like the maintenance of great military establishments or to meet municipal expenditures which should either be eliminated by government economy or supplied by taxation, they do not appear to serve a useful purpose and

ought to be discouraged. Our bankers have a great deal of responsibility in relation to the soundness of these loans when they undertake to invest the savings of our country abroad. I should regret very much to see our possession of resources which are available to meet needs in other countries be the cause of any sentiment of envy or unfriendliness toward us. It ought everywhere to be welcomed with rejoicing and considered as a part of the good fortune of the entire world that such an economic reservoir exists here which can be made available in case of need.

Everyone knows that it was our resources that saved Europe from a complete collapse immediately following the armistice. Without the benefit of our credit an appalling famine would have prevailed over great areas. In accordance with the light of all past history, disorder and revolution, with the utter breaking down of all legal restraints and the loosing of all the passions which had been aroused by four years of conflict, would have rapidly followed. Others did what they could, and no doubt made larger proportionate sacrifices, but it was the credits and food which we supplied that saved the situation.

When the work of restoring the fiscal condition of Europe began, it was accomplished again with our assistance. When Austria determined to put her financial house in order, we furnished a part of the capital. When Germany sought to establish a sound fiscal condition, we again contributed a large proportion of the necessary gold loan. Without this, the reparations plan would have utterly failed. Germany could not otherwise have paid. The armies of occupation would have gone on increasing international irritation and ill will. It was our large guarantee of credit that assisted Great Britain to return to a gold basis. What we have done for France, Italy, Belgium, Czechoslovakia, Poland, and other countries, is all a piece of the same endeavor. These efforts and accomplishments, whether they be appreciated at home or received with gratitude abroad, which have been brought about by the business interests of our country, constitute an enormous world service. Others have made plans and adopted agreements for future action which hold a rank of great importance. But when we come to the consideration of what has been done, when we turn aside from what has been promised, to examine what has been performed, no positive and constructive accomplishment of the past five years compares with the support which America has contributed to the financial stability of the world. It clearly marks a new epoch.

This holds a distinctly higher rank than a mere barter and sale. It reaches above the ordinary business transaction into a broader realm. America has disbanded her huge armies and reduced her powerful fleet, but in attempting to deal justly through the sharing of our financial resources we have done more for peace than we could have done with all our military power. Peace, we know, rests to a great extent upon justice, but it is very difficult for the public mind to divorce justice from economic opportunity. The problem for which we have been attempting a solution is in the first instance to place the people of the earth back into avenues of profitable employment. It was necessary to restore hope, to renew courage. A great contribution to this end has been made with American money. The work is not all done yet. No doubt it will develop that this has not been accomplished without some mistakes, but the important fact remains that when the world needed to be revived we did respond. As nations see their way to a safer economic existence, they will see their way to a more peaceful existence. Possessed of the means to meet personal and public obligations, people are reestablishing their self-respect. The financial strength of America has contributed to the spiritual restoration of the world. It has risen into the domain of true business. . . .

The working out of these problems of regulation, government economy, the elimination of waste in the use of human effort and of materials, conservation and the proper investment of our savings both at home and abroad, is all a part of the mighty task which was imposed upon mankind of subduing the earth. America must either perform her full share in the accomplishment of this great world destiny or fail. For almost three centuries we were intent upon our domestic development. We sought the help of the people and the wealth of other lands by which to increase our numerical strength and augment our national fortune. We have grown exceedingly great in population and in riches. This power and this prosperity we can continue for ourselves if we will but proceed with moderation. If our people will but use those resources which have been intrusted to them, whether of command over large numbers of men or of command over large investments of capital, not selfishly but generously, not to exploit others but to serve others, there will be no doubt of an increasing production and distribution of wealth. . . .

This is the land of George Washington. We can do no less than work toward the realization of his hope. It ought to be our ambition to see the institutions which he founded grow in the blessings which they bestow upon our own citizens and increase in the good which their influence casts upon all the world. He did not hesitate to meet peril or encounter danger or make sacrifices. There is no cause which can be supported by any other methods. We cannot listen to the counsels of perfection; we cannot pursue a timorous policy; we cannot avoid the obligations of a common humanity. We must meet our perils, we must encounter our dangers; we must make our sacrifices; or history will recount that the works of Washington have failed. I do not believe the future is to be dismayed by that record. The truth and faith and justice of the ancient days have not departed from us.

The Farmer and the Nation

Chicago, Illinois
December 7, 1925

THE GENERAL PROSPERITY that U.S. industry enjoyed under Coolidge was not shared by the farmers, who appealed to the government for help. Speaking to the annual convention of the American Farm Bureau Federation, Coolidge rejected proposals introduced in Congress to establish a federal agency that would maintain prices by buying surplus crops and selling them cheaply in foreign markets. Eventually he twice vetoed such legislation (the McNary-Haugen Bill), saying that "if the measure is enacted . . . the lobbies of Congress would be filled with emissaries from every momentarily distressed industry demanding similar relief of a burdensome surplus at the expense of the Treasury." His own alternative, enacted by Congress in 1929 without much effect, was to offer farmers government assistance in forming marketing and credit cooperatives.

No one can travel across the vast area that lies between the Alleghenies and the Rockies without being thoroughly impressed with the enormous expansion of American agriculture. Other sections of our country, acre for acre, are just as important and just as productive, but it is in this region that the cultivation of the land holds its most dominant position. It is to serve the farmers of this great open country that teeming cities have arisen, great stretches of navigation have been opened, a mighty network of railways has been constructed, a fast increasing mileage of highways has been laid out, and modern inventions have stretched their lines of communication among all the various communities and into nearly every home. Agriculture holds a position in this country that it was never before able to secure anywhere else on earth.

It is the development which has taken place within this area, mostly within the last 75 years, which has given agriculture a new standing in the world. By bringing the tillage of the soil under a new technique it has given to the people on the farm a new relationship to commerce, industry, and society. The ownership of land has always been a mark of privilege and distinction, but in other times and places the laborious effort of farming, the hard work of cultivating the soil—which was done almost entirely by hand—the comparative isolation of rural existence, was traditionally an unattractive life assigned to the serf and the uncultured peasant. It still partakes of that nature in most countries. But in America the farm has long since ceased to be associated with a mode of life that could be called rustic.

It has become a great industrial enterprise, requiring a broad knowledge in its management, a technical skill in its labor, intricate machinery in its processes, and trained merchandising in its marketings. Agriculture in America has been raised to the rank of a profession. It does not draw any artificial support from industry or from the government. It rests squarely on a foundation of its own. It is independent.

The place which agriculture holds today in this country, superior to that which it ever held before in time of peace in this or any other land, is by reason of its very eminence one of increasing exactions and difficulties. It does not require much talent or any great foresight to live on an inferior scale, limited and impoverished, nor does it evoke much eulogy, but to maintain freedom and independence, to rise in the economic scale to the ownership and profitable management of a great property amid all the perils of our competitive life, requires a high degree of industry and ability. Those who achieve that position in a community will always be entitled to the highest commendation. Whatever other obstacles the American people have had to meet and overcome, of every station in life, they have never permitted themselves to be hampered by a condition of dependence. As what they have had was secured not by favor or by bounty, but by their own efforts, no one else has had any power to deprive them of it. Unencumbered by any special artificial support, they have stood secure on their own foundation. America is not without a true nobility, but it is not supported by privilege. It rests on worth.

It is our farm life that is particularly representative of this standard of American citizenship. It is made up of many different types and races; it includes many different modes of thought and living. Stretching from the North, with its months of frost, to the Gulf, with its perpetual summer, it embraces a wide variety of production. But it is all a partaker of the same high measure of achievement and character. It rises in its importance above the products of the land and puts a stamp of its own upon the quality of our people. It is not merely for a supply of food that we look to the farms, but as a never-failing source, if others become exhausted, from which we can always replenish the manhood and womanhood of the nation. It is for this reason that our whole country entertains the greatest solicitude for the welfare of the people who make up our agricultural population. The importance of their continued success and progress cannot be overestimated. It affects not only the material prosperity but reaches beyond that into the moral and spiritual life of America.

It was the people of this stamp and character who were mainly instrumental in founding American institutions. It was well on into the 19th century before the great industrial development of our country began. In the old days there were some professional men and there were the clergy who exercised in a high degree an inspired leadership not only in the religion and educational, but to a marked extent in the political, life of their day. But the people were of the farm. Their living came from the soil. Their sturdy industry, their determination to be free, resulted in no small part from their occupation and mode of life. Wherever there is a farm, there is the greatest opportunity for a true home. It was the loyalty and perseverance bred for the home life of the American farmer that supported Washington through seven years of conflict and provided the necessary self-restraint to translate his victory into the abiding institutions of feedom. It is the spirit of those homes that our country must forever cherish.

But the gratitude of America, and I think of the whole world, is due not only to "the embattled farmers" who stood at Concord bridge and "fired the shot heard round the world," but to those tillers of the soil of the great prairie states, prophets and pioneers of freedom, who rose to power in time to make it possible for Lincoln to save the Union, and also to the informed, improved, and well-equipped agriculture of our own day, which, while giving generously of their own manhood and womanhood, put forth those stupendous efforts which provided food, cotton, wool, and other materials that turned the tide for the cause of liberty in the Great War. It is the existence of this superb power, both of resources and of people, which has its home in the great open country, that has made possible not only the independence and freedom of our own land and the extension of liberty throughout the world, but has furnished the foundation on which has been built the great expansion in the industrial and commercial life of the nation. Our statesmanship can be dedicated to no more worthy purpose than the perpetuation of this high standard of American farm life.

All of these results would appear to lead to the inevitable conclusion that to a very large extent the underlying support to the strength and character and greatness of America has been furnished by the strength and character and greatness of its agriculture. Our country has been developed under the influence of a new spirit. In the early beginnings of organized society the main form of wealth which was plentiful consisted of land. It was almost the sole source of production. Always in theory, and usually in practice, all land belonged to the Crown. It was the custom for the ruler to bestow upon his retainers not only landed estates, but to provide in addition the serfs who were attached to the soil, in order that they might supply the necessary labor for its productivity. The workers in the field were held in servitude, while their masters usually lived many miles from the land, sometimes in their castles, sometimes in towns and cities. This was the established condition all over the Old World. The position of the country thus became stationary. It was in the cities and towns, where opportunity came for exchange of ideas and educational advancement, that there started that progress toward freedom and self-government which marked the beginning of the modern age. The importance of the cities and towns became predominant. Even after freedom was granted to the serfs, the tillers of the soil never became a great influence. Their interests were always subordinated to the stronger, more aggressive life of the industrial population and of the ruling classes.

But America never fully came under this blighting influence. It was a different type of individual that formed the great bulk of our early settlers. They gained their livelihood by cultivating the soil, but there was no large and overmastering city or industrial population. The expansion of our country down to almost as late as 1880 was an agricultural expansion. A large majority of our inhabitants were engaged in that occupation. They not only tilled the soil, but they owned it. They not only directed the government, but they made it. The fertile lands and generous homestead laws under American institutions all worked together to produce an entirely new position of place and power for agriculture. When there was added to this the marvelous inventions of farm machinery which have come into modern life, it made it possible to establish here the first agriculture empire which did not rest upon an oppressed peasantry. This was a stupendous achievement.

Following this came the vast business growth which brought great changes. The town and industrial population for the first time began to exceed that of the farms. From the surplus of food products requiring foreign markets we began to reach something like a balance between domestic production and consumption. Before 1910, so wise a man as James J. Hill expressed the opinion that in the near future we should be importers of wheat.

Under normal conditions Mr. Hill might have been correct, but the World War intervened. The enormous demand from abroad brought the high prices which so stimulated production that it reached a new record in amount and value. Without this service, famine undoubtedly would have prevailed over wide areas. This resulted in a great inflation and in an overproduction, reaching its summit in 1919, which was followed by the inevitable deflation of 1920 and 1921. The best economic authority tells us this was inevitable. Whether it was or not, it came. It afflicted both agriculture and industry. The values of manufacturing plants and their stocks on hand went down, their orders were canceled, their operations ceased, and the buying capacity of their wage earners being greatly reduced, the consumption of food products declined, causing a fall in prices that reached back to the farm. The resulting losses have never been fully recovered either in industry or agriculture,

but starting from the low point of 1920 and 1921 both have made progress and from every indication appear to be entering an era of prosperity.

It has seemed to me desirable to consider thus briefly the development of our American agriculture, in order that by a better understanding of the method of its progress and the position it now holds we may better comprehend its needs and better estimate what the future promises for it. Everyone knows that the farmer, who is often least able to bear it, went through the most drastic deflation. Considered as a whole, his position has steadily improved since 1921. I do not mean that land values or prices have reached their former level. That was not to be expected. But I do mean that, generally speaking, the present business of farming as a whole is beginning to be profitable. Of course there are exceptions to be made of localties, individuals, and crops. Some people would grow poor on a mountain of gold, while others would make a good living on a rock. We can not bend our course to meet the exceptions; we must treat agriculture as a whole, and if, as a whole, it can be placed in a prosperous condition the exceptions will tend to eliminate themselves.

There have been discussions which seem to indicate some fear that our agriculture is becoming decadent, that it has already reached its highest point, and that, becoming unprofitable, it is likely to diminish. Nothing in the appearance of the country or of its people as I have traveled over it has seemed to indicate any deterioration, nor do I find anything in the farm census and reports that warrants this conclusion.

It is true that there is an increasing interchange of population between the city and the country. With the coming of the automobile many of the city people are moving out into the country, and with the increasing use of machinery some of those formerly employed on the farm have been released for employment in the industries. For the past 15 years urban population has been increasing, while farm population and the number of farms have slightly decreased. This has reversed the condition that existed before that period. But this is only a part of the story.

The real question is not the numbers employed but the amount of production. If that should appear to be inadequate to meet our requirements for food and raw materials, if the morale of the farmers should be breaking down, the situation might be serious. Such does not appear to be the fact. In intelligence, in education, in the general standards of living, farm life was never so well equipped as it is today. In the past 45 years, which roughly marks our great industrial development, the index number of production rose from 100 to 237, while that for population is estimated to be but 226. Production has outrun population, according to the statistics of the Harvard Service. While the number of farms and people engaged in farming was slightly less in 1924 than in 1910, production in 1923 and 1924 was 15 percent greater than in 1910. Fewer people but more production means each person on the farm will receive more.

It is not only production, however, but price that is important to the farmer. The value of his produce for 1924, excluding crops fed to animals, was about $12,136,000,000. The estimates for the present year are about the same. This compares with $3,549,000,000 in 1900. According to estimates, the number of people on farms in 1924 was about 10 percent greater than in 1900. The amount of money received was about 350 percent greater. But as the general price level of all commodities had greatly advanced, measured in purchasing power the amount received was only about 90 percent greater. This means that 110 percent of people engaged in agriculture received 190 percent more in 1924 than they did in 1900. While it is true that there was a great decline in farm prices in 1920 and 1921, and an even greater decline in the purchasing power of farm produce compared with other commodities, yet since that time farm prices have risen more rapidly than other commodities, so that the purchasing power of farm produce has risen also. The tendency appears to be to bring agriculture as a whole back to the same relative economic position that it occupied before the war. While general production, prices, and living conditions on the farm are improving, there is little ground for fear that agriculture is becoming decadent; yet some areas are still depressed; debts and taxes still remain.

Although it is gratifying to know that farm conditions as a whole are encouraging, yet we ought not to cease our efforts for their constant improvement. We cannot claim that they have reached perfection anywhere, and in too many instances there is still much distress. Various suggestions of artificial relief have been made. Production has been ample, but prices compared with the war era have been very much reduced, although they are now considerably improved. The proposals made have, therefore, had the purpose of increasing prices.

One of the methods by which this has been sought, though put forward chiefly as an emergency measure as I understand from its proponents, was to have corporations organized through which the government would directly or indirectly fix prices or engage in buying and selling farm produce. This would be a dangerous undertaking, and as the emergency is not so acute, it seems at present to have lost much of it support. No matter how it is disguised, the moment the government engages in buying and selling, by that act it is fixing prices. Moreover, it would apparently destroy cooperative associations and all other marketing machinery, for no one can compete with the government. Ultimately it would end the independence which the farmers of this country enjoy as a result of centuries of struggle and prevent the exercise of their own judgment and control in cultivating their land and marketing their produce.

Government control cannot be divorced from political control. The overwhelming interest of the consumer, not the smaller interest of the producer, would be sure to dominate in the end. I am reliably informed that the secretary of agriculture of a great foreign power has recently fixed the wages of farm labor in his country at less than $5 per week. The government price is not always a high price. Unless we fix corresponding prices for other commodities, a high fixed price for agriculture would simply stimulate overproduction that would end in complete collapse. However attractive this proposal was at first thought, careful consideration of it has led to much opposition on the part of the farmers. They realize that even the United States government is not strong enough, either directly or indirectly, to fix prices which would constantly guarantee success. They are opposed to submitting themselves to the control of a great government bureaucracy. They prefer the sound policy of maintaining their freedom and their own initiative as individuals, or to limit them only as they voluntarily form group associations. They do not wish to put the government into the farming business. . . .

If the price fixing and tariff revision do not seem to be helpful, there are other proposals that do promise improvements. For financing the farmer we are developing the farm loan and intermediate credit banks. These have put out about $1,200,000,000 of loans at moderate rates to about 350,000 farmers. In addition, there is the general banking system, national and state. All of these agencies need to give more informed attention to farm needs. They need more energy in administration. They should be equipped to supply not only credit but sound business advice, and the farmers to a much better extent should learn to use all these facilities.

For a more orderly marketing calculated to secure a better range of prices the cooperative movement promises the greatest success. Already they are handling $2,500,000,000 of farm produce, or nearly one-fifth of the annual production. The disposition of surplus produce has been discussed. If by this is meant the constant raising of a larger supply than is needed, it is difficult to conceive of any remedy except reduced production in any such commodity. But there are, of course, accidental surpluses due to more favorable weather conditions, which are unavoidable and which ought to be managed so that they can be spread over a year or two without depressing prices. The initiative of the farmers themselves, with such assistance as can be given them by the government without assuming responsibility for business management, through financing and through the cooperative movement, would appear to be a wise method of solving this problem. Of course, I should be willing to approve any plan that can be devised in accordance with sound economic principles.

To have agriculture worth anything, it must rest on an independent business basis. It cannot at the same time be part private business and part government business. I believe the government ought to give it every assistance, but it ought to leave it as the support, the benefit, and the business of the people. The interest which the national government takes in agriculture is manifest by an appropriation of about $140,000,000 a year, which is nearly one-fifth of our total expenditure, exclusive of the Post Office, prior to the war. I do not need to recount what is being done for education and good roads, for opening up our waterways, or the enormous activities of the Department of Agriculture which reach to almost every farmer in the land.

The most important development of late years has been the cooperative movement. With the economic information furnished by the department, which was of such great value to the hog and potato industries for the last year or two, with better warehouse and storage facilities and a better credit structure, much can be done to take care of the ordinary surplus. With a production influenced by information from the department, with adequate storage, supplied with necessary credit and the orderly marketing effected through cooperative action, agriculture could be placed on a sound and independent basis. While the government ought not to undertake to control or direct, it should supplement and assist all efforts in this direction. The leaders in the cooperative movement, with the advice of the Department of Agriculture, have prepared what is believed to be an adequate bill embodying these principles, which will be presented to the Congress for enactment. I propose actively and energetically to assist the farmers to promote their welfare through cooperative marketing.

Under the working out of the provisions of this bill the farmers would have the active and energetic assistance of the government in meeting the problem of surplus production. Through consultation and conference the best experts of the country would be employed as the needs require and methods of storage, credit, and marketing would be devised. The agencies created would have at their disposal the active cooperation of the great organizations of the Departments of Agriculture, Commerce, and federal banking. Their representatives at home and abroad would be engaged in locating and supplying domestic and foreign markets. The fundamental soundness of this proposal rests on the principle that it is helping the farmer to help himself. Already the cooperative effort in raisins and other products has met with marked success by adopting this plan.

It would be a great mistake to underestimate the difficulties under which the farmers labor. They are entitled to all the sympathy and help which the government can give them. But I feel they are also entitled to consider the encouraging features of their situation. Human nature is on their side. We are all consumers of food. The more prosperous we become, the more we consume of the higher priced products. In the past, farm prices have always tended to get the better of industrial prices. In the period from 1820 to 1860 there was general rise of all commodities, but farm prices increased about 50 percent more than other commodities. After the Civil War, from the 70s to 1896, there was a decline in all commodities, but farm prices declined less, so that their purchasing power actually increased. From 1896 to 1913, according to the Bureau of Labor Statistics, the index number of farm prices rose 82 percent while that of other prices rose but 37 percent. It was this great increase in the price of food products which brought about the complaint and discussion of the high cost of living, which everyone will recall became acute about 1911 and remained a problem of economic adjustment unsolved when the World War began.

With the coming of the great conflict an entire transformation took place. The price of all commodities rose and the price of land rose. There was a great temptation to expand. Farmers bought more land at very high prices. Then came the terrible world depression which left many involved in great debts and everybody with shrunken land values. Farm produce decreased in price faster than other commodities. These debts and shrunken values still remain as a great burden. On top of them are the war taxes which the nation has greatly reduced, but which the local commodities still tend to increase.

It is this burden which is causing distress, but history is again showing signs of repeating itself. In 1921 the price of farm produce reached its low point. According to the Department of Agriculture, however, the end of this four-year period sees the price of farm products substantially increased. Much of the debts and taxes remain, but with the prices now received the present business of farming is very much improved.

I believe that the past history of the relative trend of prices between farm products

and other commodities is of tremendous significance. The surplus lands of the country are exhausted. The industrial population is outstripping the farm population. Manufacturing is expanding. These must come to the farmers for their food and their raw materials. While we can produce more, the markets for food are increasing much faster than present farm productivity. The future of agriculture looks to be exceedingly secure.

The real wealth of our country, its productive capacity, its great manufacturing plants, its far-reaching railroad system, its mightly commerce, and its agriculture did not come into being all at once, but is the result of a vast multitude of small increments brought about by long, slow, and laborious toil. Whatever a few individuals may do, the nation as a whole and its great subdivisions of industry, transportation, commerce, and agriculture can increase by no other method. The percentage of yearly returns upon all the property of this country is low, but in the aggregate it is a stupendous sum. Unless all past experience is to be disregarded, notwithstanding its present embarrassments, agriculture as a whole should lead industry in future prosperity.

In all our economic discussions we must remember that we cannot stop with the mere acquisition of wealth. The ultimate result to be desired is not the making of money, but the making of people. Industry, thrift, and self-control are not sought because they create wealth, but because they create character. These are the prime product of the farm. We who have seen it, and lived it, we know.

It is this life that the nation is so solicitous to maintain and improve. It dwells in the open country, among the hills and valleys and over the great plains, in the unobstructed light of the sun, and under the glimmer of the stars. It brings its inhabitants into an intimate and true relation to nature, where they can live in harmony with the Great Purpose. It has been the life of freedom and independence, of religious convictions and abiding character. In its past it has made and saved America and helped rescue the world. In its future it holds the supreme promise of human progress.

The Kellogg-Briand Pact

Wausau, Wisconsin

August 15, 1928

In 1928, the United States and 14 other nations—later joined by 47 more—became signatories to the Kellogg-Briand Pact, also known as the Pact of Paris, which pledged them to renounce war "as an instrument of national policy in their relations with one another." Though Coolidge had little faith in the effectiveness of such an agreement, the Republican leaders saw in it an opportunity to enhance the party's foreign-policy image in an election year, especially after the collapse of the administration's Anglo-American naval disarmament conference and its failure to win American membership in the World Court. Coolidge obligingly went before a state convention of the American Legion in Wisconsin to urge ratification of the pact, and repeated his recommendations in his State of the Union message to Congress later in the year—at the same time approving an increase in defense appropriations. Congress ratified the pact in 1929.

It is now 10 years since the events were taking place which brought your organization into existence. They have been years necessarily attended by a great deal of hardship, but they have also been years when the world has made a great deal of progress. The war left the chief nations utterly exhausted. How many people directly and indirectly lost their lives by reason of that conflict will never be known. It ran into many millions. The cost in treasure was so great that it can never be counted. It ran into hundreds of billions. The material resources of several of the powers involved were so far exhausted as to require almost complete reconstruction.

Our own loss of life, happily, was comparatively small, but the cost in direct outlay to the national Treasury ran between 30 billion dollars and 40 billion dollars and is still going on. Of all the countries engaged, the United States has proceeded furthest toward recovery, although we are yet a long distance from its completion.

While the war proved a stupendous catastrophe for all those who were in it, and in 18 months destroyed values which it had taken us generations to create, on the other hand its lessons can be made a great advantage to us. It gave us an opportunity to know the world and afforded us a place in the world which we did not have before. It revealed to us to a large extent both our powers and our responsibilities. It demonstrated so clearly the interdependence of all people that we are not likely to hear again in responsible quarters that what other nations do is no concern of ours.

It is also easier for us to remember that what we do has its effect on other nations. Quite properly, under international law, one people is debarred from interfering in the strictly domestic affairs of another people. The first law of liberty, which was one of the principles for which we were fighting, requires that each people should be free to manage their own affairs so long as they observe the rights of others. In the domain of foreign relations there can be no doubt that throughout civilization a new disposition was created to discard the old rule of force and adopt more exclusively the rule of law, relying for enforcement upon its own moral power.

This has brought about among the nations of the world a new sympathy for each other and a new forbearance toward each other which did not before exist. It has eliminated a great deal of selfishness and produced a desire for mutual helpfulness, even at the cost of considerable sacrifice. In their foreign relations all over the world a very distinct manifestation can be seen in the attitude of the great powers of wholesome restraint and an effort to conclude by patient negotiation what but a short time ago would have been determined with an iron hand.

Another result which the United States very much hoped to see secured was a broader application to the peoples of the different nations of the principle of self-government. On the whole the movement may be said to be strongly in that direction. Arbitrary rule applied under a system of hereditary monarchy has almost disappeared. While it was not possible for all people at once successfully to make the transition into a republican form of government yet I believe that even among those nations which have appeared to be finding that experience very difficult they are laying the preliminary foundations, and are so strongly imbued with the spirit of nationality under freedom that ultimately they will be successful in accomplishing the desired ends.

As the nations of the earth have come to see each other in a new relationship so there has been revealed to the people of our own country the existence of a relationship which they did not before fully comprehend. During the war we heard much about man power. We found that it was a matter not only of quantity but of quality. The draft demonstrated to us our strength, but also our weakness. We found a very disquieting lack of education which reached into every state in the Union. Too many of our newer citizens did not understand the English language. These disadvantages were in some ways compensated by the wonderful spirit of loyalty and devotion that was manifest in the heart of the whole nation. We learned not only the importance which we are to each other but the necessity for individual development.

We found that we needed not only a large number of people, but a large number of trained and educated people capable of putting forth a common effort through being able to arrive at a common understanding. We came to a new sense of our dependence on the individual and a new realization of the obligation of society to him and his worth to society. This has immeasurably raised both the economic and spiritual standards of our country. A citizen of the United States holds a new position, higher than that which was ever held in any past time. The opportunities which are enjoyed by our countryman are far superior to those which ever came to any other people.

One of the most wide-reaching impressions that came out of our war experience was the duties and responsibilities of citizenship. We came to see that each citizen might be called upon by the government in time of need for his life and his property. Those who went into the armed service offered their lives and those who contributed to the wartime charities, to the purchase of liberty bonds and to the payment of taxes contributed their property. Those who possessed very large incomes paid into the national Treasury about 80 percent of it which with their state and local taxes, came very close to a taking over by the government of their entire property for use during the war. It was, in fact, a practical conscription for an indefinite time of the property of those of very large incomes. While some of our people were in the service, others were producing food, turning out munitions, looking after the affairs of government, and carrying on the necessary activities of commerce and transportation.

We saw that the individual did not belong wholly to himself, but must respond to the requirements of his government. Stated another way, the individuals who make up this nation found that for their self-preservation they must cooperate with each other under a unified leadership and control and contribute their services and their property in order to save themselves from destruction. Self-preservation meant then, as it always does, response to the call of duty.

Adequate defense meant the proper functioning of the entire organic life of the nation. That lesson carried over into our peacetime activities has been one of the chief factors in the enormous progress which the last 10 years have seen. It is a process that is as yet only in its beginnings, but which is being perfected from day to day and which ultimately holds the chief hope of our material, intellectual, and spiritual progress and prosperity. The foundation of it all rests on the extermination of waste and the waster, and on the elimination of slackness and the slacker. It means the coordination of national effort through an adequately trained citizenship, which will result in a scientific production and distribution of commodities that will raise the standard of living around every fireside in the land.

While the government can be a large contributing factor in providing the opportunities which will lead to this high ideal, yet, our whole experience during the war tells us that if it is to be attained it will come through the private enterprise of each individual. Its consummation requires that each citizen should do his duty.

Another fact which shines forth with a renewed brilliance is that many of the most precious rewards of life do not lie on the side of material gain. We have had a great deal of discussion concerning the injustice of one person going into the service at a very small remuneration, while another remained at home in the enjoyment of very high wages. But I wonder how many of you who put on the uniform and went into action overseas would not be willing to exchange that experience for the few dollars of extra compensation that someone else was able to earn at home during the latter months of the war. Which one is now in possession of the most valuable treasure—the one who was at the front or the one who was securing high wages? By reason of the draft both were doing the duty assigned to them and both lived up to the full requirements of their citizenship, but I think the conclusion must be that the one who was in the place of greater peril is really in possession of the greater reward. What we found in war we shall continue to find in peace.

As with many of our most important services, many of our greatest compensations cannot be measured in dollars and cents. You are greater men for what you have given to your country. You hold a higher place of honor in the estimation of your fellow citizens which no money could ever buy. You have a place and a name and a glory which you will hand down as a priceless heritage.

One of the most gratifying of all revelations was that the strength of character of our citizenship was universal. It was all-embracing. It was not limited to any locality, to any class, to any nationality, or to any creed. We found as sturdy and inspiring examples among the foreign-born as among the oldest native stock. It came from some obscure mountain home, some isolated dwelling on the broad prairie, or some tenement of a great metropolis, as well as from those who enjoyed the most favored circumstances. We cannot contemplate it without increasing our respect for our people and renewing our faith in our institutions. It was another demonstration that we are all Americans.

As we contemplate these past 10 years, we have every justification for increasing our sentiment of patriotism. But while we are doing that we should also remember that other nations during that period have displayed qualities of a high character. They also are entitled to our respect and admiration in their successes and our sympathy and consideration in their trials. While it is our privilege and duty as citizens to place our regard for

America first, if we are to justify that position we must make America right.

Because we believe in our country it will always be our desire and our duty to defend it. It cannot be too often stated that we cherish no sentiment of aggression toward any other people. But the obligation to resist evil, to be prepared to maintain the orderly authority of the rule of law in both our domestic and our foreign relations is one which cannot be avoided. For the government to disregard the science of national defense would expose it to the contempt of its citizens at home and of the world abroad. It would be an attempt to evade bearing our share of the burdens of civilization. For this reason we maintain according to our resources, our population, our position and our responsibilites, a moderate army and navy based on what we believe to be our requirements for national security.

While it is incumbent upon us to secure such advantages as we can from our adversity, we all recognize that we should take every precaution to prevent ourselves or the rest of the world from being involved again in such a tragedy as began in 1914. While the country's national defense should never be neglected, preparation for the maintenance of peace is likewise required by every humane impulse that stirs the hearts of men. Those of you who have seen service would be the first to say that if the country needed you, you would respond again. But you will also be the first to say that you require of your government that it should take every possible precaution that human ingenuity can devise to insure the settlement of its differences with other countries through diplomatic negotiations and mutual concessions according to the dictates of reason, rather than by appeal to force.

It is in accordance with our determination to refrain from aggression and build up a sentiment and practice among nations more favorable to peace, that we ratified a treaty for the limitation of naval armaments made in 1921, earnestly sought for a further extension of this principle in 1927, and have secured the consent of 14 important nations to the negotiation of a treaty condemning recourse to war, renouncing it is an instrument of national policy, and pledging each other to seek no solution of their disagreements except by pacific means. It is hoped other nations will join in this movement. Had an agreement of this kind been in existence in 1914, there is every reason to suppose that it would have saved the situation and delivered the world from all the misery which was inflicted by the Great War.

By taking a leading position in securing this agreement, which is fraught with so much hope for the progress of humanity, we have demonstrated that when we have said we maintained our armaments, not for aggression, but purely for defense, we were making a candid statement which we were willing to verify by our actions.

I shall not now go into a discussion of the details or the implications of this agreement other than to point out that, of course, it detracts nothing from the right and obligation of ourselves or the other high contracting parties to maintain an adequate national defense against any attack, but it does pledge ourselves not to attack others in consideration for their agreement not to attack us, and to seek a settlement of our controversies one with another through peaceful means.

While it would be too much to suppose that war has been entirely banished, yet a new and important barrier, reasonable and honorable, has been set up to prevent it. This agreement proposes a revolutionary policy among nations. It holds a greater hope for peaceful relations than was ever before given to the world. If those who are involved in it, having started it will finish it, its provisions will prove one of the greatest blessings ever bestowed upon humanity. It is a fitting consummation of the first decade of peace.

Courtesy of Herbert Hoover Library

Herbert Clark Hoover

Herbert Clark Hoover

1929–1933

ELECTED IN 1928 by a landslide, Herbert Hoover suffered the most precipitous fall from grace of any president since John Quincy Adams. It was his misfortune to hold the chief executive's office when the stock market crashed, a little more than half a year after he entered the White House.

In part, his sudden loss of the public's confidence was the result of his having been over-sold to the public during the campaign—the first real presidential public-relations blitz in the nation's history. The son of a Quaker family from Iowa, orphaned at the age of eight, Hoover had made a fortune as a globe-trotting mining engineer before turning, with great success, to the management of humanitarian government projects, including massive food relief programs in Europe during World War I. Harding and Coolidge (who called Hoover "the Wonder Boy") brought him into their cabinets as secretary of commerce. The publicity campaign of 1928, masterminded by New York advertising executives, presented him to the voters as an organizational genius, a supermanager who would run the nation efficiently. He arrived in office with a progressive plan that rested on equal opportunity for the people and fair treatment for labor and business.

The Depression tested to the limit Hoover's belief that self-sacrifice and "rugged individualism," rather than excessive government interference, would finally set the economy to rights. The suffering electorate soon lost patience with this view. Hoover did little to bolster their confidence. As a project administrator he was used to getting things accomplished behind the scenes, and he was too shy to play the public relations game himself. Criticism by the press made him angry and unresponsive. The Democratic national organization capitalized on these weaknesses in a smear campaign that cost Hoover what little popular support he had left. After his loss to Franklin D. Roosevelt in 1932—by a far greater landslide than the one that had elected him in 1928—Hoover became a spokesman for the conservatives and twice headed presidential commissions.

The high principles, devotion to duty, and progressive outlook that have rehabilitated Hoover in the eyes of many later historians might have made a stronger impression on his contemporaries if he had been a more persuasive orator. Yet though he made frequent public addresses—his bibliography lists almost 600 speeches given between the years 1917 and 1962, with 138 during his presidential years—he had a leaden delivery that bored even friendly audiences. Nor was he much more comfortable speaking on the radio. As commerce secretary he had overseen the development and regulation of the radio industry, and he appreciated its effectiveness as a molder of public opinion, so much that he distrusted it. "Propaganda over the air," he wrote in his memoirs, "raises emotion at the expense of reason far more than the printed word."

During his 1932 reelection campaign Hoover's speaking style grew even more ponderous as he tried to defend himself. His speech accepting the nomination was received with barely a ripple of applause. One observer described "the dispiriting influence of Mr. Hoover's personality, his unprepossessing exterior, his sour, puckered face of a bilious baby, his dreary, nasal monotone reading interminably, and for the most part inaudibly, from a typescript without a single inflection of voice or gesture to relieve the tedium." At the very end of the campaign he was seen to tremble at the podium.

In fact, Hoover's addresses are better read than heard. They were intended to be educational messages from the nation's leader, lectures that would teach the public something about the assessment of practical solutions to national problems and the identification of the moral and political principles at stake in each choice. Almost every speech concluded with remarks on the preservation of the nation's spiritual ideals as the ultimate goal of social and economic progress. "The things of the spirit alone persist," he told a Memorial Day crowd at Gettysburg. Occasionally a fleck of dry, subtle humor also found its way in among the slew of statistics and sober analyses that filled Hoover's addresses. Howard Runkel, in his study of Hoover's oratory, notes that his "lack of boldness in *pathos* does not signify a dearth of appeals, for the speeches are replete with emotional drive. In Hoover's speeches, however, this drive is distinctly subordinated to the argumentative development—the element of *logos.*" Once, as secretary of commerce, Hoover wrote part of a speech for Harding, but Harding found it hard going and whispered, "Damn it, Hoover, why don't you write the same English as I do?"

Hoover was the last president to eschew all use of ghostwriters. His speeches were written out in longhand and then revised again and again, first in typescript and then in proof. Theodore H. Joslin, his press secretary, remarked that he "built his public utterances as he would drive a mine shaft or construct a bridge. He would search his storehouse of words for those that would interpret his exact thought, testing each and every one for stress and strain, and then interlocking them with a fine network of minor words like the web of wires on a suspension bridge. Those that fell short of the necessary requirements he ruthlessly discarded, as he would a steel beam in which a flaw had been discovered. But the final result was the work of a craftsman. The principal criticism to make of his addresses is that each one was too correct in detail, too precise, for the casual listener or reader."

Acceptance Speech

Stanford, California
August 11, 1928

FOLLOWING TRADITION, Hoover stayed away from the Republican convention while his candidacy was debated. Once he had received formal notification of his nomination, he made his acceptance speech to an audience of 70,000 in the stadium of Stanford University, near his home in Palo Alto, on his 54th birthday. Its main theme was "progress through technology"—the eradication of poverty and the betterment of workers' lives through the proper use of America's material wealth. Afterward, Hoover said to a friend: "I wonder if this speech will help me to live down my reputation as an engineer."

Hoover's statement that "we are nearer a final triumph over poverty than in any other land at any other time" was resurrected as the target of ridicule by the Democrats as the Depression deepened. Four years later, in a campaign speech given at Madison Square Garden in New York, Hoover said of this passage: "I do not withdraw a word of it. When I look about the world even in these times of trouble and distress I find it more true in this land than anywhere else under that traveling sun. I am not ashamed of it, because I am not ashamed of holding ideals and purposes for the American people. . . . For my part, I propose to continue to strive for it, and I hope to live to see it accomplished."

You bring, Mr. Chairman, formal notice of my nomination by the Republican Party to the presidency of the United States. I accept. It is a great honor to be chosen for leadership in that party which has so largely made the history of our country in these last 70 years.

Mr. Chairman, you and your associates have in four days traveled 3,000 miles across the continent to bring me this notice. I am reminded that in order to notify George Washington of his election Charles Thomson, secretary of the Congress, spent seven days on horseback to deliver that important intelligence 230 miles from New York to Mount Vernon.

In another way, too, this occasion illuminates the milestones of progress. By the magic of the radio this nomination was heard by millions of our fellow citizens not seven days after its occurrence, nor one day, nor even one minute. They were, to all intents and purposes, present in the hall and participants in the proceedings. Today these same millions have heard your voice and now are hearing mine. We stand in their unseen presence. It is fitting, however, that the forms of our national life, hallowed by generations of usage, should be jealously preserved, and for that reason you have come to me, as similar delegations have come to other candidates through the years.

Those invisible millions have already heard from Kansas City the reading of our party principles. They would wish to hear from me not a discourse upon the platorm—in which I fully concur—but something of the spirit and ideals with which it is proposed to carry it into administration.

Our problems of the past seven years have been problems of reconstruction; our problems of the future are problems of construction. They are problems of progress. New and gigantic forces have come into our national life. The Great War released ideas of government in conflict with our principles. We have grown to financial and physical power which compels us into a new setting among nations. Science has given us new tools and a thousand inventions. Through them have come to each of us wider relationships, more neighbors, more leisure, broader vision, higher ambitions, greater problems. To insure that these tools shall not be used to limit liberty has brought a vast array of questions in government.

The points of contact between the government and the people are constantly multiplying. Every year wise governmental policies become more vital in ordinary life. As our problems grow so do our temptations grow to venture away from those principles upon which our republic was founded and upon which it has grown to greatness. Moreover, we must direct economic progress in support of moral and spiritual progress.

Our party platform deals mainly with economic problems, but our nation is not an agglomeration of railroads, of ships, of factories, of dynamos, or statistics. It is a nation of homes, a nation of men, of women, of children. Every man has a right to ask of us whether the United States is a better place for him, his wife, and his children to live in, because the Republican Party has conducted the government for nearly eight years. Every woman has a right to ask whether her life, her home, her man's job, her hopes, her happiness will be better assured by the continuance of the Republican Party in power. I propose to discuss the question before me in that light.

With this occasion we inaugurate the campaign. It shall be an honest campaign; every penny will be publicly accounted for. It shall be a true campaign. We shall use words to convey our meaning, not to hide it.

The Republican Party came into authority nearly eight years ago. It is necessary to remind ourselves of the critical conditions of that time. We were confronted with an incompleted peace and involved in violent and dangerous disputes both at home and abroad. The federal government was spending at the rate of five and a half billions per year; our national debt stood at the staggering total of 24 billions. The foreign debts were unsettled. The country was in a panic from overexpansion due to the war and the continued inflation of credit and currency after the armistice, followed by a precipitant nationwide deflation which in half a year crashed the prices of commodities by nearly one-half. Agriculture was prostrated; land was unsalable; commerce and industry were stagnated; our foreign trade ebbed away; 5 millions of unemployed walked the streets. Discontent and agitation against our democracy were rampant. Fear for the future haunted every heart.

No party ever accepted a more difficult task of reconstruction than did the Republican Party in 1921. The record of these seven and a half years constitutes a period of rare courage in leadership and constructive action. Never has a political party been able to look back upon a similar period with more satisfaction. Never could it look forward with more confidence that its record would be approved by the electorate.

Peace has been made. The healing process of good will have extinguished the fires of hate. Year by year in our relations with other nations we have advanced the ideals of law and of peace, in substitution for force. By rigorous economy federal expenses have been reduced by two billions per annum. The national debt has been reduced by six and a half billions. The foreign debts have been settled in large part and on terms which have regard for our debtors and for our taxpayers. Taxes have been reduced four successive times. These reductions have been made in the particular interest of the small taxpayers. For this purpose taxes upon articles of consumption and popular service have been removed. The income tax rolls today show a reduction of 80 percent in the total revenue collected on incomes under $10,000 per year, while they show a reduction of only 25 percent in revenues from incomes above that amount. Each successive reduction in taxes has brought a reduction in the cost of living to all our people.

Commerce and industry have revived. Although the agricultural, coal, and textile industries still lag in their recovery and still require our solicitude and assistance, yet they have made substantial progress. While other countries engaged in the war are only now regaining their prewar level in foreign trade, our exports, even if we allow for the depreciated dollar, are 58 percent greater than before the war. Constructive leadership and cooperation by the government have released and stimulated the energies of our people. Faith in the future has been restored. Confidence in our form of government has never been greater.

But it is not through the recitation of wise policies in government alone that we demonstrate our progress under Republican guidance. To me the test is the security, comfort, and opportunity that have been brought to the average American family. During this less than eight years our population has increased by 8 percent. Yet our national income has increased by over $30 billion per year or more than 45 percent. Our production—and therefore our consumption—of goods has increased by about 2,300,000; we have built more than 3,500,000 new and better homes. In this short time we have equipped nearly nine million more homes with electricity, and through it drudgery has been lifted from the lives of women. The barriers of time and distance have been swept away and life made freer and larger by the installation of six million more telephones, seven million radio sets, and the service of an additional 14 million automobiles. Our cities are growing magnificent with beautiful buildings, parks, and playgrounds. Our countryside has been knit together with splendid roads.

We have doubled the use of electrical power and with it we have taken sweat from the backs of men. The purchasing power of wages has steadily increased. The hours of labor have decreased. The 12-hour day has been abolished. Great progress has been made in stabilization of commerce and industry. The job of every man has thus been made more secure. Unemployment in the sense of distress is widely disappearing.

Most of all, I like to remember what this progress has meant to America's children. The portal of their opportunity has been ever widening. While our population has grown but 8 percent, we have increased by 11 percent the number of children in our grade schools, by *66* percent the number in our high schools, and by 75 percent the number in our institutions of higher learning.

With all our spending we have doubled savings deposits in our banks and building and loan associations. We have nearly doubled our life insurance. Nor have our people been selfish. They have met with a full hand the most sacred obligation of man—charity. The gifts of America to churches, to hospitals, and institutions for the care of the afflicted, and to relief from great disasters have surpassed by hundreds of millions any total for any similar period in all human record. One of the oldest and perhaps the noblest of human aspirations has been the abolition of poverty. By poverty I mean the grinding by undernourishment, cold, and ignorance, and fear of old age of those who have the will to work. We in America today are nearer to the final triumph over poverty than ever before in the history of any land. The poorhouse is vanishing from among us. We have not yet reached the goal, but, given a chance to go forward with the policies of the last eight years, we shall soon with the help of God be in sight of the day when poverty will be banished from this nation. There is no guarantee against poverty equal to a job for every man. That is the primary purpose of the economic policies we advocate.

I especially rejoice in the effect of our increased national efficiency upon the improvement of the American home. That is the sanctuary of our loftiest ideals, the source of the spiritual energy of our people. The bettered home surroundings, the expanded schools and playgrounds, and the enlarged leisure which have come with our economic progress have brought to the average family a fuller life, a wider outlook, a stirred imagination, and a lift in aspirations.

Economic advancement is not an end in itself. Successful democracy rests wholly upon the moral and spiritual quality of its people. Our growth in spiritual achievements must keep pace with our growth in physical accomplishments. Material prosperity and moral progress must march together if we would make the United States that commonwealth so grandly conceived by its founders. Our government, to match the expectations of our people, must have constant regard for those human values that give dignity and nobility to life. Generosity of impulse, cultivation of mind, willingness to sacrifice, spaciousness of spirit—those are the qualities whereby America, growing bigger and richer and more powerful, may become America great and noble. A people or government to which these values are not real, because they are not tangible, is in peril. Size, wealth, and power alone cannot fulfill the promise of America's opportunity.

The most urgent economic problem in our nation today is in agriculture. It must be solved if we are to bring prosperity and contentment to one-third of our people directly and to all of our people indirectly. We have pledged ourselves to find a solution.

To my mind most agricultural discussions go wrong because of two false premises. The first is that agriculture is one industry. It is a dozen distinct industries incapable of the same organization. The second false premise is that rehabilitation will be complete when it has reached a point comparable with prewar. Agriculture was not upon a satisfactory basis before the war. The abandoned farms of the Northeast bear their own testimony. Generally, there was but little profit in Midwest agriculture for many years except that derived from the slow increases in farmland values. Even of more importance is the great advance in standards of living of all occupations since the war. Some branches of agriculture have greatly recovered, but taken as a whole it is not keeping pace with the onward march in other industries.

There are many causes for failure of agriculture to win its full share of national prosperity. The afterwar deflation of prices not only brought great direct losses to the farmer, but he was often left indebted in inflated dollars to be paid in deflated dollars. Prices are often demoralized through gluts in our markets during the harvest season. Local taxes have been increased to provide the improved roads and schools. The tariff on some products is proving inadequate to protect him from imports from abroad. The increases in transportation rates since the war have greatly affected the price which he receives for his products. Over six million farmers in times of surplus engage in destructive competition with one another in the sale of their product, often depressing prices below those levels that could be maintained.

The whole tendency of our civilization during the last 50 years has been toward an increase in the size of the units of production in order to secure lower costs and a more orderly adjustment of the flow of commodities to the demand. But the organization of agriculture into larger units must not be by enlarged farms. The farmer has shown he can increase the skill of his industry without large operations. He is today producing 20 percent more than eight years ago, with about the same acreage and personnel. Farming is and must continue to be an individualistic business of small units and independent ownership. The farm is more than a business: it is a state of living. We do not wish it converted into a mass-production machine. Therefore, if the farmer's position is to be improved by larger operations it must be done not on the farm but in the field of distribution. Agriculture has partially advanced in this direction through cooperatives and pools. But the traditional cooperative is often not a complete solution.

Differences of opinion as to both causes and remedy have retarded the completion of a constructive program of relief. It is our plain duty to search out the common ground on which we may mobilize the sound forces of agricultural reconstruction. Our platform lays a solid basis upon which we can build. It offers an affirmative program.

An adequate tariff is the foundation of farm relief. Our consumers increase faster than our producers. The domestic market must be protected. Foreign products raised under lower standards of living are today competing in our home markets. I would use my office and influence to give the farmer the full benefit of our historic tariff policy.

A large portion of the spread between what the farmer receives for his products and what the ultimate consumer pays is due to increased transportation charges. Increases in railway rates has been one of the penalties of the war. These increases have been added to the cost to the farmer of reaching seaboard and foreign markets and result therefore in reduction of his prices. The farmers of foreign countires have thus been indirectly aided in their competition with the American farmer. Nature has endowed us with a great system of inland waterways. Their modernization will comprise a most substantial contribution to Midwest farm relief and to the development of 20 of our interior states. This modernization includes not only the great Mississippi system, with its joining of the Great Lakes and of the heart of Midwest agriculture to the gulf, but also a shipway from the Great Lakes to the Atlantic. These improvements would mean so large an increment in farmers' prices as to warrant their construction many times over. There is no more vital method of farm relief.

Be we must not stop here.

An outstanding proposal of the party program is the wholehearted pledge to undertake the reorganization of the marketing system upon sounder and more economical lines. We have already contributed greatly to this purpose by the acts supporting farm cooperatives, the establishment of intermediate credit banks, the regulation of stockyards and public exchange, and the expansion of the Department of Agriculture. The platform proposes to go much farther. It pledges the creation of a federal Farm Board of representative farmers to be clothed with authority and resources with which not only to still further aid farmers' cooperatives and pools and to assist generally in solution of farm problems but especially to build up, with federal finance, farmer-owned and farmer-controlled stabilization corporations which will protect the farmer from the depression and demoralization of seasonal gluts and periodical surpluses.

Objection has been made that this program, as laid down by the party platform, may require that several hundred millions of dollars of capital be advanced by the federal government without obligation upon the individual farmer. With that objection I have little patience. A nation which is spending 90 billions a year can well afford an expenditure of a few hundred millions for a workable program that will give to one-third of its population their fair share of the nation's prosperity. Nor does this proposal put the government into business except so far as it is called upon to furnish capital with which to build up the farmer to the control of his own destinies.

The program adapts itself to the variable problems of agriculture not only today but which will arise in the future. I do not believe that any single human being or any group of human beings can determine in advance all questions that will arise in so vast and complicated an industry over a term of years. The first step is to create an effective agency directly for these purposes and to give it authority and resources. These are solemn pledges and they will be fulfilled by the Republican Party. It is a definite plan of relief. It needs only the detailed elaboration of legislation and appropriations to put it into force.

During my term as secretary of commerce I have steadily endeavored to build up a system of cooperation between the government and business. Under these cooperative actions all elements interested in the problems of a particular industry such as manufacturer, distributor, worker, and consumer have been called into council together, not for a single occasion but for continuous work. These efforts have been successful beyond any expectation. They have been accomplished without interference or regulation by the government. They have secured progress in the industries, remedy for abuses, elimination of waste, reduction of cost in production and distribution, lower prices to the consumer, and more stable employment and profit. While the problem varies with every different commodity and with every different part of our great country, I should wish to apply the same method to agriculture so that the leaders of every phase of each group can advise and organize on policies and constructive measures. I am convinced that this form of action, as it has done in other industries, can greatly benefit farmer, distributor, and consumer.

The working out of agricultural relief constitutes the most important obligation of the next administration. I stand pledged to these proposals. The object of our policies is to establish for our farmers an income equal to those of other occupations; for the farmer's wife the same comforts in her home as women in other groups; for the farm boys and girls the same opportunities in life as other boys and girls. So far as my own abilities may be of service, I dedicate them to help secure prosperity and contentment in that industry where I and my forefathers were born and nearly all my family still obtain their livelihood.

The Republican Party has ever been the exponent of protection to all our people from competition with lower standards of living abroad. We have always fought for tariffs designed to establish this protection from imported goods. We also have enacted restrictions upon immigration for the protection of labor from the inflow of workers faster than we can absorb them without breaking down our wage levels.

The Republican principle of an effective control of imported goods and of immigration has contributed greatly to the prosperity of our country. There is no selfishness in the defense of our standards of living. Other countries gain nothing if the high standards of America are sunk and if we are prevented from building a civilization which sets the level of hope for the entire world. A general reduction in the tariff would admit a flood of goods from abroad. It would injure every home. It would fill our streets with idle workers. It would destroy the returns to our dairymen, our fruit, flax, and livestock growers, and our other farmers.

No man will say that any immigration or tariff law is perfect. We welcome our new immigrant citizens and their great contribution to our nation; we seek only to protect them equally with those already here. We shall amend the immigration laws to relieve unnecessary hardships upon families. As a member of the commission whose duty is to determine the quota basis under the national origins law, I have found it is impossible to do so accurately and without hardship. The basis now in effect carries out the essential principle of the law and I favor repeal of that part of the act calling for a new basis of quotas.

We have pledged ourselves to make such revisions in the tariff laws as may be necessary to provide real protection against the shiftings of economic tides in our various industries. I am sure the American people would rather entrust the perfection of the tariff to the consistent friend of the tariff than to our opponents, who have always reduced our tariffs, who voted against our present protection to the worker and the farmer, and whose whole economic theory over generations has been the destruction of the protective principle.

Having earned my living with my own hands, I cannot have other than the greatest sympathy with the aspirations of those who toil. It has been my good fortune during the past 12 years to have received the cooperation of labor in many directions, and in promotion of many public purposes.

The trade union movement in our country has maintained two departures from such movements in all other countries. They have been staunch supporters of American individualism and American institutions. They have steadfastly opposed subversive doctrines from abroad. Our freedom from foreign social and economic diseases is in large degree due to this resistance by our own labor. Our trade unions, with few exceptions, have welcomed all basic improvement in industrial methods. This largeness of mind has contributed to the advancing standards of living of the whole of our people. They properly have sought to participate—by additions to wages—in the result of improvements and savings which they have helped to make.

During these past years we have grown greatly in the mutual understanding between employer and employee. We have seen a growing realization by the employer that the highest practicable wage is the road to increased consumption and prosperity, and we have seen a growing realization by labor that the maximum use of machines, of effort, and of skill is the road to lower production costs and in the end to higher real wages. Under these impulses and the Republican protective system our industrial output has increased as never before and our wages have grown steadily in buying power. Our workers with their average weekly wages can today buy two and often three times more bread and butter than any wage earner of Europe. At one time we demanded for our workers a "full dinner pail." We have now gone far beyond that conception. Today we demand larger comfort and greater participation in life and leisure.

The Republican platform gives the pledge of the party to the support of labor. It endorses the principle of collective bargaining and freedom in labor negotiations. We stand also pledged to the curtailment of excessive use of the injunction in labor disputes.

The war and the necessary curtailment of expenditure during the reconstruction years have suspended the construction of many needed public works. Moreover, the time has arrived when we must undertake a larger-visioned development of our water resources. Every drop which runs to the sea without yielding its full economic service is a waste.

Nearly all of our greater drainages contain within themselves possibilities of cheapened transportation, irrigation, reclamation, domestic water supply, hydroelectric power, and frequently the necessities of flood control. But this development of our waters requires more definite national policies in the systematic coordination of those different works upon each drainage area. We have wasted scores of millions by projects undertaken not as a part of a whole but as the consequence of purely local demands. We cannot develop modernized water transportation by isolated projects. We must develop it as a definite and positive interconnected system of transportation. We must adjust reclamation and irrigation to our needs for more land. Where they lie together we must coordinate transportation with flood control, the development of hydroelectric power and of irrigation, else we shall as in the past commit errors that will take years and millions to remedy. The Congress has authorized and has in process of legislation great programs of public works. In addition to the works in development of water resources, we have in progress large undertakings in public roads and the construction of public buildings.

All these projects will probably require an expenditure of upward of $1,000,000 within the next four years. It comprises the largest engineering construction ever undertaken by any government. It involves three times the expenditure laid out upon the Panama Canal. It is justified by the growth, need, and wealth of our country. The organization and administration of this construction is a responsibility of the first order. For it we must provide jobs for an army of men, should so far as practicable be adjusted to take up the slack of unemployment elsewhere.

I rejoice in the completion of legislation providing adequate flood control of the

Mississippi. It marks not alone the undertaking of a great national task, but it constitutes a contribution to the development of the South. In encouragement of their economic growth lies one of the great national opportunities of the future.

I recently stated my position upon the Eighteenth Amendment [Prohibition] which I again repeat.

"I do not favor the repeal of the Eighteenth Amendment. I stand for the efficient enforcement of the laws enacted thereunder. Whoever is chosen president has under his oath the solemn duty to pursue this course.

"Our country has deliberately undertaken a great social and economic experiment, noble in motive and far-reaching in purpose. It must be worked out constructively."

Commonsense compels us to realize that grave abuses have occurred—abuses which must be remedied. An organized searching investigation of fact and causes can alone determine the wise method of correcting them. Crime and disobedience of law cannot be permitted to break down the Constitution and laws of the United States.

Modification of the enforcement laws which would permit that which the Constitution forbids is nullification. This the American people will not countenance. Change in the Constitution can and must be brought about only by the straightforward methods provided in the Constitution itself. There are those who do not believe in the purposes of several provisions of the Constitution. No one denies their right to seek to amend it. They are not subject to criticism for asserting that right. But the Republican Party does deny the right of anyone to seek to destroy the purposes of the Constitution by indirection.

Whoever is elected president takes an oath not only to faithfully execute the office of the president, but that oath provides still further that he will, to the best of his ability, preserve, protect, and defend the Constitution of the United States. I should be untrue to these great traditions, untrue to my oath of office, were I to declare otherwise.

With impressive proof on all sides of magnificent progress, no one can rightly deny the fundamental correctness of our economic system. Our preeminent advance over nations in the last eight years has been due to distinctively American accomplishments. We do not owe these accomplishments to our vast natural resources. These we have always had. They have not increased. What has changed is our ability to utilize these resources more effectively. It is our human resources that have changed. Man for man and woman for woman, we are today more capable, whether in the work of farm, factory, or business, than ever before. It lies in our magnificent educational system, in the hardworking character of our people, in the capacity of farsighted leadership in industry, the ingenuity, the daring of the pioneers of new inventions, in the abolition of the saloon, and the wisdom of our national policies.

With the growth and increasing complexity of our economic life the relations of government and business are multiplying daily. They are yearly more dependent upon each other. Where it is helpful and necessary, this relation should be encouraged. Beyond this it should not go. It is the duty of government to avoid regulation as long as equal opportunity to all citizens is not invaded and public rights violated. Government should not engage in business in competition with its citizens. Such actions extinguish the enterprise and initiative which has been the glory of America and which has been the root of its preeminence among the nations of the earth. On the other hand, it is the duty of business to conduct itself so that government regulation or government competition is unnecessary.

Business is practical, but it is founded upon faith—faith among our people in the integrity of businessmen, and faith that it will receive fair play from the government. It is the duty of government to maintain that faith. Our whole business system would break down in a day if there was not a high sense of moral responsibility in our business world. The whole practice and ethics of business has made great strides of improvement in the last quarter of a century, largely due to the effort of business and the professions themselves. One of the most helpful signs of recent years is the stronger growth of associations of workers, farmers, businessmen, and professional men with a desire to cure their own abuses and a purpose to serve public interest. Many problems can be solved through cooperation between government and these self-governing associations to improve methods and practices. When business cures its own abuses it is true self-government, which comprises more than political institutions.

One of the greatest difficulites of business with government is the multitude of unnecessary contacts with government bureaus, the uncertainty and inconsistency of government policies, and the duplication of governmental activities. A large part of this is due to the scattering of functions and the great confusion of responsibility in our federal organizations. We have, for instance, 14 different bureaus or agencies engaged in public works and construction, located in nine different departments of the government. It brings about competition between government agencies, inadequacy of control, and a total lack of coordinated policies in public works. We have eight different bureaus and agencies charged with conservation of our natural resources, located in five different departments of the government. These conditions exist in many other directions. Divided responsibility, with the absense of centralized authority, prevents constructive and consistent development of broad national policies.

Our Republican presidents have repeatedly recommended to Congress that it would not only greatly reduce expenses of business in its contacts with government, but that a great reduction could be made in governmental expenditure and more consistent and continued national policies could be developed, if we could secure the grouping of these agencies devoted to one major purpose under single responsibility and authority. I have had the good fortune to be able to carry out such reorganization in respect to the Department of Commerce. The results have amply justified its expansion to other departments and I should consider it an obligation to enlist the support of Congress to effect it.

The government can be of invaluable aid in the promotion of business. The ideal state of business is freedom from those fluctuations from boom to slump which bring on one hand the periods of unemployment and bankruptcy and, on the other, speculation and waste. Both are destructive to progress and fraught with great hardship to every home. By economy in expenditures, wise taxation, and sound fiscal finance it can relieve the burdens upon sound business and promote financial stability. By sound tariff policies it can protect our workmen, our farmers, and our manufacturers from lower standards of living abroad. By scientific research it can promote invention and improvement in methods. By economic research and statistical service it can promote the elimination of waste and contribute to stability in production and distribution. By promotion of foreign trade it can expand the markets for our manufacturers and farmers and thereby contribute greatly to stability and employment.

Our people know that the production and distribution of goods on a large scale is not wrong. Many of the most important comforts of our people are only possible by mass production and distribution. Both small and big business have their full place. The test of business is not its size—the test is whether there is honest competition, whether there is freedom from domination, whether there is integrity and usefulness of purpose. As secretary of commerce I have been greatly impressed by the fact that the foundation of American business is the independent businessman. The department by encouragement of his associations and by provision of special services has endeavored to place him in a position of equality in information and skill with larger operations. Alike with our farmers his is the stronghold of American individuality. It is here that our local communities receive their leadership. It is here that we refresh our leadership for larger enterprise. We must maintain his opportunity and his individual service. He and the public must be protected from any domination or from predatory business.

I have said that the problems before us are more than economic, that in a much greater degree they are moral and spiritual. I hold that there rests upon government many responsibilities which affect the moral and spiritual welfare of our people. The participation of women in politics means a keener realization of the importance of these questions. It means higher political standards.

One-half of our citizens fail to exercise the responsibilities of the ballot box. I would wish that the women of our country could embrace this problem in citizenship as peculiarly their own. If they could apply their higher sense of service and responsibility, their freshness of enthusiasm, their capacity for organization to this problem, it would become, as it should become, an issue of profound patriotism. The whole plane of political life would be lifted, the foundations of democracy made more secure.

In this land, dedicated to tolerance, we still find outbreaks of intolerance. I come of Quaker stock. My ancestors were persecuted for their beliefs. Here they sought and found religious freedom. By blood and conviction I stand for religious tolerance both in act and in spirit. The glory of our American ideals is the right of every man to worship God according to the dictates of his own conscience.

In the past years there has been corruption participated in by individual officials and members of both political parties in national, state, and municipal affairs. Too often this corruption has been viewed with indifference by a great number of our people. It would seem unnecessary to state the elemental requirement that government must inspire confidence not only in its ability but in its integrity. Dishonesty in government, whether national, state, or municipal, is a double wrong. It is treason to the state. It is destructive of self-government. Government in the United States rests not only upon the consent of the governed but upon the conscience of the nation. Government weakens the moment that its integrity is even doubted. Moral incompetency by those entrusted with government is a blighting wind upon private integrity. There must be no place for cynicism in the creed of America.

Our civil service has proved a great national boon. Appointive office, both North, South, East, and West, must be based solely on merit, character, and reputation in the community in which the appointee is to serve; as it is essential for the proper performance of their duties that officials shall enjoy the confidence and respect of the people with whom they serve.

For many years I have been associated with efforts to save life and health for our children. These experiences with millions of children both at home and abroad have left an indelible impression—that the greatness of any nation, its freedom from poverty and crime, its aspirations and ideals are the direct quotient of the care of its children. Racial progress marches upon the feet of healthy and instructed children. There should be no child in America that is not born and does not live under sound conditions of health; that does not have full opportunity of education from the beginning to the end of our institutions; that is not free from injurious labor; that does not have every stimulation to accomplish the fullest of its capacities. Nothing in development of childlife will ever replace the solicitude of parents and the surroundings of home, but in many aspects both parents and children are dependent upon the vigilance of government—national, state, and local.

I especially value the contribution that the youth of the country can make to the success of our American experiment in democracy. Theirs is the precious gift of enthusiasm, without which no great deeds can be accomplished. A government that does not constantly seek to live up to the ideals of its young men and women falls short of what the American people have a right to expect and demand from it. To interpret the spirit of the youth into the spirit of our government, to bring the warmth of their enthusiasm and the flame of their idealism into the affairs of the nation is to make of American government a positive and living force, a factor for greatness and nobility in the life of the nation.

I think I may say that I have witnessed as much of the horror and suffering of war as any other American. From it I have derived a deep passion for peace. We have no hates; we wish no further possessions; we harbor no military threats. The unspeakable experiences of the Great War, the narrow margin by which civilization survived its exhaustion, is still vivid in men's minds. There is no nation in the world today that does not earnestly wish for peace—that is not striving for peace.

There are two cooperating factors in the maintenance of peace—the building of goodwill by wise and sympathetic handling of international relations, and the adequate preparedness for defense. We must not only be just; we must be respected. The experiences of the war afforded final proof that we cannot isolate ourselves from the world, that the safeguarding of peace cannot be attained by negative action. Our offer of treaties open to the signature of all, renouncing war as an instrument of national policy, proves that we have every desire to cooperate with other nations for peace. But our people have determined that we can give the greatest real help—both in times of tranquillity and in times of strain—if we maintain our independence from the political exigencies of the Old World. In pursuance of this, our country has refused membership in the League of Nations, but we are glad to cooperate with the league in its endeavors to further scientific, economic, and social welfare, and to secure limitation of armament.

We believe that the foundations of peace can be strengthened by the creation of methods and agencies by which a multitude of incidents may be transferred from the realm of prejudice and force to arbitration and the determination of right and wrong based upon international law.

We have been and we are particularly desirous of furthering the limitation of armaments. But in the meantime we know that in an armed world there is only one certain guarantee of freedom—and that is preparedness for defense. It is solely to defend ourselves, for the protection of our citizens, that we maintain armament. No clearer evidence of this can exist than the unique fact that we have fewer men in army uniform today than we have in police uniforms, and that we maintain a standing invitation to the world that we are always ready to limit our naval armament in proportion as the other naval nations will do likewise. We earnestly wish that the burdens and dangers of armament upon every home in the world might be lessened. But we must and shall maintain our naval defense and our merchant marine in the strength and efficiency which will yield to us at all times the primary assurance of liberty, that is, of national safety.

There is one of the ideals of America upon which I wish at this time to lay especial emphasis. For we should constantly test our economic, social, and governmental system by certain ideals which must control them. The founders of our republic propounded the revolutionary doctrine that all men are created equal and all should have equality before the law. This was the emancipation of the individual. And since these beginnings, slowly, surely, and almost imperceptibly, this nation has added a third ideal almost unique to America—the ideal of equal opportunity. This is the safeguard of the individual. The simple life of early days in our republic found but few limitations upon equal opportunity. By the crowding of our people and the intensity and complexity of their activities it takes today a new importance.

Equality of opportunity is the right of every American—rich or poor, foreign or native-born, irrespective of faith or color. It is the right of every individual to attain that position in life to which his ability and character entitle him. By its maintenance we will alone hold open the door of opportunity to every new generation, to every boy and girl. It tolerates no privileged classes or castes or groups who would hold opportunity as their prerogative. Only from confidence that this right will be upheld can flow that unbounded courage and hope which stimulate each individual man and woman to endeavor and to achievement. The sum of their achievement is the gigantic harvest of national progress.

This ideal of individualism based upon equal opportunity to every citizen is the negation of socialism. It is the negation of anarchy. It is the negation of despotism. It is as if we set a race. We, through free and universal education, provide the training of the runners; we give to them an equal start; we provide in the government the umpire of fairness in the race. The winner is he who shows the most conscientious training, the greatest ability, and the greatest character. Socialism bids all to end the race equally. It holds back the speedy to the pace of the slowest. Anarchy would provide neither training nor umpire. Despotism picks those who should run and those who should win.

Conservative, progressive, and liberal thought and action have their only real test in whether they contribute to equal opportunity, whether they hold open the door of opportunity. If they do not they are false in their premise no matter what their name may be.

It was Abraham Lincoln who firmly enunciated this ideal as the equal chance. The Sherman Law was enacted in endeavor to hold open the door of equal opportunity in business. The commissions for regulation of public utilities were created to prevent discrimination in service and prevent extortion in rates—and thereby the destruction of equal opportunity.

Equality of opportunity is a fundamental principle of our nation. With it we must test all our policies. The success or failure of this principle is the test of our government.

Mr. Chairman, I regret that time does not permit the compass of many important questions. I hope at a later time to discuss the development of waterways, highways, aviation, irrigable lands, foreign trade and merchant marine, the promotion of education, more effective administration of our criminal laws, the relation of our government to public utilities and railways, the primary necessity of conservation of natural resources, measures for further economy in government and reduction of taxes—all of which afford problems of the first order.

I would violate my conscience and the gratitude I feel, did I not upon this occasion express appreciation of the great president who leads our party today. President Coolidge has not only given a memorable administration, he has left an imprint of rectitude and statesmanship upon the history of our country. His has been the burden of reconstruction of our country from the destruction of war. He has dignified economy to a principle of government. He has charted the course of our nation and our party over many years to come. It is not only a duty but it is the part of statesmanship that we adhere to this course.

No man who stands before the mighty forces which ramify American life has the right to promise solutions at his hand alone. All that an honest man can say is that, within the extent of his abilities and his authority and in cooperation with the Congress and with leaders of every element in our people, these problems shall be courageously met and solution will be courageously attempted.

Our purpose is to build in this nation a human society, not an economic system. We wish to increase the efficiency and productivity of our country, but its final purpose is happier homes. We shall succeed through the faith, the loyalty, the self-sacrifice, the devotion to eternal ideals which live today in every American.

The matters which I have discussed directly and deeply affect the moral and spiritual welfare of our country. No one believes these aspirations and hopes can be realized in a day. Progress or remedy lie often enough in the hands of state and local government. But the awakening of the national conscience and the stimulation of every remedial agency is indeed a function of the national government. I want to see our government great, both as an instrument and as a symbol of the nation's greatness.

The presidency is more than an administrative office. It must be the symbol of American ideals. The high and the lowly must be seen with the same eyes, met in the same spirit. It must be the instrument by which national conscience is livened and it must under the guidance of the Almighty interpret and follow that conscience.

The Veterans' Bonus

Detroit, Michigan
September 21, 1931

AFTER WORLD WAR I, Congress promised to pay the veterans a bonus in 1945. When the Depression hit, impoverished veterans demanded early payment. Hoover was a generous supporter of veterans—fully one quarter of the 1933 national budget went for veterans' benefits—but neither he nor Congress could countenance their demands. In 1931 Hoover went before a convention of the American Legion to explain his policy. He also opposed the military dictatorship proposed by some of its members to stave off national collapse.

By the summer of 1932, the "Bonus Expeditionary force," a band of veterans and their families 20,000 strong, was encamped in shacks and abandoned buildings around Washington, D.C. Late in July, Gen. Douglas MacArthur and his troops routed the squatters, and their camp was burned. Although MacArthur had acted against Hoover's orders, the spectacle of the federal government using force against its own defenders doomed what was left of Hoover's chances at reelection in November.

I wish to thank you for the heartening cordiality of your reception. It is a pleasure to accept the invitation of your commander to attend your convention. I am led to do so at a time of most pressing public duties, because I wish to lay frankly and simply before you important facts which I am sure you will wish to have, and I wish to point to an opportunity of service which you can give not alone to your members but to the country at large.

I need not recount to you that the world is passing through a great depression fraught with gruelling daily emergencies alike to individual men and to governments. This depression today flows largely from Europe through the fundamental dislocations of economic and political forces which arose from the World War in which your service brought bloodshed to an end and gave hope of reconstruction to the world. Our economic strength is such that we would have recovered long since but for these forces from abroad. Recovery of the world now rests and awaits in no small degree upon our country, the United States of America. Some individuals amongst us may have lost their nerve and faith but the real American people are digging themselves out of this depression with industry and courage. We have the self-containment, the resources, the manhood, and the intelligence, and by united action we will lead the world in recovery.

The American Legion, born of world emergency, wields a great influence throughout our country because it speaks for a generation which has proven its citizenship by offering its all to its country. You of the Legion have a peculiarly sacred stake in the future of the country which you fought to preserve. You have proven your devotion in camp and in battle. You have built up your organization to serve in peace as in war.

You are aware that during the past year our national expenditures have exceeded our income. Today the national government is faced with another large deficit in its budget. There is a decrease in the annual yield of income taxes alone from $2,400 million that we received in the years of prosperity to only $1,200 million today. Simultaneously, we are carrying a high and necessary extra burden of public works in aid to the unemployed, of aids to agriculture, and of increased benefits and services to veterans. In these circumstances I am directing the most drastic economy in every non-vital branch of government, yet the essential services must be maintained. These obviously, include the adequate and generous provision for our disabled veterans and the continuation of our present programs of work for the unemployed and our aids to agriculture. Whatever the argument made, I do not wish you to be misled by those who say that we need only to tax the rich to secure the funds which we need. We must face the absolute fact that the rich can be taxed to the point of diminishing returns, and still the deficit in our ordinary and necessary expenditures would not be covered upon a basis even of the utmost economy. Make no mistake. In these circumstances it is those who work in the fields, at the bench, and at the desk who will be forced to carry an added burden for every added cent to our expenditures.

Whatever the deficit may be and in whatever manner it may ultimately be met, every additional expenditure placed upon our government in this emergency magnifies itself out of all proportion into intolerable pressures, whether it is by taxation or by loans. Either loans or taxes beyond the very minimum necessities of government will drain the resources of industry and commerce and in turn will increase unemployment. Such action can easily defeat our hopes, our plans, and our best efforts for the recovery of our country and so indefinitely delay the return of prosperity and employment. We can carry our present expenditures without jeopardy to national stability. We cannot carry more without grave national risks.

The imperative moment has come in our history when increase in government expenditures must be avoided, whether it be ill-considered, hasty, or uninformed legislation of any kind, or whether it be for new services meritorious in themselves. Any alternative will strike down the earnest efforts of the citizenry of our nation to start us back upon the economic paths to which we must return if we and our children are to have the destiny which everyone has the right to hope and the heart to give.

During the past week your national commander and the members of the Legion's unemployment committee came to me and offered to the nation the combined strength of your million men and your 10,000 posts to help in relief over this forthcoming winter. I here accept that offer with the thanks of the nation in the fine spirit in which it is submitted. But there is today an even greater service to our country. And that is the determined opposition by you, as a great body of influential men, to any additional demands upon the nation until we have won this war against world depression. I am not speaking alone of veterans' legislation which may be but a minor part, and that may be urged before this convention, but I am speaking equally of demands for every

other project proposed in the country which would require increased federal expenditure. It is an attitude and an action in the whole field of government expenditures that is before us today. The very first stone in the foundations of stability, and I invite you to enlist in that fight. The country's need of this service is second only to war. I invite you to study the relation of their governmental finance to the daily welfare and security of every man, woman, and child in the history of Europe during these past six months alone. It is for us to observe these lessons and to be helpful but our first duty is to the people of the United States. Nothing will give a greater glow of confidence to our country today than your enlistment and the vigorous support which you are capable of bringing to this effort to prevent additional burdens on the government from whatever quarter they may come.

You would not have the president of the United States plead with any citizen or any group of citizens for any course of action. I make no plea to you. But you would have your president point out the path of service in this nation. And I am doing that now. My mind goes back to the days of the war when you and I served in our appointed tasks. At the end of those years of heart sickness over the misery of it all, when the peace came, you and I knew that the wounds of the world were unhealed and that there would be further emergencies still before our country and the world when self-denial and courageous service must be given. Your organization was born at that time and dedicated to that service by the very preamble of your magnificent constitution. No man can doubt the charter and idealism of men who have gone into the trenches in defense of their country. I have that faith. This is an emergency and these are the times for service to which we must put full heart and purpose to help and not retard the return of the happy days we know are ahead of your country and of mine.

With the guidance of the Almighty God, with the same faith, courage, and self-sacrifice with which you, backed by the nation, won victory 14 years ago, so shall we win victory today.

Agriculture and the Depression

Des Moines, Iowa

October 4, 1932

IN THE 1932 campaign the embattled Hoover came out of the White House to make nine major speeches, mostly in the Midwest, reiterating his faith in the principles of self-reliance and mutual aid that he believed would carry the nation through the Depression. In Iowa, his home state, 2,000 anti-Hoover demonstrators stood outside the hall while he defended his farm policies. H. L. Mencken, who once called Hoover "a fat Coolidge," described the speech as "very fair hokum . . . largely compounded of hooey," a panicky attempt to deceive farmers into giving him credit for policies he had only reluctantly supported. It did not help that Hoover presented himself as lonely but heroic, a master technician striving mightily in the isolation of the White House to cure the nation's troubles despite lies and ingratitude. Hoover himself, in after years, told Charles Lindbergh that he regretted the speech; a sharper politician would have known "not to say things just because they are true."

I am glad, a son of the soil of this state, to come back to where I was born and where I spent the first 10 years of my boyhood. My parents and grandparents came to Iowa in the covered wagon—pioneers in this community. They lie buried in your soil. They broke the prairie into homes of independent living. They worshiped God, they did their duty to their neighbors. They toiled to bring to their children greater comfort, better education, and to open to them a wider opportunity than theirs.

It was my destiny in the solicitude for an orphaned family to be taken by the old emigrant railway train westward to the Pacific coast and ultimately to fix my home and hopes in California. My sons fly these long journeys in a span of daylight.

These contrasts of a half century are a vivid picture of the change and progress of American life.

My experiences of later years have in no way diminished my memories and my gratitude to my native state. It was here that the doors of opportunity were first opened to me. It was here that I was given that tender care of mind and body, those first steps in education, that knowledge of poverty and struggle for family betterment which contribute to understainding of American life.

And with it all, even in those days, a boy had his first contact with the wider life of our nation. Not that childhood grasps or understands these questions, yet great forces then, as now, touched every farm in our country.

As a boy I walked alongside the torchlight procession in the Garfield campaign; I was awed by the whispered anxiety when the president was shot by an assassin, and by the genuine grief of every person in that village when the flag was placed at half-mast on his passing.

I have been accorded the greatest honor which my country can bestow—that is to lead it among the nations of the world in the paths of peace and to serve in the stern duty of the battle against the invisible forces of a great world calamity.

It was in this community that I came in contact with my first economic depression. I was born in the midst of the terrible times of the seventies, with their poverty and their, difficulties. And only in that period has our nation had to meet a situation in any degree comparable to that with which we now contend. That was the economic storm which struck us when the aftermath of the Civil War coincided with the wars in Europe. But in those days agriculture and industry were less dependent upon each other, there was far less interdependence among the nations of the world, and thus the violence of the storm in human suffering and loss was infinitely less disastrous.

Not that I would suggest that at that age I knew what an economic depression was or that I had every heard the words, but I vividly recollect a Christmas upon the farm when the sole resources of joy were popcorn balls, sorghum, and hickory nuts, when for a flock of disappointed children there were no store toys, no store clothes, when it was carefully explained that because of the hard times everything must be saved for the mortgage. The word mortgage became for me a dreaded and haunting fear from that day to this.

I know now from reading history that that Christmas was also a time when the country was coming out of that great depression. The Democratic Party was still coquetting with the great panacea of that time—greenbacks. I did not then know what greenbacks were, but I do know that the family tightened its belt and, with confidence, voted for James A. Garfield, a Republican president.

My purpose tonight is to deal with some of the problems of the day. Seldom in our history have we gone through greater dangers, or have the difficulties before the nation been of such gravity. They attain this gravity not only because of the unprecedented dislocation in our domestic life but because our problems are worldwide.

Aside from the value of truth, the causes and origins of this unparalleled storm are of importance only as they indicate the policies we must pursue for our safety. I say to you that a storm which embraces the whole world, which ramifies to every village in China, every sheep ranch in Patagonia, every factory in Germany, every mine in Australia, every counting house in England, every farm in the state of Iowa, is the result of a terrific eruption in civilization itself. Something infinitely deeper and of greater portent has happened to the world than any reaction from our own reckless speculation and exploitation. We are contending today with forces at home and abroad which still threaten the safety of civilization.

I know it seems a far cry to the village home of America from the effect of 40 million people killed, starved, and maimed in the Great War, with all its loss in skill and character. It seems a far cry from the increase in debt of governments from 20 billion dollars to 200 billion dollars, an amount two-thirds the value of everything in the whole United States. It seems a far cry from the effect of an increase in the peace armies of the world in 20 years from two million to five million of men with the hate and suspicion they excite. It seems a far cry from the last 12 years of frantic political and financial policies of foreign nations, with the ultimate collapse of governments, of revolutions and dictatorships.

You can test the part which the Great War played in the difficulties in your home and their relation to the gravity of the situation today right at your own doors.

You will recollect that the values of your land doubled and trebled under the transitory demands of the Great War. You will recollect the expansion of mortgages, the collapse in values immediately thereafter, the doubling of taxation, the aftermaths of all which are still a part of your problems. You know the stifling of your markets from the collapse of other nations under the calamities they have inherited from the war.

We have fought an unending war against the effect of these calamities upon our people. This is no time to recount the battles on a thousand fronts. We have fought the good fight to protect our people in a thousand cities from hunger and cold.

We have carried on an unceasing campaign to protect the nation from that unhealing class bitterness which arises from strikes and lockouts and industrial conflict. We have accomplished this through the willing agreement of employer and labor which placed humanity before money through the sacrifice of profits and dividends before wages.

We have defended millions from the tragic result of droughts.

We have mobilized a vast expansion of public construction to make work for the unemployed.

We fought the battle to balance the budget.

We have defended the country from being forced off the gold standard, with its crushing effect upon all who are in debt.

We have battled to provide a supply of credits to merchants and farmers and industries.

We have fought to retard falling prices.

We have struggled to save homes and farms from foreclosure of mortgages, battled to save millions of depositors and borrowers from the ruin caused by the failure of banks, fought to assure the safety of millions of policy holders from failure of their insurance companies, and fought to save commerce and employment from the failure of railways.

We have fought to secure disarmament and maintain the peace of the world, fought for stability of other countries whose failure would inevitably injure us. And, above all, we have fought to preserve the safety, the principles and ideals of American life. We have built the foundations of recovery.

All these battles, related and unrelated, have had a single strategy and a single purpose. That was to protect your living, your comfort, and the safety of your fireside. They have been waged and have succeeded in protecting you from infinitely greater harm which could have come to you.

Thousands of our people in their bitter distress and losses today are saying that "things could not be worse." No person who has any remote understanding of the forces which confronted this country during these last 18 months ever utters that remark. Had it not been for the immediate and unprecedented actions of our government things would be infinitely worse today.

Instead of moving forward we would be degenerating for years to come, even if we had not gone clear over the precipice, with the total destruction of everything we hold dear.

Let no man tell you that it could not be worse. It could be so much worse that these days now, distressing as they are, would look like veritable prosperity.

In all these great efforts there has been the constant difficulty of translating the daily action into terms of public understanding. The forces in motion have been so gigantic, so complex in their character, the instrumentalities and actions we must undertake to deal with them are so involved, the figures we must use are so astronomical as to seem to have but little relation to the family in the apartment, the cottage, or on the farm.

Many of these battles have had to be fought in silence, without the cheers of the limelight or the encouragement of public support, because the very disclosure of the forces opposed to us would have undermined the courage of the weak and induced panic in the timid, which would have destroyed the very basis of success.

Hideous misrepresentation and unjustified complaint had to be accepted in silence. It was as if a great battle in war should be fought without public knowledge of any incident except the stream of dead and wounded from the front. There has been much of tragedy, but there has been but little public evidence of the dangers and enormous risks from which a great national victory has been achieved.

I have every confidence that the whole American people know in their hearts that there has been but one test in my mind, one supreme object in the measures and policies we have forged to win in this war against depression: that test was the interest of the people in the homes and at the firesides of our country. I have had before me but one vision: that is, the vision of the millions of homes of the sort which I knew as a boy in this state.

I wish to describe one of the battles we have fought to save this nation from a defeat that would have dragged farmers and city dwellers alike down to a common ruin. This battle was fought parallel with other battles on other fronts. Much of what I will tell you has been hitherto undisclosed. It had to be fought in silence, for it will be evident to you that had the whole of the forces in motion been made public at the time there would have been no hope of victory because of the panic through fear and destruction of confidence that very disclosure would have brought.

Happily we have won this battle. There is no longer any danger from disclosure.

Our own speculative boom had weakened our own economic structure, but the critical assaults and dangers swept upon us from foreign countries. We were therefore plunged into a battle against invading forces of destruction from abroad to preserve the financial integrity of our government; to counteract the terrific forces of deflation aligned against us; to protect the debtor class who were being strangled by the contraction of credit and the demands for payment of debt; to prevent our being pushed off the gold standard, which in our country would have meant disaster to every person who owed money; and finally to preserve the savings of the American people.

We were fighting to hold the Gibraltar of world stability, because only by holding this last fortress could we be saved from a crashing world, with a decade of misery and the very destruction of our form of government and our ideals of national life.

When 18 months ago the financial systems of Europe were no longer able to stand the strain of their war inheritances and of their after-war economic and political policies, an earthquake ran through 40 nations. Financial panics; governments unable to meet their obligations; banks unable to pay their depositors; citizens, fearing inflation of currency, seeking to export their savings to foreign countries for safety; citizens of other nations demanding payment of their loans; financial and monetary systems either in collapse or remaining only in appearance. The shocks of this earthquake ran from Vienna to Berlin, from Berlin to London, from London to Asia and South America. From all those countries they came to this country, to every city and farm in the United States.

First one and then another of these 40 nations either abandoned payment in gold of their obligations to other countries, or restricted payments by their citizens to foreign countries, so as practically to amount to at least temporary or partial repudiation of public and private debts. Every one of them, in a frantic endeavor to reduce the expenditures of their citizens, imposed drastic restrictions upon their imports of goods. These events were not as children playing with blocks. They brought revolutions, mutinies, riots, downfalls of governments, and a seething of despair which threatened civilization.

In order to prevent total collapse of the German people and its inevitable effect upon us, I brought about the German moratorium and so-called German standstill agreements by which Europe was given a breathing spell in which to arrange and stabilize its affairs. But the shocks grew in violence, and finally, at the end of September a year ago, the difficulties of Europe culminated with the suspension of gold payments by the Bank of England, followed by many other nations. With no stability to foreign currencies trade again slackened, because merchants could not calculate the amount they might realize when they shipped their goods.

An amazing statement was made a few days ago in this state that the passage of the Tariff Act of 1930 "started such a drain on the gold reserves of the principal commerical countries as to force practically all of them off the gold standard." The facts are that the Tariff Act was not passed until nearly one year after the depression began.

The earthquake started in Europe; the gold of Europe was not drained; it has increased in total every year since the passage of the act— and is right now $1,500,000,000 greater than when the act was passed, and the tariff is still on. It has been my daily task to analyze and know the forces which brought these calamities. I have had to look them in the face. They require far more penetration than such assertions as this indicate.

The shocks which rocked these nations came from profound depths; their spread gave fearful blows to our own system, finally culminating last October in what, had they not been courageously met with unprecedented measures, would, because of our peculiar situation, have brought us to greater collapse than even other countries.

The first effect of these shocks on us was from foreign dumping of American securities on our markets which demoralized prices upon our exchanges, foreign buying power stagnated because of their internal paralysis and this in turn stifled the markets for our farm and factory products, increased our unemployment and by piling up our surpluses demoralized our commodity prices.

The frantic restrictive measures on exchanges and the abandonment of gold standards made it impossible for American citizens to collect billions of the moneys due to us for goods which our citizens had sold abroad, or short-term loans they had made to facilitate commerce. At the same time citizens of those countries demanded payment from our citizens of the moneys due for goods they had sold to our merchants and for securities they had sold in our country.

Before the end foreign countries drained us of nearly a billion dollars of gold and a vast amount of other exchange.

Then we had also to meet an attack upon our own flank by some of our own people, who, becoming infected with world fear and panic, withdrew vast sums from our banks and hoarded it from the use of our own people, to the amount of $1,500,000,000. This brought its own trains of failures and bankruptcies. Even worse, many of our less patriotic citizens started to export their money to foreign countries for fear we should be forced onto a paper money basis.

All this cataclysm did not develop at once; it came blow by blow; its effect upon us grew steadily, our difficulties mounted higher day by day.

This is not time to trace its effect stage by stage. No statement of mine is needed to portray the effects upon you. No statement of mine could portray the effects upon you. No statement of mine could portray the full measure of perils which threatened us.

Three of the great perils were invisible except to those who had the responsibility of dealing with the situation.

The first of these perils was the steady strangulation of credit through the removal of three billions of gold and currency by foreign drains and by hoarding from the channels of our commerce and business. And let me remind you that credit is the lifeblood of business, of prices, and of jobs.

Had the full consequences of this action been allowed to run their full extent, it would have resulted, under our system of currency and banking, in the deflation of credit anywhere from 20 to 25 billions, or the destruction of nearly half the immediate working capital of the country. There would have been almost a universal call for payment of debt which would have brought about universal bankruptcy, because property could not be coverted to cash, no matter what its value.

And there were other forces equally dangerous. The tax income of the federal government is largely based upon profits and income. As these profits and income disappeared, the federal revenues fell by nearly one half, and thus the very stability of the federal Treasury was imperiled. The government was compelled to borrow enormous sums to pay current expenses.

The third peril, which we escaped only by the most drastic action, was that of being forced off the gold standard. I would like to make clear to you what that would have meant had we failed in that sector of the battle. Going off the gold standard in the United States would have been a most crushing blow to most of those with savings and those who owed money, and it was these we were fighting to protect.

Going off the gold standard is no academic matter. By going off the gold standard, gold goes to a premium, and the currency dollar becomes depreciated. Largely as a result of fears generated by the experience after the Civil War and by the Democratic free-silver campaign in 1896 our people have long insisted upon writing a large part of their long-term debtor documents as payment in gold.

A considerable part of farm mortgages, most of our industrial and all of our government, most of our state and municipal bonds, and most other long-term obligations are written as payable in gold.

This is not the case in foreign countries. They have no such practice, their obligations are written in currency. When they abandon the gold standard, the gold goes to a premium, the relations of their domestic debtors and creditors are unchanged, because both he who pays and he who receives use the same medium. But if the United States had been forced off the gold standard, you in this city would have sold your produce for depreciated currency. You would be paid your bank deposits and your insurance policy in currency, but you would have to pay a premium on such of your debts as are written in gold. The federal government, many of the states, the municipalities, to meet their obligations, would need to increase taxes which are payable in currency, in order to pay the gold premium, provided, of course, they did not repudiate.

I believe I can make clear why we were in danger of being forced off even with our theoretically large stocks of gold. I have told you of the enormous sums of gold and exchange drained from us by foreigners. You will realize also that our citizens who hoard Federal Reserve and some other forms of currency are in effect hoarding gold, because under the law we must maintain 40 percent gold reserve behind such currency. Owing to the lack in the Federal Reserve system of the kind of securities required by the law for the additional 60 percent of coverage of the currency, the Reserve system was forced to increase their gold reserve up to 75 percent. Thus with $1,500,000,000 of hoarded currency, there was in effect over $1,000,000,000 of gold hoarded by our own citizens.

These drains had at one moment reduced the amount of gold we could spare for current payments to a point where the secretary of the Treasury informed me that unless we could put into effect a remedy, we could not hold to the gold standard more than two weeks longer because of inability to meet the demands of foreigners and our own citizens for gold.

Being forced off the gold standard in the United States meant utter chaos. Never was our nation in greater peril, not alone in banks and financial systems, money and currency, but that foreboded dangers, moral and social chaos, with years of conflict and derangement.

In the midst of this hurricane the Republican administration kept a cool head and rejected every counsel of weakness and cowardice. Some of the reactionary economists urged that we should allow the liquidation to take its course until we had found bottom. Some people talked of vast issues of paper money. Some talked of suspending payments of government issues. Some talked of setting up a Council of National Defense. Some talked foolishly of dictatorship—any of which would have produced panic itself. Some assured me that no man could propose increased taxes in the United States to balance the budget in the midst of a depression and survive an election.

We determined that we should not enter the morass of using the printing press for currency or bonds. All human experience has demonstrated that that path once taken cannot be stopped, and that the moral integrity of the government would be sacrificed, because ultimately both currency and bonds would become valueless.

We determined that we would not follow the advice of the bitter-end liquidationists and see the whole body of debtors of the United States brought to bankruptcy and the savings of our people brought to destruction.

We determined we would stand up like men and render the credit of the United States government impregnable through the drastic reduction of government expenditures and increased revenues until we balanced our budget. We determined that if necessary we should lend the full credit of the government thus made impregnable, to aid private institutions to protect the debtor and the savings of our people.

We decided upon changes in the Federal Reserve system which would make our gold active in commercial use and that we would keep the American dollar ringing true in every city in America and in the world; that we would expand credit to offset the contraction brought about by hoarding and foreign withdrawals; that we would strengthen the federal land banks and all other mortgage institutions; that we would lend to the farmers for production; that we would protect the insurance companies, the building and loan associations, the savings banks, the country banks, and every other point of weakness.

We determined to place the shield of the federal government in front of the local communities in protection of those in distress, and that we would increase employment through profitable construction work with the aid of government credit.

On the 3rd of October last year I called to Washington the leading bankers of the country and secured from them an agreement to combine the resources of the banks to stem the tide. They pledged themselves to $500,000,000 for this purpose. On October 6th I called in the leaders of both political parties. I placed before them the situation at home and abroad. I asked unity of national action. We published a united determination to the country. The people drew a breath of relief; the ship swung to a more even keel.

But by the 1st of December the storm had grown in further intensity aboard, and the menace became more serious than ever before. With the opening of Congress in December I laid before it a program of unprecedented dimensions to meet an unprecedented situation.

The battalions and regiments and armies thus mobilized for this great battle turned the tide toward victory by July. The foreigners drew out most of their money, but finding that the American dollar rang honest on every counter, in new confidence they are sending it back. Since June $275,000,000 of gold has flowed back to us from abroad. Hoarders in our own country, finding our institutions safeguarded, have returned $250,000,000 to the useful channels of business. The securities held by our insurance companies, our savings banks, and our benevolent trusts have recovered in value.

The rills of credit are expanding. The pressure on the debtor to sacrifice his all in order to pay is relaxing. Men are daily being reemployed. If we calculate the values of this year's agricultural products compared with the low points, the farmers as a whole are, despite the heartbreaking distress which still exists, a billion dollars better off. Prices have a long way to go before the farmer has an adequate return, but at least the turn is toward recovery.

I have been talking of currency, of gold, of credit, of bonds, of banks, of insurance policies, of loans. Do not think these things have no human interpretation. The happiness of 120,000,000 people was at stake in the measure to enable the government to meet its debts and obligations, in saving the gold standard, in enabling 5,500 banks, insurance companies, building and loan associations, and a multitude of other insitutions to pay their obligations and ease pressure upon thier debtors. These institutions have been rendered safe and with them their 30,000,000 depositors, policyholders, and borrowers.

More than half of all of them were in the Midwest—500 in your own state of Iowa. Had they gone down, the shock of their failure would have carried down with them every man and institution who owed money and the whole employment and marketing fabric of the United States.

I wish I were able to translate what these perils, had they not been overcome, would have meant to each person in America. The financial system is not alone intrusted with your savings. Its failure means that the manufacturer cannot pay his worker, the worker his grocer, the merchant cannot buy his stock of goods, the farmer cannot sell his products. The great clock of economic life would stop. Had we failed, disaster would have translated itself into despair in every home, every city, village, and farm.

We won this great battle to protect our people at home. We held the Gibraltar of world stability. The world today has a chance. It is growing in strength. Let that man who complains that things could not be worse thank God for this victory and make reverent acknowledgment of the courage and stamina of a great democracy.

Let him be thankful for the presence in Washington of a Republican administration. I say this with full consideration of its portent, for I wish to call your attention to the part which the dominating leadership of the Democratic Party has played in this great crisis. I wish to bring before you the real doctrines and program of the men who then and now and in the future will dominate that party.

You will recollect that the congressional election two years ago gave the control of the lower house of Congress to our opponents. They were also in position to control the policies of the Senate. After that election their leaders announced to the world that their party would present a program to restore prosperity. One year later, when the new Congress assembled last December in the midst of this crisis, they presented no program.

The administration did present a program, which has saved the country from complete disaster. That program was patriotically supported by many members of the Democratic Party, who joined in enactment of these measures. To these men, who place patriotism above party, I pay tribute, but later in the session the opposition majority of the House of Representatives could not restrain their real purposes and doctrines. It is of importance to the country to realize what that program was, for the American people are asked to intrust the future of the United States in the hands of these same men and to these policies.

At a time when the most vital need was for reduction in expenditures and balancing of the budget to preserve the stability of the federal government as the keystone of all stability, they produced a program of pork-barrel legislation in the sum of $1,200,000,000 for nonproductive and unnecessary works at the expense of the taxpayer. They produced the cash bonus bill. They passed that through the House of Representatives by their leadership. I opposed it. It failed to pass the Senate. Under that bill it was proposed to expend $2,300,000,000. Worse still, the bill they passed provided the bonus should be paid through the creation of sheer fiat money. That would have made our currency a football of every speculator and every vicious element in the financial world at the very time when we were fighting for the honesty of the American dollar. I can do no better than quote Daniel Webster, who, 100 years ago, made one of the most prophetic statements ever made when he said:

> He who tampers with the currency robs labor of its bread. He panders, indeed, to greedy capital, which is keen-sighted and may shift for itself, but he beggars labor, which is unsuspecting and too busy with the present to calculate for the future. The prosperity of the workpeople lives, moves, and has its being in established credit and steady medium of payment.

The experience of scores of governments in the world since that day has confirmed Webster's statement, and yet the dominant leadership of the Democratic Party passed that measure to issue paper money through the House of Representatives.

And, further, the administration proposed economy measures to bring about reduction in specialized government expenditures by $300,000,000. When those recommendations had passed through the filter of the Democratic majority in the House, only $50,000,000 of savings were left; yet we hear many speeches from them upon economy. They passed a bill to destroy the effectiveness of the Tariff Commission. I vetoed that bill.

They passed a price-fixing bill creating what might be colloquially called the "rubber dollar." I opposed this. It was held up in the Senate. They passed a provision for loans to corporations and everybody else, whether they were affected and guarded by public interest or not. It would have made the government the most gigantic pawnbroker of history. I vetoed this measure. They passed other measures with this same reckless disregard for the safety of the nation.

All this undermined public confidence and delayed all the efforts of the administration and the powerful instrumentalities which we had placed in action to save the country. These measures representing the dominant Democratic control brought discouragement and delay to recovery.

That recovery began the moment when it was certain that these destructive measures of this Democratic-controlled House were stopped. Had their program passed, it would have been the end of recovery. If it ever passes, it will end hope of recovery. These measures were not simply gestures for vote-catching. These ideas and measures represented the true sentiments and doctrines of the majority of the control of the Democratic Party. A small minority of Democratic members disapproved these measures, but these men obviously have no voice today. This program was passed through the Democratic House of Representatives under the leadership of the gentleman who has been nominated the Democratic candidate for vice president, and thus these measures and policies were approved by their party.

At no time in public discussion of the vital issues of this campaign has any Democratic candidate, high or low, disavowed these destructive acts, which must emerge again if they come to power. I ask you to compare this actual Democratic program and these Democratic actions with the constructive program produced by the administration to meet the emergency. Do you propose to place these men in power and subject this country to that sort of measures and policies? It is by their acts in Congress and their leadership that you shall know them.

Of vital concern to you are the difficulties of agriculture. They have been of vital concern to me for the whole of these difficult years. I have been at the post to which the first news of every disaster is delivered, to which no detail of human suffering is spared. I have heard the cries of distress, and not only as a sympathetic listener but as one oppressed by a deep sense of responsibility to do all that human ingenuity could devise.

I wish to speak directly to those of my hearers who are farmers of what is on my mind, of what is in my heart, to tell you the conclusions I have reached from this bitter experience of the years in dealing with these problems which affect agriculture at home and their relations to foreign countries.

That agriculture is prostrate needs no proof. You have saved and economized and worked to reduce costs, but with all this, yours is a story of distress and suffering.

What the farmer wants and needs is higher prices, and in the meantime to keep from being dispossessed from his farm, to have a fighting chance to keep his home. The pressing question is how these two things are to be attained. Every decent citizen wants to see the farmer receive higher prices and wants to see him hold his home. Every citizen realizes that the general recovery of the country cannot be attained unless these things are secured to the farmer.

Every thinking citizen knows that most of these low price levels and most of this distress, except in one or two commodities where there is an unwieldy surplus, are due to the decreased demand for farm products by our millions of unemployed and by foreign countires. Every citizen knows that part of this unemployment is due to the inability of the farmer to buy the products of the factory. Every thinking citizen knows that the farmer, the worker, and the businessman are in the same boat and must all come to share together.

Every citizen who stretches his vision across the United States realizes that for the last three years we have been on this downward spiral owing to the destructive forces which I have already described. If he has this vision, he today takes courage and hope because he also knows that these destructive forces have been stopped; that the spiral is moving upward; that more men are being employed and are able to consume more agricultural products.

The policies of the Republican Party and the unprecedented instrumentalities and measures which we have put in motion, many of which are designed directly for agriculture—they are winning out. If we continue to fight along these lines we shall win.

As I have stated before, in the shifting battle against depression, we shall need to adopt new measures and new tactics as the battle moves on. The essential thing is that we should build soundly and solidly for the future. My solicitude and willingness to advance and protect the interests of agriculture is shown by the record. Protection and advancement of this industry will have my continued deepest concern, for in it lies the progress of all America. It was in this industry that I was born.

The battle against depression is making progress. We are still faced with forces which render 10 million men idle and agriculture prostrate. We have forged new weapons, we have turned the tide from defense to attack. I shall continue the fight. It calls for that cooperation, that courage, that patience and fortitude with which our fathers conquered these prairies.

In conclusion, my friends, there are many other subjects of vast importance to our country. The farmers of America are not selfishly interested in their own industry alone. They are Americans with the same concern for the welfare of the nation in its multitude of other problems, both at home and abroad. Time does not permit of their exposition tonight. The issues are grave, the stake is great.

These issues rise above the concern of an ordinary campaign. Our cause is not alone the restoration of prosperity. It is to soundly and sanely correct the weaknesses in our system which this depression has brought to the surface. It is the maintenance of courageous integrity in political action and in government. It is the holding of this nation to the principles and ideals which it has had from the beginning. It is to make free men and women.

Finally, let me deal for a moment with the ultimate realities. I have had to describe the complicated processes of currencies and taxation and other such dreary things. They are but the tools we use to manage the processes by which we answer the old, old question, wherewithal shall we live? They are necessary tools, but they are not an end in themselves. Our toils and cares are for a higher purpose.

We are not a nation of 120 million solitary individuals, we are a nation of 25 million families dwelling in 25 million homes, each warmed by the fires of affection and cherishing within it a mutual solicitude for kinfolk and children. Their safety is what we are really striving for. Their happiness is our true concern. Our most solemn hope for them is that they may share richly in a spiritual life as well, that puts them not only at peace with their fellows but also in harmony with the will of a beneficent Providence.

Out of our strivings for material blessings must come safety for homes and schools and churches and holding of national ideals, the forming of national character. These are the real aspirations of our people. These are the promises of America, and those promises must be fulfilled.

The Consequences of the Proposed New Deal

October 31, 1932

New York City, New York

ON THE EVE of the 1932 presidential balloting, President Herbert Hoover was extremely unpopular and personally disenchanted with the office. However, he deeply feared that politicians from either party were far too willing to compromise to win public support. In a speech at Madison Square Garden on October 21, 1932, Hoover passionately defended his administration while attacking his opponent and the Democrats in general.

In his speech, Hoover endeavors to cast the election in ideological terms. He declares that the upcoming balloting will be a "contest between two philosophies of government." Through the speech, Hoover criticizes many of Roosevelt's campaign promises and various plans put forth by congressional Democrats. The president also points out differences with his opponent about the government's role in public utilities. Hoover steadfastly maintains that private companies should manage electric power and water services and that the government's role is to create favorable conditions for private companies to expand. Hoover also argues that during times of prosperity, people tended to pay little attention to the importance of rights and liberties. Furthermore, during difficult times, people often sought immediate government action to solve problems, even at the expense of individual rights and freedom. The result was a steady erosion of liberties and freedoms.

This campaign is more than a contest between two men. It is more than a contest between two parties. It is a contest between two philosophies of government.

We are told by the opposition that we must have a change, that we must have a new deal. It is not the change that comes from normal development of national life to which I object or you object, but the proposal to alter the whole foundations of our national life which have been built through generations of testing and struggle, and of the principles upon which we have made this Nation. The expressions of our opponents must refer to important changes in our economic and social system and our system of government; otherwise they would be nothing but vacuous words. And I realize that in this time of distress many of our people are asking whether our social and economic system is incapable of that great primary function of providing security and comfort of life to all of the firesides of 25 million homes in America, whether our social system provides for the fundamental development and progress of our people, and whether our form of government is capable of originating and sustaining that security and progress.

This question is the basis upon which our opponents are appealing to the people in their fear and their distress. They are proposing changes and so-called new deals which would destroy the very foundations of the American system of life.

Our people should consider the primary facts before they come to the judgment—not merely through political agitation, the glitter of promise, and the discouragement of temporary hardships—whether they will support changes which radically affect the whole system which has been built during these six generations of the toil of our fathers. They should not approach the question in the despair with which our opponents would clothe it.

Our economic system has received abnormal shocks during the last 3 years which have temporarily dislocated its normal functioning. These shocks have in a large sense come from without our borders, and I say to you that our system of government has enabled us to take such strong action as to prevent the disaster which would otherwise have come to this Nation. It has enabled us further to develop measures and programs which are now demonstrating their ability to bring about restoration and progress.

We must go deeper than platitudes and emotional appeals of the public platform in the campaign if we will penetrate to the full significance of the changes which our opponents are attempting to float upon the wave of distress and discontent from the difficulties through which we have passed. We can find what our opponents would do after searching the record of their appeals to discontent, to group and sectional interest. To find that, we must search for them in the legislative acts which they sponsored and passed in the Democratic-controlled House of Representatives in the last session of Congress. We must look into both the measures for which they voted and in which they were defeated. We must inquire whether or not the Presidential and Vice-Presidential candidates have disavowed those acts. If they have not, we must conclude that they form a portion and are a substantial indication of the profound changes in the new deal which is proposed.

And we must look still further than this as to what revolutionary changes have been proposed by the candidates themselves.

We must look into the type of leaders who are campaigning for the Democratic ticket, whose philosophies have been well known all their lives and whose demands for a change in the American system are frank and forceful. I can respect the sincerity of these men in their desire to change our form of government and our social and our economic system, though I shall do my best tonight to prove they are wrong. I refer particularly to Senator Norris, Senator La Follette, Senator Cutting, Senator Huey Long, Senator Wheeler, William Randolph Hearst, and other exponents of a social philosophy different from the traditional philosophies of the American people. Unless these men have felt assurance of support to their ideas they certainly would not be supporting these candidates and the Democratic Party. The zeal of these men indicates that they must have some sure confidence that they will have a voice in the administration of this Government.

I may say at once that the changes proposed from all these Democratic principals and their allies are of the most profound and penetrating character. If they are brought about, this will not be the America which we have known in the past.

Now, I may pause for a moment and examine the American system of government and of social and economic life which it is now proposed that we should alter. Our system is the product of our race and of our experience in building a Nation to heights unparalleled in the whole history of the world. It is a system peculiar to the American people. It differs essentially from all others in the world. It is an American system. It is rounded on the conception that only through ordered liberty, through freedom to the individual, and equal opportunity to the individual will his initiative and enterprise be summoned to spur the march of national progress.

It is by the maintenance of an equality of opportunity and therefore of a society absolutely fluid in the movement of its human particles that our individualism departs from the individualism of Europe. We resent class distinction because there can be no rise for the individual through the frozen strata of classes, and no stratification of classes can take place in a mass that is livened by the free rise of its human particles. Thus in our ideals the able and ambitious are able to rise constantly from the bottom to leadership in the community. We denounce any attempt to stir class feeling or class antagonisms in the United States.

This freedom of the individual creates of itself the necessity and the cheerful willingness of men to act cooperatively in a thousand ways and for every purpose as the occasion requires, and it permits such voluntary cooperations to be dissolved as soon as it has served its purpose and to be replaced by new voluntary associations for new purposes.

There has thus grown within us, to gigantic importance, a new conception. That is the conception of voluntary cooperation within the community; cooperation to perfect the social organizations; cooperation for the care of those in distress; cooperation for the advancement of knowledge, of scientific research, of education; cooperative action in a thousand directions for the advancement of economic life. This is self-government by the people outside of the Government. It is the most powerful development of individual freedom and equality of opportunity that has taken place in the century and a half since our fundamental institutions were founded.

It is in the further development of this cooperation and in a sense of its responsibility that we should find solution for many of the complex problems, and not by the extension of the Government into our economic and social life. The greatest function a government can perform is to build up that cooperation, and its most resolute action should be to deny the extension of bureaucracy. We have developed great agencies of cooperation by the assistance of the Government which do promote and protect the interests of individuals and the smaller units of business: the Federal Reserve System, in its strengthening and support of the smaller banks; the Farm Board, in its strengthening and support of the farm cooperatives; the home loan banks, in the mobilizing of building and loan associations and savings banks; the Federal land banks, in giving independence and strength to land mortgage associations; the great mobilization of relief to distress, the mobilization of business and industry in measures of recovery from this depression, and a score of other activities that are not socialism, and they are not the Government in business. They are the essence of protection to the development of free men. I wish to explore this point a little further. The primary conception of this whole American system is not the ordering of men but the cooperation of free men. It is rounded upon the conception of responsibility of the individual to the community, of the responsibility of local government to the State, of the State to the National Government.

I am exploring these questions because I propose to take up definite proposals of the opposition and test them with these realities in a few moments.

Now, our American system is rounded on a peculiar conception of self-government designed to maintain an equality of opportunity to the individual, and through decentralization it brings about and maintains these responsibilities. The centralization of government will undermine these responsibilities and will destroy the system itself.

Our Government differs from all 'previous conceptions, not only in the decentralization but also in the independence of the judicial arm of the Government.

Our Government is rounded on a conception that in times of great emergency, when forces are running beyond the control of individuals or cooperative action, beyond the control of local communities or the States, then the great reserve powers of the Federal Government should be brought into action to protect the people. But when these forces have ceased there must be a return to State, local, and individual responsibility.

The implacable march of scientific discovery with its train of new inventions presents every year new problems to government and new problems to the social order. Questions often arise whether, in the face of the growth of these new and gigantic tools, democracy can remain master in its own house and can preserve the fundamentals of our American system. I contend that it can, and I contend that this American system of our has demonstrated its validity and superiority over any system yet invented by human mind. It has demonstrated it in the face of the greatest test of peacetime history—that is the emergency which we have passed in the last 3 years.

When the political and economic weakness of many nations of Europe, the result of the World War and its aftermath, finally culminated in the collapse of their institutions, the delicate adjustments of our economic and social and governmental life received a shock unparalleled in our history. No one knows that better than you of New York. No one knows its causes better than you. That the crisis was so great that many of the leading banks sought directly or indirectly to convert their assets into gold or its equivalent with the result that they practically ceased to function as credit institutions is known to you; that many of our citizens sought flight for their capital to other countries; that many of them attempted to hoard gold in large amounts you know. These were but superficial indications of the flight of confidence and the belief that our Government could not overcome these forces.

Yet these forces were overcome—perhaps by narrow margins—and this demonstrates that our form of government has the capacity. It demonstrates what the courage of a nation can accomplish under the resolute leadership of the Republican Party. And I say the Republican Party because our opponents, before and during the crisis, proposed no constructive program, though some of their members patriotically supported ours for which they deserve on every occasion the applause of patriotism. Later on in the critical period, the Democratic House of Representatives did develop the real thought and ideas of the Democratic Party. They were so destructive that they had to be defeated. They did delay the healing of our wounds for months.

Now, in spite of all these obstructions we did succeed. Our form of government did prove itself equal to the task. We saved this Nation from a generation of chaos and degeneration;

we preserved the savings, the insurance policies, gave a fighting chance to men to hold their homes. We saved the integrity of our Government and the honesty of the American dollar. And we installed measures which today are bringing back recovery. Employment, agriculture, and business—all of these show the steady, if slow, healing of an enormous wound.

As I left Washington, our Government departments communicated to me the fact that the October statistics on employment show that since the 1st day of July, the men returned to work in the United States exceed 1 million.

I therefore contend that the problem of today is to continue these measures and policies to restore the American system to its normal functioning, to repair the wounds it has received, to correct the weaknesses and evils which would defeat that system. To enter upon a series of deep changes now, to embark upon this inchoate new deal which has been propounded in this campaign would not only undermine and destroy our American system but it will delay for months and years the possibility of recovery.

We have carried the first-line of trenches in a great national battle. It is of little difference who the commander in chief may be if the strategy and the policies and the subordinate captains and majors and colonels and generals are maintained and if the battle be continued. But that battle cannot be continued under our political system with a 4-month lapse between the election and the inauguration and a 12 month lapse thereafter while new strategies and new policies are being determined, no matter how admirable they may be.

Now, to go back to my major thesis—the thesis of the longer view. Before we enter into courses of deep-seated change and of the new deal, I would like you to consider what the results of this American system have been during the last 30 years—that is, a single generation. For if it can be demonstrated that by this means, our unequaled political, social, and economic system, we have secured a lift in the standards of living and the diffusion of comfort and hope to men and women, the growth of equality of opportunity, the widening of all opportunity such as had never been seen in the history of the world, then we should not tamper with it and destroy it, but on the contrary we should restore it and, by its gradual improvement and perfection, foster it into new performance for our country and for our children.

Now, if we look back over the last generation we find that the number of our families and, therefore, our homes, has increased from about 16 to about 25 million, or 62 percent. In that time we have built for them 15 million new and better homes. We have equipped 20 million out of these 25 million homes with electricity; thereby we have lifted infinite drudgery from women and men. The barriers of time and space have been swept away in this single generation. Life has been made freer, the intellectual vision of every individual has been expanded by the installation of 20 million telephones, 12 million radios, and the service of 20 million automobiles. Our cities have been made magnificent with beautiful buildings, parks, and playgrounds. Our countryside has been knit together with splendid roads. We have increased by 12 times the use of electrical power and thereby taken sweat from the backs of men. In the broad sweep real wages and purchasing power of men and women have steadily increased. New comforts have steadily come to them. The hours of labor have decreased, the 12-hour day has disappeared, even the 9-hour day has almost gone. We are now advocating the 5-day week. During this generation the portals of opportunity to our children have ever widened. While our population grew by but 62 percent, yet we have increased the number of children in high schools by 700 percent, and those in institutions of higher learning by 300 percent. With all our spending, we multiplied by six times the savings in our banks and in our building and loan associations. We multiplied by 1,200 percent the amount of our life insurance. With the enlargement of our leisure we have come to a fuller life; we have gained new visions of hope; we are more nearly realizing our national aspirations and giving increased scope to the creative power of every individual and expansion of every man's mind.

Now, our people in these 30 years have grown in the sense of social responsibility. There is profound progress in the relation of the employer to the employed. We have more nearly met with a full hand the most sacred obligation of man, that is, the responsibility of a man to his neighbor. Support to our schools, hospitals, and institutions for the care of the afflicted surpassed in totals by billions the proportionate service in any period in any nation in the history of the world.

Now, 3 years ago there came a break in this progress. A break of the same type we have met 15 times in a century and yet have recovered from. But 18 months later came a further blow by the shocks transmitted to us from earthquakes of the collapse of nations throughout the world as the aftermath of the World War. The workings of this system of ours were dislocated. Businessmen and farmers suffered, and millions of men and women are out of jobs. Their distress is bitter. I do not seek to minimize it, but we may thank God that in view of the storm that we have met that 30 million still have jobs, and yet this does not distract our thoughts from the suffering of the 10 million.

But I ask you what has happened. This 30 years of incomparable improvement in the scale of living, of advance of comfort and intellectual life, of security, of inspiration, and ideals did not arise without right principles animating the American system which produced them. Shall that system be discarded because vote-seeking men appeal to distress and say that the machinery is all wrong and that it must be abandoned or tampered with ? Is it not more sensible to realize the simple fact that some extraordinary force has been thrown into the mechanism which has temporarily deranged its operation? Is it not wiser to believe that the difficulty is not with the principles upon which our American system is founded and designed through all these generations of inheritance? Should not our purpose be to restore the normal working of that system which has brought to us such immeasurable gifts, and not to destroy it?

Now, in order to indicate to you that the proposals of our opponents will endanger or destroy our system, I propose to analyze a few of them in their relation to these fundamentals which I have stated.

First: A proposal of our opponents that would break down the American system is the expansion of governmental expenditure by yielding to sectional and group raids on the Public Treasury. The extension of governmental expenditures beyond the minimum limit necessary to conduct the proper functions of the Government enslaves men to work for the Government. If we combine the whole governmental expenditures—national, State, and municipal—we will find that before the World War each citizen worked, theoretically, 25 days out of each year for the Government. In 1924, he worked 46 days out of the year for the Government. Today he works, theoretically, for the support of all forms of Government 61 days out of the year.

No nation can conscript its citizens for this proportion of men's and women's time without national impoverishment and without the destruction of their liberties. Our Nation cannot do it without destruction to our whole conception of the American system. The Federal Government has been forced in this emergency to unusual expenditure, but in partial alleviation of these extraordinary and unusual expenditures the Republican administration has made a successful effort to reduce the ordinary running expenses of the Government.

Our opponents have persistently interfered with such policies. I only need recall to you that the Democratic House of Representatives passed bills in the last session that would have increased our expenditures by $3 1/2 billion, or 87 percent. Expressed in day's labor, this would have meant the conscription of 16 days' additional work from every citizen for the Government. That was stopped. Furthermore, they refused to accept recommendations from the administration in respect to 150 or 200 million of reductions in ordinary expenditures, and finally they forced upon us an increased expenditure of $322 million. In spite of this, the ordinary expenses of the Government have been reduced upwards of $200 million during the present administration. They will be decidedly further reduced. But the major point that I wish to make-the disheartening part of these proposals of our opponents—is that they represent the successful pressures of minorities. They would appeal to sectional and group political support and thereby impose terrific burdens upon every home in the country. These things can and must be resisted. But they can only be resisted if there shall be live and virile public support to a Republican administration. That support must be in opposition to the political logrolling and the sectional and group raids on the Treasury for distribution of public money, which is cardinal in the congeries of elements which make up the Democratic Party.

These expenditures proposed by the Democratic House of Representatives for the benefit of special groups and special sections of our country directly undermine the American system which I have described to you. Those who pay are, in the last analysis, the man who works at the bench, the desk, and on the farm. They take away his comfort, stifle his leisure, and destroy his equality of opportunity.

Second: Another proposal of our opponents which would destroy the American system is that of inflation of the currency. The bill which passed the last session of the Democratic House called upon the Treasury of the United States to issue $2,300 million in paper currency that would be unconvertible into solid values. Call it what you will, greenbacks or fiat money. It was the same nightmare which overhung our own country for years after the Civil War.

In our special situation today the issuance of greenbacks means the immediate departure of this country from the gold standard, as there could be no provision for the redemption of such currency into gold. The new currency must obviously go to immediate and constantly fluctuating discount when associated with currency convertible in gold.

The oldest law of currency is that bad money drives out the good, for a population—that is, every individual—will hoard good currency and endeavor to get rid of the bad. The invariable effect is the withdrawal of a vast sum of good currency from circulation, and at once the Government is forced to print more and more bad paper currency. No candidate and no speaker in this campaign has disavowed this action of the Democratic House of Representatives. In spite of this visible experience within the recollection of this generation, with all its pitiable results, fiat money is proposed by the Democratic Party as a potent measure for relief from this depression.

The use of this expedient by nations in difficulty since the war in Europe has been one of the most tragic disasters to equality of opportunity and the independence of man.

I quote from a revealing speech by Mr. Owen D. Young upon the return of the Dawes Commission from Europe. He stated:

"The currency of Germany was depreciating so rapidly that the industries paid their wages daily, and sometimes indeed twice a day. Standing with the lines of employees was another line of wives and mothers waiting for these marks. The wife grabbed the paper from her husband's hand and rushed to the nearest provision store to spend it quickly before the rapid depreciation had cut its purchasing power in two.

"When the chairman of the syndicate of the German Trade Unions, Herr Grasseman, appeared before the Dawes Commission, I put to him this question: 'What can this committee do for German labor?'

"I expected the answer to be some one of the slogans of labor: An 8-hour day, old age or disability pensions—something of that kind. Much to my surprise the answer came promptly.

"'What your committee must do for German labor is to give us a stable currency. Do you know,' Herr Grasseman said, 'that for many months it has been impossible for a wage earner in Germany to perform even of his moral obligations?

"'Knowing that a child was coming to the family at a certain time, there was no way by which the husband, through effort or sacrifice or savings, could guarantee his wife a doctor and a nurse when that event arrived. One, knowing that his mother was stricken with a fatal disease could not by any effort or sacrifice or saving be in a position to insure her a decent burial on her death.

"'Your committee must,' Herr Grasseman added, 'just as a basic human thing, assure us a stable currency 'and thereby insure to the worker that his wages will have the same purchasing power when he wants to spend them as they had when he earned them.'"

Now, I ask, is that a policy consonant with the American system? It has been proposed by the Democratic Party within 4 months and passed a Democratic House of Representatives. Is that the preservation of equality of opportunity and the protection of men by their government?

Third: In the last session of the Congress, under the personal leadership of the Democratic Vice-Presidential candidate, and their allies in the Senate, they enacted a law to extend the Government into personal banking business. I know it is always difficult to discuss banks. There seems to be much prejudice against some of them, but I was compelled to veto that bill out of fidelity to the whole American system of life and government. I may repeat a part of that veto message, and it remains unchallenged by any Democratic leader. I quote now from that veto message because that statement was not made in the heat of any political campaign. I said:

"It would mean loans against security for any conceivable purpose on any conceivable security to anybody who wants money. It would place the Government in private business in such fashion as to violate the very principle of public relations upon which we have built our Nation, and renders insecure its very foundations. Such action would make the Reconstruction Corporation the greatest banking and money-lending institution of all history. It would constitute a gigantic centralization of banking and finance to which the American people have been properly opposed over a hundred years. The purpose of the expansion is no longer in the spirit of solving a great major emergency but to establish a privilege whether it serves a great national end or not."

I further said: "It would require the setting up of a huge bureaucracy, to establish branches in every county and town in the United States. Every political pressure would be assembled for particular persons. It would be within the power of these agencies to dictate the welfare of millions of people, to discriminate between competitive business at will, and to deal favor and disaster among them. The organization would be constantly subjected to conspiracies and raids of predatory interests, individuals, and private corporations. Huge losses and great scandals must inevitably result. It would mean the squandering of public credit to be ultimately borne by the taxpayer."

I stated further that: "This proposal violates every sound principle of public finance and of our Government. Never before has so dangerous a suggestion been made to our country. Never before has so much power for evil been placed at the unlimited discretion of seven individuals."

They failed to pass this bill over my veto. But you must not be deceived. This is still in their purposes as a part of the new deal, and no responsible candidate has yet disavowed it.

Fourth: Another proposal of our opponents which would wholly alter our American system of life is to reduce the protective tariff to a competitive tariff for revenue. The protective tariff and its results upon our economic structure has become gradually embedded into our economic life since the first protective tariff act was passed by the American Congress under the administration of George Washington. There have been gaps, at times of Democratic control, when this protection has been taken away or decreased. But whether you like it or not, it has been so embedded in our economic life and structure that its removal has never failed and never will fail to bring disaster. I can conceive a Nation built without it, but we have been built with it. Whole towns, communities, and forms of agriculture with their homes, schools, and churches have been built up under this system of protection. The grass will grow in streets of a hundred cities, a thousand towns; the weeds will overrun the fields of millions of farms if that protection be taken away. Their churches, their hospitals, and their schoolhouses will decay.

Incidentally, another one of the proposals of our opponents which also would destroy equality of opportunity between both individuals and communities is their promise to repeal the independent authority of the bipartisan Tariff Commission and thereby return the determination of import duties to the old logrolling greed of group or sectional interest under congressional action in review of the tariff.

Fifth: Another proposal is that the Government go into the power business. Three years ago, in view of the extension of the use of transmission of power over State borders and the difficulties of State regulatory bodies in the face of this interstate action, I recommended to the Congress that such interstate power should be placed under regulation by the Federal Government in cooperation with the State authorities.

That recommendation was in accord with the principles of the Republican Party, over the past 50 years, to provide regulation where public interest had developed in tools of industry which was beyond control and regulation of the States.

I succeeded in creating an independent Power Commission to handle such matters, but the Democratic House declined to approve the further powers to this Commission necessary for such regulation, possibly in order that they might use it as a matter of agitation in this campaign.

I have stated unceasingly that I am opposed to the Federal Government going into the power business. I have insisted upon rigid regulation. The Democratic candidate has declared that under the same conditions which may make local action of this character desirable, he is prepared to put the Federal Government into the power business. He is being actively supported by a score of Senators in this campaign, many of whose expenses are being paid by the Democratic National Committee, who are pledged to Federal Government development and operation of electrical power.

I find in the instructions to the campaign speakers issued by the Democratic National Committee that they are instructed to criticize my action in the veto of the bill which would have put the Government permanently into the operation of power at Muscle Shoals with a capital from the Federal Treasury of over $100 million. In fact, 31 Democratic Senators, being all except 3, voted to override that veto. In that bill was the flat issue of the Federal Government permanently in competitive business. I vetoed it because of principle and not because it was especially applied to electrical power. In that veto I stated that I was firmly opposed to the Federal Government entering into any business, the major purpose of which is competition with our citizens except in major national emergencies. In that veto message, written long before the emergence of the exigencies of political campaigning, I stated:

"There are national emergencies which require that the Government should temporarily enter the field of business but that they must be emergency actions and in matters where the cost of the project is secondary to much higher consideration. There are many localities where the Federal Government is justified in the construction of great dams and reservoirs, where navigation, flood control, reclamation, or stream regulation are of dominant importance, and where they are beyond the capacity or purpose of private or local government capital to construct. In these cases, power is often a byproduct and should be disposed of by contract or lease. But for the Federal Government to deliberately go out to build up and expand such an occasion to the major purpose of a power and manufacturing business is to break down the initiative and enterprise of the American people; it is destruction of equality of opportunity among our people; it is the negation of the ideals upon which our civilization has been based.

"This bill raises one of the important issues confronting our people. That is squarely the issue of Federal Government ownership and operation of power and manufacturing business not as a minor byproduct but as a major purpose. Involved in this question is the agitation against the conduct of the power industry. The power problem is not to be solved by the Federal Government going into the power business, nor is it to be solved by the project in this bill. The remedy for abuses in the conduct of that industry lies in regulation and not by the Federal Government entering the business itself. I have recommended to the Congress on various occasions that action should be taken to establish Federal regulation of interstate power in cooperation with State authorities. This bill would launch the Federal Government on a policy of ownership of power utilities upon a basis of competition instead of by the proper Government function of regulation for the protection of all the people. I hesitate to contemplate the future of our institutions, of our Government, and of our country, if the preoccupation of its officials is to be no longer the promotion of justice and equality of opportunity but is to be devoted to barter in the markets. That is not liberalism; it is degeneration."

From their utterances in this campaign and elsewhere, it appears to me that we are justified in the conclusion that our opponents propose to put Federal Government extensively into business.

Sixth: I may cite another instance of absolutely destructive proposals to our American system by our opponents, and I am talking about fundamentals and not superficialities.

Recently there was circulated through the unemployed in this city and other cities, a letter from the Democratic candidate in which he stated that he would support measures for the inauguration of self-liquidating public works such as the utilization of water resources, flood control, land reclamation, to provide employment for all surplus labor at all times.

I especially emphasize that promise to promote "employment for all surplus labor at all times"—by the Government. I at first could not believe that anyone would be so cruel as to hold out a hope so absolutely impossible of realization to those 10 million who are unemployed and suffering. But the authenticity of that promise has been verified. And I protest against such frivolous promises being held out to a suffering people. It is easy to demonstrate that no such employment can be found. But the point that I wish to make here and now is the mental attitude and spirit of the Democratic Party that would lead them to attempt this or to make a promise to attempt it. That is another mark of the character of the new deal and the destructive changes which mean the total abandonment of every principle upon which this Government and this American system are rounded. If it were possible to give this employment to 10 million people by the Government—at the expense of the rest of the people—it would cost upwards of $9 billion a year.

The stages of this destruction would be first the destruction of Government credit, then the destruction of the value of Government securities, the destruction of every fiduciary trust in our country, insurance policies and all. It would pull down the employment of those who are still at work by the high taxes and the demoralization of credit upon which their employment is dependent. It would mean the pulling and hauling of politics for projects and measures, the favoring of localities and sections and groups. It would mean the growth of a fearful bureaucracy which, once established, could never be dislodged. If it were possible, it would mean one-third of the electorate would have Government jobs, earnest to maintain this bureaucracy and to control the political destinies of the country.

Incidentally, the Democratic candidate has said on several occasions that we must reduce surplus production of agricultural products, and yet he proposes to extend this production on a gigantic scale through expansion of reclamation and new agricultural areas under this plan to the obvious ruin of the farmer.

I have said before, and I want to repeat on this occasion, that the only method by which we can stop the suffering and unemployment is by returning our people to their normal jobs in their normal homes, carrying on their normal functions of living. This can be done only by sound processes of protecting and stimulating recovery of the existing system upon which we have built our progress thus far—preventing distress and giving such sound employment as we can find in the meantime.

Seventh: Recently, at Indianapolis, I called attention to the statement made by Governor Roosevelt in his address on October 25 with respect to the Supreme Court of the United States. He said: "After March 4, 1929, the Republican Party was in complete control of all branches of the Government—Executive, Senate, and House, and I may add, for good measure, in order to make it complete, the Supreme Court as well."

Now, I am not called upon to defend the Supreme Court of the United States from that slurring reflection. Fortunately for the American people that Court has jealously maintained over the years its high standard of integrity, impartiality, and freedom from influence of either the Executive or Congress, so that the confidence of the people in the Court is sound and unshaken.

But is the Democratic candidate really proposing his conception of the relation of the Executive with the Supreme Court? If that is his idea, he is proposing the most revolutionary new deal, the most stupendous breaking of precedent, the most destructive undermining of the very safeguard of our form of government yet proposed by any Presidential candidate.

Eighth: In order that we may get at the philosophical background of the mind which pronounces the necessity for profound change in our economic system and a new deal, I would call your attention to an address delivered by the Democratic candidate in San Francisco early in October.

He said: "Our industrial plant is built. The problem just now is whether under existing conditions it is not overbuilt. Our last frontier has long since been reached. There is practically no more free land. There is no safety valve in the Western prairies where we can go for a new start. . . . The mere building of more industrial plants, the organization of more corporations is as likely to be as much a danger as a help. . . . Our task now is not the discovery of natural resources or necessarily the production of more goods, it is the sober, less dramatic business of administering the resources and plants already in hand . . . establishing markets for surplus production, of meeting the problem of under-consumption, distributing the wealth and products more equitably and adopting the economic organization to the service of the people. . . ."

Now, there are many of these expressions with which no one would quarrel. But I do challenge the whole idea that we have ended the advance of America, that this country has reached the zenith of its power and the height of its development. That is the counsel of despair for the future of America. That is not the spirit by which we shall emerge from this depression. That is not the spirit which has made this country. If it is true, every American must abandon the road of countless progress and countless hopes and unlimited opportunity. I deny that the promise of American life has been fulfilled, for that means we have begun the decline and the fall. No nation can cease to move forward without degeneration of spirit.

I could quote from gentlemen who have emitted this same note of profound pessimism in each economic depression going back for 100 years. What the Governor has overlooked is the fact that we are yet but on the frontiers of development of science and of invention. I have only to remind you that discoveries in electricity, the internal-combustion engine, the radio—all of which have sprung into being since our land was settled—have in themselves represented the greatest advances made in America. This philosophy upon which the Governor of New York proposes to conduct the Presidency of the United States is the philosophy of stagnation and of despair. It is the end of hope. The destinies of this country cannot be dominated by that spirit in action. It would be the end of the American system.

I have recited to you some of the items in the progress of this last generation. Progress in that generation was not due to the opening up of new agricultural land; it was due to the scientific research, the opening of new invention, new flashes of light from the intelligence of our people. These brought the improvements in agriculture and in industry. There are a thousand inventions for comfort and the expansion of life yet in the lockers of science that have not yet come to light. We are only upon their frontiers. As for myself, I am confident that if we do not destroy our American system, if we continue to stimulate scientific research, if we continue to give it the impulse of initiative and enterprise, if we continue to build voluntary cooperation instead of financial concentration, if we continue to build into a system of free men, my children will enjoy the same opportunity that has come to me and to the whole 120 million of my countrymen. I wish to see American Government conducted in that faith and hope.

Now, if these sample measures and promises, which I have discussed, or these failures to disavow these projects, this attitude of mind, mean anything, they mean the enormous expansion of the Federal Government; they mean the growth of bureaucracy such as we have never seen in our history. No man who has not occupied my position in Washington can fully realize the constant battle which must be carried on against incompetence, corruption, tyranny of government expanded into business activities. If we first examine the effect on our form of government of such a program, we come at once to the effect of the most gigantic increase in expenditure ever known in history. That alone would break down the savings, the wages, the equality of opportunity among our people. These measures would transfer vast responsibilities to the Federal Government from the States, the local governments, and the individuals. But that is not all; they would break down our form of government. It will crack the timbers of our Constitution. Our legislative bodies cannot delegate their authority to any dictator, but without such delegation every member of these bodies is impelled in representation of the interest of his constituents constantly to seek privilege and demand service in the use of such agencies. Every time the Federal Government extends its arm, 531 Senators and Congressmen become actual boards of directors of that business.

Capable men cannot be chosen by politics for all the various talents that business requires. Even if they were supermen, if there were no politics in the selection of a Government official, if there were no constant pressure for this and for that, so large a number of men would be incapable as a board of directors of any institution. At once when these extensions take place by the Federal Government, the authority and responsibility of State governments and institutions are undermined. Every enterprise of private business is at once halted to know what Federal action is going to be. It destroys initiative and courage. We can do no better than quote that great statesman of labor, the late Samuel Gompers, in speaking of an exactly parallel situation. He said:

"It is a question of whether it shall be government ownership or private ownership under control. If I were a minority of one on this occasion, I would want to cast my vote so that the men of labor shall not willingly enslave themselves to government in their industrial effort."

Now, we have heard a great deal in this campaign about reactionaries, conservatives, progressives, liberals, and radicals. I think I belong to every group. I have not yet heard an attempt by any one of the orators who mouth these phrases to define the principles upon which they base these classifications. There is one thing I can say without any question of doubt—that is, that the spirit of liberalism is to create free men; it is not the regimentation of men under government. It is not the extension of bureaucracy. I have said in this city before now that you cannot extend the mastery of government over the daily life of a people without somewhere making it master of people's souls and thoughts. Expansion of government in business and otherwise means that the government, in order to protect itself from the political consequences of its errors or even its successes, is driven irresistibly without peace to greater and greater control of the Nation's press and platform. Free speech does not live many hours after free industry and free commerce die. It is a false liberalism that interprets itself into Government operation of business. Every step in that direction poisons the very roots of liberalism. It poisons political equality, free speech, free press, and equality of opportunity. It is the road not to liberty but to less liberty. True liberalism is found not in striving to spread bureaucracy, but in striving to set bounds of it. It is found in an endeavor to extend cooperation between men. True liberalism seeks all legitimate freedom first in the confident belief that without such freedom the pursuit of other blessings is vain. Liberalism is a force truly of the spirit proceeding from the deep realization that economic freedom cannot be sacrificed if political freedom is to be preserved.

Even if the Government conduct of business could give us the maximum of efficiency instead of least efficiency, it would be purchased at the cost of freedom. It would increase rather than decrease abuse and corruption, stifle initiative and invention, undermine development of leadership, cripple mental and spiritual energies of our people, extinguish equality of opportunity, and dry up the spirit of liberty and progress. Men who are going about this country announcing that they are liberals because of their promises to extend the Government are not liberals; they are the reactionaries of the United States.

Now, I do not wish to be misquoted or misunderstood. I do not mean that our Government is to part with one iota of its national resources without complete protection to the public interest. I have already stated that democracy must remain master in its own house. I have stated that it is, at times, vitally necessary for the Government to protect the people when forces run against them which they cannot control. I have stated that abuse and wrongdoing must be punished and controlled. Nor do I wish to be interpreted as stating that the United States is a free-for-all and devil-take-the-hinder most society.

The very essence of equality of opportunity in our American system is that there shall be no monopoly or domination by anybody— whether it be a group or section of the country, or whether it be business, or whether it be group interest. On the contrary, our American system demands economic justice as well as political and social justice; it is no system of laissez faire.

I am not setting up the contention that our American system is perfect. No human ideal has ever been perfectly attained, since humanity itself is not perfect. But the wisdom of our forefathers and the wisdom of the 30 men who have preceded me in this office hold to the conception that progress can be attained only as the sum of the accomplishments of free individuals, and they have held unalterably to these principles.

In the ebb and flow of economic life our people in times of prosperity and ease naturally tend to neglect the vigilance over their economic rights. Moreover, wrongdoing is obscured by an appearance of success in enterprise. Then insidious diseases and wrongdoings do grow apace. But we have in the past seen in times of distress and difficulty that wrongdoing and weakness come to the surface, and our people, in their endeavors to correct these wrongs, have been tempted to extremes which destroy rather than build.

It is men that do wrong, not our institutions. It is men who violate the laws and public rights. It is men, not institutions, that must be punished.

Now, in my acceptance speech 4 years ago at my own home town of Palo Alto I stated:

"One of the oldest aspirations of the human race is the abolition of poverty. By poverty I mean the grinding by undernourishment and cold and ignorance and fear and of old age of those who have the will to work."

I stated that: "In America today we are nearer a final triumph over poverty than in any other land at any other time. The poorhouse has vanished from among us; we have not reached that goal, but given a chance to go forward, we shall, with the help of God, be in sight of the day when poverty will be banished from this Nation."

Our Democratic friends have quoted this passage many times in this campaign. I do not withdraw a word of it. When I look about the world even in these times of trouble and distress I find it more true in this land than anywhere else under the traveling sun. I am not ashamed of it, because I am not ashamed of holding ideals and purposes for the progress of the American people. Are our Democratic opponents prepared to state in their mouthing of this statement that they do not stand for this ideal or this hope ? For my part, I propose to continue to strive for it, and I hope to live to see it accomplished.

Now, one of the most encouraging and inspiring phases of this whole campaign has been the unprecedented interest of our younger men and women. It is in this group that we find our new homes being founded and our new families in which the children are being taught these basic principles of love and faith and patriotism. It is in this group that we find the starting of business and professional careers with courage, with hopeful faces turned to the future and its promise. It is this group who must undertake the guardianship of our American system and carry it forward to its greater achievements.

Inevitably, in the progress of time, our country and its institutions will be entirely in their hands. The burdens of the depression have fallen on the younger generation, probably greater than even its severity on their elders. It has affected not only their economic well-being but has tended also to shatter many illusions. But their faith in our country and its institutions has not been shaken. I am confident that they will resist any destruction to our American system of political, economic, and social life.

It is a tribute to America and its past and present leaders, and even more a tribute to this younger generation, that, contrary to the experience of other countries, we can say tonight that the youth of America are more staunch than many of their elders. I can ask no higher tribute to the Republican Party, no greater aid in the maintenance of the American system and the program of this administration than the support being given by the younger men and women of our country. It has just been communicated to me that in every county and almost every precinct of our country, 3 million members of the Young Republican League are meeting tonight to listen to this address and to rally their support for the party on November 8. That in itself is a victory for the American system.

My countrymen, the proposals of our opponents represent a profound change in American life—less in concrete proposal, bad as that may be, than by implication and by evasion. Dominantly in their spirit they represent a radical departure from the foundations of 150 years which have made this the greatest Nation in the world. This election is not a mere shift from the ins to the outs. It means the determining of the course of our Nation over a century to come.

Now, my conception of America is a land where men and women may walk in ordered liberty, where they may enjoy the advantages of wealth not concentrated in the hands of a few but diffused through the opportunity of all, where they build and safeguard their homes, give to their children the full opportunities of American life, where every man shall be respected in the faith that his conscience and his heart direct him to follow, and where people secure in their liberty shall have leisure and impulse to seek a fuller life. That leads to the release of the energies of men and women, to the wider vision and higher hope. It leads to opportunity for greater and greater service not alone of man to man in our country but from our country to the world. It leads to health in body and a spirit unfettered, youthful, eager with a vision stretching beyond the farthest horizons with a mind open and sympathetic and generous. But that must be built upon our experience with the past, upon the foundations which have made this country great. It must be the product of the development of our truly American system.

The Bill of Rights

San Diego, California
September 17, 1935

AFTER HIS departure from the White House, Hoover, once a progressive and an admirer of Teddy Roosevelt and Woodrow Wilson, became a fervent conservative, attacking Communism and New Deal "state-ism" in books and speeches. As an alternative, he offered principles derived from his Quaker training, including "ordered liberty"—personal freedom restrained by voluntary adherence to norms of moderation and tolerance—and individualism tempered by a sense of reciprocal responsibility within the community. In 1935, at a local observance of Constitution Day, Hoover delivered this encomium to the Bill of Rights.

In the 12 minutes which I occupy in this discussion I shall refer to but one phase of the Constitution in its many bearings upon national life—that is the Bill of Rights.

Today the Constitution is indeed under more vivid discussion than at any time since the years before the Civil War. The background of that issue was Negro slavery, but in the foreground was the constitutional question of states' rights and in the final determination was the fate of the Union. The aroused interest of today is again the rights of men. Today the issue is the rights of the individual in relation to the government; this too involves the fate of the nation. If for no other reason, this discussion has been forced upon us because new philosophies and new theories of government have arisen in the world which militantly deny the validity of our principles.

Our Constitution is not alone the working plan of a great federation of states under representative government. There is embedded in it also the vital principles of the American system of liberty. That system is based upon certain inalienable freedoms and protections which not even the government may infringe and which we call the Bill of Rights. It does not require a lawyer to interpret those provisions. They are as clear as the Ten Commandments. Among others the freedom of worship, freedom of speech and of the press, the right of peaceable assembly, equality before the law, just trial for crime, freedom from unreasonable search, and security from being deprived of life, liberty, or property without due process of law, are the principles which distinguish our civilization. Herein are the invisible sentinels which guard the door of every home from invasion of coercion, of intimidation and fear.

Herein is the expression of the spirit of men who would be forever free.

These rights were no sudden discovery, no over-night inspiration. They were established by centuries of struggle in which men died fighting bitterly for their recognition. Their beginnings lie in the Magna Charta at Runnymede 570 years before the Constitution was written. Down through the centuries the Habeas Corpus, the "Petition of Rights," the "Declaration of Rights," the growth of the fundamental maxims of the Common Law, marked their expansion and security. Our forefathers migrated to America that they might attain them more fully. When they wrote the Declaration of Independence they boldly extended these rights. Before the Constitution could be ratified patriotic men who feared a return to tyranny, whose chains had been thrown off only after years of toil and bloody war, insisted that these hard-won rights should be incorporated in black and white within the Constitution— and so came the American Bill of Rights.

In the hurricane of revolutions which have swept the world since the Great War, men, struggling with the wreckage and poverty of that great catastrophe and the complications of the machine age, are in despair surrendering their freedom for false promises of economic security. Whether it be Fascist Italy, Nazi Germany, Communist Russia, or their lesser followers, the result is the same. Every day they repudiate every principle of the Bill of Rights. Freedom of worship is denied. Freedom of speech is suppressed. The press is censored and distorted with propaganda. The right of criticism is denied. Men go to jail or the gallows for honest opinion. They may not assemble for discussion. They speak of public affairs only in whispers. They are subject to search and seizure by spies and inquisitors who haunt the land. The safeguards of justice in trial or imprisonment are set aside. There is no right in one's savings or one's own home which the government need respect.

Here is a form of servitude, of slavery—a slipping back toward the Middle Ages. Whatever these governments are, they have one common denominator—the citizen has no assured rights. He is submerged into the state. Here is the most fundamental clash known to mankind—that is, free men and women, cooperating under orderly liberty, as contrasted with human beings made pawns of dictatorial government; men who are slaves of despotism, as against free men who are the masters of the state.

Even in America, where liberty blazed brightest and by its glow shed light on all the others, it is besieged from without and challenged from within. Many, in honest belief, hold that we cannot longer accommodate the growth of science, technology, and mechanical power to the Bill of Rights and our form of government. With that I do not agree. Men's inventions cannot be of more value than men themselves. But it would be better that we sacrifice something of economic efficiency than to surrender these primary liberties. In them lies a spiritual right of men. Behind them is the conception which is the highest development of the Christian faith—the conception of individual freedom with brotherhood. From them is the fullest flowering of individual human personality.

Those who proclaim that by the machine age there is created an irreconcilable conflict in which liberty must be sacrificed should not forget the battles for these rights over the centuries, for let it be remembered that in the end these are undying principles which spring from the souls of men. We imagine conflict not because the principles of liberty are unworkable in a machine age, but because we have not worked them conscientiously or have forgotten their true meaning.

Nor do I admit that sacrifice of these rights would add to economic efficiency or would gain in economic security, or would find a single job or would give a single assurance in old age. The dynamic forces which sustain economic security and progress in human comfort lie deep below the surface. They reach to those human impulses which are watered alone by freedom. The initiative of men, their enterprise, the inspiration of thought, flower in full only in the security of these rights.

And by practical experience under the American system we have tested this truth. And here I may repeat what I have said elsewhere. Down through a century and a half this American concept of human freedom has enriched the whole world. From the release of the spirit, the initiative, the cooperation and the courage of men, which alone comes of these freedoms, has been built this very machine age with all its additions of comfort, its reductions of sweat. Wherever in the world the system of individual liberty has been sustained, mankind has been better clothed, better fed, better housed, has had more leisure. Above all, men and women have had more self-respect. They have been more generous and of finer spirit. Those who scoff that liberty is of no consequence to the underprivileged and the unemployed are grossly ignorant of the primary fact that it is through the creative and the productive impulses of free men that the redemption of those sufferers and their economic security must come. Any system which curtails these freedoms and stimulants to men destroys the possibility of the full production from which economic security can alone come.

These rights and protections of the Bill of Rights are safeguarded in the Constitution through a delicate balance and separation of powers in the framework of our government. That has been founded on the experience over centuries including our own day.

Liberty is safe only by a division of powers and upon local self-government. We know full well that power feeds upon itself—partly from the greed of power and partly from the innocent belief that utopia can be attained by dictation or coercion.

Nor is respect for the Bill of Rights a fetter upon progress. It has been no dead hand that has carried the living principles of liberty over these centuries. Without violation of these principles and their safeguards we have amended the Constitution many times in the past century to meet the problems of growing civilization. We will no doubt do so many times again. Always groups of audacious men in government or out will attempt to consolidate privilege against their fellows. New invention and new ideas require the constant remolding of our civilization. The functions of government must be readjusted from time to time to restrain the strong and protect the weak. That is the preservation of liberty itself. We ofttimes interpret some provisions of the bill of rights so that they override others. They indeed jostle each other in course of changing national life—but their respective domains can be defined by virtue, reason, and law.

Liberty comes alone and lives alone where the hard-won rights of men are held inalienable, where governments themselves may not infringe, where governments are indeed but the mechanisms to protect and sustain these principles. It was this concept for which America's sons have died on a hundred battlefields.

The nation seeks for solution of many difficulties. These solutions can come alone through the constructive forces which arise from the spirit of free men and women. The purification of liberty from abuses, the restoration of confidence in the rights of men, from which come the release of the dynamic forces of initiative and enterprise, are alone the methods through which these solutions can be found and the purpose of American life assured.

Courtesy of Franklin D. Roosevelt Library

Franklin Delano Roosevelt

Franklin Delano Roosevelt

1933–1945

THE YEARS OF presidential passivity under Harding, Coolidge, and Hoover sapped the power of the executive, and the quality of presidential rhetoric fell accordingly. During his 12 years in office Franklin Roosevelt restored both power and rhetoric to a high level—the highest, many historians believe, since the presidency of Lincoln. Roosevelt, a distant cousin of Theodore Roosevelt, belonged to one of New York's oldest and wealthiest families. He served as Wilson's assistant secretary of the navy from 1913 to 1920, came to national prominence as governor of New York (1929–1933), and in 1932 easily won the presidency, carrying 42 states. With a popular mandate to bring the country out of the Great Depression, Roosevelt and his advisers embarked during his first two terms on an ambitious program of social reform called the New Deal—the creation of a vast network of government agencies to combat poverty and unemployment. Though the New Deal was only partly successful, so popular was Roosevelt and so strong was his hold on the Democratic Party that he was able to win an unprecedented third term. When the United States entered the Second World War after the Japanese attack on Pearl Harbor, Roosevelt proved himself as adept a wartime commander as Lincoln. With the end of the war in sight he was able to win a fourth term but lived only a few months after the election.

Roosevelt was charming, self-confident, a resourceful leader and administrator. His political instincts were acute and nearly always right; he maintained control over his party and the nation longer than any other individual. Despite his aristocratic upbringing, he also possessed genuine feeling for the common citizen—a streak of humanitarianism inherited from his political mentors, Theodore Roosevelt and Woodrow Wilson—and a "strong and active faith" in democracy's ability to create a fair society. His success in overcoming the polio that left him paralyzed from the waist down at the age of 39 strengthened him for the tasks of his presidency. Francis Biddle, FDR's attorney general, noted that Roosevelt's insight into the country's problems "was rooted in his own physical suffering." Like TR and Wilson, he also viewed the presidency as above all "a place of moral leadership." Once FDR quipped that he wanted to be "a *preaching president—* like my cousin," but his speeches are much more like Wilson's in eloquence, and exceed them in naturalness of expression. He was a great phrasemaker with a ready sense of humor.

Roosevelt employed speechwriters and regularly asked for assistance from such advisers as Harry Hopkins and Samuel Rosenman on important policy statements but penned the bulk of his speeches himself. Whether supported by his braces in a speaker's stand or behind a desk in his wheelchair, he was in complete command of his audience, embellishing his talk with trademark gestures—flourishing his cigarette holder, tilting up his chin, and grinning widely at his own witticisms. But his voice was perhaps his most potent political instrument. With its mixture of upper-class New York and Harvard inflections, it was patrician and authoritative, yet he never projected an image of elite intellectualism, as Wilson had. His speaking persona could be warm and paternal, as in his fireside chats; sarcastic, as when he was lambasting the Republicans; righteous, as when he asked for war against Japan.

Above all, it became, after his many years in office, a familiar voice. From long habit, people associated that voice with political leadership. In large part this can be attributed to FDR's brilliant use of radio. All of his major addresses were broadcast, and many, such as the fireside chats, were meant primarily for the radio. He understood the potential of broadcast communications to establish a direct link from the president to the people, a link that is now considered an essential aspect of presidential power. Eleanor Roosevelt recalled that people would stop her in the street after FDR's death. "They missed the way the president used to talk to them. They'd say, 'He used to talk to me about my government.' There was a real dialogue between Franklin and the people. That dialogue seems to have disappeared from the government since he died."

A New Deal

Chicago, Illinois

July 2, 1932

ROOSEVELT broke the first of many precedents by appearing in person at the Democratic National Convention to accept the presidential nomination. No previous candidate had ever addressed a nominating convention. Roosevelt, however, was determined not to wait in feigned ignorance for the party's official notification; instead he flew to Chicago to deliver this speech, electrifying the delegates and proving that his infirmity would not prevent him from campaigning vigorously.

This marked Roosevelt's first use of the phrase new deal, which he borrowed from Mark Twain's *A Connecticut Yankee in King Arthur's Court.* It was quickly picked up by the press and became the tag for Roosevelt's entire program of reform.

I appreciate your willingness after these six arduous days to remain here, for I know well the sleepless hours which you and I have had. I regret that I am late, but I have no control over the winds of heaven and could only be thankful for my navy training.

The appearance before a national convention of its nominee for president, to be formally notified of his selection, is unprecedented and unusual, but these are unprecedented and unusual times. I have started out on the tasks that lie ahead by breaking the absurd traditions that the candidate should remain in professed ignorance of what has happened for weeks until he is formally notified of that event many weeks later.

My friends, may this be the symbol of my intention to be honest and to avoid all hypocrisy or sham, to avoid all silly shutting of the eyes to the truth in this campaign. You have nominated me and I know it, and I am here to thank you for the honor.

Let it also be symbolic that in so doing I broke traditions. Let it be from now on the task of our party to break foolish traditions. We will break foolish traditions and leave it to the Republican leadership, far more skilled in that art, to break promises.

Let us now and here highly resolve to resume the country's interrupted march along the path of real progress, of real justice, of real equality for all of our citizens, great and small. Our indomitable leader in that interrupted march is no longer with us, but there still survives today his spirit. Many of his captains, thank God, are still with us, to give us wise counsel. Let us feel that in everything we do there still lives with us, if not the body, the great indomitable, unquenchable, progressive soul of our commander-in-chief, Woodrow Wilson.

I have many things on which I want to make my position clear at the earliest possible moment in this campaign. That admirable document, the platform which you have adopted, is clear. I accept it 100 percent.

And you can accept my pledge that I will leave no doubt or ambiguity on where I stand on any question of moment in this campaign.

As we enter this new battle, let us keep always present with us some of the ideals of the party: The fact that the Democratic Party by tradition and by the continuing logic of history, past and present, is the bearer of liberalism and of progress and at the same time of safety to our institutions. And if this appeal fails, remember well, my friends, that a resentment against the failure of Republican leadership—and note well that in this campaign I shall not use the words "Republican Party," but I shall use, day in and day out, the words, "Republican leadership"—the failure of Republican leaders to solve our troubles may degenerate into unreasoning radicalism.

The great social phenomenon of this depression, unlike others before it, is that it has produced but a few of the disorderly manifestations that too often attend upon such times.

Wild radicalism has made few converts, and the greatest tribute that I can pay to my countrymen is that in these days of crushing want there persists an orderly and hopeful spirit on the part of the millions of our people who have suffered so much. To fail to offer them a new chance is not only to betray their hopes but to misunderstand their patience.

To meet by reaction that danger of radicalism is to invite disaster. Reaction is no barrier to the radical. It is a challenge, a provocation. The way to meet that danger is to offer a workable program of reconstruction, and the party to offer it is the party with clean hands.

This, and this only, is a proper protection against blind reaction on the one hand and an improvised, hit-or-miss, irresponsible opportunism on the other.

There are two ways of viewing the government's duty in matters affecting economic and social life. The first sees to it that a favored few are helped and hopes that some of their prosperity will leak through, sift through, to labor, to the farmer, to the small businessman. That theory belongs to the party of Toryism, and I had hoped that most of the Tories left this country in 1776.

But it is not and never will be the theory of the Democratic Party. This is no time for fear, for reaction or for timidity. Here and now I invite those nominal Republicans who find that their conscience cannot be squared with the groping and the failure of their party leaders to join hands with us; here and now, in equal measure, I warn those nominal Democrats who squint at the future with their faces turned toward the past, and who feel no responsibility to the demands of the new time, that they are out of step with their party.

Yes, the people of this country want a genuine choice this year, not a choice between two names for the same reactionary doctrine. Ours must be a party of liberal thought, of planned action, of enlightened international outlook, and of the greatest good to the greatest number of our citizens.

Now it is inevitable—and the choice is that of the times—it is inevitable that the main issue of this campaign should revolve about the clear fact of our economic condition, a depression so deep that it is without precedent in modern history. It will not do merely to state, as do Republican leaders to explain their broken promises of continued inaction, that the depression is worldwide. That was not their explanation of the apparent prosperity of 1928. The people will not forget the claim made by them then that prosperity was only a domestic product manufactured by a Republican president and a Republican Congress. If they claim paternity for the one they cannot deny paternity for the other.

I cannot take up all the problems today. I want to touch on a few that are vital. Let us look a little at the recent history and the simple economics, the kind of economics that you and I and the average man and woman talk.

In the years before 1929 we know that this country had completed a vast cycle of building and inflation; for 10 years we expanded on the theory of repairing the wastes of the war, but actually expanding far beyond that, and also beyond our natural and normal growth. Now it is worth remembering, and the cold figures of finance prove it, that during that time there was little or no drop in the prices that the consumer had to pay, although those same figures proved that the cost of production fell very greatly; corporate profit resulting from this period was enormous; at the same time little of that profit was devoted to the reduction of prices. The consumer was forgotten. Very little of it went into increased wages; the worker was forgotten, and by no means an adequate proportion was even paid out in dividends— the stockholder was forgotten.

And, incidentally, very little of it was taken by taxation to the beneficent government of those years.

What was the result? Enormous corporate surpluses piled up—the most stupendous in history. Where, under the spell of delirious speculation, did those surpluses go? Let us talk economics that the figures prove and that we can understand. Why, they went chiefly in two directions: first, into new and unnecessary plants which now stand stark and idle; and second, into the call-money market of Wall Street, either directly by the corporations, or indirectly through the banks. Those are the facts. Why blink at them?

Then came the crash. You know the story. Surpluses invested in unnecessary plants became idle. Men lost their jobs; purchasing power dried up; banks became frightened and started calling loans. Those who had money were afraid to part with it. Credit contracted. Industry stopped. Commerce declined, and unemployment mounted.

And there we are today.

Translate that into human terms. See how the events of the past three years have come home to specific groups of people: first, the group dependent on industry; second, the group dependent on agriculture; third, and made up in large part of members of the first two groups, the people who are called "small investors and depositors." In fact, the strongest possible tie between the first two groups, agriculture and industry, is the fact that the savings and to a degree the security of both are tied together in that third group—the credit structure of the nation.

Never in history have the interests of all the people been so united in a single economic problem. Picture to yourself, for instance, the great groups of property owned by millions of our citizens, represented by credits issued in the form of bonds and mortgages—government bonds of all kinds, federal, state, county, municipal; bonds of industrial companies, of utility companies; mortgages on real estate in farms and cities, and finally the vast investments of the nation in the railroads. What is the measure of the security of each of those groups? We know well that in our complicated, interrelated credit structure if any one of these credit groups collapses they may all collapse. Danger to one is danger to all.

How, I ask, has the present administration in Washington treated the interrelationship of these credit groups? The answer is clear: It has not recognized that interrelationship existed at all. Why, the nation asks, has Washington failed to understand that all of these groups, each and every one, the top of the pyramid and the bottom of the pyramid, must be considered together, that each and every one of them is dependent on every other; each and every one of them affecting the whole financial fabric?

Statesmanship and vision, my friends, require relief to all at the same time.

Just one word or two on taxes, the taxes that all of us pay toward the cost of government of all kinds.

I know something of taxes. For three long years I have been going up and down this country preaching that government—federal and state and local—costs too much. I shall not stop that preaching. As an immediate program of action we must abolish useless offices. We must eliminate unnecessary functions of government—functions, in fact, that are not definitely essential to the continuance of government. We must merge, we must consolidate subdivisions of government, and, like the private citizen, give up luxuries which we can no longer afford.

By our example at Washington itself, we shall have the opportunity of pointing the way of economy to local government, for let us remember well that out of every tax dollar in the average state in this nation, 40 cents enter the Treasury in Washington, D. C., 10 or 12 cents only go to the state capitals, and 48 cents are consumed by the costs of local government in counties and cities and towns.

I propose to you, my friends, and through you, that government of all kinds, big and little, be made solvent and that the example be set by the president of the United States and his cabinet.

And talking about setting a definite example, I congratulate this convention for having had the courage fearlessly to write into its declaration of principles what an overwhelming majority here assembled really thinks about the Eighteenth Amendment. This convention wants repeal. Your candidate wants repeal. And I am confident that the United States of America wants repeal.

Two years ago the platform on which I ran for governor the second time contained substantially the same provision. The overwhelming sentiment of the people of my state, as shown by the vote of that year, extends, I know, to the people of many of the other states. I say to you now that from this date on the Eighteenth Amendment is doomed. When that happens, we as Democrats must and will, rightly and morally, enable the states to protect themselves against the importation of intoxicating liquor where such importation may violate their state laws. We must rightly and morally prevent the return of the saloon.

To go back to this dry subject of finance, because it all ties in together—the Eighteenth Amendment has something to do with finance, too—in a comprehensive planning for the reconstruction of the great credit groups, including government credit, I list an important place for that prize statement of principle in the platform here adopted calling for the letting in of the light of day on issues of securities, foreign and domestic, which are offered for sale to the investing public.

My friends, you and I as common-sense citizens know that it would help to protect the savings of the country from the dishonesty of crooks and from the lack of honor of some men in high financial places. Publicity is the enemy of crookedness.

And now one word about unemployment, and incidentally about agriculture. I have favored the use of certain types of public works as a further emergency means of stimulating employment and the issuance of bonds to pay for such public works, but I have pointed out that no economic end is served if we merely build without building for a necessary purpose. Such works, of course, should insofar as possible be self-sustaining if they are to be financed by the issuing of bonds. So as to spread the points of all kinds as widely as possible, we must take definite steps to shorten the working day and the working week.

Let us use common sense and business sense. Just as one example, we know that a very hopeful and immediate means of relief, both for the unemployed and for agriculture, will come from a wide plan of the converting of many millions of acres of marginal and unused land into timberland through reforestation. There are tens of millions of acres east of the Mississippi River alone in abandoned farms, in cut-over land, now growing up in worthless brush. Why, every European nation has a definite land policy, and has had one for generations. We have none. Having none, we face a future of soil erosion and timber famine. It is clear that economic foresight and immediate employment march hand in hand in the call for the reforestation of these vast areas.

In so doing, employment can be given to a million men. That is the kind of public work that is self-sustaining, and therefore capable of being financed by the issuance of bonds which are made secure by the fact that the growth of tremendous crops will provide adequate security for the investment.

Yes, I have a very definite program for providing employment by that means. I have done it, and I am doing it today in the state of New York. I know that the Democratic Party can do it successfully in the nation. That will put men to work, and that is an example of the action that we are going to have.

Now as a further aid to agriculture, we know perfectly well—but have we come out and said so clearly and distinctly?—we should repeal immediately those provisions of law that compel the federal government to go into the market to purchase, to sell, to speculate in farm products in a futile attempt to reduce farm surpluses. And they are the people who are talking of keeping government out of business. The practical way to help the farmer is by an arrangement that will, in addition to lightening some of the impoverishing burdens from his back, do something toward the reduction of the surpluses of staple commodities that hang on the market. It should be our aim to add to the world prices of staple products the amount of a reasonable tariff protection, to give agriculture the same protection that industry has today.

And in exchange for this immediately increased return I am sure that the farmers of this nation would agree ultimately to such planning of their production as would reduce the surpluses and make it unnecessary in later years to depend on dumping those surpluses abroad in order to support domestic prices. That result has been accomplished in other nations; why not in America, too?

Farm leaders and farm economists, generally, agree that a plan based on that principle is a desirable first step in the reconstruction of agriculture. It does not in itself furnish a complete program, but it will serve in great measure in the long run to remove the pall of a surplus without the continued perpetual threat of world dumping. Final voluntary reduction of surplus is a part of our objective, but the long continuance and the present burden of existing surpluses make it necessary to repair great damage of the present by immediate emergency measures.

Such a plan as that, my friends, does not cost the government any money, nor does it keep the government in business or in speculation.

As to the actual wording of a bill, I believe that the Democratic Party stands ready to be guided by whatever the responsible farm groups themselves agree on. That is a principle that is sound; and again I ask for action.

One more word about the farmer, and I know that every delegate in this hall who lives in the city knows why I lay emphasis on the farmer. It is because one-half of our population, over 50 million people, are dependent on agriculture; and, my friends, if those 50 million people have no money, no cash, to buy what is produced in the city, the city suffers to an equal or greater extent.

That is why we are going to make the voters understand this year that this nation is not merely a nation of independence, but it is, if we are to survive, bound to be a nation of interdependence—town and city, and North and South, East and West. That is our goal, and that goal will be understood by the people of this country no matter where they live.

Yes, the purchasing power of that half of our population dependent on agriculture is gone. Farm mortgages reach nearly 10 billions of dollars today and interest charges on that alone are $560,000,000 a year. But that is not all. The tax burden caused by extravagant and inefficient local government is an additional factor. Our most immediate concern should be to reduce the interest burden on these mortgages.

Rediscounting of farm mortgages under salutary restrictions must be expanded and should, in the future, be conditioned on the reduction of interest rates. Amortization payments, maturities should likewise in this crisis be extended before rediscount is permitted where the mortgagor is sorely pressed. That, my friends, is another example of practical, immediate relief: Action.

I aim to do the same thing, and it can be done, for the small homeowner in our cities and villages. We can lighten his burden and develop his purchasing power. Take away, my friends, that spectre of too high an interest rate. Take away that spectre of the due date just a short time away. Save homes; save homes for thousands of self-respecting families, and drive out that spectre of insecurity from our midst.

Out of all the tons of printed paper, out of all the hours of oratory, the recriminations, the defenses, the happy-thought plans in Washington and in every state, there emerges one great, simple, crystal-pure fact that during the past 10 years a nation of 120 million people has been led by the Republican leaders to erect an impregnable barbed wire entanglement around its borders through the instrumentality of tariffs which have isolated us from all the other human beings in all the rest of the round world. I accept that admirable tariff statement in the platform of this convention. It would protect American business and American labor. By our acts of the past we have invited and received the retaliation of other nations. I propose an invitation to them to forget the past, to sit at the table with us, as friends, and to plan with us for the restoration of the trade of the world.

Go into the home of the businessman. He knows what the tariff has done for him. Go into the home of the factory worker. He knows why goods do not move. Go into the home of the farmer. He knows how the tariff has helped to ruin him.

At last our eyes are open. At last the American people are ready to acknowledge that Republican leadership was wrong and that the democracy is right.

My program, of which I can only touch on these points, is based upon this simple moral principle: the welfare and the soundness of a nation depend first upon what the great mass of the people wish and need; and second, whether or not they are getting it.

What do the people of America want more than anything else? To my mind, they want two things: work, with all the moral and spiritual values that go with it; and with work, a reasonable measure of security—security for themselves and for their wives and children. Work and security—these are more than words. They are more than facts. They are the spiritual values, the true goal toward which our efforts of reconstruction should lead. These are the values that this program is intended to gain; these are the values we have failed to achieve by the leadership we now have.

Our Republican leaders tell us economic laws—sacred, inviolable, unchangeable—cause panics which no one could prevent. But while they prate of economic laws, men and women are starving. We must lay hold of the fact that economic laws are not made by nature. They are made by human beings.

Yes, when—not if—when we get the chance, the federal government will assume bold leadership in distress relief. For years Washington has alternated between putting its head in the sand and saying there is no large number of destitute people in our midst who need food and clothing, and then saying the states should take care of them, if there are. Instead of planning two and a half years ago to do what they are now trying to do, they kept putting it off from day to day, week to week, and month to month, until the conscience of America demanded action.

I say that while primary responsibility for relief rests with localities now, as ever, yet the federal government has always had and still has a continuing responsibility for the broader public welfare. It will soon fulfill that responsibility.

And now, just a few words about our plans for the next four months. By coming here instead of waiting for a formal notification. I have made it clear that I believe we should eliminate expensive ceremonies and that we should set in motion at once, tonight, my friends, the necessary machinery for an adequate presentation of the issues to the electorate of the nation.

I myself have important duties as governor of a great state, duties which in these times are more arduous and more grave than at any previous period. Yet I feel confident that I shall be able to make a number of short visits to several parts of the nation. My trips will have as their first objective the study at first hand, from the lips of men and women of all parties and all occupations, of the actual conditions and needs of every part of an interdependent country.

One word more: Out of every crisis, every tribulation, every disaster, mankind rises with some share of greater knowledge, of higher decency, of purer purpose. Today we shall have come through a period of loose thinking, descending morals, an era of selfishness, among individual men and women and among nations. Blame not governments alone for this. Blame ourselves in equal share. Let us be frank in acknowledgment of the truth that many amongst us have made obeisance to Mammon, that the profits of speculation, the easy road without toil, have lured us from the old barricades. To return to higher standards we must abandon the false prophets and seek new leaders of our own choosing.

Never before in modern history have the essential differences between the two major American parties stood out in such striking contrast as they do today. Republican leaders not only have failed in material things, they have failed in national vision, because in disaster they have held out no hope, they have pointed out no path for the people below to climb back to places of security and of safety in our American life.

Throughout the nation, men and women, forgotten in the political philosophy of the government of the last years, look to us here for guidance and for more equitable opportunity to share in the distribution of national wealth.

On the farms, in the large metropolitan areas, in the smaller cities and in the villages, millions of our citizens cherish the hope that their old standards of living and of thought have not gone forever. Those millions cannot and shall not hope in vain.

I pledge you, I pledge myself, to a new deal for the American people. Let us all here assembled constitute ourselves prophets of a new order of competence and of courage. This is more than a political campaign; it is a call to arms. Give me your help, not to win votes alone, but to win in this crusade to restore America to its own people.

First Inaugural Address

Washington, D.C.

March 4, 1933

THE DEPRESSION reached its lowest point over the winter of 1932–1933. Roosevelt was confident that he and his cabinet, party backers, and the "brain trusters"—a team of lawyers, economists, and political theoreticians who drafted much of the basic New Deal legislation—could still turn the situation into an unprecedented opportunity for national growth. His inaugural address exuded cheerful competence, an attitude the country desperately needed after the years of executive paralysis under Hoover.

Roosevelt was drenched by gusts of rain as he read the address outside the east wing of the Capitol, steadying himself against the sides of the inauguration stand. Though the speech included its share of vague platitudes, and one suggestion that many found alarming—that if Congress failed to act, Roosevelt would assume whatever powers he thought necessary to combat the crisis—most listeners took courage from his energy and self-assurance. Even his aides were inspired. Long-time Roosevelt associate Ray Moley noted that "he's taken the ship of state and turned it right around."

I am certain that my fellow Americans expect that on my induction into the presidency I will address them with a candor and a decision which the present situation of our nation impels. This is preeminently the time to speak the truth, the whole truth, frankly and boldly. Nor need we shrink from honestly facing conditions in our country today. This great nation will endure as it has endured, will revive and will prosper. So, first of all, let me assert my firm belief that the only thing we have to fear is fear itself—nameless, unreasoning, unjustified terror which paralyzes needed efforts to convert retreat into advance. In every dark hour of our national life a leadership of frankness and vigor had met with that understanding and support of the people themselves which is essential to victory. I am convinced that you will again give that support to leadership in these critical days.

In such a spirit on my part and on yours we face our common difficulties. They concern, thank God, only material things. Values have shrunken to fantastic levels; taxes have risen, our ability to pay has fallen; government of all kind is faced by serious curtailment of income; the means of exchange are frozen in the currents of trade; the withered leaves of industrial enterprise lies on every side; farmers find no markets for their produce; the savings of many years in thousands of families are gone.

More important, a host of unemployed citizens face the grim problem of existence, and an equally great number toil with little return. Only a foolish optimist can deny the dark realities of the moment.

Yet our distress comes from no failure of substance. We are stricken by no plagues of locusts. Compared with the perils which our forefathers conquered because they believed and were not afraid, we have still much to be thankful for. Nature still offers her bounty and human efforts have multiplied it. Plenty is at our doorstep, but a generous use of it languishes in the very sight of the supply. Primarily this is because rulers of the exchange of mankind's goods have failed through their own stubbornness and their own incompetence, have admitted their failure, and have abdicated. Practices of the unscrupulous moneychangers stand indicted in the court of public opinion, rejected by the hearts and minds of men.

True they have tried, but their efforts have been cast in the pattern of an outworn tradition. Faced by failure of credit they have proposed only the lending of more money. Stripped of the lure of profit by which to induce our people to follow their false leadership, they have resorted to exhortations, pleading tearfully for restored confidence. They know only the rules of a generation of self-seekers. They have no vision, and when there is no vision the people perish.

The moneychangers have fled from their high seats in the temple of our civilization. We may now restore that temple to the ancient truths. The measure of the restoration lies in the extent to which we apply social values more noble than mere monetary profit.

Happiness lies not in the mere possession of money; it lies in the joy of achievement, in the thrill of creative effort. The joy and moral stimulation of work no longer must be forgotten in the mad chase of evanescent profits. These dark days will be worth all they cost us if they teach us that our true destiny is not to be ministered unto but to minister to ourselves and to our fellow men.

Recognition of the falsity of material wealth as the standard of success goes hand in hand with the abandonment of the false belief that public office and high political position are to be valued only by the standards of pride of place and personal profit; and there must be an end to a conduct in banking and in business which too often has given to a sacred trust the likeness of callous and selfish wrongdoing. Small wonder that confidence languishes, for it thrives only on honesty, on honor, on the sacredness of obligations, on faithful protection, on unselfish performance; without them it cannot live.

Restoration calls, however, not for changes in ethics alone. This nation asks for action, and action now.

Our greatest primary task is to put people to work. This is no unsolvable problem if we face it wisely and courageously. It can be accomplished in part by direct recruiting by the government itself, treating the task as we would treat the emergency of a war, but at the same time, through this employment, accomplishing greatly needed projects to stimulate and reorganize the use of our natural resources.

Hand in hand with this we must frankly recognize the overbalance of population in our industrial centers and, by engaging on a national scale in a redistribution, endeavor to provide a better use of the land for those best fitted for the land. The task can be helped by definite efforts to raise the values of agricultural products and, with this, the power to purchase the output of our cities. It can be helped by preventing realistically the tragedy of the growing loss through foreclosure of our small homes and our farms. It can be helped by insistence that the federal, state, and local governments act forthwith on the demand that their cost be drastically reduced. It can be helped by the unifying of relief activities which today are often scattered, uneconomical, and unequal. It can be helped by national planning for and supervision of all forms of transportation and of communications and other utilities which have a definitely public character. There are many ways in which it can be helped, but it can never be helped merely by talking about it. We must act and act quickly.

Finally, in our progress toward a resumption of work we require two safeguards against a return of the evils of the old order: there must be a strict supervision of all banking and credits and investments, so that there will be an end to speculation with other people's money; and there must be provisions for an adequate but sound currency.

These are the lines of attack. I shall presently urge upon a new Congress, in special session, detailed measures for their fulfillment, and I shall seek the immediate assistance of the several states.

Through this program of action we address ourselves to putting our own national house in order and making income balance outgo. Our international trade relations, though vastly important, are in point of time and necessity secondary to the establishment of a sound national economy. I favor as a practical policy the putting of first things first. I shall spare no effort to restore world trade by international economic readjustment, but the emergency at home cannot wait on that accomplishment.

The basic thought that guides these specific means of national recovery is not narrowly nationalistic. It is the insistence, as a first consideration, upon the interdependence of the various elements in and parts of the United States—a recognition of the old and permanently important manifestation of the American spirit of the pioneer. It is the way to recovery. It is the immediate way. It is the strongest assurance that the recovery will endure.

In the field of world policy I would dedicate this nation to the policy of the good neighbor— the neighbor who resolutely respects himself and, because he does so, respects the rights of others—the neighbor who respects his obligations and respects the sanctity of his agreements in and with a world of neighbors.

If I read the temper of our people correctly, we now realize as we have never realized before our interdependence on each other; that we cannot merely take but we must give as well; that if we are to go forward, we must move as a trained and loyal army willing to sacrifice for the good of a common discipline, because without such discipline no progress is made, no leadership becomes effective. We are, I know, ready and willing to submit our lives and property to such discipline, because it makes possible a leadership which aims at a larger good. This I propose to offer, pledging that the larger purposes will bind upon us all as a sacred obligation with a unity of duty hitherto evoked only in time of armed strife.

With this pledge taken, I assume unhesitatingly the leadership of this great army of our people dedicated to a disciplined attack upon our common problems.

Action in this image and to this end is feasible under the form of government which we have inherited from our ancestors. Our Constitution is so simple and practical that it is possible always to meet extraordinary needs by changes in emphasis and arrangements without loss of essential form. That is why our constitutional system has proved itself the most superbly enduring political mechanism the modern world has produced. It has met every stress of vast expansion of territory, of foreign wars, of bitter internal strife, of world relations.

It is to be hoped that the normal balance of executive and legislative authority may be wholly adequate to meet the unprecedented task before us. But it may be that an unprecedented demand and need for undelayed action may call for temporary departure from that normal balance of public procedure.

I am prepared under my constitutional duty to recommend the measures that a stricken nation in the midst of a stricken world may require. These measures, or such other measures as the Congress may build out of its experience and wisdom, I shall seek, within my constitutional authority, to bring to speedy adoption.

But in the event that the Congress shall fail to take one of these two courses, and in the event that the national emergency is still critical, I shall not evade the clear course of duty that will then confront me. I shall ask the Congress for the one remaining instrument to meet the crisis—broad executive power to wage a war against the emergency, as great as the power that would be given to me if we were in fact invaded by a foreign foe.

For the trust reposed in me I will return the courage and the devotion that befit the time. I can do no less.

We face the arduous days that lie before us in the warm courage of national unity; with the clear consciousness of seeking old and precious moral values; with the clear satisfaction that comes from the stern performance of duty by old and young alike. We aim at the assurance of a rounded and permanent national life.

We do not distrust the future of essential democracy. The people of the United States have not failed. In their need they have registered a mandate that they want direct, vigorous action. They have asked for discipline and direction under leadership. They have made me the present instrument of their wishes. In the spirit of the gift I take it.

In this dedication of a nation we humbly ask the blessing of God. May he protect each and every one of us. May he guide me in the days to come.

The Good Neighbor Policy

Washington, D.C.

April 12, 1933

DURING HIS years as assistant secretary of the navy under Wilson, Roosevelt modeled himself after his imperialist cousin, Theodore Roosevelt, who had held the same position under McKinley. He blithely boasted that he knew the Haitians had an excellent constitution because he had written it himself. But by the time of his presidency he had grown out of jingoism and was ready for a more mature policy toward the other nations of the Western Hemisphere. His efforts went far toward mending the damage done to America's democratic image by the Latin American incursions of Wilson, Coolidge, and the earlier Roosevelt. Seen by many Latin Americans as a *caudillo*—a charismatic, aristocratic leader—he was much admired south of the border, where he was referred to as *"el gran democrata."*

The idea for this speech developed from Roosevelt's inaugural address, in which he first mentioned a "policy of the good neighbor." It was delivered before a meeting of the governing board of the Pan-American Union and was broadcast in English, Spanish, and Portuguese.

I rejoice in this opportunity to participate in the celebration of "Pan-American Day" and to extend on behalf of the people of the United States a fraternal greeting to our sister American republics. The celebration of "Pan-American Day" in this building, dedicated to international goodwill and cooperation, exemplifies a unity of thought and purpose among the peoples of this hemisphere. It is a manifestation of the common ideal of mutual helpfulness, sympathetic understanding, and spiritual solidarity.

There is inspiration in the thought that on this day the attention of the citizens of the 21 republics of America is focused on the common ties—historical, cultural, economic, and social—which bind them to one another. Common ideals and a community of interest, together with a spirit of cooperation, have led to the realization that the well-being of one nation depends in large measure upon the well-being of its neighbors. It is upon these foundations that Pan-Americanism has been built.

This celebration commemorates a movement based upon the policy of fraternal cooperation. In my inaugural address I stated that I would "dedicate this nation to the policy of the good neighbor—the neighbor who resolutely respects himself and, because he does so, respects the rights of others—the neighbor who respects his obligations and respects the sanctity of his agreements in and with a world of neighbors." Never before has the significance of the words good neighbor been so manifest in international relations. Never have the need and benefit of neighborly cooperation in every form of human activity been so evident as they are today.

Friendship among nations, as among individuals, calls for constructive efforts to muster the forces of humanity in order that an atmosphere of close understanding and cooperation may be cultivated. It involves mutual obligations and responsibilities, for it is only by sympathetic respect for the rights of others and a scrupulous fulfillment of the corresponding obligations by each member of the community that a true fraternity can be maintained.

The essential qualities of a true Pan-Americanism must be the same as those which constitute a good neighbor, namely, mutual understanding, and, through such understanding, a sympathetic appreciation of the other's point of view. It is only in this manner that we can hope to build up a system of which confidence, friendship, and goodwill are the cornerstones.

In this spirit the people of every republic on our continent are coming to a deep understanding of the fact that the Monroe Doctrine, of which so much has been written and spoken for more than a century, was and is directed at the maintenance of independence by the peoples of the continent. It was aimed and is aimed against the acquisition in any manner of the control of additional territory in this hemisphere by any non-American power.

Hand in hand with this Pan-American doctrine of continental self-defense, the peoples of the American republics understand more clearly, with the passing years, that the independence of each republic must recognize the independence of every other republic. Each one of us must grow by an advancement of civilization and social well-being and not by the acquisition of territory at the expense of any neighbor.

In this spirit of mutual understanding and of cooperation on this continent you and I cannot fail to be disturbed by any armed strife between neighbors. I do not hesitate to say to you, the distinguished members of the governing board of the Pan-American Union, that I regard existing conflicts between four of our sister republics as a backward step.

Your Americanism and mine must be a structure built of confidence, cemented by a sympathy which recognizes only equality and fraternity. It finds its source and being in the hearts of men and dwells in the temple of the intellect.

We all of us have peculiar problems, and, to speak frankly, the interest of our own citizens must, in each instance, come first. But is it equally true that it is of vital importance to every nation of this continent that the American governments, individually, take, without further delay, such action as may be possible to abolish all unnecessary and artificial barriers and restrictions which now hamper the healthy flow of trade between the peoples of the American republics.

I am glad to deliver this message to you, gentlemen of the governing board of the Pan-American Union, for I look upon the union as the outward expression of the spiritual unity of the Americas. It is to this unity which must be courageous and vital in its element that humanity must look for one of the great stabilizing influences in world affairs. . . .

Social Security

Washington, D.C.

January 17, 1935

THE NEW DEAL included such famous legislation as the National Recovery Act and the laws establishing the Works Progress Administration, the Civilian Conservation Corps, and the Tennessee Valley Authority. But of all the New Deal measures, Social Security, a system of unemployment compensation, old-age pensions, and other worker protections, has had the most lasting impact. Upon signing the Social Security Act in 1935, Roosevelt claimed that it would "act as a protection to future administrations against the necessity of going deeply into debt to furnish relief to the needy . . . it is, in short, a law that will take care of human needs and at the same time provide for the United States an economic structure of vastly greater soundness."

Social Security was violently opposed by Republicans and businessmen, who saw in it proof that Roosevelt was a socialist. The American Communist press, displeased with the requirement of salary donations from workers, called it "one of the biggest frauds ever perpetrated on the people of this country." It was just that aspect, however, that in FDR's mind made Social Security unassailable. "We put those payroll contributions in there so as to give the contributors a legal, moral, and political right to collect their pensions and their unemployment benefits," he said. "With those taxes in there, no damn politician can ever scrap my social security program."

In addressing you on June eighth, 1934, I summarized the main objectives of our American program. Among these was, and is, the security of the men, women, and children of the nation against certain hazards and vicissitudes of life. This purpose is an essential part of our task. In my annual message to you I promised to submit a definite program of action. This I do in the form of a report to me by a Committee on Economic Security, appointed by me for the purpose of surveying the field and of recommending the basis of legislation.

I am gratified with the work of this committee and of those who have helped it: The Technical Board on Economic Security drawn from various departments of the government, the Advisory Council on Economic Security, consisting of informed and public-spirited private citizens and a number of other advisory groups, including a committee on actuarial consultants, a medical advisory board, a dental advisory committee, a hospital advisory committee, a public-health advisory committee, a child-welfare committee and an advisory committee on employment relief. All of those who participated in this notable task of planning this major legislative proposal are ready and willing, at any time, to consult with and assist in any way the appropriate congressional committees and members, with respect to detailed aspects.

It is my best judgment that this legislation should be brought forward with a minimum of delay. Federal action is necessary to, and conditioned upon, the action of states. Forty-four legislatures are meeting or will meet soon. In order that the necessary state action may be taken promptly it is important that the federal government proceed speedily.

The detailed report of the committee sets forth a series of proposals that will appeal to the sound sense of the American people. It has not attempted the impossible, nor has it failed to exercise sound caution and consideration of all of the factors concerned: the national credit, the rights and responsibilities of states, the capacity of industry to assume financial responsibilities and the fundamental necessity of proceeding in a manner that will merit the enthusiastic support of citizens of all sorts.

It is overwhelmingly important to avoid any danger of permanently discrediting the sound and necessary policy of federal legislation for economic security by attempting to apply it on too ambitious a scale before actual experience has provided guidance for the permanently safe direction of such efforts. The place of such a fundamental in our future civilization is too precious to be jeopardized now by extravagant action. It is a sound idea—a sound ideal. Most of the other advanced countries of the world have already adopted it, and their experience affords the knowledge that social insurance can be made a sound and workable project.

Three principles should be observed in legislation on this subject. First, the system adopted, except for the money necessary to initiate it, should be self-sustaining in the sense that funds for the payment of insurance benefits should not come from the proceeds of general taxation. Second, excepting in old-age insurance, actual management should be left to the states subject to standards established by the federal government. Third, sound financial management of the funds and the reserves, and protection of the credit structure of the nation should be assured by retaining federal control over all funds through trustees in the Treasury of the United States.

At this time, I recommend the following types of legislation looking to economic security:

1. Unemployment compensation.
2. Old-age benefits; including compulsory and voluntary annuities.
3. Federal aid to dependent children through grants to states for the support of existing mothers' pension systems and for services for the protection and care of homeless, neglected, dependent, and crippled children.
4. Additional federal aid to state and local public-health agencies and the strengthening of the Federal Public Health Service. I am not at this time recommending the adoption of so-called "health insurance," although groups representing the medical profession are cooperating with the federal government in the further study of the subject and definite progress is being made.

With respect to unemployment compensation, I have concluded that the most practical proposal is the levy of a uniform federal payroll tax, 90 percent of which should be allowed as an offset to employers contributing under a compulsory state unemployment compensation act. The purpose of this is to afford a requirement of a reasonably uniform character for all states cooperating with the federal government and to promote and encourage the passage of unemployment compensation laws in the states. The 10 percent not thus offset should be used to cover the costs of federal and state administration of this broad system. Thus, states will largely administer unemployment compensation, assisted and guided by the federal government. An unemployment compensation system should be constructed in such a way as to afford every practicable aid and incentive toward the larger purpose of employment stabilization. This can be helped by the intelligent planning of both public and private employment. It also can be helped by correlating the system with public employment so that a person who has exhausted his benefits may be eligible for some form of public work as is recommended in this report. Moreover, in order to encourage the stabilization of private employment, federal legislation should not foreclose the states from establishing means for inducing industries to afford an even greater stabilization of employment.

In the important field of security for our old people, it seems necessary to adopt three principles: First, noncontributory old-age pensions for those who are now too old to build up their own insurance. It is, of course, clear that for perhaps 30 years to come funds will have to be provided by the states and the federal government to meet these pensions. Second, compulsory contributory annuities which in time will establish a self-supporting system for those now young and for future generations. Third, voluntary contributory annuities by which individual initiative can increase the annual amounts received in old age. It is proposed that the federal government assume one-half of the cost of the old-age pension plan, which ought ultimately to be supplanted by self-supporting annuity plans.

The amount necessary at this time for the initiation of unemployment compensation, old-age security, children's aid, and the promotion of public health, as outlined in the report of the Committee on Economic Security, is approximately one hundred million dollars.

The establishment of sound means toward a greater future economic security of the American people is dictated by a prudent consideration of the hazards involved in our national life. No one can guarantee this country against the dangers of future depressions but we can reduce these dangers. We can eliminate many of the factors that cause economic depressions, and we can provide the means of mitigating their results. This plan for economic security is at once a measure of prevention and a method of alleviation.

We pay now for the dreadful consequence of economic insecurity—and dearly. This plan presents a more equitable and infinitely less expensive means of meeting these costs. We cannot afford to neglect the plain duty before us. I strongly recommend action to attain the objectives sought in this report.

Second Inaugural Address

Washington, D.C.
January 20, 1937

THIS WAS the first inaugural held in January rather than in March, a change wrought by constitutional amendment. Again it was raining, but Roosevelt ordered a glass shield around the inauguration booth removed. If the people had to stand in the rain to hear him, the president insisted, he would stand in the rain to talk to them.

In his diary, Roosevelt's secretary of the interior, Harold Ickes, contrasted the mood of the nation at FDR's first two inaugurations. "Four years ago the country was in an economic collapse. Everyone was in a low state of morale. The only hope that flickered was that the new president would be able to do something about the depression. . . . Today the banks are in a better condition than they have ever been and prosperity has returned in large measure." The emphasis in the president's speech, however, was on how far the nation still had to go.

When four years ago we met to inaugurate a president, the republic, single-minded in anxiety, stood in spirit here. We dedicated ourselves to the fulfillment of a vision—to speed the time when there would be for all the people that security and peace essential to the pursuit of happiness. We of the republic pledged ourselves to drive from the temple of our ancient faith those who had profaned it; to end by action, tireless and unafraid, the stagnation and despair of that day. We did those first things first.

Our covenant with ourselves did not stop there. Instinctively we recognized a deeper need—the need to find through government the instrument of our united purpose to solve for the individual the ever-rising problems of a complex civilization. Repeated attempts at their solution without the aid of government had left us baffled and bewildered. For, without that aid, we had been unable to create those moral controls over the services of science which are necessary to make science a useful servant instead of a ruthless master of mankind. To do this we knew that we must find practical controls over blind economic forces and blindly selfish men.

We of the republic sensed the truth that democratic government has innate capacity to protect its people against disasters once considered inevitable, to solve problems once considered unsolvable. We would not admit that we could not find a way to master economic epidemics just as, after centuries of fatalistic suffering, we had found a way to master epidemics of disease. We refused to leave the problems of our common welfare to be solved by the winds of chance and the hurricanes of disaster.

In this we Americans were discovering no wholly new truth; we were writing a new chapter in our book of self-government.

This year marks the 150th anniversary of the Constitutional Convention which made us a nation. At that convention our forefathers found the way out of the chaos which followed the Revolutionary War; they created a strong government with powers of united action sufficient then and now to solve problems utterly beyond individual or local solution. A century and a half ago they established the federal government in order to promote the general welfare and secure the blessings of liberty to the American people.

Today we invoke those same powers of government to achieve the same objectives.

Four years of new experience have not belied our historic instinct. They hold out the clear hope that government within communities, government within the separate states, and government of the United States can do the things the times require, without yielding its democracy. Our tasks in the last four years did not force democracy to take a holiday.

Nearly all of us recognize that as intricacies of human relationships increase, so power to govern them also must increase—power to stop evil; power to do good. The essential democracy of our nation and the safety of our people depend not upon the absence of power, but upon lodging it with those whom the people can change or continue at stated intervals

537

through an honest and free system of elections. The Constitution of 1787 did not make our democracy impotent.

In fact, in these last four years, we have made the exercise of all power more democratic; for we have begun to bring private autocratic powers into their proper subordination to the public's government. The legend that they were invincible—above and beyond the processes of a democracy—has been shattered. They have been challenged and beaten.

Our progress out of the Depression is obvious. But that is not all that you and I mean by the new order of things. Our pledge was not merely to do a patchwork job with second-hand materials. By using the new materials of social justice we have undertaken to erect on the old foundations a more enduring structure for the better use of future generations.

In that purpose we have been helped by achievements of mind and spirit. Old truths have been relearned; untruths have been unlearned. We have always known that heedless self-interest was bad morals; we know now that it is bad economics. Out of the collapse of a prosperity whose builders boasted their practicality has come the conviction that in the long run economic morality pays. We are beginning to wipe out the line that divides the practical from the ideal; and in so doing we are fashioning an instrument of unimagined power for the establishment of a morally better world.

This new understanding undermines the old admiration of worldly success as such. We are beginning to abandon our tolerance of the abuse of power by those who betray for profit the elementary decencies of life.

In this process evil things formerly accepted will not be so easily condoned. Hard-headedness will not so easily excuse hard-heartedness. We are moving toward an era of good feeling. But we realize that there can be no era of good feeling save among men of goodwill.

For these reasons I am justified in believing that the greatest change we have witnessed has been the change in the moral climate of America.

Among men of goodwill, science and democracy together offer an ever-richer life and ever-larger satisfaction to the individual. With this change in our moral climate and our rediscovered ability to improve our economic order, we have set our feet upon the road of enduring progress.

Shall we pause now and turn our back upon the road that lies ahead? Shall we call this the promised land? Or, shall we continue on our way? For "each age is a dream that is dying, or one that is coming to birth."

Many voices are heard as we face a great decision. Comfort says, "Tarry a while." Opportunism says, "This is a good spot." Timidity asks, "How difficult is the road ahead?"

True, we have come far from the days of stagnation and despair. Vitality has been preserved. Courage and confidence have been restored. Mental and moral horizons have been extended.

But our present gains were won under the pressure of more than ordinary circumstance. Advance became imperative under the goad of fear and suffering. The times were on the side of progress.

To hold to progress today, however, is more difficult. Dulled conscience, irresponsibility, and ruthless self-interest already reappear. Such symptoms of prosperity may become portents of disaster! Prosperity already tests the persistence of our progressive purpose.

Let us ask again: Have we reached the goal of our vision of that fourth day of March, 1933? Have we found our happy valley?

I see a great nation, upon a great continent, blessed with a great wealth of natural resources. Its 130 million people are at peace among themselves; they are making their country a good neighbor among the nations. I see a United States which can demonstrate that, under democratic methods of government, national wealth can be translated into a spreading volume of human comforts hitherto unknown, and the lowest standard of living can be raised far above the level of mere subsistence.

But here is the challenge to our democracy: In this nation I see tens of millions of its citizens—a substantial part of its whole population—who at this very moment are denied the greater part of what the very lowest standards of today call the necessities of life.

I see millions of families trying to live on incomes so meager that the pall of family disaster hangs over them day by day.

I see millions whose daily lives in city and on farm continue under conditions labeled indecent by a so-called polite society half a century ago.

I see millions denied education, recreation, and the opportunity to better their lot and the lot of their children.

I see millions lacking the means to buy the products of farm and factory and by their poverty denying work and productiveness to many other millions.

I see one-third of a nation ill-housed, ill-clad, ill-nourished.

It is not in despair that I paint you that picture. I paint it for you in hope—because the nation, seeing and understanding the injustice in it, proposes to paint it out. We are determined to make every American citizen the subject of his country's interest and concern; and we will never regard any faithful, law-abiding group within our borders as superfluous. The test of our progress is not whether we add more to the abundance of those who have much; it is whether we provide enough for those who have too little.

If I know aught of the spirit and purpose of our nation, we will not listen to Comfort, Opportunism, and Timidity. We will carry on.

Overwhelmingly, we of the republic are men and women of goodwill; men and women who have more than warm hearts of dedication; men and women who have cool heads and willing hands of practical purpose as well. They will insist that every agency of popular government use effective instruments to carry our their will.

Government is competent when all who compose it work as trustees for the whole people. It can make constant progress when it keeps abreast of all the facts. It can obtain justified support and legitimate criticism when the people receive true information of all that government does.

If I know aught of the will of our people, they will demand that these conditions of effective government shall be created and maintained. They will demand a nation uncorrupted by cancers of injustice and, therefore, strong among the nations in its example of the will to peace.

Today we reconsecrate our country to long-cherished ideals in a suddenly changed civilization. In every land there are always at work forces that drive men apart and forces that draw men together. In our personal ambitions we are individualists. But in our seeking for economic and political progress as a nation, we all go up, or else we all go down, as one people.

To maintain a democracy of effort requires a vast amount of patience in dealing with differing methods, a vast amount of humility. But out of the confusion of many voices rises an understanding of dominant public need. Then political leadership can voice common ideals, and aid in their realization.

In taking again the oath of office as president of the United States, I assume the solemn obligation of leading the American people forward along the road over which they have chosen to advance.

While this duty rests upon me I shall do my utmost to speak their purpose and to do their will, seeking Divine guidance to help us each and every one to give light to them that sit in darkness and to guide our feet into the way of peace.

The Reorganization of the Judiciary

Washington, D.C.

March 9, 1937

ROOSEVELT began giving radio talks, which he called "fireside chats," during his first term as governor of New York. With radio he could reach the voters directly, circumventing the Republicans and especially the press, which, he felt, was "85 percent" against him and his programs. Roosevelt continued his fireside chats as president, giving several a year. "Read in cold newspaper print the next day," wrote his biographer James MacGregor Burns, "these talks seemed somewhat stilted and banal. Heard in the parlor, they were fresh, intimate, direct, moving." The key to his success, thought Frances Perkins, Roosevelt's labor secretary, was the president's ability to imagine himself addressing a live audience. When he spoke to the microphone, "his face would smile and light up as though he were actually sitting on the front porch or in the parlor with them."

As effective as the fireside chats were in shaping public opinion, they were of little help when Roosevelt was clearly in the wrong or when he lacked the political influence to push a plan through Congress. After the conservative members of the Supreme Court declared many New Deal measures unconstitutional, the frustrated Roosevelt tried to overwhelm them by expanding the Court with more sympathetic jurists. For once, however, Roosevelt had failed to test the political waters first; public opinion was against his Court-packing plan, and he could not muster the congressional votes needed to pass the measure. It was his worst political blunder.

Last Thursday I described in detail certain economic problems which everyone admits now face the nation. For the many messages which have come to me after that speech, and which it is physically impossible to answer individually, I take this means of saying "thank you." Tonight, sitting at my desk in the White House, I make my first radio report to the people in my second term of office.

I am reminded of that evening in March, four years ago, when I made my first radio report to you. We were then in the midst of the great banking crisis.

Soon after, with the authority of the Congress, we asked the nation to turn over all of its privately held gold, dollar for dollar, to the government of the United States.

Today's recovery proves how right that policy was.

But when, almost two years later, it came before the Supreme Court its constitutionality was upheld only by a five-to-four vote. The change of one vote would have thrown all the affairs of this great nation back into hopeless chaos. In effect, four justices ruled that the right under a private contract to exact a pound of flesh was more sacred than the main objectives of the Constitution to establish an enduring nation.

In 1933 you and I knew that we must never let our economic system get completely out of joint again—that we could not afford to take the risk of another Great Depression.

We also became convinced that the only way to avoid a repetition of those dark days was to have a government with power to prevent and to cure the abuses and the inequalities which had thrown that system out of joint.

We then began a program of remedying those abuses and inequalities—to give balance and stability to our economic system—to make it bomb-proof against the causes of 1929.

Today we are only part-way through that program—and recovery is speeding up to a point where the dangers of 1929 are again becoming possible, not this week or month perhaps, but within a year or two.

National laws are needed to complete that program. Individual or local or state effort alone cannot protect us in 1937 any better than 10 years ago.

It will take time—and plenty of time—to work out our remedies administratively even after legislation is passed. To complete our program of protection in time, therefore, we cannot delay one moment in making certain that our national government has power to carry through.

Four years ago action did not come until the eleventh hour. It was almost too late.

If we learned anything from the Depression we will not allow ourselves to run around in new circles of futile discussion and debate, always postponing the day of decision.

The American people have learned from the Depression. For in the last three national elections an overwhelming majority of them voted a mandate that the Congress and the president begin the task of providing that protection—not after long years of debate, but now.

The courts, however, have cast doubts on the ability of the elected Congress to protect us against catastrophe by meeting squarely our modern social and economic conditions.

We are at a crisis in our ability to proceed with that protection. It is a quiet crisis. There are no lines of depositors outside closed banks. But to the far-sighted it is far-reaching in its possibilities of injury to America.

I want to talk with you very simply about the need for present action in this crisis—the need to meet the unanswered challenge of one-third of a nation ill-nourished, ill-clad, ill-housed.

Last Thursday I described the American form of government as a three-horse team provided by the Constitution to the American people so that their field might be plowed. The three horses are, of course, the three branches of government—the Congress, the executive and the courts. Two of the horses are pulling in unison today; the third is not. Those who have intimated that the president of the United States is trying to drive that team, overlook the simple fact that the president, as chief executive, is himself one of the three horses.

It is the American people themselves who are in the driver's seat.

It is the American people themselves who want the furrow plowed.

It is the American people themselves who expect the third horse to pull in unison with the other two.

I hope that you have re-read the Constitution of the United States in these past few weeks. Like the Bible, it ought to be read again and again.

It is an easy document to understand when you remember that it was called into being because the Articles of Confederation under which the original 13 states tried to operate after the Revolution showed the need of a national government with power enough to handle national problems. In its preamble, the Constitution states that it was intended to form a more perfect Union and promote the general welfare; and the powers given to the Congress to carry out those purposes can be best described by saying that they were all the powers needed to meet each and every problem which then had a national character and which could not be met by merely local action.

But the framers went further. Having in mind that in succeeding generations many other problems then undreamed of would become national problems, they gave to the Congress the ample broad powers "to levy taxes . . . and provide for the common defense and general welfare of the United States."

That, my friends, is what I honestly believe to have been the clear and underlying purpose of the patriots who wrote a federal Constitution to create a national government with national power, intended as they said, "to form a more perfect Union . . . for ourselves and our posterity."

For nearly 20 years there was no conflict between the Congress and the Court. Then Congress passed a statute which, in 1803, the Court said violated an express provision of the Constitution. The Court claimed the power to declare it unconstitutional and did so declare it. But a little later the Court itself admitted that it was an extraordinary power to exercise and through Mr. Justice Washington laid down this limitation upon it: "It is but a decent respect due to the wisdom, the integrity, and the patriotism of the legislative body, by which any law is passed, to presume in favor of its validity until its violation of the Constitution is proved beyond all reasonable doubt."

But since the rise of the modern movement for social and economic progress through legislation, the Court has more and more often and more and more boldly asserted a power to veto laws passed by the Congress and state legislatures in complete disregard of this original limitation.

In the last four years the sound rule of giving statutes the benefit of all reasonable doubt has been cast aside. The Court has been acting not as a judicial body, but as a policy-making body.

When the Congress has sought to stabilize national agriculture, to improve the conditions of labor, to safeguard business against unfair competition, to protect our national resources, and in many other ways, to serve our clearly national needs, the majority of the Court has been assuming the power to pass on the wisdom of these acts of the Congress—and to approve or disapprove the public policy written into these laws.

That is not only my accusation. It is the accusation of most distinguished justices of the present Supreme Court. I have not the time to quote to you all the language used by dissenting justices in many of these cases. But in the case holding the Railroad Retirement Act unconstitutional, for instance, Chief Justice [C. Evans] Hughes said in a dissenting opinion that the majority opinion was "a departure from sound principles," and placed "an unwarranted limitation upon the commerce clause." And three other justices agreed with him.

In the case holding the A.A.A. unconstitutional, Justice [Harlan] Stone said of the majority opinion that it was a "tortured construction of the Constitution." And two other justices agreed with him.

In the case holding the New York Minimum Wage Law unconstitutional, Justice Stone said that the majority were actually reading into the Constitution their own "personal economic predilections," and that if the legislative power is not left free to choose the methods of solving the problems of poverty, subsistence, and health of large numbers in the community, then "government is to be rendered impotent." And two other justices agreed with him.

In the face of these dissenting opinions, there is no basis for the claim made by some members of the Court that something in the Constitution has compelled them regretfully to thwart the will of the people.

In the face of such dissenting opinions, it is perfectly clear, that as Chief Justice Hughes has said: "We are under a Constitution, but the Constitution is what the judges say it is."

The Court in addition to the proper use of its judicial functions has improperly set itself up as a third house of the Congress—a super-legislature, as one of the justices has called it—reading into the Constitution words and implications which are not there, and which were never intended to be there.

We have, therefore, reached the point as a nation where we must take action to save the Constitution from the Court and the Court from itself. We must find a way to take an appeal from the Supreme Court to the Constitution itself. We want a Supreme Court which will do justice under the Constitution—not over it. In our courts we want a government of laws and not of men.

I want—as all Americans want—an independent judiciary as proposed by the framers of the Constitution. That means a Supreme Court that will enforce the Constitution as written—that will refuse to amend the Constitution by the arbitrary exercise of judicial power—amendment by judicial say-so. It does not mean a judiciary so independent that it can deny the existence of facts universally recognized.

How then could we proceed to perform the mandate given us? It was said in last year's Democratic platform, "If these problems cannot be effectively solved within the Constitution, we shall seek such clarifying amendment as will assure the power to enact those laws, adequately to regulate commerce, protect public health and safety, and safeguard economic security." In other words, we said we would seek an amendment only if every other possible means by legislation were to fail.

When I commenced to review the situation with the problem squarely before me, I came by a process of elimination to the conclusion that, short of amendments, the only method which was clearly constitutional, and would at the same time carry out other much needed reforms, was to infuse new blood into all our courts. We must have men worthy and equipped to carry out impartial justice. But, at the same time, we must have judges who will bring to the courts a present-day sense of the Constitution—judges who will retain in the courts the judicial functions of a court, and reject the legislative powers which the courts have today assumed.

In 45 out of the 48 states of the Union, judges are chosen not for life but for a period of years. In many states judges must retire at the age of 70. Congress has provided financial security by offering life pensions at full pay for federal judges on all courts who are willing to retire at 70. In the case of Supreme Court justices, that pension is $20,000 a year. But all federal judges, once appointed, can, if they choose, hold office for life, no matter how old they may get to be.

What is my proposal? It is simply this: whenever a judge or justice of any federal court has reached the age of 70 and does not avail himself of the opportunity to retire on a pension, a new member shall be appointed by the president then in office, with the approval, as required by the Constitution, of the Senate of the United States.

That plan has two chief purposes. By bringing into the judicial system a steady and continuing stream of new and younger blood, I hope, first, to make the administration of all federal justice speedier and, therefore, less costly; secondly, to bring to the decision of social and economic problems younger men who have had personal experience and contact with modern facts and circumstances under which average men have to live and work. This plan will save our national Constitution from hardening of the judicial arteries.

The number of judges to be appointed would depend wholly on the decision of present judges now over 70, or those who would subsequently reach the age of 70.

If, for instance, any one of the six justices of the Supreme Court now over the age of 70 should retire as provided under the plan, no additional place would be created. Consequently, although there never can be more than 15, there may be only 14, or 13, or 12. And there may be only nine.

There is nothing novel or radical about this idea. It seeks to maintain the federal bench in full vigor. It has been discussed and approved by many persons of high authority ever since a similar proposal passed the House of Representatives in 1869.

Why was the age fixed at 70? Because the laws of many states, the practice of the civil service, the regulations of the army and navy, and the rules of many of our universities and of almost every great private business enterprise, commonly fix the retirement age at 70 years or less.

The statute would apply to all the courts in the federal system. There is general approval so far as the lower federal courts are concerned. The plan has met opposition only so far as the Supreme Court of the United States itself is concerned. If such a plan is good for the lower courts it certainly ought to be equally good for the highest Court from which there is no appeal.

Those opposing this plan have sought to arouse prejudice and fear by crying that I am seeking to "pack" the Supreme Court and that a baneful precedent will be established.

What do they mean by the words "packing the Court"?

Let me answer this question with a bluntness that will end all honest misunderstanding of my purposes.

If by that phrase "packing the Court" it is charged that I wish to place on the bench spineless puppets who would disregard the law and would decide specific cases as I wished them to be decided, I make this answer: that no president fit for his office would appoint, and no Senate of honorable men fit for their office would confirm, that kind of appointees to the Supreme Court.

But if by that phrase the charge is made that I would appoint and the Senate would confirm justices worthy to sit beside present members of the Court who understand those modern conditions, that I will appoint justices who will not undertake to override the judgment of the Congress on legislative policy, that I will appoint justices who will act as justices and not as legislators—if the appointment of such justices can be called "packing the courts," then I say that I and with me the vast majority of the American people favor doing just that thing—now.

Is it a dangerous precedent for the Congress to change the number of the justices? The Congress has always had, and will have, that power. The number of justices has been changed several times before, in the administrations of John Adams and Thomas Jefferson—both signers of the Declaration of Independence—Andrew Jackson, Abraham Lincoln and Ulysses S. Grant.

I suggest only the addition of justices to the bench in accordance with a clearly defined principle relating to a clearly defined age limit. Fundamentally, if in the future, America cannot trust the Congress it elects to refrain from abuse of our constitutional usages, democracy will have failed far beyond the importance to it of any kind of precedent concerning the judiciary.

We think it so much in the public interest to maintain a vigorous judiciary that we encourage the retirement of elderly judges by offering them a life pension at full salary. Why then should we leave the fulfillment of this public policy to chance or make it dependent upon the desire or prejudice of any individual justice?

It is the clear intention of our public policy to provide for a constant flow of new and younger blood into the judiciary. Normally every president appoints a large number of district and circuit judges and a few members of the Supreme Court. Until my first term practically every president of the United States had appointed at least one member of the Supreme Court. President Taft appointed five members and named a chief justice; President Wilson, three; President Harding, four, including a chief justice; President Coolidge, one; President Hoover, three, including a chief justice.

Such a succession of appointments should have provided a Court well-balanced as to age. But chance and the disinclination of individuals to leave the supreme bench have now given us a Court in which five justices will be over 75 years of age before next June and one over 70. Thus a sound public policy has been defeated.

I now propose that we establish by law an assurance against any such ill-balanced Court in the future. I propose that hereafter, when a judge reaches the age of 70, a new and younger judge shall be added to the Court automatically. In this way I propose to enforce a sound public policy by law instead of leaving the composition of our federal courts, including the highest, to be determined by chance or the personal decision of individuals.

If such a law as I propose is regarded as establishing a new precedent, is it not a most desirable precedent?

Like all lawyers, like all Americans, I regret the necessity of this controversy. But the welfare of the United States, and indeed of the Constitution itself, is what we all must think about first. Our difficulty with the Court today rises not from the Court as an institution but from human beings within it. But we cannot yield our constitutional destiny to the personal judgment of a few men who, being fearful of the future, would deny us the necessary means of dealing with the present.

This plan of mine is no attack on the Court; it seeks to restore the Court to its rightful and historic place in our system of constitutional government and to have it resume its high task of building anew on the Constitution "a system of living law." The Court itself can best undo what the Court has done.

I have thus explained to you the reasons that lie behind our efforts to secure results by legislation within the Constitution. I hope that thereby the difficult process of constitutional amendment may be rendered unnecessary. But let us examine that process.

There are many types of amendment proposed. Each one is radically different from the other. There is no substantial group within the Congress or outside it who are agreed on any single amendment.

It would take months or years to get substantial agreement upon the type and language of an amendment. It would take months and years thereafter to get a two-thirds majority in favor of that amendment in both houses of the Congress.

Then would come the long course of ratification by three-fourths of all the states. No amendment which any powerful economic interests or the leaders of any powerful political party have had reason to oppose has ever been ratified within anything like a reasonable time. And 13 states which contain only 5 percent of the voting population can block ratification even though the 35 states with 95 percent of the population are in favor of it.

A very large percentage of newspaper publishers, chambers of commerce, bar associations, manufacturers' associations, who are trying to give the impression that they really do want a constitutional amendment would be the first to exclaim as soon as an amendment was proposed, "Oh! I was for an amendment all right, but this amendment that you have proposed is not the kind of an amendment that I was thinking about. I am, therefore, going to spend my time, my efforts, and my money to block that amendment, although I would be awfully glad to help get some other kind of amendment ratified."

Two groups oppose my plan on the ground that they favor a constitutional amendment. The first includes those who fundamentally object to social and economic legislation along modern lines. This is the same group who during the campaign last fall tried to block the mandate of the people.

Now they are making a last stand. And the strategy of that last stand is to suggest the time-consuming process of amendment in order to kill off by delay the legislation demanded by the mandate.

To them I say: I do not think you will be able long to fool the American people as to your purposes.

The other group is composed of those who honestly believe the amendment process is the best and who would be willing to support a reasonable amendment if they could agree on one.

To them I say: we cannot rely on an amendment as the immediate or only answer to our present difficulties. When the time comes for action, you will find that many of those who pretend to support you will sabotage any constructive amendment which is proposed. Look at these strange bedfellows of yours. When before have you found them really at your side in your fights for progress?

And remember one thing more. Even if an amendment were passed, and even if in the years to come it were to be ratified, its meaning would depend upon the kind of justices who would be sitting on the Supreme Court bench. An amendment, like the rest of the Constitution, is what the justices say it is rather than what its framers or you might hope it is.

This proposal of mine will not infringe in the slightest upon the civil or religious liberties so dear to every American.

My record as governor and as president proves my devotion to those liberties. You who know me can have no fear that I would tolerate the destruction by any branch of government of any part of our heritage of freedom.

The present attempt by those opposed to progress to play upon the fears of danger to personal liberty brings again to mind that crude and cruel strategy tried by the same opposition to frighten the workers of America in a pay-envelope propaganda against the Social Security law. The workers were not fooled by that propaganda then. The people of America will not be fooled by such propaganda now.

I am in favor of action through legislation:

First, because I believe that it can be passed at this session of the Congress.

Second, because it will provide a reinvigorated, liberal-minded judiciary necessary to furnish quicker and cheaper justice from bottom to top.

Third, because it will provide a series of federal courts willing to enforce the Constitution as written, and unwilling to assert legislative powers by writing into it their own political and economic policies.

During the past half century the balance of power between the three great branches of the federal government has been tipped out of balance by the courts in direct contradiction of the high purposes of the framers of the Constitution. It is my purpose to restore that balance. You who know me will accept my solemn assurance that in a world in which democracy is under attack, I seek to make American democracy succeed. You and I will do our part.

The Arsenal of Democracy

Washington, D.C.

December 29, 1940

AS THE AXIS POWERS overran Europe, Africa, and Asia in 1939–1940, the nation's attention turned from internal problems to the threat of fascism. Great Britain, besieged by the Germans, was in desperate need of munitions, ships, and money. Winston Churchill applied continual pressure to Roosevelt to approve some form of American aid, with the unstated but obvious aim of eventually bringing the United States into the war on the side of the Allies. Although sympathetic, Roosevelt had just won his third presidential campaign by promising to keep the nation out of the war, and he was reluctant to reverse himself outright.

The aid plan finally devised by Roosevelt, called Lend-Lease, was announced to the people in this fireside chat. Lend-Lease involved giving the British munitions with payment in kind to be made after the war. This required American industry to gear up for munitions production to become "the great arsenal of democracy." As usual, FDR had correctly gauged the trend of public opinion: in the days after the announcement, the White House was flooded with approving mail.

This is not a fireside chat on war. It is a talk on national security; because the nub of the whole purpose of your president is to keep you now, and your children later, and your grandchildren much later, out of a last-ditch war for the preservation of American independence and all the things that American independence means to you and to me and to ours.

Tonight, in the presence of a world crisis, my mind goes back eight years to a night in the midst of a domestic crisis. It was a time when the wheels of American industry were grinding to a full stop, when the whole banking system of our country had ceased to function.

I well remember that while I sat in my study in the White House, preparing to talk with the people of the United States, I had before my eyes the picture of all those Americans with whom I was talking. I saw the workmen in the mills, the mines, the factories; the girl behind the counter; the small shopkeeper; the farmer doing his spring plowing; the widows and the old men wondering about their life's savings.

I tried to convey to the great mass of American people what the banking crisis meant to them in their daily lives.

Tonight, I want to do the same thing, with the same people, in this new crisis which faces America.

We met the issue of 1933 with courage and realism.

We face this new crisis—this new threat to the security of our nation—with the same courage and realism.

Never before since Jamestown and Plymouth Rock has our American civilization been in such danger as now.

For, on September 27, 1940, by an agreement signed in Berlin, three powerful nations, two in Europe and one in Asia, joined themselves together in the threat that if the United States of America interfered with or blocked the expansion program of these three nations—a program aimed at world control—they would unite in ultimate action against the United States.

The Nazi masters of Germany have made it clear that they intend not only to dominate all life and thought in their own country, but also to enslave the whole of Europe, and then to use the resources of Europe to dominate the rest of the world.

It was only three weeks ago their leader stated this: "There are two worlds that stand opposed to each other." And then in defiant reply to his opponents, he said this: "Others are correct when they say: With this world we cannot ever reconcile ourselves. . . . I can beat any other power in the world." So said the leader of the Nazis.

In other words, the Axis not merely admits but proclaims that there can be no ultimate peace between their philosophy of government and our philosophy of government.

In view of the nature of this undeniable threat, it can be asserted, properly and categorically, that the United States has no right or reason to encourage talk of peace, until the day shall come when there is a clear intention on the part of the aggressor nations to abandon all thought of dominating or conquering the world.

At this moment, the forces of the states that are leagued against all peoples who live in freedom, are being held away from our shores. The Germans and the Italians are being blocked on the other side of the Atlantic by the British, and by the Greeks, and by thousands of soldiers and sailors who were able to escape from subjugated countries. In Asia, the Japanese are being engaged by the Chinese nation in another great defense.

In the Pacific Ocean is our fleet.

Some of our people like to believe that wars in Europe and in Asia are of no concern to us. But it is a matter of most vital concern to us that European and Asiatic war-makers should not gain control of the oceans which lead to this hemisphere.

One hundred and seventeen years ago the Monroe Doctrine was conceived by our government as a measure of defense in the face of a threat against this hemisphere by an alliance in Continental Europe. Thereafter, we stood on guard in the Atlantic, with the British as neighbors. There was no treaty. There was no "unwritten agreement."

And yet, there was the feeling, proven correct by history, that we as neighbors could settle any disputes in peaceful fashion. The fact is that during the whole of this time the Western Hemisphere has remained free from aggression from Europe or from Asia.

Does anyone seriously believe that we need to fear attack anywhere in the Americas while a free Britain remains our most powerful naval neighbor in the Atlantic? Does anyone seriously believe, on the other hand, that we could rest easy if the Axis powers were our neighbors there?

If Great Britain goes down, the Axis powers will control the continents of Europe, Asia, Africa, Australasia, and the high seas—and they will be in a position to bring enormous military and naval resources against this hemisphere. It is no exaggeration to say that all of us, in all the Americas, would be living at the point of a gun—a gun loaded with explosive bullets, economic as well as military.

We should enter upon a new and terrible era in which the whole world, our hemisphere included, would be run by threats of brute force. To survive in such a world, we would have to convert ourselves permanently into a militaristic power on the basis of war economy.

Some of us like to believe that even if Great Britain falls, we are still safe, because of the broad expanse of the Atlantic and of the Pacific.

But the width of those oceans is not what it was in the days of clipper ships. At one point between Africa and Brazil the distance is less than from Washington to Denver, Colorado—five hours for the latest type of bomber. And at the north end of the Pacific Ocean America and Asia almost touch each other.

Even today we have planes that could fly from the British Isles to New England and back again without refueling. And remember that the range of the modern bomber is ever being increased.

During the past week many people in all parts of the nation have told me what they wanted me to say tonight. Almost all of them expressed a courageous desire to hear the plain truth about the gravity of the situation. One telegram, however, expressed the attitude of the small minority who want to see no evil and hear no evil, even though they know in their hearts that evil exists. That telegram begged me not to tell again of the ease with which our American cities could be bombed by any hostile power which had gained bases in this Western Hemisphere. The gist of that telegram was: "Please, Mr. President, don't frighten us by telling us the facts."

Frankly and definitely there is danger ahead—danger against which we must prepare. But we well know that we cannot escape danger, or the fear of danger, by crawling into bed and pulling the covers over our heads.

Some nations of Europe were bound by solemn nonintervention pacts with Germany. Other nations were assured by Germany that they need never fear invasion. Nonintervention pact or not, the fact remains that they were attacked, overrun, and thrown into the modern form of slavery at an hour's notice, or even without any notice at all. As an exiled leader of one of these nations said to me the other day—"The notice was a minus quantity. It was given to my government two hours after German troops had poured into my country in a hundred places."

The fate of these nations tells us what it means to live at the point of a Nazi gun.

The Nazis have justified such actions by various pious frauds. One of these frauds is the claim that they are occupying a nation for the purpose of "restoring order." Another is that they are occupying or controlling a nation on the excuse that they are "protecting it" against the aggression of somebody else.

For example, Germany has said that she was occupying Belgium to save the Belgians from the British. Would she then hesitate to say to any South American country, "We are occupying you to protect you from aggression by the United States"?

Belgium today is being used as an invasion base against Britain, now fighting for its life. Any South American country, in Nazi hands, would always constitute a jumping-off place for German attack on any one of the other republics of this hemisphere.

Analyze for yourselves the future of two other places even nearer to Germany if the Nazis won. Could Ireland hold out? Would Irish freedom be permitted as an amazing pet exception in an unfree world? Or the Islands of the Azores which still fly the flag of Portugal after five centuries? You and I think of Hawaii as an outpost of defense in the Pacific. And yet, the Azores are closer to our shores in the Atlantic than Hawaii is on the other side.

There are those who say that the Axis powers would never have any desire to attack the Western Hemisphere. That is the same dangerous form of wishful thinking which has destroyed the powers of resistance of so many conquered peoples. The plain facts are that the Nazis have proclaimed, time and again, that all other races are their inferiors and therefore subject to their orders. And most important of all, the vast resources and wealth of this American hemisphere constitute the most tempting loot in all the round world.

Let us no longer blind ourselves to the undeniable fact that the evil forces which have crushed and undermined and corrupted so many others are already within our own gates. Your government knows much about them and every day is ferreting them out.

Their secret emissaries are active in our own and in neighboring countries. They seek to stir up suspicion and dissension to cause internal strife. They try to turn capital against labor, and vice versa. They try to reawaken long slumbering racial and religious enmities which should have no place in this country. They are active in every group that promotes intolerance. They exploit for their own ends our natual abhorrence of war. These trouble-breeders have but one purpose. It is to divide our people into hostile groups and to destroy our unity and shatter our will to defend ourselves.

There are also American citizens, many of them in high places, who, unwittingly in most cases, are aiding and abetting the work of these agents. I do not charge these American citizens with being foreign agents. But I do charge them with doing exactly the kind of work that the dictators want done in the United States.

These people not only believe that we can save our own skins by shutting our eyes to the fate of other nations. Some of them go much further than that. They say that we can and should become the friends and even the partners of the Axis powers. Some of them even suggest that we should imitate the methods of the dictatorships. Americans never can and never will do that.

The experience of the past two years has proven beyond doubt that no nation can appease the Nazis. No man can tame a tiger into a kitten by stroking it. There can be no appeasement with ruthlessness. There can be no reasoning with an incendiary bomb. We know now that a nation can have peace with the Nazis only at the price of total surrender.

Even the people of Italy have been forced to become accomplices of the Nazis; but at this moment they do not know how soon they will be embraced to death by their allies.

The American appeasers ignore the warning to be found in the fate of Austria, Czechoslovakia, Poland, Norway, Belgium, the Netherlands, Denmark, and France. They tell you that the Axis powers are going to win anyway; that all this bloodshed in the world could be saved; that the United States might just as well throw its influence into the scale of a dictated peace, and get the best out of it that we can.

They call it a "negotiated peace." Nonsense! Is it a negotiated peace if a gang of outlaws surrounds your community and on threat of extermination makes you pay tribute to save your own skins?

Such a dictated peace would be no peace at all. It would be only another armistice, leading to the most gigantic armament race and the most devastating trade wars in all history. And in these contests the Americas would offer the only real resistance to the Axis powers.

With all their vaunted efficiency, with all their parade of pious purpose in this war, there are still in their background the concentration camp and the servants of God in chains.

The history of recent years proves that shootings and chains and concentration camps are not simply the transient tools but the very altars of modern dictatorships. They may talk of a "new order" in the world, but what they have in mind is only a revival of the oldest and the worst tyranny. In that there is no liberty, no religion, no hope.

The proposed "new order" is the very opposite of a United States of Europe or a United States of Asia. It is not a government based upon the consent of the governed. It is not a union of ordinary, self-respecting men and women to protect themselves and their freedom and their dignity from oppression. It is an unholy alliance of power and pelf to dominate and enslave the human race.

The British people and their allies today are conducting an active war against this unholy alliance. Our own future security is greatly dependent on the outcome of that fight. Our ability to "keep out of war" is going to be affected by that outcome.

Thinking in terms of today and tomorrow, I make the direct statement to the American people that there is far less chance of the United States getting into war, if we do all we can now to support the nations defending themselves against attack by the Axis than if we acquiesce in their defeat, submit tamely to an Axis victory, and wait our turn to be the object of attack in another war later on.

If we are to be completely honest with ourselves, we must admit that there is risk in any course we may take. But I deeply believe that the great majority of our people agree that the course that I advocate involves the least risk now and the greatest hope for world peace in the future.

The people of Europe who are defending themselves do not ask us to do their fighting. They ask us for the implements of war, the planes, the tanks, the guns, the freighters which will enable them to fight for their liberty and for our security. Emphatically we must get these weapons to them in sufficient volume and quickly enough, so that we and

our children will be saved the agony and suffering of war which others have had to endure.

Let not the defeatists tell us that it is too late. It will never be earlier. Tomorrow will be later than today.

Certain facts are self-evident.

In a military sense Great Britain and the British Empire are today the spearhead of resistance to world conquest. They are putting up a fight which will live forever in the story of human gallantry.

There is no demand for sending an American Expeditionary Force outside our own borders. There is no intention by any member of your government to send such a force. You can, therefore, nail any talk about sending armies to Europe as deliberate untruth.

Our national policy is not directed toward war. Its sole purpose is to keep war away from our country and our people.

Democracy's fight against world conquest is being greatly aided, and must be more greatly aided, by the rearmament of the United States and by sending every ounce and every ton of munitions and supplies that we can possibly spare to help the defenders who are in the front lines. It is no more unneutral for us to do that than it is for Sweden, Russia, and other nations near Germany, to send steel and ore and oil and other war materials into Germany every day in the week.

We are planning our own defense with the utmost urgency; and in its vast scale we must integrate the war needs of Britain and the other free nations which are resisting aggression.

This is not a matter of sentiment or of controversial personal opinion. It is a matter of realistic, practical military policy, based on the advice of our military experts who are in close touch with existing warfare. These military and naval experts and the members of the Congress and the administration have a single-minded purpose—the defense of the United States.

This nation is making a great effort to produce everything that is necessary in this emergency—and with all possible speed. This great effort requires great sacrifice.

I would ask no one to defend a democracy which in turn would not defend everyone in the nation against want and privation. The strength of this nation shall not be diluted by the failure of the government to protect the economic well-being of its citizens.

If our capacity to produce is limited by machines, it must ever be remembered that these machines are operated by the skill and the stamina of the workers. As the government is determined to protect the rights of the workers, so the nation has a right to expect that the men who man the machines will discharge their full responsibilities to the urgent needs of defense.

The worker possesses the same human dignity and is entitled to the same security of position as the engineer or the manager or the owner. For the workers provide the human power that turns out the destroyers, the airplanes and the tanks.

The nation expects our defense industries to continue operation without interruption by strikes or lock-outs. It expects and insists that management and workers will reconcile their differences by voluntary or legal means, to continue to produce the supplies that are so sorely needed.

And on the economic side of our great defense program, we are, as you know, bending every effort to maintain stability of prices and with that the stability of the cost of living.

Nine days ago I announced the setting up of a more effective organization to direct our gigantic efforts to increase the production of munitions. The appropriation of vast sums of money and a well-coordinated executive direction of our defense efforts are not in themselves enough. Guns, planes, ships, and many other things have to be built in the factories and arsenals of America. They have to be produced by workers and managers and engineers with the aid of machines which in turn have to be built by hundreds of thousands of workers throughout the land.

In this great work there has been splendid cooperation between the government and industry and labor; and I am very thankful.

American industrial genius, unmatched throughout the world in the solution of production problems, has been called upon to bring its resources and its talents into action. Manufacturers of watches, farm implements, linotypes, cash registers, automobiles, sewing machines, lawn mowers, and locomotives are now making fuses, bomb packing crates, telescope mounts, shells, pistols, and tanks.

But all our present efforts are not enough. We must have more ships, more guns, more planes—more of everything. This can only be accomplished if we discard the notion of "business as usual." This job cannot be done merely by superimposing on the existing productive facilities the added requirements of the nation for defense.

Our defense efforts must not be blocked by those who fear the future consequences of surplus plant capacity. The possible consequences of failure of our defense efforts now are much more to be feared.

After the present needs of our defenses are past, a proper handling of the country's peacetime needs will require all the new productive capacity—if not more.

No pessimistic policy about the future of America shall delay the immediate expansion of those industries essential to defense. We need them.

I want to make it clear that it is the purpose of the nation to build now with all possible speed every machine, every arsenal, every factory that we need to manufacture our defense material. We have the men—the skill—the wealth—and above all, the will.

I am confident that if and when production of consumer or luxury goods in certain industries requires the use of machines and raw materials that are essential for defense purposes, then such production must yield, and will gladly yield, to our primary and compelling purpose.

I appeal to the owners of plants—to the managers—to the workers—to our own government employees—to put every ounce of effort into producing these munitions swiftly and without stint. With this appeal I give you the pledge that all of us who are officers of your government will devote ourselves to the same wholehearted extent to the great task that lies ahead.

As planes and ships and guns and shells are produced, your government, with its defense experts, can then determine how best to use them to defend this hemisphere. The decision as to how much shall be sent abroad and how much shall remain at home must be made on the basis of our overall military necessities.

We must be the great arsenal of democracy. For us this is an emergency as serious as war itself. We must apply ourselves to our task with the same resolution, the same sense of urgency, the same spirit of patriotism and sacrifice as we would show were we at war.

We have furnished the British great material support and we will furnish far more in the future.

There will be no "bottlenecks" in our determination to aid Great Britain. No dictator, no combination of dictators, will weaken that determination by threats of how they will construe that determination.

The British have received invaluable military support from the heroic Greek army, and from the forces of all the governments in exile. Their strength is growing. It is the strength of men and women who value their freedom more highly than they value their lives.

I believe that the Axis powers are not going to win this war. I base that belief on the latest and best information.

We have no excuse for defeatism. We have every good reason for hope—hope for peace, hope for the defense of our civilization and for the building of a better civilization in the future.

I have the profound conviction that the American people are now determined to put forth a mightier effort than they have ever yet made to increase our production of all the implements of defense, to meet the threat to our democratic faith.

As president of the United States I call for that national effort. I call for it in the name of this nation which we love and honor and which we are privileged and proud to serve. I call upon our people with absolute confidence that our common cause will greatly succeed.

The Four Freedoms

Eighth Annual Message to Congress
Washington, D.C.
January 6, 1941

ADDRESSING THE NEW 77th Congress, Roosevelt pushed further for American opposition to fascism. This stirring speech, one of Roosevelt's finest, explicitly linked the hard choices faced by the nation in domestic and foreign policy with the very survival of democratic freedom, a situation he claimed was "unique in our history."

I address you, the members of the 77th Congress, at a moment unprecedented in the history of the Union. I use the word unprecedented, because at no previous time has American security been as seriously threatened from without as it is today.

Since the permanent formation of our government under the Constitution, in 1789, most of the periods of crisis in our history have related to our domestic affairs. Fortunately, only one of these—the four-year war between the states—ever threatened our national unity. Today, thank God, 130 million Americans, in 48 states, have forgotten points of the compass in our national unity.

It is true that prior to 1914 the United States often had been disturbed by events in other continents. We had even engaged in two wars with European nations and in a number of undeclared wars in the West Indies, in the Mediterranean, and in the Pacific for the maintenance of American rights and for the principles of peaceful commerce. In no case, however, had a serious threat been raised against our national safety or our independence.

What I seek to convey is the historic truth that the United States as a nation has at all times maintained opposition to any attempt to lock us in behind an ancient Chinese wall while the procession of civilization went past. Today, thinking of our children and their children, we oppose enforced isolation for ourselves or for any part of the Americas.

That determination of ours was proved, for example, during the quarter century of wars following the French Revolution.

While the Napoleonic struggles did threaten interests of the United States because of the French foothold in the West Indies and in Louisiana, and while we engaged in the War of 1812 to vindicate our right to peaceful trade, it is, nevertheless, clear that neither France nor Great Britain nor any other nation was aiming at domination of the whole world.

In like fashion from 1815 to 1914—99 years—no single war in Europe or in Asia constituted a real threat against our future or against the future of any other American nation.

Except in the Maximilian interlude in Mexico, no foreign power sought to establish itself in this hemisphere; and the strength of the British fleet in the Atlantic has been a friendly strength. It is still a friendly strength.

Even when the World War broke out in 1914, it seemed to contain only small threat of danger to our own American future. But, as time went on, the American people began to visualize what the downfall of democratic nations might mean to our own democracy.

We need not over-emphasize imperfections in the Peace of Versailles. We need not harp on failure of the democracies to deal with problems of world reconstruction. We should remember that the Peace of 1919 was far less unjust than the kind of "pacification" which began even before Munich, and which is being carried on under the new order of tyranny that seeks to spread over every continent today. The American people have unalterably set their faces against that tyranny.

Every realist knows that the democratic way of life is at this moment being directly assailed in every part of the world—assailed either by arms, or by secret spreading of poisonous propaganda by those who seek to destroy unity and promote discord in nations still at peace.

During 16 months this assault has blotted out the whole pattern of democratic life in an appalling number of independent nations, great and small. The assailants are still on the march, threatening other nations, great and small.

Therefore, as your president, performing my constitutional duty to "give to the Congress information of the state of the Union," I find it necessary to report that the future and the safety of our country and of our democracy are overwhelmingly involved in events far beyond our borders.

Armed defense of democratic existence is now being gallantly waged in four continents. If that defense fails, all the population and all the resources of Europe, Asia, Africa, and Australasia will be dominated by the conquerors. The total of those populations and their resources greatly exceeds the sum total of the population and resources of the whole of the Western Hemisphere—many times over.

In times like these it is immature—and incidentally untrue—for anybody to brag that an unprepared America, single-handed, and with one hand tied behind its back, can hold off the whole world.

No realistic American can expect from a dictator's peace international generosity, or return of true independence, or world disarmament, or freedom of expression, or freedom of religion—or even good business.

Such a peace would bring no security for us or for our neighbors. "Those, who would give up essential liberty to purchase a little temporary safety, deserve neither liberty nor safety."

As a nation we may take pride in the fact that we are soft-hearted; but we cannot afford to be soft-headed.

We must always be wary of those who with sounding brass and a tinkling cymbal preach the "ism" of appeasement.

We must especially beware of that small group of selfish men who would clip the wings of the American eagle in order to feather their own nests.

I have recently pointed out how quickly the tempo of modern warfare could bring into our very midst the physical attack which we must expect if the dictator nations win this war.

There is much loose talk of our immunity from immediate and direct invasion from across the seas. Obviously, as long as the British navy retains its power, no such danger exists. Even if there were no British navy, it is not probable that any enemy would be stupid enough to attack us by landing troops in the United States from across thousands of miles of ocean, until it had acquired strategic bases from which to operate.

But we learn much from the lessons of the past years in Europe—particularly the lesson of Norway, whose essential seaports were captured by treachery and surprise built up over a series of years.

The first phase of the invasion of this hemisphere would not be the landing of regular troops. The necessary strategic points would be occupied by secret agents and their dupes—and great numbers of them are already here, and in Latin America.

As long as the aggressor nations maintain the offensive, they—not we—will choose the time and the place and the method of their attack.

That is why the future of all American republics is today in serious danger.

That is why this annual message to the Congress is unique in our history.

That is why every member of the executive branch of the government and every member of the Congress faces great responsibility—and great accountability.

The need of the moment is that our actions and our policy should be devoted primarily—almost exclusively—to meeting this foreign peril. For all our domestic problems are now a part of the great emergency.

Just as our national policy in internal affairs has been based upon a decent respect for the rights and dignity of all our fellow men within our gates, so our national policy in foreign affairs has been based on a decent respect for the rights and dignity of all nations, large and small. And the justice of morality must and will win in the end.

Our national policy is this:

First, by an impressive expression of the public will and without regard to partisanship, we are committed to all-inclusive national defense.

Second, by an impressive expression of the public will and without regard to partisanship, we are committed to full support of all those resolute peoples, everywhere, who are resisting aggression and are thereby keeping war away from our hemisphere. By this support, we express our determination that the democratic cause shall prevail; and we strengthen the defense and security of our own nation.

Third, by an impressive expression of the public will and without regard to partisanship we are committed to the proposition that principles of morality and considerations for our own security will never permit us to acquiesce in a peace dictated by aggressors and sponsored by appeasers. We know that enduring peace cannot be bought at the cost of other people's freedom.

In the recent national election there was no substantial difference between the two great parties in respect to that national policy. No issue was fought out on this line before the American electorate. Today, it is abundantly evident that American citizens everywhere are demanding and supporting speedy and complete action in recognition of obvious danger.

Therefore, the immediate need is a swift and driving increase in our armament production.

Leaders of industry and labor have responded to our summons. Goals of speed have been set. In some cases these goals are being reached ahead of time; in some cases we are on schedule; in other cases there are slight but not serious delays; and in some cases—and I am sorry to say very important cases—we are all concerned by the slowness of the accomplishment of our plans.

The army and navy, however, have made substantial progress during the past year. Actual experience is improving and speeding up our methods of production with every passing day. And today's best is not good enough for tomorrow.

I am not satisfied with the progress thus far made. The men in charge of the program represent the best in training, ability, and patriotism. They are not satisfied with the progress thus far made. None of us will be satisfied until the job is done.

No matter whether the original goal was set too high or too low, our objective is quicker and better results.

To give two illustrations:

We are behind schedule in turning out finished airplanes; we are working day and night to solve the innumerable problems and to catch up.

We are ahead of schedule in building warships; but we are working to get even further ahead of schedule.

To change a whole nation from a basis of peacetime production of implements of peace to a basis of wartime production of implements of war is no small task. And the greatest difficulty comes at the beginning of the program, when new tools and plant facilities and new assembly lines and ship ways must first be constructed before the actual material begins to flow steadily and speedily from them.

The Congress, of course, must rightly keep itself informed at all times of the progress of the program. However, there is certain information, as the Congress itself will readily recognize, which, in the interests of our own security and those of the nations we are supporting, must needs be kept in confidence.

New circumstances are constantly begetting new needs for our safety. I shall ask this Congress for greatly increased new appropriations and authorizations to carry on what we have begun.

I also ask this Congress for authority and for funds sufficient to manufacture additional munitions and war supplies of many kinds, to be turned over to those nations which are now in actual war with aggressor nations.

Our most useful and immediate role is to act as an arsenal for them as well as for ourselves. They do not need man power They do need billions of dollars worth of the weapons of defense.

The time is near when they will not be able to pay for them in ready cash. We cannot, and will not, tell them they must surrender, merely because of present inability to pay for the weapons which we know they must have.

I do not recommend that we make them a loan of dollars with which to pay for these weapons—a loan to be repaid in dollars.

I recommend that we make it possible for those nations to continue to obtain war materials in the United States, fitting their orders into our own program. Nearly all of their matériel would, if the time ever came, be useful for our own defense.

Taking counsel of expert military and naval authorities, considering what is best for our own security, we are free to decide how much should be kept here and how much should be sent abroad to our friends who by their determined and heroic resistance are giving us time in which to make ready our own defense.

For what we send abroad, we shall be repaid, within a reasonable time following the close of hostilities, in similar materials, or, at our option, in other goods of many kinds which they can produce and which we need.

Let us say to the democracies: "We Americans are vitally concerned in your defense of freedom. We are putting forth our energies, our resources and our organizing powers to give you the strength to regain and maintain a free world. We shall send you, in ever-increasing numbers, ships, planes, tanks, guns. This is our purpose and our pledge."

In fulfillment of this purpose we will not be intimidated by the threats of dictators that they will regard as a breach of international law and as an act of war our aid to the democracies which dare to resist their aggression. Such aid is not an act of war, even if a dictator should unilaterally proclaim it so to be.

When the dictators are ready to make war upon us, they will not wait for an act of war on our part. They did not wait for Norway or Belgium or the Netherlands to commit an act of war.

Their only interest is in a new one-way international law, which lacks mutuality in its observance, and, therefore, becomes an instrument of oppression.

The happiness of future generations of Americans may well depend upon how effective and how immediate we can make our aid felt. No one can tell the exact character of the emergency situations that we may be called upon to meet. The nation's hands must not be tied when the nation's life is in danger.

We must all prepare to make the sacrifices that the emergency—as serious as war itself—demands. Whatever stands in the way of speed and efficiency in defense preparations must give way to the national need.

A free nation has the right to expect full cooperation from all groups. A free nation has the right to look to the leaders of business, of labor, and of agriculture to take the lead in stimulating effort, not among other groups but within their own groups.

The best way of dealing with the few slackers or trouble makers in our midst is, first, to shame them by patriotic example, and, if that fails, to use the sovereignty of government to save government.

As men do not live by bread alone, they do not fight by armaments alone. Those who man our defenses, and those behind them who build our defenses, must have the stamina and courage which come from an unshakeable belief in the manner of life which they are defending. The mighty action which we are calling for,

cannot be based on a disregard of all things worth fighting for.

The nation takes great satisfaction and much strength from the things which have been done to make its people conscious of their individual stake in the preservation of democratic life in America. Those things have toughened the fibre of our people, have renewed their faith and strengthened their devotion to the institutions we make ready to protect.

Certainly this is no time to stop thinking about the social and economic problems which are the root cause of the social revolution which is today a supreme factor in the world.

There is nothing mysterious about the foundations of a healthy and strong democracy. The basic things expected by our people of their political and economic systems are simple. They are:

- Equality of opportunity for youth and for others.
- Jobs for those who can work.
- Security for those who need it.
- The ending of special privilege for the few.
- The preservation of civil liberties for all.
- The enjoyment of the fruits of scientific progress in a wider and constantly rising standard of living.

These are the simple and basic things that must never be lost sight of in the turmoil and unbelievable complexity of our modern world. The inner and abiding strength of our economic and political systems is dependent upon the degree to which they fulfill these expectations.

Many subjects connected with our social economy call for immediate improvement.

As examples:

We should bring more citizens under the coverage of old-age pensions and unemployment insurance.

We should widen the opportunities for adequate medical care.

We should plan a better system by which persons deserving or needing gainful employment may obtain it.

I have called for personal sacrifice. I am assured of the willingness of almost all Americans to respond to that call.

A part of the sacrifice means the payment of more money in taxes. In my budget message I recommend that a greater portion of this great defense program be paid for from taxation than we are paying today. No person should try, or be allowed, to get rich out of this program; and the principle of tax payments in accordance with ability to pay should be constantly before our eyes to guide our legislation.

If the Congress maintains these principles, the voters, putting patriotism ahead of pocketbooks, will give you their applause.

In the future days, which we seek to make secure, we look forward to a world founded upon four essential human freedoms.

The first is freedom of speech and expression—everywhere in the world.

The second is freedom of every person to worship God in his own way—everywhere in the world.

The third is freedom from want—which, translated into world terms, means economic understandings which will secure to every nation a healthy peacetime life for its inhabitants—everywhere in the world.

The fourth is freedom from fear—which, translated into world terms, means a worldwide reduction of armaments to such a point and in such a thorough fashion that no nation will be in a position to commit an act of physical aggression against any neighbor—anywhere in the world.

That is no vision of a distant millennium. It is a definite basis for a kind of world attainable in our own time and generation. That kind of world is the very antithesis of the so-called new order of tyranny which the dictators seek to create with the crash of a bomb.

To that new order we oppose the greater conception—the moral order. A good society is able to face schemes of world domination and foreign revolutions alike without fear.

Since the beginning of our American history we have been engaged in change—in a perpetual peaceful revolution—a revolution which goes on steadily, quietly adjusting itself to changing conditions—without the concentration camp or the quick-lime in the ditch. The world order which we seek is the cooperation of free countries, working together in a friendly, civilized society.

This nation has placed its destiny in the hands and heads and hearts of its millions of free men and women; and its faith in freedom under the guidance of God. Freedom means the supremacy of human rights everywhere. Our support goes to those who struggle to gain those rights or keep them. Our strength is in our unity of purpose.

To that high concept there can be no end save victory.

Day of Infamy

Washington, D.C.

December 8, 1941

THE JAPANESE ATTACK on Pearl Harbor on December 7 stunned Roosevelt. A great admirer and booster of the navy since his tenure as assistant naval secretary (he sometimes signed his letters to Churchill "the Former Naval Person"), the president was shocked at how vulnerable the service had allowed itself to become—most of the capital ships had been lost while still at their moorings. And although it had long been clear that Japanese expansionism posed a threat to the U.S. presence in the Pacific, that threat had been consistently underestimated by the administration. No one, including the president, had taken the possibility of a Japanese attack seriously.

Roosevelt drafted this famous speech to Congress himself, with some assistance from his chief aide, Harry Hopkins. The president was met with a standing ovation as he appeared in the House chamber. After half an hour of deliberation, Congress declared war on Japan. In Berlin, Hitler promptly issued a declaration of war against the United States, contemptuously calling Roosevelt "mad" and "the main culprit of this war." Congress answered this with its own unanimous call for war on Germany. The United States, reeling from its defeats in the Pacific and still not at full wartime production capacity, now faced a two-front conflict.

Yesterday, December 7, 1941—a date which will live in infamy—the United States of America was suddenly and deliberately attacked by naval and air forces of the Empire of Japan.

The United States was at peace with that nation and, at the solicitation of Japan, was still in conversation with its government and its emperor looking toward the maintenance of peace in the Pacific. Indeed, one hour after Japanese air squadrons had commenced bombing in Oahu, the Japanese ambassador to the United States and his colleague delivered to the secretary of state a formal reply to a recent American message. While this reply stated that it seemed useless to continue the existing diplomatic negotiations, it contained no threat or hint of war or armed attack.

It will be recorded that the distance of Hawaii from Japan makes it obvious that the attack was deliberately planned many days or even weeks ago. During the intervening time the Japanese government had deliberately sought to deceive the United States by false statements and expressions of hope for continued peace.

The attack yesterday on the Hawaiian Islands has caused severe damage to American naval and military forces. Very many American lives have been lost. In addition American ships have been reported torpedoed on the high seas between San Francisco and Honolulu.

Yesterday the Japanese government also launched an attack against Malaya.

Last night Japanese forces attacked Hong Kong.

Last night Japanese forces attacked Guam.

Last night Japanese forces attacked the Philippine Islands.

Last night the Japanese attacked Wake Island.

This morning the Japanese attacked Midway Island.

Japan has, therefore, undertaken a surprise offensive extending throughout the Pacific area. The facts of yesterday speak for themselves. The people of the United States have already formed their opinions and well understand the implications to the very life and safety of our nation.

As commander in chief of the army and navy I have directed that all measures be taken for our defense.

Always will we remember the character of the onslaught against us.

No matter how long it may take us to overcome this premeditated invasion, the American people in their righteous might will win through to absolute victory.

I believe I interpret the will of the Congress and of the people when I assert that we will not only defend ourselves to the uttermost but will make very certain that this form of treachery shall never endanger us again.

Hostilities exist. There is no blinking at the fact that our people, our territory, and our interests are in grave danger.

With confidence in our armed forces—with the unbounded determination of our people—we will gain the inevitable triumph—so help us God.

I ask that the Congress declare that since the unprovoked and dastardly attack by Japan on Sunday, December 7, a state of war has existed between the United States and the Japanese Empire.

Gearing for War

Ninth Annual Message to Congress
Washington, D.C.
January 6, 1942

A MONTH AFTER Pearl Harbor the country was just awakening to what a full war effort would entail. Roosevelt brought it home in his ninth annual message. Describing the war in biblical terms as a struggle between good and evil, freedom and perpetual bondage, he asked for major and continuous increases in the manufacture of armaments, increased taxes and new bond issues, and self-sacrifice by every citizen.

In fulfilling my duty to report upon the state of the Union, I am proud to say to you that the spirit of the American people was never higher than it is today—the Union was never more closely knit together—this country was never more deeply determined to face the solemn tasks before it.

The response of the American people has been instantaneous. It will be sustained until our security is assured.

Exactly one year ago today I said to this Congress: "When the dictators are ready to make war upon us, they will not wait for an act of war on our part. They—not we—will choose the time and the place and the method of their attack."

We now know their choice of the time. A peaceful Sunday morning—December 7, 1941.

We know their choice of the place. An American outpost in the Pacific.

We know their choice of the method. The method of Hitler himself.

Japan's scheme of conquest goes back half a century. It was not merely a policy of seeking living room; it was a plan which included the subjugation of all the peoples in the Far East and in the islands of the Pacific, and the domination of that ocean by Japanese military and naval control of the western coasts of North, Central, and South America.

The development of this ambitious conspiracy was marked by the war against China in 1894; the subsequent occupation of Korea; the war against Russia in 1904; the illegal fortification of the mandated Pacific Islands following 1920; the seizure of Manchuria in 1931; and the invasion of China in 1937.

A similar policy of criminal conquest was adopted by Italy. The fascists first revealed their imperial designs in Libya and Tripoli. In 1935 they seized Abyssinia. Their goal was the domination of all North Africa, Egypt, parts of France, and the entire Mediterranean world.

But the dreams of empire of the Japanese and fascist leaders were modest in comparison with the gargantuan aspirations of Hitler and his Nazis. Even before they came to power in 1933, their plans for conquest had been drawn. Those plans provided for ultimate domination, not of any one section of the world, but of the whole earth and all the oceans on it.

With Hitler's formation of the Berlin-Rome-Tokyo alliance, all these plans of conquest became a single plan. Under this, in addition to her own schemes of conquest, Japan's role was to cut off our supply of weapons of war to Britain, Russia, and China—weapons which increasingly were speeding the day of Hitler's doom. The act of Japan at Pearl Harbor was intended to stun us—to terrify us to such an extent that we would divert our industrial and military strength to the Pacific area, or even to our own continental defense.

The plan failed in its purpose. We have not been stunned. We have not been terrified or confused. This reassembling of the 77th Congress is proof of that; for the mood of quiet, grim resolution which here prevails, bodes ill for those who conspired and collaborated to murder world peace.

That mood is stronger than any mere desire for revenge. It expresses the will of the American people to make very certain that the world will never so suffer again.

Admittedly, we have been faced with hard choices. It was bitter, for example, not to be able to relieve the heroic and historic defenders of Wake Island. It was bitter for us not to be able to land a million men and a thousand ships in the Philippine Islands.

But this adds only to our determination to see to it that the Stars and Stripes will fly again over Wake and Guam; and that the brave people of the Philippines will be rid of Japanese imperialism; and will live in freedom, security, and independence.

Powerful and offensive actions must and will be taken in proper time. The consolidation of the United Nations' total war effort against our common enemies is being achieved.

That is the purpose of conferences which have been held during the past two weeks in Washington, in Moscow, and in Chungking. That is the primary objective of the declaration of solidarity signed in Washington on January 1, 1942, by 26 nations united against the Axis powers.

Difficult choices may have to be made in the months to come. We will not shrink from such decisions. We and those united with us will make those decisions with courage and determination.

Plans have been laid here and in the other capitals for coordinated and cooperative action by all the united nations—military action and economic action. Already we have established unified command of land, sea, and air forces in the southwestern Pacific theater of war. There will be a continuation of conferences and consultations among military staffs, so that the plans and operations of each will fit into a general strategy designed to crush the enemy. We shall not fight isolated wars—each nation going its own way. These 26 nations are united—not in spirit and determination alone, but in the broad conduct of the war in all its phases.

For the first time since the Japanese and the fascists and the Nazis started along their bloodstained course of conquest they now face the fact that superior forces are assembling against them. Gone forever are the days when the aggressors could attack and destroy their victims one by one without unity of resistance. We of the united nations will so dispose our forces that we can strike at the common enemy wherever the greatest damage can be done.

The militarists in Berlin and Tokyo started this war. But the massed, angered forces of common humanity will finish it.

Destruction of the material and spiritual centers of civilization—this has been and still is the purpose of Hitler and his Italian and Japanese chessmen. They would wreck the power of the British Commonwealth and Russia and China and the Netherlands—and then combine all their forces to achieve their ultimate goal, the conquest of the United States.

They know that victory for us means victory for freedom.

They know that victory for us means victory for the institution of democracy—the ideal of the family, the simple principles of common decency and humanity.

They know that victory for us means victory for religion.

And they could not tolerate that. The world is too small to provide adequate "living room" for both Hitler and God. In proof of that, the Nazis have now announced their plan for enforcing their new German, pagan religion throughout the world—the plan by which the Holy Bible and the Cross of Mercy would be displaced by Mein Kampf and the swastika and the naked sword.

Our own objectives are clear; the objective of smashing the militarism imposed by war lords upon their enslaved peoples—the objective of liberating the subjugated nations—the objective of establishing and securing freedom of speech, freedom of religion, freedom from want, and freedom from fear everywhere in the world.

We shall not stop short of these objectives—nor shall we be satisfied merely to gain them and then call it a day. I know that I speak for the American people—and I have good reason to believe I speak also for all the other peoples who fight with us—when I say that this time we are determined not only to win the war, but also to maintain the security of the peace which will follow.

But modern methods of warfare make it a task, not only of shooting and fighting, but an even more urgent one of working and producing.

Victory requires the actual weapons of war and the means of transporting them to a dozen points of combat.

It will not be sufficient for us and the other united nations to produce a slightly superior supply of munitions to that of Germany, Japan, Italy, and the stolen industries in the countries which they have overrun.

The superiority of the united nations in munitions and ships must be overwhelming—so overwhelming that the Axis nations can never hope to catch up with it. In order to attain this overwhelming superiority the

United States must build planes and tanks and guns and ships to the utmost limit of our national capacity. We have the ability and capacity to produce arms not only for our own forces, but also for the armies, navies, and air forces fighting on our side.

And our overwhelming superiority of armament must be adequate to put weapons of war at the proper time into the hands of those men in the conquered nations, who stand ready to seize the first opportunity to revolt against their German and Japanese oppressors, and against the traitors in their own ranks, known by the already infamous name of "Quislings." As we get guns to the patriots in those lands, they, too, will fire shots heard round the world.

This production of ours in the United States must be raised far above its present levels, even though it will mean the dislocation of the lives and occupations of millions of our own people. We must raise our sights all along the production line. Let no man say it cannot be done. It must be done—and we have undertaken to do it.

I have just sent a letter of directive to the appropriate departments and agencies of our government, ordering that immediate steps be taken:

1. To increase our production rate of airplanes so rapidly that in this year, 1942, we shall produce 60,000 planes, 10,000 more than the goal set a year and a half ago. This includes 45,000 combat planes—bombers, dive-bombers, pursuit planes. The rate of increase will be continued, so that next year, 1943, we shall produce 125,000 airplanes, including 100,000 combat planes.

2. To increase our production rate of tanks so rapidly that in this year, 1942, we shall produce 45,000 tanks; and to continue that increase so that next year, 1943, we shall produce 75,000 tanks.

3. To increase our production rate of antiaircraft guns so rapidly that in this year, 1942, we shall produce 20,000 of them; and to continue that increase so that next year, 1943, we shall produce 35,000 antiaircraft guns.

4. To increase our production rate of merchant ships so rapidly that in this year, 1942, we shall build 8,000,000 deadweight tons as compared with a 1941 production of 1,100,000. We shall continue that increase so that next year, 1943, we shall build 10,000,000 tons.

These figures and similar figures for a multitude of other implements of war will give the Japanese and Nazis a little idea of just what they accomplished in the attack on Pearl Harbor.

Our task is hard—our task is unprecedented—and the time is short. We must strain every existing armament-producing facility to the utmost. We must convert every available plant and tool to war production. That goes all the way from the greatest plants to the smallest—from the huge automobile industry to the village machine shop.

Production for war is based on men and women—the human hands and brains which collectively we call Labor. Our workers stand ready to work long hours; to turn out more in a day's work; to keep the wheels turning and the fires burning 24 hours a day, and seven days a week. They realize well that on the speed and efficiency of their work depend the lives of their sons and their brothers on the fighting fronts.

Production for war is based on metals and raw materials—steel, copper, rubber, aluminum, zinc, tin. Greater and greater quantities of them will have to be diverted to war purposes. Civilian use of them will have to be cut further and still further—and, in many cases, completely eliminated.

War costs money. So far, we have hardly even begun to pay for it. We have devoted only 15 percent of our national income to national defense. As will appear in my budget message tomorrow, our war program for the coming fiscal year will cost 56 billion dollars, or, in other words, more than one-half of the estimated annual national income. This means taxes and bonds and bonds and taxes. It means cutting luxuries and other nonessentials. In a word, it means an "all-out" war by individual effort and family effort in a united country.

Only this all-out scale of production will hasten the ultimate all-out victory. Speed will count. Lost ground can always be regained—lost time never. Speed will save lives; speed will save this nation which is in peril; speed will save our freedom and civilization—and slowness has never been an American characteristic.

As the United States goes into its full stride, we must always be on guard against misconceptions which will arise naturally or which will be planted among us by our enemies.

We must guard against complacency. We must not underrate the enemy. He is powerful and cunning—and cruel and ruthless. He will stop at nothing which gives him a chance to kill and to destroy. He has trained his people to believe that their highest perfection is achieved by waging war. For many years he has prepared for this very conflict—planning, plotting, training, arming, fighting. We have already tasted defeat. We may suffer further setbacks. We must face the fact of a hard war, a long war, a bloody war, a costly war.

We must, on the other hand, guard against defeatism. That has been one of the chief weapons of Hitler's propaganda machine— used time and again with deadly results. It will not be used successfully on the American people.

We must guard against divisions among ourselves and among all the other united nations. We must be particularly vigilant against racial discrimination in any of its ugly forms. Hitler will try again to breed mistrust and suspicion between one individual and another, one group and another, one race and another, one government and another. He will try to use the same technique of falsehood and rumormongering with which he divided France from Britain. He is trying to do this with us even now. But he will find a unity of will and purpose against him, which will persevere until the destruction of all his black designs upon the freedom and safety of the people of the world.

We cannot wage this war in a defensive spirit. As our power and our resources are fully mobilized, we shall carry the attack against the enemy—we shall hit him and hit him again wherever and whenever we can reach him.

We must keep him far from our shores, for we intend to bring this battle to him on his own home grounds.

American armed forces must be used at any place in all the world where it seems advisable to engage the forces of the enemy. In some cases these operations will be defensive, in order to protect key positions. In other cases, these operations will be offensive, in order to strike at the common enemy, with a view to his complete encirclement and eventual total defeat.

American armed forces will operate at many points in the Far East.

American armed forces will be on all the oceans—helping to guard the essential communications which are vital to the united nations.

American land and air and sea forces will take stations in the British Isles—which constitute an essential fortress in this world struggle.

American armed forces will help to protect this hemisphere—and also bases outside this hemisphere, which could be used for an attack on the Americas.

If any of our enemies, from Europe or from Asia, attempt long-range raids by "suicide" squadrons of bombing planes, they will do so only in the hope of terrorizing our people and disrupting our morale. Our people are not afraid of that. We know that we may have to pay a heavy price for freedom. We will pay this price with a will. Whatever the price, it is a thousand times worth it. No matter what our enemies in their desperation may attempt to do to us—we will say, as the people of London have said, "We can take it." And what's more, we can give it back—and we will give it back— with compound interest.

When our enemies challenged our country to stand up and fight, they challenged each and every one of us. And each and every one of us has accepted the challenge—for himself and for the nation.

There were only some 400 United States marines who in the heroic and historic defense of Wake Island inflicted such great losses on the enemy. Some of those men were killed in action: and others are now prisoners of war. When the survivors of that great fight are liberated and restored to their homes, they will learn that 130 million of their fellow citizens have been inspired to render their own full share of service and sacrifice.

Our men on the fighting fronts have already proved that Americans today are just as rugged and just as tough as any of the heroes whose exploits we celebrate on the Fourth of July.

Many people ask, "When will this war end?" There is only one answer to that. It will end just as soon as we make it end, by our combined efforts, our combined strength, our combined determination to fight through and work through until the end—the end of militarism in Germany and Italy and Japan. Most certainly we shall not settle for less.

That is the spirit in which discussions have been conducted during the visit of the British prime minister to Washington. Mr. Churchill and I understand each other, our motives, and our purposes. Together, during the past two weeks, we have faced squarely the major military and economic problems of this greatest world war.

All in our nation have been cheered by Mr. Churchill's visit. We have been deeply stirred by his great message to us. We wish him a safe return to his home. He is welcome in our midst, now and in days to come.

We are fighting on the same side with the British people, who fought alone for long, terrible months, and withstood the enemy with fortitude and tenacity and skill.

We are fighting on the same side with the Russian people who have seen the Nazi hordes swarm up to the very gates of Moscow, and who with almost superhuman will and courage have forced the invaders back into retreat.

We are fighting on the same side as the brave people of China who for four and a half long years have withstood bombs and starvation and have whipped the invaders time and again in spite of superior Japanese equipment and arms.

We are fighting on the same side as the indomitable Dutch.

We are fighting on the same side as all the other governments in exile, whom Hitler and all his armies and all his Gestapo have not been able to conquer.

But we of the united nations are not making all this sacrifice of human effort and human lives to return to the kind of world we had after the last World War.

We are fighting today for security, for progress, and for peace, not only for ourselves, but for all men, not only for one generation but for all generations. We are fighting to cleanse the world of ancient evils, ancient ills.

Our enemies are guided by brutal cynicism, by unholy contempt for the human race. We are inspired by a faith which goes back through all the years to the first chapter of the Book of Genesis: "God created man in His own image."

We on our side are striving to be true to that divine heritage. We are fighting as our fathers have fought, to uphold the doctrine that all men are equal in the sight of God. Those on the other side are striving to destroy this deep belief and to create a world in their own image—a world of tyranny and cruelty and serfdom.

That is the conflict that day and night now pervades our lives. No compromise can end that conflict. There never has been—there never can be—successful compromise between good and evil. Only total victory can reward the champions of tolerance and decency and freedom and faith.

Campaign Speech

Washington, D.C.

September 23, 1944

As THE 1944 PRESIDENTIAL contest gathered momentum, rumors began to circulate that Roosevelt was too ill to campaign—rumors that had some basis in truth. After 12 years in the executive office, his health was failing. For most of the summer the president showed little enthusiasm for or interest in the forthcoming election. Immediately after the Democratic convention he left on an extended tour of the Pacific theater. But by September he realized that his urbane Republican opponent, Thomas E. Dewey, was gaining ground. FDR disliked Dewey and was stung by a number of false stories put out by the Republicans, especially one that claimed he had sent a destroyer back to pick up his dog, Fala, who had been left behind on one of the Aleutian Islands during the president's recent trip.

This speech, the first of five major campaign speeches, was given at a dinner for the International Teamsters Union. Roosevelt rebutted the rumors and stories with characteristic showmanship. Samuel Rosenman noted that the impact of this speech was "smashing." It "left little doubt in the minds of the president's friends, and his enemies, that he had lost none of his skill as a campaigner and political speaker. Roosevelt in this speech was at his vigorous best—taunting his opposition for their reactionary record, ridiculing their misstatements, and inspiring his followers."

Well, here we are together again—after four years—and what years they have been! You know, I am actually four years older, which is a fact that seems to annoy some people. In fact, in the mathematical field there are millions of Americans who are more than 11 years older than when we started in to clear up the mess that was dumped in our laps in 1933.

We all know that certain people who make it a practice to depreciate the accomplishments of labor—who even attack labor as unpatriotic—they keep this up usually for three years and six months in a row. But then, for some strange reason they change their tune—every four years—just before election day. When votes are at stake, they suddenly discover that they really love labor and that they are anxious to protect labor from its old friends.

I got quite a laugh, for example—and I am sure that you did—when I read this plank in the Republican platform adopted at their National Convention in Chicago last July:

The Republican Party accepts the purposes of the National Labor Relations Act, the Wage and Hour Act, the Social Security Act, and all other federal statutes designed to promote and protect the welfare of American working men and women, and we promise a fair and just administration of these laws.

You know, many of the Republican leaders and Congressmen and candidates, who shouted enthusiastic approval of that plank in that Convention Hall would not even recognize these progressive laws if they met them in broad daylight. Indeed, they have personally spent years of effort and energy—and much money—in fighting every one of those laws in the Congress, and in the press, and in the courts, ever since this administration began to advocate them and enact them into legislation. That is a fair example of their insincerity and of their inconsistency.

The whole purpose of Republican oratory these days seems to be to switch labels. The object is to persuade the American people that the Democratic Party was responsible for the 1929 crash and the Depression, and that the Republican Party was responsible for all social progress under the New Deal.

Now, imitation may be the sincerest form of flattery—but I am afraid that in this case it is the most obvious common or garden variety of fraud.

Of course, it is perfectly true that there are enlightened, liberal elements in the Republican Party, and they have fought hard and honorably to bring the party up to date and to get it in step with the forward march of American progress. But these liberal elements were not able to drive the Old Guard Republicans from their entrenched positions.

Can the Old Guard pass itself off as the New Deal?

I think not.

We have all seen many marvelous stunts in the circus but no performing elephant could turn a hand-spring without falling flat on his back.

I need not recount to you the centuries of history which have been crowded into these four years since I saw you last.

There were some—in the Congress and out—who raised their voices against our preparations for defense—before and after 1939—objected to them, raised their voices against them as hysterical war mongering, who cried out against our help to the Allies as provocative and dangerous. We remember the voices. They would like to have us forget them now. But in 1940 and 1941—my, it seems a long time ago—they were loud voices. Happily they were a minority and—fortunately for ourselves, and for the world—they could not stop America.

There are some politicians who kept their heads buried deep in the sand while the storms of Europe and Asia were headed our way, who said that the Lend-Lease bill "would bring an end to free government in the United States," and who said, "only hysteria entertains the idea that Germany, Italy, or Japan contemplates war on us." These very men are now asking the American people to intrust to them the conduct of our foreign policy and our military policy.

What the Republican leaders are now saying in effect is this: "Oh, just forget what we used to say, we have changed our minds now—we have been reading the public opinion polls about these things and now we know what the American people want." And they say: "Don't leave the task of making the peace to those old men who first urged it and who have already laid the foundations for it, and who have had to fight all of us inch by inch during the last five years to do it. Why, just turn it all over to us. We'll do it so skillfully that we won't lose a single isolationist vote or a single isolationist campaign contribution."

I think there is one thing that you know: I am too old for that. I cannot talk out of both sides of my mouth at the same time.

The government welcomes all sincere supporters of the cause of effective world collaboration in the making of a lasting peace. Millions of Republicans all over the nation are with us—and have been with us—in our unshakable determination to build the solid structure of peace. And they too will resent this campaign talk by those who first woke up to the facts of international life a few short months ago when they began to study the polls of public opinion.

Those who today have the military responsibility for waging this war in all parts of the globe are not helped by the statements of men who, without reponsibility and without the knowledge of the facts, lecture the Chiefs of Staff of the United States as to the best means of dividing our armed forces and our military resources between the Atlantic and Pacific, between the army and the navy, and among the commanding generals of the different theaters of war. And I may say that those commanding generals are making good in a big way.

When I addressed you four years ago, I said, "I know that America will never be disappointed in its expectation that labor will always continue to do its share of the job we now face and do it patriotically and effectively and unselfishly."

Today we know that America has not been disappointed. In his Order of the Day when the Allied armies first landed in Normandy two months ago, General Eisenhower said: "Our home fronts have given us overwhelming superiority in weapons and munitions of war."

The country knows that there is a breed of cats, luckily not too numerous, called labor-baiters. I know that there are labor-baiters among the opposition who, instead of calling attention to the achievements of labor in this war, prefer to pick on the occasional strikes that have occurred—strikes that have been condemned by every responsible national labor leader. I ought to say, parenthetically, all but one. And that one labor leader, incidentally, is certainly not conspicuous among my supporters.

Labor-baiters forget that at our peak American labor and management have turned out airplanes at the rate of 109,000 a year; tanks—57,000 a year; combat vessels—573 a year; landing vessels, to get the troops ashore—31,000 a year; cargo ships—19 million tons a year—and Henry Kaiser is here tonight, I am glad to say; and small arms ammunition—oh, I can't understand it, I don't believe you can either—23 billion rounds a year.

But a strike is news, and generally appears in shrieking headlines—and, of course, they say labor is always to blame. The fact is that since Pearl Harbor only one-tenth of one percent of man-hours have been lost by strikes. Can you beat that?

But, you know, even those candidates who burst out in election-year affection for social legislation and for labor in general, still think that you ought to be good boys and stay out of politics. And above all, they hate to see any working man or woman contribute a dollar bill to any wicked political party. Of course, it is all right for large financiers and industrialists and monopolists to contribute tens of thousands of dollars—but their solicitude for that dollar which the men and women in the ranks of labor contribute is always very touching.

They are, of course, perfectly willing to let you vote—unless you happen to be a soldier or a sailor overseas, or a merchant seaman carrying the munitions of war. In that case they have made it pretty hard for you to vote at all—for there are some political candidates who think that they may have a chance of election, if only the total vote is small enough.

And while I am on the subject of voting, let me urge every American citizen—man and woman—to use your sacred privilege of voting, no matter which candidate you expect to support. Our millions of soldiers and sailors and merchant seamen have been handicapped or prevented from voting by those politicians and candidates who think that they stand to lose by such votes. You here at home have the freedom of the ballot. Irrespective of party, you should register and vote this November. I think that is a matter of plain good citizenship.

Words come easily, but they do not change the record. You are, most of you, old enough to remember what things were like for labor in 1932.

You remember the closed banks and the breadlines and the starvation wages; the foreclosures of homes and farms, and the bankruptcies of business; the "Hoovervilles," and the young men and women of the nation facing a hopeless, jobless future; the closed factories and mines and mills; the ruined and abandoned farms; the stalled railroads and the empty docks; the blank despair of a whole nation—and the utter impotence of the federal government.

You remember the long, hard road, with its gains and its setbacks, which we have traveled together ever since those days.

Now there are some politicians who do not remember that far back, and there are some who remember but find it convenient to forget. No, the record is not to be washed away that easily.

The opposition in this year has already imported into this campaign a very interesting thing, because it is foreign. They have imported the propaganda technique invented by the dictators abroad. Remember, a number of years ago, there was a book, *Mein Kampf,* written by Hitler himself. The technique was all set out in Hitler's book—and it was copied by the aggressors of Italy and Japan. According to that technique, you should never use a small falsehood; always a big one, for its very fantastic nature would make it more credible—if only you keep repeating it over and over and over again.

Well, let us take some simple illustrations that come to mind. For example, although I rubbed my eyes when I read it, we have been told that it was not a Republican Depression, but a Democratic Depression from which this nation was saved in 1933—that this administration—this one—today—is responsible for all the suffering and misery that the history books and the American people have always thought had been brought about during the 12 ill-fated years when the Republican Party was in power.

Now, there is an old and somewhat lugubrious adage which says: "Never speak of rope in the house of a man who has been hanged." In the same way, if I were a Republican leader speaking to a mixed audience, the last word in the whole dictionary that I think I would use is that word depression.

You know, they pop up all the time. For another example, I learned—much to my amazement—that the policy of this administration was to keep men in the army when the war was over, because there might be no jobs for them in civil life.

Well, the very day that this fantastic charge was first made, a formal plan for the method of speedy discharge from the army had already been announced by the War Department—a plan based on the wishes of the soldiers themselves.

This callous and brazen falsehood about demobilization did, of course, a very simple thing; it was an effort to stimulate fear among American mothers and wives and sweethearts. And, incidentally, it was hardly calculated to bolster the morale of our soldiers and sailors and airmen who are fighting our battles all over the world.

But perhaps the most ridiculous of these campaign falsifications is the one that this administration failed to prepare for the war that was coming. I doubt whether even Goebbels would have tried that one. For even he would never have dared hope that the voters of America had already forgotten that many of the Republican leaders in the Congress and outside the Congress tried to thwart and block nearly every attempt that this administration made to warn our people and to arm our nation. Some of them called our 50,000 airplane program fantastic. Many of those very same leaders who fought every defense measure that we proposed are still in control of the Republican Party—look at their names—were in control of its National Convention in Chicago, and would be in control of the machinery of the Congress and of the Republican Party, in the event of a Republican victory this fall.

These Republican leaders have not been content with attacks on me, or my wife, or on my sons. No, not content with that, they now include my little dog, Fala. Well, of course, I don't resent attacks, and my family doesn't resent attacks, but Fala does resent them. You know, Fala is Scotch, and being a Scottie, as soon as he learned that the Republican fiction writers in Congress and out had concocted a story that I had left him behind on the Aleutian Islands and had sent a destroyer back to find him—at a cost to the taxpayers of two or three, or eight or 20 million dollars—his Scotch soul was furious. He has not been the same dog since. I am accustomed to hearing malicious falsehoods about myself—such as that old, worm-eaten chestnut that I have represented myself as indispensable. But I think I have a right to resent, to object to libelous statements about my dog.

Well, I think we all recognize the old technique. The people of this country know the past too well to be deceived into forgetting. Too much is at stake to forget. There are tasks ahead of us which we must now complete with the same will and the same skill and intelligence and devotion that have already led us so far along the road to victory.

There is the task of finishing victoriously this most terrible of all wars as speedily as possible and with the least cost in lives.

There is the task of setting up international machinery to assure that the peace, once established, will not again be broken.

And there is the task that we face here at home—the task of reconverting our economy from the purposes of war to the purposes of peace.

These peace-building tasks were faced once before, nearly a generation ago. They were botched by a Republican administration. That must not happen this time. We will not let it happen this time.

Fortunately, we do not begin from scratch. Much has been done. Much more is under way. The fruits of victory this time will not be apples sold on street corners.

Many months ago, this administration set up the necessary machinery for an orderly peacetime demobilization. The Congress has passed much more legislation continuing the agencies needed for demobilization—with additional powers to carry out their functions.

I know that the American people—business and labor and agriculture—have the same will to do for peace what they have done for war. And I know that they can sustain a national income that will assure full production and full employment under our democratic system of private enterprise, with government encouragement and aid whenever and wherever that is necessary.

The keynote of all that we propose to do in reconversion can be found in the one word jobs.

We shall lease or dispose of our government-owned plants and facilities and our surplus war property and land, on the basis of how they can best be operated by private enterprise to give jobs to the greatest number.

We shall follow a wage policy that will sustain the purchasing power of labor—for that means more production and more jobs.

You and I know that the present policies on wages and prices were conceived to serve the needs of the great masses of the people. They stopped inflation. They kept prices on a relatively stable level. Through the demobilization period, policies will be carried out with the same objective in mind—to serve the needs of the great masses of the people.

This is not the time in which men can be forgotten as they were in the Republican catastrophe that we inherited. The returning soldiers, the workers by their machines, the farmers in the field, the miners, the men and women in offices and shops, do not intend to be forgotten.

No, they know that they are not surplus. Because they know that they are America.

We must set targets and objectives for the future which will seem impossible—like the airplanes—to those who live in and are weighted down by the dead past.

We are even now organizing the logistics of the peace, just as Marshall and King and Arnold, MacArthur, Eisenhower, and Nimitz are organizing the logistics of this war.

I think that the victory of the American people and their allies in this war will be far more than a victory against fascism and reaction and the dead hand of despotism of the past. The victory of the American people and their allies in this war will be a victory for democracy. It will constitute such an affirmation of the strength and power and vitality of government by the people as history has never before witnessed.

And so, my friends, we have had affirmation of the vitality of democratic government behind us, that demonstration of its resilience and its capacity for decision and for action— we have that knowledge of our own strength and power—we move forward with God's help to the greatest epoch of free achievement by free men that the world has ever known.

The Yalta Conference

Washington, D.C.

March 1, 1945

THE END OF the European war was at hand. Roosevelt had just returned from a meeting with Churchill and Stalin at Yalta on the Black Sea. There the "Big Three" had worked out the preliminary details of the postwar partition of Germany, the dismantling of the Nazi war machine, the disposition of Poland, and the proposed United Nations, successor to Wilson's League of Nations. In this address to Congress, Roosevelt reported the results of the meeting and pleaded for rapid and decisive support for his peace plan.

Observers remarked on how tired and ill Roosevelt looked. Dean Acheson noted that the president's voice had "lost its timbre." His reading of the text was uncertain and hesitant; several passages were ad-libbed. It was thought by many that Roosevelt had lacked the physical strength to deal effectively with Stalin. Indeed, the carefully negotiated balance of power between the Kremlin and the West fell apart within weeks.

I hope that you will pardon me for an unusual posture of sitting down during the presentation of what I want to say, but I know that you will realize it makes it a lot easier for me in not having to carry about ten pounds of steel around on the bottom of my legs and also because of the fact that I have just completed a 14,000-mile trip.

First of all, I want to say that it is good to be home. It has been a long journey and I hope you also will agree that it has been, so far, a fruitful one.

Speaking in all frankness, the question of whether it is entirely fruitful or not lies to a great extent in your hands. For unless you here, in the halls of the American Congress—with the support of the American people—concur in the general conclusions reached in the place called Yalta, and give them your active support, the meeting will not have produced lasting results.

And that is why I have come before you at the earliest hour I could after my return. I want to make a personal report to you, and at the same time to the people of the country. Many months of earnest work are ahead of us all, and I should like to feel that when the last stone is laid on the structure of international peace, it will be an achievement for which all of us in America have worked steadfastly and unselfishly—together.

I am returning from this trip, which took me so far, refreshed and inspired. I was well the entire time. I was not ill for a second until I arrived back in Washington. And I heard all of the humors which occurred in my absence. Yes, I returned from the trip refreshed and inspired—the Roosevelts are not, as you may suspect, averse to travel; we seem to thrive on it.

And far away as I was, I was kept constantly informed of affairs in the United States. The modern miracle of rapid communications has made this world very small; we must always bear in mind that fact when we speak or think of international relations. I received a steady stream of messages from Washington, I might say not only from the executive branch with all its departments, but also from the legislative branch—its two departments. And, except where radio silence was necessary for security purposes, I could continuously send messages any place in the world. And, of course, in a grave emergency we could even have risked the breaking of the security rule.

I come from the Crimean Conference with a firm belief that we have made a good start on the road to a world of peace.

There were two main purposes in this Crimean Conference. The first was to bring defeat to Germany with the greatest possible speed and with the smallest possible loss of Allied men. That purpose is now being carried out in great force. The German army, and the German people, are feeling the ever-increasing might of our fighting men of the Allied armies and every hour gives us added pride in the heroic advance of our troops in Germany, on German soil, toward a meeting with the gallant Red Army.

The second purpose was to continue to build the foundation for an international accord which would bring order and security after the chaos of the war and would give some assurance of lasting peace among the nations of the world. In that goal, toward that goal, a tremendous stride was made.

After Teheran, a little over a year ago, there were long-range military plans laid by the chiefs of staff of the three most powerful nations. Among the civilian leaders at Teheran, however, at that time, there were only exchanges of views and expressions of opinion. No political arrangements were made and none was attempted.

At the Crimean Conference, however, the time had come for getting down to specific cases in the political field. There was on all sides at this conference an enthusiastic effort to reach an agreement. Since the time of Teheran, a year ago, there had developed among all of us a—what shall I call it—a greater facility in negotiating with each other, which augurs well for the peace of the world. We know each other better.

I have never for an instant wavered in my belief that an agreement to insure world peace and security can be reached. There are a number of things that we did at the conference that were definite. For instance, the lapse of time between Teheran and Yalta without conferences of civilian representatives of the three major powers have proved to be too long—14 months. During this long period local problems were permitted to become acute in places like Poland and Greece and Italy and Yugoslavia.

Therefore we decided at Yalta that, even if circumstances made it impossible for the heads of the three governments to do it, to meet more often in the future, and to make that sure by arranging that there would be frequent personal contacts for the exchange of views between the secretaries of state, the foreign ministers of these three powers.

We arranged for periodic meetings, at intervals of three or four months. I feel very confident that under this arrangement there will be no recurrence of the incidents which this winter disturbed the friends of worldwide cooperation and collaboration.

When we met at Yalta, in addition to laying our strategic and tactical plans for the complete, final military victory over Germany, there were other problems of vital political consequence.

For instance, there were the problems of occupational control of Germany after victory, the complete destruction of her military power, and the assurance that neither the Nazis nor Prussian militarism could again be revived to threaten the peace and the civilization of the world.

Secondly, again for example, there was the settlement of the few differences which remained among us with respect to the international security organization after the Dumbarton Oaks Conference. As you remember, at that time, I said afterward we had agreed 90 percent. That's a pretty good percentage. I think the other 10 percent was ironed out at Yalta.

Thirdly, there were the general political and economic problems common to all of the areas that would be in the future, or which had been, liberated from the Nazi yoke. There are special problems—we over here find it difficult to understand the ramifications of many of these problems in foreign lands. But we are trying to.

Fourth, there were the special problems created by a few instances, such as Poland and Yugoslavia.

Days were spent in discussing these momentous matters. We argued freely and frankly across the table. But at the end, on every point, unanimous agreement was reached. And more important even than the agreement of words, I may say we achieved a unity of thought and a way of getting along together.

Of course we know that it was Hitler's hope—and German war lords—that we would not agree, that some slight crack might appear in the solid wall of Allied unity, a crack that would give him and his fellow-gangsters one last hope of escaping their just doom. That is the objective for which his propaganda machine has been working for many months.

But Hitler has failed.

Never before have the major Allies been more closely united—not only in the war aims but also in their peace aims. And they are determined to continue to be united— to be united with each other—and with all peace-loving nations—so that the ideal of lasting peace will become a reality.

The Soviet, British, and United States Chiefs of Staff held daily meetings with each other, they conferred frequently with Marshal Stalin, with Prime Minister Churchill and with me, on the problem of coordinating the strategic and tactical efforts of the Allied powers. They completed their plans for the final knockout blow to Germany.

At the time of the Teheran Conference the Russian front, for instance, was removed so far from the American and British fronts that, while certain long-range strategic cooperation was possible, there could be no tactical, day-by-day coordination. They were too far apart.

But Russian troops have now crossed Poland, they are fighting on the eastern soil of Germany herself, British and American troops are now on German soil close to the Rhine River in the west. It is a different situation today from what it was 14 months ago. A closer tactical liaison has become possible—for the first time in Europe—and, in the Crimean Conference, that was something else that was accomplished.

Provision was made for daily exchange of information between the armies under command of General Eisenhower, on the western front, and those armies under the command of the Soviet marshals on that long eastern front, and also with our armies in Italy—without the necessity of going through the Chiefs of Staff in Washington or London, as in the past.

You have seen one result of this exchange of information in the recent bombing by American and English aircraft of points which are directly related to the Russian advance on Berlin.

From now on, American and British heavy bombers will be used-in the day-by-day tactics of the war—and we have begun to realize, I think, that there is all the difference in the world between tactics on the one side and strategy on the other. Day-by-day tactical war, in direct support of the Soviet armies, as well as in the support of our own in the western front.

They are now engaged in bombing and strafing in order to hamper the movement of German reserves, German materials, to the eastern and western fronts from other parts of Germany or from Italy.

Arrangements have been made for the most effective distribution of all available material and transportation to the places where they can best be used in the combined war effort—American, British and Russian.

Details of these plans and arrangements are military secrets, of course. But they are going to hasten—this kind of working together is going to hasten—the day of the final collapse of Germany. The Nazis are learning about some of them already, to their sorrow, and I think all three of us at the conference felt that they will learn more about them tomorrow and the next day—and the day after that.

There will be no respite for these attacks. We will not desist for one moment until unconditional surrender. You know I have always felt that common sense prevails in the long run, quiet overnight thinking. I think that's true in Germany, just as much as it is here. The German people, as well as the German soldier, must realize, the sooner, the sooner they give up and surrender, surrender by groups or by individuals, the sooner their present agony will be over. They must realize that only with complete surrender can they begin to reestablish themselves as people whom the world might accept as decent neighbors.

We made it clear again at Yalta, and I now repeat—that unconditional surrender does not mean the destruction or the enslavement of the German people. The Nazi leaders have deliberately withheld that part of the Yalta declaration from the German press and radio. They seek to convince the people of Germany that the Yalta declaration does mean slavery and destruction for them—they are working at it day and night—for that is how the Nazis hope to save their own skins, how to deceive their people into continued and useless resistance.

We did, however, make it clear at the conference just what unconditional surrender does mean for Germany.

It means the temporary control of Germany by Great Britain, Russia, France, and the United States. Each of these nations will occupy and control a separate zone of Germany—and the administration of the four zones will be coordinated—coordinated in Berlin by a control council composed of representatives of the four nations.

Unconditional surrender means something else. It means the end of Nazism. It means the end of the Nazi Party—and all of its barbaric laws and institutions.

It means the termination of all militaristic influence in public, private, and cultural life of Germany.

It means for the Nazi war criminals a punishment that is speedy and just—and severe.

It means the complete disarmament of Germany, the destruction of its militarism, of its military equipment; the end of its production of armament; the dispersal of all armed forces; the permanent dismemberment of the German General Staff, which has so often shattered the peace of the world.

It means that Germany will have to make reparations—reparations in kind for the damage which has been done to the innocent victims of its aggression.

By compelling reparations in kind—in plants, in machinery, in rolling stock and raw materials—we shall avoid the mistake that we and other people—other nations—made after the last war, the demanding of reparations in the form of money, which Germany could never pay.

We do not want the German people to starve, or to become a burden on the rest of the world.

Our objective in handling Germany is simple—it is to secure the peace of the rest of the world, now and in the future. Too much experience has shown that that objective is impossible if Germany is allowed to retain any ability to wage aggressive warfare.

Now these objectives will not hurt German people. On the contrary it will protect them from a repetition of the fate which the General Staff and Kaiserism imposed on them before and which Hitlerism is now imposing upon them again a hundredfold. It will be removing a cancer from the German body politic, which for generations has produced only misery and only pain for the whole world.

During my stay in Yalta I saw the kind of reckless, senseless fury, this terrible destruction, that comes out of German militarism. Yalta, on the Black Sea, had no military significance of any kind. It had no defense.

Before the last war it had been a resort, a resort for people like czars, princes, and aristocracy, and their hanger-ons. However, after the war, after the Red Revolution, until the attack on the Soviet Union by Hitler a few years ago, the palaces, the villas of Yalta had been used as a rest and recreation center by the Russian people.

The Nazi officers took these former palaces and villas, took them over for their own use. They are the only reasons that the so-called former palace of the czar was still habitable when we got there. It had been given, or had thought to have been given, to a German general for his own property and his own use. And when Yalta was so destroyed he kept soldiers there to protect what he thought would become his own nice villa.

It was a useful rest and recreation center for hundreds of thousands of Russian workers, farmers, and their families, up to the time it was taken again by the Germans.

The Nazi officers took these places for their own use, and when the Red Army forced the Nazis out of the Crimea, just almost a year ago—last April, I think it was—all the villas were looted by the Nazis, and then nearly all of them were destroyed by bombs placed on the inside. And even the humblest of homes of Yalta were not spared.

There was little left of it except blank walls, ruins, destruction.

Sevastopol, the weather-fortified port, about 40 or 50 miles away—there again was a scene of utter destruction—a large city with its great navy yards, its fortifications. I think less than a dozen buildings were left intact in the entire city.

I had read about Warsaw and Lidice and Rotterdam and Coventry—but I saw Sevastopol and Yalta. And I know that there is not room enough on earth for both German militarism and Christian decency.

Of equal importance with the military arrangements at the Crimean Conference were the agreements reached with respect to a general international organization for lasting world peace.

The foundations were laid at Dumbarton Oaks. There was one point, however, on which agreement was not reached. It involved the procedure of voting, of voting in the Security Council. I want to try to make it clear by making it simple. It took me hours and hours to get the thing straight in my own mind at many conferences. At the Crimea Conference the Americans made a proposal on this subject which, after full discussion, I am glad to say, was unanimously adopted by the other two nations.

It is not yet possible to announce the terms of it publicly, but it will be in a short time.

With respect to voting, when the conclusions reached are made known, I think and I hope, that you will find them a fair solution of this complicated and difficult problem. You might almost say it's a legislative problem. They are founded in justice, and will go far to assure international cooperation in the maintenance of peace.

There is going to be held—as you know—after we have straightened that voting matter out, there is going to be held in San Francisco a meeting of all the united nations of the world, on the 25th of April, next month. There, we all hope, and confidently expect, to execute a definite charter of organization upon which the peace of the world will be preserved and the forces of aggression permanently outlawed.

This time we are not making the mistake of waiting until the end of the war to set up the machinery of peace. This time, as we fight together to win the war finally, we work together to keep it from happening again.

As you know, I have always been a believer in the document called the Constitution of the United States. I spent a good deal of time in educating two other nations of the world in regard to the Constitution of the United States.

The charter has to be, and should be, approved by the Senate of the United States under the Constitution. I think the other nations all know it now—I am aware of that fact, and now all the other nations are, and we hope that the Senate will approve of what is set forth as the charter of the United Nations, when they all come together in San Francisco, next month.

The Senate of the United States, through its appropriate representatives, has been kept continuously advised of the program of this government in the creation of the International Security Organization.

The Senate and the House will both be represented at the San Francisco Conference. The congressional delegates will consist of an equal number, and the senatorial will consist of an equal number of Republican and Democratic members. The American delegation is—in every sense of the word—bipartisan.

But I think that world peace is not exactly a party question—I think that Republicans want peace just as much as Democrats. It is not a party question any more than is military victory—the winning of the war.

When our republic was threatened, first by the Nazi clutch for world conquest back in 1939 and 1940, and then by the Japanese treachery in 1941, partisanship and politics were laid aside by nearly every American; and every resource was dedicated to our common safety. The same consecration to the cause of peace will be expected, I think, by every patriotic American, by every human soul overseas, too.

The structure of world peace cannot be the work of one man, or one party, or one nation, it cannot be just an American peace, or British peace, or a Russian, or a French, or a Chinese peace. It cannot be a peace of large nations—or of small nations. It must be a peace which rests on the cooperative effort of the whole world.

It cannot be what some people think—a structure of complete perfection at first. But it can be a peace, and it will be a peace, based on the sound and just principles of the Atlantic Charter—on the concept of the dignity of the human being—and on the guarantees of tolerance and freedom of religious worship.

As the Allied armies have marched to military victory, they have liberated peoples whose liberties had been crushed by the Nazis for four long years, whose economy had been reduced to ruins by Nazi despoilers.

There have been instances of political confusion and unrest in these liberated areas—that is not unexpected—as in Greece or in Poland or in Yugoslavia, and maybe more. Worse than that, there actually began to grow in some of these places queer ideas of "spheres of influence"—which were incompatible with the basic principles of international collaboration. If allowed to go on unchecked these developments might have had tragic results, in time.

It is fruitless to try to place the blame for this situation on one particular nation or on another. It is the kind of development which is almost inevitable unless the major powers of the world continue without interruption to work together and assume joint responsibility for the solution of problems that may arise to endanger the peace of the world.

We met in the Crimea determined to settle this matter of liberated areas. Things that might happen that we can't see at this moment might happen suddenly, unexpectedly, next week or next month. And I am happy to confirm to the Congress that we did arrive at a settlement—and incidentally, a unanimous settlement.

The three most powerful nations have agreed that the political and economic problems of any area liberated from Nazi conquest, or any former Axis satellite, are a joint responsibility of all three governments. They will join together during the temporary period of instability after hostilities, to help the people of any liberated area, or of any former satellite state, to solve their own problems through firmly established democratic processes.

They will endeavor to see—to see to it that interim governing, and the people who carry on the interim government between occupation by Germany and true independence— that such an interim government will be as representative as possible of all democratic elements in the population, and that free elections are held as soon as possible thereafter.

Responsibility for political conditions thousands of miles away can no longer be avoided, I think, by this great nation. Certainly, I don't want to live to see another war. As I have said, the world is smaller—smaller every year. The United States now exerts a tremendous influence on the cause of peace.

What we people over here are thinking and talking about is in the interest of peace, because it's known all over the world. The slightest remark in either house of the Congress is known all over the world the following day. We will continue to exert that influence only if we are willing to continue to share in the responsibility for keeping the peace. It would be our own tragic loss, I think, if we were to shirk that responsibility.

Final decisions in these areas are going to be made jointly, therefore, and therefore they will often be a result of give-and-take compromise.

The United States will not always have its way 100 percent, nor will Russia, nor Great Britain. We shall not always have ideal answers, solutions to complicated international problems, even though we are determined continuously to strive toward that ideal. But I am sure that under the agreements reached at Yalta there will be a more stable political Europe than ever before.

Of course, once there has been a true expression out of the people's will in any country, our immediate responsibility ends, with the exception only of such action as may be agreed on by the international security organization we will set up.

The united nations must also begin to help these liberated areas adequately to reconstruct their economy—I don't want them starving to death—so that they are ready to resume their places in the world. The Nazi war machine has stripped them of raw materials and machine tools, and trucks and locomotives and things like that. They have left the industry of these places stagnant, and much of the agricultural areas are unproductive—the Nazis have left a complete ruin, or a partial ruin, in their wake.

To start the wheels running again is not a mere matter of relief. It is to the national interest that all of us see to it that these liberated areas are again made self-supporting and productive, so that they do not need continuous relief from us. I can say that as an argument based on plain common sense.

One outstanding example of joint action by the three major Allied powers was the solution reached on Poland. The whole Polish question was a potential source of trouble in postwar Europe, as it had been some time before, and we came to the conference determined to find a common ground for its solution, and we did, even though everybody doesn't agree with us, obviously.

Our objective was to help create a strong, independent, and prosperous nation. That's the thing we must always remember, those words, agreed to by Russia, by Britain, and by me, the objective of making Poland a strong, independent, and prosperous nation, with a government ultimately to be selected by the Polish people themselves.

To achieve that objective it is necessary to provide for the formation of a new government, much more representative than had been possible while Poland was enslaved. Accordingly, steps were taken at Yalta to reorganize the existing provisional government in Poland on a broader democratic basis, so as to include democratic leaders now in Poland and those abroad. This new reorganized government will be recognized by all of us as the temporary government of Poland. Poland needs a temporary government in the worst way. An ad interim government, I think, is another way of putting it.

However, the new Polish provisional government of national unity will be pledged to holding a free election as soon as possible on the basis of universal suffrage and a secret ballot.

Throughout history Poland has been the corridor through which attacks on Russia have been made. Twice in this generation Germany has struck at Russia through this corridor. To insure European security and world peace a strong and independent Poland is necessary to prevent that from happening again.

The decision with respect to the boundaries of Poland was practically a compromise. I didn't agree with all of it by any means, but we didn't go as far as Britain wanted in certain areas, go as far as Russia wanted in certain areas, and we didn't go so far as I wanted in certain areas. It was a compromise. The decision was a compromise under which the Poles will receive compensation in territory in the north and west in exchange for what they lose by the Curzon Line in the east.

The limits of the western border will be permanently fixed in the final peace conference. We know roughly that it will include in the new strong Poland quite a large slice of what now is called Germany. And it was agreed also that the new Poland will have a large and long coastline and many a new harbor. Also that East Prussia, most of it, will go to Poland and the corner of it will go to Russia. Also (what shall I call it) that the anomaly of the Free State of Danzig, I think Danzig would be a lot better if it were Polish.

It is well known that the people east of the Curzon Line are predominantly White Russian and Ukrainian. They are not Polish, to a very great majority. And the people west of the line are predominantly Polish, except in that part of East Prussia and East Germany which will go to new Poland. As far back as 1919 the representatives of the Allies agreed that the Curzon Line represented a fair boundary between the two peoples. You must remember also there was no Poland before, there had not been any Polish government, before 1919, for a great many generations.

I am convinced that this agreement on Poland, under the circumstances, is the most hopeful agreement possible for a free, independent, and prosperous Polish state.

Now the Crimean conference was a meeting of the three major military powers on whose shoulders rest the chief responsibility and burden of the war. Although, for this reason, another nation was not included—France was not a participant in the conference—no one should detract from the recognition that was accorded there to her role in the future of Europe and the future of the world.

France has been invited to accept (on second thought, this was on my motion), France has been invited to accept a zone of control in

Germany, and to participate as a fourth member of the Allied control council of Germany.

She has been invited to join as a sponsor of the international conference at San Francisco next month.

She will be a permanent member of the International Security Council together with the other four major powers.

And, finally, we have asked that she be associated with us in our joint responsibility over the liberated areas of Europe. Of course there are a number of smaller things which I haven't got time to go into on which argument was had. We hope these things will straighten out.

Agreement was reached on Yugoslavia, as announced in the communiqué, and we hope that it is in process of fulfillment. But it is not only there, but in some other places we have to remember there are a great number of prima donnas in the world, who all wish to be heard. Before anything becomes fact, we may have a little delay while we listen to more prima donnas.

Quite naturally, this conference concerned itself only with the European war and with the political problems of Europe, and not with the Pacific war.

In Malta, however, our combined British and American staffs made their plans to increase the attack against Japan.

The Japanese war lords know that they are not being overlooked. They have felt the force of our B-29s, and our carrier planes. They have felt the naval might of the United States, and do not appear very anxious to come out and try it again.

The Japs now know what it means to hear that "The United States Marines have landed." And I think I can add, having Iwo Jima in mind, that "the situation is well in hand."

They also know what is in store for the homeland of Japan now that General MacArthur has completed his magnificent march back to Manila, and that Admiral Nimitz is establishing his air bases right in their own back yard.

But, lest somebody else lay off work in the United States, I can repeat what I have said, a short sentence, even in my sleep, "We haven't won the wars yet," with an s on wars.

It is a long tough road to Tokyo. It is longer to go to Tokyo than it is to Berlin, in every sense of the word.

The defeat of Germany will not mean the end of the war against Japan. On the contrary, we must be prepared for a long and costly struggle in the Pacific. But the unconditional surrender of Japan is as essential as the defeat of Germany. I say that advisedly, with the thought in mind that that is especially true if our plans for world peace are to succeed. For Japanese militarism must be wiped out as thoroughly as German militarism.

On the way back from the Crimea I made arrangements to meet personally King Farouk of Egypt, Haile Selassie, the emperor of Ethiopia, and King Ibn Saud of Saudi Arabia. Our conversations had to do with matters of common interest. They will be of great mutual advantage because they gave me and a good many of us an opportunity of meeting and talking face to face, and of exchanging views in personal conversation instead of formal correspondence.

Of the problems of Arabia, I learned more about that whole problem, the Moslem problem, the Jewish problem, by talking with Ibn Saud for five minutes than I could have learned in exchange of two or three dozen letters.

On my voyage, I had the benefit of seeing the army and navy and air force at work.

All Americans, I think, would feel proud, as proud of our armed forces as I am, if they could see and hear what I did.

Against the most efficient professional leaders, sailors, and airmen of all history, our men stood and fought and won.

I think that this is our chance to see to it that the sons and grandsons of these gallant fighting men do not have to do it all over again in a few years.

The conference in the Crimea was a turning point, I hope, in our history, and therefore in the history of the world. It will soon be presented to the Senate and the American people, a great decision that will determine the fate of the United States, and I think therefore of the world, for generations to come.

There can be no middle ground here. We shall have to take the responsibility for world collaboration, or we shall have to bear the responsibility for another world conflict.

I know that the word planning is not looked upon with favor in some circles. In domestic affairs, tragic mistakes have been made by reason of lack of planning, and, on the other hand, many great improvements in living, and many benefits to the human race, have been accomplished as a result of adequate, intelligent planning—reclamations of desert areas, developments of whole river valleys, provision for adequate housing, and a dozen different topics.

The same will be true in relations between nations. For the second time in the lives of most of us, this generation is face to face with the objective of preventing wars. To meet that objective, the nations of the world will either have a plan or they will not. The groundwork of a plan has now been furnished, and has been submitted to humanity for discussion and decision.

No plan is perfect. Whatever is adopted at San Francisco will doubtless have to be amended time and again over the years, just as our own Constitution has been.

No one can say exactly how long any plan will last. Peace can endure only so long as humanity really insists upon it and is willing to work for it and sacrifice for it.

Twenty-five years ago American fighting men looked to the statesmen of the world to finish the work of peace for which they fought and suffered. We failed them then. We cannot fail them again, and expect the world to survive again.

I think the Crimean conference was a successful effort by the three leading nations to find a common ground of peace. It spells, it ought to spell, the end of the system of unilateral action and exclusive alliances and spheres of influence and balances of power and all the other expedients that have been tried for centuries, and have always failed.

We propose to substitute for all these a universal organization in which all peace-loving nations will finally have a chance to join.

And I am confident that the Congress and the American people will accept the results of this conference as the beginning of a permanent structure of peace upon which we can begin to build, under God, that better world in which our children and grandchildren, yours and mine, the children and grandchildren of the whole world, must live and can live.

And that, my friends, is the only message I can give you, but I feel very deeply, and I know that all of you are feeling it today and are going to feel it in the future.

Strong and Active Faith

Warm Springs, Georgia

April 11, 1945

ROOSEVELT DICTATED this address while resting at his Warm Springs retreat. It was to be delivered on April 13, Jefferson Day. On April 12, Roosevelt died from a massive cerebral hemorrhage. These were "the truest words he ever wrote," claimed James MacGregor Burns. "He had a strong and active faith, a huge and unprovable faith, in the possibilities of human understanding, trust, and love."

Americans are gathered together this evening in communities all over the country to pay tribute to the living memory of Thomas Jefferson—one of the greatest of all democrats; and I want to make it clear that I am spelling that word democrats with a small d.

I wish I had the power, just for this evening, to be present at all these gatherings.

In this historic year, more than ever before, we do well to consider the character of Thomas Jefferson as an American citizen of the world.

As minister to France, then as our first secretary of state and as our third president, Jefferson was instrumental in the establishment of the United States as a vital factor in international affairs.

It was he who first sent our navy into far distant waters to defend our rights. And the promulgation of the Monroe Doctrine was the logical development of Jefferson's far-seeing foreign policy.

Today this nation which Jefferson helped so greatly to build is playing a tremendous part in the battle for the rights of man all over the world.

Today we are part of the vast Allied force—a force composed of flesh and blood and steel and spirit—which is today destroying the makers of war, the breeders of hate, in Europe and in Asia.

In Jefferson's time our navy consisted of only a handful of frigates—but that tiny navy taught nations across the Atlantic that piracy in the Mediterranean—acts of aggression against peaceful commerce and the enslavement of their crews was one of those things which, among neighbors, simply was not done.

Today we have learned in the agony of war that great power involves great responsibility. Today we can no more escape the consequence of German and Japanese aggression than could we avoid the consequences of attacks by the Barbary corsairs a century and a half before.

We, as Americans, do not choose to deny our responsibility.

Nor do we intend to abandon our determination that, within the lives of our children and our children's children, there will not be a third world war.

We seek peace—enduring peace. More than an end to war, we want an end to the beginnings of all wars—yes, an end to this brutal, inhuman, and thoroughly impractical method of settling the differences between governments.

The once powerful, malignant Nazi state is crumbling, the Japanese war lords are receiving, in their homeland, the retribution for which they asked when they attacked Pearl Harbor.

But the mere conquest of our enemies is not enough.

We must go on to do all in our power to conquer the doubts and the fears, the ignorance and the greed, which made this horror possible.

Thomas Jefferson, himself a distinguished scientist, once spoke of the "brotherly spirit of science, which unites into one family all its votaries of whatever grade, and however widely dispersed throughout the different quarters of the globe."

Today, science has brought all the different quarters of the globe so close together that it is impossible to isolate them one from another.

Today we are faced with the preeminent fact that, if civilization is to survive, we must cultivate the science of human relationships—the ability of all peoples, of all kinds, to live together and work together in the same world, at peace.

Let me assure you that my hand is the steadier for the work that is to be done, that

I move more firmly into the task, knowing that you—millions and millions of you—are joined with me in the resolve to make this work endure.

The work, my friends, is peace more than an end of this war—an end to the beginning of all wars, yes, an end, forever, to this impractical, unrealistic settlement of the differences between governments by the mass killing of peoples.

Today as we move against the terrible scourge of war—as we go forward toward the greatest contribution that any generation of human beings can make in this world—the contribution of lasting peace, I ask you to keep up your faith. I measure the sound, solid achievement that can be made at this time by the straight edge of your confidence and your resolve. And to you, and to all Americans who dedicate themselves with us to the making of an abiding peace, I say:

The only limit to our realization of tomorrow will be our doubts of today. Let us move forward with strong and active faith.

Franklin D. Roosevelt's gravesite in Hyde Park, New York.
(Courtesy of PresidentsUSA.net)

Courtesy of Leo Stern

Harry S Truman

Harry S Truman

1945–1953

HARRY TRUMAN, born and raised in the archetypally Middle American small town of Independence, Missouri, was a hard worker and plain speaker in the Missouri tradition. He was a farmer, bank clerk, and haberdasher, and an army artillery officer in World War I, before he was elected to a county judgeship at the age of 35 with the help of the Kansas City Democratic machine. A senator from 1935, Truman distinguished himself during World War II as the tireless head of a special committee to investigate waste, mismanagement, and fraud in the war production effort. The Democratic Party bosses convinced Franklin D. Roosevelt to choose Truman as his running mate in 1944; the following year the stunned Missourian succeeded to the presidency on Roosevelt's death. He was reelected in 1948.

When it came to speechmaking, the contrast between Truman and his predecessor could not have been greater. "People had seen something of him fleetingly in the last [1944] campaign," wrote Truman historian Cabell Phillips, "had heard his flat Missouri diction, his earthy and unpretentious rhetoric, and it had sounded like a muffled gong—whether you liked Roosevelt or hated his guts—against the majestic sonorities to which the public ear had become attuned in the last 12 years." Phillips further characterized Truman the speaker as failing to project "any of the outward attributes of forcefulness or dignity or command out of which the popular image of leadership is compounded." Even Truman was modest about his own speaking abilities: "As for style in speaking and writing, I never had any."

Yet Truman's writing style—he did indeed have one—was effective and well-suited to him. What he lacked in majesty he made up for in directness. Better-read than most modern presidents, especially in history, Truman admired and learned from such disparate sources as Mark Twain's *Tom Sawyer* and the King James Bible; among orators, he thought highly of Cicero (whom he read in Latin) and tried to imitate him. When it came to writing his own speeches, simplicity was the goal—"facts and supporting data to prove those facts, and that is it."

When Truman stuck to a prepared text—as he did for major statements—his delivery was usually strained. Truman outlined those speeches and carefully corrected the many drafts prepared for him by his chief speechwriter, George Elsey, and a research staff, but he went over the material so many times that it lost its freshness, making it difficult for him to give the words natural emphasis. Margaret Truman wrote that her father "was so acutely conscious of the historical importance of what a president said, he hesitated to use anything but prepared texts. The result was continuous erosion of his public support. He read a speech badly, always seeming, as one man said, to be 'rushing for the period.'" When he allowed himself to speak off the cuff, as he did increasingly during and after the presidential campaign of 1948, he was more comfortable, and his speeches more successful. In his second term, Truman spoke only from a set of notes, even for important speeches. "When I have no text in front of me," he told one interviewer, "and I'm free to talk as I would to you across the table, then I do better." He would buttress the succinct factual core of these impromptu speeches with down-to-earth jokes (often at his own expense), good-natured boasting, salty repartee with the audience, and energetic attacks on his opponents. Truman knew how to coin telling phrases: the Republican-controlled 80th Congress was the "do-nothing" Congress, and the smooth-talking Republican candidate in the 1948 presidential contest, Thomas Dewey, was waging a "soothing-syrup campaign" for the "gluttons of privilege."

Audiences saw him as an ordinary American like themselves, which FDR never was seen to be. There is little doubt that Truman, whose public approval at the beginning of the 1948 campaign was quite low, would have lost the election if he hadn't embarked on a whistle-stop tour, giving extemporaneous speeches from the back of his train to crowds of farmers and laborers in hundreds of small towns. The crowds liked his scrappiness, cheering him on with shouts of "Give 'em hell, Harry!", and warmed to his obvious understanding and affection for the rural way of life. Even the Washington establishment appreciated his bluntness and honesty. After Truman retired from public service in 1953, political columnist Mary McGrory wrote: "Since Harry Truman left town almost nobody has spoken his mind. Mr. Truman took the tradition of plain speaking back to Missouri with him."

The Destruction of Hiroshima

Shipboard

August 6, 1945

AT THE POTSDAM Conference the Allies issued a demand for Japan's complete and unconditional surrender by August 30, 1945. As the deadline approached with no official reaction from the Japanese, Truman ordered the Air Force to make preparations to drop an atomic bomb on Japan, a measure that the United States hoped would obviate the need for a costly and bloody invasion. On August 6 a bomb was detonated over Hiroshima, causing 135,000 casualties and leveling the greater part of the city. Truman, enroute from Potsdam aboard the cruiser *Augusta,* made this address to the nation via radio the same day. The Japanese asked for an armistice after a second bomb was dropped on Nagasaki on August 9.

Truman was jubilant on hearing of the successful bombing and claimed later to have gotten "a sound night's sleep" that evening. A president, he said, could not afford to be "constantly worrying about what history and future generations would say about decisions he has to make. He must live in the present, do what he thinks is right at the time, and history will take care of itself." Yet he later denied Gen. Douglas MacArthur's request to bomb North Korea during the Korean War and always believed that "starting an atomic war is totally unthinkable for rational men."

Sixteen hours ago an American airplane dropped one bomb on Hiroshima, an important Japanese army base. That bomb had more power than 20,000 tons of TNT. It had more than 2,000 times the blast power of the British "Grand Slam," which is the largest bomb ever yet used in the history of warfare.

The Japanese began the war from the air at Pearl Harbor. They have been repaid manyfold. And the end is not yet. With this bomb we have now added a new and revolutionary increase in destruction to supplement the growing power of our armed forces. In their present form these bombs are now in production, and even more powerful forms are in development.

It is an atomic bomb. It is a harnessing of the basic power of the universe. The force from which the sun draws its power has been loosed against those who brought war to the Far East.

Before 1939, it was the accepted belief of scientists that it was theoretically possible to release atomic energy. But no one knew any practical method of doing it. By 1942, however, we knew that the Germans were working feverishly to find a way to add atomic energy to the other engines of war with which they hoped to enslave the world. But they failed. We may be grateful to Providence that the Germans got the V-1s and V-2s late and in limited quantities and

even more grateful that they did not get the atomic bomb at all.

The battle of the laboratories held fateful risks for us as well as the battles of the air, land, and sea, and we have now won the battle of the laboratories as we have won the other battles.

Beginning in 1940, before Pearl Harbor, scientific knowledge useful in war was pooled between the United States and Great Britain, and many priceless helps to our victories have come from that arrangement. Under that general policy the research on the atomic bomb was begun. With American and British scientists working together we entered the race of discovery against the Germans.

The United States had available the large number of scientists of distinction in the many needed areas of knowledge. It had the tremendous industrial and financial resources necessary for the project, and they could be devoted to it without undue impairment of other vital war work. In the United States the laboratory work and the production plants, on which a substantial start had already been made, would be out of reach of enemy bombing, while at that time Britain was exposed to constant air attack and was still threatened with the possibility of invasion. For these reasons Prime Minister Churchill and President Roosevelt agreed that it was wise to carry on the project here.

We now have two great plants and many lesser works devoted to the production of atomic power. Employment during peak construction numbered 125,000 and over 65,000 individuals are even now engaged in operating the plants. Many have worked there for two and a half years. Few know what they have been producing. They see great quantities of material going in and they see nothing coming out of these plants, for the physical size of the explosive charge is exceedingly small. We have spent $2,000,000 on the greatest scientific gamble in history—and won.

But the greatest marvel is not the size of the enterprise, its secrecy, nor its cost, but the achievement of scientific brains in putting together infinitely complex pieces of knowledge held by many men in different fields of science into a workable plan. And hardly less marvelous has been the capacity of industry to design, and of labor to operate, the machines and methods to do things never done before so that the brainchild of many minds came forth in physical shape and performed as it was supposed to do. Both science and industry worked under the direction of the United States Army, which achieved a unique success in managing so diverse a problem in the advancement of knowledge in an amazingly short time. It is doubtful if such another combination could be got together in the world. What has been done is the greatest achievement of organized science in history. It was done under high pressure and without failure.

We are now prepared to obliterate more rapidly and completely every productive enterprise the Japanese have above ground in any city. We shall destroy their docks, their factories, and their communications. Let there be no mistake; we shall completely destroy Japan's power to make war.

It was to spare the Japanese people from utter destruction that the ultimatum of July 26 was issued at Potsdam. Their leaders promptly rejected that ultimatum. If they do not now accept our terms they may expect a rain of ruin from the air, the like of which has never been seen on this earth. Behind this air attack will follow sea and land forces in such numbers and power as they have not yet seen and with the fighting skill of which they are already well aware.

The secretary of war, who has kept in personal touch with all phases of the project, will immediately make public a statement giving further details.

His statement will give facts concerning the sites at Oak Ridge near Knoxville, Tennessee, and at Richland near Pasco, Washington, and an installation near Santa Fe, New Mexico. Although the workers at the sites have been making materials to be used in producing the greatest destructive force in history, they have not themselves been in danger beyond that of many other occupations, for the utmost care has been taken of their safety.

The fact that we can release atomic energy ushers in a new era in man's understanding of nature's forces. Atomic energy may in the future supplement the power that now comes from coal, oil, and falling water, but at present it cannot be produced on a basis to compete with them commercially. Before that comes there must be a long period of intensive research.

It has never been the habit of the scientists of this country or the policy of this government to withhold from the world scientific knowledge. Normally, therefore, everything about the work with atomic energy would be made public.

But under present circumstances it is not intended to divulge the technical processes of production or all the military applications, pending further examination of possible methods of protecting us and the rest of the world from the danger of sudden destruction.

I shall recommend that the Congress of the United States consider promptly the establishment of an appropriate commission to control the production and use of atomic power within the United States. I shall give further consideration and make further recommendations to the Congress as to how atomic power can become a powerful and forceful influence towards the maintenance of world peace.

The Truman Doctrine

Washington, D.C.

March 12, 1947

IN 1947 TRUMAN joined the long list of presidents who have adapted the Monroe Doctrine to the political crises of the moment. The situation Truman faced was a serious one. The Soviet Union, expanding into the power vacuum left by the postwar collapse of British influence in the eastern Mediterranean, was sponsoring a Communist insurgency in Greece and was also putting pressure on Turkey to share control of the Dardanelles (the straits between the Aegean and the Sea of Marmara), the Russian navy's only outlet to the Mediterranean. With the British retreating from the scene, it was up to the United States to strengthen Greece and Turkey and contain Soviet expansion into the region. Truman had grown increasingly distrustful of Stalin, and did not hesitate, as he wrote, "to put the world on notice that it would be our policy to support the cause of freedom wherever it was threatened"—a significant expansion of the Monroe Doctrine from hemispheric to global scope. He announced a plan of aid to Greece and Turkey in this speech before a joint session of Congress. The Greek-Turkish aid bill, as it was known, was passed by Congress in May.

Truman's major accomplishments were mainly in foreign affairs—the conclusion of the Pacific War, the Marshall Plan, the formation of NATO, the Berlin airlift, the beginning of the Korean War—even though this was the area in which he had the least experience when he assumed the presidency. This very success may have cost him popular support at home. When addressing the American people on the volatile and dangerous postwar situation, wrote historian Robert H. Ferrell, Truman "forthrightly described what was happening and what was necessary," even though most people were tired of foreign problems. "Many Americans," claimed Ferrell, "sought some single person to blame for their new responsibilities abroad. Harry S. Truman focused their unease, their discontent."

The gravity of the situation which confronts the world today necessitates my appearance before a joint session of the Congress. The foreign policy and the national security of this country are involved.

One aspect of the present situation which I wish to present to you at this time for your consideration and decision concerns Greece and Turkey. The United States has received from the Greek government an urgent appeal for financial and economic assistance. Preliminary reports from the American economic mission now in Greece and reports from the American ambassador in Greece corroborate the statement of the Greek government that assistance is imperative if Greece is to survive as a free nation.

I do not believe that the American people and the Congress wish to turn a deaf ear to the appeal of the Greek government.

Greece is not a rich country. Lack of sufficient natural resources has always forced the Greek people to work hard to make both ends meet. Since 1940, this industrious and peace-loving country has suffered invasion, four years of cruel enemy occupation, and bitter internal strife.

When forces of liberation entered Greece they found that the retreating Germans had destroyed virtually all the railways, roads, port facilities, communications, and merchant marine. More than a thousand villages had been burned. Eighty-five percent of the children were tubercular. Livestock, poultry, and draft animals had almost disappeared. Inflation had wiped out practically all savings. As a result of these tragic conditions, a militant minority, exploiting human want and misery, was able to create political chaos which, until now, has made economic recovery impossible.

Greece is today without funds to finance the importation of those goods which are essential to bare subsistence. Under these circumstances the people of Greece cannot make progress in solving their problems of reconstruction. Greece is in desperate need of financial and economic assistance to enable it to resume purchases of food, clothing, fuel, and seeds. These are indispensable for the subsistence of its people and are obtainable only from abroad. Greece must have help to import the goods necessary to restore internal order and security so essential for economic and political recovery.

The Greek government has also asked for the assistance of experienced American administrators, economists, and technicians to insure that the financial and other aid given to Greece shall be used effectively in creating a stable and self-sustaining economy and in improving its public administration.

The very existence of the Greek state is today threatened by the terrorist activities of several thousand armed men, led by Communists, who defy the government's authority at a number of points, particularly along the northern boundaries. A commission appointed by the United Nations Security Council is at present investigating disturbed conditions in northern Greece and alleged border violations along the frontier between Greece, on the one hand, and Albania, Bulgaria, and Yugoslavia on the other. Meanwhile, the Greek government is unable to cope with the situation. The Greek army is small and poorly equipped. It needs supplies and equipment if it is to restore the authority of the government throughout Greek territory.

Greece must have assistance if it is to become a self-supporting and self-respecting democracy. The United States must supply this assistance. We have already extended to Greece certain types of relief and economic aid but these are inadequate. There is no other country to which democratic Greece can turn. No other nation is willing and able to provide the necessary support for a democratic Greek government.

The British government, which has been helping Greece, can give no further financial or economic aid after March 31. Great Britain finds itself under the necessity of reducing or liquidating its commitments in several parts of the world, including Greece.

We have considered how the United Nations might assist in this crisis. But the situation is an urgent one requiring immediate action, and the United Nations and its related organizations are not in a position to extend help of the kind that is required.

It is important to note that the Greek government has asked for our aid in utilizing effectively the financial and other assistance we may give to Greece and in improving its public administration. It is of the utmost importance that we supervise the use of any funds made available to Greece in such a manner that each dollar spent will count toward making Greece self-supporting and will help to build an economy in which a healthy democracy can flourish.

No government is perfect. One of the chief virtues of a democracy, however, is that its defects are always visible and under democratic processes can be pointed out and corrected. The government of Greece is not perfect. Nevertheless, it represents 35 percent of the members of the Greek Parliament who were chosen in an election last year. Foreign observers, including 692 Americans, considered this election to be a fair expression of the views of the Greek people.

The Greek government has been operating in an atmosphere of chaos and extremism. It has made mistakes. The extension of aid by this country does not mean that the United States condones everything that the Greek government has done or will do. We have condemned in the past, and we condemn now, extremist measures of the right or the left. We have in the past advised tolerance, and we advise tolerance now.

Greece's neighbor, Turkey, also deserves our attention. The future of Turkey as an independent and economically sound state is clearly no less important to the freedom-loving peoples of the world than the future of Greece. The circumstances in which Turkey finds itself today are considerably different from those of Greece. Turkey has been spared the disasters that have beset Greece. And during the war, the United States and Great Britain furnished Turkey with material aid. Nevertheless, Turkey now needs our support.

Since the war, Turkey has sought financial assistance from Great Britain and the United States for the purpose of effecting that modernization necessary for the maintenance of its national integrity. That integrity is essential to the preservation of order in the Middle East.

The British government has informed us that, owing to its own difficulties, it can no longer extend financial or economic aid to Turkey. As in the case of Greece, if Turkey is to have the assistance it needs, the United States must supply it. We are the only country able to provide that help.

I am fully aware of the broad implications involved if the United States extends assistance to Greece and Turkey, and I shall discuss these implications with you at this time.

One of the primary objectives of the foreign policy of the United States is the creation of conditions in which we and other nations will be able to work out a way of life free from coercion. This was a fundamental issue in the war with Germany and Japan. Our victory was won over countries which sought to impose their will and their way of life upon other nations.

To insure the peaceful development of nations, free from coercion, the United States has taken a leading part in establishing the United Nations. The United Nations is designed to make possible lasting freedom and independence for all its members. We shall not realize our objectives, however, unless we are willing to help free peoples to maintain their free institutions and their national integrity against aggressive movements that seek to impose upon them totalitarian regimes. This is no more than a frank recognition that totalitarian regimes imposed on free peoples, by direct or indirect aggression, undermine the foundations of international peace and hence the security of the United States.

The peoples of a number of countries of the world have recently had totalitarian regimes forced upon them against their will. The government of the United States has made frequent protests against coercion and intimidation, in violation of the Yalta Agreement, in Poland, Rumania, and Bulgaria. I must also state that in a number of other countries there have been similar developments.

At the present moment in world history nearly every nation must choose between alternative ways of life. The choice is too often not a free one.

One way of life is based upon the will of the majority, and is distinguished by free institutions, representative government, free elections, guarantees of individual liberty, freedom of speech and religion, and freedom from political oppression. The second way of life is based upon the will of a minority forcibly imposed upon the majority. It relies upon terror and oppression, a controlled press and radio, fixed elections, and the suppression of personal freedoms.

I believe that it must be the policy of the United States to support free peoples who are resisting attempted subjugation by armed minorities or by outside pressures. I believe that we must assist free peoples to work out their own destinies in their own way. I believe that our help should be primarily through economic and financial aid, which is essential to economic stability and orderly political processes.

The world is not static and the status quo is not sacred. But we cannot allow changes in the status quo in violation of the Charter of the United Nations by such methods as coercion or by such subterfuges as political infiltration. In helping free and independent nations to maintain their freedom, the United States will be giving effect to the principles of the Charter of the United Nations.

It is necessary only to glance at a map to realize that the survival and integrity of the Greek nation are of grave importance in a much wider situation. If Greece should fall under the control of an armed minority, the effect upon its neighbor, Turkey, would be immediate and serious. Confusion and disorder might well spread throughout the entire Middle East. Moreover, the disappearance of Greece as an independent state would have a profound effect upon those countries in Europe whose peoples are struggling against great difficulties to maintain their freedoms and their independence while they repair the damages of war.

It would be an unspeakable tragedy if these countries, which have struggled so long against overwhelming odds, should lose that victory for which they sacrificed so much. Collapse of free institutions and loss of independence would be disastrous not only for them but for the world. Discouragement and possibly failure would quickly be the lot of neighboring peoples striving to maintain their freedom and independence.

Should we fail to aid Greece and Turkey in this fateful hour, the effect will be far-reaching to the West as well as to the East. We must take immediate and resolute action.

I therefore ask the Congress to provide authority for assistance to Greece and Turkey in the amount of $400 million for the period ending June 30, 1948. In requesting these funds, I have taken into consideration the maximum amount of relief assistance which would be furnished to Greece out of the $350 million which I recently requested that the Congress authorize for the prevention of starvation and suffering in countries devastated by the war.

In addition to funds, I ask the Congress to authorize the detail of American civilian and military personnel to Greece and Turkey, at the request of those countries, to assist in the tasks of reconstruction, and for the purpose of supervising the use of such financial and material assistance as may be furnished. I recommend that authority also be provided for the instruction and training of selected Greek and Turkish personnel.

Finally, I ask that the Congress provide authority which will permit the speediest and most effective use, in terms of needed commodities, supplies, and equipment, of such funds as may be authorized.

If further funds, or further authority, should be needed for purposes indicated in this message, I shall not hesitate to bring the situation before the Congress. On this subject the executive and legislative branches of the government must work together.

This is a serious course upon which we embark. I would not recommend it except that the alternative is much more serious.

The United States contributed $341 billion toward winning World War II. This is an investment in world freedom and world peace. The assistance that I am recommending for Greece and Turkey amounts to little more than one-tenth of 1 percent of this investment. It is only common sense that we should safeguard this investment and make sure that it was not in vain.

The seeds of totalitarian regimes are nurtured by misery and want. They spread and grow in the evil soil of poverty and strife. They reach their full growth when the hope of a people for a better life has died. We must keep that hope alive.

The free peoples of the world look to us for support in maintaining their freedoms. If we falter in our leadership, we may endanger the peace of the world—and we shall surely endanger the welfare of our own nation.

Great responsibilities have been placed upon us by the swift movement of events. I am confident that the Congress will face these responsibilities squarely.

Whistle-Stop Talks

THE POLLSTERS, the press, and the Republican Party were all confident that Truman would be defeated by the Republican challenger, Thomas Dewey, in the 1948 presidential election. The only person who appeared to think Truman could win was Truman himself. As the election approached, the president took his campaign to the people through a nationwide whistle-stop tour, traveling 21,928 miles and giving 275 short speeches between Labor Day and election day. Four representative whistle-stop speeches are reprinted below.

Colorado Springs, Colorado
September 20, 1948

I am very happy to be in Colorado Springs again. I have been here on numerous occasions. It's a lovely place, beautifully situated, and you don't dare talk about the climate of Colorado Springs in California—or Florida either, for that matter.

One of the reasons you are prosperous and happy is because you've learned how to use your resources to the very best advantage, especially your water resources.

You know, the Reclamation Act has been on the books for more than 30 years, but nothing much was done about it or the development of this part of the world until 1932, when you elected Franklin D. Roosevelt.

Most of you in 1932 had given up hope and were thinking of going somewhere else, along with the Okies and the other people who were moving around the country; but much to your satisfaction you didn't do that.

At that time the income of the great state of Colorado was about $35 million. Do you know what it was last year? It was a 1,500 billion dollars. And that wasn't due to any accident. That was due to the development of the resources of this great state.

It's a wonderful thing that has happened to this part of the world in the last decade, and I am wondering whether you are going to let the present propaganda machine fool you into turning the clock back to 1932 again. I am very sure you won't do that. If you'll just study the facts and the figures, you can't do anything else but keep an administration in power that has been trying to do things for this part of the world.

I made a speech in Denver at noon, in which I made the statement that due to the example of that terrible 80th Republican Congress elected in 1946, I could say definitely that the Republicans are trying to sabotage the West.

In 1946, you know, two-thirds of you stayed at home and didn't vote. You wanted a change. Well, you got it. You got the change. You got just exactly what you deserved.

If you stay at home on November the 2d and let this same gang get control of the government, I won't have any sympathy with you. But if you go out to the polls on that day and do your duty as you should I won't have to worry about moving out of the White House; and you won't have to worry about what happens to the welfare of the West. Those two things go together.

I have been most happy today to travel around over Colorado with your Democratic candidate for Congress and your Democratic candidate for the Senate, Ed Johnson, and with your wonderful and able Democratic governor who introduced me up in Denver today. It's been a pleasure to be with those gentlemen, and I want to see Colorado come out of the kinks entirely and send us a Democratic delegation in toto to the Congress.

Eldorado, Illinois
September 30, 1948

Thank you very much. I never had a more cordial welcome on the whole trip. I appreciate it very much. I had the pleasure of riding with your mayor, and with your Mr. Powell, who has entertained me most highly on this trip, and he told me all about Illinois and this part of the state—a great Democratic stronghold, this is. I am certainly glad to be here in this great Democratic stronghold, and I wish I had all afternoon to discuss with you the issues that are before us in this campaign; but the issues are clearly drawn.

It is merely the people against the special interests. The Democratic Party has always represented the people in these fights with the special interests, and the Republican

589

Party has been the special interest party. And this 80th Congress—I call it the "do-nothing" 80th Congress—has conclusively proven that they are still for that viewpoint of the public servant.

Now, the way you can cure that is to elect a Democratic Congress, and if you do that, of course you will return me to the White House, and I won't have any trouble with the housing shortage.

I want to see Illinois come back into the fold and go Democratic, as it should. I want to see you elect John Upchurch here to the Congress of the United States, and Paul Douglas to the United States Senate; and then you ought to elect Adlai Stevenson to be the governor of Illinois. You know, Mr. Stevenson comes of a line of public servants. His father was vice president of the United States with Grover Cleveland, and he has rendered tremendous public service during this emergency through which we have just passed. He is a good administrator, and I am sure you can't do better than to make him governor of Illinois.

If you will send Paul Douglas and John Upchurch to the Congress, and if Illinois will go down the line and give us a Democratic delegation in the Congress of the United States, we won't have any more 80th "do-nothing" Congresses.

Here are just a few examples to prove it to you that this Congress is a special interest Congress. The first thing they did when they got there was to vote themselves a rich man's tax bill, which I vetoed. Then they took it back and modified it, and I vetoed it again. Then they passed it over my veto. It is a rich man's tax bill, if you analyze it.

Then the next thing they did was to take some freedom away from labor, and to pass the Taft-Hartley Act which tried to emasculate the Wagner Act. Now labor got its magna charta from President Roosevelt under the Wagner Act back in 1935, the act that gives to labor the right to free collective bargaining, and guarantees that right. Well, this Taft-Hartley law endeavored to take that right away from labor.

And if the laboringmen stay at home, as they did in 1946, I have just received information as to what the Republicans intend to do further to labor.

Then they took on the farmer, and they are going right down the line to undo everything that has been done to keep his income on an even keel, to evenly distribute the income so that everybody will have his fair share. Then, on the price support program, they almost wrecked it by a joker which they put into the recharter of the CCC, which does not allow the government to furnish storage space for the grain on which they make loans.

Corn, right now, in this vicinity is selling 45 percent below the support price just for that reason, and the speculators will get the benefit of the Republican change in that Commodity Credit law. And it isn't fair. It isn't right.

I have been going up and down this country pointing out specific examples of what happened. We wanted to build a steamplant—a standby plant for TVA, which would be of some benefit to you people right here and cost $4 million. They knocked that out. I asked them to put it in again at the special session, but they never did it. They did not intend to do anything for the welfare and benefit of the people. The power trust lobby stood out here at the rathole and wouldn't let them do it. There are bigger lobbies in Congress this time—in that 80th Congress—than ever before in history.

We have been making a crusade up and down this country, trying to convince the people that their interests are with the Democratic Party, and if you believe that, you will send me back to the White House, and you will elect a Democratic Congress to take the place of this "do-nothing," good-for-nothing 80th Congress.

Thank you.

Elizabeth, New Jersey
October 7, 1948

I appreciate very much this very cordial welcome which you have accorded me. This is my first stop in the great state of New Jersey, and it is right in line with the other first stops. In every state, through which I have been, they were all just like this. People want to see their president, they want to hear what their president has to say; and I can't tell you how very much I thank you for that interest.

You are here because you are interested in the issues of this campaign. You know, as all the citizens of this great country know, that the election is not all over but the shouting. That is what they would like to have you believe, but it isn't so—it isn't so at all. The

Republicans are trying to hide the truth from you in a great many ways. They don't want you to know the truth about the issues in this campaign. The big fundamental issue in this campaign is the people against the special interests. The Democratic Party stands for the people. The Republican Party stands, and always has stood, for special interests. They have proved that conclusively in the record that they made in this "do-nothing" Congress.

The Republican Party candidates are going around talking to you in high-sounding platitudes trying to make you believe that they themselves are the best people to run the government. Well now, you have had experience with them running the government. In 1920 to 1932, they had complete control of the government. Look what they did to it!

They started again in 1946, when two-thirds of the people in the United States stayed at home and allowed a third of the people to send that Congress which we now have down to Washington. They immediately began to try to undo all the good things that the Democrats have been doing for you for the last 14 years.

You get the truth if you listen to your candidates—Archie Alexander, one of the finest young men I know, is going all over this state telling you the facts. You ought to send him to the Senate. He is the Democratic candidate for the Senate from this great state, and he is so good that the Republican paper, the New York *Herald Tribune,* said about Mr. Alexander, that he possesses superior qualifications.

Of course, I think all the candidates on the Democratic ticket always do have superior qualifications, or they wouldn't be on the Democratic ticket. This country is enjoying the greatest prosperity it has ever known because we have been following for 16 years the policies inaugurated by Franklin D. Roosevelt. Everybody benefited from these policies—labor, the farmer, businessmen, and white-collar workers.

We want to keep that prosperity. We cannot keep that if we don't lick the biggest problem facing us today, and that is high prices.

I have been trying to get the Republicans to do something about high prices and housing ever since they came to Washington. They are responsible for that situation, because they killed price control, and they killed the housing bill. That Republican 80th "do-nothing"

Congress absolutely refused to give any relief whatever in either one of those categories.

What do you suppose the Republicans think you ought to do about high prices?

Senator Taft, one of the leaders in the Republican Congress, said, "If consumers think the price is too high today, they will wait until the price is lower. I feel that in time the law of supply and demand will bring prices into line."

There is the Republican answer to the high cost of living.

If it costs too much, just wait.

If you think 15 cents is too much for a loaf of bread, just do without it and wait until you can afford to pay 15 cents for it.

If you don't want to pay 60 cents a pound for hamburger, just wait.

That is what the Republican Congress thought you ought to do, and that is the same Congress that the Republican candidate for president said did a good job.

Some people say I ought not to talk so much about the Republican 80th "do-nothing" Congress in this campaign. I will tell you why I will talk about it. If two-thirds of the people stay at home again on election day as they did in 1946, and if we get another Republican Congress like the 80th Congress, it will be controlled by the same men who controlled that 80th Congress—the Tabers, and the Tafts, the Martins and the Hallecks would be the bosses. The same men would be the bosses, the same as those who passed the Taft-Hartley Act, and passed the rich man's tax bill, and took social security away from a million workers.

Do you want that kind of administration? I don't believe you do—I don't believe you do.

I don't believe you would be out here interested in listening to my outline of what the Republicans are trying to do to you if you intended to put them back in there.

When a bunch of Republican reactionaries are in control of the Congress, then the people get reactionary laws. The only way you can get the kind of government you need is by going to the polls and voting the straight Democratic ticket on November 2d. Then you will get a Democratic Congress and I will get a Congress that will work with me. Then we will get good housing at prices we can afford to pay; and repeal of that vicious Taft-Hartley Act; and more social security coverage; and prices that will be fair to everybody; and we can go on and keep 61 million people at work; we can have an income of more than $217 billion, and that income will be distributed so that the farmer, the workingman, the white-collar worker, and the businessman get their fair share of that income.

That is what I stand for.

That is what the Democratic Party stands for.

Vote for that, and you will be safe!

Framingham, Massachusetts
October 27, 1948

Thank you, thank you very much. I certainly appreciate most highly that cordial introduction. I have had a most wonderful reception in this great state, and I certainly wish I could visit every corner of New England and every town in it.

Now, this city of Framingham has a reputation of being a forward-looking community. I had heard about it long before I ever arrived here. I know that you want to keep right on going forward along the lines laid down by the Democratic Party in the last 16 years. You proved that in 1946 when you sent a fine Democrat to Congress, Harold D. Donohue. If more cities and congressional districts had followed your example, how much better off we would all be! We would never have had that backward-looking 80th Congress if every city and community had done what you did the last time.

I am satisfied that the American people are very sorry that they let so many moss-back Republicans slip into that 80th Congress. I believe the voters all over the country are going to send those reactionary Republicans back to private life in November. I believe the voters are going to turn thumbs down on the Republican candidate for president, a candidate who won't tell you where he stands or what he believes in. He goes around preaching platitudes. You know, he has given "G.O.P." another meaning. It now means "Grand Old Platitudes." I believe the American people are entitled to hear from the Republican leaders the full and honest convictions of the candidate.

You certainly know where the leaders of the Democratic Party stand. I have gone all over the country, from one end to the other—north and south and east and west—and you understand exactly where I stand; and I have tried to make it perfectly clear to you where the Republicans stand too. I defy you to say what the Republicans stand for—what the Republican candidate for president stands for except for the Republican Party. And if he can stand for that, he can stand for anything!

In the last 16 years your government has been headed by men who have done everything possible to promote the welfare of the people as a whole. By "the people" I mean all the citizens of the United States. We don't restrict our sympathies to the people who make $100,000 a year. We mean everybody in the country. We want to build millions of low-priced houses for workingmen and their families. We want to get rid of the vicious Taft-Hartley law, passed by the Republican Congress under the whip of the millionaire manufacturers. We want to provide federal aid to education so that all our children will have a chance to get a decent schooling. We want to put a national health program into effect so that all Americans can get good medical care and good dental care.

We can do all these things if everybody goes to the polls and votes the Democratic ticket straight in November. You can vote for a federal housing program, a federal aid to education program, a federal health program, by marking your ballot for the Democratic candidates.

You have a stake in this election. It will affect your job, your chance to get a raise, your chance to get a better home, your chance to control the high prices that rob you of all gains you had before those prices went up. It will mean the difference between moving ahead and going backward.

The people's campaign is rolling to victory. I can assure you of that. The West is with us, the central states are with us, and the East is swinging into line. If you would see the people I have been talking to since I came East, you would understand what I mean when I say the East is beginning to find out what side its bread is buttered on.

All I ask you to do is vote for yourself, vote for your family. When you come right down to the analysis of our government, our government is the people, and when the people exercise their right to vote on election day they control that government. When they don't exercise that right then you get—then you get an 80th Congress. So, two-thirds of the people of the United

States entitled to vote in 1946 stayed at home. They didn't have energy enough to go and look after their political interests on election day—and they got the 80th Congress. Don't do that again. Don't do that again.

The Democrats are not afraid of the people. The Democrats know that when the people exercise their rights the country is safe.

I am urging you with everything I have: on November 2d, everyone of you, get up early and go to the polls and vote the Democratic ticket straight—and then you'll have a Democratic president, a Democratic Congress, and a Democratic organization and government here in this great Commonwealth of Massachusetts.

I appreciate your coming out very much.

The Fair Deal

Pittsburgh, Pennsylvania
September 5, 1949

THE FAIR DEAL (the tag was picked up by the press from Truman's 1949 State of the Union Message) was a loose program of liberal reforms meant to solidify and extend the New Deal, especially in the areas of civil rights, social welfare, health insurance, and labor legislation. Truman outlined the philosophy and goals of the Fair Deal in this speech on Labor Day at the Allegheny County Fair. But as political historian Robert Donovan has pointed out, "the public had been indifferent toward further reforms in Truman's first term, and no sudden new stirring was apparent." Only a fraction of Truman's Fair Deal agenda ever became law.

I am very happy to be here today at the Allegheny County Free Fair. . . .

I notice that this is called "the world's largest county fair." I have attended county fairs for 60 years, and I'm glad to be a guest at the biggest one of all today.

My first visit to a county fair was when I was about five years old. My old grandfather took me in a cart with a strawberry roan horse and drove me six miles to the Cass County Fair at Belton, Mo. And I went with him all six days, and sat with him in the judges' stand when the races were called. It was a great event in my young life, and I have been going to county fairs ever since. And here I am now at the biggest one.

I am particularly impressed by this fair, because it is both a farm show and an industrial exposition. Farmers and industrial workers together are showing their best products here today.

Farmers and industrial workers—agriculture and industry—ought to show their products together. For these two groups depend upon each other. Together, they are responsible for the tremendous production of this country's economic system. No program for prosperity in the country can ignore the interests of either group.

In recent years some people have been telling farmers, out of one corner of their mouths, that the labor unions are bad for farmers. Out of the other corner of their mouths, these same people have been telling industrial workers that programs to benefit farmers are bad for labor. If you ever meet anybody like that, you can be sure he is not interested in the welfare of either the farmer or the industrial worker. Those who are trying to set these two great groups against each other just have axes of their own to grind.

Now, about this time last year, if you remember, the country was engaged in a great political campaign. I covered a good deal of the United States in the course of that campaign, and I put the plain facts, as I saw them, before the people. I also offered a program to meet the needs of all groups in this country for growth and prosperity. The votes of the people showed that they wanted that kind of program. They were not misled by the newspapers and the magazines and the so-called experts who tried to convince them that they did not want that kind of program.

The people knew what they wanted.

Their votes showed that the farmers and the workers stand together in demanding a government that works for the benefit of all our citizens.

It is now almost a year since that campaign, and I think it is time to take stock of the situation and see what progress we have made in carrying out the program the people voted for.

I am happy to be able to report to you that we have made progress; and we are continuing to make progress.

As a result of last fall's election, we have a new Congress in Washington. And this new 81st Congress has an entirely different approach to the needs and desires of the people from that of the 80th Congress.

The 80th Congress was a threat to almost every bit of forward-looking legislation passed during recent years. For example, it repealed the Wagner Labor Relations Act and replaced it with an unfair and restrictive Taft-Hartley Act. It took social security benefits from hundreds of thousands of people. It weakened our farm programs. It attacked our national policy for making the benefits of electric power available to the public-to all the people-instead of just the privileged few.

If the 80th Congress had not been repudiated, this tearing down process would have gone on and on. But now the new 81st Congress has reversed this backward trend.

The 81st Congress has put a stop to the piecemeal destruction of the hard-won protections and benefits that the people have built up for themselves. It has done more than that. The 81st Congress has moved forward.

Some people are trying to make you believe that the 81st Congress has been a "do-nothing" Congress. That simply is not true. The fact is the 81st Congress has already passed many important measures for the good of the people-and it will pass many more progressive laws.

The 81st Congress has taken wise and important steps in foreign policy by extending the European recovery program and ratifying the North Atlantic Treaty. It has enacted a far-reaching housing program that will benefit millions of our citizens. It has extended rent control. It has taken action to make low-cost electricity available to more of our people. It has strengthened the soil conservation and reclamation programs. This congress has restored the government's power to acquire grain storage facilities necessary to carry out the farm-price support program. This Congress has approved an International Wheat Agreement which will give our farmers a fair share of the world wheat markets at fair prices. This Congress has strengthened and improved our organization for national defense.

My friends, this is real progress. And this session is not over yet. Other important measures, such as those raising the minimum wage and extending the Reciprocal Trade Agreements Act, are well on their way to final passage.

The 81st Congress has taken these actions over the fierce opposition of the selfish interests. The organized conspiracy of the selfish interests has gone right on working against the common good, in spite of the election returns.

One of the things that the special interests have managed to do up until this time is to prevent the repeal of the Taft-Hartley law. But that issue is far from settled. We are going to continue to fight for the repeal of that repressive law until it is wiped off the statute books.

The selfish interests have always been working against the common good, since the beginning of our history. Our fathers and our grandfathers had to fight against them every step of the way to make progress. They had to fight for a free public school system. They had to fight for the right of homesteaders to settle on the public lands. They had to fight for laws to protect the health and safety of industrial workers. They had to fight for labor's right to organize.

We face the same situation today. We still have a fight on our hands.

The special interests always fail to see that the way of progress, the way of greater prosperity for themselves, as well as others, lies in the direction of a fuller and happier life for all.

Too many people who can afford big insurance policies for themselves are not concerned over the need of expanding social security. Too many who are making money out of the rents from slums are not in favor of expanding public housing to provide decent shelter for low-income families. Too many with big incomes are not interested in raising minimum wages. Too many who can freely organize themselves in business associations or employers' groups are not anxious to protect the same right to organize among industrial workers.

It is hard, perhaps, for the people in comfortable circumstances to see the need for improving the well-being of the less fortunate. Furthermore, they are always being stirred up and misled by the spokesmen and lobbyists for organized selfish interests. There are a lot of paid agitators, promoters, and so-called publicity experts who make a fat living by frightening the people in the higher income groups about forward-looking legislation, and by organizing campaigns against that forward-looking legislation.

Ever since the election those spokesmen have been very busy stirring up opposition to our legislative program.

The hue and cry that has resulted, in the press, and on the air, and through the mail, has been deafening.

These propagandists do not argue the merits of our program. They know that the American people will always decide against the selfish interests if all the facts are before them. So they have adopted the age-old device to hide the weakness of their case.

This is the device of the "scare-word" campaign.

It is a device that has been used in every country and every age by the propagandists for selfish interests. They invent slogans in an effort to scare the people. They apply frightening labels to anything they happen to oppose. These scare words are intended to confuse the people and turn them against their own best interests.

Scare words change with the times.

When Franklin D. Roosevelt and the New Deal saved our country from the great depression, the selfish interests raised the scare words of "socialism" and "regimentation."

But the American people didn't scare.

Year after year the selfish interests kept up their refrain. They tried new words-"bureaucracy" and "bankruptcy."

But the American people still didn't scare.

Last November the people gave the selfish interests the surprise of their lives. The people just didn't believe that programs designed to assure them decent housing, adequate wages, improved medical care, and better education were "socialism" or "regimentation."

So the selfish interests retired to a backroom with their high-priced advertising experts and thought things over. They decided that the old set of scare words had become a little mildewed. Maybe it was time for a change.

So they came up with a new set of scare words. Now they're talking about "collectivism," and "statism," and "the welfare state."

The selfish interests don't know-in fact, they don't care-what those words mean. They are using those words only because they want to turn the American people against the programs which the people want, and need, and for which the people voted last fall.

Let's see how the selfish interests are using these scare words.

The people want public housing for low-income families. The selfish interests are opposed to this because they think it will cut down their own incomes; so they call it "collectivism."

Well, we don't care what they call it.

We are for public housing. It is the democratic way to provide decent homes in place of slums.

The people want fair laws for labor. The selfish interests are against these laws because

they mistakenly fear that their profits will be reduced; so they call that "statism."

Well, we don't care what they call it.

We believe that the workers in this country have a fundamental right to square treatment from employers.

The people want a fair program for the farmers, including an effective price support system. The selfish interests fight against this because it keeps them from profiteering at the farmers' expense; so they call this "socialism."

Well, we don't care what they call it.

We know that the well-being of the country depends upon the well-being of the farmers, and that farm prosperity must be protected in the interest of all of us.

The people want a better social security system, improved education, and a national health program. The selfish interests are trying to sabotage these programs because they have no concern about helping the little fellow; and so they call this the "welfare state."

Well, we don't care what they call it.

We know that the little fellow is the backbone of this country, and we are dedicated to the principle that the government should promote the welfare of all the people.

The spokesmen for these special interests say that these programs make the government too powerful and cause the people to lose their freedom. Well now, that just is not so. Programs like these make the people more independent-independent of the government, independent of big business and corporate power.

People who have opportunity to work and earn, and who have an assured income in their old age, are free. They are free of the fear of poverty. They are free of public or private charity. They can live happier, more useful lives. That's real freedom. And that is something we should be proud of-that's not something to be slandered by trumped-up slogans.

Along with this campaign of scare words, we hear another argument against adopting any forward-looking legislation. It is to the effect that even if these programs are good things, we can't adopt them now, because they cost too much and we can't afford them.

The selfish interests say we can't afford these programs during a boom because that would be inflationary. They say we can't afford them during a recession because that would be deflationary. They say we can't afford them during a war because we are too busy with defense, we can't afford them in time of peace because that would discourage business. So, according to the selfish interests, we never can afford them.

But the truth is, we can't afford not to put these programs into effect. We can afford them, we ought to have them, and we will have them.

The sooner we have them the better it will be for the country, and the more we will save.

Take our programs for resource development, for example. If we fail to conserve our soil, we lose our most valuable resource. If we fail to build electric power facilities, we hamper the development of industry.

Take our social security system. Shall we force our old people to turn to charity? Or shall we let them have an independent and self-respecting existence through an up-to-date old-age insurance system, paid for during their working years?

Take housing. If we don't go forward with our housing and slum-clearance programs, we shall have to pay the rising costs of disease, immorality, and crime bred in slums.

Consider our schools. The hidden costs of poor education, lost opportunity, and poverty resulting from inadequate schools are costs the nation can no longer afford. Federal aid to education will be a lot less expensive than ignorance and illiteracy.

If we are to have a healthy and prosperous United States, we must have better schools, better housing, better medical care, better use of our resources, stronger social security, and the other improvements in our democracy that the people need.

Those who oppose these improvements refuse to face the facts of today's world. They don't understand the overriding urgency of proving the value of the democratic way of life, not just with words, but with deeds. They don't see that the very survival of free enterprise depends upon a rising standard of living and an expanding economy. They don't recognize that to work for the increasing security and liberty of the people of the United States is the key not only to our own prosperity, but to the prosperity and peace of the whole world.

But the people of the United States do understand these things. When they have the facts before them, they always choose progress-not reaction.

They made this clear again last fall. They chose the very same programs that are now being attacked by the selfish interests with their campaign scare words. The people were not misled about those programs then. They will not be misled about them now.

The people know that the second half of the 20th century is going to be a time of challenge to the way of freedom and progress that our democracy represents. As we meet that challenge, we shall have to fight, as we have always fought, the selfish forces of reaction and special privilege.

The people of the United States have been winning that fight for 160 years. I am convinced that we will continue to win that fight through the years to come.

Slandermongers and Real Americans

Washington, D.C.

August 14, 1951

TRUMAN WAS deeply disturbed by the witch-hunts masterminded by Sen. Joseph McCarthy, who had become one of the most powerful men in Congress by accusing the administration of fostering subversion in every corner of the government. With anti-Communist hysteria at its height, efforts to discredit McCarthy not only failed but appeared to bolster the senator's claim that "reds" in the government were out to get him.

Truman himself spoke out vehemently against McCarthy's "lies, slander, [and] mudslinging." This speech to the American Legion was his most eloquent on the subject. McCarthy immediately recognized it as an attack on him and retorted that "it ill-befits the president of this great nation to try to protect the dupes and stooges of the Kremlin by using his high office to attack—not the facts—but whoever attempts to bring the facts to the attention of the American people."

I am happy to be here this afternoon to dedicate the new Washington headquarters of the American Legion. I wish the legion every success in its new home.

I have been thinking back to the early days of the American Legion, right after World War I. You know, I was pretty active in legion affairs, back in those days. I helped to establish four different legion posts in Missouri.

We didn't start this organization just to look out for our own interests as veterans or to give us an excuse for reminiscing about what heroes we had been. We started this organization so we could work together as patriotic citizens for the good of all Americans.

That is what we have been trying to do for the last 30 years.

Not everything we have done has been perfect, but the record is one to make us proud. The American Legion has been a powerful and constructive force in American life.

The legion has been in the forefront of the fight to establish the best system of help and care for veterans that any country ever had.

The legion has done wonderful work for the welfare of children. It established a national child welfare division in 1925, and since then it has carried on a full-fledged program helping to provide home care for needy children.

Another of the legion's principal objectives has been to help in achieving a sound national defense. At its first national convention in 1919 the legion adopted a resolution urging a policy of universal military training. It has consistently supported that policy from that day until this. I appreciate that support very much because I have recommended universal training to the Congress at least seven times. I am glad to be able to say that we have finally made some real progress on this issue. On June 13 I signed into law the Universal Military and Service Act. This is a great step toward a sensible, long-range military manpower program for our country.

The legion's interest in national defense has extended far beyond universal training—it has extended to all the measures needed for the protection of our country. In recent years, the organization has supported unification of the armed services. It has supported the North Atlantic Treaty and military aid for Europe and our own rearmament program.

This participation by the legion in our national defense activities is a very healthy thing. The members of the legion who have served their country as citizen-soldiers know how important it is to defend our country from its enemies. And they know that citizens must take an active part in these matters if we are to maintain our tradition of civilian control over the military establishment.

It is natural for the legion to be especially concerned with veterans' affairs and national defense. But I am glad to say that the American Legion has never considered its responsibilities to be limited to those fields. It has recognized from the beginning that its members are not only veterans; but, more important, they are also citizens of a great republic with all of a citizen's duties and responsibilities.

In the preamble to the legion's constitution, its members pledged themselves—among other things—to "uphold and defend the Constitution of the United States . . . to foster and perpetuate a 100 percent Americanism . . . to safeguard and transmit to posterity the principles of justice, freedom, and democracy."

At the present time, it is especially important for us to understand what these words mean and to live up to them.

The keystone of our form of government is the liberty of the individual. The Bill of Rights, which protects our individual liberties, is the most fundamental part of our Constitution.

When the legion pledged itself to uphold the Constitution, and to foster 100 percent Americanism, it pledged itself to protect the rights and liberties of all our citizens.

Real Americanism means that we will protect freedom of speech—we will defend the right of people to say what they think, regardless of how much we may disagree with them.

Real Americanism means freedom of religion. It means that we will not discriminate against a man because of his religious faith.

Real Americanism means fair opportunities for all our citizens. It means that none of our citizens should be held back by unfair discrimination and prejudice.

Real Americanism means fair play. It means that a man who is accused of a crime shall be considered innocent until he has been proved guilty. It means that people are not to be penalized and persecuted for exercising their constitutional liberties.

Real Americanism means also that liberty is not license. There is no freedom to injure others. The Constitution does not protect free speech to the extent of permitting conspiracies to overthrow the government. Neither does the right of free speech authorize slander or character assassination. These limitations are essential to keep us working together in one great community.

Real Americanism includes all these things. And it takes all of them together to make 100 percent Americanism—the kind the legion is pledged to support.

I'm glad the legion has made that pledge. For true Americanism is under terrible attack today. True Americanism needs defending— here and now. It needs defending by every decent human being in this country.

Americanism is under attack by Communism, at home and abroad. We are defending it against that attack. We are protecting our country from spies and saboteurs. We are breaking up the Communist conspiracy in the United States. We are building our defenses, and making our country strong, and helping our allies to help themselves.

If we keep on doing these things—if we put our best into the job—we can protect ourselves from the attack of Communism.

But Americanism is also under another kind of attack. It is being undermined by some people in this country who are loudly proclaiming that they are its chief defenders. These people claim to be against Communism. But they are chipping away our basic freedoms just as insidiously and far more effectively than the Communists have ever been able to do.

These people have attacked the basic principle of fair play that underlies our Constitution. They are trying to create fear and suspicion among us by the use of slander, unproved accusations, and just plain lies.

They are filling the air with the most irresponsible kinds of accusations against other people. They are trying to get us to believe that our government is riddled with Communism and corruption—when the fact is that we have the finest and most loyal body of civil servants in the world. These slandermongers are trying to get us so hysterical that no one will stand up to them for fear of being called a Communist.

Now, this is an old Communist trick in reverse. Everybody in Russia lives in terror of being called an anti-Communist. For once that charge is made against anybody in Russia—no matter what the facts are—he is on the way out.

In a dictatorship, everybody lives in fear and terror of being denounced and slandered. Nobody dares stand up for his rights.

We must never let such a condition come to pass in this country.

Yet this is exactly what the scaremongers and hatemongers are trying to bring about. Character assassination is their stock in trade. Guilt by association is their motto. They have created such a wave of fear and uncertainty that their attacks upon our liberties go almost unchallenged. Many people are growing frightened—and frightened people don't protest.

Stop and think. Stop and think where this is leading us.

The growing practice of character assassination is already curbing free speech and it is threatening all our other freedoms. I daresay there are people here today who have reached the point where they are afraid to explore a new idea. How many of you are afraid to come right out in public and say what you think about a controversial issue? How many of you feel that you must "play it safe" in all things—and on all occasions?

I hope there are not many, but from all that I have seen and heard, I am afraid of what your answers might be.

For I know you have no way of telling when some unfounded accusation may be hurled at you, perhaps straight from the halls of Congress.

Some of you have friends or neighbors who have been singled out for the pitiless publicity that follows accusations of this kind—accusations that are made without any regard for the actual guilt or innocence of the victim.

That is not playing fair. That is not Americanism. It is not the American way to slur the loyalty and besmirch the character of the innocent and the guilty alike. We have always considered it just as important to protect the innocent as it is to punish the guilty.

We want to protect the country against disloyalty—of course we do. We have been punishing people for disloyal acts, and we are going to keep on punishing the guilty whenever we have a case against them. But we don't want to destroy our whole system of justice in the process. We don't want to injure innocent people. And yet the scurrilous work of the scandalmongers gravely threatens the whole idea of protection for the innocent in our country today.

Perhaps the Americans who live outside of Washington are less aware of this than you and I. If that is so I want to warn them all. Slander, lies, character assassination—these things are a threat to every single citizen everywhere in this country. When even one American—who has done nothing wrong—is forced by fear to shut his mind and close his mouth, then all Americans are in peril.

It is the job of all of us—of every American who loves his country and his freedom—to rise up and put a stop to this terrible business. This is one of the greatest challenges we face today. We have got to make a fight for real 100 percent Americanism.

You Legionnaires, living up to your constitution as I know you want to do, can help lead the way. You can set an example of fair play. You can raise your voices against hysteria. You can expose the rotten motives of those people who are trying to divide us and confuse us and tear up the Bill of Rights.

No organization ever had the opportunity to do a greater service for America. No organization was ever better suited or better equipped to do the job.

I know the legion. I know what a tremendous force for good it can be.

Now go to it.

And God bless you.

The Struggle for Civil Rights

New York City, New York

October 11, 1952

A PASSIONATE and vocal advocate of civil rights, Truman was the first modern president to draft legislation to help secure the civil rights of blacks. During his administration, he introduced bills against lynching, segregation in interstate transportation, and the poll tax. These bills were a decade or more ahead of the times, and none passed Congress. One civil rights measure that Truman did achieve was the integration of the armed forces, completed during the Korean War. The president enumerated these and other accomplishments while stumping in Harlem for Adlai Stevenson, the 1952 Democratic presidential candidate.

I deeply appreciate the Franklin Delano Roosevelt award you have just given me. I appreciate it all the more because I received the same award here in Dorrance Brooks Park four years ago this month.

That was an occasion I shall never forget. The deep feeling that poured forth from the hearts of the many thousands of people who were assembled in this park four years ago, was one of the most moving experiences of my whole life. Mrs. Truman remarked that it was the greatest and most dignified meeting she had ever attended. That is something for her to say.

You, of course, know that Dorrance Brooks Park is named after a very gallant youth who was a private in the army of the United States. He gave his life for his country in the best American tradition. It is to the credit of the people of this great city of New York that his heroism has been appreciated and acknowledged.

That meeting was the high point of the 1948 campaign. I knew then that you had placed your trust in me. We pledged ourselves that day to a great enterprise—the end of racial injustice and unfair discrimination. I am here to say to you now that fight will never cease with me as long as I live.

I am very proud of this award. Franklin Roosevelt beat back depression, he led us to victory in war, he gave us the chance to create a world order based on the equal worth and dignity of every individual. It is up to us to make good on the chance he gave us.

Today I am winding up a trip across this great country in which I have urged the American people to elect Adlai Stevenson as president. There are a great many reasons why you should do that.

The Democratic Party under Adlai Stevenson offers you the best hope of peace in the world. The Democratic Party offers you the best protection against depression. And not least, it offers you continued progress toward full civil rights for all Americans.

Now, many people have wondered how I came to have such a deep interest in civil rights. I want to tell you about that. Right after World War II, religious and racial intolerance began to show up just as it did in 1919. There were a good many incidents of violence and friction, but two of them in particular made a very deep impression on me. One was when a Negro veteran, still wearing this country's uniform, was arrested, and beaten and blinded. Not long after that, two Negro veterans with their wives lost their lives at the hands of a mob.

It is the duty of the state and local government to prevent such tragedies. But, as president of the United States, I felt I ought to do everything in my power to find what caused such crimes and to root out the causes. It was for that reason that I created the President's Committee on Civil Rights. I asked its members to study the situation and recommend to the whole country what we should do.

Their report is one of our great American documents. When it was handed to me, I said that it was a new charter of human freedom. Five years have passed, but I have never seen anything to make me change my mind. These five years have seen some hard fighting by those who believe in civil rights for all our people—women like that great lady, Mrs. Eleanor Roosevelt, men like your own good senators, Herbert Lehman and Bob Wagner—and the fine Democrats you have sent from

New York to the House of Representatives. These five years have seen a lot of progress—progress in spite of obstacles that have been placed in our way.

I want to review that progress for you today.

Right after the Committee on Civil Rights made its report to me, I sent to the Congress a special message making 10 recommendations for new legislation. Only two of those 10 recommendations have been approved by the Congress. The opponents of civil rights in the Congress have blocked every effort to enact such important legislation as a fair employment practices law, an antipoll tax law, and an antilynch law. Not only that, they have succeeded in changing the rules under which Congress operates, so as to make it impossible to stop a filibuster.

Who are the opponents of civil rights? All you have to do is to look at the record. Read the Congressional Record, and you'll find them. I sent a good FEPC bill to Congress; but the Republicans introduced the McConnell amendment—a toothless substitute for FEPC. And the Republicans in the House voted two to one for that amendment—beating the Democratic majority that wanted FEPC. The Republicans also introduced and got passed in the Senate the Wherry rule making it next to impossible to stop these filibusters. That is rule 22 that Governor Lehman was talking to you about.

It is no accident that these anti-civil rights measures bear the names of Republican legislators. Republicans introduced them, and Republicans approved them. The Republicans deserve this recognition, for they are always on tap to provide just enough votes to insure the defeat of civil rights measures.

When the Congress refused to act, I went ahead to do what I could within the executive branch itself. This fight of ours cannot stop just because we have been blocked in the United States Congress.

First, I acted to stop racial discrimination in the armed services. The navy and the air force have now eliminated all racial distinctions. And for over two years, every soldier coming into an army training unit in this country has been assigned on the basis of his individual merit—regardless of race or color. All the troops in Korea are now integrated, and integration is going forward elsewhere overseas.

I also had a Fair Employment Board set up in the Civil Service Commission. Today,

every federal agency has a fair employment practices program that is working. Any federal employee, or applicant for federal employment, who feels he has been discriminated against because of race can now ask for and receive justice.

At my request, the solicitor general of the United States went before the Supreme Court to argue that Negro citizens have the right to enter state colleges and universities on exactly the same basis as any other citizens. And we won that fight. And more than a thousand Negro graduate and professional students have been accepted by state universities that had barred their doors to Negroes before. This means that this country will have more men like Louis T. Wright and Ralph Bunche.

At my request, the Solicitor General again went before the Supreme Court and argued against the vicious, restrictive covenants that had prevented houses in many places from being sold to Negroes and to Jews. It was a great day in the history of civil rights when we won that case, also, before the Supreme Court.

As one result of that decision, more Negroes are homeowners today than ever before in American history.

Our locally—operated public housing projects are increasingly open to families of all races and creeds. The number of integrated projects has increased eightfold in eight years. In the last few years, nine states and eight cities have forbidden discrimination or segregation in public housing.

In the last few years, 11 states and 20 cities have enacted fair employment practice laws. This is where the greatest gap exists in our federal laws on civil rights, and I have repeatedly urged the Congress to pass the kind of law we need. Such a statute must have enforcement powers if it is to mean anything. To talk about voluntary compliance with fair employment practice is just plain nonsense. Federal fair employment legislation with enforcement power is greatly needed and it ought to be on the books. And I am going to keep fighting for it, come hell or high water!

Progress has been made in assuring Negroes the opportunity to exercise their right to vote as citizens. The courts have made the infamous "white primary" a thing of the past. Thank God for that. And there are only five poll tax states left in this Union. Nevertheless, we still need laws to abolish the poll tax and otherwise protect the right to vote where intimidation or restrictions still exist.

In the last five years, two states have enacted antilynch laws. Five states and 45 cities have passed laws against wearing masks in public—which will strip the hoods off the Ku Klux Klan. One of the finest things that has happened recently was the conviction and prosecution of those Ku Kluxers down in North Carolina and southern states. This is splendid progress in the fight to guarantee our citizens' protection against mob violence, but it is not enough. It is the clear duty of the federal government to stand behind local law enforcement agencies, and to step in if they fail to control mob action. That is exactly what we have been doing through the FBI and through the civil rights section of the Department of Justice.

Last year, a mob formed in Cicero, Illinois, and prevented a Negro veteran and his family from moving into an apartment house. Fortunately, Illinois was blessed with a great governor, who is now your Democratic candidate for president.

Governor Stevenson, who believes in action in these matters, restored law and order with the National Guard. But a local grand jury did the incredible thing of indicting—not the ringleaders of the mob—but the Negro veteran's lawyer and the property owner. At this point the federal government stepped in to prevent a gross miscarriage of justice. It obtained an indictment of the city officials who had failed in their duty to assure equal justice under the law. And the officials who had abetted the mob were tried and convicted in a federal court.

It was also last year that the nation was shocked by the bomb murder in Florida of Harry T. Moore and his wife. These tragic deaths came shortly after the bombings of synagogues and Catholic churches and of the housing project at Carver Village. For several months the FBI has been gathering evidence on the mobs responsible for these outrages. And this week the United States government began to present that evidence to a federal grand jury at Miami.

These are examples of how your federal government—under a Democratic president—stands behind the constitutional guarantees of human rights. The federal government could do a better job if we had stronger civil rights laws—and we must never let down in fighting for those laws.

Now, the progress we have been making in the field of human rights is in grave danger. Make no mistake about that.

We are menaced by the forces of reaction which would have our government turn its back upon the common man. These forces of reaction are organized in the Republican Party. They would have our government cease to be what it has been for 20 years, under the Democrats—the protector of the weak against the mighty. And these policies, as sure as you are standing here, would lead us back to the dark days of the depression—and depression is always a breeder of hate among human beings.

You and I are not going to let this happen. We are not going to turn the clock back. We are not going to turn the country over to the greedy interests that control the Republican Party. They're not interested in equal rights.

Now remember this. One person in this country has to think of all the people all the time; that person is the president of the United States. If you want this civil rights program to continue, you must make the right man president this year.

Now every special interest in the United States has a highly paid lobby at Washington who spend their time banqueting the legislators and trying to force legislation through for the special interests. And the only lobbyist that the 150 million people have who can't afford to hire one, is the president of the United States.

Now on the one hand, there is the Republican candidate for president. He is the front man for the party that adopted the Wherry rule in the Senate—making it harder to stop a filibuster than at any time in history. His party is the one that produced a watered-down version of the FEPC in the House—and would not permit even that version to come to a vote in the Senate. His is the party that beat a retreat this year in the civil rights plank of its platform. That's the lousiest platform you ever read on the subject.

And while the Republican candidate was in uniform, he told the Armed Services Committee of the Senate that a certain amount of segregation is necessary in the army. You and I know that this is morally wrong. And what's more, it's even militarily wrong. Our troops in Korea are demonstrating, every day, that Americans can stand side by side, regardless of color, and fight better because of it.

Now, the Republican candidate, and his party, and his party's platform have refused to pledge effective action for assuring equal rights for all our citizens. You could not even depend on them to save what we have now—and goodness knows that isn't enough.

And now, while the Republican candidate is whispering promises to you, he has been touring the South to woo the Dixiecrats into the Republican fold. What do you think the Republican candidate and a Dixiecrat governor talk about when they sit down together for lunch? Do you think they talk about civil rights? I think maybe they talk about taking them away.

You can draw your own conclusion when the Dixiecrat governor announces, after the lunch, he's going to vote Republican this year.

I am afraid, my friends, that the Republican candidate does not offer you much hope so far as civil rights are concerned.

On the other hand, there is the Democratic Party—the party of proven performance. This is the party that has taken the great forward steps I have just described—the greatest since the abolition of slavery.

The Democratic platform this year contains the strongest civil rights plank ever adopted by any political party in this country. Our candidates have taken their stand firmly on that platform. You can count on them to fight to carry it out.

You placed your trust in me four years ago when I dedicated myself to our great cause, and I have tried not to let you down. I am here today to tell you that you can place the same trust in the Democratic candidates in this election year. And I assure you with all the sincerity I have, that they will fulfill your trust in exactly the same way.

Adlai Stevenson has shown by everything he has done and said that he believes deeply in the equality of human beings. He will bring new courage and new energy to the fight for civil rights.

He has the courage to say the same things about civil rights in New York and in Richmond, Virginia. He has been a great civil rights governor and he will make a great civil rights president.

Let me tell you some of the things he has done. When he gave his inaugural address as governor in 1949, he listed the matters he wanted the Illinois legislature to take up. High on that list was an FEPC. But Adlai Stevenson was not asking for the toothless kind of FEPC, so you can imagine what happened to his request. It passed the Democratic House only to be killed by that Illinois Republican senate. In the following session, both houses of the Illinois legislature were Republican-controlled. That year, the house bill died in committee. But get this one. This is really a good one. The Republican-controlled senate committee reported out Adlai Stevenson's FEPC, but they brought it out with a recommendation that it not be passed.

That is an example of the same kind of Republican doubletalk we get in Washington all the time.

Now let me tell you some other things about Stevenson, and what he did. He didn't make a lot of noise about them. He just quietly issued an executive order ending segregation in the Illinois National Guard. And he issued another executive order taking race out of the Illinois Employment Service forms. And it was during his administration that segregation was finally wiped out in the Illinois public schools. Now I think some of our generals could take lessons from him in how to get things done.

Adlai Stevenson also helped make it possible for Negro sailors to have duties other than as messmen. That was during the war when he was assistant to the secretary of the navy.

You people know that if there is one thing I have fought for as president of the United States, it has been the protection of the God-given rights of every citizen of this great country. I solemnly pledged myself to that task at a meeting like this four years ago. Today, I have listed some of the things we have accomplished in the great fight. And Adlai Stevenson has shown by his record that he will continue the fight with renewed vigor.

Now, it's not enough to nod your heads in agreement when we talk about this fight we have been making together. You must go to the polls in such numbers that you can defeat the forces of reaction. You have until 10:30 tonight to register. And you are not worth a hoot to the Democratic Party unless you are registered. Make sure your name is on the books—and that your friends' and neighbors' names are on the books—by the time those books close tonight. And on November 4, let's roll up a great majority for Adlai Stevenson and a Democratic Congress and we will support him in his battle for civil rights.

Farewell Address

Washington, D.C.

January 15, 1953

THIS FIRESIDE CHAT was Truman's last major speech as president. His speechwriters worked hard on this address, but the outline and final wording were Truman's own. He delivered it in a personal tone more reminiscent of his off-the-cuff speeches than of his readings from prepared texts.

The American people gave Truman a remarkably affectionate farewell, considering the low esteem in which he was held during most of his presidency. Thousands of well-wishers cheered Truman and his family in Washington and at every train stop along the route home to Independence.

I am happy to have this opportunity to talk to you once more before I leave the White House.

Next Tuesday, General Eisenhower will be inaugurated as president of the United States. A short time after the new president takes his oath of office, I will be on the train going back home to Independence, Missouri. I will once again be a plain, private citizen of this great republic.

That is as it should be. Inauguration day will be a great demonstration of our democratic process. I am glad to be a part of it—glad to wish General Eisenhower all possible success, as he begins his term—glad the whole world will have a chance to see how simply and how peacefully our American system transfers the vast power of the presidency from my hands to his. It is a good object lesson in democracy. I am very proud of it. And I know you are, too.

During the last two months I have done my best to make this transfer an orderly one. I have talked with my successor on the affairs of the country, both foreign and domestic, and my cabinet officers have talked with their successors. I want to say that General Eisenhower and his associates have cooperated fully in this effort. Such an orderly transfer from one party to another has never taken place before in our history. I think a real precedent has been set.

In speaking to you tonight, I have no new revelations to make—no political statements—no policy announcements. There are simply a few things in my heart that I want to say to you. I want to say "good-bye" and "thanks for your help." And I want to talk to you a little while about what has happened since I became your president.

I am speaking to you from the room where I have worked since April 12, 1945. This is the president's office in the West Wing of the White House. This is the desk where I have signed most of the papers that embodied the decisions I have made as president. It has been the desk of many presidents, and will be the desk of many more.

Since I became president, I have been to Europe, Mexico, Canada, Brazil, Puerto Rico, and the Virgin Islands—Wake Island and Hawaii. I have visited almost every state in the Union. I have traveled 135,000 miles by air, 77,000 by rail, and 17,000 by ship. But the mail always followed me, and wherever I happened to be, that's where the office of the president was.

The greatest part of the president's job is to make decisions—big ones and small ones, dozens of them almost every day. The papers may circulate around the government for a while but they finally reach this desk. And then, there's no place else for them to go. The president—whoever he is—has to decide. He can't pass the buck to anybody. No one else can do the deciding for him. That's his job.

That's what I've been doing here in this room, for almost eight years. And over in the main part of the White House, there's a study on the second floor—a room much like this one—where I have worked at night and early in the morning on the papers I couldn't get to at the office.

Of course, for more than three years Mrs. Truman and I were not living in the White House. We were across the street in the Blair House. That was when the White House almost fell down on us and had to be rebuilt. I had a study over at the Blair House, too, but living in the Blair House was not as convenient as living in the White House. The Secret Service wouldn't let me walk across the street, so I had to get in a car every morning to cross the street to the White House office, again at noon to go to the Blair House for lunch, again to go back to the office after lunch, and finally take an automobile at night to return to the Blair House. Fantastic, isn't it? But necessary, so my guards thought—and they are the bosses on such matters as that.

Now, of course, we're back in the White House. It is in very good condition, and General Eisenhower will be able to take up his residence in the house and work right here. That will be much more convenient for him, and I'm very glad the renovation job was all completed before his term began.

Your new president is taking office in quite different circumstances than when I became president eight years ago. On April 12, 1945, I had been presiding over the Senate in my capacity as vice president. When the Senate recessed about five o'clock in the afternoon, I walked over to the office of the Speaker of the House, Mr. Rayburn, to discuss pending legislation. As soon as I arrived, I was told that Mr. Early, one of President Roosevelt's secretaries, wanted me to call. I reached Mr. Early, and he told me to come to the White House as quickly as possible, to enter by way of the Pennsylvania Avenue entrance, and to come to Mrs. Roosevelt's study.

When I arrived, Mrs. Roosevelt told me the tragic news, and I felt the shock that all of you felt a little later—when the word came over the radio and appeared in the newspapers. President Roosevelt had died. I offered to do anything I could for Mrs. Roosevelt, and then I asked the secretary of state to call the cabinet together.

At 7:09 p.m. I was sworn in as president by Chief Justice Stone in the Cabinet Room.

Things were happening fast in those days. The San Francisco conference to organize the United Nations had been called for April 25th. I was asked if that meeting would go forward. I announced that it would. That was my first decision.

After attending President Roosevelt's funeral, I went to the Hall of the House of Representatives and told a joint session of the Congress that I would carry on President Roosevelt's policies.

On May 7th, Germany surrendered. The announcement was made on May 8th, my 61st birthday.

Mr. Churchill called me shortly after that and wanted a meeting with me and Prime Minister Stalin of Russia. Later on, a meeting was agreed upon, and Churchill, Stalin, and I met at Potsdam in Germany.

Meanwhile, the first atomic explosion took place out in the New Mexico desert.

The war against Japan was still going on. I made the decision that the atomic bomb had to be used to end it. I made that decision in the conviction it would save hundreds of thousands of lives—Japanese as well as American. Japan surrendered, and we were faced with the huge problems of bringing the troops home and reconverting the economy from war to peace.

All these things happened within just a little over four months—from April to August 1945. I tell you this to illustrate the tremendous scope of the work your president has to do.

And all these emergencies and all the developments to meet them have required the president to put in long hours—usually 17 hours a day, with no payment for overtime. I sign my name, on the average, 600 times a day, see and talk to hundreds of people every month, shake hands with thousands every year, and still carry on the business of the largest going concern in the whole world. There is no job like it on the face of the earth—in the power which is concentrated here at this desk, and in the responsibility and difficulty of the decisions.

I want all of you to realize how big a job, how hard a job, it is—not for my sake, because I am stepping out of it—but for the sake of my successor. He needs the understanding and the help of every citizen. It is not enough for you to come out once every four years and vote for a candidate, and then go back home and say, "Well, I've done my part, now let the new president do the worrying." He can't do the job alone.

Regardless of your politics, whether you are Republican or Democrat, your fate is tied up with what is done here in this room. The president is president of the whole country. We must give him our support as citizens of the United States. He will have mine, and I want you to give him yours.

I suppose that history will remember my term in office as the years when the "cold war" began to overshadow our lives. I have had hardly a day in office that has not been dominated by this all-embracing struggle—this conflict between those who love freedom and those who would lead the world back into slavery and darkness. And always in the background there has been the atomic bomb.

But when history says that my term of office saw the beginning of the cold war, it will also say that in those eight years we have set the course that can win it. We have succeeded in carving out a new set of policies to attain peace—positive policies, policies of world leadership, policies that express faith in other free people. We have averted World War III up to now, and we may already have succeeded in establishing conditions which can keep that war from happening as far ahead as man can see.

These are great and historic achievements that we can all be proud of. Think of the difference between our course now and our course 30 years ago. After the First World War we withdrew from world affairs—we failed to act in concert with other peoples against aggression—we helped to kill the League of Nations—and we built up tariff barriers that strangled world trade. This time, we avoided those mistakes. We helped to found and sustain the United Nations. We have welded alliances that include the greater part of the free world. And we have gone ahead with other free countries to help build their economies and link us all together in a healthy world trade.

Think back for a moment to the 1930s and you will see the difference. The Japanese moved into Manchuria, and free men did not act. The fascists moved into Ethiopia, and we did not act. The Nazis marched into the Rhineland, into Austria, into Czechoslovakia, and free men were paralyzed for lack of strength and unity and will.

Think about those years of weakness and indecision, and the World War II which was their evil result. Then think about the speed and courage and decisiveness with which we have moved against the Communist threat since World War II.

The first crisis came in 1945 and 1946, when the Soviet Union refused to honor its agreement to remove its troops from Iran. Members of my cabinet came to me and asked if we were ready to take the risk that a firm stand involved. I replied that we were. So we took our stand—we made it clear to the Soviet Union that we expected them to honor their agreement—and the Soviet troops were withdrawn from Iran.

Then, in early 1947, the Soviet Union threatened Greece and Turkey. The British sent me a message saying they could no longer keep their forces in that area. Something had to be done at once, or the eastern Mediterranean would be taken over by the Communists. On March 12th, I went before the Congress and stated our determination to help the people of Greece and Turkey maintain their independence. Today, Greece is still free and independent; and Turkey is a bulwark of strength at a strategic corner of the world.

Then came the Marshall Plan which saved Europe, the heroic Berlin airlift, and our military aid programs.

We inaugurated the North Atlantic Pact, the Rio Pact binding the Western Hemisphere together, and the defense pacts with countries of the Far Pacific.

Most important of all, we acted in Korea.

I was in Independence, Missouri, in June 1950, when Secretary Acheson telephoned me and gave me the news about the invasion of Korea. I told the secretary to lay the matter at once before the United Nations, and I came on back to Washington.

Flying back over the flatlands of the Middle West and over the Appalachians that summer afternoon, I had a lot of time to think. I turned the problem over in my mind in many ways, but my thoughts kept coming back to the 1930's—to Manchuria, to Ethiopia, the Rhineland, Austria, and finally to Munich.

Here was history repeating itself. Here was another probing action, another testing action. If we let the republic of Korea go under, some other country would be next, and then another. And all the time, the courage and confidence of the free world would be ebbing away, just as it did in the 1930s. And the United Nations would go the way of the League of Nations.

When I reached Washington, I met immediately with the secretary of state, the secretary of defense, and General Bradley, and the other civilian and military officials who had information and advice to help me decide on what to do. We talked about the problems long and hard. We considered those problems very carefully.

It was not easy to make the decision to send American boys again into battle. I was a soldier in the First World War, and I know what a soldier goes through. I know well the anguish that mothers and fathers and families go through. So I knew what was ahead if we acted in Korea.

But after all this was said, we realized that the issue was whether there would be fighting in a limited area now or on a much larger scale later on—whether there would be some casualties now or many more casualties later.

So a decision was reached—the decision I believe was the most important in my time as president of the United States.

In the days that followed, the most heartening fact was that the American people clearly agreed with the decision.

And in Korea, our men are fighting as valiantly as Americans have ever fought—because they know they are fighting in the same cause of freedom in which Americans have stood ever since the beginning of the republic.

Where free men had failed the test before, this time we met the test.

We met it firmly. We met it successfully. The aggression has been repelled. The Communists have seen their hopes of easy conquest go down the drain. The determination of free people to defend themselves has been made clear to the Kremlin.

As I have thought about our worldwide struggle with the Communists these past eight years—day in and day out—I have never once doubted that you, the people of our country, have the will to do what is necessary to win this terrible fight against Communism. I know the people of this country have that will and determination, and I have always depended on it. Because I have been sure of that, I have been able to make necessary decisions even though they called for sacrifices by all of us. And I have not been wrong in my judgment of the American people.

That same assurance of our people's determination will be General Eisenhower's greatest source of strength in carrying on this struggle.

Now, once in a while, I get a letter from some impatient person asking, why don't we get it over with? Why don't we issue an ultimatum, make all-out war, drop the atomic bomb?

For most Americans, the answer is quite simple: We are not made that way. We are a moral people. Peace is our goal, with justice and freedom. We cannot, of our own free will,

violate the very principles that we are striving to defend. The whole purpose of what we are doing is to prevent World War III. Starting a war is no way to make peace.

But if anyone still thinks that just this once, bad means can bring good ends, then let me remind you of this: We are living in the eighth year of the atomic age. We are not the only nation that is learning to unleash the power of the atom. A third world war might dig the grave not only of our Communist opponents but also of our own society, our world as well as theirs.

Starting an atomic war is totally unthinkable for rational men.

Then, some of you may ask, when and how will the cold war end? I think I can answer that simply. The Communist world has great resources, and it looks strong. But there is a fatal flaw in their society. Theirs is a godless system, a system of slavery; there is no freedom in it, no consent. The Iron Curtain, the secret police, the constant purges, all these are symptoms of a great basic weakness—the rulers' fear of their own people.

In the long run the strength of our free society, and our ideals, will prevail over a system that has respect for neither God nor man.

Last week, in my State of the Union message to the Congress—and I hope you will all take the time to read it—I explained how I think we will finally win through.

As the free world grows stronger, more united, more attractive to men on both sides of the Iron Curtain—and as the Soviet hopes for easy expansion are blocked—then there will have to come a time of change in the Soviet world. Nobody can say for sure when that is going to be, or exactly how it will come about, whether by revolution, or trouble in the satellite states, or by a change inside the Kremlin.

Whether the Communist rulers shift their policies of their own free will—or whether the change comes about in some other way—I have not a doubt in the world that a change will occur.

I have a deep and abiding faith in the destiny of free men. With patience and courage, we shall some day move on into a new era—a wonderful golden age—an age when we can use the peaceful tools that science has forged for us to do away with poverty and human misery everywhere on earth.

Think what can be done, once our capital, our skills, our science—most of all atomic energy—can be released from the tasks of defense and turned wholly to peaceful purposes all around the world.

There is no end to what can be done.

I can't help but dream out loud just a little here.

The Tigris and Euphrates Valley can be made to bloom as it did in the times of Babylon and Nineveh. Israel can be made the country of milk and honey as it was in the time of Joshua.

There is a plateau in Ethiopia some 6,000 to 8,000 feet high, that has 65,000 square miles of land just exactly like the corn belt in northern Illinois. Enough food can be raised there to feed a hundred million people.

There are places in South America—places in Colombia and Venezuela and Brazil—just like that plateau in Ethiopia—places where food could be raised for millions of people.

These things can be done, and they are self-liquidating projects. If we can get peace and safety in the world under the United Nations, the developments will come so fast we will not recognize the world in which we now live.

This is our dream of the future—our picture of the world we hope to have when the Communist threat is overcome.

I've talked a lot tonight about the menace of Communism—and our fight against it—because that is the overriding issue of our time. But there are some other things we've done that history will record. One of them is that we in America have learned how to attain real prosperity for our people.

We have 62 1/2 million people at work. Businessmen, farmers, laborers, white-collar people, all have better incomes and more of the good things of life than ever before in the history of the world.

There hasn't been a failure of an insured bank in nearly nine years. No depositor has lost a cent in that period.

And the income of our people has been fairly distributed, perhaps more so than at any other time in recent history.

We have made progress in spreading the blessings of American life to all of our people. There has been a tremendous awakening of the American conscience on the great issues of civil rights—equal economic opportunities, equal rights of citizenship, and equal educational opportunities for all our people, whatever their race or religion or status of birth.

So, as I empty the drawers of this desk, and as Mrs. Truman and I leave the White House, we have no regret. We feel we have done our best in the public service. I hope and believe we have contributed to the welfare of this nation and to the peace of the world.

When Franklin Roosevelt died, I felt there must be a million men better qualified than I, to take up the presidential task. But the work was mine to do, and I had to do it. And I have tried to give it everything that was in me.

Through all of it, through all the years that I have worked here in this room, I have been well aware I did not really work alone—that you were working with me.

No president could ever hope to lead our country, or to sustain the burdens of this office, save as the people helped with their support. I have had that help—you have given me that support-on all our great essential undertakings to build the free world's strength and keep the peace.

Those are the big things. Those are the things we have done together.

For that I shall be grateful, always.

And now, the time has come for me to say good night—and God bless you all.

Dwight David Eisenhower

Dwight David Eisenhower

1953–1961

SEVEN YEARS AFTER he led the Allied forces to victory in World War II, Dwight D. Eisenhower was swept into the presidency on a wave of popular admiration, the latest in a series of war hero presidents that began with Washington. The image he presented to the public during his two terms in office was that of a battle-seasoned Boy Scout—virtuous, honest, strong enough to govern through influence and example rather than confrontation.

Eisenhower was not a natural orator, but as a military leader he knew how to command the attention of an audience and how to conduct himself with authority. His flat Kansas accent fell in a monotone, but he could add some drama to his speeches with a flash of his intense blue eyes or his famous grin. When he entered the 1952 presidential race against Adlai Stevenson, a far more accomplished orator, Eisenhower had speechwriting expertise going back to his days as an aide to Generals Pershing and MacArthur. During the festivities and tributes that followed victory in World War II he made several speeches in Europe, including a much-publicized one at the Guildhall in London when he received the honorary Freedom of the City; back in the United States, as army chief of staff, he made speeches on the average of one a week, promoting military preparedness and an active role for the United States in European affairs. By 1951, when he went to Paris as supreme commander of NATO, he had assembled a public relations staff to help him with speechwriting tasks.

Eisenhower spent most of the 1952 presidential race aboard a campaign train that took him through 45 states. In his memoirs, he recalled in detail "the urgent, whirling grind that is the daily and hourly portion of such a barnstorming organization. . . . The instant the wheels cease turning, the candidate, who lives in the rearmost section of the last car on the train, steps blithely out to face the crowd, doing his best to conceal with a big grin the ache in his bones, the exhaustion in his mind. . . . But quickly he feels within himself a transformation. Although as he came out to the platform he was bored, resentful, or even sorry for himself, invariably the excitement generated by the crowd buoys him up—suddenly he is anxious to make his planned points; he strives for new thoughts; he speaks enthusiastically of Congressman Blank; he seeks for lucidity, conciseness, and logic in the exposition of his policies. . . . Then, out of sight once more, he stumbles back into the car, to an inviting couch where he tries, for a moment, to revitalize himself for the next chore." This was, in fact, the last of the whistle-stop campaign tours. Four years later, Eisenhower was able to limit himself to half a dozen major speeches with the aid of plane travel and television.

The 1952 election was clinched on October 24 by Eisenhower's famous "I shall go to Korea" speech, in which he promised personally to visit the battlefields of Korea. The result was a landslide for the Republicans. Eisenhower brought to the White House a speechwriting team that included Emmett Hughes, Arthur Larson, Bryce Harlow, Kevin McCann, and Gabriel Hauge; he appointed as press secretary James Hagerty, who, by masterful stage-management, helped to keep relations between the president and the journalists on a friendly basis.

The trick for the speechwriters was to find clear, forceful, accurate ways to articulate Eisenhower's ideas while avoiding the oratorical devices and inflated rhetoric he disliked. "There were no screaming trumpets in his rhetoric," commentator Garry Wills observed. "He preferred drums." Most of Eisenhower's addresses were drafted by the staff writers, sometimes with the assistance of outside experts, and given to Eisenhower two weeks ahead of schedule for his changes, since, as Eisenhower admitted, "I have never been able to accept a draft of a suggested talk and deliver it intact as my own." Hughes, for one, thought him a good editor who functioned best when a draft was read aloud to him: "For him, the ear was keener than the eye, the spoken word more persuasive than the written."

The concern with grammar and sentence structure that Eisenhower displayed while editing texts was not evident in his press conferences. His garbled syntax was legendary among the White House press corps. The journalist Marquis Childs gives this example (on the subject of the Tennessee Valley Authority as an agent of what Eisenhower called "creeping socialism"): "So we get to this curious thing in the socialistic theory, that we all of us, provide cheap power, such cheap power for one region that it cannot only—apparently it is subsidized by taxes from all of us all over the country—but then it can appeal and take away the industries from the other sections of the country." Some observers attribute his tongue-tangling to ineptitude, but others consider it deliberate, a way of avoiding any statement that might cause trouble for the administration—"skilled obfuscation," as Wills called it. Eisenhower himself explained it by saying that he "focused on ideas rather than phrasing."

Although Eisenhower was the first president to have regular access to television, he did not like being made up for the camera, nor did he like the idea of intruding into people's lives by machine. "I can think of nothing more boring, for the American public, than to have to sit in their living rooms for a whole half hour looking at my face on their television screens," he told his aides. Nonetheless, he appreciated the power of a good speech to change public opinion. Of his "Atoms for Peace" speech to the United Nations, Eisenhower wrote that his motivation was "the clear conviction that as of that moment, the world, as it still is, was courting disaster in the armaments race, that something must be done to put a brake on this momentum. Certainly there were few so foolish as to think that the brake could be composed only of words and protestations, however eloquent or sincere. But ideas expressed in words must certainly have an effect in getting people to think of specific ways by which future disaster can be avoided." For, as the former general reminded his audience in a 1956 campaign speech, "the only way to win World War III is to prevent it."

First Inaugural Address

Washington, D.C.
January 20, 1953

EISENHOWER'S INAUGURATION was the first to be televised and thus the first to be seen live by a mass audience. The address, written in collaboration with Emmett Hughes, had undergone innumerable changes nearly up to the last minute. Hughes recalled: "Words, phrases, paragraphs—spirited exhortations and sweeping affirmations—had been shuttled in and out of the speech so often, so excitedly, and so confusedly that, quite often, the derided deletion of yesterday ended as the prized text of tomorrow." The final version described the role of the United States in the postwar world in strongly religious, almost apocalyptic terms, as an all-consuming crusade against the satanic forces of Communism.

The prayer that opens the address was composed by Eisenhower himself. His biographer, Peter Lyon, observed that this prayer "had none of the poetic magic that suffuses Christian ceremony with beauty; rather it suggested George F. Babbitt before a session of the local Rotary," though "it sparkled with the earnest sincerity that was Eisenhower's own personal magic." Eisenhower, whose family was descended from the River Brethren branch of the Mennonite Church, but who had had no formal religious connection for years, had joined the National Presbyterian Church just before his inauguration.

Before I begin the expression of those thoughts which I deem appropriate to this moment, would you permit me the privilege of uttering a little private prayer of my own, and I ask that you bow your heads.

Almighty God, as we stand here, at this moment, my future associates in the executive branch of government join me in beseeching that Thou wilt make full and complete our dedication to the service of the people in this throng and their fellow citizens everywhere. Give us, we pray, the power to discern clearly right from wrong and allow all our words and actions to be governed thereby and by the laws of this land.

Especially we pray that our concern shall be for all the people—regardless of station, race, or calling. May cooperation be permitted and be the mutual aim of those who, under the concepts of our Constitution, hold to differing political beliefs, so that all may work for the good of our beloved country and for Thy glory. Amen.

My fellow citizens, the world and we have passed the midway point of a century of continuing challenge. We sense with all our faculties that forces of good and evil are massed and armed and opposed as rarely before in history.

This fact defines the meaning of this day. We are summoned, by this honored and historic ceremony, to witness more than the act of one citizen swearing his oath of service, in the presence of his God. We are called as a people, to give testimony, in the sight of the world, to our faith that the future shall belong to the free.

Since this century's beginning, a time of tempest has seemed to come upon the continents of the earth. Masses of Asia have wakened to strike off shackles of the past. Great nations of Europe have waged their bloodiest wars. Thrones have toppled and their vast empires have disappeared. New nations have been born.

For our own country, it has been a time of recurring trial. We have grown in power and in responsibility. We have passed through the anxieties of depression and of war to a summit unmatched in man's history. Seeking to secure peace in the world, we have had to fight through the forests of the Argonne, to the shores of Iwo Jima, and to the cold mountains of Korea.

In the swift rush of great events, we find ourselves groping to know the full sense and meaning of the times in which we live. In our quest of understanding, we beseech God's guidance. We summon all our knowledge of the past and we scan all signs of the future. We bring all our wit and will to meet the question: how far have we come in man's long pilgrimage from darkness toward light? Are we nearing the light—a day of freedom and of peace for all mankind? Or are the shadows of another night closing in upon us?

Great as are the preoccupations absorbing us at home, concerned as we are with matters that deeply affect our livelihood today and our vision of the future, each of these domestic problems is dwarfed by, and often even created by, this question that involves all human kind.

This trial comes at a moment when man's power to achieve good or to inflict evil surpasses the brightest hopes and the sharpest fears of all ages. We can turn rivers in their courses, level mountains to the plains. Ocean and land and sky are avenues for our colossal commerce. Disease diminishes and life lengthens.

Yet the promise of this life is imperiled by the very genius that has made it possible. Nations amass wealth. Labor sweats to create—and turns out devices to level not only mountains but also cities. Science seems ready to confer upon us, as its final gift, the power to erase human life from this planet.

At such a time in history, we, who are free, must proclaim anew our faith.

This faith is the abiding creed of our fathers. It is our faith in the deathless dignity of man, governed by eternal moral and natural laws.

This faith defines our full view of life. It establishes, beyond debate, those gifts of the Creator that are man's inalienable rights, and that make all men equal in His sight!

In the light of this equality, we know that the virtues most cherished by free peoples—love of truth, pride of work, devotion to country—all are treasures equally precious in the lives of the most humble and of the most exalted. The men who mine coal and fire furnaces and balance ledgers and turn lathes and pick cotton and heal the sick and plant corn—all serve as proudly, and as profitably, for America as the statesmen who draft treaties or the legislators who enact laws.

This faith rules our whole way of life. It decrees that we, the people, elect leaders not to rule but to serve. It asserts that we have the right to choice of our own work and to the reward of our own toil. It inspires the initiative that makes our productivity the wonder of the world. And it warns that any man who seeks to deny equality in all his brothers betrays the spirit of the free and invites the mockery of the tyrant.

It is because we, all of us, hold to these principles that the political changes accomplished this day do not imply turbulence, upheaval, or disorder. Rather this change expresses a purpose of strengthening our dedication and devotion to the precepts of our founding documents, a conscious renewal of faith in our country and in the watchfulness of a divine Providence.

The enemies of this faith know no god but force, no devotion but its use. They tutor men in treason. They feed upon the hunger of others. Whatever defies them, they torture, especially the truth.

Here, then, is joined no pallid argument between slightly differing philosophies. This conflict strikes directly at the faith of our fathers and the lives of our sons. No principle or treasure that we hold, from the spiritual knowledge of our free schools and churches to the creative magic of free labor and capital, nothing lies safely beyond the reach of the struggle.

Freedom is pitted against slavery; light against dark.

The faith we hold belongs not to us alone but to the free of all the world. This common bond binds the grower of rice in Burma and the planter of wheat in Iowa, the shepherd in southern Italy and the mountaineer in the Andes. It confers a common dignity upon the French soldier who dies in Indo-China, the British soldier killed in Malaya, the American life given in Korea.

We know, beyond this, that we are linked to all free peoples not merely by a noble idea but by a simple need. No free people can for long cling to any privilege or enjoy any safety in economic solitude. For all our own material might, even we need markets in the world for the surpluses of our farms and of our factories. Equally, we need for these same farms and factories vital materials and products of distant lands. This basic law of interdependence, so manifest in the commerce of peace, applies with thousand-fold intensity in the event of war.

So are we persuaded by necessity and by belief that the strength of all free peoples lies in unity, their danger in discord.

To produce this unity, to meet the challenge of our time, destiny has laid upon our country the responsibility of the free world's leadership. So it is proper that we assure our friends once again that, in the discharge of this responsibility, we Americans know and observe the difference between world leadership and imperialism; between firmness and truculence; between a thoughtfully calculated goal and spasmodic reaction to the stimulus of emergencies.

We wish our friends the world over to know this above all: we face the threat—not with dread and confusion—but with confidence and conviction.

We feel this moral strength because we know that we are not helpless prisoners of history. We are free men. We shall remain free, never to be proven guilty of the one capital offense against freedom, a lack of staunch faith.

In pleading our just cause before the bar of history and in pressing our labor for world peace, we shall be guided by certain fixed principles.

These principles are:

1. Abhorring war as a chosen way to balk the purposes of those who threaten us, we hold it to be the first task of statesmanship to develop the strength that will deter the forces of aggression and promote the conditions of peace. For, as it must be the supreme purpose of all free men, so it must be the dedication of their leaders, to save humanity from preying upon itself.

   In the light of this principle, we stand ready to engage with any and all others in joint effort to remove the causes of mutual fear and distrust among nations, and so to make possible drastic reductions of armaments. The sole requisites for undertaking such effort are that—in their purpose—they be aimed logically and honestly toward secure peace for all; and that—in their result—they provide methods by which every participating nation will prove good faith in carrying out its pledge.

2. Realizing that common sense and common decency alike dictate the futility of appeasement, we shall never try to placate an aggressor by the false and wicked bargain of trading honor for security. For in the final choice a soldier's pack is not so heavy a burden as a prisoner's chains.

3. Knowing that only a United States that is strong and immensely productive can help defend freedom in our world, we view our nation's strength and security as a trust upon which rests the hope of free men everywhere. It is the firm duty of each of our free citizens and of every free citizen everywhere to place the cause of his country before the comfort and convenience of himself.

4. Honoring the identity and heritage of each nation of the world, we shall never use our strength to try to impress upon another people our own cherished political and economic institutions.

5. Assessing realistically the needs and capacities of proven friends of freedom, we shall strive to help them to achieve their own security and well-being. Likewise, we shall count upon them to assume, within the limits of their resources, their full and just burdens in the common defense of freedom.

6. Recognizing economic health as an indispensable basis of military strength and the free world's peace, we shall strive to foster everywhere, and to practice ourselves, policies that encourage productivity and profitable trade. For the impoverishment of any single people in the world means danger to the well-being of all other peoples.

7. Appreciating that economic need, military security, and political wisdom combine to suggest regional groupings of free peoples, we hope, within the framework of the United Nations, to help strengthen such special bonds the world over. The nature of these ties must vary with the different problems of different areas.

   In the Western Hemisphere, we enthusiastically join with all our neighbors in the work of perfecting a community of fraternal trust and common purpose.

   In Europe, we ask that enlightened and inspired leaders of the Western nations strive with renewed vigor to make the unity of their peoples a reality. Only as free Europe unitedly marshals its strength can it effectively safeguard, even with our help, its spiritual and cultural heritages.

8. Conceiving the defense of freedom, like freedom itself, to be one and indivisible, we hold all continents and peoples in equal regard and honor. We reject any insinuation that one race or another, one people or another, is in any sense inferior or expendable.

9. Respecting the United Nations as the living sign of all people's hope for peace, we shall strive to make it not merely an eloquent symbol but an effective force. And in our quest of honorable peace, we shall neither compromise, nor tire, nor ever cease.

By these rules of conduct, we hope to be known to all peoples.

By their observance, an earth of peace may become not a vision but a fact.

This hope—this supreme aspiration—must rule the way we live.

We must be ready to dare all for our country. For history does not long entrust the care of freedom to the weak or the timid. We must acquire proficiency in defense and display stamina in purpose.

We must be willing, individually and as a nation, to accept whatever sacrifices may be required of us. A people that values its privileges above its principles soon loses both.

These basic precepts are not lofty abstractions, far removed from matters of daily living. They are laws of spiritual strength that generate and define our material strength. Patriotism means equipped forces and prepared citizenry. Moral stamina means more energy and more productivity, on the farm and in the factory. Love of liberty means the guarding of every resource that makes freedom possible—from the sanctity of our families and the wealth of our soil to the genius of our scientists.

So each citizen plays an indispensable role. The productivity of our heads, our hands, and our hearts is the source of all the strength we can command for both the enrichment of our lives and the winning of peace.

No person, no home, no community can be beyond the reach of this call. We are summoned to act in wisdom and in conscience, to work with industry, to teach with persuasion, to preach with conviction, to weigh our every deed with care and with compassion. For this truth must be clear before us: whatever America hopes to bring to pass in the world must first come to pass in the heart of America.

The peace we seek, then, is nothing less than the practice and fulfillment of our whole faith, among ourselves and in our dealings with others. It signifies more than stilling the guns, easing the sorrow of war.

More than an escape from death, it is a way of life.

More than a haven for the weary, it is a hope for the brave.

This is the hope that beckons us onward in this century of trial. This is the work that awaits us all, to be done with bravery, with charity—and with prayer to Almighty God.

A Chance for Peace

Washington, D.C.

April 16, 1953

THE DEATH OF Joseph Stalin in March 1953, less than three months after Eisenhower's inauguration, provided the new administration with an opportunity to break the long impasse in Soviet-American relations. At a meeting of the American Society of Newspaper Editors in Washington, Eisenhower—so weak from an intestinal disorder that he could barely stand—asked for mutual understanding and peaceful coexistence between the free world and the U.S.S.R., citing in concrete and vivid terms the human cost of the cold war.

Written by Emmett Hughes over the course of several weeks, the address came close to being scuttled by Secretary of State John Foster Dulles, who did not want Eisenhower to commit himself to any policy that would preclude military action by the United States in China and Korea, and by Winston Churchill, who advised Eisenhower to wait for further Soviet developments. But once delivered, it instantly won worldwide praise. Sherman Adams, Eisenhower's chief of staff, observed that "it was the most effective speech of Eisenhower's public career. . . . We heard later that people behind the Iron Curtain prayed and wept as they listened to it, and Winston Churchill sent a personal message in praise of it to [Soviet leader] Vyacheslav Molotov."

In this spring of 1953 the free world weighs one question above all others: the chance for a just peace for all peoples.

To weigh this chance is to summon instantly to mind another recent moment of great decision. It came with that yet more hopeful spring of 1945, bright with the promise of victory and of freedom. The hope of all just men in that moment too was a just and lasting peace.

The eight years that have passed have seen that hope waver, grow dim, and almost die. And the shadow of fear again has darkly lengthened across the world.

Today the hope of free men remains stubborn and brave, but it is sternly disciplined by experience. It shuns not only all crude counsel of despair but also the self-deceit of easy illusion. It weighs the chance for peace with sure, clear knowledge of what happened to the vain hope of 1945.

In that spring of victory the soldiers of the Western Allies met the soldiers of Russia in the center of Europe. They were triumphant comrades in arms. Their peoples shared the joyous prospect of building, in honor of their dead, the only fitting monument—an age of just peace. All these war-weary peoples shared too this concrete, decent purpose: to guard vigilantly against the domination ever again of any part of the world by a single, unbridled aggressive power.

This common purpose lasted an instant and perished. The nations of the world divided to follow two distinct roads.

The United States and our valued friends, the other free nations, chose one road.

The leaders of the Soviet Union chose another.

The way chosen by the United States was plainly marked by a few clear precepts, which govern its conduct in world affairs.

First: No people on earth can be held, as a people, to be an enemy, for all humanity shares the common hunger for peace and fellowship and justice.

Second: No nation's security and well-being can be lastingly achieved in isolation but only in effective cooperation with fellow-nations.

Third: Any nation's right to a form of government and an economic system of its own choosing is inalienable.

Fourth: Any nation's attempt to dictate to other nations their form of government is indefensible.

And fifth: A nation's hope of lasting peace cannot be firmly based upon any race in armaments but rather upon just relations and honest understanding with all other nations.

In the light of these principles the citizens of the United States defined the way they proposed to follow, through the aftermath of war, toward true peace.

This way was faithful to the spirit that inspired the United Nations: to prohibit strife, to relieve tensions, to banish fears. This way was to control and to reduce armaments. This way was to allow all nations to devote their energies and resources to the great and good tasks of healing the war's wounds, of clothing and feeding and housing the needy, of perfecting a just political life, of enjoying the fruits of their own free toil.

The Soviet government held a vastly different vision of the future.

In the world of its design, security was to be found, not in mutual trust and mutual aid but in force: huge armies, subversion, rule of neighbor nations. The goal was power superiority at all cost. Security was to be sought by denying it to all others.

The result has been tragic for the world and, for the Soviet Union, it has also been ironic.

The amassing of Soviet power alerted free nations to a new danger of aggression. It compelled them in self-defense to spend unprecedented money and energy for armaments. It forced them to develop weapons of war now capable of inflicting instant and terrible punishment upon any aggressor.

It instilled in the free nations—and let none doubt this—the unshakable conviction that, as long as there persists a threat to freedom, they must, at any cost, remain armed, strong, and ready for the risk of war.

It inspired them—and let none doubt this— to attain a unity of purpose and will beyond the power of propaganda or pressure to break, now or ever.

There remained, however, one thing essentially unchanged and unaffected by Soviet conduct: the readiness of the free nations to welcome sincerely any genuine evidence of peaceful purpose enabling all peoples again to resume their common quest of just peace.

The free nations, most solemnly and repeatedly, have assured the Soviet Union that their firm association has never had any aggressive purpose whatsoever. Soviet leaders, however, have seemed to persuade themselves, or tried to persuade their people, otherwise.

And so it has come to pass that the Soviet Union itself has shared and suffered the very fears it has fostered in the rest of the world.

This has been the way of life forged by eight years of fear and force.

What can the world, or any nation in it, hope for if no turning is found on this dread road?

The worst to be feared and the best to be expected can be simply stated.

The worst is atomic war.

The best would be this: a life of perpetual fear and tension; a burden of arms draining the wealth and the labor of all peoples; a wasting of strength that defies the American system or the Soviet system or any system to achieve true abundance and happiness for the peoples of this earth.

Every gun that is made, every warship launched, every rocket fired signifies, in the final sense, a theft from those who hunger and are not fed, those who are cold and are not clothed.

This world in arms is not spending money alone.

It is spending the sweat of its laborers, the genius of its scientists, the hopes of its children.

The cost of one modern heavy bomber is this: a modern brick school in more than 30 cities.

It is two electric power plants, each serving a town of 60,000 population.

It is two fine, fully equipped hospitals.

It is some 50 miles of concrete highway.

We pay for a single fighter plane with a half million bushels of wheat.

We pay for a single destroyer with new homes that could have housed more than 8,000 people.

This, I repeat, is the best way of life to be found on the road the world has been taking.

This is not a way of life at all, in any true sense. Under the cloud of threatening war, it is humanity hanging from a cross of iron.

These plain and cruel truths define the peril and point the hope that come with this spring of 1953.

This is one of those times in the affairs of nations when the gravest choices must be made, if there is to be a turning toward a just and lasting peace.

It is a moment that calls upon the governments of the world to speak their intentions with simplicity and with honesty.

It calls upon them to answer the question that stirs the hearts of all sane men: is there no other way the world may live?

The world knows that an era ended with the death of Joseph Stalin. The extraordinary 30-year span of his rule saw the Soviet Empire expand to reach from the Baltic Sea to the Sea of Japan, finally to dominate 800 million souls.

The Soviet system shaped by Stalin and his predecessors was born of one World War. It survived with stubborn and often amazing courage a second World War. It has lived to threaten a third.

Now a new leadership has assumed power in the Soviet Union. Its links to the past, however strong, cannot bind it completely. Its future is, in great part, its own to make.

This new leadership confronts a free world aroused, as rarely in its history, by the will to stay free.

This free world knows, out of the bitter wisdom of experience, that vigilance and sacrifice are the price of liberty.

It knows that the defense of Western Europe imperatively demands the unity of purpose and action made possible by the North Atlantic Treaty Organization, embracing a European Defense Community.

It knows that Western Germany deserves to be a free and equal partner in this community and that this, for Germany, is the only safe way to full, final unity.

It knows that aggression in Korea and in Southeast Asia are threats to the whole free community to be met by united action.

This is the kind of free world which the new Soviet leadership confronts. It is a world that demands and expects the fullest respect of its rights and interests. It is a world that will always accord the same respect to all others.

So the new Soviet leadership now has a precious opportunity to awaken, with the rest of the world, to the point of peril reached and to help turn the tide of history.

Will it do this?

We do not yet know. Recent statements and gestures of Soviet leaders give some evidence that they may recognize this critical moment.

We welcome every honest act of peace.

We care nothing for mere rhetoric.

We are only for sincerity of peaceful purpose attested by deeds. The opportunities for such deeds are many. The performance of a great number of them waits upon no complex protocol but upon the simple will to do them. Even a few such clear and specific acts, such as the Soviet Union's signature upon an Austrian treaty or its release of thousands of prisoners still held from World War II, would be impressive signs of sincere intent. They would carry a power of persuasion not to be matched by any amount of oratory.

This we do know: a world that begins to witness the rebirth of trust among nations can find its way to a peace that is neither partial nor punitive.

With all who will work in good faith toward such a peace, we are ready, with renewed resolve, to strive to redeem the near-lost hopes of our day.

The first great step along this way must be the conclusion of an honorable armistice in Korea.

This means the immediate cessation of hostilities and the prompt initiation of political discussions leading to the holding of free elections in a united Korea.

It should mean, no less importantly, an end to the direct and indirect attacks upon the security of Indo-china and Malaya. For any armistice in Korea that merely released aggressive armies to attack elsewhere would be a fraud.

We seek, throughout Asia as throughout the world, a peace that is true and total.

Out of this can grow a still wider task—the achieving of just political settlements for the other serious and specific issues between the free world and the Soviet Union.

None of these issues, great or small, is insoluble—given only the will to respect the rights of all nations.

Again we say: the United States is ready to assume its just part.

We have already done all within our power to speed conclusion of a treaty with Austria, which will free that country from economic exploitation and from occupation by foreign troops.

We are ready not only to press forward with the present plans for closer unity of the nations of Western Europe but also, upon that foundation, to strive to foster a broader European community, conducive to the free movement of persons, of trade, and of ideas.

This community would include a free and united Germany, with a government based upon free and secret elections.

This free community and the full independence of the East European nations could mean the end of the present unnatural division of Europe.

As progress in all these areas strengthens world trust, we could proceed concurrently with the next great work—the reduction of the burden of armaments now weighing upon the world. To this end we would welcome and enter into the most solemn agreements. These could properly include:

1. The limitation, by absolute numbers or by an agreed international ratio, of the sizes of the military and security forces of all nations.
2. A commitment by all nations to set an agreed limit upon that proportion of total production of certain strategic materials to be devoted to military purposes.
3. International control of atomic energy to promote its use for peaceful purposes only and to insure the prohibition of atomic weapons.
4. A limitation or prohibition of other categories of weapons of great destructiveness.
5. The enforcement of all these agreed limitations and prohibitions by adequate safeguards, including a practical system of inspection under the United Nations.

The details of such disarmament programs are manifestly critical and complex. Neither the United States nor any other nation can properly claim to possess a perfect, immutable formula. But the formula matters less than the faith—the good faith without which no formula can work justly and effectively.

The fruit of success in all these tasks would present the world with the greatest task, and the greatest opportunity, of all. It is this: the dedication of the energies, the resources, and the imaginations of all peaceful nations to a new kind of war. This would be a declared total war, not upon any human enemy but upon the brute forces of poverty and need.

The peace we seek, founded upon decent trust and cooperative effort among nations, can be fortified, not by weapons of war but by wheat and by cotton, by milk and by wool, by meat and by timber and by rice. These are words that translate into every language on earth. These are needs that challenge this world in arms.

This idea of a just and peaceful world is not new or strange to us. It inspired the people of the United States to initiate the European Recovery Program in 1947. That program was prepared to treat, with like and equal concern, the needs of Eastern and Western Europe.

We are prepared to reaffirm, with the most concrete evidence, our readiness to help build a world in which all peoples can be productive and prosperous.

This government is ready to ask its people to join with all nations in devoting a substantial percentage of the savings achieved by disarmament to a fund for world aid and reconstruction. The purposes of this great work would be to help other peoples to develop the undeveloped areas of the world, to stimulate profitable and fair world trade, to assist all peoples to know the blessings of productive freedom.

The monuments to this new kind of war would be these: roads and schools, hospitals and homes, food and health.

We are ready, in short, to dedicate our strength to serving the needs, rather than the fears, of the world.

We are ready, by these and all such actions, to make of the United Nations an institution that can effectively guard the peace and security of all peoples.

I know of nothing I can add to make plainer the sincere purpose of the United States.

I know of no course, other than that marked by these and similar actions, that can be called the highway of peace.

I know of only one question upon which progress waits. It is this:

What is the Soviet Union ready to do?

Whatever the answer be, let it be plainly spoken.

Again we say: the hunger for peace is too great, the hour in history too late, for any government to mock men's hopes with mere words and promises and gestures.

The test of truth is simple. There can be no persuasion but by deeds.

Is the new leadership of the Soviet Union prepared to use its decisive influence in the Communist world, including control of the flow of arms, to bring not merely an expedient truce in Korea but genuine peace in Asia?

Is it prepared to allow other nations, including those of Eastern Europe, the free choice of their own forms of government?

Is it prepared to act in concert with others upon serious disarmament proposals to be made firmly effective by stringent UN control and inspection?

If not, where then is the concrete evidence of the Soviet Union's concern for peace?

The test is clear.

There is, before all peoples, a precious chance to turn the black tide of events. If we failed to strive to seize this chance, the judgment of future ages would be harsh and just.

If we strive but fail and the world remains armed against itself, it at least need be divided no longer in its clear knowledge of who has condemned humankind to this fate.

The purpose of the United States, in stating these proposals, is simple and clear.

These proposals spring, without ulterior purpose or political passion, from our calm conviction that the hunger for peace is in the hearts of all peoples—those of Russia and of China no less than of our own country.

They conform to our firm faith that God created men to enjoy, not destroy, the fruits of the earth and of their own toil.

They aspire to this: the lifting, from the backs and from the hearts of men, of their burden of arms and of fears, so that they may find before them a golden age of freedom and of peace.

Don't Join the Bookburners

Hanover, New Hampshire

June 14, 1953

As a POLITICIAN, Eisenhower conducted himself in accordance with the motto engraved on a plaque on his Oval Office desk: *Suaviter in modo, fortiter in re* ["gentle in manner, strong in deed"]— the Latin equivalent of Teddy Roosevelt's "Speak softly and carry a big stick." Despite frequent promptings by his advisers, Eisenhower refused to publicly denounce Joseph McCarthy, the senator whose claims of Communist infiltration into American society were destroying many reputations and keeping much of the nation in a state of paranoia. McCarthy was a fellow Republican, and the internationalist president felt he could not afford to alienate his party's isolationist Old Guard, whose support he needed in the Senate. "McCarthyism was a much larger issue than McCarthy," Eisenhower wrote in his memoirs. "Lashing back at one man, which is easy enough for a president, was not as important to me as the long-term value of restraint, the due process of law, and the basic rights of free men." One of Eisenhower's rare replies to McCarthy's tactics, though it did not mention him by name, was made extemporaneously during commencement exercises at Dartmouth College. It is an oblique reference to McCarthy's demand for a purge of "subversive" books from American overseas libraries.

[The] president [of Dartmouth] possesses a brash bravery approaching fool-hardiness when he gives to me this platform in front of such an audience, with no other admonition except to speak informally, and giving me no limits of any other kind.

He has forgotten, I think, that old soldiers love to reminisce, and that they are, in addition, notoriously garrulous. But I have certain limitations of my own I learned throughout these many years, and I think they will serve to keep me from offending too deeply. But even if I do offend, I beg, in advance, the pardon of those families and friends, sweethearts that are waiting to greet these new graduates with a chaste handshake of congratulations, and assure you that any overstaying of my time was unintentional and just merely a product of my past upbringing. . . .

Now, with your permission, I want to talk about two points—two qualities—today that are purely personal. I am not going to be an exhorter. . . . I want to talk about these two things and merely suggest to you certain ideas concerning them.

I am going to talk about fun—joy— happiness, just fun in life. I am going to talk a little about courage.

Now, as to fun: to get myself straight at once, for fear that in my garrulous way I might stray from my point, I shall say this: unless each day can be looked back upon by an individual as one in which he has had some fun, some joy, some real satisfaction, that day is a loss. It is un-Christian and wicked, in my opinion, to allow such a thing to occur.

Now, there are many, many different things and thoughts and ideas that will contribute— any acts of your own—that will contribute to the fun you have out of life. You can go along the bank of a stream in the tropics, and there is a crocodile lying in the sun. He looks the picture of contentment. They tell me that often they live to be a great age—a hundred years or more— and still lying in the sun and that is all they do.

Now, by going to Dartmouth, by coming this far along the road, you have achieved certain standards. One of those standards is: it is no longer so easy for you to have fun, and you can't be like a crocodile and sleep away your life and be satisfied. You must do something, and normally it must involve others, something you do for them. The satisfaction—it's trite but it's true—the satisfaction of a clear conscience, no matter what happens.

You can get a lot of fun out of shooting a good game of golf. But you wouldn't have the slightest fun out of it if you knew to achieve that first 79—you broke 80 today—if you did it by teeing up in the rough or taking the slightest advantage anywhere, and no one else in the world but you knew it. That game would never be a 79 to you, and so it was not worthwhile because you had no fun doing it.

Whatever you do—a little help to someone along the road—something you have achieved because you worked hard for it, like your graduation diploma today, those things have become worthwhile, and in your own estimation will contribute to your happiness. They will measure up to your standards because your standards have become those that only you know, but they have become very high. And if you do those things, they are the kind of things that will satisfy you and make life something that is joyous, that will cause your face to spread out a little, instead of going this way [indicating a long face]. There's too much of that in the world, anyway.

You are leaders. You are bound to be leaders because you have had advantages that make you leader to someone, whether you know it or not. There will be tough problems to solve. You have heard about them. You can't solve them with long faces—they don't solve problems, not when they deal with humans. Humans have to have confidence. You have got to help give it to them.

This brings me up to my second little topic, which is courage. I forget the author, but one many years ago, you know, uttered that famous saying, "The coward dies a thousand deaths, but the brave man dies but once." In other words, you can live happily if you have courage, because you are not fearing something that you can't help.

You must have courage to look at all about you with honest eyes—above all, yourself. And we go back to our standards. Have you actually measured up? If you have, it is that courage to look at yourself and say, well, I failed miserably there, I hurt someone's feelings needlessly, I lost my temper—which you must never do except deliberately. You did not measure up to your own standards.

Now, if you have the courage to look at yourself, soon you begin to achieve a code or a pattern that is closer to your own standards. By the same token, look at all that is dear to you: your own family. Of course, your children are going to be the greatest, the most extraordinary that ever lived. But, also, look at them as they are, occasionally.

Look at your country. Here is a country of which we are proud, as you are proud of Dartmouth and all about you, and the families to which you belong. But this country is a long way from perfection—a long way. We have the disgrace of racial discrimination, or we have prejudice against people because of their religion. We have crime on the docks. We have not had the courage to uproot these things, although we know they are wrong. And we with our standards, the standards given us at places like Dartmouth, we know they are wrong.

Now, that courage is not going to be satisfied—your sense of satisfaction is not going to be satisfied, if you haven't the courage to look at these things and do your best to help correct them, because that is the contribution you shall make to this beloved country in your time. Each of us, as he passes along, should strive to add something.

It is not enough merely to say I love America, and to salute the flag and take off your hat as it goes by, and to help sing the Star Spangled Banner. Wonderful! We love to do them, and our hearts swell with pride, because those who went before you worked to give to us today, standing here, this pride.

And this is a pride in an institution that we think has brought great happiness, and we know has brought great contentment and freedom of soul to many people. But it is not yet done. You must add to it.

Don't join the bookburners. Don't think you are going to conceal faults by concealing evidence that they ever existed. Don't be afraid to go in your library and read every book, as long as that document does not offend our own ideas of decency. That should be the only censorship.

How will we defeat Communism unless we know what it is, and what it teaches, and why does it have such an appeal for men, why are so many people swearing allegiance to it? It is almost a religion, albeit one of the nether regions.

And we have got to fight it with something better, not try to conceal the thinking of our own people. They are part of America. And even if they think ideas that are contrary to ours, their right to say them, their right to record them, and their right to have them at places where they are accessible to others is unquestioned, or it isn't America.

I fear I have already violated my promise not to stay too long and not to exhort. I could not, though, go back to that chair without saying that my sense of distinction in Dartmouth's honorary doctorate, in the overgenerous—extravagantly overgenerous—remarks of your president in awarding me that doctorate, in the present of the cane from the young men of the graduating class—all of these things are very precious to me.

I have been fortunate in that my life has been spent with America's young men, probably one of the finest things that has happened to me in a very long life.

I thank you again for this.

Atoms for Peace

New York City, New York
December 8, 1953

EISENHOWER'S APPEAL to the Soviet Union of April 1953 received no direct reply, but four months later came the news that the Soviet Union had succeeded in building a hydrogen bomb. From this point on, every confrontation between the superpowers carried with it the prospect of a world-engulfing nuclear war. At the White House, a project called Operation Candor, headed by C. ID. Jackson, was organized to formulate a presidential speech on the subject. In December Eisenhower went before the United Nations General Assembly to propose that the United States and the U.S.S.R. cooperate in the development of humanitarian uses for nuclear power. The idea was Eisenhower's own. It received a wildly enthusiastic response from the UN audience, but reluctance on the part of the Kremlin and of some members of the Eisenhower administration nearly killed all progress on it. The final result was the creation by the United States, the Soviet Union, and 10 other nations of the International Atomic Energy Association.

Although Operation Candor had been at work for some months on Eisenhower's suggestion, the decision to present it before the United Nations was made at the last minute—so late, in fact, that Eisenhower had to interrupt a meeting in Bermuda with the prime ministers of England and France in order to be in New York on time. Even so, the plane had to circle the airport for 15 minutes while the speech was finished, typed, mimeographed, and collated by Eisenhower's aides and secretaries.

When Secretary-General Hammarskjold's invitation to address this General Assembly reached me in Bermuda, I was just beginning a series of conferences with the prime ministers and foreign ministers of Great Britain and of France. Our subject was some of the problems that beset our world.

During the remainder of the Bermuda Conference, I had constantly in mind that ahead of me lay a great honor. That honor is mine today as I stand here, privileged to address the General Assembly of the United Nations.

At the same time that I appreciate the distinction of addressing you, I have a sense of exhilaration as I look upon this Assembly.

Never before in history has so much hope for so many people been gathered together in a single organization. Your deliberations and decisions during these somber years have already realized part of those hopes.

But the great tests and the great accomplishments still lie ahead. And in the confident expectation of those accomplishments, I would use the office which, for the time being, I hold, to assure you that the government of the United States will remain steadfast in its support of this body. This we shall do in the conviction that you will provide a great share of the wisdom, the courage, and the faith which can bring to this world lasting peace for all nations, and happiness and well-being for all men.

Clearly, it would not be fitting for me to take this occasion to present to you a unilateral American report on Bermuda. Nevertheless, I assure you that in our deliberations on that lovely island we sought to invoke those same great concepts of universal peace and human dignity which are so clearly etched in your Charter.

Neither would it be a measure of this great opportunity merely to recite, however hopefully, pious platitudes.

I therefore decided that this occasion warranted my saying to you some of the things that have been on the minds and hearts of my legislative and executive associates and on mine for a great many months—thoughts I had originally planned to say primarily to the American people.

I know that the American people share my deep belief that if a danger exists in the world, it is a danger shared by all—and equally, that if hope exists in the mind of one nation, that hope should be shared by all.

Finally, if there is to be advanced any proposal designed to ease even by the smallest measure the tensions of today's world, what more appropriate audience could there be than the members of the General Assembly of the United Nations?

I feel impelled to speak today in a language that in a sense is new—one which I, who have spent so much of my life in the military profession, would have preferred never to use.

That new language is the language of atomic warfare.

The atomic age has moved forward at such a pace that every citizen of the world should have some comprehension, at least in comparative terms, of the extent of this development of the utmost significance to every one of us. Clearly, if the peoples of the world are to conduct an intelligent search for peace, they must be armed with the significant facts of today's existence.

My recital of atomic danger and power is necessarily stated in United States terms, for these are the only incontrovertible facts that I know. I need hardly point out to this Assembly, however, that this subject is global, not merely national in character.

On July 16, 1945, the United States set off the world's first atomic explosion. Since that date in 1945, the United States of America has conducted 42 test explosions.

Atomic bombs today are more than 25 times as powerful as the weapons with which the atomic age dawned, while hydrogen weapons are in the ranges of millions of tons of TNT equivalent.

Today, the United States' stockpile of atomic weapons, which, of course, increases daily, exceeds by many times the explosive equivalent of the total of all bombs and all shells that came from every plane and every gun in every theater of war in all of the years of World War II.

A single air group, whether afloat or land-based, can now deliver to any reachable target a destructive cargo exceeding in power all the bombs that fell on Britain in all of World War II.

In size and variety, the development of atomic weapons has been no less remarkable. The development has been such that atomic weapons have virtually achieved conventional status within our armed services. In the United States, the army, the navy, the air force, and the marine corps are all capable of putting this weapon to military use.

But the dread secret, and the fearful engines of atomic might, are not ours alone.

In the first place, the secret is possessed by our friends and allies, Great Britain and Canada, whose scientific genius made a tremendous contribution to our original discoveries, and the designs of atomic bombs.

The secret is also known by the Soviet Union.

The Soviet Union has informed us that, over recent years, it has devoted extensive resources to atomic weapons. During this period, the Soviet Union has exploded a series of atomic devices, including at least one involving thermonuclear reactions.

If at one time the United States possessed what might have been called a monopoly of atomic power, that monopoly ceased to exist several years ago. Therefore, although our earlier start has permitted us to accumulate what is today a great quantitative advantage, the atomic realities of today comprehend two facts of even greater significance.

First, the knowledge now possessed by several nations will eventually be shared by others—possibly all others.

Second, even a vast superiority in numbers of weapons, and a consequent capability of devastating retaliation, is no preventive, of itself, against the fearful material damage and toll of human lives that would be inflicted by surprise aggression.

The free world, at least dimly aware of these facts, has naturally embarked on a large program of warning and defense systems. That program will be accelerated and expanded.

But let no one think that the expenditure of vast sums for weapons and systems of defense can guarantee absolute safety for the cities and citizens of any nation. The awful arithmetic of the atomic bomb does not permit of any such easy solution. Even against the most powerful defense, an aggressor in possession of the effective minimum number of atomic bombs for a surprise attack could probably place a sufficient number of his bombs on the chosen targets to cause hideous damage.

Should such an atomic attack be launched against the United States, our reactions would be swift and resolute. But for me to say that the defense capabilities of the United States are such that they could inflict terrible losses upon an aggressor—for me to say that the retaliation capabilities of the United States are so great that such an aggressor's land would be laid waste—all this, while fact, is not the true expression of the purpose and the hope of the United States.

To pause there would be to confirm the hopeless finality of a belief that two atomic colossi are doomed malevolently to eye each other indefinitely across a trembling world. To stop there would be to accept helplessly the probability of civilization destroyed—the annihilation of the irreplaceable heritage of mankind handed down to us generation from generation—and the condemnation of mankind to begin all over again the age-old struggle upward from savagery toward decency, and right, and justice.

Surely no sane member of the human race could discover victory in such desolation. Could anyone wish his name to be coupled by history with such human degradation and destruction.

Occasional pages of history do record the faces of the "Great Destroyers" but the whole book of history reveals mankind's never-ending quest for peace, and mankind's God-given capacity to build.

It is with the book of history, and not with isolated pages, that the United States will ever wish to be identified. My country wants to be constructive, not destructive. It wants agreements, not wars, among nations. It wants itself to live in freedom, and in the confidence that the people of every other nation enjoy equally the right of choosing their own way of life.

So my country's purpose is to help us move out of the dark chamber of horrors into the light, to find a way by which the minds of men, the hopes of men, the souls of men everywhere, can move forward toward peace and happiness and well being.

In this quest, I know that we must not lack patience.

I know that in a world divided, such as ours today, salvation cannot be attained by one dramatic act.

I know that many steps will have to be taken over many months before the world can look at itself one day and truly realize that a new climate of mutually peaceful confidence is abroad in the world.

But I know, above all else, that we must start to take these steps—now.

The United States and its allies, Great Britain and France, have over the past months tried to take some of these steps. Let no one say that we shun the conference table.

On the record has long stood the request of the United States, Great Britain, and France to negotiate with the Soviet Union the problems of a divided Germany.

On that record has long stood the request of the same three nations to negotiate an Austrian Peace Treaty.

On the same record still stands the request of the United Nations to negotiate the problems of Korea.

Most recently, we have received from the Soviet Union what is in effect an expression of willingness to hold a Four Power Meeting. Along with our allies, Great Britain and France, we were pleased to see that this note did not contain the unacceptable preconditions previously put forward.

As you already know from our joint Bermuda communique, the United States, Great Britain, and France have agreed promptly to meet with the Soviet Union.

The government of the United States approaches this conference with hopeful sincerity. We will bend every effort of our minds to the single purpose of emerging from that conference with tangible results toward peace—the only true way of lessening international tension.

We never have, we never will, propose or suggest that the Soviet Union surrender what is rightfully theirs.

We will never say that the peoples of Russia are an enemy with whom we have no desire ever to deal or mingle in friendly and fruitful relationship.

On the contrary, we hope that this coming conference may initiate a relationship with the Soviet Union which will eventually bring about a free intermingling of the peoples of the East and of the West—the one sure, human way of developing the understanding required for confident and peaceful relations.

Instead of the discontent which is now settling upon Eastern Germany, occupied Austria, and the countries of Eastern Europe, we seek a harmonious family of free European nations, with none a threat to the other, and least of all a threat to the peoples of Russia.

Beyond the turmoil and strife and misery of Asia, we seek peaceful opportunity for these peoples to develop their natural resources and to elevate their lives.

These are not idle words or shallow visions. Behind them lies a story of nations lately come to independence, not as a result of war, but through free grant or peaceful negotiation. There is a record, already written, of assistance gladly given by nations of the West to needy peoples, and to those suffering the temporary effects of famine, drought, and natural disaster.

These are deeds of peace. They speak more loudly than promises or protestations of peaceful intent.

But I do not wish to rest either upon the reiteration of past proposals or the restatement of past deeds. The gravity of the time is such that every new avenue of peace, no matter how dimly discernible, should be explored.

There is at least one new avenue of peace which has not yet been well explored—an avenue now laid out by the General Assembly of the United Nations.

In its resolution of November 18th, 1953, this General Assembly suggested—and I quote—"that the Disarmament Commission study the desirability of establishing a sub-committee consisting of representatives of the Powers principally involved, which should seek in private an acceptable solution . . . and report on such a solution to the General Assembly and to the Security Council not later than 1 September 1954."

The United States, heeding the suggestion of the General Assembly of the United Nations, is instantly prepared to meet privately with such other countries as may be "principally involved," to seek "an acceptable solution" to the atomic armaments race which overshadows not only the peace, but the very life, of the world.

We shall carry into these private or diplomatic talks a new conception.

The United States would seek more than the mere reduction or elimination of atomic materials for military purposes.

It is not enough to take this weapon out of the hands of the soldiers. It must be put into the hands of those who will know how to strip its military casing and adapt it to the arts of peace.

The United States knows that if the fearful trend of atomic military buildup can be reversed, this greatest of destructive forces can be developed into a great boon, for the benefit of all mankind.

The United States knows that peaceful power from atomic energy is no dream of the future. That capability, already proved, is here—now—today. Who can doubt, if the entire body of the world's scientists and engineers had adequate amounts of fissionable material with which to test and develop their ideas, that this capability would rapidly be transformed into universal, efficient, and economic usage.

To hasten the day when fear of the atom will begin to disappear from the minds of people, and the governments of the East and West, there are certain steps that can be taken now.

I therefore make the following proposals:

The governments principally involved, to the extent permitted by elementary prudence, to begin now and continue to make joint contributions from their stockpiles of normal uranium and fissionable materials to an International Atomic Energy Agency. We would expect that such an agency would be set up under the aegis of the United Nations.

The ratios of contributions, the procedures and other details would properly be within the scope of the "private conversations" I have referred to earlier.

The United States is prepared to undertake these explorations in good faith. Any partner of the United States acting in the same good faith will find the United States a not unreasonable or ungenerous associate.

Undoubtedly initial and early contributions to this plan would be small in quantity. However, the proposal has the great virtue that it can be undertaken without the irritations and mutual suspicions incident to any attempt to set up a completely acceptable system of worldwide inspection and control.

The Atomic Energy Agency could be made responsible for the impounding, storage, and protection of the contributed fissionable and other materials. The ingenuity of our scientists will provide special safe conditions under which such a bank of fissionable material can be made essentially immune to surprise seizure.

The more important responsibility of this Atomic Energy Agency would be to devise methods whereby this fissionable material would be allocated to serve the peaceful pursuits of mankind. Experts would be mobilized to apply atomic energy to the needs of agriculture, medicine, and other peaceful activities. A special purpose would be to provide abundant electrical energy in the power-starved areas of the world. Thus the contributing powers would be dedicating some of their strength to serve the needs rather than the fears of mankind.

The United States would be more than willing—it would be proud to take up with others "principally involved" the development of plans whereby such peaceful use of atomic energy would be expedited.

Of those "principally involved" the Soviet Union must, of course, be one.

I would be prepared to submit to the Congress of the United States, and with every expectation of approval, any such plan that would:

First—encourage worldwide investigation into the most effective peacetime uses of fissionable material, and with the certainty that they had all the material needed for the conduct of all experiments that were appropriate;

Second—begin to diminish the potential destructive power of the world's atomic stockpiles;

Third—allow all peoples of all nations to see that, in this enlightened age, the great powers of the earth, both of the East and of the West, are interested in human aspirations first, rather than in building up the armaments of war;

Fourth—open up a new channel for peaceful discussion, and initiate at least a new approach to the many difficult problems that must be solved in both private and public conversations, if the world is to shake off the inertia imposed by fear, and is to make positive progress toward peace.

Against the dark background of the atomic bomb, the United States does not wish merely to present strength, but also the desire and the hope for peace.

The coming months will be fraught with fateful decisions. In this Assembly; in the capitals and military headquarters of the world; in the hearts of men everywhere, be they governors or governed, may they be the decisions which will lead this world out of fear and into peace.

To the making of these fateful decisions, the United States pledges before you—and therefore before the world—its determination to help solve the fearful atomic dilemma—to devote its entire heart and mind to find the way by which the miraculous inventiveness of man shall not be dedicated to his death, but consecrated to his life.

I again thank the delegates for the great honor they have done me, in inviting me to appear before them, and in listening to me so courteously. Thank you.

The Double Crisis

Washington, D.C.

October 31, 1956

THE FINAL WEEKS of Eisenhower's 1956 reelection campaign were dominated not by the campaign itself—Eisenhower's victory was a foregone conclusion—but by two major developments in foreign affairs: the Hungarian rebellion against the Soviet Union and the attack on Egypt by Britain, France, and Israel, which had as its aim to recapture control of the recently nationalized Suez Canal. Six days before the election, Eisenhower made a televised report to the nation about both events. The speech, written under great pressure while Eisenhower coolly practiced his golf swing on the White House lawn, had to be worded with unusual care, so delicate was the situation. In the first case, Eisenhower had to welcome the possibility of freedom for Hungary while reassuring the Soviet Union of U.S. neutrality; in the second, he had to reject as illegal the attack on Egypt without offending the aggressors, who were also America's allies. Tact was difficult to come by in the White House, where many officials had worked themselves into near-hysteria over the Suez crisis and the likelihood of war, but Eisenhower, despite his own anxiety, delivered the speech with an air of calm and confidence. By election eve, the Soviet Union had recaptured control of Hungary and a cease-fire had gone into effect in the Middle East.

Tonight I report to you as your president.

We all realize that the full and free debate of a political campaign surrounds us. But the events and issues I wish to place before you this evening have no connection whatsoever with matters of partisanship. They are concerns of every American—his present and his future.

I wish, therefore, to give you a report of essential facts so that you—whether belonging to either one of our two great parties, or to neither—may give thoughtful and informed consideration to this swiftly changing world scene.

The changes of which I speak have come in two areas of the world—Eastern Europe and the Mideast.

I.

In Eastern Europe there is the dawning of a new day. It has not been short or easy in coming.

After World War II, the Soviet Union used military force to impose on the nations of Eastern Europe, governments of Soviet choice—servants of Moscow.

It has been consistent United States policy—without regard to political party—to seek to end this situation. We have sought to fulfill the wartime pledge of the United Nations that these countries, overrun by wartime armies, would once again know sovereignty and self-government.

We could not, of course, carry out this policy by resort to force. Such force would have been contrary both to the best interests of the Eastern European peoples and to the abiding principles of the United Nations. But we did help to keep alive the hope of these peoples for freedom.

Beyond this, they needed from us no education in the worth of national independence and personal liberty—for, at the time of the American Revolution, it was many of them who came to our land to aid our cause. Now, recently the pressure of the will of these peoples for national independence has become more and more insistent.

A few days ago, the people of Poland—with their proud and deathless devotion to freedom—moved to secure a peaceful transition to a new government. And this government, it seems, will strive genuinely to serve the Polish people.

And, more recently, all the world has been watching dramatic events in Hungary where this brave people, as so often in the past, have offered their very lives for independence from foreign masters. Today, it appears, a new Hungary is rising from this struggle, a Hungary which we hope from our hearts will know full and free nationhood.

We have rejoiced in all these historic events.

Only yesterday the Soviet Union issued an important statement on its relations with all the countries of Eastern Europe. This statement recognized the need for review of Soviet policies, and the amendment of these policies to meet the demands of the people for greater national independence and personal freedom. The Soviet Union declared its readiness to consider the withdrawal of Soviet "advisers"—who have been, as you know, the effective ruling force in Soviet occupied countries—and also to consider withdrawal of Soviet forces from Poland, Hungary and Rumania.

We cannot yet know if these avowed purposes will be truly carried out.

But two things are clear.

First, the fervor and the sacrifice of the peoples of these countries, in the name of freedom, have themselves brought real promise that the light of liberty soon will shine again in this darkness.

And second, if the Soviet Union indeed faithfully acts upon its announced intention, the world will witness the greatest forward stride toward justice, trust and understanding among nations in our generation.

These are the facts. How has your government responded to them?

The United States has made clear its readiness to assist economically the new and independent governments of these countries. We have already—some days since—been in contact with the new government of Poland on this matter. We have also publicly declared that we do not demand of these governments their adoption of any particular form of society as a condition upon our economic assistance. Our one concern is that they be free—for their sake, and for freedom's sake.

We have also—with respect to the Soviet Union—sought clearly to remove any false fears that we would look upon new governments in these Eastern European countries as potential military allies. We have no such ulterior purpose. We see these peoples as friends, and we wish simply that they be friends who are free.

II.

I now turn to that other part of the world where, at this moment, the situation is somber. It is not a situation that calls for extravagant fear or hysteria. But it invites our most serious concern.

I speak, of course, of the Middle East. This ancient crossroads of the world was, as we all know, an area long subject to colonial rule. This rule ended after World War II, when all countries there won full independence. Out of the Palestinian mandated territory was born the new state of Israel.

These historic changes could not, however, instantly banish animosities born of the ages. Israel and her Arab neighbors soon found themselves at war with one another. And the Arab nations showed continuing anger toward their former colonial rulers, notably France and Great Britain.

The United States—through all the years since the close of World War II—has labored tirelessly to bring peace and stability to this area.

We have considered it a basic matter of United States policy to support the new state of Israel and—at the same time—to strengthen our bonds both with Israel and with the Arab countries. But, unfortunately through all these years, passion in the area threatened to prevail over peaceful purposes, and in one form or another, there has been almost continuous fighting.

This situation recently was aggravated by Egyptian policy including rearmament with Communist weapons. We felt this to be a misguided policy on the part of the government of Egypt. The state of Israel, at the same time, felt increasing anxiety for its safety. And Great Britain and France feared more and more that Egyptian policies threatened their "life line" of the Suez Canal.

These matters came to a crisis on July 26th of this year, when the Egyptian government seized the Universal Suez Canal Company. For 90 years—ever since the inauguration of the Canal—that company has operated the Canal, largely under British and French technical supervision.

Now there were some among our allies who urged an immediate reaction to this event by use of force. We insistently urged otherwise, and our wish prevailed—through a long succession of conferences and negotiations for weeks—even months—with participation by the United Nations. And there, in the United Nations, only a short while ago, on the basis of agreed principles, it seemed that an acceptable accord was within our reach.

But the direct relations of Egypt with both Israel and France kept worsening to a point at which first Israel—then France—and Great

Britain also—determined that, in their judgment, there could be no protection of their vital interests without resort to force.

Upon ths decision, events followed swiftly. On Sunday the Israeli government ordered total mobilization. On Monday, their armed forces penetrated deeply into Egypt and to the vicinity of the Suez Canal, nearly 100 miles away. And on Tuesday, the British and French governments delivered a 12-hour ultimatum to Israel and Egypt—now followed up by armed attack against Egypt.

The United States was not consulted in any way about any phase of these actions. Nor were we informed of them in advance.

As it is the manifest right of any of these nations to take such decisions and actions, it is likewise our right—if our judgment so dictates—to dissent. We believe these actions to have been taken in error. For we do not accept the use of force as a wise or proper instrument for the settlement of international disputes.

To say this—in this particular instance—is in no way to minimize our friendship with these nations—nor our determination to maintain those friendships.

And we are fully aware of the grave anxieties of Israel, of Britain and of France. We know that they have been subjected to grave and repeated provocations.

The present fact, nonetheless, seems clear: the action taken can scarcely be reconciled with the principles and purposes of the United Nations to which we have all subscribed. And, beyond this, we are forced to doubt that resort to force and war will for long serve the permanent interest of the attacking nations.

Now—we must look to the future.

In the circumstances I have described, there will be no United States involvement in these present hostilities. I therefore have no plan to call the Congress in Special Session. Of course, we shall continue to keep in contact with congressional leaders of both parties.

I assure you, your government will remain alert to every possibility of this situation, and keep in close contact and coordination with the legislative branch of this government.

At the same time it is—and it will remain—the dedicated purpose of your government to do all in its power to localize the fighting and to end the conflict.

We took our first measure in this action yesterday. We went to the United Nations with a request that the forces of Israel return to their own land and that hostilities in the area be brought to a close. This proposal was not adopted—because it was vetoed by Great Britain and by France.

The processes of the United Nations, however, are not exhausted. It is our hope and intent that this matter will be brought before the United Nations General Assembly. There—with no veto operating—the opinion of the world can be brought to bear in our quest for a just end to this tormenting problem. In the past the United Nations has proved able to find a way to end bloodshed. We believe it can and that it will do so again.

My fellow citizens, as I review the march of world events in recent years, I am ever more deeply convinced that the processes of the United Nations represent the soundest hope for peace in the world. For this very reason, I believe that the processes of the United Nations need further to be developed and strengthened. I speak particularly of increasing its ability to secure justice under international law.

In all the recent troubles in the Middle East, there have indeed been injustices suffered by all nations involved. But I do not believe that another instrument of injustice—war—is the remedy for these wrongs.

There can be no peace—without law. And there can be no law—if we were to invoke one code of international conduct for those who oppose us—and another for our friends.

The society of nations has been slow in developing means to apply this truth.

But the passionate longing for peace—on the part of all peoples of the earth—compels us to speed our search for new and more effective instruments of justice.

The peace we seek and need means much more than mere absence of war. It means the acceptance of law, and the fostering of justice, in all the world.

To our principles guiding us in this quest we must stand fast. In so doing we can honor the hopes of all men for a world in which peace will truly and justly reign.

I thank you, and goodnight.

The Situation in Little Rock

Washington, D.C.

September 24, 1957

EISENHOWER DID HIS BEST to avoid becoming involved in the inflammatory issue of school desegregation, which had been mandated by the Supreme Court's 1954 *Brown v. Board of Education of Topeka* decision. The apparent threat to social stability posed by desegregation troubled him, and he did not agree with those who "believe that you are going to reform the human heart by law." When Orval Faubus, the governor of Arkansas, sent the National Guard to bar black students from entering a high school in the city of Little Rock, Eisenhower continued his golfing vacation and tried in vain to work out a behind-the-scenes compromise with the governor. Eventually the white mobs in the city became so violent that the mayor cabled the White House with an urgent request for federal protection. Eisenhower immediately ordered 1,000 army paratroopers into the city, put the state's National Guard under federal authority, and returned to Washington to broadcast this address, in which he stressed that he had acted not to promote integration but to defend the rule of law.

It was the first time since Reconstruction that black civil rights in the South had been defended by federal troops. They remained in place through November; the federalized National Guard stayed until June.

For a few minutes this evening I want to speak to you about the serious situation that has arisen in Little Rock. To make this talk I have come to the president's office in the White House. I could have spoken from Rhode Island, where I have been staying recently, but I felt that, in speaking from the house of Lincoln, of Jackson, and of Wilson, my words would better convey both the sadness I feel in the action I was compelled today to take and the firmness with which I intend to pursue this course until the orders of the federal court at Little Rock can be executed without unlawful interference.

In that city, under the leadership of demagogic extremists, disorderly mobs have deliberately prevented the carrying out of proper orders from a federal court. Local authorities have not eliminated that violent opposition and, under the law, I yesterday issued a proclamation calling upon the mob to disperse.

This morning the mob again gathered in front of the Central High School of Little Rock, obviously for the purpose of again preventing the carrying out of the Court's order relating to the admission of Negro children to that school.

Whenever normal agencies prove inadequate to the task and it becomes necessary for the executive branch of the federal government to use its powers and authority to uphold federal courts, the president's responsibility is inescapable.

In accordance with that responsibility, I have today issued an Executive Order directing the use of troops under federal authority to aid in the execution of federal law at Little Rock, Arkansas. This became necessary when my proclamation of yesterday was not observed, and the obstruction of justice still continues.

It is important that the reasons for my action be understood by all our citizens.

As you know, the Supreme Court of the United States has decided that separate public educational facilities for the races are inherently unequal and therefore compulsory school segregation laws are unconstitutional.

Our personal opinions about the decision have no bearing on the matter of enforcement; the responsibility and authority of the Supreme Court to interpret the Constitution are very clear. Local federal courts were instructed by the Supreme Court to issue such orders and decrees as might be necessary to achieve admission to public schools without regard to race-and with all deliberate speed.

During the past several years, many communities in our southern states have instituted public school plans for gradual progress in the enrollment and attendance of schoolchildren of all races in order to bring themselves into compliance with the law of the land.

They thus demonstrated to the world that we are a nation in which laws, not men, are supreme.

I regret to say that this truth—the cornerstone of our liberties—was not observed in this instance.

It was my hope that this localized situation would be brought under control by city and state authorities. If the use of local police powers had been sufficient, our traditional method of leaving the problems in those hands would have been pursued. But when large gatherings of obstructionists made it impossible for the decrees of the court to be carried out, both the law and the national interest demanded that the president take action.

Here is the sequence of events in the development of the Little Rock school case.

In May of 1955, the Little Rock School Board approved a moderate plan for the gradual desegregation of the public schools in that city. It provided that a start toward integration would be made at the present term in the high school, and that the plan would be in full operation by 1963. Here I might say that in a number of communities in Arkansas integration in the schools has already started and without violence of any kind. Now this Little Rock plan was challenged in the courts by some who believed that the period of time as proposed in the plan was too long.

The United States Court at Little Rock, which has supervisory responsibility under the law for the plan of desegregation in the public schools, dismissed the challenge, thus approving a gradual rather than an abrupt change from the existing system. The court found that the school board had acted in good faith in planning for a public school system free from racial discrimination.

Since that time, the court has on three separate occasions issued orders directing that the plan be carried out. All persons were instructed to refrain from interfering with the efforts of the school board to comply with the law.

Proper and sensible observance of the law then demanded the respectful obedience which the nation has a right to expect from all its people. This, unfortunately, has not been the case at Little Rock. Certain misguided persons, many of them imported into Little Rock by agitators, have insisted upon defying the law and have sought to bring it into disrepute. The orders of the court have thus been frustrated.

The very basis of our individual rights and freedoms rests upon the certainty that the president and the executive branch of government will support and insure the carrying out of the decisions of the federal courts, even, when necessary with all the means at the president's command.

Unless the president did so, anarchy would result.

There would be no security for any except that which each one of us could provide for himself.

The interest of the nation in the proper fulfillment of the law's requirements cannot yield to opposition and demonstrations by some few persons.

Mob rule cannot be allowed to override the decisions of our courts.

Now, let me make it very clear that federal troops are not being used to relieve local and state authorities of their primary duty to preserve the peace and order of the community. Nor are the troops there for the purpose of taking over the responsibility of the School Board and the other responsible local officials in running Central High School. The running of our school system and the maintenance of peace and order in each of our states are strictly local affairs and the federal government does not interfere except in a very few special cases and when requested by one of the several states. In the present case the troops are there, pursuant to law, solely for the purpose of preventing interference with the orders of the court.

The proper use of the powers of the executive branch to enforce the orders of a federal court is limited to extraordinary and compelling circumstances. Manifestly, such an extreme situation has been created in Little Rock. This challenge must be met and with such measures as will preserve to the people as a whole their lawfully protected rights in a climate permitting their free and fair exercise.

The overwhelming majority of our people in every section of the country are united in their respect for observance of the law—even in those cases where they may disagree with that law.

They deplore the call of extremists to violence.

The decision of the Supreme Court concerning school integration, of course, affects the South more seriously than it does other sections of the country. In that region I have many warm friends, some of them in the city of Little Rock. I have deemed it a great personal privilege to spend in our southland tours of duty while in the military service and enjoyable recreational periods since that time.

So from intimate personal knowledge, I know that the overwhelming majority of the people in the South—including those of Arkansas and of Little Rock—are of goodwill, united in their efforts to preserve and respect the law even when they disagree with it.

They do not sympathize with mob rule. They, like the rest of our nation, have proved in two great wars their readiness to sacrifice for America.

A foundation of our American way of life is our national respect for law.

In the South, as elsewhere, citizens are keenly aware of the tremendous disservice that has been done to the people of Arkansas in the eyes of the nation, and that has been done to the nation in the eyes of the world.

At a time when we face grave situations abroad because of the hatred that Communism bears toward a system of government based on human rights, it would be difficult to exaggerate the harm that is being done to the prestige and influence, and indeed to the safety, of our nation and the world.

Our enemies are gloating over this incident and using it everywhere to misrepresent our whole nation. We are portrayed as a violator of those standards of conduct which the peoples of the world united to proclaim in the Charter of the United Nations. There they affirmed "faith in fundamental human rights" and "in the dignity and worth of the human person" and they did so "without distinction as to race, sex, language or religion."

And so, with deep confidence, I call upon the citizens of the state of Arkansas to assist in bringing to an immediate end all interference with the law and its processes. If resistance to the federal court orders ceases at once, the further presence of federal troops will be unnecessary and the city of Little Rock will return to its normal habits of peace and order and a blot upon the fair name and high honor of our nation in the world will be removed.

Thus will be restored the image of America and of all its parts as one nation, indivisible, with liberty and justice for all.

Good night, and thank you very much.

The Eisenhower Doctrine in Lebanon

Washington, D.C.

July 15, 1958

IN MARCH 1957 Congress passed a resolution, originally proposed by Eisenhower, that autho-rized the president to offer economic aid, weapons, and armed intervention to any nation that requested it. The Eisenhower Doctrine, as it was known, was meant to give the administration a freer hand in dealing with the Arab nations in order to advance Western interests and reduce Soviet influence in the Middle East.

The provision for military intervention was put into practice by Eisenhower only once, in July 1958, when the assassination of the Iraqi royal family by members of the anti-Western pan-Arabist movement threatened to set off revolutions across the Middle East. At the request of Lebanon's president, Eisenhower sent the Marine Corps to Beirut, where they remained until October. On the evening following the marine landing, Eisenhower explained his decision in a radio and television address. In the opinion of his biographer, Stephen E. Ambrose, "In justifying the intervention . . . Eisenhower overstated his reasons. He linked Lebanon in 1958 with Greece in 1947, Czechoslovakia in 1948, the Chinese Communist victory in 1949, and the Korean inva-sion of 1950. But then he could hardly have said that he was sending in the marines in order to impress [Egyptian President] Nasser, [Saudi Arabian King] Saud, and the others, or to show that the American armed forces were not muscle-bound, or to protect feudal monarchies."

Yesterday was a day of grave developments in the Middle East. In Iraq a highly organized military blow struck down the duly constituted government and attempted to put in its place a committee of army officers. The attack was con-ducted with great brutality. Many of the leading personalities were beaten to death or hanged and their bodies dragged through the streets.

At about the same time there was discov-ered a highly organized plot to overthrow the lawful government of Jordan.

Warned and alarmed by these developments, President Chamoun of Lebanon sent me an urgent plea that the United States station some military units in Lebanon to evidence our con-cern for the independence of Lebanon, that little country, which itself has for about two months been subjected to civil strife. This has been actively fomented by Soviet and Cairo broad-casts and abetted and aided by substantial amounts of arms, money, and personnel infil-trated into Lebanon across the Syrian border.

President Chamoun stated that without an immediate show of United States support, the government of Lebanon would be unable to survive against the forces which had been set loose in the area.

The plea of President Chamoun was sup-ported by the unanimous action of the Leba-nese cabinet.

After giving this plea earnest thought and after taking advice from leaders of both the executive and congressional branches of the government, I decided to comply with the plea of the government of Lebanon. A few hours ago a battalion of United States Marines landed and took up stations in and about the city of Beirut.

The mission of these forces is to protect American lives—there are about 2,500 Amer-icans in Lebanon—and by their presence to assist the government of Lebanon to pre-serve its territorial integrity and political independence.

The United States does not, of course, intend to replace the United Nations which has a primary responsibility to maintain international peace and security. We reacted as we did within a matter of hours because the situation was such that only prompt action would suffice. We have, however, with equal promptness moved in the United Nations. This morning there was held at our request an emergency meeting of the United Nations Security Council. At this meeting we reported the action which we had taken. We stated the reasons therefor. We expressed the hope that the United Nations would itself take measures which would be adequate to preserve the inde-pendence of Lebanon and permit of the early withdrawal of the United States forces.

I should like now to take a few minutes to explain the situation in Lebanon.

Lebanon is a small country, a little less than the size of Connecticut, with a population of about one and one half million. It has always had close and friendly relations with the United States. Many of you no doubt have heard of the American University at Beirut which has a distinguished record. Lebanon has been a prosperous, peaceful country, thriving on trade largely with the West. A little over a year ago there were general elections, held in an atmosphere of total calm, which resulted in the establishment, by an overwhelming popular vote, of the present Parliament for a period of four years. The term of the president, however, is of a different duration and would normally expire next September. The president, Mr. Chamoun, has made clear that he does not seek reelection.

When the attacks on the government of Lebanon began to occur, it took the matter to the United Nations Security Council, pointing out that Lebanon was the victim of indirect aggression from without. As a result, the Security Council sent observers to Lebanon in the hope of thereby insuring that hostile intervention would cease. Secretary-General Hammarskjold undertook a mission to the area to reinforce the work of the observers.

We believe that his efforts and those of the United Nations observers were helpful. They could not eliminate arms or ammunition or remove persons already sent into Lebanon. But we believe they did reduce such aid from across the border. It seemed, last week, that the situation was moving toward a peaceful solution which would preserve the integrity of Lebanon, and end indirect aggression from without.

Those hopes were, however, dashed by the events of yesterday in Iraq and Jordan. These events demonstrate a scope of aggressive purpose which tiny Lebanon could not combat without further evidence of support. That is why Lebanon's request for troops from the United States was made. That is why we have responded to that request.

Some will ask, does the stationing of some United States troops in Lebanon involve any interference in the internal affairs of Lebanon? The clear answer is no.

First of all we have acted at the urgent plea of the government of Lebanon, a government which has been freely elected by the people only a little over a year ago. It is entitled, as are we, to join in measures of collective security for self-defense. Such action, the United Nations Charter recognizes, is an "inherent right."

In the second place what we now see in the Middle East is the same pattern of conquest with which we became familiar during the period of 1945 to 1950. This involves taking over a nation by means of indirect aggression; that is, under the cover of a fomented civil strife the purpose is to put into domestic control those whose real loyalty is to the aggressor.

It was by such means that the Communists attempted to take over Greece in 1947. That effort was thwarted by the Truman Doctrine.

It was by such means that the Communists took over Czechoslovakia in 1948.

It was by such means that the Communists took over the mainland of China in 1949.

It was by such means that the Communists attempted to take over Korea and Indochina, beginning in 1950.

You will remember at the time of the Korean War that the Soviet government claimed that this was merely a civil war, because the only attack was by North Koreans upon South Koreans. But all the world knew that the North Koreans were armed, equipped, and directed from without for the purpose of aggression.

This means of conquest was denounced by the United Nations General Assembly when it adopted in November 1950 its resolution entitled, "Peace through Deeds." It thereby called upon every nation to refrain from "fomenting civil strife in the interest of a foreign power" and denounced such action as "the gravest of all crimes against peace and security throughout the world."

We had hoped that these threats to the peace and to the independence and integrity of small nations had come to an end. Unhappily, now they reappear. Lebanon was selected to become a victim.

Last year, the Congress of the United States joined with the president to declare that "the United States regards as vital to the national interest and world peace the preservation of the independence and integrity of the nations of the Middle East."

I believe that the presence of the United States forces now being sent to Lebanon will have a stabilizing effect which will preserve the independence and integrity of Lebanon. It will also afford an increased measure of security to the thousands of Americans who reside in Lebanon.

We know that stability and well-being cannot be achieved purely by military measures. The economy of Lebanon has been gravely strained by civil strife. Foreign trade and tourist traffic have almost come to a standstill. The United States stands ready, under its Mutual Security Program, to cooperate with the government of Lebanon to find ways to restore its shattered economy. Thus we shall help to bring back to Lebanon a peace which is not merely the absence of fighting but the well-being of the people.

I am well aware of the fact that landing of United States troops in Lebanon could have some serious consequences. That is why this step was taken only after the most serious consideration and broad consultation. I have, however, come to the sober and clear conclusion that the action taken was essential to the welfare of the United States. It was required to support the principles of justice and international law upon which peace and a stable international order depend.

That, and that alone, is the purpose of the United States. We are not actuated by any hope of material gain or by any emotional hostility against any person or any government. Our dedication is to the principles of the United Nations Charter and to the preservation of the independence of every state. That is the basic pledge of the United Nations Charter.

Yet indirect aggression and violence are being promoted in the Near East in clear violation of the provisions of the United Nations Charter.

There can be no peace in the world unless there is fuller dedication to the basic principles of the United Nations Charter. If ever the United States fails to support these principles the result would be to open the floodgates to direct and indirect aggression throughout the world.

In the 1930s the members of the League of Nations became indifferent to direct and indirect aggression in Europe, Asia, and Africa. The result was to strengthen and stimulate aggressive forces that made World War II inevitable.

The United States is determined that that history shall not now be repeated. We are hopeful that the action which we are taking will both preserve the independence of Lebanon and check international violations which, if they succeeded, would endanger world peace.

We hope that this result will quickly be attained and that our forces can be promptly withdrawn. We must, however, be prepared to meet the situation, whatever be the consequences. We can do so, confident that we strive for a world in which nations, be they great or be they small, can preserve their independence. We are striving for an ideal which is close to the heart of every American and for which in the past many Americans have laid down their lives.

To serve these ideals is also to serve the cause of peace, security, and well-being, not only for us, but for all men everywhere.

The U-2 Incident

Washington, D.C.

May 25, 1960

To MONITOR the Russians' building of intercontinental ballistic missiles, Eisenhower ordered the CIA to conduct a secret surveillance program using U-2 photographic planes in illegal flights over Soviet airspace. On May 1, 1960, two weeks before the scheduled start of a summit conference between the United States and the U.S.S.R., the final U-2 flight was shot down by the Russians. The White House, which had been assured by the CIA that neither plane nor pilot could survive an attack, at first issued a statement declaring that the U-2 had been on a weather research mission. The announcement by Soviet premier Nikita Khrushchev that the pilot, Gary Powers, had been captured alive, along with what remained of the plane, so embarrassed Eisenhower that he had the State Department issue a second statement denying that he had authorized the spying mission. But the idea that a top-secret espionage program was controlled by low-ranking subordinates was even more damaging to Eisenhower. Additional contradictory statements followed.

The Soviet leaders exploited the U-2 incident to the fullest, ending Eisenhower's hopes for a disarmament agreement in Paris. After the summit ended, he made a radio and television speech explaining the espionage program, the reasons for the cover-up, and the disastrous effects on relations between the superpowers. Powers was repatriated as part of a "spy swap" in 1962.

Tonight I want to talk with you about the remarkable events last week in Paris, and their meaning to our future.

First, I am deeply grateful to the many thousands of you, and to representatives in Congress, who sent me messages of encouragement and support while I was in Paris, and later upon my return to Washington. Your messages clearly revealed your abiding loyalty to America's great purpose—that of pursuing, from a position of spiritual, moral, and material strength—a lasting peace with justice.

You recall, of course, why I went to Paris 10 days ago.

Last summer and fall I had many conversations with world leaders; some of these were with Chairman Khrushchev, here in America. Over those months a small improvement in relations between the Soviet Union and the West seemed discernible. A possibility developed that the Soviet leaders might at last be ready for serious talks about our most persistent problems—those of disarmament, mutual inspection, atomic control, and Germany, including Berlin.

To explore that possibility, our own and the British and French leaders met together, and later we agreed, with the Soviet leaders, to gather in Paris on May 16.

Of course we had no indication or thought that basic Soviet policies had turned about.

But when there is even the slightest chance of strengthening peace, there can be no higher obligation than to pursue it.

Nor had our own policies changed. We did hope to make some progress in a summit meeting, unpromising though previous experiences had been. But as we made preparations for this meeting, we did not drop our guard nor relax our vigilance.

Our safety, and that of the free world, demand, of course, effective systems for gathering information about the military capabilities of other powerful nations, especially those that make a fetish of secrecy. This involves many techniques and methods. In these times of vast military machines and nuclear-tipped missiles, the ferreting out of this information is indispensable to free world security.

This has long been one of my most serious preoccupations. It is part of my grave responsibility, within the over-all problem of protecting the American people, to guard ourselves and our allies against surprise attack.

During the period leading up to World War II we learned from bitter experience the imperative necessity of a continuous gathering of intelligence information, the maintenance of military communications and contact, and alertness of command.

An additional word seems appropriate about this matter of communications and command. While the secretary of defense and I were in Paris, we were, of course, away from our normal command posts. He recommended that under the circumstances we test the continuing readiness of our military communications. I personally approved. Such tests are valuable and will be frequently repeated in the future.

Moreover, as president, charged by the Constitution with the conduct of America's foreign relations, and as commander in chief, charged with the direction of the operations and activities of our armed forces and their supporting services, I take full responsibility for approving all the various programs undertaken by our government to secure and evaluate military intelligence.

It was in the prosecution of one of these intelligence programs that the widely publicized U-2 incident occurred.

Aerial photography has been one of many methods we have used to keep ourselves and the free world abreast of major Soviet military developments. The usefulness of this work has been well established through four years of effort. The Soviets were well aware of it. Chairman Khrushchev has stated that he became aware of these flights several years ago. Only last week, in his Paris press conference, Chairman Khrushchev confirmed that he knew of these flights when he visited the United States last September.

Incidentally, this raises the natural question—why all the furor concerning one particular flight? He did not, when in America last September charge that these flights were any threat to Soviet safety. He did not then see any reason to refuse to confer with American representatives.

This he did only about the flight that unfortunately failed, on May 1, far inside Russia.

Now, two questions have been raised about this particular flight; first, as to its timing, considering the imminence of the summit meeting; second, our initial statements when we learned the flight had failed.

As to the timing, the question was really whether to halt the program and thus forego the gathering of important information that was essential and that was likely to be unavailable at a later date. The decision was that the program should not be halted.

The plain truth is this: when a nation needs intelligence activity, there is no time when vigilance can be relaxed. Incidentally, from Pearl Harbor we learned that even negotiation itself can be used to conceal preparations for a surprise attack.

Next, as to our government's initial statement about the flight, this was issued to protect the pilot, his mission, and our intelligence processes, at a time when the true facts were still undetermined.

Our first information about the failure of this mission did not disclose whether the pilot was still alive, was trying to escape, was avoiding interrogation, or whether both plane and pilot had been destroyed. Protection of our intelligence system and the pilot, and concealment of the plane's mission, seemed imperative. It must be remembered that over a long period, these flights had given us information of the greatest importance to the nation's security. In fact, their success has been nothing short of remarkable.

For these reasons, what is known in intelligence circles as a "covering statement" was issued. It was issued on assumptions that were later proved incorrect. Consequently, when later the status of the pilot was definitely established, and there was no further possibility of avoiding exposure of the project, the factual details were set forth.

I then made two facts clear to the public: first, our program of aerial reconnaissance had been undertaken with my approval; second, this government is compelled to keep abreast, by one means or another, of military activities of the Soviets, just as their government has for years engaged in espionage activities in our country and throughout the world. Our necessity to proceed with such activities was also asserted by our secretary of state who, however, had been careful—as was I—not to say that these particular flights would be continued.

In fact, before leaving Washington, I had directed that these U-2 flights be stopped. Clearly their usefulness was impaired. Moreover, continuing this particular activity in these new circumstances could not but complicate the relations of certain of our allies with the Soviets. And of course, new techniques, other than aircraft, are constantly being developed.

Now I wanted no public announcement of this decision until I could personally disclose it at the summit meeting in conjunction with certain proposals I had prepared for the conference.

At my first Paris meeting with Mr. Khrushchev, and before his tirade was made public, I informed him of this discontinuance and the character of the constructive proposals I planned to make. These contemplated the establishment of a system of aerial surveillance operated by the United Nations.

The day before the first scheduled meeting, Mr. Khrushchev had advised President de Gaulle and Prime Minister Macmillan that he would make certain demands upon the United States as a precondition for beginning a summit conference.

Although the United States was the only power against which he expressed his displeasure, he did not communicate this information to me. I was, of course, informed by our allies.

At the four-power meeting on Monday morning, he demanded of the United States four things: first, condemnation of U-2 flights as a method of espionage; second, assurance that they would not be continued; third, a public apology on behalf of the United States; and, fourth, punishment of all those who had any responsibility respecting this particular mission.

I replied by advising the Soviet leader that I had, during the previous week, stopped these flights and that they would not be resumed. I offered also to discuss the matter with him in personal meetings, while the regular business of the summit might proceed. Obviously, I would not respond to his extreme demands. He knew, of course, by holding to those demands the Soviet Union was scuttling the summit conference.

In torpedoing the conference, Mr. Khrushchev claimed that he acted as the result of his own high moral indignation over alleged American acts of aggression. As I said earlier, he had known of these flights for a long time. It is apparent that the Soviets had decided even before the Soviet delegation left Moscow that my trip to the Soviet Union should be cancelled and that nothing constructive from their viewpoint would come out of the summit conference.

In evaluating the results, however, I think we must not write the record all in red ink.

There are several things to be written in the black. Perhaps the Soviet action has turned the clock back in some measure, but it should be noted that Mr. Khrushchev did not go beyond invective—a timeworn Soviet device to achieve an immediate objective. In this case, the wrecking of the conference.

On our side, at Paris, we demonstrated once again America's willingness, and that of her allies, always to go the extra mile in behalf of peace. Once again, Soviet intransigence reminded us all of the unpredictability of despotic rule, and the need for those who work for freedom to stand together in determination and in strength.

The conduct of our allies was magnificent. My colleagues and friends—President de Gaulle and Prime Minister Macmillan—stood sturdily with the American delegation in spite of persistent Soviet attempts to split the Western group. The NATO meeting after the Paris Conference showed unprecedented unity and support for the alliance and for the position taken at the summit meeting. I salute our allies for us all.

And now, most importantly, what about the future?

All of us know that, whether started deliberately or accidentally, global war would leave civilization in a shambles. This is as true of the Soviet system as of all others. In a nuclear war there can be no victors—only losers. Even despots understand this. Mr. Khrushchev stated last week that he well realizes that general nuclear war would bring catastrophe for both sides. Recognition of this mutual destructive capability is the basic reality of our present relations. Most assuredly, however, this does not mean that we shall ever give up trying to build a more sane and hopeful reality—a better foundation for our common relations.

To do this, here are the policies we must follow, and to these I am confident the great majority of our people, regardless of party, give their support:

First. We must keep up our strength, and hold it steady for the long pull—a strength not neglected in complacency nor overbuilt in hysteria. So doing, we can make it clear to everyone that there can be no gain in the use of pressure tactics or aggression against us and our Allies.

Second. We must continue businesslike dealings with the Soviet leaders on outstanding issues, and improve the contacts between our own and the Soviet peoples, making clear that the path of reason and common sense is still open if the Soviets will but use it.

Third. To improve world conditions in which human freedom can flourish, we must continue to move ahead with positive programs at home and abroad, in collaboration with free nations everywhere. In doing so, we shall continue to give our strong support to the United Nations and the great principles for which it stands.

Now as to the first of these purposes—our defenses are sound. They are tailored to the situation confronting us.

Their adequacy has been my primary concern for these past seven years—indeed throughout my adult life.

In no respect have the composition and size of our forces been based on or affected by any Soviet blandishment. Nor will they be. We will continue to carry forward the great improvements already planned in these forces. They will be kept ready—and under constant review.

Any changes made necessary by technological advances or world events will be recommended at once.

This strength—by far the most potent on earth—is, I emphasize, for deterrent, defensive, and retaliatory purposes only, without threat or aggressive intent toward anyone.

Concerning the second part of our policy— relations with the Soviets—we and all the world realize, despite our recent disappointment, that progress toward the goal of mutual understanding, easing the causes of tensions, and reduction of armaments is as necessary as ever.

We shall continue these peaceful efforts, including participation in the existing negotiations with the Soviet Union. In these negotiations we have made some progress. We are prepared to preserve and build on it. The Allied Paris communiqué and my own statement on returning to the United States should have made this abundantly clear to the Soviet government.

We conduct these negotiations not on the basis of surface harmony nor are we deterred by any bad deportment we meet. Rather we approach them as a careful search for common interests between the Western allies and the Soviet Union on specific problems.

I have in mind, particularly, the nuclear test and disarmament negotiations. We shall not back away, on account of recent events, from the efforts or commitments that we have undertaken.

Nor shall we relax our search for new means of reducing the risk of war by miscalculation, and of achieving verifiable arms control.

A major American goal is a world of open societies.

Here in our country anyone can buy maps and aerial photographs showing our cities, our dams, our plants, our highways—indeed, our whole industrial and economic complex. We know that Soviet attachés regularly collect this information. Last fall Chairman Khrushchev's train passed no more than a few hundred feet from an operational ICBM, in plain view from his window. Our thousands of books and scientific journals, our magazines, newspapers, and official publications, our radio and television, all openly describe to all the world every aspect of our society.

This is as it should be. We are proud of our freedom.

Soviet distrust, however, does still remain. To allay these misgivings I offered five years ago to open our skies to Soviet reconnaissance aircraft on a reciprocal basis. The Soviets refused. That offer is still open. At an appropriate time America will submit such a program to the United Nations, together with the recommendation that the United Nations itself conduct this reconnaissance. Should the United Nations accept this proposal, I am prepared to propose that America supply part of the aircraft and equipment required.

This is a photograph of the North Island Naval Station in San Diego, California. It was taken from an altitude of more than 70 thousand feet. You may not perhaps be able to see them on your television screens, but the white lines in the parking strips around the field are clearly discernible from 13 miles up. Those lines are just six inches wide.

Obviously most of the details necessary for a military evaluation of the airfield and its aircraft are clearly distinguishable.

I show you this photograph as an example of what could be accomplished through United Nations aerial surveillance.

Indeed, if the United Nations should undertake this policy, this program, and the great nations of the world should accept it, I am convinced that not only can all humanity be assured that they are safe from any surprise attack from any quarter, but indeed the greatest tensions of all, the fear of war, would be removed from the world. I sincerely hope that the United Nations may adopt such a program.

As far as we in America are concerned, our programs for increased contacts between all peoples will continue. Despite the suddenly expressed hostility of the men in the Kremlin, I remain convinced that the basic longings of the Soviet people are much like our own. I believe that Soviet citizens have a sincere friendship for the people of America. I deeply believe that above all else they want a lasting peace and a chance for a more abundant life in place of more and more instruments of war.

Finally, turning to the third part of America's policy—the strengthening of freedom—we must do far more than concern ourselves with military defense against, and our relations with, the Communist bloc. Beyond this, we must advance constructive programs throughout the world for the betterment of peoples in the newly developing nations.

The zigs and zags of the Kremlin cannot be allowed to disturb our worldwide programs and purposes. In the period ahead, these programs could well be the decisive factor in our persistent search for peace in freedom.

To the peoples in the newly developing nations urgently needed help will surely come.

If it does not come from us and our friends, these peoples will be driven to seek it from the enemies of freedom. Moreover, those joined with us in defense partnerships look to us for proof of our steadfastness. We must not relax our common security efforts.

As to this, there is something specific all of us can do, and right now. It is imperative that crippling cuts not be made in the appropriations recommended for mutual security, whether economic or military. We must support this program with all of our wisdom and all of our strength. We are proud to call this a nation of the people. With the people knowing the importance of this program, and making their voices heard in its behalf throughout the land, there can be no doubt of its continued success.

Fellow Americans, long ago I pledged to you that I would journey anywhere in the world to promote the cause of peace. I remain pledged to pursue a peace of dignity, of friendship, of honor, of justice.

Operating from the firm base of our spiritual and physical strength, and seeking wisdom from the Almighty, we and our allies together will continue to work for the survival of mankind in freedom—and for the goal of mutual respect, mutual understanding, and openness among all nations.

Thank you, and good night.

Farewell Address

Washington, D.C.

January 17, 1961

BY THE END of his second term, Eisenhower was convinced that the cold war rivalry with the Soviet Union was exacting a terrible price from American society—the destruction of the ideals that Eisenhower had all along thought he was acting to protect. Every year during his administration (as well as every year up to the present) a large portion of the nation's scientific, educational, and material resources was sacrificed to the urgent need to "stay ahead of the Russians." There was no foreseeable limit to the growth of the armed services and the extension of their influence, in the form of federal contracts for weapons production, on legislators and voters. No doubt Eisenhower's own military background and connections to Big Business helped him see sooner than others the trend toward technocracy and its inexorable intrusion into all aspects of the nation's life. In his last television and radio address to the American people, in January 1961, Eisenhower surprised his audience with a warning to beware of the "military-industrial complex" (the phrase was invented by the speechwriter, Malcolm Moos). Of this speech, historian Walter A. McDougall wrote: "It reads like prophecy now, its phrases sagging with future memories."

Three days from now, after half a century in the service of our country, I shall lay down the responsibilities of office as, in traditional and solemn ceremony, the authority of the presidency is vested in my successor.

This evening I come to you with a message of leave-taking and farewell, and to share a few final thoughts with you, my countrymen.

Like every other citizen, I wish the new president, and all who will labor with him, Godspeed. I pray that the coming years will be blessed with peace and prosperity for all.

I.

Our people expect their president and the Congress to find essential agreement on issues of great moment, the wise resolution of which will better shape the future of the nation.

My own relations with the Congress, which began on a remote and tenuous basis when, long ago, a member of the Senate appointed me to West Point, have since ranged to the intimate during the war and immediate postwar period, and, finally, to the mutually interdependent during these past eight years.

In this final relationship, the Congress and the administration have, on most vital issues, cooperated well, to serve the national good rather than mere partisanship, and so have assured that the business of the nation should go forward. So, my official relationship with the Congress ends in a feeling, on my part, of gratitude that we have been able to do so much together.

II.

We now stand 10 years past the midpoint of a century that has witnessed four major wars among great nations. Three of these involved our own country. Despite these holocausts America is today the strongest, the most influential and most productive nation in the world. Understandably proud of this preeminence, we yet realize that America's leadership and prestige depend, not merely upon our unmatched material progress, riches, and military strength, but on how we use our power in the interests of world peace and human betterment.

III.

Throughout America's adventure in free government, our basic purposes have been to keep the peace; to foster progress in human achievement, and to enhance liberty, dignity, and integrity among people and among nations. To strive for less would be unworthy of a free and religious people. Any failure traceable to arrogance, or our lack of comprehension or readiness to sacrifice would inflict upon us grievous hurt both at home and abroad.

Progress toward these noble goals is persistently threatened by the conflict now engulfing the world. It commands our whole attention, absorbs our very beings. We face a hostile ideology—global in scope, atheistic in character, ruthless in purpose, and insidious in method. Unhappily the danger it poses promises to be of indefinite duration. To meet it successfully, there is called for, not so much the emotional and transitory sacrifices of crisis, but rather those which enable us to carry forward steadily, surely, and without complaint the burdens of a prolonged and complex struggle—with liberty the stake. Only thus shall we remain, despite every provocation, on our charted course toward permanent peace and human betterment.

Crises there will continue to be. In meeting them, whether foreign or domestic, great or small, there is a recurring temptation to feel that some spectacular and costly action could become the miraculous solution to all current difficulties. A huge increase in newer elements of our defense; development of unrealistic programs to cure every ill in agriculture; a dramatic expansion in basic and applied research—these and many other possibilities, each possibly promising in itself, may be suggested as the only way to the road we wish to travel.

But each proposal must be weighed in the light of a broader consideration: the need to maintain balance in and among national programs—balance between the private and the public economy; balance between cost and hoped for advantage; balance between the clearly necessary and the comfortably desirable; balance between our essential requirements as a nation and the duties imposed by the nation upon the individual; balance between actions of the moment and the national welfare of the future. Good judgment seeks balance and progress; lack of it eventually finds imbalance and frustration.

The record of many decades stands as proof that our people and their government have, in the main, understood these truths and have responded to them well, in the face of stress and threat. But threats, new in kind or degree, constantly arise. I mention two only.

IV.

A vital element in keeping the peace is our military establishment. Our arms must be mighty, ready for instant action, so that no potential aggressor may be tempted to risk his own destruction.

Our military organization today bears little relation to that known by any of my predecessors in peacetime, or indeed by the fighting men of World War II or Korea.

Until the latest of our world conflicts, the United States had no armaments industry. American makers of plowshares could, with time and as required, make swords as well. But now we can no longer risk emergency improvisation of national defense; we have been compelled to create a permanent armaments industry of vast proportions. Added to this, three and a half million men and women are directly engaged in the defense establishment. We annually spend on military security more than the net income of all United States corporations.

This conjunction of an immense military establishment and a large arms industry is new in the American experience. The total influence—economic, political, even spiritual—is felt in every city, every statehouse, every office of the federal government. We recognize the imperative need for this development. Yet we must not fail to comprehend its grave implications. Our toil, resources, and livelihood are all involved; so is the very structure of our society.

In the councils of government, we must guard against the acquisition of unwarranted influence, whether sought or unsought, by the military-industrial complex. The potential for the disastrous rise of misplaced power exists and will persist.

We must never let the weight of this combination endanger our liberties or democratic processes. We should take nothing for granted. Only an alert and knowledgeable citizenry can compel the proper meshing of the huge industrial and military machinery of defense with our peaceful methods and goals, so that security and liberty may prosper together.

Akin to, and largely responsible for the sweeping changes in our industrial-military posture, has been the technological revolution during recent decades.

In this revolution, research has become central; it also becomes more formalized, complex, and costly. A steadily increasing share is conducted for, by, or at the direction of, the federal government.

Today, the solitary inventor, tinkering in his shop, has been overshadowed by task forces of scientists in laboratories and testing fields. In the same fashion, the free university, historically the fountainhead of free ideas and scientific discovery, has experienced a revolution in the conduct of research.

Partly because of the huge costs involved, a government contract becomes virtually a substitute for intellectual curiosity. For every old blackboard there are now hundreds of new electronic computers.

The prospect of domination of the nation's scholars by federal employment, project allocations, and the power of money is ever present—and is gravely to be regarded.

Yet, in holding scientific research and discovery in respect, as we should, we must also be alert to the equal and opposite danger that public policy could itself become the captive of a scientific-technological elite.

It is the task of statesmanship to mold, to balance, and to integrate these and other forces, new and old, within the principles of our democratic system—ever aiming toward the supreme goals of our free society.

V.

Another factor in maintaining balance involves the element of time. As we peer into society's future, we—you and I, and our government—must avoid the impulse to live only for today, plundering, for our own ease and convenience, the precious resources of tomorrow. We cannot mortgage the material assets of our grandchildren without risking the loss also of their political and spiritual heritage. We want democracy to survive for all generations to come, not to become the insolvent phantom of tomorrow.

VI.

Down the long lane of the history yet to be written America knows that this world of ours, ever growing smaller, must avoid becoming a community of dreadful fear and hate, and be, instead, a proud confederation of mutual trust and respect.

Such a confederation must be one of equals. The weakest must come to the conference table with the same confidence as do we, protected as we are by our moral, economic, and military strength. That table, though scarred by many past frustrations, cannot be abandoned for the certain agony of the battlefield.

Disarmament, with mutual honor and confidence, is a continuing imperative. Together we must learn how to compose differences, not with arms, but with intellect and decent purpose. Because this need is so sharp and apparent I confess that I lay down my official responsibilities in this field with a definite sense of disappointment. As one who has witnessed the horror and the lingering sadness of war—as one who knows that another war could utterly destroy this civilization which has been so slowly and painfully built over thousands of years—I wish I could say tonight that a lasting peace is in sight.

Happily, I can say that war has been avoided. Steady progress toward our ultimate goal has been made. But, so much remains to be done. As a private citizen, I shall never cease to do what little I can to help the world advance along that road.

VII.

So—in this my last good night to you as your president—I thank you for the many opportunities you have given me for public service in war and peace. I trust that in that service you find some things worthy; as for the rest of it, I know you will find ways to improve performance in the future.

You and I—my fellow citizens—need to be strong in our faith that all nations, under God, will reach the goal of peace with justice. May we be ever unswerving in devotion to principle, confident but humble with power, diligent in pursuit of the nation's great goals.

To all the peoples of the world, I once more give expression to America's prayerful and continuing aspiration:

We pray that peoples of all faiths, all races, all nations, may have their great human needs satisfied; that those now denied opportunity shall come to enjoy it to the full; that all who yearn for freedom may experience its spiritual blessings; that those who have freedom will understand, also, its heavy responsibilities; that all who are insensitive to the needs of others will learn charity; that the scourges of poverty, disease, and ignorance will be made to disappear from the earth, and that, in the goodness of time, all peoples will come to live together in a peace guaranteed by the binding force of mutual respect and love.

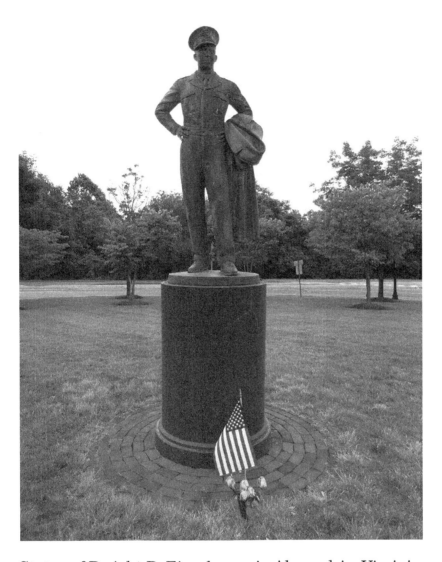

Statue of Dwight D. Eisenhower in Alexandria, Virginia.
(Courtesy of PresidentsUSA.net)

Courtesy of Library of Congress

John Fitzgerald Kennedy

John Fitzgerald Kennedy

1961–1963

STYLE AND IMAGE played a major role in the presidency and in the mythology that developed after Kennedy's assassination. Theodore Sorensen characterized the Kennedy style as "cool, convincing, self-confident. . . [it] spoke to and for the young at heart, cut through cant, overrode trivia, and elevated eloquence and gallantry and wit." It was just the kind of rhetoric that the country needed to carry it into the Space Age, into an era of rapid change, strange new technologies, and unprecedented political realignments. But the sense of hope, intelligence, and vitality that the public derived from Kennedy's speeches evaporated almost as soon as his voice was stilled.

Kennedy was the second son of one of the wealthiest and most ambitious families in Massachusetts. Educated at Harvard, a war hero in World War II, he came early to Democratic politics and rose quickly. He was elected a representative from his home state in 1946, went to the Senate in 1952, nearly captured the vice-presidential nomination in 1956, and gained the Democratic presidential nomination in 1960. The highlight of the campaign was a series of televised debates with his Republican opponent, Richard Nixon. Nixon, who appeared tired and defensive on camera, lost the "image war," and thus the election, to the confident, attractive Kennedy.

The first president born in the 20th century and the youngest ever to be elected, Kennedy presented himself as a new kind of leader, an activist president able to transcend conventional politics and achieve a national consensus through sheer force of character. "His personality," wrote Arthur M. Schlesinger Jr., the historian and Kennedy biographer, "was the most potent instrument he had to awaken a national desire for something new and better." For this reason, Kennedy preferred foreign policy to domestic problems, since foreign affairs can more often be handled by unencumbered executive action. He was less inclined to engage in the politicking required to push innovative domestic programs through Congress; instead, he created public pressure on Congress through direct appeals to the electorate.

Maintaining this rapport with the public was a priority at the Kennedy White House. The president managed his audiences expertly. As adroitly as any professional actor, he projected a "warm" persona that many viewers found immensely appealing, especially after eight years of Eisenhower's blandness. Never at a loss for a remark, even in the hurly-burly of his press conferences (the first to be televised), Kennedy always appeared cool, capable, and intelligent. He possessed, according to the historian Harold H. Martin, "an intangible, an indefinable charm, a warmth which [made] voters feel instinctively that, whatever they believed, he believed in too." So effective was Kennedy's charm that he managed to recover from political disasters, like the invasion of Cuba at the Bay of Pigs, that might have brought down a different kind of president.

Television was one of the keys to his success. He avoided long speeches in favor of short, pithy, polished statements that would sound well on television; his Massachusetts accent, staccato speech, and emphatic right hand gave him a memorable screen presence. Not only did he deliver most of his major speeches on television, but he frequently allowed network cameras into the White House to view his daily activities and meetings for "news" specials. Kennedy's talent for nurturing his television image was unsurpassed even by Ronald Reagan; Herbert S. Parmet called him "the first picture star in the White House," and Garry Wills wrote that the Kennedy years marked the inauguration "of something new—not so much the Imperial Presidency as the Appearances Presidency." In fact, his advisers worried that he appeared on television too often and would lose political effectiveness by overexposure.

Kennedy did much of his own speech writing, and often spoke extemporaneously. For major policy statements he employed a team of talented speechwriters, chief among them Theodore Sorensen. Sorensen, a long-time Kennedy adviser, had a gift for crafting striking phrases; he refined and extended Kennedy's penchant for portentous exhortation and for what Kennedy scholar Henry Fairlie called his "rich imperial symbolism"—the recurrent use of such concepts as "helping the poor nations to help themselves," "opposing aggression and subversion wherever they may be found," and "exploring the New Frontier." This imperial tone, in Fairlie's view, colored the president's entire image. "Kennedy spoke in public as Byzantine emperors appeared on state occasions: sheathed in gold, suspended between earth and heaven." In the mouth of a less charming or an older president, some of Kennedy's speeches would have sounded pompous or alarmingly militaristic—for example, his inaugural call, in peacetime, for the nation "to pay any price, bear any burden, meet any hardship, support any friend, oppose any foe, in order to assure the survival and the success of liberty." But Kennedy counteracted this with a dispassionate delivery that was self-aware and witty. Audiences found this combination of inspirational language and rationalistic style nearly irresistible; many accepted Kennedy's own valuation of himself as a new FDR, the best hope for an uncertain future. His assassination in 1963 made it even more difficult for Americans to grasp that his rhetoric was too exalted to be translated into political reality.

The New Frontier

Los Angeles, California
July 15, 1960

THE 1960 PRESIDENTIAL contest matched the young, charismatic Kennedy, anxious to build an image of competent, experienced statesmanship, with the dour Richard Nixon, anxious to shed his previous image as a political mudslinger. Kennedy stole a march on Nixon by starting his campaign for the nomination immediately following the 1956 election. Difficult political problems like Kennedy's Catholicism and youth were defused with the typical Kennedy wit and forthrightness. He easily won all seven Democratic primaries on the strength of his commitment to "get the country moving again" after the stasis of the Eisenhower years.

At the Democratic convention in Los Angeles, Kennedy won the nomination on the first ballot, garnering twice as many votes as his closest rival, Lyndon Johnson, who then became his running mate. In his acceptance speech, reprinted below, he first used the famous phrase "the new frontier"; this became the name for his program, and his circle of advisers became "New Frontiersmen." The New Frontier, in Kennedy's conception, was not a physical territory, but rather the outer reaches of personal commitment, where could be found "the opportunity for all of us to be of service to this great republic in difficult and dangerous times."

With a deep sense of duty and high resolve, I accept your nomination.

I accept it with a full and grateful heart—without reservation—and with only one obligation—the obligation to devote every effort of body, mind, and spirit to lead our party back to victory and our nation back to greatness.

I am grateful, too, that you have provided me with such an eloquent statement of our party's platform. Pledges which are made so eloquently are made to be kept. "The Rights of Man"—the civil and economic rights essential to the human dignity of all men—are indeed our goal and our first principles. This is a platform on which I can run with enthusiasm and conviction.

And I am grateful, finally, that I can rely in the coming months on so many others—on a distinguished runningmate who brings unity to our ticket and strength to our platform, Lyndon Johnson—on one of the most articulate statesmen of our time, Adlai Stevenson—on a guest spokesman for our needs as a nation and a people, Stuart Symington—and on that fighting campaigner whose support I welcome, President Harry S Truman.

I feel a lot safer now that they are on my side again. And I am proud of the contrast with our Republican competitors. For their ranks are apparently so thin that not one challenger has come forth with both the competence and the courage to make theirs an open convention.

I am fully aware of the fact that the Democratic Party, by nominating someone of my faith, has taken on what many regard as a new and hazardous risk—new, at least, since 1928. But I look at it this way: the Democratic Party has once again placed its confidence in the American people, and in their ability to render a free, fair judgment. And you have, at the same time, placed your confidence in me, and in my ability to render a free, fair judgment—to uphold the Constitution and my oath of office—and to reject any kind of religious pressure or obligation that might directly or indirectly interfere with my conduct of the presidency in the national interest. My record of 14 years supporting public education—supporting complete separation of church and state—and resisting pressure from any source on any issue should be clear by now to everyone.

I hope that no American, considering the really critical issues facing this country, will waste his franchise by voting either for me or against me solely on account of my religious affiliation. It is not relevant, I want to stress, what some other political or religious leader may have said on this subject. It is not relevant what abuses may have existed in other countries or in other times. It is not relevant what pressures, if any, might conceivably be brought to bear on me. I am telling you now what you are entitled to know: that my decisions on every public policy will be my own— as an American, a Democrat and a free man.

Under any circumstances, however, the victory we seek in November will not be easy. We all know that in our hearts. We recognize the power of the forces that will be aligned against us. We know they will invoke the name of Abraham Lincoln on behalf of their candidate—despite the fact that his political career has often seemed to show charity toward none and malice for all.

We know that it will not be easy to campaign against a man who has spoken or voted on every known side of every known issue. Mr. Nixon may feel it is his turn now, after the New Deal and the Fair Deal—but before he deals, someone had better cut the cards.

That "someone" may be the millions of Americans who voted for President Eisenhower but balk at his would-be, self-appointed successor. For just as historians tell us that Richard I was not fit to fill the shoes of bold Henry II—and that Richard Cromwell was not fit to wear the mantle of his uncle—they might add in future years that Richard Nixon did not measure to the footsteps of Dwight D. Eisenhower.

Perhaps he could carry on the party policies—the policies of Nixon, Benson, Dirksen, and Goldwater. But this nation cannot afford such a luxury. Perhaps we could afford a Coolidge following Harding. And perhaps we could afford a Pierce following Fillmore. But after Buchanan, this nation needed a Lincoln—after Taft we needed a Wilson—after Hoover we needed Franklin Roosevelt. . . . And after eight years of drugged and fitful sleep, this nation needs strong, creative Democratic leadership in the White House.

But we are not merely running against Mr. Nixon. Our task is not merely one of itemizing Republican failures. Nor is that wholly necessary. For the families forced from the farm will know how to vote without our telling them. The unemployed miners and textile workers will know how to vote. The old people without medical care—the families without a decent home—the parents of children without adequate food or schools—they all know that it's time for a change.

But I think the American people expect more from us than cries of indignation and attack. The times are too grave, the challenge too urgent, and the stakes too high—to permit the customary passions of political debate. We are not here to curse the darkness, but to light the candle that can guide us through that darkness to a safe and sane future. As Winston Churchill said on taking office some 20 years ago: if we open a quarrel between the present and the past, we shall be in danger of losing the future.

Today our concern must be with that future. For the world is changing. The old era is ending. The old ways will not do.

Abroad, the balance of power is shifting. There are new and more terrible weapons— new and uncertain nations—new pressures of population and deprivation. One-third of the world, it has been said, may be free-but one-third is the victim of cruel repression—and the other one-third is rocked by the pangs of poverty, hunger, and envy. More energy is released by the awakening of these new nations than by the fission of the atom itself.

Meanwhile, Communist influence has penetrated further into Asia, stood astride the Middle East and now festers some 90 miles off the coast of Florida. Friends have slipped into neutrality—and neutrals into hostility. As our keynoter reminded us, the president who began his career by going to Korea ends it by staying away from Japan.

The world has been close to war before— but now man, who has survived all previous threats to his existence, has taken into his mortal hands the power to exterminate the entire species seven times over.

Here at home, the changing face of the future is equally revolutionary. The New Deal and the Fair Deal were bold measures for their generations—but this is a new generation.

A technological revolution on the farm has led to an output explosion—but we have not yet learned to harness that explosion usefully, while protecting our farmers' right to full parity income.

An urban population revolution has overcrowded our schools, cluttered up our suburbs, and increased the squalor of our slums.

A peaceful revolution for human rights— demanding an end to racial discrimination in all parts of our community life—has strained at the leashes imposed by timid executive leadership.

A medical revolution has extended the life of our elder citizens without providing the dignity and security those later years deserve. And a revolution of automation finds machines replacing men in the mines and mills of America, without replacing their income or their training or their need to pay the family doctor, grocer, and landlord.

There has also been a change—a slippage—in our intellectual and moral strength. Seven lean years of drouth and famine have withered the field of ideas. Blight has descended on our regulatory agencies—and a dry rot, beginning in Washington, is seeping into every corner of America—in the payola mentality, the expense account way of life, the confusion between what is legal and what is right. Too many Americans have lost their way, their will and their sense of historic purpose.

It is time, in short, for a new generation of leadership—new men to cope with new problems and new opportunities.

All over the world, particularly in the newer nations, young men are coming to power—men who are not bound by the traditions of the past—men who are not blinded by the old fears and hates and rivalries—young men who can cast off the old slogans and delusions and suspicions.

The Republican nominee-to-be, of course, is also a young man. But his approach is as old as McKinley. His party is the party of the past. His speeches are generalities from *Poor Richard's Almanac.* Their platform, made up of leftover Democratic planks, has the courage of our old convictions. Their pledge is a pledge to the status quo—and today there can be no status quo.

For I stand tonight facing west on what was once the last frontier. From the lands that stretch 3,000 miles behind me, the pioneers of old gave up their safety, their comfort, and sometimes their lives to build a new world here in the West. They were not the captives of their own doubts, the prisoners of their own price tags. Their motto was not "every man for himself"—but "all for the common cause." They were determined to make that new world strong and free, to overcome its hazards and its hardships, to conquer the enemies that threatened from without and within.

Today some would say that those struggles are all over—that all the horizons have been explored—that all the battles have been won—that there is no longer an American frontier.

But I trust that no one in this vast assemblage will agree with those sentiments. For the problems are not all solved and the battles are not all won—and we stand today on the edge of a New Frontier—the frontier of the 1960s—a frontier of unknown opportunities and perils—a frontier of unfulfilled hopes and threats.

Woodrow Wilson's New Freedom promised our nation a new political and economic framework. Franklin Roosevelt's New Deal promised security and succor to those in need. But the New Frontier of which I speak is not a set of promises—it is a set of challenges. It sums up not what I intend to offer the American people, but what I intend to ask of them. It appeals to their pride, not their pocketbook—it holds out the promise of more sacrifice instead of more security.

But I tell you the New Frontier is here, whether we seek it or not. Beyond that frontier are uncharted areas of science and space, unsolved problems of peace and war, unconquered pockets of ignorance and prejudice, unanswered questions of poverty and surplus. It would be easier to shrink back from that frontier, to look to the safe mediocrity of the past, to be lulled by good intentions and high rhetoric—and those who prefer that course should not cast their votes for me, regardless of party.

But I believe the times demand invention, innovation, imagination, decision. I am asking each of you to be new pioneers on that New Frontier. My call is to the young in heart, regardless of age—to the stout in spirit, regardless of party—to all who respond to the scriptural call: "Be strong and of good courage; be not afraid, neither be thou dismayed."

For courage—not complacency, is our need today—leadership—not salesmanship. And the only valid test of leadership is the ability to lead, and lead vigorously. A tired nation, said David Lloyd George, is a Tory nation—and the United States today cannot afford to be either tired or Tory.

There may be those who wish to hear more—more promises to this group or that—more harsh rhetoric about the men in the Kremlin—more assurances of a golden future, where taxes are always low and subsidies ever high. But my promises are in the platform you have adopted—our ends will not be won by rhetoric and we can have faith in the future only if we have faith in ourselves.

For the harsh facts of the matter are that we stand on this frontier at a turning-point in history. We must prove all over again whether this nation—or any nation so conceived—can long endure—whether our society—with its freedom of choice, its breadth of opportunity, its range of alternatives—can compete with the single-minded advance of the Communist system.

Can a nation organized and governed such as ours endure? That is the real question. Have we the nerve and the will? Can we carry through in an age where we will witness not only new breakthroughs in weapons of destruction—but also a race for mastery of the sky and the rain, the ocean and the tides, the far side of space and the inside of men's minds?

Are we up to the task—are we equal to the challenge? Are we willing to match the Russian sacrifice of the present for the future—or must we sacrifice our future in order to enjoy the present?

That is the question of the New Frontier. That is the choice our nation must make—a choice that lies not merely between two men or two parties but between the public interest and private comfort—between national greatness and national decline—between the fresh air of progress and the stale, dank atmosphere of "normalcy"—between determined dedication and creeping mediocrity.

All mankind waits upon our decision. A whole world looks to see what we will do. We cannot fail their trust, we cannot fail to try.

It has been a long road from that first snowy day in New Hampshire to this crowded convention city. Now begins another long journey, taking me into your cities and homes all over America. Give me your help, your hand, your voice, your vote. Recall with me the words of Isaiah: "They that wait upon the Lord shall renew their strength; they shall mount up with wings as eagles; they shall run, and not be weary."

As we face the coming challenge, we too, shall wait upon the Lord, and ask that He renew our strength. Then shall we be equal to the test. Then we shall not be weary. And then we shall prevail.

Inaugural Address

Washington, D.C.

January 20, 1961

GENERALLY CONSIDERED to be one of the handful of great inaugural addresses, this short speech reveals the heavy influence of Theodore Sorensen, JFK's chief speechwriter, in its biblical phraseology and its frequent use of contrapuntal clauses—"United there is little we cannot do . . . divided, there is little we can do"—a style derived from Lincoln's use of parallelism in his speeches. Adlai Stevenson, Walter Lippmann, John Kenneth Galbraith, and Arthur Schlesinger all had a hand in its creation as well. But the address's exclusive concentration on foreign affairs, and the near-religious fervor with which it appealed for national sacrifice in the cause of liberty, were Kennedy's own.

The popular response to the address was overwhelmingly favorable. Kennedy had shown himself to be a commanding, intelligent speaker offering fresh inspiration to the nation, even if it was not immediately clear what the "historic effort" he called for really was or where it might lead. Columnist James Reston called the speech "a revolutionary document," and Sam Rayburn, Speaker of the House and an old New Dealer, thought it better than anything FDR or Lincoln had written. Later commentators have found in the nationalistic language of the address a strong measure of cold war bellicosity.

We observe today not a victory of party but a celebration of freedom—symbolizing an end as well as a beginning—signifying renewal as well as change. For I have sworn before you and Almighty God the same solemn oath our forebears prescribed nearly a century and three quarters ago.

The world is very different now. For man holds in his mortal hands the power to abolish all forms of human poverty and all forms of human life. And yet the same revolutionary beliefs for which our forebears fought are still at issue around the globe—the belief that the rights of man come not from the generosity of the state but from the hand of God.

We dare not forget today that we are the heirs of that first revolution. Let the word go forth from this time and place, to friend and foe alike, that the torch has been passed to a new generation of Americans—born in this century, tempered by war, disciplined by a hard and bitter peace, proud of our ancient heritage—and unwilling to witness or permit the slow undoing of those human rights to which this nation has always been committed, and to which we are committed today at home and around the world.

Let every nation know, whether it wishes us well or ill, that we shall pay any price, bear any burden, meet any hardship, support any friend, oppose any foe to assure the survival and the success of liberty.

This much we pledge—and more.

To those old allies whose cultural and spiritual origins we share, we pledge the loyalty of faithful friends. United, there is little we cannot do in a host of cooperative ventures. Divided, there is little we can do—for we dare not meet a powerful challenge at odds and split asunder.

To those new states whom we welcome to the ranks of the free, we pledge our word that one form of colonial control shall not have passed away merely to be replaced by a far more iron tyranny. We shall not always expect to find them supporting our view. But we shall always hope to find them strongly supporting their own freedom—and to remember that, in the past, those who foolishly sought power by riding the back of the tiger ended up inside.

To those peoples in the huts and villages of half the globe struggling to break the bonds of mass misery, we pledge our best efforts to help them help themselves, for whatever period is required—not because the Communists may be doing it, not because we seek their votes, but because it is right. If a free society cannot help the many who are poor, it cannot save the few who are rich.

To our sister republics south of our border, we offer a special pledge—to convert our good words into good deeds—in a new alliance for progress—to assist free men and free governments in casting off the chains of poverty. But this peaceful revolution of hope cannot become the prey of hostile powers. Let all our neighbors know that we shall join with them to oppose aggression or subversion anywhere in the Americas. And let every other power know that this hemisphere intends to remain the master of its own house.

To that world assembly of sovereign states, the United Nations, our last best hope in an age where the instruments of war have far outpaced the instruments of peace, we renew our pledge of support—to prevent it from becoming merely a forum for invective—to strengthen its shield of the new and the weak—and to enlarge the area in which its writ may run.

Finally, to those nations who would make themselves our adversary, we offer not a pledge but a request: that both sides begin anew the quest for peace, before the dark powers of destruction unleashed by science engulf all humanity in planned or accidental self-destruction.

We dare not tempt them with weakness. For only when our arms are sufficient beyond doubt can we be certain beyond doubt that they will never be employed.

But neither can two great and powerful groups of nations take comfort from our present course—both sides overburdened by the cost of modern weapons, both rightly alarmed by the steady spread of the deadly atom, yet both racing to alter that uncertain balance of terror that stays the hand of mankind's final war.

So let us begin anew—remembering on both sides that civility is not a sign of weakness, and sincerity is always subject to proof. Let us never negotiate out of fear. But let us never fear to negotiate.

Let both sides explore what problems unite us instead of belaboring those problems which divide us.

Let both sides, for the first time, formulate serious and precise proposals for the inspection and control of arms—and bring the absolute power to destroy other nations under the absolute control of all nations.

Let both sides seek to invoke the wonders of science instead of its terrors. Together let us explore the stars, conquer the deserts, eradicate disease, tap the ocean depths, and encourage the arts and commerce.

Let both sides unite to heed in all corners of the earth the command of Isaiah—to "undo the heavy burdens . . . [and] let the oppressed go free."

And if a beachhead of cooperation may push back the jungles of suspicion, let both sides join in creating a new endeavor—not a new balance of power, but a new world of law, where the strong are just and the weak secure and the peace preserved.

All this will not be finished in the first hundred days. Nor will it be finished in the first thousand days, nor in the life of this administration, nor even perhaps in our lifetime on this planet. But let us begin.

In your hands, my fellow citizens, more than mine, will rest the final success or failure of our course. Since this country was founded, each generation of Americans has been summoned to give testimony to its national loyalty. The graves of young Americans who answered the call to service surround the globe.

Now the trumpet summons us again—not as a call to bear arms, though arms we need—not as a call to battle, though embattled we are—but a call to bear the burden of a long twilight struggle, year in and year out, "rejoicing in hope, patient in tribulation"—a struggle against the common enemies of man: tyranny, poverty, disease, and war itself.

Can we forge against these enemies a grand and global alliance, north and south, east and west, that can assure a more fruitful life for all mankind? Will you join in that historic effort?

In the long history of the world, only a few generations have been granted the role of defending freedom in its hour of maximum danger. I do not shrink from this responsibility—I welcome it. I do not believe that any of us would exchange places with any other people or any other generation. The energy, the faith, the devotion which we bring to this endeavor will light our country and all who serve it—and the glow from the fire can truly light the world.

And so, my fellow Americans; ask not what your country can do for you—ask what you can do for your country.

My fellow citizens of the world; ask not what America will do for you, but what together we can do for the freedom of man.

Finally, whether you are citizens of America or citizens of the world, ask of us here the same high standards of strength and sacrifice which we ask of you. With a good conscience our only sure reward, with history the final judge of our deeds, let us go forth to lead the land we love, asking His blessing and His help, but knowing that here on earth God's work must truly be our own.

Putting a Man on the Moon

Washington, D.C.

May 25, 1961

ON APRIL 12, 1961, Soviet cosmonaut Yuri Gagarin became the first human being to orbit the earth, much to the embarrassment of NASA and the chagrin of President Kennedy, who had been preoccupied with the idea of putting a man in space since before his election. After Gagarin's flight, many in Washington called for the cancellation of the space program, but Alan Shepard's successful sub-orbital trip on May 5 galvanized the president. Kennedy was further encouraged to announce a major American space initiative—a moon-landing mission—by newly appointed NASA chief James E. Webb and Vice President Lyndon Johnson, head of the National Space Council, who foresaw a huge bonanza in the multi-billion-dollar program for his home state of Texas.

Such a bold adventure—and major political risk—also served in part to distract from a recession at home, communist incursions abroad, and especially the disastrous Bay of Pigs invasion of April 17. Kennedy addressed those issues in this speech before he memorably proposed "the goal, before this decade is out, of landing a man on the moon and returning him safely to the earth." Kennedy's closest aides "could tell he was nervous—by the way he kept playing with the pages of his speech, creasing them, smoothing them," according to space historian Andrew Chaikin. "They sensed that Kennedy wasn't sure he was doing the right thing, to ask for such an enormous sum of money for something so audacious."

There was no assurance that NASA could in fact achieve this goal—the announcement came as a shock to many of the engineers who would be responsible for inventing the necessary technologies—but after Kennedy's assassination in 1963, the space agency felt honor-bound to achieve his dream. It did so on July 20, 1969, six months before the end of the decade.

Mr. Speaker, Mr. Vice President, my copartners in Government, gentlemen, and ladies:

The Constitution imposes upon me the obligation to "from time to time give to the Congress information of the State of the Union." While this has traditionally been interpreted as an annual affair, this tradition has been broken in extraordinary times.

These are extraordinary times. And we face an extraordinary challenge. Our strength as well as our convictions have imposed upon this nation the role of leader in freedom's cause.

No role in history could be more difficult or more important. We stand for freedom.

That is our conviction for ourselves—that is our only commitment to others. No friend, no neutral and no adversary should think otherwise. We are not against any man—or any nation—or any system—except as it is hostile to freedom. Nor am I here to present a new military doctrine, bearing any one name or aimed at any one area. I am here to promote the freedom doctrine.

I.

The great battleground for the defense and expansion of freedom today is the whole southern half of the globe—Asia, Latin America, Africa, and the Middle East—the lands of the rising peoples. Their revolution is the greatest in human history. They seek an end to injustice, tyranny, and exploitation. More than an end, they seek a beginning.

And theirs is a revolution which we would support regardless of the Cold War, and regardless of which political or economic route they should choose to freedom.

For the adversaries of freedom did not create the revolution; nor did they create the conditions which compel it. But they are seeking to ride the crest of its wave—to capture it for themselves.

Yet their aggression is more often concealed than open. They have fired no missiles; and their troops are seldom seen. They send arms, agitators, aid, technicians, and propaganda to every troubled area. But where fighting is required, it is usually done by others—by guerrillas striking at night, by assassins striking alone—assassins who have taken the lives of four thousand civil officers in the last twelve months in Vietnam alone—by subversives and saboteurs and insurrectionists, who in some cases control whole areas inside of independent nations.

With these formidable weapons, the adversaries of freedom plan to consolidate their territory—to exploit, to control, and finally to destroy the hopes of the world's newest nations; and they have ambition to do it before the end of this decade. It is a contest of will and purpose as well as force and violence—a battle for minds and souls as well as lives and territory. And in that contest, we cannot stand aside.

We stand, as we have always stood from our earliest beginnings, for the independence and equality of all nations. This nation was born of revolution and raised in freedom. And we do not intend to leave an open road for despotism.

There is no single simple policy which meets this challenge. Experience has taught us that no one nation has the power or the wisdom to solve all the problems of the world or manage its revolutionary tides—that extending our commitments does not always increase our security—that any initiative carries with it the risk of a temporary defeat—that nuclear weapons cannot prevent subversion—that no free people can be kept free without will and energy of their own—and that no two nations or situations are exactly alike.

Yet there is much we can do—and must do. The proposals I bring before you are numerous and varied. They arise from the host of special opportunities and dangers which have become increasingly clear in recent months. Taken together, I believe that they can mark another step forward in our effort as a people. I am here to ask the help of this Congress and the nation in approving these necessary measures.

II. Economic and Social Progress at Home

The first and basic task confronting this nation this year was to turn recession into recovery. An affirmative anti-recession program, initiated with your cooperation, supported the natural forces in the private sector; and our economy is now enjoying renewed confidence and energy. The recession has been halted. Recovery is under way.

But the task of abating unemployment and achieving a full use of our resources does remain a serious challenge for us all. Large-scale unemployment during a recession is bad enough, but large-scale unemployment during a period of prosperity would be intolerable.

I am therefore transmitting to the Congress a new Manpower Development and Training program, to train or retrain several hundred thousand workers, particularly in those areas where we have seen chronic unemployment as a result of technological factors in new occupational skills over a four-year period, in order to replace those skills made obsolete by automation and industrial change with the new skills which the new processes demand. . . .

III. Economic and Social Progress Abroad

I stress the strength of our economy because it is essential to the strength of our nation. And what is true in our case is true in the case of other countries. Their strength in the struggle for freedom depends on the strength of their economic and their social progress.

We would be badly mistaken to consider their problems in military terms alone. For no amount of arms and armies can help stabilize those governments which are unable or unwilling to achieve social and economic reform and development. Military pacts cannot help nations whose social injustice and economic chaos invite insurgency and penetration and subversion. The most skillful counter-guerrilla efforts cannot succeed where the local population is too caught up in its own misery to be concerned about the advance of communism.

But for those who share this view, we stand ready now, as we have in the past, to provide generously of our skills, and our capital, and our food to assist the peoples of the less-developed nations to reach their goals in freedom—to help them before they are engulfed in crisis.

This is also our great opportunity in 1961. If we grasp it, then subversion to prevent its success is exposed as an unjustifiable attempt to keep these nations from either being free or equal. But if we do not pursue it, and if they do not pursue it, the bankruptcy of unstable governments, one by one, and of unfilled hopes will surely lead to a series of totalitarian receiverships. . . .

IV.

All that I have said makes it clear that we are engaged in a world-wide struggle in which we bear a heavy burden to preserve and promote the ideals that we share with all mankind, or have alien ideals forced upon them. That struggle has highlighted the role of our Information

Agency. It is essential that the funds previously requested for this effort be not only approved in full, but increased by 2 million, 400 thousand dollars, to a total of 121 million dollars.

This new request is for additional radio and television to Latin America and Southeast Asia. These tools are particularly effective and essential in the cities and villages of those great continents as a means of reaching millions of uncertain peoples to tell them of our interest in their fight for freedom. In Latin America, we are proposing to increase our Spanish and Portuguese broadcasts to a total of 154 hours a week, compared to 42 hours today, none of which is in Portuguese, the language of about one-third of the people of South America. The Soviets, Red Chinese and satellites already broadcast into Latin America more than 134 hours a week in Spanish and Portuguese. Communist China alone does more public information broadcasting in our own hemisphere than we do. Moreover, powerful propaganda broadcasts from Havana now are heard throughout Latin America, encouraging new revolutions in several countries.

Similarly, in Laos, Vietnam, Cambodia, and Thailand, we must communicate our determination and support to those upon whom our hopes for resisting the communist tide in that continent ultimately depend. Our interest is in the truth.

V. Our Partnership for Self-Defense

But while we talk of sharing and building and the competition of ideas, others talk of arms and threaten war. So we have learned to keep our defenses strong—and to cooperate with others in a partnership of self-defense. The events of recent weeks have caused us to look anew at these efforts.

The center of freedom's defense is our network of world alliances, extending from NATO, recommended by a Democratic President and approved by a Republican Congress, to SEATO, recommended by a Republican President and approved by a Democratic Congress. These alliances were constructed in the 1940's and 1950's—it is our task and responsibility in the 1960's to strengthen them.

To meet the changing conditions of power—and power relationships have changed—we have endorsed an increased emphasis on NATO's conventional strength. At the same time we are affirming our conviction that the NATO nuclear deterrent must also be kept strong. I have made clear our intention to commit to the NATO command, for this purpose, the 5 Polaris submarines originally suggested by President Eisenhower, with the possibility, if needed, of more to come.

Second, a major part of our partnership for self-defense is the Military Assistance Program. The main burden of local defense against local attack, subversion, insurrection or guerrilla warfare must of necessity rest with local forces. Where these forces have the necessary will and capacity to cope with such threats, our intervention is rarely necessary or helpful. Where the will is present and only capacity is lacking, our Military Assistance Program can be of help.

But this program, like economic assistance, needs a new emphasis. It cannot be extended without regard to the social, political and military reforms essential to internal respect and stability. The equipment and training provided must be tailored to legitimate local needs and to our own foreign and military policies, not to our supply of military stocks or a local leader's desire for military display. And military assistance can, in addition to its military purposes, make a contribution to economic progress, as do our own Army Engineers.

In an earlier message, I requested 1.6 billion dollars for Military Assistance, stating that this would maintain existing force levels, but that I could not foresee how much more might be required. It is now clear that this is not enough. The present crisis in Southeast Asia, on which the vice president has made a valuable report—the rising threat of communism in Latin America—the increased arms traffic in Africa—and all the new pressures on every nation found on the map by tracing your fingers along the borders of the Communist bloc in Asia and the Middle East—all make clear the dimension of our needs.

I therefore request the Congress to provide a total of 1.885 billion dollars for Military Assistance in the coming fiscal year—an amount less than that requested a year ago—but a minimum which must be assured if we are to help those nations make secure their independence. This must be prudently and wisely spent—and that will be our common endeavor. Military and economic assistance has been a heavy burden on our citizens for a long time, and I recognize the strong pressures against it;

but this battle is far from over, it is reaching a crucial stage, and I believe we should participate in it. We cannot merely state our opposition to totalitarian advance without paying the price of helping those now under the greatest pressure.

VI. Our Own Military and Intelligence Shield

In line with these developments, I have directed a further reinforcement of our own capacity to deter or resist non-nuclear aggression. In the conventional field, with one exception, I find no present need for large new levies of men. What is needed is rather a change of position to give us still further increases in flexibility.

Therefore, I am directing the Secretary of Defense to undertake a reorganization and modernization of the army's divisional structure, to increase its non-nuclear firepower, to improve its tactical mobility in any environment, to insure its flexibility to meet any direct or indirect threat, to facilitate its coordination with our major allies, and to provide more modern mechanized divisions in Europe and bring their equipment up to date, and new airborne brigades in both the Pacific and Europe.

And secondly, I am asking the Congress for an additional 100 million dollars to begin the procurement task necessary to re-equip this new army structure with the most modern material. New helicopters, new armored personnel carriers, and new howitzers, for example, must be obtained now.

Third, I am directing the Secretary of Defense to expand rapidly and substantially, in cooperation with our Allies, the orientation of existing forces for the conduct of non-nuclear war, paramilitary operations and sub-limited or unconventional wars.

In addition our special forces and unconventional warfare units will be increased and reoriented. Throughout the services new emphasis must be placed on the special skills and languages which are required to work with local populations.

Fourth, the army is developing plans to make possible a much more rapid deployment of a major portion of its highly trained reserve forces. When these plans are completed and the reserve is strengthened, two combat-equipped divisions, plus their supporting forces, a total

of 89,000 men, could be ready in an emergency for operations with but 3 weeks' notice—2 more divisions with but 5 weeks' notice—and six additional divisions and their supporting forces, making a total of 10 divisions, could be deployable with less than 8 weeks' notice. In short, these new plans will allow us to almost double the combat power of the army in less than two months, compared to the nearly nine months heretofore required.

Fifth, to enhance the already formidable ability of the Marine Corps to respond to limited war emergencies, I am asking the Congress for 60 million dollars to increase the Marine Corps strength to 190,000 men. This will increase the initial impact and staying power of our three Marine divisions and three air wings, and provide a trained nucleus for further expansion, if necessary for self-defense.

Finally, to cite one other area of activities that are both legitimate and necessary as a means of self-defense in an age of hidden perils, our whole intelligence effort must be reviewed, and its coordination with other elements of policy assured. The Congress and the American people are entitled to know that we will institute whatever new organization, policies, and control are necessary.

VII. Civil Defense

One major element of the national security program which this nation has never squarely faced up to is civil defense. This problem arises not from present trends but from national inaction in which most of us have participated. In the past decade we have intermittently considered a variety of programs, but we have never adopted a consistent policy. Public considerations have been largely characterized by apathy, indifference and skepticism; while, at the same time, many of the civil defense plans have been so far-reaching and unrealistic that they have not gained essential support.

This Administration has been looking hard at exactly what civil defense can and cannot do. It cannot be obtained cheaply. It cannot give an assurance of blast protection that will be proof against surprise attack or guaranteed against obsolescence or destruction. And it cannot deter a nuclear attack.

We will deter an enemy from making a nuclear attack only if our retaliatory power is so strong and so invulnerable that he knows he would be destroyed by our response. If we have that strength, civil defense is not needed to deter an attack. If we should ever lack it, civil defense would not be an adequate substitute.

But this deterrent concept assumes rational calculations by rational men. And the history of this planet, and particularly the history of the 20th century, is sufficient to remind us of the possibilities of an irrational attack, a miscalculation, an accidental war, [or a war of escalation in which the stakes by each side gradually increase to the point of maximum danger] which cannot be either foreseen or deterred. It is on this basis that civil defense can be readily justifiable—as insurance for the civilian population in case of an enemy miscalculation. It is insurance we trust will never be needed—but insurance which we could never forgive ourselves for foregoing in the event of catastrophe.

Once the validity of this concept is recognized, there is no point in delaying the initiation of a nation-wide long-range program of identifying present fallout shelter capacity and providing shelter in new and existing structures. Such a program would protect millions of people against the hazards of radioactive fallout in the event of large-scale nuclear attack. Effective performance of the entire program not only requires new legislative authority and more funds, but also sound organizational arrangements.

Therefore, under the authority vested in me by Reorganization Plan No. 1 of 1958, I am assigning responsibility for this program to the top civilian authority already responsible for continental defense, the Secretary of Defense. It is important that this function remain civilian, in nature and leadership; and this feature will not be changed.

The Office of Civil and Defense Mobilization will be reconstituted as a small staff agency to assist in the coordination of these functions. To more accurately describe its role, its title should be changed to the Office of Emergency Planning.

As soon as those newly charged with these responsibilities have prepared new authorization and appropriation requests, such requests will be transmitted to the Congress for a much strengthened Federal-State civil defense program. Such a program will provide Federal funds for identifying fallout shelter capacity in existing, structures, and it will include, where appropriate, incorporation of shelter in Federal buildings, new requirements for shelter in buildings constructed with Federal assistance, and matching grants and other incentives for constructing shelter in State and local and private buildings.

Federal appropriations for civil defense in fiscal 1962 under this program will in all likelihood be more than triple the pending budget requests; and they will increase sharply in subsequent years. Financial participation will also be required from State and local governments and from private citizens. But no insurance is cost-free; and every American citizen and his community must decide for themselves whether this form of survival insurance justifies the expenditure of effort, time and money. For myself, I am convinced that it does.

VIII. Disarmament

I cannot end this discussion of defense and armaments without emphasizing our strongest hope: the creation of an orderly world where disarmament will be possible. Our aims do not prepare for war—they are efforts to discourage and resist the adventures of others that could end in war.

That is why it is consistent with these efforts that we continue to press for properly safeguarded disarmament measures. At Geneva, in cooperation with the United Kingdom, we have put forward concrete proposals to make clear our wish to meet the Soviets halfway in an effective nuclear test ban treaty—the first significant but essential step on the road towards disarmament. Up to now, their response has not been what we hoped, but Mr. Dean returned last night to Geneva, and we intend to go the last mile in patience to secure this gain if we can.

Meanwhile, we are determined to keep disarmament high on our agenda—to make an intensified effort to develop acceptable political and technical alternatives to the present arms race. To this end I shall send to the Congress a measure to establish a strengthened and enlarged Disarmament Agency.

IX. Space

Finally, if we are to win the battle that is now going on around the world between freedom and tyranny, the dramatic achievements in space which occurred in recent weeks should have made clear to us all, as did the *Sputnik* in 1957, the impact of this adventure on the minds of men everywhere, who are attempting to make a determination of which road they should take. Since early in my term, our efforts in space have been under review. With the advice of the vice president, who is chairman of the National Space Council, we have examined where we are strong and where we are not, where we may succeed and where we may not. Now it is time to take longer strides—time for a great new American enterprise—time for this nation to take a clearly leading role in space achievement, which in many ways may hold the key to our future on earth.

I believe we possess all the resources and talents necessary. But the facts of the matter are that we have never made the national decisions or marshalled the national resources required for such leadership. We have never specified long-range goals on an urgent time schedule, or managed our resources and our time so as to insure their fulfillment.

Recognizing the head start obtained by the Soviets with their large rocket engines, which gives them many months of lead-time, and recognizing the likelihood that they will exploit this lead for some time to come in still more impressive successes, we nevertheless are required to make new efforts on our own. For while we cannot guarantee that we shall one day be first, we can guarantee that any failure to make this effort will make us last. We take an additional risk by making it in full view of the world, but as shown by the feat of astronaut Shepard, this very risk enhances our stature when we are successful. But this is not merely a race. Space is open to us now; and our eagerness to share its meaning is not governed by the efforts of others. We go into space because whatever mankind must undertake, free men must fully share.

I therefore ask the Congress, above and beyond the increases I have earlier requested for space activities, to provide the funds which are needed to meet the following national goals:

First, I believe that this nation should commit itself to achieving the goal, before this decade is out, of landing a man on the moon and returning him safely to the earth. No single space project in this period will be more impressive to mankind, or more important for the long- range exploration of space; and none will be so difficult or expensive to accomplish. We propose to accelerate the development of the appropriate lunar space craft. We propose to develop alternate liquid and solid fuel boosters, much larger than any now being developed, until certain which is superior. We propose additional funds for other engine development and for unmanned explorations—explorations which are particularly important for one purpose which this nation will never overlook: the survival of the man who first makes this daring flight. But in a very real sense, it will not be one man going to the moon—if we make this judgment affirmatively, it will be an entire nation. For all of us must work to put him there.

Secondly, an additional 23 million dollars, together with 7 million dollars already available, will accelerate development of the Rover nuclear rocket. This gives promise of some day providing a means for even more exciting and ambitious exploration of space, perhaps beyond the moon, perhaps to the very end of the solar system itself.

Third, an additional 50 million dollars will make the most of our present leadership, by accelerating the use of space satellites for world-wide communications.

Fourth, an additional 75 million dollars—of which 53 million dollars is for the Weather Bureau—will help give us at the earliest possible time a satellite system for world-wide weather observation.

Let it be clear—and this is a judgment which the Members of the Congress must finally make—let it be clear that I am asking the Congress and the country to accept a firm commitment to a new course of action, a course which will last for many years and carry very heavy costs: 531 million dollars in fiscal '62—an estimated seven to nine billion dollars additional over the next five years. If we are to go only half way, or reduce our sights in the face of difficulty, in my judgment it would be better not to go at all.

Now this is a choice which this country must make, and I am confident that under the leadership of the Space Committees of the Congress, and the Appropriating Committees, that you will consider the matter carefully.

It is a most important decision that we make as a nation. But all of you have lived through the last four years and have seen the significance of space and the adventures in space, and no one can predict with certainty what the ultimate meaning will be of mastery of space.

I believe we should go to the moon. But I think every citizen of this country as well as the Members of the Congress should consider the matter carefully in making their judgment, to which we have given attention over many weeks and months, because it is a heavy burden, and there is no sense in agreeing or desiring that the United States take an affirmative position in outer space, unless we are prepared to do the work and bear the burdens to make it successful. If we are not, we should decide today and this year.

This decision demands a major national commitment of scientific and technical manpower, material and facilities, and the possibility of their diversion from other important activities where they are already thinly spread. It means a degree of dedication, organization and discipline which have not always characterized our research and development efforts. It means we cannot afford undue work stoppages, inflated costs of material or talent, wasteful interagency rivalries, or a high turnover of key personnel.

New objectives and new money cannot solve these problems. They could in fact, aggravate them further—unless every scientist, every engineer, every serviceman, every technician, contractor, and civil servant gives his personal pledge that this nation will move forward, with the full speed of freedom, in the exciting adventure of space.

X. Conclusion

In conclusion, let me emphasize one point. It is not a pleasure for any president of the United States, as I am sure it was not a pleasure for my predecessors, to come before the Congress and ask for new appropriations which place burdens on our people. I came to this conclusion with some reluctance. But in my judgment, this is a most serious time in the life of our country and in the life of freedom around the globe, and it is the obligation, I believe, of the president of the United States to at least make his recommendations to the members of the Congress, so that they can reach their own conclusions with that judgment before them. You must decide yourselves, as I have decided, and I am confident that whether you finally decide in the way that I have decided or not, that your judgment—as my judgment—is reached on what is in the best interests of our country.

In conclusion, let me emphasize one point: that we are determined, as a nation in 1961 that freedom shall survive and succeed—and whatever the peril and setbacks, we have some very large advantages. . . .

The Quest for Peace

New York City, New York

September 25, 1961

KENNEDY'S ADDRESS to the opening session of the United Nations General Assembly on disarmament and peace included proposals to ban nuclear testing and to establish a permanent UN peacekeeping force.

Underlying his appeal to the world body were two power struggles between the United States and the U. S. S. R. One was over control of the UN itself. Moscow was vigorously pressing for the replacement of the office of secretary-general (left vacant by the recent death of Dag Hammarskjold) with a *troika* of leaders, including one from each of the superpowers. Kennedy rejected this plan (in Section II of this speech) as undermining the UN's neutrality. The other contest involved nuclear testing and disarmament, with both powers playing to world opinion. In the welter of proposals and counterproposals, each side sought to appear more peaceloving than the other while retaining all its important military prerogatives. Though the verbal battles of nuclear arms negotiations between the superpowers have since become commonplace, Kennedy's administration was the first to engage in them wholeheartedly. Ultimately, a test-ban treaty was signed (see "A Step Toward Peace").

I.

We meet in an hour of grief and challenge. Dag Hammarskjold is dead. But the United Nations lives. His tragedy is deep in our hearts, but the task for which he died is at the top of our agenda. A noble servant of peace is gone. But the quest for peace lies before us.

The problem is not the death of one man—the problem is the life of this organization. It will either grow to meet the challenges of our age, or it will be gone with the wind, without influence, without force, without respect. Were we to let it die, to enfeeble its vigor, to cripple its powers, we would condemn our future.

For in the development of this organization rests the only true alternative to war—and war appeals no longer as a rational alternative. Unconditional war can no longer lead to unconditional victory. It can no longer serve to settle disputes. It can no longer concern the great powers alone. For a nuclear disaster, spread by wind and water and fear, could well engulf the great and the small, the rich and the poor, the committed and the uncommitted alike. Mankind must put an end to war—or war will put an end to mankind.

So let us here resolve that Dag Hammarskjold did not live, or die, in vain. Let us call a truce to terror. Let us invoke the blessings of peace. And, as we build an international capacity to keep peace, let us join in dismantling the national capacity to wage war.

II.

This will require new strength and new roles for the United Nations. For disarmament without checks is but a shadow—and a community without law is but a shell. Already the United Nations has become both the measure and the vehicle of man's most generous impulses. Already it has provided—in the Middle East, in Asia, in Africa this year in the Congo—a means of holding man's violence within bounds.

But the great question which confronted this body in 1945 is still before us: whether man's cherished hopes for progress and peace are to be destroyed by terror and disruption, whether the "foul winds of war" can be tamed in time to free the cooling winds of reason, and whether the pledges of our Charter are to be fulfilled or defied—pledges to secure peace, progress, human rights, and world law.

In this Hall, there are not three forces, but two. One is composed of those who are trying to build the kind of world described in Articles I and II of the Charter. The other, seeking a far different world, would undermine this organization in the process.

Today of all days our dedication to the Charter must be maintained. It must be strengthened first of all by the selection of an outstanding civil servant to carry forward the responsibilities of the secretary-general—a man endowed with both the wisdom and the power to make meaningful the moral force of the world community. The late secretary-general nurtured and sharpened the United Nations' obligation to act. But he did not invent it. It was there in the Charter. It is still there in the Charter.

However difficult it may be to fill Mr. Hammarskjold's place, it can better be filled by one man rather than by three. Even the three horses of the troika did not have three drivers, all going in different directions. They had only one—and so must the United Nations executive. To install a triumvirate, or any panel, or any rotating authority, in the United Nations administrative offices would replace order with anarchy, action with paralysis, confidence with confusion.

The secretary-general, in a very real sense, is the servant of the General Assembly. Diminish his authority and you diminish the authority of the only body where all nations, regardless of power, are equal and sovereign. Until all the powerful are just, the weak will be secure only in the strength of this Assembly.

Effective and independent executive action is not the same question as balanced representation. In view of the enormous change in membership in this body since its founding, the American delegation will join in any effort for the prompt review and revision of the composition of United Nations bodies.

But to give this organization three drivers—to permit each great power to decide its own case, would entrench the cold war in the headquarters of peace. Whatever advantages such a plan may hold out to my own country, as one of the great powers, we reject it. For we far prefer world law, in the age of self-determination, to world war, in the age of mass extermination.

III.

Today, every inhabitant of this planet must contemplate the day when this planet may no longer be habitable. Every man, woman, and child lives under a nuclear sword of Damocles, hanging by the slenderest of threads, capable of being cut at any moment by accident or miscalculation or by madness. The weapons of war must be abolished before they abolish us.

Men no longer debate whether armaments are a symptom or a cause of tension. The mere existence of modern weapons—10 million times more powerful than any that the world has ever seen, and only minutes away from any target on earth—is a source of horror, and discord and distrust. Men no longer maintain that disarmament must await the settlement of all disputes—for disarmament must be a part of any permanent settlement. And men may no longer pretend that the quest for disarmament is a sign of weakness—for in a spiraling arms race, a nation's security may well be shrinking even as its arms increase.

For 15 years this organization has sought the reduction and destruction of arms. Now that goal is no longer a dream—it is a practical matter of life or death. The risks inherent in disarmament pale in comparison to the risks inherent in an unlimited arms race.

It is in this spirit that the recent Belgrade Conference—recognizing that this is no longer a Soviet problem or an American problem, but a human problem—endorsed a program of "general, complete and strictly an internationally controlled disarmament." It is in this same spirit that we in the United States have labored this year, with a new urgency, and with a new, now statutory agency fully endorsed by the Congress, to find an approach to disarmament which would be so far-reaching yet realistic, so mutually balanced and beneficial, that it could be accepted by every nation. And it is in this spirit that we have presented with the agreement of the Soviet Union—under the label both nations now accept of "general and complete disarmament"—a new statement of newly agreed principles for negotiation.

But we are well aware that all issues of principle are not settled, and that principles alone are not enough. It is therefore our intention to challenge the Soviet Union, not to an arms race, but to a peace race—to advance together step by step, stage by stage, until general and complete disarmament has been achieved. We invite them now to go beyond agreement in principle to reach agreement on actual plans.

The program to be presented to this assembly—for general and complete disarmament under effective international control—moves to bridge the gap between those who insist on a gradual approach and those who talk only of the final and total achievement. It would create machinery to keep the peace as it destroys the machinery of war. It would proceed through balanced and safeguarded stages designed to give no state a military advantage over another. It would place the final responsibility for verification and control where it belongs, not with the big powers alone, not with one's adversary or one's self, but in an international organization within the framework of the United Nations. It would assure that indispensable condition of disarmament—true inspection—and apply it in stages proportionate to the stage of disarmament. It would cover delivery systems as well as weapons. It would ultimately halt their production as well as their testing, their transfer as well as their possession. It would achieve, under the eyes of an international disarmament organization, a steady reduction in force, both nuclear and conventional, until it has abolished all armies and all weapons except those needed for internal order and a new United Nations Peace Force. And it starts that process now, today, even as the talks begin.

In short, general and complete disarmament must no longer be a slogan, used to resist the first steps. It is no longer to be a goal without means of achieving it, without means of verifying its progress, without means of keeping the peace. It is now a realistic plan, and a test—a test of those only willing to talk and a test of those willing to act.

Such a plan would not bring a world free from conflict and greed—but it would bring a world free from the terrors of mass destruction. It would not usher in the era of the super state—but it would usher in an era in which no state could annihilate or be annihilated by another.

In 1945, this nation proposed the Baruch Plan to internationalize the atom before other nations even possessed the bomb or demilitarized their troops. We proposed with our allies the Disarmament Plan of 1951 while still at war in Korea. And we make our proposals today, while building up our defenses over Berlin, not because we are inconsistent or insincere or intimidated, but because we know the rights of free men will prevail—because while we are compelled against our will to rearm, we look confidently beyond Berlin to the kind of disarmed world we all prefer.

I therefore propose, on the basis of this plan, that disarmament negotiations resume promptly, and continue without interruption until an entire program for general and complete disarmament has not only been agreed but has been actually achieved.

IV.

The logical place to begin is a treaty assuring the end of nuclear tests of all kinds, in every environment, under workable controls. The United States and the United Kingdom have proposed such a treaty that is both reasonable, effective, and ready for signature. We are still prepared to sign that treaty today.

We also proposed a mutual ban on atmospheric testing, without inspection or controls, in order to save the human race from the poison of radioactive fallout. We regret that that offer has not been accepted.

For 15 years we have sought to make the atom an instrument of peaceful growth rather than of war. But for 15 years our concessions have been matched by obstruction, our patience by intransigence. And the pleas of mankind for peace have met with disregard.

Finally, as the explosions of others beclouded the skies, my country was left with no alternative but to act in the interests of its own and the free world's security. We cannot endanger that security by refraining from testing while others improve their arsenals. Nor can we endanger it by another long, uninspected ban on testing. For three years we accepted those risks in our open society while seeking agreement on inspection. But this year, while we were negotiating in good faith in Geneva, others were secretly preparing new experiments in destruction.

Our tests are not polluting the atmosphere. Our deterrent weapons are guarded against accidental explosion or use. Our doctors and scientists stand ready to help any nation measure and meet the hazards of health which inevitably result from the tests in the atmosphere.

But to halt the spread of these terrible weapons, to halt the contamination of the air, to halt the spiralling nuclear arms race, we remain ready to seek new avenues of agreement; our new Disarmament Program thus includes the following proposals:

—First, signing the test-ban treaty by all nations. This can be done now. Test ban negotiations need not and should not await general disarmament.

—Second, stopping the production of fissionable materials for use in weapons, and preventing their transfer to any nation now lacking in nuclear weapons.

—Third, prohibiting the transfer of control over nuclear weapons to states that do not own them.

—Fourth, keeping nuclear weapons from seeding new battlegrounds in outer space.

—Fifth, gradually destroying existing nuclear weapons and converting their materials to peaceful uses; and

—Finally, halting the unlimited testing and production of strategic nuclear delivery vehicles, and gradually destroying them as well.

V.

To destroy arms, however, is not enough. We must create even as we destroy—creating worldwide law and law enforcement as we outlaw worldwide war and weapons. In the world we seek, the United Nations Emergency Forces which have been hastily assembled, uncertainly supplied, and inadequately financed, will never be enough.

Therefore, the United States recommends that all member nations earmark special peacekeeping units in their armed forces—to be on call of the United Nations, to be specially trained and quickly available, and with advance provision for financial and logistic support.

In addition, the American delegation will suggest a series of steps to improve the United Nations' machinery for the peaceful settlement of disputes—for on-the-spot fact-finding, mediation, and adjudication—for extending the rule of international law. For peace is not solely a matter of military or technical problems—it is primarily a problem of politics and people. And unless man can match his strides in weaponry and technology with equal strides in social and political development, our great strength, like that of the dinosaur, will become incapable of proper control—and like the dinosaur vanish from the earth.

VI.

As we extend the rule of law on earth, so must we also extend it to man's new domain—outer space.

All of us salute the brave cosmonauts of the Soviet Union. The new horizons of outer space must not be driven by the old bitter concepts of imperialism and sovereign claims. The cold reaches of the universe must not become the new arena of an even colder war.

To this end, we shall urge proposals extending the United Nations Charter to the limits of man's exploration in the universe, reserving outer space for peaceful use, prohibiting weapons of mass destruction in space or on celestial bodies, and opening the mysteries and benefits of space to every nation. We shall propose further cooperative efforts between all nations in weather prediction and eventually in weather control.

We shall propose, finally, a global system of communications satellites linking the whole world in telegraph and telephone and radio and television. The day need not be far away when such a system will televise the proceedings of this body to every corner of the world for the benefit of peace.

VII.

But the mysteries of outer space must not divert our eyes or our energies from the harsh realities that face our fellow men. Political sovereignty is but a mockery without the means of meeting poverty and illiteracy and disease. Self-determination is but a slogan if the future holds no hope.

That is why my nation, which has freely shared its capital and its technology to help others help themselves, now proposes officially designating this decade of the 1960s as the United Nations Decade of Development. Under the framework of that resolution, the United Nations' existing efforts in promoting economic growth can be expanded and coordinated. Regional surveys and training institutes can now pool the talents of many. New research, technical assistance, and pilot projects can unlock the wealth of less developed lands and untapped waters. And development can become a cooperative and not a competitive enterprise—to enable all nations, however diverse in their systems and beliefs, to become in fact as well as in law free and equal nations.

VIII.

My country favors a world of free and equal states. We agree with those who say that colonialism is a key issue in this Assembly. But let the full facts of that issue be discussed in full.

On the one hand is the fact that, since the close of World War II, a worldwide declaration of independence has transformed nearly one billion people and nine million square miles into 42 free and independent states. Less than 2 percent of the world's population now lives in "dependent" territories.

I do not ignore the remaining problems of traditional colonialism which still confront this body. Those problems will be solved, with patience, goodwill, and determination. Within the limits of our responsibility in such matters, my country intends to be a participant and not merely an observer, in the peaceful, expeditious movement of nations from the status of colonies to the partnership of equals. That continuing tide of self-determination, which runs so strong, has our sympathy and our support.

But colonialism in its harshest forms is not only the exploitation of new nations by old, of dark skins by light, or the subjugation of the poor by the rich. My nation was once a colony, and we know what colonialism means; the exploitation and subjugation of the weak by the powerful, of the many by the few, of the governed who have given no consent to be governed, whatever their continent, their class, or their color.

And that is why there is no ignoring the fact that the tide of self-determination has not reached the Communist empire where a population far larger than that officially termed "dependent" lives under governments installed by foreign troops instead of free institutions—under a system which knows only one party and one belief—which suppresses free debate, and free elections, and free newspapers, and free books, and free trade unions—and which builds a wall to keep truth a stranger and its own citizens prisoners. Let us debate colonialism in full—and apply the principle of free choice and the practice of free plebiscites in every corner of the globe.

IX.

Finally, as president of the United States, I consider it my duty to report to this Assembly on two threats to the peace which are not on your crowded agenda, but which causes us, and most of you, the deepest concern.

The first threat on which I wish to report is widely misunderstood: the smoldering coals of war in Southeast Asia. South Vietnam is already under attack—sometimes by a single assassin, sometimes by a band of guerrillas, recently by full battalions. The peaceful borders of Burma, Cambodia, and India have been repeatedly violated. And the peaceful people of Laos are in danger of losing the independence they gained not so long ago.

No one can call these "wars of liberation." For these are free countries living under their own governments. Nor are these aggressions any less real because men are knifed in their homes and not shot in the fields of battle.

The very simple question confronting the world community is whether measures can be devised to protect the small and the weak from such tactics. For if they are successful in Laos and South Vietnam, the gates will be opened wide.

The United States seeks for itself no base, no territory, no special position in this area of any kind. We support a truly neutral and independent Laos, its people free from outside interference, living at peace with themselves and with their neighbors, assured that their territory will not be used for attacks on others, and under a government comparable (as Mr. Khrushchev and I agreed at Vienna) to Cambodia and Burma.

But now the negotiations over Laos are reaching a crucial stage. The cease-fire is at best precarious. The rainy season is coming to an end. Laotian territory is being used to infiltrate South Vietnam. The world community must recognize—and all those who are involved—that this potent threat to Laotian peace and freedom is indivisible from all other threats to their own.

Secondly, I wish to report to you on the crisis over Germany and Berlin. This is not the time or the place for immoderate tones, but the world community is entitled to know the very simple issues as we see them. If there is a crisis it is because an existing peace is under threat, because an existing island of free people is under pressure, because solemn agreements are being treated with indifference. Established international rights are being threatened with unilateral usurpation. Peaceful circulation has been interrupted by barbed wire and concrete blocks.

One recalls the order of the czar in Pushkin's "Boris Godunov": "Take steps at this very hour that our frontiers be fenced in by barriers. . . . That not a single soul pass o'er the border, that not a hare be able to run or a crow to fly."

It is absurd to allege that we are threatening a war merely to prevent the Soviet Union and East Germany from signing a so-called "treaty" of peace. The Western Allies are not concerned with any paper arrangement the

Soviets may wish to make with a regime of their own creation, on territory occupied by their own troops and governed by their own agents. No such action can affect either our rights or our responsibilities.

If there is a dangerous crisis in Berlin—and there is—it is because of threats against the vital interests and the deep commitments of the Western powers, and the freedom of West Berlin. We cannot yield these interests. We cannot fail these commitments. We cannot surrender the freedom of these people for whom we are responsible. A "peace treaty" which carried with it the provisions which destroy the peace would be a fraud. A "free city" which was not genuinely free would suffocate freedom and would be an infamy.

For a city or a people to be truly free, they must have the secure right, without economic, political, or police pressure, to make their own choice and to live their own lives. And as I have said before, if anyone doubts the extent to which our presence is desired by the people of West Berlin, we are ready to have that question submitted to a free vote in all Berlin and, if possible, among all the German people.

The elementary fact about this crisis is that it is unnecessary. The elementary tools for a peaceful settlement are to be found in the Charter. Under its law, agreements are to be kept, unless changed by all those who made them. Established rights are to be respected. The political disposition of peoples should rest upon their own wishes, freely expressed in plebiscites or free elections. If there are legal problems, they can be solved by legal means. If there is a threat of force, it must be rejected. If there is desire for change, it must be a subject for negotiation and if there is negotiation, it must be rooted in mutual respect and concern for the rights of others.

The Western powers have calmly resolved to defend, by whatever means are forced upon them, their obligations and their access to the free citizens of West Berlin and the self-determination of those citizens. This generation learned from bitter experience that either brandishing or yielding to threats can only lead to war. But firmness and reason can lead to the kind of peaceful solution in which my country profoundly believes.

We are committed to no rigid formula. We see no perfect solution. We recognize that troops and tanks can, for a time, keep a nation divided against its will, however unwise that policy may seem to us. But we believe a peaceful agreement is possible which protects the freedom of West Berlin and Allied presence and access, while recognizing the historic and legitimate interests of others in assuring European security.

The possibilities of negotiation are now being explored; it is too early to report what the prospects may be. For our part, we would be glad to report at the appropriate time that a solution has been found. For there is no need for a crisis over Berlin, threatening the peace—and if those who created this crisis desire peace, there will be peace and freedom in Berlin.

X.

The events and decisions of the next 10 months may well decide the fate of man for the next 10,000 years. There will be no avoiding those events. There will be no appeal from these decisions. And we in this hall shall be remembered either as part of the generation that turned this planet into a flaming funeral pyre or the generation that met its vow "to save succeeding generations from the scourge of war."

In the endeavor to meet that vow, I pledge you every effort this nation possesses. I pledge you that we shall neither commit nor provoke aggression, that we shall neither flee nor invoke the threat of force, that we shall never negotiate out of fear, we shall never fear to negotiate.

Terror is not a new weapon. Throughout history it has been used by those who could not prevail, either by persuasion or example. But inevitably they fail, either because men are not afraid to die for a life worth living, or because the terrorists themselves came to realize that free men cannot be frightened by threats, and that aggression would meet its own response. And it is in the light of that history that every nation today should know, be he friend or foe, that the United States has both the will and the weapons to join free men in standing up to their responsibilities.

But I come here today to look across this world of threats to a world of peace. In that search we cannot expect any final triumph—for new problems will always arise. We cannot expect that all nations will adopt like systems—for conformity is the jailor of freedom, and the enemy of growth. Nor can we expect to reach our goal by contrivance, by fiat, or even by the wishes of all.

But however close we sometimes seem to that dark and final abyss, let no man of peace and freedom despair. For he does not stand alone. If we all can persevere, if we can in every land and office look beyond our own shores and ambitions, then surely the age will dawn in which the strong are just and the weak secure and the peace preserved.

Ladies and gentlemen of this Assembly, the decision is ours. Never have the nations of the world had so much to lose, or so much to gain. Together we shall save our planet, or together we shall perish in its flames. Save it we can—and save it we must—and then shall we earn the eternal thanks of mankind and, as peacemakers, the eternal blessing of God.

The Cuban Missile Crisis

Washington, D.C.

October 22, 1962

THE BAY OF PIGS disaster, in which CIA-backed anti-Castro Cuban rebels failed in an attempt to invade the island, was Kennedy's first Cuban crisis. In October 1962 Cuba was again the focus of national concern when the United States discovered that the Soviets were secretly installing in Cuba nuclear missiles that could attack a wide range of Western Hemisphere targets, including every major American city. As Schlesinger has noted, this was (and remains) "the supreme Soviet probe of American intentions . . . a staggering project—staggering in its recklessness, staggering in its misconception of the American response, staggering in its rejection of the ground rules for coexistence among the superpowers which Kennedy had offered."

The president and his advisers chose a naval blockade of the island as the most flexible response to the threat. From his office, Kennedy outlined the situation to the nation in a major radio and television address, "his expression grave, his voice firm and calm, the evidence set forth without emotion, the conclusion unequivocal," in Schlesinger's description. As Moscow issued angry denials, world apprehension grew; a clash between the superpowers seemed imminent. Finally the Soviet premier, Nikita Khrushchev, backed down, ordering the missiles removed in exchange for a United States pledge not to invade Cuba.

This government, as promised, has maintained the closest surveillance of the Soviet military buildup on the island of Cuba. Within the past week, unmistakable evidence has established the fact that a series of offensive missile sites is now in preparation on that imprisoned island. The purpose of these bases can be none other than to provide a nuclear strike capability against the Western Hemisphere.

Upon receiving the first preliminary hard information of this nature last Tuesday morning at 9 a.m., I directed that our surveillance be stepped up. And having now confirmed and completed our evaluation of the evidence and our decision on a course of action, this government feels obliged to report this new crisis to you in fullest detail.

The characteristics of these new missile sites indicate two distinct types of installations. Several of them include medium-range ballistic missiles, capable of carrying a nuclear warhead for a distance of more than 1,000 nautical miles. Each of these missiles, in short, is capable of striking Washington, D.C., the Panama Canal, Cape Canaveral, Mexico City, or any other city in the southeastern part of the United States, in Central America, or in the Caribbean area.

Additional sites not yet completed appear to be designed for intermediate-range ballistic missiles—capable of traveling more than twice as far—and thus capable of striking most of the major cities in the Western Hemisphere, ranging as far north as Hudson Bay, Canada, and as far south as Lima, Peru. In addition, jet bombers, capable of carrying nuclear weapons, are now being uncrated and assembled in Cuba, while the necessary air bases are being prepared.

This urgent transformation of Cuba into an important strategic base—by the presence of these large, long-range, and clearly offensive weapons of sudden mass destruction—constitutes an explicit threat to the peace and security of all the Americas, in flagrant and deliberate defiance of the Rio Pact of 1947, the traditions of this nation and hemisphere, the joint resolution of the 87th Congress, the Charter of the United Nations, and my own public warnings to the Soviets on September 4 and 13. This action also contradicts the repeated assurances of Soviet spokesmen, both publicly and privately delivered, that the arms buildup in Cuba would retain its original defensive character, and that the Soviet Union had no need or desire to station strategic missiles on the territory of any other nation.

The size of this undertaking makes clear that it has been planned for some months. Yet only last month, after I had made clear the distinction between any introduction of ground-to-ground missiles and the existence of defensive antiaircraft missiles, the Soviet government publicly stated on September 11 that, and I quote, "the armaments and military equipment sent to Cuba are designed exclusively for defensive purposes," that, and I quote the Soviet government, "there is no need for the Soviet government to shift its weapons . . . for a retaliatory blow to any other country, for instance Cuba," and that, and I quote their government, "the Soviet Union has so powerful rockets to carry these nuclear warheads that there is no need to search for sites for them beyond the boundaries of the Soviet Union." That statement was false.

Only last Thursday, as evidence of this rapid offensive buildup was already in my hand, Soviet foreign minister Gromyko told me in my office that he was instructed to make it clear once again, as he said his government had already done, that Soviet assistance to Cuba, and I quote, "pursued solely the purpose of contributing to the defense capabilities of Cuba," that, and I quote him, "training by Soviet specialists of Cuban nationals in handling defensive armaments was by no means offensive, and if it were otherwise," Mr. Gromyko went on, "the Soviet government would never become involved in rendering such assistance." That statement also was false.

Neither the United States of America nor the world community of nations can tolerate deliberate deception and offensive threats on the part of any nation, large or small. We no longer live in a world where only the actual firing of weapons represents a sufficient challenge to a nation's security to constitute maximum peril. Nuclear weapons are so destructive and ballistic missiles are so swift, that any substantially increased possibility of their use or any sudden change in their deployment may well be regarded as a definite threat to peace.

For many years, both the Soviet Union and the United States, recognizing this fact, have deployed strategic nuclear weapons with great care, never upsetting the precarious status quo which insured that these weapons would not be used in the absence of some vital challenge. Our own strategic missiles have never been transferred to the territory of any other nation under a cloak of secrecy and deception; and our history—unlike that of the Soviets since the end of World War II—demonstrates that we have no desire to dominate or conquer any other nation or impose our system upon its people. Nevertheless, American citizens have become adjusted to living daily on the bull's-eye of Soviet missiles located inside the U.S.S.R. or in submarines.

In that sense, missiles in Cuba add to an already clear and present danger—although it should be noted the nations of Latin America have never previously been subjected to a potential nuclear threat.

But this secret, swift, and extraordinary buildup of Communist missiles—in an area well known to have a special and historical relationship to the United States and the nations of the Western Hemisphere, in violation of Soviet assurances, and in defiance of American and hemispheric policy—this sudden, clandestine decision to station strategic weapons for the first time outside of Soviet soil—is a deliberately provocative and unjustified change in the status quo which cannot be accepted by this country, if our courage and our commitments are ever to be trusted again by either friend or foe.

The 1930s taught us a clear lesson; aggressive conduct, if allowed to go unchecked and unchallenged, ultimately leads to war. This nation is opposed to war. We are also true to our word. Our unswerving objective, therefore, must be to prevent the use of these missiles against this or any other country, and to secure their withdrawal or elimination from the Western Hemisphere.

Our policy has been one of patience and restraint, as befits a peaceful and powerful nation, which leads a worldwide alliance. We have been determined not to be diverted from our central concerns by mere irritants and fanatics. But now further action is required— and it is under way; and these actions may only be the beginning. We will not prematurely or unnecessarily risk the costs of worldwide nuclear war in which even the fruits of victory would be ashes in our mouth—but neither will we shrink from that risk at any time it must be faced.

Acting, therefore, in the defense of our own security and of the entire Western Hemisphere, and under the authority entrusted to me by the Constitution as endorsed by the resolution of the Congress, I have directed that the following initial steps be taken immediately:

First: To halt this offensive buildup, a strict quarantine on all offensive military equipment under shipment to Cuba is being initiated. All ships of any kind bound for Cuba from whatever nation or port will, if found to contain cargoes of offensive weapons, be turned back. This quarantine will be extended, if needed, to other types of cargo and carriers. We are not at this time, however, denying the necessities of life as the Soviets attempted to do in their Berlin blockade of 1948.

Second: I have directed the continued and increased close surveillance of Cuba and its military buildup. The foreign ministers of the OAS, in their communiqué of October 6, rejected secrecy on such matters in this hemisphere. Should these offensive military preparations continue, thus increasing the threat to the hemisphere, further action will be justified. I have directed the armed forces to prepare for any eventualities; and I trust that in the interest of both the Cuban people and the Soviet technicians at the sites, the hazards to all concerned of continuing this threat will be recognized.

Third: It shall be the policy of this nation to regard any nuclear missile launched from Cuba against any nation in the Western Hemisphere as an attack by the Soviet Union on the United States, requiring a full retaliatory response upon the Soviet Union.

Fourth: As a necessary military precaution, I have reinforced our base at Guantanamo, evacuated today the dependents of our personnel there, and ordered additional military units to be on a standby alert basis.

Fifth: We are calling tonight for an immediate meeting of the Organ of Consultation under the Organization of American States, to consider this threat to hemispheric security and to invoke Articles 6 and 8 of the Rio Treaty in support of all necessary action. The United Nations Charter allows for regional security arrangements—and the nations of this hemisphere decided long ago against the military presence of outside powers. Our other allies around the world have also been alerted.

Sixth: Under the Charter of the United Nations, we are asking tonight that an emergency meeting of the Security Council be convoked without delay to take action against this latest Soviet threat to world peace. Our resolution will call for the prompt dismantling and withdrawal of all offensive weapons in Cuba, under the supervision of UN observers, before the quarantine can be lifted.

Seventh and finally: I call upon Chairman Khrushchev to halt and eliminate this clandestine, reckless, and provocative threat to world peace and to stable relations between our two nations. I call upon him further to abandon this course of world domination, and to join in an historic effort to end the perilous arms race and to transform the history of man. He has an opportunity now to move the world back from the abyss of destruction—by returning to his government's own words that it had no need to station missiles outside its own territory, and withdrawing these weapons from Cuba—by refraining from any action which will widen or deepen the present crisis—and then by participating in a search for peaceful and permanent solutions.

This nation is prepared to present its case against the Soviet threat to peace, and our own proposals for a peaceful world, at any time and in any forum—in the OAS, in the United Nations, or in any other meeting that could be useful—without limiting our freedom of action. We have in the past made strenuous efforts to limit the spread of nuclear weapons. We have proposed the elimination of all arms and military bases in a fair and effective disarmament treaty. We are prepared to discuss new proposals for the removal of tensions on both sides—including the possibilities of a genuinely independent Cuba, free to determine its own destiny. We have no wish to war with the Soviet Union—for we are a peaceful people who desire to live in peace with all other peoples.

But it is difficult to settle or even discuss these problems in an atmosphere of intimidation. That is why this latest Soviet threat—or any other threat which is made either independently or in response to our actions this week—must and will be met with determination. Any hostile move anywhere in the world against the safety and freedom of peoples to whom we are committed—including in particular the brave people of West Berlin—will be met by whatever action is needed.

Finally, I want to say a few words to the captive people of Cuba, to whom this speech is being directly carried by special radio facilities. I speak to you as a friend, as one who knows of your deep attachment to your fatherland, as one who shares your aspirations for liberty and justice for all. And I have watched and the American people have watched with deep sorrow how your nationalist revolution was betrayed—and how your fatherland fell under foreign domination: Now your leaders are no longer Cuban leaders inspired by Cuban ideals. They are puppets and agents of an international conspiracy which has turned Cuba against your friends and neighbors in the Americas—and turned it into the first Latin American country to become a target for nuclear war—the first Latin American country to have these weapons on its soil.

These new weapons are not in your interest. They contribute nothing to your peace and well-being. They can only undermine it. But this country has no wish to cause you to suffer or to impose any system upon you. We know that your lives and land are being used as pawns by those who deny your freedom.

Many times in the past, the Cuban people have risen to throw out tyrants who destroyed their liberty. And I have no doubt that most Cubans today look forward to the time when they will be truly free—free from foreign domination, free to choose their own leaders, free to select their own system, free to own their own land, free to speak and write and worship without fear or degradation. And then shall Cuba be welcomed back to the society of free nations and to the associations of this hemisphere.

My fellow citizens: let no one doubt that this is a difficult and dangerous effort on which we have set out. No one can foresee precisely what course it will take or what costs or casualties will be incurred. Many months of sacrifice and self-discipline lie ahead—months in which both our patience and our will will be tested—months in which many threats and denunciations will keep us aware of our dangers. But the greatest danger of all would be to do nothing.

The path we have chosen for the present is full of hazards, as all paths are—but it is the one most consistent with our character and courage as a nation and our commitments around the world. The cost of freedom is always high—but Americans have always paid it. And one path we shall never choose, and that is the path of surrender or submission.

Our goal is not the victory of might, but the vindication of right—not peace at the expense of freedom, but both peace and freedom, here in this hemisphere, and, we hope, around the world. God willing, that goal will be achieved.

Thank you and good night.

Civil Rights and National Morality

Washington, D.C.

June 11, 1963

THE BLACK CIVIL RIGHTS movement gathered momentum during the early 1960s. By 1963 the struggle for political and social equality was moving into the streets, and many commentators, black and white, foresaw widespread disruption if progress was not made. In the spring of 1963, white police in Birmingham, Alabama, beat black demonstrators, including children, and blacks rioted in protest. It appeared to many to be the beginning of a race war.

Kennedy, having campaigned for black civil rights during the election, had since neglected the issue, despite the appointment of several blacks to government posts. But when the governor of Alabama, George Wallace, promised to "stand in the schoolhouse door" to block the court-ordered admission of two blacks to the all-white University of Alabama, the president decided to act. Federal marshals were provided to protect the students. Wallace, under pressure from the White House, challenged the students at the university on June 11 but stepped aside after a symbolic confrontation. That evening Kennedy read this speech on national television. The administration then moved quickly to introduce a civil rights bill into Congress. It was passed shortly after Kennedy's death.

This afternoon, following a series of threats and defiant statements, the presence of Alabama National Guardsmen was required on the University of Alabama to carry out the final and unequivocal order of the U.S. District Court of the Northern District of Alabama. That order called for the admission of two clearly qualified young Alabama residents who happened to have been born Negro.

That they were admitted peacefully on the campus is due in good measure to the conduct of the students of the University of Alabama, who met their responsibilities in a constructive way.

I hope that every American, regardless of where he lives, will stop and examine his conscience about this and other related incidents. This nation was founded by men of many nations and backgrounds. It was founded on the principle that all men are created equal and that the rights of every man are diminished when the rights of one man are threatened.

Today we are committed to a worldwide struggle to promote and protect the rights of all who wish to be free, and when Americans are sent to Vietnam or West Berlin, we do not ask for whites only. It ought to be possible, therefore, for American students of any color to attend any public institution they select without having to be backed up by troops.

It ought to be possible for American consumers of any color to receive equal service in places of public accommodation, such as hotels and restaurants and theaters and retail stores, without being forced to resort to demonstrations in the street; and it ought to be possible for American citizens of any color to register and to vote in a free election without interference or fear of reprisal.

It ought to be possible, in short, for every American to enjoy the privileges of being American without regard to his race or his color. In short, every American ought to have the right to be treated as he would wish to be treated, as one would wish his children to be treated. But this is not the case.

The Negro baby born in America today, regardless of the section of the nation in which he is born, has about one-half as much chance of completing a high school as a white baby born in the same place on the same day, one-third as much chance of completing college, one-third as much chance of becoming a professional man, twice as much chance of becoming unemployed, about one-seventh as much chance of earning $10,000 a year, a life expectancy which is seven years shorter, and the prospects of earning only half as much.

This is not a sectional issue. Difficulties over segregation and discrimination exist in every city in every state of the Union, producing in many cities a rising tide of discontent that threatens the public safety. Nor is this a partisan issue in a time of domestic crisis.

Men of goodwill and generosity should be able to unite regardless of party or politics. This is not even a legal or legislative issue alone. It is better to settle these matters in the courts than on the streets, and new laws are needed at every level, but law alone cannot make men see right.

We are confronted primarily with a moral issue. It is as old as the Scriptures and is as clear as the American Constitution.

The heart of the question is whether all Americans are to be afforded equal rights and equal opportunities, whether we are going to treat our fellow Americans as we want to be treated. If an American, because his skin is dark, cannot eat lunch in a restaurant opened to the public, if he cannot send his children to the best public school available, if he cannot vote for the public officials who represent him, if, in short, he cannot enjoy the full and free life which all of us want, then who among us would be content to have the color of his skin changed and stand in his place? Who among us would then be content with the counsels of patience and delay?

One hundred years of delay have passed since President Lincoln freed the slaves, yet their heirs, their grandsons, are not fully free. They are not yet freed from the bonds of injustice. They are not yet freed from social and economic oppression, and this nation, for all its hopes and all its boasts, will not be fully free until all its citizens are free.

We preach freedom around the world, and we mean it, and we cherish our freedom here at home; but are we to say to the world, and much more importantly, to each other that this is a land of the free except for the Negroes; that we have no second-class citizens except Negroes; that we have no class or caste system, no ghettoes, no master race except with respect to Negroes?

Now the time has come for this nation to fulfill its promise. The events in Birmingham and elsewhere have so increased the cries for equality that no city or state or legislative body can prudently choose to ignore them. The fires of frustration and discord are burning in every city, North and South, where legal remedies are not at hand. Redress is sought in the streets, in demonstrations, parades, and protests, which create tensions and threaten violence and threaten lives.

We face, therefore, a moral crisis as a country and as a people. It cannot be met by repressive police action. It cannot be left to increased demonstrations in the streets. It cannot be quieted by token moves or talk. It is a time to act in the Congress, in your state and local legislative body and, above all, in all of our daily lives.

It is not enough to pin the blame on others, to say this is a problem of one section of the country or another, or deplore the fact that we face. A great change is at hand, and our task, our obligation, is to make that revolution, that change, peaceful and constructive for all. Those who do nothing are inviting shame as well as violence. Those who act boldly are recognizing right as well as reality.

Next week I shall ask the Congress of the United States to act, to make a commitment it has not fully made in this century to the proposition that race has no place in American life or law. The federal judiciary has upheld that proposition in a series of forthright cases. The executive branch has adopted that proposition in the conduct of its affairs, including the employment of federal personnel, the use of federal facilities, and the sale of federally financed housing.

But there are other necessary measures which only the Congress can provide, and they must be provided at this session. The old code of equity law under which we live commands for every wrong a remedy, but in too many communities, in too many parts of the country, wrongs are inflicted on Negro citizens as there are no remedies at law. Unless the Congress acts, their only remedy is in the street.

I am therefore asking the Congress to enact legislation giving all Americans the right to be served in facilities which are open to the public—hotels, restaurants, theaters, retail stores, and similar establishments. This seems to me to be an elementary right. Its denial is an arbitrary indignity that no American in 1963 should have to endure, but many do.

I have recently met with scores of business leaders urging them to take voluntary action to end this discrimination and I have been encouraged by their response; and in the last two weeks over 75 cities have seen progress made in desegregating these kinds of facilities. But many are unwilling to act alone, and for this reason nationwide legislation is needed if we are to move this problem from the streets to the courts.

I am also asking Congress to authorize the federal government to participate more fully in lawsuits designed to end segregation in public education. We have succeeded in persuading many districts to desegregate voluntarily. Dozens have admitted Negroes without violence. Today a Negro is attending a state-supported institution in every one of our 50 states, but the pace is very slow.

Too many Negro children entering segregated grade schools at the time of the Supreme Court's decision nine years ago will enter segregated high schools this fall, having suffered a loss which can never be restored. The lack of an adequate education denies the Negro a chance to get a decent job. The orderly implementation of the Supreme Court decision, therefore, cannot be left solely to those who may not have the economic resources to carry the legal action or who may be subject to harassment.

Other features will be also requested, including greater protection for the right to vote. But legislation, I repeat, cannot solve this problem alone. It must be solved in the homes of every American in every community across our country.

In this respect, I want to pay tribute to those citizens north and south who have been working in their communities to make life better for all. They are acting not out of a sense of legal duty but out of a sense of human decency. Like our soldiers and sailors in all parts of the world, they are meeting freedom's challenge on the firing line, and I salute them for their honor and their courage.

My fellow Americans, this is a problem which faces us all—in every city of the North as well as the South. Today there are Negroes unemployed two or three times as many compared to whites, inadequate in education, moving into the large cities, unable to find work, young people particularly out of work without hope, denied equal rights, denied the opportunity to eat at a restaurant or lunch counter or go to a movie theater, denied the right to a decent education, denied almost today the right to attend a state university even though qualified. It seems to me that these are matters which concern us all, not merely presidents or congressmen or governors, but every citizen of the United States.

This is one country. It has become one country because all of us and all the people who came here had an equal chance to develop their talents. We cannot say to 10 percent of the population that you can't have that right; that your children can't have the chance to develop whatever talents they have; that the only way that they are going to get their rights is to go into the streets and demonstrate. I think we owe them and we owe ourselves a better country than that. Therefore, I am asking for your help in making it easier for us to move ahead and to provide the kind of equality of treatment which we would want ourselves; to give a chance for every child to be educated to the limit of his talents.

As I have said before, not every child has an equal talent or an equal ability or an equal motivation, but they should have the equal right to develop their talent and their ability and their motivation to make something of themselves. We have a right to expect that the Negro community will be responsible, will uphold the law, but they have a right to expect that the law will be fair; that the Constitution will be color blind, as Justice Harlan said at the turn of the century.

This is what we are talking about and this is a matter which concerns this country and what it stands for, and in meeting it I ask the support of all of our citizens.

Ich Bin Ein Berliner

West Berlin, West Germany

June 26, 1963

BERLIN WAS another critical friction point between Washington and Moscow. In August 1961, the city, divided politically into eastern and western sectors since 1945, was divided physically by a masonry and barbed-wire barrier erected by the Russians and the East Germans. The Berlin Wall, intended primarily to stop the massive outflow of East Berliners to the western part of the city, symbolized the self-imprisonment of the Communist bloc and the vulnerability and distrust that characterized East-West relations.

Kennedy's tour of West Berlin in June 1963 was met with a tumultuous welcome. Tens of thousands followed his entourage as he viewed the Berlin Wall. The Brandenburg Gate, just on the east side of the wall, had been veiled with red cloth by the East Germans so that the president could not see in, and more important, so that he could not be seen by the East Berliners. Angered, he gave this famous speech at the Rudolph Wilde Platz outside the city hall. The throng reached such a fever pitch of excitement that, the president later remarked, he believed that if he had given the command "March to the wall—tear it down!" the crowd would have done so.

I am proud to come to this city as the guest of your distinguished mayor [Willy Brandt], who has symbolized throughout the world the fighting spirit of West Berlin. And I am proud to visit the Federal Republic with your distinguished chancellor [Konrad Adenauer] who for so many years has committed Germany to democracy and freedom and progress, and to come here in the company of my fellow American, General [Lucius] Clay, who has been in this city during its great moments of crisis and will come again if ever needed.

Two thousand years ago the proudest boast was "civis Romanus sum." Today, in the world of freedom, the proudest boast is "Ich bin ein Berliner."

I appreciate my interpreter translating my German!

There are many people in the world who really don't understand, or say they don't, what is the great issue between the free world and the Communist world. Let them come to Berlin. There are some who say that Communism is the wave of the future. Let them come to Berlin. And there are some who say in Europe and elsewhere we can work with the Communists. Let them come to Berlin. And there are even a few who say that it is true that Communism is an evil system, but it permits us to make economic progress. Lass' sie nach Berlin kommen. Let them come to Berlin.

Freedom has many difficulties and democracy is not perfect, but we have never had to put a wall up to keep our people in, to prevent them from leaving us. I want to say, on behalf of my countrymen, who live many miles away on the other side of the Atlantic, who are far distant from you, that they take the greatest pride that they have been able to share with you, even from a distance, the story of the last 18 years. I know of no town, no city, that has been besieged for 18 years that still lives with the vitality and the force, and the hope and the determination of the city of West Berlin. While the wall is the most obvious and vivid demonstration of the failures of the Communist system, for all the world to see, we take no satisfaction in it, for it is, as your mayor has said, an offense not only against history but an offense against humanity, separating families, dividing husbands and wives and brothers and sisters, and dividing a people who wish to be joined together.

What is true of this city is true of Germany—real, lasting peace in Europe can never be assured as long as one German out of four is denied the elementary right of free men, and that is to make a free choice. In 18 years of peace and good faith, this generation of Germans has earned the right to be free, including the right to unite their families and their nation in lasting peace, with goodwill to all people. You live in a defended island of freedom, but your life is part of the main. So let me ask you, as I close, to lift your eyes beyond the dangers of today, to the hopes of tomorrow, beyond the freedom merely of this city of Berlin, or your country of Germany, to the advance of freedom everywhere, beyond the wall to the day of peace with justice, beyond yourselves and ourselves to all mankind.

Freedom is indivisible, and when one man is enslaved, all are not free. When all are free, then we can look forward to that day when this city will be joined as one and this country and this great continent of Europe in a peaceful and hopeful globe. When that day finally comes, as it will, the people of West Berlin can take sober satisfaction in the fact that they were in the front lines for almost two decades.

All free men, wherever they may live, are citizens of Berlin, and, therefore, as a free man, I take pride in the words "Ich bin ein Berliner."

A Step Toward Peace

Washington, D.C.

July 26, 1963

AFTER THE Berlin and Cuban crises Kennedy was eager to find ways to ease the superpower rivalry. One of these, long favored by the United States and Britain, was a treaty banning atmospheric and oceanic testing of nuclear weapons. The Soviets had several times refused to adhere to such an agreement, but in a speech at the commencement ceremonies of American University on June 10, 1963, Kennedy announced that he would broach the subject with the Russians again in negotiations the following month.

On July 25, American, Russian, and British representatives concluded a test-ban treaty, considered by many historians to be the Kennedy administration's most significant foreign-policy achievement. Kennedy explained the treaty's provisions to the nation the next day. The treaty was ratified by Congress in September.

I speak to you tonight in a spirit of hope. Eighteen years ago the advent of nuclear weapons changed the course of the world as well as the war. Since that time, all mankind has been struggling to escape from the darkening prospect of mass destruction on earth. In an age when both sides have come to possess enough nuclear power to destroy the human race several times over, the world of Communism and the world of free choice have been caught up in a vicious circle of conflicting ideology and interest. Each increase of tension has produced an increase of arms; each increase of arms has produced an increase of tension.

In these years, the United States and the Soviet Union have frequently communicated suspicion and warnings to each other, but very rarely hope. Our representatives have met at the summit and at the brink; they have met in Washington and in Moscow; in Geneva and at the United Nations. But too often these meetings have produced only darkness, discord, or disillusion.

Yesterday a shaft of light cut into the darkness. Negotiations were concluded in Moscow on a treaty to ban all nuclear tests in the atmosphere, in outer space, and under water. For the first time, an agreement has been reached on bringing the forces of nuclear destruction under international control—a goal first sought in 1946 when Bernard Baruch presented a comprehensive control plan to the United Nations.

That plan, and many subsequent disarmament plans, large and small, have all been blocked by those opposed to international inspection. A ban on nuclear tests, however, requires on-the-spot inspection only for underground tests. This nation now possesses a variety of techniques to detect the nuclear tests of other nations which are conducted in the air or under water. For such tests produce unmistakable signs which our modern instruments can pick up.

The treaty initialed yesterday, therefore, is a limited treaty which permits continued underground testing and prohibits only those tests that we ourselves can police. It requires no control posts, no on-site inspection, no international body.

We should also understand that it has other limits as well. Any nation which signs the treaty will have an opportunity to withdraw if it finds that extraordinary events related to the subject matter of the treaty have jeopardized its supreme interests; and no nation's right of self-defense will in any way be impaired. Nor does this treaty mean an end to the threat of nuclear war. It will not reduce nuclear stockpiles; it will not halt the production of nuclear weapons; it will not restrict their use in time of war.

Nevertheless, this limited treaty will radically reduce the nuclear testing which would otherwise be conducted on both sides; it will prohibit the United States, and United Kingdom, the Soviet Union, and all others who sign it, from engaging in the atmospheric tests which have so alarmed mankind; and it offers to all the world a welcome sign of hope.

For this is not a unilateral moratorium, but a specific and solemn legal obligation. While it will not prevent this nation from testing underground, or from being ready to conduct atmospheric tests if the acts of others so require, it gives us a concrete opportunity to extend its coverage to other nations and later to other forms of nuclear tests.

This treaty is in part the product of Western patience and vigilance. We have made clear—most recently in Berlin and Cuba—our deep resolve to protect our security and our freedom against any form of aggression. We have also made clear our steadfast determination to limit the arms race. In three administrations, our soldiers and diplomats have worked together to this end, always supported by Great Britain. Prime Minister [Harold] Macmillan joined with President Eisenhower in proposing a limited test ban in 1959, and again with me in 1961 and 1962.

But the achievement of this goal is not a victory for one side—it is a victory for mankind. It reflects no concessions either to or by the Soviet Union. It reflects simply our common recognition of the dangers in further testing.

This treaty is not the millennium. It will not resolve all conflicts, or cause the Communists to forgo their ambitions, or eliminate the dangers of war. It will not reduce our need for arms or allies or programs of assistance to others. But it is an important first step—a step towards peace—a step towards reason—a step away from war.

Here is what this step can mean to you and to your children and your neighbors.

First, this treaty can be a step towards reduced world tension and broader areas of agreement. The Moscow talks have reached no agreement on any other subject, nor is this treaty conditioned on any other matter. Under Secretary [W. Averell] Harriman made it clear that any nonaggression arrangements across the division in Europe would require full consultation with our allies and full attention to their interests. He also made clear our strong preference for a more comprehensive treaty banning all tests everywhere, and our ultimate hope for general and complete disarmament. The Soviet government however, is still unwilling to accept the inspection such goals require.

No one can predict with certainty, therefore, what further agreements, if any, can be built on the foundations of this one. They could include controls on preparations for surprise attack, or on numbers and type of armaments. There could be further limitations on the spread of nuclear weapons. The important point is that efforts to seek new agreements will go forward.

But the difficulty of predicting the next step is no reason to be reluctant about this step. Nuclear test-ban negotiations have long been a symbol of East-West disagreement. If this treaty can also be a symbol—if it can symbolize the end of one era and the beginning of another—if both sides can by this treaty gain confidence and experience in peaceful collaboration—then this short and simple treaty may well become an historic mark in man's age-old pursuit of peace.

Western policies have long been designed to persuade the Soviet Union to renounce aggression, direct or indirect, so that their people and all people may live and let live in peace. The unlimited testing of new weapons of war cannot lead towards that end—but this treaty, if it can be followed by further progress, can clearly move in that direction.

I do not say that a world without aggression or threats of war would be an easy world. It will bring new problems, new challenges from the Communists, new dangers of relaxing our vigilance or of mistaking their intent.

But those dangers pale in comparison to those of the spiraling arms race and collision course towards war. Since the beginning of history, war has been mankind's constant companion. It has been the rule, not the exception. Even a nation as young and as peace-loving as our own has fought through eight wars. And three times in the last two years and a half I have been required to report to you as president that this nation and the Soviet Union stood on the verge of direct military confrontation—in Laos, in Berlin, and in Cuba.

A war today or tomorrow, if it led to nuclear war, would not be like any war in history. A full-scale nuclear exchange, lasting less than 60 minutes, with the weapons now in existence, could wipe out more than 300 million Americans, Europeans, and Russians, as well as untold numbers elsewhere. And the survivors, as Chairman Khrushchev warned the Communist Chinese, "The survivors would envy the dead." For they would inherit a world so devastated by explosions and poison and fire that today we cannot even conceive of its horrors. So let us try to turn the world from war. Let us make the most of this opportunity, and every opportunity, to reduce tension, to slow down the perilous nuclear arms race, and to check the world's slide toward final annihilation.

Second, this treaty can be a step towards freeing the world from the fears and dangers of radioactive fallout. Our own atmospheric tests last year were conducted under conditions which restricted such fallout to an absolute minimum. But over the years the number and the yield of weapons tested have rapidly increased and so have the radioactive hazards from such testing. Continued unrestricted testing by the nuclear powers, joined in time by other nations which may be less adept in limiting pollution, will increasingly contaminate the air that all of us must breathe.

Even then, the number of children and grandchildren with cancer in their bones, with leukemia in their blood, or with poison in their lungs might seem statistically small to some, in comparison with natural health hazards. But this is not a natural health hazard—and it is not a statistical issue. The loss of even one human life, or the malformation of even one baby—who may be born long after we are gone—should be of concern to us all. Our children and grandchildren are not merely statistics toward which we can be indifferent.

Nor does this affect the nuclear powers alone. These tests befoul the air of all men and all nations, the committed and the uncommitted alike, without their knowledge and without their consent. That is why the continuation of atmospheric testing causes so many countries to regard all nuclear powers as equally evil; and we can hope that its prevention will enable those countries to see the world more clearly, while enabling all the world to breathe more easily.

Third, this treaty can be a step toward preventing the spread of nuclear weapons to nations not now possessing them. During the next several years, in addition to the four current nuclear powers, a small but significant number of nations will have the intellectual, physical, and financial resources to produce both nuclear weapons and the means of delivering them. In time, it is estimated, many other nations will have either this capacity or other ways of obtaining nuclear warheads, even as missiles can be commercially purchased today.

I ask you to stop and think for a moment what it would mean to have nuclear weapons in so many hands, in the hands of countries large and small, stable and unstable, responsible and irresponsible, scattered throughout the world. There would be no rest for anyone then, no stability, no real security, and no chance of effective disarmament. There would only be the increased chance of accidental war, and an increased necessity for the great powers to involve themselves in what otherwise would be local conflicts.

If only one thermonuclear bomb were to be dropped on any American, Russian, or any other city, whether it was launched by accident or design, by a madman or by an enemy, by a large nation or by a small, from any corner of the world, that one bomb could release more destructive power on the inhabitants of that one helpless city than all the bombs dropped in the Second World War.

Neither the United States nor the Soviet Union nor the United Kingdom nor France can look forward to that day with equanimity. We have a great obligation, all four nuclear powers have a great obligation, to use whatever time remains to prevent the spread of nuclear weapons, to persuade other countries not to test, transfer, acquire, possess, or produce such weapons.

This treaty can be the opening wedge in that campaign. It provides that none of the parties will assist other nations to test in the forbidden environments. It opens the door for further agreements on the control of nuclear weapons, and it is open for all nations to sign, for it is in the interest of all nations, and already we have heard from a number of countries who wish to join with us promptly.

Fourth and finally, this treaty can limit the nuclear arms race in ways which, on balance, will strengthen our nation's security far more than the continuation of unrestricted testing. For in today's world, a nation's security does not always increase as its arms increase, when its adversary is doing the same, and unlimited competition in the testing and development of new types of destructive nuclear weapons will not make the world safer for either side. Under this limited treaty, on the other hand, the testing of other nations could never be sufficient to offset the ability of our strategic forces to deter or survive a nuclear attack and to penetrate and destroy an aggressor's homeland.

We have, and under this treaty we will continue to have, the nuclear strength that we need. It is true that the Soviets have tested nuclear weapons of a yield higher than that which we thought to be necessary, but the hundred-megaton bomb of which they spoke two years ago does not and will not change the balance of strategic power. The United States has chosen, deliberately, to concentrate on more mobile and more efficient weapons, with lower but entirely sufficient yield, and our security is, therefore, not impaired by the treaty I am discussing.

It is also true, as Mr. Khrushchev would agree, that nations cannot afford in these matters to rely simply on the good faith of their adversaries. We have not, therefore, overlooked the risk of secret violations. There is at present a possibility that deep in outer space, that hundreds and thousands and millions of miles away from the earth illegal tests might go undetected. But we already have the capability to construct a system of observation that would make such tests almost impossible to conceal, and we can decide at any time whether such a system is needed in the light of the limited risk to us and the limited reward to others of violations attempted at that range. For any tests which might be conducted so far out in space, which cannot be conducted more easily and efficiently and legally underground, would necessarily be of such a magnitude that they would be extremely difficult to conceal. We can also employ new devices to check on the testing of smaller weapons in the lower atmosphere. Any violation, moreover, involves, along with the risk of detection, the end of the treaty and the worldwide consequences for the violator.

Secret violations are possible and secret preparations for a sudden withdrawal are possible, and, thus, our own vigilance and strength must be maintained, as we remain ready to withdraw and to resume all forms of testing, if we must. But it would be a mistake to assume that this treaty will be quickly broken. The gains of illegal testing are obviously slight compared to their cost, and the hazard of discovery, and the nations which have initialed and will sign this treaty prefer it, in my judgment, to unrestricted testing as a matter of their own self-interest, for these nations, too, and all nations, have a stake in limiting the arms race, in holding the spread of nuclear weapons, and in breathing air that is not radioactive. While it may be theoretically possible to demonstrate the risks inherent in any treaty, and such risks in this treaty are small, the far greater risks to our security are the risks of unrestricted testing, the risk of a nuclear arms race, the risk of new nuclear powers, nuclear pollution, and nuclear war.

This limited test ban, in our most careful judgment, is safer by far for the United States than an unlimited nuclear arms race. For all these reasons, I am hopeful that this nation will promptly approve the limited test-ban treaty. There will, of course, be debate in the country and in the Senate. The Constitution wisely requires the advice and consent of the Senate to all treaties, and that consultation has already begun. All this is as it should be. A document which may mark an historic and constructive opportunity for the world deserves an historic and constructive debate.

It is my hope that all of you will take part in that debate, for this treaty is for all of us. It is particularly for our children and our grandchildren, and they have no lobby here in Washington. This debate will involve military, scientific, and political experts, but it must be not left to them alone. The right and the responsibility are yours.

If we are to open new doorways to peace, if we are to seize this rare opportunity for progress, if we are to be as bold and far-sighted in our control of weapons as we have been in their invention, then let us now show all the world on this side of the wall and the other that a strong America also stands for peace. There is no cause for complacency.

We have learned in times past that the spirit of one moment or place can be gone in the next. We have been disappointed more than once, and we have no illusions now that there are short cuts on the road to peace. At many points around the globe the Communists are continuing their efforts to exploit weakness and poverty. Their concentration of nuclear and conventional arms must still be deterred.

The familiar contest between choice and coercion, the familiar places of danger and conflict, are still there, in Cuba, in Southeast Asia, in Berlin, and all around the globe, still requiring all the strength and the vigilance that we can muster. Nothing could more greatly damage our cause than if we and our allies were to believe that peace has already been achieved, and that our strength and unity were no longer required.

But now, for the first time in many years, the path of peace may be open. No one can be certain what the future will bring. No one can say whether the time has come for an easing of the struggle. But history and our own conscience will judge us harsher if we do not now make every effort to test our hopes by action, and this is the place to begin. According to the ancient Chinese proverb, "A journey of a thousand miles must begin with a single step."

My fellow Americans, let us take that first step. Let us, if we can, get back from the shadows of war and seek out the way of peace. And if that journey is one thousand miles, or even more, let history record that we, in this land at this time, took the first step.

John F. Kennedy gravesite at Arlington National Cemetery,
Washington, D.C. (Courtesy of PresidentsUSA.net)

Lyndon Baines Johnson

Lyndon Baines Johnson

1963–1969

LYNDON JOHNSON was "a man steeped in politics," according to his vice president, Hubert Humphrey. "Politics was not an avocation with him. It was It." Ironically, this consummate manipulator, who ran the Senate for years and who could be enormously persuasive in person (when dealing with politicians), was spectacularly unsuccessful in managing the press and public opinion. He never warmed to the television cameras and often appeared awkward and insincere in the televised speeches that had become an integral link between the president and the electorate during the Kennedy administration.

Johnson was born in the hardscrabble Hill Country of Texas. The eldest of five children, he inherited a taste for politics from his father, a Texas legislator, and his mother, a part-time newspaper reporter and editor. At Southwest Texas Teachers College Johnson was active in the debating club and student politics. In 1937, running on a New Deal platform, he was elected to the U.S. House of Representatives, where he learned to be a skilled backroom negotiator and compromiser. After six successive terms he went to the Senate, becoming Democratic majority leader in 1955, the youngest ever. In 1960 he was elected as Kennedy's vice president.

After Kennedy's assassination, Johnson smoothly picked up the reins of government, continuing most of his predecessor's programs. Johnson's own domestic reforms, including voting and civil rights legislation, antipoverty programs, Medicare, Medicaid, and consumer and environmental measures, were the most extensive since the New Deal. But these achievements were overshadowed by the Vietnam War, which under Johnson escalated from a limited military action to a major conflict. Unable to win the war by conventional means, and unable to quell growing domestic opposition, LBJ lost the public's confidence—he suffered from the first presidential "credibility gap"—and declined to run for reelection in 1968.

Johnson was a complex and contradictory president, part wheeler-dealer, part country boy, and part visionary statesman. Arthur M. Schlesinger Jr. called him "a proud and testy man, well-known for his sensitivity and egotism." He alternately flattered and browbeat his opponents, his supporters, and his closest aides, using whatever technique necessary to get his way. "He was primarily an actor," recalled political columnist Marianne Means, "and a good one, with all the requisite body gestures and facial expressions, and he gave a real performance." Johnson's oratorical range was wide; he could confide in and plead with his audience at one moment, then roar at them the next. He had a large frame, which he often used to intimidate recalcitrant congressmen, grabbing them by the shoulders and propelling them bodily along; it helped him create an air of authority on the podium as well.

Johnson warmed to small crowds, the smaller the better, and he gave his most convincing performances to them. These speeches, which he often made up on the spot, were enlivened with a fund of colorful Texas stories from his childhood. "His speech was filled with country rhythms, country similes, metaphors that came from people who are born on the land and live on the land," according to publisher John Dodds. But little of this skill and confidence with small crowds came through in his major televised addresses, which were all that most Americans saw of him. Johnson was stiff and ill-at-ease on television. Fundamentally an insecure man, he feared that his natural earthiness would alienate the electorate if it ever escaped on camera, but the dull, statesmanlike image he preferred to project rang false. Bill Moyers, his press secretary, noted that LBJ "studied too much his effect on the audience" and thus "worried too much about how he was appearing." At press conferences and major forums he would shield himself behind a bulky podium that reporters nicknamed "Mother."

Johnson's major speeches, while containing some striking phrases, lacked his personal fire. They were written by his aides, mainly Richard Goodwin (who had written for JFK) and Moyers, and, according to Johnson historian Doris Kearns Goodwin, reinforced his image of "feigned propriety, dullness, and dishonesty." He was most effective in moments of crisis—speaking to the people for the first time after Kennedy's assassination, or announcing that he would step down—when his emotions showed through.

Let Us Continue

Washington, D.C.

November 27, 1963

FIVE DAYS after Kennedy's assassination, President Johnson spoke to the assembled Senate, House, and Supreme Court (and, via television, to the public) for the first time. It was one of the few times that Johnson struck exactly the right chord in a major address. He reassured the grieving nation that political continuity was preserved and that he would push forward with the most important efforts of the Kennedy administration. Most Americans knew little about the former vice president aside from his name; this speech provided their first good look at him, and in general the reaction was one of gratitude for his tact and steadfastness.

Doris Kearns Goodwin makes the point that Johnson repeatedly invoked Kennedy in his early public addresses, more often than anyone or anything else. "In this way," wrote Kearns, "Johnson was able to act both as apprentice and caretaker—faithful agent of Kennedy's intentions and the healing leader of a stunned and baffled nation."

All I have I would have given gladly not to be standing here today.

The greatest leader of our time has been struck down by the foulest deed of our time. Today John Fitzgerald Kennedy lives on in the immortal words and works that he left behind. He lives on in the mind and memories of mankind. He lives on in the hearts of his countrymen.

No words are sad enough to express our sense of loss. No words are strong enough to express our determination to continue the forward thrust of America that he began.

The dream of conquering the vastness of space—the dream of partnership across the Atlantic—and across the Pacific as well—the dream of a Peace Corps in less developed nations—the dream of education for all of our children—the dream of jobs for all who seek them and need them—the dream of care for our elderly—the dream of an all-out attack on mental illness—and above all, the dream of equal rights for all Americans, whatever their race or color—these and other American dreams have been vitalized by his drive and by his dedication.

And now the ideas and the ideals which he so nobly represented must and will be translated into effective action.

Under John Kennedy's leadership, this nation has demonstrated that it has the courage to seek peace, and it has the fortitude to risk war. We have proved that we are a good and reliable friend to those who seek peace and freedom. We have shown that we can also

be a formidable foe to those who reject the path of peace and those who seek to impose upon us or our allies the yoke of tyranny.

This nation will keep its commitments from South Vietnam to West Berlin. We will be unceasing in the search for peace; resourceful in our pursuit of areas of agreement even with those with whom we differ; and generous and loyal to those who join with us in common cause.

In this age when there can be no losers in peace and no victors in war, we must recognize the obligation to match national strength with national restraint. We must be prepared at one and the same time for both the confrontation of power and the limitation of power. We must be ready to defend the national interest and to negotiate the common interest. This is the path that we shall continue to pursue. Those who test our courage will find it strong, and those who seek our friendship will find it honorable. We will demonstrate anew that the strong can be just in the use of strength; and the just can be strong in the defense of justice.

And let all know we will extend no special privilege and impose no persecution. We will carry on the fight against poverty and misery, and disease and ignorance, in other lands and in our own.

We will serve all the nation, not one section or one sector, or one group, but all Americans. These are the United States—a united people with a united purpose.

Our American unity does not depend upon unanimity. We have differences; but now, as in the past, we can derive from those differences strength, not weakness, wisdom, not despair. Both as a people and a government, we can unite upon a program, a program which is wise and just, enlightened and constructive.

For 32 years Capitol Hill has been my home. I have shared many moments of pride with you, pride in the ability of the Congress of the United States to act, to meet any crisis, to distill from our differences strong programs of national action.

An assassin's bullet has thrust upon me the awesome burden of the presidency. I am here today to say I need your help; I cannot bear this burden alone. I need the help of all Americans, and all America. This nation has experienced a profound shock, and in this critical moment, it is our duty, yours and mine, as the government of the United States, to do away with uncertainty and doubt and delay, and to show that we are capable of decisive action; that from the brutal loss of our leader we will derive not weakness, but strength; that we can and will act and act now.

From this chamber of representative government, let all the world know and none misunderstand that I rededicate this government to the unswerving support of the United Nations, to the honorable and determined execution of our commitments to our allies, to the maintenance of military strength second to none, to the defense of the strength and the stability of the dollar, to the expansion of our foreign trade, to the reinforcement of our programs of mutual assistance and cooperation in Asia and Africa, and to our Alliance for Progress in this hemisphere.

On the 20th day of January, in 1961, John F. Kennedy told his countrymen that our national work would not be finished "in the first thousand days, nor in the life of this administration, nor even perhaps in our lifetime on this planet. But," he said, "let us begin."

Today, in this moment of new resolve, I would say to all my fellow Americans, let us continue.

This is our challenge—not to hesitate, not to pause, not to turn about and linger over this evil moment, but to continue on our course so that we may fulfill the destiny that history has set for us. Our most immediate tasks are here on this Hill.

First, no memorial oration or eulogy could more eloquently honor President Kennedy's memory than the earliest possible passage of the civil rights bill for which he fought so long. We have talked long enough in this country about equal rights. We have talked for one hundred years or more. It is time now to write the next chapter, and to write it in the books of law.

I urge you again, as I did in 1957 and again in 1960, to enact a civil rights law so that we can move forward to eliminate from this nation every trace of discrimination and oppression that is based upon race or color. There could be no greater source of strength to this nation both at home and abroad.

And second, no act of ours could more fittingly continue the work of President Kennedy than the early passage of the tax bill for which he fought all this long year. This is a bill designed to increase our national income and federal revenues, and to provide insurance against recession. That bill, if passed without delay, means more security for those now working, more jobs for those now without them, and more incentive for our economy.

In short, this is no time for delay. It is a time for action—strong, forward-looking action on the pending education bills to help bring the light of learning to every home and hamlet in America—strong, forward-looking action on youth employment opportunities; strong, forward-looking action on the pending foreign aid bill, making clear that we are not forfeiting our responsibilities to this hemisphere or to the world, nor erasing executive flexibility in the conduct of our foreign affairs—and strong, prompt, and forward-looking action on the remaining appropriation bills.

In this new spirit of action, the Congress can expect the full cooperation and support of the executive branch. And in particular, I pledge that the expenditures of your government will be administered with the utmost thrift and frugality. I will insist that the government get a dollar's value for a dollar spent. The government will set an example of prudence and economy. This does not mean that we will not meet our unfilled needs or that we will not honor our commitments. We will do both.

As one who has long served in both houses of the Congress, I firmly believe in the independence and the integrity of the legislative branch. And I promise you that I shall always respect this. It is deep in the marrow of my bones. With equal firmness, I believe in the capacity and I believe in the ability of the

Congress, despite the divisions of opinions which characterize our nation, to act—to act wisely, to act vigorously, to act speedily when the need arises.

The need is here. The need is now. I ask your help.

We meet in grief, but let us also meet in renewed dedication and renewed vigor. Let us meet in action, in tolerance, and in mutual understanding. John Kennedy's death commands what his life conveyed—that America must move forward. The time has come for Americans of all races and creeds and political beliefs to understand and to respect one another. So let us put an end to the teaching and the preaching of hate and evil and violence. Let us turn away from the fanatics of the far left and the far right, from the apostles of bitterness and bigotry, from those defiant of law, and those who pour venom into our nation's bloodstream.

I profoundly hope that the tragedy and the torment of these terrible days will bind us together in new fellowship, making us one people in our hour of sorrow. So let us here highly resolve that John Fitzgerald Kennedy did not live—or die—in vain. And on this Thanksgiving eve, as we gather together to ask the Lord's blessing, and give Him our thanks, let us unite in those familiar and cherished words:

America, America,
God shed His grace on thee,
And crown thy good
With brotherhood
From sea to shining sea.

The War on Poverty

Washington, D.C.

March 16, 1964

JOHNSON acquired an understanding of real poverty from the Mexican-American children he taught in Texas in the late 1920s. When he learned that Kennedy had planned to introduce antipoverty measures in his second term, Johnson embraced the idea wholeheartedly. According to Elizabeth Goldschmidt, an administrator of social service organizations during the Johnson years, "The whole idea of declaring a big war on poverty and ending it for all time, all the rhetoric of it, appealed to him very much. In fact, I think he built the rhetoric far beyond that which had been planned by his advisers." The specifics of Johnson's war on poverty were spelled out in this special message to Congress.

We are citizens of the richest and most fortunate nation in the history of the world.

One hundred and eighty years ago we were a small country struggling for survival on the margin of a hostile land.

Today we have established a civilization of free men which spans an entire continent.

With the growth of our country has come opportunity for our people—opportunity to educate our children, to use our energies in productive work, to increase our leisure—opportunity for almost every American to hope that through work and talent he could create a better life for himself and his family.

The path forward has not been an easy one.

But we have never lost sight of our goal: an America in which every citizen shares all the opportunities of his society, in which every man has a chance to advance his welfare to the limit of his capacities.

We have come a long way toward this goal.

We still have a long way to go.

The distance which remains is the measure of the great unfinished work of our society.

To finish that work I have called for a national war on poverty. Our objective: total victory.

There are millions of Americans—one-fifth of our people—who have not shared in the abundance which has been granted to most of us, and on whom the gates of opportunity have been closed.

What does this poverty mean to those who endure it?

It means a daily struggle to secure the necessities for even a meager existence. It means that the abundance, the comforts, the opportunities they see all around them are beyond their grasp.

Worst of all, it means hopelessness for the young.

The young man or woman who grows up without a decent education, in a broken home, in a hostile and squalid environment, in ill health, or in the face of racial injustice—that young man or woman is often trapped in a life of poverty.

He does not have the skills demanded by a complex society. He does not know how to acquire those skills. He faces a mounting sense of despair which drains initiative and ambition and energy.

Our tax cut will create millions of new jobs—new exits from poverty.

But we must also strike down all the barriers which keep many from using those exits.

The war on poverty is not a struggle simply to support people, to make them dependent on the generosity of others.

It is a struggle to give people a chance.

It is an effort to allow them to develop and use their capacities, as we have been allowed to develop and use ours, so that they can share, as others share, in the promise of this nation.

We do this, first of all, because it is right that we should.

From the establishment of public education and land grant colleges through agricultural extension and encouragement to industry, we have pursued the goal of a nation with full and increasing opportunities for all its citizens.

The war on poverty is a further step in that pursuit.

We do it also because helping some will increase the prosperity of all.

Our fight against poverty will be an investment in the most valuable of our resources—the skills and strength of our people.

And in the future, as in the past, this investment will return its cost manyfold to our entire economy.

If we can raise the annual earnings of 10 million among the poor by only $1,000 we will have added 14 billion dollars a year to our national output. In addition we can make important reductions in public assistance payments which now cost us four billion dollars a year, and in the large costs of fighting crime and delinquency, disease and hunger.

This is only part of the story.

Our history has proved that each time we broaden the base of abundance, giving more people the chance to produce and consume, we create new industry, higher production, increased earnings, and better income for all.

Giving new opportunity to those who have little will enrich the lives of all the rest.

Because it is right, because it is wise, and because, for the first time in our history, it is possible to conquer poverty, I submit, for the consideration of the Congress and the country, the Economic Opportunity Act of 1964.

The act does not merely expand old programs or improve what is already being done.

It charts a new course.

It strikes at the causes, not just the consequences of poverty.

It can be a milestone in our 180-year search for a better life for our people.

This act provides five basic opportunities.

It will give almost half a million underprivileged young Americans the opportunity to develop skills, continue education, and find useful work.

It will give every American community the opportunity to develop a comprehensive plan to fight its own poverty—and help them to carry out their plans.

It will give dedicated Americans the opportunity to enlist as volunteers in the war against poverty.

It will give many workers and farmers the opportunity to break through particular barriers which bar their escape from poverty.

It will give the entire nation the opportunity for a concerted attack on poverty through the establishment, under my direction, of the Office of Economic Opportunity, a national headquarters for the war against poverty.

This is how we propose to create these opportunities.

First we will give high priority to helping young Americans who lack skills, who have not completed their education or who cannot complete it because they are too poor.

The years of high school and college age are the most critical stage of a young person's life. If they are not helped then, many will be condemned to a life of poverty which they, in turn, will pass on to their children.

I therefore recommend the creation of a Job Corps, a Work-Training Program, and a Work-Study Program.

A new national Job Corps will build toward an enlistment of 100,000 young men. They will be drawn from those whose background, health, and education make them least fit for useful work.

Those who volunteer will enter more than 100 camps and centers around the country.

Half of these young men will work, in the first year, on special conservation projects to give them education, useful work experience and to enrich the natural resources of the country.

Half of these young men will receive, in the first year, a blend of training, basic education, and work experience in Job Training Centers.

These are not simply camps for the underprivileged. They are new educational institutions, comparable in innovation to the land grant colleges. Those who enter them will emerge better qualified to play a productive role in American society.

A new national Work-Training Program operated by the Department of Labor will provide work and training for 200,000 American men and women between the ages of 16 and 21. This will be developed through state and local governments and nonprofit agencies.

Hundreds of thousands of young Americans badly need the experience, the income, and the sense of purpose which useful full or part-time work can bring. For them such work may mean the difference between finishing school or dropping out. Vital community activities from hospitals and playgrounds to libraries and settlement houses are suffering because there are not enough people to staff them.

We are simply bringing these needs together.

A new national Work-Study Program operated by the Department of Health, Education, and Welfare will provide federal funds for part-time jobs for 140,000 young Americans who do not go to college because they cannot afford it.

There is no more senseless waste than the waste of the brainpower and skill of those who are kept from college by economic circumstance. Under this program they will, in a great American tradition, be able to work their way through school.

They and the country will be richer for it.

Second, through a new Community Action Program we intend to strike at poverty at its source—in the streets of our cities and on the farms of our countryside among the very young and the impoverished old.

This program asks men and women throughout the country to prepare long-range plans for the attack on poverty in their own local communities.

These are not plans prepared in Washington and imposed upon hundreds of different situations.

They are based on the fact that local citizens best understand their own problems, and know best how to deal with those problems.

These plans will be local plans striking at the many unfilled needs which underlie poverty in each community, not just one or two. Their components and emphasis will differ as needs differ.

These plans will be local plans calling upon all the resources available to the community—federal and state, local and private, human and material.

And when these plans are approved by the Office of Economic Opportunity, the federal government will finance up to 90 percent of the additional cost for the first two years.

The most enduring strength of our nation is the huge reservoir of talent, initiative, and leadership which exists at every level of our society.

Through the Community Action Program we call upon this, our greatest strength, to overcome our greatest weakness.

Third, I ask for the authority to recruit and train skilled volunteers for the war against poverty.

Thousands of Americans have volunteered to serve the needs of other lands.

They should have that chance to serve the needs of their own land.

Thousands more want the chance to serve the needs of their own land.

They should have that chance.

Among older people who have retired, as well as among the young, among women as well as men, there are many Americans who are ready to enlist in our war against poverty.

They have skills and dedication. They are badly needed.

If the state requests them, if the community needs and will use them, we will recruit and train them and give them the chance to serve.

Fourth, we intend to create new opportunities for certain hard-hit groups to break out of the pattern of poverty.

Through a new program of loans and guarantees we can provide incentives to those who will employ the unemployed.

Through programs of work and retraining for unemployed fathers and mothers we can help them support their families in dignity while preparing themselves for new work.

Through funds to purchase needed land, organize cooperatives, and create new and adequate family farms we can help those whose life on the land has been a struggle without hope.

Fifth, I do not intend that the war against poverty become a series of uncoordinated and unrelated efforts—that it perish for lack of leadership and direction.

Therefore this bill creates, in the executive office of the president, a new Office of Economic Opportunity. Its director will be my personal chief of staff for the war against poverty. I intend to appoint Sargent Shriver to this post.

He will be directly responsible for these new programs. He will work with and through existing agencies of the government.

This program—the Economic Opportunity Act—is the foundation of our war against poverty. But it does not stand alone.

For the past three years this government has advanced a number of new proposals which strike at important areas of need and distress. I ask the Congress to extend those which are already in action, and to establish those which have already been proposed.

There are programs to help badly distressed areas such as the Area Redevelopment Act, and the legislation now being prepared to help Appalachia.

There are programs to help those without training find a place in today's complex society—such as the Manpower Development Training Act and the Vocational Education Act for youth.

There are programs to protect those who are specially vulnerable to the ravages of poverty—hospital insurance for the elderly, protection for migration farm workers, a food stamp program for the needy, coverage for millions not now protected by a minimum wage, new and expanded unemployment benefits for men out of work, a housing and community development bill for those seeking decent homes.

Finally there are programs which help the entire country, such as aid to education which, by raising the quality of schooling available to every American child, will give a new chance for knowledge to the children of the poor.

I ask immediate action on all these programs.

What you are being asked to consider is not a simple or an easy program. But poverty is not a simple or an easy enemy.

It cannot be driven from the land by a single attack on a single front. Were this so we would have conquered poverty long ago.

Nor can it be conquered by government alone.

For decades American labor and American business, private institutions and private individuals have been engaged in strengthening our economy and offering new opportunity to those in need.

We need their help, their support, and their full participation.

Through this program we offer new incentives and new opportunities for cooperation, so that all the energy of our nation, not merely the efforts of government, can be brought to bear on our common enemy.

Today, for the first time in our history, we have the power to strike away the barriers to full participation in our society. Having the power, we have the duty.

The Congress is charged by the constitution to "provide . . . for the general welfare of the United States." Our present abundance is a measure of its success in fulfilling that duty. Now Congress is being asked to extend that welfare to all our people.

The president of the United States is president of all the people in every section of the country. But this office also holds a special responsibility to the distressed and disinherited, the hungry and the hopeless of this abundant nation.

It is in pursuit of that special responsibility that I submit this message to you today.

The new program I propose is within our means. Its cost of 970 million dollars is one percent of our national budget—and every dollar I am requesting for this program is already included in the budget I sent to Congress in January.

But we cannot measure its importance by its cost.

For it charts an entirely new course of hope for our people.

We are fully aware that this program will not eliminate all the poverty in America in a few months or a few years. Poverty is deeply rooted and its causes are many.

But this program will show the way to new opportunities for millions of our fellow citizens.

It will provide a lever with which we can begin to open the door to our prosperity for those who have been kept outside.

It will also give us the chance to test our weapons, to try our energy and ideas and imagination for the many battles yet to come. As conditions change, and as experience illuminates our difficulties, we will be prepared to modify our strategy.

And this program is much more than a beginning.

Rather it is a commitment. It is a total commitment by this president, and this Congress, and this nation, to pursue victory over the most ancient of mankind's enemies.

On many historic occasions the president has requested from Congress the authority to move against forces which were endangering the well-being of our country.

This is such an occasion.

On similar occasions in the past we have often been called upon to wage war against foreign enemies which threatened our freedom. Today we are asked to declare war on a domestic enemy which threatens the strength of our nation and the welfare of our people.

If we now move forward against this enemy—if we can bring to the challenges of peace the same determination and strength which has brought us victory in war—then this day and this Congress will have won a secure and honorable place in the history of the nation, and the enduring gratitude of generations of Americans yet to come.

The Great Society

Ann Arbor, Michigan

May 22, 1964

THE MAIN DOMESTIC GOAL of Johnson's administration was the establishment of what he called "the Great Society," a new social order that would go beyond the New Deal to guarantee "abundance and liberty for all" and "an end to poverty and injustice." America's growing wealth would be rationally deployed to better the lives of all Americans through an unprecedented series of progressive reforms, including federal funding of medical care, antipoverty measures, and educational improvement. He outlined his ideas in this commencement address before a crowd of 80,000 at the University of Michigan.

After the 20-minute speech, Johnson was euphoric. It was one of his more successful performances—he was interrupted by applause at least 27 times—and the one, he believed, in which he finally separated himself from the Kennedy legacy.

It is a great pleasure to be here today. This university has been coeducational since 1870, but I do not believe it was on the basis of your accomplishments that a Detroit high school girl said, "In choosing a college, you first have to decide whether you want a coeducational school or an educational school."

Well, we can find both here at Michigan, although perhaps at different hours.

I came out here today very anxious to meet the Michigan student whose father told a friend of mine that his son's education had been a real value. It stopped his mother from bragging about him.

I have come today from the turmoil of your capital to the tranquility of your campus to speak about the future of your country.

The purpose of protecting the life of our nation and preserving the liberty of our citizens is to pursue the happiness of our people. Our success in that pursuit is the test of our success as a nation.

For a century we labored to settle and to subdue a continent. For half a century we called upon unbounded invention and untiring industry to create an order of plenty for all of our people.

The challenge of the next half century is whether we have the wisdom to use that wealth to enrich and elevate our national life, and to advance the quality of our American civilization.

Your imagination, your initiative, and your indignation will determine whether we build a society where progress is the servant of our needs, or a society where old values and new visions are buried under unbridled growth. For in your time we have the opportunity to move not only toward the rich society and the powerful society, but upward to the Great Society.

The Great Society rests on abundance and liberty for all. It demands an end to poverty and racial injustice, to which we are totally committed in our time. But that is just the beginning.

The Great Society is a place where every child can find knowledge to enrich his mind and to enlarge his talents. It is a place where leisure is a welcome chance to build and reflect, not a feared cause of boredom and restlessness. It is a place where the city of man serves not only the needs of the body and the demands of commerce but the desire for beauty and the hunger for community.

It is a place where man can renew contact with nature. It is a place which honors creation for its own sake and for what it adds to the understanding of the race. It is a place where men are more concerned with the quality of their goals than the quantity of their goods.

But most of all, the Great Society is not a safe harbor, a resting place, a final objective, a finished work. It is a challenge constantly renewed, beckoning us toward a destiny where the meaning of our lives matches the marvelous products of our labor.

So I want to talk to you today about three places where we begin to build the Great Society—in our cities, in our countryside, and in our classrooms.

Many of you will live to see the day, perhaps 50 years from now, when there will be

400 million Americans—four-fifths of them in urban areas. In the remainder of this century urban population will double, city land will double, and we will have to build homes, highways, and facilities equal to all those built since this country was first settled. So in the next 40 years we must rebuild the entire urban United States.

Aristotle said: "Men come together in cities in order to live, but they remain together in order to live the good life." It is harder and harder to live the good life in American cities today.

The catalog of ills is long: there is the decay of the centers and the despoiling of the suburbs. There is not enough housing for our people or transportation for our traffic. Open land is vanishing and old landmarks are violated.

Worst of all expansion is eroding the precious and time-honored values of community with neighbors and communion with nature. The loss of these values breeds loneliness and boredom and indifference.

Our society will never be great until our cities are great. Today the frontier of imagination and innovation is inside those cities and not beyond their borders.

New experiments are already going on. It will be the task of your generation to make the American city a place where future generations will come, not only to live but to live the good life.

I understand that if I stayed here tonight I would see that Michigan students are really doing their best to live the good life.

This is the place where the Peace Corps was started. It is inspiring to see how all of you, while you are in this country, are trying so hard to live at the level of the people.

A second place where we begin to build the Great Society is in our countryside. We have always prided ourselves on being not only America the strong and America the free, but America the beautiful. Today that beauty is in danger. The water we drink, the food we eat, the very air that we breathe, are threatened with pollution. Our parks are overcrowded, our seashores overburdened. Green fields and dense forests are disappearing.

A few years ago we were greatly concerned about the "Ugly American." Today we must act to prevent an ugly America.

For once the battle is lost, once our natural splendor is destroyed, it can never be recaptured. And once man can no longer walk with beauty or wonder at nature his spirit will wither and his sustenance be wasted.

A third place to build the Great Society is in the classrooms of America. There your children's lives will be shaped. Our society will not be great until every young mind is set free to scan the farthest reaches of thought and imagination. We are still far from that goal.

Today, eight million adult Americans, more than the entire population of Michigan, have not finished five years of school. Nearly 20 million have not finished eight years of school. Nearly 54 million—more than one-quarter of all America—have not even finished high school.

Each year more than 100,000 high school graduates, with proved ability, do not enter college because they cannot afford it. And if we cannot educate today's youth, what will we do in 1970 when elementary school enrollment will be five million greater than 1960? And high school enrollment will rise by five million. College enrollment will increase by more than three million.

In many places, classrooms are overcrowded and curricula are outdated. Most of our qualified teachers are underpaid, and many of our paid teachers are unqualified. So we must give every child a place to sit and a teacher to learn from. Poverty must not be a bar to learning, and learning must offer an escape from poverty.

But more classrooms and more teachers are not enough. We must seek an educational system which grows in excellence as it grows in size. This means better training for our teachers. It means preparing youth to enjoy their hours of leisure as well as their hours of labor. It means exploring new techniques of teaching, to find new ways to stimulate the love of learning and the capacity for creation.

These are three of the central issues of the Great Society. While our government has many programs directed at those issues, I do not pretend that we have the full answer to those problems.

But I do promise this: We are going to assemble the best thought and the broadest knowledge from all over the world to find those answers for America. I intend to establish working groups to prepare a series of White House conferences and meetings—on the cities, on natural beauty, on the quality of education, and on other emerging challenges. And from these meetings and from this inspiration and from these studies we will begin to set our course toward the Great Society.

The solution to these problems does not rest on a massive program in Washington, nor can it rely solely on the strained resources of local authority. They require us to create new concepts of cooperation, a creative federalism, between the national capital and the leaders of local communities.

Woodrow Wilson once wrote: "Every man sent out from his university should be a man of his nation as well as a man of his time."

Within your lifetime powerful forces, already loosed, will take us toward a way of life beyond the realm of our experience, almost beyond the bounds of our imagination.

For better or for worse, your generation has been appointed by history to deal with those problems and to lead America toward a new age. You have the chance never before afforded to any people in any age. You can help build a society where the demands of morality, and the needs of the spirit, can be realized in the life of the nation.

So, will you join in the battle to give every citizen the full equality which God enjoins and the law requires, whatever his belief, or race, or the color of his skin?

Will you join in the battle to give every citizen an escape from the crushing weight of poverty?

Will you join in the battle to make it possible for all nations to live in enduring peace—as neighbors and not as mortal enemies?

Will you join in the battle to build the Great Society, to prove that our material progress is only the foundation on which we will build a richer life of mind and spirit?

There are those timid souls who say this battle cannot be won; that we are condemned to a soulless wealth. I do not agree. We have the power to shape the civilization that we want. But we need your will, your labor, your hearts, if we are to build that kind of society.

Those who came to this land sought to build more than just a new country. They sought a new world. So I have come here today to your campus to say that you can make their vision our reality. So let us from this moment begin our work so that in the future men will look back and say: It was then, after a long and weary way, that man turned the exploits of his genius to the full enrichment of his life.

Thank you. Good-bye.

We Shall Overcome

Washington, D.C.
March 15, 1965

JOHNSON and his advisers were drafting what was to become the Voting Rights Act of 1965 when the issue of black voting rights suddenly came to national attention. The Southern Christian Leadership Conference, led by Martin Luther King Jr., had chosen Selma, Alabama, as the site of nonviolent protest marches against the general abridgment of voting rights for blacks throughout the South. Alabama police used tear gas and cavalry charges to disperse the marchers—the scene was viewed by millions on the evening television news—and Gov. George Wallace refused to guarantee the marchers' safety from marauding groups of whites.

On March 15, Johnson went before the nation and both houses of Congress to announce the voting rights legislation in a speech that is regarded as one of his most eloquent. Doris Kearns Goodwin called the address "Lyndon Johnson at his best—homely, compassionate, audacious, and noble—[conveying] a hard, practical appeal and a strong moral statement. . . . [It] was that rare thing in politics, rarer still for Lyndon Johnson—a speech that shaped the course of events. For once, Americans would honor him for a greatness of spirit as well as a mastery of technique. For on this issue he was more than a giver of gifts, he had become a moral leader."

Four days later Johnson ordered the Alabama National Guard to protect the marchers, who left for Montgomery the next day.

I speak tonight for the dignity of man and the destiny of democracy.

I urge every member of both parties, Americans of all religions and of all colors, from every section of this country, to join me in that cause.

At times history and fate meet at a single time in a single place to shape a turning point in man's unending search for freedom. So it was at Lexington and Concord. So it was a century ago at Appomattox. So it was last week in Selma, Alabama.

There, long-suffering men and women peacefully protested the denial of their rights as Americans. Many were brutally assaulted. One good man, a man of God, was killed.

There is no cause for pride in what has happened in Selma. There is no cause for self-satisfaction in the long denial of equal rights of millions of Americans. But there is cause for hope and for faith in our democracy in what is happening here tonight.

For the cries of pain and the hymns and protests of oppressed people have summoned into convocation all the majesty of this great government—the government of the greatest nation on earth.

Our mission is at once the oldest and the most basic of this country: to right wrong, to do justice, to serve man.

In our time we have come to live with moments of great crisis. Our lives have been marked with debate about great issues; issues of war and peace, issues of prosperity and depression. But rarely in any time does an issue lay bare the secret heart of America itself. Rarely are we met with a challenge, not to our growth or abundance, our welfare or our security, but rather to the values and the purposes and the meaning of our beloved nation.

The issue of equal rights for American Negroes is such an issue. And should we defeat every enemy, should we double our wealth and conquer the stars, and still be unequal to this issue, then we will have failed as a people and as a nation.

For with a country as with a person, "What is a man profited, if he shall gain the whole world, and lose his own soul?"

There is no Negro problem. There is no southern problem. There is no northern problem. There is only an American problem. And we are met here tonight as Americans—not as Democrats or Republicans—we are met here as Americans to solve that problem.

This was the first nation in the history of the world to be founded with a purpose. The great phrases of that purpose still sound in every American heart, North and South: "All men are created equal"—"government by consent of the governed"—"give me liberty or give me death." Well, those are not just clever words, or those are not just empty theories. In their name Americans have fought and died for two centuries, and tonight around the world they stand there as guardians of our liberty, risking their lives.

Those words are a promise to every citizen that he shall share in the dignity of man. This dignity cannot be found in a man's possessions; it cannot be found in his power, or in his position. It really rests on his right to be treated as a man equal in opportunity to all others. It says that he shall share in freedom, he shall choose his leaders, educate his children, and provide for his family according to his ability and his merits as a human being.

To apply any other test—to deny a man his hopes because of his color or race, his religion or the place of his birth—is not only to do injustice, it is to deny America and to dishonor the dead who gave their lives for American freedom.

The Right to Vote

Our fathers believed that if this noble view of the rights of man was to flourish, it must be rooted in democracy. The most basic right of all was the right to choose your own leaders. The history of this country, in large measure, is the history of the expansion of that right to all of our people.

Many of the issues of civil rights are very complex and most difficult. But about this there can and should be no argument. Every American citizen must have an equal right to vote. There is no reason which can excuse the denial of that right. There is no duty which weighs more heavily on us than the duty we have to ensure that right.

Yet the harsh fact is that in many places in this country men and women are kept from voting simply because they are Negroes.

Every device of which human ingenuity is capable has been used to deny this right. The Negro citizen may go to register only to be told that the day is wrong, or the hour is late, or the official in charge is absent. And if he persists, and if he manages to present himself to the registrar, he may be disqualified because he did not spell out his middle name or because he abbreviated a word on the application.

And if he manages to fill out an application he is given a test. The registrar is the sole judge of whether he passes this test. He may be asked to recite the entire Constitution, or explain the most complex provisions of state law. And even a college degree cannot be used to prove that he can read and write.

For the fact is that the only way to pass these barriers is to show a white skin.

Experience has clearly shown that the existing process of law cannot overcome systematic and ingenious discrimination. No law that we now have on the books—and I have helped to put three of them there—can ensure the right to vote when local officials are determined to deny it.

In such a case our duty must be clear to all of us. The Constitution says that no person shall be kept from voting because of his race or his color. We have all sworn an oath before God to support and to defend that Constitution. We must now act in obedience to that oath.

Guaranteeing the Right to Vote

Wednesday I will send to Congress a law designed to eliminate illegal barriers to the right to vote.

The broad principles of that bill will be in the hands of the Democratic and Republican leaders tomorrow. After they have reviewed it, it will come here formally as a bill. I am grateful for this opportunity to come here tonight at the invitation of the leadership to reason with my friends, to give them my views, and to visit with my former colleagues.

I have had prepared a more comprehensive analysis of the legislation which I had intended to transmit to the clerk tomorrow but which I will submit to the clerks tonight. But I want to really discuss with you now briefly the main proposals of this legislation.

This bill will strike down restrictions to voting in all elections—federal, state, and local—which have been used to deny Negroes the right to vote.

This bill will establish a simple, uniform standard which cannot be used, however ingenious the effort, to flout our Constitution.

It will provide for citizens to be registered by officials of the United States government if the state officials refuse to register them.

It will eliminate tedious, unnecessary lawsuits which delay the right to vote.

Finally, this legislation will ensure that properly registered individuals are not prohibited from voting.

I will welcome the suggestions from all of the members of Congress—I have no doubt that I will get some—on ways and means to strengthen this law and to make it effective. But experience has plainly shown that this is the only path to carry out the command of the Constitution.

To those who seek to avoid action by their national government in their own communities; who want to and who seek to maintain purely local control over elections, the answer is simple:

Open your polling places to all your people.

Allow men and women to register and vote whatever the color of their skin.

Extend the rights of citizenship to every citizen of this land.

The Need for Action

There is no Constitutional issue here. The command of the Constitution is plain.

There is no moral issue. It is wrong—deadly wrong—to deny any of your fellow Americans the right to vote in this country.

There is no issue of states rights or national rights. There is only the struggle for human rights.

I have not the slightest doubt what will be your answer.

The last time a president sent a civil rights bill to the Congress it contained a provision to protect voting rights in federal elections. That civil rights bill was passed after eight long months of debate. And when that bill came to my desk from the Congress for my signature, the heart of the voting provision had been eliminated.

This time, on this issue, there must be no delay, no hesitation and no compromise with our purpose.

We cannot, we must not, refuse to protect the right of every American to vote in every election that he may desire to participate in. And we ought not and we cannot and we must not wait another eight months before we get a bill. We have already waited a hundred years and more, and the time for waiting is gone.

So I ask you to join me in working long hours—nights and weekends, if necessary—to pass this bill. And I don't make that request

lightly. For from the window where I sit with the problems of our country I recognize that outside this chamber is the outraged conscience of a nation, the grave concern of many nations, and the harsh judgment of history on our acts.

We Shall Overcome

But even if we pass this bill, the battle will not be over. What happened in Selma is part of a far larger movement which reaches into every section and state of America. It is the effort of American Negroes to secure for themselves the full blessings of American life.

Their cause must be our cause too. Because it is not just Negroes, but really it is all of us, who must overcome the crippling legacy of bigotry and injustice.

And we shall overcome.

As a man whose roots go deeply into Southern soil I know how agonizing racial feelings are. I know how difficult it is to reshape the attitudes and the structure of our society.

But a century has passed, more than a hundred years, since the Negro was freed. And he is not fully free tonight.

It was more than a hundred years ago that Abraham Lincoln, a great president of another party, signed the Emancipation Proclamation, but emancipation is a proclamation and not a fact.

A century has passed, more than a hundred years, since equality was promised. And yet the Negro is not equal.

A century has passed since the day of promise. And the promise is unkept.

The time of justice has now come. I tell you that I believe sincerely that no force can hold it back. It is right in the eyes of man and God that it should come. And when it does, I think that day will brighten the lives of every American.

For Negroes are not the only victims. How many white children have gone uneducated, how many white families have lived in stark poverty, how many white lives have been scarred by fear, because we have wasted our energy and our substance to maintain the barriers of hatred and terror?

So I say to all of you here, and to all in the nation tonight, that those who appeal to you to hold on to the past do so at the cost of denying you your future.

This great, rich, restless country can offer opportunity and education and hope to all: black and white, North and South, sharecropper and city dweller. These are the enemies: poverty, ignorance, disease. They are the enemies and not our fellow man, not our neighbor. And these enemies too, poverty, disease, and ignorance, we shall overcome.

An American Problem

Now let none of us in any sections look with prideful righteousness on the troubles in another section, or on the problems of our neighbors. There is really no part of America where the promise of equality has been fully kept. In Buffalo as well as in Birmingham, in Philadelphia as well as in Selma, Americans are struggling for the fruits of freedom.

This is one nation. What happens in Selma or in Cincinnati is a matter of legitimate concern to every American. But let each of us look within our own hearts and our own communities, and let each of us put our shoulder to the wheel to root out injustice wherever it exists.

As we meet here in this peaceful, historic chamber tonight, men from the South, some of whom were at Iwo Jima, men from the North who have carried Old Glory to far corners of the world and brought it back without a stain on it, men from the East and from the West, are all fighting together without regard to religion, or color, or region, in Vietnam. Men from every region fought for us across the world 20 years ago.

And in these common dangers and these common sacrifices the South made its contribution of honor and gallantry no less than any other region of the great republic—and in some instances, a great many of them, more.

And I have not the slightest doubt that good men from everywhere in this country, from the Great Lakes to the Gulf of Mexico, from the Golden Gate to the harbors along the Atlantic, will rally together now in this cause to vindicate the freedom of all Americans. For all of us owe this duty; and I believe that all of us will respond to it.

Your president makes that request of every American.

Progress through the Democratic Process

The real hero of this struggle is the American Negro. His actions and protests, his courage to risk safety and even to risk his life, have awakened the conscience of this nation. His demonstrations have been designed to call attention to injustice, designed to provoke change, designed to stir reform.

He has called upon us to make good the promise of America. And who among us can say that we would have made the same progress were it not for his persistent bravery, and his faith in American democracy.

For at the real heart of battle for equality is a deep-seated belief in the democratic process. Equality depends not on the force of arms or tear gas but upon the force of moral right; not on recourse to violence but on respect for law and order.

There have been many pressures upon your president and there will be others as the days come and go. But I pledge you tonight that we intend to fight this battle where it should be fought: in the courts, and in the Congress, and in the hearts of men.

We must preserve the right of free speech and the right of free assembly. But the right of free speech does not carry with it, as has been said, the right to holler fire in a crowded theater. We must preserve the right to free assembly, but free assembly does not carry with it the right to block public thoroughfares to traffic.

We do have a right to protest, and a right to march under conditions that do not infringe the constitutional rights of our neighbors. And I intend to protect all those rights as long as I am permitted to serve in this office.

We will guard against violence, knowing it strikes from our hands the very weapons which we seek—progress, obedience to law, and belief in American values.

In Selma as elsewhere we seek and pray for peace. We seek order. We seek unity. But we will not accept the peace of stifled rights, or the order imposed by fear, or the unity that stifles protest. For peace cannot be purchased at the cost of liberty.

In Selma tonight, as in every—and we had a good day there—as in every city, we are working for just and peaceful settlement. We must all remember that after this speech I am making tonight, after the police and the FBI and the marshals have all gone, and after you have promptly passed this bill, the people of Selma and the other cities of the nation must still live and work together. And when the attention of the nation has gone elsewhere they must try to heal the wounds and to build a new community.

This cannot be easily done on a battleground of violence, as the history of the South itself shows. It is in recognition of this that men of both races have shown such an outstandingly impressive responsibility in recent days—last Tuesday, again today.

Rights Must Be Opportunities

The bill that I am presenting to you will be known as a civil rights bill. But, in a larger sense, most of the program I am recommending is a civil rights program. Its object is to open the city of hope to all people of all races.

Because all Americans must have the right to vote. And we are going to give them that right.

All Americans must have the privileges of citizenship regardless of race. And they are going to have those privileges of citizenship regardless of race.

But I would like to caution you and remind you that to exercise these privileges takes much more than just legal right. It requires a trained mind and a healthy body. It requires a decent home, and the chance to find a job, and the opportunity to escape from the clutches of poverty.

Of course, people cannot contribute to the nation if they are never taught to read or write, if their bodies are stunted from hunger, if their sickness goes untended, if their life is spent in hopeless poverty just drawing a welfare check.

So we want to open the gates to opportunity. But we are also going to give all our people, black and white, the help that they need to walk through those gates.

The Purpose of This Government

My first job after college was as a teacher in Cotulla, Texas, in a small Mexican-American school. Few of them could speak English, and I couldn't speak much Spanish. My students were poor and they often came to class without breakfast, hungry. They knew even in their youth the pain of prejudice. They never seemed to know why people disliked them. But they knew it was so, because I saw it in their eyes. I often walked home late in the afternoon, after the classes were finished, wishing there was more that I could do. But all I knew was to teach them the little that I knew, hoping that it might help them against the hardships that lay ahead.

Somehow you never forget what poverty and hatred can do when you see its scars on the hopeful face of a young child.

I never thought then, in 1928, that I would be standing here in 1965. It never even occurred to me in my fondest dreams that I might have the chance to help the sons and daughters of those students and to help people like them all over this country.

But now I do have that chance-and I'll let you in on a secret—I mean to use it. And I hope that you will use it with me.

This is the richest and most powerful country which ever occupied the globe. The might of past empires is little compared to ours. But I do not want to be the president who built empires, or sought grandeur, or extended dominion.

I want to be the president who educated young children to the wonders of their world. I want to be the president who helped to feed the hungry and to prepare them to be taxpayers instead of taxeaters.

I want to be the president who helped the poor to find their own way and who protected the right of every citizen to vote in every election.

I want to be the president who helped to end hatred among his fellow men and who promoted love among the people of all races and all regions and all parties.

I want to be the president who helped to end war among the brothers of this earth.

And so at the request of your beloved Speaker and the senator from Montana, the majority leader; the senator from Illinois, the minority leader; Mr. McCulloch, and other members of both parties, I came here tonight—not as President Roosevelt came down one time in person to veto a bonus bill, not as President Truman came down one time to urge the passage of a railroad bill—but I came down here to ask you to share this task with me and to share it with the people that we both work for. I want this to be the Congress, Republicans and Democrats alike, which did all these things for all these people.

Beyond this great chamber, out yonder in 50 states, are the people that we serve. Who can tell what deep and unspoken hopes are in their hearts tonight as they sit there and listen. We all can guess, from our own lives, how difficult they often find their own pursuit of happiness, how many problems each little family has. They look most of all to themselves for their futures. But I think that they also look to each of us.

Above the pyramid on the great seal of the United States it says—in Latin—"God has favored our undertaking."

God will not favor everything that we do. It is rather our duty to divine His will. But I cannot help believing that He truly understands and that He really favors the undertaking that we begin here tonight.

Peace Without Compromise

Baltimore, Maryland

April 7, 1965

WITHOUT THE VIETNAM WAR, as Johnson observed in his retirement, he would have been remembered as one of the great presidents for his domestic reforms. Because of it, he became a tragic figure. The cost of the war, which deepened under Kennedy and escalated rapidly after the Gulf of Tonkin Resolution by Congress in March 1965, crippled his Great Society programs and left a legacy of inflation and deficit spending.

In this speech at Johns Hopkins University, Johnson envisioned a Tennessee Valley Authority-style development of Vietnam's Mekong River delta—a massive agricultural project that Johnson assumed the Vietnamese would find irresistible—and called for unconditional discussions with the North Vietnamese. But a few days later Hanoi issued its conditions for peace, including the complete withdrawal of all U.S. troops from the south. Johnson responded by sending 50,000 more troops to Vietnam in late July.

Last week 17 nations sent their views to some two dozen countries having an interest in Southeast Asia. We are joining those 17 countries and stating our American policy tonight which we believe will contribute toward peace in this area of the world.

I have come here to review once again with my own people the views of the American government.

Tonight Americans and Asians are dying for a world where each people may choose its own path to change.

This is the principle for which our ancestors fought in the valleys of Pennsylvania. It is the principle for which our sons fight tonight in the jungles of Vietnam.

Vietnam is far away from this quiet campus. We have no territory there, nor do we seek any. The war is dirty and brutal and difficult. And some 400 young men, born into an America that is bursting with opportunity and promise, have ended their lives on Vietnam's steaming soil.

Why must we take this painful road?

Why must this nation hazard its ease, and its interest, and its power for the sake of a people so far away?

We fight because we must fight if we are to live in a world where every country can shape its own destiny. And only in such a world will our own freedom be finally secure.

This kind of world will never be built by bombs or bullets. Yet the infirmities of man are such that force must often precede reason, and the waste of war, the works of peace.

We wish that this were not so. But we must deal with the world as it is, if it is ever to be as we wish.

The Nature of the Conflict

The world as it is in Asia is not a serene or peaceful place.

The first reality is that North Vietnam has attacked the independent nation of South Vietnam. Its object is total conquest.

Of course, some of the people of South Vietnam are participating in attack on their own government. But trained men and supplies, orders and arms, flow in a constant stream from north to south.

This support is the heartbeat of the war.

And it is a war of unparalleled brutality. Simple farmers are the targets of assassination and kidnapping. Women and children are strangled in the night because their men are loyal to their government. And helpless villages are ravaged by sneak attacks. Large-scale raids are conducted on towns, and terror strikes in the heart of cities.

The confused nature of this conflict cannot mask the fact that it is the new face of an old enemy.

Over this war—and all Asia—is another reality: the deepening shadow of Communist China. The rulers in Hanoi are urged on by Peking. This is a regime which has destroyed freedom in Tibet, which has attacked India, and has been condemned by the United Nations for aggression in Korea. It is a nation which is helping the forces of violence in almost every continent. The contest in Vietnam is part of a wider pattern of aggressive purposes.

Why Are We in Vietnam?

Why are these realities our concern? Why are we in South Vietnam?

We are there because we have a promise to keep. Since 1954 every American president has offered support to the people of South Vietnam. We have helped to build, and we have helped to defend. Thus, over many years, we have made a national pledge to help South Vietnam defend its independence.

And I intend to keep that promise.

To dishonor that pledge, to abandon this small and brave nation to its enemies, and to the terror that must follow, would be an unforgivable wrong.

We are also there to strengthen world order. Around the globe, from Berlin to Thailand, are people whose well-being rests, in part, on the belief that they can count on us if they are attacked. To leave Vietnam to its fate would shake the confidence of all these people in the value of an American commitment and in the value of America's word. The result would be increased unrest and instability, and even wider war.

We are also there because there are great stakes in the balance. Let no one think for a moment that retreat from Vietnam would bring an end to conflict. The battle would be renewed in one country and then another. The central lesson of our time is that the appetite of aggression is never satisfied. To withdraw from one battlefield means only to prepare for the next. We must say in Southeast Asia—as we did in Europe—in the words of the Bible: "Hitherto shalt thou come, but no further."

There are those who say that all our effort there will be futile—that China's power is such that it is bound to dominate all Southeast Asia. But there is no end to that argument until all of the nations of Asia are swallowed up.

There are those who wonder why we have a responsibility there. Well, we have it there for the same reason that we have a responsibility for the defense of Europe. World War II was fought in both Europe and Asia, and when it ended we found ourselves with continued responsibility for the defense of freedom.

Our Objective in Vietnam

Our objective is the independence of South Vietnam, and its freedom from attack. We want nothing for ourselves—only that the people of South Vietnam be allowed to guide their own country in their own way.

We will do everything necessary to reach that objective. And we will do only what is absolutely necessary.

In recent months attacks on South Vietnam were stepped up. Thus, it became necessary for us to increase our response and to make attacks by air. This is not a change of purpose. It is a change in what we believe that purpose requires.

We do this in order to slow down aggression.

We do this to increase the confidence of the brave people of South Vietnam who have bravely borne this brutal battle for so many years with so many casualties.

And we do this to convince the leaders of North Vietnam—and all who seek to share their conquest—of a very simple fact:

We will not be defeated.

We will not grow tired.

We will not withdraw, either openly or under the cloak of a meaningless agreement.

We know that air attacks alone will not accomplish all of these purposes. But it is our best and prayerful judgment that they are a necessary part of the surest road to peace.

We hope that peace will come swiftly. But that is in the hands of others besides ourselves. And we must be prepared for a long continued conflict. It will require patience as well as bravery, the will to endure as well as the will to resist.

I wish it were possible to convince others with words of what we now find it necessary to say with guns and planes: Armed hostility is futile. Our resources are equal to any challenge. Because we fight for values and we fight for principles, rather than territory or colonies, our patience and our determination are unending.

Once this is clear, then it should also be clear that the only path for reasonable men is the path of peaceful settlement.

Such peace demands an independent South Vietnam—securely guaranteed and able to shape its own relationships to all others—free from outside interference—tied to no alliance—a military base for no other country.

These are the essentials of any final settlement.

We will never be second in the search for such a peaceful settlement in Vietnam.

There may be many ways to this kind of peace: in discussion or negotiation with the governments concerned; in large groups or in small ones; in the reaffirmation of old agreements or their strengthening with new ones.

We have stated this position over and over again, fifty times and more, to friend and foe alike. And we remain ready, with this purpose, for unconditional discussions.

And until that bright and necessary day of peace we will try to keep conflict from spreading. We have no desire to see thousands die in battle—Asians or Americans. We have no desire to devastate that which the people of North Vietnam have built with toil and sacrifice. We will use our power with restraint and with all the wisdom that we can command.

But we will use it.

This war, like most wars, is filled with terrible irony. For what do the people of North Vietnam want? They want what their neighbors also desire: food for their hunger; health for their bodies; a chance to learn; progress for their country; and an end to the bondage of material misery. And they would find all these things far more readily in peaceful association with others than in the endless course of battle.

A Cooperative Effort for Development

These countries of southeast Asia are homes for millions of impoverished people. Each day these people rise at dawn and struggle through until the night to wrestle existence from the soil. They are often wracked by disease, plagued by hunger, and death comes at the early age of 40.

Stability and peace do not come easily in such a land. Neither independence nor human dignity will ever be won, though, by arms alone. It also requires the work of peace. The American people have helped generously in times past in these works. Now there must be a much more massive effort to improve the life of man in that conflict-torn corner of our world.

The first step is for the countries of southeast Asia to associate themselves in a greatly expanded cooperative effort for development.

We would hope that North Vietnam would take its place in the common effort just as soon as peaceful cooperation is possible.

The United Nations is already actively engaged in development in this area. As far back as 1961 I conferred with our authorities in Vietnam in connection with their work there. And I would hope tonight that the Secretary General of the United Nations could use the prestige of his great office, and his deep knowledge of Asia, to initiate, as soon as possible, with the countries of that area, a plan for cooperation in increased development.

For our part I will ask the Congress to join in a billion dollar American investment in this effort as soon as it is underway.

And I would hope that all other industrialized countries, including the Soviet Union, will join in this effort to replace despair with hope, and terror with progress.

The task is nothing less than to enrich the hopes and the existence of more than a hundred million people. And there is much to be done.

The vast Mekong River can provide food and water and power on a scale to dwarf even our own TVA.

The wonders of modern medicine can be spread through villages where thousands die every year from lack of care.

Schools can be established to train people in the skills that are needed to manage the process of development.

And these objectives, and more, are within the reach of a cooperative and determined effort.

I also intend to expand and speed up a program to make available our farm surpluses to assist in feeding and clothing the needy Asia. We should not allow people to go hungry and wear rags while our own warehouses overflow with an abundance of wheat and corn, rice and cotton.

So I will very shortly name a special team of outstanding, patriotic, distinguished Americans to inaugurate our participation in these programs. This team will be headed by Mr. Eugene Black, the very able former president of the World Bank.

In areas that are still ripped by conflict, of course development will not be easy. Peace will be necessary for final success. But we cannot and must not wait for peace to begin this job.

The Dream of World Order

This will be a disorderly planet for a long time. In Asia, as elsewhere, the forces of the modern world are shaking old ways and uprooting ancient civilizations. There will be turbulence and struggle and even violence. Great social change—as we see in our own country now—does not always come without conflict.

We must also expect that nations will on occasion be in dispute with us. It may be because we are rich, or powerful; or because we have made some mistakes; or because they honestly fear our intentions. However, no nation need ever fear that we desire their land, or to impose our will, or to dictate their institutions.

But we will always oppose the effort of one nation to conquer another nation.

We will do this because our own security is at stake.

But there is more to it than that. For our generation has a dream. It is a very old dream. But we have the power and now we have the opportunity to make that dream come true.

For centuries nations have struggled among each other. But we dream of a world where disputes are settled by law and reason. And we will try to make it so.

For most of history men have hated and killed one another in battle. But we dream of an end to war. And we will try to make it so.

For all existence most men have lived in poverty, threatened by hunger. But we dream of a world where all are fed and charged with hope. And we will help to make it so.

The ordinary men and women of North Vietnam and South Vietnam—of China and India—of Russia and America—are brave people. They are filled with the same proportions of hate and fear, of love and hope. Most of them want the same things for themselves and their families. Most of them do not want their sons to ever die in battle, or to see their homes, or the homes of others, destroyed.

Well, this can be their world yet. Man now has the knowledge—always before denied—to make this planet serve the real needs of the people who live on it.

I know this will not be easy. I know how difficult it is for reason to guide passion, and love to master hate. The complexities of this world do not bow easily to pure and consistent answers.

But the simple truths are there just the same. We must all try to follow them as best we can.

Conclusion

We often say how impressive power is. But I do not find it impressive at all. The guns and the bombs, the rockets and the warships, are all symbols of human failure. They are necessary symbols. They protect what we cherish. But they are witness to human folly.

A dam built across a great river is impressive.

In the countryside where I was born, and where I live, I have seen the night illuminated, and the kitchens warmed, and the homes heated, where once the cheerless night and the ceaseless cold held sway. And all this happened because electricity came to our area along the humming wires of the REA. Electrification of the countryside—yes, that, too, is impressive.

A rich harvest in a hungry land is impressive.

The sight of healthy children in a classroom is impressive.

These—not mighty arms—are the achievements which the American nation believes to be impressive.

And, if we are steadfast, the time may come when all other nations will also find it so.

Every night before I turn out the lights to sleep I ask myself this question: Have I done everything that I can do to unite this country? Have I done everything I can to help unite the world, to try to bring peace and hope to all the peoples of the world? Have I done enough?

Ask yourselves that question in your homes—and in this hall tonight. Have we, each of us, all done all we could? Have we done enough?

We may well be living in the time foretold many years ago when it was said: "I call heaven and earth to record this day against you, that I have set before you life and death, blessing and cursing: therefore choose life, that both thou and thy seed may live."

This generation of the world must choose: destroy or build, kill or aid, hate or understand.

We can do all these things on a scale never dreamed of before.

Well, we will choose life. In so doing we will prevail over the enemies within man, and over the natural enemies of all mankind.

Why Are We in Vietnam?

San Antonio, Texas
September 29, 1967

BY 1967 THE WAR—never formally declared by Congress—had created deep divisions in the nation. American military efforts in Vietnam were not yielding the kind of successes predicted by the administration, yet government officials continued to assure the increasingly skeptical public that the war was progressing satisfactorily. The president found it necessary to give repeated explanations of America's mission in Vietnam, as in this address before the National Legislative Conference.

I deeply appreciate this opportunity to appear before an organization whose members contribute every day such important work to the public affairs of our state and of our country.

This evening I came here to speak to you about Vietnam.

I do not have to tell you that our people are profoundly concerned about that struggle.

There are passionate convictions about the wisest course for our nation to follow. There are many sincere and patriotic Americans who harbor doubts about sustaining the commitment that three presidents and a half a million of our young men have made.

Doubt and debate are enlarged because the problems of Vietnam are quite complex. They are a mixture of political turmoil—of poverty—of religious and factional strife—of ancient servitude and modern longing for freedom. Vietnam is all of these things.

Vietnam is also the scene of a powerful aggression that is spurred by an appetite for conquest.

It is the arena where Communist expansionism is most aggressively at work in the world today—where it is crossing international frontiers in violation of international agreements; where it is killing and kidnapping; where it is ruthlessly attempting to bend free people to its will.

Into this mixture of subversion and war, of terror and hope, America has entered—with its material power and with its moral commitment.

Why?

Why should three presidents and the elected representatives of our people have chosen to defend this Asian nation more than 10,000 miles from American shores?

We cherish freedom—yes. We cherish self-determination for all people—yes. We abhor the political murder of any state by another, and the bodily murder of any people by gangsters of whatever ideology. And for 27 years—since the days of Lend-Lease—we have sought to strengthen free people against domination by aggressive foreign powers.

But the key to all that we have done is really our own security. At times of crisis—before asking Americans to fight and die to resist aggression in a foreign land—every American president has finally had to answer this question:

Is the aggression a threat—not only to the immediate victim—but to the United States of America and to the peace and security of the entire world of which we in America are a very vital part?

That is the question which Dwight Eisenhower and John Kennedy and Lyndon Johnson had to answer in facing the issue in Vietnam.

That is the question that the Senate of the United States answered by a vote of 82 to 1 when it ratified and approved the SEATO treaty in 1955, and to which the members of the United States Congress responded in a resolution that it passed in 1964 by a vote of 504 to 2: "the United States is, therefore, prepared, as the president determines, to take all necessary steps, including the use of armed force, to assist any member or protocol state of the Southeast Asia Collective Defense Treaty requesting assistance in defense of its freedom."

Those who tell us now that we should abandon our commitment—that securing South Vietnam from armed domination is not worth the price we are paying—must also answer this question. And the test they must meet is this: What would be the consequences of letting armed aggression against South Vietnam succeed? What would follow in the time ahead? What kind of world are they prepared to live in five months or five years from tonight?

For those who have borne the responsibility for decision during these past 10 years, the stakes to us have seemed clear—and have seemed high.

President Dwight Eisenhower said in 1959:

Strategically, South Vietnam's capture by the Communists would bring their power several hundred miles into a hitherto free region. The remaining countries in Southeast Asia would be menaced by a great flanking movement. The freedom of 12 million people would be lost immediately, and that of 150 million in adjacent lands would be seriously endangered. The loss of South Vietnam would set in motion a crumbling process that could, as it progressed, have grave consequences for us and for freedom.

And President John F. Kennedy said in 1962: "withdrawal in the case of Vietnam and the case of Thailand might mean a collapse of the entire area."

A year later, he reaffirmed that: "We are not going to withdraw from that effort. In my opinion, for us to withdraw from that effort would mean a collapse not only of South Vietnam, but Southeast Asia. So we are going to stay there," said President Kennedy.

This is not simply an American viewpoint, I would have you legislative leaders know. I am going to call the roll now of those who live in that part of the world—in the great arc of Asian and Pacific nations—and who bear the responsibility for leading their people, and the responsibility for the fate of their people.

The president of the Philippines had this to say:

Vietnam is the focus of attention now. . . . It may happen to Thailand or the Philippines, or anywhere, wherever there is misery, disease, ignorance. . . . For you to renounce your position of leadership in Asia is to allow the Red Chinese to gobble up all of Asia.

The foreign minister of Thailand said: "(The American) decision will go down in history as the move that prevented the world from having to face another major conflagration."

The prime minister of Australia said: "We are there because while Communist aggression persists the whole of Southeast Asia is threatened."

President Park of Korea said:

For the first time in our history, we decided to dispatch our combat troops overseas . . . because in our belief any aggression against the republic of Vietnam represented a direct and grave menace against the security and peace of free Asia, and therefore directly jeopardized the very security and freedom of our own people.

The prime minister of Malaysia warned his people that if the United States pulled out of South Vietnam, it would go to the Communists, and after that, it would be only a matter of time until they moved against neighboring states.

The prime minister of New Zealand said: "We can thank God that America at least regards aggression in Asia with the same concern as it regards aggression in Europe—and is prepared to back up its concern with action."

The prime minister of Singapore said: "I feel the fate of Asia—South and Southeast Asia—will be decided in the next few years by what happens in Vietnam."

I cannot tell you tonight as your president—with certainty—that a Communist conquest of South Vietnam would be followed by a Communist conquest of Southeast Asia. But I do know there are North Vietnamese troops in Laos. I do know that there are North Vietnamese-trained guerrillas tonight in northeast Thailand. I do know that there are Communist-supported guerrilla forces operating in Burma. And a Communist coup was barely averted in Indonesia, the fifth largest nation in the world.

So your American president cannot tell you—with certainty—that a Southeast Asia dominated by Communist power would bring a third world war much closer to terrible reality. One could hope that this would not be so.

But all that we have learned in this tragic century strongly suggests to me that it would be so. As president of the United States, I am not prepared to gamble on the chance that it is not so. I am not prepared to risk the security—indeed, the survival—of this American nation on mere hope and wishful thinking. I am convinced that by seeing this struggle through now, we are greatly reducing the chances of a much larger war—perhaps a nuclear war. I would rather stand in Vietnam, in our time, and by meeting this danger now, and facing up to it, thereby reduce the danger for our children and for our grandchildren.

I want to turn now to the struggle in Vietnam itself.

There are questions about this difficult war that must trouble every really thoughtful person. I am going to put some of these questions. And I am going to give you the very best answers that I can give you.

First, are the Vietnamese—with our help, and that of their other allies—really making any progress? Is there a forward movement? The reports I see make it clear that there is. Certainly there is a positive movement toward constitutional government. Thus far the Vietnamese have met the political schedule that they laid down in January 1966.

The people wanted an elected, responsive government. They wanted it strongly enough to brave a vicious campaign of Communist terror and assassination to vote for it. It has been said that they killed more civilians in four weeks trying to keep them from voting before the election than our American bombers have killed in the big cities of North Vietnam in bombing military targets.

On November 1, subject to the action, of course, of the Constituent Assembly, an elected government will be inaugurated and an elected senate and legislature will be installed. Their responsibility is clear: To answer the desires of the South Vietnamese people for self-determination and for peace, for an attack on corruption, for economic development, and for social justice.

There is progress in the war itself, steady progress considering the war that we are fighting; rather dramatic progress considering the situation that actually prevailed when we sent our troops there in 1965; when we intervened to prevent the dismemberment of the country by the Vietcong and the North Vietnamese.

The campaigns of the last year drove the enemy from many of their major interior bases. The military victory almost within Hanoi's grasp in 1965 has now been denied them. The grip of the Vietcong on the people is being broken.

Since our commitment of major forces in July 1965 the proportion of the population living under Communist control has been reduced to well under 20 percent. Tonight the secure proportion of the population has grown from about 45 percent to 65 percent—and in the contested areas, the tide continues to run with us.

But the struggle remains hard. The South Vietnamese have suffered severely, as have we—particularly in the First Corps area in the north, where the enemy has mounted his heaviest attacks, and where his lines of communication to North Vietnam are shortest. Our casualties in the war have reached about 13,500 killed in action, and about 85,000 wounded. Of those 85,000 wounded, we thank God that 79,000 of the 85,000 have been returned, or will return to duty shortly. Thanks to our great American medical science and the helicopter.

I know there are other questions on your minds, and on the minds of many sincere, troubled Americans: "Why not negotiate now?" so many ask me. The answer is that we and our South Vietnamese allies are wholly prepared to negotiate tonight.

I am ready to talk with Ho Chi Minh, and other chiefs of state concerned, tomorrow.

I am ready to have Secretary [Dean] Rusk meet with their foreign minister tomorrow.

I am ready to send a trusted representative of America to any spot on this earth to talk in public or private with a spokesman of Hanoi.

We have twice sought to have the issue of Vietnam dealt with by the United Nations—and twice Hanoi has refused.

Our desire to negotiate peace—through the United Nations or out—has been made very, very clear to Hanoi—directly and many times through third parties.

As we have told Hanoi time and time and time again, the heart of the matter is really this: The United States is willing to stop all aerial and naval bombardment of North Vietnam when this will lead promptly to productive discussions. We, of course, assume that while discussions proceed, North Vietnam would not take advantage of the bombing cessation or limitation.

But Hanoi has not accepted any of these proposals.

So it is by Hanoi's choice—and not ours, and not the rest of the world's—that the war continues.

Why, in the face of military and political progress in the South, and the burden of our bombing in the North, do they insist and persist with the war?

From many sources the answer is the same. They still hope that the people of the United States will not see this struggle through to the very end. As one Western diplomat reported to me only this week—he had just been in Hanoi—"They believe their staying power is greater than ours and that they can't lose." A visitor from a Communist capital had this to say: They expect the war to be long, and that the Americans in the end will be defeated by a breakdown in morale, fatigue, and psychological factors." The premier of North Vietnam said as far back as 1962: "Americans do not like long, inconclusive war. . . . Thus we are sure to win in the end."

Are the North Vietnamese right about us?

I think not. No. I think they are wrong. I think it is the common failing to totalitarian regimes that they cannot really understand the nature of our democracy:

—They mistake dissent for disloyalty.
—They mistake restlessness for a rejection of policy.
—They mistake a few committees for a country.
—They misjudge individual speeches for public policy.

They are no better suited to judge the strength and perseverance of America than the Nazi and the Stalinist propagandists were able to judge it. It is a tragedy that they must discover these qualities in the American people, and discover them through a bloody war.

And, soon or late, they will discover them.

In the meantime, it shall be our policy to continue to seek negotiations—confident that reason will some day prevail; that Hanoi will realize that it just can never win; that it will turn away from fighting and start building for its own people.

Since World War II, this nation has met and has mastered many challenges—challenges in Greece and Turkey, in Berlin, in Korea, in Cuba.

We met them because brave men were willing to risk their lives for their nation's security. And braver men have never lived than those who carry our colors in Vietnam at this very hour.

The price of these efforts, of course, has been heavy. But the price of not having made them at all, not having seen them through, in my judgment would have been vastly greater.

Our goal has been the same—in Europe, in Asia, in our own hemisphere. It has been—and it is now—peace.

And peace cannot be secured by wishes; peace cannot be preserved by noble words and pure intentions. "Enduring peace," Franklin D. Roosevelt said, "cannot be bought at the cost of other people's freedom."

The late President Kennedy put it precisely in November 1961, when he said: "We are neither warmongers nor appeasers, neither hard nor soft. We are Americans determined to defend the frontiers of freedom by an honorable peace if peace is possible but by arms if arms are used against us."

The true peacekeepers in the world tonight are not those who urge us to retire from the field in Vietnam—who tell us to try to find the quickest, cheapest exit from that tormented land, no matter what the consequences to us may be.

The true peacekeepers are those men who stand out there on the DMZ at this very hour, taking the worst that the enemy can give. The true peacekeepers are the soldiers who are breaking the terrorists' grip around the villages of Vietnam—the civilians who are bringing medical care and food and education to people who have already suffered a generation of war.

And so I report to you that we are going to continue to press forward. Two things we must do. Two things we shall do.

First, we must not mislead the enemy. Let him not think that debate and dissent will produce wavering and withdrawal. For I can assure you they won't. Let him not think that protests will produce surrender. Because they won't. Let him not think that he will wait us out. For he won't.

Second, we will provide all that our brave men require to do the job that must be done. And that job is going to be done.

These gallant men have our prayers—have our thanks—have our heart-felt praise—and our deepest gratitude.

Let the world know that the keepers of peace will endure through every trial—and that with the full backing of their countrymen, they are going to prevail.

Announcement of Refusal to Seek Reelection

Washington, D.C.

March 31, 1968

DEFEATED BY the war, which took a dismal turn after the Viet Cong mounted a massive offensive in January 1968, and facing continuing unrest at home, Johnson decided not to seek the Democratic presidential nomination in 1968. His decision was made public in a nationally televised address that also announced an unconditional end to the bombing of North Vietnam.

 The news hit like a bombshell—Johnson had not even told his cabinet before the speech began. Though many people had hoped that he would step down, few expected it. Not surprisingly, public sympathy for the president, who had appeared exhausted and beaten on camera, rose significantly after the speech. As journalist Tom Wicker noted, Johnson's most moving speeches were "his first and last. . . . Johnson came into office seeking a great society in America and found instead an ugly little war that consumed him."

Tonight I want to speak to you of peace in Vietnam and Southeast Asia.

No other question so preoccupies our people. No other dream so absorbs the 250 million human beings who live in that part of the world. No other goal motivates American policy in Southeast Asia.

For years, representatives of our government and others have traveled the world—seeking to find a basis for peace talks.

Since last September, they have carried the offer that I made public at San Antonio.

That offer was this:

That the United States would stop its bombardment of North Vietnam when that would lead promptly to productive discussions—and that we would assume that North Vietnam would not take military advantage of our restraint.

Hanoi denounced this offer, both privately and publicly. Even while the search for peace was going on, North Vietnam rushed their preparations for a savage assault on the people, the government, and the allies of South Vietnam.

Their attack—during the Tet holidays—failed to achieve its principal objectives.

It did not collapse the elected government of South Vietnam or shatter its army—as the Communists had hoped.

It did not produce a "general uprising" among the people of the cities as they had predicted.

The Communists were unable to maintain control of any of the more than 30 cities that they attacked. And they took very heavy casualties.

But they did compel the South Vietnamese and their allies to move certain forces from the countryside into the cities.

They caused widespread disruption and suffering. Their attacks, and the battles that followed, made refugees of half a million human beings.

The Communists may renew their attack any day.

They are, it appears, trying to make 1968 the year of decision in South Vietnam—the year that brings, if not final victory or defeat, at least a turning point in the struggle.

This much is clear:

If they do mount another round of heavy attacks, they will not succeed in destroying the fighting power of South Vietnam and its allies.

But tragically, this is also clear: Many men—on both sides of the struggle—will be lost. A nation that has already suffered 20 years of warfare will suffer once again. Armies on both sides will take new casualties. And the war will go on.

There is no need for this to be so.

There is no need to delay the talks that could bring an end to this long and this bloody war.

Tonight, I renew the offer I made last August—to stop the bombardment of North Vietnam. We ask that talks begin promptly, that they be serious talks on the substance of peace. We assume that during those talks Hanoi will not take advantage of our restraint.

We are prepared to move immediately toward peace through negotiations.

So, tonight, in the hope that this action will lead to early talks, I am taking the first step to deescalate the conflict. We are reducing—substantially reducing—the present level of hostilities.

And we are doing so unilaterally, and at once.

Tonight, I have ordered our aircraft and our naval vessels to make no attacks on North Vietnam, except in the area north of the demilitarized zone where the continuing enemy buildup directly threatens allied forward positions and where the movements of their troops and supplies are clearly related to that threat.

The area in which we are stopping our attacks includes almost 90 percent of North Vietnam's population, and most of its territory. Thus there will be no attacks around the principal populated areas, or in the food-producing areas of North Vietnam.

Even this very limited bombing of the North could come to an early end—if our restraint is matched by restraint in Hanoi. But I cannot in good conscience stop all bombing so long as to do so would immediately and directly endanger the lives of our men and our allies. Whether a complete bombing halt becomes possible in the future will be determined by events.

Our purpose in this action is to bring about a reduction in the level of violence that now exists.

It is to save the lives of brave men—and to save the lives of innocent women and children. It is to permit the contending forces to move closer to a political settlement.

And tonight, I call upon the United Kingdom and I call upon the Soviet Union—as cochairmen of the Geneva Conferences, and as permanent members of the United Nations Security Council—to do all they can to move from the unilateral act of deescalation that I have just announced toward genuine peace in Southeast Asia.

Now, as in the past, the United States is ready to send its representatives to any forum, at any time, to discuss the means of bringing this ugly war to an end.

I am designating one of our most distinguished Americans, Ambassador Averell Harriman, as my personal representative for such talks. In addition, I have asked Ambassador Llewellyn Thompson, who returned from Moscow for consultation, to be available to join Ambassador Harriman at Geneva or any other suitable place—just as soon as Hanoi agrees to a conference.

I call upon President Ho Chi Minh to respond positively, and favorably, to this new step toward peace.

But if peace does not come now through negotiations, it will come when Hanoi understands that our common resolve is unshakable, and our common strength is invincible.

Tonight, we and the other allied nations are contributing 600,000 fighting men to assist 700,000 South Vietnamese troops in defending their little country.

Our presence there has always rested on this basic belief: The main burden of preserving their freedom must be carried out by them—by the South Vietnamese themselves.

We and our allies can only help to provide a shield behind which the people of South Vietnam can survive and can grow and develop. On their efforts—on their determination and resourcefulness—the outcome will ultimately depend.

That small, beleaguered nation has suffered terrible punishment for more than 20 years.

I pay tribute once again tonight to the great courage and endurance of its people. South Vietnam supports armed forces tonight of almost 700,000 men—and I call your attention to the fact that this is the equivalent of more than 10 million in our own population. Its people maintain their firm determination to be free of domination by the North.

There has been substantial progress, I think, in building a durable government during these last three years. The South Vietnam of 1965 could not have survived the enemy's Tet offensive of 1968. The elected government of South Vietnam survived that attack—and is rapidly repairing the devastation that it wrought.

The South Vietnamese know that further efforts are going to be required:
—to expand their own armed forces,
—to move back into the countryside as quickly as possible,
—to increase their taxes,
—to select the very best men that they have for civil and military responsibility,
—to achieve a new unity within their constitutional government, and
—to include in the national effort all those groups who wish to preserve South

Vietnam's control over its own destiny. Last week President Thieu ordered the mobilization of 135,000 additional South Vietnamese. He plans to reach—as soon as possible—a total military strength of more than 800,000 men.

To achieve this, the government of South Vietnam started the drafting of 19-year-olds on March 1st. On May 1st, the government will begin the drafting of 18-year-olds.

Last month, 10,000 men volunteered for military service—that was two and a half times the number of volunteers during the same month last year. Since the middle of January, more than 48,000 South Vietnamese have joined the armed forces—and nearly half of them volunteered to do so.

All men in the South Vietnamese armed forces have had their tours of duty extended for the duration of the war, and reserves are now being called up for immediate active duty.

President Thieu told his people last week: "We must make greater efforts and accept more sacrifices because, as I have said many times, this is our country. The existence of our nation is at stake, and this is mainly a Vietnamese responsibility."

He warned his people that a major national effort is required to root out corruption and incompetence at all levels of government.

We applaud this evidence of determination on the part of South Vietnam. Our first priority will be to support their effort.

We shall accelerate the reequipment of South Vietnam's armed forces—in order to meet the enemy's increased firepower. This will enable them progressively to undertake a larger share of combat operations against the Communist invaders.

On many occasions I have told the American people that we would send to Vietnam those forces that are required to accomplish our mission there. So, with that as our guide, we have previously authorized a force level of approximately 525,000.

Some weeks ago—to help meet the enemy's new offensive—we sent to Vietnam about 11,000 additional marine and airborne troops. They were deployed by air in 48 hours, on an emergency basis. But the artillery, tank, aircraft, medical, and other units that were needed to work with and to support these infantry troops in combat could not then accompany them by air on that short notice.

In order that these forces may reach maximum combat effectiveness, the Joint Chiefs of Staff have recommended to me that we should prepare to send—during the next five months—support troops totaling approximately 13,500 men.

A portion of these men will be made available from our active forces. The balance will come from reserve component units which will be called up for service.

The actions that we have taken since the beginning of the year
—to reequip the South Vietnamese forces,
—to meet our responsibilities in Korea, as well as our responsibilities in Vietnam,
—to meet price increases and the cost of activating and deploying reserve forces,
—to replace helicopters and provide the other military supplies we need, all of these actions are going to require additional expenditures.

The tentative estimate of those additional expenditures is $2.5 billion in this fiscal year, and $2.6 billion in the next fiscal year.

These projected increases in expenditures for our national security will bring into sharper focus the nation's need for immediate action: action to protect the prosperity of the American people and to protect the strength and the stability of our American dollar.

On many occasions I have pointed out that, without a tax bill or decreased expenditures, next year's deficit would again be around 20 billion dollars. I have emphasized the need to set strict priorities in our spending. I have stressed that failure to act and to act promptly and decisively would raise very strong doubts throughout the world about America's willingness to keep its financial house in order.

Yet Congress has not acted. And tonight we face the sharpest financial threat in the postwar era—a threat to the dollar's role as the keystone of international trade and finance in the world.

Last week, at the monetary conference in Stockholm, the major industrial countries decided to take a big step toward creating a new international monetary asset that will strengthen the international system. I am very proud of the very able work done by Secretary Fowler and Chairman Martin of the Federal Reserve Board.

But to make this system work the United States just must bring its balance of payments to—or very close to—equilibrium. We must have a responsible fiscal policy in this country. The passage of a tax bill now, together with expenditure control that the Congress may desire and dictate, is absolutely necessary to protect this nation's security, to continue our prosperity, and to meet the needs of our people.

What is at stake is seven years of unparalleled prosperity. In those seven years, the real income of the average American, after taxes, rose by almost 30 percent—a gain as large as that of the entire preceding 19 years.

So the steps that we must take to convince the world are exactly the steps we must take to sustain our own economic strength here at home. In the past eight months, prices and interest rates have risen because of our inaction.

We must, therefore, now do everything we can to move from debate to action—from talking to voting. There is, I believe—I hope there is—in both houses of the Congress-a growing sense of urgency that this situation just must be acted upon and must be corrected.

My budget in January was, we thought, a tight one. It fully reflected our evaluation of most of the demanding needs of this nation.

But in these budgetary matters, the president does not decide alone. The Congress has the power and the duty to determine appropriations and taxes.

The Congress is now considering our proposals and they are considering reductions in the budget that we submitted.

As part of a program of fiscal restraint that includes the tax surcharge, I shall approve appropriate reductions in the January budget when and if Congress so decides that that should be done.

One thing is unmistakably clear, however: Our deficit just must be reduced. Failure to act could bring on conditions that would strike hardest at those people that all of us are trying so hard to help.

These times call for prudence in this land of plenty. I believe that we have the character to provide it, and tonight I plead with the Congress and with the people to act promptly to serve the national interest, and thereby serve all of our people.

Now let me give you my estimate of the chances for peace:
—the peace that will one day stop the bloodshed in South Vietnam,
—that will permit all the Vietnamese people to rebuild and develop their land,
—that will permit us to turn more fully to our own tasks here at home.

I cannot promise that the initiative that I have announced tonight will be completely successful in achieving peace any more than the 30 others that we have undertaken and agreed to in recent years.

But it is our fervent hope that North Vietnam, after years of fighting that have left the issue unresolved, will now cease its efforts to achieve a military victory and will join with us in moving toward the peace table.

And there may come a time when South Vietnamese—on both sides—are able to work out a way to settle their own differences by free political choice rather than by war.

As Hanoi considers its course, it should be in no doubt of our intentions. It must not miscalculate the pressures within our democracy in this election year.

We have no intention of widening this war.

But the United States will never accept a fake solution to this long and arduous struggle and call it peace.

No one can foretell the precise terms of an eventual settlement.

Our objective in South Vietnam has never been the annihilation of the enemy. It has been to bring about a recognition in Hanoi that its objective—taking over the South by force—could not be achieved.

We think that peace can be based on the Geneva Accords of 1954—under political conditions that permit the South Vietnamese—all the South Vietnamese—to chart their course free of any outside domination or interference, from us or from anyone else.

So tonight I reaffirm the pledge that we made at Manila—that we are prepared to withdraw our forces from South Vietnam as the other side withdraws its forces to the north, stops the infiltration, and the level of violence thus subsides.

Our goal of peace and self-determination in Vietnam is directly related to the future of all of Southeast Asia—where much has happened to inspire confidence during the past 10 years. We have done all that we knew how to do to contribute and to help build that confidence.

A number of its nations have shown what can be accomplished under conditions of security. Since 1966, Indonesia, the fifth largest nation in all the world, with a population of more than one hundred million people, has had a government that is dedicated to peace with its neighbors and improved conditions for its own people. Political and economic cooperation between nations has grown rapidly.

I think every American can take a great deal of pride in the role that we have played in bringing this about in Southeast Asia. We can rightly judge—as responsible Southeast Asians themselves do—that the progress of the past three years would have been far less likely—if not completely impossible—if America's sons and others had not made their stand in Vietnam.

At Johns Hopkins University, about three years ago, I announced that the United States would take part in the great work of developing Southeast Asia, including the Mekong Valley, for all the people of that region. Our determination to help build a better land—a better land for men on both sides of the present conflict—has not diminished in the least. Indeed, the ravages of war, I think, have made it more urgent than ever.

So, I repeat on behalf of the United States again tonight what I said at Johns Hopkins— that North Vietnam could take its place in this common effort just as soon as peace comes.

Over time, a wider framework of peace and security in Southeast Asia may become possible. The new cooperation of the nations of the area could be a foundation-stone. Certainly friendship with the nations of such a Southeast Asia is what the United States seeks— and that is all that the United States seeks.

One day, my fellow citizens, there will be peace in Southeast Asia.

It will come because the people of Southeast Asia want it—those whose armies are at war tonight, and those who, though threatened, have thus far been spared.

Peace will come because Asians were willing to work for it—and to sacrifice for it—and to die by the thousands for it.

But let it never be forgotten: Peace will come also because America sent her sons to help secure it.

It has not been easy—far from it. During the past four and a half years, it has been my fate and my responsibility to be commander in chief. I have lived—daily and nightly—with the cost of this war. I know the pain that it has inflicted. I know, perhaps better than anyone, the misgivings that it has aroused.

Throughout this entire, long period, I have been sustained by a single principle: that what we are doing now, in Vietnam, is vital not only to the security of Southeast Asia, but it is vital to the security of every American.

Surely we have treaties which we must respect. Surely we have commitments that we are going to keep. Resolutions of the Congress testify to the need to resist aggression in the world and in Southeast Asia.

But the heart of our involvement in South Vietnam—under three different presidents, three separate administrations—has always been America's own security.

And the larger purpose of our involvement has always been to help the nations of Southeast Asia become independent and stand alone, self-sustaining, as members of a great world community—at peace with themselves, and at peace with all others.

With such an Asia, our country—and the world—will be far more secure than it is tonight.

I believe that a peaceful Asia is far nearer to reality because of what America has done in Vietnam. I believe that the men who endure the dangers of battle—fighting there for us tonight—are helping the entire world avoid far greater conflicts, far wider wars, far more destruction, than this one.

The peace that will bring them home someday will come. Tonight I have offered the first in what I hope will be a series of mutual moves toward peace.

I pray that it will not be rejected by the leaders of North Vietnam. I pray that they will accept it as a means by which the sacrifices of their own people may be ended. And I ask your help and your support, my fellow citizens, for this effort to reach across the battlefield toward an early peace.

Finally, my fellow Americans, let me say this:

Of those to whom much is given, much is asked. I cannot say and no man could say that no more will be asked of us.

Yet, I believe that now, no less than when the decade began, this generation of Americans is willing to "pay any price, bear any burden, meet any hardship, support any friend, oppose any foe to assure the survival and the success of liberty."

Since those words were spoken by John F. Kennedy, the people of America have kept that compact with mankind's noblest cause.

And we shall continue to keep it.

Yet, I believe that we must always be mindful of this one thing, whatever the trials and the tests ahead. The ultimate strength of our country and our cause will lie not in powerful weapons or infinite resources or boundless wealth, but will lie in the unity of our people.

This I believe very deeply.

Throughout my entire public career I have followed the personal philosophy that I am a free man, an American, a public servant, and a member of my party, in that order always and only.

For 37 years in the service of our nation, first as a congressman, as a senator, and as vice president, and now as your president, I have put the unity of the people first. I have put it ahead of any divisive partisanship.

And in these times as in times before, it is true that a house divided against itself by the spirit of faction, of party, of region, of religion, of race, is a house that cannot stand.

There is division in the American house now. There is divisiveness among us all tonight. And holding the trust that is mine, as president of all the people, I cannot disregard the peril to the progress of the American people and the hope and the prospect of peace for all peoples.

So, I would ask all Americans, whatever their personal interests or concern, to guard against divisiveness and all its ugly consequences.

Fifty-two months and 10 days ago, in a moment of tragedy and trauma, the duties of this office fell upon me. I asked then for your help and God's, that we might continue America on its course, binding up our wounds, healing our history, moving forward in new unity, to clear the American agenda and to keep the American commitment for all of our people.

United we have kept that commitment. United we have enlarged that commitment.

Through all time to come, I think America will be a stronger nation, a more just society, and a land of greater opportunity and fulfillment because of what we have all done together in these years of unparalleled achievement.

Our reward will come in the life of freedom, peace, and hope that our children will enjoy through ages ahead.

What we won when all of our people united just must not now be lost in suspicion, distrust, selfishness, and politics among any of our people.

Believing this as I do, I have concluded that I should not permit the presidency to become involved in the partisan divisions that are developing in this political year.

With America's sons in the fields far away, with America's future under challenge right here at home, with our hopes and the world's hopes for peace in the balance every day, I do not believe that I should devote an hour or a day of my time to any personal partisan causes or to any duties other than the awesome duties of this office—the presidency of your country.

Accordingly, I shall not seek, and I will not accept, the nomination of my party for another term as your president.

But let men everywhere know, however, that a strong, a confident, and a vigilant America stands ready tonight to seek an honorable peace—and stands ready tonight to defend an honored cause—whatever the price, whatever the burden, whatever the sacrifice that duty may require.

Thank you for listening.

Good night and God bless all of you.

Courtesy of National Archives and Records Administration

Richard Milhous Nixon

Richard Milhous Nixon

1969–1974

IN THE DRAMA of Richard Nixon's rise to the presidency and departure in disgrace, speechmaking played a pivotal role. The famous "Checkers" speech of 1952 saved him from being thrown off the Republican ticket into political oblivion. His debates with John F. Kennedy in 1960 very probably cost him the election. During his administration his speeches were incorporated into the massive public-relations campaign orchestrated by the White House. Finally there came the resignation speech, marking the first time, and so far the only time, that a president left office to avoid impeachment.

In a sense, Nixon's ascendancy to the presidency began with the Checkers speech, which, though it was intended by some Eisenhower advisers as an act of public humiliation, actually gave Nixon his first national audience (via television) and brought him new sources of support. Nixon was then a young California lawyer with six years' experience in the House and Senate and a reputation as an implacable anti-Communist. His place as Eisenhower's running mate was jeopardized by accusations that he had an illegal campaign contribution fund. Under pressure to resign, the exhausted Nixon went on television to defend himself and produced a tour de force. His talk, partially improvised and containing some maudlin outbursts, provoked a deluge of letters and telegrams demanding that the Republicans keep him on the ticket. It also revealed to politicians and voters alike the possibilities of television as a new political art form. Politics as spectacle became a standard element of Nixon's style in his presidential years, but by then it was the product of expert contrivance rather than of his own skill and nerve.

In general, Nixon when campaigning relied on a method developed by political campaign manager Murray Chotiner: keep opponents on the defensive by publicizing potentially damaging aspects of their views and voting records while giving away as little information as possible about one's own. The failure of this strategy in the 1960 presidential race, which Nixon lost by a mere tenth of a percent of the popular vote, was partly due to Nixon's poor showing in the first of four televised debates with Kennedy. Nixon had been a top debater since his college days, but bad lighting and lack of makeup gave him a most unflattering appearance. As he remarked in his book *Six Crises,* "One bad camera angle on television can have far more effect on the election outcome than a major mistake in writing a speech."

Defeated in this election and the 1962 race for governor of California, Nixon left politics to practice law on Wall Street until 1968, when he ran again for president against Hubert Humphrey. There were no debates in this campaign, and most of Nixon's speeches were attacks on the Johnson administration's escalation of the Vietnam War and on the social disruption caused by the antiwar movement. At his inauguration he promised to be the bringer of unity.

From the beginning of his term, Nixon showed a high degree of concern for building and preserving the right image—his own and that of his administration. The White House staff was expanded to include a public relations department called the Office of Communications for the Executive Branch, and among Nixon's aides and speechwriters were many with experience in advertising, public relations, and television production. While the previous presidents of the electronic age had made most of their television appearances in the daytime to ensure good coverage in the evening newspapers, Nixon preferred the "primetime" hours, which gave him a larger direct audience. His summit trip to the People's Republic of China in 1972 was the first large-scale presidential "media event." The president was accompanied by 70 tons of transmitting equipment that allowed the television networks to produce almost continuous coverage of the trip, which was arranged to begin and end in prime time.

The objective of the White House public relations operation was to present Nixon as a man of dignity, moral strength, and honesty. His director of communications declared that "truth will become the hallmark of the Nixon administration. . . . We will be able to eliminate any possibility of a credibility gap in this administration." Yet while the administration was pursuing important goals, especially in foreign policy, it was also covertly engaged in a host of illegal activities, including secret military actions, spying on citizens, the use of government agencies to intimidate opponents, forgery, and burglary—the crime whose discovery brought about the wreck of the administration.

Speechmaking was used by the White House to reinforce the president's image of authority and moral probity and to deflect attention from its covert activities, as well as to solicit support for its policies. This applied both to Nixon's speeches and those by Vice President Spiro Agnew, who for a time was assigned to deliver attacks on antiwar protesters in his speeches so that Nixon could take a more statesmanlike approach in his. Nixon aides wrote a script for the entire 1972 Republican convention that was followed in minute detail, including a prearranged ovation at the moment of Nixon's renomination. They were also put to work at such tasks as manufacturing pro-administration letters and telegrams under assumed names.

The White House speechwriting staff included two chief writers, a moderate (Raymond Price) to inspire the general public and a conservative (Patrick J. Buchanan) to arouse the hard-line Republicans. But, as journalist Richard Wilson pointed out, Nixon, who thought of himself as a statesman and intellectual in the Woodrow Wilson mode, "has written hundreds of his own speeches and is one of the few men in public life capable of delivering an hour-long television presentation with reference only to notes as if he were reading from text." His typical method of preparing a major speech was to draft a series of outlines, incorporating material from one or more staff writers; the final version was typed by his secretary as a formal, numbered outline, which he kept before him during the delivery. Though various phrases might be contributed by staff writers, the overall shape of the speech—its transitions, crescendos, and rhythms—was likely to be the work of the president, who once remarked that "politics is poetry." William Safire, one of Nixon's speechwriters, described his style as conversational, "designed to be heard rather than read," with vocabulary and sentence formation kept simple enough to allow the average listener to follow the argument.

Nixon excelled at performing before live audiences and was a master of the extemporaneous speech. "Nixon on a platform was one of the most adept speakers to have practiced the art in our time," says Safire. The mannerisms that made him the frequent butt of caricaturists—awkward gestures, forced smiles, hunched postures—were more pronounced on television, where, as if too conscious of the audience passing judgment, he rarely seemed at ease. He reportedly refused ever to watch himself on television.

The playwright Arthur Miller once observed that "if Mr. Nixon produces one fundamental effect it is his defensiveness, his caution, even his suspiciousness. Of course he speaks of confidence and bids us to share it, but this in theater is what we call acting against the words. The human truth is not in what he is saying but in what his body and soul are doing and it is the latter—the actor rather than the script, which penetrates to the people."

Checkers Speech

Los Angeles, California
September 23, 1952

ON SEPTEMBER 18, 1952, the *New York Post* ran a front-page article alleging that Senator Nixon, the Republican Party's vice-presidential candidate, had been the recipient of a secret slush fund to which rich Californians had donated more than $18,000, and that he was using the money to maintain himself in luxurious style. To restore his credibility, Nixon made a bold move: he bought airtime on network television, just after the popular *Milton Eerie Show,* and treated the nation to a bravura performance in which he re-created himself as a goodhearted, mistreated family man. It was the first time that a politician used television to put "spin" on an event, and one of the deftest examples ever. In the Checkers speech, wrote journalist Garry Wills, "Nixon electronically entered the average man's home, mingled his own cares with the problems of that family living room, hung his wife's cloth coat in the closet, rustled his own mortgages in among the house-holder's debts and bills, parked his two-year-old car in the garage, and boarded Checkers in the backyard doghouse." The speech was a public relations triumph for Nixon and was even reviewed in *Variety,* the magazine of the entertainment industry.

I come before you tonight as a candidate for the vice-presidency and as a man whose honesty and integrity has been questioned.

Now, the usual political thing to do when charges are made against you is to either ignore them or to deny them without giving details. I believe we have had enough of that in the United States, particularly with the present administration in Washington, D.C.

To me the office of the vice presidency of the United States is a great office, and I feel that the people have got to have confidence in the integrity of the men who run for that office and who might attain them.

I have a theory, too, that the best and only answer to a smear or an honest misunderstanding of the facts is to tell the truth. And that is why I am here tonight. I want to tell you my side of the case.

I am sure that you have read the charges, and you have heard it, that I, Senator Nixon, took $18,000 from a group of my supporters.

Now, was that wrong? And let me say that it was wrong. I am saying it, incidentally, that it was wrong, just not illegal, because it isn't a question of whether it was legal or illegal, that isn't enough. The question is, was it morally wrong. I say that it was morally wrong—if any of that $18,000 went to Senator Nixon, for my personal use. I say that it was morally wrong if it was secretly given and secretly handled.

And I say that it was morally wrong if any of the contributors got special favors for the contributions that they made.

And to answer those questions let me say this: not a cent of the $18,000 or any other money of that type ever went to me for my personal use. Every penny of it was used to pay for political expenses that I did not think should be charged to the taxpayers of the United States.

It was not a secret fund. As a matter of fact, when I was on Meet the Press—some of you may have seen it last Sunday—Peter Edson came up to me, after the program, and he said, "Dick, what about this fund we hear about?" And I said, "Well, there is no secret about it. Go out and see Dana Smith who was the administrator of the fund," and I gave him his address. And I said you will find that the purpose of the fund simply was to defray political expenses that I did not feel should be charged to the government.

And third, let me point out, and I want to make this particularly clear, that no contributor to this fund, no contributor to any of my campaigns, has ever received any consideration that he would not have received as an ordinary constituent.

I just don't believe in that, and I can say that never, while I have been in the Senate of the United States, as far as the people that contributed to this fund are concerned, have I made a telephone call to an agency, nor have I gone down to an agency on their behalf.

And the records will show that, the records which are in the hands of the administration.

Well, then, some of you will say, and rightly, "Well, what did you use the fund for, Senator? Why did you have to have it?"

Let me tell you in just a word how a Senate office operates. First of all, the senator gets $15,000 a year in salary. He gets enough money to pay for one trip a year, a round trip, that is, for himself, and his family between his home and Washington, D.C., and then he gets an allowance to handle the people that work in his office to handle his mail.

And the allowance for my state of California is enough to hire 13 people. And let me say, incidentally, that this allowance is not paid to the senator.

It is paid directly to the individuals, that the senator puts on his payroll, but all of these people and all of these allowances are for strictly official business; business, for example, when a constituent writes in and wants you to go down to the Veteran's Administration and get some information about his GI policy—items of that type for example. But there are other expenses that are not covered by the government. And I think I can best discuss those expenses by asking you some questions.

Do you think that when I or any other senator makes a political speech, has it printed, should charge the printing of that speech and the mailing of that speech to the taxpayers?

Do you think, for example, when I or any other senator makes a trip to his home state to make a purely political speech that the cost of that trip should be charged to the taxpayers?

Do you think when a senator makes political broadcasts or political television broadcasts, radio or television, that the expense of those broadcasts should be charged to the taxpayers?

I know what your answer is: It is the same answer that audiences give me whenever I discuss this particular problem.

The answer is no. The taxpayers should not be required to finance items which are not official business but which are primarily political business.

Well, then the question arises, you say, "Well, how do you pay for these and how can you do it legally?" And there are several ways that it can be done, incidentally, and it is done legally in the United States Senate and in the Congress.

The first way is to be a rich man. So I couldn't use that.

Another way that is used is to put your wife on the payroll. Let me say, incidentally, that my opponent, my opposite number for the vice presidency on the Democratic ticket, does have his wife on the payroll and has had her on his payroll for the past 10 years. Now let me just say this: That is his business, and I am not critical of him for doing that. You will have to pass judgment on that particular point, but I have never done that for this reason:

I have found that there are so many deserving stenographers and secretaries in Washington that needed the work that I just didn't feel it was right to put my wife on the payroll.—My wife sitting over there.

She is a wonderful stenographer. She used to teach stenography and she used to teach shorthand in high school. That was when I met her. And I can tell you folks that she has worked many hours on Saturdays and Sundays in my office, and she has done a fine job, and I am proud to say tonight that in the six years I have been in the Senate of the United States Pat Nixon has never been on the government payroll.

What are the other ways that these finances can be taken care of? Some who are lawyers, and I happen to be a lawyer, continue to practice law, but I haven't been able to do that.

I am so far away from California and I have been so busy with my senatorial work that I have not engaged in any legal practice, and, also, as far as law practice is concerned, it seemed to me that the relationship between an attorney and the client was so personal that you couldn't possibly represent a man as an attorney and then have an unbiased view when he presented his case to you in the event that he had one before government.

And so I felt that the best way to handle these necessary political expenses of getting my message to the American people and the speeches I made—the speeches I had printed for the most part concerned this one message of exposing this administration, the Communism in it, the corruption in it—the only way I could do that was to accept the aid which people in my home state of California, who contributed to my campaign and who continued to make these contributions after I was elected, were glad to make.

And let me say that I am proud of the fact that not one of them has ever asked me for a special favor. I am proud of the fact that not one of them has ever asked me to vote on a bill other than my own conscience would dictate. And I am proud of the fact that the taxpayers by subterfuge or otherwise have never paid one dime for expenses which I thought were political and should not be charged to the taxpayers.

Let me say, incidentally, that some of you may say, "Well, that is all right, Senator, that is your explanation, but have you got any proof?" And I would like to tell you this evening that just an hour ago we received an independent audit of this entire fund. I suggested to Governor Sherman Adams, who is the chief of staff of the Eisenhower campaign, that an independent audit and legal report be obtained, and I have that audit in my hand.

It is an audit made by Price Waterhouse & Company firm, and the legal opinion by Gibson, Dunn & Crutcher, lawyers in Los Angeles, the biggest law firm, and incidentally, one of the best ones in Los Angeles.

I am proud to report to you tonight that this audit and legal opinion is being forwarded to General Eisenhower and I would like to read to you the opinion that was prepared by Gibson, Dunn & Crutcher, based on all the pertinent laws, and statutes, together with the audit report prepared by the certified public accountants:

It is our conclusion that Senator Nixon did not obtain any financial gain from the collection and disbursement of the funds by Dana Smith; that Senator Nixon did not violate any federal or state law by reason of the operation of the fund; and that neither the portion of the fund paid by Dana Smith directly to third persons, nor the portion paid to Senator Nixon, to reimburse him for office expenses, constituted income in a sense which was either reportable or taxable as income under income tax laws.
(signed)
Gibson, Dunn & Crutcher,
by Elmo Conley

That is not Nixon speaking, but it is an independent audit which was requested because I want the American people to know all the facts and I am not afraid of having

independent people go in and check the facts, and that is exactly what they did.

But then I realized that there are still some who may say, and rightly so—and let me say that I recognize that some will continue to smear regardless of what the truth may be—but that there has been understandably, some honest misunderstanding on this matter, and there are some that will say, "well, maybe you were able, Senator, to fake the thing. How can we believe what you say—after all, is there a possibility that maybe you got some sums in cash? Is there a possibility that you might have feathered your own nest?" And so now, what I am going to do—and incidentally this is unprecedented in the history of American politics—I am going at this time to give to this television and radio audience a complete financial history, everything I have earned, everything I have spent, and everything I own, and I want you to know the facts.

I will have to start early, I was born in 1913. Our family was one of modest circumstances, and most of my early life was spent in a store out in East Whittier. It was a grocery store, one of those family enterprises.

The only reason we were able to make it go was because my mother and dad had five boys, and we all worked in the store. I worked my way through college, and, to a great extent, through law school. And then in 1940, probably the best thing that ever happened to me happened. I married Pat who is sitting over here.

We had a rather difficult time after we were married, like so many of the young couples who might be listening to us. I practiced law. She continued to teach school.

Then, in 1942, I went into the service. Let me say that my service record was not a particularly unusual one. I went to the South Pacific. I guess I'm entitled to a couple of battle stars. I got a couple of letters of commendation. But I was just there when the bombs were falling. And then I returned. I returned to the United States, and in 1946, I ran for Congress. When we came out of the war—Pat and I—Pat during the war had worked as a stenographer, and in a bank, and as an economist for a government agency—and when we came out, the total of our savings, from both my law practice, her teaching, and all the time I was in the war, the total for that entire period was just less than $10,000—every cent of that, incidentally, was in government bonds—well, that's where we start, when I go into politics.

Now, whatever I earned since I went into politics—well, here it is. I jotted it down. Let me read the notes.

First of all, I have had my salary as a congressman and as a senator.

Second, I have received a total in this past six years of $1,600 from estates which were in my law firm at the time that I severed my connection with it. And, incidentally, as I said before, I have not engaged in any legal practice, and have not accepted any fees from business that came into the firm after I went into politics.

I have made an average of approximately $1,500 a year from nonpolitical speaking engagements and lectures.

And then, unfortunately, we have inherited little money. Pat sold her interest in her father's estate for $3,000, and I inherited $1,500 from my grandfather. We lived rather modestly.

For four years we lived in an apartment in Parkfairfax, Alexandria, Virginia. The rent was $80 a month. And we saved for a time when we could buy a house. Now that was what we took in.

What did we do with this money? What do we have today to show for it? This will surprise you because it is so little, I suppose, as standards generally go of people in public life.

First of all, we've got a house in Washington, which cost $41,000 and on which we owe $20,000. We have a house in Whittier, California, which cost $13,000 and on which we owe $3,000. My folks are living there at the present time.

I have just $4,000 in life insurance, plus my GI policy, which I have never been able to convert, and which will run out in two years.

I have no life insurance whatever on Pat. I have no life insurance on our two youngsters, Patricia and Julie.

I own a 1950 Oldsmobile car. We have our furniture. We have no stocks and bonds of any type. We have no interest, direct or indirect, in any business. Now that is what we have. What do we owe?

Well, in addition to the mortgages, the $20,000 mortgage on the house in Washington and the $10,000 mortgage on the house in Whittier, I owe $4,000 to the Riggs Bank in Washington, D.C., with an interest at 4 percent.

I owe $3,500 to my parents, and the interest on that loan, which I pay regularly, because it is a part of the savings they made through the years they were working so hard—I pay regularly 4 percent interest. And then I have a $500 loan, which I have on my life insurance.

Well, that's about it. That's what we have. And that's what we owe. It isn't very much. But Pat and I have the satisfaction that every dime that we have got is honestly ours.

I should say this, that Pat doesn't have a mink coat. But she does have a respectable Republican cloth coat, and I always tell her she would look good in anything.

One other thing I should probably tell you, because if I don't they will probably be saying this about me, too. We did get something, a gift, after the election.

A man down in Texas heard Pat on the radio mention that our two youngsters would like to have a dog, and, believe it or not, the day we left before this campaign trip we got a message from Union Station in Baltimore, saying they had a package for us. We went down to get it. You know what it was?

It was a little cocker spaniel dog, in a crate that he had sent all the way from Texas, black and white, spotted, and our little girl Tricia, the six-year-old, named it Checkers.

And you know, the kids, like all kids, loved the dog, and I just want to say this, right now, that regardless of what they say about it, we are going to keep it.

It isn't easy to come before a nationwide audience and bare your life, as I have done. But I want to say some things before I conclude, that I think most of you will agree on.

Mr. Mitchell, the chairman of the Democratic National Committee, made this statement that if a man couldn't afford to be in the United States Senate, he shouldn't run for the Senate. And I just want to make my position clear.

I don't agree with Mr. Mitchell when he says that only a rich man should serve his government in the United States Senate or Congress. I don't believe that represents the thinking of the Democratic Party, and I know it doesn't represent the thinking of the Republican Party.

I believe that it's fine that a man like Governor Stevenson, who inherited a fortune from his father, can run for president. But I also feel that it is essential in this country of ours that a man of modest means can also run for president, because, you know—remember Abraham Lincoln—you remember what he said—"God must have loved the common people, he made so many of them."

And now I'm going to suggest some courses of conduct.

First of all, you have read in the papers about other funds; now, Mr. Stevenson apparently had a couple. One of them in which a group of business people paid and helped to supplement the salaries of state employees. Here is where the money went directly into their pockets, and I think that what Mr. Stevenson should do should be to come before the American people, as I have, give the names of the people that contributed to that fund, give the names of the people who put this money into their pockets, at the same time that they were receiving money from their state government and see what favors, if any, they gave out for that.

I don't condemn Mr. Stevenson for what he did, but until the facts are in there is a doubt that would be raised. And as far as Mr. Sparkman is concerned, I would suggest the same thing. He's had his wife on the payroll. I don't condemn him for that, but I think that he should come before the American people and indicate what outside sources of income he has had. I would suggest that under the circumstances both Mr. Sparkman and Mr. Stevenson should come before the American people, as I have, and make a complete financial statement as to their financial history, and if they don't it will be an admission that they have something to hide.

And I think you will agree with me— because, folks, remember, a man that's to be president of the United States, a man that is to be vice president of the United States, must have the confidence of all the people. And that's why I'm doing what I'm doing and that is why I suggest that Mr. Stevenson and Mr. Sparkman, if they are under attack, that should be what they are doing.

Now let me say this: I know this is not the last of the smears. In spite of my explanation tonight, other smears will be made. Others have been made in the past. And the purpose of the smears, I know, is this, to silence me, to make me let up.

Well, they just don't know who they are dealing with. I'm going to tell you this: I remember in the dark days of the Hiss trial some of the same columnists, some of the same radio commentators who are attacking me now and misrepresenting my position, were violently opposing me at the time I was after Alger Hiss. But I continued to fight because I knew I was right, and I can say to this great television and radio audience that I have no apologies to the American people for my part in putting Alger Hiss where he is today. And as far as this is concerned, I intend to continue to fight.

Why do I feel so deeply? Why do I feel that in spite of the smears, the misunderstanding, the necessity for a man to come up here and bare his soul? And I want to tell you why.

Because, you see, I love my country. And I think my country is in danger. And I think the only man that can save America at this time is the man that's running for president on my ticket, Dwight Eisenhower.

You say, why do I think it is in danger? And I say look at the record. Seven years of the Truman-Acheson administration, and what's happened? Six hundred million people lost to the Communists. And a war in Korea in which we have lost 117,000 American casualties, and I say that those in the State Department that made the mistakes which caused that war and which resulted in those losses should be kicked out of the State Department just as fast as we can get them out of there.

And let me say that I know Mr. Stevenson won't do that because he defends the Truman policy, and I know that Dwight Eisenhower will do that, and he will give America the leadership that it needs.

Take the problem of corruption. You have read about the mess in Washington. Mr. Stevenson can't clean it up because he was picked by the man, Truman, under whose administration the mess was made.

You wouldn't trust the man who made the mess to clean it up. That is Truman. And by the same token you can't trust the man who was picked by the man who made the mess to clean it up and that's Stevenson. And so I say, Eisenhower who owes nothing to Truman, nothing to the big city bosses—he is the man who can clean up the mess in Washington.

Take Communism. I say as far as that subject is concerned the danger is greater to America. In the Hiss case they got the secrets which enabled them to break the American secret State Department code.

They got secrets in the atomic-bomb case which enabled them to get the secret of the atomic bomb five years before they would have gotten it by their own devices. And I say that any man who called the Alger Hiss case a red herring isn't fit to be president of the United States.

I say that a man who, like Mr. Stevenson, has pooh-poohed and ridiculed the Communist threat in the United States—he has accused us, that they have attempted to expose the Communists, of looking for Communists in the Bureau of Fisheries and Wildlife. I say that a man who says that isn't qualified to be president of the United States.

And I say that the only man who can lead us into this fight to rid the government of both those who are Communists and those who have corrupted this government is Eisenhower, because General Eisenhower, you can be sure, recognizes the problem, and knows how to handle it.

Let me say this, finally. This evening I want to read to you just briefly excerpts from a letter that I received, a letter which after all this is over no one can take away from us. It reads as follows:

Dear Senator Nixon, since I am only 19 years of age, I can't vote in this presidential election, but believe me if I could you and General Eisenhower would certainly get my vote. My husband is in the Fleet Marines in Korea. He is in the front lines. And we have a two-month-old son he has never seen. And I feel confident that with great Americans like you and General Eisenhower in the White House, lonely Americans like myself will be united with their loved ones now in Korea. I only pray to God that you won't be too late. Enclosed is a small check to help you with your campaign. Living on $85 a month it is all I can do.

Folks, it is a check for $10, and it is one that I shall never cash. And let me just say this: We hear a lot about prosperity these days, but I say why can't we have prosperity built on peace, rather than prosperity built on war? Why can't we have prosperity and an honest government in Washington, D.C., at the same time?

Believe me, we can. And Eisenhower is the man that can lead the crusade to bring us that kind of prosperity.

And now, finally, I know that you wonder whether or not I am going to stay on the Republican ticket or resign. Let me say this: I don't believe that I ought to quit, because I am not a quitter. And, incidentally, Pat is not a quitter. After all, her name is Patricia Ryan and she was born on St. Patrick's Day, and you know the Irish never quit.

But the decision, my friends, is not mine. I would do nothing that would harm the possibilities of Dwight Eisenhower to become president of the United States. And for that reason I am submitting to the Republican National Committee tonight through this television broadcast the decision which it is theirs to make. Let them decide whether my position on the ticket will help or hurt. And I am going to ask you to help them decide. Wire and write the Republican National Committee whether you think I should stay on or whether I should get off. And whatever their decision, I will abide by it.

But let me just say this last word. Regardless of what happens, I am going to continue this fight. I am going to campaign up and down America until we drive the crooks and the Communists and those that defend them out of Washington, and remember folks, Eisenhower is a great man. Folks, he is a great man, and a vote for Eisenhower is a vote for what is good for America.

First Inaugural Address

Washington, D.C.
January 20, 1969

NIXON WON ELECTION in 1968 by the thinnest of margins. In the campaign he had promised to be a peacemaker who would end both the war in Vietnam and the breakdown of the social order at home. Ray Price, the speechwriter who assisted Nixon in the composition of his inaugural address, has written that the new president intended it "as a place to signal directions, to suggest priorities, to lay a healing hand on the nation's fevered brow, and, importantly, to seek to enlist the people themselves in the 'high adventure' that he saw ahead." As if to remind the nation of the difficulties entailed in this task, a crowd of antiwar protesters attacked Nixon's car with rocks and bottles as he left the Capitol after the swearing-in ceremony.

I ask you to share with me today the majesty of this moment. In the orderly transfer of power, we celebrate the unity that keeps us free.

Each moment in history is a fleeting time, precious and unique. But some stand out as moments of beginning, in which courses are set that shape decades or centuries.

This can be such a moment.

Forces now are converging that make possible, for the first time, the hope that many of man's deepest aspirations can at last be realized. The spiraling pace of change allows us to contemplate, within our own lifetime, advances that once would have taken centuries.

In throwing wide the horizons of space, we have discovered new horizons on earth.

For the first time, because the people of the world want peace, and the leaders of the world are afraid of war, the times are on the side of peace.

Eight years from now America will celebrate its 200th anniversary as a nation. Within the lifetime of most people now living, mankind will celebrate that great new year which comes only once in a thousand years—the beginning of the third millennium.

What kind of a nation we will be, what kind of a world we will live in, whether we shape the future in the image of our hopes, is ours to determine by our actions and our choices.

The greatest honor history can bestow is the title of peacemaker. This honor now beckons America—the chance to help lead the world at last out of the valley of turmoil and onto that high ground of peace that man has dreamed of since the dawn of civilization.

If we succeed, generations to come will say of us now living that we mastered our moment, that we helped make the world safe for mankind.

This is our summons to greatness.

I believe the American people are ready to answer this call.

The second third of this century has been a time of proud achievement. We have made enormous strides in science and industry and agriculture. We have shared our wealth more broadly than ever. We have learned at last to manage a modern economy to assure its continued growth.

We have given freedom new reach. We have begun to make its promise real for black as well as for white.

We see the hope of tomorrow in the youth of today. I know America's youth. I believe in them. We can be proud that they are better educated, more committed, more passionately driven by conscience than any generation in our history.

No people has ever been so close to the achievement of a just and abundant society, or so possessed of the will to achieve it. And because our strengths are so great, we can afford to appraise our weaknesses with candor and to approach them with hope.

Standing in this same place a third of a century ago, Franklin Delano Roosevelt addressed a nation ravaged by depression and gripped in fear. He could say in surveying the nation's troubles: "They concern, thank God, only material things."

Our crisis today is in reverse.

We find ourselves rich in goods, but ragged in spirit; reaching with magnificent precision for the moon, but falling into raucous discord on earth.

We are caught in war, wanting peace. We are torn by division, wanting unity. We see around us empty lives, wanting fulfillment. We see tasks that need doing, waiting for hands to do them.

To a crisis of the spirit, we need an answer of the spirit.

And to find that answer, we need only look within ourselves.

When we listen to "the better angels of our nature," we find that they celebrate the simple things, the basic things—such as goodness, decency, love, kindness.

Greatness comes in simple trappings.

The simple things are the ones most needed today if we are to surmount what divides us, and cement what unites us.

To lower our voices would be a simple thing.

In these difficult years, America has suffered from a fever of words; from inflated rhetoric that promises more than it can deliver; from angry rhetoric that fans discontents into hatreds; from bombastic rhetoric that postures instead of persuading.

We cannot learn from one another until we stop shouting at one another—until we speak quietly enough so that our words can be heard as well as our voices.

For its part, government will listen. We will strive to listen in new ways—to the voices of quiet anguish, the voices that speak without words, the voices of the heart—to the injured voices, the anxious voices, the voices that have despaired of being heard.

Those who have been left out, we will try to bring in.

Those left behind, we will help to catch up.

For all of our people, we will set as our goal the decent order that makes progress possible and our lives secure.

As we reach toward our hopes, our task is to build on what has gone before—not turning away from the old, but turning toward the new.

In this past third of a century, government has passed more laws, spent more money, initiated more programs than in all our previous history.

In pursuing our goals of full employment, better housing, excellence in education; in rebuilding our cities and improving our rural areas; in protecting our environment and enhancing the quality of life—in all these

and more, we will and must press urgently forward.

We shall plan now for the day when our wealth can be transferred from the destruction of war abroad to the urgent needs of our people at home.

The American dream does not come to those who fall asleep.

But we are approaching the limits of what government alone can do.

Our greatest need now is to reach beyond government, to enlist the legions of the concerned and the committed.

What has to be done, has to be done by government and people together or it will not be done at all. The lesson of past agony is that without the people we can do nothing—with the people we can do everything.

To match the magnitude of our tasks, we need the energies of our people—enlisted not only in grand enterprises, but more importantly in those small, splendid efforts that make headlines in the neighborhood newspaper instead of the national journal.

With these, we can build a great cathedral of the spirit—each of us raising it one stone at a time, as he reaches out to his neighbor, helping, caring, doing.

I do not offer a life of uninspiring ease. I do not call for a life of grim sacrifice. I ask you to join in a high adventure—one as rich as humanity itself, and exciting as the times we live in.

The essence of freedom is that each of us shares in the shaping of his own destiny.

Until he has been part of a cause larger than himself, no man is truly whole.

The way to fulfillment is in the use of our talents. We achieve nobility in the spirit that inspires that use.

As we measure what can be done, we shall promise only what we know we can produce; but as we chart our goals, we shall be lifted by our dreams.

No man can be fully free while his neighbor is not. To go forward at all is to go forward together.

This means black and white together, as one nation, not two. The laws have caught up with our conscience. What remains is to give life to what is in the law; to insure at last that as all are born equal in dignity before God, all are born equal in dignity before man.

As we learn to go forward together at home, let us also seek to go forward together with all mankind.

Let us take as our goal: Where peace is unknown, make it welcome; where peace is fragile, make it strong; where peace is temporary, make it permanent.

After a period of confrontation, we are entering an era of negotiation.

Let all nations know that during this administration our lines of communication will be open.

We seek an open world—open to ideas, open to the exchange of goods and people—a world in which no people, great or small, will live in angry isolation.

We cannot expect to make everyone our friend, but we can try to make no one our enemy.

Those who would be our adversaries, we invite to a peaceful competition—not in conquering territory or extending dominion, but in enriching the life of man.

As we explore the reaches of space, let us go to the new worlds together—not as new worlds to be conquered, but as a new adventure to be shared.

With those who are willing to join, let us cooperate to reduce the burden of arms, to strengthen the structure of peace, to lift up the poor and the hungry.

But to all those who would be tempted by weakness, let us leave no doubt that we will be as strong as we need to be for as long as we need to be.

Over the past 20 years, since I first came to this capital as a freshman congressman, I have visited most of the nations of the world. I have come to know the leaders of the world and the great forces, the hatreds, the fears that divide the world.

I know that peace does not come through wishing for it—that there is no substitute for days and even years of patient and prolonged diplomacy.

I also know the people of the world.

I have seen the hunger of a homeless child, the pain of a man wounded in battle, the grief of a mother who has lost her son. I know these have no ideology, no race.

I know America. I know the heart of America is good.

I speak from my own heart, and the heart of my country, the deep concern we have for those who suffer and those who sorrow.

I have taken an oath today in the presence of God and my countrymen to uphold and defend the Constitution of the United States. To that oath I now add this sacred commitment: I shall consecrate my office, my energies, and all the wisdom I can summon to the cause of peace among nations.

Let this message be heard by strong and weak alike:

The peace we seek—the peace we seek to win—is not victory over any other people, but the peace that comes "with healing in its wings"; with compassion for those who have suffered; with understanding for those who have opposed us; with the opportunity for all the peoples of this earth to choose their own destiny.

Only a few short weeks ago we shared the glory of man's first sight of the world as God sees it, as a single sphere reflecting light in the darkness.

As the Apollo astronauts flew over the Moon's gray surface on Christmas Eve, they spoke to us of the beauty of Earth—and in that voice so clear across the lunar distance, we heard them invoke God's blessing on its goodness.

In that moment, their view from the Moon moved poet Archibald MacLeish to write: "To see the Earth as it truly is, small and blue and beautiful in that eternal silence where it floats, is to see ourselves as riders on the Earth together, brothers on that bright loveliness in the eternal cold—brothers who know now they are truly brothers."

In that moment of surpassing technological triumph, men turned their thoughts toward home and humanity—seeing in that far perspective that man's destiny on Earth is not divisible; telling us that however far we reach into the cosmos, our destiny lies not in the stars but on Earth itself, in our own hands, in our own hearts.

We have endured a long night of the American spirit. But as our eyes catch the dimness of the first rays of dawn, let us not curse the remaining dark. Let us gather the light.

Our destiny offers not the cup of despair, but the chalice of opportunity. So let us seize it not in fear, but in gladness—and "riders on the Earth together," let us go forward, firm in our faith, steadfast in our purpose, cautious of the dangers, but sustained by our confidence in the will of God and the promise of man.

The Pursuit of Peace

Washington, D.C.
November 3, 1969

THE ROLE OF healer and unifier that Nixon adopted at his inauguration was soon undermined by his refusal to put a quick end to the war in Vietnam. The antiwar movement again began to gather momentum. A nationwide day of protest, the Moratorium, was held on October 15 but was diluted by the president's announcement on October 13 that he was preparing a major address on the situation.

The speech, said to have been written by Nixon without the aid of his staff writers, was a rejection both of North Vietnam's intransigence and of the peace movement's call for a negotiated withdrawal. The strategy he advocated for ending the war was "Vietnamization," or the gradual transfer of military efforts to the South Vietnamese armed forces under the supervision of a reduced American occupation force. Columnist James Reston spoke for many opponents of the war when he wrote: "If his policy is to stick with the South Vietnamese until they demonstrate that they are secure, all they have to do is prolong their inefficiency in order to guarantee that we will stay in the battle indefinitely."

The final paragraphs were widely thought to be a deliberate attempt to polarize the nation further by characterizing all critics of the war as defeatists and extremists. As Jonathan Schell notes, the president "had identified a foe within the United States more dangerous to the country than the one it was fighting in Vietnam."

The speech was broadcast on television and radio to an audience estimated at 72 million people. According to Richard Wilson, "No more effective single speech ever was made by a president, certainly in this century." Columnist Joseph Alsop called it "one of the most successful technical feats of political leadership in many, many years." The peace movement, after staging a huge demonstration in Washington, went into decline, and the "great silent majority" to whom Nixon directed his speech appeared to unite behind him to await the end of the war, which finally came, for the Americans, in 1973.

Tonight I want to talk to you on a subject of deep concern to all Americans and to many people in all parts of the world—the war in Vietnam.

I believe that one of the reasons for the deep division about Vietnam is that many Americans have lost confidence in what their government has told them about our policy. The American people cannot and should not be asked to support a policy which involves the overriding issues of war and peace unless they know the truth about that policy.

Tonight, therefore, I would like to answer some of the questions that I know are on the minds of many of you listening to me.

How and why did America get involved in Vietnam in the first place?

How has this administration changed the policy of the previous administration?

What has really happened in the negotiations in Paris and on the battlefront in Vietnam?

What choices do we have if we are to end the war?

What are the prospects for peace?

Now, let me begin by describing the situation I found when I was inaugurated on January 20.

- The war had been going on for four years.
- 31,000 Americans had been killed in action.
- The training program for the South Vietnamese was behind schedule.
- 540,000 Americans were in Vietnam with no plans to reduce the number.
- No progress had been made at the negotiations in Paris, and the United States had not put forth a comprehensive peace proposal.
- The war was causing deep division at home and criticism from many of our friends as well as our enemies abroad.

In view of these circumstances there were some who urged that I end the war at once by ordering the immediate withdrawal of all American forces.

From a political standpoint this would have been a popular and easy course to follow. After all, we became involved in the war while my predecessor was in office. I could blame the defeat which would be the result of my action on him and come out as the peacemaker. Some put it to me quite bluntly: This was the only way to avoid allowing Johnson's war to become Nixon's war.

But I had a greater obligation than to think only of the years of my administration and of the next election. I had to think of the effect of my decision on the next generation and on the future of peace and freedom in America and in the world.

Let us all understand that the question before us is not whether some Americans are for peace and some Americans are against peace. The question at issue is not whether Johnson's war becomes Nixon's war.

The great question is: How can we win America's peace?

Well, let us turn now to the fundamental issue. Why and how did the United States become involved in Vietnam in the first place?

Fifteen years ago North Vietnam, with the logistical support of Communist China and the Soviet Union, launched a campaign to impose a Communist government on South Vietnam by instigating and supporting a revolution.

In response to the request of the government of South Vietnam, President Eisenhower sent economic aid and military equipment to assist the people of South Vietnam in their efforts to prevent a Communist takeover. Seven years ago, President Kennedy sent 16,000 military personnel to Vietnam as combat advisers. Four years ago, President Johnson sent American combat forces to South Vietnam.

Now, many believe that President Johnson's decision to send American combat forces to South Vietnam was wrong. And many others—I among them—have been strongly critical of the way the war has been conducted.

But the question facing us today is: Now that we are in the war, what is the best way to end it?

In January I could only conclude that the precipitate withdrawal of American forces from Vietnam would be a disaster not only for South Vietnam but for the United States and for the cause of peace.

For the South Vietnamese, our precipitate withdrawal would inevitably allow the Communists to repeat the massacres which followed their takeover in the North 15 years before.

- They then murdered more than 50,000 people, and hundreds of thousands more died in slave labor camps.
- We saw a prelude of what would happen in South Vietnam when the Communists entered the city of Hue last year. During their brief rule there, there was a bloody reign of terror in which 3,000 civilians were clubbed, shot to death, and buried in mass graves.
- With the sudden collapse of our support, these atrocities of Hue would become the nightmare of the entire nation—and particularly for the million and a half Catholic refugees who fled to South Vietnam when the Communists took over in the North.

For the United States, this first defeat in our nation's history would result in a collapse of confidence in American leadership, not only in Asia but throughout the world.

Three American presidents have recognized the great stakes involved in Vietnam and understood what had to be done.

In 1963 President Kennedy, with his characteristic eloquence and clarity, said:

> . . . we want to see a stable government there, carrying on a struggle to maintain its national independence. We believe strongly in that. We are not going to withdraw from that effort. In my opinion, for us to withdraw from that effort would mean a collapse not only of South Vietnam, but Southeast Asia. So we are going to stay there.

President Eisenhower and President Johnson expressed the same conclusion during their terms of office.

For the future of peace, precipitate withdrawal would thus be a disaster of immense magnitude.

- A nation cannot remain great if it betrays its allies and lets down its friends.
- Our defeat and humiliation in South Vietnam without question would promote recklessness in the councils of those great

powers who have not yet abandoned their goals of world conquest.

- This would spark violence wherever our commitments help maintain the peace—in the Middle East, in Berlin, eventually even in the Western Hemisphere.

Ultimately, this would cost more lives.

It would not bring peace; it would bring more war.

For these reasons, I rejected the recommendation that I should end the war by immediately withdrawing all of our forces. I chose instead to change American policy on both the negotiating front and battle-front.

In order to end a war fought on many fronts, I initiated a pursuit for peace on many fronts.

In a television speech on May 14, in a speech before the United Nations, and on a number of other occasions I set forth our peace proposals in great detail.

- We have offered the complete withdrawal of all outside forces within one year.
- We have proposed a cease-fire under international supervision.
- We have offered free elections under international supervision with the Communists participating in the organization and conduct of the elections as an organized political force. And the Saigon government has pledged to accept the result of the elections.

We have not put forth our proposals on a take-it-or-leave-it basis. We have indicated that we are willing to discuss the proposals that have been put forth by the other side. We have declared that anything is negotiable except the right of the people of South Vietnam to determine their own future. At the Paris Peace Conference, Ambassador Lodge has demonstrated our flexibility and good faith in 40 public meetings.

Hanoi has refused even to discuss our proposals. They demand our unconditional acceptance of their terms, which are that we withdraw all American forces immediately and unconditionally and that we overthrow the government of South Vietnam as we leave.

We have not limited our peace initiatives to public forums and public statements. I recognized, in January, that a long and bitter war like this usually cannot be settled in a public forum. That is why in addition to the public statements and negotiations I have explored every possible private avenue that might lead to a settlement.

Tonight I am taking the unprecedented step of disclosing to you some of our other initiatives for peace—initiatives we undertook privately and secretly because we thought we thereby might open a door which publicly would be closed.

I did not wait for my inauguration to begin my quest for peace.

- Soon after my election, through an individual who is directly in contact on a personal basis with the leaders of North Vietnam, I made two private offers for a rapid, comprehensive settlement. Hanoi's replies called in effect for our surrender before negotiations.
- Since the Soviet Union furnishes most of the military equipment for North Vietnam, Secretary of State Rogers, my assistant for National Security Affairs, Dr. Kissinger, Ambassador Lodge, and I, personally, have met on a number of occasions with representatives of the Soviet government to enlist their assistance in getting meaningful negotiations started. In addition, we have had extended discussions directed toward that same end with representatives of other governments which have diplomatic relations with North Vietnam. None of these initiatives have to date produced results.
- In mid-July, I became convinced that it was necessary to make a major move to break the deadlock in the Paris talks. I spoke directly in this office, where I am now sitting, with an individual who had known Ho Chi Minh [president, Democratic Republic of Vietnam] on a personal basis for 25 years. Through him I sent a letter to Ho Chi Minh.

I did this outside of the usual diplomatic channels with the hope that with the necessity of making statements for propaganda removed, there might be constructive progress toward bringing the war to an end. Let me read from that letter to you now.

Dear Mr. President:

I realize that it is difficult to communicate meaningfully across the gulf of four years of war. But precisely because of this gulf, I wanted to take this opportunity to reaffirm in all solemnity my desire to work for a just peace. I deeply believe that the war in Vietnam has gone on too long and delay in bringing it to an end can benefit no one—least of all the people of Vietnam. . . .

The time has come to move forward at the conference table toward an early resolution of this tragic war. You will find us forthcoming and open-minded in a common effort to bring the blessings of peace to the brave people of Vietnam. Let history record that at this critical juncture, both sides turned their face toward peace rather than toward conflict and war.

I received Ho Chi Minh's reply on August 30, three days before his death. It simply reiterated the public position North Vietnam had taken at Paris and flatly rejected my initiative.

The full text of both letters is being released to the press.

- In addition to the public meetings that I have referred to, Ambassador Lodge has met with Vietnam's chief negotiator in Paris in 11 private sessions.
- We have taken other significant initiatives which must remain secret to keep open some channels of communication which may still prove to be productive.

But the effect of all the public, private, and secret negotiations which have been undertaken since the bombing halt a year ago and since this administration came into office on January 20, can be summed up in one sentence: No progress whatever has been made except agreement on the shape of the bargaining table.

Well now, who is at fault?

It has become clear that the obstacle in negotiating an end to the war is not the president of the United States. It is not the South Vietnamese government.

The obstacle is the other side's absolute refusal to show the least willingness to join us in seeking a just peace. And it will not do so while it is convinced that all it has to do is to wait for our next concession, and our next concession after that one, until it gets everything it wants.

There can now be no longer any question that progress in negotiation depends only on Hanoi's deciding to negotiate, to negotiate seriously.

I realize that this report on our efforts on the diplomatic front is discouraging to the American people, but the American people are entitled to know the truth—the bad news as well as the good news—where the lives of our young men are involved.

Now let me turn, however, to a more encouraging report on another front.

At the time we launched our search for peace I recognized we might not succeed in bringing an end to the war through negotiation. I, therefore, put into effect another plan to bring peace—a plan which will bring the war to an end regardless of what happens on the negotiating front.

It is in line with a major shift in U.S. foreign policy which I described in my press conference at Guam on July 25. Let me briefly explain what has been described as the Nixon Doctrine—a policy which not only will help end the war in Vietnam, but which is an essential element of our program to prevent future Vietnams.

We Americans are a do-it-yourself people. We are an impatient people. Instead of teaching someone else to do a job, we like to do it ourselves. And this trait has been carried over into our foreign policy.

In Korea and again in Vietnam, the United States furnished most of the money, most of the arms, and most of the men to help the people of those countries defend their freedom against Communist aggression.

Before any American troops were committed to Vietnam, a leader of another Asian country expressed this opinion to me when I was traveling in Asia as a private citizen. He said: "When you are trying to assist another nation defend its freedom, U.S. policy should be to help them fight the war but not to fight the war for them."

Well, in accordance with this wise counsel, I laid down in Guam three principles as guidelines for future American policy toward Asia:

- First, the United States will keep all of its treaty commitments.
- Second, we shall provide a shield if a nuclear power threatens the freedom of a nation allied with us or of a nation whose survival we consider vital to our security.
- Third, in cases involving other types of aggression, we shall furnish military and economic assistance when requested in accordance

with our treaty commitments. But we shall look to the nation directly threatened to assume the primary responsibility of providing the manpower for its defense.

After I announced this policy, I found that the leaders of the Philippines, Thailand, Vietnam, South Korea, and other nations which might be threatened by Communist aggression, welcomed this new direction in American foreign policy.

The defense of freedom is everybody's business—not just America's business. And it is particularly the responsibility of the people whose freedom is threatened. In the previous administration, we Americanized the war in Vietnam. In this administration, we are Vietnamizing the search for peace.

The policy of the previous administration not only resulted in our assuming the primary responsibility for fighting the war, but even more significantly did not adequately stress the goal of strengthening the South Vietnamese so that they could defend themselves when we left.

The Vietnamization plan was launched following Secretary Laird's visit to Vietnam in March. Under the plan, I ordered first a substantial increase in the training and equipment of South Vietnamese forces.

In July, on my visit to Vietnam, I changed General Abrams's orders so that they were consistent with the objectives of our new policies. Under the new orders, the primary mission of our troops is to enable the South Vietnamese forces to assume the full responsibility for the security of South Vietnam.

Our air operations have been reduced by over 20 percent.

And now we have begun to see the results of this long overdue change in American policy in Vietnam.

- After five years of Americans going into Vietnam, we are finally bringing American men home. By December 15, over 60,000 men will have been withdrawn from South Vietnam—including 20 percent of all of our combat forces.
- The South Vietnamese have continued to gain in strength. As a result they have been able to take over combat responsibilities from our American troops.

Two other significant developments have occurred since this administration took office.

- Enemy infiltration, infiltration which is essential if they are to launch a major attack, over the last three months is less than 20 percent of what it was over the same period last year.
- Most important—United States casualties have declined during the last two months to the lowest point in three years.

Let me now turn to our program for the future.

We have adopted a plan which we have worked out in cooperation with the South Vietnamese for the complete withdrawal of all U.S. combat ground forces, and their replacement by South Vietnamese forces on an orderly scheduled timetable. This withdrawal will be made from strength and not from weakness. As South Vietnamese forces become stronger, the rate of American withdrawal can become greater.

I have not and do not intend to announce the timetable for our program. And there are obvious reasons for this decision which I am sure you will understand. As I have indicated on several occasions, the rate of withdrawal will depend on developments on three fronts.

One of these is the progress which can be or might be made in the Paris talks. An announcement of a fixed timetable for our withdrawal would completely remove any incentive for the enemy to negotiate an agreement. They would simply wait until our forces had withdrawn and then move in.

The other two factors on which we will base our withdrawal decisions are the level of enemy activity and the progress of the training programs of the South Vietnamese forces. And I am glad to be able to report tonight progress on both of these fronts has been greater than we anticipated when we started the program in June for withdrawal. As a result, our timetable for withdrawal is more optimistic now than when we made our first estimates in June. Now, this clearly demonstrates why it is not wise to be frozen in on a fixed timetable.

We must retain the flexibility to base each withdrawal decision on the situation as it is at that time rather than on estimates that are no longer valid.

Along with this optimistic estimate, I must—in all candor—leave one note of caution.

If the level of enemy activity significantly increases we might have to adjust our timetable accordingly.

However, I want the record to be completely clear on one point.

At the time of the bombing halt just a year ago, there was some confusion as to whether there was an understanding on the part of the enemy that if we stopped the bombing of North Vietnam they would stop the shelling of cities in South Vietnam. I want to be sure that there is no misunderstanding on the part of the enemy with regard to our withdrawal program.

We have noted the reduced level of infiltration, the reduction of our casualties, and are basing our withdrawal decisions partially on those factors.

If the level of infiltration or our casualties increase while we are trying to scale down the fighting, it will be the result of a conscious decision by the enemy.

Hanoi could make no greater mistake than to assume that an increase in violence will be to its advantage. If I conclude that increased enemy action jeopardizes our remaining forces in Vietnam, I shall not hesitate to take strong and effective measures to deal with that situation.

This is not a threat. This is a statement of policy, which as commander in chief of our armed forces, I am making in meeting my responsibility for the protection of American fighting men wherever they may be.

My fellow Americans, I am sure you can recognize from what I have said that we really only have two choices open to us if we want to end this war.

- I can order an immediate, precipitate withdrawal of all Americans from Vietnam without regard to the effects of that action.
- Or we can persist in our search for a just peace through a negotiated settlement if possible, or through continued implementation of our plan for Vietnamization if necessary—a plan in which we will withdraw all of our forces from Vietnam on a schedule in accordance with our program, as the South Vietnamese become strong enough to defend their own freedom.

I have chosen this second course.
It is not the easy way.
It is the right way.

It is a plan which will end the war and serve the cause of peace—not just in Vietnam but in the Pacific and in the world.

In speaking of the consequences of a precipitate withdrawal, I mentioned that our allies would lose confidence in America.

Far more dangerous, we would lose confidence in ourselves. Oh, the immediate reaction would be a sense of relief that our men were coming home. But as we saw the consequences of what we had done, inevitable remorse and divisive recrimination would scar our spirit as a people.

We have faced other crises in our history and have become stronger by rejecting the easy way out and taking the right way in meeting our challllenges. Our greatness as a nation has been our capacity to do what had to be done when we knew our course was right.

I recognize that some of my fellow citizens disagree with the plan for peace I have chosen. Honest and patriotic Americans have reached different conclusions as to how peace should be achieved.

In San Francisco a few weeks ago, I saw demonstrators carrying signs reading: "Lose in Vietnam, bring the boys home."

Well, one of the strengths of our free society is that any American has a right to reach that conclusion and to advocate that point of view. But as president of the United States, I would be untrue to my oath of office if I allowed the policy of this nation to be dictated by the minority who hold that point of view and who try to impose it on the nation by mounting demonstrations in the street.

For almost 200 years, the policy of this nation has been made under our Constitution by those leaders in the Congress and the White House elected by all of the people. If a vocal minority, however fervent its cause, prevails over reason and the will of the majority, this nation has no future as a free society.

And now I would like to address a word, if I may, to the young people of this nation who are particularly concerned, and I understand why they are concerned, about this war.

I respect your idealism.
I share your concern for peace.
I want peace as much as you do.

There are powerful personal reasons I want to end this war. This week I will have to sign 83 letters to mothers, fathers, wives, and loved ones of men who have given their lives for America in Vietnam. It is very little satisfaction to me that this is only one-third as many letters as I signed the first week in office. There is nothing I want more than to see the day come when I do not have to write any of those letters.

- I want to end the war to save the lives of those brave young men in Vietnam.
- But I want to end it in a way which will increase the chance that their young brothers and their sons will not have to fight in some future Vietnam someplace in the world.
- And I want to end the war for another reason. I want to end it so that the energy and dedication of you, our young people, now too often directed into bitter hatred against those responsible for the war, can be turned to the great challenges of peace, a better life for all Americans, a better life for all people on this earth.

I have chosen a plan for peace. I believe it will succeed.

If it does succeed, what the critics say now won't matter. If it does not succeed, anything I say then won't matter.

I know it may not be fashionable to speak of patriotism or national destiny these days. But I feel it is appropriate to do so on this occasion.

Two hundred years ago this nation was weak and poor. But even then, America was the hope of millions in the world. Today we have become the strongest and richest nation in the world. And the wheel of destiny has turned so that any hope the world has for the survival of peace and freedom will be determined by whether the American people have the moral stamina and the courage to meet the challenge of free world leadership.

Let historians not record that when America was the most powerful nation in the world we passed on the other side of the road and allowed the last hopes for peace and freedom of millions of people to be suffocated by the forces of totalitarianism.

And so tonight—to you, the great silent majority of my fellow Americans—I ask for your support.

I pledged in my campaign for the presidency to end the war in a way that we could win the peace. I have initiated a plan of action which will enable me to keep that pledge.

The more support I can have from the American people, the sooner that pledge can be redeemed; for the more divided we are at home, the less likely the enemy is to negotiate at Paris.

Let us be united for peace. Let us also be united against defeat. Because let us understand: North Vietnam cannot defeat or humiliate the United States. Only Americans can do that.

Fifty years ago, in this room and at this very desk, President Woodrow Wilson spoke words which caught the imagination of a war-weary world. He said: 'This is the war to end war." His dream for peace after World War I was shattered on the hard realities of great power politics, and Woodrow Wilson died a broken man.

Tonight I do not tell you that the war in Vietnam is the war to end wars. But I do say this: I have initiated a plan which will end this war in a way that will bring us closer to that great goal to which Woodrow Wilson and every American president in our history has been dedicated—the goal of a just and lasting peace.

As president I hold the responsibility for choosing the best path to that goal and then leading the nation along it.

I pledge to you tonight that I shall meet this responsibility with all of the strength and wisdom I can command in accordance with your hopes, mindful of your concerns, sustained by your prayers.

Thank you and goodnight.

The Invasion of Cambodia

Washington, D.C.

April 30, 1970

THREE MONTHS after taking office, Nixon ordered the extension of bombing raids into Vietnam's neighbor, Cambodia. This operation was kept secret from the public, from Congress, and even from some military leaders. In April of 1970 Nixon went on national television to announce that he had ordered a ground invasion of Cambodia to attack Communist supply bases there. The speech, writes Schell, was "the most comprehensive statement of the doctrine of credibility that had ever been made by an American president"—the doctrine, that is, that any defeat, or even the appearance of defeat, in American foreign policy would decrease the nation's power to affect world affairs.

The reaction on college campuses was one of outrage. A few days after the speech was delivered, four students attending a demonstration at Kent State University in Ohio were shot to death by National Guardsmen. Within a week, nearly 450 colleges and universities had been shut down by protesters. The bitterness over these killings lasted longer than the invasion, which was over within two months.

Ten days ago, in my report to the nation on Vietnam, I announced a decision to withdraw an additional 150,000 Americans from Vietnam over the next year. I said then that I was making that decision despite our concern over increased enemy activity in Laos, in Cambodia, and in South Vietnam.

At that time, I warned that if I concluded that increased enemy activity in any of these areas endangered the lives of Americans remaining in Vietnam, I would not hesitate to take strong and effective measures to deal with that situation.

Despite that warning, North Vietnam has increased its military aggression in all these areas, and particularly in Cambodia.

After full consultation with the National Security Council, Ambassador Bunker, General Abrams, and my other advisers, I have concluded that the actions of the enemy in the last 10 days clearly endanger the lives of Americans who are in Vietnam now and would constitute an unacceptable risk to those who will be there after withdrawal of another 150,000.

To protect our men who are in Vietnam and to guarantee the continued success of our withdrawal and Vietnamization programs, I have concluded that the time has come for action.

Tonight, I shall describe the actions of the enemy, the actions I have ordered to deal with that situation, and the reasons for my decision.

Cambodia, a small country of seven million people, has been a neutral nation since the Geneva Agreement of 1954—an agreement, incidentally, which was signed by the government of North Vietnam.

American policy since then has been to scrupulously respect the neutrality of the Cambodian people. We have maintained a skeleton diplomatic mission of fewer than 15 in Cambodia's capital, and that only since last August. For the previous four years, from 1965 to 1969, we did not have any diplomatic mission whatever in Cambodia. And for the past five years, we have provided no military assistance whatever and no economic assistance to Cambodia.

North Vietnam, however, has not respected that neutrality.

For the past five years—as indicated on this map that you see here—North Vietnam has occupied military sanctuaries all along the Cambodian frontier with South Vietnam. Some of these extend up to 20 miles into Cambodia. The sanctuaries are in red and, as you note, they are on both sides of the border. They are used for hit and run attacks on American and South Vietnamese forces in South Vietnam.

These Communist-occupied territories contain major base camps, training sites, logistics facilities, weapons and ammunition factories, air strips, and prisoner-of-war compounds.

For five years, neither the United States nor South Vietnam has moved against these enemy sanctuaries because we did not wish to violate the territory of a neutral nation. Even after the Vietnamese Communists began to expand these sanctuaries four weeks ago, we counseled patience to our South Vietnamese allies and imposed restraints on our own commanders.

In contrast to our policy, the enemy in the past two weeks has stepped up his guerrilla actions, and he is concentrating his main forces in these sanctuaries that you see on this map where they are building up to launch massive attacks on our forces and those of South Vietnam.

North Vietnam in the last two weeks has stripped away all pretense of respecting the sovereignty or the neutrality of Cambodia. Thousands of their soldiers are invading the country from the sanctuaries; they are encircling the capital of Phnom Penh. Coming from these sanctuaries, as you see here, they have moved into Cambodia and are encircling the capital.

Cambodia, as a result of this, has sent out a call to the United States, to a number of other nations, for assistance. Because if this enemy effort succeeds, Cambodia would become a vast enemy staging area and a springboard for attacks on South Vietnam along 600 miles of frontier—a refuge where enemy troops could return from combat without fear of retaliation.

North Vietnamese men and supplies could then be poured into that country, jeopardizing not only the lives of our own men but the people of South Vietnam as well.

Now confronted with this situation, we have three options.

First, we can do nothing. Well, the ultimate result of that course of action is clear. Unless we indulge in wishful thinking, the lives of Americans remaining in Vietnam after our next withdrawal of 150,000 would be gravely threatened.

Let us go to the map again. Here is South Vietnam. Here is North Vietnam. North Vietnam already occupies this part of Laos. If North Vietnam also occupied this whole band in Cambodia, or the entire country, it would mean that South Vietnam was completely outflanked and the forces of Americans in this area, as well as the South Vietnamese, would be in an untenable military position.

Our second choice is to provide massive military assistance to Cambodia itself. Now unfortunately, while we deeply sympathize with the plight of seven million Cambodians whose country is being invaded, massive amounts of military assistance could not be rapidly and effectively utilized by the small Cambodian army against the immediate threat.

With other nations, we shall do our best to provide the small arms and other equipment which the Cambodian army of 40,000 needs and can use for its defense. But the aid we will provide will be limited to the purpose of enabling Cambodia to defend its neutrality and not for the purpose of making it an active belligerent on one side or the other.

Our third choice is to go to the heart of the trouble. That means cleaning out major North Vietnamese and Vietcong occupied territories, these sanctuaries which serve as bases for attacks on both Cambodia and American and South Vietnamese forces in South Vietnam. Some of these, incidentally, are as close to Saigon as Baltimore is to Washington.

This one, for example, is called the Parrot's Beak. It is only 33 miles from Saigon.

Now faced with these three options, this is the decision I have made.

In cooperation with the armed forces of South Vietnam, attacks are being launched this week to clean out major enemy sanctuaries on the Cambodian-Vietnam border.

A major responsibility for the ground operations is being assumed by South Vietnamese forces. For example, the attacks in several areas, including the Parrot's Beak that I referred to a moment ago, are exclusively South Vietnamese ground operations under South Vietnamese command with the United States providing air and logistical support.

There is one area, however, immediately above Parrot's Beak, where I have concluded that a combined American and South Vietnamese operation is necessary.

Tonight, American and South Vietnamese units will attack the headquarters for the entire Communist military operation in South Vietnam. This key control center has been occupied by the North Vietnamese and Vietcong for five years in blatant violation of Cambodia's neutrality.

This is not an invasion of Cambodia. The areas in which these attacks will be launched are completely occupied and controlled by North Vietnamese forces. Our purpose is not to occupy the areas. Once enemy forces are driven out of these sanctuaries and once their military supplies are destroyed, we will withdraw.

These actions are in no way directed at the security interests of any nation. Any government that chooses to use these actions as a pretext for harming relations with the United States will be doing so on its own responsibility, and on its own initiative, and we will draw the appropriate conclusions.

Now let me give you the reasons for my decision.

A majority of the American people, a majority of you listening to me, are for the withdrawal of our forces from Vietnam. The action I have taken tonight is indispensable for the continuing success of that withdrawal program.

A majority of the American people want to end this war rather than to have it drag on interminably. The action I have taken tonight will serve that purpose.

A majority of the American people want to keep the casualties of our brave men in Vietnam at an absolute minimum. The action I take tonight is essential if we are to accomplish that goal.

We take this action not for the purpose of expanding the war into Cambodia but for the purpose of ending the war in Vietnam and winning the just peace we all desire. We have made and we will continue to make every possible effort to end this war through negotiation at the conference table rather than through more fighting on the battlefield.

Let us look again at the record. We have stopped the bombing of North Vietnam. We have cut air operations by over 20 percent. We have announced withdrawal of over 250,000 of our men. We have offered to withdraw all of our men if they will withdraw theirs. We have offered to negotiate all issues with only one condition—and that is that the future of South Vietnam be determined not by North Vietnam, not by the United States, but by the people of South Vietnam themselves.

The answer of the enemy has been intransigence at the conference table, belligerence in Hanoi, massive military aggression in Laos and Cambodia, and stepped-up attacks in South Vietnam, designed to increase American casualties.

This attitude has become intolerable. We will not react to this threat to American lives merely by plaintive diplomatic protests. If we did, the credibility of the United States would be destroyed in every area of the world where only the power of the United States deters aggression.

Tonight, I again warn the North Vietnamese that if they continue to escalate the fighting when the United States is withdrawing its forces, I shall meet my responsibility as commander in chief of our armed forces to take the action I consider necessary to defend the security of our American men.

The action that I have announced tonight puts the leaders of North Vietnam on notice that we will be patient in working for peace, we will be conciliatory at the conference table, but we will not be humiliated. We will not be defeated. We will not allow American men by the thousands to be killed by an enemy from privileged sanctuaries.

The time came long ago to end this war through peaceful negotiations. We stand ready for those negotiations. We have made major efforts, many of which must remain secret. I say tonight that all the offers and approaches made previously remain on the conference table whenever Hanoi is ready to negotiate seriously.

But if the enemy response to our most conciliatory offers for peaceful negotiation continues to be to increase its attacks and humiliate and defeat us, we shall react accordingly.

My fellow Americans, we live in an age of anarchy both abroad and at home. We see mindless attacks on all the great institutions which have been created by free civilizations in the last 500 years. Even here in the United States, great universities are being systematically destroyed. Small nations all over the world find themselves under attack from within and from without.

If, when the chips are down, the world's most powerful nation, the United States of America, acts like a pitiful, helpless giant, the forces of totalitarianism and anarchy will threaten free nations and free institutions throughout the world.

It is not our power but our will and character that is being tested tonight. The question all Americans must ask and answer tonight is this: Does the richest and strongest nation in the history of the world have the character to meet a direct challenge by a group which rejects every effort to win a just peace, ignores our warning, tramples on solemn agreements, violates the neutrality of an unarmed people, and uses our prisoners as hostages?

If we fail to meet this challenge, all other nations will be on notice that despite its overwhelming power the United States, when a real crisis comes, will be found wanting.

During my campaign for the presidency, I pledged to bring Americans home from Vietnam. They are coming home.

I promised to end this war. I shall keep that promise.

I promised to win a just peace. I shall keep that promise.

We shall avoid a wider war. But we are also determined to put an end to this war.

In this room, Woodrow Wilson made the great decisions which led to victory in World War I. Franklin Roosevelt made the decisions which led to our victory in World War II. Dwight D. Eisenhower made decisions which ended the war in Korea and avoided war in the Middle East. John F. Kennedy, in his finest hour, made the great decision which removed Soviet nuclear missiles from Cuba and the Western Hemisphere.

I have noted that there has been a great deal of discussion with regard to this decision that I have made, and I should point out that I do not contend that it is in the same magnitude as these decisions that I have just mentioned. But between those decisions and this decision there is a difference that is very fundamental. In those decisions, the American people were not assailed by counsels of doubt and defeat from some of the most widely known opinion leaders of the nation.

I have noted, for example, that a Republican senator has said that this action I have taken means that my party has lost all chance of winning the November elections. And others are saying today that this move against enemy sanctuaries will make me a one-term president.

No one is more aware than I am of the political consequences of the action I have taken. It is tempting to take the easy political path: to blame this war on previous administrations and to bring all of our men home immediately, regardless of the consequences, even though

that would mean defeat for the United States; to desert 18 million South Vietnamese people, who have put their trust in us and to expose them to the same slaughter and savagery which the leaders of North Vietnam inflicted on hundreds of thousands of North Vietnamese who chose freedom when the Communists took over North Vietnam in 1954; to get peace at any price now, even though I know that a peace of humiliation for the United States would lead to a bigger war or surrender later.

I have rejected all political considerations in making this decision.

Whether my party gains in November is nothing compared to the lives of 400,000 brave Americans fighting for our country and for the cause of peace and freedom in Vietnam. Whether I may be a one-term president is insignificant compared to whether by our failure to act in this crisis the United States proves itself to be unworthy to lead the forces of freedom in this critical period in world history. I would rather be a one-term president and do what I believe is right than to be a two-term president at the cost of seeing America become a second-rate power and to see this nation accept the first defeat in its proud 190-year history.

I realize that in this war there are honest and deep differences in this country about whether we should have become involved, that there are differences as to how the war should have been conducted. But the decision I announce tonight transcends those differences.

For the lives of American men are involved. The opportunity for 150,000 Americans to come home in the next 12 months is involved. The future of 18 million people in South Vietnam and seven million people in Cambodia is involved. The possibility of winning a just peace in Vietnam and in the Pacific is at stake.

It is customary to conclude a speech from the White House by asking support for the president of the United States. Tonight, I depart from that precedent. What I ask is far more important. I ask for your support for our brave men fighting tonight halfway around the world—not for territory—not for glory—but so that their younger brothers and their sons and your sons can have a chance to grow up in a world of peace and freedom and justice.

The New American Revolution

From the Second State of the Union Message
Washington, D.C.
January 22, 1971

ALTHOUGH HE KEPT his conservative backers happy by denouncing Lyndon Johnson's Great Society programs, undercutting civil rights legislation, and proposing drastic law enforcement measures, Nixon also put forward a number of progressive proposals, including support for welfare reform, the arts, environmental protection, and worker safety. One of his pet projects was the "New Federalism," a plan to return some federal funding and decision-making powers to state and local authorities. He outlined his ideas, and his intention to reorganize the executive branch accordingly, in his 1971 State of the Union message to Congress.

. . . Mr. Speaker, this 92d Congress has a chance to be recorded as the greatest Congress in America's history.

In these troubled years just past, America has been going through a long nightmare of war and division, of crime and inflation. Even more deeply, we have gone through a long, dark night of the American spirit. But now that night is ending. Now we must let our spirits soar again. Now we are ready for the lift of a driving dream.

The people of this nation are eager to get on with the quest for new greatness. They see challenges, and they are prepared to meet those challenges. It is for us here to open the doors that will set free again the real greatness of this nation—the genius of the American people.

How shall we meet this challenge? How can we truly open the doors, and set free the full genius of our people?

The way in which the 92d Congress answers these questions will determine its place in history. More importantly, it can determine this nation's place in history as we enter the third century of our independence.

Tonight I shall present to the Congress six great goals. I shall ask not simply for more new programs in the old framework. I shall ask to change the framework of government itself—to reform the entire structure of American government so we can make it again fully responsive to the needs and the wishes of the American people.

If we act boldly—if we seize this moment and achieve these goals—we can close the gap between promise and performance in American government. We can bring together the resources of this nation and the spirit of the American people.

In discussing these great goals, I shall deal tonight only with matters on the domestic side of the nation's agenda. I shall make a separate report to the Congress and the nation next month on developments in foreign policy.

The first of these great goals is already before the Congress.

I urge that the unfinished business of the 91st Congress be made the first priority business of the 92d Congress.

Over the next two weeks, I will call upon Congress to take action on more than 35 pieces of proposed legislation on which action was not completed last year.

The most important is welfare reform.

The present welfare system has become a monstrous, consuming outrage—an outrage against the community, against the taxpayer, and particularly against the children it is supposed to help.

We may honestly disagree, as we do, on what to do about it. But we can all agree that we must meet the challenge, not by pouring more money into a bad program, but by abolishing the present welfare system and adopting a new one.

So let us place a floor under the income of every family with children in America—and without those demeaning, soul-stifling affronts to human dignity that so blight the lives of welfare children today. But let us also establish an effective work incentive and an effective work requirement.

Let us provide the means by which more can help themselves. This shall be our goal.

Let us generously help those who are not able to help themselves. But let us stop helping those who are able to help themselves but refuse to do so.

The second great goal is to achieve what Americans have not enjoyed since 1957—full prosperity in peacetime.

The tide of inflation has turned. The rise in the cost of living, which had been gathering dangerous momentum in the late sixties, was reduced last year. Inflation will be further reduced this year.

But as we have moved from runaway inflation toward reasonable price stability and at the same time as we have been moving from a wartime economy to a peacetime economy, we have paid a price in increased unemployment.

We should take no comfort from the fact that the level of unemployment in this transition from a wartime to a peacetime economy is lower than in any peacetime year of the sixties.

This is not good enough for the man who is unemployed in the seventies. We must do better for workers in peacetime and we will do better.

To achieve this, I will submit an expansionary budget this year—one that will help stimulate the economy and thereby open up new job opportunities for millions of Americans.

It will be a full employment budget, a budget designed to be in balance if the economy were operating at its peak potential. By spending as if we were at full employment, we will help to bring about full employment.

I ask the Congress to accept these expansionary policies—to accept the concept of a full employment budget. At the same time, I ask the Congress to cooperate in resisting expenditures that go beyond the limits of the full employment budget. For as we wage a campaign to bring about a widely shared prosperity, we must not reignite the fires of inflation and so undermine that prosperity.

With the stimulus and the discipline of a full employment budget, with the commitment of the independent Federal Reserve System to provide fully for the monetary needs of a growing economy, and with a much greater effort on the part of labor and management to make their wage and price decisions in the light of the national interest and their own self-interest—then for the worker, the farmer, the consumer, for Americans everywhere we shall gain the goal of a new prosperity: more jobs, more income, more profits, without inflation and without war.

This is a great goal, and one that we can achieve together.

The third great goal is to continue the effort so dramatically begun last year: to restore and enhance our natural environment.

Building on the foundation laid in the 37-point program that I submitted to Congress last year, I will propose a strong new set of initiatives to clean up our air and water, to combat noise, and to preserve and restore our surroundings.

I will propose programs to make better use of our land, to encourage a balanced national growth—growth that will revitalize our rural heartland and enhance the quality of life in America.

And not only to meet today's needs but to anticipate those of tomorrow, I will put forward the most extensive program ever proposed by a president of the United States to expand the nation's parks, recreation areas, open spaces, in a way that truly brings parks to the people where the people are. For only if we leave a legacy of parks will the next generation have parks to enjoy.

As a fourth great goal, I will offer a far-reaching set of proposals for improving America's health care and making it available more fairly to more people.

I will propose:

- A program to insure that no American family will be prevented from obtaining basic medical care by inability to pay.
- I will propose a major increase in and redirection of aid to medical schools, to greatly increase the number of doctors and other health personnel.
- Incentives to improve the delivery of health services, to get more medical care resources into those areas that have not been adequately served, to make greater use of medical assistants, and to slow the alarming rise in the costs of medical care.
- New programs to encourage better preventive medicine, by attacking the causes of disease and injury, and by providing incentives to doctors to keep people well rather than just to treat them when they are sick.

I will also ask for an appropriation of an extra $100 million to launch an intensive campaign to find a cure for cancer, and I will ask later for whatever additional funds can effectively be used. The time has come in America when the same kind of concentrated effort that split the atom and took man to the Moon should be turned toward conquering this dread disease. Let us make a total national commitment to achieve this goal.

America has long been the wealthiest nation in the world. Now it is time we became the healthiest nation in the world.

The fifth great goal is to strengthen and to renew our state and local governments.

As we approach our 200th anniversary in 1976, we remember that this nation launched itself as a loose confederation of separate states, without a workable central government. At that time, the mark of its leaders' vision was that they quickly saw the need to balance the separate powers of the states with a government of central powers.

And so they gave us a constitution of balanced powers, of unity with diversity—and so clear was their vision that it survives today as the oldest written constitution still in force in the world.

For almost two centuries since—and dramatically in the 1930s—at those great turning points when the question has been between the states and the federal government, that question has been resolved in favor of a stronger central federal government.

During this time the nation grew and the nation prospered. But one thing history tells us is that no great movement goes in the same direction forever. Nations change, they adapt, or they slowly die.

The time has now come in America to reverse the flow of power and resources from the states and communities to Washington, and start power and resources flowing back from Washington to the states and communities and, more important, to the people all across America.

The time has come for a new partnership between the federal government and the states and localities—a partnership in which we entrust the states and localities with a larger share of the nation's responsibilities, and in which we share our federal revenues with them so that they can meet those responsibilities.

To achieve this goal, I propose to the Congress tonight that we enact a plan of revenue sharing historic in scope and bold in concept.

All across America today, states and cities are confronted with a financial crisis. Some have already been cutting back on essential services—for example, just recently San Diego and Cleveland cut back on trash collections. Most are caught between the prospects of bankruptcy on the one hand and adding to an already crushing tax burden on the other.

As one indication of the rising costs of local government, I discovered the other day that my home town of Whittier, California—which has a population of 67,000—has a larger budget for 1971 than the entire federal budget was in 1791.

Now the time has come to take a new direction, and once again to introduce a new and more creative balance to our approach to government.

So let us put the money where the needs are. And let us put the power to spend it where the people are.

I propose that the Congress make a $16 billion investment in renewing state and local government. Five billion dollars of this will be in new and unrestricted funds to be used as the states and localities see fit. The other $11 billion will be provided by allocating $1 billion of new funds and converting one-third of the money going to the present narrow-purpose aid programs into federal revenue-sharing funds for six broad purposes—for urban development, rural development, education, transportation, job training, and law enforcement—but with the states and localities making their own decisions on how it should be spent within each category.

For the next fiscal year, this would increase total federal aid to the states and localities more than 25 percent over the present level.

The revenue-sharing proposals I send to the Congress will include the safeguards against discrimination that accompany all other federal funds allocated to the states. Neither the president nor the Congress nor the conscience of this nation can permit money which comes from all the people to be used in a way which discriminates against some of the people.

The federal government will still have a large and vital role to play in achieving our national progress. Established functions that are clearly and essentially federal in nature will still be performed by the federal government. New functions that need to be sponsored or performed by the federal government—such

743

as those I have urged tonight in welfare and health—will be added to the federal agenda. Whenever it makes the best sense for us to act as a whole nation, the federal government should and will lead the way. But where states or local governments can better do what needs to be done, let us see that they have the resources to do it there.

Under this plan, the federal government will provide the states and localities with more money and less interference—and by cutting down the interference the same amount of money will go a lot further.

Let us share our resources.

Let us share them to rescue the states and localities from the brink of financial crisis.

Let us share them to give homeowners and wage earners a chance to escape from ever-higher property taxes and sales taxes.

Let us share our resources for two other reasons as well.

The first of these reasons has to do with government itself, and the second has to do with each of us, with the individual.

Let's face it. Most Americans today are simply fed up with government at all levels. They will not—and they should not—continue to tolerate the gap between promise and performance in government.

The fact is that we have made the federal government so strong it grows musclebound and the states and localities so weak they approach impotence.

If we put more power in more places, we can make government more creative in more places. That way we multiply the number of people with the ability to make things happen—and we can open the way to a new burst of creative energy throughout America.

The final reason I urge this historic shift is much more personal, for each and for everyone of us.

As everything seems to have grown bigger and more complex in America, as the forces that shape our lives seem to have grown more distant and more impersonal, a great feeling of frustration has crept across this land.

Whether it is the workingman who feels neglected, the black man who feels oppressed, or the mother concerned about her children, there has been a growing feeling that "Things are in the saddle, and ride mankind."

Millions of frustrated young Americans today are crying out—asking not what will government do for me, but what can I do, how can I contribute, how can I matter?

And so let us answer them. Let us say to them and let us say to all Americans, "We hear you. We will give you a chance. We are going to give you a new chance to have more to say about the decisions that affect your future—a chance to participate in government—because we are going to provide more centers of power where what you do can make a difference that you can see and feel in your own life and the life of your whole community."

The further away government is from people, the stronger government becomes and the weaker people become. And a nation with a strong government and a weak people is an empty shell.

I reject the patronizing idea that government in Washington, D.C., is inevitably more wise, more honest, and more efficient than government at the local or state level. The honesty and efficiency of government depends on people. Government at all levels has good people and bad people. And the way to get more good people into government is to give them more opportunity to do good things.

The idea that a bureaucratic elite in Washington knows best what is best for people everywhere and that you cannot trust local governments is really a contention that you cannot trust people to govern themselves. This notion is completely foreign to the American experience. Local government is the government closest to the people, it is most responsive to the individual person. It is people's government in a far more intimate way than the government in Washington can ever be.

People came to America because they wanted to determine their own future rather than to live in a country where others determined their future for them.

What this change means is that once again in America we are placing our trust in people.

I have faith in people. I trust the judgment of people. Let us give the people of America a chance, a bigger voice in deciding for themselves those questions that so greatly affect their lives.

The sixth great goal is a complete reform of the federal government itself.

Based on a long and intensive study with the aid of the best advice obtainable, I have concluded that a sweeping reorganization of the executive branch is needed if the government is to keep up with the times and with the needs of the people.

I propose, therefore, that we reduce the present 12 cabinet departments to eight.

I propose that the Departments of State, Treasury, Defense, and Justice remain, but that all the other departments be consolidated into four: Human Resources, Community Development, Natural Resources, and Economic Development.

Let us look at what these would be:

- First, a department dealing with the concerns of people—as individuals, as members of a family—a department focused on human needs.
- Second, a department concerned with the community—rural communities and urban communities—and with all that it takes to make a community function as a community.
- Third, a department concerned with our physical environment, with the preservation and balanced use of those great natural resources on which our nation depends.
- And fourth, a department concerned with our prosperity—with our jobs, our businesses, and those many activities that keep our economy running smoothly and well.

Under this plan, rather than dividing up our departments by narrow subjects, we would organize them around the great purposes of government. Rather than scattering responsibility by adding new levels of bureaucracy, we would focus and concentrate the responsibility for getting problems solved.

With these four departments, when we have a problem we will know where to go—and the department will have the authority and the resources to do something about it.

Over the years we have added departments and created agencies at the federal level, each to serve a new constituency, to handle a particular task—and these have grown and multiplied in what has become a hopeless confusion of form and function.

The time has come to match our structure to our purposes—to look with a fresh eye, to organize the government by conscious, comprehensive design to meet the new needs of a new era.

One hundred years ago, Abraham Lincoln stood on a battlefield and spoke of a "government of the people, by the people, for the people." Too often since then, we have become a nation of the government, by the government, for the government.

By enacting these reforms, we can renew that principle that Lincoln stated so simply and so well.

By giving everyone's voice a chance to be heard, we will have government that truly is of the people.

By creating more centers of meaningful power, more places where decisions that really count can be made, by giving more people a chance to do something, we can have government that truly is by the people.

And by setting up a completely modern, functional system of government at the national level, we in Washington will at last be able to provide government that is truly for the people.

I realize that what I am asking is that not only the executive branch in Washington but that even this Congress will have to change by giving up some of its power.

Change is hard. But without change there can be no progress. And for each of us the question then becomes, not "Will change cause me inconvenience?" but "Will change bring progress for America?"

Giving up power is hard. But I would urge all of you, as leaders of this country, to remember that the truly revered leaders in world history are those who gave power to people, and not those who took it away.

As we consider these reforms we will be acting, not for the next two years or for the next 10 years, but for the next 100 years.

So let us approach these six great goals with a sense not only of this moment in history but also of history itself.

Let us act with the willingness to work together and the vision and the boldness and the courage of those great Americans who met in Philadelphia almost 190 years ago to write a constitution.

Let us leave a heritage as they did—not just for our children but for millions yet unborn—of a nation where every American will have a chance not only to live in peace and to enjoy prosperity and opportunity but to participate in a system of government where he knows not only his votes but his ideas count—a system of government which will provide the means for America to reach heights of achievement undreamed of before.

Those men who met at Philadelphia left a great heritage because they had a vision—not only of what the nation was but of what it could become.

As I think of that vision, I recall that America was founded as the land of the open door—as a haven for the oppressed, a land of opportunity, a place of refuge, of hope.

When the first settlers opened the door of America three and a half centuries ago, they came to escape persecution and to find opportunity—and they left wide the door of welcome for others to follow.

When the 13 colonies declared their independence almost two centuries ago, they opened the door to a new vision of liberty and of human fulfillment—not just for an elite but for all.

To the generations that followed, America's was the open door that beckoned millions from the old world to the new in search of a better life, a freer life, a fuller life, and in which, by their own decisions, they could shape their own destinies.

For the black American, the Indian, the Mexican-American, and for those others in our land who have not had an equal chance, the nation at last has begun to confront the need to press open the door of full and equal opportunity, and of human dignity.

For all Americans, with these changes I have proposed tonight we can open the door to a new era of opportunity. We can open the door to full and effective participation in the decisions that affect their lives. We can open the door to a new partnership among governments at all levels, between those governments and the people themselves. And by so doing, we can open wide the doors of human fulfillment for millions of people here in America now and in the years to come.

In the next few weeks I will spell out in greater detail the way I propose that we achieve these six great goals. I ask this Congress to be responsive. If it is, then the 92d Congress, your Congress, our Congress, at the end of its term, will be able to look back on a record more splendid than any in our history.

This can be the Congress that helped us end the longest war in the nation's history, and end it in a way that will give us at last a genuine chance to enjoy what we have not had in this century: a full generation of peace.

This can be the Congress that helped achieve an expanding economy, with full employment and without inflation—and without the deadly stimulus of war.

This can be the Congress that reformed a welfare system that has robbed recipients of their dignity and robbed states and cities of their resources.

This can be the Congress that pressed forward the rescue of our environment, and established for the next generation an enduring legacy of parks for the people.

This can be the Congress that launched a new era in American medicine, in which the quality of medical care was enhanced while the costs were made less burdensome.

But above all, what this Congress can be remembered for is opening the way to a new American revolution—a peaceful revolution in which power was turned back to the people—in which government at all levels was refreshed and renewed and made truly responsive. This can be a revolution as profound, as far-reaching, as exciting as that first revolution almost 200 years ago—and it can mean that just five years from now America will enter its third century as a young nation new in spirit, with all the vigor and the freshness with which it began its first century.

My colleagues in the Congress, these are great goals. They can make the sessions of this Congress a great moment for America. So let us pledge together to go forward together—by achieving these goals to give America the foundation today for a new greatness tomorrow and in all the years to come, and in so doing to make this the greatest Congress in the history of this great and good country.

The New Economic Policy

Washington, D.C.

August 15, 1971

THE YEAR 1971 was notable for three actions that became known as the "Nixon shocks"—the announcement that the fiercely anti-Communist Nixon would visit the People's Republic of China; the announcement that he would go to Moscow for a summit conference; and the announcement that he would impose wage and price controls. It had long been a tenet of Nixon's economic philosophy that such controls were anathema in a society based on free trade. But with the 1972 election approaching, the Treasury's gold reserves diminishing, and inflation and unemployment rising despite a massive budget deficit, Nixon decided to take drastic steps. A conference of his economic advisers at his Camp David retreat produced a program of restraints that Nixon outlined to the nation in a televised speech. (William Safire, who contributed to the speech, notes that the title was, ironically, identical to a slogan used by Lenin.) Most of the restraints were lifted within 18 months.

I have addressed the nation a number of times over the past two years on the problems of ending a war. Because of the progress we have made toward achieving that goal, this Sunday evening is an appropriate time for us to turn our attention to the challenges of peace.

America today has the best opportunity in this century to achieve two of its greatest ideals: to bring about a full generation of peace, and to create a new prosperity without war.

This not only requires bold leadership ready to take bold action—it calls forth the greatness in a great people.

Prosperity without war requires action on three fronts: We must create more and better jobs; we must stop the rise in the cost of living; we must protect the dollar from the attacks of international money speculators.

We are going to take that action—not timidly, not half-heartedly, and not in piecemeal fashion. We are going to move forward to the new prosperity without war as befits a great people—all together, and along a broad front.

The time has come for a new economic policy for the United States. Its targets are unemployment, inflation, and international speculation. And this is how we are going to attack those targets.

First, on the subject of jobs. We all know why we have an unemployment problem. Two million workers have been released from the armed forces and defense plants because of our success in winding down the war in Vietnam. Putting those people back to work is one of the challenges of peace, and we have begun to make progress. Our unemployment rate today is below the average of the four peacetime years of the 1960s.

But we can and we must do better than that.

The time has come for American industry, which has produced more jobs at higher real wages than any other industrial system in history, to embark on a bold program of new investment in production for peace.

To give that system a powerful new stimulus, I shall ask the Congress, when it reconvenes after its summer recess, to consider as its first priority the enactment of the Job Development Act of 1971.

I will propose to provide the strongest short-term incentive in our history to invest in new machinery and equipment that will create new jobs for Americans: a 10 percent Job Development Credit for one year, effective as of today, with a 5 percent credit after August 15, 1972. This tax credit for investment in new equipment will not only generate new jobs; it will raise productivity; it will make our goods more competitive in the years ahead.

Second, I will propose to repeal the 7 percent excise tax on automobiles, effective today. This will mean a reduction in price of about $200 per car. I shall insist that the American auto industry pass this tax reduction on to the nearly eight million customers who are buying automobiles this year. Lower prices will mean that more people will be able to afford new cars, and every additional 100,000 cars sold means 25,000 new jobs.

Third, I propose to speed up the personal income tax exemptions scheduled for January 1, 1973, to January 1, 1972—so that taxpayers can deduct an extra $50 for each exemption one year earlier than planned. This increase in consumer spending power will provide a strong boost to the economy in general and to employment in particular.

The tax reductions I am recommending, together with this broad upturn of the economy which has taken place in the first half of this year, will move us strongly forward toward a goal this nation has not reached since 1956, 15 years ago: prosperity with full employment in peacetime.

Looking to the future, I have directed the secretary of the treasury to recommend to the Congress in January new tax proposals for stimulating research and development of new industries and new techniques to help provide the 20 million new jobs that America needs for the young people who will be coming into the job market in the next decade.

To offset the loss of revenue from these tax cuts which directly stimulate new jobs, I have ordered today a $4.7 billion cut in federal spending.

Tax cuts to stimulate employment must be matched by spending cuts to restrain inflation. To check the rise in the cost of government, I have ordered a postponement of pay raises and a 5 percent cut in government personnel.

I have ordered a 10 percent cut in foreign economic aid.

In addition, since the Congress has already delayed action on two of the great initiatives of this administration, I will ask Congress to amend my proposals to postpone the implementation of revenue sharing for three months and welfare reform for one year.

In this way, I am reordering our budget priorities so as to concentrate more on achieving our goal of full employment.

The second indispensable element of the new prosperity is to stop the rise in the cost of living.

One of the cruelest legacies of the artificial prosperity produced by war is inflation. Inflation robs every American, every one of you. The 20 million who are retired and living on fixed incomes—they are particularly hard hit. Homemakers find it harder than ever to balance the family budget. And 80 million American wage earners have been on a treadmill.

For example, in the four war years between 1965 and 1969, your wage increases were completely eaten up by price increases. Your paychecks were higher, but you were no better off.

We have made progress against the rise in the cost of living. From the high point of 6 percent a year in 1969, the rise in consumer prices has been cut to 4 percent in the first half of 1971. But just as is the case in our fight against unemployment, we can and we must do better than that.

The time has come for decisive action—action that will break the vicious circle of spiraling prices and costs.

I am today ordering a freeze on all prices and wages throughout the United States for a period of 90 days. In addition, I call upon corporations to extend the wage-price freeze to all dividends.

I have today appointed a Cost of Living Council within the government. I have directed this Council to work with leaders of labor and business to set up the proper mechanism for achieving continued price and wage stability after the 90-day freeze is over.

Let me emphasize two characteristics of this action: First, it is temporary. To put the strong, vigorous American economy into a permanent straitjacket would lock in unfairness; it would stifle the expansion of our free enterprise system. And second, while the wage-price freeze will be backed by government sanctions, if necessary, it will not be accompanied by the establishment of a huge price control bureaucracy. I am relying on the voluntary cooperation of all Americans—each one of you: workers, employers, consumers—to make this freeze work.

Working together, we will break the back of inflation, and we will do it without the mandatory wage and price controls that crush economic and personal freedom.

The third indispensable element in building the new prosperity is closely related to creating new jobs and halting inflation. We must protect the position of the American dollar as a pillar of monetary stability around the world.

In the past seven years, there has been an average of one international monetary crisis every year. Now who gains from these crises? Not the workingman; not the investor; not the real producers of wealth. The gainers are the international money speculators. Because they thrive on crises, they help to create them.

In recent weeks, the speculators have been waging an all-out war on the American dollar. The strength of a nation's currency is based on the strength of that nation's economy—and the American economy is by far the strongest in the world. Accordingly, I have directed the secretary of the treasury to take the action necessary to defend the dollar against the speculators.

I have directed Secretary Connally to suspend temporarily the convertibility of the dollar into gold or other reserve assets, except in amounts and conditions determined to be in the interest of monetary stability and in the best interests of the United States.

Now, what is this action—which is very technical—what does it mean for you?

Let me lay to rest the bugaboo of what is called devaluation.

If you want to buy a foreign car or take a trip abroad, market conditions may cause your dollar to buy slightly less. But if you are among the overwhelming majority of Americans who buy American-made products in America, your dollar will be worth just as much tomorrow as it is today.

The effect of this action, in other words, will be to stabilize the dollar.

Now, this action will not win us any friends among the international money traders. But our primary concern is with the American workers, and with fair competition around the world.

To our friends abroad, including the many responsible members of the international banking community who are dedicated to stability and the flow of trade, I give this assurance: The United States has always been, and will continue to be, a forward-looking and trustworthy trading partner. In full cooperation with the International Monetary Fund and those who trade with us, we will press for the necessary reforms to set up an urgently needed new international monetary system. Stability and equal treatment is in everybody's best interest. I am determined that the American dollar must never again be a hostage in the hands of international speculators.

I am taking one further step to protect the dollar, to improve our balance of payments, and to increase jobs for Americans. As a temporary measure, I am today imposing an additional tax of 10 percent on goods imported into the United States. This is a better solution for international trade than direct controls on the amount of imports.

This import tax is a temporary action. It isn't directed against any other country. It is an action to make certain that American products will not be at a disadvantage because of unfair exchange rates. When the unfair treatment is ended, the import tax will end as well.

As a result of these actions, the product of American labor will be more competitive, and the unfair edge that some of our foreign competition has will be removed. This is a major reason why our trade balance has eroded over the past 15 years.

At the end of World War II the economies of the major industrial nations of Europe and Asia were shattered. To help them get on their feet and to protect their freedom, the United States has provided over the past 25 years $143 billion in foreign aid. That was the right thing for us to do.

Today, largely with our help, they have regained their vitality. They have become our strong competitors, and we welcome their success. But now that other nations are economically strong, the time has come for them to bear their fair share of the burden of defending freedom around the world. The time has come for exchange rates to be set straight and for the major nations to compete as equals. There is no longer any need for the United States to compete with one hand tied behind her back.

The range of actions I have taken and proposed tonight—on the job front, on the inflation front, on the monetary front—is the most comprehensive new economic policy to be undertaken in this nation in four decades.

We are fortunate to live in a nation with an economic system capable of producing for its people the highest standard of living in the world; a system flexible enough to change its ways dramatically when circumstances call for change; and, most important, a system resourceful enough to produce prosperity with freedom and opportunity unmatched in the history of nations.

The purposes of the government actions I have announced tonight are to lay the basis for renewed confidence, to make it possible for us to compete fairly with the rest of the world, to open the door to new prosperity.

But government, with all of its powers, does not hold the key to the success of a people. That key, my fellow Americans, is in your hands.

A nation, like a person, has to have a certain inner drive in order to succeed. In economic affairs, that inner drive is called the competitive spirit.

Every action I have taken tonight is designed to nurture and stimulate that competitive spirit, to help us snap out of the self-doubt, the self-disparagement that saps our energy and erodes our confidence in ourselves.

Whether this nation stays number one in the world's economy or resigns itself to second, third, or fourth place; whether we as a people have faith in ourselves, or lose that faith; whether we hold fast to the strength that makes peace and freedom possible in this world, or lose our grip—all that depends on you, on your competitive spirit, your sense of personal destiny, your pride in your country and in yourself.

We can be certain of this: As the threat of war recedes, the challenge of peaceful competition in the world will greatly increase.

We welcome competition, because America is at her greatest when she is called on to compete.

As there always have been in our history, there will be voices urging us to shrink from that challenge of competition, to build a protective wall around ourselves, to crawl into a shell as the rest of the world moves ahead.

Two hundred years ago a man wrote in his diary these words: "Many thinking people believe America has seen its best days." That was written in 1775, just before the American Revolution—the dawn of the most exciting era in the history of man. And today we hear the echoes of those voices, preaching a gospel of gloom and defeat, saying the same thing: "We have seen our best days."

I say, let Americans reply: "Our best days lie ahead."

As we move into a generation of peace, as we blaze the trail toward the new prosperity, I say to every American: Let us raise our spirits. Let us raise our sights. Let all of us contribute all we can to this great and good country that has contributed so much to the progress of mankind.

Let us invest in our nation's future, and let us revitalize that faith in ourselves that built a great nation in the past and that will shape the world of the future.

Thank you and good evening.

The Moscow Summit

Moscow, U.S.S.R.

May 28, 1972

NIXON'S VISIT to Moscow in May of 1972 was the first by any American president and came only three months after his biggest diplomatic coup—his trip to China (again, the first by an American president) to formally renew relations after two decades of hostility. He accomplished both feats by virtue of his own record of extreme anti-Communism, which served to protect him from criticism by the American right wing.

The agenda at the Moscow summit included discussions on trade, joint scientific ventures, and human rights. Most important, Nixon and Henry Kissinger, his national security adviser, negotiated agreements limiting the deployment of antiballistic missile systems (the SALT I accords). To emphasize the symbolic unity of the occasion, Nixon delivered an address, broadcast from the Kremlin, that reached American and Soviet viewers simultaneously. Ray Price, Nixon's speechwriter, observed: "Being directed at the Soviet people, in making its points the speech drew heavily on the sort of homespun analogies and simple folk tales so popular in Russian tradition. It also played to the strong emotional feelings the Russians still have about World War II, and particularly to the intense concern for children which is characteristically Russian."

But this high point of Nixon's presidency coincided with the beginning of his downfall. On the same night that this speech was delivered, the Washington offices of the Democratic National Committee, in the Watergate complex, were burglarized by a hit team working for the Committee for the Re-Election of the President. Two weeks later, another break-in team was arrested in the same offices. A scheme to obstruct justice by covering up the administration's illegal operations was quickly initiated by the White House.

Dobryy vecher. [Good evening.]

I deeply appreciate this opportunity your government has given me to speak directly with the people of the Soviet Union, to bring you a message of friendship from all the people of the United States and to share with you some of my thoughts about the relations between our two countries and about the way to peace and progress in the world.

This is my fourth visit to the Soviet Union. On these visits I have gained a great respect for the peoples of the Soviet Union, for your strength, your generosity, your determination, for the diversity and richness of your cultural heritage, for your many achievements.

In the three years I have been in office, one of my principal aims has been to establish a better relationship between the United States and the Soviet Union. Our two countries have much in common. Most important of all, we have never fought one another in war. On the contrary, the memory of your soldiers and ours embracing at the Elbe, as allies, in 1945, remains strong in millions of hearts in both of our countries. It is my hope that that memory can serve as an inspiration

for the renewal of Soviet-American cooperation in the 1970s.

As great powers, we shall sometimes be competitors, but we need never be enemies.

Thirteen years ago, when I visited your country as vice president, I addressed the people of the Soviet Union on radio and television, as I am addressing you tonight. I said then:

> Let us have peaceful competition not only in producing the best factories but in producing better lives for our people.

> Let us cooperate in our exploration of outer space. . . . Let our aim be not victory over other peoples but the victory of all mankind over hunger, want, misery, and disease, wherever it exists in the world.

In our meetings this week, we have begun to bring some of those hopes to fruition. Shortly after we arrived here on Monday afternoon, a brief rain fell on Moscow, of a kind that I am told is called a mushroom rain, a warm rain, with sunshine breaking through, that makes the mushrooms grow and is therefore

751

considered a good omen. The month of May is early for mushrooms, but as our talks progressed this week, what did grow was even better: a far-reaching set of agreements that can lead to a better life for both of our peoples, to a better chance for peace in the world.

We have agreed on joint ventures in space. We have agreed on ways of working together to protect the environment, to advance health, to cooperate in science and technology. We have agreed on means of preventing incidents at sea. We have established a commission to expand trade between our two nations.

Most important, we have taken an historic first step in the limitation of nuclear strategic arms. This arms control agreement is not for the purpose of giving either side an advantage over the other. Both of our nations are strong, each respects the strength of the other, each will maintain the strength necessary to defend its independence.

But in an unchecked arms race between two great nations, there would be no winners, only losers. By setting this limitation together, the people of both of our nations, and of all nations, can be winners. If we continue in the spirit of serious purpose that has marked our discussions this week, these agreements can start us on a new road of cooperation for the benefit of our people, for the benefit of all peoples.

There is an old proverb that says, "Make peace with man and quarrel with your sins." The hardships and evils that beset all men and all nations, these and these alone are what we should make war upon.

As we look at the prospects for peace, we see that we have made significant progress at reducing the possible sources of direct conflict between us. But history tells us that great nations have often been dragged into war without intending it, by conflicts between smaller nations. As great powers, we can and should use our influence to prevent this from happening. Our goal should be to discourage aggression in other parts of the world and particularly among those smaller nations that look to us for leadership and example.

With great power goes great responsibility. When a man walks with a giant tread, he must be careful where he sets his feet. There can be true peace only when the weak are as safe as the strong. The wealthier and more powerful our own nations become, the more we have to

lose from war and the threat of war, anywhere in the world.

Speaking for the United States, I can say this: We covet no one else's territory, we seek no dominion over any other people, we seek the right to live in peace, not only for ourselves but for all the peoples of this earth. Our power will only be used to keep the peace, never to break it, only to defend freedom, never to destroy it. No nation that does not threaten its neighbors has anything to fear from the United States.

Soviet citizens have often asked me, "Does America truly want peace?"

I believe that our actions answer that question far better than any words could do. If we did not want peace, we would not have reduced the size of our armed forces by a million men, by almost one-third, during the past three years. If we did not want peace, we would not have worked so hard at reaching an agreement on the limitation of nuclear arms, at achieving a settlement of Berlin, at maintaining peace in the Middle East, at establishing better relations with the Soviet Union, with the People's Republic of China, with other nations of the world.

Mrs. Nixon and I feel very fortunate to have had the opportunity to visit the Soviet Union, to get to know the people of the Soviet Union, friendly and hospitable, courageous and strong. Most Americans will never have a chance to visit the Soviet Union, and most Soviet citizens will never have a chance to visit America. Most of you know our country only through what you read in your newspapers and what you hear and see on radio and television and motion pictures. This is only a part of the real America.

I would like to take this opportunity to try to convey to you something of what America is really like, not in terms of its scenic beauties, its great cities, its factories, its farms, or its highways, but in terms of its people.

In many ways, the people of our two countries are very much alike. Like the Soviet Union, ours is a large and diverse nation. Our people, like yours, are hard working. Like you, we Americans have a strong spirit of competition, but we also have a great love of music and poetry, of sports, and of humor. Above all, we, like you, are an open, natural, and friendly people. We love our country. We love our children. And we want for you and for your children the same peace and abundance that we want for ourselves and for our children.

We Americans are idealists. We believe deeply in our system of government. We cherish our personal liberty. We would fight to defend it, if necessary, as we have done before. But we also believe deeply in the right of each nation to choose its own system. Therefore, however much we like our own system for ourselves, we have no desire to impose it on anyone else.

As we conclude this week of talks, there are certain fundamental premises of the American point of view which I believe deserve emphasis. In conducting these talks, it has not been our aim to divide up the world into spheres of influence, to establish a condominium, or in any way to conspire together against the interests of any other nation. Rather we have sought to construct a better framework of understanding between our two nations, to make progress in our bilateral relationships, to find ways of insuring that future frictions between us would never embroil our two nations, and therefore the world, in war.

While ours are both great and powerful nations, the world is no longer dominated by two superpowers. The world is a better and safer place because its power and resources are more widely distributed.

Beyond this, since World War II, more than 70 new nations have come into being. We cannot have true peace unless they, and all nations, can feel that they share it.

America seeks better relations, not only with the Soviet Union but with all nations. The only sound basis for a peaceful and progressive international order is sovereign equality and mutual respect. We believe in the right of each nation to chart its own course, to choose its own system, to go its own way, without interference from other nations.

As we look to the longer term, peace depends also on continued progress in the developing nations. Together with other advanced industrial countries, the United States and the Soviet Union share a twofold responsibility in this regard: on the one hand, to practice restraint in those activities, such as the supply of arms, that might endanger the peace of developing nations; and second, to assist them in their orderly economic and social development, without political interference.

Some of you may have heard an old story told in Russia of a traveler who was walking to another village. He knew the way, but not the distance. Finally he came upon a woodsman chopping wood by the side of the road and he asked the woodsman, "How long will it take to reach the village?"

The woodsman replied, "I don't know."

The traveler was angry, because he was sure the woodsman was from the village and therefore knew how far it was. And so he started off down the road again. After he had gone a few steps, the woodsman called out, "Stop. It will take you about 15 minutes."

The traveler turned and demanded, "Why didn't you tell me that in the first place?"

The woodsman replied, "Because then I didn't know the length of your stride."

In our talks this week with the leaders of the Soviet Union, both sides have had a chance to measure the length of our strides toward peace and security. I believe that those strides have been substantial and that now we have well begun the long journey which will lead us to a new age in the relations between our two countries. It is important to both of our peoples that we continue those strides.

As our two countries learn to work together, our people will be able to get to know one another better. Greater cooperation can also mean a great deal in our daily lives. As we learn to cooperate in space, in health and the environment, in science and technology, our cooperation can help sick people get well. It can help industries produce more consumer goods. It can help all of us enjoy cleaner air and water. It can increase our knowledge of the world around us.

As we expand our trade, each of our countries can buy more of the other's goods and market more of our own. As we gain experience with arms control, we can bring closer the day when further agreements can lessen the arms burden of our two nations and lessen the threat of war in the world.

Through all the pages of history, through all the centuries, the world's people have struggled to be free from fear, whether fear of the elements or fear of hunger or fear of their own rulers or fear of their neighbors in other countries. And yet, time and again, people have vanquished the source of one fear only to fall prey to another.

753

Let our goal now be a world free of fear—a world in which nation will no longer prey upon nation, in which human energies will be turned away from production for war and toward more production for peace, away from conquest and toward invention, development, creation; a world in which together we can establish that peace which is more than the absence of war, which enables man to pursue those higher goals that the spirit yearns for.

Yesterday, I laid a wreath at the cemetery which commemorates the brave people who died during the siege of Leningrad in World War II. At the cemetery, I saw the picture of a 12-year-old girl. She was a beautiful child. Her name was Tanya. The pages of her diary tell the terrible story of war. In the simple words of a child, she wrote of the deaths of the members of her family: Zhenya in December. Grannie in January. Leka the next. Then Uncle Vasya. Then Uncle Lyosha. Then Mama. And then the Savichevs. And then finally, these words, the last words in her diary: "All are dead. Only Tanya is left."

As we work toward a more peaceful world, let us think of Tanya and of the other Tanyas and their brothers and sisters everywhere. Let us do all that we can to insure that no other children will have to endure what Tanya did and that your children and ours, all the children of the world can live their full lives together in friendship and in peace.

Spasibo y do svidaniye. [Thank you and good-bye.]

The Watergate Case

Washington, D.C.

April 30, 1973

WITH THE PRESIDENT denying all knowledge of the affair, the arrest of the Watergate burglars in June 1972 did nothing to stop Nixon's landslide reelection in November. But by the following spring, a full-scale investigation was under way in the Senate and seven defendants in the burglary case were on trial in U.S. District Court; their testimony implicated several high-level White House aides. In late April Nixon spoke to the nation by radio and television to reaffirm his own innocence and to announce the resignations of three aides who were under suspicion and the dismissal of a fourth—John Dean, special counsel to the president—who had already implicated Nixon in the cover-up scheme.

I want to talk to you tonight from my heart on a subject of deep concern to every American.

In recent months, members of my administration and officials of the Committee for the Re-Election of the President—including some of my closest friends and most trusted aides—have been charged with involvement in what has come to be known as the Watergate affair. These include charges of illegal activity during and preceding the 1972 presidential election and charges that responsible officials participated in efforts to cover up that illegal activity.

The inevitable result of these charges has been to raise serious questions about the integrity of the White House itself. Tonight I wish to address those questions.

Last June 17, while I was in Florida trying to get a few days rest after my visit to Moscow, I first learned from news reports of the Watergate break-in. I was appalled at this senseless, illegal action, and I was shocked to learn that employees of the Re-Election Committee were apparently among those guilty. I immediately ordered an investigation by appropriate government authorities. On September 15, as you will recall, indictments were brought against seven defendants in the case.

As the investigations went forward, I repeatedly asked those conducting the investigation whether there was any reason to believe that members of my administration were in any way involved. I received repeated assurances that there were not. Because of these continuing reassurances, because I believed the reports I was getting, because I had faith in the persons from whom I was getting them, I discounted the stories in the press that appeared to implicate members

of my administration or other officials of the campaign committee.

Until March of this year, I remained convinced that the denials were true and that the charges of involvement by members of the White House staff were false. The comments I made during this period, and the comments made by my press secretary in my behalf, were based on the information provided to us at the time we made those comments. However, new information then came to me which persuaded me that there was a real possibility that some of these charges were true, and suggesting further that there had been an effort to conceal the facts both from the public, from you, and from me.

As a result, on March 21, I personally assumed the responsibility for coordinating intensive new inquiries into the matter, and I personally ordered those conducting the investigations to get all the facts and to report them directly to me, right here in this office.

I again ordered that all persons in the government or at the Re-Election Committee should cooperate fully with the FBI, the prosecutors, and the grand jury. I also ordered that anyone who refused to cooperate in telling the truth would be asked to resign from government service. And, with ground rules adopted that would preserve the basic constitutional separation of powers between the Congress and the presidency, I directed that members of the White House staff should appear and testify voluntarily under oath before the Senate committee which was investigating Watergate.

I was determined that we should get to the bottom of the matter, and that the truth should be fully brought out—no matter who was involved.

At the same time, I was determined not to take precipitate action and to avoid, if at all possible, any action that would appear to reflect on innocent people. I wanted to be fair. But I knew that in the final analysis, the integrity of this office—public faith in the integrity of this office—would have to take priority over all personal considerations.

Today, in one of the most difficult decisions of my presidency, I accepted the resignations of two of my closet associates in the White House—Bob Haldeman, John Ehrlichman—two of the finest public servants it has been my privilege to know.

I want to stress that in accepting these resignations, I mean to leave no implication whatever of personal wrongdoing on their part, and I leave no implication tonight of implication on the part of others who have been charged in this matter. But in matters as sensitive as guarding the integrity of our democratic process, it is essential not only that rigorous legal and ethical standards be observed but also that the public, you, have total confidence that they are both being observed and enforced by those in authority and particularly by the president of the United States. They agreed with me that this move was necessary in order to restore that confidence.

Because Attorney General Kleindienst—though a distinguished public servant, my personal friend for 20 years, with no personal involvement whatever in this matter—has been a close personal and professional associate of some of those who are involved in this case, he and I both felt that it was also necessary to name a new attorney general.

The counsel to the president, John Dean, has also resigned.

As the new attorney general, I have today named Elliot Richardson, a man of unimpeachable integrity and rigorously high principle. I have directed him to do everything necessary to ensure that the Department of Justice has the confidence and the trust of every law-abiding person in this country.

I have given him absolute authority to make all decisions bearing upon the prosecution of the Watergate case and related matters. I have instructed him that if he should consider it appropriate, he has the authority to name a special supervising prosecutor for matters arising out of the case.

Whatever may appear to have been the case before, whatever improper activities may yet be discovered in connection with this whole sordid affair, I want the American people, I want you to know beyond the shadow of a doubt that during my term as president, justice will be pursued fairly, fully, and impartially, no matter who is involved. This office is a sacred trust and I am determined to be worthy of that trust.

Looking back at the history of this case, two questions arise:

How could it have happened?

Who is to blame?

Political commentators have correctly observed that during my 27 years in politics I have always previously insisted on running my own campaigns for office.

But 1972 presented a very different situation. In both domestic and foreign policy, 1972 was a year of crucially important decisions, of intense negotiations, of vital new directions, particularly in working toward the goal which has been my overriding concern throughout my political career—the goal of bringing peace to America, peace to the world.

That is why I decided, as the 1972 campaign approached, that the presidency should come first and politics second. To the maximum extent possible, therefore, I sought to delegate campaign operations, to remove the day-to-day campaign decisions from the president's office and from the White House. I also, as you recall, severely limited the number of my own campaign appearances.

Who, then, is to blame for what happened in this case?

For specific criminal actions by specific individuals, those who committed those actions must, of course, bear the liability and pay the penalty.

For the fact that alleged improper actions took place within the White House or within my campaign organization, the easiest course would be for me to blame those to whom I delegated the responsibility to run the campaign. But that would be a cowardly thing to do.

I will not place the blame on subordinates—on people whose zeal exceeded their judgment and who may have done wrong in a cause they deeply believed to be right.

In any organization, the man at the top must bear the responsibility. That responsibility, therefore, belongs here, in this office. I accept it. And I pledge to you tonight, from this office, that I will do everything in my power to ensure that the guilty are brought to justice and that such abuses are purged from our political processes in the years to come, long after I have left this office.

Some people, quite properly appalled at the abuses that occurred, will say that Watergate demonstrates the bankruptcy of the American political system. I believe precisely the opposite is true. Watergate represented a series of illegal acts and bad judgments by a number of individuals. It was the system that has brought the facts to light and that will bring those guilty to justice—a system that in this case has included a determined grand jury, honest prosecutors, a courageous judge, John Sirica, and a vigorous free press.

It is essential now that we place our faith in that system—and especially in the judicial system. It is essential that we let the judicial process go forward, respecting those safeguards that are established to protect the innocent as well as to convict the guilty. It is essential that in reacting to the excesses of others, we not fall into excesses ourselves.

It is also essential that we not be so distracted by events such as this that we neglect the vital work before us, before this nation, before America, at a time of critical importance to America and the world.

Since March, when I first learned that the Watergate affair might in fact be far more serious than I had been led to believe, it has claimed far too much of my time and my attention.

Whatever may now transpire in the case, whatever the actions of the grand jury, whatever the outcome of any eventual trials, I must now turn my full attention—and I shall do so—once again to the larger duties of this office. I owe it to this great office that I hold, and I owe it to you—to my country.

I know that as attorney general, Elliot Richardson will be both fair and he will be fearless in pursuing this case wherever it leads. I am confident that with him in charge, justice will be done.

There is vital work to be done toward our goal of a lasting structure of peace in the world—work that cannot wait, work that I must do.

Tomorrow, for example, Chancellor Brandt of West Germany will visit the White House for talks that are a vital element of "The Year of Europe," as 1973 has been called. We are already preparing for the next Soviet-American summit meeting later this year.

This is also a year in which we are seeking to negotiate a mutual and balanced reduction of armed forces in Europe, which will reduce our defense budget and allow us to have funds for other purposes at home so desperately needed. It is the year when the United States and Soviet negotiators will seek to work out the second and even more important round of our talks on limiting nuclear arms and of reducing the danger of a nuclear war that would destroy civilization as we know it. It is a year in which we confront the difficult tasks of maintaining peace in Southeast Asia and in the potentially explosive Middle East.

There is also vital work to be done right here in America: to ensure prosperity, and that means a good job for everyone who wants to work; to control inflation, that I know worries every housewife, everyone who tries to balance a family budget in America; to set in motion new and better ways of ensuring progress toward a better life for all Americans.

When I think of this office—of what it means—I think of all the things that I want to accomplish for this nation, of all the things I want to accomplish for you.

On Christmas Eve, during my terrible personal ordeal of the renewed bombing of North Vietnam, which after 12 years of war finally helped to bring America peace with honor, I sat down just before midnight. I wrote out some of my goals for my second term as president.

Let me read them to you.

- To make it possible for our children, and for our children's children, to live in a world of peace.
- To make this country be more than ever a land of opportunity—of equal opportunity, full opportunity for every American.
- To provide jobs for all who can work, and generous help for those who cannot work.
- To establish a climate of decency and civility, in which each person respects the feelings and the dignity and the God-given rights of his neighbor.
- To make this a land in which each person can dare to dream, can live his dreams—not in fear, but in hope—proud of his community, proud of his country, proud of what America has meant to himself and to the world.

These are great goals. I believe we can, we must work for them. We can achieve them. But we cannot achieve these goals unless we dedicate ourselves to another goal.

We must maintain the integrity of the White House, and that integrity must be real, not transparent. There can be no whitewash at the White House.

We must reform our political process—ridding it not only of the violations of the law but also of the ugly mob violence and other inexcusable campaign tactics that have been too often practiced and too readily accepted in the past, including those that may have been a response by one side to the excesses or expected excesses of the other side. Two wrongs do not make a right.

I have been in public life for more than a quarter of a century. Like any other calling, politics has good people and bad people. And let me tell you, the great majority in politics—in the Congress, in the federal government, in the state government—are good people. I know that it can be very easy, under the intensive pressures of a campaign, for even well-intentioned people to fall into shady tactics—to rationalize this on the grounds that what is at stake is of such importance to the nation that the end justifies the means. And both of our great parties have been guilty of such tactics in the past.

In recent years, however, the campaign excesses that have occurred on all sides have provided a sobering demonstration of how far this false doctrine can take us. The lesson is clear: America, in its political campaigns, must not again fall into the trap of letting the end, however great that end is, justify the means.

I urge the leaders of both political parties, I urge citizens, all of you, everywhere, to join in working toward a new set of standards, new rules and procedures to ensure that future elections will be as nearly free of such abuses as they possibly can be made. This is my goal. I ask you to join in making it America's goal.

When I was inaugurated for a second time this past January 20, I gave each member of my cabinet and each member of my senior White House staff a special four-year calendar, with each day marked to show the number of days remaining to the administration. In the inscription on each calendar, I wrote these words: "The presidential term which begins today consists of 1,461 days—no more, no less. Each can be a day of strengthening and renewal for America; each can add depth and dimension to the American experience. If we strive together, if we make the most of the challenge and the opportunity that these days offer us, they can stand out as great days for America, and great moments in the history of the world."

I looked at my own calendar this morning up at Camp David as I was working on this speech. It showed exactly 1,361 days remaining in my term. I want these to be the best days in America's history, because I love America. I deeply believe that America is the hope of the world. And I know that in the quality and wisdom of the leadership America gives lies the only hope for millions of people all over the world that they can live their lives in peace and freedom. We must be worthy of that hope, in every sense of the word. Tonight, I ask for your prayers to help me in everything that I do throughout the days of my presidency to be worthy of their hopes and of yours.

God bless America and God bless each and every one of you.

The Resignation Speech

Washington, D.C.

August 8, 1974

REVELATIONS OF White House misconduct continued to pour out of trial proceedings and congressional hearings during 1973–1974. The president resisted all attempts by Congress and the courts to force him to turn over evidence, especially tapes he had made of conversations held in the White House. By the summer of 1974 a number of his close associates, as well as his former attorney general, had been convicted of a variety of charges, including perjury and conspiracy, and Nixon himself had been named as a co-conspirator by a federal grand jury. In July the Supreme Court, in a unanimous decision, directed Nixon to surrender the tapes to the Watergate special prosecutor, and the House of Representatives began impeachment proceedings. Tapes released on August 5 made it clear that Nixon had been involved in blocking the investigation of the Watergate scandal almost from the beginning. His remaining support in Congress disappeared. On August 8, before a nationwide audience torn between relief and shock, and without admitting guilt, Nixon announced that he would resign the following day.

This is the 37th time I have spoken to you from this office, where so many decisions have been made that shaped the history of this nation. Each time I have done so to discuss with you some matter that I believe affected the national interest.

In all the decisions I have made in my public life, I have always tried to do what was best for the nation. Throughout the long and difficult period of Watergate, I have felt it was my duty to persevere, to make every possible effort to complete the term of office to which you elected me.

In the past few days, however, it has become evident to me that I no longer have a strong enough political base in the Congress to justify continuing that effort. As long as there was such a base, I felt strongly that it was necessary to see the constitutional process through to its conclusion, that to do otherwise would be unfaithful to the spirit of that deliberately difficult process and a dangerously destabilizing precedent for the future.

But with the disappearance of that base, I now believe that the constitutional purpose has been served, and there is no longer a need for the process to be prolonged.

I would have preferred to carry through to the finish, whatever the personal agony it would have involved, and my family unanimously urged me to do so. But the interests of the nation must always come before any personal considerations.

From the discussions I have had with congressional and other leaders, I have concluded that because of the Watergate matter, I might not have the support of the Congress that I would consider necessary to back the very difficult decisions and carry out the duties of this office in the way the interests of the nation will require.

I have never been a quitter. To leave office before my term is completed is abhorrent to every instinct in my body. But as president, I must put the interests of America first. America needs a full-time president and a full-time Congress, particularly at this time with problems we face at home and abroad.

To continue to fight through the months ahead for my personal vindication would almost totally absorb the time and attention of both the president and the Congress in a period when our entire focus should be on the great issues of peace abroad and prosperity without inflation at home.

Therefore, I shall resign the presidency effective at noon tomorrow. Vice President Ford will be sworn in as president at that hour in this office.

As I recall the high hopes for America with which we began this second term, I feel a great sadness that I will not be here in this office working on your behalf to achieve those hopes in the next two and a half years. But in turning over direction of the government to Vice President Ford, I know, as I told the nation when I nominated him for that office 10 months ago, that the leadership of America will be in good hands.

In passing this office to the vice president, I also do so with the profound sense of the weight of responsibility that will fall on his shoulders tomorrow and, therefore, of the understanding, the patience, the cooperation he will need from all Americans.

As he assumes that responsibility, he will deserve the help and the support of all of us. As we look to the future, the first essential is to begin healing the wounds of this nation, to put the bitterness and divisions of the recent past behind us and to rediscover those shared ideals that lie at the heart of our strength and unity as a great and as a free people.

By taking this action, I hope that I will have hastened the start of that process of healing which is so desperately needed in America.

I regret deeply any injuries that may have been done in the course of the events that led to this decision. I would say only that if some of my judgments were wrong—and some were wrong—they were made in what I believed at the time to be the best interest of the nation.

To those who have stood with me during these past difficult months—to my family, my friends, to many others who joined in supporting my cause because they believed it was right—I will be eternally grateful for your support.

And to those who have not felt able to give me your support, let me say I leave with no bitterness toward those who have opposed me, because all of us, in the final analysis, have been concerned with the good of the country, however our judgments might differ.

So, let us all now join together in affirming that common commitment and in helping our new president succeed for the benefit of all Americans.

I shall leave this office with regret at not completing my term, but with gratitude for the privilege of serving as your president for the past five and a half years. These years have been a momentous time in the history of our nation and the world. They have been a time of achievement in which we can all be proud, achievements that represent the shared efforts of the administration, the Congress, and the people.

But the challenges ahead are equally great, and they, too, will require the support and the efforts of the Congress and the people working in cooperation with the new administration.

We have ended America's longest war, but in the work of securing a lasting peace in the world, the goals ahead are even more far-reaching and more difficult. We must complete a structure of peace so that it will be said of this generation, our generation of Americans, by the people of all nations, not only that we ended one war but that we prevented future wars.

We have unlocked the doors that for a quarter of a century stood between the United States and the People's Republic of China.

We must now ensure that the one-quarter of the world's people who live in the People's Republic of China will be and remain not our enemies, but our friends.

In the Middle East, 100 million people in the Arab countries, many of whom have considered us their enemy for nearly 20 years, now look on us as their friends. We must continue to build on that friendship so that peace can settle at last over the Middle East and so that the cradle of civilization will not become its grave.

Together with the Soviet Union, we have made the crucial breakthroughs that have begun the process of limiting nuclear arms. But we must set as our goal not just limiting but reducing and, finally, destroying these terrible weapons so that they cannot destroy civilization and so that the threat of nuclear war will no longer hang over the world and the people.

We have opened the new relation with the Soviet Union. We must continue to develop and expand that new relationship so that the two strongest nations of the world will live together in cooperation, rather than confrontation.

Around the world—in Asia, in Africa, in Latin America, in the Middle East—there are millions of people who live in terrible poverty, even starvation. We must keep as our goal turning away from production for war and expanding production for peace so that people everywhere on this earth can at last look forward in their children's time, if not in our own time, to having the necessities for a decent life.

Here in America, we are fortunate that most of our people have not only the blessings of liberty but also the means to live full and good and, by the world's standards, even abundant lives. We must press on, however, toward a goal, not only of more and better jobs but of full opportunity for every American and of what we are striving so hard right now to achieve, prosperity without inflation.

For more than a quarter of a century in public life, I have shared in the turbulent history of this era. I have fought for what I believed in. I have tried, to the best of my ability, to discharge those duties and meet those responsibilities that were entrusted to me.

Sometimes I have succeeded and sometimes I have failed, but always I have taken heart from what Theodore Roosevelt once said about the man in the arena, "whose face is marred by dust and sweat and blood, who strives valiantly, who errs and comes short again and again because there is not effort without error and shortcoming, but who does actually strive to do the deed, who knows the great enthusiasms, the great devotions, who spends himself in a worthy cause, who at the best knows in the end the triumphs of high achievements and who at the worst, if he fails, at least fails while daring greatly."

I pledge to you tonight that as long as I have a breath of life in my body, I shall continue in that spirit. I shall continue to work for the great causes to which I have been dedicated throughout my years as a congressman, a senator, vice president, and president, the cause of peace, not just for America but among all nations—prosperity, justice, and opportunity for all of our people.

There is one cause above all to which I have been devoted and to which I shall always be devoted for as long as I live.

When I first took the oath of office as president five and a half years ago, I made this sacred commitment: to "consecrate my office, my energies, and all the wisdom I can summon to the cause of peace among nations."

I have done my very best in all the days since to be true to that pledge. As a result of these efforts, I am confident that the world is a safer place today, not only for the people of America but for the people of all nations, and that all of our children have a better chance than before of living in peace rather than dying in war.

This, more than anything, is what I hoped to achieve when I sought the presidency. This, more than anything, is what I hope will be my legacy to you, to our country, as I leave the presidency.

To have served in this office is to have felt a very personal sense of kinship with each and every American. In leaving it, I do so with this prayer: May God's grace be with you in all the days ahead.

Gerald Rudolph Ford

Gerald Rudolph Ford

1974–1977

GERALD FORD'S presidency was really a "stewardship," as he himself admitted. His greatest accomplishment was shepherding the nation out of the turmoil of the Nixon years. Compared with his predecessor, Ford appeared upright, honest, and loyal, a "nice guy" with no political enemies. Nonetheless, the majority of Americans were not convinced that he was of presidential caliber.

Ford grew up in Grand Rapids, Michigan. His stepfather was a paint-store owner and active Republican. He practiced law in Grand Rapids until 1949, then ran successfully for the congressional seat from Michigan's fifth district. Ford served as House minority leader from 1965 to 1973, when, as a dependable moderate with a clean record, he was chosen by Nixon to replace Vice President Spiro Agnew, who resigned after bribery charges were brought against him stemming from his years as governor of Maryland. When Nixon himself was forced to resign less than a year later, Ford became the first president to attain the office without having been elected either president or vice president. Unable to construct a national constituency of his own, and damaged politically by his pardon of Nixon, the energy crisis, and the worst recession in years, he lost the 1976 presidential contest to Jimmy Carter.

During his brief term—a little more than two years—Ford delivered more than one thousand speeches, totaling in excess of two million official words. The Ford speechwriting operation, though not as large as Nixon's, was still considerable: six full-time speechwriters, headed by Robert T. Hartmann, a long-time aide, and backed up by 35 researchers and clerical workers. For all this effort and support, Ford is not remembered as an effective orator. Bitter power struggles among Ford's advisers and speechwriters sometimes resulted in patched-together speeches that lacked coherence and bite. Though the president edited and revised some of his material, he lacked a personal literary style that would have given his speeches distinction. As William Safire remarked, there is not a single memorable phrase to be found among all of Ford's presidential utterances.

At his best, Ford spoke with the kind of directness that Harry Truman used to good effect. He favored short words and plain sentences, sometimes peppering his speeches with football terminology acquired in his days as an all-American center at the University of Michigan and as a coach at Yale. This may have worked to his disadvantage as well; Ford found it hard to shake his image as a slightly dull former jock. And his effectiveness as an orator was not enhanced by his flat, monotonous voice and general impassiveness on the podium. Recognizing this, the president sought professional help in polishing his performances. Hartmann recalled that Ford used a vocal coach to rehearse his acceptance speech at the 1976 Republican convention. Ford viewed and reviewed his reading on videotape until "he could say every word right, and, once again, with *feeling.*" Overall, however, he had, according to *Newsday,* "a lackluster career before the microphone" and was widely regarded as plodding and lacking in charisma. Admitting the partial justice of such criticism, Ford offered this defense: "I'd rather be plodding and get something done than have charisma and accomplish nothing."

First Presidential Address

Washington, D.C.

August 9, 1974

MOMENTS AFTER Nixon's helicopter lifted off from the White House grounds, Ford took the oath of office in the East Room. He then gave this speech, showing what one reporter called "a new sense of self-assurance." As Ford wrote in his 1979 autobiography: "At this historic moment I was aware of kinship with my predecessors. It was almost as if all of America's past presidents were praying for me to succeed." The blunt, unadorned style of the following remarks is typical of Ford's rhetoric.

The oath that I have taken is the same oath that was taken by George Washington and by every president under the Constitution. But I assume the presidency under extraordinary circumstances never before experienced by Americans. This is an hour of history that troubles our minds and hurts our hearts.

Therefore, I feel it is my first duty to make an unprecedented compact with my countrymen. Not an inaugural address, not a fireside chat, not a campaign speech—just a little straight talk among friends. And I intend it to be the first of many.

I am acutely aware that you have not elected me as your president by your ballots, and so I ask you to confirm me as your president with your prayers. And I hope that such prayers will also be the first of many.

If you have not chosen me by secret ballot, neither have I gained office by any secret promises. I have not campaigned either for the presidency or the vice presidency. I have not subscribed to any partisan platform. I am indebted to no man, and only to one woman—my dear wife—as I begin this very difficult job.

I have not sought this enormous responsibility, but I will not shirk it. Those who nominated and confirmed me as vice president were my friends and are my friends. They were of both parties, elected by all the people and acting under the Constitution in their name. It is only fitting then that I should pledge to them and to you that I will be the president of all the people.

Thomas Jefferson said the people are the only sure reliance for the preservation of our liberty. And down the years, Abraham Lincoln renewed this American article of faith asking, "Is there any better way or equal hope in the world?"

I intend, on Monday next, to request of the Speaker of the House of Representatives and the president pro tempore of the Senate the privilege of appearing before the Congress to share with my former colleagues and with you, the American people, my views on the priority business of the nation and to solicit your views and their views. And may I say to the Speaker and the others, if I could meet with you right after these remarks, I would appreciate it.

Even though this is late in an election year, there is no way we can go forward except together and no way anybody can win except by serving the people's urgent needs. We cannot stand still or slip backwards. We must go forward now together.

To the peoples and the governments of all friendly nations, and I hope that could encompass the whole world, I pledge an uninterrupted and sincere search for peace. America will remain strong and united, but its strength will remain dedicated to the safety and sanity of the entire family of man, as well as to our own precious freedom.

I believe that truth is the glue that holds government together, not only our government but civilization itself. That bond, though strained, is unbroken at home and abroad.

In all my public and private acts as your president, I expect to follow my instincts of openness and candor with full confidence that honesty is always the best policy in the end.

My fellow Americans, our long national nightmare is over.

Our Constitution works; our great republic is a government of laws and not of men. Here the people rule. But there is a higher power, by whatever name we honor Him, who ordains not only righteousness but love, not only justice but mercy.

As we bind up the internal wounds of Watergate, more painful and more poisonous than those of foreign wars, let us restore the golden rule to our political process, and let brotherly love purge our hearts of suspicion and of hate.

In the beginning, I asked you to pray for me. Before closing, I ask again your prayers, for Richard Nixon and for his family. May our former president, who brought peace to millions, find it for himself. May God bless and comfort his wonderful wife and daughters, whose love and loyalty will forever be a shining legacy to all who bear the lonely burdens of the White House.

I can only guess at those burdens, although I have witnessed at close hand the tragedies that befell three presidents and the lesser trials of others.

With all the strength and all the good sense I have gained from life, with all the confidence my family, my friends, and my dedicated staff impart to me, and with the goodwill of countless Americans I have encountered in recent visits to 40 states, I now solemnly reaffirm my promise I made to you last December 6: to uphold the Constitution, to do what is right as God gives me to see the right, and to do the very best I can for America.

God helping me, I will not let you down.

Thank you.

The Pardon for Nixon

Washington, D.C.

September 8, 1974

WHATEVER GOODWILL Ford had accrued in his first month in office was abruptly dissipated when the president, in a surprise move, pardoned Nixon for any acts he had "committed or may have committed" in the Watergate cover-up. Ford sincerely believed that the pardon would mean that he "could now proceed without being harassed by Nixon or his problems anymore." But the opposite was true: the press and the public were outraged by the pardon, and even Ford's press secretary, Jerald terHorst, resigned in protest. Many people suspected that a deal had been worked out with Nixon before his resignation, despite Ford's frequent denials under oath, and this seriously damaged Ford's reputation for honesty and fairness. It was the pardon, more than any other factor, that cost Ford the 1976 election.

I have come to a decision which I felt I should tell you and all of my fellow American citizens, as soon as I was certain in my own mind and in my own conscience that it is the right thing to do.

I have learned already in this office that the difficult decisions always come to this desk. I must admit that many of them do not look at all the same as the hypothetical questions that I have answered freely and perhaps too fast on previous occasions.

My customary policy is to try and get all the facts and to consider the opinions of my countrymen and to take counsel with my most valued friends. But these seldom agree, and in the end, the decision is mine. To procrastinate, to agonize, and to wait for a more favorable turn of events that may never come or more compelling external pressures that may as well be wrong as right, is itself a decision of sorts and a weak and potentially dangerous course for a president to follow.

I have promised to uphold the Constitution, to do what is right as God gives me to see the right, and to do the very best that I can for America.

I have asked your help and your prayers, not only when I became president but many times since. The Constitution is the supreme law of our land and it governs our actions as citizens. Only the laws of God, which govern our consciences, are superior to it.

As we are a nation under God, so I am sworn to uphold our laws with the help of God. And I have sought such guidance and searched my own conscience with special diligence to determine the right thing for me to do

with respect to my predecessor in this place, Richard Nixon, and his loyal wife and family.

Theirs is an American tragedy in which we all have played a part. It could go on and on and on, or someone must write the end to it. I have concluded that only I can do that, and if I can, I must.

There are no historic or legal precedents to which I can turn in this matter, none that precisely fit the circumstances of a private citizen who has resigned the presidency of the United States. But it is common knowledge that serious allegations and accusations hang like a sword over our former president's head, threatening his health as he tries to reshape his life, a great part of which was spent in the service of this country and by the mandate of its people.

After years of bitter controversy and divisive national debate, I have been advised, and I am compelled to conclude that many months and perhaps more years will have to pass before Richard Nixon could obtain a fair trial by jury in any jurisdiction of the United States under governing decisions of the Supreme Court.

I deeply believe in equal justice for all Americans, whatever their station or former station. The law, whether human or divine, is no respecter of persons; but the law is a respecter of reality.

The facts, as I see them, are that a former president of the United States, instead of enjoying equal treatment with any other citizen accused of violating the law, would be cruelly and excessively penalized either in preserving the presumption of his innocence or in obtaining a speedy determination of his guilt in order to repay a legal debt to society.

During this long period of delay and potential litigation, ugly passions would again be aroused. And our people would again be polarized in their opinions. And the credibility of our free institutions of government would again be challenged at home and abroad.

In the end, the courts might well hold that Richard Nixon had been denied due process, and the verdict of history would even more be inconclusive with respect to those charges arising out of the period of his presidency, of which I am presently aware.

But it is not the ultimate fate of Richard Nixon that most concerns me, though surely it deeply troubles every decent and every compassionate person. My concern is the immediate future of this great country.

In this, I dare not depend upon my personal sympathy as a long-time friend of the former president, nor my professional judgment as a lawyer, and I do not.

As president, my primary concern must always be the greatest good of all the people of the United States whose servant I am. As a man, my first consideration is to be true to my own convictions and my own conscience.

My conscience tells me clearly and certainly that I cannot prolong the bad dreams that continue to reopen a chapter that is closed. My conscience tells me that only I, as president, have the constitutional power to firmly shut and seal this book. My conscience tells me it is my duty, not merely to proclaim domestic tranquillity but to use every means that I have to insure it.

I do believe that the buck stops here, that I cannot rely upon public opinion polls to tell me what is right.

I do believe that right makes might and that if I am wrong, 10 angels swearing I was right would make no difference.

I do believe, with all my heart and mind and spirit, that I, not as president but as a humble servant of God, will receive justice without mercy if I fail to show mercy.

Finally, I feel that Richard Nixon and his loved ones have suffered enough and will continue to suffer, no matter what I do, no matter what we, as a great and good nation, can do together to make his goal of peace come true.

[Reading from the proclamation granting the pardon:] Now, therefore, I, Gerald R. Ford, president of the United States, pursuant to the pardon power conferred upon me by Article II, Section 2, of the Constitution, have granted and by these presents do grant a full, free, and absolute pardon unto Richard Nixon for all offenses against the United States which he, Richard Nixon, has committed or may have committed or taken part in during the period from July [January] 20, 1969, through August 9, 1974.

In witness whereof, I have hereunto set my hand this eighth day of September, in the year of our Lord nineteen hundred and seventy-four, and of the Independence of the United States of America the 199th.

Whip Inflation Now

Washington, D.C.

October 8, 1974

REELING FROM the effects of the OPEC oil embargo and the billions spent on the Vietnam War, the U.S. economy was undergoing a damaging cycle of double-digit wage and price inflation. Ford and his advisers decided that one of the best ways to fight inflation, which Ford called "Public Enemy Number One," was a national campaign to support volunteer anti-inflation measures. Businesses and unions were asked to freeze prices and wages; individuals were asked to conserve petroleum by carpooling and lowering their thermostats. The slogan for the program was "Whip Inflation Now"—WIN—and millions of WIN buttons, posters, and bumper stickers were printed at the taxpayers' expense. Ford wore a WIN button as he launched the program with these remarks before a joint session of Congress.

Critics immediately pegged WIN as naive, ineffective, and laughable, and the program "melted with the summer snow," according to Robert Hartmann. Ford himself later described WIN as "probably too gimmicky."

In his first inaugural address, President Franklin D. Roosevelt said, and I quote: "The people of the United States have not failed. . . . They want direct, vigorous action, and they have asked for discipline and direction under our leadership."

Today, though our economic difficulties do not approach the emergency of 1933, the message from the American people is exactly the same. I trust that you are getting the very same message that I am receiving: Our constituents want leadership, our constituents want action.

All of us have heard much talk on this very floor about Congress recovering its rightful share of national leadership. I now intend to offer you that chance.

The 73d Congress responded to FDR's appeal in five days. I am deeply grateful for the cooperation of the 93d Congress and the Conference on Inflation, which ended 10 days ago.

Mr. Speaker, many—but not all—of your recommendations on behalf of your party's caucus are reflected in some of my proposals here today. The distinguished majority leader of the Senate offered a nine-point program. I seriously studied all of them and adopted some of his suggestions.

I might add, I have also listened very hard to many of our former colleagues in both bodies and of both the majority and the minority, and have been both persuaded and dissuaded. But in the end, I had to make the decision, I had to decide, as each of you do when the rollcall is called.

I will not take your time today with the discussion of the origins of inflation and its bad effect on the United States, but I do know where we want to be in 1976—on the 200th birthday of a United States of America that has not lost its way, nor its will, nor its sense of national purpose.

During the meetings on inflation, I listened carefully to many valuable suggestions. Since the summit, I have evaluated literally hundreds of ideas, day and night.

My conclusions are very simply stated. There is only one point on which all advisers have agreed: We must whip inflation right now.

None of the remedies proposed, great or small, compulsory or voluntary, stands a chance unless they are combined in a considered package, in a concerted effort, in a grand design.

I have reviewed the past and the present efforts of our federal government to help the economy. They are simply not good enough, nor sufficiently broad, nor do they pack the punch that will turn America's economy on.

A stable American economy cannot be sustained if the world's economy is in chaos. International cooperation is absolutely essential and vital. But while we seek agreements with other nations, let us put our own economic house in order.

Today, I have identified 10 areas for our joint action, the executive and the legislative branches of our government.

Number one: food. America is the world's champion producer of food. Food prices and petroleum prices in the United States are primary inflationary factors. America today partially depends on foreign sources for petroleum, but we can grow more than enough food for ourselves.

To halt higher food prices, we must produce more food, and I call upon every farmer to produce to full capacity. And I say to you and to the farmers, they have done a magnificent job in the past, and we should be eternally grateful.

This government, however, will do all in its power to assure him—that farmer—he can sell his entire yield at reasonable prices. Accordingly, I ask the Congress to remove all remaining acreage limitations on rice, peanuts, and cotton.

I also assure America's farmers here and now that I will allocate all the fuel and ask authority to allocate all the fertilizer they need to do this essential job.

Agricultural marketing orders and other federal regulations are being reviewed to eliminate or modify those responsible for inflated prices.

I have directed our new Council on Wage and Price Stability to find and to expose all restrictive practices, public or private, which raise food prices. The administration will also monitor food production, margins, pricing, and exports. We can and we shall have an adequate supply at home, and through cooperation, meet the needs of our trading partners abroad.

Over this past weekend, we initiated a voluntary program to monitor grain exports. The Economic Policy Board will be responsible for determining the policy under this program.

In addition, in order to better allocate our supplies for export, I ask that a provision be added to Public Law 480 under which we ship food to the needy and friendly countries. The president needs authority to waive certain of the restrictions on shipments based on national interest or humanitarian grounds.

Number two: energy. America's future depends heavily on oil, gas, coal, electricity, and other resources called energy. Make no mistake, we do have a real energy problem.

One-third of our oil—17 percent of America's total energy—now comes from foreign sources that we cannot control, at high cartel prices costing you and me $16 billion—$16 billion more than just a year ago.

The primary solution has to be at home. If you have forgotten the shortages of last winter, most Americans have not.

I have ordered today the reorganization of our national energy effort and the creation of a national energy board. It will be chaired with developing—or I should say charged with developing—a single national energy policy and program. And I think most of you will be glad to know that our former colleague, Rog Morton, our secretary of interior, will be the overall boss of our national energy program.

Rog Morton's marching orders are to reduce imports of foreign oil by one million barrels per day by the end of 1975, whether by savings here at home, or by increasing our own sources.

Secretary Morton, along with his other responsibility, is also charged with increasing our domestic energy supply by promptly utilizing our coal resources and expanding recovery of domestic oil still in the ground in old wells.

New legislation will be sought after your recess to require use of cleaner coal processes and nuclear fuel in new electric plants, and the quick conversion of existing oil plants. I propose that we, together, set a target date of 1980 for eliminating oil-fired plants from the nation's base-loaded electrical capacity.

I will use the Defense Production Act to allocate scarce materials for energy development, and I will ask you, the House and Senate, for whatever amendments prove necessary.

I will meet with top management of the automobile industry to assure, either by agreement or by law, a firm program aimed at achieving a 40 percent increase in gasoline mileage within a four-year development deadline.

Priority legislation—action, I should say—to increase energy supply here at home requires the following:

—One, long-sought deregulation of natural gas supplies,

—Number two, responsible use of our naval petroleum reserves in California and Alaska,

—Number three, amendments to the Clean Air Act; and

—Four, passage of surface mining legislation to ensure an adequate supply with common-sense environmental protection.

Now, if all of these steps fail to meet our current energy-saving goals, I will not hesitate to ask for tougher measures. For the long range, we must work harder on coal gasification.

We must push with renewed vigor and talent research in the use of non-fossil fuels. The power of the atom, the heat of the sun and the steam stored deep in the earth, the force of the winds and water must be main sources of energy for our grandchildren, and we can do it.

Number three: restrictive practices. To increase productivity and contain prices, we must end restrictive and costly practices whether instituted by government, industry, labor, or others. And I am determined to return to the vigorous enforcement of antitrust laws.

The administration will zero in on more effective enforcement of laws against price fixing and bid rigging. For instance, noncompetitive professional fee schedules and real estate settlement fees must be eliminated. Such violations will be prosecuted by the Department of Justice to the full extent of the law.

Now, I ask Congress for prompt authority to increase maximum penalties for antitrust violations from $50,000 to $1 million for corporations, and from $50,000 to $100,000 for individual violators.

At the Conference on Inflation we found, I would say, very broad agreement that the federal government imposes too many hidden and too many inflationary costs on our economy. As a result, I propose a four-point program aimed at a substantial purging process.

Number one, I have ordered the Council on Wage and Price Stability to be the watchdog over inflationary costs of all governmental actions.

Two, I ask the Congress to establish a National Commission on Regulatory Reform to undertake a long-overdue total reexamination of the independent regulatory agencies. It will be a joint effort by the Congress, the executive branch, and the private sector to identify and eliminate existing federal rules and regulations that increase costs to the consumer without any good reason in today's economic climate.

Three: Hereafter, I will require that all major legislative proposals, regulations, and rules emanating from the executive branch of the government will include an inflation impact statement that certifies we have carefully weighed the effect on the nation. I respectfully request that the Congress require a similar advance inflation impact statement for its own legislative initiatives.

Finally, I urge state and local units of government to undertake similar programs to reduce inflationary effects of their regulatory activities.

At this point, I thank the Congress for recently revitalizing the National Commission on Productivity and Work Quality. It will initially concentrate on problems of productivity in government—federal, state, and local. Outside of government, it will develop meaningful blueprints for labor-management cooperation at the plant level. It should look particularly at the construction and the health service industries.

The Council on Wage and Price Stability will, of course, monitor wage and price increases in the private sector. Monitoring will include public hearings to justify either price or wage increases. I emphasize, in fact reemphasize, that this is not a compulsory wage and price control agency.

Now, I know many Americans see federal controls as the answer. But I believe from past experience controls show us that they never really stop inflation—not the last time, not even during and immediately after World War II when, as I recall, prices rose despite severe and enforceable wartime rationing.

Now, peacetime controls actually, we know from recent experience, create shortages, hamper production, stifle growth, and limit jobs. I do not ask for such powers, however politically tempting, as such a program could cause the fixer and the black marketeer to flourish while decent citizens face empty shelves and stand in long waiting lines.

Number four: we need more capital. We cannot "eat up our seed corn." Our free enterprise system depends on orderly capital markets through which the savings of our people become productively used. Today, our capital markets are in total disarray. We must restore their vitality. Prudent monetary restraint is essential.

You and the American people should know, however, that I have personally been assured by the chairman of the independent Federal Reserve Board that the supply of money and credit will expand sufficiently to meet the needs of our economy and that in no event will a credit crunch occur.

The prime lending rate is going down. To help industry to buy more machines and create more jobs, I am recommending a liberalized 10 percent investment tax credit. This credit should be especially helpful to capital-intensive industries such as primary metals, public utilities, where capacity shortages have developed.

I am asking Congress to enact tax legislation to provide that all dividends on preferred stocks issued for cash be fully deductible by the issuing company. This should bring in more capital, especially for energy-producing utilities. It will also help other industries shift from debt to equity, providing a sounder capital structure.

Capital gains tax legislation must be liberalized as proposed by the tax reform bill currently before the Committee on Ways and Means. I endorse this approach and hope that it will pass promptly.

Number five: helping the casualties. And this is a very important part of the overall speech. The Conference on Inflation made everybody even more aware of who is suffering most from inflation. Foremost are those who are jobless through no fault of their own.

Three weeks ago, I released funds which, with earlier actions, provide public service employment for some 170,000 who need work. I now propose to the Congress a two-step program to augment this action.

First, 13 weeks of special unemployment insurance benefits would be provided to those who have exhausted their regular and extended unemployment insurance benefits, and 26 weeks of special unemployment insurance benefits to those who qualify but are not now covered by regular unemployment insurance programs. Funding in this case would come from the general Treasury, not from taxes on employers as is the case with the established unemployment programs.

Second, I ask the Congress to create a brand new Community Improvement Corps to provide work for the unemployed through short-term useful work projects to improve, beautify, and enhance the environment of our cities, our towns, and our countryside.

This standby program would come alive whenever unemployment exceeds 6 percent nationally. It would be stopped when unemployment drops below 6 percent. Local labor markets would each qualify for grants whenever their unemployment rate exceeds 6.5 percent.

State and local government contractors would supervise these projects and could hire only those who had exhausted their

unemployment insurance benefits. The goal of this new program is to provide more constructive work for all Americans, young or old, who cannot find a job.

The purpose really follows this formula: Short-term problems require short-term remedies. I therefore request that these programs be for a one-year period.

Now, I know that low- and middle-income Americans have been hardest hit by inflation. Their budgets are most vulnerable because a larger part of their income goes for the highly inflated costs of food, fuel, and medical care.

The tax reform bill now in the House Committee on Ways and Means, which I favor, already provides approximately $1.6 billion of tax relief to these groups. Compensating new revenues are provided in this prospective legislation by a windfall tax, profits tax on oil producers, and by closing other loopholes. If enacted, this will be a major contribution by the Congress in our common effort to make our tax system fairer to all.

Number six: stimulating housing. Without question, credit is the lifeblood of housing. The United States, unfortunately, is suffering the longest and the most severe housing recession since the end of World War II. Unemployment in the construction trades is twice the national average.

One of my first acts as president was to sign the Housing and Community Development Act of 1974. I have since concluded that still more help is needed, help that can be delivered very quickly and with minimum inflationary impact.

I urge the Congress to enact before recess additional legislation to make most home mortgages eligible for purchase by an agency of the federal government. As the law stands now, only FHA or VA home mortgages, one-fifth of the total, are covered.

I am very glad that the Senate, thanks to the leadership of Senator Brooke and Senator Cranston, has already made substantial progress on this legislation. As soon as it comes to me, I will make at least $3 billion immediately available for mortgage purchases, enough to finance about 100,000 more American homes.

Number seven: thrift institutions. Savings and loan and similar institutions are hard hit by inflation and high interest rates. They no longer attract, unfortunately, adequate deposits. The executive branch, in my judgment, must join with the Congress in giving critically needed attention to the structure and the operation of our thrift institutions which now find themselves for the third time in eight years in another period of serious mortgage credit scarcity.

Passage of the pending financial institution bill will help, but no single measure has yet appeared, as I see it, to solve feast or famine in mortgage credit. However, I promise to work with you individually and collectively to develop additional specific programs in this area in the future.

Number eight: international interdependency. The United States has a responsibility not only to maintain a healthy economy at home, but also to seek policies which complement rather than disrupt the constructive efforts of others.

Essential to U.S. initiatives is the early passage of an acceptable trade reform bill. My special representative for trade negotiations [William D. Eberle] departed earlier this afternoon to Canada, Europe, Japan, to brief foreign friends on my proposals.

We live in an interdependent world and, therefore, must work together to resolve common economic problems.

Number nine: federal taxes and spending. To support programs, to increase production and share inflation-produced hardships, we need additional tax revenues.

I am aware that any proposal for new taxes just 4 weeks before a national election is, to put it mildly, considered politically unwise. And I am frank to say that I have been earnestly advised to wait and talk about taxes anytime after November 5. But I do say in sincerity that I will not play politics with America's future.

Our present inflation to a considerable degree comes from many years of enacting expensive programs without raising enough revenues to pay for them. The truth is that 19 out of the 25 years I had the honor and the privilege to serve in this chamber, the federal government ended up with federal deficits. That is not a very good batting average.

By now, almost everybody—almost everybody else, I should say—has stated my position on federal gasoline taxes. This time I will do it myself. I am not—emphasizing not—asking you for any increase in gas taxes.

I am—I *am* asking you to approve a one-year temporary tax surcharge of 5 percent on corporate and upper-level individual incomes. This would generally exclude from the surcharge those families with gross incomes below $15,000 a year. The estimated $5 billion in extra revenue to be raised by this inflation-fighting tax should pay for the new programs I have recommended in this message.

I think, and I suspect each of you know, this is the acid test of our joint determination to whip inflation in America. I would not ask this if major loopholes were not now being closed by the Committee on Ways and Means' tax reform bill.

I urge you to join me before your recess, in addition to what I have said before, to join me by voting to set a target spending limit—let me emphasize it—a target spending limit of $300 billion for the federal fiscal budget of 1975.

When Congress agrees to this spending target, I will submit a package of budget deferrals and rescissions to meet this goal. I will do the tough job of designating for congressional action, on your return, those areas which I believe can and must be reduced. These will be hard choices and every one of you in this chamber know it as well as I. They will be hard choices, but no federal agency, including the Defense Department, will be untouchable.

It is my judgment that fiscal discipline is a necessary weapon in any fight against inflation. While this spending target is a small step, it is a step in the right direction, and we need to get on that course without any further delay. I do not think that any of us in this chamber today can ask the American people to tighten their belts if Uncle Sam is unwilling to tighten his belt first.

And now, if I might, I would like to say a few words directly to your constituents and, incidentally, mine.

My fellow Americans, 10 days ago I asked you to get things started by making a list of 10 ways to fight inflation and save energy, to exchange your list with your neighbors, and to send me a copy.

I have personally read scores of the thousands of letters received at the White House, and incidentally, I have made my economic experts read some of them, too. We all benefited, at least I did, and I thank each and every one of you for this cooperation.

Some of the good ideas from your home to mine have been cranked into the recommendations I have just made to the Congress and the steps I am taking as president to whip inflation right now. There were also firm warnings on what government must not do, and I appreciated those, too. Your best suggestions for voluntary restraint and self-discipline showed me that a great degree of patriotic determination and unanimity already exists in this great land.

I have asked Congress for urgent specific actions it alone can take. I advised Congress of the initial steps that I am taking as president. Here is what only you can do: Unless every able American pitches in, Congress and I cannot do the job. Winning our fight against inflation and waste involves total mobilization of America's greatest resources—the brains, the skills, and the willpower of the American people.

Here is what we must do, what each and every one of you can do: To help increase food and lower prices, grow more and waste less; to help save scarce fuel in the energy crisis, drive less, heat less. Every housewife knows almost exactly how much she spent for food last week. If you cannot spare a penny from your food budget—and I know there are many—surely you can cut the food that you waste by 5 percent.

Every American motorist knows exactly how many miles he or she drives to work or to school every day and about how much mileage she or he runs up each year. If we all drive at least 5 percent fewer miles, we can save, almost unbelievably, 250,000 barrels of foreign oil per day. By the end of 1975, most of us can do better than 5 percent by carpooling, taking the bus, riding bikes, or just plain walking. We can save enough gas by self-discipline to meet our one million barrels per day goal.

I think there is one final thing that all Americans can do, rich or poor, and that is share with others. We can share burdens as we can share blessings. Sharing is not easy, not easy to measure like mileage and family budgets, but I am sure that 5 percent more is not nearly enough to ask, so I ask you to share everything you can and a little bit more. And it will strengthen our spirits as well as our economy.

Today I will not take more of the time of this busy Congress, for I vividly remember the rush before every recess, and the clock is already running on my specific and urgent requests for legislative action. I also remember how much Congress can get done when it puts its shoulder to the wheel.

One week from tonight I have a longstanding invitation in Kansas City to address the Future Farmers of America, a fine organization of wonderful young people whose help, with millions of others, is vital in this battle. I will elaborate then how volunteer inflation fighters and energy savers can further mobilize their total efforts.

Since asking Miss Sylvia Porter, the well-known financial writer, to help me organize an all-out nationwide volunteer mobilization, I have named a White House coordinator and have enlisted the enthusiastic support and services of some 17 other distinguished Americans to help plan for citizen and private group participation.

There will be no big federal bureaucracy set up for this crash program. Through the courtesy of such volunteers from the communication and media fields, a very simple enlistment form will appear in many of tomorrow's newspapers along with the symbol of this new mobilization, which I am wearing on my lapel. It bears the single word WIN. I think that tells it all. I will call upon every American to join in this massive mobilization and stick with it until we do win as a nation and as a people.

Mr. Speaker and Mr. President, I stand on a spot hallowed by history. Many presidents have come here many times to solicit, to scold, to flatter, to exhort the Congress to support them in their leadership. Once in a great while, presidents have stood here and truly inspired the most skeptical and the most sophisticated audience of their co-equal partners in government. Perhaps once or twice in a generation is there such a joint session. I don't expect this one to be.

Only two of my predecessors have come in person to call upon Congress for a declaration of war, and I shall not do that. But I say to you with all sincerity that our inflation, our public enemy number one, will, unless whipped, destroy our country, our homes, our liberties, our property, and finally our national pride, as surely as any well-armed wartime enemy.

I concede there will be no sudden Pearl Harbor to shock us into unity and to sacrifice, but I think we have had enough early warnings. The time to intercept is right now. The time to intercept is almost gone.

My friends and former colleagues, will you enlist now? My friends and fellow Americans, will you enlist now? Together with discipline and determination, we will win.

I thank you very much.

The Energy and Economic Crisis

Washington, D.C.
January 13, 1975

FORD AIRED a series of complex proposals for energy conservation and antirecession measures in a televised speech delivered from the Lincoln Library, on the ground floor of the White House. Although those parts of his proposals that passed the Congress had no measurable effect on the energy crisis or the recession, Ford did score a coup over congressional Democrats, who lacked an alternative program.

This was one of Ford's most successful speeches; in the informal setting of the library he looked more at ease, and his matter-of-fact approach to the problems addressed was rhetorically appropriate. The press felt that he had regained some of the appearance of "presidentiality" that he had lost after the Nixon pardon. The television commentator Eric Sevareid claimed to see a "vigor and decisiveness" that Ford had not shown before.

Without wasting words, I want to talk with you tonight about putting our domestic house in order. We must turn America in a new direction. We must reverse the current recession, reduce unemployment, and create more jobs.

We must restore the confidence of consumers and investors alike. We must continue an effective plan to curb inflation. We must, without any delay, take firm control of our progress as a free people.

Together we can and will do this job. Our national character is strong on self-discipline and the will to win. Americans are at their very best when the going is rough. Right now, the going is rough, and it may get rougher. But if we do what must be done, we will be on our way to better days. We have an historic opportunity.

On Wednesday, I will report to the new Congress on the state of the Union and ask for its help to quickly improve it. But neither Congress nor the president can pass laws or issue orders to assure economic improvement and instant prosperity. The government can help by equalizing unfair burdens, by setting an example of sound economic actions, and by exerting leadership through clear and coordinated national recovery programs.

Tonight, I want to talk to you about what must be done. After all, you are the people most affected.

Since becoming your president five months ago, economic problems have been my foremost concern. Two elements of our problem are long-range—inflation and energy. Both are affected not only by our actions but also by international forces beyond our direct control.

The new and disturbing element in the economic picture is our worsening recession and the unemployment that goes with it.

We have made some progress in slowing the upward spiral of inflation and getting interest rates started down, but we have suffered sudden and serious setbacks in sales and unemployment. Therefore, we must shift our emphasis from inflation to recession, but in doing so, we must not lose sight of the very real and deadly dangers of rising prices and declining domestic energy supplies.

Americans are no longer in full control of their own national destiny when that destiny depends on uncertain foreign fuel at high prices fixed by others. Higher energy costs compound both inflation and recession, and dependence on others for future energy supplies is intolerable to our national security.

Therefore, we must wage a simultaneous three-front campaign against recession, inflation, and energy dependence. We have no choice. We need, within 90 days, the strongest and most far-reaching energy conservation program we have ever had.

Yes, gasoline and oil will cost even more than they do now, but this program will achieve two important objectives: It will discourage the unnecessary use of petroleum products, and it will encourage the development and substitution of other fuels and newer sources of energy.

To get started immediately on an urgent national energy plan, I will use the presidential emergency powers to reduce our dependence on foreign oil by raising import fees on each barrel of foreign crude oil by $1 to $3 over the next three months.

A more comprehensive program of energy conservation taxes on oil and natural gas to reduce consumption substantially must be enacted by the Congress. The revenues derived from such taxes will be returned to the economy. In addition, my energy conservation program contains oil allocation authority to avoid undue hardships in any one geographic area, such as New England, or in any specific industries or areas of human need where oil is essential.

The plan prevents windfall profits by producers. There must also be volunteer efforts to cut gasoline and other energy use.

My national energy conservation plan will urge Congress to grant a five-year delay on higher automobile pollution standards in order to achieve a 40 percent improvement in miles per gallon.

Stronger measures to speed the development of other domestic energy resources, such as coal, geothermal, solar, and nuclear power, are also essential.

This plan requires personal sacrifice. But if we all pitch in, we will meet our goal of reducing foreign oil imports by one million barrels a day by the end of this year and by two million barrels before the end of 1977. The energy conservation measures I have outlined tonight will be supplemented by use of presidential powers to limit oil imports as necessary to fully achieve these goals.

By 1985—10 years from now—the United States will be invulnerable to foreign energy disruptions or oil embargoes such as we experienced last year. Of course, our domestic needs come first. But our gains in energy independence will be fully coordinated with our friends abroad. Our efforts should prompt similar action by our allies.

If Congress speedily enacts this national energy program, there will be no need for compulsory rationing or long waiting lines at the service station. Yes, gasoline prices will go up, though not as much as with a 20-cent-a-gallon tax. Furthermore, the burden of the conservation taxes on oil will be shared by all petroleum users, not just motorists.

Now, let me talk about the problem of unemployment. This country needs an immediate federal income tax cut of $16 billion. Twelve billion dollars, or three-fourths of the total of this cut, should go to individual taxpayers

in the form of a cash rebate amounting to 12 percent of their 1974 tax payments—up to a $1,000 rebate. If Congress acts by April 1, you will get your first check for half the rebate in May and the rest by September.

The other one-fourth of the cut, about $4 billion, will go to business taxpayers, including farmers, to promote plant expansion and create more jobs. This will be in the form of an increase in the investment tax credit to 12 percent for one year. There will be special provisions to assist essential public utilities to step up their energy capacity. This will encourage capital spending and productivity, the key to recovery and growth.

As soon as the new revenues from energy conservation taxes are received, we will be able to return $30 billion to the economy in the form of additional payments and credits to individuals, business, and state and local governments. Cash payments from this total also will be available to those who pay no income taxes because of low earnings. They are the hardest hit by inflation and higher energy costs. This combined program adds up to $46 billion—$30 billion in returned energy tax revenues to compensate for higher fuel costs and $16 billion in tax cuts to help provide more jobs. And the energy conservation tax revenues will continue to be put back into the economy as long as the emergency lasts.

This economic program is different in emphasis from the proposals I put forward last October. The reason is that the situation has changed. You know it, and I know it. What we most urgently need today is more spending money in your pockets rather than in the Treasury in Washington.

Let's face it, a tax cut to bolster the economy will mean a bigger federal deficit temporarily, and I have fought against deficits all my public life. But unless our economy revives rapidly, federal tax revenues will shrink so much that future deficits will be even larger. But I have not abandoned my lifelong belief in fiscal restraint. In the long run, there is no other real remedy for our economic troubles.

While wrestling with the budgets for this year and next, I found that at least three-quarters of all federal expenditures are required by laws already on the books. The president cannot, by law, cut spending in an ever-growing list of programs which provide mandatory formulas for payments to state and local governments and to families and to individuals. Unless these laws are changed, I can tell you there are only two ways to go—still higher federal taxes or the more ruinous hidden tax of inflation. Unchecked, federal programs mandated by law will be prime contributors to federal deficits of $30 to $50 billion this year and next. Deficits of this magnitude are wrong—except on a temporary basis in the most extenuating circumstances.

Reform of these costly, mandated federal spending programs will take time. Meanwhile, in order to keep the budget deficit as low as possible, I will do what I can.

In my State of the Union and subsequent messages, I will not propose any new federal spending programs except for energy. And the Congress—your representatives in Washington—share an equal responsibility to see that no new spending programs are enacted. I will not hesitate to veto any new spending programs that Congress sends to me. Many proposed federal spending programs are desirable and have had my support in the past. But they cost money—*your* tax dollars. Plainly, it is time to declare a one-year moratorium on new federal spending programs.

I need your support in this. It is vital that your representatives in Congress know that you share this concern about inflation.

I believe the federal government ought to show all Americans it practices what it preaches about sacrifice and self-restraint. Therefore, I will insist on a 5 percent limit on any federal pay increases in 1975, and I will ask Congress to put the same temporary 5 percent ceiling on automatic cost-of-living increases in government and military retirement pay and social security.

Government alone cannot bring the cost of living down but until it does start down, government can refrain from pushing it up. For only when the cost of living comes down can everybody get full value from a pension or a paycheck. I want to hasten that day.

Tonight I have summarized the highlights of my energy and my economic programs. They must go hand-in-hand, as I see it.

On Wednesday I will spell out these proposals to the Congress. There will be other recommendations, both short-term and long-range, to make our program as fair to all as possible.

I will press for prompt action and responsible legislation. The danger of doing nothing is great; the danger of doing too much is just as great. We cannot afford to throw monkey wrenches into our complex economic machine just because it isn't running at full speed.

We are in trouble, but we are not on the brink of another Great Depression.

Our political and economic system today is many times stronger than it was in the 1930s. We have income safeguards and unemployment cushions built into our economy. I have taken and will continue to take whatever steps are needed to prevent massive dislocations and personal hardships and, in particular, the tragedy of rising unemployment.

But sound solutions to our economic difficulties depend primarily on the strong support of each one of you. Self-restraint must be exercised by big and small business, by organized and unorganized labor, by state and local governments as well as by the federal government.

No one will be allowed to prosper from the temporary hardships most of us willingly bear, nor can we permit any special interests to gain from our common distress.

To improve the economic outlook we must rekindle faith in ourselves. Nobody is going to pull us out of our troubles but ourselves—and by our own bootstraps.

In 200 years as a nation, we have triumphed over external enemies and internal conflicts, and each time we have emerged stronger than before. This has called for determined leaders and dedicated people, and this call has never gone unheeded.

In every crisis, the American people have closed ranks, rolled up their sleeves, and rallied to do whatever had to be done.

I ask you and those who represent you in the Congress to work to turn our economy around, declare our energy independence, and resolve to make our free society again the wonder of the world.

The beginning of our bicentennial is a good time to reaffirm our pride and purpose as Americans who help themselves and help their neighbors no matter how tough the task. For my part, I will do what I believe is right for all our people—to do my best for America as long as I occupy this historic house.

We know what must be done. The time to act is now. We have our nation to preserve and our future to protect. Let us act together. May God bless our endeavors.

Thank you, and good night.

Farewell Address

From the State of the Union Address
Washington, D.C.
January 12, 1977

THE ELECTION of 1976 was close, with Carter edging out Ford by only 2 percent of the vote. Ford's pardon of Nixon hurt him badly, but so did Ronald Reagan, who battled Ford for the Republican nomination and then refused to campaign for him in the general election. In addition, Ford made a serious blunder in the second of three televised debates with Carter when he claimed that Eastern Europe was not under Soviet domination, a misstatement that called into question his grasp of foreign policy.

In his final State of the Union address, Ford included a farewell, written by Hartmann, that was meant to recall his remarks on taking the oath of office in 1974.

In accordance with the Constitution, I come before you once again to report on the state of the Union.

This report will be my last—maybe—[laughter]—but for the Union it is only the first of such reports in our third century of independence, the close of which none of us will ever see. We can be confident, however, that 100 years from now a freely elected president will come before a freely elected Congress chosen to renew our great republic's pledge to the government of the people, by the people, and for the people.

For my part I pray the third century we are beginning will bring to all Americans, our children and their children's children, a greater measure of individual equality, opportunity, and justice, a greater abundance of spiritual and material blessings, and a higher quality of life, liberty, and the pursuit of happiness.

The state of the Union is a measurement of the many elements of which it is composed—a political union of diverse states, an economic union of varying interests, an intellectual union of common convictions, and a moral union of immutable ideals.

Taken in sum, I can report that the state of the Union is good. There is room for improvement, as always, but today we have a more perfect Union than when my stewardship began.

As a people we discovered that our bicentennial was much more than a celebration of the past; it became a joyous reaffirmation of all that it means to be Americans, a confirmation before all the world of the vitality and durability of our free institutions. I am proud to have been privileged to preside over the affairs of our federal government during these eventful years when we proved, as I said in my first words upon assuming office, that "our Constitution works; our great republic is a government of laws and not of men. Here the people rule." . . .

As I look to the future—and I assure you I intend to go on doing that for a good many years—I can say with confidence that the state of the Union is good, but we must go on making it better and better.

This gathering symbolizes the constitutional foundation which makes continued progress possible, synchronizing the skills of three independent branches of government, reserving fundamental sovereignty to the people of this great land. It is only as the temporary representatives and servants of the people that we meet here; we bring no hereditary status or gift of infallibility, and none follows us from this place.

Like President Washington, like the more fortunate of his successors, I look forward to the status of private citizen with gladness and gratitude. To me, being a citizen of the United States of America is the greatest honor and privilege in this world.

From the opportunities which fate and my fellow citizens have given me, as a member of the House, as vice president and president of the Senate, and as president of all the people, I have come to understand and place the highest value on the checks and balances which our founders imposed on government through the separation of powers among co-equal legislative, executive, and judicial branches. This often results in difficulty and delay, as I well know, but it also places supreme authority under God, beyond any one person, any one branch, any majority great or small, or any one party. The Constitution is the bedrock of all our freedoms. Guard and cherish it, keep honor and order in your own house, and the republic will endure.

It is not easy to end these remarks. In this chamber, along with some of you, I have experienced many, many of the highlights of my life. It was here that I stood 28 years ago with my freshman colleagues, as Speaker Sam Rayburn administered the oath. I see some of you now—Charlie Bennett, Dick Boiling, Carl Perkins, Pete Rodino, Harley Staggers, Tom Steed, Sid Yates, Clem Zablocki—and I remember those who have gone to their rest. It was here

we waged many, many a lively battle—won some, lost some, but always remaining friends. It was here, surrounded by such friends, that the distinguished chief justice swore me in as vice president on December 6, 1973. It was here I returned eight months later as your president to ask not for a honeymoon, but for a good marriage.

I will always treasure those memories and your many, many kindnesses. I thank you for them all.

My fellow Americans, I once asked you for your prayers, and now I give you mine: May God guide this wonderful country, its people, and those they have chosen to lead them. May our third century be illuminated by liberty and blessed with brotherhood, so that we and all who come after us may be the humble servants of thy peace. Amen.

Gerald F. Ford Museum in Grand Rapids, Michigan.
(Courtesy of PresidentsUSA.net)

Courtesy of Jimmy Carter Library

Jimmy Carter

Jimmy Carter

1977–1981

WHEN JIMMY CARTER ran for the presidency in 1976, he was perceived by many of his most ardent supporters not so much as a politician but as a political magician who could reconcile within himself, and symbolically for the nation, the contradictions and conflicts in American life. He was a white southerner who hung Martin Luther King Jr.'s portrait in the Georgia statehouse when he was governor; a businessman and engineer who had grown up in the backwoods; a former naval officer with a strong pacifist bent; above all, an evangelical Christian who sought to make every action, personal and public, consistent with a moral standard derived from his religion. His presidency was intended to be a kind of pastorate, even a prophetic mission, as is reflected in the quote from the theologian Reinhold Niebuhr that opened his campaign autobiography: "The sad duty of politics is to establish justice in a sinful world."

Good oratory is essential for any preacher, whether churchly or secular. Carter's softvoiced pitch and personal charm served him well during his candidacy, when he made an appealing contrast to both Ford and Nixon. Kandy Stroud, a journalist who followed the 1976 campaign, wrote: "At one moment, he seemed unimpressive, small, average, pleasant enough, but hardly presidential. At another moment he could be the statesman, grappling with the most complex issues of our day. He could put an audience of labor leaders to sleep, stir an audience of blacks to tears." When there was rapport between Carter and his audience, the feeling of communion was said to be almost palpable. "He has one truly remarkable platform gift," wrote journalist Helen Dewar, "the ability to establish a sense of intimacy with each member of the audience." He was also adept at accommodating different points of view without committing himself too deeply in any direction. According to one of his biographers, Betty Glad, candidate Carter sent out "complex messages that various listeners could interpret according to their own dispositions. From the multitude of signals—a word, a condition, a posture—Carter was able to send different people different signals about his positions."

The relaxed, friendly tone of Carter's extemporaneous campaign speeches was lost, for the most part, when he moved to Washington. His style of delivery was not well served by television, which made him seem rather too earnest, and his formal presidential speeches, which were prepared by staff members and substantially edited by Carter, lacked inspiration. Their basic format was the list, a point-by-point recitation of ideas, proposals, or events. James Fallows, his chief speechwriter, attributed this to the analytical, managerial cast of Carter's mind.

So did William Lee Miller, who wrote: "Though verbally agile, he uses words as instruments only, to convey facts, points, arguments. . . . In a particularly un-southern way, his speeches have no rhythm. Big words pop out in unexpected places. Complex formulations intrude when he is trying to be simple. Parallels don't parallel." Jody Powell, Carter's press secretary, notes that the president had a "bias against rhetoric"—he did not want to present a slickly manufactured image to the electorate—and would cut out language when he did not consider it direct, simple, and to the point. In moments of crisis, though, his phrasing could be solemn, even apocalyptic, as when he warned that the Soviet invasion of Afghanistan "could pose the most serious threat to peace since the Second World War," or when he tried to galvanize the national will to combat the energy crisis by calling such an effort "the moral equivalent of war."

Betty Glad remarks that "in his speeches Carter has been unusually self-referent, interlacing his discussions of issues with personal recollections about his boyhood and interpretations of his own personality." When he appeared before the nation in a televised speech, he seemed to be offering himself less as a maker of policy than as a kind of Sunday school teacher (which, indeed, he was in private life) who excelled in searching out the right path and guiding his listeners to follow it. In his presidency, therefore, much depended on his credibility as a moral leader. He was the first president since Johnson to give real attention to issues of social justice and civil rights. But the public's lack of patience with his efforts to deal with the hostage situation in Iran and economic problems at home undermined his position. He lost the 1980 election to another emphatically moral candidate who was, however, a more satisfying television performer.

Fireside Chat

Washington, D.C.

February 2, 1977

IN HIS election campaign, Carter presented himself as a new kind of populist, not in the traditional economic sense—he was by no means an enemy of business or finance—but in a mystical sense that made him the representative of "the people" in their struggle against the distant federal bureaucracy. His inauguration was pointedly plain and folksy, with none of the regalia of the imperial presidency. A few weeks later he went on the air with the first of a series of "fireside chats." The term was literal: Carter, dressed in a warm sweater, sat near a cozy fire in the White House library, under the Gilbert Stuart portrait of George Washington, while he discussed his plans and proposals with the voters in their living rooms. The following month he introduced a new media technique, the call-in show, which allowed him to answer questions from ordinary citizens, a format he preferred to the press conference.

Good evening.

Tomorrow will be two weeks since I became president. I have spent a lot of time deciding how I can be a good president. This talk, which the broadcast networks have agreed to bring to you, is one of several steps that I will take to keep in close touch with the people of our country, and to let you know informally about our plans for the coming months.

When I was running for president, I made a number of commitments. I take them very seriously. I believe that they were the reason that I was elected. And I want you to know that I intend to carry them out. As you probably noticed already, I have acted on several of my promises.

I will report to you from time to time about our government—both our problems and our achievements—but tonight I want to tell you how I plan to carry out some of my other commitments.

Some of our obvious goals can be achieved very quickly—for example, through executive orders and decisions made directly by me. But in many other areas, we must move carefully, with full involvement by the Congress, allowing time for citizens to participate in careful study, in order to develop predictable, long-range programs that we can be sure are affordable and that we know will work.

Some of these efforts will also require dedication—perhaps even some sacrifice—from you. But I don't believe that any of us are afraid to learn that our national goals require cooperation and mutual effort.

One of our most urgent projects is to develop a national energy policy. As I pointed out during the campaign, the United States is the only major industrial country without a comprehensive, long-range energy policy.

The extremely cold weather this winter has dangerously depleted our supplies of natural gas and fuel oil and forced hundreds of thousands of workers off the job. I congratulate the Congress for its quick action on the Emergency Natural Gas Act, which was passed today and signed just a few minutes ago. But the real problem—our failure to plan for the future or to take energy conservation seriously—started long before this winter, and it will take much longer to solve.

I realize that many of you have not believed that we really have an energy problem. But this winter has made all of us realize that we have to act.

Now, the Congress has already made many of the preparations for energy legislation. Presidential Assistant Dr. James Schlesinger is beginning to direct an effort to develop a national energy policy. Many groups of Americans will be involved. On April 20, we will have completed the planning for our energy program and will immediately then ask the Congress for its help in enacting comprehensive legislation.

Our program will emphasize conservation. The amount of energy being wasted which could be saved is greater than the total energy that we are importing from foreign countries. We will also stress development of our rich coal reserves in an environmentally sound way; we will emphasize research on solar energy and other renewable energy sources;

and we will maintain strict safeguards on necessary atomic energy production.

The responsibility for setting energy policy is now split among more than 50 different agencies, departments, and bureaus in the federal government. Later this month, I will ask the Congress for its help in combining many of these agencies in a new energy department to bring order out of chaos. Congressional leaders have already been working on this for quite a while.

We must face the fact that the energy shortage is permanent. There is no way we can solve it quickly. But if we all cooperate and make modest sacrifices, if we learn to live thriftily and remember the importance of helping our neighbors, then we can find ways to adjust and to make our society more efficient and our own lives more enjoyable and productive. Utility companies must promote conservation and not consumption. Oil and natural gas companies must be honest with all of us about their reserves and profits. We will find out the difference between real shortages and artificial ones. We will ask private companies to sacrifice, just as private citizens must do.

All of us must learn to waste less energy. Simply by keeping our thermostats, for instance, at 65 degrees in the daytime and 55 degrees at night we could save half the current shortage of natural gas.

There is no way that I, or anyone else in the government, can solve our energy problems if you are not willing to help. I know that we can meet this energy challenge if the burden is borne fairly among all our people—and if we realize that in order to solve our energy problems we need not sacrifice the quality of our lives.

The Congress has made great progress toward responsible strip-mining legislation, so that we can produce more energy without unnecessary destruction of our beautiful lands. My administration will support these efforts this year. We will also ask Congress for its help with legislation which will reduce the risk of future oil tanker spills and help deal with those that do occur.

I also stated during my campaign that our administration would do everything possible to restore a healthy American economy.

Our nation was built on the principle of work and not welfare; productivity and not stagnation. But I took office a couple of weeks ago in the middle of the worst economic slowdown of the last 40 years. More than seven and a half million people who want to work cannot find it according to the latest statistics. Because of high unemployment and idle factories the average American family like yours has been losing $1,800 a year in income, and many billions of dollars have been added to the federal deficit.

Also, inflation hurts us all. In every part of the country, whether we have a job or whether we are looking for a job, we must race just to keep up with the constant rise in prices. Inflation has hit us hardest, not in luxuries, but in the essentials—food, energy, health, housing. You see it every time you go shopping.

I understand that unemployment and inflation are very real, and have done great harm to many American families. Nothing makes it harder to provide decent health, housing, and education for our people, protect our environment, or to realize our goal of a balanced budget, than a stagnant economy.

As soon as I was elected, the leaders of the Congress and my own advisers began to work with me to develop a proposal for economic recovery. We were guided by the principle that everyone who is able to work ought to work; that our economic strength is based on a healthy, productive, private business sector; that we must provide the greatest help to those with the greatest need; and that there must be a predictable and a steady growth in our economy.

Two days ago, I presented this plan to the Congress. It is a balanced plan, with many elements, to meet the many causes of our economic problems.

One element that I am sure you will like is reducing taxes. This year the one-time tax benefits to the average family of four with $10,000 in income will be $200—a 30 percent reduction in income taxes.

But my primary concern is still jobs, and these one-time tax rebates are the only quick, effective way to get money into the economy and create those jobs.

But at the same time, we are reducing taxes permanently by increasing the standard deduction, which most taxpayers claim. Again, this family of four earning $10,000 will save $133 on a permanent basis—about 20 percent—on future income taxes. This will also be a major step toward tax simplification, allowing 75 percent of all taxpayers to take the standard deduction and to file a very simple tax return, quite different from the one that you will file this year.

We will also provide tax incentives to business firms to encourage them to fight inflation by expanding output and to hire more of our people who are eager to work. I think it makes more sense for the government to help workers stay on the payroll than to force them onto unemployment benefits or welfare payments.

We have several proposals, too, in this legislation to help our cities, which have been especially hard hit by nationwide economic problems. Communities where unemployment is worst will be eligible for additional money through the revenue-sharing program. A special program of public service employment will enable those who are now unemployed to contribute to their communities in hospitals, nursing homes, parks and recreation programs, and other related activities. A strong public works program will permit the construction of selected projects which are needed most.

These will not be make-work projects. They will be especially valuable in communities where budget cutbacks have reduced municipal services, and they will also help to prevent local tax increases.

Now, because unemployment is most severe among special groups of our people—the young, the disabled, minority groups—we will focus our training programs on them.

The top priority in our job training programs will go to young veterans of the Vietnam War. Unemployment is much higher among veterans than among others of the same age who did not serve in the military. I hope that putting many thousands of veterans back to work will be one more step toward binding up the wounds of the war years and toward helping those who have helped our country in the past.

I realize that very few people will think that this total economic plan is perfect. Many groups would like to see more of one kind of aid and less of another. But I am confident that this is the best balanced plan that we can produce for the overall economic health of the nation. It will produce steady, balanced, sustainable growth. It does not ignore inflation to solve unemployment or vice versa.

It does not ask one group of people to sacrifice solely for the benefit of another group.

It asks all of us to contribute, participate, and share to get the country back on the road to work again. It is an excellent investment in the future.

I also said many times during the campaign that we must reform and reorganize the federal government. I have often used the phrase "competent and compassionate" to describe what our government should be. When the government must perform a function, it should do it efficiently. Wherever free competition would do a better job of serving the public, the government should stay out. Ordinary people should be able to understand how our own government works, and to get satisfactory answers to questions.

Our confused and wasteful system that took so long to grow will take a long time to change. The place to start is at the top in the White House. I am reducing the size of the White House staff by nearly one-third, and I have asked the members of the cabinet to do the same at their top staff level. Soon, I will put a ceiling on the number of people employed by the federal government agencies so we can bring the growth of government under control.

We are now reviewing the government's 1,250 advisory committees and commissions to see how many could be abolished without harm to the public.

We have eliminated some expensive and unnecessary luxuries, such as door-to-door limousine service for many top officials, including all members of the White House staff. Government officials can't be sensitive to your problems if we are living like royalty here in Washington. While I am deeply grateful for the good wishes that lie behind them, I would like to ask that people not send gifts to me or to my family or to anyone else who serves in my administration.

We will cut down also on government regulations, and we will make sure that those that are written are in plain English for a change. Whenever a regulation is issued, it will carry its author's name. And I will request the cabinet members to read all regulations personally before they are released.

This week, I will ask the Congress for enabling legislation to let me reorganize the government. The passage of this legislation, which will give me the same authority extended to every president from Franklin Roosevelt through Richard Nixon, and used by many governors across the country, is absolutely crucial to a successful reorganization effort. So far, news from the Congress, because of their support, is very encouraging.

The Office of Management and Budget is now working on this plan, which will include zero-based budgeting, removal of unnecessary government regulations, sunset laws to cancel programs that have outlived their purpose, and elimination of overlap and duplication among government services.

We will not propose changes until we have done our best to be sure they are right. But we will be eager to learn from experience. If a program does not work, we will end it instead of just starting another to conceal our first mistakes.

We will also move quickly to reform our tax system and welfare system.

I said in the campaign that our income tax system was a disgrace because it is so arbitrary, complicated, and unfair. I made a commitment to a total overhaul of the income tax laws.

The economic program that I have already mentioned earlier will, by enabling more taxpayers to use the standard deduction, be just a first step toward a much better tax system.

My advisers have already started working with the Congress on a study of a more complete tax reform which will give us a fairer, simpler system. We will outline the study procedures very soon and, after consultation with many American citizens and with the Congress, we will present a comprehensive tax reform package before the end of this year.

The welfare system also needs a complete overhaul. Welfare waste robs both the taxpayers of our country and those who really and genuinely need help. It often forces families to split. It discourages people from seeking work.

The secretary of labor and the secretary of health, education, and welfare, and others have already begun a review of the entire welfare system. They will, of course, work with the Congress to develop proposals for a new system which will minimize abuse, strengthen the family, and emphasize adequate support for those who cannot work and training and jobs for those who can work. We expect their first report to be ready within 90 days.

In the meantime, I will support the Congress in its efforts to deal with the widespread fraud and waste and abuse of our Medicaid system.

Reforming the government also means making the government as open and honest as it can be. Congress is moving strongly on ethics legislation.

I've asked the people appointed by me to high positions in government to abide by strict rules of financial disclosure and to avoid all conflicts of interest. I intend to make those rules permanent. And I will select my appointees in such a way which will close the revolving door between government regulatory agencies on the one hand and the businesses they regulate on the other.

My cabinet members and I will conduct an open administration, with frequent press conferences and reports to the people and with "Town Hall" meetings all across the nation, where you can criticize, make suggestions, and ask questions.

We are also planning with some of the radio networks live, call-in sessions in the Oval Office during which I can accept your phone calls and answer the questions that are on your mind. I have asked the members of the cabinet to travel regularly around the country to stay in close touch with you out in your communities where government services are delivered.

There are many other areas of domestic policy—housing, health, crime, education, agriculture, and others—that will concern me as president but which I do not have time to discuss tonight.

All of these projects will take careful study and close cooperation with the Congress. Many will take longer than I would like. But we are determined to work on all of them. Later, through other reports, I will explain how, with your help and the help of Congress, we can carry them out.

I have also made commitments about our nation's foreign policy. As commander in chief of the armed forces, I am determined to have a strong, lean, efficient fighting force. Our policy should be based on close cooperation with our allies and worldwide respect for human rights, a reduction in world armaments, and it must always reflect our own moral values. I want our nation's actions to make you proud.

Yesterday, Vice President Mondale returned from his 10-day visit with leaders of Western Europe and Japan. I asked him to make this trip to demonstrate our intention to consult our traditional allies and friends on all important questions. I have been very pleased with his report. Vice President Mondale will be a constant and close adviser for me.

In a spirit of international friendship we will soon welcome here in the United States the leaders of several nations, beginning with our neighbors, Canada and Mexico.

This month the secretary of state, Cyrus Vance, will go to the Middle East, seeking ways to achieve a genuine peace between Israel and its Arab neighbors.

Our ambassador to the United Nations, Andrew Young, left last night on a visit to Africa to demonstrate our friendship for its peoples and our commitment to peaceful change toward majority rule in southern Africa.

I will also strive to improve our relations with the Soviet Union and the People's Republic of China, ensuring our security while seeking to reduce the risks of conflict.

We will continue to express our concern about violations of human rights, as we have during this past week, without upsetting our efforts toward friendly relationships with other countries.

Later, on another program, I will make a much more complete report to you on foreign-policy matters.

I would like to tell you now about one of the things that I have already learned in my brief time in office. I have learned that there are many things that a president cannot do. There is no energy policy that we can develop that would do more good than voluntary conservation. There is no economic policy that will do as much as shared faith in hard work, efficiency, and in the future of our system.

I know that both the Congress and the administration, as partners in leadership, have limited powers. That's the way it ought to be. But in the months in which I have campaigned, prepared to take office, and now

begun to serve as your president, I have found a reason for optimism.

With the help of my predecessor, we have come through a very difficult period in our nation's history. But for almost 10 years, we have not had a sense of a common national interest. We have lost faith in joint efforts and mutual sacrifices. Because of the divisions in our country many of us cannot remember a time when we really felt united.

But I remember another difficult time in our nation's history when we felt a different spirit. During World War II we faced a terrible crisis—but the challenge of fighting Nazism drew us together.

Those of us old enough to remember know that they were dark and frightening times—but many of our memories are of people ready to help each other for the common good.

I believe that we are ready for that same spirit again—to plan ahead, to work together, and to use common sense. Not because of war, but because we realize that we must act together to solve our problems, and because we are ready to trust one another.

As president, I will not be able to provide everything that every one of you might like. I am sure to make many mistakes. But I can promise that your needs will never be ignored, nor will we forget who put us in office.

We will always be a nation of differences—business and labor, blacks and whites, men and women, people of different regions and religions and different ethnic backgrounds—but with faith and confidence in each other our differences can be a source of personal fullness and national strength, rather than a cause of weakness and division.

If we are a united nation, then I can be a good president. But I will need your help to do it. I will do my best. I know you will do yours.

Thank you very much, and good night.

Human Rights and Foreign Policy

Notre Dame, Indiana

May 22, 1977

ACCORDING TO one of Carter's speechwriters, Hendrik Hertzberg, Carter's human rights campaign was "pure Jimmy," "a reflection of . . . strong moral impulses tethered somewhat loosely to a set of political goals." It was also a sure-fire issue with which to court public opinion at home. Carter discussed his stance on human rights and his eagerness to develop a nonconfrontational style in international relations at the 1977 commencement exercises at Notre Dame University. But translating this concern into a functioning policy and reconciling it with competing interests such as national security were problems that the administration could not resolve.

In an interview, Carter said: "I think my Notre Dame speech expresses my feeling about the power of words as clearly as I can. It's obvious that in our society the most significant action that can be taken is the evocation of a concept or an idea by words. In totalitarian governments the people who are being punished or condemned for illegal actions—that action is almost always words. I think, just to constantly keep it in the forefront of the world consciousness, a concern about the freedom of expression, is something that I can do, and we've had remarkable success so far. I don't believe there's a world leader on earth now who doesn't have a constant preoccupation with the concept of human rights."

Thank you for that welcome. I'm very glad to be with you. You may have started a new graduation trend which I don't deplore, that is, throwing peanuts on graduation day. The more that are used or consumed the higher the price goes.

I really did appreciate the great honor bestowed upon me this afternoon. My other degree is blue and gold from the navy, and I want to let you know that I do feel a kinship with those who are assembled here this afternoon. I was a little taken aback by the comment that I had brought a new accent to the White House. In the minds of many people in our country, for the first time in almost 150 years, there is no accent.

I tried to think of a story that would illustrate two points simultaneously and also be brief, which is kind of a difficult assignment. I was sitting on the Truman Balcony the other night with my good friend, Charles Kirbo, who told me about a man who was arrested and taken in to court for being drunk and for setting a bed on fire. When the judge asked him how to plead, he said, "not guilty." He said, "I was drunk but the bed was on fire when I got in it."

I think most of the graduates can draw the parallel between that statement and what you are approaching after this graduation exercise. But there are two points to that, and I'll come to the other one in just a few minutes.

In his 25 years as president of Notre Dame, Father Hesburgh has spoken more consistently and more effectively in the support of the rights of human beings than any other person I know. His interest in the Notre Dame Center for Civil Rights has never wavered. And he played an important role in broadening the scope of the center's work—and I visited there last fall—to see this work include, now, all people in the world, as shown by last month's conference here on human rights and American foreign policy.

And that concern has been demonstrated again today in a vivid fashion by the selection of Bishop Donal Lamont, Paul Cardinal Arns, and Stephen Cardinal Kim to receive honorary degrees. In their fight for human freedoms in Rhodesia, Brazil, and South Korea, these three religious leaders typify all that is best in their countries and in our church. I'm honored to join you in recognizing their dedication, their personal sacrifice, and their supreme courage.

Quite often, brave men like these are castigated and sometimes punished, sometimes even put to death, because they enter the realm where human rights is a struggle. And sometimes they are blamed for the very circumstance which they helped to dramatize, but it's been there for a long time. And the flames which they seek to extinguish concern us all and are increasingly visible around the world.

Last week, I spoke in California about the domestic agenda for our nation: to provide more efficiently for the needs of our people, to demonstrate—against the dark faith of our times—that our government can be both competent and more humane.

But I want to speak to you today about the strands that connect our actions overseas with our essential character as a nation. I believe we can have a foreign policy that is democratic, that is based on fundamental values, and that uses power and influence, which we have, for humane purposes. We can also have a foreign policy that the American people both support and, for a change, know about and understand.

I have a quiet confidence in our own political system. Because we know that democracy works, we can reject the arguments of those rulers who deny human rights to their people.

We are confident that democracy's example will be compelling, and so we seek to bring that example closer to those from whom in the past few years we have been separated and who are not yet convinced about the advantages of our kind of life.

We are confident that the democratic methods are the most effective, and so we are not tempted to employ improper tactics here at home or abroad.

We are confident of our own strength, so we can seek substantial mutual reductions in the nuclear arms race.

And we are confident of the good sense of American people, and so we let them share in the process of making foreign-policy decisions. We can thus speak with the voices of 215 million, and not just of an isolated handful.

Democracy's great recent successes—in India, Portugal, Spain, Greece—show that our confidence in this system is not misplaced. Being confident of our own future, we are now free of that inordinate fear of Communism which once led us to embrace any dictator who joined us in that fear. I'm glad that that's being changed.

For too many years, we've been willing to adopt the flawed and erroneous principles and tactics of our adversaries, sometimes abandoning our own values for theirs. We've fought fire with fire, never thinking that fire is better quenched with water. This approach failed, with Vietnam the best example of its intellectual and moral poverty. But through failure we have now found our way back to our own principles and values, and we have regained our lost confidence.

By the measure of history, our nation's 200 years are very brief, and our rise to world eminence is briefer still. It dates from 1945, when Europe and the old international order lay in ruins. Before then, America was largely on the periphery of world affairs. But since then, we have inescapably been at the center of world affairs.

Our policy during this period was guided by two principles: a belief that Soviet expansion was almost inevitable but that it must be contained, and the corresponding belief in the importance of an almost exclusive alliance among non-Communist nations on both sides of the Atlantic. That system could not last forever unchanged. Historical trends have weakened its foundation. The unifying threat of conflict with the Soviet Union has become less intensive, even though the competition has become more extensive.

The Vietnamese war produced a profound moral crisis, sapping worldwide faith in our own policy and our system of life, a crisis of confidence made even more grave by the covert pessimism of some of our leaders.

In less than a generation, we've seen the world change dramatically. The daily lives and aspirations of most human beings have been transformed. Colonialism is nearly gone. A new sense of national identity now exists in almost one hundred new countries that have been formed in the last generation. Knowledge has become more widespread. Aspirations are higher. As more people have been freed from traditional constraints, more have been determined to achieve, for the first time in their lives, social justice.

The world is still divided by ideological disputes, dominated by regional conflicts, and threatened by danger that we will not resolve the differences of race and wealth without violence or without drawing into combat the major military powers. We can no longer separate the traditional issues of war and peace from the new global questions of justice, equity, and human rights.

It is a new world, but America should not fear it. It is a new world, and we should help to shape it. It is a new world that calls for a new American foreign policy—a policy based on constant decency in its values and on optimism in our historical vision.

We can no longer have a policy solely for the industrial nations as the foundation of global stability, but we must respond to the new reality of a politically awakening world.

We can no longer expect that the other 150 nations will follow the dictates of the powerful, but we must continue—confidently—our efforts to inspire, to persuade, and to lead.

Our policy must reflect our belief that the world can hope for more than simple survival and our belief that dignity and freedom are fundamental spiritual requirements. Our policy must shape an international system that will last longer than secret deals.

We cannot make this kind of policy by manipulation. Our policy must be open; it must be candid; it must be one of constructive global involvement, resting on five cardinal principles.

I've tried to make these premises clear to the American people since last January. Let me review what we have been doing and discuss what we intend to do.

First, we have reaffirmed America's commitment to human rights as a fundamental tenet of our foreign policy. In ancestry, religion, color, place of origin, and cultural background, we Americans are as diverse a nation as the world has even seen. No common mystique of blood or soil unites us. What draws us together, perhaps more than anything else, is a belief in human freedom. We want the world to know that our nation stands for more than financial prosperity.

This does not mean that we can conduct our foreign policy by rigid moral maxims. We live in a world that is imperfect and which will always be imperfect—a world that is complex and confused and which will always be complex and confused.

I understand fully the limits of moral suasion. We have no illusion that changes will come easily or soon. But I also believe that it is a mistake to undervalue the power of words and of the ideas that words embody. In our own history, that power has ranged from Thomas Paine's "Common Sense" to Martin Luther King Jr.'s "I Have a Dream."

In the life of the human spirit, words are action, much more so than many of us may realize who live in countries where freedom of expression is taken for granted. The leaders of totalitarian nations understand this very well. The proof is that words are precisely the action for which dissidents in those countries are being persecuted.

Nonetheless, we can already see dramatic, worldwide advances in the protection of the individual from the arbitrary power of the state. For us to ignore this trend would be to lose influence and moral authority in the world. To lead it will be to regain the moral stature that we once had.

The great democracies are not free because we are strong and prosperous. I believe we are strong and influential and prosperous because we are free.

Throughout the world today, in free nations and in totalitarian countries as well, there is a preoccupation with the subject of human freedom, human rights. And I believe it is incumbent on us in this country to keep that discussion, that debate, that contention alive. No other country is as well-qualified as we to set an example. We have our own shortcomings and faults, and we should strive constantly and with courage to make sure that we are legitimately proud of what we have.

Second, we've moved deliberately to reinforce the bonds among our democracies. In our recent meetings in London, we agreed to widen our economic cooperation, to promote free trade, to strengthen the world's monetary system, to seek ways of avoiding nuclear proliferation. We prepared constructive proposals for the forthcoming meetings on North-South problems of poverty, development, and global well-being. And we agreed on joint efforts to reinforce and to modernize our common defense.

You may be interested in knowing that at this NATO meeting, for the first time in more than 25 years, all members are democracies. Even more important, all of us reaffirmed our basic optimism in the future of the democratic system. Our spirit of confidence is spreading. Together, our democracies can help to shape the wider architecture of global cooperation.

Third, we've moved to engage the Soviet Union in a joint effort to halt the strategic arms race. This race is not only dangerous, it's morally deplorable. We must put an end to it.

I know it will not be easy to reach agreements. Our goal is to be fair to both sides, to produce reciprocal stability, parity, and security. We desire a freeze on further modernization and production of weapons and a continuing, substantial reduction of strategic nuclear weapons as well. We want a comprehensive ban on all nuclear testing, a prohibition against all chemical warfare, no attack capability against space satellites, and arms limitations in the Indian Ocean.

We hope that we can take joint steps with all nations toward a final agreement eliminating nuclear weapons completely from our arsenals of death. We will persist in this effort.

Now, I believe in détente with the Soviet Union. To me it means progress toward peace. But the effects of détente should not be limited to our own two countries alone. We hope to persuade the Soviet Union that one country cannot impose its system of society upon another, either through direct military intervention or through the use of a client state's military force, as was the case with Cuban intervention in Angola.

Cooperation also implies obligation. We hope that the Soviet Union will join with us and other nations in playing a larger role in aiding the developing world, for common aid efforts will help us build a bridge of mutual confidence in one another.

Fourth, we are taking deliberate steps to improve the chances of lasting peace in the Middle East. Through wide-ranging consultation with leaders of the countries involved—Israel, Syria, Jordan, and Egypt—we have found some areas of agreement and some movement toward consensus. The negotiations must continue.

Through my own public comments, I've also tried to suggest a more flexible framework for the discussion of the three key issues which have so far been so intractable: the nature of a comprehensive peace—what is peace; what does it mean to the Israelis; what does it mean to their Arab neighbors; secondly, the relationship between security and borders—how can the dispute over border delineations be established and settled with a feeling of security on both sides; and the issue of the Palestinian homeland.

The historic friendship that the United States has with Israel is not dependent on domestic politics in either nation; it's derived from our common respect for human freedom and from a common search for permanent peace.

We will continue to promote a settlement which all of us need. Our own policy will not be affected by changes in leadership in any of the countries in the Middle East. Therefore, we expect Israel and her neighbors to continue to be bound by United Nations Resolutions 242 and 338, which they have previously accepted.

This may be the most propitious time for a genuine settlement since the beginning of the Arab-Israeli conflict almost 30 years ago. To let this opportunity pass could mean disaster not only for the Middle East but, perhaps, for the international political and economic order as well.

And fifth, we are attempting, even at the risk of some friction with our friends, to reduce the danger of nuclear proliferation and the worldwide spread of conventional weapons.

At the recent summit, we set in motion an international effort to determine the best ways of harnessing nuclear energy for peaceful use while reducing the risks that its products will be diverted to the making of explosives.

We've already completed a comprehensive review of our own policy on arms transfers. Competition in arms sales is inimical to peace and destructive of the economic development of the poorer countries.

We will, as a matter of national policy now in our country, seek to reduce the annual dollar volume of arms sales, to restrict the transfer of advanced weapons, and to reduce the extent of our coproduction arrangements about weapons with foreign states. And just as important, we are trying to get other nations, both free and otherwise, to join us in this effort.

But all of this that I've described is just the beginning. It's a beginning aimed towards a clear goal: to create a wider framework of international cooperation suited to the new and rapidly changing historical circumstances.

We will cooperate more closely with the newly influential countries in Latin America, Africa, and Asia. We need their friendship and cooperation in a common effort as the structure of world power changes.

More than one hundred years ago, Abraham Lincoln said that our nation could not exist half slave and half free. We know a peaceful world cannot long exist one-third rich and two-thirds hungry.

Most nations share our faith that, in the long run, expanded and equitable trade will best help the developing countries to help themselves. But the immediate problems of hunger, disease, illiteracy, and repression are here now.

The Western democracies, the OPEC nations, and the developed Communist countries can cooperate through existing international institutions in providing more effective aid. This is an excellent alternative to war.

We have a special need for cooperation and consultation with other nations in this hemisphere—to the north and to the south. We do not need another slogan. Although these are our close friends and neighbors, our links with them are the same links of equality that we forge for the rest of the world. We will be dealing with them as part of a new, worldwide mosaic of global, regional, and bilateral relations.

It's important that we make progress toward normalizing relations with the People's Republic of China. We see the American and Chinese relationship as a central element of our global policy and China as a key force for global peace. We wish to cooperate closely with the creative Chinese people on the problems that confront all mankind. And we hope to find a formula which can bridge some of the difficulties that still separate us.

Finally, let me say that we are committed to a peaceful resolution of the crisis in southern Africa. The time has come for the principle of majority rule to be the basis for political order, recognizing that in a democratic system the rights of the minority must also be protected.

To be peaceful, change must come promptly. The United States is determined to work together with our European allies and with the concerned African states to shape a congenial international framework for the rapid and progressive transformation of southern African society and to help protect it from unwarranted outside interference.

Let me conclude by summarizing: Our policy is based on an historical vision of America's role. Our policy is derived from a larger view of global change. Our policy is rooted in our moral values, which never change. Our policy is reinforced by our material wealth and by our military power. Our policy is designed to serve mankind. And it is a policy that I hope will make you proud to be Americans.

Thank you.

The Panama Canal

Washington, D.C.

February 1, 1978

THE TRANSFER to Panama of control over the Panama Canal was the centerpiece of Carter's Latin American policy. Two treaties were signed in September 1977, one providing for joint control until 1999, the other providing for American military defense of the canal after Panama assumed full control in the year 2000. The American right wing regarded the agreements as practically treasonous and mounted a campaign to scuttle them. Just before the Senate began its debate over ratification, Carter gave this televised explanation of his purpose in seeking the new arrangement, in a tone that Terence Smith described as "subdued, as though he was trying to convince his audience of the merits of the treaties more by gentle persuasion than exhortation." After intense arm-twisting by both sides, the Senate approved the treaties by the slimmest of margins.

Seventy-five years ago, our nation signed a treaty which gave us rights to build a canal across Panama, to take the historic step of joining the Atlantic and Pacific Oceans. The results of the agreement have been of great benefit to ourselves and to other nations throughout the world who navigate the high seas.

The building of the canal was one of the greatest engineering feats of history. Although massive in concept and construction, it's relatively simple in design and has been reliable and efficient in operation. We Americans are justly and deeply proud of this great achievement.

The canal has also been a source of pride and benefit to the people of Panama—but a cause of some continuing discontent. Because we have controlled a 10-mile-wide strip of land across the heart of their country and because they considered the original terms of the agreement to be unfair, the people of Panama have been dissatisfied with the treaty. It was drafted here in our country and was not signed by any Panamanian. Our own secretary of state who did sign the original treaty said it was "vastly advantageous to the United States and . . . not so advantageous to Panama."

In 1964, after consulting with former Presidents Truman and Eisenhower, President Johnson committed our nation to work towards a new treaty with the republic of Panama. And last summer, after 14 years of negotiation under two Democratic presidents and two Republican presidents, we reached and signed an agreement that is fair and beneficial to both countries. The United States Senate will soon be debating whether these treaties should be ratified.

Throughout the negotiations, we were determined that our national security interests would be protected; that the canal would always be open and neutral and available to ships of all nations; that in time of need or emergency our warships would have the right to go to the head of the line for priority passage through the canal; and that our military forces would have the permanent right to defend the canal if it should ever be in danger. The new treaties meet all of these requirements.

Let me outline the terms of the agreement. There are two treaties—one covering the rest of this century, and the other guaranteeing the safety, openness, and neutrality of the canal after the year 1999, when Panama will be in charge of its operation.

For the rest of this century, we will operate the canal through a nine-person board of directors. Five members will be from the United States and four will be from Panama. Within the area of the present Canal Zone, we have the right to select whatever lands and waters our military and civilian forces need to maintain, to operate, and to defend the canal.

About 75 percent of those who now maintain and operate the canal are Panamanians; over the next 22 years, as we manage the canal together, this percentage will increase. The Americans who work on the canal will continue to have their rights of employment, promotion, and retirement carefully protected.

We will share with Panama some of the fees paid by shippers who use the canal. As in the past, the canal should continue to be self-supporting.

This is not a partisan issue. The treaties are strongly backed by President Gerald Ford and by former Secretaries of State Dean Rusk and Henry Kissinger. They are endorsed by our business and professional leaders, especially those who recognize the benefits of goodwill and trade with other nations in this hemisphere. And they were endorsed overwhelmingly by the Senate Foreign Relations Committee which, this week, moved closer to ratification by approving the treaties, although with some recommended changes which we do not feel are needed.

And the treaties are supported enthusiastically by every member of the Joint Chiefs of Staff—General George Brown, the chairman, General Bernard Rogers, chief of staff of the army, Admiral James Holloway, chief of naval operations, General David Jones, chief of staff of the air force, and General Lewis Wilson, commandant of the marine corps—responsible men whose profession is the defense of this nation and the preservation of our security.

The treaties also have been overwhelmingly supported throughout Latin America, but predictably, they are opposed abroad by some who are unfriendly to the United States and who would like to see disorder in Panama and a disruption of our political, economic, and military ties with our friends in Central and South America and in the Caribbean.

I know that the treaties also have been opposed by many Americans. Much of that opposition is based on misunderstanding and misinformation. I've found that when the full terms of the agreement are known, most people are convinced that the national interests of our country will be served best by ratifying the treaties.

Tonight, I want you to hear the facts. I want to answer the most serious questions and tell you why I feel that Panama Canal treaties should be approved.

The most important reason—the only reason—to ratify the treaties is that they are in the highest national interest of the United States and will strengthen our position in the world. Our security interests will be stronger. Our trade opportunities will be improved. We will demonstrate that as a large and powerful country, we are able to deal fairly and honorably with a proud but smaller sovereign nation. We will honor our commitment to those engaged in world commerce that the Panama Canal will be open and available for use by their ships—at a reasonable and competitive cost—both now and in the future.

Let me answer specifically the most common questions about the treaties.

Will our nation have the right to protect and defend the canal against any armed attack or threat to the security of the canal or of ships going through it?

The answer is yes, and is contained in both treaties and also in the statement of understanding between the leaders of our two nations.

The first treaty says, and I quote: "The United States of America and the republic of Panama commit themselves to protect and defend the Panama Canal. Each party shall act, in accordance with its constitutional processes, to meet the danger resulting from an armed attack or other actions which threaten the security of the Panama Canal or [of] ships transiting it."

The neutrality treaty says, and I quote again: "The United States of America and the republic of Panama agree to maintain the regime of neutrality established in this treaty which shall be maintained in order that the canal shall remain permanently neutral."

And to explain exactly what that means, the statement of understanding says, and I quote again: "Under (the Neutrality Treaty), Panama and the United States have the responsibility to assure that the Panama Canal will remain open and secure to ships of all nations. The correct interpretation of this principle is that each of the two countries shall, in accordance with their respective constitutional processes, defend the canal against any threat to the regime of neutrality, and consequently [shall] have the right to act against the canal or against the peaceful transit of vessels through the canal."

It is obvious that we can take whatever military action is necessary to make sure that the canal always remains open and safe.

Of course, this does not give the United States any right to intervene in the internal affairs of Panama, nor would our military action ever be directed against the territorial integrity or the political independence of Panama.

Military experts agree that even with the Panamanian armed forces joined with us as brothers against a common enemy, it would take a large number of American troops to ward off a heavy attack. I, as president, would not hesitate to deploy whatever armed forces are necessary to defend the canal, and I have no doubt that even in a sustained combat, that we would be successful. But there is a much better way than sending our sons and grandsons to fight in the jungles of Panama.

We would serve our interests better by implementing the new treaties, an action that will help to avoid any attack on the Panama Canal.

What we want is the permanent right to use the canal—and we can defend this right through the treaties—through real cooperation with Panama. The citizens of Panama and their government have already shown their support of the new partnership, and a protocol to the neutrality treaty will be signed by many other nations, thereby showing their strong approval.

The new treaties will naturally change Panama from a passive and sometimes deeply resentful bystander into an active and interested partner, whose vital interests will be served by a well-operated canal. This agreement leads to cooperation and not confrontation between our country and Panama.

Another question is: Why should we give away the Panama Canal Zone? As many people say, "We bought it; we paid for it; it's ours."

I must repeat a very important point: We do not own the Panama Canal Zone. We have never had sovereignty over it. We have only had the right to use it.

The Canal Zone cannot be compared with United States territory. We bought Alaska from the Russians, and no one has ever doubted that we own it. We bought the Louisiana Purchases—territories from France, and that's an integral part of the United States.

From the beginning, we have made an annual payment to Panama to use their land. You do not pay rent on your own land. The Panama Canal Zone has always been Panamanian territory. The U.S. Supreme Court and previous American presidents have repeatedly acknowledged the sovereignty of Panama over the Canal Zone.

We've never needed to own the Panama Canal Zone, any more than we need to own a 10-mile-wide strip of land all the way through Canada from Alaska when we build an international gas pipeline.

The new treaties give us what we do need—not ownership of the canal but the right to use it and to protect it. As the chairman of the

Joint Chiefs of Staff has said, "The strategic value of the canal lies in its use."

There's another question: Can our naval ships, our warships, in time of need or emergency, get through the canal immediately instead of waiting in line?

The treaties answer that clearly by guaranteeing that our ships will always have expeditious transit through the canal. To make sure that there could be no possible disagreement about what these words mean, the joint statement says that expeditious transit, and I quote, "is intended. . . to assure the transit of such vessels through the Canal as quickly as possible, without any impediment, with expedited treatment, and in case of need or emergency, to go to the head of the line of vessels in order to transit the canal rapidly."

Will the treaties affect our standing in Latin America? Will they create a so-called power vacuum, which our enemies might move in to fill? They will do just the opposite. The treaties will increase our nation's influence in this hemisphere, will help to reduce any mistrust and disagreement, and they will remove a major source of anti-American feeling.

The new agreement has already provided vivid proof to the people of this hemisphere that a new era of friendship and cooperation is beginning and that what they regard as the last remnant of alleged American colonialism is being removed.

Last fall, I met individually with the leaders of 18 countries in this hemisphere. Between the United States and Latin America there is already a new sense of equality, a new sense of trust and mutual respect that exists because of the Panama Canal treaties. This opens up a fine opportunity for us in goodwill, trade, jobs, exports, and political cooperation.

If the treaties should be rejected, this would all be lost, and disappointment and despair among our good neighbors and traditional friends would be severe.

In the peaceful struggle against alien ideologies like Communism, these treaties are a step in the right direction. Nothing could strengthen our competitors and adversaries in this hemisphere more than for us to reject this agreement.

What if a new sea-level canal should be needed in the future? This question has been studied over and over throughout this century, from before the time the canal was built up through the last few years. Every study has reached the same conclusion—that the best place to build a sea-level canal is in Panama.

The treaties say that if we want to build such a canal, we will build it in Panama, and if any canal is to be built in Panama, that we, the United States, will have the right to participate in the project.

This is a clear benefit to us, for it ensures that, say, 10 or 20 years from now, no unfriendly but wealthy power will be able to purchase the right to build a sea-level canal, to bypass the existing canal, perhaps leaving that other nation in control of the only usable waterway across the isthmus.

Are we paying Panama to take the canal? We are not. Under the new treaty, any payments to Panama will come from tolls paid by ships which use the canal.

What about the present and the future stability and the capability of the Panamanian government? Do the people of Panama themselves support the agreement?

Well, as you know, Panama and her people have been our historical allies and friends. The present leader of Panama has been in office for more than nine years, and he heads a stable government which has encouraged the development of free enterprise in Panama. Democratic elections will be held this August to choose the members of the Panamanian Assembly, who will in turn elect a president and a vice president by majority vote. In the past, regimes have changed in Panama, but for 75 years, no Panamanian government has ever wanted to close the canal.

Panama wants the canal open and neutral—perhaps even more than we do. The canal's continued operation is very important to us, but it is much more than that to Panama. To Panama, it's crucial. Much of her economy flows directly or indirectly from the canal. Panama would be no more likely to neglect or to close the canal than we would be to close the Interstate Highway System here in the United States.

In an open and free referendum last October, which was monitored very carefully by the United Nations, the people of Panama gave the new treaties their support.

The major threat to the canal comes not from any government of Panama but from misguided persons who may try to fan the flames of dissatisfaction with the terms of the old treaty.

There's a final question—about the deeper meaning of the treaties themselves, to us and to Panama.

Recently, I discussed the treaties with David McCullough, author of The Path Between the Seas, the great history of the Panama Canal. He believes that the canal is something that we built and have looked after these many years; it is "ours" in that sense, which is very different from just ownership.

So, when we talk of the canal, whether we are old, young, for or against the treaties, we are talking about very deep and elemental feelings about our own strength.

Still, we Americans want a more humane and stable world. We believe in goodwill and fairness, as well as strength. This agreement with Panama is something we want because we know it is right. This is not merely the surest way to protect and save the canal; it's a strong, positive act of a people who are still confident, still creative, still great.

This new partnership can become a source of national pride and self-respect in much the same way that building the canal was 75 years ago. It's the spirit in which we act that is so very important.

Theodore Roosevelt, who was president when America built the canal, saw history itself as a force, and the history of our own time and the changes it has brought would not be lost on him. He knew that change was inevitable and necessary. Change is growth. The true conservative, he once remarked, keeps his face to the future.

But if Theodore Roosevelt were to endorse the treaties, as I'm quite sure he would, it would be mainly because he could see the decision as one by which we are demonstrating the kind of great power we wish to be.

"We cannot avoid meeting great issues," Roosevelt said. "All that we can determine for ourselves is whether we shall meet them well or ill."

The Panama Canal is a vast, heroic expression of that age-old desire to bridge the divide and to bring people closer together. This is what the treaties are all about.

We can sense what Roosevelt called "the lift toward nobler things which marks a great and generous people."

In this historic decision, he would join us in our pride for being a great and generous people, with the national strength and wisdom to do what is right for us and what is fair to others.

Peace in the Middle East

Washington, D.C.

March 26, 1979

CARTER'S MOST sustained piece of personal diplomacy, and the one that brought him the greatest acclaim, was his involvement in negotiations resulting in a peace treaty between Egypt and Israel. For two weeks during the month of September 1978 he and his aides closeted themselves in the president's mountain retreat at Camp David, Maryland, with Egypt's President Anwar Sadat and Israel's Prime Minister Menachem Begin, who were not even on speaking terms. Exercising his famous charm to the limit, Carter maneuvered the two adversaries into agreement on two "frameworks," one for a general peace plan in the Middle East, the other for a peace treaty between their own nations. After further intervention by Carter to prevent the parties from reneging, the treaty was signed at the White House in March 1979.

During the past 30 years, Israel and Egypt have waged war. But for the past 16 months, these same two great nations have waged peace. Today we celebrate a victory—not of a bloody military campaign, but of an inspiring peace campaign. Two leaders who will loom large in the history of nations, President Anwar al-Sadat and Prime Minister Menahem Begin, have conducted this campaign with all the courage, tenacity, brilliance, and inspiration of any generals who have ever led men and machines onto the field of battle.

At the end of this campaign, the soil of the two lands is not drenched with young blood. The country sides of both lands are free from the litter and the carnage of a wasteful war. Mothers in Egypt and Israel are not weeping today for their children fallen in senseless battle. The dedication and determination of these two world statesmen have borne fruit. Peace has come to Israel and to Egypt.

I honor these two leaders and their government officials who have hammered out this peace treaty which we have just signed. But most of all, I honor the people of these two lands whose yearning for peace kept alive the negotiations which today culminate in this glorious event.

We have won at last the first step of peace, a first step on a long and difficult road. We must not minimize the obstacles which still lie ahead. Differences still separate the signatories to this treaty from one another, and also from some of their neighbors who fear what they have just done. To overcome these differences, to dispel these fears, we must rededicate ourselves to the goal of a broader peace with justice for all who have lived in a state of conflict in the Middle East.

We have no illusions—we have hopes, dreams, and prayers, yes, but no illusions.

There now remains the rest of the Arab world, whose support and whose cooperation in the peace process is needed and honestly sought. I am convinced that other Arab people need and want peace. But some of their leaders are not yet willing to honor these needs and desires for peace. We must now demonstrate the advantages of peace and expand its benefits to encompass all those who have suffered so much in the Middle East.

Obviously, time and understanding will be necessary for people, hitherto enemies, to become neighbors in the best sense of the word.

Just because a paper is signed, all the problems will not automatically go away. Future days will require the best from us to give reality to these lofty aspirations.

Let those who would shatter peace, who would callously spill more blood, be aware that we three and all others who may join us will vigorously wage peace.

So let history record that deep and ancient antagonism can be settled without bloodshed and without staggering waste of precious lives, without rapacious destruction of the land.

It has been said, and I quote, "Peace has one thing in common with its enemy, with the fiend it battles, with war; peace is active, not passive; peace is doing, not waiting; peace is aggressive—attacking; peace plans its strategy and encircles the enemy; peace marshals its forces and storms the gates; peace gathers its weapons and pierces the defense; peace, like war, is waged."

It is true that we cannot enforce trust and cooperation between nations, but we can use all our strength to see that nations do not again go to war.

All our religious doctrines give us hope. In the Koran, we read: "But if the enemy incline towards peace, do thou also incline towards peace, and trust in God; for He is the One that heareth and knoweth all things."

And the prophet Isaiah said: "Nations shall beat their swords into plowshares and their spears into pruning hooks: nation shall not lift up sword against nation, neither shall they learn war any more."

So let us now lay aside war. Let us now reward all the children of Abraham who hunger for a comprehensive peace in the Middle East. Let us now enjoy the adventure of becoming fully human, fully neighbors, even brothers and sisters. We pray God, we pray God together, that these dreams will come true. I believe they will.

Thank you very much.

Energy and National Goals

Washington, D.C.

July 15, 1979

IN JULY 1979 Carter held a second marathon talk session at Camp David. The subject this time was how to combat the domestic energy crisis brought on by the revolution in Iran and steep price increases by the oil-producing Arab states. More than one hundred people were flown to the compound to share their counsel with the president. The 32-minute speech that Carter delivered at the end of this period was about energy in two senses of the word—about his new program for developing alternatives to foreign oil, and about the general crisis in self-confidence and trust that he perceived in the nation.

The language of this speech, which is probably Carter's most famous, was unmistakably that of a sermon in which the preacher, after confessing his own inadequacies and exposing the weaknesses of his congregation, rededicates the community to its original goals. Journalists John Tebbel and Sarah Miles Watts observed that, "like Moses, Carter came down from the mountain eventually, but without exactly having talked to God. . . . He had rehearsed [the speech] several times beforehand, even to practicing clenching a visible fist as a symbol of determined leadership." (That in itself was rare for Carter, who usually eschewed oratorical practice.) The speech reached an estimated television and radio audience of 60 million people.

This is a special night for me. Exactly three years ago, on July 15, 1976, I accepted the nomination of my party to run for president of the United States. I promised you a president who is not isolated from the people, who feels your pain, and who shares your dreams and who draws his strength and his wisdom from you.

During the past three years I've spoken to you on many occasions about national concerns, the energy crisis, reorganizing the government, our nation's economy, and issues of war and especially peace. But over those years the subjects of the speeches, the talks, and the press conferences have become increasingly narrow, focused more and more on what the isolated world of Washington thinks is important. Gradually, you've heard more and more about what the government thinks or what the government should be doing and less and less about our nation's hopes, our dreams, and our vision of the future.

Ten days ago I had planned to speak to you again about a very important subject—energy. For the fifth time I would have described the urgency of the problem and laid out a series of legislative recommendations to the Congress. But as I was preparing to speak, I began to ask myself the same question that I now know has been troubling many of you. Why have we not been able to get together as a nation to resolve our serious energy problem?

It's clear that the true problems of our nation are much deeper—deeper than gasoline lines or energy shortages, deeper even than inflation or recession. And I realize more than ever that as president I need your help. So, I decided to reach out and listen to the voices of America.

I invited to Camp David people from almost every segment of our society—business and labor, teachers and preachers, governors, mayors, and private citizens. And then I left Camp David to listen to other Americans, men and women like you. It has been an extraordinary 10 days, and I want to share with you what I've heard.

First of all, I got a lot of personal advice. Let me quote a few of the typical comments that I wrote down.

This from a southern governor: "Mr. President, you are not leading this nation—you're just managing the government."

"You don't see the people enough any more."

"Some of your cabinet members don't seem loyal. There is not enough discipline among your disciples."

"Don't talk to us about politics or the mechanics of government, but about an understanding of our common good."

"Mr. President, we're in trouble. Talk to us about blood and sweat and tears."

"If you lead, Mr. President, we will follow."

Many people talked about themselves and about the condition of our nation. This from a young woman in Pennsylvania: " I feel so far from government. I feel like ordinary people are excluded from political power."

And this from a young Chicano: "Some of us have suffered from recession all our lives."

"Some people have wasted energy, but others haven't had anything to waste."

And this from a religious leader: "No material shortage can touch the important things like God's love for us or our love for one another."

And I like this one particularly from a black woman who happens to be the mayor of a small Mississippi town: "The big-shots are not the only ones who are important. Remember, you can't sell anything on Wall Street unless someone digs it up somewhere else first."

This kind of summarized a lot of other statements: "Mr. President, we are confronted with a moral and a spiritual crisis."

Several of our discussions were on energy, and I have a notebook full of comments and advice. I'll read just a few.

"We can't go on consuming 40 percent more energy than we produce. When we import oil we are also importing inflation plus unemployment."

"We've got to use what we have. The Middle East has only 5 percent of the world's energy, but the United States has 24 percent."

And this is one of the most vivid statements: "Our neck is stretched over the fence and OPEC has a knife."

"There will be other cartels and other shortages. American wisdom and courage right now can set a path to follow in the future."

This was a good one: "Be bold, Mr. President. We may make mistakes, but we are ready to experiment."

And this one from a labor leader got to the heart of it: "The real issue is freedom. We must deal with the energy problem on a war footing."

And the last that I'll read: "When we enter the moral equivalent of war, Mr. President, don't issue us BB guns."

These 10 days confirmed my belief in the decency and the strength and the wisdom of the American people, but it also bore out some of my longstanding concerns about our nation's underlying problems.

I know, of course, being president, that government actions and legislation can be very important. That's why I've worked hard to put my campaign promises into law—and I have to admit, with just mixed success. But after listening to the American people I have been reminded again that all the legislation in the world can't fix what's wrong with America. So, I want to speak to you first tonight about a subject even more serious than energy or inflation. I want to talk to you right now about a fundamental threat to American democracy.

I do not mean our political and civil liberties. They will endure. And I do not refer to the outward strength of America, a nation that is at peace tonight everywhere in the world, with unmatched economic power and military might.

The threat is nearly invisible in ordinary ways. It is a crisis of confidence. It is a crisis that strikes at the very heart and soul and spirit of our national will. We can see this crisis in the growing doubt about the meaning of our own lives and in the loss of a unity of purpose for our nation.

The erosion of our confidence in the future is threatening to destroy the social and the political fabric of America.

The confidence that we have always had as a people is not simply some romantic dream or a proverb in a dusty book that we read just on the Fourth of July. It is the idea which founded our nation and has guided our development as a people. Confidence in the future has supported everything else— public institutions and private enterprise, our own families, and the very Constitution of the United States. Confidence has defined our course and has served as a link between generations. We've always believed in something called progress. We've always had a faith that the days of our children would be better than our own.

Our people are losing that faith, not only in government itself but in the ability as citizens to serve as the ultimate rulers and shapers of our democracy. As a people we know our past and we are proud of it. Our progress has been part of the living history of America, even the world. We always believed that we were part of a great movement of humanity itself called democracy, involved in the search for freedom, and that belief has always strengthened us in our purpose. But just as we are losing our confidence in the future, we are also beginning to close the door on our past.

In a nation that was proud of hard work, strong families, close-knit communities, and our faith in God, too many of us now tend to worship self-indulgence and consumption. Human identity is no longer defined by what one does, but by what one owns. But we've discovered that owning things and consuming things does not satisfy our longing for meaning. We've learned that piling up material goods cannot fill the emptiness of lives which have no confidence or purpose.

The symptoms of this crisis of the American spirit are all around us. For the first time in the history of our country a majority of our people believe that the next five years will be worse than the past five years. Two-thirds of our people do not even vote. The productivity of American workers is actually dropping, and the willingness of Americans to save for the future has fallen below that of all other people in the Western world.

As you know, there is a growing disrespect for government and for churches and for schools, the news media, and other institutions. This is not a message of happiness or reassurance, but it is the truth and it is a warning.

These changes did not happen overnight. They've come upon us gradually over the last generation, years that were filled with shocks and tragedy.

We were sure that ours was a nation of the ballot, not the bullet, until the murders of John Kennedy and Robert Kennedy and Martin Luther King Jr. We were taught that our armies were always invincible and our causes were always just, only to suffer the agony of Vietnam. We respected the presidency as a place of honor until the shock of Watergate.

We remember when the phrase "sound as a dollar" was an expression of absolute dependability, until 10 years of inflation began to shrink our dollar and our savings. We believed that our nation's resources were limitless until 1973, when we had to face a growing dependence on foreign oil.

These wounds are still very deep. They have never been healed.

Looking for a way out of this crisis, our people have turned to the federal government and found it isolated from the mainstream of our nation's life. Washington, D.C., has become an island. The gap between our citizens and our government has never been so wide. The people are looking for honest answers, not easy answers; clear leadership, not false claims and evasiveness and politics as usual.

What you see too often in Washington and elsewhere around the country is a system of government that seems incapable of action. You see a Congress twisted and pulled in every direction by hundreds of well-financed and powerful special interests. You see every extreme position defended to the last vote, almost to the last breath by one unyielding group or another. You often see a balanced and a fair approach that demands sacrifice, a little sacrifice from everyone, abandoned like an orphan without support and without friends.

Often you see paralysis and stagnation and drift. You don't like it, and neither do I. What can we do?

First of all, we must face the truth, and then we can change our course. We simply must have faith in each other, faith in our ability to govern ourselves, and faith in the future of this nation. Restoring that faith and that confidence to America is now the most important task we face. It is a true challenge of this generation of Americans.

One of the visitors to Camp David last week put it this way: "We've got to stop crying and start sweating, stop talking and start walking, stop cursing and start praying. The strength we need will not come from the White House, but from every house in America."

We know the strength of America. We are strong. We can regain our unity. We can regain our confidence. We are the heirs of generations who survived threats much more powerful and awesome than those that challenge us now. Our fathers and mothers were strong men and women who shaped a new society during the Great Depression, who fought world wars, and who carved out a new charter of peace for the world.

We ourselves are the same Americans who just 10 years ago put a man on the Moon. We are the generation that dedicated our society to the pursuit of human rights and equality. And we are the generation that will win the war on the energy problem and in that process rebuild the unity and confidence of America.

We are at a turning point in our history. There are two paths to choose. One is a path I've warned about tonight, the path that leads to fragmentation and self-interest. Down that road lies a mistaken idea of freedom, the right to grasp for ourselves some advantage over others. That path would be one of constant conflict between narrow interests ending in chaos and immobility. It is a certain route to failure.

All the traditions of our past, all the lessons of our heritage, all the promises of our future point to another path, the path of common purpose and the restoration of American values. That path leads to true freedom for our nation and ourselves. We can take the first steps down that path as we begin to solve our energy problem.

Energy will be the immediate test of our ability to unite this nation, and it can also be the standard around which we rally. On the battlefield of energy we can win for our nation a new confidence, and we can seize control again of our common destiny.

In little more than two decades we've gone from a position of energy independence to one in which almost half the oil we use comes from foreign countries, at prices that are going through the roof. Our excessive dependence on OPEC has already taken a tremendous toll on our economy and our people. This is the direct cause of the long lines which have made millions of you spend aggravating hours waiting for gasoline. It's a cause of the increased inflation and unemployment that we now face. This intolerable dependence on foreign oil threatens our economic independence and the very security of our nation.

The energy crisis is real. It is worldwide. It is a clear and present danger to our nation. These are facts and we simply must face them.

What I have to say to you now about energy is simple and vitally important.

Point one: I am tonight setting a clear goal for the energy policy of the United States. Beginning this moment, this nation will never use more foreign oil than we did in 1977—never. From now on, every new addition to our demand for energy will be met from our own production and our own conservation. The generation-long growth in our dependence on foreign oil will be stopped dead in its tracks right now and then reversed as we move through the 1980s, for I am tonight setting the further goal of cutting our dependence on foreign oil by one-half by the end of the next decade—a saving of over four and one-half million barrels of imported oil per day.

Point two: To ensure that we meet these targets, I will use my presidential authority to set import quotas. I'm announcing tonight that for 1979 and 1980, I will forbid the entry into this country of one drop of foreign oil more than these goals allow. These quotas will ensure a reduction in imports even below the ambitious levels we set at the recent Tokyo summit.

Point three: To give us energy security, I am asking for the most massive peacetime commitment of funds and resources in our nation's history to develop America's own alternative sources of fuel—from coal, from oil shale, from plant products for gasohol, from unconventional gas, from the sun.

I propose the creation of an energy security corporation to lead this effort to replace two and one-half million barrels of imported oil per day by 1990. The corporation will issue up to five billion dollars in energy bonds, and I especially want them to be in small denominations so that average Americans can invest directly in America's energy security.

Just as a similar synthetic rubber corporation helped us win World War II, so will we mobilize American determination and ability to win the energy war. Moreover, I will soon submit legislation to Congress calling for the creation of this nation's first solar bank, which will help us achieve the crucial goal of 20 percent of our energy coming from solar power by the year 2000.

These efforts will cost money, a lot of money, and that is why Congress must enact the windfall profits tax without delay. It will be money well spent. Unlike the billions of dollars that we ship to foreign countries to pay for foreign oil, these funds will be paid by Americans to Americans. These funds will go to fight, not to increase, inflation and unemployment.

Point four: I'm asking Congress to mandate, to require as a matter of law, that our nation's utility companies cut their massive use of oil by 50 percent within the next decade and switch to other fuels, especially coal, our most abundant energy source.

Point five: To make absolutely certain that nothing stands in the way of achieving these goals, I will urge Congress to create an energy mobilization board which, like the War Production Board in World War II, will have the responsibility and authority to cut through the red tape, the delays, and the endless roadblocks to completing key energy projects.

We will protect our environment. But when this nation critically needs a refinery or a pipeline, we will build it.

Point six: I'm proposing a bold conservation program to involve every state, country, and city, every average American in our energy battle. This effort will permit you to build conservation into your homes and your lives at a cost you can afford.

I ask Congress to give me authority for mandatory conservation and for standby gasoline rationing. To further conserve energy, I'm proposing tonight an extra 10 billion dollars over the next decade to strengthen our public transportation systems. And I'm asking you for your good and for your nation's security to take no unnecessary trips, to use carpools or public transportation whenever you can, to park your car one extra day per week, to obey the speed limit, and to set your thermostats to save fuel. Every act of energy conservation like this is more than just common sense—I tell you it is an act of patriotism.

Our nation must be fair to the poorest among us, so we will increase aid to needy Americans to cope with rising energy prices. We often think of conservation only in terms of sacrifice. In fact, it is the most painless and immediate way of rebuilding our nation's strength. Every gallon of oil each one of us saves is a new form of production. It gives us more freedom, more confidence, that much more control over our own lives.

So, the solution of our energy crisis can also help us to conquer the crisis of the spirit in our country. It can rekindle our sense of unity, our confidence in the future, and give our nation and all of us individually a new sense of purpose.

You know we can do it. We have the natural resources. We have more oil in our shale alone than several Saudi Arabias. We have more coal than any nation on Earth. We have the world's highest level of technology. We have the most skilled workforce, with innovative genius, and I firmly believe that we have the national will to win this war.

I do not promise you that this struggle for freedom will be easy. I do not promise a quick way out of our nation's problems, when the truth is that the only way out is an all-out effort. What I do promise you is that I will lead our fight, and I will enforce fairness in our struggle, and I will ensure honesty. And above all, I will act.

We can manage the short-term shortages more effectively and we will, but there are no short-term solutions to our long-range problems. There is simply no way to avoid sacrifice.

Twelve hours from now I will speak again in Kansas City, to expand and to explain further our energy program. Just as the search for solutions to our energy shortages has now led us to a new awareness of our nation's deeper problems, so our willingness to work for those solutions in energy can strengthen us to attack those deeper problems.

I will continue to travel this country, to hear the people of America. You can help me to develop a national agenda for the 1980s. I will listen and I will act. We will act together. These were the promises I made three years ago, and I intend to keep them.

Little by little we can and we must rebuild our confidence. We can spend until we empty our treasuries, and we may summon all the wonders of science. But we can succeed only if we tap our greatest resources—America's people, America's values, and America's confidence.

I have seen the strength of America in the inexhaustible resources of our people. In the days to come, let us renew that strength in the struggle for an energy-secure nation.

In closing, let me say this: I will do my best, but I will not do it alone. Let your voice be heard. Whenever you have a chance, say something good about our country. With God's help and for the sake of our nation, it is time for us to join hands in America. Let us commit ourselves together to a rebirth of the American spirit. Working together with our common faith we cannot fail.

Thank you and good night.

The Carter Doctrine

Third State of the Union Message
Washington, D.C.
January 23, 1980

THE SEARCH for moral regeneration promised by Carter in his July 1979 energy speech was soon superseded by the need to "get tough" in world affairs. In November, 52 American citizens were taken prisoner in Iran by terrorists acting in the name of the revolutionary government that had overthrown Carter's ally, the shah. This was followed a month later by the invasion of Afghanistan by the Soviet Union. In his next State of the Union message, Carter warned the Soviets that "any attempt by any outside force to gain control of the Persian Gulf [and thus of America's oil supply] . . . will be repelled by any means necessary, including military force." According to historian Gaddis Smith, this address "marked his full conversion to military strength as the nation's highest priority and resistance to the Soviet Union as the dominant objective. . . . He invoked history, not, as during the campaign of 1976, to list American wrongdoing for which repentence was necessary, but to celebrate the ways in which the United States has stood up to the Soviet Union." The phrasing of the statement, which came to be known as the Carter Doctrine, echoed previous statements by Truman and Eisenhower.

This last few months has not been an easy time for any of us. As we meet tonight, it has never been more clear that the state of our Union depends on the state of the world. And tonight, as throughout our own generation, freedom and peace in the world depend on the state of our Union.

The 1980s have been born in turmoil, strife, and change. This is a time of challenge to our interests and our values and it's a time that tests our wisdom and our skills.

At this time in Iran, 50 Americans are still held captive, innocent victims of terrorism and anarchy. Also at this moment, massive Soviet troops are attempting to subjugate the fiercely independent and deeply religious people of Afghanistan. These two acts—one of international terrorism and one of military aggression—present a serious challenge to the United States of America and indeed to all the nations of the world. Together, we will meet these threats to peace.

I'm determined that the United States will remain the strongest of all nations, but our power will never be used to initiate a threat to the security of any nation or to the rights of any human being. We seek to be and to remain secure—a nation at peace in a stable world. But to be secure we must face the world as it is.

Three basic developments have helped to shape our challenges: the steady growth and increased projection of Soviet military power

beyond its own borders; the overwhelming dependence of the Western democracies on oil supplies from the Middle East; and the press of social and religious and economic and political change in the many nations of the developing world, exemplified by the revolution in Iran.

Each of these factors is important in its own right. Each interacts with the others. All must be faced together, squarely and courageously. We will face these challenges, and we will meet them with the best that is in us. And we will not fail.

In response to the abhorrent act in Iran, our nation has never been aroused and unified so greatly in peacetime. Our position is clear. The United States will not yield to blackmail.

We continue to pursue these specific goals: first, to protect the present and long-range interests of the United States; secondly, to preserve the lives of the American hostages and to secure, as quickly as possible, their safe release, if possible, to avoid bloodshed which might further endanger the lives of our fellow citizens; to enlist the help of other nations in condemning this act of violence, which is shocking and violates the moral and the legal standards of a civilized world; and also to convince and to persuade the Iranian leaders that the real danger to their nation lies in the north, in the Soviet Union and from the Soviet troops now in Afghanistan, and that the unwarranted Iranian quarrel with the United States hampers their response to this far greater danger to them.

If the American hostages are harmed, a severe price will be paid. We will never rest until every one of the American hostages are released.

But now we face a broader and more fundamental challenge in this region because of the recent military action of the Soviet Union.

Now, as during the last three and a half decades, the relationship between our country, the United States of America, and the Soviet Union is the most critical factor in determining whether the world will live at peace or be engulfed in global conflict.

Since the end of the Second World War, America has led other nations in meeting the challenge of mounting Soviet power. This has not been a simple or a static relationship. Between us there has been cooperation, there has been competition, and at times there has been confrontation.

In the 1940s we took the lead in creating the Atlantic Alliance in response to the Soviet Union's suppression and then consolidation of its East European empire and the resulting threat of the Warsaw Pact to Western Europe.

In the 1950s we helped to contain further Soviet challenges in Korea and in the Middle East, and we rearmed to assure the continuation of that containment.

In the 1960s we met the Soviet challenges in Berlin, and we faced the Cuban missile crisis. And we sought to engage the Soviet Union in the important task of moving beyond the cold war and away from confrontation.

And in the 1970s three American presidents negotiated with the Soviet leaders in attempts to halt the growth of the nuclear arms race. We sought to establish rules of behavior that would reduce the risks of conflict, and we searched for areas of cooperation that could make our relations reciprocal and productive, not only for the sake of our two nations but for the security and peace of the entire world.

In all these actions, we have maintained two commitments: to be ready to meet any challenge by Soviet military power, and to develop ways to resolve disputes and to keep the peace.

Preventing nuclear war is the foremost responsibility of the two superpowers. That's

why we've negotiated the strategic arms limitation treaties—SALT I and SALT II. Especially now, in a time of great tension, observing the mutual constraints imposed by the terms of these treaties will be in the best interest of both countries and will help to preserve world peace. I will consult very closely with the Congress on this matter as we strive to control nuclear weapons. That effort to control nuclear weapons will not be abandoned.

We superpowers also have the responsibility to exercise restraint in the use of our great military force. The integrity and the independence of weaker nations must not be threatened. They must know that in our presence they are secure.

But now the Soviet Union has taken a radical and an aggressive new step. It's using its great military power against a relatively defenseless nation. The implications of the Soviet invasion of Afghanistan could pose the most serious threat to the peace since the Second World War.

The vast majority of nations on Earth have condemned this latest Soviet attempt to extend its colonial domination of others and have demanded the immediate withdrawal of Soviet troops. The Moslem world is especially and justifiably outraged by this aggression against an Islamic people. No action of a world power has ever been so quickly and so overwhelmingly condemned. But verbal condemnation is not enough. The Soviet Union must pay a concrete price for their aggression.

While this invasion continues, we and the other nations of the world cannot conduct business as usual with the Soviet Union. That's why the United States has imposed stiff economic penalties on the Soviet Union. I will not issue any permits for Soviet ships to fish in the coastal waters of the United States. I've cut Soviet access to high-technology equipment and to agricultural products. I've limited other commerce with the Soviet Union, and I've asked our allies and friends to join with us in restraining their own trade with the Soviets and not to replace our own embargoed items. And I have notified the Olympic Committee that with Soviet invading forces in Afghanistan, neither the American people nor I will support sending an Olympic team to Moscow.

The Soviet Union is going to have to answer some basic questions: Will it help promote a more stable international environment in which its own legitimate, peaceful concerns can be pursued? Or will it continue to expand its military power far beyond its genuine security needs, and use that power for colonial conquest? The Soviet Union must realize that its decision to use military force in Afghanistan will be costly to every political and economic relationship it values.

The region which is now threatened by Soviet troops in Afghanistan is of great strategic importance: It contains more than two-thirds of the world's exportable oil. The Soviet effort to dominate Afghanistan has brought Soviet military forces to within 300 miles of the Indian Ocean and close to the Straits of Hormuz, a waterway through which most of the world's oil must flow. The Soviet Union is now attempting to consolidate a strategic position, therefore, that poses a grave threat to the free movement of Middle East oil.

This situation demands careful thought, steady nerves, and resolute action, not only for this year but for many years to come. It demands collective efforts to meet this new threat to security in the Persian Gulf and in Southwest Asia. It demands the participation of all those who rely on oil from the Middle East and who are concerned with global peace and stability. And it demands consultation and close cooperation with countries in the area which might be threatened.

Meeting this challenge will take national will, diplomatic and political wisdom, economic sacrifice, and, of course, military capability. We must call on the best that is in us to preserve the security of this crucial region.

Let our position be absolutely clear: An attempt by any outside force to gain control of the Persian Gulf region will be regarded as an assault on the vital interests of the United States of America, and such an assault will be repelled by any means necessary, including military force.

During the past three years, you have joined with me to improve our own security and the prospects for peace, not only in the vital oil-producing area of the Persian Gulf region but around the world. We've increased annually our real commitment for defense, and we will sustain this increase of effort throughout the Five-Year Defense Program. It's imperative that Congress approve this strong defense budget for 1981, encompassing a 5 percent real growth in authorizations, without any reduction.

We are also improving our capability to deploy U.S. military forces rapidly to distant areas. We've helped to strengthen NATO and our other alliances, and recently we and other NATO members have decided to develop and to deploy modernized, intermediate-range nuclear forces to meet an unwarranted and increased threat from the nuclear weapons of the Soviet Union.

We are working with our allies to prevent conflict in the Middle East. The peace treaty between Egypt and Israel is a notable achievement which represents a strategic asset for America and which also enhances prospects for regional and world peace. We are now engaged in further negotiations to provide full autonomy for the people of the West Bank and Gaza, to resolve the Palestinian issue in all its aspects, and to preserve the peace and security of Israel. Let no one doubt our commitment to the security of Israel. In a few days we will observe an historic event when Israel makes another major withdrawal from the Sinai and when ambassadors will be exchanged between Israel and Egypt.

We've also expanded our own sphere of friendship. Our deep commitment to human rights and to meeting human needs has improved our relationship with much of the Third World. Our decision to normalize relations with the People's Republic of China will help to preserve peace and stability in Asia and in the Western Pacific.

We've increased and strengthened our naval presence in the Indian Ocean, and we are now making arrangements for key naval and air facilities to be used by our forces in the region of northeast Africa and the Persian Gulf.

We've reconfirmed our 1959 agreement to help Pakistan preserve its independence and its integrity. The United States will take action consistent with our own laws to assist Pakistan in resisting any outside aggression. And I'm asking the Congress specifically to reaffirm this agreement. I'm also working, along with the leaders of other nations, to provide additional military and economic aid for Pakistan. That request will come to you in just a few days.

In the weeks ahead, we will further strengthen political and military ties with other nations in the region. We believe that there are no irreconcilable differences between us and any Islamic nation. We respect the faith of Islam, and we are ready to cooperate with all Moslem countries.

Finally, we are prepared to work with other countries in the region to share a cooperative security framework that respects differing values and political beliefs, yet which enhances the independence, security, and prosperity of all.

All these efforts combined emphasize our dedication to defend and preserve the vital interests of the region and of the nation which we represent and those of our allies—in Europe and the Pacific, and also in the parts of the world which have such great strategic importance to us, stretching especially through the Middle East and Southwest Asia. With your help, I will pursue these efforts with vigor and with determination. You and I will act as necessary to protect and to preserve our nation's security.

The men and women of America's armed forces are on duty tonight in many parts of the world. I'm proud of the job they are doing, and I know you share that pride. I believe that our volunteer forces are adequate for current defense needs, and I hope that it will not become necessary to impose a draft. However, we must be prepared for that possibility. For this reason, I have determined that the Selective Service System must now be revitalized. I will send legislation and budget proposals to the Congress next month so that we can begin registration and then meet future mobilization needs rapidly if they arise.

We also need clear and quick passage of a new charter to define the legal authority and accountability of our intelligence agencies. We will guarantee that abuses do not recur, but we must tighten our controls on sensitive intelligence information, and we need to remove unwarranted restraints on America's ability to collect intelligence.

The decade ahead will be a time of rapid change, as nations everywhere seek to deal with new problems and age-old tensions. But America need have no fear. We can thrive in a world of change if we remain true to our values and actively engaged in promoting world peace. We will continue to work as we have for peace in the Middle East and southern Africa. We will continue to build our ties with developing nations, respecting and helping to strengthen their national independence which they have struggled so hard to achieve. And we will continue to support the growth of democracy and the protection of human rights.

In repressive regimes, popular frustrations often have no outlet except through violence. But when peoples and their governments can approach their problems together through open, democratic methods, the basis for stability and peace is far more solid and far more enduring. That is why our support for human rights in other countries is in our own national interest as well as part of our own national character.

Peace—a peace that preserves freedom—remains America's first goal. In the coming years, as a mighty nation we will continue to pursue peace. But to be strong abroad we must be strong at home. And in order to be strong, we must continue to face up to the difficult issues that confront us as a nation today.

The crises in Iran and Afghanistan have dramatized a very important lesson: Our excessive dependence on foreign oil is a clear and present danger to our nation's security. The need has never been more urgent. At long last, we must have a clear, comprehensive energy policy for the United States.

As you well know, I have been working with the Congress in a concentrated and persistent way over the past three years to meet this need. We have made progress together. But Congress must act promptly now to complete final action on this vital energy legislation. Our nation will then have a major conservation effort, important initiatives to develop solar power, realistic pricing based on the true value of oil, strong incentives for the production of coal and other fossil fuels in the United States, and our nation's most massive peacetime investment in the development of synthetic fuels.

The American people are making progress in energy conservation. Last year we reduced overall petroleum consumption by 8 percent and gasoline consumption by 5 percent below what it was the year before. Now we must do more.

After consultation with the governors, we will set gasoline conservation goals for each of the 50 states, and I will make them mandatory if these goals are not met.

I've established an import ceiling for 1980 of 8.2 million barrels a day—well below the level of foreign oil purchases in 1977. I expect our imports to be much lower than this, but the ceiling will be enforced by an oil import fee if necessary. I'm prepared to lower these imports still further if the other oil-consuming countries will join us in a fair and mutual reduction. If we have a serious shortage, I will not hesitate to impose mandatory gasoline rationing immediately.

The single biggest factor in the inflation rate last year, the increase in the inflation rate last year, was from one cause: the skyrocketing prices of OPEC oil. We must take whatever actions are necessary to reduce our dependence on foreign oil—and at the same time reduce inflation.

As individuals and as families, few of us can produce energy by ourselves. But all of us can conserve energy—every one of us, every day of our lives. Tonight I call on you—in fact, all the people of America—to help our nation. Conserve energy. Eliminate waste. Make 1980 indeed a year of energy conservation.

Of course, we must take other actions to strengthen our nation's economy.

First, we will continue to reduce the deficit and then to balance the federal budget.

Second, as we continue to work with business to hold down prices, we'll build also on the historic national accord with organized labor to restrain pay increases in a fair fight against inflation.

Third, we will continue our successful efforts to cut paperwork and to dismantle unnecessary government regulation.

Fourth, we will continue our progress in providing jobs for America, concentrating on a major new program to provide training and work for our young people, especially minority youth. It has been said that "a mind is a terrible thing to waste." We will give our young people new hope for jobs and a better life in the 1980s.

And fifth, we must use the decade of the 1980s to attack the basic structural weaknesses and problems in our economy through measures to increase productivity, savings, and investment.

With these energy and economic policies, we will make America even stronger at home in this decade—just as our foreign and defense policies will make us stronger and safer throughout the world. We will never abandon our struggle for a just and a decent society here at home. That's the heart of America—and it's the source of our ability to inspire other people to defend their own rights abroad.

Our material resources, great as they are, are limited. Our problems are too complex for simple slogans or for quick solutions. We cannot solve them without effort and sacrifice. Walter Lippmann once reminded us, "You took the good things for granted. Now you must earn them again. For every right that you cherish, you have a duty which you must fulfill. For every good which you wish to preserve, you will have to sacrifice your comfort and your ease. There is nothing for nothing any longer."

Our challenges are formidable. But there's a new spirit of unity and resolve in our country. We move into the 1980s with confidence and hope and a bright vision of the America we want: an America strong and free, an America at peace, an America with equal rights for all citizens—and for women, guaranteed in the United States Constitution—an America with jobs and good health and good education for every citizen, an America with a clean and bountiful life in our cities and on our farms, an America that helps to feed the world, an America secure in filling its own energy needs, an America of justice, tolerance, and compassion. For this vision to come true, we must sacrifice, but this national commitment will be an exciting enterprise that will unify our people.

Together as one people, let us work to build our strength at home, and together as one indivisible Union, let us seek peace and security throughout the world.

Together let us make of this time of challenge and danger a decade of national resolve and of brave achievement.

Thank you very much.

Rescue Attempt

Washington, D.C.

April 25, 1980

THE LAST 14 months of Carter's presidency were almost totally preoccupied with the crisis in Iran. The administration's inability to negotiate effectively amid the turbulence of Iranian politics cast over all its activities an aura of frustration and helplessness. There was irony also in the sight of an evangelical Christian denounced as the leader of the "Great Satan" by the leaders of a militant theocracy.

Despite his earlier resistance to the use of force in settling international conflicts, Carter ordered a rescue attempt in the spring of 1980. After months of planning, the mission had to be aborted at the last moment because of equipment failure. As the rescue team prepared to withdraw from its landing area in the Iranian desert, a helicopter crashed into a transport plane, and the mission ended in a fiery disaster that cost eight lives (and probably doomed Carter's aspirations to a second term). The following morning, at 7 a.m., he announced the news to the nation in a brief televised statement.

Late yesterday I canceled a carefully planned operation which was under way in Iran to position our rescue team for a later withdrawal of American hostages who have been held captive there since November 4.

Equipment failure in the rescue helicopter made it necessary to end the mission. As our team was withdrawing after my order to do so, two of our American aircraft collided on the ground following a refueling operation in a remote desert location in Iran.

Other information about this rescue mission will be made available to the American people when it is appropriate to do so.

There was no fighting. There was no combat. But to my deep regret eight of the crewmen of the two aircraft which collided were killed and several other Americans were hurt in the accident.

Our people were immediately airlifted from Iran. Those who were injured have gotten medical treatment and all of them are expected to recover.

No knowledge of this operation by any Iranian officials or authorities was evident to us until several hours after all Americans were withdrawn from Iran.

Our rescue team knew and I knew that the operation was certain to be difficult and it was certain to be dangerous. We were all convinced that if and when the rescue operation had been commenced, that it had an excellent chance of success.

They were all volunteers. They were all highly trained. I met with their leaders before they went on this operation. They knew then what hopes of mine and of all Americans they carried with them.

To the families of those who died and who were wounded, I want to express the admiration I feel for the courage of their loved ones and the sorrow that I feel personally for their sacrifice.

The mission on which they were involved was a humanitarian mission. It was not directed against Iran. It was not directed against the people of Iran. It was not undertaken with any feeling of hostility toward Iran or its people. It has caused no Iranian casualties.

Planning for this rescue effort began shortly after our embassy was seized, but for a number of reasons I waited until now to put those rescue plans into effect.

To be feasible this complex operation had to be the product of intensive planning and intensive training and repeated rehearsal.

However, a resolution of this crisis through negotiations and with voluntary action on the part of Iranian officials was obviously then, has been, and will be, preferable.

This rescue attempt had to await my judgment that the Iranian authorities could not or would not resolve this crisis on their own initiative.

With the steady unraveling of authority in Iran and the mounting dangers that were posed to the safety of the hostages themselves and the growing realization that their early release was highly unlikely, I made a decision to commence the rescue operations plans.

This attempt became a necessity and a duty. The readiness of our team to undertake the rescue made it completely practical. Accordingly, I made a decision to set our long-developed plans into operation.

I ordered this rescue mission prepared in order to safeguard American lives and protect America's national interests and to reduce the tensions in the world that have been caused among many nations as this crisis has continued.

It was my decision to attempt the rescue operation. It was my decision to cancel it when problems developed in the placement of our rescue team for a future rescue operation. The responsibility is fully my own.

In the aftermath of the attempt, we continue to hold the government of Iran responsible for the safety and for the early release of the American hostages who have been held so long.

The United States remains determined to bring about their safe release at the earliest date possible.

As president I know that our entire nation feels deep gratitude for the brave men who were prepared to rescue their fellow Americans from captivity. And as president I also know that the nation shares not only my disappointment that the rescue effort could not be mounted because of mechanical difficulties, but also my determination to persevere and to bring all of our hostages home to freedom.

We have been disappointed before. We will not give up in our efforts.

Throughout this extraordinarily difficult period, we have pursued and will continue to pursue every possible avenue to secure the release of the hostages.

In these efforts, the support of the American people and of our friends throughout the world has been a most crucial element. That support of other nations is even more important now. We will seek to continue along with other nations and the officials of Iran a prompt resolution of the crisis without any loss of life and through peaceful and diplomatic means.

Farewell Address

Washington, D.C.

January 14, 1981

A WEEK BEFORE his departure from the White House, with the pressures of the reelection campaign lifted, Carter delivered a televised farewell address that was more genuinely moving than any of his previous speeches. As journalist Charles Krauthammer wrote, "Carter's speech, intended for the future, revealed what for years we had been clamoring for—his vision of the present." Its main theme was not the problems that had beset his administration, but an issue that unites all administrations, the prevention of nuclear war.

Good evening. In a few days, I will lay down my official responsibilities in this office to take up once more the only title in our democracy superior to that of president, the title of citizen.

Of Vice President Mondale, my cabinet, and the hundreds of others who have served with me during these four years, I wish to say publicly what I have said in private. I thank them for the dedication and competence they have brought to the service of our country.

But I owe my deepest thanks to you, the American people, because you gave me this extraordinary opportunity to serve. We have faced great challenges together. We know that future problems will also be difficult, but I am now more convinced than ever that the United States—better than any other nation—can meet successfully whatever the future might bring.

These last four years have made me more certain than ever of the inner strength of our country—the unchanging value of our principles and ideals, the stability of our political system, the ingenuity and decency of our people.

Tonight I would like first to say a few words about this most special office, the presidency of the United States.

This is at once the most powerful office in the world—and among the most severely constrained by law and custom. The president is given a broad responsibility to lead—but cannot do so without the support and consent of the people, expressed formally through the Congress and informally through a whole range of public and private institutions.

This is as it should be. Within our system of government every American has a right and duty to help shape the future course of the United States. Thoughtful criticism and close scrutiny of all government officials by the press and the public are an important part of our democratic society. Now as in our past, only the understanding and involvement of the people through full and open debate can help to avoid mistakes and assure the continued dignity and safety of the nation.

Today we are asking our political system to do things of which the founding fathers never dreamed. The government they designed for a few hundred thousand people now serves a nation of almost 230 million people. Their small coastal republic now spans beyond a continent, and we now have the responsibility to help lead much of the world through difficult times to a secure and prosperous future.

Today, as people have become more doubtful of the ability of the government to deal with our problems, we are increasingly drawn to single-issue groups and special-interest organizations to insure that whatever else happens our own personal views and our own private interests are protected. This is a disturbing factor in American political life. It tends to distort our purposes because the national interest is not always the sum of all our single or special interests. We are all Americans together and we must not forget that the common good is our common interest and our individual responsibility.

Because of the fragmented pressures of special interests, it is very important that the office of the president be a strong one, and that its constitutional authority be preserved. The president is the only elected official charged with representing all the people. In the moments of decision, after the different and conflicting views have been aired, it is the president who then must speak to the nation and for the nation.

I understand, as few others can, how formidable is the task the president-elect is about to undertake. To the very limits of conscience and conviction, I pledge to support him in that task. I wish him success and Godspeed.

I know from experience that presidents have to face major issues that are controversial, broad in scope, and which do not arouse the natural support of a political majority.

For a few minutes now, I want to lay aside my role as a leader of one nation and speak to you as a fellow citizen of the world about three such issues: the threat of nuclear destruction, our stewardship of the physical resources of our planet and the preeminence of the basic rights of human beings.

It has now been 35 years since the first atomic bomb fell on Hiroshima. The great majority of the world's people cannot remember a time when the nuclear shadow did not hang over the earth. Our minds have adjusted to it, as after a time our eyes adjust to the dark.

Yet the risk of a nuclear conflagration has not lessened. It has not happened yet, but that can give us little comfort—for it only has to happen once.

The danger is becoming greater. As the arsenals of the superpowers grow in size and sophistication and as other governments acquire these weapons, it may only be a matter of time before madness, desperation, greed, or miscalculation lets loose this terrible force.

In an all-out nuclear war, more destructive power than in all of World War II would be unleashed every second for the long afternoon it would take for all the missiles and bombs to fall. A World War II every second—more people killed in the first few hours than all the wars of history put together. The survivors, if any, would live in despair amid the poisoned ruins of a civilization that had committed suicide.

National weakness—real or perceived—can tempt aggression and thus cause war. That is why the United States cannot neglect its military strength. We must and we will remain strong. But with equal determination, the United States and all countries must find ways to control and reduce the horrifying danger that is posed by the world's stockpiles of nuclear arms.

This has been a concern of every American president since the moment we first saw what these weapons could do. Our leaders will require our understanding and support as they grapple with this difficult but crucial challenge. There is no disagreement on the goals or the basic approach to controlling this enormous destructive force. The answer lies not just in the attitudes or actions of world leaders, but in the concern and demands of all of us as we continue our struggle to preserve the peace.

Nuclear weapons are an expression of one side of our human character. But there is another side. The same rocket technology that delivers nuclear warheads has also taken us peacefully into space. From that perspective, we see our earth as it really is—a small and fragile and beautiful blue globe, the only home we have. We see no barriers of race or religion or country. We see the essential unity of our species and our planet; and with faith and common sense that bright vision will ultimately prevail.

Another major challenge is to protect the quality of this world within which we live. The shadows that fall across the future are cast not only by the kinds of weapons we have built but by the kind of world we will either nourish or neglect. There are real and growing dangers to our simple and most precious possessions: the air we breathe, the water we drink, and the land which sustains us. The rapid depletion of irreplaceable minerals, the erosion of topsoil, the destruction of beauty, the blight of pollution, the demands of increasing billions of people all combine to create problems which are easy to observe and predict but difficult to resolve. If we do not act, the world of the year 2000 will be much less able to sustain life than it is now.

But there is no reason for despair. Acknowledging the physical realities of our planet does not mean a dismal future of endless sacrifice. In fact, acknowledging these realities is the first step in dealing with them. We can meet the resource problems of the world—water, food, minerals, farmlands, forests, overpopulation, pollution—if we tackle them with courage and foresight.

I have just been talking about forces of potential destruction that mankind has developed and how we might control them. It is equally important that we remember the beneficial forces that we have evolved over the ages and hold fast to them.

One of those constructive forces is enhancement of individual human freedoms through the strengthening of democracy, and the fight against deprivation, torture, terrorism, and the persecution of people throughout the world. The struggle for human rights overrides all differences of color, nation, or language.

Those who hunger for freedom, who thirst for human dignity, and who suffer for the sake of justice—they are the patriots of this cause.

I believe with all my heart that America must always stand for these basic human rights—at home and abroad. That is both our history and our destiny.

America did not invent human rights. In a very real sense it is the other way around. Human rights invented America.

Ours was the first nation in the history of the world to be founded explicitly on such an idea. Our social and political progress has been based on one fundamental principle—the value and importance of the individual. The fundamental force that unites us is not kinship or place of origin or religious preference. The love of liberty is the common blood that flows in our American veins.

The battle for human rights—at home and abroad—is far from over. We should never be surprised nor discouraged because the impact of our efforts has had varied results. Rather we should take pride that the ideals which gave birth to our nation still inspire the hopes of oppressed people around the world. We have no cause for self-righteousness or complacency. But we have every reason to persevere, both in our own country and beyond our borders.

If we are to serve as a beacon for human rights we must continue to perfect here at home the rights and values we espouse around the world: a decent education for our children, adequate medical care for all Americans, an end to discrimination against minorities and women, a job for those able to work, and freedom from injustice and religious intolerance.

We live in a time of transition, an uneasy era which is likely to endure for the rest of this century. It will be a period of tensions both within nations and between nations—of competition for scarce resources, of social, political, and economic stresses and strains. During this period we may be tempted to abandon some of the time-honored principles and commitments which have been proven during the difficult times of past generations.

We must never yield to this temptation. Our American values are not luxuries but necessities—not the salt in our bread but the bread itself. Our common vision of a free and just society is our greatest source of cohesion at home and strength abroad—greater even than the bounty of our material blessings.

Remember these words. "We hold these truths to be self-evident, that all men are created equal; that they are endowed by their creator with certain inalienable rights; that among these are life, liberty, and the pursuit of happiness."

This vision still grips the imagination of the world. But we know that democracy is always an unfinished creation. Each generation must renew its foundations. Each generation must rediscover the meaning of this hallowed vision in the light of its own modern challenges. For this generation, life is nuclear survival; liberty is human rights; the pursuit of happiness is a planet whose resources are devoted to the physical and spiritual nourishment of its inhabitants.

As I return home to the South where I was born and raised, I am looking forward to the opportunity to reflect and further to assess—I hope with accuracy—the circumstances of our times. I intend to give our new president my support, and I intend to work as a citizen, as I have worked as president, for the values this nation was founded to secure.

Again, from the bottom of my heart, I want to express to you the gratitude I feel. Thank you, fellow citizens, and farewell.

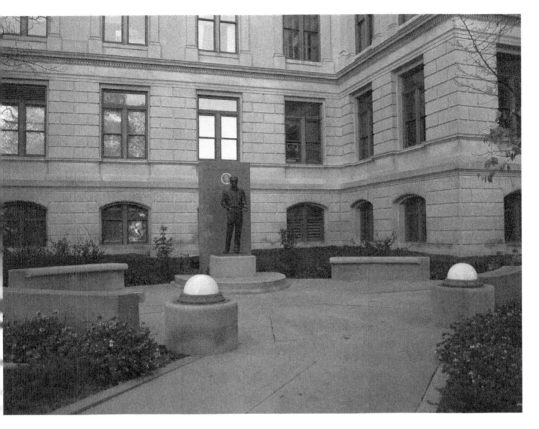

Statue of Jimmy Carter at the Georgia State Capital in Atlanta,
Georgia. (Courtesy of PresidentsUSA.net)

Courtesy of Ronald Reagan Library

Ronald Wilson Reagan

Ronald Wilson Reagan

1981–1989

THE GREATEST PERFORMER ever to occupy the White House, Ronald Reagan, labeled "the Great Communicator" by journalists, built his political success on expert exploitation of the electronic media. Drawing on skills he learned in his first career as a Hollywood actor, television series host, and corporate spokesman, he promoted an undiluted conservative ideology with a flair that brought him enormous public goodwill as well as two landslide victories in his presidential campaigns.

Born in Illinois, Reagan became a movie actor by way of radio sports announcing. Never one of Hollywood's major stars, he was a capable actor popular for playing himself— a virtuous, blandly amiable, all-American, next-door-neighbor sort of guy—one who made a fairly smooth transition to television. After his transformation, in the 1950s, from liberal Democrat to staunch conservative Republican, he became a spokesman for the General Electric Corporation and served two terms as governor of California (1966–1974). Though Reagan lost the Republican presidential nomination to Gerald Ford in 1976, he was easily nominated and elected in 1980. Reelected by a landslide in 1984, he received the most electoral votes (525) of any president up to that time.

Reagan's speeches—his "star performances"—were his vital link to the mass of voters who liked him personally even when they did not like his programs. These crowd-pleasing addresses were crafted by a large staff that included (until 1987) the ultraconservative Pat Buchanan, a former Nixon speechwriter; Reagan never drafted his own speeches, although he often contributed homilies and anecdotes to include in them. Robert Dallek describes the typical Reagan speech as "pure symbolic politics: a celebration of middle-class America and its values, an expression of regard for middle-class citizens whose conventional beliefs he wishes to restore to the center of American life." The president cast his speeches to appeal to the broadest audience, with frequent recourse to pious and patriotic phrases given energy by advertising buzzwords (new and free are among the most common words in his speeches). Typically, complex issues were reduced to or deflected by simple but often effective slogans—for example, the president's tongue-clucking scold to Carter in the 1980 presidential debates, "There you go again," when the incumbent accused him of opposing Medicare in 1965 (Reagan did oppose it); his shorthand description for the fiscal habits of Congress as "tax and tax, spend and spend"; or his characterization of the Soviet Union as the "evil empire." Ironically, on those occasions when Reagan and his speechwriters tried for a lofty style, they often adapted the cadences and metaphors of Franklin D. Roosevelt, Reagan's political idol until the late 1940s and the president whose accomplishments he tried his best to dismantle.

As James Reston noted, "President Reagan has a story for every occasion and an excuse for every disaster." A skillful raconteur with a comedian's gift for split-second timing, Reagan often inserted a story or anecdote based on his personal experience (and, on at least one occasion, taken unattributed from a war film he had seen) to drive home his point, discussing even the most abstract issues in terms of his own feelings, experience, capacity for growth, and so on. This had the useful effect of making his speeches seem more like intimate conversation with a friend than an expression of policy by the most powerful man in the world. Alexander Haig, Reagan's first secretary of state, commented that one key to Reagan's success was the "impression he gives of *liking* the person [audience] he is talking to." Most audiences could not help but like him back. Sometimes Reagan chose to appear as "a bewildered ordinary guy, vulnerable, blundering at times, but aw shucks," as the journalist Anthony Lewis wrote. At other times he played the part of a stern but forgiving father figure. To the chagrin of many political analysts and of his opponents in the Congress, Reagan's adoring public was unconcerned with the vast numbers of errors, half-truths, or outright fabrications that peppered his remarks, whether prepared or off-the-cuff. These were usually contributed, presumably in innocence, by the president himself. (Reagan's biographer Lou Cannon quipped that Reagan "never met a statistic he didn't like.")

Though he was the oldest president ever to hold office, the broad-shouldered, cowboy-rugged Reagan was the first executive with sex appeal since Kennedy. He made the most of this by posing for the cameras on horseback, chopping wood with his sleeves rolled up, and wearing a worn leather flight jacket when using the presidential helicopter. His carefully stage-managed official gestures seemed to paint in bold outlines a portrait of what the public wanted a chief executive to look and act like. The president's natural aptitude for role-playing and his ample self-confidence were enhanced by teams of behavior-modification experts and Hollywood imagemakers (he was also assisted by his wife, Nancy, herself a former actress). Reagan, wrote Garry Wills, "was the first candidate to be engineered by professionals . . . his larger confidence in his capacity is unshakable because not entirely dependent on his own achievement." During his gubernatorial and presidential campaigns, Reagan was packaged for mass consumption with the same methods used to sell consumer goods, particularly the "sentimental sell," an appeal to the nostalgic vision of America that Reagan routinely invoked in his speeches.

Under the Reagan administration, the White House apparatus for projecting and polishing the electronic presidential image, especially during speechmaking, attained near perfection. Journalist Steven Weisman observed that Reagan and his aides had achieved "a new level of control over the mechanics of modern communication—the staging of news events for maximum press coverage, the timing of announcements to hit the largest television audience. . . . From the beginning of his presidency, Mr. Reagan and his aides have understood and exploited what they acknowledged to be the built-in tendency of television to emphasize appearance and impressions more than information." The combination of these factors made Reagan the most effective speaker in presidential history, if effectiveness is measured by audience applause. The speeches themselves, when detached from his performance of them, are unlikely to endure.

First Inaugural Address

Washington, D.C.
January 20, 1981

REAGAN'S 20-MINUTE inaugural address was held, contrary to tradition, on the West Front of the Capitol rather than on the East Front to honor Reagan's western connections. The president signaled with this speech that he intended to undertake revolutionary changes in the nation's economic policies. In the address can be found the basic tenets of Reaganomics, drawn from the "supply-side" economic theories of Arthur Laffer: decrease the size and expense of government by trimming social spending; cut taxes; return fiscal responsibilities to the states; reduce the trade deficit and national debt. One of the president's first official acts was to enact a freeze on all government hiring. Inauguration day also marked the end of the Iranian hostage affair, a matter of deliberate timing by the Iranian government. As Reagan concluded his address, the hostages were finally allowed to leave Iran after 444 days of captivity.

To a few of us here today this is a solemn and most momentous occasion, and yet in the history of our nation it is a commonplace occurrence. The orderly transfer of authority as called for in the Constitution routinely takes place, as it has for almost two centuries, and few of us stop to think how unique we really are. In the eyes of many in the world, this every-four-year-ceremony we accept as normal is nothing less than a miracle.

Mr. President, I want our fellow citizens to know how much you did to carry on this tradition. By your gracious cooperation in the transition process, you have shown a watching world that we are a united people pledged to maintaining a political system which guarantees individual liberty to a greater degree than any other, and I thank you and your people for all your help in maintaining the continuity which is the bulwark of our republic.

The business of our nation goes forward. These United States are confronted with an economic affliction of great proportions. We suffer from the longest and one of the worst sustained inflations in our national history. It distorts our economic decisions, penalizes thrift, and crushes the struggling young and the fixed-income elderly alike. It threatens to shatter the lives of millions of our people.

Idle industries have cast workers into unemployment, human misery, and personal indignity. Those who do work are denied a fair return for their labor by a tax system which penalizes successful achievement and keeps us from maintaining full productivity.

But great as our tax burden is, it has not kept pace with public spending. For decades we have piled deficit upon deficit, mortgaging our future and our children's future for the temporary convenience of the present. To continue this long trend is to guarantee tremendous social, cultural, political, and economic upheavals.

You and I, as individuals, can, by borrowing, live beyond our means, but for only a limited period of time. Why, then, should we think that collectively, as a nation, we're not bound by that same limitation? We must act today in order to preserve tomorrow. And let there be no misunderstanding: We are going to begin to act, beginning today.

The economic ills we suffer have come upon us over several decades. They will not go away in days, weeks, or months, but they will go away. They will go away because we as Americans have the capacity now, as we've had in the past, to do whatever needs to be done to preserve this last and greatest bastion of freedom.

In this present crisis, government is not the solution to our problem; government is the problem. From time to time we've been tempted to believe that society has become too complex to be managed by self-rule, that government by an elite group is superior to government for, by, and of the people. Well, if no one among us is capable of governing himself, then who among us has the capacity to govern someone else? All of us together, in and out of government, must bear the burden. The solutions we seek must be equitable, with no one group singled out to pay a higher price.

We hear much of special interest groups. Well, our concern must be for a special interest group that has been too long neglected. It knows no sectional boundaries or ethnic and racial divisions, and it crosses political party lines. It is made up of men and women who raise our food, patrol our streets, man our mines and factories, teach our children, keep our homes, and heal us when we're sick—professionals, industrialists, shopkeepers, clerks, cabbies, and truck-drivers. They are, in short, "We the people," this breed called Americans.

Well, this administration's objective will be a healthy, vigorous, growing economy that provides equal opportunities for all Americans, with no barriers born of bigotry or discrimination. Putting America back to work means putting all Americans back to work. Ending inflation means freeing all Americans from the terror of runaway living costs. All must share in the productive work of this "new beginning," and all must share in the bounty of a revived economy. With the idealism and fair play which are the core of our system and our strength, we can have a strong and prosperous America, at peace with itself and the world.

So, as we begin, let us take inventory. We are a nation that has a government— not the other way around. And this makes us special among the nations of the earth. Our government has no power except that granted it by the people. It is time to check and reverse the growth of government, which shows signs of having grown beyond the consent of the governed.

It is my intention to curb the size and influence of the federal establishment and to demand recognition of the distinction between the powers granted to the federal government and those reserved to the states or to the people. All of us need to be reminded that the federal government did not create the states; the states created the federal government.

Now, so there will be no misunderstanding, it's not my intention to do away with government. It is rather to make it work— work with us, not over us; to stand by our side, not ride on our back. Government can and must provide opportunity, not smother it; foster productivity, not stifle it.

If we look to the answer as to why for so many years we achieved so much, prospered as no other people on earth, it was because here in this land we unleashed the energy and individual genius of man to a greater extent than has ever been done before. Freedom and the dignity of the individual have been more available and assured here than in any other place on earth. The price for this freedom at times has been high, but we have never been unwilling to pay that price.

It is no coincidence that our present troubles parallel and are proportionate to the intervention and intrusion in our lives that result from unnecessary and excessive growth of government. It is time for us to realize that we're too great a nation to limit ourselves to small dreams. We're not, as some would have us believe, doomed to an inevitable decline. I do not believe in a fate that will fall on us no matter what we do. I believe in a fate that will fall on us if we do nothing, So, with all the creative energy at our command, let us begin an era of national renewal. Let us renew our determination, our courage, and our strength. And let us renew our faith and our hope.

We have every right to dream heroic dreams. Those who say that we're in a time when there are not heroes, they just don't know where to look. You can see heroes every day going in and out of factory gates. Others, a handful in number, produce enough food to feed all of us and then the world beyond. You meet heroes across a counter, and they're on both sides of that counter. There are entrepreneurs with faith in themselves and faith in an idea who create new jobs, new wealth and opportunity. They're individuals and families whose taxes support the government and whose voluntary gifts support church, charity, culture, art, and education. Their patriotism is quiet, but deep. Their values sustain our national life.

Now, I have used the words they and their in speaking of these heroes. I could say you and your, because I'm addressing the heroes of whom I speak—you, the citizens of this blessed land. Your dreams, your hopes, your goals are going to be the dreams, the hopes, and the goals of this administration, so help me God.

We shall reflect the compassion that is so much a part of your makeup. How can we love our country and not love our countrymen; and loving them, reach out a hand when they fall, heal them when they're sick, and provide opportunity to make them self-sufficient so they will be equal in fact and not just in theory?

Can we solve the problems confronting us? Well, the answer is an unequivocal and emphatic "yes." To paraphrase Winston Churchill, I did not take the oath I've just taken with the intention of presiding over the dissolution of the world's strongest economy.

In the days ahead I will propose removing the roadblocks that have slowed our economy and reduced productivity. Steps will be taken aimed at restoring the balance between the various levels of government. Progress may be slow, measured in inches and feet, not miles, but we will progress. It is time to reawaken this industrial giant, to get government back within its means, and to lighten our punitive tax burden. And these will be our first priorities, and on these principles there will be no compromise.

On the eve of our struggle for independence a man who might have been one of the greatest among the founding fathers, Dr. Joseph Warren, president of the Massachusetts Congress, said to his fellow Americans, "Our country is in danger, but not to de despaired of. . . . On you depend the fortunes of America. You are to decide the important questions upon which rests the happiness and the liberty of millions yet unborn. Act worthy of yourselves."

Well, I believe we, the Americans of today, are ready to act worthy of ourselves, ready to do what must be done to ensure happiness and liberty for ourselves, our children, and our children's children. And as we renew ourselves here in our own land, we will be seen as having greater strength throughout the world. We will again be the exemplar of freedom and a beacon of hope for those who do not now have freedom.

To those neighbors and allies who share our freedom, we will strengthen our historic ties and assure them of our support and firm commitment. We will match loyalty with loyalty. We will strive for mutually beneficial relations. We will not use our friendship to impose on their sovereignty, for our own sovereignty is not for sale.

As for the enemies of freedom, those who are potential adversaries, they will be reminded that peace is the highest aspiration of the American people. We will negotiate for it, sacrifice for it; we will not surrender for it, now or ever.

Our forbearance should never be misunderstood. Our reluctance for conflict should not be misjudged as a failure of will. When action is required to preserve our national security, we will act. We will maintain sufficient strength to prevail if need be, knowing that if we do so we have the best chance of never having to use that strength.

Above all, we must realize that no arsenal or no weapon in the arsenals of the world is so formidable as the will and moral courage of free men and women. It is a weapon our adversaries in today's world do not have. It is a weapon that we as Americans do have. Let that be understood by those who practice terrorism and prey upon their neighbors.

I'm told that tens of thousands of prayer meetings are being held on this day, and for that I'm deeply grateful. We are a nation under God, and I believe God intended for us to be free. It would be fitting and good, I think, if on each inaugural day in future years it should be declared a day of prayer.

This is the first time in our history that this ceremony has been held, as you've been told, on this West Front of the Capitol. Standing here, one faces a magnificent vista, opening up on this city's special beauty and history. At the end of this open mall are those shrines to the giants on whose shoulders we stand.

Directly in front of me, the monument to a monumental man, George Washington, father of our country. A man of humility who came to greatness reluctantly. He led America out of revolutionary victory into infant nationhood. Off to one side, the stately memorial to Thomas Jefferson. The Declaration of Independence flames with his eloquence. And then, beyond the Reflecting Pool, the dignified columns of the Lincoln Memorial. Whoever would understand in his heart the meaning of America will find it in the life of Abraham Lincoln.

Beyond those monuments to heroism is the Potomac River, and on the far shore the sloping hills of Arlington National Cemetery, with its row upon row of simple white markers bearing crosses or Stars of David. They add up to only a tiny fraction of the price that has been paid for our freedom.

Each one of those markers is a monument to the kind of hero I spoke of earlier. Their lives ended in places called Belleau Wood, the Argonne, Omaha Beach, Salerno, and halfway around the world on Guadalcanal, Tarawa, Pork Chop Hill, the Chosin Reservoir, and in a hundred rice paddies and jungles of a place called Vietnam.

Under one such marker lies a young man, Martin Treptow, who left his job in a small town barbershop in 1917 to go to France with the famed Rainbow Division. There, on the western front, he was killed trying to carry a message between battalions under heavy artillery fire.

We're told that on his body was found a diary. On the flyleaf under the heading, "My Pledge," he had written these words: "America must win this war. Therefore I will work, I will save, I will sacrifice, I will endure, I will fight cheerfully and do my utmost, as if the issue of the whole struggle depended on me alone."

The crisis we are facing today does not require of us the kind of sacrifice that Martin Treptow and so many thousands of others were called upon to make. It does require, however, our best effort and our willingness to believe in ourselves and to believe in our capacity to perform great deeds, to believe that together with God's help we can and will resolve the problems which now confront us.

And after all, why shouldn't we believe that? We are Americans.

God bless you, and thank you.

The New Federalism

First State of the Union Address
Washington, D.C.
January 26, 1982

THE THEME of this address was the effort by the Reagan administration to transfer many federal responsibilities—notably welfare, education, and health-care payments—to the states. This was part of Reagan's overall plan to reduce the size of the federal government by shrinking or eliminating most Great Society social programs. Unlike the tax cuts of Reagan's first year, which Congress endorsed, there were few supporters for the New Federalism in Congress or the state capitols. The states feared that they would be unable to make up the shortfall if federal funds were withdrawn or restructured as "block grants." Nor was Reagan's call for private charities to make up for the cuts in federal services taken seriously. Many organizations made good-faith efforts, but it was obvious that charity alone could not close the gap and take care of the burgeoning numbers of unemployed, hungry, and homeless people. Reagan's failure to match the lost revenue from the tax cuts of his first year with spending cuts in his second resulted in the most massive debt ever accumulated by the United States. By 1983 Reagan was forced to enact billions of dollars in new taxes—although the administration never called them that—to reduce the threatening deficit, which reached nearly $200 billion by the following year.

Today marks my first State of the Union address to you, a constitutional duty as old as our republic itself.

President Washington began this tradition in 1790 after reminding the nation that the destiny of self-government and the "preservation of the sacred fire of liberty" is "finally staked on the experiment entrusted to the hands of the American people." For our friends in the press, who place a high premium on accuracy, let me say: I did not actually hear George Washington say that. But it is a matter of historic record.

But from this podium, Winston Churchill asked the free world to stand together against the onslaught of aggression. Franklin Delano Roosevelt spoke of a day of infamy and summoned a nation to arms. Douglas MacArthur made an unforgettable farewell to a country he loved and served so well. Dwight Eisenhower reminded us that peace was purchased only at the price of strength. And John F. Kennedy spoke of the burden and glory that is freedom.

When I visited this chamber last year as a newcomer to Washington, critical of past policies which I believed had failed, I proposed a new spirit of partnership between this Congress and this administration and between Washington and our state and local governments. In forging this new partnership for America, we could achieve the oldest hopes of our republic—prosperity for our nation, peace for the world, and the blessings of individual liberty for our children and, something for all of humanity.

It's my duty to report to you tonight on the progress that we have made in our relations with other nations, on the foundation we've carefully laid for our economic recovery, and finally, on a bold and spirited initiative that I believe can change the face of American government and make it again the servant of the people.

Seldom have the stakes been higher for America. What we do and say here will make all the difference to auto workers in Detroit, lumberjacks in the Northwest, steelworkers in Steubenville who are in the unemployment lines; to black teenagers in Newark and Chicago; to hard-pressed farmers and small businessmen; and to millions of everyday Americans who harbor the simple wish of a safe and financially secure future for their children. To understand the state of the Union, we must look not only at where we are and where we're going but where we've been. The situation at this time last year was truly ominous.

The last decade has seen a series of recessions. There was a recession in 1970, in 1974, and again in the spring of 1980. Each time, unemployment increased and inflation soon turned up again. We coined the word stagflation to describe this.

Government's response to these recessions was to pump up the money supply and increase spending. In the last six months of 1980, as an example, the money supply increased at the fastest rate in postwar history—13 percent. Inflation remained in double digits, and government spending increased at an annual rate of 17 percent. Interest rates reached a staggering 21 1/2 percent. There were eight million unemployed.

Late in 1981 we sank into the present recession, largely because continued high interest rates hurt the auto industry and construction. And there was a drop in productivity, and the already high unemployment increased.

This time, however, things are different. We have an economic program in place, completely different from the artificial quick-fixes of the past. It calls for a reduction of the rate of increase in government spending, and already that rate has been cut nearly in half. But reduced spending alone isn't enough. We've just implemented the first and smallest phase of a three-year tax-rate reduction designed to stimulate the economy and create jobs. Already interest rates are down to 15 3/4 percent, but they must still go lower. Inflation is down from 12.4 percent to 8.9, and for the month of December it was running at an annualized rate of 5.2 percent. If we had not acted as we did, things would be far worse for all Americans than they are today. Inflation, taxes, and interest rates would all be higher.

A year ago, American's faith in their governmental process was steadily declining. Six out of ten Americans were saying they were pessimistic about their future. A new kind of defeatism was heard. Some said our domestic problems were uncontrollable, that we had to learn to live with this seemingly endless cycle of high inflation and high unemployment.

There were also pessimistic predictions about the relationship between our administration and this Congress. It was said we could never work together. Well, those predictions were wrong. The record is clear, and I believe that history will remember this as an era of American renewal, remember this administration as an administration of change, and remember this Congress as a Congress of destiny.

Together, we not only cut the increase in government spending nearly half, we brought about the largest tax reductions and the most sweeping changes in our tax structure since the beginning of this century. And because we indexed future taxes to the rate of inflation, we took away government's built-in profit on inflation and its hidden incentive to grow larger at the expense of American workers.

Together, after 50 years of taking power away from the hands of the people in their states and local communities, we have started returning power and resources to them.

Together, we have cut the growth of the new federal regulations nearly in half. In 1981 there were 23,000 fewer pages in the *Federal Register*, which lists new regulations, than there were in 1980. By deregulating oil we've come closer to achieving energy independence and helped bring down the cost of gasoline and heating fuel.

Together, we have created an effective federal strike force to combat waste and fraud in government. In just six months it has saved the taxpayers more than $2 billion, and it's only getting started.

Together we've begun to mobilize the private sector, not to duplicate wasteful and discredited programs, but to bring thousands of Americans into a volunteer effort to help solve many of America's social problems.

Together we've begun to restore that margin of military safety that ensures peace. Our country's uniform is being worn once again with pride.

Together we have made a New Beginning, but we have only begun.

No one pretends that the way ahead will be easy. In my inaugural address last year, I warned that the "ills we suffer have come upon us over several decades. They will not go away in days, weeks, or months, but they will go away . . . because we as Americans have the capacity now, as we've had it in the past, to do whatever needs to be done to preserve this last and greatest bastion of freedom."

The economy will face difficult moments in the months ahead. But the program for economic recovery that is in place will pull the economy out of its slump and put us on the road to prosperity and stable growth by the latter half of this year. And that is why I can report to you tonight that in the near future the state of the Union and the economy will be better—much better—if we summon the strength to continue on the course that we've charted.

And so, the question: If the fundamentals are in place, what now? Well, two things. First, we must understand what's happening at the moment to the economy. Our current problems are not the product of the recovery program that's only just now getting under way, as some would have you believe; they are the inheritance of decades of tax and tax and spend and spend.

Second, because our economic problems are deeply rooted and will not respond to quick political fixes, we must stick to our carefully integrated plan for recovery. That plan is based on four commonsense fundamentals: continued reduction of the growth in federal spending; preserving the individual and business tax reductions that will stimulate saving and investment; removing unnecessary federal regulations to spark productivity; and maintaining a healthy dollar and a stable monetary policy, the latter a responsibility of the Federal Reserve System.

The only alternative being offered to this economic program is a return to the policies that gave us a trillion-dollar debt, runaway inflation, runaway interest rates and unemployment. The doubters would have us turn back the clock with tax increases that would offset the personal tax-rate reductions already passed by this Congress. Raise present taxes to cut future deficits, they tell us. Well, I don't believe we should buy that argument.

There are too many imponderables for any one to predict deficits or surpluses several years ahead with any degree of accuracy. The budget in place, when I took office, had been projected as balanced. It turned out to have one of the biggest deficits in history. Another example of the imponderables that can make deficit projections highly questionable—a change of only one percentage point in unemployment can alter a deficit up or down by some $25 billion.

As it now stands, our forecast, which we're required by law to make, will show major deficits starting at less than a hundred billion dollars and declining, but still too high. More important, we're making progress with the three keys to reducing deficits: economic growth, lower interest rates, and spending control. The policies we have in place will reduce the deficit steadily, surely, and in time, completely.

Higher taxes would not mean lower deficits. If they did, how would we explain that tax revenues more than doubled just since 1976; yet in that same six-year period we ran the largest series of deficits in our history. In 1980 tax revenues increased by $54 billion and in 1980 we had one of our all-time biggest deficits. Raising taxes won't balance the budget; it will encourage more government spending and less private investment. Raising taxes will slow economic growth, reduce production, and destroy future jobs, making it more difficult for those without jobs to find them and more likely that those who now have jobs could lose them. So, I will not ask you to try to balance the budget on the backs of the American taxpayers.

I will seek no tax increases this year, and I have no intention of retreating from our basic program of tax relief. I promise to bring the American people—to bring their tax rates down and to keep them down, to provide them incentives to rebuild our economy, to save, to invest in America's future. I will stand by my word. Tonight I'm urging the American people: Seize these new opportunities to produce, to save, to invest, and together we'll make this economy a mighty engine of freedom, hope, and prosperity again.

Now, the budget deficit this year will exceed our earlier expectations. The recession did that. It lowered revenues and increased costs. To some extent, we're also victims of our own success. We've brought inflation down faster than we though we could, and in doing this, we've deprived government of those hidden revenues that occur when inflation pushes people into higher income tax brackets. And the continued high interest rates last year cost the government about $5 billion more than anticipated.

We must cut out more nonessential government spending and root out more waste, and we will continue our efforts to reduce the number of employees in the federal work force by 75,000.

The budget plan I submit to you on February 8th will realize major savings by dismantling the Departments of Energy and Education and by eliminating ineffective subsidies for business. We'll continue to redirect our resources to our two highest budget priorities—a strong national defense to keep America free and at peace and a reliable safety net of social programs for those who have contributed and those who are in need.

Contrary to some of the wild charges you may have heard, this administration has not and will not turn its back on America's elderly or America's poor. Under the new budget, funding for social insurance programs will be more than double the amount spent only six years ago. But it would be foolish to pretend that these or any programs cannot be made more efficient and economical.

The entitlement programs that make up our safety net for the truly needy have worthy goals and many deserving recipients. We will protect them. But there's only one way to see to it that these programs really help those whom they were designed to help. And that is to bring their spiraling costs under control.

Today we face the absurd situation of a federal budget with three-quarters of its expenditures routinely referred to as "uncontrollable." And a large part of this goes to entitlement programs.

Committee after committee of this Congress has heard witness after witness describe many of these programs as poorly administered and rife with waste and fraud. Virtually every American who shops in a local supermarket is aware of the daily abuses that take place in the food stamp program, which has grown by 16,000 percent in the last 15 years. Another example is Medicare and Medicaid—programs with worthy goals but whose costs have increased from 11.2 billion to almost 60 billion, more than five times as much, in just 10 years.

Waste and fraud are serious problems. Back in 1980, federal investigators testified before one of your committees that "corruption has permeated virtually every area of the Medicare and Medicaid healthcare industry." One official said many of the people who are cheating the system were "very confident that nothing was going to happen to them." Well, something is going to happen. Not only the taxpayers are defrauded; the people with real dependency on these programs are deprived of what they need, because available resources are going not to the needy, but to the greedy.

The time has come to control the uncontrollable. In August we made a start. I signed a bill to reduce the growth of these programs by $44 billion over the next three years while at the same time preserving essential services for the truly needy. Shortly you will receive from me a message on further reforms we intend to install— some new, but others long recommended by your own congressional committees. I ask you to help make these savings for the American taxpayer.

The savings we propose in entitlement programs will total some $63 billion over four years and will, without affecting Social Security, go a long way toward bringing federal spending under control.

But don't be fooled by those who proclaim that spending cuts will deprive the elderly, the needy, and the helpless. The federal government will still subsidize 95 million meals every day. That's one out of seven of all the meals served in America. Head Start, senior nutrition programs, and child welfare programs will not be cut from the levels we proposed last year. More than one-half billion dollars has been proposed for minority business assistance. And research at the National Institute of Health will be increased by over $100 million. While meeting all these needs, we intend to plug unwarranted tax loopholes and strengthen the law which requires all large corporations to pay a minimum tax.

I am confident the economic program we've put into operation will protect the needy while it triggers a recovery that will benefit all Americans. it will stimulate the economy, result in increased savings and provide capital for expansion, mortgages for homebuilding, and jobs for the unemployed.

Now that the essentials of that program are in place, our next major undertaking must be a program—just as bold, just as innovative— to make government again accountable to the people, to make our system of federalism work again.

Our citizens feel they've lost control of even the most basic decisons made about the essential services of government, such as schools, welfare, roads, and even garbage collection. And they're right. A maze of interlocking jurisdictions and levels of government confronts average citizens in trying to solve even the simplest of problems. They don't know where to turn for answers, who to hold accountable, who to praise, who to blame, who to vote for or against. The main reason for this is the overpowering growth of federal grants-in-aid programs during the past few decades.

In 1960 the federal government had 132 categorical grant programs, costing $7 billion. When I took office, there were approximately

500, costing nearly a hundred billion dollars—13 programs for energy, 36 for pollution control, *66* for social services, 90 for education. And here in the Congress, it takes at least 166 committees just to try to keep track of them.

You know and I know that neither the president nor the Congress can properly oversee this jungle of grants-in-aid; indeed, the growth of these grants has led to the distortion in the vital functions of government. As one Democratic governor put it recently: The national government should be worrying about "arms control, not potholes."

The growth in these federal programs has—in the words of one intergovernmental commission—made the federal government "more pervasive, more intrusive, more unmanageable, more ineffective and costly, and above all, more (un)accountable." Let's solve this problem with a single, bold stroke: the return of some $47 billion in federal programs to state and local government, together with the means to finance them and a transition period of nearly 10 years to avoid unnecessary disruption.

I will shortly send this Congress a message describing this program. I want to emphasize, however, that its full details will have been worked out only after close consultation with congressional, state, and local officials.

Starting in fiscal 1984, the federal government will assume full responsibility for the cost of the rapidly growing Medicaid program to go along with its existing responsibility for Medicare. As part of a financially equal swap, the states will simultaneously take full responsibility for Aid to Families with Dependent Children and food stamps. This will make welfare less costly and more responsive to genuine need, because it'll be designed and administered closer to the grass roots and the people it serves.

In 1984 the federal government will apply the full proceeds from certain excise taxes to a grassroots trust fund that will belong in fair shares to the 50 states. The total amount flowing into this fund will be $28 billion a year. Over the next four years the states can use this money in either of two ways. If they want to continue receiving federal grants in such areas as transportation, education, and social services, they can use their trust fund money to pay for the grants. Or to the extent they choose to forgo the federal grant programs,

they can use their trust fund money on their own for those or other purposes. There will be a mandatory pass-through of part of these funds to local governments.

By 1988 the states will be in complete control of over 40 federal grant programs. The trust fund will start to phase out, eventually to disappear, and the excise taxes will be turned over to the states. They can then preserve, lower, or raise taxes on their own and fund and manage these programs as they see fit.

In a single stroke we will be accomplishing a realignment that will end cumbersome administration and spiraling costs at the federal level while we ensure these programs will be more responsive to both the people they're meant to help and the people who pay for them.

Hand-in-hand with this program to strengthen the discretion and flexibility of state and local governments, we're proposing legislation for an experimental effort to improve and develop our repressed urban areas in the 1980s and '90s. This legislation will permit states and localities to apply to the federal government for designation as urban enterprise zones. A broad range of special economic incentives in the zones will help attract new business, new jobs, new opportunity to America's inner cities and rural towns. Some will say our mission is to save free enterprise. Well, I say we must free enterprise so that together we can save America.

Some will also say our states and local communities are not up to the challenge of a new and creative partnership. Well, that might have been true 20 years ago before reforms like reapportionment and the Voting Rights Act, the 10-year extension of which I strongly support. It's no longer true today. This administration has faith in state and local governments and the constitutional balance envisioned by the founding fathers. We also believe in the integrity, decency, and sound, good sense of grassroots Americans.

Our faith in the American people is reflected in another major endeavor. Our Private Sector Initiatives Task Force is seeking our successful community models of school, church, business, union, foundation, and civic programs that help community needs. Such groups are almost invariably far more efficient than government in running social programs.

We're not asking them to replace discarded and often discredited government programs dollar for dollar, service for service. We just want to help them perform the good works they choose and help others to profit by their example. Three hundred and eighty-five thousand corporations and private organizations are already working on social programs ranging from drug rehabilitation to job training, and thousands more Americans have written us asking how they can help. The volunteer spirit is still alive and well in America. . . .

We have made pledges of a new frankness in our public statements and worldwide broadcasts. In the face of a climate of falsehood and misinformation, we've promised the world a season of truth—the truth of our great civilized ideas: Individual liberty, representative government, the rule of law under God. We've never needed walls or minefields or barbed wire to keep our people in. Nor do we declare martial law to keep our people from voting for the kind of government they want.

Yes, we have our problems; yes, we're in a time of recession. And it's true, there's no quick fix, as I said, to instantly end the tragic pain of unemployment. But we will end it. The process has already begun and we'll see its effect as the year goes on.

We speak with pride and admiration of that little band of Americans who overcame insuperable odds to set this nation on course 200 years ago. But our glory didn't end with them. Americans ever since have emulated their deeds.

We don't have to turn to our history books for heroes. They're all around us. One who sits among you here tonight epitomized that heroism at the end of the longest imprisonment ever inflicted on men of our armed forces. Who will ever forget that night when we waited for television to bring us the scene of that first plane landing at Clark Field in the Philippines, bringing our POWs home? The plane door opened and Jeremiah Denton came slowly down the ramp. He caught sight of our flag, saluted it, said, "God bless America," and then thanked us for bringing him home.

Just two weeks ago, in the midst of a terrible tragedy on the Potomac, we saw again the spirit of American heroism at its finest—the heroism of dedicated rescue workers saving crash victims from icy waters. And we saw the heroism of one of our young government employees, Lenny Skutnik, who, when he saw a woman lose her grip on the helicopter line, dived into the water and dragged her to safety.

And then there are countless, quiet, everyday heroes of American life—parents who sacrifice long and hard so their children will know a better life than they've known: church and civic volunteers who help to feed, clothe, nurse, and teach the needy; millions who've made our nation and our nation's destiny so very special— unsung heroes who may not have realized their own dreams themselves but then who reinvest those dreams in their children. Don't let anyone tell you that America's best days are behind her, that the American spirit has been vanquished. We've seen it triumph too often in our lives to stop believing in it now.

A hundred and twenty years ago, the greatest of all our presidents delivered his second State of the Union message in this chamber. "We cannot escape history," Abraham Lincoln warned. "We of this Congress and this administration will be remembered in spite of ourselves." The "trial through which we pass will light us down, in honor or dishonor, to the latest generation."

Well, that president and that Congress did not fail the American people. Together they weathered the storm and preserved the Union. Let it be said of us that we, too, did not fail; that we, too, worked together to bring America through difficult times. Let us so conduct ourselves that two centuries from now, another Congress and another president, meeting in this chamber as we are meeting, will speak of us with pride, saying that we met the test and preserved for them in their day the sacred flame of liberty—this last, best hope of man on Earth.

God bless you, and thank you.

The Evil Empire

Orlando, Florida

March 8, 1983

RIGHT-WING EVANGELICAL Christians composed a key element of Reagan's support, and they welcomed his conservative views on such issues as abortion, school prayer, sex education, and creationism. This address to the National Association of Evangelists was delivered as a sermon rather than as a policy statement, complete with extensive quotations from the Bible. The theme of the speech was evil in the modern world, whose source Reagan identified as the Soviet Union. His remarks (which were not nationally televised) were received with enthusiasm by the audience, but with dismay by the Left and by America's allies. In the *New York Times,* Henry Steele Commager called this speech the worst ever given by a president. To the New Right, however, this was only "Reagan being Reagan," that is, the symbol of American moral superiority in its pure manifestation, untrammeled by considerations for any other point of view.

The speech nonetheless hit home hard with the Soviets, where it counted. Nor was Reagan afraid to express his moral indignation directly to Russian leaders. The refusenik Anatoly Sharansky, who served nine harsh years in KGB prisons, credited his release in 1986 to a scolding Reagan gave Mikhail Gorbachev in November 1985.

This administration is motivated by a political philosophy that sees the greatness of America in you, her people, and in your families, churches, neighborhoods, communities—the institutions that foster and nourish values like concern for others and respect for the rule of law under God.

Now I don't have to tell you that this puts us in opposition to, or at least out of step with, a prevailing attitude of many who have turned to a modern-day secularism, discarding the tried and time-tested values upon which our very civilization is based.

No matter how well-intentioned, their value system is radically different from that of most Americans.

And, while they proclaim they are freeing us from superstitions of the past, they have taken upon themselves the job of superintending us by government rule and regulation. Sometimes their voices are louder than ours, but they are not yet a majority.

An example of that vocal superiority is evident in a controversy now going on in Washington. Since I'm involved, I've been waiting to hear from the parents of young America. How far are they willing to go in giving to government their prerogatives as parents?

Let me state the case as briefly and simply as I can. An organization of citizens sincerely motivated and deeply concerned about the increase in illegitimate births and abortions involving girls well below the age of consent established clinics nationwide to offer help to these girls and hopefully alleviate this situation.

Again let me say, I do not fault their intent. However, in their well-intentioned effort, these clinics provide advice and birth control drugs and devices to underage girls without the knowledge of their parents.

For some years now, the federal government has helped with funds to subsidize these clinics. In providing for this, the Congress decreed that every effort would be made to maximize parental participation. Nevertheless, the drugs and devices are prescribed without getting parental consent or giving notification. Girls termed "sexually active"—that has replaced the word promiscuous—are given this help in order to prevent illegitimate birth or abortion.

We have ordered clinics receiving federal funds to notify the parents such help has been given. One of the nation's leading newspapers has created the term squeal rule in editorializing against us, and we are being criticized for violating the privacy of young people. A judge has granted an injunction against enforcement of our rule. I have watched TV panel shows discuss this issue, have read columns pontificating on our error, but no one seems to mention morality as playing a part in the subject of sex.

Is all of Judeo-Christian tradition wrong? Are we to believe that something so sacred can be looked upon as a purely physical thing with no potential for emotional and psychological harm? And isn't it the parents' right to give counsel and advice to keep their children from making mistakes that may affect their entire lives?

Many of us in government would like to know what parents think about this intrusion in their family by government. We are going to fight in the courts. The rights of parents and the rights of family take precedence over those of Washington-based bureaucrats and social engineers.

But the fight against parental notification is really only one example of many attempts to water down traditonal values and even abrogate the original terms of American democracy. Freedom prospers when religion is vibrant and the rule of law under God acknowledged.

When our founding fathers passed the First Amendment, they sought to protect churches from government interference. They never meant to construct a wall of hostility between government and the concept of religious belief itself.

The evidence of this permeates our history and our government: The Declaration of Independence mentions the Supreme Being no less than four times; "In God We Trust" is engraved on our coinage; the Supreme Court opens its proceedings with a religious invocation; and the members of Congress open their sessions with a prayer.

I just happen to believe the school-children of the United States are entitled to the same privileges as Supreme Court justices and congressmen. Last year, I sent the Congress a constitutional amendment to restore prayer to public schools. This week I am resubmitting that amendment and calling on the Congress to act speedily to pass it.

Let our children pray. Perhaps some of you read recently about the Lubbock school case where a judge actually ruled that it was unconstitutional for a school district to give equal treatment to religious and non-religious student groups, even when the group meetings were held during the students' own time.

The First Amendment never intended to require government to discriminate against religious speech. Senators Denton and Hatfield have proposed legislation in the Congress on the whole question of prohibiting discrimination against religious forms of student speech. Such legislation could go far to restore freedom of religious speech for public school students and I hope the Congress considers these bills quickly. And with your help, I think it's possible we can get the constitutional amendment through the Congress this year.

More than a decade ago, a Supreme Court decision literally wiped off the books of 50 states statutes protecting the rights of unborn children. "Abortion on demand" now takes the lives of up to one and a half million unborn children a year.

Human life legislation ending this tragedy will someday pass the Congress—and you and I must never rest until it does. Unless and until it can be proven that the unborn child is not a living entity, then its right to life, liberty, and the pursuit of happiness must be protected.

You may remember that when abortion on demand began many, indeed, I'm sure many of you warned, that the practice would lead to a decline in respect for human life, that the philosophical premises used to justify abortion on demand would ultimately be used to justify other attacks on the sacredness of human life, infanticide or mercy killing. Tragically enough, those warnings proved all too true: Only last year a court permitted the death by starvation of a handicapped infant.

I have directed the Health and Human Services Department to make clear to every health-care facility in the United States that the Rehabilitation Act of 1973 protects all handicapped persons against discrimination based on handicaps, including infants.

And we have taken the further step of requiring that each and every recipient of federal funds who provides health-care services to infants must post and keep posted in a conspicuous place a notice stating that "discriminatory failure to feed and care for handicapped infants in this facility is prohibited by federal law." It also lists a 24-hour, toll-free number so that nurses and others may report violations in time to save the infant's life.

In addition, recent legislation introduced in the Congress by Representative Henry Hyde not only increased restrictions on publicly financed abortions, it also addresses this whole problem of infanticide.

I urge the Congress to begin hearings and to adopt legislation that will protect the right of life to all children, including the disabled or handicapped.

I'm sure you must get discouraged at times, but there is a great spiritual awakening in America, a renewal of the traditional values that have been the bedrock of America's goodness and greatness.

One recent survey by a Washington-based research council concluded that Americans were far more religious than the people of other nations; 95 percent of those surveyed expressed a belief in God and a huge majority believed the Ten Commandments had real meaning for their lives.

Another study has found that an overwhelming majority of Americans disapprove of adultery, teenage sex, pornography, abortion, and hard drugs. And this same study showed a deep reverence for the importance of family ties and religious belief.

I think the items we have discussed here today must be a key part of the nation's political agenda. For the first time the Congress is openly and seriously debating and dealing with the prayer and abortion issues—that's enormous progress right there.

I repeat: America is in the midst of a spiritual awakening and moral renewal. With your biblical keynote, I say today let "justice roll on like a river, righteousness like a never-failing stream."

Now, obviously, much of this new political and social consensus I have talked about is based on a positive view of American history, one that takes pride in our country's accomplishments and record. But we must never forget that no government schemes are going to perfect man; we know that living in this world means dealing with what philosophers would call the phenomenology of evil or, as theologians would put it, the docrine of sin.

There is sin and evil in the world, and we are enjoined by Scripture and the Lord Jesus to oppose it with all our might. Our nation, too, has a legacy of evil with which it must deal. The glory of this land has been its capacity for transcending the moral evils of our past.

For example, the long struggle of minority citizens for equal rights, once a source of disunity and civil war, is now a point of pride for all Americans. We must never go back.

There is no room for racism, anti-Semitism, or other forms of ethnic and racial hatred in this country. I know you have been horrified, as have I, by the resurgence of some hate groups preaching bigotry and prejudice. Use the mighty voice of your pulpits and the powerful standing of your churches to denounce and isolate these hate groups in our midst. The commandment given us is clear and simple: "Thou shalt love thy neighbor as thyself."

But whatever sad episodes exist in our past, any objective observer must hold a positive view of American history, a history that has been the story of hopes fulfilled and dreams made into reality. Especially in this century, America has kept alight the torch of freedom—not just for ourselves but for millions of others around the world. And this brings me to my final point today.

During my first press conference as president, in answer to a direct question, I pointed out that as good Marxist-Leninists the Soviet leaders have openly and publicly declared that the only morality they recognize is that which will further their cause, which is world revolution.

I think I should point out I was only quoting Lenin, their guiding spirit, who said in 1920 that they repudiate all morality that proceeds from supernatural ideas or ideas that are outside class conceptions; morality is entirely subordinate to the interests of class war; and everything is moral that is necessary for the annihilation of the old exploiting social order and for uniting the proletariat.

I think the refusal of many influential people to accept this elementary fact of Soviet doctrine illustrates an historical reluctance to see totalitarian powers for what they are. We saw this phenomenon in the 1930s; we see it too often today. This does not mean we should isolate ourselves and refuse to seek an understanding with them.

I intend to do everything I can to persuade them of our peaceful intent; to remind them that it was the West that refused to use its nuclear monopoly in the '40s and '50s for territoral gain and which now proposes 50 percent cuts in strategic ballistic missiles and the elimination of an entire class of land-based, intermediate-range nuclear missiles.

At the same time, however, they must be made to understand we will never compromise our principles and standards. We will never give way our freedom. We will never abandon our belief in God.

And we will never stop searching for a genuine peace. But we can assure none of these things America stands for through the so-called nuclear freeze solutions proposed by some. The truth is that a freeze now would be a very dangerous fraud, for that is merely the illusion of peace. The reality is that we must find peace through strength.

I would agree to a freeze if only we could freeze the Soviets' global desires. A freeze at current levels of weapons would remove any incentive for the Soviets to negotiate seriously in Geneva, and virtually end our chances to achieve the major arms reductions which we have proposed. Instead, they would achieve their objectives through the freeze.

A freeze would reward the Soviet Union for its enormous and unparalleled military buildup. It would prevent the essential and long overdue modernization of United States and allied defenses and would leave our aging forces increasingly vulnerable. And an honest freeze would require extensive prior negotiations on the systems and numbers to be limited and on the measures to insure effective verification and compliance.

And the kind of freeze that has been suggested would be virtually impossible to verify. Such a major effort would divert us completely from our current negotiations on achieving substantial reductions.

Let us pray for the salvation of all those who live in totalitarian darkness, pray they will discover the joy of knowing God.

But until they do, let us be aware that while they preach the supremacy of the state, declare its omnipotence over individual man, and predict its eventual domination of all peoples of the earth—they are the focus of evil in the modern world.

It was C. S. Lewis who, in his unforgettable "Screwtape Letters," wrote:

"The greatest evil is not now done in those sordid 'dens of crime' that Dickens loved to paint. It is not done even in concentration camps and labor camps. In those we see its final result. But it is conceived and ordered (moved, seconded, carried, and minuted) in clear, carpeted, warmed, and well-lighted offices, by quiet men with white collars and cut fingernails and smooth shaven cheeks who do not need to raise their voice."

Because these "quiet men" do not "raise their voices," because they sometimes speak in soothing tones of brotherhood and peace, because, like other dictators before them, they are always making "their final territorial demand," some would have us accept them at their word and accommodate ourselves to their aggressive impulses.

But, if history teaches anything, it teaches: Simple-minded appeasement or wishful thinking about our adversaries is folly—it means the betrayal of our past, the squandering of our freedom.

So I urge you to speak out against those who would place the United States in a position of military and moral inferiority. You know, I have always believed that old Screwtape reserves his best efforts for those of you in the church.

So in your discussions of the nuclear freeze proposals, I urge you to beware the temptation of pride—the temptation blithely to declare yourselves above it all and label both sides equally at fault, to ignore the facts of history and the aggressive impulses of an evil empire, to simply call the arms race a giant misunderstanding and thereby remove yourself from the struggle between right and wrong, good and evil.

I ask you to resist the attempts of those who would have you withhold your support for this administration's efforts to keep America strong and free, while we negotiate real and verifiable reductions in the world's nuclear arsenals and one day, with God's help, their total elimination.

While America's military strength is important, let me add here that I have always maintained that the struggle now going on for the world will never be decided by bombs or rockets, by armies or military might.

The real crisis we face today is a spiritual one; at root, it is a test of moral will and faith.

Whittaker Chambers, the man whose own religious conversion made him a "witness" to one of the terrible traumas of our age, the Hiss-Chambers case, wrote that the crisis of the Western world exists to the degree in which the West is indifferent to God, the degree to which it collaborates in Communism's attempt to make man stand alone without God.

For Marxism-Leninism is actually the second oldest faith, he said, first proclaimed in the Garden of Eden with the words of temptation: "Ye shall be as gods." The Western world can answer this challenge, he wrote, "but only provided that its faith in God and the freedom He enjoins is as great as Communism's faith in man."

I believe we shall rise to this challenge; I believe that Communism is another sad, bizarre chapter in human history whose last pages even now are being written. I believe this because the source of our strength in the quest for human freedom is not material but spiritual, and, because it knows no limitation, it must terrify and ultimately triumph over those who would enslave their fellow man.

For, in the words of Isaiah:

"He giveth power to the faint; and to them that have no might He increased strength. But they that wait upon the Lord shall renew their strength; they shall mount up with wings as eagles; they shall run, and not be weary."

Star Wars

Washington, D.C.

March 23, 1983

REAGAN'S announcement, during a nationally televised speech on peace and national security, that the United States would develop a space-based defense against nuclear ballistic missiles came as a surprise not only to the world in general but also to most of his administration and the military establishment. The president had discussed the Strategic Defense Initiative (SDI), as the program was officially called, with few of his advisers; he took most aspects of the proposal from "High Frontier: A New National Strategy," a report prepared by the Heritage Foundation, an influential conservative think tank. Making the United States invulnerable to nuclear missile attack with a protective shield of exotic weapons straight out of the Star Wars movies was an irresistible idea to Reagan, who saw it as the perfect way to end the current system of deterrence based on mutually assured destruction (MAD) without having to trust the Soviets in an arms limitation agreement. But in this speech the president gave only the vaguest hints as to how the SDI was to be accomplished; most of the hard questions on deployment, cost, and political and technological feasibility went unanswered. Nonetheless, SDI marked a major change in U.S. strategic policy, one that the Pentagon and its contractors soon embraced wholeheartedly and the Soviets took very seriously.

SDI proved unexpectedly to be one of the most significant and enduring initiatives of the Reagan presidency. It revealed the U.S.S.R.'s crucial strategic weakness—its inability to pay for high-technology initiatives like SDI—and did immeasurable harm to Soviet prestige, both internally and globally. Ironically, SDI also proved too costly and unreliable for the United States, but by the time President Bill Clinton vetoed the program in the year 2000, the Soviet empire had been dead for almost a decade.

... Thus far tonight I have shared with you my thoughts on the problems of national security we must face together. My predecessors in the Oval Office have appeared before you on other occasions to describe the threat posed by Soviet power and have proposed steps to address that threat. But since the advent of nuclear weapons, those steps have been directed toward deterrence of aggression thorugh the promise of retaliation—the notion that no rational nation would launch an attack that would inevitably result in unacceptable losses to themselves. This approach to stability through offensive threat has worked. We and our allies have succeeded in preventing nuclear war for three decades. In recent months, however, my advisers, including in particular the Joint Chiefs of Staff, have underscored the bleakness of the future before us.

Over the course of these discussions, I have become more and more deeply convinced that the human spirit must be capable of rising above dealing with other nations and human beings by threatening their existence. Feeling this way, I believe we must thoroughly examine every opportunity for reducing tensions and for introducing greater stability into the strategic calculus on both sides. One of the most important contributions we can make is, of course, to lower the level of all arms, and particularly nuclear arms. We are engaged right now in several negotiations with the Soviet Union to bring about a mutual reduction of weapons. I will report to you a week from tomorrow my thoughts on that score. But let me just say I am totally committed to this course.

If the Soviet Union will join us in our effort to achieve major arms reduction we will have succeeded in stabilizing the nuclear balance. Nevertheless it will still be necessary to rely on the specter of retaliation—on mutual threat, and that is a sad commentary on the human condition.

Would it not be better to save lives than to avenge them? Are we not capable of demonstrating our peaceful intentions by applying all our abilities and our ingenuity to achieving a truly lasting stability? I think we are—indeed, we must!

After careful consultation with my advisers, including the Joint Chiefs of Staff, I believe there is a way. Let me share with you a vision of the future which offers hope. It is that we embark on a program to counter the awesome Soviet missile threat with measures that are defensive. Let us turn to the very strengths in technology that spawned our great industrial base and that have given us the quality of life we enjoy today.

Up until now we have increasingly based our strategy of deterrence upon the threat of retaliation. But what if free people could live secure in the knowledge that their security did not rest upon the threat of instant U.S. retaliation to deter a Soviet attack; that we could intercept and destroy strategic ballistic missiles before they reached our own soil or that of our allies?

I know this is a formidable technical task, one that may not be accomplished before the end of this century. Yet, current technology has attained a level of sophistication where it is reasonable for us to begin this effort. It will take years, probably decades, of effort on many fronts. There will be failures and setbacks just as there will be successes and breakthroughs. And as we proceed we must remain constant in preserving the nuclear deterrent and maintaining a solid capability for flexible response. But is it not worth every investment necessary to free the world from the threat of nuclear war? We know it is!

In the meantime, we will continue to pursue real reductions in nuclear arms, negotiating from a position of strength that can be insured only by modernizing our strategic forces. At the same time, we must take steps to reduce the risk of a convential military conflict escalating to nuclear war by improving our nonnuclear capabilities. America does possess—now—the technologies to attain very significant improvements in the effectiveness of our conventional, nonnuclear forces. Proceeding boldly with these new technologies, we can significantly reduce any incentive that the Soviet Union may have to threaten attack against the United States or its allies.

As we pursue our goal of defensive technologies, we recognize that our allies rely upon our strategic offensive power to deter attacks against them. Their vital interests and ours are inextricably linked—their safety and ours are one. And no change in technology can or will alter that reality. We must and shall continue to honor our commitments.

I clearly recognize that defensive systems have limitations and raise certain problems and ambiguities. If paired with offensive systems, they can be viewed as fostering an aggressive policy, and no one wants that.

But with these considerations firmly in mind, I call upon the scientific community who gave us nuclear weapons to turn their great talents to the cause of mankind and world peace: to give us the means of rendering these nuclear weapons impotent and obsolete.

Tonight, consistent with our obligations under the ABM treaty and recognizing the need for close consultation with our allies, I am taking an important first step. I am directing a comprehensive and intensive effort to define a long-term research and development program to begin to achieve our ultimate goal of eliminating the threat posed by strategic nuclear missiles. This could pave the way for arms control measures to eliminate the weapons themselves. We seek neither military superiority nor political advantage. Our only purpose—one all people share—is to search for ways to reduce the danger of nuclear war.

My fellow Americans, tonight we are launching an effort which holds the purpose of changing the course of human history. There will be risks, and results take time. But with your support, I believe we can do it.

The Central American Threat

Washington, D.C.

April 27, 1983

AN ABIDING foreign-policy theme of the Reagan presidency was the presumed threat posed to the United States by Marxist movements in Central America. The president's specific target was usually Nicaragua's Sandinista regime, which came to power in 1979. Reagan repeatedly asked Congress for increased U.S. military aid for the contras (Nicaraguan guerrillas fighting an insurrectionist war against the Sandinistas), as he did in this long speech before Congress. At this point the president was still assuring Congress that the United States was "not doing anything to try and overthrow the Nicaraguan government." Most observers agree, however, that CIA-backed covert operations against the Sandinistas had been under way for some time and that it was the administration's unofficial policy to destabilize the current government by any available means, whether authorized by Congress or not.

A number of times in past years, members of Congress and a president have come together in meetings like this to resolve a crisis. I have asked for this meeting in the hope that we can prevent one.

It would be hard to find many Americans who are not aware of our stake in the Middle East, the Persian Gulf, or the NATO line dividing the free world from the Communist bloc. And the same could be said for Asia.

But in spite of, or maybe because of, a flurry of stories about places like Nicaragua and EL Salvador and, yes, some concerted propaganda, many of us find it hard to believe we have a stake in problems involving those countries. Too many have thought of Central America as just a place way down below Mexico that cannot possibly constitute a threat to our well-being.

And that is why I have asked for this session. Central America's problems do directly affect the security and the well-being of our own people. And Central America is much closer to the United States than many of the world trouble spots that concern us. So as we work to restore our own economy, we cannot afford to lose sight of our neighbors to the south.

El Salvador is nearer to Texas than Texas is to Massachusetts. Nicaragua is just as close to Miami, San Antonio, San Diego, and Tucson as those cities are to Washington, where we are gathered tonight.

Bur nearness on the map does not even begin to tell the strategic importance of Central America, bordering as it does on the Caribbean—our lifeline to the outside world. Two-thirds of all our foreign trade and petroleum pass through the Panama Canal and the Caribbean. In a European crisis, at least half of our supplies for NATO would go through these areas by sea. It is well to remember that in early 1942 a handful of Hitler's submarines sank more tonnage there than in all of the Atlantic Ocean. And they did this without a single naval base anywhere in the area.

And today, the situation is different. Cuba is host to a Soviet combat brigade, a submarine base capable of servicing Soviet submarines and military air bases visited regularly by Soviet military aircraft.

Because of its importance, the Caribbean Basin is a magnet for adventurism. We are all aware of the Libyan cargo planes refueling in Brazil a few days ago on their way to deliver medical supplies to Nicaragua. Brazilian authorities discovered the so-called medical supplies were actually munitions and prevented their delivery. You may remember that last month, speaking on national television, I showed an aerial photo of an airfield being built on the island of Grenada. Well, if that airfield had been completed, those planes could have refueled there and completed their journey.

If the Nazis during World War II and the Soviets today could recognize the Caribbean and Central America as vital to our interests, shouldn't we also?

For several years now, under two administrations, the United States has been increasing its defense of freedom in the Caribbean

Basin. And I can tell you tonight, democracy is beginning to take root in El Salvador, which, until a short time ago, knew only dictatorship. The new government is now delivering on its promises of democracy, reforms, and free elections. It was not easy and there was resistance to many of the attempted reforms with assassinations of some of the reformers. Guerrilla bands and urban terrorists were portrayed in a worldwide propaganda campaign as freedom fighters representative of the people. Ten days before I came into office, the guerrillas launched what they called a "final offensive" to overthrow the government. And their radio boasted that our new administration would be too late to prevent their victory. Well they learned democracy cannot be so easily defeated.

President Carter did not hesitate. He authorized arms and munitions to El Salvador. The guerrilla offensive failed, but not America's will. Every president since this country assumed global responsibilities has known that those responsibilities could only be met if we pursued a bipartisan foreign policy.

As I said a moment ago, the government of El Salvador has been keeping its promise, like the land reform program which is making thousands of farm tenants farm owners. In a little over three years, 20 percent of the arable land in El Salvador has been redistributed to more than 450,000 people. That's one in 10 Salvadorans who has directly benefitted from this program.

El Salvador has continued to strive toward an orderly and democratic society. The government promised free elections. On March 28th, little more than a year ago, after months of campaigning by a variety of candidates, the suffering people of El Salvador were offered a chance to vote—to choose the kind of government they wanted. And suddenly the so-called freedom fighters in the hills were exposed for what they really are—a small minority who want power for themselves and their backers—not democracy for the people. The guerrillas threatened death to anyone who voted. They destroyed hundreds of buses and trucks to keep the people from getting to the polling places. Their slogan was brutal: "Vote today, die tonight." But on election day, an unprecedented 80 percent of the electorate braved ambush and gunfire and trudged for miles, many of them, to vote for freedom. And that's

truly fighting for freedom. We can never turn our backs on that.

Members of this Congress who went there as observers told me of a woman who was wounded by rifle fire on the way to the polls, who refused to leave the line to have her wound treated until after she had voted. Another woman had been told by the guerrillas that she would be killed when she returned from the polls, and she told the guerrillas, "You can kill me, you can kill my family, kill my neighbors, you can't kill us all." The real freedom fighters of El Salvador turned out to be the people of that country—the young, the old, the in-between—more than a million of them out of a population of less than five million. The world should respect this courage, and not allow it to be belittled or forgotten. And again, I say in good conscience, we can never turn our backs on that.

The democratic political parties and factions in El Salvador are coming together around the common goal of seeking a political solution to their country's problems. New national elections will be held this year and they will be open to all political parties. The government has invited the guerrillas to participate in the election and is preparing an amnesty law. The people of El Salvador are earning their freedom and they deserve our moral and material support to protect it.

Yes, there are still major problems regarding human rights, the criminal justice system, and violence against noncombatants. And, like the rest of Central America, El Salvador also faces severe economic problems. But, in addition to recession-depressed prices for major agricultural exports, El Salvador's economy is being deliberately sabotaged.

Tonight in El Salvador—because of ruthless guerrilla attacks—much of the fertile land cannot be cultivated; less than half the rolling stock of the railways remains operational; bridges, water facilities, telephone and electrical systems have been destroyed and damaged. In one 22-month period, there were 5,000 interruptions of electrical power. One region was without electricity for a third of a year.

I think Secretary of State Shultz put it very well the other day; "Unable to win the free loyalty of El Salvador's people, the guerrillas," he said, "are deliberately and systematically depriving them of food, water, transportation, light, sanitation, and jobs. And these are the people who claim they want to help the common people."

They do not want elections because they know they would be defeated. But, as the previous election showed, the Salvadoran people's desire for democracy will not be defeated.

The guerrillas are not embattled peasants armed with muskets. They are professional, sometimes with better training and weaponry than the government's soldier. The Salvadoran battalions that have received U.S. training have been conducting themselves well on the battlefield and with the civilian population. But, so far, we have only provided enough money to train one Salvadoran soldier out of 10, fewer than the number of guerrillas that are trained by Nicaragua and Cuba.

And let me set the record straight on Nicaragua, a country next to El Salvador. In 1979, when the new government took over in Nicaragua after a revolution which overthrew the authoritarian rule of Somoza, everyone hoped for the growth of democracy. We in the United States did, too. By January of 1981, our emergency relief and recovery aid to Nicaragua totaled $118 million—more than provided by any other developed country. In fact, in the first two years of Sandinista rule, the United States directly or indirectly sent five times more aid to Nicaragua than it had in the two years prior to the revolution. Can anyone doubt the generosity and good faith of the American people?

These were hardly the actions of a nation implacably hostile to Nicaragua. Yet the government of Nicaragua has treated us as an enemy. It has rejected our repeated peace efforts. It has broken its promises to us, to the Organization of American States and, most important of all, to the people of Nicaragua.

No sooner was victory achieved than a small clique ousted others who had been part of the revolution from having any voice in the government. Humberto Ortega, the minister of defense, declared Marxism-Leninism would be their guide, and so it is.

The government of Nicaragua has imposed a new dictatorship; it has refused to hold the elections it promised; it has seized control of most media and subjects all media to heavy prior censorship; it denied the bishops and priests of the Roman Catholic Church the right to say mass on radio during Holy Week; it insulted and mocked the pope; it has driven the Miskito Indians from their homelands—burning their villages, destroying their crops, and forcing them into involuntary internment camps far from home; it has moved against the private sector and free labor unions; it condoned mob action against Nicaragua's independent human rights commission and drove the director of that commission into exile.

In short, after all these acts of repression by the government, is it any wonder that opposition has formed? Contrary to propaganda, the opponents of the Sandinistas are not die-hard supporters of the previous Somoza regime. In fact, many are anti-Somoza heroes who fought beside the Sandinistas to bring down the Somoza government. Now they have been denied any part in the new government because they truly wanted democracy for Nicaragua and they still do. Others are Miskito Indians fighting for their homes, their lands and their lives.

The Sandinista revolution in Nicaragua turned out to be just an exchange of one set of autocratic rulers for another, and the people still have no freedom, no democratic rights, and more poverty. Even worse than its predecessor, it is helping Cuba and the Soviets to destabilize our hemisphere.

Meanwhile, the government of El Salvador, making every effort to guarantee democracy, free labor unions, freedom of religion, and a free press, is under attack by guerrillas dedicated to the same philosophy that prevails in Nicaragua, Cuba, and, yes, the Soviet Union. Violence has been Nicaragua's most important export to the world. It is the ultimate in hypocrisy for the unelected Nicaraguan government to charge that we seek their overthrow when they are doing everything they can to bring down the elected government of El Salvador. The guerrilla attacks are directed from a headquarters in Managua, the capital of Nicaragua.

But let us be clear as to the American attitude toward the government of Nicaragua. We do not seek its overthrow. Our interest is to insure that it does not infect its neighbors through the export of subversion and violence. Our purpose, in conformity with American and international law, is to prevent the flow of arms to El Salvador, Honduras, Guatemala, and Costa Rica. We have attempted to have a dialogue with the government of Nicaragua but it persists in its efforts to spread violence.

We should not—and we will not—protect the Nicaraguan government from the anger of its own people. But we should, through diplomacy, offer an alternative. And, as Nicaragua ponders its options we can and will—with all the resources of diplomacy—protect each country of Central America from the danger of war.

Even Costa Rica, Central America's oldest and strongest democracy, a government so peaceful it doesn't even have an army, is the object of bullying and threats from Nicaragua's dictators.

Nicaragua's neighbors know that Sandinista promises of peace, nonalliance, and nonintervention have not been kept. Some 36 new military bases have been built— there were only 13 during the Somoza years.

Nicaragua's new army numbers 25,000 men supported by a militia of 50,000. It is the largest army in Central America supplemented by 2,000 Cuban military and security advisers. It is equipped with the most modern weapons, dozens of Soviet-made tanks, 800 Soviet-bloc trucks, Soviet 152-millimeter howitzers, 100 antiaircraft guns plus planes and helicopters. There are additional thousands of civilian advisers from Cuba, the Soviet Union, East Germany, Libya, and the PLO And we are attacked because we have 55 military trainers in El Salvador.

The goal of the professional guerrilla movements in Central America is as simple as it is sinister—to destablilize the entire region from the Panama Canal to Mexico. And if you doubt me on this point, just consider what Cayetano Carpio, the now-deceased Salvadoran guerrilla leader, said earlier this month. Carpio said that after El Salvador falls, El Salvador and Nicaragua would be "arm-in-arm and struggling for the total liberation of Central America."

Nicaragua's dictatorial junta, who themselves made war and won power operating from bases in Honduras and Costa Rica, like to pretend that they are today being attacked by forces based in Honduras. The fact is, it is Nicaragua's government that threatens Honduras, not the reverse.

It is Nicaragua who has moved heavy tanks close to the border and Nicaragua who speaks of war. It was Nicaraguan radio that announced on April 18th the creation of a new, unified revolutionary coordinating board to push forward the Marxist struggle in Honduras.

Nicaragua, supported by weapons and military resources provided by the Communist bloc, represses its own people, refuses to make peace, and sponsors a guerrilla war against El Salvador.

President Truman's words are as apt today as they were in 1947, when he, too, spoke before a joint session of the Congress:

At the present moment in world history nearly every nation must choose between alternative ways of life. The choice is not too often a free one.

One way of life is based upon the will of the majority and is distinguished by free institutions representative government, free elections, guarantees of individual liberty, freedom of speech and religion, and freedom political oppression. "The second way of life is based upon the will of a minority forcibly imposed upon the majority. It relies upon terror and oppression, a controlled press and radio, fixed elections, and the suppression of personal freedoms.

I believe that it must be the policy of the United States to support free peoples who are resisting attempted subjugation by armed minorities or by outside pressures.

I believe that we must assist free peoples to work out their own destinies in their own way.

I believe that our help should be primarily through economic and financial aid, which is essential to economic stability and orderly political processes.

Collapse of free institutions and loss of independence would be disastrous not only for them but for the world. Discouragement and possibly failure would quickly be the lot of neighboring peoples striving to maintain their freedom and independence.

The countries of Central America are smaller than the nations that prompted President Truman's message. But the political and strategic stakes are the same. Will our response—economic, social, military—be as appropriate and successful as Mr. Truman's bold solutions to the problems of postwar Europe?

Some people have forgotten the successes of those years—and the decades of peace, prosperity, and freedom they secured.

Some people talk as though the United States were incapable of acting effectively in international affairs without risking war or damaging those we seek to help.

Are democracies required to remain passive while threats to their security and prosperity accumulate?

Must we just accept the destabilization of an entire region from the Panama Canal to Mexico on our southern border?

Must we sit by while independent nations of this hemisphere are integrated into the most aggressive empire the modern world has seen?

Must we wait while Central Americans are driven from their homes, like the more than a million who have sought refuge out of Afghanistan or the one and a half million who fled Indochina or the more than one million Cubans who have fled Castro's Caribbean utopia? Must we, by default, leave the people of El Salvador no choice but to flee their homes, creating another tragic human exodus?

I do not believe there is a majority in the Congress or the country that counsels passivity, resignation, defeatism in the face of this challenge to freedom and security in our own hemisphere.

I do not believe that a majority of the Congress or the country is prepared to stand by passively while the people of Central America are delivered to totalitarianism and we ourselves are left vulnerable to new dangers.

Only last week an official of the Soviet Union reiterated Brezhnev's threat to station nuclear missiles in this hemisphere— five minutes from the United States. Like an echo, Nicaragua's commandante, Daniel Ortega, confirmed that, if asked, his country would consider accepting those missiles. I understand that today they may be having second thoughts.

Now, before I go any further, let me say to those who invoke the memory of Vietnam: There is no thought of sending American combat troops to Central America. They are not needed—indeed, they have not been requested there. All our neighbors ask of us is assistance in training and arms to protect themselves while they build a better, freer life.

We must continue to encourage peace among the nations of Central America. We must support the regional efforts now under way to promote solutions to regional problems.

We cannot be certain that the Marxist-Leninist bands who believe war is an instrument of politics will be readily discouraged. It is crucial that we not become discouraged before they do. Otherwise the region's freedom will be lost and our security damaged in ways that can hardly be calculated.

If Central America were to fall, what would the consequences be for our position in Asia, Europe, and for alliances such as NATO? If the United States cannot respond to a threat near our own borders, why should Europeans or Asians believe that we are seriously concerned about threats to them? If the Soviets can assume that nothing short of an actual attack on the United States will provoke an American response, which ally, which friend will trust us then?

The Congress shares both the power and the responsibility for our foreign policy.

Tonight I ask you, the Congress, to join me in a bold, generous approach to the problems of peace and poverty, democracy and dictatorship in the region. Join me in a program that prevents Communist victory in the short run but goes beyond to produce, for the deprived people of the area, the reality of present progress and the promise of more to come.

Let us lay the foundation for a bipartisan approach to sustain the independence and freedom of the countries of Central America. We in the administration reach out to you in this spirit.

We will pursue four basic goals in Central America:

First, in response to decades of inequity and indifference, we will support democracy, reform, and human freedom. This means using our assistance, our powers of persuasion and our legitimate leverage to bolster humane democratic systems where they already exist and to help countries on their way to that goal complete the process as quickly as human institutions can be changed. Elections—in El Salvador and also in Nicaragua—must be open to all, fair and safe. The international community must help. We will work at human rights problems, not walk away from them.

Second, in response to the challenge of world recession and, in the case of El Salvador, to the unrelenting campaign of economic sabotage by the guerrillas, we will support economic development. By a margin of 2-to-1, our aid is economic now, not military. Seventy-seven cents out of every dollar we will spend in the area this year goes for food, fertilizers, and other essentials for economic growth and development. And our economic program goes beyond traditional aid: The Caribbean Initiative introduced in the House earlier today will provide powerful trade and investment incentives to help these countries achieve self-sustaining economic growth without exporting U.S. jobs. Our goal must be to focus our immense and growing technology to enhance health care, agriculture, industry and to insure that we who inhabit this interdependent region come to know and understand each other better, retaining our diverse identities, respecting our diverse traditions and institutions.

And third, in response to the military challenge from Cuba and Nicaragua—to their deliberate use of force to spread tyranny—we will support the security of the region's threatened nations. We do not view security assistance as an end in itself but as a shield for democratization, economic development, and diplomacy. No amount of reform will bring peace so long as guerrillas believe they will win by force. No amount of economic help will suffice if guerrilla units can destroy roads and bridges and power stations and crops again and again with impugnity. But with better training and material help, our neighbors can hold off the guerrillas and give democratic reform time to take root.

Fourth, we will support dialogue and negotiations—both among the countries of the region and within each country. The terms and conditions of participation in elections are negotiable. Costa Rica is a shining example of democracy. Honduras has made the move from military rule to democratic government. Guatemala is pledged to the same course. The United States will work toward a political solution in Central America which will serve the interests of the democratic process.

To support these diplomatic goals, I offer these assurances:

The United States will support any agreement among Central American countries for the withdrawal—under fully verifiable and reciprocal conditions—of all foreign military and security advisers and troops.

We want to help opposition groups join the political process in all countries and compete by ballots instead of bullets.

We will support any verifiable, reciprocal agreement among Central American countries on the renunciation of support of insurgencies on neighbors' territory.

And, finally, we desire to help Central America end its costly arms race and will support any verifiable, reciprocal agreements on the nonimportation of offensive weapons.

To move us toward these goals more rapidly, I am tonight announcing my intention to name an ambassador-at-large as my special envoy to Central America. He or she will report to me through the secretary of state. The ambassador's responsibilities will be to lend U.S. support to the efforts of regional governments to bring peace to this troubled area and to work closely with the Congress to assure the fullest possible bipartisan coordination of our policies toward the region.

What I am asking for is prompt congressional approval for the full reprogramming of funds for key current economic and security programs so that the people of Central America can hold the line against externally supported aggression. In addition, I am asking for prompt action on the supplemental request in these same areas to carry us through the current fiscal year and for early and favorable congressional action on my requests for fiscal year 1984. And finally, I am asking that the bipartisan consensus, which last year acted on the trade and tax provisions of the Caribbean Basin Initiative in the House, again take the lead to move this vital proposal to the floor of both chambers. And, as I said before, the greatest share of these requests is targeted toward economic and humanitarian aid, not military.

What the administration is asking for on behalf of freedom in Central America is so small, so minimal—considering what is at stake. The total amount requested for aid to all of Central America in 1984 is about $60 million; that is less than one-tenth of what Americans will spend this year on coin-operated video games.

In summation, I say to you that tonight there can be no question: The national security of all the Americas is at stake in Central America. If we cannot defend ourselves there, we cannot expect to prevail elsewhere. Our credibility would collapse, our alliances would crumble and the safety of our homeland would be put in jeopardy.

We have a vital interest, a moral duty and a solemn responsibility.

This is not a partisan issue. It is a question of our meeting our moral responsibility to ourselves, our friends and our posterity. It is a duty that falls to all of us—the president, the Congress, and the people. We must perform it together. Who among us would wish to bear responsibility for failing to meet our shared obligation?

Thank you.

Lebanon and Grenada

Washington, D.C.

October 27, 1983

IN THIS TELEVISED speech Reagan discussed the worst foreign policy-disaster of his first term—the bombing of the U.S. Marine compound in Beirut, Lebanon, on October 23, 1983—and his one military success—the invasion of Grenada on October 25. The Beirut bombing resulted from the administration's lack of a solid policy aim in Lebanon and its failure to comprehend the real conditions in Beirut. The marine peacekeeping force, sent after the assassination of Lebanon's president and the massacre of Palestinian refugees by Lebanese Christian Phalangists, occupied an exposed position near the Beirut airport, yet for political reasons the marine commander was not allowed to maintain a completely secure perimeter. A Muslim terrorist was able to drive a truck filled with explosives right into the compound; the blast killed 241 marines. In the first part of this speech, Reagan explained his decision to keep the marines in Lebanon (four months later, he ordered their withdrawal). The entire incident, which might have irreparably damaged a less popular president, appeared to do little permanent harm to Reagan. In part this was because the Beirut incident was partially obscured by news of the invasion of Grenada, which Reagan discusses in the second half of this speech. This minor military action, undertaken ostensibly to protect American citizens on the tiny island from violence following a Marxist coup, was a no-lose situation for the United States (the polar opposite of the no-win situation in Beirut). The press, excluded from the Grenada action, could not contradict the president's assertion that the marines arrived "just in time" to forestall a Cuban-Soviet occupation of the Caribbean. Reagan ended his remarks with an anecdote about a wounded marine, a surefire sentimental touch reminiscent of the closing scenes of 1940s war films.

My fellow Americans, some two months ago we were shocked by the brutal massacre of 269 men, women, and children, in the shooting down of a Korean airliner. Now, in these past several days, violence has erupted again, in Lebanon and Grenada.

In Lebanon we have some 1,600 marines, part of a multinational force that's trying to help the people of Lebanon restore order and stability to that troubled land. Our marines are assigned to the south of the city of Beirut near the only airport operating in Lebanon. Just a mile or so to the north is the Italian contingent and not far from them the French and a company of British soldiers.

This past Sunday, at 22 minutes after six, Beirut time, with dawn just breaking, a truck looking like a lot of other vehicles in the city approached the airport on a busy main road. There was nothing in its appearance to suggest it was any different than the truck or cars that were normally seen on and around the airport. But this one was different.

At the wheel was a young man on a suicide mission. The truck carried some 2,000 pounds of explosives, but there was no way our marine

guard could know this. Their first warning that something was wrong came when the truck crashed through a series of barriers, including a chain link fence and barbed wire entanglements. The guards opened fire, but it was too late.

The truck smashed through the doors of the headquarters building in which our marines were sleeping and instantly exploded. The four-story concrete building collapsed in a pile of rubble.

More than 200 of the sleeping men were killed in that one hideous insane attack. Many others suffered injury and are hospitalized here or in Europe. This was not the end of the horror.

At almost the same instant another vehicle on a suicide and murder mission crashed into the headquarters of the French peacekeeping force, an eight-story building, destroying and killing more than 50 French soldiers.

Prior to this day of horror there had been several tragedies for our men in the multinational force; attacks by snipers and mortar fire had taken their toll. I called the bereaved parents and/or widows of the victims to express on behalf of all of us our sorrow and sympathy. Sometimes there were questions. And now many of you are asking: Why should our young men be dying in Lebanon? Why is Lebanon important to us?

Well, it's true Lebanon is a small country more than five and a half thousand miles from our shores, on the edge of what we call the Middle East. But every president who has occupied this office in recent years has recognized that peace in the Middle East is of vital concern to our nation and, indeed, to our allies in Western Europe and Japan. We've been concerned because the Middle East is a powder keg. Four times in the last 30 years the Arabs and Israelis have gone to war and each time the world has teetered near the edge of catastrophe. The area is key to the economic and political life of the West. Its strategic importance, its energy resources, the Suez Canal, the well-being of the nearly 200 million people living there; all are vital to us and to world peace.

If that key should fall into the hands of a power or powers hostile to the free world, there would be a direct threat to the United States and to our allies.

We have another reason to be involved. Since 1948, our nation has recognized and accepted a moral obligation to assure the continued existence of Israel as a nation. Israel shares our democratic values and is a formidable force an invader of the Middle East would have to reckon with. For several years, Lebanon has been torn by internal strife. Once a prosperous, peaceful nation, its government had become ineffective in controlling the militias that warred on each other.

Sixteen months ago we were watching on our TV screens the shelling and bombing of Beirut, which was being used as a fortress by PLO bands. Hundreds and hundreds of civilians were being killed and wounded in the daily battles. Syria, which makes no secret of its claim that Lebanon should be part of a greater Syria, was occupying a large part of Lebanon. Today, Syria has become a home for 7,000 Soviet advisers and technicians who man a massive amount of Soviet weaponry, including SS-2 ground-to-ground missiles capable of reaching vital areas of Israel.

A little over a year ago, hoping to build on the Camp David accords, which have led to peace between Israel and Egypt, I proposed a peace plan for the Middle East to end the wars between the Arab states and Israel. It was based on UN Resolutions 242 and 338 and called for a fair and just solution to the Palestinian problem, as well as a fair and just settlement of issues between the Arab states and Israel.

Before the necessary negotiations could begin, it was essential to get all foreign forces out of Lebanon and to end the fighting there. So why are we there? Well, the answer is straightforward: to help bring peace to Lebanon and stability to the vital Middle East. To that end the multinational force was created to help stabilize the situation in Lebanon until a government could be established and the Lebanese army mobilized to restore Lebanese sovereignty over its own soil as the foreign forces withdrew.

Israel agreed to withdraw as did Syria. But Syria then reneged on its promise. Over 10,000 Palestinians who had been bringing ruin down on Beirut, however, did leave the country. Lebanon has formed a government under the leadership of President Gemayel and that government, with our assistance and training, has set up its own army. In only a year's time that army has been rebuilt. It's a good army composed of Lebanese of all factions.

A few weeks ago the Israeli army pulled back to the Awali River in southern Lebanon. Despite fierce resistance by Syrian-backed forces, the Lebanese army was able to hold the lines and maintain the defensive perimeter around Beirut. In the year that our marines have been there Lebanon has made important steps toward stability and order. The physical presence of the marines lends support to both the Lebanese government and its army. It allows the hard work of diplomacy to go forward. Indeed without peacekeepers from the U.S., France, Italy, and Britain, the efforts to find a peaceful solution in Lebanon would collapse.

As for that narrower question, what exactly is the operational mission of the marines, the answer is to secure a piece of Beirut; to keep order in their sector and to prevent the area from becoming a battlefield. Our marines are not just sitting in an airport. Part of their task is to guard that airport. Because of their presence the airport has remained operational. In addition they patrol the surrounding area. This is their part—a limited but essential part—in a larger effort that I described.

If our marines must be there, I'm asked, why can't we make them safer? Who committed this latest atrocity against them and why? Well, we'll do everything we can to insure that our men are as safe as possible. We ordered the battleship New Jersey to join our naval forces offshore. Without even firing them, the threat of its 16-inch guns silenced those who once fired down on our marines from the hills. And they're a good part of the reason we suddenly had a cease-fire. We're doing our best to make our forces less vulnerable to those who want to snipe at them or send in future suicide missions.

Secretary Shultz called me today from Europe, where he was meeting with the foreign ministers of our allies, and the multinational force. They remain committed to our task, and plans were made to share information as to how we can improve security for all our men.

We have strong circumstantial evidence that the attack on the marines was directed by terrorists who used the same method to destroy our embassy in Beirut. Those who directed this atrocity must be dealt justice, and they will be. The obvious purpose behind the sniping and now this attack was to weaken American will and force the withdrawal of U.S. and French forces from Lebanon.

The clear intent of the terrorists was to limit our support of the Lebanese government and to destroy the ability of the Lebanese people to determine their own destiny. To answer those who ask if we're serving any purpose in being there, let me answer a question with a question: would the terrorists have launched their suicide attacks against the multinational force if it were not doing its job?

The multinational force was attacked precisely because it is doing the job it was sent to do in Beirut. It is accomplishing its mission.

Now then, where do we go from here?

What can we do now to help Lebanon gain greater stability so that our marines can come home? I believe we can take three steps now that will make a difference.

First, we will accelerate the search for peace and stability in that region. Little attention is being paid to the fact that we have had special envoys there working literally around the clock to bring the warring factions together. This coming Monday in Geneva President Gemayel of Lebanon will sit down with other factions from his country to see if national reconciliation can be achieved. He has our firm support.

I will soon be announcing a replacement for Bud McFarlane who was preceded by Phil Habib. Both worked tirelessly and must be credited for much, if not most, of the progress we've made.

Second, we'll work even more closely with our allies in providing support for the government of Lebanon and for the rebuilding of a national consensus.

Third, we will insure that the multinational peacekeeping forces, our marines, are given the greatest possible protection. Our commandant of the marine corps, General Kelley, returned from Lebanon today and will be advising us on steps we can take to improve security.

Vice President Bush returned just last night from Beirut and gave me a full report of his brief visit.

Beyond our progress in Lebanon let us remember that our main goal and purpose is to achieve a broader peace in all of the Middle East. The factions and bitterness that we see in Lebanon are just a microcosm of the difficulties that are spread across much of that region. A peace initiative for the entire Middle East, consistent with the Camp David accord, and UN Resolutions 242 and 338, still offers the best hope for bringing peace to the region.

Let me ask those who say we should get out of Lebanon: If we were to leave Lebanon now, what message would that send to those who foment instability and terrorism? If Americans were to walk away from Lebanon, what chance would there be for a negotiated settlement producing the unified, democratic Lebanon? If we turned our backs on Lebanon now, what would be the future of Israel? At stake is the fate of only the second Arab country to negotiate a major agreement with Israel. That's another accomplishment of this past year, the May 17 accord signed by Lebanon and Israel.

If terrorism and intimidation succeed, it'll be a devastating blow to the peace process and to Israel's search for genuine security. It won't just be Lebanon sentenced to a future of chaos. Can the United States, or the free world, for that matter, stand by and see the Middle East incorporated into the Soviet bloc? What of Western Europe and Japan's dependence on Middle East oil for the energy to fuel their industries? The Middle East is, as I said, vital to our national security and economic well-being.

Brave young men have been taken from us. Many others have been grievously wounded. Are we to tell them their sacrifice was wasted or that they gave their lives in defense of our national security every bit as much as any man who ever died fighting in a war?

We must not strip every ounce of meaning and purpose from their courageous sacrifice. We are a nation with global responsibilities, we're not somewhere else in the world protecting someone else's interest. We're there protecting our own.

I received a message from the father of a marine in Lebanon. He told me: "In a world where we speak of human rights, there is a sad lack of acceptance of responsibility. My son has chosen the acceptance of responsibility for the privilege of living in this country."

Certainly in this country one does not inherently have rights unless the responsibility for these rights is accepted.

Dr. Kenneth Morrison said that while he was waiting to learn if his son was one of the dead. I was thrilled for him to learn today that his son, Ross, is alive and well and carrying on his duties in Lebanon.

Let us meet our responsibilities. For longer than any of us can remember, the people of the Middle East have lived from war to war with no prospect for any other future. That dreadful cycle must be broken.

Why are we there? Well, a Lebanese mother told one of our ambassadors that her little girl had only attended school two of the last eight years. Now, because of our presence there, she said her daughter could live a normal life. With patience and firmness we can help bring peace to that strife-torn region and make our own lives more secure.

Our role is to help the Lebanese put their country together, not to do it for them.

Now I know another part of the world is very much on our minds. A place much closer to our shores. Grenada. The island is only twice the size of the District of Columbia with a total population of about 110,000 people. Grenada and a half-dozen other Caribbean islands here were, until recently, British colonies. They are not independent states and members of the British Commonwealth.

While they respect each other's independence they also feel a kinship with each other and think of themselves as one people. In 1979 trouble came to Grenada. Maurice Bishop, a protégé of Fidel Castro, staged a military coup and overthrew the government which had been elected under the constitution left to the people by the British.

He sought the help of Cuba in building an airport, which he claimed was for tourist trade, but which looked suspiciously suitable for military aircraft, including Soviet-built long-range bombers. The six sovereign countries and one remaining colony are joined together in what they call the Organization of Eastern Caribbean States. The six became increasingly alarmed as Bishop built an army greater than all of theirs combined.

Obviously it was not purely for defense. In this last year or so, Prime Minister Bishop gave indications that he might like better relations with the United States. He even made a trip to our country and met with senior officials at the White House and the State Department. Whether he was serious or not we'll never know.

On October 12, a small group of his militia seized him and put him under arrest. They were, if anything, even more radical and more devoted to Castro's Cuba than he had been. Several days later, a crowd of citizens appeared before Bishop's home, freed him, and escorted him toward the headquarters of the Military Council. They were fired upon. A number, including some children, were killed and Bishop was seized. He and several members of his cabinet were subsequently executed and a 24-hour shoot-to-kill curfew was put in effect. Grenada was without a government, its only authority exercised by a self-proclaimed band of military men.

There were then about 1,000 of our citizens on Grenada, 800 of them students in St. George's University Medical School. Concern that they'd be harmed or held as hostages, I ordered a flotilla of ships then on its way to Lebanon with marines—part of our regular rotation program—to circle south on a course that would put them somewhere in the vicinity of Grenada in case there should be a need to evacuate our people.

Last weekend I was awakened in the early morning hours and told that six members of the Organization of Eastern Caribbean States joined by Jamaica and Barbados had sent an urgent request that we join them in a military operation to restore order and democracy to Grenada.

They were proposing this action under the terms of a treaty, a mutual assistance pact that existed among them. These small peaceful nations needed our help. Three of them don't have armies at all and the others have very limited forces.

The legitimacy of their request plus my own concern for our citizens dictated my decision. I believe our government has a responsibility to go to the aid of its citizens if their right to life and liberty is threatened. The nightmare of our hostages in Iran must never be repeated.

We knew we had little time and that complete secrecy was vital to insure both the safety of the young men who would undertake this mission and the Americans they were about to rescue.

The joint chiefs worked around the clock to come up with a plan. They had little intelligence information about conditions on the island. We had to assume that several hundred Cubans working on the airport could be military reserves. As it turned out the number was much larger, and they were a military force. Six hundred of them have been taken prisoner, and we have discovered a complete base with weapons and communications equipment, which makes it clear a Cuban occupation of the island had been planned.

Two hours ago we released the first photos from Grenada. They included pictures of a warehouse of military equipment—one of three we've uncovered so far. This warehouse contained weapons and ammunition stacked almost to the ceiling, enough to supply thousands of terrorists.

Grenada, we were told, was a friendly island paradise for tourism. Well it wasn't. It was a Soviet-Cuban colony being readied as a major military bastion to export terror and undermine democracy.

We got there just in time.

I can't say enough in praise of our military. Army rangers and paratroopers, navy, marine, and air force personnel, those who planned a brilliant campaign and those who carried it out.

Almost instantly our military seized the two airports, secured the campus where most of our students were, and they're now in the mopping-up phase.

It should be noted that in all the planning, a top priority was to minimize risk, to avoid casualties to our own men and also the Grenadian forces as much as humanly possible. But there were casualties. And we all owe a debt to those who lost their lives or were wounded. They were few in number but even one is a tragic price to pay.

It's our intention to get our men out as soon as possible.

Prime Minister Eugenia Charles of Dominica—I called that wrong, she pronounces it Dom-in-EEE-kuh—she is chairman of OECS She's calling for help from Commonwealth nations in giving the people their right to establish a constitutional government on Grenada. We anticipate that the governor general, a Grenadian, will participate in setting up a provisional government in the interim.

The events in Lebanon and Grenada, though oceans apart, are closely related. Not only has Moscow assisted and encouraged the violence in both countries, but it provides direct support through a network of surrogates and terrorists. It is no coincidence that when the thugs tried to wrest control of Grenada, there were 30 Soviet advisers and hundreds of Cuban military and paramilitary forces on the island. At the moment of our landing we communicated with the governments of Cuba and the Soviet Union and told them we would offer shelter and security to their people on Grenada. Regrettably, Castro ordered his men to fight to the death and some did. The others will be sent to their homelands.

Now there was a time when our national security was based on a standing army here within our own borders and shore, batteries of artillery along our coast, and of course a navy to keep the sea-lanes open for the shipping of things necessary to our well-being. The world has changed. Today our national security can be threatened in faraway places. It's up to all of us to be aware of the strategic importance of such places and to be able to identify them.

Sam Rayburn once said that freedom is not something a nation can work for once and win forever. He said it's like an insurance policy; its premiums must be kept up-to-date. In order to keep it we have to keep working for it and sacrificing for it just as long as we live. If we do not, our children may not know the pleasure of working to keep it for it may not be theirs to keep.

In these last few days, I've been more sure than I've ever been that we Americans of today will keep freedom and maintain peace. I've been made to feel that by the magnificent spirit of our young men and women in uniform, and by something here in our nation's capital.

In this city, where political strife is so much a part of our lives, I've seen Democratic leaders in the Congress join their Republican colleagues, send a message to the world that we're all Americans before we're anything else, and when our country is threatened, we stand shoulder to shoulder in support of men and women in the armed forces.

May I share something with you I think you'd like to know? It's something that happened to the commandant of our marine corps, General Paul Kelley, while he was visiting our critically injured marines in an air force hospital. It says more than any of us could ever hope to say about the gallantry and heroism of these young men, young men who served so willingly so that others might have a chance at peace and freedom in their own lives and in the life of their country.

I'll let General Kelley's words describe the incident. He spoke of a "young marine with more tubes going in and out of his body than I have ever seen in one body. He couldn't see very well. He reached up and grabbed my four stars just to make sure I was who I said I was. He held my hand with a firm grip. He was making signals and we realized he wanted to to tell me something. We put a pad of paper in his hand and he wrote, 'semper fi.'"

Well, if you've been a marine, or if, like myself, you're an admirer of the marines, you know those words are a battle cry, a greeting, and a legend in the marine corps. They're marine shorthand for the motto of the corps: Semper Fidelis, Always Faithful.

General Kelley has a reputation for being a very sophisticated general and a very tough marine, but he cried when he saw those words, and who can blame him. That marine, and all those like him living and dead, have been faithful to their ideals. They've given willingly of themselves so that a nearly defenseless people in a region of great strategic importance to the free world will have a chance someday to live lives free of murder and mayhem and terrorism. I think that young marine and all of his comrades have given every one of us something to live up to.

They were not afraid to stand up for their country or no matter how difficult and slow the journey might be, to give to others that last best hope of a better future.

We cannot and will not dishonor them now and the sacrifices they made by failing to remain as faithful to the cause of freedom and the pursuit of peace as they have been.

I will not ask you to pray for the dead because they are safe in God's loving arms and beyond need of our prayers.

I would like to ask you all, wherever you may be in this blessed land, to pray for these wounded young men and to pray for the bereaved families of those who gave their lives for our freedom.

God bless you and God bless America.

Terrorist States

Washington, D.C.

July 7, 1985

STUNG BY a sharp increase in terrorist acts against Americans, especially in the Middle East, Reagan spoke out against "a confederation of terrorist states," including Libya, Nicaragua, Cuba, North Korea, and the Soviet Union, accusing them of "acts of war against the government and people of the United States." The threat of retaliation that he delivered in this speech before the American Bar Association had no immediate effect on the accused states. Indeed, the pugnacity of these remarks contrasted sharply with the administration's obvious inability to protect citizens abroad. Nine months later, in April 1986, U.S. planes bombed Tripoli in retaliation for a terrorist incident in West Germany, apparently with the intention of killing Libya's leader, Col. Muammar Qaddafi, a vociferous supporter of anti-American terrorism.

My purpose today goes even beyond our concern over the recent outrages in Beirut, El Salvador—or the Air-India tragedy, the Narita bombing, or the Jordanian Airlines hijacking. We must look beyond these events because I feel it is vital not to allow them, as terrible as they are, to obscure an even larger and darker terrorist menace.

There is a temptation to see the terrorist act as simply an erratic work of a small group of fanatics. We make this mistake at great peril; for the attacks on America, her citizens, her allies, and other democratic nations in recent years do form a pattern of terrorism that has strategic implications and political goals. And only by moving our focus from the tactical to the strategic perspective, only by identifying the pattern of terror and those behind it, can we hope to put into force a strategy to deal with it.

In recent years, the Mideast has been one principal point of focus for these attacks, attacks directed at the United States, Israel, France, Jordan, and the United Kingdom. Beginning in the summer of 1984 and culminating in January and February of this year, there was also a series of apparently coordinated attacks and assassinations by left-wing terrorist groups in Belgium, West Germany, and France—attacks directed against American and NATO installations or military and industrial officials of those nations.

Now what do we know about the sources of those attacks and the whole pattern of terrorist assaults in recent years? In 1983 alone, the Central Intelligence Agency either confirmed or found strong evidence of Iranian involvement in 57 terrorist attacks. While most of these attacks occurred in Lebanon, an increase in activity by terrorists sympathetic to Iran was seen throughout Europe: Spain and France have such incidents, and in Italy, seven pro-Iranian Lebanese students were arrested for plotting an attack on the U.S. Embassy, and this violence continues.

It will not surprise any of you to know that, in addition to Iran, we have identified another nation, Libya, as deeply involved in terrorism. We have evidence which links Libyan agents or surrogates to at least 25 incidents last year.

Colonel Qaddafi's outrages against civilized conduct are, of course, as infamous as those of the Ayatollah Khomeini: The gunning down last year—from inside the Libyan Embassy—of a British policewoman is only one of many examples.

Since September 1984, Iranian-backed terrorist groups have been responsible for almost 30 attacks, and, most recently, the Egyptian government aborted a Libyan-backed plot to bomb our embassy in Cairo. It was this pattern of state-approved assassination and terrorism by Libya that led the United States, a few years ago to expel Libyan diplomats and has forced other nations to take similar steps since then.

Now three other governments, along with Iran and Libya, are actively supporting a campaign of international terrorism against the United States, her allies, and moderate Third World states.

First, North Korea. The extent and crudity of North Korean violence against the United States and our ally, South Korea, are a matter of record. Our aircraft have been shot down;

our servicemen have been murdered in border incidents; and two years ago, four members of the South Korean cabinet were blown up in a bombing in Burma by North Korean terrorists— a failed attempt to assassinate President Chun. This incident was just one more of an unending series of attacks directed against the Republic of Korea by North Korea.

What is not readily known or understood is North Korea's wider links to the international terrorist network: There is no time today to recount all of North Korea's efforts to foster separatism, violence, and subversion in other lands well beyond its immediate borders; but to cite one example: North Korea's efforts to spread separatism and terrorism in the free and prosperous nation of Sri Lanka are a deep and continuing source of tension in South Asia.

And this is not even to mention North Korea's involvement here in our own hemisphere, including a secret arms agreement with the former Communist government in Grenada. I will also have something to say about North Korea's involvement in Central America in a moment.

And then there is Cuba, a nation whose government has since the 1960s, openly armed, trained, and directed terrorists operating on at least three continents.

This has occurred in Latin America; the OAS has repeatedly passed sanctions against Castro for sponsoring terrorism in places and countries too numerous to mention. This has also occurred in Africa; President Carter openly accused the Castro government of supporting and training Katangan terrorists from Angola in their attacks on Zaire.

And even in the Middle East, Castro himself has acknowledged that he actively assisted the Sandinistas in the early '70s when they were training in the Middle East with terrorist factions of the PLO.

And finally, there is the latest partner of Iran, Libya, North Korea, and Cuba in a campaign of international terror—the Communist regime in Nicaragua. The Sandinistas not only sponsor terror in El Salvador, Costa Rica, and Honduras—terror that led recently to the murder of four U.S. marines, two civilians, and seven Latin Americans—they provide one of the world's principal refuges for international terrorists.

Members of the Italian government have openly charged that Nicaragua is harboring some of Italy's worst terrorists; and we have evidence that in addition to Italy's Red Brigades, other elements of the world's most vicious terrorist groups—West Germany's Baader-Meinhof gang; the Basque ETA; the PLO; the Tupamaros; and the IRA—have found a haven in Nicaragua and support from that country's Communist dictatorship.

During his state visit to North Korea, Nicaragua's Sandinista leader Daniel Ortega heard Kim Il Sung say this about the mutual objectives of North Korea and Nicaragua: "if the peoples of the revolutionary countries of the world put pressure on and deal blows at U.S. imperialism in all places where it stretches its talons of aggression, they will make it powerless and impossible to behave as dominator any longer."

And Colonel Qaddafi, who has a formal alliance with North Korea, echoed Kim Il Sung's words, when he laid out the agenda for the terrorist network: "We must force America to fight on 100 fronts all over the earth. We must force it to fight in Lebanon, to fight in Chad, to fight in Sudan, and to fight in El Salvador."

So there we have it, Iran, Libya, North Korea, Cuba, Nicaragua—continents away, tens of thousands of miles apart—but the same goals and objectives.

I submit to you that the growth in terrorism in recent years results from the increasing involvement of these states in terrorism in every region of the world. This is terrorism that is part of a pattern—the work of a confederation of terrorist states.

Most of the terrorists who are kidnapping and murdering American citizens and attacking American installations are being trained, financed, and directly or indirectly controlled by a core group of radical and totalitarian governments, a new, international version of Murder Inc.—and all of these states are united by one simple, criminal phenomenon—their fanatical hatred of the United States, our people, our way of life, our international stature.

And the strategic purpose behind the terrorism sponsored by these outlaw states is clear: to disorient the United States, to disrupt or alter our foreign policy, to sow discord between ourselves and our allies, to frighten friendly Third World nations working with us for peaceful settlements of regional conflicts and, finally, to remove American influence from those areas of the world where we are working to bring stable and democratic government.

In short, to cause us to retreat, retrench, to become "Fortress America." Yes, their real goal is to expel America from the world.

That is the real reason these terrorist nations are arming, training, and supporting attacks against this nation. And that is why we can be clear on one point; these terrorist states are now engaged in acts of war against the government and people of the United States. And under international law, any state which is the victim of acts of war has the right to defend itself.

The American people are not—I repeat, not—going to tolerate intimidation, terror, and outright acts of war against this nation and its people. And we are especially not going to tolerate these attacks from outlaw states run by the strangest collection of misfits, Looney Tunes, and squalid criminals since the advent of the Third Reich.

Do not for a moment think that this discussion has been all-inclusive. First of all—though their strength does not match that of the groups supported by the terrorist network I have already mentioned—there are some terrorist organizations that are indigenous to certain localities or countries which are not necessarily tied to this international network.

And second, the countries I have mentioned today are not necessarily the only ones that support terrorism against the United States and its allies. Those which I have described are simply ones that can be most directly implicated.

Now, the question of the Soviet Union's close relationship with almost all of the terrorist states I have mentioned and the implications of these Soviet ties on bilateral relations with the United States and other democratic nations must be recognized.

So, too, Secretary of State Shultz in his speech of June 24 of last year openly raised the question of Soviet support for terrorist organizations, as did Secretary Haig before him.

Now much needs to be done by all of us in the community of civilized nations. We must act against the criminal menace of terrorism with the full weight of the law— both domestic and international. We will act to indict, apprehend, and prosecute those who commit the kind of atrocities the world has witnessed in recent weeks.

We can act together as free peoples who wish not to see our citizens kidnapped, or shot, or blown out of the skies—just as we acted together to rid the seas of piracy at the turn of the last century. There can be no place on earth left where it is safe for these monsters to rest, or train, or practice their cruel and deadly skills. We must act together, or unilaterally if necessary, to ensure that terrorists have no sanctuary— anywhere.

The United Nations' 40th Anniversary

New York City, New York

October 24, 1985

REAGAN never had a high regard for the United Nations, calling it morally bankrupt in 1971 and recommending U.S. withdrawal from the organization several times in the late 1970s. As president, Reagan backed a plan to quit UNESCO, the UN's cultural arm, which the administration claimed had become "politicized," and refused to sign the Law of the Seas treaty even after years of difficult negotiations. The president's speech to the General Assembly on the occasion of the UN's 40th anniversary began with criticism of the world body, then continued in the pattern of his domestic speeches: quick points for a treasured domestic program (the SDI), an attack on the Soviet Union, a vague plan for further action (the peace proposals), and a life-affirming anecdote to uplift his listeners at the end.

Forty years ago, the world awoke daring to believe hatred's unyielding grip had finally been broken, daring to believe the torch of peace would be protected in liberty's firm grasp.

Forty years ago, the world yearned to dream again innocent dreams, to believe in ideals with innocent trust. Dreams of trust are worthy, but in these 40 years too many dreams have been shattered, too many promises have been broken, too many lives have been lost. The painful truth is that the use of violence to take, to exercise, and to preserve power remains a persistent reality in much of the world.

The vision of the UN Charter—to spare succeeding generations this scourge of war—remains real. It still stirs our souls and warms our hearts. But it also demands of us a realism that is rock-hard, clear-eyed, steady and sure, a realism that understands the nations of the United Nations are not united.

I come before you this morning preoccupied with peace, with insuring that the differences between some of us not be permitted to degenerate into open conflict. And I come offering from my own country a new commitment, a fresh start.

On this UN anniversary we acknowledge its successes: the decisive action during the Korean War, negotiation of the Nonproliferation Treaty, strong support for decolonization, and the laudable achievements by the United Nations High Commissioner for Refugees.

Nor must we close our eyes to this organization's disappointments: its failure to deal with real security issues, the total inversion of morality in the infamous Zionism-is-racism resolution. . . . We recognize that. But let us remember: from those first days, one guiding star was supposed to light our path toward the UN vision of peace and progress—the star of freedom.

What kind of people will we be 40 years from today? May we answer: free people, worthy of freedom and firm in the conviction that freedom is not the sole prerogative of a chosen few, but the universal right of all God's children.

This is the Universal Declaration of Human Rights set forth in 1948. And this is the affirming flame the United States has held high to a watching world. We champion freedom not only because it is practical and beneficial, but because it is morally right and just.

Free people, whose governments rest upon the consent of the governed, do not wage war on their neighbors. Free people, blessed by economic opportunity, and protected by laws that respect the dignity of the individual, are not driven toward the domination of others.

We readily acknowledge that the United States is far from perfect. Yet we have endeavored earnestly to carry out our responsibilities to the Charter these past 40 years, and we take national pride in our contributions to peace.

We take pride in 40 years of helping avert a new world war and pride in our alliances that protect and preserve us and our friends from aggression. We take pride in the Camp David agreements and our efforts for peace in the Middle East rooted in Resolutions 242 and 338; in supporting Pakistan, target of outside intimidation; in assisting El Salvador's struggle to carry forward its democratic revolution; in answering the appeal of our Caribbean friends in Grenada; in seeing Grenada's representative here today, voting the will of its own people. And we take pride in our proposals to reduce the weapons of war.

We submit this history as evidence of our sincerity of purpose. But today it is more important to speak to you about what my country proposes to do in these closing years of the 20th century, to bring about a safer, a more peaceful, a more civilized world.

Let us begin with candor, with words that rest on plain and simple facts. The differences between America and the Soviet Union are deep and abiding.

The United States is a democratic nation. Here the people rule. We build no walls to keep them in, nor organize any system of police to keep them mute. We occupy no country. The only land abroad we occupy is beneath the grave where our heroes rest. What is called the West is a voluntary association of free nations, all of whom fiercely value their independence and their sovereignty. And as deeply as we cherish our beliefs, we do not seek to compel others to share them.

When we enjoy these vast freedoms as we do, it's difficult for us to understand the restrictions of dictatorships which seek to control each institution and every fact of the people's lives, the expression of their beliefs, their movements, and their contacts with the outside world. It's difficult for us to understand the ideological premise that force is an acceptable way to expand a political system.

Americans do not accept that any government has the right to command and order the lives of its people, that any nation has a, an historic right to use force to export its ideology. This belief, regarding the nature of man and the limitations of government, is at the core of our deep and abiding differences with the Soviet Union, differences that put us into natural conflict and competition with one another.

Now, we would welcome enthusiastically a true competition of ideas, welcome a competition of economic strength and scientific and artistic creativity, and yes, welcome a competition for the goodwill of the world's people. But we cannot accommodate ourselves to the use of force and subversion to consolidate and expand the reach of totalitarianism.

When Mr. Gorbachev and I meet in Geneva next month, I look to a fresh start in the relationship of our two nations. We can and should meet in the spirit that we can deal with our differences peacefully. That is what we expect.

The only way to resolve differences is to understand them. We must have candid and complete discussions of where dangers exist and where peace is being disrupted. Make no mistake; our policy of open and vigorous competition rests on a realistic view of the world. And therefore, at Geneva, we must review the reasons for the current level of mistrust.

For example, in 1972 the international community negotiated in good faith a ban on biological and toxin weapons; in 1975 we negotiated the Helsinki accords on human rights and freedoms; and during the decade just past, the United States and the Soviet Union negotiated several agreements on strategic weapons. And yet, we feel it will be necessary at Geneva to discuss with the Soviet Union what we believe are violations of a number of the provisions in all of these agreements. Indeed, this is why it is important that we have this opportunity to air our differences through face-to-face meetings, to let frank talk substitute for anger and tension.

The United States has never sought treaties merely to paper over differences. We continue to believe that a nuclear war is one that cannot be won and must never be fought. And that is why we have sought, for nearly 10 years, still seek, and will discuss in Geneva radical, equitable, verifiable reductions in these vast arsenals of offensive nuclear weapons.

At the beginning of the latest round of the ongoing negotiations in Geneva, the Soviet Union presented a specific proposal involving numerical values. We are studying the Soviet counterproposal carefully. I believe that within their proposal there are seeds which we should nurture, and in the coming weeks we will seek to establish a genuine process of give and take.

The United States is also seeking to discuss with the Soviet Union in Geneva the vital relationship between offensive and defensive systems, including the possibility of moving toward a more stable and secure world in which defenses play a growing role.

The ballistic missile is the most awesome, threatening, and destructive weapon in the history of man. Thus, I welcome the interest of the new Soviet leadership in the reduction of offensive strategic forces. Ultimately, we must remove this menace, once and for all, from the face of the earth.

Until that day, the United States seeks to escape the prison of mutual terror by research and testing that could, in time, enable us to neutralize the threat of these ballistic missiles and, ultimately, render them obsolete.

How is Moscow threatened if the capitals of other nations are protected? We do not ask that the Soviet leaders—whose country has suffered so much from war—to leave their people defenseless against foreign attack. Why then do they insist that we remain undefended? Who is threatened if Western research and Soviet research that is itself well advanced should develop a nonnuclear system which would threaten not human beings, but only ballistic missiles?

Surely, the world will sleep more secure when these missiles have been rendered useless, militarily and politically, when the Sword of Damocles that has hung over our planet for too many decades is lifted by Western and Russian scientists working to shield their citizens and one day shut down space as an avenue of weapons of mass destruction.

If we're destined by history to compete, militarily, to keep the peace, then let us compete in systems that defend our societies rather than weapons which can destroy us both, and much of God's creation along with us.

Some 18 years ago, then-Premier Aleksei Kosygin was asked about a moratorium on the development of an antimissile defense system. The official news agency, Tass, reported that he replied with these words:

"I believe that defensive systems, which prevent attack, are not the cause of the arms race, but constitute a factor preventing the death of people. Maybe an antimissile system is more expensive than an offensive system, but it is designed not to kill people but to preserve human lives." Quoting Aleksei Kosygin.

Preserving lives. No peace is more fundamental than that. Great obstacles lie ahead, but they should not deter us. Peace is God's commandment. Peace is the holy shadow cast by men treading on the path of virtue.

But just as we all know what peace is, we certainly know what peace is not.

A peace based on repression cannot be true peace and is secure only when individuals are free to direct their own governments.

Peace based on partition cannot be true peace. Put simply: Nothing can justify the continuing and permanent division of the European continent. Walls of partition and distrust must give way to greater communication for an open world. Before leaving for Geneva, I shall make new proposals to achieve this goal.

Peace based on mutual fear cannot be true peace because staking our future on a precarious balance of terror is not good enough. The world needs a balance of safety.

And finally, a peace based on averting our eyes from trouble cannot be true peace. The consequences of conflict are every bit as tragic when the destruction is contained within one country.

Real peace is what we seek, and that is why today the United States is presenting an initiative that addresses what will be a central issue in Geneva: the issue of regional conflicts in Africa, Asia and Central America.

Our own position is clear: As the oldest nation of the New World, as the first anti-colonial power, the United States rejoiced when decolonization gave birth to so many new nations after World War II. We have always supported the right of the people of each nation to define their own destiny. We have given $300 billion since 1945 to help people of other countries. And we've tried to help friendly governments defend against aggression, subversion and terror.

We have noted with great interest similar expressions of peaceful intent by leaders of the Soviet Union. I am not here to challenge the good faith of what they say. But isn't it important for us to weigh the record, as well?

In Afghanistan, there are 118,000 Soviet troops prosecuting war against the Afghan people.

In Cambodia, 140,000 Soviet-backed Vietnamese soldiers wage a war of occupation.

In Ethiopia, 1,700 Soviet advisers are involved in military planning and support operations along with 2,500 Cuban combat troops.

In Angola, 1,200 Soviet military advisers involved in planning and supervising combat operations, along with 35,000 Cuban troops.

In Nicaragua, some 8,000 Soviet bloc and Cuban personnel, including about 3,500 military and secret police personnel.

All of these conflicts, some of them under way for a decade, originate in local disputes but they share a common characteristic: they are the consequence of an ideology imposed from without, dividing nations and creating regimes that are, almost from the day they take power, at war with their own people. And in each case, Marxism-Leninism's war with the people becomes war with their neighbors.

These wars are exacting a staggering human toll and threaten to spill across national boundaries and trigger dangerous confrontations. Where is it more appropriate than right here at the United Nations to call attention to Article 2 of our Charter, which instructs members to refrain "from the use, or threat of use of force against the territorial integrity or political independence of any state"?

During the past decade these wars played a large role in building suspicions and tensions in my country over the purpose of Soviet policy. This gives us an extra reason to address them seriously today.

Last year I proposed from this podium that the United States and Soviet Union hold discussions on some of these issues, and we have done so. But I believe these problems need more than talk.

For that reason, we are proposing, and are fully committed to support, a regional peace process that seeks progress on three levels:

First, we believe the starting point must be a process of negotiation among the warring parties in each country I've mentioned, which, in the case of Afghanistan, includes the Soviet Union. The form of these talks may and should vary, but negotiations and an improvement of internal political conditions are essential to achieving an end to violence, the withdrawal of foreign troops and national reconciliation.

There is a second level: Once negotiations take hold and the parties directly involved are making real progress, representatives of the United States and the Soviet Union should sit down together. It is not for us to impose any solutions in this separate set of talks. Such solutions would not last. But the issue we should address is how best to support the ongoing talks among the warring parties. In some cases, it might well be appropriate to consider guarantees for any agreements already reached. But in every case the primary task is to promote this goal: verified elimination of the foreign military presence and restraint on the flow of outside arms.

And finally, if these first two steps are successful, we could move on to the third;

welcoming each country back into the world economy so its citizens can share in the dynamic growth that other developing countries, countries that are at peace, enjoy. Despite past differences with these regimes, the United States would respond generously to their democratic reconciliation with their own people, their respect for human rights, and their return to the family of free nations.

Of course, until such time as these negotiations result in definitive progress America's support for struggling democratic resistance forces must not and shall not cease.

This plan is bold. It is realistic, it is not a substitute for existing peacemaking efforts; it complements them. We're not trying to solve every conflcit in every region of the globe, and we recognize that each conflict has its own character. Naturally other regional problems will require different approaches. But we believe that the recurrent pattern of conflict that we see in these five cases ought to be broken as soon as possible.

We must begin somewhere, so let us begin where there is great need and great hope. This will be a clear step forward to help people choose their future more freely. Moreover, this is an extraordinary opportunity for the Soviet side to make a contribution to regional peace which in turn can promote future dialogue and negotiations on other critical issues.

With hard work and imagination, there is no limit to what, working together, our nations can achieve. Gaining a peaceful resolution of these conflicts will open whole new vistas of peace and progress, the discovery that the promise of the future lies not in measures of military defense, or the control of weapons, but in the expansion of individual freedom and human rights.

Only when the human spirit can worship, create, and build, only when people are given a personal stake in determining their own destiny and benefiting from their own risks do societies become prosperous, progressive, dynamic and free. We need only open our eyes to the economic evidence all around us. Nations that deny their people opportunity, in Eastern Europe, Indochina, southern Africa, and Latin America, without exception are dropping further behind in the race for the future.

But where we see enlightened leaders who understand that economic freedom and personal incentive are key to development, we see economies striding forward. Singapore, Taiwan and South Korea, India, Botswana, and China. These are among the current and emerging success stories because they have the courage to give economic incentives a chance.

Let us all heed the simple eloquence in Andrei Sakharov's Nobel Peace Prize message: "International trust, mutual understanding, disarmament, and international security are inconceivable without an open society with freedom of conscience, the right to publish, and the right to travel and choose the country in which one wishes to live."

At the core, this is an eternal truth. Freedom works. That is the promise of the open world and awaits only our collective grasp. Forty years ago, hope came alive again for a world that hungered for hope. I believe fervently that hope is still alive.

The United States has spoken with candor and conviction today, but that does not lessen these strong feelings held by every American: It's in the nature of Americans to hate war and its destructiveness. We would rather wage our struggle to rebuild and renew, not to tear down. We would rather fight against hunger, disease, and catastrophe. We would rather engage our adversaries in the battle of ideals and ideas for the future.

These principles emerge from the innate openness and good character of our people. And from our long struggle and sacrifice for our liberties and the liberties of others. Americans always yearn for peace. They have a passion for life. They carry in their hearts a deep capacity for reconciliation.

Last year at this General Assembly, I indicated there was every reason for the United States and the Soviet Union to shorten the distance between us. In Geneva, the first meeting between our heads of government in more than six years, Mr. Gorbachev and I will have that opportunity.

So, yes, let us go to Geneva with both sides committed to dialogue. Let both sides go committed to a world with fewer nuclear weapons and some day with none. Let both sides go committed to walk together on a safer path into the 21st century and to lay the foundation for enduring peace.

It is time, indeed to do more than just talk of a better world. It is time to act. And we will act when nations cease to try to impose their ways upon others. And we will act when they

realize that we, for whom the achievement of freedom has come dear, will do what we must to preserve it from assault.

America is committed to the world because so much of the world is inside America. After all, only a few miles from this very room is our Statue of Liberty, past which life began anew for millions, where the peoples from nearly every country in this had joined to build these United States.

The blood of each nation courses through the American vein, and feeds the spirits that compel us to involve ourselves in the fate of this good earth. It is the same spirit that warms our heart in concern to help ease the desperate hunger that grip proud people on the African continent.

It is the internationalist spirit that came together last month when our neighbor, Mexico, was struck suddenly by an earthquake. Even as the Mexican nation moved vigorously into action, there were heartwarming offers by other nations offering to help and glimpses of people working together, without concern for national self-interest or gain.

And if there was any meaning to salvage out of that tragedy, it was found one day in a huge mound of rubble that was once the Juarez Hospital in Mexico City.

A week after that terrible event and as another day of despair unfolded, a team of workers heard a faint sound coming from somewhere in the heart of the crushed concrete. Hoping beyond hope, they quickly burrowed toward it.

And as the late afternoon light faded, and racing against time, they found what they had heard and the first of three baby girls—newborn infants—emerged to the safety of the rescue team.

And let me tell you the scene through the eyes of one who was there. "Everyone was so quiet when they lowered that little baby down in a basket covered with blankets. The baby didn't make a sound, either. But the minute they put her in the Red Cross ambulance everybody just got up and cheered."

Well, amidst all that hopelessness and debris came a timely—and timeless—lesson for us all. We witnessed the miracle of life.

It is on this that I believe our nations can make a renewed commitment. The miracle of life is given by one greater than ourselves. But once given, each life is ours to nurture and preserve, to foster not only for today's world but for a better one to come.

There is no purpose more noble than for us to sustain and celebrate life in a turbulent world. And that is what we must do now. We have no higher duty, no greater cause as humans. Life and the preservation of freedom to live it in dignity is what we are on this earth do to.

Everything we work to achieve must seek that end so that some day our prime ministers, our premiers, our presidents and our general secretaries will talk not of war and peace, but only of peace.

We've had 40 years to begin. Let us not waste one more moment to give back to the world all that we can in return for this miracle of life.

Thank you all. God bless you all.

The *Challenger* Disaster

Washington, D.C.
January 28, 1986

PRESIDENT REAGAN'S 1986 State of the Union address, scheduled to be delivered on January 28, was preempted by the disaster that took place early that morning, when the space shuttle *Challenger* exploded off the coast of Florida barely a minute after it was launched. The accident took the lives of six astronauts and a civilian, schoolteacher Christa McAuliffe. Postponing his address to Congress, Reagan delivered instead a brief eulogy that consoled the nation in fatherly tones. He later appointed a commission of inquiry which concluded that NASA, trying to meet an overbooked schedule of launch dates, had relaxed its own safety regulations and had allowed the shuttle to take off in dangerously cold weather.

Ladies and Gentlemen, I'd planned to speak to you tonight to report on the state of the Union, but the events of earlier today have led me to change those plans. Today is a day for mourning and remembering. Nancy and I are pained to the core by the tragedy of the shuttle *Challenger*. We know we share this pain with all of the people of our country. This is truly a national loss.

Nineteen years ago, almost to the day, we lost three astronauts in a terrible accident on the ground. But, we've never lost an astronaut in flight; we've never had a tragedy like this. And perhaps we've forgotten the courage it took for the crew of the shuttle; but they, the *Challenger* Seven, were aware of the dangers but overcame them and did their jobs brilliantly. We mourn seven heroes: Michael Smith, Dick Scobee, Judith Resnik, Ronald McNair, Ellison Onizuka, Gregory Jarvis, and Christa McAuliffe. We mourn their loss as a nation together.

For the families of the seven, we cannot bear, as you do, the full impact of this tragedy. But we feel the loss, and we're thinking about you so very much. Your loved ones were daring and brave, and they had that special grace, that special spirit that says, "Give me a challenge and I'll meet it with joy." They had a hunger to explore the universe and discover its truths. They wished to serve, and they did. They served all of us.

We've grown used to wonders in this century. It's hard to dazzle us. But for 25 years the United States space program has been doing just that. We've grown used to the idea of space, and perhaps we forget that we've only just begun. We're still pioneers. They, the members of the *Challenger* crew, were pioneers.

And I want to say something to the schoolchildren of America who were watching the live coverage of the shuttle's takeoff. I know it is hard to understand, but sometimes painful things like this happen. It's all part of the process of exploration and discovery. It's all part of taking a chance and expanding man's horizons. The future doesn't belong to the fainthearted; it belongs to the brave. The *Challenger* crew was pulling us into the future, and we'll continue to follow them. . . .

There's a coincidence today. On this day 390 years ago, the great explorer Sir Francis Drake died aboard ship off the coast of Panama. In his lifetime the great frontiers were the oceans, and a historian later said, "He lived by the sea, died on it, and was buried in it." Well, today we can say of the *Challenger* crew: Their dedication was, like Drake's, complete.

The crew of the space shuttle *Challenger* honored us by the manner in which they lived their lives. We will never forget them, nor the last time we saw them, this morning, as they prepared for the journey and waved good-bye and "slipped the surly bonds of earth" to "touch the face of God."

The Iceland Summit

Washington, D.C.

October 13, 1986

THE PRESIDENT'S two summits with Mikhail Gorbachev in 1984 and 1986 were unproductive. Reagan refused to meet with a Soviet leader until late in his first term, and then, as Garry Wills has noted, he ensured that the press knew that substantial issues were not going to be discussed so that no one's hopes would be raised. The second summit, held in Reykjavik, Iceland, was a bona fide failure. The U.S. negotiators, apparently poorly prepared, could not come to grips with radical Soviet proposals for massive arms reductions, or follow through on Reagan's suggestion to eliminate all ballistic missiles over a fixed period. Nor could the Soviets, falling behind in strategic defense technology, accept Reagan's firm intention to test and deploy a Star Wars defense. So disappointing was the whole event that top Reagan aides, especially Secretary of State George Shultz, could not conceal their anger and dismay. (This was attributed by the White House to "fatigue.") In this national address, the president sought to deflect criticism of the summit, laying most of the blame for the lack of results on the Soviets (in a parallel statement, Gorbachev blamed the United States) and insisting that radical arms reductions were still possible.

Good evening. As most of you know, I have just returned from meetings in Iceland with the leader of the Soviet Union, General Secretary Gorbachev. As I did last year when I returned from the summit conference in Geneva, I want to take a few moments tonight to share with you what took place in these discussions.

The implications of these talks are enormous and only just beginning to be understood.

We proposed the most sweeping and generous arms control proposal in history. We offered the complete elimination of all ballistic missiles—Soviet and American— from the face of the earth by 1996. While we parted company with this American offer still on the table, we're closer than ever before to agreements that could lead to a safer world without nuclear weapons.

But first, let me tell you that, from the start of my meetings with Mr. Gorbachev, I have always regarded you, the American people, as full participants. Believe me, without your support, none of these talks could have been held, nor could the ultimate aims of American foreign policy— world peace and freedom—be pursued. And it's for these aims I went the, went the extra mile to Iceland.

Before I report on our talks though, allow me to set the stage by explaining two things that were very much a part of our talks, one a treaty and the other a defense against nuclear missiles which we're trying to develop. Now you've heard their titles a thousand times—the

ABM treaty and SDI Well, those letters stand for ABM, anti-ballistic missile, SDI, Strategic Defense Initiative.

Some years ago, the United States and the Soviet Union agreed to limit any defense against nuclear missile attacks to the emplacement in one location in each country of a small number of missiles capable of intercepting and shooting down incoming nuclear missiles. Thus leaving our real defense a policy called Mutual Assured Destruction, meaning if one side launched a nuclear attack, the other side could retaliate. And this mutual threat of destruction was believed to be a deterrent against either side striking first.

So here we sit with thousands of nuclear warheads targeted on each other and capable of wiping out both our countries. The Soviets deployed the few anti-ballistic missiles around Moscow as the treaty permitted. Our country didn't bother deploying because the threat of nationwide annihilation made such a limited defense seem useless.

For some years now we've been aware that the Soviets may be developing a nationwide defense. They have installed a large modern radar at Krashnoyarsk which we believe is a critical part of a radar system designed to provide radar guidance for anti-ballistic missiles protecting the entire nation. Now this is a violation of the ABM treaty.

Believing that a policy of mutual destruction and slaughter of their citizens and ours was uncivilized, I asked our military a few years ago to study and see if there was a practical way to destroy nuclear missiles after their launch but before they can reach their targets rather than to just destroy people. Well this is the goal for what we call SDI, and our scientists researching such a system are convicned it is practical and that several years down the road we can have such a system ready to deploy. Incidentally we are not violating the ABM treaty, which permits such research. If and when we deploy, the treaty also allows withdrawal from the treaty upon six months' notice. SDI, let me make it clear, is a nonnuclear defense.

So here we are at Iceland for our second such meeting. In the first and in the months in between, we have discussed ways to reduce and in fact eliminate nuclear weapons entirely. We and the Soviets have had teams of negotiators in Geneva trying to work out a mutual agreement on how we could reduce or eliminate nuclear weapons. And so far, no success.

On Saturday and Sunday, General Secretary Gorbachev and his Foreign Minister Shevardnadze and Secretary of State George Shultz and I met for nearly 10 hours. We didn't limit ourselves to just arms reductions; we discussed what we call violation of human rights on the part of the Soviets, refusal to let people emigrate from Russia so they can practice their religion without being persecuted, letting people go to rejoin their families, husbands and wives separated by national borders being allowed to reunite. In much of this the Soviet Union is violating another agreement—the Helsinki accords they had signed in 1975. Yuri Orlov, whose freedom we just obtained, was imprisoned for pointing out to his government its violations of that pact, its refusal to let citizens leave their country or return.

We also discussed regional matters such as Afghanistan, Angola, Nicaragua, and Cambodia.

But by their choice the main subject was arms control. We discussed the emplacement of intermediate-range missiles in Europe and Asia and seemed to be in agreement they could be drastically reduced. Both sides seemed willing to find a way to reduce even to zero the strategic ballistic missiles we have aimed at each other. This then brought up the subject of SDI.

I offered a proposal that we continue our present research and if and when we reached the stage of testing we would sign now a treaty that would permit Soviet observation of such tests. And if the program was practical we would both eliminate our offensive missiles, and then we would share the benefits of advanced defenses.

I explained that even though we would have done away with our offensive ballistic missiles, having the defense would protect against cheating or the possibility of a madman sometime decideing to create nuclear missiles. After all, the world now knows how to make them. I likened it to our keeping our gas masks even though the nations of the world had outlawed poison gas after World War I.

We seemed to be making progress on reducing weaponry, although the general secretary was registering opposition to SDI and proposing a pledge to observe ABM for a number of years as the day was ending.

Secretary Shultz suggested we turn over the notes our note-takers had been making of everything we'd said to our respective teams and let them work through the night to put them together and find just where we were in agreement and what differences separated us. With respect and gratitude, I can inform you those teams worked through the night till 6:30 A.M.

Yesterday, Sunday morning, Mr. Gorbachev and I, with our foreign ministers, came together again and took up the report of our two teams. It was most promising. The Soviets had asked for a 10-year delay in the deployment of SDI programs. In an effort to see how we could satisfy their concerns while protecting our principles and security, we proposed a 10-year period in which we began with the reduction of all strategic nuclear arms, bombers, air-launched cruise missiles, intercontinental ballistic missiles, submarine-launched ballistic missiles and the weapons they carry.

They would be reduced 50 percent in the first five years. During the next five years, we would continue by eliminating all remaining offensive ballistic missiles, of all ranges. And during that time we would proceed with research development and testing of SDI. All done in conformity with ABM provisions. At the 10-year point, with all ballistic missiles eliminated, we could proceed to deploy advanced defenses, at the same time permitting the Soviets to do likewise.

And here the debate began. The general secretary wanted wording that in effect would have kept us from developing the SDI for the entire 10 years. In effect, he was killing SDI. and unless I agreed, all that work toward eliminating nuclear weapons would go down the drain—canceled.

I told him I had pledged to the American people that I would not trade away SDI. There was no way I could tell our people their government would not protect them against nuclear destruction. I went to Reykjavik determined that everything was negotiable except two things, our freedom and our future.

I'm still optimistic that a way will be found. The door is open and the opportunity to begin eliminating the nuclear threat is within reach.

So you can see we made progress in Iceland. And we will continue to make progress if we pursue a prudent, deliberate, and, above all, realistic approach with the Soviets. From the earliest days of our administration, this has been our policy. We made it clear we had no illusions about the Soviets or their ultimate intentions. We were publicly candid about the critical moral distinctions between totalitarianism and democracy. We declared the principal objective of American foreign policy to be not just the prevention of war but the extension of freedom. And, we stressed our commitment to the growth of democratic government and democratic institutions around the world. And that's why we assisted freedom fighters who are resisting the imposition of totalitarian rule in Afghanistan, Nicaragua, Angola, Cambodia, and elsewhere. And, finally, we began work on what I believe most spurred the Soviets to negotiate seriously—rebuilding our military strength, reconstructing our strategic deterrence, and, above all, beginning work on the Strategic Defense Initiative.

And yet at the same time we set out these foreign-policy goals and began working toward them, we pursued another of our major objectives: that of seeking means to lessen tensions with the Soviets, and ways to prevent war and keep the peace.

Now, this policy is now paying dividends—one sign of this in Iceland was the progress on the issue of arms control. For the first time in a long while, Soviet-American negotiations in the area of arms reduction are moving, and moving in the right direction: not just toward arms *control*, but toward arms *reduction*.

But for all the progress we made on arms reductions, we must remember there was other issues on the table in Iceland, issues that are fundamental.

As I mentioned, one such issue is human rights. As President Kennedy once said, "And, is not peace, in the last analysis, basically a matter of human rights?"

I made it plain that the United States would not seek to exploit improvement in these matters for purposes of propaganda. But I also made it plain, once again, that an improvement of the human condition within the Soviet Union is indispensable for an improvement in bilateral relations with the United States. For a government that will break faith with its own people cannot be trusted to keep faith with foreign powers. So, I told Mr. Gorbachev—again in Reykjavik as I had in Geneva—we Americans place far less weight upon the words that are spoken at meetings such as these, than upon the deeds that follow. When it comes to human rights and judging Soviet intentions, we're all from Missouri: you gotta show us.

Another subject area we took up in Iceland also lies at the heart of the differences between the Soviet Union and America. This is the issue of regional conflicts. Summit meetings cannot make the American people forget what Soviet actions have meant for the peoples of Afghanistan, Central America, Africa, and Southeast Asia. Until Soviet policies change, we will make sure that our friends in these areas—those who fight for freedom and independence— will have the support they need.

Finally, there was a fourth item. And this area was that of bilateral relations, people-to-people contacts. In Geneva last year, we welcomed several cultural exchange accords; in Iceland, we saw indications of more movement in these areas. But let me say now the United States remains committed to people-to-people programs that could lead to exchanges between not just a few elite but thousands of everyday citizens from both our countries.

So I think then that you can see that we did make progress in Iceland on a broad range of topics. We reaffirmed our four-point agenda; we discovered major new grounds of agreement; we probed again some old areas of disagreement.

And let me return again to the SDL issue.

I realize some Americans may be asking tonight: Why not accept Mr. Gorbachev's demand? Why not give up SDI for this agreement?

Well, the answer, my friends, is simple. SDI is America's insurance policy that the Soviet Union would keep the commitments made at Reykjavik. SDI is America's security guarantee—if the Soviets should—as they have done too often in the past—fail to comply with their solemn commitments. SDI is what brought the Soviets back to arms control talks at Geneva and Iceland. SDI is the key to a world without nuclear weapons.

The Soviets understand this. They have devoted far more resources for a lot longer time than we, to *their own* SDI. The world's only operational missile defense today surrounds Moscow, the capital of the Soviet Union. What Mr. Gorbachev was demanding at Reykjavik was that the United States agree to a new version of a 14-year-old ABM treaty that the Soviet Union has already violated. I told him we don't make those kind of deals in the United States.

And the American people should reflect on these critical questions.

How does a defense of the United States threaten the Soviet Union or anyone else? Why are the Soviets so adamant that America remain forever vulnerable to Soviet rocket attack? As of today, all free nations are utterly defenseless against Soviet missiles—fired either by accident or design. Why does the Soviet Union insist that we remain so forever?

So, my fellow Americans, I cannot promise, nor can any president promise, that the talks in Iceland or any future discussions with Mr. Gorbachev will lead inevitably to great breakthroughs or momentous treaty signings.

We will not abandon the guiding principle we took to Reykjavik. We prefer no agreement than to bring home a bad agreement to the United States.

And on this point, I know you're also interested in the question of whether there will be another summit. There was no indication by Mr. Gorbachev as to when or whether he plans to travel to the United States, as we agreed he would last year in Geneva. I repeat tonight that our invitation stands and that we continue to believe additional meetings would be useful. But that's a decision the Soviets must make.

But whatever the immediate prospects, I can tell you that I'm ultimately hopeful about the prospects for progress at the summit and for world peace and freedom. You see, the current summit process is very different from that of previous decades; it's different because the world is different; and the world is different because of the hard work and sacrifice of the American people during the past five and a half years.

Your energy has restored and expanded our economic might; your support has restored our military strength. Your courage and sense of national unity in times of crisis have given pause to our adversaries, heartened our friends, and inspired the world. The Western democracies and the NATO alliance are revitalized and all across the world nations are turning to democratic ideas and the principles of the free market. So because the American people stood guard at the critical hour, freedom has gathered its forces, regained its strength, and is on the march.

So, if there's one impression I carry away with me from these October talks, it is that, unlike the past, we are dealing now from a position of strength, and for that reason we have it within our grasp to move speedily with the Soviets toward even more breakthroughs.

Our ideas are out there on the table. They won't go away. We're ready to pick up where we left off. Our negotiators are heading back to Geneva, and we're prepared to go forward whenever and wherever the Soviets are ready. So, there's reason—good reason—for hope.

I saw evidence of this in the progress we made in the talks with Mr. Gorbachev. And I saw evidence of it when we left Iceland yesterday, and I spoke to our young men and women at our naval installation at Keflavik—a critically important base far closer to Soviet naval bases than to our own coastline. As always, I was proud to spend a few moments with them and thank them for their sacrifices and devotion to country. They represent America at ther finest: committed to defend not only our own freedom but the freedom of others who would be living in a far more frightening world— were it not for the strength and resolve of the United States.

"Whenever the standard of freedom and independence has been . . . unfurled, there will be America's heart, her benedictions, and her prayers," John Quincy Adams once said. He spoke well of our destiny as a nation. My fellow Americans, we are honored by history, entrusted by destiny with the oldest dream of humanity—the dream of lasting peace and human freedom.

Another president, Harry Truman, noted that our century has seen two of the most frightful wars in history. And that "the supreme need of our time is for man to learn to live together in peace and harmony."

It's in pursuit of that ideal I went to Geneva a year ago and to Iceland last week. And it's in pursuit of that ideal that I thank you now for all the support you've given me, and I again ask for your help and your prayers as we continue our journey toward a world where peace reigns and freedom is enshrined.

Thank you and God bless you.

The Iran-Contra Affair

Washington, D.C.

March 4, 1987

In October 1986 reports began to circulate that the Reagan administration had secretly sold arms to Iran in the hope of securing the release of American hostages held in Beirut by Iranian-backed terrorists—in effect, offering ransom for hostages, in direct contradiction to the president's oft-expressed policy of not negotiating with terrorists. Shortly afterward, the administration revealed that some of the money paid by Iran for the arms had been diverted to the Nicaraguan contras by members of the National Security Council (NSC) at a time when direct funding of contra military activities was banned by Congress. The president, who claimed to have approved the arms sales only after they took place, and who claimed to have no knowledge at all of the diversion of funds, authorized a special commission headed by former Senator John Tower to investigate the affair. The Tower report, released in late February 1987, was a scathing indictment of many Reagan aides and sharply criticized the "management style" of the president himself. With public opinion turning against him, Reagan went on nationwide television to demonstrate that he was still in command of himself and of the government, and he brought it off with great skill. The speech was a masterful piece of image-building. Appearing earnest and a touch chastened, Reagan presented the entire affair as a simple matter of poor judgment—a regrettable error that had made him a sadder but wiser president.

My fellow Americans, I've spoken to you from this historic office on many occasions and about many things. The power of the presidency is often thought to reside within this Oval Office. Yet it doesn't rest here; it rests in you, the American people, and in your trust.

Your trust is what gives a president his powers of leadership and his personal strength, and it's what I want to talk to you about this evening.

For the past three months, I've been silent on the revelations about Iran. You must have been thinking, "Well, why doesn't he tell us what's happening? Why doesn't he just speak to us as he has in the past when we've faced troubles or tragedies?" Others of you, I guess, were thinking, "What's he doing hiding out in the White House?"

The reason I haven't spoken to you before now is this: You deserved the truth. And, as frustrating as the waiting has been, I felt it was improper to come to you with sketchy reports, or possibly even erroneous statements, which would then have to be corrected, creating even more doubt and confuston. There's been enough of that.

I've paid a price for my silence in terms of your trust and confidence. But I have had to wait, as have you, for the complete story.

That's why I appointed Ambassador David Abshire as my special counselor to help get out the thousands of documents to the various investigations. And I appointed a special review board, the Tower board, which took on the core of pulling the truth together for me and getting to the bottom of things. It has now issued its findings.

I'm often accused of being an optimist, and it's true I had to hunt pretty hard to find any good news in the board's report. As you know, it's well-stocked with criticisms, which I'll discuss in a moment, but I was very relieved to read this sentence: "The board is convinced that the president does indeed want the full story to be told."

And that will continue to be my pledge to you as the other investigations go forward.

I want to thank the members of the panel—former Senator John Tower, former Secretary of State Edmund Muskie, and former National Security Adviser Brent Scowcroft. They have done the nation, as well as me personally, a great service by submitting a report of such integrity and depth. They have my genuine and enduring gratitude.

I've studied the board's report. Its findings are honest, convincing and highly critical, and I accept them. Tonight I want to share with you my thoughts on these findings and report to you on the actions I'm taking to implement the board's recommendations.

First, let me say I take full responsibility for my own actions and for those of my administration. As angry as I may be about activities undertaken without my knowledge, I am still accountable for those activities. As disappointed as I may be in some who served me, I am still the one who must answer to the American people for this behavior. And as personally distastful as I find sceret bank accounts and diverted funds, as the navy would say, this happened on my watch.

Let's start with the part that is the most controversial. A few months ago I told the American people I did not trade arms for hostages. My heart and my best intentions still tell me that is true, but the fact and the evidence tell me it is not.

As the Tower board reported, what began as a strategic opening to Iran deteriorated in its implementation into trading arms for hostages. This runs counter to my own beliefs, to administration policy and to the original strategy we had in mind. There are reasons why it happened but no excuses. It was a mistake.

I undertook the original Iran initiative in order to develop relations with those who might assume leadership in a post-Khomeini government. It's clear from the board's report, however, that I let my personal concern for the hostages spill over into the geopolitical strategy of reaching out to Iran. I asked so many questions about the hostages' welfare that I didn't ask enough about the specifics of the total Iran plan.

Let me say to the hostage families, we have not given up. We never will, and I promise you we'll use every legitimate means to free your loved ones from captivity. But I must also caution that those Americans who freely remain in such dangerous areas must know that they're responsible for their own safety.

Now, another major aspect of the board's findings regards the transfer of funds to the Nicaraguan contras. The Tower board wasn't able to find out what happened to this money, so the facts here will be left to the continuing investigations of the court-appointed independent counsel and the two congressional investigating committees. I'm confident the truth will come out about this matter as well.

As I told the Tower board, I didn't know about any diversion of funds to the contras. But as president, I cannot escape responsibility.

Much has been said about my management style, a style that's worked successfully for me during eight years as governor of California and for most of my presidency. The way I work is to identify the problem, find the right individuals to do the job, and then let them go to it. I've found this invariably brings out the best in people. They seem to rise to their full capability, and in the long run you get more done.

When it came to managing the NSC staff, let's face it, my style didn't match its previous track record. I've already begun correcting this. As a start, yesterday I met with the entire professional staff of the National Security Council. I defined for them the values I want to guide the national security policies of this country. I told them that I wanted a policy that was as justifiable and understandable in public as it was in secret. I wanted a policy that reflected the will of the Congress as well as the White House. And I told them that there'll be no more freelancing by individuals when it comes to our national security.

You've heard a lot about the staff of the National Security Council in recent months. I can tell you, they are good and dedicated government employees, who put in long hours for the nation's benefit. They are eager and anxious to serve their country.

One thing still upsetting me, however, is that no one kept proper records of meetings or decisions. This led to my failure to recollect whether I approved an arms shipment before or after the fact. I did approve it; I just can't say specifically when. Rest assured, there's plenty of record keeping now going on at 1600 Pennsylvania Avenue.

For nearly a week now, I've been studying the board's report. I want the American people to know that this wrenching ordeal of recent months has not been in vain. I endorse every one of the Tower board's recommendations. In fact, I'm going beyond its recommendations, so as to put the house in even better order.

I'm taking action in three basic areas— personnel, national security policy and the process for making sure that the system works.

First, personnel. I've brought in an accomplished and highly respected new team here at the White House. They bring new blood, new energy, and new credibility and experience.

Former Senator Howard Baker, my new chief of staff, possesses a breadth of legislative and foreign affairs skills that's impossible to match. I'm hopeful that his experience as minority and majority leader of the

Senate can help us forge a new partnership with the Congress, especially on foreign and national security policies. I'm genuinely honored that he's given up his own presidential aspirations to serve the country as my chief of staff.

Frank Carlucci, my new national security adviser, is respected for his experience in government and trusted for his judgment and counsel. Under him, the NSC staff is being rebuilt with proper management discipline. Already almost half the NSC professional staff is comprised of new people.

Yesterday I nominated William Webster, a man of sterling reputation, to be director of the Central Intelligence Agency. Mr. Webster has served as Director of the FBI and as a U.S. District Court judge. He understands the meaning of "Rule of Law."

So that his knowledge of national security matters can be available to me on a continuing basis, I will also appoint John Tower to serve as a member of my Foreign Intelligence Advisory Board.

I am considering other changes in personnel, and I will move more furniture as I see fit in the weeks and months ahead.

Second, in the area of national security policy, I have ordered the NSC to begin a comprehensive review of all covert operations.

I have also directed that any covert activity be in support of clear policy objectives and in compliance with American values. I expect a covert policy that if Americans saw it on the front page of their newspaper, they'd say, "that makes sense."

I have had issued a directive prohibiting the NSC staff itself from undertaking covert operations—no if's and's or but's.

I have asked Vice President Bush to reconvene his task force on terrorism to review our terrorist policy in light of the events that have occurred.

Third, in terms of the process of reaching national security decisions, I am adopting in total the Tower report's model of how the NSC process and staff should work. I am directing Mr. Carlucci to take the necessary steps to make that happen. He will report back to me on further reforms that might be needed.

I've created the post of NSC legal adviser to assure a greater sensitivity to matters of law.

I am also determined to make the congressional oversight process work. Proper procedures for consultation with the Congress will be followed, not only in letter but in spirit.

Before the end of March I will report to the Congress on all the steps I've taken in line with the Tower board's conclusions.

Now what should happen when you make a mistake is this: You take your knocks, you learn your lessons and then you move on. That's the healthiest way to deal with a problem. This in no way diminishes the importance of the other continuing investigations, but the business of our country and our people must proceed. I've gotted this message from Republicans and Democrats in Congress, from allies around the world—and if we're reading the signals right, even from the Soviets. And, of course, I've heard the message from you, the American people.

You know, by the time you reach my age, you've made plenty of mistakes if you've lived your life properly. So you learn. You put things in perspective. You pull your energies together. You change. You go forward.

My fellow Americans, I have a great deal that I want to accomplish with you and for you over the next two years, and, the Lord willing, that's exactly what I intend to do. Goodnight and God bless you.

Remarks on East-West Relations at the Brandenburg Gate

June 12, 1987

West Berlin, Germany

ON JUNE 12, 1987, President Ronald Reagan delivered his historic speech "Remarks on East-West Relations at the Brandenburg Gate" in Berlin, West Germany. The Brandenburg Gate, a Berlin landmark, had been commissioned by Friedrich Wilhelm II as a symbol of peace, but at the time of Reagan's speech it was part of the infamous Berlin Wall, a brick-and-mortar line dividing democratic West Germany and communist East Germany. Although the bulk of Reagan's remarks have been largely forgotten, one line—"Mr. Gorbachev, tear down this wall!"—has survived as an expression of Reagan's implacable opposition to communism.

Reagan opens by highlighting the division in Europe. Throughout his address, he emphasizes that the divisions in Berlin and throughout Europe affect all people, not just Germans, and that the issue is not just the freedom of Germany but that of all humankind. Reagan continues with a historical survey. He refers to the dark days at the end of World War II, when Berlin was in chaos. He then turns his attention to the Soviet Union and the Eastern Bloc, noting that the Soviet Union was implementing new policies of openness and liberalization. Reagan concludes by urging the nations of Europe, including the Soviet Union, to find ways to bring East and West closer together.

Twenty four years ago, President John F. Kennedy visited Berlin, speaking to the people of this city and the world at the city hall. Well, since then two other presidents have come, each in his turn, to Berlin. And today I, myself, make my second visit to your city.

We come to Berlin, we American Presidents, because it's our duty to speak, in this place, of freedom. But I must confess, we're drawn here by other things as well: by the feeling of history in this city, more than 500 years older than our own nation; by the beauty of the Grunewald and the Tiergarten; most of all, by your courage and determination. Perhaps the composer, Paul Lincke, understood something about American Presidents. You see, like so many Presidents before me, I come here today because wherever I go, whatever I do: "Ich hab noch einen koffer in Berlin." [I still have a suitcase in Berlin.]

Our gathering today is being broadcast throughout Western Europe and North America. I understand that it is being seen and heard as well in the East. To those listening throughout Eastern Europe, I extend my warmest greetings and the good will of the American people. To those listening in East Berlin, a special word: Although I cannot be with you, I address my remarks to you just as surely as to those standing here before me. For I join you, as I join your fellow countrymen in the West, in this firm, this unalterable belief: Es gibt nur ein Berlin. [There is only one Berlin.]

Behind me stands a wall that encircles the free sectors of this city, part of a vast system of barriers that divides the entire continent of Europe. From the Baltic, south, those barriers cut across Germany in a gash of barbed wire, concrete, dog runs, and guard towers. Farther south, there may be no visible, no obvious wall. But there remain armed guards and checkpoints all the same–still a restriction on the right to travel, still an instrument to impose upon ordinary men and women the will of a totalitarian state. Yet it is here in Berlin where the wall emerges most clearly; here, cutting across your city, where the news photo and the television screen have imprinted this brutal division of a continent upon the mind of the world. Standing before the Brandenburg Gate, every man is a German, separated from his fellow men. Every man is a Berliner, forced to look upon a scar.

President von Weizsacker has said: "The German question is open as long as the Brandenburg Gate is closed." Today I say: As long as this gate is closed, as long as this scar of a wall is permitted to stand, it is not the German question alone that remains open, but the question of freedom for all mankind. Yet I do not come here to lament. For I find in Berlin a message of hope, even in the shadow of this wall, a message of triumph.

In this season of spring in 1945, the people of Berlin emerged from their air raid shelters to find devastation. Thousands of miles away, the people of the United States reached out to help. And in 1947 Secretary of State–as you've been told–George Marshall announced the creation of what would become known as the Marshall plan. Speaking precisely 40 years ago this month, he said: "Our policy is directed not against any country or doctrine, but against hunger, poverty, desperation, and chaos."

In the Reichstag a few moments ago, I saw a display commemorating this 40th anniversary of the Marshall plan. I was struck by the sign on a burnt-out, gutted structure that was being rebuilt. I understand that Berliners of my own generation can remember seeing signs like it dotted throughout the Western sectors of the city. The sign read simply: "The Marshall plan is helping here to strengthen the free world." A strong, free world in the West, that dream became real. Japan rose from ruin to become an economic giant. Italy, France, Belgium–virtually every nation in Western Europe saw political and economic rebirth; the European Community was founded.

In West Germany and here in Berlin, there took place an economic miracle, the Wirtschaftswunder. Adenauer, Erhard, Reuter, and other leaders understood the practical importance of liberty–that just as truth can flourish only when the journalist is given freedom of speech, so prosperity can come about only when the farmer and businessman enjoy economic freedom. The German leaders reduced tariffs, expanded free trade, lowered taxes. From 1950 to 1960 alone, the standard of living in West Germany and Berlin doubled.

Where four decades ago there was rubble, today in West Berlin there is the greatest industrial output of any city in Germany-busy office blocks, fine homes and apartments, proud avenues, and the spreading lawns of park land. Where a city's culture seemed to have been destroyed, today there are two great universities, orchestras and an opera, countless theaters, and museums. Where there was

want, today there's abundance–food, clothing, automobiles-the wonderful goods of the Ku'damm. From devastation, from utter ruin, you Berliners have, in freedom, rebuilt a city that once again ranks as one of the greatest on Earth. The Soviets may have had other plans. But, my friends, there were a few things the Soviets didn't count on: Berliner herz, Berliner humor, ja, und Berliner schnauze. [Berliner heart, Berliner humor, yes, and a Berliner schnauze.]

In the 1950's, Khrushchev predicted: "We will bury you." But in the West today, we see a free world that has achieved a level of prosperity and well-being unprecedented in all human history. In the Communist world, we see failure, technological backwardness, declining standards of health, even want of the most basic kind-too little food. Even today, the Soviet Union still cannot feed itself. After these four decades, then, there stands before the entire world one great and inescapable conclusion: Freedom leads to prosperity. Freedom replaces the ancient hatreds among the nations with comity and peace. Freedom is the victor.

And now the Soviets themselves may, in a limited way, be coming to understand the importance of freedom. We hear much from Moscow about a new policy of reform and openness. Some political prisoners have been released. Certain foreign news broadcasts are no longer being jammed. Some economic enterprises have been permitted to operate with greater freedom from state control. Are these the beginnings of profound changes in the Soviet state? Or are they token gestures, intended to raise false hopes in the West, or to strengthen the Soviet system without changing it? We welcome change and openness; for we believe that freedom and security go together, that the advance of human liberty can only strengthen the cause of world peace.

There is one sign the Soviets can make that would be unmistakable, that would advance dramatically the cause of freedom and peace. General Secretary Gorbachev, if you seek peace, if you seek prosperity for the Soviet Union and Eastern Europe, if you seek liberalization: Come here to this gate! Mr. Gorbachev, open this gate! Mr. Gorbachev, tear down this wall!

I understand the fear of war and the pain of division that afflict this continent–and I pledge to you my country's efforts to help overcome these burdens. To be sure, we in the West must resist Soviet expansion. So we must maintain defenses of unassailable strength. Yet we seek peace; so we must strive to reduce arms on both sides. Beginning 10 years ago, the Soviets challenged the Western alliance with a grave new threat, hundreds of new and more deadly SS-20 nuclear missiles, capable of-striking every capital in Europe. The Western alliance responded by committing itself to a counter deployment unless the Soviets agreed to negotiate a better solution; namely, the elimination of such weapons on both sides. For many months, the Soviets refused to bargain in earnestness. As the alliance, in turn, prepared to go forward with its counter deployment, there were difficult days–days of protests like those during my 1982 visit to this city–and the Soviets later walked away from the table.

But through it all, the alliance held firm. And I invite those who protested then–I invite those who protest today–to mark this fact: Because we remained strong, the Soviets came back to the table. And because we remained strong, today we have within reach the possibility, not merely of limiting the growth of arms, but of eliminating, for the first time, an entire class of nuclear weapons from the face of the Earth. As I speak, NATO ministers are meeting in Iceland to review the progress of our proposals for eliminating these weapons. At the talks in Geneva, we have also proposed deep cuts in strategic offensive weapons. And the Western allies have likewise made far-reaching proposals to reduce the danger of conventional war and to place a total ban on chemical weapons.

While we pursue these arms reductions, I pledge to you that we will maintain the capacity to deter Soviet aggression at any level at which it might occur. And in cooperation with many of our allies, the United States is pursuing the Strategic Defense Initiative-research to base deterrence not on the threat of offensive retaliation, but on defenses that truly defend; on systems, in short, that will not target populations, but shield them. By these means we seek to increase the safety of Europe and all the world. But we must remember a crucial fact: East and West do not mistrust each other because we are armed; we are armed because we mistrust each other. And our differences are not about weapons but about liberty. When President Kennedy spoke at the City Hall those 24 years ago, freedom was encircled, Berlin was under siege. And today, despite all the pressures upon this city, Berlin stands secure in its liberty. And freedom itself is transforming the globe.

In the Philippines, in South and Central America, democracy has been given a rebirth. Throughout the Pacific, free markets are working miracle after miracle of economic growth. In the industrialized nations, a technological revolution is taking place–a revolution marked by rapid, dramatic advances in computers and telecommunications.

In Europe, only one nation and those it controls refuse to join the community of freedom. Yet in this age of redoubled economic growth, of information and innovation, the Soviet Union faces a choice: It must make fundamental changes, or it will become obsolete. Today thus represents a moment of hope. We in the West stand ready to cooperate with the East to promote true openness, to break down barriers that separate people, to create a safer, freer world.

And surely there is no better place than Berlin, the meeting place of East and West, to make a start. Free people of Berlin: Today, as in the past, the United States stands for the strict observance and full implementation of all parts of the Four Power Agreement of 1971. Let us use this occasion, the 750th anniversary of this city, to usher in a new era, to seek a still fuller, richer life for the Berlin of the future. Together, let us maintain and develop the ties between the Federal Republic and the Western sectors of Berlin, which is permitted by the 1971 agreement.

And I invite Mr. Gorbachev: Let us work to bring the Eastern and Western parts of the city closer together, so that all the inhabitants of all Berlin can enjoy the benefits that come with life in one of the great cities of the world. To open Berlin still further to all Europe, East and West, let us expand the vital air access to this city, finding ways of making commercial air service to Berlin more convenient, more comfortable, and more economical. We look to the day when West Berlin can become one of the chief aviation hubs in all central Europe.

With our French and British partners, the United States is prepared to help bring international meetings to Berlin. It would be only fitting for Berlin to serve as the site of United Nations meetings, or world conferences on human rights and arms control or other issues that call for international cooperation. There is no better way to establish hope for the future than to enlighten young minds, and we would be honored to sponsor summer youth exchanges, cultural events, and other programs for young Berliners from the East. Our French and British friends, I'm certain, will do the same. And it's my hope that an authority can be found in East Berlin to sponsor visits from young people of the Western sectors.

One final proposal, one close to my heart: Sport represents a source of enjoyment and ennoblement, and you many have noted that the Republic of Korea–South Korea–has offered to permit certain events of the 1988 Olympics to take place in the North. International sports competitions of all kinds could take place in both parts of this city. And what better way to demonstrate to the world the openness of this city than to offer in some future year to hold the Olympic Games here in Berlin, East and West?

In these four decades, as I have said, you Berliners have built a great city. You've done so in spite of threats–the Soviet attempts to impose the East-mark, the blockade. Today the city thrives in spite of the challenges implicit in the very presence of this wall. What keeps you here? Certainly there's a great deal to be said for your fortitude, for your defiant courage. But I believe there's something deeper, something that involves Berlin's whole look and feel and way of life–not mere sentiment. No one could live long in Berlin without being completely disabused of illusions. Something instead, that has seen the difficulties of life in Berlin but chose to accept them, that continues to build this good and proud city in contrast to a surrounding totalitarian presence that refuses to release human energies or aspirations. Something that speaks with a powerful voice of affirmation, that says yes to this city, yes to the future, yes to freedom. In a word, I would submit that what keeps you in Berlin is love–love both profound and abiding.

Perhaps this gets to the root of the matter, to the most fundamental distinction of all between East and West. The totalitarian world produces backwardness because it does such violence to the spirit, thwarting the human impulse to create, to enjoy, to worship. The totalitarian world finds even symbols of love and of worship an affront. Years ago, before the East Germans began rebuilding their churches, they erected a secular structure: the television tower at Alexander Platz. Virtually ever since, the authorities have been working to correct what they view as the tower's one major flaw, treating the glass sphere at the top with paints and chemicals of every kind. Yet even today when the Sun strikes that sphere–that sphere that towers over all Berlin–the light makes the sign of the cross. There in Berlin, like the city itself, symbols of love, symbols of worship, cannot be suppressed.

As I looked out a moment ago from the Reichstag, that embodiment of German unity, I noticed words crudely spray-painted upon the wall, perhaps by a young Berliner, "This wall will fall. Beliefs become reality." Yes, across Europe, this wall will fall. For it cannot withstand faith; it cannot withstand truth. The wall cannot withstand freedom.

And I would like, before I close, to say one word. I have read, and I have been questioned since I've been here about certain demonstrations against my coming. And I would like to say just one thing, and to those who demonstrate so. I wonder if they have ever asked themselves that if they should have the kind of government they apparently seek, no one would ever be able to do what they're doing again.

Thank you and God bless you all.

Farewell Address

Washington, D.C.

January 11, 1989

REAGAN'S lyrical, meditative farewell address was crafted by Peggy Noonan, a veteran White House speechwriter who was also responsible for George Bush's acceptance speech at the 1988 Republican convention and for his inaugural address. In her memoir of the Reagan administration, she described the torments suffered by presidential speechwriters whose work was constantly being revised by tin-eared State Department bureaucrats. "It was a constant struggle over speeches, a constant struggle over who was in charge and what view would prevail and which group would triumph. Each speech was a battle in a never-ending war; when the smoke cleared there was Reagan, holding the speech and saying the words as the mist curled about his feet."

My fellow Americans, this is the 34th time I'll speak to you from the Oval Office, and the last. We have been together eight years now, and soon it will be time for me to go. But before I do, I wanted to share some thoughts, some of which I have been saving for a long time.

It has been the honor of my life to be your president. So many of you have written the past few weeks to say thanks, but I could say as much to you. Nancy and I are grateful for the opportunity you gave us to serve.

One of the things about the presidency is that you're always somewhat apart. You spend a lot of time going by too fast in a car someone else is driving, and seeing the people through tinted glass—the parents holding up a child, and the wave you saw too late and couldn't return. And so many times I wanted to stop, and reach out from behind the glass, to connect. And maybe I can do a little of that tonight.

People ask how I feel about leaving, and the fact is parting is "such sweet sorrow." The sweet part is California, and the ranch, and freedom. The sorrow? The goodbyes, of course, and leaving this beautiful place.

You know, down the hall and up the stairs from this office is the part of the White House where the president and his family live. There are a few favorite windows I have up there that I like to stand and look out of early in the morning. The view is over the grounds here to the Washington Monument, and then the Mall, and the Jefferson Memorial. But on mornings when the humidity is low, you can see past the Jefferson to the river, the Potomac, and the Virginia shore. Someone said that's the view Lincoln had when he saw the smoke rising from the battle of Bull Run. I see more prosaic things: the grass on the banks, the morning traffic as people make their way to work, now and then a sailboat on the river.

I have been thinking a bit at that window. I have been reflecting on what the past eight years have meant, and mean. And the image that comes to mind like a refrain is a nautical one—a small story about a big ship, and a refugee, and a sailor.

It was back in the early eighties, at the height of the boat people, and the sailor was hard at work on the carrier Midway, which was patrolling the South China Sea. The sailor, like most American servicemen, was young, smart, and fiercely observant. The crew spied on the horizon a leaky little boat—and crammed inside were refugees from Indochina hoping to get to America. The Midway sent a small launch to bring them to the ship, and safety. As the refugees made their way through the choppy seas, one spied the sailor on deck, and stood up and called out to him. He yelled, "Hello American sailor—Hello Freedom Man."

A small moment with a big meaning, a moment the sailor, who wrote it in a letter, couldn't get out of his mind. And, when I saw it, neither could I.

Because that's what it was to be an American in the 1980s. We stood, again, for freedom. I know we always have but in the past few years the world—again, in a way, we ourselves rediscovered it.

It has been quite a journey this decade, and we held together through some stormy seas. And at the end, together, we are reaching our destination.

The fact is, from Grenada to the Washington and Moscow Summits, from the recession of '81 and '82 to the expansion that began in late '82 and continues to this day, we've made a difference.

The way I see it, there were two great triumphs, two things that I'm proudest of. One is the economic recovery, in which the people of America created—and filled—19 million new jobs. The other is the recovery of our morale: America is respected again in the world, and looked to for leadership.

Something that happened to me a few years ago reflects some of this. It was back in 1981, and I was attending my first big economic summit, which was held that year in Canada. The meeting place rotates among the member countries. The opening meeting was a formal dinner for the heads of government of the seven industrialized nations. I sat there like the new kid in school and listened, and it was all François this and Helmut that. They dropped titles and spoke to one another on a first-name basis. At one point I sort of leaned and said, "My name's Ron."

In that same year, we began the actions we felt would ignite an economic comeback: cut taxes and regulation, started to cut spending. Soon the recovery began.

Two years later, another economic summit, with pretty much the same cast. At the big opening meeting, we all got together, and all of a sudden just for a moment I saw that everyone was looking at me. Then one of them broke the silence. "Tell us about the American miracle," he said.

Back in 1980, when I was running for president, it was all so different. Some pundits said our programs would result in catastrophe. Our views on foreign affairs would cause war, our plans for the economy would cause inflation to soar and bring about economic collapse. I even remember one highly respected economist saying, back in 1982, that "The engines of economic growth have shut down here and across the globe and they are likely to stay that way for years to come."

Well, he—and the other "opinion leaders"— were wrong. The fact is, what they called "radical" really was "right"; what they called "dangerous" was just "desperately needed."

And in all that time I won a nickname—"The Great Communicator." But I never thought it was my style or the words I used that made a difference—it was the content. I wasn't a great communicator, but I communicated great

things, and they didn't spring full blown from my brow, they came from the heart of a great nation—from our experience, our wisdom, and our belief in the principles that have guided us for two centuries.

They call it the Reagan Revolution, and I'll accept that, but for me it always seemed more like the Great Rediscovery: a rediscovery of our values and our common sense.

Common sense told us that when you put a big tax on something, the people will produce less of it. So we cut the people's tax rates, and the people produced more than ever before. The economy bloomed like a plant that had been cut back and could now grow quicker and stronger. Our economic program brought about the longest peacetime expansion in our history: real family income up, the poverty rate down, entrepreneurship booming and an explosion in research and new technology. We are exporting more than ever because American industry became more competitive, and at the same time we summoned the national will to knock down protectionist walls abroad instead of erecting them at home.

Common sense also told us that to preserve the peace we'd have to become strong again after years of weakness and confusion. So we rebuilt our defenses—and this New Year we toasted the new peacefulness around the globe. Not only have the superpowers actually begun to reduce their stockpiles of nuclear weapons—and hope for even more progress is bright—but the regional conflicts that rock the globe are also beginning to cease. The Persian Gulf is no longer a war zone, the Soviets are leaving Afghanistan, the Vietnamese are preparing to pull out of Cambodia, and an American-mediated accord will soon send 50,000 Cuban troops home from Angola.

The lesson of all this was, of course, that because we are a great nation, our challenges seem complex. It will always be this way. But as long as we remember our first principles and believe in ourselves, the future will always be ours.

And something else we learned: once you begin a great movement, there's no telling where it will end. We meant to change a nation, and instead, we changed a world.

Countries across the globe are turning to free markets and free speech—and turning away from the ideologies of the past. For them, the Great Discovery of the 1980s has been that, lo and behold, the moral way of government is the practical way of government. Democracy, the profoundly good, is also the profoundly productive.

When you've got to the point where you can celebrate the anniversaries of your 39th birthday you can sit back sometimes, review your life, and see it flowing before you. For me, there was a fork in the river, and it was right in the middle of my life.

I never meant to go into politics; it wasn't my intention when I was young. But I was raised to believe you had to pay your way for the blessings bestowed on you. I was happy with my career in the entertainment world, but I ultimately went into politics because I wanted to protect something precious.

Ours was the first revolution in the history of mankind that truly reversed the course of government, and with three little words: "We the people."

"We the people" tell the government what to do, it doesn't tell us. "We the people" are the driver—the government is the car. And we decide where it should go, and by what route, and how fast. Almost all the world's constitutions are documents in which government tells the people what their privileges are. Our Constitution is a document in which "We the people" tell the government what it is allowed to do. "We the people" are free.

This belief has been the underlying basis for everything I have tried to do these past eight years.

But back in the 1960s when I began, it seemed to me that we had begun reversing the order of things—that through more and more rules and regulations and confiscatory taxes, the government was taking more of our money, more of our options, and more of our freedom. I went into politics in part to put up my hand and say, "Stop!" I was a citizen-politician, and it seemed the right thing for a citizen to do.

I think we have stopped a lot of what needed stopping. And I hope we have once again reminded people that man is not free unless government is limited. There's a clear cause and effect here that is as neat and predictable as a law of physics: as government expands, liberty contracts.

Nothing is less free than pure Communism, and yet we have, the past few years, forged a satisfying new closeness with the Soviet Union. I've been asked if this isn't a gamble, and my answer is no, because we're basing our actions not on words but on deeds.

The détente of the 1970s was based not on actions but promises. They'd promise to treat their own people and the people of the world better, but the gulag was still the gulag, and the state was still expansionist, and they still waged proxy wars in Africa, Asia, and Latin America.

This time, so far, it's different: President Gorbachev has brought about some internal democratic reforms and begun the withdrawal from Afghanistan. He has also freed prisoners whose names I've given him every time we've met.

But life has a way of reminding you of big things through small incidents. Once, during the heady days of the Moscow Summit, Nancy and I decided to break off from the entourage one afternoon to visit the shops on Arbat Street, a little street just off Moscow's main shopping area.

Even though our visit was a surprise, every Russian there immediately recognized us, and called out our names, and reached for our hands. We were just about swept away by the warmth—you could almost feel the possibilities in all that joy. But within seconds, a KGB detail pushed their way toward us and began pushing and shoving the people in the crowd. It was an interesting moment. It reminded me that while the man on the street in the Soviet Union yearns for peace, the government is Communist—those that run it are Communists—and that means we and they view such issues as freedom and human rights very differently.

We must keep up our guard—but we must also continue to work together to lessen and eliminate tension and mistrust.

My view is that President Gorbachev is different from previous Soviet leaders. I think he knows some of the things wrong with his society and is trying to fix them. We wish him well. And we'll continue to work to make sure that the Soviet Union that eventually emerges from this process is a less threatening one.

What it all boils down to is this: I want the new closeness to continue. And it will be, as long as we make it clear that we will continue to act in a certain way as long as they continue to act in a helpful manner. If and when they don't—at first pull your punches. If they persist, pull the plug.

It's still trust—but verify.

It's still play—but cut the cards.

It's still watch closely—and don't be afraid to see what you see.

I've been asked if I have any regrets. I do.

The deficit is one. I've been talking a great deal about that lately, but tonight isn't for arguments, and I'm going to hold my tongue.

But an observation: I've had my share of victories in the Congress, but what few people noticed is that I never won anything you didn't win for me. They never saw my troops; they never saw Reagan's Regiments, the American people. You won every battle with every call you made and letter you wrote demanding action.

Well, action is still needed. If we're to finish the job, Reagan's Regiments will have to become the Bush Brigades. Soon he'll be the chief, and he'll need you every bit as much as I did.

Finally, there is a great tradition of warnings in presidential farewells, and I've got one that's been on my mind for some time.

But oddly enough it starts with one of the things I'm proudest of the past eight years: the resurgence of national pride that I called "the new patriotism." This national feeling is good, but it won't count for much, and it won't last unless it's grounded in thoughtfulness and knowledge.

An informed patriotism is what we want. And are we doing a good enough job teaching our children what America is and what she represents in the long history of the world?

Those of us who are over 35 or so years of age grew up in a different America. We were taught, very directly, what it means to be an American, and we absorbed almost in the air a love of country and an appreciation of its institutions. If you didn't get these things from your family you got them from the neighborhood, from the father down the street who fought in Korea or the family who lost someone at Anzio. Or you could get a sense of patriotism from school. And if all else failed, you could get a sense of patriotism from the popular culture. The movies celebrated democratic values and implicitly reinforced the idea that America was special. TV was like that, too, through the mid-sixties.

But now we're about to enter the nineties, and some things have changed. Younger parents aren't sure that an unambivalent appreciation of America is the right thing to teach modern children. And as for those who create the popular culture, well-grounded patriotism is no longer the style.

Our spirit is back, but we haven't reinstitutionalized it. We've got to do a better job of getting across that America is freedom—freedom of speech, freedom of religion, freedom of enterprise—and freedom is special and rare. It's fragile; it needs protection.

We've got to teach history based not on what's in fashion but what's important: why the Pilgrims came here, who Jimmy Doolittle was, and what those 30 seconds over Tokyo meant. You know, four years ago, on the 40th anniversary of D day, I read a letter from a young woman writing to her late father, who'd fought on Omaha Beach. Her name was Lisa Zanatta Henn, and she said, we will always remember, we will never forget what the boys of Normandy did. Well, let's help her keep her word.

If we forget what we did, we won't know who we are. I am warning of an eradication of the American memory that could result, ultimately, in an erosion of the American spirit.

Let's start with some basics—more attention to American history and a greater emphasis on civil ritual. And let me offer lesson number one about America: all great change in America begins at the dinner table. So tomorrow night in the kitchen I hope the talking begins. And children, if your parents haven't been teaching you what it means to be an American—let 'em know and nail 'em on it. That would be a very American thing to do.

And that's about all I have to say tonight. Except for one thing.

The past few days when I've been at the window upstairs, I've thought a bit of the shining "city upon a hill." The phrase comes from John Winthrop, who wrote it to describe the America he imagined. What he imagined was important, because he was an early Pilgrim—an early "Freedom Man." He journeyed here on what today we'd call a little wooden boat; and, like the other Pilgrims, he was looking for a home that would be free.

I've spoken of the shining city all my political life, but I don't know if I ever quite communicated what I saw when I said it. But in my mind, it was a tall proud city built on rocks stronger than oceans, windswept, God-blessed, and teeming with people of all kinds living in harmony and peace—a city with free ports that hummed with commerce and creativity, and if there had to be city walls, the walls had doors, and the doors were open to anyone with the will and the heart to get here.

That's how I saw it, and see it still.

And how stands the city on this winter night? More prosperous, more secure and happier than it was eight years ago. But more than that: after 200 years, two centuries, she still stands strong and true on the granite ridge, and her glow has held steady no matter what storm.

And she's still a beacon, still a magnet for all who must have freedom, for all the Pilgrims from all the lost places who are hurtling through the darkness, toward home.

We've done our part. And as I "walk off into the city streets," a final word to the men and women of the Reagan Revolution—the men and women across America who for eight years did the work that brought America back:

My friends, we did it. We weren't just marking time, we made a difference. We made the city stronger—we made the city freer—and we left her in good hands.

All in all, not bad. Not bad at all.

And so, good-bye.

God bless you. And God bless the United States of America.

Statue of Ronald Reagan in Newport Beach, California.
(Courtesy of PresidentsUSA.net)

Courtesy of The George Bush Library

George Herbert Walker Bush

George Herbert Walker Bush

1989–1993

THE REAGAN REVOLUTION of 1980 was intended by the Republican Party to last indefinitely. Reagan's ability to attract voters from a wide variety of political camps—fiscal conservatives, the old-money elite, evangelical Christians, disaffected Democrats, in fact nearly every group but diehard liberals—appeared to be a reproducible phenomenon that could be sustained through successive presidential terms as long as the Democratic Party adhered to its new identity as the party of special interests and radical social engineering. The experience of George Bush, who came to the Oval Office in 1988 after eight years as Reagan's vice president and heir apparent, showed that the game of holding on to the presidency was not going to be quite so easy. After a single term Bush was ousted by an electorate angered over an economic recession and looking for someone capable of more active leadership.

Part of Bush's difficulty was the stark contrast between himself and Reagan in presenting a public image that commanded respect. Reagan had the advantage of his training as an actor and his man-of-the-people style. Bush had no such training and was patently not a man of the people. He came from a rich Yankee family, attended a prestigious prep school and an Ivy League university, and made a fortune in his own right as founder of a Texas oil company before going into politics, first as a congressman, later as ambassador to the United Nations and director of the Central Intelligence Agency. Although he was known as a friendly, sociable, humorous man, he was completely lacking in the gifts of quick wit and easy rapport that had given Reagan and Kennedy much of their appeal. In fact, whenever he spoke without a prepared text, he showed himself to be inept at the simple task of articulating his thoughts. He interrupted himself frequently, mixed his metaphors, and got lost midway through his sentences, making himself sound more like a confused teenager than a statesman.

Stories of Bush's verbal slips abounded. During one press conference in the Oval Office, a reporter who persisted too long with a particular line of questioning received this reply: "Please don't ask me to do that which I've said I'm not going to do, because you're burning up time; the meter is running through the sand on you, and I am now filibustering." To a group of students visiting the White House, he remarked: "And I guess with these cameras listening, be sure never to end your sentence with a—without—end a sentence with a preposition because it will be duly reported all across the country by these guardians of the—[sentence unfinished]." Sometimes his meandering would take him into the realm of the absurd. Remembering his ordeal as a Navy fighter pilot during World War II, when his plane was shot down in the Pacific, he said: "I thought of my family, my mom and dad, and the strength I got from them. I thought of my faith, the separation of church and state." This lack of competence in using the English language gave the impression that Bush was a man with nothing to say, a president who didn't care enough about any subject to think hard about it and make a coherent case for it.

This impression was bolstered by the Bush administration's dismissive attitude toward speechmaking. Early in Bush's term, the speechwriting team was moved out of its former quarters in the West Wing of the White House to an office building. Instead of crafting persuasive statements of public policy, the writers were given the job of putting into Bush's mouth high-sounding cliches that avoided all controversy and promised nothing specific. If, while delivering a speech, Bush chanced on phrases that were meant to add drama or emotion, he simply left them out. His favorite part of every speech was the first paragraph, in which he acknowledged friends and colleagues in the audience.

According to journalists Michael Duffy and Dan Goodgame, Bush from the outset intended to downsize the presidency and convince the American public to expect less of it. "Winking at the political stunts expected of a president became, for Bush, a kind of theater in itself—a new kind of political pantomime. For nearly every time Bush noted the respect he had for the office, he would do or say something that suggested, sometimes explicitly, that he didn't take the job too seriously."

Undermining the tradition of White House speechmaking was one way to help Bush shrink the presidency and its responsibilities to a manageable size.

As Bush progressed further into his term, it became ever more obvious that he used value-laden words like justice, freedom, and democracy in his speeches purely for effect and that he had no intention of pursuing any program of action to advance those ideas. When pro-democracy demonstrators were massacred in Beijing in June 1989, for example, Bush refused to take a hard line with China's leaders for fear of making their totalitarian government less stable. His penchant for exaggeration reached its peak in 1991, when he justified his decision to take military action against Iraq by casting Saddam Hussein as another Hitler, himself as another Churchill, and the Gulf War as a miniature version of World War II. The voters, long accustomed to this kind of manipulation, went along with Bush on that one but finally lost sympathy with his transparent posturing.

Bush himself realized that he had not made sufficient use of the opportunity speechmaking offered to inform his countrymen about the debates and issues of the day and to put new spirit in them. "I think sometimes that I as a person—as the president—perhaps underestimate the bully pulpit aspect of the presidency," he said in February 1990. "Or perhaps the fact that the presidency has a very special and thus specific role in exhorting or encouraging people to do whatever it is."

Acceptance Speech

New Orleans, Louisiana

August 18, 1988

THE HIGH POINT of Bush's oratorical career was his speech at the 1988 Republican Convention in which he accepted the party's nomination as its candidate for the presidency. It is remembered for three phrases in particular. The first is the "thousand points of light" with which he described the diversity of American volunteer and communal organizations. The second is the reference to his hope that the United States would become "a kinder, gentler nation." Both phrases were afterwards used by editorial writers and cartoonists to rebuke Bush for his various attempts to deregulate industries and cut social-service spending. The third is the now-famous invitation "Read my lips: no new taxes." Bush's promise to keep taxes level was one that he had very little chance of keeping; the federal deficit had doubled during Reagan's two terms and stood in 1988 at a staggering 155 billion dollars, increasing all the time. Two years later, Bush reached a deal with Congress in which he agreed to raise taxes in exchange for a restructuring of government expenditures. The headline in the *New York Post* spoke for millions of outraged voters: "Read My Lips—I Lied."

I have many friends to thank tonight. I thank the voters who supported me. I thank the gallant men who entered the contest for this presidency this year, and who've honored me with their support. And, for their kind and stirring words, I thank Governor Tom Kean of New Jersey, Senator Phil Gramm of Texas, President Gerald Ford—and my friend President Ronald Reagan.

I accept your nomination for president. I mean to run hard, to fight hard, to stand on the issues—and I mean to win.

There are a lot of great stories in politics about the underdog winning, and this is going to be one of them.

And we're going to win with the help of Senator Dan Quayle of Indiana, a young leader who has become a forceful voice in preparing America's workers for the labor force of the future. What a superb job he did here tonight. Born in the middle of the century, in the middle of America, and holding the promise of the future—I'm proud to have Dan Quayle at my side.

Many of you have asked, "When will this campaign really begin?" Well, I've come to this hall to tell you, and to tell America: tonight is the night.

For seven and a half years I have helped the president conduct the most difficult job on earth. Ronald Reagan asked for, and received, my candor. He never asked for, but he did receive, my loyalty. And those of you who saw the president's speech this week, and listened to the simple truth of his words, will understand my loyalty all these years.

But now, now you must see me for what I am: the Republican candidate for president of the United States. And now I turn to the American people to share my hopes and intentions, and why and where I wish to lead.

And so tonight is for big things. But I'll try to be fair to the other side. I'll try to hold my charisma in check. And you know, I reject the temptation to engage in personal references. My approach this evening is, as Sergeant Joe Friday used to say, "Just the facts, ma'am."

And after all, the facts are on our side.

I seek the presidency for a single purpose, a purpose that has motivated millions of Americans across the years and the ocean voyages. I seek the presidency to build a better America. It's that simple, and that big.

I'm a man who sees life in terms of missions—missions defined and missions completed. And when I was a torpedo bomber pilot they defined the mission for us. And before we took off we all understood that no matter what, you try to reach the target. And there've been other missions for me—Congress and China, the CIA. But I am here tonight, and I am your candidate, because the most important work of my life is to complete the mission that we started in 1980. And how do we complete it? We build on it.

The stakes are high this year and the choice is crucial, for the differences between the two candidates are as deep and wide as they have ever been in our long history.

Not only two very different men, but two very different ideas of the future will be voted on this election day.

And what it all comes down to is this: my opponent's view of the world sees a long slow decline for our country, an inevitable fall mandated by impersonal historical forces.

But America is not in decline. America is a rising nation.

He sees America as another pleasant country on the UN roll call, somewhere between Albania and Zimbabwe. And I see America as the leader, a unique nation with a special role in the world.

And this has been called the American century, because in it we were the dominant force for good in the world. We saved Europe, cured polio, went to the Moon and lit the world with our culture. And now we're on the verge of a new century, and what country's name will it bear? I say it will be another American century.

Our work is not done; our force is not spent.

There are those who say there isn't much of a difference this year. But America, don't let 'em fool ya.

Two parties this year ask for your support. Both will speak of growth and peace. But only one has proved it can deliver. Two parties this year ask for your trust, but only one has earned it.

Eight years ago, I stood here with Ronald Reagan and we promised, together, to break with the past and return America to her greatness. Eight years later, look at what the American people have produced: the highest level of economic growth in our entire history, and the lowest level of world tensions in more than 50 years.

Some say this isn't an election about ideology, that it's an election about competence. Well, it's nice of them to want to play on our field. But this election isn't only about competence, for competence is a narrow ideal. Competence makes the trains run on time but doesn't know where they're going. Competence is the creed of the technocrat who makes sure the gears mesh but doesn't for a second understand the magic of the machine.

The truth is, this election is about the beliefs we share, the values that we honor, and the principles that we hold dear.

But since someone brought up competence—consider the size of our triumph: a record number of Americans at work, a record high percentage of our people with jobs, a record high of new businesses, a record high rate of real personal income.

These are facts. And one way you know our opponents know the facts is that to attack our record they have to misrepresent it. They call it a "Swiss cheese economy." Well, that's the way it may look to the three blind mice. But when they were in charge it was all holes and no cheese.

You know the litany. Inflation was 13 percent when we came in. We got it down to 4. Interest rates were more than 21. And we cut them in half. Unemployment was up and climbing, and now it's the lowest in 14 years.

My friends, eight years ago this economy was flat on its back—intensive care. And we came in and gave it emergency treatment—got the temperature down by lowering regulation, and got the blood pressure down when we lowered taxes. And pretty soon the patient was up, back on his feet, and stronger than ever.

And now who do we hear knocking on the door but the same doctors who made him sick. And they're telling us to put them in charge of the case again. My friends, they're lucky we don't hit them with a malpractice suit!

We've created 17 million new jobs the past five years, more than twice as many as Europe and Japan combined. And they're good jobs. The majority of them created in the past six years paid an average of more than $22,000 a year. And someone better take a message to Michael: tell him that we have been creating good jobs at good wages. The fact is, they talk and we deliver. They promise and we perform.

And there are millions of young Americans in their 20s who barely remember the days of gas lines and unemployment lines. And now they're marrying and starting careers. And to those young people I say, "You have the opportunity you deserve, and I'm not going to let them take it away from you."

The leaders of this expansion have been the women of America, who helped create the new jobs and filled two out of every three of them.

And to the women of America I say: "You know better than anyone that equality begins with economic empowerment. You're gaining economic power, and I'm not going to let them take it away from you."

There are millions of Americans who were brutalized by inflation. We arrested it, and we're not going to let it out on furlough. And we're going to keep that Social Security trust fund sound and out of reach of the big spenders. To America's elderly I say, "Once again you have the security that is your right, and I'm not going to let them take it away from you."

I know the liberal Democrats are worried about the economy. They're worried it's going to remain strong. And they're right, it is. With the right leadership it will remain strong.

But let's be frank. Things aren't perfect in this country. There are people who haven't tasted the fruits of the expansion. I've talked to farmers about the bills they can't pay. And I've been to the factories that feel the strain of change. And I've seen the urban children who play amid the shattered glass and the shattered lives. And there are the homeless. And you know, it doesn't do any good to debate endlessly which policy mistake of the '70s is responsible. They're there. And we have to help them.

But what we must remember, if we're to be responsible and compassionate, is that economic growth is the key to our endeavors.

I want growth that stays, that broadens, that touches, finally, all Americans, from the hollows of Kentucky to the sunlit streets of Denver, from the suburbs of Chicago to the broad avenues of New York, and from the oil fields of Oklahoma to the farms of the Great Plains.

And can we do it? Of course we can. We know how. We've done it. And if we continue to grow at our current rate, we will be able to produce 30 million jobs in the next eight years. And we will do it—by maintaining our commitment to free and fair trade, by keeping government spending down and by keeping taxes down.

Our economic life is not the only test of our success. One issue overwhelms all the others, and that's the issue of peace.

And look at the world on this bright August night. The spirit of democracy is sweeping the Pacific rim. China feels the winds of change.

New democracies assert themselves in South America. And one by one the unfree places fall, not to the force of arms but to the force of an idea: Freedom works.

And we have a new relationship with the Soviet Union—the INF treaty, the beginning of the Soviet withdrawal from Afghanistan, the beginning of the end of the Soviet proxy war in Angola, and with it the independence of Namibia. Iran and Iraq move toward peace.

It's a watershed. It is no accident.

It happened when we acted on the ancient knowledge that strength and clarity lead to peace; weakness and ambivalence lead to war. You see, weakness tempts aggressors. Strength stops them. I will not allow this country to be made weak again. Never.

The tremors in the Soviet world continue. The hard earth there has not yet settled. Perhaps what is happening will change our world forever. And perhaps not. A prudent skepticism is in order. And so is hope. But either way, we're in an unprecedented position to change the nature of our relationship. Not by preemptive concession, but by keeping our strength. Not by yielding up defense systems with nothing won in return, but by hard, cool engagement in the tug and pull of diplomacy.

My life has been lived in the shadow of war. I almost lost my life in one.

And I hate war. Love peace. And we have peace. And I am not going to let anyone take it away from us.

Our economy is strong but not invulnerable, and the peace is broad but can be broken. And now we must decide. We will surely have change this year, but will it be change that moves us forward, or change that risks retreat?

In 1940, when I was barely more than a boy, Franklin Roosevelt said we shouldn't change horses in midstream. My friends, these days the world moves even more quickly, and now, after two great terms, a switch will be made. But when you have to change horses in midstream, doesn't it make sense to switch to one who's going the same way?

An election that's about ideas and values is also about philosophy. And I have one.

At the bright center is the individual. And radiating out from him or her is the family, the essential unit of closeness and of love. For it's the family that communicates to our children—to the 21st century—our culture, our religious faith, our traditions and history.

From the individual to the family to the community, and then on out to the town, to the church, and the school and, still echoing out, to the county, the state, and the nation—each doing only what it does well, and no more. And I believe that power must always be kept close to the individual, close to the hands that raise the family and run the home.

I am guided by certain traditions. One is that there's a God and He is good, and His love, while free, has a self-imposed cost: we must be good to one another.

I believe in another tradition that is, by now, imbedded in the national soul. It's that learning is good in and of itself. You know, the mothers of the Jewish ghettoes of the East would pour honey on a book so the children would know that learning is sweet. And the parents who settled hungry Kansas would take their children in from the fields when a teacher came. That is our history.

And there is another tradition. And that's the idea of community—a beautiful word with a big meaning, though liberal Democrats have an odd view of it. They see community as a limited cluster of interest groups, locked in odd conformity. And in this view, the country waits passive while Washington sets the rules.

But that's not what community means, not to me. For we are a nation of communities, of thousands and tens of thousands of ethnic, religious, social, business, labor union, neighborhood, regional, and other organizations, all of them varied, voluntary, and unique.

This is America: the Knights of Columbus, the Grange, Hadassah, the Disabled American Veterans, the Order of Ahepa, the Business and Professional Women of America, the union hall, the Bible study group, LULAC, Holy Name—a brilliant diversity spread like stars, like a thousand points of light in a broad and peaceful sky.

Does government have a place? Yes. Government that remembers that the people are its master is a good and needed thing.

And I respect old-fashioned common sense, and I have no great love for the imaginings of the social planners. You see, I like what's been tested and found to be true. For instance:

Should public school teachers be required to lead our children in the Pledge of Allegiance? My opponent says no—and I say yes.

Should society be allowed to impose the death penalty on those who commit crimes of extraordinary cruelty and violence? My opponent says no—but I say yes.

And should our children—should our children have the right to say a voluntary prayer, or even observe a moment of silence, in the schools? My opponent says no—but I say yes.

And should free men and women have the right to own a gun to protect their home? My opponent says no—but I say yes.

And is it right to believe in the sanctity of life and protect the lives of innocent children? My opponent says no—but I say yes. You see, we must, we must change—we've got to change from abortion to adoption. And let me tell you this—Barbara and I have an adopted granddaughter. On the day of her christening we wept with joy. I thank God that her parents chose life.

I'm the one who believes it is a scandal to give a weekend furlough to a hardened first-degree killer who hasn't even served enough time to be eligible for parole.

I'm the one who says a drug dealer who is responsible for the death of a policeman should be subject to capital punishment.

And I'm the one who will not raise taxes. My opponent now says he'll raise them as a last resort, or a third resort. But when a politician talks like that, you know that's one resort he'll be checking into. And my opponent won't rule out raising taxes. But I will. And the Congress will push me to raise taxes, and I'll say no, and they'll push, and I'll say no, and they'll push again. And I'll say to them, read my lips, no new taxes.

Let me tell you more, let me just tell you more about the mission on jobs. My mission is: 30 in eight—30 million jobs in the next eight years.

Every one of our children deserves a first-rate school. The liberal Democrats want power in the hands of the federal government and I want power in the hands of the parents. And I will encourage merit schools. I will give more kids a Head Start. And I'll make it easier to save for college.

I want a drug-free America, and this will not be easy to achieve. But I want to enlist the help of some people who are rarely included. Tonight I challenge the young people of our country to shut down the drug dealers around the world. Unite with us, work with us.

Zero tolerance isn't just a policy, it's an attitude. Tell them what you think of people who underwrite the dealers who put poison in our society. And while you're doing that, my administration will be telling the dealers, "Whatever we have to do we'll do, but your day is over, you are history."

I'm going to do whatever it takes to make sure the disabled are included in the mainstream. For too long they've been left out. But they're not going to be left out any more.

And I am going to stop ocean dumping. Our beaches should not be garbage dumps and our harbors should not be cesspools. And I'm going to have the FBI trace the medical wastes and we're going to punish the people who dump those infected needles into our oceans, lakes, and rivers.

Let's clean the air. We must reduce the harm done by acid rain.

And I'll put incentives back into the domestic energy industry, for I know from personal experience there is no security for the United States in further dependence on foreign oil.

In foreign affairs, I'll continue our policy of peace through strength. I'll move toward further cuts in strategic and conventional arsenals of both the United States and the Soviet Union and the Eastern bloc and NATO. I'll modernize and preserve our technological edge and that includes strategic defense. And a priority: ban chemical and biological weapons from the face of the earth. That will be a priority with me. And I intend to speak for freedom, stand for freedom, be a patient friend to anyone, East or West, who will fight for freedom.

It seems to me the presidency provides an incomparable opportunity for "gentle persuasion."

And I hope to stand for a new harmony, a greater tolerance. We've come far, but I think we need a new harmony among the races in our country. And we're on a journey into a new century, and we've got to leave that tired old baggage of bigotry behind.

Some people who are enjoying our prosperity are forgetting what it's for. But they diminish our triumph when they act as if wealth is an end in itself.

And there are those who've dropped their standards along the way, as if ethics were too heavy and slowed their rise to the top. There's graft in City Hall and there's greed on Wall Street and there's influence-peddling in Washington, and the small corruptions of everyday ambition.

But you see, I believe public service is honorable. And every time I hear that someone has breached the public trust, it breaks my heart.

And I wonder sometimes if we've forgotten who we are. But we're the people who sundered a nation rather than allow a sin called slavery—and we're the people who rose from the ghettoes and the deserts.

And we weren't saints, but we lived by standards. We celebrated the individual, but we weren't self-centered. We were practical, but we didn't live only for material things. We believed in getting ahead, but blind ambition wasn't our way.

The fact is, prosperity has a purpose. It's to allow us to pursue the "better angels," to give us time to think and grow. Prosperity with a purpose means taking your idealism and making it concrete by certain acts of goodness. It means helping a child from an unhappy home learn how to read—and I thank my wife, Barbara, for all her work in helping people to read and all her work for literacy in this country. It means teaching troubled children through your presence that there is such a thing as reliable love. Some would say it's soft and insufficiently tough to care about these things. But where is it written that we must act as if we do not care, as if we're not moved? Well, I am moved. I want a kinder and gentler nation.

Two men this year ask for your support. And you must know us.

As for me, I've held high office and done the work of democracy day by day. Yes, my parents were prosperous, and their children sure were lucky. But there were lessons we had to learn about life. John Kennedy discovered poverty when he campaigned in West Virginia; there were children who had no milk. And young Teddy Roosevelt met the new America when he roamed the immigrant streets of New York. And I learned a few things about life in a place called Texas. And when I was working on this part of the speech, Barbara came in and asked what I was doing and I looked up and I said I'm working hard. And she said, Oh, dear, don't worry. Relax. Sit back. Take off your shoes and put up your silver foot.

Now, we moved to West Texas 40 years ago, 40 years ago this year. And the war was over, and we wanted to get out and make it on our own. And those were exciting days. We lived in a little shotgun house, one room for the three of us. Worked in the oil business and then started on my own.

And in time we had six children. Moved from the shotgun to a duplex apartment to a house. And lived the dream—high school football on Friday nights, Little League, neighborhood barbecue.

People don't see their own experience as symbolic of an era, but of course we were. And so was everyone else who was taking a chance and pushing into unknown territory with kids and a dog and a car. But the big thing I learned is the satisfaction of creating jobs, which meant creating opportunity, which meant happy families, who in turn could do more to help others and enhance their own lives. I learned that the good done by a single good job could be felt in ways you can't imagine.

It's been said that I'm not the most compelling speaker, and there are actually those who claim that I don't always communicate in the clearest, most concise way. But I dare them to keep it up. Go ahead, make my 24-hour time period. Now I may be—may not be the most eloquent, but I learned early on that eloquence won't draw oil from the ground. And I may sometimes be a little awkward, but there's nothing self-conscious in my love of country. And I'm a quiet man, but I hear the quiet people others don't—the ones who raise the family, pay the taxes, meet the mortgage. And I hear them and I am moved, and their concerns are mine.

A president must be many things. He must be a shrewd protector of America's interests, and he must be an idealist who leads those who move for a freer and more democratic planet.

And he must see to it that government intrudes as little as possible in the lives of the people; and yet remember that it is right and proper that a nation's leader take an interest in the nation's character. And he must be able to define—and lead—a mission.

For seven and a half years I've worked with a president. I've seen what crosses that big desk. I've seen the unexpected crisis that arrives in a cable in a young aide's hand. And I've seen the problems that simmer on for decades and suddenly demand resolution. And I've seen modest decisions made with anguish, and crucial decisions made with dispatch.

And so I know that what it all comes down to, this election—what it all comes down to, after all the shouting and the cheers—is the man at the desk. And who should sit at that desk.

My friends, I am that man.

I say it—I say it without boast or bravado. I've fought for my country, I've served, I've built—and I'll go from the hills to the hollows, from the cities to the suburbs to the loneliest town on the quietest street to take our message of hope and growth for every American to every American.

I will keep America moving forward, always forward—for a better America, for an endless, enduring dream and a thousand points of light.

This is my mission. And I will complete it.

Thank you. You know, it is customary to end an address with a pledge, or saying, that holds a special meaning. And I've chosen one that we all know by heart, one that we all learned in school. And I ask everyone in this great hall to stand and join me in this. We all know it.

I pledge allegiance to the flag of the United States of America and to the republic for which it stands, one nation, under God, indivisible, with liberty and justice for all.

Thank you. God bless you.

Inaugural Address

Washington, D.C.

January 20, 1989

BUSH'S INAUGURAL ADDRESS was intended to demonstrate his worthiness to succeed the immensely popular Reagan without subscribing to Reagan's ideology. Its use of religious symbolism was a public reminder that the two presidents shared the same values; at the same time, the speech contained hints of compromise and cooperation that were not at all in the fiercely partisan tradition of Reagan. William Safire called it "a good speech, suitably solemn and unifying, coherent and appropriately brief. It did not soar and cause listeners to tingle, but that is not the Bush style." Stephen R. Graubard, on the other hand, said the address was "maudlin when it was not positively embarrassing" and "resembled no other in the long history of the republic" in its substitution of inspirational buzzwords for a real statement of principles.

Mr. Chief Justice, Mr. President, Vice President Quayle, Senator Mitchell, Speaker Wright, Senator Dole, Congressman Michel, and fellow citizens, neighbors, and friends. There is a man here who has earned a lasting place in our hearts and in our history. President Reagan, on behalf of our nation I thank you for the wonderful things that you have done for America.

I've just repeated, word for word, the oath taken by George Washington 200 years ago, and the Bible on which I placed my hand is the Bible on which he placed his. It is right that the memory of Washington be with us today, not only because this is our bicentennial inauguration but because Washington remains the father of our country. And he would, I think, be gladdened by this day. For today is the concrete expression of a stunning fact: our continuity these 200 years since our government began.

We meet on democracy's front porch, a good place to talk as neighbors and as friends. For this is a day when our nation is made whole, when our differences for a moment are suspended. And my first act as president is a prayer—I ask you to bow your heads.

Heavenly Father, we bow our heads and thank You for Your love. Accept our thanks for the peace that yields this day and the shared faith that makes its continuance likely. Make us strong to do Your work, willing to heed and hear Your will, and write on our hearts these words: "Use power to help people." For we are given power not to advance our own purposes nor to make a great show in the world, nor a name. There is but one just use of power and it is to serve people. Help us remember, Lord. Amen.

I come before you and assume the presidency at a moment rich with promise. We live in a peaceful, prosperous time but we can make it better. For a new breeze is blowing and a world refreshed by freedom seems reborn; for in man's heart, if not in fact, the day of the dictator is over. The totalitarian era is passing, its old ideas blown away like leaves from an ancient, lifeless tree.

A new breeze is blowing—and a national refreshed by freedom stands ready to push on. There's new ground to be broken and new action to be taken. There are times when the future seems thick as a fog; you sit and wait, hoping the mist will lift and reveal the right path.

But this is a time when the future seems a door you can walk right through—into a room called Tomorrow. Great nations of the world are moving toward democracy— through the door to freedom. Men and women of the world move toward free markets—through the door to prosperity. The people of the world agitate for free expression and free thought—through the door to the moral and intellectual satisfactions that only liberty allows.

We know what works: Freedom works. We know what's right: Freedom is right. We know how to secure a more just and prosperous life for man on earth: through free markets, free speech, free elections and the exercise of free will unhampered by the state.

For the first time in this century—for the first time in perhaps all history—man does not have to invent a system by which to live. We don't have to talk late into the night about which form of government is better. We don't have to wrest justice from the kings—we have only to summon it from within ourselves.

We must act on what we know. I take as my guide the hope of a saint: in crucial things, unity—in important things, diversity—in all things, generosity.

American today is a proud, free nation, decent and civil—a place we cannot help but love. We know in our hearts, not loudly and proudly but as a simple fact, that this country has meaning beyond what we see, and that our strength is a force for good.

Have we changed as a nation even in our time? Are we enthralled with material things, less appreciative of the nobility of work and sacrifice? My friends, we are not the sum of our possessions. They are not the measure of our lives. In our hearts we know what matters. We cannot hope only to leave our children a bigger car, a bigger bank account. We must hope to give them a sense of what it means to be a loyal friend, a loving parent, a citizen who leaves his home, his neighborhood, and town better than he found it.

And what do we want the men and women who work with us to say when we're no longer there? That we were more driven to succeed than anyone around us? Or do we stop to ask if a sick child had gotten better, and stayed a moment there to trade a word of friendship.

No president, no government can teach us to remember what is best in what we are. But if the man you have chosen to lead this government can help make a difference, if he can celebrate the quieter, deeper successes that are made not of gold and silk but of better hearts and finer souls; if he can do these things, then he must.

America is never wholly herself unless she is engaged in high moral principle. We as a people have such a purpose today. It is to make kinder the face of the nation and gentler the face of the world.

My friends, we have work to do. There are the homeless, lost and roaming. There are the children who have nothing—no love, no normalcy. There are those who cannot free themselves of enslavement to whatever addiction—drugs, welfare, the demoralization that rules the slums. There is crime to be conquered, the rough crime of the streets. There are young women to be helped who are about to become mothers of children they can't care for and might not love. They need our care, our guidance, and our education, though we bless them for choosing life.

The old solution, the old way, was to think that public money alone could end these problems. But we have learned that that is not so. And in any case, our funds are low. We have a deficit to bring down. We have more will than wallet; but will is what we need.

We will make the hard choices, looking at what we have, perhaps allocating it differently, making our decisions based on honest need and prudent safety. And then we will do the wisest thing of all: We will turn to the only resource we have that in times of need always grows: the goodness and the courage of the American people.

And I am speaking of a new engagement in the lives of others—a new activism, hands-on and involved, that gets the job done. We must bring in the generations, harnessing the unused talent of the elderly and the unfocused energy of the young. For not only leadership is passed from generation to generation, but so is stewardship. And the generation born after the Second World War has come of age.

I've spoken of a thousand points of light—of all the community organizations that are spread like stars throughout the nation doing good. We will work hand in hand, encouraging, sometimes leading, sometimes being led, rewarding. We will work on this in the White House, in the cabinet agencies. I will go to the people and the programs that are the brighter points of light, and I'll ask every member of my government to become involved. The old ideas are new again because they're not old, they are timeless: duty, sacrifice, commitment, and a patriotism that finds its expression in taking part and pitching in.

And we need a new engagement, too, between the executive and the Congress. The challenges before us will be thrashed out with the White—with the House and the Senate. And we must bring the federal budget into balance. And we must insure that America stands before the world united: strong, at peace, and fiscally sound. But, of course, things may be difficult.

We need compromise; we've had dissension. We need harmony; we've had a chorus of discordant voices. For Congress, too, has changed in our time. There's grown a certain divisiveness. We've seen the hard looks and heard the statements in which not each other's ideas are challenged, but each other's motives. And our great parties have too often been far apart and untrusting of each other.

It's been this way since Vietnam. That war cleaves us still. But, friends, that war began in earnest a quarter of a century ago; and surely the statute of limitations has been reached. This is a fact: The final lesson of Vietnam is that no great nation can long afford to be sundered by a memory.

A new breeze is blowing—and the old bipartisanship must be made new again.

To my friends—and yes, I do mean friends—in the loyal opposition—and yes, I mean loyal—I put out my hand. I'm putting out my hand to you, Mr. Speaker. I'm putting out my hand to you, Mr. Majority Leader. For this is the thing: this is the age of the offered hand. And we can't turn back clocks, and I don't want to. But when our fathers were young, Mr. Speaker, our differences ended at the water's edge. And we don't wish to turn back time, but when our mothers were young, Mr. Majority Leader, the Congress and the executive were capable of working together to produce a budget on which this nation could live. Let us negotiate soon and hard, but in the end let us produce.

The American people await action. They didn't send us here to bicker. They asked us to rise above the merely partisan. In crucial things, unity—and this, my friends, is crucial.

To the world, too, we offer new engagement and a renewed vow: We will stay strong to protect the peace. The "offered hand" is a reluctant fist; but the fist, once made, is strong and can be used with great effect.

There are today Americans who are held against their will in foreign lands, and Americans who are unaccounted for. Assistance can be shown here and will be long remembered. Goodwill begets goodwill. Good faith can be a spiral that endlessly moves on.

"Great nations like great men must keep their word." When America says something, America means it, whether a treaty or an agreement or a vow made on marble steps. We will always try to speak clearly, for candor is a compliment. But subtlety, too, is good and has its place.

While keeping our alliances and friendships around the world strong, ever strong, we will continue our new closeness with the Soviet Union, consistent both with our security and with progress. One might say that our new relationship in part reflects the triumph of hope and strength over experience. But hope is good. And so is strength, and vigilance.

Here today are tens of thousands of our citizens who feel the understandable satisfaction of those who have taken part in democracy and seen their hopes fulfilled. But my thoughts have been turning the past few days to those who would be watching at home—to an older fellow who will throw a salute by himself when the flag goes by, and the woman who will tell her sons the words of the battle hymns. I don't mean this to be sentimental. I mean that on days like this we remember that we are all part of a continuum, inescapably connected by the ties that bind.

Our children are watching in schools throughout our great land. And to them I say, thank you for watching democracy's big day. For democracy belongs to us all and freedom is like a beautiful kite that can go higher and higher with the breeze. And to all I say: No matter what your circumstances or where you are, you are part of this day. You are part of the life of our great nation.

A president is neither prince nor pope, and I don't seek "a window on men's souls." In fact, I yearn for a greater tolerance, an easygoingness about each other's attitudes and way of life.

There are a few clear areas in which we as a society must rise up united and express our intolerance and the most obvious now is drugs. And when that first cocaine was smuggled in on a ship, it may as well have been a deadly bacteria, so much has it hurt the body, the soul of our country. And there is much to be done and to be said, but take my word for it: This scourge will stop.

And so, there is much to do; and tomorrow the work begins. And I do not mistrust the future; I do not fear what is ahead. For our problems are large, but our heart is larger. Our challenges are great, but our will is greater. And if our flaws are endless, God's love is truly boundless.

Some see leadership as high drama, and the sound of trumpets calling. And sometimes it is that. But I see history as a book with many pages—and each day we fill a page with acts of hopefulness and meaning.

A new breeze blows, a page turns, the story unfolds—and so today a chapter begins: a small and stately story of unity, diversity, and generosity—shared and written together.

Thank you. God bless you and God bless the United States of America.

The Invasion of Panama

Washington, D.C.

December 20, 1989

In 1989 the White House found itself in a quandary over the political crisis developing in Panama, where Manuel Antonio Noriega, the army general who had ruled Panama for six years, was refusing to make way for an elected civilian government. For more than three decades Noriega had received money from American intelligence officials. Since coming to power, he had used terror tactics to control Panama and was accused of making multi-million-dollar profits from drug trafficking, gambling and prostitution rackets, and the sale of U.S. military secrets to Cuba and the Soviet Union. Economic sanctions by the United States and a coup attempt in October 1989 failed to dislodge him.

On December 20, five days after Noriega declared his nation to be in a state of war with the United States, Bush went on the air to announce Operation Just Cause, the invasion of Panama by a strike force of airborne Army troops. The fighting, which cost the lives of 23 American soldiers and several hundred Panamanians, lasted only a few days. Noriega, after eluding capture for two weeks, surrendered to U.S. authorities and was eventually convicted on charges of racketeering and conspiracy.

Last night I ordered U.S. military forces to Panama. No president takes such action lightly. This morning, I want to tell you what I did and why I did it. For nearly two years, the United States, nations of Latin America and the Caribbean have worked together to resolve the crisis in Panama. The goals of the United States have been to safeguard the lives of Americans, to defend democracy in Panama, to combat drug trafficking, and to protect the integrity of the Panama Canal Treaty. Many attempts have been made to resolve this crisis through diplomacy and negotiations. All were rejected by the dictator of Panama, General Manuel Noriega, an indicted drug trafficker.

Last Friday, Noriega declared his military dictatorship to be in a state of war with the United States and publicly threatened the lives of Americans in Panama. The very next day, forces under his command shot and killed an unarmed American serviceman, wounded another, arrested and brutally beat a third American serviceman and then brutally interrogated his wife, threatening her with sexual abuse. That was enough.

General Noriega's reckless threats and attacks upon Americans in Panama created an eminent danger to the 35,000 American citizens in Panama. As president, I have no higher obligation than to safeguard the lives of American citizens. And that is why I directed our armed forces to protect the lives of American citizens in Panama, and to bring General Noriega to justice in the United States. I contacted the bipartisan leadership of Congress last night and informed them of this decision, and after taking this action, I also talked with leaders in Latin America, the Caribbean, and those of other U.S. allies.

At this moment, U.S. forces, including forces deployed from the United States last night, are engaged in action in Panama. The United States intends to withdraw the forces newly deployed to Panama as quickly as possible. All forces have conducted themselves courageously and self-lessly, and as commander in chief, I salute every one of them and thank them on behalf of our country.

Tragically, some Americans have lost their lives in defense of their fellow citizens, in defense of democracy, and my heart goes out to their families. We also regret and mourn the loss of innocent Panamanians.

The brave Panamanians elected by the people of Panama in the elections last May, President Guillermo Endara and Vice Presidents Calderón and Ford, have assumed the rightful leadership of their country. You remember those horrible pictures of newly elected Vice President Ford covered head to toe with blood, beaten mercilessly by so-called dignity battalions. Well, the United States today recognizes the democratically elected government of

President Endara. I will send our ambassador back to Panama immediately.

Key military objectives have been achieved. Most organized resistance has been eliminated. But the operation is not over yet. General Noriega is in hiding. And nevertheless, yesterday, a dictator ruled Panama, and today, constitutionally elected govern—elected leaders govern.

I have today directed the secretary of the treasury and the secretary of state to lift the economic sanctions with respect to the democratically elected government of Panama, and in cooperation with that government, to take steps to effect an orderly unblocking of Panamanian government assets in the United States.

I am fully committed to implement the Panama Canal Treaty and turn over the Canal to Panama in the year 2000. The actions we have taken and the cooperation of a new democratic government in Panama will permit us to honor these commitments. As soon as the new government recommends a qualified candidate, Panamanian, to be administrator of the Canal, as called for in the treaties, I will submit this nominee to the Senate for expedited consideration.

I am committed to strengthening our relationship with the democratic nations in this hemisphere. I will continue to seek solutions to the problems of this region through dialogue and multilateral diplomacy.

I took this action only after reaching the conclusion that every other avenue was closed and the lives of American citizens were in grave danger.

I hope that the people of Panama will put this dark chapter of dictatorship behind them and will move forward together as citizens of a democratic Panama with this government that they themselves have elected.

The United States is eager to work with the Panamanian people in partnership and friendship to rebuild their economy. The Panamanian people want democracy, peace, and the chance for a better life in dignity and freedom. The people of the United States seek only to support them in pursuit of these noble goals.

Thank you very much.

The Gulf War

Washington, D.C.

January 16, 1991

"I JUST AM not one who flamboyantly believes in throwing words around," Bush remarked to reporters on one occasion. "I'm more interested in action." Iraq's attempt to annex neighboring Kuwait in August 1990 gave him a reason to undertake military action on a far grander scale than the invasion of Panama two years earlier. At stake, in addition to Kuwait's independence, was the price structure of the world's supply of oil. When a trade embargo imposed by the United Nations Security Council failed to persuade Iraq's dictator, Saddam Hussein, a coalition of 28 Western and Middle Eastern nations went on the attack. The massive air bombardment of Iraq—the heaviest bombardment in history—was only a few hours old when Bush, looking calmer and more composed than usual, delivered this televised address from the Oval Office.

The air bombardment was followed by Operation Desert Storm, a combined air and ground war. It began on February 24 with an invasion by 270,000 American, British, and French troops. Iraq's surrender a mere four days later gave Bush the highest popularity rating among American presidents since Franklin Roosevelt after Pearl Harbor. But Bush's decision to end the war without removing Saddam Hussein from power cost him considerable goodwill. When an economic recession hit the United States the following year, many cars sported bumper stickers that read: "Saddam Hussein still has his job. How about you?"

Just two hours ago, allied air forces began an attack on military targets in Iraq and Kuwait. These attacks continue as I speak. Ground forces are not engaged. This conflict started August 2, when the dictator of Iraq invaded a small and helpless neighbor. Kuwait, a member of the Arab League and a member of the United Nations, was crushed, its people brutalized. Five months ago, Saddam Hussein started this cruel war against Kuwait; tonight, the battle has been joined.

This military action, taken in accord with United States resolutions and with the consent of the United States Congress, follows months of constant and virtually endless diplomatic activity on the part of the United Nations, the United States, and many, many other countries.

Arab leaders sought what became known as an Arab solution, only to conclude that Saddam Hussein was unwilling to leave Kuwait. Others traveled to Baghdad in a variety of efforts to restore peace and justice. Our secretary of state, James Baker, held an historic meeting in Geneva, only to be totally rebuffed.

This past weekend, in a last-ditch effort, the secretary-general of the United Nations went to the Middle East with peace in his heart—his second such mission. And he came back from Baghdad with no progress at all in getting Saddam Hussein to withdraw from Kuwait.

Now, the 28 countries with forces in the Gulf area have exhausted all reasonable efforts to reach a peaceful resolution and have no choice but to drive Saddam from Kuwait by force. We will not fail.

As I report to you, air attacks are under way against military targets in Iraq. We are determined to knock out Saddam Hussein's nuclear bomb potential. We will also destroy his chemical weapons facilities. Much of Saddam's artillery and tanks will be destroyed. Our operations are designed to best protect the lives of all the coalition forces by targeting Saddam's vast military arsenal.

Initial reports from General Schwartzkopf are that our operations are proceeding according to plan. Our objectives are clear: Saddam Hussein's forces will leave Kuwait. The legitimate government of Kuwait will be restored to its rightful place, and Kuwait will once again be free.

Iraq will eventually comply with all relevant United Nations resolutions, and then, when peace is restored, it is our hope that Iraq will live as a peaceful and cooperative member of the family of nations, thus enhancing the security and stability of the Gulf.

Some may ask, why act now? Why not wait? The answer is clear. The world could wait no longer. Sanctions, though having some effect, showed no signs of accomplishing their objective. Sanctions were tried for well over five months, and we and our allies concluded that sanctions alone would not force Saddam from Kuwait.

While the world waited, Saddam Hussein systematically raped, pillaged, and plundered a tiny nation no threat to his own. He subjected the people of Kuwait to unspeakable atrocities, and among those maimed and murdered, innocent children.

While the world waited, Saddam sought to add to the chemical weapons arsenal he now possesses, an infinitely more dangerous weapon of mass destruction—a nuclear weapon. And while the world waited, while the world talked peace and withdrawal, Saddam Hussein dug in and moved massive forces into Kuwait.

While the world waited, while Saddam stalled, more damage was being done to the fragile economies of the Third World, emerging democracies of Eastern Europe, to the entire world, including to our own economy.

The United States, together with the United Nations, exhausted every means at our disposal to bring this crisis to a peaceful end. However, Saddam clearly felt that by stalling and threatening and defying the United Nations, he could weaken the forces arrayed against him.

While the world waited, Saddam Hussein met every overture of peace with open contempt. While the world prayed for peace, Saddam prepared for war.

I had hoped that when the United States Congress, in historic debate, took its resolute action, Saddam would realize he could not prevail, and would move out of Kuwait in accord with the United Nations resolutions. He did not do that. Instead, he remained intransigent, certain that time was on his side.

Saddam was warned over and over again to comply with the will of the United Nations, leave Kuwait, or be driven out. Saddam has arrogantly rejected all warnings. Instead he tried to make this a dispute between Iraq and the United States of America.

Well, he failed. Tonight 28 nations-countries from five continents, Europe and Asia, Africa and the Arab League—have forces in the Gulf area standing shoulder to shoulder against Saddam Hussein. These countries had hoped the use of force could be avoided. Regrettably, we now believe that only force will make him leave.

Prior to ordering our forces into battle, I instructed our military commanders to take every necessary step to prevail as quickly as possible, and with the greatest degree of protection possible for American and allied servicemen and women. I've told the American people before that this will not be another Vietnam, and I repeat this here tonight. Our troops will have the best possible support in the entire world, and they will not be asked to fight with one hand tied behind their back. I'm hopeful that this fighting will not go on for long and that casualties will be held to an absolute minimum.

This is an historic moment. We have in this past year made great progress in ending the long era of conflict and cold war. We have before us the opportunity to forge for ourselves and for future generations a new world order, a world where the rule of law, not the law of the jungle, governs the conduct of nations.

When we are successful, and we will be, we have a real chance at this new world order, an order in which a credible United Nations can use its peacekeeping role to fulfill the promise and vision of the UN's founders. We have no argument with the people of Iraq. Indeed, for the innocents caught in this conflict, I pray for their safety.

Our goal is not the conquest of Iraq. It is the liberation of Kuwait. It is my hope that somehow the Iraqi people can, even now, convince their dictator that he must lay down his arms, leave Kuwait, and let Iraq itself rejoin the family of peace-loving nations.

Thomas Paine wrote many years ago: "These are the times that try men's souls." Those well-known words are so very true today. But even as planes of the multinational forces attack Iraq, I prefer to think of peace, not war. I am convinced not only that we will prevail, but that out of the horror of combat will come the recognition that no nation can stand against a world united. No nation will be permitted to brutally assault its neighbor.

No president can easily commit our sons and daughters to war. They are the nation's finest. Ours is an all-volunteer force, magnificently trained, highly motivated. The troops know why they're there. And listen to what they say, because they've said it better than any president or prime minister ever could. Listen to Hollywood Huddleston, marine lance corporal. He says: "Let's free these people so we can go home and be free again." And he's right. The terrible crimes and tortures committed by Saddam's henchmen against the innocent people of Kuwait are an affront to mankind and a challenge to the freedom of all.

Listen to one of our great officers out there, marine Lieutenant General Walter Boomer. He said: "There are things worth fighting for. A world in which brutality and lawlessness are allowed to go unchecked isn't the kind of world we're going to want to live in."

Listen to Master Sergeant J. P. Kendall of the 82nd Airborne: 'We're here for more than just the price of a gallon of gas. What we're doing is going to chart the future of the world for the next hundred years. It's better to deal with this guy now than five years from now."

And finally, we should all sit up and listen to Jackie Jones, an army lieutenant, when she says, "If we let him get away with this, who knows what's going to be next."

I've called upon Hollywood and Walter and J. P. and Jackie and all their courageous comrades-in-arms to do what must be done. Tonight, America and the world are deeply grateful to them and to their families.

And let me say to everyone listening or watching tonight: When the troops we've sent in finish their work, I'm determined to bring them home as soon as possible. Tonight, as our forces fight, they and their families are in our prayers.

May God bless each and every one of them, and the coalition forces at our side in the Gulf, and may He continue to bless our nation, the United States of America.

The New World Order

Montgomery, Alabama

April 13, 1991

DESPITE THE GULF WAR'S unpleasant aftermath, in which Iraq massacred its Kurdish and Shi'ite Muslim minorities, the White House saw in it the greatest triumph of American world leadership since World War II. This, coupled with the rapid breakdown of the Soviet Union and the sudden independence of the European nations it had dominated, gave rise to the notion that the "good guys" had finally won the long standoff between the superpowers and that the world was poised to enter a new era. In an address to a joint session of Congress on March 6 celebrating the war's end, Bush invoked Winston Churchill's idea of a new world order in which "the principles of justice and fair play . . . protect the weak against the strong." He expanded on this idea a few weeks later in a speech at Maxwell Air Force Base in Alabama. Both speeches were constructed largely of insubstantial platitudes, allowing Bush to describe a variety of challenges without explaining how, in concrete terms, he proposed to meet them.

It is my great pleasure to look out across what essentially is a sea of blue, to meet this morning with the men and women of the Air University—the Air War College, the Air Command and Staff School, the Squadron Officers School, and of course, the NCO Academy. And I'm glad to see democracy in action. I see a navy guy here or there, or maybe a coast guardsman, maybe the marines, maybe the army over here. And I think I recognize some friends from overseas, members of our coalition who helped us so much in achieving our objectives halfway around the world. They're more than welcome.

The history of aviation has been shaped here since the Wright brothers brought their strange new mechanical bird to Montgomery and housed it in a hangar not far from where we stand. This institution from its early days as the Air Corps Tactical School has defined the nation's air strategy and tactics that have guided our operations over the fields of Europe and the seas of the Pacific, from the First World War to the thousand hours of Desert Storm.

It falls to all of you to derive the lessons learned from this war. Desert Storm demonstrated the true strength of joint operations. Not the notion that each service must participate in equal parts in every operation in every war, but that we use the proper tools at the proper time. In Desert Storm, a critical tool was certainly air power. And every one of you can take pride in that fact. Our technology and training ensured minimal losses, and our precision, your precision, spared the lives of innocent civilians.

But our victory also showed that technology alone is insufficient. A warrior's heart must burn with the will to fight. And if he fights but does not believe, no technology in the world can save him. We and our allies had more than superior weapons, we had the will to win.

I might say parenthetically, this will is personified by the man who leads you. I know that General Boyd often speaks about what he calls the unlimited liability of the military profession. He knows because he's put it all on the line. As a veteran of Vietnam, he flew 105 combat missions before being shot down over Hanoi. And he spent almost seven years, 2,500 cruel days, in captivity. And yet he emerged brave, unbroken. He kept the faith to himself and his nation.

And let me just say a word about this man over here on my left, General McPeak. I remember early on a meeting up at Camp David with Tony McPeak. Secretary Cheney was there; General Powell was there; Brent Scowcroft, other chiefs. The other chiefs, I believe, were with us, Tony. And in a very laid-back way, typical of him with his modesty, but with total confidence, he told me exactly what he felt air power could do. And after he left, I don't mean to show my naive skepticism, but I turned to my trusted national security adviser, who's standing over here, General

Brent Scowcroft, and I said, "Brent, does this guy really know what he's talking about?"

And Lieutenant General Scowcroft—Air Force Lieutenant General—said, "Yes."

And General McPeak did.

And to be doubly sure then, and he'll remember this, just before the war started, I invited General McPeak and Secretary Cheney to join me and General Scowcroft upstairs at the residence in the White House—quiet lunch there. And I asked Tony, I think he'd just come back then from the theater, the other theater. And I put the question to him—I think this is exactly what I said: "Are you as certain now as you were up at Camp David?"

And he said, "Even more so."

And the war started just a few days later, and history will record that General McPeak was 100 percent right, right on target.

Here at Air University it's your business to read the lessons of the past with an eye on the far horizon. And that's why I wanted to speak to you today about the new world taking shape around us, about the prospects for a new world order now within our reach. For more than four decades we've lived in a world divided, East from West; a world locked in a conflict of arms and ideas called the cold war. Two systems, two superpowers, separated by mistrust and unremitting hostility.

For more than four decades, America's energies were focused on containing the threat to the free world from the forces of Communism. That war is over. East Germany has vanished from the map as a separate entity. Today in Berlin, the wall that once divided a continent, divided a world in two, has been pulverized, turned into souvenirs. And the sections that remain standing are but museum pieces. The Warsaw Pact passed into the pages of history last week. Not with a bang, but with a whimper, its demise reported in a story reported on page A16 of the Washington Post.

In the coming weeks I'll be talking in some detail about the possibility of a new world order emerging after the cold war. And in recent weeks I've been focusing not only on the Gulf, but on free trade, on the North American Free Trade Agreement, the Uruguay Round trade negotiations, and the essentiality of obtaining from the United States Congress a renewal of fasttrack authority to achieve our goals. But today I want to discuss another aspect of that order, our relations with Europe and the Soviet Union.

Twice this century, a dream born on the battlefields of Europe died after the shooting stopped—the dream of a world in which major powers worked together to ensure peace, to settle their disputes through cooperation, not confrontation. Today a transformed Europe stands closer than ever before to its free and democratic destiny. At long last, Europe is moving forward, moving toward a new world of hope.

At the same time, we and our European allies have moved beyond containment to a policy of active engagement in a world no longer driven by cold war tensions and animosities. You see, as the cold war drew to an end we saw the possibilities of a new order in which nations worked together to promote peace and prosperity. I'm not talking here of a blueprint that will govern the conduct of nations or some supernatural structure or institution. The new world order does not mean surrendering our national sovereignty imposed by our successes. It really describes a responsibility imposed by our successes. It refers to new ways of working with other nations to deter aggression and to achieve stability, to achieve prosperity and, above all, to achieve peace.

It springs from hopes for a world based on a shared commitment among nations large and small to a set of principles that undergird our relations: peaceful settlements of disputes, solidarity against aggression, reduced and controlled arsenals, and just treatment of all peoples.

This order, this ability to work together, got its first real test in the Gulf War. For the first time, a regional conflict, the aggression against Kuwait, did not serve as a proxy for superpower confrontation. For the first time, the United Nations Security Council, free from the clash of cold war ideologies, functioned as its designers intended, a force for conflict resolution in collective security.

In the Gulf, nations from Europe and North America, Asia and Africa, and the Arab world joined together to stop aggression and sent a signal to would-be tyrants everywhere in the world. By joining forces to defend one small nation, we showed that we can work together against aggressors in defense of principle.

We also recognize that the cold war's end didn't deliver us into an era of perpetual peace. As old threats recede, new threats emerge. The quest for the new world order is, in part, a challenge to keep the dangers of disorder at bay.

Today, thank God, Kuwait is free. But turmoil in that tormented region of the world continues. Saddam's continued savagery has placed his regime outside the international order. We will not interfere in Iraq's civil war. Iraqi people must decide their own political future.

Looking out here at you and thinking of your families, let me comment a little further. We set our objectives. These objectives, sanctioned by international law, have been achieved. I made very clear that when our objectives were obtained that our troops would be coming home. And yes, we want the suffering of those refugees to stop, and in keeping with our nation's compassion and concern, we are massively helping. But, yes, I want our troops out of Iraq and back home as soon as possible.

Internal conflicts have been raging in Iraq for many years. And we're helping out and we're going to continue to help these refugees. But I do not want one single soldier or airman shoved into a civil war in Iraq that's been going on for ages. And I'm not going to have that.

I know the coalition's historic effort destroyed Saddam's ability to undertake aggression against any neighbor. You did that job. But now the international community will further guarantee that Saddam's ability to threaten his neighbors is completely eliminated by destroying Iraq's weapons of mass destructions.

And as I just mentioned, we will continue to help the Iraqi refugees, the hundreds and thousands of victims of this man's, Saddam Hussein's, brutality, see food and shelter and safety and the opportunity to return unharmed to their homes. We will not tolerate any interference in this massive international relief effort. Iraq can return to the community of nations only when its leaders abandon the brutality and repression that is destroying their country. With Saddam in power, Iraq will remain a pariah nation, its people denied moral contacts with most of the outside world.

We must build on the successes of Desert Storm to give new shape and momentum to this new world order, to use force wisely and extend the hand of compassion wherever we can. Today we welcome Europe's willingness to shoulder a large share of this responsibility. This new sense of responsibility on the part of our European allies is most evident and most critical in Europe's eastern half.

The nations of Eastern Europe, for so long the other Europe, must take their place now alongside their neighbors to the west. Just as we've overcome Europe's political division, we must help to ease crossover from poverty into prosperity.

The United States will do its part. We always have, as we have already in reducing Poland's official debt burden to the United States by 70 percent, increasing our assistance this year to Eastern Europe by 50 percent. But the key, the key to helping these new democracies develop is trade and investment.

The new entrepreneurs of Czechoslovakia and Poland and Hungary aren't looking to government, their own or others, to shower them with riches. They're looking for new opportunities, a new freedom for the productive genius strangled by 40 years of state control.

Yesterday, my esteemed friend, a man we all honor and salute, President Vaclav Havel of Czechoslovakia, called me up. He wanted to request advice and help from the West. He faces enormous problems. You see, Czechoslovakia wants to be democratic. This man is leading them towards perfecting their fledgling democracy. Its economy is moving from a failed socialist model to a market economy.

We all must help. It's not easy to convert state-owned and-operated weapons plants into market-driven plants to produce consumer goods. But these new democracies can do just that with the proper advice and help from the West. It is in our interest, it is in the interest of the United States of America, that Czechoslovakia, Poland, and Hungary strengthen those fledgling democracies and strengthen their fledgling market economies.

We recognize that new roles and even new institutions are natural outgrowths of the new

Europe. Whether it's the European Community or a broadened mandate for the CSCE, the U.S. supports all efforts to forge a European approach to common challenges on the Continent and in the world beyond, with the understanding that Europe's long-term security is intertwined with America's and that NATO remains the best means to assure it.

And we look to Europe to act as a force for stability outside its own borders. In a world as interdependent as ours, no industrialized nation can maintain membership in good standing in the global community without assuming its fair share of responsibility for peace and security.

But even in the face of such welcome change, Americans will remain in Europe in support of history's most successful alliance, NATO. America's commitment is the best guarantee of a secure Europe, and a secure Europe is vital to American interests and vital to world peace. This is the essential logic of the Atlantic alliance which anchors America in Europe.

This century's history shows that America's destiny and interests cannot be separate from Europe's. Through the long years of cold war and conflict, the United States stood fast for freedom in Europe. And now, as Eastern Europe is opening up to democratic ideals, true progress becomes possible.

The Soviet Union is engaged in its own dramatic transformation. The policies of confrontation abroad, like the discredited dogma of Communism from which those policies sprang, lies dormant, if not mortally wounded. Much has changed. The path of international cooperation fostered by President Gorbachev and manifested most clearly in the Persian Gulf marks a radical change in Soviet behavior. And yet, the course of change within the Soviet Union is far less clear.

Economic and political reform there is under severe challenge. Soviet citizens, facing the collapse of the old order while the new still struggles to be born, confront desperate economic conditions, their hardwon freedoms in peril. Ancient ethnic enmities, conflict between republics and between republics and the central government add to these monumental challenges that they face.

America's policy toward the Soviet Union in these troubled times is, first and foremost, to continue our efforts to build the cooperative relationship that has allowed our nations and so many others to strengthen international peace and stability. At the same time, we will continue to support a reform process within the Soviet Union aimed at political and economic freedom, a process we believe must be built on peaceful dialogue and negotiation. This is a policy that we will advocate steadfastly, both in our discussions with the central Soviet government and with all elements active in Soviet political life.

Let there be no misunderstanding. The path ahead for the Soviet Union will be difficult and, at times, extraordinarily painful. History weighs heavily on all the peoples of the U.S.S.R., liberation from 70 years of Communism, from a thousand years of autocracy. It's going to be slow. There will be setbacks. But this process of reform, this transformation from within, must proceed. If external cooperation and our progress toward true international peace is to endure, it must succeed. Only when this transformation is complete will we be able to take full measure of the opportunities presented by this new and evolving world order.

The new world order really is a tool for addressing a new world of possibilities. This order gains its mission and shape not just from shared interests, but from shared ideals. And the ideals that have spawned new freedoms throughout the world have received their boldest and clearest expression in our great country, the United States. Never before has the world looked more to the American example. Never before have so many millions drawn hope from the American idea.

And the reason is simple: Unlike any other nation in the world, as Americans, we enjoy profound and mysterious bonds of affection and idealism. We feel our deep connections to community, to families, to our faiths. But what defines this nation? What makes us American is not our ties to a piece of territory or bonds of blood; what makes us American is our allegiance to an idea that all people everywhere must be free. This idea is as old and enduring as this nation itself, as deeply rooted, and what we are is a promise implicit to all the world in the words of our own Declaration of Independence.

The new world facing us, and I wish I were your age, it's a wonderful world of discovery. A world devoted to unlocking the promise of freedom. It's no more structured than a dream; no more regimented than an innovator's burst of inspiration. If we trust ourselves and our values; if we retain the pioneer's enthusiasm for exploring the world beyond our shores; if we strive to engage in the world that beckons us; then and only then will America be true to all that is best in us.

May God bless our great nation, the United States of America. And thank you all for what you have done for freedom and for our fundamental values. Thank you very much.

The Los Angeles Riots

Washington, D.C.

May 1, 1992

FOR SEVERAL WEEKS in the spring of 1992, the American public was preoccupied with the case of Rodney King, a black motorist who had been beaten and kicked by state troopers after he led them on a high-speed chase on a California freeway. Four officers charged with assault in the case were acquitted. Within hours after the verdict was announced, South-Central, an inner-city black neighborhood of Los Angeles, erupted in riots that the police were unable to quell. Forty-four people were killed and hundreds of businesses were burned and looted. Two days later, with the city still in flames, Bush made a televised speech to say that he was sending federal troops to help restore order and that he had directed the Justice Department to prosecute the four officers for violating King's civil rights.

Tonight I want to talk to you about violence in our cities and justice for our citizens, two big issues that have collided on the streets of Los Angeles. First, an update on where matters stand in Los Angeles.

Fifteen minutes ago I talked to California's Governor Pete Wilson and Los Angeles mayor Tom Bradley. They told me that last night was better than the night before; today, calmer than yesterday. But there were still incidents of random terror and lawlessness this afternoon.

In the wake of the first night's violence I spoke directly to both Governor Wilson and Mayor Bradley to assess the situation and to offer assistance. There are two very different issues at hand: one is the urgent need to restore order. What followed Wednesday's jury verdict in the Rodney King case was a tragic series of events for the city of Los Angeles: nearly 4,000 fires, staggering property damage, hundreds of injuries, and the senseless deaths of over 30 people.

To restore order right now, there are 3,000 National Guardsmen on duty in the city of Los Angeles. Another 2,200 stand ready to provide immediate support. To supplement this effort I've taken several additional actions. First, this morning I've ordered the Justice Department to dispatch 1,000 federal riot-trained law enforcement officials to help restore order in Los Angeles beginning tonight. These officials include FBI SWAT teams, special riot control units of the U.S. Marshals Service, the Border Patrol, and other federal law enforcement agencies. Second, another 1,000 federal law enforcement officials are on standby alert,

should they be needed. Third, early today I directed 3,000 members of the 7th Infantry and 1,500 marines to stand by at El Toro Air Station, California.

Tonight, at the request of the governor and the mayor, I have committed these troops to help restore order. I'm also federalizing the National Guard and I'm instructing General Colin Powell to place all those troops under a central command.

What we saw last night and the night before in Los Angeles is not about civil rights. It's not about the great cause of equality that all Americans must uphold. It's not a message of protest. It's been the brutality of a mob, pure and simple. And let me assure you: I will use whatever force is necessary to restore order.

What is going in L.A. must—and will—stop. As your president I guarantee you this violence will end.

And now let's talk about the beating of Rodney King. Because beyond the urgent need to restore order is the second issue, the issue of justice: whether Rodney King's federal civil rights were violated. What you saw and what I saw on the TV video was revolting. I felt anger. I felt pain. I thought: how can I explain this to my grandchildren?

Civil rights leaders just plain fearful of, and sometimes victimized by, police brutality were deeply hurt. And I know good and decent policemen who were equally appalled.

I spoke this morning to many leaders of the civil rights community. And they saw the video, as we all did. For 14 months they waited patiently, hopefully. They waited for the system to work. And when the verdict came in, they felt betrayed. Viewed from outside the trial, it was hard to understand how the verdict could possibly square with the video. Those civil rights leaders with whom I met were stunned. And so was I and so was Barbara and so were my kids.

But the verdict Wednesday was not the end of the process. The Department of Justice had started its own investigation immediately after the Rodney King incident and was monitoring the state investigation and trial. And so let me tell you what actions we are taking on the federal level to ensure that justice is served.

Within one hour of the verdict, I directed the Justice Department to move into high gear on its own independent criminal investigation into the case. And next, on Thursday, five federal prosecutors were on their way to Los Angeles. Our Justice Department has consistently demonstrated its ability to investigate fully a matter like this.

Since 1988, the Justice Department has successfully prosecuted over 100 law enforcement officials for excessive violence. I am confident that in this case, the Department of Justice will act as it should. Federal grand jury action is under way today in Los Angeles. Subpoenas are being issued. Evidence is being reviewed. The federal effort in this case will be expeditious and it will be fair. It will not be driven by mob violence, but by respect for due process and the rule of law.

We owe it to all Americans who put their faith in the law to see that justice is served. But as we move forward on this or any other case, we must remember the fundamental tenet of our legal system. Every American, whether accused or accuser, is entitled to protection of his or her rights.

In this highly controversial court case, a verdict was handed down by a California jury. To Americans of all races who were shocked by the verdict, let me say this: you must understand that our system of justice provides for the peaceful, orderly means of addressing this frustration. We must respect the process of law whether or not we agree with the outcome. There's a difference between frustration with the law and direct assaults upon our legal system.

In a civilized society, there can be no excuse—no excuse—for the murder, arson, theft, and vandalism that have terrorized the law-abiding citizens of Los Angeles. Mayor Bradley, just a few minutes ago, mentioned to me his particular concern, among others, regarding the safety of the Korean community. My heart goes out to them and all others who have suffered losses.

The wanton destruction of life and property is not a legitimate expression of outrage with injustice—it is itself injustice. And no rationalization, no matter how heartfelt, no matter how eloquent, can make it otherwise.

Television has become a medium that often brings us together. But its vivid display of Rodney King's beating shocked us. And the America it has shown us on our screens these last 48 hours has appalled us. None of this is what we wish to think of as America. It's as if we were looking in a mirror that distorted our better selves and turned us ugly. We cannot let that happen. We cannot do that to ourselves.

We've seen images in the last 48 hours that we will never forget. Some were horrifying almost beyond belief. But there were other acts—small but significant acts—in all this ugliness that gave us hope.

I'm one who respects our police. They keep the peace. They face danger every day. They help kids. They don't make a lot of money—but they care about their communities and their country. Thousands of police officers and firefighters are risking their lives right now on the streets of L.A. and they deserve our support.

And then there are the people who have spent each night not in the streets but in the churches of Los Angeles, praying that man's gentler instincts be revealed in the hearts of people driven by hate.

And finally, there were the citizens who showed great personal responsibility, who ignored the mob, who at great personal danger helped the victims of violence— regardless of race.

Among the many stories I've seen and heard about these past few days, one sticks in my mind—the story of one savagely beaten white truck driver, alive tonight because four strangers, four black strangers, came to his aid. Two were men who had been watching television and saw the beating as it was happening and came out into the street to help. Another was a woman on her way home from work, and the fourth, a young man whose name we may never know. The injured driver was able to get behind the wheel of his truck and tried to drive away. But his eyes were swollen shut. The woman asked him if he could see. He answered no. She said, "Well then, I will be your eyes."

Together, those four people braved the mob and drove that truck driver to the hospital. He's alive today—only because they stepped in to help.

It is for every one of them that we must rebuild the community of Los Angeles—for these four people and the others like them who in the midst of this nightmare acted with simple human decency.

We must understand that no one in Los Angeles or any other city has rendered a verdict on America. If we are to remain the most vibrant and hopeful nation on Earth, we must allow our diversity to bring us together, not drive us apart. This must be the rallying cry of good and decent people.

For their sake, for all our sakes, we must build a future where, in every city across this country, empty rage gives way to hope, where poverty and despair give way to opportunity. After peace is restored to Los Angeles, we must then turn again to the underlying causes of such tragic events. We must keep on working to create a climate of understanding and tolerance, a climate that refuses to accept racism, bigotry, anti-Semitism, and hate of any kind, anytime, anywhere.

Tonight, I ask all Americans to lend their hearts, their voices, and their prayers to the healing of hatred. As president, I took an oath to preserve, protect, and defend the Constitution, an oath that requires every president to establish justice and ensure domestic tranquility. That duty is foremost in my mind tonight.

Let me say to the people saddened by the spectacle of the past few days—to the good people of Los Angeles, caught at the center of this senseless suffering: the violence will end. Justice will be served. Hope will return.

Thank you, and may God bless the United States of America.

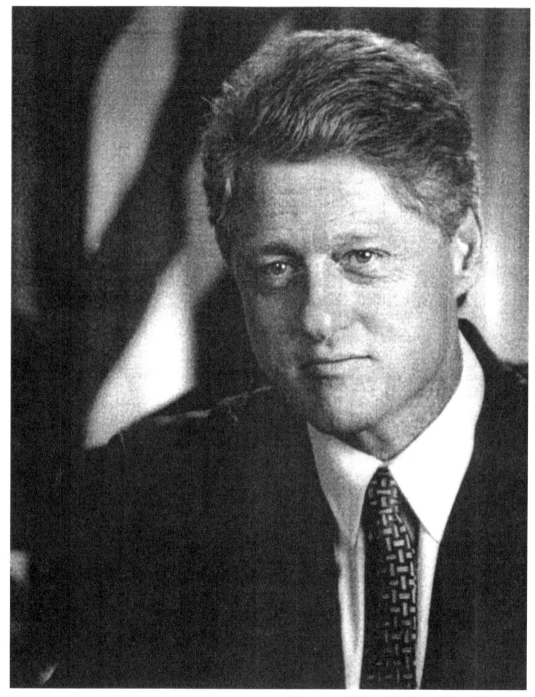

Courtesy of Clinton Presidential Materials Project

William Jefferson Clinton

William Jefferson Clinton

1993–2001

BILL CLINTON'S PRESIDENTIAL VICTORY in 1992 symbolized the success of the upwardly mobile baby boomers of whom he was the paragon. His life story seemed to have been scripted for a political soap opera. Only 46 years old, he was the first president to be born after World War II. He had suffered hardships in childhood: his father had died before his birth, and he had grown up in a troubled family with an alcoholic stepfather. He had raised himself from poverty through education, winning a Rhodes Scholarship to Oxford University before attending law school. His ambition—coupled with that of his wife, Hillary Rodham Clinton, a lawyer and social activist—had put him in the Arkansas statehouse when he was barely in his 30s. After he lost his reelection bid, he had staged a comeback that kept him in the governor's seat for 12 years. He also had an interesting character flaw—a tendency to self-indulgence and fibbing—that would eventually give his two terms in the White House all the plot twists and bathos of a real soap opera.

Clinton appeared to see the presidency as a kind of funneling device, with citizens pouring their stories of pain, discrimination, and injustice into one end of it, and socially healing legislation emerging from the other end. Speechmaking was his chief way of demonstrating his sensitivity to other people and their problems. On the 1992 campaign trail, he introduced the use of the "electronic town hall," an intimate format in which he conversed with a studio audience while a much bigger audience listened in via satellite. Talking to his questioners individually, standing close to them, making prolonged eye contact with them, thanking them, and acknowledging them, he succeeded in giving voters the impression that here was a candidate who cared about them and who would fight their battles.

Once in office, Clinton threw himself and his inexperienced staff into the task of passing one major piece of legislation after another. He gave hundreds of brief talks in his first year alone, including a regular Saturday morning radio address but found himself competing for public attention with a multitude of news shows and media distractions. He changed his approach in 1995, when the Republicans took over both houses of Congress. As he observed at a press conference, "I have spent so much time trying to pass bills through Congress that I haven't spent as much time as I was able to when I was running for president making sure people understood, were in on, and felt part of, the process by which we make decisions." Countering the Republican "Contract with America" with his own "New Covenant," he directed his speechmaking toward broad issues, including racial reconciliation and support for families.

Ironically—since their political agendas were complete opposites—Clinton's speechmaking was modeled on Ronald Reagan's. What Clinton admired in Reagan was his ability to control the terms of debate, his ability to get his ideas understood and appreciated by ordinary people as well as by politicians. Reagan, however, was a by-the-book orator who placed his confidence in his speechwriting staff and happily read what they composed. Clinton, on the contrary, was an erudite thinker with a head full of ideas who could speak extemporaneously on almost any question of public policy, was accustomed to writing his own speeches, and generally preferred to use an outline rather than a finished text. As one of his aides remarked, "He's a jazz improviser who riffs all over the place." So great was his pleasure in talking that he sometimes kept going far too long. Indeed, he nearly killed his career in 1988 when his nominating speech for the presidential candidacy of Michael Dukakis went on for more than an hour.

Though a thorough command of his subject matter was usually an asset to Clinton, in the case of major addresses it proved to be a hindrance. In his memoir of the White House, Clinton's longtime adviser George Stephanopoulos described the agonizing and messy process by which the president's major addresses were tortured into life. The speechwriting staff would consult with policy specialists and come up with a draft which was then torn apart by Clinton's advisers, the First Lady, and Clinton himself. Arguments broke out over statistics, objectives, intentions. Trial runs in the White House "family theater" resulted in further drastic revisions. The president would stay awake most of the night, editing and re-editing, and would still be wielding his black magic marker right up until it was time to deliver the speech. This frenzied approach to composition resulted in near-disasters on more than one occasion (see, for example, Clinton's address to Congress on health care, printed below). Former White House speechwriter Tony Snow warned Stephanopoulos, "George, you guys are bungee jumping without a rope."

In part, the Clinton administration's speechwriting woes were the result of poor organization in the White House staff. Initially, there were two separate teams, one producing the speeches on domestic policy, the other the speeches on foreign policy. The foreign-policy writers were experts from the National Security Council who had ready access to the president, but the domestic-policy writers were mainly professional wordsmiths who needed far more guidance from the Oval Office than they received. Eventually, under Director of Communications Donald Baer, the situation improved. Among the members of Baer's department was Terry Edmonds, the first African-American speechwriter ever hired by the White House. Clinton was also the first president to appoint a woman—Dee Dee Myers—as his press secretary.

Clinton's speaking style, already highly practiced when he took office, was given added polish with the help of a coach. Even more important than his speaking was his acting, a skill that evidently came naturally to him. His stock of gestures included lip biting, lip pursing, jaw clenching, eye watering, and head shaking. The theater critic Robert Brustein, writing in the *New Republic,* compared him favorably with Ronald Reagan, saying that "the current president almost makes the Great Communicator look like he was acting in silents." Clinton, he continued, had "the patent sincerity of a Method actor" and particularly excelled in reading smoothly from the TelePrompTer. "If most people are unaware that he is reading his part, it is because, like all good actors who inhabit their characters, he seems to be making up his lines as he goes along. This is impressive enough in relatively short Shakespearean soliloquies; but it is absolutely dazzling in an 87-minute monologue. To achieve this effect, of course, you have to believe completely in what you are saying at the moment you are saying it—even if your part demands that you say (and believe) the exact opposite a moment later."

It was Clinton's penchant for considering the truth to be elastic and stretching it farther than it could go that ultimately brought about his disgrace and very nearly caused his dismissal from office. When his extramarital affair with a 22-year-old intern became the subject of dangerous rumors, Clinton attempted to save himself by giving legally accurate but factually misleading statements to a federal grand jury. He also made a direct appeal to a credulous public at a press conference, saying emphatically: "I did not have sexual relations with that woman." Little more than half a year later, he was making his famous four-minute apology, reluctantly admitting to having had an "inappropriate relationship" with the intern. The Republicans in Congress impeached him for having perjured himself but were unable to muster enough support to remove him from power. By the time the scandal and its aftermath had played themselves out, the nation was exhausted, Clinton had earned himself a reputation as one of history's boldest liars, and his administration, which had arrived in Washington in a flurry of plans and promises, was coasting to its end.

On the last full day of his term, Clinton signed an agreement with the federal prosecutor's office. The settlement gave him protection from criminal liability in all matters that had been under investigation in exchange for a five-year suspension of his license to practive law, payment of a 25 thousand dollar fine to the Arkansas Bar Association, and a public admission that he had, in fact, given false testimony under oath.

Among the 140 pardons he issued just before leaving the White House were those for several of his friends who had been convicted in the Whitewater case.

First Inaugural Address

Washington, D.C.

January 21, 1993

ALTHOUGH CLINTON WON 70 percent of the electoral vote in the election of 1992, he received only 43 percent of the popular vote—not enough to constitute a strong mandate for his political and social agenda. His inaugural speech was intended to be a conclusive demonstration of his fitness to lead the nation. It was also intended to counteract the public perception of Clinton as an unfocused, windy orator, a perception bolstered by his hour-long acceptance speech at the Democratic National Convention the previous August.

The speech's main metaphor, that of "forcing the spring"—embracing change and bringing it about by serving others—was contributed posthumously by Father Tim Healy, president of the New York Public Library. (Though Healy had died several weeks after the election, his ideas concerning the speech were retrieved from his word processor.)

Clinton and his close advisers thrashed out the text in several all-night sessions at their headquarters in Washington's Blair House, revising right up until the wee hours of the morning of inauguration day. The final version, a pithy 14 minutes, was handed to the TelePrompTer operators at the Capitol with only half an hour to spare before the start of the ceremony.

Today we celebrate the mystery of American renewal.

This ceremony is held in the depth of winter. But, by the words we speak and the faces we show the world, we force the spring. A spring reborn in the world's oldest democracy, that brings forth the vision and courage to reinvent America.

When our founders boldly declared America's independence to the world and our purposes to the Almighty, they knew that America, to endure, would have to change.

Not change for change's sake, but change to preserve America's ideals—life, liberty, the pursuit of happiness. Though we march to the music of our time, our mission is timeless.

Each generation of Americans must define what it means to be an American.

On behalf of our nation, I salute my predecessor, President Bush, for his half-century of service to America. And I thank the millions of men and women whose steadfastness and sacrifice triumphed over Depression, fascism, and Communism.

Today, a generation raised in the shadows of the cold war assumes new responsibilities in a world warmed by the sunshine of freedom but threatened still by ancient hatreds and new plagues.

Raised in unrivaled prosperity, we inherit an economy that is still the world's strongest, but is weakened by business failures, stagnant wages, increasing inequality, and deep divisions among our people.

When George Washington first took the oath I have just sworn to uphold, news traveled slowly across the land by horseback and across the ocean by boat. Now, the sights and sounds of this ceremony are broadcast instantaneously to billions around the world. Communications and commerce are global; investment is mobile; technology is almost magical; and ambition for a better life is now universal. We earn our livelihood in peaceful competition with people all across the earth.

Profound and powerful forces are shaking and remaking our world, and the urgent question of our time is whether we can make change our friend and not our enemy.

This new world has already enriched the lives of millions of Americans who are able to compete and win in it. But when most people are working harder for less; when others cannot work at all; when the cost of health care devastates families and threatens to bankrupt many of our enterprises, great and small; when fear of crime robs law-abiding citizens of their freedom; and when millions of poor children cannot even imagine the lives we are calling them to lead—we have not made change our friend.

We know we have to face hard truths and take strong steps. But we have not done so. Instead, we have drifted, and that drifting has eroded our resources, fractured our economy, and shaken our confidence.

Though our challenges are fearsome, so are our strengths. And Americans have ever been a restless, questing, hopeful people. We must bring to our task today the vision and will of those who came before us.

From our revolution, the Civil War, to the Great Depression to the civil rights movement, our people have always mustered the determination to construct from these crises the pillars of our history.

Thomas Jefferson believed that to preserve the very foundations of our nation, we would need dramatic change from time to time. Well, my fellow citizens, this is our time. Let us embrace it.

Our democracy must be not only the envy of the world but the engine of our own renewal. There is nothing wrong with America that cannot be cured by what is right with America.

And so today, we pledge an end to the era of deadlock and drift—a new season of American renewal has begun.

To renew America, we must be bold. We must do what no generation has had to do before. We must invest more in our own people, in their jobs, in their future, and at the same time cut our massive debt. And we must do so in a world in which we must compete for every opportunity.

It will not be easy; it will require sacrifice. But it can be done, and done fairly, not choosing sacrifice for its own sake, but for our own sake. We must provide for our nation the way a family provides for its children.

Our founders saw themselves in the light of posterity. We can do no less. Anyone who has ever watched a child's eyes wander into sleep knows what posterity is. Posterity is the world to come—the world for whom we hold our ideals, from whom we have borrowed our planet, and to whom we bear sacred responsibility.

We must do what America does best: offer more opportunity to all and demand responsibility from all.

It is time to break the bad habit of expecting something for nothing, from our government or from each other. Let us all take more responsibility, not only for ourselves and our families but for our communities and our country.

To renew America, we must revitalize our democracy.

This beautiful capital, like every capital since the dawn of civilization, is often a place of intrigue and calculation. Powerful people maneuver for position and worry endlessly about who is in and who is out, who is up and who is down, forgetting those people whose toil and sweat sends us here and pays our way.

Americans deserve better, and in this city today, there are people who want to do better. And so I say to all of us here, let us resolve to reform our politics, so that power and privilege no longer shout down the voice of the people. Let us put aside personal advantage so that we can feel the pain and see the promise of America.

Let us resolve to make our government a place for what Franklin Roosevelt called "bold, persistent experimentation," a government for our tomorrows, not our yesterdays. Let us give this capital back to the people to whom it belongs.

To renew America, we must meet challenges abroad as well as at home. There is no longer division between what is foreign and what is domestic—the world economy, the world environment, the world AIDS crisis, the world arms race—they affect us all.

Today, as an old order passes, the new world is more free but less stable. Communism's collapse has called forth old animosities and new dangers. Clearly America must continue to lead the world we did so much to make.

While America rebuilds at home, we will not shrink from the challenges, nor fail to seize the opportunities, of this new world. Together with our friends and allies, we will work to shape change, lest it engulf us.

When our vital interests are challenged, or the will and conscience of the international community is defied, we will act— with peaceful diplomacy whenever possible, with force when necessary. The brave Americans serving our nation today in the Persian Gulf, in Somalia, and wherever else they stand are testament to our resolve.

But our greatest strength is the power of our ideas, which are still new in many lands. Across the world, we see them embraced—and we rejoice. Our hopes, our hearts, our hands, are with those on every continent who are building democracy and freedom. Their cause is America's cause.

The American people have summoned the change we celebrate today. You have raised your voices in an unmistakable chorus. You have cast your votes in historic numbers. And you have changed the face of Congress, the presidency, and the political process itself. Yes, you, my fellow Americans, have forced the spring. Now, we must do the work the season demands.

To that work I now turn, with all the authority of my office. I ask the Congress to join with me. But no president, no Congress, no government, can undertake this mission alone. My fellow Americans, you, too, must play your part in our renewal. I challenge a new generation of young Americans to a season of service—to act on your idealism by helping troubled children, keeping company with those in need, reconnecting our torn communities. There is so much to be done— enough indeed for millions of others who are still young in spirit to give of themselves in service, too. In serving, we recognize a simple but powerful truth—we need each other. And we must care for one another.

Today, we do more than celebrate America; we rededicate ourselves to the very idea of America. An idea born in revolution and renewed through two centuries of challenge. An idea tempered by the knowledge that, but for fate, we—the fortunate and the unfortunate—might have been each other. An idea ennobled by the faith that our nation can summon from its myriad diversity the deepest measure of unity. An idea infused with the conviction that America's long heroic journey must go forever upward.

And so, my fellow Americans, at the edge of the 21st century, let us begin with energy and hope, with faith and discipline, and let us work until our work is done. The scripture says, "And let us not be weary in well-doing, for in due season, we shall reap, if we faint not."

From this joyful mountaintop of celebration, we hear a call to service in the valley. We have heard the trumpets. We have changed the guard. And now, each in our way, and with God's help, we must answer the call.

Thank you and God bless you all.

The Oslo Accords

Washington, D.C.
September 13, 1993

IN THE SPRING of 1993, negotiators for Israel and the Palestine Liberation Organization reached an agreement that called for mutual recognition and set forth a framework for future peace talks. Though the pact had been brokered by Norway and was known as the Oslo accords, it was decided, for symbolic reasons, that the signing ceremony should be held at the White House. The staff had only a few days' notice to prepare for the event, which was to feature a handshake between two mortal enemies, Prime Minister Yitzhak Rabin of Israel and Chairman Yasir Arafat of the PLO. The preparations for the ceremony included a session in which Clinton's aides choreographed not only the handshake but also the application of an arm grip by the president to prevent Arafat from kissing him.

Clinton awakened at 3 a.m. on the morning of the ceremony to read from the biblical Book of Joshua and to put the finishing touches on his address, which included quotations from both the Koran and the Jewish prayerbook. The ceremony, broadcast worldwide, was held on the South Lawn before an audience of 3,000. Clinton's remarks, reprinted here, were followed by those of Israel's foreign minister, Shimon Peres; Mahmoud Abbas of the PLO Executive Council; U.S. secretary of state Warren Christopher; Andrei Kozyrev, the foreign minister of Russia; Rabin; and Arafat.

The signing of the Oslo accords earned Rabin, Peres, and Arafat the 1994 Nobel Peace Prize, but so flawed was the agreement that by 2000 the region was again on the verge of war and Rabin was in his grave, the victim of an assassin.

Prime Minister Rabin, Chairman Arafat, Foreign Minister Peres, Mr. Abbas, President Carter, President Bush, distinguished guests.

On behalf of the United States and Russia, cosponsors of the Middle East peace process, welcome to this great occasion of history and hope.

Today, we bear witness to an extraordinary act in one of history's defining dramas, a drama that began in the time of our ancestors when the word went forth from a sliver of land between the river Jordan and the Mediterranean Sea. That hallowed piece of earth, that land of light and revelation is the home to the memories and dreams of Jews, Muslims, and Christians throughout the world.

As we all know, devotion to that land has also been the source of conflict and bloodshed for too long. Throughout this century, bitterness between the Palestinian and Jewish people has robbed the entire region of its resources, its potential, and too many of its sons and daughters. The land has been so drenched in warfare and hatred, the conflicting claims of history etched so deeply in the souls of the combatants there, that many

believe the past would always have the upper hand.

Then, 14 years ago, the past began to give way when, at this place and upon this desk, three men of great vision signed their names to the Camp David accords. Today we honor the memories of Menachem Begin and Anwar Sadat. And we salute the wise leadership of President Jimmy Carter.

Then, as now, we heard from those who said that conflict would come again soon. But the peace between Egypt and Israel has endured, just so this bold new venture today, this brave gamble that the future can be better than the past, must endure.

Two years ago in Madrid, another president took a major step on the road to peace by bringing Israel and all her neighbors together to launch direct negotiations. And today we also express our deep thanks for the skillful leadership of President George Bush.

Ever since Harry Truman first recognized Israel, every American president—Democrat and Republican—has worked for peace between Israel and her neighbors. Now the efforts of all who have labored before us bring us to this moment—a moment when we dare to pledge what for so long seemed difficult even to imagine: that the security of the Israeli people will be reconciled with the hopes of the Palestinian people and there will be more security and more hope for all.

Today, the leadership of Israel and the Palestine Liberation Organization will sign a declaration of principles on interim Palestinian self-government. It charts a course toward reconciliation between two peoples who have both known the bitterness of exile. Now both pledge to put old sorrows and antagonisms behind them and to work for a shared future, shaped by the values of the Torah, the Koran, and the Bible.

Let us salute, also, today the government of Norway for its remarkable role in nurturing this agreement. But above all, let us today pay tribute to the leaders who had the courage to lead their people toward peace, away from the scars of battle, the wounds and the losses of the past toward a brighter tomorrow. The world today thanks Prime Minister Rabin, Foreign Minister Peres and Chairman Arafat.

Their tenacity and vision has given us the promise of a new beginning. What these leaders have done now must be done by others. Their achievement must be a catalyst for progress in all aspects of the peace process. And those of us who support them must be there to help in all aspects. For the peace must render the people who make it more secure. A peace of the brave is within our reach. Throughout the Middle East, there is a great yearning for the quiet miracle of a normal life.

We know a difficult road lies ahead. Every peace has its enemies—those who still prefer the easy habits of hatred to the hard labors of reconciliation. But Prime Minister Rabin has reminded us that you do not have to make peace with your friends. And the Koran teaches that if the enemy inclines toward peace, do thou also incline toward peace.

Therefore, let us resolve that this new mutual recognition will be a continuing process in which the parties transform the very way they see and understand each other. Let the skeptics of this peace recall what once existed among these people. There was a time when the traffic of ideas in commerce and pilgrims flowed uninterrupted among the cities of the fertile crescent. In Spain and the Middle East, Muslims and Jews once worked together to write brilliant chapters in the history of literature and science. All this can come to pass again.

Mr. Prime Minister, Mr. Chairman: I pledge the active support of the United States of America to the difficult work that lies ahead.

The United States is committed to ensuring that the people who are affected by this agreement will be made more secure by it and to leading the world in marshaling the sources necessary to implement the difficult details that will make real the principles to which you commit yourselves today.

Together let us imagine what can be accomplished if all the energy and ability the Israelis and the Palestinians have invested into your struggle can now be channeled into cultivating the land and freshening the waters, into ending the boycotts and creating new industry, into building a land as bountiful and peaceful as it is holy. Above all, let us dedicate ourselves today to your region's next generation. In this entire assembly, no one is more important than the group of Israeli and Arab children who are seated here with us today.

Mr. Prime Minister, Mr. Chairman: this day belongs to you. And because of what you have done, tomorrow belongs to them.

We must not leave them prey to the politics of extremism and despair, to those who would derail this process because they cannot overcome the fears and hatreds of the past. We must not betray their future. For too long, the young of the Middle East have been caught in a web of hatred, not of their own making. For too long they have been taught from the chronicles of war. Now, we can give them the chance to know the season of peace. For them we must realize the prophecy of Isaiah, that the cry of violence shall no more be heard in your land, nor wrack nor ruin within your borders. The children of Abraham, the descendants of Isaac and Ishmael, have embarked together on a bold journey. Together, today, with all our hearts and all our souls, we bid them shalom, salaam, peace.

[Following speeches by six other dignitaries:]

We have been granted the great privilege of witnessing this victory for peace. Just as the Jewish people this week celebrate the dawn of a new year, let us all go from this place to celebrate the dawn of a new era not. only for the Middle East, but for the entire world.

The sound we heard today, once again, as in ancient Jericho, was the trumpets toppling walls. The walls of anger and suspicion between Israeli and Palestinian, between Arab and Jew. This time, praise God, the trumpets herald not the destruction of that city, but its new beginning.

Now let each of us here today return to our portion of that effort, uplifted by the spirit of the moment, refreshed in our hopes and guided by the wisdom of the Almighty, who has brought us to this joyous day.

Go in peace. Go as peacemakers.

Reform of the Health Care System

Washington, D.C.

September 22, 1993

BY THE 1990s, the skyrocketing costs of health care, and particularly of prescription drugs, had put medical insurance beyond the financial reach of some 40 million Americans. A succession of presidents, beginning with Franklin Delano Roosevelt, had tried in various ways to fix the problem, without success. Reform of the health care system was at the top of the Clintons' agenda when they entered the White House, and Mrs. Clinton personally took direction of the effort to develop new legislation. After many months of hearings, proposals, arguments, and media events, she settled on an ambitious, complex plan to achieve universal coverage by completely reorganizing the way in which health services are delivered and paid for, with new levels of state and federal bureaucratic oversight.

President Clinton's appearance before the Congress to pitch the plan nearly resulted in disaster. In typical Clinton White House style, the speech underwent revision after revision, with aides and officials fighting endlessly over the language. Frantic rewriting continued all day on September 22, starting before sunrise, and came to a halt only when the president entered his limousine in the evening to appear before Congress. The text was downloaded into the Capitol's TelePrompTer at the last possible moment. In the confusion the operator made an error and the wrong speech appeared on the screen. For seven full minutes, while his aides rushed to download the correct speech from a spare diskette, Clinton delivered his talk from memory, ignoring both the written text—he had forgotten his reading glasses—and the distracting rush of unintelligible words from the TelePrompTer.

Despite Clinton's bravura performance, everyone from doctors to senior citizens to economists to company executives found reason to dislike the plan. Its defeat was a major blow to the administration.

Mr. Speaker, Mr. President, members of Congress, distinguished guests, my fellow Americans. Before I begin my words tonight I would like to ask that we all bow in a moment of silent prayer for the memory of those who were killed and those who have been injured in the tragic train accident in Alabama today. [A moment of silence is observed.] Amen.

My fellow Americans, tonight we come together to write a new chapter in the American story. Our forebears enshrined the American Dream—life, liberty, the pursuit of happiness. Every generation of Americans has worked to strengthen that legacy, to make our country a place of freedom and opportunity, a place where people who work hard can rise to their full potential, a place where their children can have a better future.

From the settling of the frontier to the landing on the Moon, ours has been a continuous story of challenges defined, obstacles overcome, new horizons secured. That is what makes America what it is and Americans what we are. Now we are in a time of profound change and opportunity. The end of the cold war, the information age, the global economy have brought us both opportunity and hope and strife and uncertainty. Our purpose in this dynamic age must be to change—to make change our friend and not our enemy.

To achieve that goal, we must face all our challenges with confidence, with faith, and with discipline—whether we're reducing the deficit, creating tomorrow's jobs and training our people to fill them, converting from a high-tech defense to a hightech domestic economy, expanding trade, reinventing government, making our streets safer, or rewarding work over idleness. All these challenges require us to change.

If Americans are to have the courage to change in a difficult time, we must first be secure in our most basic needs. Tonight I want to talk to you about the most critical thing we can do to build that security. This health care system of ours is badly broken and it is time to fix it.

Despite the dedication of literally millions of talented health care professionals, our health care is too uncertain and too expensive, too bureaucratic and too wasteful. It has too much fraud and too much greed.

At long last, after decades of false starts, we must make this our most urgent priority, giving every American health security; health care that can never be taken away; health care that is always there. That is what we must do tonight.

On this journey, as on all others of true consequence, there will be rough spots in the road and honest disagreements about how we should proceed. After all, this is a complicated issue. But every successful journey is guided by fixed stars. And if we can agree on some basic values and principles we will reach this destination, and we will reach it together.

So tonight I want to talk to you about the principles that I believe must embody our efforts to reform America's health care system—security, simplicity, savings, choice, quality, and responsibility.

When I launched our nation on this journey to reform the health care system I knew we needed a talented navigator, someone with a rigorous mind, a steady compass, a caring heart. Luckily for me and for our nation, I didn't have to look very far.

Over the last eight months, Hillary and those working with her have talked to literally thousands of Americans to understand the strengths and the frailties of this system of ours. They met with over 1,100 health care organizations. They talked with doctors and nurses, pharmacists and drug company representatives, hospital administrators, insurance company executives, and small and large businesses. They spoke with self-employed people. They talked with people who had insurance and people who didn't. They talked with union members and older Americans and advocates for our children. The First Lady also consulted, as all of you know, extensively with governmental leaders in both parties in the states of our nation, and especially here on Capitol Hill.

Hillary and the Task Force received and read over 700,000 letters from ordinary citizens. What they wrote and the bravery with which they told their stories is really what calls us all here tonight.

Every one of us knows someone who's worked hard and played by the rules and still been hurt by this system that just doesn't work for too many people. But I'd like to tell you about just one.

Kerry Kennedy owns a small furniture store that employs seven people in Titusville, Florida. Like most small business owners, he's poured his heart and soul, his sweat and blood into that business for years. But over the last several years, again like most small business owners, he's seen his health care premiums skyrocket, even in years when no claims were made. And last year, he painfully discovered he could no longer afford to provide coverage for all his workers because his insurance company told him that two of his workers had become high risks because of their advanced age. The problem was that those two people were his mother and father, the people who founded the business and still worked in the store.

This story speaks for millions of others. And from them we have learned a powerful truth. We have to preserve and strengthen what is right with the health care system, but we have got to fix what is wrong with it.

Now, we all know what's right. We're blessed with the best health care professionals on earth, the finest health care institutions, the best medical research, the most sophisticated technology. My mother is a nurse. I grew up around hospitals. Doctors and nurses were the first professional people I ever knew or learned to look up to. They are what is right with this health care system. But we also know that we can no longer afford to continue to ignore what is wrong.

Millions of Americans are just a pink slip away from losing their health insurance, and one serious illness away from losing all their savings. Millions more are locked into the jobs they have now just because they or someone in their family has once been sick and they have what is called the preexisting condition. And on any given day, over 37 million Americans—most of them working people and their little children—have no health insurance at all.

And in spite of all this, our medical bills are growing at over twice the rate of inflation, and the United States spends over a third more of its income on health care than any other nation on Earth. And the gap is growing, causing many of our companies in global competition severe disadvantage. There is no excuse for this kind of system. We know other people have done better. We know people in our own country are doing better. We have no excuse. My fellow Americans, we must fix this system and it has to begin with congressional action.

I believe as strongly as I can say that we can reform the costliest and most wasteful system on the face of the earth without enacting new broad-based taxes. I believe it because of the conversations I have had with thousands of health care professionals around the country; with people who are outside this city, but are inside experts on the way this system works and wastes money.

The proposal that I describe tonight borrows many of the principles and ideas that have been embraced in plans introduced by both Republicans and Democrats in this Congress. For the first time in this century, leaders of both political parties have joined together around the principle of providing universal, comprehensive health care. It is a magic moment and we must seize it.

I want to say to all of you I have been deeply moved by the spirit of this debate, by the openness of all people to new ideas and argument and information. The American people would be proud to know that earlier this week when a health care university was held for members of Congress just to try to give everybody the same amount of information, over 320 Republicans and Democrats signed up and showed up for two days just to learn the basic facts of the complicated problem before us.

Both sides are willing to say we have listened to the people. We know the cost of going forward with this system is far greater than the cost of change. Both sides, I think, understand the literal ethical imperative of doing something about the system we have now. Rising above these difficulties and our past differences to solve this problem will go a long way toward defining who we are and who we intend to be as a people in this difficult and challenging era. I believe we all understand that.

And so tonight, let me ask all of you— every member of the House, every member of the Senate, each Republican and each Democrat— let us keep this spirit and let us keep this commitment until this job is done. We owe it to the American people.

Now, if I might, I would like to review the six principles I mentioned earlier and describe how we think we can best fulfill those principles.

First and most important, security. This principle speaks to the human misery, to the costs, to the anxiety we hear about every day—all of us—when people talk about their problems with the present system. Security means that those who do not now have health care coverage will have it; and for those who have it, it will never be taken away. We must achieve that security as soon as possible.

Under our plan, every American would receive a health care security card that will guarantee a comprehensive package of benefits over the course of an entire lifetime, roughly comparable to the benefit package offered by most Fortune 500 companies. This health care security card will offer this package of benefits in a way that can never be taken away.

So let us agree on this: whatever else we disagree on, before this Congress finishes its work next year, you will pass and I will sign legislation to guarantee this security to every citizen of this country.

With this card, if you lose your job or you switch jobs, you're covered. If you leave your job to start a small business, you're covered. If you're an early retiree, you're covered. If someone in your family has, unfortunately, had an illness that qualifies as a preexisting condition, you're still covered. If you get sick or a member of your family gets sick, even if it's a life-threatening illness, you're covered. And if an insurance company tries to drop you for any reason, you will still be covered, because that will be illegal. This card will give comprehensive coverage. It will cover people for hospital care, doctor visits, emergency and lab services, diagnostic services like Pap smears and mammograms and cholesterol tests, substance abuse, and mental health treatment.

And equally important, for both health care and economic reasons, this program for the first time would provide a broad range of preventive services including regular checkups and well-baby visits.

Now, it's just common sense. We know— any family doctor will tell you that people will stay healthier and long-term costs of the health system will be lower if we have comprehensive preventive services. You know how all of our mothers told us that an ounce of prevention was worth a pound of cure? Our mothers were right. And it's a lesson, like so many lessons from our mothers, that we have waited too long to live by. It is time to start doing it.

Health care security must also apply to older Americans. This is something I imagine all of us in this room feel very deeply about. The first thing I want to say about that is that we must maintain the Medicare program. It works to provide that kind of security. But this time and for the first time, I believe Medicare should provide coverage for the cost of prescription drugs.

Yes, it will cost some more in the beginning. But, again, any physician who deals with the elderly will tell you that there are thousands of elderly people in every state who are not poor enough to be on Medicaid, but just above that line and on Medicare, who desperately need medicine, who makes decisions every week between medicine and food. Any doctor who deals with the elderly will tell you that there are many elderly people who don't get medicine, who get sicker and sicker and eventually go to the doctor and wind up spending more money and draining more money from the health care system than they would if they had regular treatment in the way that only adequate medicine can provide.

I also believe that over time, we should phase in long-term care for the disabled and the elderly on a comprehensive basis.

As we proceed with this health care reform, we cannot forget that the most rapidly growing percentage of Americans are those over 80. We cannot break faith with them. We have to do better by them.

The second principle is simplicity. Our health care system must be simpler for the patients and simpler for those who actually deliver health care—our doctors, our nurses, our other medical professionals. Today we have more than 1,500 insurers, with hundreds and hundreds of different forms. No other nation has a system like this. These forms are time consuming for health care providers, they're expensive for health care consumers, they're exasperating for anyone who's ever tried to sit down around a table and wade through them and figure them out.

The medical care industry is literally drowning in paperwork. In recent years, the number of administrators in our hospitals has grown by four times the rate that the number of doctors has grown. A hospital ought to be a house of healing, not a monument to paperwork and bureaucracy.

Just a few days ago, the vice president and I had the honor of visiting the Children's Hospital here in Washington where they do wonderful, often miraculous things for very sick children. A nurse named Debbie Freiberg told us that she was in the cancer and bone marrow unit. The other day a little boy asked her just to stay at his side during his chemotherapy. And she had to walk away from that child because she had been instructed to go to yet another class to learn how to fill out another form for something that didn't have a lick to do with the health care of the children she was helping. That is wrong, and we can stop it, and we ought to do it.

We met a very compelling doctor named Lillian Beard, a pediatrician, who said that she didn't get into her profession to spend hours and hours—some doctors up to 25 hours a week—just filling out forms. She told us she became a doctor to keep children well and to help save those who got sick. We can relieve people like her of this burden. We learned—the vice president and I did—that in the Washington Children's Hospital alone, the administrators told us they spend $2 million a year in one hospital filling out forms that have nothing whatever to do with keeping up with the treatment of the patients.

And the doctors there applauded when I was told and I related to them that they spend so much time filling out paperwork, that if they only had to fill out those paperwork requirements necessary to monitor the health of the children, each doctor on that one hospital staff—200 of them— could see another 500 children a year. That is 10,000 children a year. I think we can save money in this system if we simplify it. And we can make the doctors and the nurses and the people that are giving their lives to help us all be healthier a whole lot happier, too, on their jobs.

Under our proposal there would be one standard insurance form—not hundreds of them. We will simplify also—and we must— the government's rules and regulations, because they are a big part of this problem. This is one of those cases where the physician should heal thyself. We have to reinvent the way we relate to the health care system, along with reinventing government. A doctor should not have to check with a bureaucrat in an office thousands of miles away before ordering a simple blood test. That's not right, and we can change it. And doctors, nurses, and consumers shouldn't have to worry about the fine print. If we have this one simple form, there won't be any fine print. People will know what it means.

The third principle is savings. Reform must produce savings in this health care system. It has to. We're spending over 14 percent of our income on health care—Canada's at 10; nobody else is over 9. We're competing with all these people for the future. And the other major countries, they cover everybody and they cover them with services as generous as the best company policies here in this country.

Rampant medical inflation is eating away at our wages, our savings, our investment capital, our ability to create new jobs in the private sector and this public Treasury. You know the budget we just adopted had steep cuts in defense, a five-year freeze on the discretionary spending, so critical to reeducating America and investing in jobs and helping us to convert from a defense to a domestic economy. But we passed a budget which has Medicaid increases of between 16 and 11 percent a year over the next five years, and Medicare increases of between 11 and 9 percent in an environment where we assume inflation will be at 4 percent or less.

We cannot continue to do this. Our competitiveness, our whole economy, the integrity of the way the government works and, ultimately, our living standards depend upon our ability to achieve savings without harming the quality of health care.

Unless we do this, our workers will lose $655 in income each year by the end of the decade. Small businesses will continue to face skyrocketing premiums. And a full third of small businesses now covering their employees say they will be forced to drop their insurance. Large corporations will bear vivid disadvantages in global competition. And health care costs will devour more and more and more of our budget. Pretty soon all of you or the people who succeed you will be showing up here, and writing out checks for health care and interest on the debt and worrying about whether we've got enough defense, and that will be it, unless we have the courage to achieve the savings that are plainly there before us. Every state and local government will continue to cut back on everything from education to law enforcement to pay more and more for the same health care.

These rising costs are a special nightmare for our small businesses—the engine of our entrepreneurship and our job creation in America today. Health care premiums for small businesses are 35 percent higher than those of large corporations today. And they will keep rising at double-digit rates unless we act.

So how will we achieve these savings? Rather than looking at price control, or looking away as the price spiral continues; rather than using the heavy hand of government to try to control what's happening, or continuing to ignore what's happening, we believe there is a third way to achieve these savings. First, to give groups of consumers and small businesses the same market bargaining power that large corporations and large groups of public employees now have. We want to let market forces enable plans to compete. We want to force these plans to compete on the basis of price and quality, not simply to allow them to continue making money by turning people away who are sick or old or performing mountains of unnecessary procedures. But we also believe we should back this system up with limits on how much plans can raise their premiums year in and year out, forcing people, again, to continue to pay more for the same health care, without regard to inflation or the rising population needs.

We want to create what has been missing in this system for too long, and what every successful nation who has dealt with this problem has already had to do: to have a combination of private market forces and a sound public policy that will support that competition, but limit the rate at which prices can exceed the rate of inflation and population growth, if the competition doesn't work, especially in the early going.

The second thing I want to say is that unless everybody is covered—and this is a very important thing—unless everybody is covered, we will never be able to fully put the breaks on health care inflation. Why is that? Because when people don't have any health insurance, they still get health care, but they get it when it's too late, when it's too expensive, often from the most expensive place of all, the emergency room. Usually by the time they show up, their illnesses are more severe and their mortality rates are much higher in our hospitals than those who have insurance. So they cost us more.

And what else happens? Since they get the care but they don't pay, who does pay? All the rest of us. We pay in higher hospital bills and higher insurance premiums. This cost shifting is a major problem.

The third thing we can do to save money is simply by simplifying the system—what we've already discussed. Freeing the health care providers from these costly and unnecessary paperwork and administrative decisions will save tens of billions of dollars. We spend twice as much as any other major country does on paperwork. We spend at least a dime on the dollar more than any other major country. That is a stunning statistic. It is something that every Republican and every Democrat ought to be able to say, we agree that we're going to squeeze this out. We cannot tolerate this. This has nothing to do with keeping people well or helping them when they're sick. We should invest the money in something else.

We also have to crack down on fraud and abuse in the system. That drains billions of dollars a year. It is a very large figure, according to every health care expert I've ever spoken with. So I believe we can achieve large savings. And that large savings can be used to cover the unemployed uninsured, and will be used for people who realize those savings in the private sector to increase their ability to invest and grow, to hire new workers or to give their workers pay raises, many of them for the first time in years.

Now, nobody has to take my word for this. You can ask Dr. Koop. He's up here with us tonight, and I thank him for being here. Since he left his distinguished tenure as our surgeon general, he has spent an enormous amount of time studying our health care system, how it operates, what's right and wrong with it. He says we could spend $200 billion every year, more than 20 percent of the total budget, without sacrificing the high quality of American medicine.

Ask the public employees in California, who have held their own premiums down by adopting the same strategy that I want every American to be able to adopt—bargaining within the limits of a strict budget. Ask Xerox, which saved an estimated $1,000 per worker on their health insurance premium. Ask the staff of the Mayo Clinic, who we all agree provides some of the finest health care in the world. They are holding their cost increases to less than half the national average. Ask the people of Hawaii, the only state that covers virtually all of their citizens and has still been able to keep costs below the national average.

People may disagree over the best way to fix this system. We may all disagree about how quickly we can do what—the thing that we have to do. But we cannot disagree that we can find tens of billions of dollars in savings in what is clearly the most costly and the most bureaucratic system in the entire world. And we have to do something about that, and we have to do it now.

The fourth principle is choice. Americans believe they ought to be able to choose their own health care plan and keep their own doctors. And I think all of us agree. Under any plan we pass, they ought to have that right. But today, under our broken health care system, in spite of the rhetoric of choice, the fact is that that power is slipping away for more and more Americans.

Of course, it is usually the employer, not the employee, who makes the initial choice of what health care plan the employee will be in. And if your employer offers only one plan, as nearly three-quarters of small or medium-sized firms do today, you're stuck with that plan, and the doctors that it covers.

We propose to give every American a choice among high-quality plans. You can stay with your current doctor, join a network of doctors and hospitals, or join a health maintenance organization. If you don't like your plan, every year you'll have the chance to choose a new one. The choice will be left to the American citizen, the worker—not the boss, and certainly not some government bureaucrat.

We also believe that doctors should have a choice as to what plans they practice in. Otherwise, citizens may have their own choices limited. We want to end the discrimination that is now growing against doctors, and to permit them to practice in several different plans. Choice is important for doctors, and it is absolutely critical for our consumers. We've got to have it in whatever plan we pass.

The fifth principle is quality. If we reformed everything else in health care, but failed to preserve and enhance the high quality of our medical care, we will have taken a step backward, not forward. Quality is something that we simply can't leave to chance. When you board an airplane, you feel better knowing that the plane had to meet standards designed to protect your safety. And we can't ask any less of our health care system.

Our proposal will create report cards on health plans, so that consumers can choose the highest quality health care providers and reward them with their business. At the same time, our plan will track quality indicators, so that doctors can make better and smarter choices of the kind of care they provide. We have evidence that more efficient delivery of health care doesn't decrease quality. In fact, it may enhance it.

Let me just give you one example of one commonly performed procedure, the coronary bypass operation. Pennsylvania discovered that patients who were charged $21,000 for this surgery received as good or better care as patients who were charged $84,000 for the same procedure in the same state. High prices simply don't always equal good quality. Our plan will guarantee that high-quality information is available in even the most remote areas of this country so that we can have high-quality service, linking rural doctors, for example, with hospitals with high-tech urban medical centers. And our plan will ensure the quality of continuing progress on a whole range of issues by speeding the search on effective prevention and treatment measures for cancer, for AIDS, for Alzheimer's, for heart disease, and for other chronic diseases. We have to safeguard the finest medical research establishment in the entire world. And we will do that with this plan. Indeed, we will even make it better.

The sixth and final principle is responsibility. We need to restore a sense that we're all in this together and that we all have a responsibility to be a part of the solution. Responsibility has to start with those who profit from the current system. Responsibility means insurance companies should no longer be allowed to cast people aside when they get sick. It should apply to laboratories that submit fraudulent bills, to lawyers who abuse malpractice claims, to doctors who order unnecessary procedures. It means drug companies should no longer charge three times more per prescription drugs made in America here in the United States than they charge for the same drugs overseas.

In short, responsibility should apply to anybody who abuses this system and drives up the cost for honest, hard-working citizens and undermines confidence in the honest, gifted health care providers we have.

Responsibility also means changing some behaviors in this country that drive up our costs like crazy. And without changing it we'll never have the system we ought to have. We will never.

Let me just mention a few and start with the most important—the outrageous costs of violence in this country stem in large measure from the fact that this is the only country in the world where teenagers can rout the streets at random with semiautomatic weapons and be better armed than the police.

But let's not kid ourselves, it's not that simple. We also have higher rates of AIDS, of smoking and excessive drinking, of teen pregnancy, of low birth weight babies. And we have the third worst immunization rate of any nation in the Western Hemisphere. We have to change our ways if we ever really want to be healthy as a people and have an affordable health care system. And no one can deny that.

But let me say this—and I hope every American will listen, because this is not an easy thing to hear—responsibility in our health care system isn't just about them, it's about you, it's about me, it's about each of us. Too many of us have not taken responsibility for our own health care and for our own relations to the health care system. Many of us who have had fully paid health care plans have used the system whether we needed it or not without thinking what the costs were. Many people who use this system don't pay a penny for their care even though they can afford to. I think those who don't have any health insurance should be responsible for paying a portion of their new coverage. There can't be any something for nothing, and we have to demonstrate that to people. This is not a free system. Even small contributions, as small as the $10 copayment when you visit a doctor, illustrates that this is something of value. There is a cost to it. It is not free.

And I want to tell you that I believe that all of us should have insurance. Why should the rest of us pick up the tab when a guy who doesn't think he needs insurance or says he can't afford it gets in an accident, winds up in an emergency room, gets good care, and everybody else pays? Why should the small businesspeople who are struggling to keep afloat and take care of their employees have to pay to maintain this wonderful health care infrastructure for those who refuse to do anything?

If we're going to produce a better health care system for every one of us, every one of us is going to have to do our part. There cannot be any such thing as a free ride. We have to pay for it. We have to pay for it.

Tonight I want to say plainly how I think we should do that. Most of the money we will—will come under my way of thinking, as it does today, from premiums paid by employers and individuals. That's the way it happens today. But under this health care security plan, every employer and every individual will be asked to contribute something to health care.

This concept was first conveyed to the Congress about 20 years ago by President Nixon. And today, a lot of people agree with the concept of shared responsibility between employers and employees, and that the best thing to do is to ask every employer and every employee to share that. The Chamber of Commerce has said that, and they're not in the business of hurting small business. The American Medical Association has said that.

Some call it an employer mandate, but I think it's the fairest way to achieve responsibility in the health care system. And it's the easiest for ordinary Americans to understand, because it builds on what we already have and what already works for so many Americans. It is the reform that is not only easiest to understand, but easiest to implement in a way that is fair to small business, because we can give a discount to help struggling small businesses meet the cost of covering their employees. We should require the least bureaucracy or disruption, and create the cooperation we need to make the system cost-conscious, even as we expand coverage. And we should do it in a way that does not cripple small businesses and low-wage workers.

Every employer should provide coverage, just as three-quarters do now. Those that pay are picking up the tab for those who don't today. I don't think that's right. To finance the rest of reform, we can achieve new savings, as I have outlined, in both the federal government and the private sector, through better decision making and increased competition. And we will impose new taxes on tobacco.

I don't think that should be the only source of revenues. I believe we should also ask for a modest contribution from big employers who opt out of the system to make up for what those who are in the system pay for medical research, for health education centers, for all the subsidies to small business, for all the things that everyone else is contributing to. But between those two things, we believe we can pay for this package of benefits and universal coverage and a subsidy program that will help small business.

These sources can cover the cost of the proposal that I have described tonight. We subjected the numbers in our proposal to the scrutiny of not only all the major agencies in government—I know a lot of people don't trust them, but it would be interesting for the American people to know that this was the first time that the financial experts on health care in all of the different government agencies have ever been required to sit in the room together and agree on numbers. It had never happened before.

But, obviously, that's not enough. So then we gave these numbers to actuaries from major accounting firms and major Fortune 500 companies who have no stake in this other than to see that our efforts succeed. So I believe our numbers are good and achievable.

Now, what does this mean to an individual American citizen? Some will be asked to pay more. If you're an employer and you aren't insuring your workers at all, you'll have to pay more. But if you're a small business with fewer than 50 employees, you'll get a subsidy. If you're a firm that provides only very limited coverage, you may have to pay more. But some firms will pay the same or less for more coverage.

If you're a young, single person in your 20s and you're already insured, your rates may go up somewhat because you're going to go into a big pool with middle-aged people and older people, and we want to enable people to keep their insurance even when someone in their family gets sick. But I think that's fair because when the young get older, they will benefit from it, first, and secondly, even those who pay a little more today will benefit four, five, six, seven years from now by our bringing health care costs closer to inflation. Over the long run, we can all win. But some will have to pay more in the short run. Nevertheless, the vast majority of the Americans watching this tonight will pay the same or less for health care coverage that will be the same or better than the coverage they have tonight. That is the central reality.

If you currently get your health insurance through your job, under our plan you still will. And for the first time, everybody will get to choose from among at least three plans to belong to. If you're a small business owner who wants to provide health insurance to your family and your employees, but you can't afford it because the system is stacked against you, this plan will give you a discount that will finally make insurance affordable. If you're already providing insurance, your rates may well drop because we'll help you as a small business person join thousands of others to get the same benefits big corporations get at the same price they get those benefits. If you're self-employed, you'll pay less and you will get to deduct from your taxes 100 percent of your health care premiums.

If you're a large employer, your health care costs won't go up as fast, so that you will have more money to put into higher wages and new jobs and to put into the work of being competitive in this tough global economy.

Now, these, my fellow Americans, are the principles on which I think we should base our efforts: security, simplicity, savings, choice, quality, and responsibility. These are the guiding stars that we should follow on our journey toward health care reform.

Over the coming months, you'll be bombarded with information from all kinds of sources. There will be some who will stoutly disagree with what I have proposed—and with all other plans in the Congress, for that matter. And some of the arguments will be genuinely sincere and enlightening. Others may simply be scare tactics by those who are motivated by the self-interest they have in the waste the system now generates, because that waste is providing jobs, incomes and money for some people.

I ask you only to think of this when you hear all of these arguments: Ask yourself whether the cost of staying on this same course isn't greater than the cost of change. And ask yourself when you hear the arguments whether the arguments are in your interest or someone else's. This is something we have got to try to do together.

I want also to say to the representatives in Congress, you have a special duty to look beyond these arguments. I ask you instead to look into the eyes of the sick child who needs care; to think of the face of the woman who's been told not only that her condition is malignant, but not covered by her insurance. To look at the bottom lines of the businesses driven to bankruptcy by health care costs. To look at the "for sale" signs in front of the homes of families who have lost everything because of their health care costs.

I ask you to remember the kind of people I met over the last year and a half—the elderly couple in New Hampshire that broke down and cried because of their shame at having an empty refrigerator to pay for their drugs; a woman who lost a $50,000 job that she used to support her six children because her youngest child was so ill that she couldn't keep health insurance, and the only way to get care for the child was to get public assistance; a young couple that had a sick child and could only get insurance from one of the parents' employers that was a nonprofit corporation with 20 employees, and so they had to face the question of whether to let this poor person with a sick child go or raise the premiums of every employee in the firm by $200. And on and on and on.

I know we have differences of opinion, but we are here tonight in a spirit that is animated by the problems of those people, and by the sheer knowledge that if we can look into our heart, we will not be able to say that the greatest nation in the history of the world is powerless to confront this crisis.

Our history and our heritage tell us that we can meet this challenge. Everything about America's past tells us we will do it. So I say to you, let us write that new chapter in the American story. Let us guarantee every American comprehensive health benefits that can never be taken away.

In spite of all the work we've done together and all the progress we've made, there's still a lot of people who say it would be an outright miracle if we passed health care reform. But my fellow Americans, in a time of change, you have to have miracles. And miracles do happen. I mean, just a few days ago we saw a simple handshake shatter decades of deadlock in the Middle East. We've seen the walls crumble in Berlin and South Africa. We see the ongoing brave struggle of the people of Russia to seize freedom and democracy.

And now, it is our turn to strike a blow for freedom in this country. The freedom of

Americans to live without fear that their own nation's health care system won't be there for them when they need it. It's hard to believe that there was once a time in this century when that kind of fear gripped old age. When retirement was nearly synonymous with poverty, and older Americans died in the street. That's unthinkable today, because over a half a century ago Americans had the courage to change—to create a Social Security system that ensures that no Americans will be forgotten in their later years.

Forty years from now, our grandchildren will also find it unthinkable that there was a time in this country when hardworking families lost their homes, their savings, their businesses, lost everything simply because their children got sick or because they had to change jobs. Our grandchildren will find such things unthinkable tomorrow if we have the courage to change today.

This is our chance. This is our journey. And when our work is done, we will know that we have answered the call of history and met the challenge of our time.

Thank you very much. And God bless America.

What Would Martin Luther King Say?

Memphis, Tennessee
November 13, 1993

CLINTON GOT A CHANCE to exercise his favorite kind of oratory—the ringing call to moral action—when he spoke to a convocation of 5,000 African-American ministers of the Church of God in Christ who were gathered at a convention in Memphis, Tennessee. Adopting the emotional, cadenced style of southern preachers, Clinton asked his audience to help put a stop to the violence and drug-related crime that was plaguing black urban neighborhoods and setting back the nation's painfully won gains in racial equality. The speech, delivered from notes drafted by Carolyn Curiel, was the more affecting because it was delivered in the church where Martin Luther King Jr. preached on the night before he was assassinated. Clinton afterward remarked, "I've just had the most moving day of my presidency."

. . . Proverbs says, "A happy heart doeth good like medicine, but a broken spirit dryeth the bone." This is a happy place, and I'm happy to be here. I thank you for your spirit.

By the grace of God and your help, last year I was elected president of this great country. I never dreamed that I would ever have a chance to come to this hallowed place where Martin Luther King gave his last sermon. I ask you to think today about the purpose for which I ran and the purpose for which so many of you worked to put me in this great office. I have worked hard to keep faith with our common efforts: to restore the economy, to reverse the politics of helping only those at the top of our totem pole and not the hard-working middle class or the poor; to bring our people together across racial and regional and political lines, to make a strength out of our diversity instead of letting it tear us apart; to reward work and family and community and try to move us forward into the 21st century. I have tried to keep faith.

Thirteen percent of all my presidential appointments are African-Americans, and there are five African-Americans in the cabinet of the United States, two and a half times as many as have ever served in the history of this great land. I have sought to advance the right to vote with the motor voter bill, supported so strongly by all the churches in our country. And next week it will be my great honor to sign the Restoration of Religious Freedoms Act, a bill supported widely by people across all religions and political philosophies to put back the real meaning of the Constitution, to give you and every other American the freedom to do what is most important in your life, to worship God as your spirit leads you.

I say to you, my fellow Americans, we have made a good beginning. Inflation is down. Interest rates are down. The deficit is down. Investment is up. Millions of Americans, including, I bet, some people in this room, have refinanced their homes or their business loans just in the last year. And in the last 10 months, this economy has produced more jobs in the private sector than in the previous four years.

We have passed a law called the Family Leave Law, which says you can't be fired if you take a little time off when a baby is born or a parent is sick. We know that most Americans have to work, but you ought not to have to give up being a good parent just to take a job. If you can't succeed as a worker and a parent, this country can't make it.

We have radically reformed the college loan program, as I promised, to lower the cost of college loans and broaden the availability of it and make the repayment terms easier. And we have passed the national service law that will give in three years, three years from now, 100,000 young Americans the chance to serve their communities at home, to repair the frayed bonds of community, to build up the needs of people at the grass roots, and at the same time, earn some money to pay for a college education. It is a wonderful idea.

On April 15th when people pay their taxes, somewhere between 15 million and 18 million working families on modest incomes, families with children and incomes of under $23,000, will get a tax cut, not a tax increase, in the most important effort to ensure that we reward work and family in the last 20 years. Fifty million American parents and their children will be advantaged by putting the Tax Code back on the side of working American parents for a change.

Under the leadership of the First Lady, we have produced a comprehensive plan to guarantee health care security to all Americans. How can we expect the American people to work and to live with all the changes in a global economy, where the average 18-year-old will change work seven times in a lifetime, unless we can simply say we have joined the ranks of all the other advanced countries in the world, you can have decent health care that's always there, that can never be taken away? It is time we did that, long past time. I ask you to help its achieve that.

But we have so much more to do. You and I know that most people are still working harder for the same or lower wages, that many people are afraid that their job will go away. We have to provide the education and training our people need, not just for our children but for our adults, too. If we cannot close this country up to the forces of change sweeping throughout the world, we have to at least guarantee people the security of being employable. They have to be able to get a new job if they're going to have to get a new job. We don't do that today, and we must, and we intend to proceed until that is done.

We have a guarantee that there will be some investment in those areas of our country, in the inner cities and in the destitute rural areas in the Mississippi Delta, of my home state and this state and Louisiana and Mississippi and other places like it throughout America. It's all very well to train people, but if they don't have a job, they can be trained for nothing. We must get investment into those places where the people are dying for work.

And finally, let me say, we must find people who will buy what we have to produce. We are the most productive people on Earth. That makes us proud. But what that means is that every year one person can produce more in the same amount of time. Now, if fewer and fewer people can produce more and more things, and yet you want to create more jobs and raise people's incomes, you have to have more customers for what it is you're making. And that is why I have worked so hard to sell more

American products around the world; why I have asked that we be able to sell billions of dollars of computers we used not to sell to foreign countries and foreign interests, to put our people to work; why next week I am going all the way to Washington State to meet with the president of China and the prime minister of Japan and the heads of 13 other Asian countries, the fastest growing part of the world, to say, "We want to be your partners. We will buy your goods, but we want you to buy ours, too, if you please." That is why.

That is why I have worked so hard for this North American trade agreement that Congressman Ford endorsed today and Congressman Jefferson endorsed and Congressman Cooper and Congressman Clement, because we know that Americans can compete and win only if people will buy what it is we have to sell. There are 90 million people in Mexico. Seventy cents of every dollar they spend on foreign goods, they spend on American goods.

People worry fairly about people shutting down plants in America and going not just to Mexico but to any place where the labor is cheap. It has happened. What I want to say to you, my fellow Americans, is nothing in this agreement makes that more likely. That has happened already. It may happen again. What we need to do is keep the jobs here by finding customers there. That's what this agreement does. It gives us a chance to create opportunity for people. I have friends in this audience, people who are ministers from my state, fathers and sons, people—I've looked out all over this vast crowd and I see people I've known for years. They know I spent my whole life working to create jobs. I would never knowingly do anything that would take a job away from the American people. This agreement will make more jobs. Now, we can also leave it if it doesn't work in six months. But if we don't take it, we'll lose it forever. We need to take it, because we have to do better.

But I guess what I really want to say to you today, my fellow Americans, is that we can do all of this and still fail unless we meet the great crisis of the spirit that is gripping America today.

When I leave you, Congressman Ford and I are going to a Baptist church near here to a town meeting he's having on health care and violence. I tell you, unless we do something about crime and violence and drugs that is ravaging the community, we will not be able to repair this country.

If Martin Luther King, who said, "Like Moses, I am on the mountaintop, and I can see the promised land, but I'm not going to be able to get there with you, but we will get there"— if he were to reappear by my side today and give us a report card on the last 25 years, what would be say? You did a good job, he would say, voting and electing people who formerly were not electable because of the color of their skin. You have more political power, and that is good. You did a good job, he would say, letting people who have the ability to do so live wherever they want to live, go wherever they want to go in this great country. You did a good job, he would say, elevating people of color into the ranks of the United States Armed Forces to the very top or into the very top of our government. You did a very good job, he would say. He would say, you did a good job creating a black middle class of people who really are doing well, and the middle class is growing more among African-Americans than among non-African-Americans. You did a good job; you did a good job in opening opportunity.

But he would say, I did not live and die to see the American family destroyed. I did not live and die to see 13-year-old boys get automatic weapons and gun down nine-year-olds just for the kick of it. I did not live and die to see young people destroy their own lives with drugs and then build fortunes destroying the lives of others. That is not what I came here to do. I fought for freedom, he would say, but not for the freedom of people to kill each other with reckless abandon, not for the freedom of children to have children and the fathers of the children walk away from them and abandon them as if they don't amount to anything. I fought for people to have the right to work but not to have whole communities and people abandoned. This is not what I lived and died for.

My fellow Americans, he would say, I fought to stop white people from being so filled with hate that they would wreak violence on black people. I did not fight for the right of black people to murder other black people with reckless abandon.

The other day the mayor of Baltimore, a dear friend of mine, told me a story of visiting the family of a young man who had been killed—18 years old—on Halloween.

He always went out with little bitty kids so they could trick-or-treat safely. And across the street from where they were walking on Halloween, a 14-year-old boy gave a 13-year-old boy a gun and dared him to shoot the 18-year-old boy, and he shot him dead. And the mayor had to visit the family.

In Washington, D.C., where I live, your nation's capital, the symbol of freedom throughout the world, look how that freedom is being exercised. The other night a man came along the street and grabbed a one-year-old child and put the child in his car. The child may have been the child of the man. And two people were after him, and they chased him in the car, and they just kept shooting with reckless abandon, knowing that baby was in the car. And they shot the man dead, and a bullet went through his body into the baby's body, and blew the little bootie off the child's foot.

The other day on the front page of our paper, the nation's capital, are we talking about world peace or world conflict? No, big article on the front page of the *Washington Post* about an 11-year-old child planning her funeral: "These are the hymns I want sung. This is the dress I want to wear. I know I'm not going to live very long." That is not the freedom, the freedom to die before you're a teenager is not what Martin Luther King lived and died for.

More than 37,000 people die from gunshot wounds in this country every year. Gunfire is the leading cause of death in young men. And now that we've all gotten so cool that everybody can get a semiautomatic weapon, a person shot now is three times more likely to die than 15 years ago, because they're likely to have three bullets in them. A hundred and sixty thousand children stay home from school every day because they are scared they will be hurt in their schools.

The other day I was in California at a town meeting, and a handsome young man stood up and said, "Mr. President, my brother and I, we don't belong to gangs. We don't have guns. We don't do drugs. We want to go to school. We want to be professionals. We want to work hard. We want to do well. We want to have families. And we changed our school because the school we were in was so dangerous. So when we showed up to the new school to register, my brother and I were standing in line and somebody ran into the school and started shooting a gun. My brother was shot down standing right in front of me at the safer school." The freedom to do that kind of thing is not what Martin Luther King lived and died for, not what people gathered in this hallowed church for the night before he was assassinated in April of 1968. If you had told anybody who was here in that church on that night that we would abuse our freedom in that way, they would have found it hard to believe. And I tell you, it is our moral duty to turn it around.

And now I think finally we have a chance. Finally, I think, we have a chance. We have a pastor here from New Haven, Connecticut. I was in his church with Reverend Jackson when I was running for president on a snowy day in Connecticut to mourn the death of children who had been killed in that city. And afterward we walked down the street for more than a mile in the snow. Then, the American people were not ready. People would say, "Oh, this is a terrible thing, but what can we do about it?"

Now when we read that foreign visitors come to our shores and are killed at random in our fine state of Florida, when we see our children planning their funerals, when the American people are finally coming to grips with the accumulated weight of crime and violence and the breakdown of family and community and the increase in drugs and the decrease in jobs, I think finally we may be ready to do something about it.

And there is something for each of us to do. There are changes we can make from the outside in; that's the job of the president and the Congress and the governors and the mayors and the social service agencies. And then there's some changes we're going to have to make from the inside out, or the others won't matter. That's what that magnificent song was about, isn't it? Sometimes there are no answers from the outside in; sometimes all the answers have to come from the values and the stirrings and the voices that speak to us from within.

So we are beginning. We are trying to pass a bill to make our people safer, to put another 100,000 police officers on the street, to provide boot camps instead of prisons for young people who can still be rescued, to provide more safety in our schools, to restrict the availability of these awful assault weapons, to pass the Brady Bill and at least require people to have their criminal background checked before they get a gun, and to say, if you're not old enough to vote and you're not old enough to go to war, you ought not to own a handgun, and you ought not to use one unless you're on a target range.

We want to pass a health care bill that will make drug treatment available for everyone. And we also have to do it, we have to have drug treatment and education available to everyone and especially those who are in prison who are coming out. We have a drug czar now in Lee Brown, who was the police chief of Atlanta, of Houston, of New York, who understands these things. And when the Congress comes back next year, we will be moving forward on that.

We need this crime bill now. We ought to give it to the American people for Christmas. And we need to move forward on all these other fronts. But I say to you, my fellow Americans, we need some other things as well. I do not believe we can repair the basic fabric of society until people who are willing to work have work. Work organizes life. It gives structure and discipline to life. It gives meaning and self-esteem to people who are parents. It gives a role model to children.

The famous African-American sociologist William Julius Wilson has written a stunning book called *The Truly Disadvantaged* in which he chronicles in breathtaking terms how the inner cities of our country have crumbled as work has disappeared. And we must find a way, through public and private sources, to enhance the attractiveness of the American people who live there to get investment there. We cannot, I submit to you, repair the American community and restore the American family until we provide the structure, the values, the discipline, and the reward that work gives.

I read a wonderful speech the other day given at Howard University in a lecture series funded by Bill and Camille Cosby, in which the speaker said, "I grew up in Anacostia years ago. Even then it was all black, and it was a very poor neighborhood. But you know, when I was a child in Anacostia, a 100 percent African-American neighborhood, a very poor neighborhood, we had a crime rate that was lower than the average of the crime rate of our city. Why? Because we had coherent families. We had coherent communities. The people who filled the church on Sunday lived in the same place they went to church. The guy that owned the drugstore lived down the street. The person that owned the grocery store lived in our community. We were whole." And I say to you, we have to make our people whole again.

This church has stood for that. Why do you think you have 5 million members in this country? Because people know you are filled with the spirit of God to do the right thing in this life by them. So I say to you, we have to make a partnership, all the government agencies, all the business folks; but where there are no families, where there is no order, where there is no hope, where we are reducing the size of our armed services because we have won the cold war, who will be there to give structure, discipline, and love to these children? You must do that. And we must help you. Scripture says, you are the salt of the earth and the light of the world, that if your light shines before men they will give glory to the Father in heaven. That is what we must do.

That is what we must do. How would we explain it to Martin Luther King if he showed up today and said, yes, we won the cold war. Yes, the biggest threat that all of us grew up under, Communism and nuclear war, Communism gone, nuclear war receding. Yes, we developed all these miraculous technologies. Yes, we all have got a VCR in our home; it's interesting. Yes, we get 50 channels on the cable. Yes, without regard to race, if you work hard and play by the rules, you can get into a service academy or a good college, you'll do just great. How would we explain to him all these kids getting killed and killing each other? How would we justify the things that we permit that no other country in the world would permit? How could we explain that we gave people the freedom to succeed, and we created conditions in which millions abuse that freedom to destroy the things that make life worth living and life itself? We cannot.

And so I say to you today, my fellow Americans, you gave me this job, and we're making progress on the things you hired me to do. But unless we deal with the ravages of crime and drugs and violence and unless we recognize that it's due to the breakdown of the family, the community, and the disappearance of jobs, and unless we say some of this cannot be done by government, because we have to reach deep inside to the values, the spirit, the soul, and the truth of human nature, none of the other things we seek to do will ever take us where we need to go.

So in this pulpit, on this day, let me ask all of you in your heart to say: We will honor the life and the work of Martin Luther King. We will honor the meaning of our church. We will, somehow, by God's grace, we will turn this around. We will give these children a future. We will take away their guns and give them books. We will take away their despair and give them hope. We will rebuild the families and the neighborhoods and the communities. We won't make all the work that has gone on here benefit just a few. We will do it together by the grace of God.

Thank you.

Condemning the Militias

East Lansing, Michigan

May 5, 1995

ON APRIL 19, 1995, the Alfred R. Murrah Federal Building in Oklahoma City, OK, was destroyed by a truck bomb that had been planted by terrorists with ties to the radically antigovernment militia movement. The explosion killed 168 people, including young children in the building's day care center, and wounded hundreds of others. The date of April 19 had been chosen by the terrorists to retaliate for the federal government's raid on the Branch Davidian cult in Waco, TX, two years earlier.

President Clinton spoke to the nation in a brief television address late in the afternoon on the day of the bombing. He eulogized the victims at a memorial service in Oklahoma City a few days later and continued to talk about the event in speech after speech over the next month. His most vigorous expression of outrage and concern came in a commencement speech at Michigan State University.

I'm honored to be your speaker today and to be back on this wonderful campus, the site of one of the great presidential debates in 1992.

I have fond memories of Michigan State. And I was sitting there thinking of all the uses to which I might put my honorary degree. Maybe I will get more respect in Washington now. Regardless, now I know who I'm supposed to root for in the Big 10.

Speaking of sports, I want to take a moment of personal privilege to offer my very best wishes on his retirement to your distinguished basketball coach, Judd Heathcote.

And as a person who never, ever, would have had an opportunity to be here today, doing what I am doing, I want to thank President McPherson, the present and past governors of Michigan, and all others who have supported the remarkable set of educational opportunities for young people in Michigan, especially in higher education. The tuition guarantee program to keep tuition increases here to the rate of inflation for five years is a standard I wish other universities all across America would follow.

I also hope that other states will follow the example of the Michigan Education Trust, and of Michigan State in entering into the direct loan program, which will lower the cost of college loans for young people and improve their repayment options so more people can afford to go to college and stay there until they get their degrees.

I also want to say that I am deeply honored to be joined today by another Michigan State alumnist who spoke from this platform last year, my friend and fellow Arkansan, Ernest Green. He was one of the Little Rock Nine, a brave group of Americans who staked their lives for the cause of school integration and equal opportunity in education in my state almost 40 years ago. He made the right choice at the right moment in his life. He is a good model for you, and I hope you will do the same.

As I was reminded by your president and others when we gathered just a few moments ago, the last sitting president to address this assembly was Theodore Roosevelt in 1907. There were fewer than 100 graduates in the senior class then. But it was a time not unlike this time. We are on the edge of a new century; they had just begun a new century. We are on the edge of a new era; they had just begun the dawn of the industrial age. Like us now, they had many, many opportunities, but profound problems. And people were full of hope mixed with fear.

But President Roosevelt and his generation of Americans were optimistic, aggressive in facing the challenges of the day, and determined to solve the problems before them. They launched the progressive era, using the power of government to free the market forces of our country from the heavy hand of monopoly, beginning to protect our environment for future generations, to keep our children out of sweatshops, to stand strong for America's role in the world.

Theodore Roosevelt and the Americans of his generation made the right choices at the right moment. They met the challenges of the present, paved the way for a better future, and redeemed the promise of America.

Our journey as a nation has never been an automatic march to freedom and opportunity. In every generation there has come a point of challenge in change. When critical decisions are made by our people to go forward to turn back, to reach out or turn inward, to unify or divide, to believe or doubt.

Today, we stand at the end of the cold war and the industrial age, at the onset of the global economy and the information age. Throughout all 219 years of our republic, times of great change like this have unleashed forces of promise and threat, forces that uplift us and unsettle us.

This time is not different. You are walking into a future of unlimited possibilities. But more than half your fellow citizens are working harder, spending less time with their children, and earning about the same they did 15 years ago.

You can look forward to bringing your children into an exciting world, freer of the dangers of war and nuclear annihilation, but the dangers here at home are still profound. Too many of our children are not born into stable families. Our streets are still too violent. And new forces threaten the order and security which free people everywhere cherish.

And so, my fellow Americans, it falls to your generation to make your historic choices for America. This is a very new and different time. But the basic question before us is as old as our country: Will we face up to the problems and seize our opportunities with confidence and courage? It is our responsibility to make that choice again.

Because you have a fine education, with all its power and potential, when you leave this stadium your responsibility to your families, your community, and your country will be greater than ever before. With your lives fully before you, you, too, must once again redeem the promise of America.

On the homefront there is reason for optimism. Though income stagnation and economic uncertainty plague too many of our people, unemployment is down, inflation is low, our deficit is declining, trade is up, and most importantly of all, educational opportunities are increasing. Though crime and violence, drug abuse and welfare dependency and out-of-wedlock pregnancies are still too high and threaten our social fabric, we are making a serious assault on all of them, and we can make progress on all of them. Though government is still too cumbersome and outdated, it is growing smaller, more flexible, less wasteful, and more effective.

In all these endeavors you must demand higher standards and more personal responsibility. But you must know that progress is possible.

Beyond our borders there is also reason for hope. Since the end of the cold war the bonds among nations and the forces of commerce have grown stronger. There is now a greater understanding of our world's environmental challenges, and a willingness to do something about them. Freedom, democracy, and free enterprise are on the march. Large countries are much less likely to go to war with one another. I am very proud to say that for the first time since the dawn of the nuclear age, no Russian missiles are pointed at the people of the United States.

And I am equally proud to say that next week I will become the first American president in nearly 40 years to visit Russia when no American missiles are pointed at the people of Russia.

Therefore, you who graduate today will have the chance to live in the most exciting, the most prosperous, the most diverse and interesting world in the entire history of humanity. Still you must face the fact that no time is free of problems, and we have new and grave security challenges.

In this, the 20th century, millions of lives were lost in wars between nations, and in efforts by totalitarian dictatorships to stamp out the light of liberty among their subjects. In the 21st century, bloody wars of ethnic and tribal hatred will be fought still in some parts of the world. But with freedom and democracy advancing, the real threat to our security will be rooted in the fact that all the forces that are lifting us up and opening unparalleled opportunity for us contain a dark underside. For open societies are characterized by free and rapid movements of people and technology and information. And that very wonder makes them very, very vulnerable to the forces of organized destruction and evil. So the great security challenge for your future in the 21st century will be to determine how to beat back the dangers while keeping the benefits of this new time.

The dark possibilities of our age are visible now in the smoke, the horror, and the heartbreak of Oklahoma City. As the long and painful search and rescue effort comes to an end with 165 dead, 467 injured, and two still unaccounted for, our prayers are with those who lost their loved ones, and with the brave and good people of Oklahoma City, who have moved with such strength and character to deal with this tragedy. But that threat is not isolated. And you must not believe it is. We see that threat again in the bombing of the World Trade Center in New York; in the nerve gas attack in the Tokyo subway; in the terrorist assault on innocent civilians in the Middle East; in the organized crime plaguing the former Soviet Union now that the heavy hand of Communism has been lifted. We see it even on the Internet, where people exchange information about bombs and terrorism, even as children learn from sources all around the world.

My fellow Americans, we must respond to this threat in ways that preserve both our security and our freedoms. Appeasement of organized evil is not an option for the next century any more than it was in this century. Like the vigilant generations that brought us victory in World War II and the cold war, we must stand our ground. In this high-tech world, we must make sure that we have the high-tech tools to confront the high-tech forces of destruction and evil.

That is why I have insisted that Congress pass strong antiterrorism legislation immediately—to provide for more than 1,000 new law enforcement personnel solely to fight terrorism; to create a domestic antiterrorism center; to make available the most up-to-date technology to trace the source of any bomb that goes off; and to provide tough new punishment for carrying stolen explosives, selling those explosives for use in a violent crime, and for attacking members of the uniformed services or federal workers.

To their credit, the leaders of Congress have promised to put a bill on my desk by Memorial Day. I applaud them for that. This is not, and must never be, a partisan issue. This is about America's future. It is about your future.

We can do this without undermining our constitutional rights. In fact, the failure to act will undermine those rights. For no one is free in America where parents have to worry when they drop off their children for day care, or when you are the target of assassination simply because you work for our government. No one is free in America when large numbers of our fellow citizens must always be looking over their shoulders.

It is with this in mind that I would like to say something to the paramilitary groups and to others who believe the greatest threat to America comes not from terrorists from within our country or beyond our borders, but from our own government.

I want to say this to the militias and to others who believe this, to those nearby and those far away: I am well aware that most of you have never violated the law of the land. I welcome the comments that some of you have made recently condemning the bombing in Oklahoma City. I believe you have every right, indeed you have the responsibility, to question our government when you disagree with its policies. And I will do everything in my power to protect your right to do so.

But I also know there have been lawbreakers among those who espouse your philosophy. I know from painful personal experience as a governor of a state who lived through the cold-blooded killing of a young sheriff and a young African-American state trooper who were friends of mine by people who espouse the view that the government was the biggest problem in America and that people had a right to take violence into their own hands. So I ask you to hear me now. It is one thing to believe that the federal government has too much power and to work within the law to reduce it. It is quite another to break the law of the land and threaten to shoot officers of the law if all they do is their duty to uphold it.

It is one thing to believe we are taxed too much and work to reduce the tax burden. It is quite another to refuse to pay your taxes, though your neighbor pays his. It is one thing to believe we are over-regulated and to work to lessen the burden of regulation. It is quite another to slander our dedicated public servants, our brave police officers, even our rescue workers who have been called a hostile army of occupation.

This is a very free country. Those of you in the militia movements have broader rights here than you would in any other country in the entire world.

Do people who work for the government sometimes make mistakes? Of course they do. They are human. Almost every American has some experience with this—a rude tax collector, an arbitrary regulator, an insensitive social worker, an abusive law officer. As long as human beings make up our government there will be mistakes. But our Constitution was established by Americans determined to limit those abuses. And think of the limits—the Bill of Rights, the separation of powers, access to the courts, the right to take your case to the country through the media, and the right to vote people in or out of office on a regular basis.

But there is no right to resort to violence when you don't get your way. There is no right to kill people. There is no right to kill people who are doing their duty, or minding their own business, or children who are innocent in every way. Those are the people who perished in Oklahoma City. And those who claim such rights are wrong and un-American.

Whenever in our history people have believed that violence is a legitimate extension of politics they have been wrong. In the 1960s, as your distinguished alumni said, many good things happened and there was much turmoil. But the Weathermen of the radical Left who resorted to violence in the 1960s were wrong. Today, the gang members who use life on the mean streets of America, as terrible as it is, to justify taking the law into their own hands and taking innocent life are wrong. The people who came to the United States to bomb the World Trade Center were wrong.

Freedom of political speech will never justify violence—never. Our founding fathers created a system of laws in which reason could prevail over fear. Without respect for this law there is no freedom.

So I say this to the militias and all others who believe that the greatest threat to freedom comes from the government instead of from those who would take away our freedom: If you say violence is an acceptable way to make change, you are wrong. If you say that government is in a conspiracy to take your freedom away, you are just plain wrong.

If you treat law enforcement officers who put their lives on the line for your safety every day like some kind of enemy army to be suspected, derided, and, if they should enforce the law against you, to be shot, you are wrong. If you appropriate our sacred symbols for paranoid purposes and compare yourselves to colonial militias who fought for the democracy you now rail against, you are wrong.

How dare you suggest that we in the freest nation on earth live in tyranny. How dare you call yourselves patriots and heroes.

I say to you, all of you, the members of the Class of 1995, there is nothing patriotic about hating your country, or pretending that you can love your country but despise your government. There is nothing heroic about turning your back on America, or ignoring your own responsibilities. If you want to preserve your own freedom, you must stand up for the freedom of others with whom you disagree. But you also must stand up for the rule of law. You cannot have one without the other.

The real American heroes today are the citizens who get up every morning and have the courage to work hard and play by the rules—the mother who stays up the extra half hour after a long day's work to read her child a story; the rescue worker who digs with his hands in the rubble as the building crumbles about him; the neighbor who lives side-by-side with people different from himself; the government worker who quietly and efficiently labors to see to it that the programs we depend on are honestly and properly carried out; most of all, the parent who works long years for modest pay and sacrifices so that his or her children can have the education that you have had, and the chances you are going to have. I ask you never to forget that.

And I would like to say one word to the people of the United States. I know you have heard a lot of publicity in recent days about Michigan and militias. But what you have seen and heard is not the real Michigan. This is the real Michigan.

This is the real Michigan in this stadium today. The real Michigan is Michigan State. It's the astonishing revival of the automobile industry, with the remarkable partnership between the autoworkers and the management. Real Michigan is Kellogg's Corn Flakes and the best cherries in the world. The real Michigan is the Great Lakes and the UP [Upper Peninsula].

And the real Michigan—most of all, the real Michigan was presented to me when I got off the plane and one of your local officials told me that here in mid-Michigan in only five days, the people of this area raised $70,000 to pay for the help that people need in Oklahoma City. And that money is now on its way to Oklahoma City in a 27-car caravan, led by members of 27 different law enforcement agencies from this part of your wonderful state. That is what I want America to know about the real Michigan.

So, my fellow Americans and members of the Class of 1995, let me close by reminding you once again that you live in a very great country. When we are united by our humanity and our civic virtue, nothing can stop us. Let me remind you once again that our best days as a nation still lie before us. But we must not give in to fear or use the frustrations of the moment as an excuse to walk from the obligations of citizenship.

Remember what our founding fathers built. Remember the victories won for us in the cold war and in World War II, 50 years ago next week. Remember the blood and sweat and triumph that enabled us to come to this, the greatest moment of possibility in our history.

Go out and make the most of the potential God has given you. Make the most of the opportunities and freedoms America has given to you. Be optimistic; be strong. Make the choices that Theodore Roosevelt made, that Ernest Green made. Seize your moment. Build a better future. And redeem once again the promise of America.

Thank you, and God bless you all.

Affirmative Action

Washington, D.C.

July 19, 1995

AFTER THE DEVASTATING midterm elections of 1994, when the Republicans took control of both houses of Congress, President Clinton began moving toward the political center and away from liberal positions that appeared too extreme. A particularly fraught issue was affirmative action for minority ethnic groups and for women, which was under attack by conservatives opposed to the idea that governments should enforce compensatory discrimination. A White House task force headed by George Stephanopoulos and Harvard professor Christopher Edley undertook a four-month review and concluded that affirmative action programs had to be retained as a matter of social justice, though reform was needed to prevent abuses.

On July 19, 1995, Clinton went to the rotunda of the National Archives to defend affirmative action from a podium set between the Declaration of Independence and the Constitution. According to Daniel Seligman, writing in *Fortune,* the speech was "repetitive, disorganized, klutzily written, and relentlessly evasive on all the big questions." Nonetheless, it shored up Clinton's standing with the liberal wing of his party, and just in time: one week earlier, the Supreme Court, in *Adarand Constructors, Inc. v. Pena,* had ordered the Justice Department to evaluate all federal affirmative action programs for compliance with strict constitutional tests.

Thank you very much. To the members of Congress who are here, members of the cabinet and the administration, my fellow Americans: In recent weeks I have begun a conversation with the American people about our fate and our duty to prepare our nation not only to meet the new century, but to live and lead in a world transformed to a degree seldom seen in all of our history. Much of this change is good, but it is not all good, and all of us are affected by it. Therefore, we must reach beyond our fears and our divisions to a new time of great and common purpose.

Our challenge is twofold: first, to restore the American dream of opportunity and the American value of responsibility; and second, to bring our country together amid all our diversity into a stronger community, so that we can find common ground and move forward as one.

More than ever these two endeavors are inseparable. I am absolutely convinced we cannot restore economic opportunity or solve our social problems unless we find a way to bring the American people together. To bring our people together we must openly and honestly deal with the issues that divide us. Today I want to discuss one of those issues: affirmative action.

It is, in a way, ironic that this issue should be divisive today, because affirmative action began 25 years ago by a Republican president with bipartisan support. It began simply as a means to an end of enduring national purpose—equal opportunity for all Americans.

So let us today trace the roots of affirmative action in our never-ending search for equal opportunity. Let us determine what it is and what it isn't. Let us see where it's worked and where it hasn't, and ask ourselves what we need to do now. Along the way, let us remember always that finding common ground as we move toward the 21st century depends fundamentally on our shared commitment to equal opportunity for all Americans. It is a moral imperative, a constitutional mandate, and a legal necessity.

There could be no better place for this discussion than the National Archives, for within these walls are America's bedrocks of our common ground—the Declaration of Independence, the Constitution, the Bill of Rights. No paper is as lasting as the words these documents contain. So we put them in these special cases to protect the parchment from the elements. No building is as solid as the principles these documents embody, but we sure tried to build one with these metal doors 11 inches thick to keep them safe, for these documents are America's only crown jewels. But the best place of all to hold these words and these principles is the one place in which they can never fade and never grow old—in the stronger chambers of our hearts.

Beyond all else, our country is a set of convictions: We hold these truths to be self-evident that all men are created equal; that they are endowed by their Creator with certain inalienable rights; that among these are life, liberty, and the pursuit of happiness.

Our whole history can be seen first as an effort to preserve these rights, and then as an effort to make them real in the lives of all our citizens. We know that from the beginning, there was a great gap between the plain meaning of our creed and the meaner reality of our daily lives. Back then, only white male property owners could vote. Black slaves were not even counted as whole people, and Native Americans were regarded as little more than an obstacle to our great national progress. No wonder Thomas Jefferson, reflecting on slavery, said he trembled to think God is just.

On the 200th anniversary of our great Constitution, Justice Thurgood Marshall, the grandson of a slave, said, "The government our founders devised was defective from the start, requiring several amendments, a civil war, and momentous social transformation to attain the system of constitutional government and its respect for the individual freedoms and human rights we hold as fundamental today."

Emancipation, women's suffrage, civil rights, voting rights, equal rights, the struggle for the rights of the disabled—all these and other struggles are milestones on America's often rocky, but fundamentally righteous journey to close the gap between the ideals enshrined in these treasures here in the National Archives and the reality of our daily lives.

I first came to this very spot where I'm standing today 32 years ago this month. I was a 16-year-old delegate to the American Legion Boys Nation. Now, that summer was a high-water mark for our national journey. That was the summer that President Kennedy ordered Alabama National Guardsmen to enforce a court order to allow two young blacks to enter the University of Alabama. As he told our nation, "Every American ought to have the right to be treated as he would wish to be treated; as one would wish his children to be treated."

Later that same summer, on the steps of the Lincoln Memorial, Martin Luther King told Americans of his dream that one day the sons of former slaves and the sons of former slaveowners would sit down together at the table of brotherhood; that one day his four little children would be judged not by the color of their skin, but by the content of their character. His words captured the hearts and steeled the wills of millions of Americans. Some of them sang with him in the hot sun that day. Millions more like me listened and wept in the privacy of their homes.

It's hard to believe where we were just three decades ago. When I came up here to Boys Nation and we had this mock congressional session I was one of only three or four southerners who would even vote for the civil rights plank. That's largely because of my family. My grandfather had a grade school education and ran a grocery store across the street from the cemetery in Hope, Arkansas, where my parents and my grandparents are buried. Most of his customers were black, were poor, and were working people. As a child in that store I saw that people of different races could treat each other with respect and dignity.

But I also saw that the black neighborhood across the street was the only one in town where the streets weren't paved. And when I returned to that neighborhood in the late '60s to see a woman who had cared for me as a toddler, the streets still weren't paved. A lot of you know that I am an ardent movie-goer. As a child I never went to a movie where I could sit next to a black American. They were always sitting upstairs.

In the 1960s, believe it or not, there were still a few courthouse squares in my state where the rest rooms were marked "white" and "colored." I graduated from a segregated high school seven years after President Eisenhower integrated Little Rock Central High School. And when President Kennedy barely carried my home state in 1960, the poll tax system was still alive and well there.

Even though my grandparents were in a minority, being poor, southern whites who were pro–civil rights, I think most other people knew better than to think the way they did. And those who were smart enough to act differently, discovered a lesson that we ought to remember today: Discrimination is not just morally wrong, it hurts everybody.

In 1960, Atlanta, Georgia, in reaction to all the things that were going on all across the

South, adopted the motto, "The city too busy to hate." And however imperfectly over the years, they tried to live by it. I am convinced that Atlanta's success—it now is home to more foreign corporations than any other American city, and one year from today it will begin to host the Olympics— that that success all began when people got too busy to hate.

The lesson we learned was a hard one. When we allow people to pit us against one another or spend energy denying opportunity based on our differences, everyone is held back. But when we give all Americans a chance to develop and use their talents, to be full partners in our common enterprise, then everybody is pushed forward.

My experiences with discrimination are rooted in the South and in the legacy slavery left. I also lived with a working mother and a working grandmother when women's work was far rarer and far more circumscribed than it is today. But we all know there are millions of other stories— those of Hispanics, Asian Americans, Native Americans, people with disabilities, others against whom fingers have been pointed. Many of you have your own stories, and that's why you're here today— people who were denied the right to develop and use their full human potential. And their progress, too, is a part of our journey to make the reality of America consistent with the principles just behind me here.

Thirty years ago in this city, you didn't see many people of color or women making their way to work in the morning in business clothes, or serving in substantial numbers in powerful positions in Congress or at the White House, or making executive decisions every day in businesses. In fact, even the employment want ads were divided, men on one side and women on the other.

It was extraordinary then to see women or people of color as television news anchors, or, believe it or not, even in college sports. There were far fewer women or minorities as job supervisors, or firefighters, or police officers, or doctors, or lawyers, or college professors, or in many other jobs that offer stability and honor and integrity to family life.

A lot has changed, and it did not happen as some sort of random evolutionary drift. It took hard work and sacrifices and countless acts of courage and conscience by millions of Americans. It took the political courage and

statesmanship of Democrats and Republicans alike, the vigilance and compassion of courts and advocates in and out of government committed to the Constitution and to equal protection and to equal opportunity. It took the leadership of people in business who knew that in the end we would all be better. It took the leadership of people in labor unions who knew that working people had to be reconciled.

Some people, like Congressman Lewis there, put their lives on the line. Other people lost their lives. And millions of Americans changed their own lives and put hate behind them. As a result, today all our lives are better. Women have become a major force in business and political life, and far more able to contribute to their families' incomes. A true and growing black middle class has emerged. Higher education has literally been revolutionized, with women and racial and ethnic minorities attending once overwhelmingly white and sometimes all-male schools.

In communities across our nation police departments now better reflect the makeup of those whom they protect. A generation of professionals now serve as role models for young women and minority youth. Hispanics and newer immigrant populations are succeeding in making America stronger.

For an example of where the best of our future lies just think about our space program and the stunning hook-up with the Russian space station this month. Let's remember that that program, the world's finest, began with heroes like Alan Shepard and Senator John Glenn, but today it's had American heroes like Sally Ride, Ellen Ochoa, Leroy Child, Guy Bluford, and other outstanding, completely qualified women and minorities.

How did this happen? Fundamentally, because we opened our hearts and minds and changed our ways. But not without pressure— the pressure of court decisions, legislation, executive action, and the power of examples in the public and private sector. Along the way we learned that laws alone do not change society; that old habits and thinking patterns are deeply ingrained and die hard; that more is required to really open the doors of opportunity. Our search to find ways to move more quickly to equal opportunity led to the development of what we now call affirmative action.

The purpose of affirmative action is to give our nation a way to finally address the systemic exclusion of individuals of talent on the basis of their gender or race from opportunities to develop, perform, achieve, and contribute. Affirmative action is an effort to develop a systematic approach to open the doors of education, employment, and business development opportunities to qualified individuals who happen to be members of groups that have experienced longstanding and persistent discrimination.

It is a policy that grew out of many years of trying to navigate between two unacceptable pasts. One was to say simply that we declared discrimination illegal and that's enough. We saw that that way still relegated blacks with college degrees to jobs as railroad porters, and kept women with degrees under a glass ceiling with a lower paycheck.

The other path was simply to try to impose change by leveling draconian penalties on employers who didn't meet certain imposed, ultimately arbitrary, and sometimes unachievable quotas. That, too, was rejected out of a sense of fairness.

So a middle ground was developed that would change an inequitable status quo gradually, but firmly, by building the pool of qualified applicants for college, for contracts, for jobs, and giving more people the chance to learn, work, and earn. When affirmative action is done right, it is flexible, it is fair, and it works.

I know some people are honestly concerned about the times affirmative action doesn't work, when it's done in the wrong way. And I know there are times when some employers don't use it in the right way. They may cut corners and treat a flexible goal as a quota. They may give opportunities to people who are unqualified instead of those who deserve it. They may, in so doing, allow a different kind of discrimination. When this happens, it is also wrong. But it isn't affirmative action, and it is not legal.

So when our administration finds cases of that sort, we will enforce the law aggressively. The Justice Department files hundreds of cases every year, attacking discrimination in employment, including suits on behalf of white males. Most of these suits, however, affect women and minorities for a simple reason—because the vast majority of discrimination in America is still discrimination against them. But the law does require fairness for

everyone and we are determined to see that that is exactly what the law delivers.

Let me be clear about what affirmative action must not mean and what I won't allow it to be. It does not mean—and I don't favor—the unjustified preference of the unqualified over the qualified of any race or gender. It doesn't mean—and I don't favor—numerical quotas. It doesn't mean—and don't favor—rejection or selection of any employee or student solely on the basis of race or gender without regard to merit.

Like many business executives and public servants, I owe it to you to say that my views on this subject are, more than anything else, the product of my personal experience. I have had experience with affirmative action, nearly 20 years of it now, and I know it works.

When I was attorney general of my home state, I hired a record number of women and African-American lawyers— every one clearly qualified and exceptionally hardworking. As governor, I appointed more women to my cabinet and state boards than any other governor in the state's history, and more African-Americans than all the governors in the state's history combined. And no one ever questioned their qualifications or performance. And our state was better and stronger because of their service.

As president, I am proud to have the most diverse administration in history in my cabinet, my agencies, and my staff. And I must say, I have been surprised at the criticism I have received from some quarters in my determination to achieve this.

In the last two and a half years, the most outstanding example of affirmative action in the United States, the Pentagon, has opened 260,000 positions for women who serve in our armed forces. I have appointed more women and minorities to the federal bench than any other president, more than the last two combined. And yet, far more of our judicial appointments have received the highest rating from the American Bar Association than any other administration since those ratings have been given.

In our administration many government agencies are doing more business with qualified firms run by minorities and women. The Small Business Administration has reduced its budget by 40 percent, doubled its loan outputs, dramatically increased the number of loans to women and minority small business-people, without reducing the number of loans to white businessowners who happen to be male, and without changing the loan standards for a single, solitary application. Quality and diversity can go hand in hand, and they must.

Let me say that affirmative action has also done more than just open the doors of opportunity to individual Americans. Most economists who study it agree that affirmative action has also been an important part of closing gaps in economic opportunity in our society, thereby strengthening the entire economy.

A group of distinguished business leaders told me just a couple of days ago that their companies are stronger and their profits are larger because of the diversity and the excellence of their work-forces achieved through intelligent and fair affirmative action programs. And they said we have gone far beyond anything the government might require us to do because managing diversity and individual opportunity and being fair to everybody is the key to our future economic success in the global marketplace.

Now, there are those who say, my fellow Americans, that even good affirmative action programs are no longer needed; that it should be enough to resort to the courts or the Equal Employment Opportunity Commission in cases of actual, provable, individual discrimination because there is no longer any systematic discrimination in our society. In deciding how to answer that let us consider the facts.

The unemployment rate for African-Americans remains about twice that of whites. The Hispanic rate is still much higher. Women have narrowed the earnings gap, but still make only 72 percent as much as men do for comparable jobs. The average income for an Hispanic woman with a college degree is still less than the average income of a white man with a high school diploma.

According to the recently completed Glass Ceiling Report, sponsored by Republican members of Congress, in the nation's largest companies only six-tenths of one percent of senior management positions are held by African-Americans, four-tenths of a percent by Hispanic Americans, three-tenths of a percent by Asian Americans; women hold between 3 and 5 percent of these positions. White males make up 43 percent of our workforce, but hold 95 percent of these jobs.

Just last week, the Chicago Federal Reserve Bank reported that black home loan applicants are more than twice as likely to be denied credit as whites with the same qualifications; and that Hispanic applicants are more than one and a half times as likely to be denied loans as whites with the same qualifications.

Last year alone the federal government received more than 90,000 complaints of employment discrimination based on race, ethnicity, or gender. Less than 3 percent were for reverse discrimination.

Evidence abounds in other ways of the persistence of the kind of bigotry that can affect the way we think even if we're not conscious of it, in hiring and promotion and business and educational decisions.

Crimes and violence based on hate against Asians, Hispanics, African-Americans and other minorities are still with us. And, I'm sorry to say, that the worst and most recent evidence of this involves a recent report of federal law enforcement officials in Tennessee attending an event literally overflowing with racism—a sickening reminder of just how pervasive these kinds of attitudes still are.

By the way, I want to tell you that I am committed to finding the truth about what happened there and to taking appropriate action. And I want to say that if anybody who works in federal law enforcement thinks that that kind of behavior is acceptable, they ought to think about working someplace else.

Now, let's get to the other side of the argument. If affirmative action has worked and if there is evidence that discrimination still exists on a wide scale in ways that are conscious and unconscious, then why should we get rid of it as many people are urging? Some question the effectiveness or the fairness of particular affirmative action programs. I say to all of you, those are fair questions, and they prompted the review of our affirmative action programs, about which I will talk in a few moments.

Some question the fundamental purpose of the effort. There are people who honestly believe that affirmative action always amounts to group preferences over individual merit; that affirmative action always leads to reverse discrimination; that ultimately, therefore, it demeans those who benefit from it and discriminates against those who are not helped by it.

I just have to tell you that all of you have to decide how you feel about that, and all of our fellow countrymen and women have to decide as well. But I believe if there are no quotas, if we give no opportunities to unqualified people, if we have no reverse discrimination, and if, when the problem ends—the program ends, that criticism is wrong. That's what I believe. But we should have this debate and everyone should ask the question.

Now let's deal with what I really think is behind so much of this debate today. There are a lot of people who oppose affirmative action today who supported it for a very long time. I believe they are responding to the sea change in the experiences that most Americans have in the world in which we live.

If you say now you're against affirmative action because the government is using its power or the private sector is using its power to help minorities at the expense of the majority, that gives you a way of explaining away the economic distress that a majority of Americans honestly feel. It gives you a way of turning their resentment against the minorities or against a particular government program, instead of having an honest debate about how we all got into the fix we're in and what we're all going to do together to get out of it.

That explanation, the affirmative action explanation for the fix we're in is just wrong. It is just wrong. Affirmative action did not cause the great economic problems of the American middle-class. And because most minorities or women are either members of that middle class or people who are poor who are struggling to get into it, we must also admit that affirmative action alone won't solve the problems of minorities and women who seek to be a part of the American Dream. To do that, we have to have an economic strategy that reverses the decline in wages and the growth of poverty among working people. Without that, women, minorities, and white males will all be in trouble in the future.

But it is wrong to use the anxieties of the middle class to divert the American people from the real causes of their economic distress—the sweeping historic changes taking all the globe in its path, and the specific policies or lack of them in our own country which have aggravated those challenges. It is simply wrong to play politics with the issue of affirmative action and divide our country at a time when, if we're really going to change things, we have to be united.

I must say, I think it is ironic that some of those—not all, but some of those who call for an end to affirmative action also advocate policies which will make the real economic problems of the anxious middle class even worse. They talk about opportunity and being for equal opportunity for everyone, and then they reduce investment in equal opportunity on an evenhanded basis. For example, if the real goal is economic opportunity for all Americans, why in the world would we reduce our investment in education from Head Start to affordable college loans? Why don't we make college loans available to every American instead?

If the real goal is empowering all middle-class Americans and empowering poor people to work their way into the middle class without regard to race or gender, why in the world would the people who advocate that turn around and raise taxes on our poorest working families, or reduce the money available for education and training when they lose their jobs or they're living on poverty wages, or increase the cost of housing for lower-income, working people with children?

Why would we do that? If we're going to empower America, we have to do more than talk about it, we have to do it. And we surely have learned that we cannot empower all Americans by a simple strategy of taking opportunity away from some Americans.

So to those who use this as a political strategy to divide us, we must say, no. We must say, no. But to those who raise legitimate questions about the way affirmative action works, or who raise the larger question about the genuine problems and anxieties of all the American people and their sense of being left behind and treated unfairly, we must say, yes, you are entitled to answers to your questions. We must say yes to that.

Now, that's why I ordered this review of all of our affirmative action programs; a review to look at the facts, not the politics of affirmative action. This review concluded that affirmative action remains a useful tool for widening economic and educational opportunity. The model used by the military, the army in particular—and I'm delighted to have the Commanding General of the Army here today because he set such a fine example—has been especially successful because it emphasizes education and training, ensuring that it has a wide pool of qualified candidates for every level of promotion. That approach has given us the most racially diverse and best-qualified military in our history. There are more opportunities for women and minorities there than ever before. And now there are over 50 generals and admirals who are Hispanic, Asian, or African-Americans.

We found that the Education Department targeted on—had programs targeted—on underrepresented minorities that do a great deal of good with the tiniest of investments. We found that these programs comprised 40 cents of every $1,000 in the Education Department's budget.

Now, college presidents will tell you that the education their schools offer actually benefit from diversity colleges where young people get the education and make the personal and professional contacts that will shape their lives. If their colleges look like the world they're going to live and work in, and they learn from all different kinds of people things that they can't learn in books, our systems of higher education are stronger.

Still, I believe every child needs the chance to go to college. Every child. That means every child has to have a chance to get affordable and repayable college loans, Pell Grants for poor kids and a chance to do things like join AmeriCorps and work their way through school. Every child is entitled to that. That is not an argument against affirmative action, it's an argument for more opportunity for more Americans until everyone is reached.

As I said a moment ago, the review found that the Small Business Administration last year increased loans to minorities by over two-thirds, loans to women by over 80 percent, did not decrease loans to white men, and not a single loan went to a unqualified person. People who never had a chance before to be part of the American system of free enterprise now have it. No one was hurt in the process. That made America stronger.

This review also found that the executive order on employment practices of large federal contractors also has helped to bring more fairness and inclusion into the workforce.

Since President Nixon was here in my job, America has used goals and timetables to preserve opportunity and to prevent discrimination, to urge businesses to set higher expectations for themselves and to realize those expectations. But we did not and we will not use rigid quotas to mandate outcomes.

We also looked at the way we award procurement contracts under the programs known as set-asides. There's no question that these programs have helped to build up firms owned by minorities and women, who historically had been excluded from the old-boy networks in these areas. It has helped a new generation of entrepreneurs to flourish, opening new paths to self-reliance and an economic growth in which all of us ultimately share. Because of the set-asides, businesses ready to compete have had a chance to compete, a chance they would not have otherwise had.

But as with any government program, set-asides can be misapplied, misused, even intentionally abused. There are critics who exploit that fact as an excuse to abolish all these programs, regardless of their effects. I believe they are wrong, but I also believe, based on our factual review, we clearly need some reform. So first, we should crack down on those who take advantage of everyone else through fraud and abuse. We must crack down on fronts and pass-throughs, people who pretend to be eligible for these programs and aren't. That is wrong.

We also, in offering new businesses a leg up, must make sure that the set-asides go to businesses that need them most. We must really look and make sure that our standard for eligibility is fair and defensible. We have to tighten the requirement to move businesses out of programs once they've had a fair opportunity to compete. The graduation requirement must mean something—it must mean graduation. There should be no permanent set-aside for any company.

Second, we must, and we will, comply with the Supreme Court's Adarand decision of last month. Now, in particular, that means focusing set-aside programs on particular regions and business sectors where the problems of discrimination or exclusion are provable and are clearly requiring affirmative action. I have directed the attorney general and the agencies to move forward with compliance with Adarand expeditiously.

But I also want to emphasize that the Adarand decision did not dismantle affirmative action and did not dismantle set-asides. In fact, while setting stricter standards to mandate reform of affirmative action, it actually reaffirmed the need for affirmative action and reaffirmed the continuing existence of systematic discrimination in the United States.

What the Supreme Court ordered the federal government to do was to meet the same more rigorous standard for affirmative action programs that state and local governments were ordered to meet several years ago. And the best set-aside programs under that standard have been challenged and have survived.

Third, beyond discrimination we need to do more to help disadvantaged people and distressed communities, no matter what their race or gender. There are places in our country where the free enterprise system simply doesn't reach. It simply isn't working to provide jobs and opportunity. Disproportionately, these areas in urban and rural America are highly populated by racial minorities, but not entirely. To make this initiative work, I believe the government must become a better partner for people in places in urban and rural America that are caught in a cycle of poverty. And I believe we have to find ways to get the private sector to assume their rightful role as a driver of economic growth.

It has always amazed me that we have given incentives to our business-people to help to develop poor economies in other parts of the world, our neighbors in the Caribbean, our neighbors in other parts of the world—I have supported this when not subject to their own abuses—but we ignore the biggest source of economic growth available to the American economy, the poor economies isolated within the United States of America.

There are those who say, well, even if we made the jobs available people wouldn't work. They haven't tried. Most of the people in disadvantaged communities work today, and most of them who don't work have a very strong desire to do so. In central Harlem, 14 people apply for every single minimum-wage job opening. Think how many more would apply if there were good jobs with a good future. Our job has to connect disadvantaged people and disadvantaged communities to economic opportunity so that everybody who wants to work can do so.

We've been working at this through our empowerment zones and community develop

banks, through the initiatives of Secretary Cisneros of the Housing and Urban Development Department and many other things that we have tried to do to put capital where it is needed. And now I have asked Vice President Gore to develop a proposal to use our contracting to support businesses that locate themselves in these distressed areas or hire a large percentage of their workers from these areas—not to substitute what we're doing in affirmative action, but to supplement it, to go beyond it, to do something that will help to deal with the economic crisis of America. We want to make our procurement system more responsive to people in these areas who need help.

My fellow Americans, affirmative action has to be made consistent with our highest ideals of personal responsibility and merit, and our urgent need to find common ground, and to prepare all Americans to compete in the global economy of the next century.

Today, I am directing all our agencies to comply with the Supreme Court's Adarand decision, and also to apply the four standards of fairness to all our affirmative action programs that I have already articulated: No quotas in theory or practice; no illegal discrimination of any kind, including reverse discrimination; no preference for people who are not qualified for any job or other opportunity; and as soon as a program has succeeded, it must be retired. Any program that doesn't meet these four principles must be eliminated or reformed to meet them.

But let me be clear: Affirmative action has been good for America.

Affirmative action has not always been perfect, and affirmative action should not go on forever. It should be changed now to take care of those things that are wrong, and it should be retired when its job is done. I am resolved that that day will come. But the evidence suggests, indeed, screams that that day has not come.

The job of ending discrimination in this country is not over. That should not be surprising. We had slavery for centuries before the passage of the Thirteenth, Fourteenth, and Fifteenth Amendments. We waited another hundred years for the civil rights legislation. Women have had the vote less than a hundred years. We have always had difficulty with these things, as most societies do. But we are making more progress than many people.

Based on the evidence, the job is not done. So here is what I think we should do. We should reaffirm the principle of affirmative action and fix the practices. We should have a simple slogan: Mend it, but don't end it.

Let me ask all Americans, whether they agree or disagree with what I have said today, to see this issue in the larger context of our times. President Lincoln said, we cannot escape our history. We cannot escape our future, either. And that future must be one in which every American has the chance to live up to his or her God-given capacities.

The new technology, the instant communications, the explosion of global commerce have created enormous opportunities and enormous anxieties for Americans. In the last two and a half years, we have seen seven million new jobs, more millionaires and new businesses than ever before, high corporate profits, and a booming stock market. Yet, most Americans are working harder for the same or lower pay. And they feel more insecurity about their jobs, their retirement, their health care, and their children's education. Too many of our children are clearly exposed to poverty and welfare, violence and drugs.

These are the great challenges for our whole country on the homefront at the dawn of the 21st century. We've got to find the wisdom and the will to create family-wage jobs for all the people who want to work; to open the door of college to all Americans; to strengthen families and reduce the awful problems to which our children are exposed; to move poor Americans from welfare to work.

This is the work of our administration— to give the people the tools they need to make the most of their own lives, to give families and communities the tools they need to solve their own problems. But let us not forget affirmative action didn't cause these problems. It won't solve them. And getting rid of affirmative action certainly won't solve them.

If properly done, affirmative action can help us come together, go forward, and grow together. It is in our moral, legal, and practical interest to see that every person can make the most of his life. In the fight for the future, we need all hands on deck and some of those hands still need a helping hand.

In our national community we're all different, we're all the same. We want liberty and freedom. We want the embrace of family and community. We want to make the most of our own lives and we're determined to give our children a better one. Today there are voices of division who would say forget all that. Don't you dare. Remember we're still closing the gap between our founders' ideals and our reality. But every step along the way has made us richer, stronger, and better. And the best is yet to come.

Thank you very much. And God bless you.

Second Inaugural Address

Washington, D.C.

January 20, 1997

DESPITE THE TROUBLES of his first term, President Clinton rebounded in time for his reelection bid in 1996 and succeeded in defeating Republican challenger Bob Dole, gaining 49 percent of the popular vote. At his swearing-in ceremony, he took the oath of office on a Bible that was opened to a page in the book of Isaiah: "Those from among you shall build the old waste place; you shall raise up the foundations of many generations; and you shall be called the Repairer of the Breach, the Restorer of Streets to Dwell In." Clinton made reference to this verse in his 22-minute address, which unfolded a utopian view of the future, though with little mention of specific ways to achieve it. It was, as commentator Daniel Schorr put it, "long on dreams and short on program." It also referred to the United States as "the indispensable nation," a phrase that recurred many times during his second term as his administration tried to ameliorate one foreign conflict and crisis after another.

At this last presidential inauguration of the 20th century, let us lift our eyes toward the challenges that await us in the next century.

It is our great good fortune that time and chance have put us not only at the edge of a new century, in a new millennium, but on the edge of a bright new prospect in human affairs—a moment that will define our course, and our character, for decades to come.

We must keep our old democracy forever young. Guided by the ancient vision of a promised land, let us set our sights upon a land of new promise.

The promise of America was born in the 18th century out of the bold conviction that we are all created equal. It was extended and preserved in the 19th century, when our nation spread across the continent, saved the union, and abolished the awful scourge of slavery. Then, in turmoil and triumph, that promise exploded onto the world stage to make this the American Century.

And what a century it has been. America became the world's mightiest industrial power; saved the world from tyranny in two world wars and a long cold war; and time and again, reached out across the globe to millions who, like us, longed for the blessings of liberty.

Along the way, Americans produced a great middle class and security in old age; built unrivaled centers of learning and opened public schools to all; split the atom and explored the heavens; invented the computer and the microchip; and deepened the wellspring of justice by making a revolution in civil rights for African-Americans and all minorities and extending the circle of citizenship, opportunity, and dignity to women.

Now, for the third time, a new century is upon us, and another time to choose. We began the 19th century with a choice, to spread our nation from coast to coast. We began the 20th century with a choice, to harness the Industrial Revolution to our values of free enterprise, conservation, and human decency. Those choices made all the difference. At the dawn of the 21st century a free people must now choose to shape the forces of the information age and the global society, to unleash the limitless potential of all our people, and, yes, to form a more perfect union.

When last we gathered, our march to this new future seemed less certain than it does today. We vowed then to set a clear course to renew our nation. In these four years, we have been touched by tragedy, exhilarated by challenge, strengthened by achievement. America stands alone as the world's indispensable nation.

Once again, our economy is the strongest on earth. Once again, we are building stronger families, thriving communities, better educational opportunities, a cleaner environment. Problems that once seemed destined to deepen now bend to our efforts: our streets are safer and record numbers of our fellow citizens have moved from welfare to work.

And once again, we have resolved for our time a great debate over the role of government. Today we can declare: Government is not the problem, and government is not the solution. We—the American people—we are the solution. Our founders understood that well and gave us a democracy strong enough to endure for centuries, flexible enough to face our common challenges and advance our common dreams in each new day.

As times change, so government must change. We need a new government for a new century—humble enough not to try to solve all our problems for us, but strong enough to give us the tools to solve our problems for ourselves; a government that is smaller, lives within its means, and does more with less. Yet where it can stand up for our values and interests in the world, and where it can give Americans the power to make a real difference in their everyday lives, government should do more, not less. The preeminent mission of our new government is to give all Americans an opportunity—not a guarantee, but a real opportunity—to build better lives.

Beyond that, my fellow citizens, the future is up to us. Our founders taught us that the preservation of our liberty and our union depends upon responsible citizenship. And we need a new sense of responsibility for a new century. There is work to do, work that government alone cannot do: teaching children to read; hiring people off welfare rolls; coming out from behind locked doors and shuttered windows to help reclaim our streets from drugs and gangs and crime; taking time out of our own lives to serve others.

Each and every one of us, in our own way, must assume personal responsibility—not only for ourselves and our families, but for our neighbors and our nation. Our greatest responsibility is to embrace a new spirit of community for a new century. For any one of us to succeed, we must succeed as one America.

The challenge of our past remains the challenge of our future—will we be one nation, one people, with one common destiny, or not? Will we all come together, or come apart?

The divide of race has been America's constant curse. And each new wave of immigrants gives new targets to old prejudices. Prejudice and contempt, cloaked in the pretense of religious or political conviction, are no different. These forces have nearly destroyed our nation in the past. They plague us still. They fuel the fanaticism of terror. And they torment the lives of millions in fractured nations all around the world.

These obsessions cripple both those who hate and, of course, those who are hated, robbing both of what they might become. We cannot, we will not, succumb to the dark impulses that lurk in the far regions of the soul everywhere. We shall overcome them. And we shall replace them with the generous spirit of a people who feel at home with one another.

Our rich texture of racial, religious and political diversity will be a godsend in the 21st century. Great rewards will come to those who can live together, learn together, work together, forge new ties that bind together.

As this new era approaches we can already see its broad outlines. Ten years ago, the Internet was the mystical province of physicists; today, it is a commonplace encyclopedia for millions of schoolchildren. Scientists now are decoding the blueprint of human life. Cures for our most feared illnesses seem close at hand.

The world is no longer divided into two hostile camps. Instead, now we are building bonds with nations that once were our adversaries. Growing connections of commerce and culture give us a chance to lift the fortunes and spirits of people the world over. And for the very first time in all of history, more people on this planet live under democracy than dictatorship.

My fellow Americans, as we look back at this remarkable century, we may ask, can we hope not just to follow, but even to surpass the achievements of the 20th century in America and to avoid the awful bloodshed that stained its legacy? To that question, every American here and every American in our land today must answer a resounding "Yes."

This is the heart of our task. With a new vision of government, a new sense of responsibility, a new spirit of community, we will sustain America's journey. The promise we sought in a new land we will find again in a land of new promise.

In this new land, education will be every citizen's most prized possession. Our schools will have the highest standards in the world, igniting the spark of possibility in the eyes of every girl and every boy. And the doors of higher education will be open to all. The knowledge and power of the information age will be within reach not just of the few, but of every classroom, every library, every child. Parents and children will have time not only to work, but to read and play together. And the plans they make at their kitchen table will be those of a better home, a better job, the certain chance to go to college.

Our streets will echo again with the laughter of our children, because no one will try to shoot them or sell them drugs anymore. Everyone who can work, will work, with today's permanent under-class part of tomorrow's growing middle class. New miracles of medicine at last will reach not only those who can claim care now, but the children and hard-working families too long denied.

We will stand mighty for peace and freedom, and maintain a strong defense against terror and destruction. Our children will sleep free from the threat of nuclear, chemical, or biological weapons. Ports and airports, farms and factories will thrive with trade and innovation and ideas. And the world's greatest democracy will lead a whole world of democracies.

Our land of new promise will be a nation that meets its obligations—a nation that balances its budget, but never loses the balance of its values. A nation where our grandparents have secure retirement and health care, and their grandchildren know we have made the reforms necessary to sustain those benefits for their time. A nation that fortifies the world's most productive economy even as it protects the great natural bounty of our water, air, and majestic land.

And in this land of new promise, we will have reformed our politics so that the voice of the people will always speak louder than the din of narrow interests—regaining the participation and deserving the trust of all Americans.

Fellow citizens, let us build that America, a nation ever moving forward toward realizing the full potential of all its citizens. Prosperity and power—yes, they are important, and we must maintain them. But let us never forget: The greatest progress we have made, and the greatest progress we have yet to make, is in the human heart. In the end, all the world's wealth and a thousand armies are no match for the strength and decency of the human spirit.

Thirty-four years ago, the man whose life we celebrate today spoke to us down there, at the other end of this Mall, in words that moved the conscience of a nation. Like a prophet of old, he told of his dream that one day America would rise up and treat all its citizens as equals before the law and in the heart. Martin Luther King's dream was the American Dream. His quest is our quest: the ceaseless striving to live out our true creed. Our history has been built on such dreams and labors.

And by our dreams and labors we will redeem the promise of America in the 21st century.

To that effort I pledge all my strength and every power of my office. I ask the members of Congress here to join in that pledge. The American people returned to office a president of one party and a Congress of another. Surely, they did not do this to advance the politics of petty bickering and extreme partisanship they plainly deplore. No, they call on us instead to be repairers of the breach, and to move on with America's mission.

America demands and deserves big things from us—and nothing big ever came from being small. Let us remember the timeless wisdom of Cardinal Bernardin, when facing the end of his own life. He said: "It is wrong to waste the precious gift of time on acrimony and division."

Fellow citizens, we must not waste the precious gift of this time. For all of us are on that same journey of our lives, and our journey, too, will come to an end. But the journey of our America must go on.

And so, my fellow Americans, we must be strong, for there is much to dare. The demands of our time are great and they are different. Let us meet them with faith and courage, with patience and a grateful and happy heart. Let us shape the hope of this day into the noblest chapter in our history. Yes, let us build our bridge. A bridge wide enough and strong enough for every American to cross over to a blessed land of new promise.

May those generations whose faces we cannot yet see, whose names we may never know, say of us here that we led our beloved land into a new century with the American Dream alive for all her children; with the American promise of a more perfect union a reality for all her people; with America's bright flame of freedom spreading throughout all the world.

From the height of this place and the summit of this century, let us go forth. May God strengthen our hands for the good work ahead—and always, always bless our America.

Gay Rights

Washington, D.C.
November 8, 1997

AMONG THE CONTROVERSIES that caused the Clinton administration to get off to a rocky start in 1993 was that of "gays in the military." During his election campaign, Clinton promised to overturn the armed forces' refusal to allow military service by people who were known to be, or suspected of being, homosexual. When the Joint Chiefs of Staff and key congressional leaders opposed his plan to revise the Uniform Code of Military Justice, Clinton settled for a lukewarm compromise policy—"don't ask, don't tell"—that was considered by many gays and lesbians as a betrayal. They were also angered by the president's decision in 1996 to sign the Defense of Marriage Act, which defined marriage in federal law as a union between a woman and a man.

Still, Clinton went much further than previous presidents in advancing the goal of social equality for homosexuals and in addressing their concerns. He appointed more than 100 openly gay people to senior government posts, invited leaders of the movement to the White House, and increased government spending on AIDS research and treatment. In November 1997 he set another precedent by delivering the keynote speech at a fund-raising dinner for the Human Rights Campaign, a gay rights organization.

A little more than six years ago, I had this crazy idea that I ought to run for president. Only my mother thought I could win. And at the time, I was so obsessed with what I thought had to be done I thought winning would take care of itself. What bothered me was that our country seemed to be drifting and divided as we moved into a new and exciting and challenging area where we were living differently, working differently, relating to each other and the rest of the world in very different ways on the edge of a new century.

And I sat down alone before I decided to do this and asked myself, what is it that you want America to look like when you're done if you win? My vision for the 21st century, now, I have said hundreds and hundreds of times, but I still think about it every day—I want this to be a country where every child and every person who is responsible enough to work for it can live the American Dream. I want this country to embrace the wider world and continue to be the strongest force for peace and freedom and prosperity, and I want us to come together across all our lines of difference into one America.

That is my vision. It drives me every day. I think if we really could create a society where there is opportunity for all and responsibility from all and we believed in a community of all Americans, we could truly meet every problem we have and seize every opportunity we have.

For more than two centuries now, our country has had to meet challenge after challenge after challenge. We have had to continue to lift ourselves beyond what we thought America meant. Our ideals were never meant to be frozen in stone or time. Keep in mind, when we started out with Thomas Jefferson's credo that all of us are created equal by God, what that really meant in civic political terms was that you had to be white, you had to be male, and that wasn't enough—you had to own property, which would have left my crowd out when I was a boy.

Over time, we have had to redefine the words that we started with, not because there was anything wrong with them and their universal power and strength of liberty and justice, but because we were limited in our imaginations about how we could live and what we were capable of and how we should live. Indeed, the story of how we kept going higher and higher and higher to new and higher definitions—and more meaningful definitions—of equality and dignity and freedom is in its essence the fundamental story of our country.

Fifty years ago, President Truman stood at a new frontier in our defining struggle on civil rights. Slavery had ended a long time before, but segregation remained. Harry Truman stood before the Lincoln Memorial and said, "It is more important today than ever to ensure that all Americans enjoy the rights [of freedom and equality]. When I say all Americans, I mean all Americans."

Well, my friends, all Americans still means all Americans. We all know that it is an ideal and not perfectly real now. We all know that some of the old kinds of discrimination we have sought to rid ourselves of by law and purge our spirits of still exist in America today. We all know that there is continuing discrimination against gays and lesbians. But we also know that if we're ever going to build one America, then all Americans—including you and those whom you represent—have got to be a part of it.

To be sure, no president can grant rights. Our ideals and our history hold that they are inalienable, embedded in our Constitution, amplified over time by our courts and legislature. I cannot grant them—but I am bound by my oath of office and the burden of history to reaffirm them.

All America loses if we let prejudice and discrimination stifle the hopes or deny the potential of a single American. All America loses when any person is denied or forced out of a job because of sexual orientation. Being gay, the last time I thought about it, seemed to have nothing to do with the ability to read a balance book, fix a broken bone, or change a spark plug.

For generations, the American Dream has represented a fundamental compact among our people. If you take responsibility and work hard, you have the right to achieve a better life for yourself and a better future for your family. Equal opportunity for all, special privileges for none—a fate shared by Americans regardless of political views. We believe—or we all say we believe—that all citizens should have the chance to rise as far as their God-given talents will take them. What counts is energy and honesty and talent. No arbitrary distinctions should bar the way.

So when we deny opportunity because of ancestry or religion, race or gender, disability or sexual orientation, we break the compact. It is wrong. And it should be illegal. Once again I call upon Congress to honor our most cherished principles and make the Employment Non-Discrimination Act the law of the land.

I also come here tonight to ask you for another favor. Protecting the civil rights of all Americans—

[Heckler: "People with AIDS are dying." Audience members: "Sit down."]

Wait, wait, wait. I would have been disappointed if you hadn't been here tonight. I'm kind of used to this. People with AIDS are dying. But since I've become president we're spending 10 times as much per fatality on people with AIDS as people with breast cancer or prostate cancer. And the drugs are being approved more quickly. And a lot of people are living normal lives. We just have to keep working on it.

I thank you, but this, too, is part of what makes America great. We all have our say, and nobody has to be afraid when he or she screams at the president. That's a good thing. That's a good thing. And at a time when so many people feel their voices will never be heard, that's a good thing.

What is not a good thing, however, is when people believe their free speech rights trump yours. That's not good. That's not.

Now, I want to ask you for a favor. You want us to pass the Employment Non-Discrimination Act. You know when we do— and I believe it will pass—you know when we do it will have to be enforced. The law on the books only works if it is also a law in the life of America.

Let me say, I thank you very much for your support of my nominee for the Office of Civil Rights, Bill Lee. I thank you for that. But he, too, comes from a family that has known discrimination and now he is being discriminated against, not because there is anything wrong with his qualifications, not because anybody believes he is not even-tempered, but because some members of the Senate disagree with his views on affirmative action.

Now, if I have to appoint a head of the Office of Civil Rights who is against affirmative action, it's going to be vacant a long time. That office is not there to advocate or promote—primarily to advocate or promote—the policies of the government when it comes to affirmative action; it's there to enforce the existing laws against discrimination. You hope someday you will have one of those existing laws. We need somebody to enforce the laws, and Bill Lee should be confirmed, and I ask you to help me to get him confirmed.

I'd like to say just one more word. There are some people who aren't in this room tonight who aren't comfortable yet with you and won't be comfortable with me for being here.

[Audience member: "We love you, Bill."]

Wait a minute. This is serious. On issue after issue involving gays and lesbians, survey after survey shows that the most important determinant of people's attitudes is whether they are aware—whether they knowingly have had a family or a friendship or a work relation with a gay person.

Now, I hope that we will embrace good people who are trying to overcome their fears. After all, all of us can look back in history and see what the right thing to do was. It is quite another thing to look ahead and light the way. Most people are preoccupied with the burdens of daily living. Most of us, as we grow older, become—whether we like it or not—somewhat more limited in our imaginations. So I think one of the greatest things we have to do still is just to increase the ability of Americans who do not yet know that gays and lesbians are their fellow Americans in every sense of the word to feel that way. I think it's very important.

When I say, "I believe all Americans means all Americans," I see the faces of the friends of 35 years. When I say, "all Americans means all Americans," I see the faces of the people who stood up when I asked the people who are part of our administration to stand tonight. When I say, "all Americans means all Americans," I see kind, unbelievably generous, giving people back in my home state who helped my family and my friends when they were in need. It is a different story when you know what you are seeing.

So I say to you tonight, should we change the law? You bet. Should we keep fighting discrimination? Absolutely. Is this Hate Crimes Conference important? It is terribly important. But we have to broaden the imagination of America. We are redefining, in practical terms, the immutable ideals that have guided us from the beginning. Again I say, we have to make sure that for every single person in our country, all Americans means all Americans.

After experiencing the horrors of the Civil War and witnessing the transformation of the previous century, Walt Whitman said that our greatest strength was that we are an embracing nation. In his words, a "Union, holding all, fusing, absorbing, tolerating all." Let us move forward in the spirit of that one America. Let us realize that this is a good obligation that has been imposed upon our generation, and a grand opportunity once again to lift America to a higher level of unity, once again to redefine and to strengthen, and to ensure one America for a new century and a new generation of our precious children.

Thank you and God bless you.

Address to Arkansas Democrats

Washington, D.C.

December 13, 1997

As HIS SECOND term progressed, President Clinton demonstrated a remarkable ability to weather scandals without endangering his public approval ratings. Though the nickname "Teflon president" was not applied to him, he deserved it even more than did Ronald Reagan, for whom it was coined. In large part, his popularity was the result of his persuasive charm with individuals—he had a veteran politician's knack for remembering faces, names, favors, and debts—and his skillful handling of audiences. The rapport he could achieve with a friendly crowd is well illustrated by the following speech, which was delivered by President Clinton at a dinner for Democratic activists from his home state of Arkansas.

I probably shouldn't do this, but I'm going to try to acknowledge the Arkansans in the administration who are here. If I omit you and you quit, I will never speak to you again. I am doing my best. Normally, presidents don't have to remember this stuff. But I think it's important. I just want you to get a feel for how many people are here: Mack and Donna McLarty, of course; Bruce Lindsey; Nancy Hernreich; Marsha Scott; Bob Nash and Janis Kearney; Stephanie Streett; Mary Streett; Catherine Grundin; Patsy Thomasson; Anne and Grady McCoy. Ben Johnson told me he was from Arkansas tonight, that he was born in Marion and his wife, Jacqueline, said she was born in Joiner, and I'd say that qualifies. Steve and Jennifer Ronnel; Darren and Vivian Peters. And in the administration, of course, Secretary Slater and Cassandra; James Lee and Lea Ellen Witt; Hershel Gober and Mary Lou Keener; Harold and Arlee Gist; Wilbur Peer; Gloria Cabe has done great work for us; and in the DNC, Carol and Joyce Willis; Lottie Shackleford; Mary Anne Salmon. I'm so glad they're here. There are others I wish were here tonight. I wish Maurice Smith and Betsy Wright and Bill Clark and David Matthews and Linda Dixon and a host of other people could be here. But I want to thank you, all of you—those of you in the administration, those of you who have been in the administration, and, most of all, those of you without whom there never would have been an administration. I thank you very much.

I don't want to embarrass him, but about two hours before I came over here tonight I was finishing up some paper work in my office. And Nancy always collects interesting letters

that come from people from home and puts them in a little folder for me, and I get them at least once a week. And at the top of the folder was a letter that Richard Mason just wrote to the Wall Street Journal. And it said, I got about as much chance of getting this letter printed as Dan Quayle does of getting elected president.

But he went on to say he was a businessman, he had read the Journal faithfully for years. He said, for five years I've watched you bad-mouth my president and my state and say things that weren't true. And if your advice on business is as bad as your understanding of politics, I'll be in deep trouble if I keep reading this newspaper. Please cancel my subscription.

I did what I always do. You know, I was saying, but, Richard, you know, you can't blame the editorial page, they have good articles, all that kind of stuff. I was making my good government argument. He said, look, the economy is better, the world is at peace, the crime rate is down, the country is in great shape—sooner or later some of those people that are trying to tear your guts out and lying about our state are going to have to fess up and admit it. Get over it, the country is in better shape. This is working.

Since under our new policy all these are covered by the press, they may have to run your letter now, Richard. We'll see.

Let me say to all of you, when I was getting ready to come over here tonight—and I'm sorry Hillary is not here, but she is, to put it mildly, under the weather, and she said to send you her love. But when I was getting ready to come over here, I was reliving many of the things that have happened since October the third of 1991 when I declared for president.

I remember how people sneeringly referred to me as the governor of a small southern state. I remember how people talked about how we had failed to do all these things. I remember when I was pronounced dead before arrival in New Hampshire. And the Arkansas Travelers, who had been traveling all around the country anyway and then all of a sudden, 150 people just dropped everything they were doing at home and came to New Hampshire and went around knocking on people's doors, total strangers, introducing themselves, saying, this is my governor; you cannot do this. Don't let them stampede you into this. Don't one more time let the kind of negative, hateful, personality-destroying politics that has kept our country back, don't do it one more time.

One hundred fifty people up there in colder weather, some of them, than they had ever been in their lives, knocking on doors in New Hampshire.

I remember when that great ad appeared in the Manchester Union Leader, with hundreds of Arkansans names and their phone numbers, saying, instead of believing what they're saying about him, if you want to know about this guy, call me. I will never forget that.

I remember how surprised—the people that ran against me in '92 by and large are good friends of mine now, and I remember how surprised they were that we kept doing well in odd places. And it took them a long time to figure out that 25 percent of the voters in Chicago were from Arkansas. That there was something to be said for being poor throughout the '30s, '40s, '50s, and '60s. I keep waiting any day now for all of them to be subpoenaed by Mr. Starr. You know, a 50-year-old conspiracy to take over the White House which started with our running people out of Arkansas back in the '30s and '40s in a dark and devious way.

I came upon a little town outside Flint, Michigan, one day full of auto workers. And literally 90 percent of them had roots in Arkansas, and I thought to myself today, those people are going to be called to testify any minute now. There's a presumption there's something wrong with them; it was some dark plot.

I was in the Bronx—did you see the pictures? Where I went back to the Bronx to the place where president Reagan said it looked like London during the blitz and now it looks like a neighborhood any American would be proud to live in—to celebrate what this community organization had done. They're called the Mid-Bronx Desperados, because they were so desperate to turn their community around years and years ago. Half the housing this particular group has built has been built since I have been president because of our approach, which is to basically support community groups and people that are working together and let them define their own future.

So I get out, I shake hands with Ralph Porter; he's the current president of the Mid-Bronx Desperados and we are walking down the street in the Bronx. He looked at me and he said, you know, my wife worked with your mother at Washita Hospital for 15 years. And I graduated from Langston High School in Hot Springs. I said, no, they'll never believe this. I hope Ralph doesn't get a subpoena.

And he went on to tell me that his mother was living in the Bronx and was ill and he'd been living in—he grew up in Hot Springs and his wife worked in the hospital with Mother; and that he went to see about his mother and he decided the Bronx is in terrible shape and that God wanted him to be in the Bronx and help turn it around. And I'm telling you, it will take your breath away if you could walk down some of these streets—not just nice houses, but safe streets, clean streets, going to remodeled schools that are working where communities that were given up for dead are working. And sometimes I think what our adversaries, that are almost pathologically obsessed with personal destruction, don't get is that that's what politics is about. That's what you taught me. That's why we're all here after five years and that's why the country is in better shape. Politics is about real people and their hopes and their dreams. So, to me, all this stuff—you all always say, gosh, I don't know how you put up with it. How do you put up with mosquitoes in summertime in Arkansas? You just swat them and go on, it's a part of living. That's what you do.

If rice farmers thought farming rice was about mosquitoes, we'd all starve. It's about planting rice and bringing it in when harvest comes. Politics is about people and their dreams, and building a better future. And that's what you taught me.

All the stories—I saw a great little special on one of the television networks the other night, that the state of Tennessee is now sponsoring a story-telling contest every year. And there was a very, very large African-American woman telling stories and all these East Tennessee hill people were sitting around the circle listening to her and their eyes were big as dollars, and they were all—and they were taking turns telling stories and then they'd pick a winner. And I thought to myself, it would do this town a lot of good if we had a storytelling contest every year to remind people about what life is all about.

So they were telling their story. You want to know why we survived up here? Because I still remember the stories. I got to telling some of the young people that work for me the other day in the White House stories about my first two or three campaigns in Arkansas; they were laughing so hard they had tears in their eyes. When David Pryor and I started, you had to know that kind of stuff. I mean, you were expected to know people and you cared about their parents and their children and their brothers and their sisters. You knew that misfortune happened. It wasn't a denigrating thing to say you felt someone's pain; that just meant you were a real live human being with blood flowing in your veins and you had some imagination about what life was all about. And I just want you to know that that's what we've tried to do here. If I hadn't been governor of Arkansas in the time I was—and keep in mind, until the year I ran for president every single month I was governor but one, the unemployment rate in our state was higher than the national average—every single month. And I stood on those factory lines when people came off the line for the very last time before they shut down in the recession of the '80s. I knew farmers that had gone broke. I understood what things happened to people when older people couldn't buy medicine and younger people couldn't afford to send their children to the dentist. I understood those things because you taught me them, and I knew what politics was about. And I ran for a very clear reason: I thought our country was divided and drifting; that we were not succeeding; that we were clearly the greatest country in human history; and that we were too dominated, completely paralyzed and in the grip of the mosquitoes instead of the planting. That's what I thought then. And so we decided that we would endure the mosquitoes so that we

could plant and reap. And I think it's been worth the effort.

When you go home tonight I want you to think about this: you were standing and freezing your feet off in New Hampshire in '92, or you had to do some other kind of service above and beyond the call since then— you gave us the chance to serve and your country has the lowest unemployment rate in 24 years. That's the statistic. The story is there's 14 million people out there with jobs who didn't have them before, and every one of them has got a story. There's 3.8 million people who were on welfare when I became president, who are now living in homes with paychecks, and they've got a different story. There are over 13 million people who got to claim the benefits of the Family and Medical Leave law when a baby was born or a parent was sick. There are 8.5 million people whose pensions were gone that were rescued in one of Senator Pryor's last legislative acts, great legislative acts, when we reformed the pension system—and we saved 40 million other people's pensions from having to worry about it—8 million people who saved their retirement. That's a story. There's 250,000 people with criminal records or mental health histories who couldn't buy handguns because we passed the Brady Bill— and we don't know how many people are alive because of that, and they're out telling stories tonight of their lives because we did that.

We set aside more land—I'd forgotten this until I read Richard's letter—we set aside more land in national trusts in one form or another than any administration in the history of America, except the two Roosevelts. And there will be millions and millions of people just before the end of this decade that will be someplace or another having an experience with nature and God and their families because of that, that they would not have had. And that will become part of their story.

The air is cleaner, the water is cleaner, the food is safer, there are fewer little children living next to toxic waste dumps. And every one of them will have a different story now.

We're about to pass another Christmas in Bosnia, where we no longer have the bloodiest conflict since the end of World War II. We've made another year in Haiti. We're on the verge of seeing a profound and permanent peace, I hope, in Ireland this coming year. We've made real steps in making the world less likely to be subject to chemical warfare last year—this year, when we ratified the Chemical Weapons Treaty. This Race Initiative—a lot of people say it's just talk—I'd rather see people talking than fighting. It's not just talk, it's a lot more than that. But there's something to be said for that. The more complicated and different this country gets, and the more contentious and conflict-oriented the larger means of communication get, the more important it is for people who are different to sit down and talk to one another and understand their stories, and understand that we have things that bind us together that are even more important than the very interesting things about us which are different, one from another. And that's what this whole Race Initiative is all about. We've got a lot of challenges in the world. The challenge in Iraq, the general challenge of weapons of mass destruction, the chemical and biological weapons. They could bother our kids a lot and we're going to work hard to see that they don't. We've got financial upheavals in Asia now. And since Thanksgiving, Secretary Rubin and I have been talking at all kinds of odd hours because of the time difference in Asia and here. I was on the phone last night at 11:00 p.m. to Asia. But we're managing the best we can.

And there are lots of other things we have to deal with—the challenge of the entitlement, the challenge of educational excellence in our public schools, the challenge of extending health care further. But you just look at this balanced budget. All the other politicians, I heard them all talk about balancing the budget up here for years; it just got worse. The deficit has been cut by 92 percent before we passed the balanced budget act. Now we've got a balanced budget bill that gives a tax credit or a scholarship to virtually every person who needs to go to college in America. We can literally say we've opened the doors of college to everyone. The balanced budget has the biggest increase in aid to go to college since the G.I. Bill passed in 1945. That will make a lot of different stories.

It has the biggest increase in health care for children since Medicaid was enacted in 1965. Five million more kids in working families with modest incomes will be able to get health insurance. Who knows how many of them will live to be adults because of it. Who knows how many of them will be healthier intellectually and physically and emotionally because of it. They'll all have a slightly different story and it will be better. That's what I want you to think about. The reason it's important for you to be here is that part of the counter-battle, the mosquito biting, this year was a calculated, determined effort to use the hearing process and the legal process to force all the Democrats—and especially people associated with the party—to hire a lawyer every 15 seconds in the hope that we'd never have another penny to spend on campaigns. Somebody pointed out I'd been to so many fund-raisers in the last year that I'd gotten tired a time or two, and I plead guilty to that. It's okay to get tired, you just can't give in.

So when you go home and people ask you why you did this, say because they tried to end the two-party system in America by forcing the Democrats to spend all their money hiring lawyers, and you think the two-party system is a pretty good idea, especially since one party, the one you belong to, was right about the deficit, was right about the economy, was right about crime, was right about welfare, was right about so many things, and that's why this country is in better shape today, and you think that's a pretty good indication about which party ought to be able to lead us into the new century. That's why you're here and that's why I'm very proud of you.

Let me just say, lastly, I want you to go back home and tell the people who aren't here what I said tonight. And remind them—because they're a long way away— never to get confused between the mosquitoes and the planting, because as soon as you do you won't be able to bring in the crop. We have brought in the crop and you made it possible and I'm very, very proud of you. Thank you and God bless you.

Confession in the Lewinsky Affair

Washington, D.C.

August 17, 1998

IN ARKANSAS, where he occupied the statehouse from 1978 to 1980 and again from 1982 to 1992, Bill Clinton gained a reputation among insiders as an enthusiastic philanderer. He passed up the chance to run for the Democratic presidential nomination in 1988 for fear that his adulteries would come to light and had to bluff his way out of rumors that nearly wrecked his 1992 presidential campaign bid. Halfway through his first term in the White House, he was named as a defendant in a sexual harassment case that eventually came under the purview of Kenneth Starr, the independent federal prosecutor who had been appointed to investigate the Clintons' involvement in a failed Arkansas land-development deal known as Whitewater. Starr's office developed evidence suggesting that President Clinton had carried on an extramarital affair with a young White House intern, Monica Lewinsky; had urged her to lie in order to keep the affair a secret; and had used his influence to find her a high-paying job.

Testifying under oath in the harassment lawsuit in January 1998, the president denied the accusations. He repeated his denial publicly at a press conference and privately to his aides and cabinet members, whose active support he solicited. Seven months later, however, the revelation of the existence of DNA evidence linking him to Lewinsky caused him to reverse himself. On August 17, during four hours of questioning before a federal grand jury, he admitted that he had been intimate with her in a relationship that lasted over a year. This was the first time in history that a sitting president testified before a grand jury in a matter in which he himself was under investigation.

Clinton then went before TV cameras to deliver a brief speech to the nation that had been drafted with the help of his wife. Still on the defensive, he refused to offer a real apology, instead insisting that the matter was private and attacking the independent counsel for persecuting him. Former White House speechwriter Peggy Noonan called it "four minutes of petulance and prevarication," and most of the nation's newspaper editorialists agreed with her.

This afternoon in this room, from this chair, I testified before the Office of Independent Counsel and the grand jury.

I answered their questions truthfully, including questions about my private life, questions no American citizen would ever want to answer.

Still, I must take complete responsibility for all my actions, both public and private. And that is why I am speaking to you tonight.

As you know, in a deposition in January, I was asked questions about my relationship with Monica Lewinsky. While my answers were legally accurate, I did not volunteer information.

Indeed, I did have a relationship with Ms. Lewinsky that was not appropriate. In fact, it was wrong. It constituted a critical lapse in judgment and a personal failure on my part for which I am solely and completely responsible.

But I told the grand jury today and I say to you now that at no time did I ask anyone to lie, to hide or destroy evidence, or to take any other unlawful action.

I know that my public comments and my silence about this matter gave a false impression. I misled people, including even my wife. I deeply regret that.

I can only tell you I was motivated by many factors. First, by a desire to protect myself from the embarrassment of my own conduct.

I was also very concerned about protecting my family. The fact that these questions were being asked in a politically inspired lawsuit, which has since been dismissed, was a consideration, too.

In addition, I had real and serious concerns about an independent counsel investigation that began with private business dealings 20 years ago—dealings, I might add, about which an independent federal agency found no evidence of any wrongdoing by me or my wife over two years ago.

The independent counsel investigation moved on to my staff and friends, then into my private life. And now the investigation itself is under investigation.

This has gone on too long, cost too much, and hurt too many innocent people.

Now, this matter is between me, the two people I love most—my wife and our daughter—and our God. I must put it right, and I am prepared to do whatever it takes to do so.

Nothing is more important to me personally. But it is private, and I intend to reclaim my family life for my family. It's nobody's business but ours.

Even presidents have private lives. It is time to stop the pursuit of personal destruction and the prying into private lives and get on with our national life.

Our country has been distracted by this matter for too long, and I take my responsibility for my part in all of this. That is all I can do.

Now it is time—in fact, it is past time to move on.

We have important work to do—real opportunities to seize, real problems to solve, real security matters to face.

And so tonight, I ask you to turn away from the spectacle of the past seven months, to repair the fabric of our national discourse, and to return our attention to all the challenges and all the promise of the next American century.

Thank you for watching. And good night.

Statement on Impeachment

Washington, D.C.

December 11, 1998

THE REPORT OF independent counsel Kenneth Starr was delivered to the House of Representatives on September 8, 1998, and was released to the public three days later. It described in massive detail the results of his investigation into the Clinton-Lewinsky relationship and formed the basis for four articles of impeachment approved by the Judiciary Committee of the House of Representatives on December 11. Eight days later, after a tremendous partisan fight, the House adopted two of these articles, the first charging President Clinton with committing perjury before a federal grand jury in his testimony about the relationship and the second charging him with obstruction of justice. Clinton thus became the first elected president in the history of the United States to face an impeachment trial in the Senate. The trial, which Clinton did not attend, was presided over by William Rehnquist, the chief justice of the Supreme Court, with 13 members of the House acting as prosecutors, and resulted in acquittal on both charges on February 12.

A few minutes before the House Judiciary Committee's vote, President Clinton entered the White House's Rose Garden and made a short televised statement in which he said he was sorry for having misled people and expressed his willingness to accept Congress's punishment in the form of rebuke and censure. For legal reasons, and perhaps for personal ones as well, the president never conceded that he had told lies.

As anyone close to me knows, for months I have been grappling with how best to reconcile myself to the American people, to acknowledge my own wrongdoing and still to maintain my focus on the work of the presidency.

Others are presenting my defense on the facts, the law, and the Constitution. Nothing I can say now can add to that.

What I want the American people to know, what I want the Congress to know is that I am profoundly sorry for all I have done wrong in words and deeds.

I never should have misled the country, the Congress, my friends, or my family. Quite simply, I gave in to my shame. I have been condemned by my accusers with harsh words.

And while it's hard to hear yourself called deceitful and manipulative, I remember Ben Franklin's admonition that our critics are our friends, for they do show us our faults.

Mere words cannot fully express the profound remorse I feel for what our country is going through and for what members of both parties in Congress are now forced to deal with. These past months have been a torturous process of coming to terms with what I did. I understand that accountability demands consequences, and I'm prepared to accept them.

Painful as the condemnation of the Congress would be, it would pale in comparison to the consequences of the pain I have caused my family. There is no greater agony.

Like anyone who honestly faces the shame of wrongful conduct, I would give anything to go back and undo what I did.

But one of the painful truths I have to live with is the reality that that is simply not possible. An old and dear friend of mine recently sent me the wisdom of a poet who wrote, "The moving finger writes and having writ, moves on. Nor all your piety nor wit shall lure it back to cancel half a line. Nor all your tears wash out a word of it."

So nothing, not piety, nor tears, nor wit, nor torment can alter what I have done. I must make my peace with that.

I must also be at peace with the fact that the public consequences of my actions are in the hands of the American people and their representatives in the Congress. Should they determine that my errors of word and deed require their rebuke and censure, I am ready to accept that.

Meanwhile, I will continue to do all I can to reclaim the trust of the American people and to serve them well.

We must all return to the work, the vital work, of strengthening our nation for the new century. Our country has wonderful opportunities and daunting challenges ahead. I intend to seize those opportunities and meet those challenges with all the energy and ability and strength God has given me.

That is simply all I can do—the work of the American people.

Thank you very much.

Air Strikes Against Iraq

Washington, D.C.

December 16, 1998

IN THE MIDST of the crisis over impeachment, President Clinton went on the air to announce that he had ordered air strikes against targets in Iraq. The purpose of the strikes was to punish Iraq's dictator, Saddam Hussein, for preventing United Nations inspectors from doing their job—searching Iraq to uncover facilities for making and storing weapons of mass destruction, including biological, chemical, and nuclear weapons. The entire campaign, called Operation Desert Fox, lasted for 72 hours, during which an estimated 100 targets were hit by cruise missiles and American and British bomber planes. As he had done previously in Haiti, Sudan, Afghanistan, and other places, president Clinton did not ask for congressional permission to make war, asserting that the use of limited military force was within his power to order as commander in chief of the armed forces.

The president made his announcement only a few hours before the impeachment debate in the House of Representatives was scheduled to start. The timing was considered suspicious by many disillusioned people who believed Clinton quite capable of acting to save himself by creating a distraction. More trusting observers were willing to see it as a coincidence. The *New Republic* editorialized: "The address in which the president explained the nature and the justification of the attack . . . was so clear and unmisleading that it almost made you melancholy about the presidency that might have been. . . . In the middle of the greatest political excruciation in its modern history, the United States is doing the noble and necessary thing beyond its borders."

Earlier today, I ordered America's armed forces to strike military and security targets in Iraq. They are joined by British forces. Their mission is to attack Iraq's nuclear, chemical, and biological programs, and its military capacity to threaten its neighbors. Their purpose is to protect the national interest of the United States and, indeed, the interest of people throughout the Middle East and around the world. Saddam Hussein must not be allowed to threaten his neighbors or the world with nuclear arms, poison gas, or biological weapons.

I want to explain why I have decided, with the unanimous recommendation of my national security team, to use force in Iraq, why we have acted now, and what we aim to accomplish.

Six weeks ago, Saddam Hussein announced that he would no longer cooperate with the United Nations weapons inspectors, called UNSCOM. They are highly professional experts from dozens of countries. Their job is to oversee the elimination of Iraq's capability to retain, create, and use weapons of mass destruction, and to verify that Iraq does not attempt to rebuild that capability. The inspectors undertook this mission, first, seven and a half years ago, at the end of the Gulf War,

when Iraq agreed to declare and destroy its arsenal as a condition of the cease-fire.

The international community had good reason to set this requirement. Other countries possess weapons of mass destruction and ballistic missiles. With Saddam, there's one big difference: he has used them, not once but repeatedly—unleashing chemical weapons against Iranian troops during a decade-long war, not only against soldiers, but against civilians; firing Scud missiles at the citizens of Israel, Saudi Arabia, Bahrain, and Iran—not only against a foreign enemy, but even against his own people, gassing Kurdish civilians in northern Iraq.

The international community had little doubt then, and I have no doubt today, that left unchecked, Saddam Hussein will use these terrible weapons again.

The United States has patiently worked to preserve UNSCOM, as Iraq has sought to avoid its obligation to cooperate with the inspectors. On occasion, we've had to threaten military force, and Saddam has backed down. Faced with Saddam's latest act of defiance in late October, we built intensive diplomatic pressure on Iraq, backed by overwhelming military force in the region. The UN Security Council voted 15 to zero to condemn Saddam's actions and to demand that he immediately come into compliance. Eight Arab nations—Egypt, Syria, Saudi Arabia, Kuwait, Bahrain, Qatar, United Arab Emirates, and Oman—warned that Iraq alone would bear responsibility for the consequences of defying the UN.

When Saddam still failed to comply, we prepared to act militarily. It was only then, at the last possible moment, that Iraq backed down. It pledged to the UN that it had made—and I quote—"a clear and unconditional decision to resume cooperation with the weapons inspectors."

I decided then to call off the attack, with our airplanes already in the air, because Saddam had given in to our demands. I concluded then that the right thing to do was to use restraint and give Saddam one last chance to prove his willingness to cooperate.

I made it very clear at that time what "unconditional cooperation" meant, based on existing UN resolutions and Iraq's own commitments. And along with Prime Minister Blair of Great Britain, I made it equally clear that if Saddam failed to cooperate fully, we would be prepared to act without delay, diplomacy or warning.

Now, over the past three weeks, the UN weapons inspectors have carried out their plan for testing Iraq's cooperation. The testing period ended this weekend, and last night, UNSCOM's chairman, Richard Butler, reported the results to UN Secretary-General Annan. The conclusions are stark, sobering, and profoundly disturbing.

In four out of the five categories set forth, Iraq has failed to cooperate. Indeed, it actually has placed new restrictions on the inspectors. Here are some of the particulars:

Iraq repeatedly blocked UNSCOM from inspecting suspect sites. For example, it shut off access to the headquarters of its ruling party and said it will deny access to the party's other offices, even though UN resolutions make no exception for them and UNSCOM has inspected them in the past.

Iraq repeatedly restricted UNSCOM's ability to obtain necessary evidence. For example, Iraq obstructed UNSCOM's effort to photograph bombs related to its chemical weapons program. It tried to stop an UNSCOM biological weapons team from videotaping a site and photocopying documents, and prevented Iraqi personnel from answering UNSCOM's questions.

Prior to the inspection of another site, Iraq actually emptied out the building, removing not just documents, but even the furniture and the equipment. Iraq has failed to turn over virtually all the documents requested by the inspectors; indeed, we know that Iraq ordered the destruction of weapons-related documents in anticipation of an UNSCOM inspection.

So Iraq has abused its final chance. As the UNSCOM report concludes—and again I quote—"Iraq's conduct ensured that no progress was able to be made in the fields of disarmament. In light of this experience, and in the absence of full cooperation by Iraq, it must, regrettably, be recorded again that the commission is not able to conduct the work mandated to it by the Security Council with respect to Iraq's prohibited weapons program."

In short, the inspectors are saying that, even if they could stay in Iraq, their work would be a sham. Saddam's deception has defeated their effectiveness. Instead of the inspectors disarming Saddam, Saddam has disarmed the inspectors.

This situation presents a clear and present danger to the stability of the Persian Gulf and the safety of people everywhere. The international community gave Saddam one last chance to resume cooperation with the weapons inspectors. Saddam has failed to seize the chance.

And so we had to act, and act now. Let me explain why.

First, without a strong inspections system, Iraq would be free to retain and begin to rebuild its chemical, biological, and nuclear weapons programs—in months, not years.

Second, if Saddam can cripple the weapons inspections system and get away with it, he would conclude that the international community, led by the United States, has simply lost its will. He will surmise that he has free rein to rebuild his arsenal of destruction. And some day, make no mistake, he will use it again, as he has in the past.

Third, in halting our air strikes in November, I gave Saddam a chance, not a license. If we turn our backs on his defiance, the credibility of U.S. power as a check against Saddam will be destroyed. We will not only have allowed Saddam to shatter the inspections system that controls his weapons of mass destruction program, we also will have fatally undercut the fear of force that stops Saddam from acting to gain domination in the region.

That is why, on the unanimous recommendation of my national security team, including the vice president, secretary of defense, the chairman of the Joint Chiefs of Staff, the secretary of state, and the national security adviser, I have ordered a strong, sustained series of air strikes against Iraq. They are designed to degrade Saddam's capacity to develop and deliver weapons of mass destruction, and to degrade his ability to threaten his neighbors. At the same time, we are delivering a powerful message to Saddam: If you act recklessly, you will pay a heavy price.

We acted today because, in the judgment of my military advisers, a swift response would provide the most surprise and the least opportunity for Saddam to prepare. If we had delayed for even a matter of days from Chairman Butler's report, we would have given Saddam more time to disperse forces and protect his weapons.

Also, the Muslim holy month of Ramadan begins this weekend. For us to initiate military action during Ramadan would be profoundly offensive to the Muslim world, and therefore, would damage our relations with Arab countries and the progress we have made in the Middle East. That is something we wanted very much to avoid without giving Iraq a month's head start to prepare for potential action against it.

Finally, our allies, including Prime Minister Tony Blair of Great Britain, concurred that now is the time to strike.

I hope Saddam will come into cooperation with the inspection system now and comply with the relevant UN Security Council resolutions. But we have to be prepared that he will not, and we must deal with the very real danger he poses. So we will pursue a long-term strategy to contain Iraq and its weapons of mass destruction, and work toward the day when Iraq has a government worthy of its people.

First, we must be prepared to use force again if Saddam takes threatening actions, such as trying to reconstitute his weapons of mass destruction or their delivery systems, threatening his neighbors, challenging allied aircraft over Iraq, or moving against his own Kurdish citizens. The credible threat to use force and, when necessary, the actual use of force, is the surest way to contain Saddam's

weapons of mass destruction program, curtail his aggression, and prevent another Gulf War.

Second, so long as Iraq remains out of compliance, we will work with the international community to maintain and enforce economic sanctions. Sanctions have caused Saddam more than $120 billion—resources that would have been used to rebuild his military. The sanctions system allows Iraq to sell oil for food, for medicine, for other humanitarian supplies for the Iraqi people. We have no quarrel with them. But without the sanctions, we would see the oil-for-food program become oil-for-tanks, resulting in a greater threat to Iraq's neighbors and less food for its people.

The hard fact is that so long as Saddam remains in power, he threatens the well-being of his people, the peace of his region, the security of the world. The best way to end that threat once and for all is with the new Iraqi government, a government ready to live in peace with its neighbors, a government that respects the rights of its people.

Bringing change in Baghdad will take time and effort. We will strengthen our engagement with the full range of Iraqi opposition forces and work with them effectively and prudently.

The decision to use force is never cost-free. Whenever American forces are placed in harm's way, we risk the loss of life. And while our strikes are focused on Iraq's military capabilities, there will be unintended Iraqi casualties. Indeed, in the past, Saddam has intentionally placed Iraqi civilians in harm's way in a cynical bid to sway international opinion. We must be prepared for these realities. At the same time, Saddam should have absolutely no doubt: If he lashes out at his neighbors, we will respond forcefully.

Heavy as they are, the costs of action must be weighed against the price of inaction. If Saddam defies the world and we fail to respond, we will face a far greater threat in the future. Saddam will strike again at his neighbors; he will make war on his own people. And mark my words, he will develop weapons of mass destruction. He will deploy them, and he will use them. Because we are acting today, it is less likely that we will face these dangers in the future.

Let me close by addressing one other issue. Saddam Hussein and the other enemies of peace may have thought that the serious debate currently before the House of Representatives would distract Americans or weaken our resolve to face him down. But once more, the United States has proven that, although we are never eager to use force, when we must act in America's vital interests, we will do so.

In the century we're leaving, America has often made the difference between chaos and community; fear and hope. Now, in a new century, we'll have a remarkable opportunity to shape a future more peaceful than the past—but only if we stand strong against the enemies of peace.

Tonight, the United States is doing just that.

May God bless and protect the brave men and women who are carrying out this vital mission, and their families. And may God bless America.

Postponement of the Nuclear Missile Shield

Washington, D.C.

September 1, 2000

ALTHOUGH MOST AMERICANS associate the idea of a national missile shield with Ronald Reagan's Strategic Defense Initiative (better known as "Star Wars"), such a system was first proposed by President Dwight D. Eisenhower in the late 1950s. Despite billions of dollars spent in research and testing, however, no feasible system was ever developed, and at the turn of the millennium, the United States remained vulnerable to long-range missile attack.

During the Clinton administration, the federal government attempted to develop a ground-based "smart" interceptor, the Exo-Atmospheric Kill Vehicle, but the technology failed a series of tests, the last one in July 2000. The following September, speaking at Georgetown University, Clinton announced that he had decided not to go ahead with construction of the system, leaving its final disposition to be handled by his Successor in the White House. Among his reasons was the existence of the 1972 Anti-ballistic Missile treaty, which prohibits missile shields (although some experts said that the disappearance of the treaty's other signatory—the Soviet Union—rendered it invalid). Clinton's decision was hailed as a prudent one by Russia and China, whose leaders opposed the possibility of another arms race, and by the United States' European allies, none of whom would receive protection under the system.

I came today to talk about a subject that is not fraught with applause lines, but one that is very, very important to your future: the defense of our nation. At this moment of unprecedented peace and prosperity, with no immediate threat to our security or our existence, with our democratic values ascendant and our alliances strong, with the great forces of our time, globalization and the revolution in information technology so clearly beneficial to a society like ours, with our diversity and our openness, and our entrepreneurial spirit; at a time like this, it is tempting, but wrong, to believe there are no serious long-term challenges to our security.

The rapid spread of technology across increasingly porous borders raises the specter that more and more states, terrorists, and criminal syndicates could gain access to chemical, biological, or even nuclear weapons, and to the means of delivering them—whether in small units deployed by terrorists within our midst, or ballistic missiles capable of hurtling those weapons halfway around the world.

Today I want to discuss these threats with you, because you will live with them a lot longer than I will. Especially, I want to talk about the ballistic missile threat. It is real and growing, and has given new urgency to the debate about national missile defenses, known in the popular jargon as NMD.

When I became president, I put our effort to stop the proliferation of weapons of mass destruction at the very top of our national security agenda. Since then, we have carried out a comprehensive strategy to reduce and secure nuclear arsenals, to strengthen the international regime against biological and chemical weapons and nuclear testing, and to stop the flow of dangerous technology to nations that might wish us harm.

At the same time, we have pursued new technologies that could strengthen our defenses against a possible attack, including a terrorist attack here at home.

None of these elements of our national security strategy can be pursued in isolation. Each is important, and we have made progress in each area. For example, Russia and the United States already have destroyed about 25,000 nuclear weapons in the last decade. And we have agreed that in a START III treaty, we will go 80 percent below the level of a decade ago.

In 1994, we persuaded Ukraine, Kazakhstan, and Belarus, three of the former Soviet Republics, to give up their nuclear weapons entirely. We have worked with Russia and its neighbors to dispose of hundreds of tons of dangerous nuclear materials, to strengthen controls on a list of exports, and to keep weapon scientists from selling their services to the highest bidder.

We extended the nuclear nonproliferation treaty indefinitely. We were the very first nation to sign the comprehensive test ban treaty, an idea first embraced by Presidents Kennedy and Eisenhower. Sixty nations now have ratified the test ban treaty. I believe the United States Senate made a serious error in failing to ratify it last year, and I hope it will do so next year.

We also negotiated and ratified the international convention to ban chemical weapons, and strengthened the convention against biological weapons. We've used our export controls to deny terrorists and potential adversaries access to materials and equipment needed to build these kinds of weapons.

We've imposed sanctions on those who contribute to foreign chemical and biological weapons programs, we've invested in new equipment and medical countermeasures to protect people from exposure. And we're working with state and local medical units all over our country to strengthen our preparedness in case of a chemical or biological terrorist attack, which many people believe is the most likely new security threat of the 21st century.

We have also acted to reduce the threat posed by states that have sought weapons of mass destruction and ballistic missiles, while pursuing activities that are clearly hostile to our long-term interests. For over a decade—for almost a decade, excuse me—we have diverted about 90 percent of Iraq's oil revenues from the production of weapons to the purchase of food and medicine.

This is an important statistic for those who believe that our sanctions are only a negative for the people, and particularly the children, of Iraq. In 1989, Iraq earned $15 billion from oil exports, and spent $13 billion of that money on its military. This year, Iraq is projected to earn $19 billion from its legal oil-for-food exports that can spend none of those revenues on the military.

We worked to counter Iran's efforts to develop nuclear weapons and missile technology, convincing China to provide no new assistance to Iran's nuclear program, and pressing Russia to strengthen its controls on the export of sensitive technologies.

In 1994, six years after the United States first learned that North Korea had a nuclear weapons program, we negotiated the agreement that verifiably has frozen its production of plutonium for nuclear weapons. Now, in the context of the United States negotiations with the North, the diplomatic efforts by former Defense Secretary Bill Perry and, most lately, the summit between the leaders of North and South Korea, North Korea has refrained from flight testing a new missile that could pose a threat to America.

We should be clear: North Korea's capability remains a serious issue and its intentions remain unclear. But its missile testing moratorium is a good development worth pursuing.

These diplomatic efforts to meet the threat of proliferation are backed by the strong and global reach of our armed forces. Today, the United States enjoys overwhelming military superiority over any potential adversary. For example, in 1985, we spent about as much on defense as Russia, China, and North Korea combined. Today, we spend nearly three times as much, nearly $300 billion a year. And our military technology clearly is well ahead of the rest of the world.

The principle of deterrence served us very well in the cold war, and deterrence remains imperative. The threat of overwhelming retaliation deterred Saddam Hussein from using weapons of mass destruction during the Gulf War. Our forces in South Korea have deterred North Korea in aggression for 47 years.

The question is, can deterrence protect us against all those who might wish us harm in the future? Can we make America even more secure? The effort to answer these questions is the impetus behind the search for NMD. The issue is whether we can do more, not to meet today's threat, but to meet tomorrow's threat to our security.

For example, there is the possibility that a hostile state with nuclear weapons and long-range missiles may simply disintegrate, with command over missiles falling into unstable hands; or that in a moment of desperation, such a country might miscalculate, believing it could use nuclear weapons to intimidate us from defending our vital interests, or from coming to the aid of our allies, or others who are defenseless and clearly in need.

In the future, we cannot rule out that terrorist groups could gain the capability to strike us with nuclear weapons if they seized even temporary control of a state with an existing nuclear weapons establishment.

Now, no one suggests that NMD would ever substitute for diplomacy or for deterrence. But such a system, if it worked properly, could give us an extra dimension of insurance in a world where proliferation has complicated the task of preserving the peace. Therefore, I believe we have an obligation to determine the feasibility, the effectiveness, and the impact of a national missile defense on the overall security of the United States.

The system now under development is designed to work as follows. In the event of an attack, American satellites would protect the launch of missiles. Our radar would track the enemy warhead and highly accurate, high-speed, ground-based interceptors would destroy them before they could reach their target in the United States.

We have made substantial progress on a system that would be based in Alaska and that, when operational, could protect all 50 states from the near-term missile threats we face, those emanating from North Korea and the Middle East. The system could be deployed sooner than any of the proposed alternatives.

Since last fall, we've been conducting flight tests to see if this NMD system actually can reliably intercept a ballistic missile. We've begun to show that the different parts of this system can work together.

Our Defense Department has overcome daunting technical obstacles in a remarkably short period of time, and I'm proud of the work that Secretary Cohen, General Shelton, and their teams have done.

One test proved that it is, in fact, possible to hit a bullet with a bullet. Still, though the technology for NMD is promising, the system as a whole is not yet proven. After the initial test succeeded, our two most recent tests failed, for different reasons, to achieve an intercept. Several more tests are planned. They will tell us whether NMD can work reliably under realistic conditions. Critical elements of the program, such as the booster rocket for the missile interceptor, have yet to be tested.

There are also questions to be resolved about the ability of the system to deal with countermeasures. In other words, measures by those firing the missiles to confuse the missile defense into thinking it is hitting a target when it is not.

There is a reasonable chance that all these challenges can be met in time. But I simply cannot conclude with the information I have today that we have enough confidence in the technology, and the operational effectiveness of the entire NMD system, to move forward to deployment.

Therefore, I have decided not to authorize deployment of a national missile defense at this time. Instead, I have asked Secretary Cohen to continue a robust program of development and testing. That effort still is at an early stage. Only three of the 19 planned intercept tests have been held so far. We need more tests against more challenging targets, and more simulations before we can responsibly commit our nation's resources to deployment.

We should use this time to ensure that NMD, if deployed, would actually enhance our overall national security. And I want to talk about that in a few moments.

I want you to know that I have reached this decision about not deploying the NMD after careful deliberation. My decision will not have a significant impact on the date the overall system could be deployed in the next administration, if the next president decides to go forward.

The best judgment of the experts who have examined this question is that if we were to commit today to construct the system, it most likely would be operational about 2006 or 2007. If the next president decides to move forward next year, the system still could be ready in the same time frame.

In the meantime, we will continue to work with our allies and with Russia to strengthen their understanding and support for our efforts to meet the emerging ballistic missile threat, and to explore creative ways that we can cooperate to enhance their security against this threat, as well.

An effective NMD could play an important part of our national security strategy, but it could not be the sum total of that strategy. It can never be the sum total of that strategy for dealing with nuclear and missile threats.

Moreover, ballistic missiles, armed with nuclear weapons, as I said earlier, do not represent the sum total of the threats we face. Those include chemical, and biological weapons, and a range of deadly technologies for deploying them. So it would be folly to base the defense of our nation solely on a strategy of waiting until missiles are in the air, and then trying to shoot them down.

We must work with our allies, and with Russia, to prevent potential adversaries from ever threatening us with nuclear, chemical, and biological weapons of mass destruction in the first place, and to make sure they know the devastating consequences of doing so.

The elements of our strategy cannot be allowed to undermine one another. They must reinforce one another, and contribute to our national defense in all its dimensions. That includes the profoundly important dimension of arms control.

Over the past 30 years, Republican and Democratic presidents alike have negotiated an array of arms control treaties with Russia. We and our allies have relied on these treaties to ensure strategic stability and predictability with Russia, to get on with the job of dismantling the legacy of the cold war, and to further the transition from confrontation to cooperation with our former adversary in the most important arena, nuclear weapons.

A key part of the international security structure we have built with Russia and, therefore, a key part of our national security, is the Anti-Ballistic Missile treaty signed by President Nixon in 1972. The ABM treaty limits anti-missile defenses according to a simple principle: neither side should deploy defenses that would undermine the other side's nuclear deterrent, and thus tempt the other side to strike first in a crisis or to take counter-measures that would make both our countries less secure.

Strategic stability, based on mutual deterrence, is still important, despite the end of the cold war. Why? Because the United States and Russia still have nuclear arsenals that can devastate each other. And this is still a period of transition in our relationship.

We have worked together in many ways. Signed an agreement of cooperation between Russia and NATO. Served with Russian troops in Bosnia and Kosovo. But while we are no longer adversaries, we are not yet real allies. Therefore, for them as well as for us, maintaining strategic stability increases trust and confidence on both sides. It reduces the risk of confrontation. It makes it possible to build an even better partnership and an even safer world.

Now, here's the issue: NMD, if deployed, would require us either to adjust the treaty or to withdraw from it—not because NMD poses a challenge to the strategic stability I just discussed, but because by its very words, NMD prohibits any national missile defense.

What we should want is to both explore the most effective defenses possible, not only for ourselves, but for all other law-abiding states, and to maintain our strategic stability with Russia. Thus far, Russia has been reluctant to agree, fearing I think, frankly, that in some sense, this system or some future incarnation of it could threaten the reliability of its deterrence and, therefore, strategic stability.

Nevertheless, at our summit in Moscow in June, President Putin and I did agree that the world has changed since the ABM treaty was signed 28 years ago, and that the proliferation of missile technology has resulted in new threats that may require amending that treaty. And again, I say, these threats are not threats to the United States alone.

Russia agrees that there is an emerging missile threat. In fact, given its place on the map, it is particularly vulnerable to this emerging threat. In time, I hope the United States can narrow our differences with Russia on this issue. The course I have chosen today gives the United States more time to pursue that, and we will use it.

President Putin and I have agreed to intensify our work on strategic defense, while pursuing, in parallel, deeper arms reductions in START III. He and I have instructed our experts to develop further cooperative initiatives in areas such as theater missile defense, early warning, and missile threat discussions for our meeting just next week in New York.

Apart from the Russians, another critical diplomatic consideration in the NMD decision is the view of our NATO allies. They have all made clear that they hope the United States will pursue strategic defense in a way that preserves, not abrogates, the ABM treaty. If we decide to proceed with NMD deployment we must have their support, because key components of NMD would be based on their territories.

The decision I have made also gives the United States time to answer our allies' questions and consult further on the path ahead.

Finally, we must consider the impact of a decision to deploy on security in Asia. As the next president makes a deployment decision, he will need to avoid stimulating an already dangerous regional nuclear capability from China to South Asia. Now, let me be clear: no nation can ever have a veto over American security, even if the United States and Russia cannot reach agreement; even if we cannot secure the support of our allies at first; even if we conclude that the Chinese will respond to NMD by increasing their arsenal of nuclear weapons substantially with a corollary, inevitable impact in India and then in Pakistan.

The next president may nevertheless decide that our interest in security in the 21st century dictates that we go forward with deployment of NMD. But we can never afford to overlook the fact that the actions and reactions of others in this increasingly interdependent world do bear on our security.

Clearly, therefore, it would be far better to move forward in the context of the ABM treaty and allied support. Our efforts to make that possible have not been completed. For me, the bottom line on this decision is this: because the emerging missile threat is real, we have an obligation to pursue a missile defense system that could enhance our security.

We have made progress, but we should not move forward until we have absolute confidence that the system will work, and until we have made every reasonable diplomatic effort to minimize the cost of deployment, and maximize the benefit, as I said, not only to America's security, but to the security of law abiding nations everywhere subject to the same threat.

I am convinced that America and the world will be better off if we explore the frontiers of strategic defenses, while continuing to pursue arms control, to stand with our allies, and to work with Russia and others to stop the spread of deadly weapons.

I strongly believe this is the best course for the United States, and therefore the decision I have reached today, is in the best security interest of the United States. In short, we need to move forward with realism, with steadiness, and with prudence, not dismissing the threat we face, or assuming we can meet it, while ignoring our overall strategic environment, including the interests and concerns of our allies, friends, and other nations. A national missile defense, if deployed, should be part of a larger strategy to preserve and enhance the peace, strength, and security we now enjoy, and to build an even safer world.

I have tried to maximize the ability of the next president to pursue that strategy. In so doing, I have tried to maximize the chance that all you young students will live in a safer, more humane, more positively interdependent world. I hope I have done so. I believe I have.

Thank you very much.

Farewell Address

Washington, D.C.
January 18, 2001

As HE PREPARED to leave office, President Clinton gave a series of farewell speeches in various locations. On Wednesday, January 18, he paid a visit to his home state of Arkansas— the last out-of-town trip of his presidency—to deliver an hour-long talk to a joint session of the legislature. The following day, he made his final address to the nation from the Oval Office. This speech, televised by all major broadcasting networks, was unusually brief for the president—a mere 10 minutes—but was composed in classic Clinton style, with the president making revisions until the last moment. In addition to presenting a favorable assessment of his administration's economic and foreign-policy achievements, Clinton hinted at trouble to come if his successor in the White House, George W. Bush, failed to follow his lead in these areas. He ended his remarks by pumping the air with his fist.

My fellow citizens, tonight is my last opportunity to speak to you from the Oval Office as your president.

I am profoundly grateful to you for twice giving me the honor to serve, to work for you and with you to prepare our nation for the 21st century. And I'm grateful to Vice President Gore, to my cabinet secretaries, and to all those who served with me for the last eight years.

This has been a time of dramatic transformation. And you have risen to every new challenge. You have made our social fabric stronger, our families healthier and safer, our people more prosperous. You, the American people, have made our passage into the global information age an era of great American renewal.

In all the work I have done as president, every decision I have made, every executive action I have taken, every bill I have proposed and signed, I've tried to give all Americans the tools and conditions to build a future of our dreams in a good society with a strong economy, a cleaner environment, and a freer, safer, more prosperous world.

I have steered my course by our enduring values: opportunity for all, responsibility from all, a community of all Americans. I have sought to give America a new kind of government: smaller, more modern, more effective, full of ideas and policies appropriate to this new time, always putting people first, always focusing on the future.

Working together, America has done well. Our economy is breaking records with more than 22 million new jobs, the lowest unemployment in 30 years, the highest home ownership ever, the longest expansion in history. Our families and communities are stronger. Thirty-five million Americans have used the family leave law; eight million have moved off welfare; crime is at a 25-year low.

Over 10 million Americans received more college aid and more people than ever are going to college. Our schools are better: higher standards, greater accountability, and larger investments have brought higher test scores and higher graduation rates.

More than three million children have health insurance now and more than seven million Americans have been lifted out of poverty. Incomes are rising across the board.

Our air and water are cleaner, our food and drinking water are safer, and more of our precious land has been preserved in the continental United States than at any time in a hundred years.

America has been a force for peace and prosperity in every corner of the globe.

I'm very grateful to be able to turn over the reins of leadership to a new president with America in such a strong position to meet the challenges of the future.

Tonight I want to leave you with three thoughts about our future.

First, America must maintain our record of fiscal responsibility. Through our last four budgets, we've turned record deficits to record surpluses and we've been able to pay down $600 billion of our national debt, on track to be debt-free by the end of the decade for the first time since 1835. Staying on that course will bring lower interest rates, greater prosperity, and the opportunity to meet our big challenges.

If we choose wisely, we can pay down the debt, deal with the retirement of the baby boomers, invest more in our future, and provide tax relief.

Second, because the world is more connected every day in every way, America's security and prosperity require us to continue to lead in the world. At this remarkable moment in history, more people live in freedom than ever before. Our alliances are stronger than ever. People all around the world look to America to be a force for peace and prosperity, freedom and security.

The global economy is giving more of our own people and millions around the world the chance to work and live and raise their families with dignity. But the forces of integration that have created these good opportunities also make us more subject to global forces of destruction, to terrorism, organized crime and narcotrafficking, the spread of deadly weapons and disease, the degradation of the global environment. The expansion of trade hasn't fully closed the gap between those of us who live on the cutting edge of the global economy and the billions around the world who live on the knife's edge of survival. This global gap requires more than compassion. It requires action. Global poverty is a powder keg that could be ignited by our indifference.

In his first inaugural address, Thomas Jefferson warned of entangling alliances. But in our times, America cannot and must not disentangle itself from the world. If we want the world to embody our shared values, then we must assume a shared responsibility.

If the wars of the 20th century, especially the recent ones in Kosovo and Bosnia, have taught us anything, it is that we achieve our aims by defending our values and leading the forces of freedom and peace. We must embrace boldly and resolutely that duty to lead, to stand with our allies in word and deed and to put a human face on the global economy so that expanded trade benefits all peoples in all nations, lifting lives and hopes all across the world.

Third, we must remember that America cannot lead in the world unless here at home we weave the threads of our coat of many colors into the fabric of one America. As we become ever more diverse, we must work harder to unite around our common values and our common humanity. We must work harder to overcome our differences in our hearts and in our laws. We must treat all our people with fairness and dignity, regardless of their race, religion, gender, or sexual orientation and regardless of when they arrived in our country, always moving toward the more perfect union of our founders' dreams.

Hillary, Chelsea, and I join all Americans in wishing our very best to the next president, George W. Bush, to his family and his administration, in meeting these challenges and in leading freedom's march in this new century.

As for me, I'll leave the presidency more idealistic, more full of hope, than the day I arrived, and more confident than ever that America's best days lie ahead.

My days in this office are nearly through. But my days of service, I hope, are not. In the years ahead I will never hold a position higher or a covenant more sacred than that of president of the United States. But there is no title I will wear more proudly than that of citizen.

Thank you. God bless you, and God bless America.

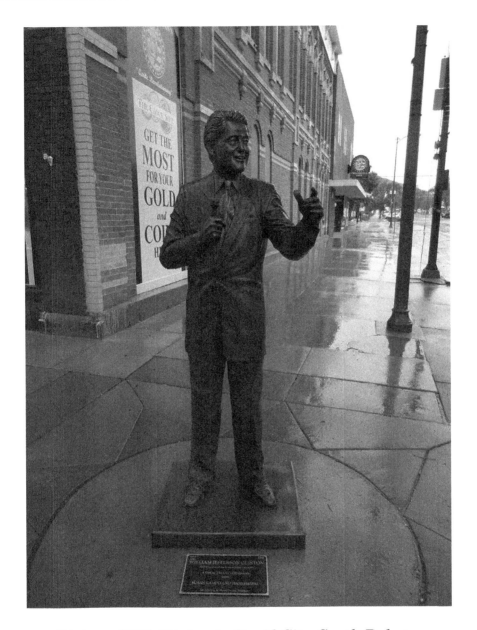

Statue of Bill Clinton in Rapid City, South Dakota.
(Courtesy of PresidentsUSA.net)

Courtesy of www.georgewbush.com

George Walker Bush

George Walker Bush

2001–2009

THE PRESIDENTIAL CAMPAIGN of 2000 was, for most of its duration, a singularly unexciting race. The major parties presented the voters with two mild-mannered gentlemen—Al Gore, the outgoing Democratic vice president, who combined an addiction to policy micro-management with a zeal for progressive ideology, and George W. Bush, the Republican governor of Texas, a social and fiscal moderate conservative with an amiable demeanor and no intellectual pretensions. Neither was able to gain much of an advantage, and election day arrived with the pollsters unable to predict who the winner would be. The result was a national nightmare—a virtually even split in the popular vote and an inconclusive electoral vote that could not be resolved without protracted litigation. The recounting of faulty ballots in the state of Florida, and the partisan court battles over the recount's legitimacy, dragged on for 36 days, until the Supreme Court put an end to them in a 5-to-4 decision on December 12. The Florida House of Representatives then appointed a slate of Republican electors, giving George W. Bush the support he needed to win the electoral college by a single vote. He thus gained the presidency despite the fact that he had lost the popular vote by a thin margin (50.46 million to 50.99 million).

The new president came to his position with only six years of political experience. Though he was the grandson of Senator Prescott Bush and the son of the 41st president, George Herbert Walker Bush, George W. Bush had spent most of his adult life as a Texas oilman and as part-owner of a baseball team. Apart from one unsuccessful run for Congress in 1978, he had remained aloof from politics until 1994, when he surprised nearly everyone by defeating the incumbent governor, Ann Richards. In the statehouse, he built a reputation as a good manager, a bridge-builder eager to work with the Democrats to promote a bipartisan agenda headed by aid to education. His landslide reelection victory in 1998 propelled him into the Republican presidential primaries two years later.

Although a smoother orator than the first President Bush, George W. Bush inherited his father's penchant for tripping over his tongue. (An often-quoted example was his remark to a group in Wisconsin: "Families is where our nation takes hope, where wings take dream.") Audiences on the campaign trail appeared to like him nonetheless. Despite his status as the scion of a wealthy family, he came across in his speeches as an unpretentious, humorous, down-to-earth fellow who was more interested in people than in the kind of policy minutiae that thrilled Al Gore. Part of his appeal was undoubtedly the religious faith that had helped him overcome a drinking problem and subdue a notoriously quick temper. His self-control was certain to be tested during his term in office, for many disappointed Democrats made it clear that they thought Gore had been robbed of the presidency. President Bush also faced a tough situation in Congress—a very slim Republican majority in the House and a 50–50 split in the Senate, whose Democratic members included the outgoing First Lady, Hillary Clinton, now the freshman senator from New York.

From the first days of his presidency, however, Bush gave clear indications that his presidency would be very different from that of Clinton—and even from that of his father, George H. W. Bush. He proposed a domestic agenda that pushed tax cuts and education reform. More significantly, however, his administration charted a unilateralist course for American foreign policy that placed its faith in American power—economic and military. As a result Bush pushed for the development of a domestic missile defense system resembling the Reagan-era Strategic Defense Initiative (SDI, also known as Star Wars). When critics pointed out that implementation of the new defense system would violate the 1972 Anti-Ballistic Missile Treaty with the Soviet Union signed by President Nixon, Bush simply withdrew the United States from the treaty.

Everything changed for Bush at 8:46 a.m. on September 11, 2001, when a band of hijackers crashed a jet aircraft into the north tower of the World Trade Center in New York City. Eighteen minutes later another group of hijackers flew another plane into the south tower, bringing both to the ground within two hours of the initial impact. In addition, slightly more than an hour after the first impact, a third craft crashed into the Pentagon. A fourth plane was also hijacked, but its passengers stormed the cockpit and brought it down before it could reach its intended target. In all, almost three thousand victims were killed in the attacks—more than were killed in the assault on Pearl Harbor in 1941.

For Bush, 9/11 refocused his administration's attention firmly on national defense. The powers he called for—and received—to act against American enemies had not been used since the middle of the Vietnam War. He assured the nation that everything possible would be done to bring the persons who planned the attacks to justice and to relentlessly pursue anyone, and any country, that tried to shelter them. In a reiteration of his administration's unilateralism, he also warned the world that "either you are with us or you are against us."

Bush's first target was the fundamentalist Islamist government in Afghanistan called the Taliban, which had sheltered the al-Qaeda terrorists who perpetrated the 9/11 attacks. Within a month the United States began bombing Taliban and al-Qaeda targets in Afghanistan. By December, the Taliban had been driven from power—although many Taliban leaders and Osama bin Laden, head of al-Qaeda, were neither captured nor killed.

Bush's quick and deliberate actions led Americans to understand that their interests were being protected. That unanimity, however, was shattered in 2002, when Bush called for further sanctions against Iraq, claiming that the country's leader, Saddam Hussein, had concealed weapons of mass destruction from United Nations inspectors. As a result Bush, with support from Great Britain, launched an invasion of Iraq early in 2003. Although U.S. troops quickly overran the country and captured Baghdad, American occupation of the country led to abuses of power that culminated in the release of photographs of Iraqi prisoners being abused by American captors at Abu Ghraib prison. Despite these problems, Bush won reelection in 2004 over his Democratic challenger John Kerry, a veteran of the Vietnam War.

The suggestions of administrative incompetence suggested by the abuses of Abu Ghraib were compounded when Hurricane Katrina struck the Gulf Coast in August 2005. The hurricane, one of the worst to hit the United States, washed out the levees that protected New Orleans and flooded the city. By the time the storm ended, four-fifths of the city was under water, and more than eighteen hundred people, most of them poor and black, were dead. The administration's weak response—a week went by before the National Guard arrived to assist with civilian evacuations—led to accusations that racial bias was still rampant in twenty-first-century America.

The Bush administration also reaped the whirlwind of years of financial deregulation dating to the Reagan era when the market for subprime mortgages collapsed in 2007. Unregulated speculation in the housing market—augmented by unethical practices by some financial firms—led to a housing bubble that burst when people who had obtained unaffordable mortgages defaulted on them in large numbers. As a result, credit markets froze, businesses laid off employees, and the crisis deepened, becoming the worst financial downturn in the United States since the Great Depression. Efforts by the Bush administration to prop up financial markets were perceived as directed at the same individuals and institutions that had caused the crisis in the first place. As a result, Bush left the White House in 2009 as he had come into it—under a cloud of doubt.

First Inaugural Address

Washington, D.C.
January 20, 2001

THE SWEARING-IN CEREMONY of George W. Bush was the first presidential inauguration to be designated a "national special security event" and placed under the supervision of the Secret Service. With thousands of protesters converging on Washington, the police closed off two subway stations and a large section of the Mall and established a series of checkpoints where bags could be inspected for weapons.

Against this backdrop of serious division, Bush's 14-minute inaugural address, written by Mike Gerson, asked the nation to unite behind common ideals and to adopt an ethic of mutual service and responsibility. Former White House speechwriter William Safire noted approvingly, "There was more philosophy in Bush's well-delivered speech than met the ear."

Thank you all. Chief Justice Rehnquist, President Carter, President Bush, President Clinton, distinguished guests, and my fellow citizens. The peaceful transfer of authority is rare in history, yet common in our country. With a simple oath, we affirm old traditions and make new beginnings. As I begin, I thank President Clinton for his service to our nation. And I thank Vice President Gore for a contest conducted with spirit and ended with grace.

I am honored and humbled to stand here, where so many of America's leaders have come before me, and so many will follow.

We have a place, all of us, in a long story, a story we continue, but whose end we will not see. It is the story of a new world that became a friend and liberator of the old. The story of a slaveholding society that became a servant of freedom. The story of a power that went into the world to protect but not possess, to defend but not to conquer. It is the American story, a story of flawed and fallible people, united across the generations by grand and enduring ideals.

The grandest of these ideals is an unfolding American promise: that everyone belongs, that everyone deserves a chance, that no insignificant person was ever born. Americans are called to enact this promise in our lives and in our laws. And though our nation has sometimes halted, and sometimes delayed, we must follow no other course.

Through much of the last century, America's faith in freedom and democracy was a rock in a raging sea. Now it is a seed upon the wind, taking root in many nations. Our democratic faith is more than the creed of our country, it is the inborn hope of our humanity, an ideal we carry but do not own, a trust we bear and pass along. And even after nearly 225 years, we have a long way yet to travel.

While many of our citizens prosper, others doubt the promise N even the justice N of our own country. The ambitions of some Americans are limited by failing schools and hidden prejudice and the circumstances of their birth. And sometimes our differences run so deep, it seems we share a continent, but not a country.

We do not accept this, and we will not allow it. Our unity, our union, is the serious work of leaders and citizens in every generation. And this is my solemn pledge: I will work to build a single nation of justice and opportunity. I know this is in our reach, because we are guided by a power larger than ourselves, who creates us equal in his image. And we are confident in principles that unite and lead us onward.

America has never been united by blood or birth or soil. We are bound by ideals that move us beyond our backgrounds, lift us above our interests, and teach us what it means to be citizens. Every child must be taught these principles. Every citizen must uphold them. And every immigrant, by embracing these ideals, makes our country more, not less, American.

Today we affirm a new commitment to live out our nation's promise through civility, courage, compassion, and character.

America, at its best, matches a commitment to principle with a concern for civility. A civil society demands from each of us goodwill and respect, fair dealing and forgiveness.

Some seem to believe that our politics can afford to be petty because in a time of peace the stakes of our debates appear small. But the stakes for America are never small. If our country does not lead the cause of freedom, it will not be led. If we do not turn the hearts of children toward knowledge and character, we will lose their gifts and undermine their idealism. If we permit our economy to drift and decline, the vulnerable will suffer most.

We must live up to the calling we share. Civility is not a tactic or a sentiment. It is the determined choice of trust over cynicism, of community over chaos. And this commitment, if keep it, is a way to shared accomplishment.

America at its best is also courageous. Our national courage has been clear in times of depression and war, when defeating common dangers defined our common good. Now we must chose if the example of our fathers and mothers will inspire us or condemn us. We must show courage in a time of blessing, by confronting problems instead of passing them on to future generations.

Together, we will reclaim America's schools before ignorance and apathy claim more young lives. We will reform Social Security and Medicare, sparing our children from struggles we have the power to prevent. And we will reduce taxes to recover the momentum of our economy and reward the effort and enterprise of working Americans. We will build our defenses beyond challenge, lest weakness invite challenge. We will confront weapons of mass destruction, so that a new century is spared new horrors.

The enemies of liberty and our country should make no mistake, America remains engaged in the world, by history and by choice, shaping a balance of power that favors freedom. We will defend our allies and our interests. We will show purpose without arrogance. We will meet aggression and bad faith with resolve and strength. And to all nations, we will speak for the values that gave our nation birth.

America at its best is compassionate.

In the quiet of American conscience, we know that deep, persistent poverty is unworthy of our nation's promise. And whatever our views of its cause, we can agree that children at risk are not at fault. Abandonment and abuse are not acts of God, they are failures of love. And the proliferation of prisons, however necessary, is no substitute for hope and order in our souls.

Where there is suffering, there is duty. Americans in need are not strangers, they are citizens; not problems, but priorities; and all of us are diminished when any are hopeless.

Government has great responsibilities, for public safety and public health, for civil rights and common schools. Yet compassion is the work of a nation, not just a government. And some needs and hurts are so deep they will only respond to a mentor's touch or a pastor's prayer. Church and charity, synagogue and mosque, lend our communities their humanity and they will have an honored place in our plans and in our laws.

Many in our country do not know the pain of poverty. But we can listen to those who do. And I can pledge our nation to a goal: When we see that wounded traveler on the road to Jericho, we will not pass to the other side.

America at its best is a place where personal responsibility is valued and expected. Encouraging responsibility is not a search for scapegoats, it is a call to conscience. And though it requires sacrifice, it brings a deeper fulfillment. We find the fullness of life, not only in options, but in commitments. And we find that children and community are the commitments that set us free.

Our public interest depends on private character, on civic duty and family bonds and basic fairness, on uncounted, unhonored acts of decency which give direction to our freedom.

Sometimes in life we are called to do great things. But as a saint of our times has said, every day we are called to do small things with great love. The most important tasks of a democracy are done by everyone.

I will live and lead by these principles: to advance my convictions with civility, to pursue the public interest with courage, to speak for greater justice and compassion, to call for responsibility and try to live it as well. In all these ways, I will bring the values of our history to the care of our times.

What you do is as important as anything government does. I ask you to seek a common good beyond your comfort, to defend needed reforms against easy attacks, to serve your nation, beginning with your neighbor. I ask you to be citizens. Citizens, not spectators. Citizens, not subjects. Responsible citizens, building communities of service and a nation of character.

Americans are generous and strong and decent, not because we believe in ourselves, but because we hold beliefs beyond ourselves. When this spirit of citizenship is missing, no government program can replace it. When this spirit is present, no wrong can stand against it.

After the Declaration of Independence was signed, Virginia statesman John Page wrote to Thomas Jefferson: "We know the race is not to the swift, nor the battle to the strong. Do you not think an angel rides in the whirlwind and directs this storm?"

Much time has passed since Jefferson arrived for his inauguration. The years and changes accumulate. But the themes of this day he would know: our nation's grand story of courage, and its simple dream of dignity. We are not this story's author, who fills time and eternity with his purpose. Yet his purpose is achieved in our duty and our duty is fulfilled in service to one another.

Never tiring, never yielding, never finishing, we renew that purpose today: to make our country more just and generous, to affirm the dignity of our lives and every life.

This work continues. This story goes on. And an angel still rides in the whirlwind and directs this storm.

God bless you all, and God bless America.

Address to the Nation on September 11, 2001

Washington, D.C.

September 11, 2001

ON THE evening of September 11, 2001, President George W. Bush spoke to the nation about the events that occurred that morning in New York, Washington, DC, and rural Pennsylvania. In doing so, he addressed the fears of an uncertain nation and demonstrated firm leadership in response to a national emergency. His determination and confidence during the address rallied the American people and bolstered public support for the coming war on terror and Bush's domestic security initiatives.

President Bush points out that with the exception of the attack on Pearl Harbor in 1941, the United States had fought its wars on foreign soil since the end of the Civil War. After identifying the attacks as terrorist sponsored, he suggests that America was targeted largely because it stands for freedom, opportunity, and values that are antithetical to those held by the terrorist organizations responsible for the 9/11 attacks. He reassures the nation that its military and emergency response forces are fully prepared to detect, prevent, and, if necessary, respond to further acts of terrorism. He then calls for the support of other nations in the fight against terrorism. Most significantly, he declares that states that harbor terrorists will be held responsible for crimes committed by those terrorists.

Good evening. Today our fellow citizens, our way of life, our very freedom came under attack in a series of deliberate and deadly terrorist acts. The victims were in airplanes or in their offices: secretaries, business men and women, military and Federal workers, moms and dads, friends and neighbors. Thousands of lives were suddenly ended by evil, despicable acts of terror.

The pictures of airplanes flying into buildings, fires burning, huge structures collapsing have filled us with disbelief, terrible sadness, and a quiet, unyielding anger. These acts of mass murder were intended to frighten our Nation into chaos and retreat, but they have failed. Our country is strong.

A great people has been moved to defend a great nation. Terrorist attacks can shake the foundations of our biggest buildings, but they cannot touch the foundation of America. These acts shattered steel, but they cannot dent the steel of American resolve. America was targeted for attack because we're the brightest beacon for freedom and opportunity in the world. And no one will keep that light from shining.

Today our Nation saw evil, the very worst of human nature. And we responded with the best of America, with the daring of our rescue workers, with the caring for strangers and neighbors who came to give blood and help in any way they could.

Immediately following the first attack, I implemented our Government's emergency response plans. Our military is powerful, and it's prepared. Our emergency teams are working in New York City and Washington, DC, to help with local rescue efforts.

Our first priority is to get help to those who have been injured and to take every precaution to protect our citizens at home and around the world from further attacks.

The functions of our Government continue without interruption. Federal agencies in Washington which had to be evacuated today are reopening for essential personnel tonight and will be open for business tomorrow. Our financial institutions remain strong, and the American economy will be open for business as well.

The search is underway for those who are behind these evil acts. I've directed the full resources of our intelligence and law enforcement communities to find those responsible and to bring them to justice. We will make no distinction between the terrorists who committed these acts and those who harbor them.

I appreciate so very much the Members of Congress who have joined me in strongly condemning these attacks. And on behalf of the American people, I thank the many world leaders who have called to offer their condolences and assistance.

America and our friends and allies join with all those who want peace and security in the world, and we stand together to win the war against terrorism.

Tonight I ask for your prayers for all those who grieve, for the children whose worlds have been shattered, for all whose sense of safety and security has been threatened. And I pray they will be comforted by a power greater than any of us, spoken through the ages in Psalm 23: "Even though I walk through the valley of the shadow of death, I fear no evil, for You are with me."

This is a day when all Americans from every walk of life unite in our resolve for justice and peace. America has stood down enemies before, and we will do so this time. None of us will ever forget this day. Yet, we go forward to defend freedom and all that is good and just in our world.

Thank you. Good night, and God bless America.

Second State of the Union Address

Washington, D.C.

January 29, 2002

IN HIS SECOND STATE of the Union Address, delivered on January 29, 2002, George W. Bush calls for an ongoing war on terror in response to the attacks of September 11, 2001, which destroyed the World Trade Center in New York, NY, damaged the Pentagon, and killed thousands of people. He identifies Iran, Iraq, and North Korea as members of an axis of evil that threatens world peace, and he promises to take action to prevent terrorist strikes against the United States. He also notes that the regime in Iraq defied weapons inspections by the United Nations and used chemical weapons against its own people—an early indication of future action against Iraq. The president discusses the continuing threat posed to the United States and other nations by global terrorism and highlights some of the operations that the nation and its allies were undertaking to counter the danger. He also asserts what will become known as the Bush Doctrine, declaring that the United States will act unilaterally and launch preemptive strikes to stop terrorist activities if it believes its interests or its safety are threatened. Bush's so-called axis of evil speech led to a new codification of national security, a war with Iraq, and the destruction of Saddam Hussein's regime.

As we gather tonight, our Nation is at war; our economy is in recession; and the civilized world faces unprecedented dangers. Yet, the state of our Union has never been stronger.

We last met in an hour of shock and suffering. In 4 short months, our Nation has comforted the victims, begun to rebuild New York and the Pentagon, rallied a great coalition, captured, arrested, and rid the world of thousands of terrorists, destroyed Afghanistan's terrorist training camps, saved a people from starvation, and freed a country from brutal oppression.

The American flag flies again over our Embassy in Kabul. Terrorists who once occupied Afghanistan now occupy cells at Guantanamo Bay. And terrorist leaders who urged followers to sacrifice their lives are running for their own.

America and Afghanistan are now allies against terror. We'll be partners in rebuilding that country. And this evening we welcomed the distinguished interim leader of a liberated Afghanistan, Chairman Hamid Karzai.

The last time we met in this Chamber, the mothers and daughters of Afghanistan were captives in their own homes, forbidden from working or going to school. Today, women are free and are part of Afghanistan's new Government. And we welcome the new Minister of Women's Affairs, Dr. Sima Samar.

Our progress is a tribute to the spirit of the Afghan people, to the resolve of our coalition, and to the might of the United States military. When I called our troops into action, I did so with complete confidence in their courage and skill. And tonight, thanks to them, we are winning the war on terror. The men and women of our Armed Forces have delivered a message now clear to every enemy of the United States: Even 7,000 miles away, across oceans and continents, on mountaintops and in caves, you will not escape the justice of this Nation.

For many Americans, these 4 months have brought sorrow and pain that will never completely go away. Every day a retired firefighter returns to Ground Zero to feel closer to his two sons who died there. At a memorial in New York, a little boy left his football with a note for his lost father: "Dear Daddy, please take this to heaven. I don't want to play football until I can play with you again some day."

Last month, at the grave of her husband, Micheal, a CIA officer and marine who died in Mazar-e-Sharif, Shannon Spann said these words of farewell, "Semper Fi, my love." Shannon is with us tonight. Shannon, I assure you and all who have lost a loved one that our cause is just, and our country will never forget the debt we owe Micheal and all who gave their lives for freedom.

Our cause is just, and it continues. Our discoveries in Afghanistan confirmed our worst fears and showed us the true scope of the task ahead. We have seen the depth of our enemies' hatred in videos where they laugh about the loss of innocent life. And the depth of their hatred is equaled by the madness of the destruction they design. We have found diagrams of American nuclear power plants and public water facilities, detailed instructions for making chemical weapons, surveillance maps of American cities, and thorough descriptions of landmarks in America and throughout the world.

What we have found in Afghanistan confirms that, far from ending there, our war against terror is only beginning. Most of the 19 men who hijacked planes on September the 11th were trained in Afghanistan's camps, and so were tens of thousands of others. Thousands of dangerous killers, schooled in the methods of murder, often supported by outlaw regimes, are now spread throughout the world like ticking time bombs, set to go off without warning.

Thanks to the work of our law enforcement officials and coalition partners, hundreds of terrorists have been arrested. Yet, tens of thousands of trained terrorists are still at large. These enemies view the entire world as a battlefield, and we must pursue them wherever they are. So long as training camps operate, so long as nations harbor terrorists, freedom is at risk. And America and our allies must not and will not allow it.

Our Nation will continue to be steadfast and patient and persistent in the pursuit of two great objectives. First, we will shut down terrorist camps, disrupt terrorist plans, and bring terrorists to justice. And second, we must prevent the terrorists and regimes who seek chemical, biological, or nuclear weapons from threatening the United States and the world.

Our military has put the terror training camps of Afghanistan out of business, yet camps still exist in at least a dozen countries. A terrorist underworld, including groups like Hamas, Hizballah, Islamic Jihad, Jaish-e-Mohammed, operates in remote jungles and deserts and hides in the centers of large cities.

While the most visible military action is in Afghanistan, America is acting elsewhere. We now have troops in the Philippines, helping to train that country's armed forces to go after terrorist cells that have executed an American and still hold hostages. Our soldiers, working with the Bosnian Government, seized terrorists who were plotting to bomb our Embassy. Our Navy is patrolling the coast of Africa to block the shipment of weapons and the establishment of terrorist camps in Somalia.

My hope is that all nations will heed our call and eliminate the terrorist parasites who threaten their countries and our own. Many nations are acting forcefully. Pakistan is now cracking down on terror, and I admire the strong leadership of President Musharraf. But some governments will be timid in the face of terror. And make no mistake about it: If they do not act, America will.

Our second goal is to prevent regimes that sponsor terror from threatening America or our friends and allies with weapons of mass destruction. Some of these regimes have been pretty quiet since September the 11th, but we know their true nature.

North Korea is a regime arming with missiles and weapons of mass destruction, while starving its citizens.

Iran aggressively pursues these weapons and exports terror, while an unelected few repress the Iranian people's hope for freedom.

Iraq continues to flaunt its hostility toward America and to support terror. The Iraqi regime has plotted to develop anthrax and nerve gas and nuclear weapons for over a decade. This is a regime that has already used poison gas to murder thousands of its own citizens, leaving the bodies of mothers huddled over their dead children. This is a regime that agreed to international inspections, then kicked out the inspectors. This is a regime that has something to hide from the civilized world.

States like these and their terrorist allies constitute an axis of evil, arming to threaten the peace of the world. By seeking weapons of mass destruction, these regimes pose a grave and growing danger. They could provide these arms to terrorists, giving them the means to match their hatred. They could attack our allies or attempt to blackmail the United States. In any of these cases, the price of indifference would be catastrophic.

We will work closely with our coalition to deny terrorists and their state sponsors the materials, technology, and expertise to make and deliver weapons of mass destruction. We will develop and deploy effective missile defenses to protect America and our allies from sudden attack. And all nations should know: America will do what is necessary to ensure our Nation's security.

We'll be deliberate; yet, time is not on our side. I will not wait on events while dangers gather. I will not stand by as peril draws closer and closer. The United States of America will not permit the world's most dangerous regimes to threaten us with the world's most destructive weapons.

Our war on terror is well begun, but it is only begun. This campaign may not be finished on our watch; yet, it must be and it will be waged on our watch. We can't stop short. If we stop now, leaving terror camps intact and terrorist states unchecked, our sense of security would be false and temporary. History has called America and our allies to action, and it is both our responsibility and our privilege to fight freedom's fight.

Our first priority must always be the security of our Nation, and that will be reflected in the budget I send to Congress. My budget supports three great goals for America: We will win this war; we will protect our homeland; and we will revive our economy.

September the 11th brought out the best in America and the best in this Congress. And I join the American people in applauding your unity and resolve. Now Americans deserve to have this same spirit directed toward addressing problems here at home. I'm a proud member of my party. Yet as we act to win the war, protect our people, and create jobs in America, we must act, first and foremost, not as Republicans, not as Democrats but as Americans.

It costs a lot to fight this war. We have spent more than a billion dollars a month, over $30 million a day, and we must be prepared for future operations. Afghanistan proved that expensive precision weapons defeat the enemy and spare innocent lives, and we need more of them. We need to replace aging aircraft and make our military more agile to put our troops anywhere in the world quickly and safely. Our men and women in uniform deserve the best weapons, the best equipment, the best training, and they also deserve another pay raise.

My budget includes the largest increase in defense spending in two decades, because while the price of freedom and security is high, it is never too high. Whatever it costs to defend our country, we will pay.

The next priority of my budget is to do everything possible to protect our citizens and strengthen our Nation against the ongoing threat of another attack. Time and distance from the events of September the 11th will not make us safer unless we act on its lessons. America is no longer protected by vast oceans. We are protected from attack only by vigorous action abroad and increased vigilance at home.

My budget nearly doubles funding for a sustained strategy of homeland security, focused on four key areas: bioterrorism, emergency response, airport and border security, and improved intelligence. We will develop vaccines to fight anthrax and other deadly diseases. We'll increase funding to help States and communities train and equip our heroic police and firefighters. We will improve intelligence collection and sharing, expand patrols at our borders, strengthen the security of air travel, and use technology to track the arrivals and departures of visitors to the United States.

Homeland security will make America not only stronger but, in many ways, better. Knowledge gained from bioterrorism research will improve public health. Stronger police and fire departments will mean safer neighborhoods. Stricter border enforcement will help combat illegal drugs. And as government works to better secure our homeland, America will continue to depend on the eyes and ears of alert citizens.

A few days before Christmas, an airline flight attendant spotted a passenger lighting a match. The crew and passengers quickly subdued the man, who had been trained by Al Qaida and was armed with explosives. The people on that plane were alert and, as a result, likely saved nearly 200 lives. And tonight we welcome and thank flight attendants Hermis Moutardier and Christina Jones.

Once we have funded our national security and our homeland security, the final great priority of my budget is economic security for the American people. To achieve these great national objectives—to win the war, protect the homeland, and revitalize our economy—our budget will run a deficit that will be small and short term, so long as Congress restrains spending and acts in a fiscally responsible manner. We have clear priorities, and we must act at home with the same purpose and resolve we have shown overseas. We'll prevail in the war, and we will defeat this recession.

Americans who have lost their jobs need our help, and I support extending unemployment benefits and direct assistance for health care coverage. Yet, American workers want more than unemployment checks; they want a steady paycheck. When America works, America prospers, so my economic security plan can be summed up in one word: jobs.

Good jobs begin with good schools, and here we've made a fine start. Republicans and Democrats worked together to achieve historic education reform so that no child is left behind. I was proud to work with members of both parties: Chairman John Boehner and Congressman George Miller; Senator Judd Gregg. And I was so proud of our work, I even had nice things to say about my friend Ted Kennedy. I know the folks at the Crawford coffee shop couldn't believe I'd say such a thing but our work on this bill shows what is possible if we set aside posturing and focus on results.

There is more to do. We need to prepare our children to read and succeed in school with improved Head Start and early childhood development programs. We must upgrade our teacher colleges and teacher training and launch a major recruiting drive with a great goal for America, a quality teacher in every classroom.

Good jobs also depend on reliable and affordable energy. This Congress must act to encourage conservation, promote technology, build infrastructure, and it must act to increase energy production at home so America is less dependent on foreign oil.

Good jobs depend on expanded trade. Selling into new markets creates new jobs, so I ask Congress to finally approve trade promotion authority.

On these two key issues, trade and energy, the House of Representatives has acted to create jobs, and I urge the Senate to pass this legislation.

Good jobs depend on sound tax policy. Last year, some in this Hall thought my tax relief plan was too small; some thought it was too big. But when the checks arrived in the mail, most Americans thought tax relief was just about right. Congress listened to the people and responded by reducing tax rates, doubling the child credit, and ending the death tax. For the sake of long-term growth and to help Americans plan for the future, let's make these tax cuts permanent.

The way out of this recession, the way to create jobs, is to grow the economy by encouraging investment in factories and equipment and by speeding up tax relief so people have more money to spend. For the sake of American workers, let's pass a stimulus package.

Good jobs must be the aim of welfare reform. As we reauthorize these important reforms, we must always remember the goal is to reduce dependency on government and offer every American the dignity of a job.

Americans know economic security can vanish in an instant without health security. I ask Congress to join me this year to enact a patients' bill of rights, to give uninsured workers credits to help buy health coverage, to approve an historic increase in the spending for veterans' health, and to give seniors a sound and modern Medicare system that includes coverage for prescription drugs.

A good job should lead to security in retirement. I ask Congress to enact new safeguards for 401(k) and pension plans. Employees who have worked hard and saved all their lives should not have to risk losing everything if their company fails. Through stricter accounting standards and tougher disclosure requirements, corporate America must be made more accountable to employees and shareholders and held to the highest standards of conduct.

Retirement security also depends upon keeping the commitments of Social Security, and we will. We must make Social Security financially stable and allow personal retirement accounts for younger workers who choose them.

Members, you and I will work together in the months ahead on other issues: productive farm policy; a cleaner environment; broader homeownership, especially among minorities; and ways to encourage the good work of charities and faith-based groups. I ask you to join me on these important domestic issues in the same spirit of cooperation we've applied to our war against terrorism.

During these last few months, I've been humbled and privileged to see the true character of this country in a time of testing. Our enemies believed America was weak and materialistic, that we would splinter in fear and selfishness. They were as wrong as they are evil.

The American people have responded magnificently, with courage and compassion, strength and resolve. As I have met the heroes, hugged the families, and looked into the tired faces of rescuers, I have stood in awe of the American people.

And I hope you will join me—I hope you will join me in expressing thanks to one American for the strength and calm and comfort she brings to our Nation in crisis, our First Lady, Laura Bush.

None of us would ever wish the evil that was done on September the 11th. Yet, after America was attacked, it was as if our entire country looked into a mirror and saw our better selves. We were reminded that we are citizens with obligations to each other, to our country, and to history. We began to think less of the goods we can accumulate and more about the good we can do.

For too long our culture has said, "If it feels good, do it." Now America is embracing a new ethic and a new creed, "Let's roll." In the sacrifice of soldiers, the fierce brotherhood of firefighters, and the bravery and generosity of ordinary citizens, we have glimpsed what a new culture of responsibility could look like. We want to be a nation that serves goals larger than self. We've been offered a unique opportunity, and we must not let this moment pass.

My call tonight is for every American to commit at least 2 years, 4,000 hours over the rest of your lifetime, to the service of your neighbors and your Nation. Many are already serving, and I thank you. If you aren't sure how to help, I've got a good place to start. To sustain and extend the best that has emerged in America, I invite you to join the new USA Freedom Corps. The Freedom Corps will focus on three areas of need: responding in case of crisis at home; rebuilding our communities; and extending American compassion throughout the world.

One purpose of the USA Freedom Corps will be homeland security. America needs retired doctors and nurses who can be mobilized in major emergencies, volunteers to help police and fire departments, transportation and utility workers well-trained in spotting danger.

Our country also needs citizens working to rebuild our communities. We need mentors to love children, especially children whose parents are in prison. And we need more talented teachers in troubled schools. USA Freedom Corps will expand and improve the good efforts of AmeriCorps and Senior Corps to recruit more than 200,000 new volunteers.

And America needs citizens to extend the compassion of our country to every part of the world. So we will renew the promise of the Peace Corps, double its volunteers over the next 5 years, and ask it to join a new effort to encourage development and education and opportunity in the Islamic world.

This time of adversity offers a unique moment of opportunity, a moment we must seize to change our culture. Through the gathering momentum of millions of acts of service and decency and kindness, I know we can overcome evil with greater good.

And we have a great opportunity during this time of war to lead the world toward the values that will bring lasting peace. All fathers and mothers, in all societies, want their children to be educated and live free from poverty and violence. No people on Earth yearn to be oppressed or aspire to servitude or eagerly await the midnight knock of the secret police. If anyone doubts this, let them look to Afghanistan, where the Islamic "street" greeted the fall of tyranny with song and celebration. Let the skeptics look to Islam's own rich history, with its centuries of learning and tolerance and progress. America will lead by defending liberty and justice because they are right and true and unchanging for all people everywhere.

No nation owns these aspirations, and no nation is exempt from them. We have no intention of imposing our culture. But America will always stand firm for the nonnegotiable demands of human dignity: the rule of law; limits on the power of the state; respect for women; private property; free speech; equal justice; and religious tolerance.

America will take the side of brave men and women who advocate these values around the world, including the Islamic world, because we have a greater objective than eliminating threats and containing resentment. We seek a just and peaceful world beyond the war on terror.

In this moment of opportunity, a common danger is erasing old rivalries. America is working with Russia and China and India, in ways we have never before, to achieve peace and prosperity. In every region, free markets and free trade and free societies are proving their power to lift lives. Together with friends and allies from Europe to Asia and Africa to Latin America, we will demonstrate that the forces of terror cannot stop the momentum of freedom.

The last time I spoke here, I expressed the hope that life would return to normal. In some ways, it has. In others, it never will. Those of us who have lived through these challenging times have been changed by them. We've come to know truths that we will never question: Evil is real, and it must be opposed. Beyond all differences of race or creed, we are one country, mourning together and facing danger together. Deep in the American character, there is honor, and it is stronger than cynicism. And many have discovered again that even in tragedy—especially in tragedy— God is near.

In a single instant, we realized that this will be a decisive decade in the history of liberty, that we've been called to a unique role in human events. Rarely has the world faced a choice more clear or consequential.

Our enemies send other people's children on missions of suicide and murder. They embrace tyranny and death as a cause and a creed. We stand for a different choice, made long ago on the day of our founding. We affirm it again today. We choose freedom and the dignity of every life.

Steadfast in our purpose, we now press on. We have known freedom's price. We have shown freedom's power. And in this great conflict, my fellow Americans, we will see freedom's victory.

Thank you all. May God bless.

Address to the Nation on Military Operations in Iraq

Washington, D.C.

March 19, 2003

AFTER THE TERRORIST attacks of September 2001, the Bush administration accused the Iraqi regime of Saddam Hussein of having an ongoing program for weapons of mass destruction, of supporting terrorism, and of violating a range of United Nations Security Council resolutions enacted in the aftermath of the 1991 Gulf War. On March 19, 2003, Bush went on television to explain to the American people why the United States was launching military strikes against Iraq.

Bush opens the address by declaring that the war was being initiated "to disarm Iraq, to free its people and to defend the world from grave danger." To counter criticism that the conflict lacked international support, Bush notes that the U.S.-led anti–Saddam Hussein coalition included thirty-five nations (although at first only four contributed troops to the invasion force). He further declares that the United States has no territorial ambitions in Iraq and only seeks to remove a tyrannical regime and bring freedom to the Iraqi people.

Although the Iraq War was popular when it began, it quickly lost support when an anti-U.S. insurgency spread through Iraq, eventually costing the lives of thousands of servicepersons. Subsequent inspections failed to produce any Iraqi weapons of mass destruction. By 2008, only approximately one-third of Americans continued to support the war.

My fellow citizens, at this hour, American and coalition forces are in the early stages of military operations to disarm Iraq, to free its people, and to defend the world from grave danger.

On my orders, coalition forces have begun striking selected targets of military importance to undermine Saddam Hussein's ability to wage war. These are opening stages of what will be a broad and concerted campaign. More than 35 countries are giving crucial support, from the use of naval and air bases, to help with intelligence and logistics, to the deployment of combat units. Every nation in this coalition has chosen to bear the duty and share the honor of serving in our common defense.

To all the men and women of the United States Armed Forces now in the Middle East, the peace of a troubled world and the hopes of an oppressed people now depend on you. That trust is well-placed. The enemies you confront will come to know your skill and bravery. The people you liberate will witness the honorable and decent spirit of the American military.

In this conflict, America faces an enemy who has no regard for conventions of war or rules of morality. Saddam Hussein has placed Iraqi troops and equipment in civilian areas, attempting to use innocent men, women, and children as shields for his own military, a final atrocity against his people. I want Americans and all the world to know that coalition forces will make every effort to spare innocent civilians from harm.

A campaign on the harsh terrain of a nation as large as California could be longer and more difficult than some predict. And helping Iraqis achieve a united, stable, and free country will require our sustained commitment. We come to Iraq with respect for its citizens, for their great civilization, and for the religious faiths they practice. We have no ambition in Iraq except to remove a threat and restore control of that country to its own people.

I know that the families of our military are praying that all those who serve will return safely and soon. Millions of Americans are praying with you for the safety of your loved ones and for the protection of the innocent. For your sacrifice, you have the gratitude and respect of the American people. And you can know that our forces will be coming home as soon as their work is done.

Our Nation enters this conflict reluctantly. Yet our purpose is sure. The people of the United States and our friends and allies will not live at the mercy of an outlaw regime that threatens the peace with weapons of mass murder. We will meet that threat now with our Army, Air Force, Navy, Coast Guard, and Marines, so that we do not have to meet it later with armies of firefighters and police and doctors on the streets of our cities.

Now that conflict has come, the only way to limit its duration is to apply decisive force. And I assure you, this will not be a campaign of half measures, and we will accept no outcome but victory.

My fellow citizens, the dangers to our country and the world will be overcome. We will pass through this time of peril and carry on the work of peace. We will defend our freedom. We will bring freedom to others, and we will prevail.

May God bless our country and all who defend her.

Second Inaugural Address

Washington, D.C

January 20, 2005

GEORGE W. BUSH'S first term was dominated by the terrorist attacks of September 11, 2001. At the beginning of his second term, he reminds Americans that for most of the twentieth century the United States was engaged in struggles meant to defend democracy and freedom. Bush asserts that the demise of Soviet communism ushered in "years of repose, years of sabbatical" that were superseded by the war on terror. He says that in the post-9/11 era the only way to ensure freedom in the United States is to extend liberty around the world. He pledges to support democratic movements anywhere in the world while assuring Americans that such efforts would not be conducted mainly through military action. Instead, a variety of economic, diplomatic, and social efforts would be coordinated to pressure antidemocratic regimes. Bush promises that the United States would "not impose our own style of government on the unwilling," but would try to aid other nations in the development of governments and political systems that would match their individual cultural and historical backgrounds. Bush notes that any attempt to expand democracy is a multiyear process. Like the war on terror, the campaign to spread democracy would continue after the end of his presidency.

On this day, prescribed by law and marked by ceremony, we celebrate the durable wisdom of our Constitution and recall the deep commitments that unite our country. I am grateful for the honor of this hour, mindful of the consequential times in which we live, and determined to fulfill the oath that I have sworn and you have witnessed.

At this second gathering, our duties are defined not by the words I use but by the history we have seen together. For a half a century, America defended our own freedom by standing watch on distant borders. After the shipwreck of communism came years of relative quiet, years of repose, years of sabbatical, and then there came a day of fire.

We have seen our vulnerability, and we have seen its deepest source. For as long as whole regions of the world simmer in resentment and tyranny, prone to ideologies that feed hatred and excuse murder, violence will gather and multiply in destructive power and cross the most defended borders and raise a mortal threat. There is only one force of history that can break the reign of hatred and resentment and expose the pretensions of tyrants and reward the hopes of the decent and tolerant, and that is the force of human freedom.

We are led, by events and common sense, to one conclusion: The survival of liberty in our land increasingly depends on the success of liberty in other lands. The best hope for peace in our world is the expansion of freedom in all the world.

America's vital interests and our deepest beliefs are now one. From the day of our founding, we have proclaimed that every man and woman on this Earth has rights and dignity and matchless value, because they bear the image of the Maker of heaven and Earth. Across the generations, we have proclaimed the imperative of self-government, because no one is fit to be a master and no one deserves to be a slave. Advancing these ideals is the mission that created our Nation. It is the honorable achievement of our fathers. Now, it is the urgent requirement of our Nation's security and the calling of our time.

So it is the policy of the United States to seek and support the growth of democratic movements and institutions in every nation and culture, with the ultimate goal of ending tyranny in our world. This is not primarily the task of arms, though we will defend ourselves and our friends by force of arms when necessary. Freedom, by its nature, must be chosen and defended by citizens and sustained by the rule of law and the protection of minorities. And when the soul of a nation finally speaks, the institutions that arise may reflect customs and traditions very different from our own. America will not impose our own style of government on the unwilling. Our goal instead is to help others find their own voice, attain their own freedom, and make their own way.

The great objective of ending tyranny is the concentrated work of generations. The difficulty of the task is no excuse for avoiding it. America's influence is not unlimited, but fortunately for the oppressed, America's influence is considerable and we will use it confidently in freedom's cause.

My most solemn duty is to protect this Nation and its people from further attacks and emerging threats. Some have unwisely chosen to test America's resolve and have found it firm. We will persistently clarify the choice before every ruler and every nation, the moral choice between oppression, which is always wrong, and freedom, which is eternally right.

America will not pretend that jailed dissidents prefer their chains or that women welcome humiliation and servitude or that any human being aspires to live at the mercy of bullies. We will encourage reform in other governments by making clear that success in our relations will require the decent treatment of their own people. America's belief in human dignity will guide our policies. Yet rights must be more than the grudging concessions of dictators. They are secured by free dissent and the participation of the governed. In the long run, there is no justice without freedom and there can be no human rights without human liberty.

Some, I know, have questioned the global appeal of liberty, though this time in history, four decades defined by the swiftest advance of freedom ever seen, is an odd time for doubt. Americans, of all people, should never be surprised by the power of our ideals. Eventually, the call of freedom comes to every mind and every soul. We do not accept the existence of permanent tyranny because we do not accept the possibility of permanent slavery. Liberty will come to those who love it.

Today, America speaks anew to the peoples of the world. All who live in tyranny and hopelessness can know: The United States will not ignore your oppression or excuse your oppressors. When you stand for your liberty, we will stand with you.

Democratic reformers facing repression, prison, or exile can know: America sees you for who you are, the future leaders of your free country.

The rulers of outlaw regimes can know that we still believe as Abraham Lincoln did: "Those who deny freedom to others deserve it not for themselves and, under the rule of a just God, cannot long retain it."

The leaders of governments with long habits of control need to know: To serve your people, you must learn to trust them. Start on this journey of progress and justice, and America will walk at your side.

And all the allies of the United States can know: We honor your friendship; we rely on your counsel; and we depend on your help. Division among free nations is a primary goal of freedom's enemies. The concerted effort of free nations to promote democracy is a prelude to our enemies' defeat.

Today I also speak anew to my fellow citizens. From all of you I have asked patience in the hard task of securing America, which you have granted in good measure. Our country has accepted obligations that are difficult to fulfill and would be dishonorable to abandon. Yet because we have acted in the great liberating tradition of this Nation, tens of millions have achieved their freedom. And as hope kindles hope, millions more will find it. By our efforts, we have lit a fire as well, a fire in the minds of men. It warms those who feel its power. It burns those who fight its progress. And one day this untamed fire of freedom will reach the darkest corners of our world.

A few Americans have accepted the hardest duties in this cause, in the quiet work of intelligence and diplomacy, the idealistic work of helping raise up free governments, the dangerous and necessary work of fighting our enemies. Some have shown their devotion to our country in deaths that honored their whole lives, and we will always honor their names and their sacrifice.

All Americans have witnessed this idealism and some for the first time. I ask our youngest citizens to believe the evidence of your eyes. You have seen duty and allegiance in the determined faces of our soldiers. You have seen that life is fragile and evil is real and courage triumphs. Make the choice to serve in a cause larger than your wants, larger than yourself, and in your days you will add not just to the wealth of our country but to its character.

America has need of idealism and courage because we have essential work at home, the unfinished work of American freedom. In a world moving toward liberty, we are determined to show the meaning and promise of liberty.

In America's ideal of freedom, citizens find the dignity and security of economic independence instead of laboring on the edge of subsistence. This is the broader definition of liberty that motivated the Homestead Act, the Social Security Act, and the GI bill of rights. And now we will extend this vision by reforming great institutions to serve the needs of our time. To give every American a stake in the promise and future of our country, we will bring the highest standards to our schools and build an ownership society. We will widen the ownership of homes and businesses, retirement savings, and health insurance, preparing our people for the challenges of life in a free society. By making every citizen an agent of his or her own destiny, we will give our fellow Americans greater freedom from want and fear and make our society more prosperous and just and equal.

In America's ideal of freedom, the public interest depends on private character, on integrity and tolerance toward others and the rule of conscience in our own lives. Self-government relies, in the end, on the governing of the self. That edifice of character is built in families, supported by communities with standards, and sustained in our national life by the truths of Sinai, the Sermon on the Mount, the words of the Koran, and the varied faiths of our people. Americans move forward in every generation by reaffirming all that is good and true that came before, ideals of justice and conduct that are the same yesterday, today, and forever.

In America's ideal of freedom, the exercise of rights is ennobled by service and mercy and a heart for the weak. Liberty for all does not mean independence from one another. Our Nation relies on men and women who look after a neighbor and surround the lost with love. Americans, at our best, value the life we see in one another and must always remember that even the unwanted have worth. And our country must abandon all the habits of racism, because we cannot carry the message of freedom and the baggage of bigotry at the same time.

From the perspective of a single day, including this day of dedication, the issues and questions before our country are many. From the viewpoint of centuries, the questions that come to us are narrowed and few: Did our generation advance the cause of freedom? And did our character bring credit to that cause?

These questions that judge us also unite us, because Americans of every party and background, Americans by choice and by birth are bound to one another in the cause of freedom. We have known divisions, which must be healed to move forward in great purposes, and I will strive in good faith to heal them. Yet those divisions do not define America. We felt the unity and fellowship of our Nation when freedom came under attack, and our response came like a single hand over a single heart. And we can feel that same unity and pride whenever America acts for good and the victims of disaster are given hope and the unjust encounter justice and the captives are set free.

We go forward with complete confidence in the eventual triumph of freedom, not because history runs on the wheels of inevitability—it is human choices that move events; not because we consider ourselves a chosen nation—God moves and chooses as He wills. We have confidence because freedom is the permanent hope of mankind, the hunger in dark places, the longing of the soul. When our Founders declared a new order of the ages, when soldiers died in wave upon wave for a union based on liberty, when citizens marched in peaceful outrage under the banner "Freedom Now," they were acting on an ancient hope that is meant to be fulfilled. History has an ebb and flow of justice, but history also has a visible direction, set by liberty and the Author of Liberty.

When the Declaration of Independence was first read in public and the Liberty Bell was sounded in celebration, a witness said, "It rang as if it meant something." In our time, it means something still. America, in this young century, proclaims liberty throughout all the world and to all the inhabitants thereof. Renewed in our strength, tested but not weary, we are ready for the greatest achievements in the history of freedom.

May God bless you, and may He watch over the United States of America.

George W. Bush and George H.W. Bush Monument located at the George W. Bush Presidential Library and Museum in Dallas, Texas. (Courtesy of PresidentsUSA.net)

Courtesy of Library of Congress

Barack Hussein Obama

Barack Hussein Obama

2009–2017

WHEN HE WON election over his Republican rival John McCain in November 2008, Barack Hussein Obama was a relative newcomer to national politics. A young man—he was only forty-seven when he won election to the presidency—he was also the first African American to take the nation's highest office. He had earned headlines in major outlets in 2002 with a speech opposing President Bush's war in Iraq, and he gave a stirring keynote speech at the 2004 Democratic national convention. The ideas that became the keywords of his campaign—hope and change—offered Americans reeling from the partisanship of the Bush era a chance to believe in a new unified future.

Obama was one of the most cosmopolitan figures ever to win the presidency. The son of a white American college professor mother and a Kenyan economist father, he was born in Hawaii and raised in Honolulu and Seattle, Washington. His early years are chronicled in his memoir *Dreams from My Father* (1995). His parents divorced when he was two. Both of them remarried and raised families in different corners of the world, so Obama had relatives in Kenya and in Jakarta, Indonesia, where his mother had married an Indonesian geographer. Obama spent some years in Jakarta, where he received his elementary schooling. Later he returned to Hawaii, where he lived with his grandparents until he graduated from high school in 1979. He graduated from Columbia University before moving to Chicago to work as a community organizer. He then attended Harvard Law School, becoming editor of the prestigious *Harvard Law Review* before receiving his degree and returning to Illinois as a faculty member at the University of Chicago.

Obama is regarded as one of the greatest modern orators. He worked as a writer and editor before he began his political career in the Illinois senate in 1997, representing the South Side Chicago communities he had served in his organizing days. He stayed in the state senate until he ran for Illinois's newly empty U.S. Senate seat in 2004. By that time, Obama had already earned a reputation as a rising star for his outspoken opposition to the Bush administration's invasion of Iraq in 2002. Obama's overwhelming victory in the senate election, in which he won 70 percent of the vote, led to his selection as the keynote speaker at the 2004 Democratic national convention. Some of the ideas expressed in the speech emerged in his 2006 book *The Audacity of Hope.*

An extremely articulate man, Obama wrote many of his speeches himself. In general, he projected a thoughtful, reflective image—one that critics occasionally labeled professorial—that countered the emotional resolve of the Bush years. On occasion, however, Obama's native rhetorical brilliance shone through. One of his most famous speeches was delivered on the campaign trail after his loss to Hillary Rodham Clinton in the New Hampshire Democratic primary in 2007. Out of that speech emerged the slogan "Yes we can," which helped propel Obama to the presidency.

By 2007, Obama had recruited Jon Favreau, a recent college graduate who became Obama's director of speechwriting for about four years. Favreau focused Obama's speeches on stories that appealed to the average citizen disillusioned by administrations that seemed to care more for business interests than for voters and taxpayers. Favreau contributed to some of candidate Obama's most important speeches, including "A More Perfect Union," delivered in Philadelphia during the 2008 campaign.

Candidate Obama promised the American people change, and President Obama moved to fulfill that promise was soon as he entered office. He inherited a faltering economy—the worst the United States had seen since the Great Depression—and two ongoing wars (in Afghanistan and Iraq) and a huge federal deficit. Within a month of his inauguration, Obama had signed legislation for an economic stimulus package intended to boost domestic spending. He extended the bailout program (the Troubled Asset Relief Program, or TARP) to the major American automobile manufacturers General Motors and Chrysler. Although leading economic indicators suggested that the recession was ending in 2009, unemployment remained high into 2010 and helped lead to a Republican takeover of the House of Representatives in the midterm elections.

Perhaps Obama's most significant legislation was the Affordable Care Act (ACA, or Obamacare), which promised to provide the most sweeping health care reforms since the 1960s. The ACA took a market-based approach to controlling the high costs of health care in the United States. It created a series of exchanges to help individuals select their health insurance providers but also required all Americans to have health care insurance or pay a penalty. Although the ACA had a number of serious problems, it nonetheless helped provide health insurance to millions of Americans who could not have previously afforded it.

The ACA was controversial among conservatives, who saw it as an example of government overreach and as a means of making middle-class Americans pay for health insurance for non-working Americans. In 2010, resistance to the ACA provided a major boost for conservative Republicans. They were invigorated by a new conservative movement that called itself the Tea Party, which was made up mostly of middle-class voters but with essential funding provided by wealthy conservatives.

Obama also faced setbacks in trying to end the wars in Iraq and Afghanistan. He declared the U.S. mission in Iraq over in December 2011, but the long-sought political stability in the country remained out of reach. At the same time, the Afghanistan war heated up instead of cooling down. In 2009, Obama ordered a surge in American troops to help stabilize the situation—a surge that lasted until 2012. Ironically, for someone who had been awarded the Nobel Peace Prize, Obama was at war for most of his presidency.

At the time of his election in 2008, Obama was hailed as a harbinger of a new, post-racial America—a country that, it was believed, had finally outgrown the legacy of slavery, racism, and injustice that had plagued it throughout the nineteenth and twentieth centuries. That proved not to be the case. Despite Obama's status as the first African American president, his election and the conservative reaction to it gave a kind of license to racism and hatred that had only been driven underground after the tumult of the 1960s. What this would mean for the United States emerged in the election of 2016.

First Inaugural Address

January 20, 2009

Washington, D.C

BARACK OBAMA'S first inaugural address, delivered on January 20, 2009, was the most anticipated political speech of the first decade of the twenty-first century. Obama delivered the address before a crowd of 1.8 million people, more than had ever before seen a president take the oath of office. Obama inspired millions of Americans with his eloquence and his promise to bring change at a time when economic collapse was devastating individual lives and when American forces were engaged in two long and controversial wars. In his inaugural address, Obama offered the American people hope that the nation would meet these serious challenges, but he stated frankly that success would not come easily or quickly.

Obama quickly introduces the two main themes of his address. The first is that America faces a crisis brought about by a faltering economy and two wars. He links the symptoms of economic recession to longer-term problems, such as expensive health care, ineffective schools, and wasteful energy consumption. The second theme is that enduring national principles and values will enable the nation to meet the challenges it faces. Obama hails traditional values that have accounted for progress throughout American history. In words recalling those of John F. Kennedy, Obama calls for the American people to accept obligations to themselves, their country, and the world.

My fellow citizens, I stand here today humbled by the task before us, grateful for the trust you have bestowed, mindful of the sacrifices borne by our ancestors. I thank President Bush for his service to our Nation, as well as the generosity and cooperation he has shown throughout this transition.

Forty-four Americans have now taken the Presidential oath. The words have been spoken during rising tides of prosperity and the still waters of peace. Yet every so often, the oath is taken amidst gathering clouds and raging storms. At these moments, America has carried on not simply because of the skill or vision of those in high office, but because we the people have remained faithful to the ideals of our forebears and true to our founding documents.

So it has been; so it must be with this generation of Americans.

That we are in the midst of crisis is now well understood. Our Nation is at war against a far-reaching network of violence and hatred. Our economy is badly weakened, a consequence of greed and irresponsibility on the part of some, but also our collective failure to make hard choices and prepare the Nation for a new age. Homes have been lost, jobs shed, businesses shuttered. Our health care is too costly. Our schools fail too many. And each day brings further evidence that the ways we use energy strengthen our adversaries and threaten our planet.

These are the indicators of crisis, subject to data and statistics. Less measurable but no less profound is a sapping of confidence across our land, a nagging fear that America's decline is inevitable, that the next generation must lower its sights. Today I say to you that the challenges we face are real. They are serious, and they are many. They will not be met easily or in a short span of time. But know this, America: They will be met.

On this day, we gather because we have chosen hope over fear, unity of purpose over conflict and discord. On this day, we come to proclaim an end to the petty grievances and false promises, the recriminations and worn-out dogmas that for far too long have strangled our politics.

We remain a young nation, but in the words of Scripture, the time has come to set aside childish things. The time has come to reaffirm our enduring spirit, to choose our better history, to carry forward that precious gift, that noble idea passed on from generation to generation: the God-given promise that all are equal, all are free, and all deserve a chance to pursue their full measure of happiness.

In reaffirming the greatness of our Nation, we understand that greatness is never a given. It must be earned. Our journey has never been one of shortcuts or settling for less. It has not been the path for the fainthearted, for those who prefer leisure over work or seek only the pleasures of riches and fame. Rather, it has been the risk-takers, the doers, the makers of things—some celebrated, but more often men and women obscure in their labor—who have carried us up the long, rugged path toward prosperity and freedom.

For us, they packed up their few worldly possessions and traveled across oceans in search of a new life. For us, they toiled in sweatshops and settled the West, endured the lash of the whip, and plowed the hard Earth. For us, they fought and died in places like Concord and Gettysburg, Normandy and Khe Sanh.

Time and again, these men and women struggled and sacrificed and worked 'til their hands were raw so that we might live a better life. They saw America as bigger than the sum of our individual ambitions, greater than all the differences of birth or wealth or faction.

This is the journey we continue today. We remain the most prosperous, powerful nation on Earth. Our workers are no less productive than when this crisis began. Our minds are no less inventive. Our goods and services no less needed than they were last week or last month or last year. Our capacity remains undiminished. But our time of standing pat, of protecting narrow interests and putting off unpleasant decisions, that time has surely passed. Starting today, we must pick ourselves up, dust ourselves off, and begin again the work of remaking America.

For everywhere we look, there is work to be done. The state of the economy calls for action, bold and swift, and we will act not only to create new jobs but to lay a new foundation for growth. We will build the roads and bridges, the electric grids and digital lines that feed our commerce and bind us together. We will restore science to its rightful place and wield technology's wonders to raise health care's quality and lower its cost. We will harness the sun and the winds and the soil to fuel our cars and run our factories. And we will transform our schools and colleges and universities to meet the demands of a new age. All this we can do. All this we will do.

Now, there are some who question the scale of our ambitions, who suggest that our system cannot tolerate too many big plans. Their memories are short, for they have forgotten what this country has already done, what free men and women can achieve when imagination is joined to common purpose and necessity to courage.

What the cynics fail to understand is that the ground has shifted beneath them, that the stale political arguments that have consumed us for so long no longer apply. The question we ask today is not whether our Government is too big or too small, but whether it works; whether it helps families find jobs at a decent wage, care they can afford, a retirement that is dignified. Where the answer is yes, we intend to move forward. Where the answer is no, programs will end. And those of us who manage the public's dollars will be held to account to spend wisely, reform bad habits, and do our business in the light of day, because only then can we restore the vital trust between a people and their government.

Nor is the question before us whether the market is a force for good or ill. Its power to generate wealth and expand freedom is unmatched. But this crisis has reminded us that without a watchful eye, the market can spin out of control. The Nation cannot prosper long when it favors only the prosperous. The success of our economy has always depended not just on the size of our gross domestic product, but on the reach of our prosperity, on our ability to extend opportunity to every willing heart, not out of charity, but because it is the surest route to our common good.

As for our common defense, we reject as false the choice between our safety and our ideals. Our Founding Fathers, faced with perils that we can scarcely imagine, drafted a charter to assure the rule of law and the rights of man, a charter expanded by the blood of generations. Those ideals still light the world, and we will not give them up for expedience's sake. And so to all the other peoples and governments who are watching today, from the grandest capitals to the small village where my father was born, know that America is a friend of each nation and every man, woman, and child who seeks a future of peace and dignity, and we are ready to lead once more.

Recall that earlier generations faced down fascism and communism not just with missiles and tanks but with sturdy alliances and enduring convictions. They understood that our power alone cannot protect us, nor does it entitle us to do as we please. Instead, they knew that our power grows through its prudent use. Our security emanates from the justness of our cause, the force of our example, the tempering qualities of humility and restraint.

We are the keepers of this legacy. Guided by these principles once more, we can meet those new threats that demand even greater effort, even greater cooperation and understanding between nations. We will begin to responsibly leave Iraq to its people and forge a hard-earned peace in Afghanistan. With old friends and former foes, we will work tirelessly to lessen the nuclear threat and roll back the specter of a warming planet. We will not apologize for our way of life, nor will we waver in its defense. And for those who seek to advance their aims by inducing terror and slaughtering innocents, we say to you now that our spirit is stronger and cannot be broken. You cannot outlast us, and we will defeat you.

For we know that our patchwork heritage is a strength, not a weakness. We are a nation of Christians and Muslims, Jews and Hindus and nonbelievers. We are shaped by every language and culture, drawn from every end of this Earth. And because we have tasted the bitter swill of civil war and segregation and emerged from that dark chapter stronger and more united, we cannot help but believe that the old hatreds shall someday pass, that the lines of tribe shall soon dissolve; that as the world grows smaller, our common humanity shall reveal itself, and that America must play its role in ushering in a new era of peace.

To the Muslim world, we seek a new way forward based on mutual interest and mutual respect. To those leaders around the globe who seek to sow conflict or blame their society's ills on the West, know that your people will judge you on what you can build, not what you destroy. To those who cling to power through corruption and deceit and the silencing of dissent, know that you are on the wrong side of history, but that we will extend a hand if you are willing to unclench your fist.

To the people of poor nations, we pledge to work alongside you to make your farms flourish and let clean waters flow, to nourish starved bodies and feed hungry minds. And to those nations like ours that enjoy relative plenty, we say we can no longer afford indifference to suffering outside our borders, nor can we consume the world's resources without regard to effect, for the world has changed, and we must change with it.

As we consider the road that unfolds before us, we remember with humble gratitude those brave Americans who, at this very hour, patrol far-off deserts and distant mountains. They have something to tell us today, just as the fallen heroes who lie in Arlington whisper through the ages. We honor them not only because they are guardians of our liberty, but because they embody the spirit of service, a willingness to find meaning in something greater than themselves. And yet at this moment, a moment that will define a generation, it is precisely this spirit that must inhabit us all.

For as much as Government can do and must do, it is ultimately the faith and determination of the American people upon which this Nation relies. It is the kindness to take in a stranger when the levees break, the selflessness of workers who would rather cut their hours than see a friend lose their job, which sees us through our darkest hours. It is the firefighter's courage to storm a stairway filled with smoke, but also a parent's willingness to nurture a child, that finally decides our fate.

Our challenges may be new. The instruments with which we meet them may be new. But those values upon which our success depends—honesty and hard work, courage and fair play, tolerance and curiosity, loyalty and patriotism—these things are old. These things are true. They have been the quiet force of progress throughout our history. What is demanded then is a return to these truths. What is required of us now is a new era of responsibility, a recognition on the part of every American that we have duties to ourselves, our Nation, and the world. Duties that we do not grudgingly accept but, rather, seize gladly, firm in the knowledge that there is nothing so satisfying to the spirit, so defining of our character, than giving our all to a difficult task.

This is the price and the promise of citizenship. This is the source of our confidence, the knowledge that God calls on us to shape an uncertain destiny. This is the meaning of our liberty and our creed; why men and women and children of every race and every faith can join in celebration across this magnificent Mall, and why a man whose father less than 60 years ago might not have been served at a local restaurant can now stand before you to take a most sacred oath.

So let us mark this day with remembrance of who we are and how far we have traveled. In the year of America's birth, in the coldest of months, a small band of patriots huddled by dying campfires on the shores of an icy river. The Capital was abandoned. The enemy was advancing. The snow was stained with blood. At a moment when the outcome of our Revolution was most in doubt, the Father of our Nation ordered these words be read to the people:

"Let it be told to the future world . . . that in the depth of winter, when nothing but hope and virtue could survive . . . that the city and the country, alarmed at one common danger, came forth to meet [it]."

America, in the face of our common dangers, in this winter of our hardship, let us remember these timeless words. With hope and virtue, let us brave once more the icy currents and endure what storms may come. Let it be said by our children's children that when we were tested, we refused to let this journey end; that we did not turn back, nor did we falter. And with eyes fixed on the horizon and God's grace upon us, we carried forth that great gift of freedom and delivered it safely to future generations.

Thank you. God bless you, and God bless the United States of America.

Address to the NAACP Centennial Convention

July 16, 2009

New York City, New York

IN 2009 President Barack Obama addressed the centennial meeting of the NAACP. The address was eagerly anticipated as a celebration of African Americans' aspirations and a promise of things to come. Obama comments on the origins of the NAACP, commemorating the organization's successes and its support of civil rights. He speaks of the courage of activists who risked their lives to demand an end to lynching and segregation. He reminds his listeners that those involved risked their lives to combat racism. Obama builds toward the most extraordinary victory—his election as president of the United States.

The president adds, however, that many inequalities still plague African Americans, including disproportionate suffering in the realm of economics, health care, the prison system, and HIV/AIDS. He argues that because these obstacles are different from the ones fought in the 1930s and 1940s, the steps to overcome them must be different as well—but they must be met with the same sense of urgency and aspiration. His solution for suffering of black Americans is to better the lives of all Americans. By example, Obama suggests that anyone, regardless of skin color or socioeconomic status, can aspire to become president of the United States.

What an extraordinary night, capping off an extraordinary week, capping off an extraordinary 100 years at the NAACP. To Chairman Bond, Brother Justice, I am so grateful to all of you for being here. And it's just good to be among friends.

It is an extraordinary honor to be here, in the city where the NAACP was formed, to mark its centennial. What we celebrate tonight is not simply the journey the NAACP has traveled, but the journey that we as Americans have traveled over the past 100 years.

It's a journey that takes us back to a time before most of us was—were born, long before the Voting Rights Act and the Civil Rights Act and Brown v. Board of Education, back to an America just a generation past slavery. It was a time when Jim Crow was a way of life, when lynchings were all too common, when race riots were shaking cities across a segregated land.

It was in this America where an Atlanta scholar named W.E.B. Du Bois, a man of towering intellect and a fierce passion for justice, sparked what became known as the Niagara movement, where reformers united not by color but by cause, where an association was born that would, as its charter says, promote equality and eradicate prejudice among citizens of the United States.

From the beginning, these founders understood how change would come, just as King and all the civil rights giants did later. They understood that unjust laws needed to be overturned, that legislation needed to be passed, and that Presidents needed to be pressured into action. They knew that the stain of slavery and the sin of segregation had to be lifted in the courtroom and in the Legislature and in the hearts and the minds of Americans.

They also knew that here in America change would have to come from the people. It would come from people protesting lynchings, rallying against violence, all those women who decided to walk instead of taking the bus, even though they were tired after a long day of doing somebody else's laundry, looking after somebody else's children. It would come from men and women of every age and faith and every race and region taking Greyhounds on freedom rides, sitting down at Greensboro lunch counters, registering voters in rural Mississippi, knowing they would be harassed, knowing they would be beaten, knowing that some of them might never return.

Because of what they did, we are a more perfect Union. Because Jim Crow laws were overturned, Black CEOs today run Fortune 500 companies. Because civil rights laws were passed, Black mayors and Black Governors, Members of Congress serve in places where they might once have been able, not just to vote but even take a sip of water. And because ordinary people did such ordinary—extraordinary things, because they made the civil rights movement their own, even though there may not be a plaque or their names might not be in the history books, because of their efforts, I made a little trip to Springfield, Illinois, a couple of years ago, where Lincoln once lived, and race riots once raged, and began the journey that has led me to be here tonight as the 44th President of the United States of America.

Because of them I stand here tonight, on the shoulders of giants. And I'm here to say thank you to those pioneers and thank you to the NAACP.

And yet even as we celebrate the remarkable achievements of the past 100 years, even as we inherit extraordinary progress that cannot be denied, even as we marvel at the courage and determination of so many plain folk, we know that too many barriers still remain.

We know that even as our economic crisis batters Americans of all races, African Americans are out of work more than just about anybody else, a gap that's widening here in New York City, as a detailed report this week by Comptroller Bill Thompson laid out. We know that even as spiraling health care costs crush families of all races, African Americans are more likely to suffer from a host of diseases, but less likely to own health insurance than just about anybody else. We know that even as we imprison more people of all races than any nation in the world, an African American child is roughly five times as likely as a White child to see the inside of a prison. We know that even as the scourge of HIV/AIDS devastates nations abroad, particularly in Africa, it is devastating the African American community here at home with disproportionate force. We know these things.

These are some of the barriers of our time. They're very different from the barriers faced by earlier generations. They're very different from the ones faced when fire hoses and dogs were being turned on young marchers, when Charles Hamilton Houston and a group of young Howard lawyers were dismantling segregation case by case across the land.

But what's required today, what's required to overcome today's barriers is the same as what was needed then. The same commitment, the same sense of urgency, the same sense of sacrifice, the same sense of community, the same willingness to do our part for ourselves and one another that has always defined America at its best and the African American experience at its best. And so the question is, where do we direct our efforts? What steps do we take to overcome these barriers? How do we move forward in the next 100 years?

Now, the first thing we need to do is to make real the words of the NAACP Charter and eradicate prejudice, bigotry, and discrimination among citizens of the United States. I understand there may be a temptation among some to think that discrimination is no longer a problem in 2009. And I believe that overall, there probably has never been less discrimination in America than there is today. I think we can say that.

But make no mistake, the pain of discrimination is still felt in America: by African American women paid less for doing the same work as colleagues of a different color and a different gender; by Latinos made to feel unwelcome in their own country; by Muslim Americans viewed with suspicion simply because they kneel down to pray to their God; by our gay brothers and sisters, still taunted, still attacked, still denied their rights.

On the 45th anniversary of the Civil Rights Act, discrimination cannot stand, not on account of color or gender, how you worship, or who you love. Prejudice has no place in the United States of America. That's what the NAACP stands for. That's what the NAACP will continue to fight for as long as it takes.

But we also know that prejudice and discrimination—at least, the most blatant types of prejudice and discrimination—are not even the steepest barriers to opportunity today. The most difficult barriers include structural inequalities that our Nation's legacy of discrimination has left behind, inequalities still plaguing too many communities and too often the object of national neglect.

These are barriers we are beginning to tear down one by one by rewarding work with an expanded tax credit, by making housing more affordable, by giving ex-offenders a second chance. These are barriers we're targeting through our White House Office on Urban Affairs, through programs like Promise Neighborhoods that builds on Geoffrey Canada's success with the Harlem Children's Zone that foster a comprehensive approach to ending poverty by putting all children on a pathway to college and giving them the schooling and after-school support that they need to get there.

Now, I think all of us understand that our task of reducing these structural inequalities has been made more difficult by the state and structure of our broader economy, an economy that for the last decade has been fueled by a cycle of boom and bust, an economy where the rich got really, really rich, but ordinary folks didn't see their incomes or their wages go up, an economy built on credit cards and shady mortgage loans, an economy built not on a rock but on sand.

That's why my administration is working so hard not only to create and save jobs in the short term, not only to extend unemployment insurance and help for people who have lost their health care in this crisis, not just to stem the immediate economic wreckage, but to lay a new foundation for growth and prosperity that will put opportunity within the reach of not just African Americans, but all Americans. All Americans, of every race, of every creed, from every region of the country, we want everybody to participate in the American Dream. That's what the NAACP is all about.

Now, one pillar of this new foundation is health insurance for everybody. Health insurance reform that cuts costs and makes quality health coverage affordable for all and it closes health care disparities in the process. Another pillar is energy reform that makes clean energy profitable, freeing America from the grip of foreign oil, putting young people to work upgrading low-income homes, weatherizing them, creating jobs that can't be outsourced. Another pillar is financial reform with consumer protections that crackdown on mortgage fraud and stop predatory lenders from targeting Black and Latino communities all across the country.

All these things will make America stronger and more competitive. They will drive innovation; they will create jobs; they will provide families with more security. And yet even if we do all that, the African American community will still fall behind in the United States and the United States will fall behind in the world unless we do a far better job than we have been doing of educating our sons and daughters.

I hope you don't mind, I want to go into a little detail here about education. In the 21st century, when so many jobs will require a bachelor's degree or more, when countries that outeducate us today will outcompete us

tomorrow, a world-class education is a prerequisite for success.

There's no two ways about it. There's no way to avoid it. You know what I'm talking about. There's a reason the story of the civil rights movement was written in our schools. There's a reason Thurgood Marshall took up the cause of Linda Brown. There's a reason why the Little Rock Nine defied a Governor and a mob. It's because there is no stronger weapon against inequality and no better path to opportunity than an education that can unlock a child's God-given potential.

And yet more than half a century after Brown v. Board, the dream of a world-class education is still being deferred all across the country. African American students are lagging behind White classmates in reading and math, an achievement gap that is growing in States that once led the way in the civil rights movement. Over half of all African American students are dropping out of school in some places. There are overcrowded classrooms and crumbling schools and corridors of shame in America filled with poor children, not just Black children, Brown and White children as well.

The state of our schools is not an African American problem; it is an American problem, because if Black and Brown children cannot compete, then America cannot compete. And let me say this: If Al Sharpton, Mike Bloomberg, and Newt Gingrich can agree that we need to solve the education problem, then that's something all of America can agree we can solve. Those guys came into my office. Just sitting in the Oval Office—I kept on doing a double take. But that's a sign of progress and it is a sign of the urgency of the education problem. All of us can agree that we need to offer every child in this country every child in this country the best education the world has to offer from cradle through a career.

That's our responsibility as leaders. That's the responsibility of the United States of America. And we, all of us in Government, have to work to do our part by not only offering more resources but also demanding more reform. Because when it comes to education, we've got to get past this old paradigm, this outdated notion that somehow it's just money, or somehow it's just reform, but no money, and embrace what Dr. King called the "both-and" philosophy. We need more money, and we need more reform.

When it comes to higher education, we're making college and advanced training more affordable and strengthening community colleges that are the gateway to so many with an initiative that will prepare students not only to earn a degree but to find a job when they graduate, an initiative that will help us meet the goal I have set of leading the world in college degrees by 2020. We used to rank number one in college graduates. Now we are in the middle of the pack. And since we are seeing more and more African American and Latino youth in our population, if we are leaving them behind, we cannot achieve our goal, and America will fall further behind. And that is not a future that I accept, and that is not a future that the NAACP is willing to accept.

We're creating a Race to the Top fund that will reward States and public school districts that adopt 21st-century standards and assessments. We're creating incentives for States to promote excellent teachers and replace bad ones, because the job of a teacher is too important for us to accept anything less than the best.

We also have to explore innovative approaches such as those being pursued here in New York City, innovations like Bard High School Early College and Medgar Evers College Preparatory School that are challenging students to complete high school and earn a free associate's degree or college credit in just 4 years.

And we should raise the bar when it comes to early learning programs. It's not enough just to have a babysitter. We need our young people stimulated and engaged and involved. And we need our folks involved in child development to understand the latest science. Today, some early learning programs are excellent, some are mediocre, and some are wasting what studies show are by far a child's most formative years.

That's why I've issued a challenge to America's Governors: If you match the success of States like Pennsylvania and develop an effective model for early learning, if you focus reform on standards and results in early learning programs, if you demonstrate how you will prepare the lowest income children to meet the highest standards of success, then you can compete for an Early Learning Challenge Grant that will help prepare all our children to enter kindergarten all ready to learn.

So these are some of the laws we're passing. These are some of the policies we are enacting. We are busy in Washington. Folks in Congress are getting a little tuckered out. But I'm telling them we can't rest; we've got a lot of work to do. The American people are counting on us. These are some of the ways we're doing our part in Government to overcome the inequities, the injustices, the barriers that still exist in our country.

But all these innovative programs and expanded opportunities will not, in and of themselves, make a difference if each of us, as parents and as community leaders, fail to do our part by encouraging excellence in our children. Government programs alone won't get our children to the promised land. We need a new mindset, a new set of attitudes, because one of the most durable and destructive legacies of discrimination is the way we've internalized a sense of limitation, how so many in our community have come to expect so little from the world and from themselves.

We've got to say to our children, yes, if you're African American, the odds of growing up amid crime and gangs are higher. Yes, if you live in a poor neighborhood, you will face challenges that somebody in a wealthy suburb does not have to face. But that's not a reason to get bad grades, that's not a reason to cut class, that's not a reason to give up on your education and drop out of school. No one has written your destiny for you. Your destiny is in your hands, you cannot forget that. That's what we have to teach all of our children. No excuses—no excuses. You get that education, all those hardships will just make you stronger, better able to compete. Yes we can.

To parents: We can't tell our kids to do well in school and then fail to support them when they get home. You can't just contract out parenting. For our kids to excel, we have to accept our responsibility to help them learn. That means putting away the Xbox, putting our kids to bed at a reasonable hour. It means attending those parent-teacher conferences and reading to our children and helping them with their homework.

And by the way, it means we need to be there for our neighbors' sons and daughters. We need to go back to the time, back to the day when parents saw somebody, saw some kid fooling around, and it wasn't your child, but they'll whup you anyway. Or at least they'll tell your parents, and the parents will. You know. That's the meaning of community. That's how we can reclaim the strength and the determination and the hopefulness that helped us come so far, helped us make a way out of no way.

It also means pushing our children to set their sights a little bit higher. They might think they've got a pretty good jump shot or a pretty good flow, but our kids can't all aspire to be LeBron or Lil' Wayne. I want them aspiring to be scientists and engineers, doctors and teachers, not just ballers and rappers. I want them aspiring to be a Supreme Court Justice. I want them aspiring to be the President of the United States of America. I want their horizons to be limitless. I don't—don't tell them they can't do something. Don't feed our children with a sense of—that somehow because of their race that they cannot achieve.

Yes, Government must be a force for opportunity. Yes, Government must be a force for equality. But ultimately, if we are to be true to our past, then we also have to seize our own future, each and every day.

And that's what the NAACP is all about. The NAACP was not founded in search of a handout. The NAACP was not founded in search of favors. The NAACP was founded on a firm notion of justice, to cash the promissory note of America that says all of our children, all God's children, deserve a fair chance in the race of life.

It's a simple dream and yet one that all too often has been denied and is still being denied to so many Americans. It's a painful thing, seeing that dream denied. I remember visiting a Chicago school in a rough neighborhood when I was a community organizer, and some of the children gathered round me. And I remember thinking how remarkable it was that all of these children seemed so full of hope, despite being born into poverty, despite being delivered, in some cases, into addiction, despite all the obstacles they were already facing, you could see that spark in their eyes. They were the equal of children anywhere.

And I remember the principal of the school telling me that soon that sparkle would begin to dim, that things would begin to change, that soon the laughter in their eyes would begin to fade, that soon something would shut off inside, as it sunk in—because kids are smarter than we give them credit for—as it sunk in that their hopes would not come to

pass, not because they weren't smart enough, not because they weren't talented enough, not because of anything about them inherently, but because, by accident of birth, they had not received a fair chance in life.

I know what can happen to a child who doesn't have that chance. But I also know what can happen to a child that does. I was raised by a single mom. I didn't come from a lot of wealth. I got into my share of trouble as a child. My life could have easily taken a turn for the worse. When I drive through Harlem or I drive through the south side of Chicago and I see young men on the corners, I say, there but for the grace of God go I. They're no less gifted than me. They're no less talented than me.

But I had some brakes. That mother of mine, she gave me love; she pushed me; she cared about my education; she took no lip; she taught me right from wrong. Because of her, I had a chance to make the most of my abilities. I had the chance to make the most of my opportunities. I had the chance to make the most of life.

The same story holds true for Michelle. The same story holds true for so many of you. And I want all the other Barack Obamas out there, all the other Michelle Obamas out there to have the same chance, the chance that my mother gave me, that my education gave me, that the United States of America has given me. That's how our Union will be perfected and our economy rebuilt. That is how America will move forward in the next 100 years.

And we will move forward. This I know, for I know how far we have come. Some, you saw, last week in Ghana, Michelle and I took Malia and Sasha and my mother-in-law to Cape Coast Castle in Ghana. Some of you may have been there. This is where captives were once imprisoned before being auctioned, where, across an ocean, so much of the African American experience began.

We went down into the dungeons where the captives were held. There was a church above one of the dungeons, which tells you something about saying one thing and doing another. I was—we walked through the door of no return. I was reminded of all the pain and all the hardships, all the injustices and all the indignities on the voyage from slavery to freedom.

But I was reminded of something else. I was reminded that no matter how bitter the rod, how stony the road, we have always persevered. We have not faltered, nor have we grown weary. As Americans, we have demanded and strived for and shaped a better destiny. And that is what we are called on to do once more. NAACP, it will not be easy. It will take time. Doubts may rise, and hopes may recede.

But if John Lewis could brave billy clubs to cross a bridge, then I know young people today can do their part to lift up our community. If Emmet Till's uncle, Mose Wright, could summon the courage to testify against the men who killed his nephew, I know we can be better fathers and better brothers and better mothers and sisters in our own families. If three civil rights workers in Mississippi—Black,

White, Christian and Jew, city born and country bred—could lay down their lives in freedom's cause, I know we can come together to face down the challenges of our own time. We can fix our schools; we can heal our sick; we can rescue our youth from violence and despair.

And 100 years from now, on the 200th anniversary of the NAACP, let it be said that this generation did its part, that we too ran the race, that full of faith that our dark past has taught us, full of the hope that the present has brought us, we faced in our lives and all across this Nation the rising sun of a new day begun.

Thank you. God bless you. God bless the United States of America.

Remarks on Health Care Reform

September 9, 2009
Washington, D.C.

ON SEPTEMBER 9, 2009, in the final stages of the health insurance reform debate, President Barack Obama delivered his remarks on health care reform to a joint session of Congress. Health care reform was a contentious political issue during the first years of Obama's administration. During his campaign for the presidency in 2008, Obama pledged to make health care reform one of his top priorities because of the increasing cost of health care (and health insurance) and the large number of Americans who did not have health insurance. Eventually, Obama's efforts resulted in the Patient Protection and Affordable Care Act, which the president signed into law on March 23, 2010. The law became one of the widest-reaching pieces of social legislation signed in decades.

The president begins his address by referring to the nation's deep recession. He indicates that in addition to responding to crises, the goal of his administration is to build a better future, including a better health care system. He states that his goal is to end partisan bickering by offering his vision of what health care reform would look like. His plan would ensure that health insurance companies could not decline coverage because of preexisting medical conditions, could not drop people from coverage, and could not place arbitrary caps on benefits.

Madam Speaker, Vice President Biden, members of Congress, and the American people:

When I spoke here last winter, this nation was facing the worst economic crisis since the Great Depression. We were losing an average of 700,000 jobs per month. Credit was frozen. And our financial system was on the verge of collapse.

As any American who is still looking for work or a way to pay their bills will tell you, we are by no means out of the woods. A full and vibrant recovery is still many months away. And I will not let up until those Americans who seek jobs can find them; until those businesses that seek capital and credit can thrive; until all responsible homeowners can stay in their homes. That is our ultimate goal. But thanks to the bold and decisive action we've taken since January, I can stand here with confidence and say that we have pulled this economy back from the brink.

I want to thank the members of this body for your efforts and your support in these last several months, and especially those who've taken the difficult votes that have put us on a path to recovery. I also want to thank the American people for their patience and resolve during this trying time for our nation.

But we did not come here just to clean up crises. We came here to build a future. So tonight, I return to speak to all of you about an issue that is central to that future; and that is the issue of health care.

I am not the first President to take up this cause, but I am determined to be the last. It has now been nearly a century since Theodore Roosevelt first called for health care reform. And ever since, nearly every President and Congress, whether Democrat or Republican, has attempted to meet this challenge in some way. A bill for comprehensive health reform was first introduced by John Dingell Sr. in 1943. Sixty-five years later, his son continues to introduce that same bill at the beginning of each session.

Our collective failure to meet this challenge; year after year, decade after decade; has led us to the breaking point. Everyone understands the extraordinary hardships that are placed on the uninsured, who live every day just one accident or illness away from bankruptcy. These are not primarily people on welfare. These are middle-class Americans. Some can't get insurance on the job. Others are self-employed, and can't afford it, since buying insurance on your own costs you three times as much as the coverage you get from your employer. Many other Americans who are willing and able to pay are still denied insurance due to previous illnesses or conditions that insurance companies decide are too risky or too expensive to cover.

We are the only democracy; the only advanced democracy on Earth; the only wealthy nation; that allows such hardship for millions of its people. There are now more than 30 million American citizens who cannot get coverage. In just a two-year period, one in every three Americans goes without health care coverage at some point. And every day, 14,000 Americans lose their coverage. In other words, it can happen to anyone.

But the problem that plagues the health care system is not just a problem for the uninsured. Those who do have insurance have never had less security and stability than they do today. More and more Americans worry that if you move, lose your job, or change your job, you'll lose your health insurance too. More and more Americans pay their premiums, only to discover that their insurance company has dropped their coverage when they get sick, or won't pay the full cost of care. It happens every day.

One man from Illinois lost his coverage in the middle of chemotherapy because his insurer found that he hadn't reported gallstones that he didn't even know about. They delayed his treatment, and he died because of it. Another woman from Texas was about to get a double mastectomy when her insurance company canceled her policy because she forgot to declare a case of acne. By the time she had her insurance reinstated, her breast cancer had more than doubled in size. That is heart-breaking, it is wrong, and no one should be treated that way in the United States of America.

Then there's the problem of rising cost. We spend one and a half times more per person on health care than any other country, but we aren't any healthier for it. This is one of the reasons that insurance premiums have gone up three times faster than wages. It's why so many employers; especially small businesses; are forcing their employees to pay more for insurance, or are dropping their coverage entirely. It's why so many aspiring entrepreneurs cannot afford to open a business in the first place, and why American businesses that compete internationally; like our automakers; are at a huge disadvantage. And it's why those of us with health insurance are also paying a hidden and growing tax for those without it; about $1,000 per year that pays for somebody else's emergency room and charitable care.

Finally, our health care system is placing an unsustainable burden on taxpayers. When health care costs grow at the rate they have, it puts greater pressure on programs like Medicare and Medicaid. If we do nothing to slow these skyrocketing costs, we will eventually be spending more on Medicare and Medicaid than every other government program combined. Put simply, our health care problem is our deficit problem. Nothing else even comes close. Nothing else

Now, these are the facts. Nobody disputes them. We know we must reform this system. The question is how.

There are those on the left who believe that the only way to fix the system is through a single-payer system like Canada's, where we would severely restrict the private insurance market and have the government provide coverage for everybody. On the right, there are those who argue that we should end employer-based systems and leave individuals to buy health insurance on their own.

I've said; I have to say that there are arguments to be made for both these approaches. But either one would represent a radical shift that would disrupt the health care most people currently have. Since health care represents one-sixth of our economy, I believe it makes more sense to build on what works and fix what doesn't, rather than try to build an entirely new system from scratch. And that is precisely what those of you in Congress have tried to do over the past several months.

During that time, we've seen Washington at its best and at its worst.

We've seen many in this chamber work tirelessly for the better part of this year to offer thoughtful ideas about how to achieve reform. Of the five committees asked to develop bills, four have completed their work, and the Senate Finance Committee announced today that it will move forward next week. That has never happened before. Our overall efforts have been supported by an unprecedented coalition of doctors and nurses; hospitals, seniors; groups, and even drug companies; many of whom opposed reform in the past. And there is agreement in this chamber on about 80 percent of what needs to be done, putting us closer to the goal of reform than we have ever been.

But what we've also seen in these last months is the same partisan spectacle that only hardens the disdain many Americans have towards their own government. Instead of honest debate, we've seen scare tactics. Some have dug into unyielding ideological camps that offer no hope of compromise. Too many have used this as an opportunity to score short-term political points, even if it robs the country of our opportunity to solve a long-term challenge. And out of this blizzard of charges and counter-charges, confusion has reigned.

Well, the time for bickering is over. The time for games has passed. Now is the season for action. Now is when we must bring the best ideas of both parties together, and show the American people that we can still do what we were sent here to do. Now is the time to deliver on health care. Now is the time to deliver on health care.

The plan I'm announcing tonight would meet three basic goals. It will provide more security and stability to those who have health insurance. It will provide insurance for those who don't. And it will slow the growth of health care costs for our families, our businesses, and our government. It's a plan that asks everyone to take responsibility for meeting this challenge; not just government, not just insurance companies, but everybody including employers and individuals. And it's a plan that incorporates ideas from senators and congressmen, from Democrats and Republicans; and yes, from some of my opponents in both the primary and general election.

Here are the details that every American needs to know about this plan. First, if you are among the hundreds of millions of Americans who already have health insurance through your job, or Medicare, or Medicaid, or the VA, nothing in this plan will require you or your employer to change the coverage or the doctor you have. Let me repeat this: Nothing in our plan requires you to change what you have.

What this plan will do is make the insurance you have works better for you. Under this plan, it will be against the law for insurance companies to deny you coverage because of a preexisting condition. As soon as I sign this bill, it will be against the law for insurance companies to drop your coverage when you get sick or water it down when you need it the most. They will no longer be able to place some arbitrary cap on the amount of coverage you can receive in a given year or in a lifetime. We will place a limit on how much you can be charged for out-of-pocket expenses, because in the United States of America, no one should go broke because they get sick. And insurance companies will be required to cover, with no extra charge, routine checkups and preventive care, like mammograms and colonoscopies because there's no reason we shouldn't be catching diseases like breast cancer and colon cancer before they get worse. That makes sense, it saves money, and it saves lives.

Now, that's what Americans who have health insurance can expect from this plan; more security and more stability.

Now, if you're one of the tens of millions of Americans who don't currently have health insurance, the second part of this plan will finally offer you quality, affordable choices. If you lose your job or you change your job, you'll be able to get coverage. If you strike out on your own and start a small business, you'll be able to get coverage. We'll do this by creating a new insurance exchange; a marketplace where individuals and small businesses will be able to shop for health insurance at competitive prices. Insurance companies will have an incentive to participate in this exchange because it lets them compete for millions of new customers. As one big group, these customers will have greater leverage to bargain with the insurance companies for better prices and quality coverage. This is how large companies and government employees get affordable insurance. It's how everyone in this Congress gets affordable insurance. And it's time to give every American the same opportunity that we give ourselves.

Now, for those individuals and small businesses who still can't afford the lower-priced insurance available in the exchange, we'll provide tax credits, the size of which will be based on your need. And all insurance companies that want access to this new marketplace will have to abide by the consumer protections I already mentioned. This exchange will take effect in four years, which will give us time to do it right. In the meantime, for those Americans who can't get insurance today because they have preexisting medical conditions, we will immediately offer low-cost coverage that will protect you against financial ruin if you become seriously ill. This was a good idea when Senator John McCain proposed it in the campaign, it's a good idea now, and we should all embrace it.

Now, even if we provide these affordable options, there may be those; especially the young and the healthy; who still want to take the risk and go without coverage. There may still be companies that refuse to do right by their workers by giving them coverage. The problem is, such irresponsible behavior costs all the rest of us money. If there are affordable options and people still don't sign up for health insurance, it means we pay for these people's expensive emergency room visits. If some businesses don't provide workers health care, it forces the rest of us to pick up the tab when their workers get sick, and gives those businesses an unfair advantage over their competitors. And unless everybody does their part, many of the insurance reforms we seek; especially requiring insurance companies to cover preexisting conditions; just can't be achieved.

And that's why under my plan, individuals will be required to carry basic health insurance; just as most states require you to carry auto insurance. Likewise, businesses will be required to either offer their workers health care, or chip in to help cover the cost of their workers. There will be a hardship waiver for those individuals who still can't afford coverage, and 95 percent of all small businesses, because of their size and narrow profit margin, would be exempt from these requirements. But we can't have large businesses and individuals who can afford coverage game the system by avoiding responsibility to themselves or their employees. Improving our health care system only works if everybody does their part.

And while there remain some significant details to be ironed out, I believe a broad consensus exists for the aspects of the plan I just outlined: consumer protections for those with insurance, an exchange that allows individuals and small businesses to purchase affordable coverage, and a requirement that people who can afford insurance get insurance.

And I have no doubt that these reforms would greatly benefit Americans from all walks of life, as well as the economy as a whole. Still, given all the misinformation that's been spread over the past few months, I realize that many Americans have grown nervous about reform. So tonight I want to address some of the key controversies that are still out there.

Some of people's concerns have grown out of bogus claims spread by those whose only agenda is to kill reform at any cost. The best example is the claim made not just by radio and cable talk show hosts, but by prominent politicians, that we plan to set up panels of bureaucrats with the power to kill off senior citizens. Now, such a charge would be laughable if it weren't so cynical and irresponsible. It is a lie, plain and simple.

There are also those who claim that our reform efforts would insure illegal immigrants. This, too, is false. The reforms I'm proposing would not apply to those who are here illegally.

And one more misunderstanding I want to clear up; under our plan, no federal dollars will be used to fund abortions, and federal conscience laws will remain in place.

Now, my health care proposal has also been attacked by some who oppose reform as a government takeover of the entire health care system. As proof, critics point to a provision in our plan that allows the uninsured and small businesses to choose a publicly sponsored insurance option, administered by the government just like Medicaid or Medicare.

So let me set the record straight here. My guiding principle is, and always has been, that consumers do better when there is choice and competition. That's how the market works. Unfortunately, in 34 states, 75 percent of the insurance market is controlled by five or fewer companies. In Alabama, almost 90 percent is controlled by just one company. And without competition, the price of insurance goes up and quality goes down. And it makes it easier for insurance companies to treat their customers badly; by cherry-picking the healthiest individuals and trying to drop the sickest, by overcharging small businesses who have no leverage, and by jacking up rates.

Insurance executives don't do this because they're bad people; they do it because it's profitable. As one former insurance executive testified before Congress, insurance companies are not only encouraged to find reasons to drop the seriously ill, they are rewarded for it. All of this is in service of meeting what this former executive called "Wall Street's relentless profit expectations."

Now, I have no interest in putting insurance companies out of business. They provide a legitimate service, and employ a lot of our friends and neighbors. I just want to hold them accountable. And the insurance reforms that I've already mentioned would do just that. But an additional step we can take to keep insurance companies honest is by making a not-for-profit public option available in the insurance exchange. Now, let me be clear. Let me be clear. It would only be an option for those who don't have insurance. No one would be forced to choose it, and it would not impact those of you who already have insurance. In fact, based on Congressional Budget Office estimates, we believe that less than 5 percent of Americans would sign up.

Despite all this, the insurance companies and their allies don't like this idea. They argue that these private companies can't fairly compete with the government. And they'd be right if taxpayers were subsidizing this public insurance option. But they won't be. I've insisted that like any private insurance company, the public insurance option would have to be self-sufficient and rely on the premiums it collects. But by avoiding some of the overhead that gets eaten up at private companies by profits and excessive administrative costs and executive salaries, it could provide a good deal for consumers, and would also keep pressure on private insurers to keep their policies affordable and treat their customers better, the same way public colleges and universities provide additional choice and competition to students without in any way inhibiting a vibrant system of private colleges and universities.

Now, it is worth noting that a strong majority of Americans still favor a public insurance option of the sort I've proposed tonight. But its impact shouldn't be exaggerated; by the left or the right or the media. It is only one part of my plan, and shouldn't be used as a handy excuse for the usual Washington ideological battles. To my progressive friends, I would remind you that for decades, the driving idea behind reform has been to end insurance company abuses and make coverage available for those without it. The public option is only a means to that end; and we should remain open to other ideas that accomplish our ultimate goal. And to my Republican friends, I say that rather than making wild claims about a government takeover of health care, we should work together to address any legitimate concerns you may have.

For example, some have suggested that the public option go into effect only in those markets where insurance companies are not providing affordable policies. Others have proposed a co-op or another non-profit entity to administer the plan. These are all constructive ideas worth exploring. But I will not back down on the basic principle that if Americans can't find affordable coverage, we will provide you with a choice. And I will make sure that no government bureaucrat or insurance company bureaucrat gets between you and the care that you need.

Finally, let me discuss an issue that is a great concern to me, to members of this chamber, and to the public; and that's how we pay for this plan.

And here's what you need to know. First, I will not sign a plan that adds one dime to our deficits; either now or in the future. I will not sign it if it adds one dime to the deficit, now or in the future, period. And to prove that I'm serious, there will be a provision in this plan that requires us to come forward with more spending cuts if the savings we promised don't materialize. Now, part of the reason I faced a trillion-dollar deficit when I walked in the door of the White House is because too many initiatives over the last decade were not paid for; from the Iraq war to tax breaks for the wealthy. I will not make that same mistake with health care.

Second, we've estimated that most of this plan can be paid for by finding savings within the existing health care system, a system that is currently full of waste and abuse. Right now, too much of the hard-earned savings and tax dollars we spend on health care don't make us any healthier. That's not my judgment; it's the judgment of medical professionals across this country. And this is also true when it comes to Medicare and Medicaid.

In fact, I want to speak directly to seniors for a moment, because Medicare is another issue that's been subjected to demagoguery and distortion during the course of this debate.

More than four decades ago, this nation stood up for the principle that after a lifetime of hard work, our seniors should not be left to struggle with a pile of medical bills in their later years. That's how Medicare was born. And it remains a sacred trust that must be passed down from one generation to the next. And that is why not a dollar of the Medicare trust fund will be used to pay for this plan.

The only thing this plan would eliminate is the hundreds of billions of dollars in waste and fraud, as well as unwarranted subsidies in

Medicare that go to insurance companies; subsidies that do everything to pad their profits but don't improve the care of seniors. And we will also create an independent commission of doctors and medical experts charged with identifying more waste in the years ahead.

Now, these steps will ensure that you; America's seniors; get the benefits you've been promised. They will ensure that Medicare is there for future generations. And we can use some of the savings to fill the gap in coverage that forces too many seniors to pay thousands of dollars a year out of their own pockets for prescription drugs. That's what this plan will do for you. So don't pay attention to those scary stories about how your benefits will be cut, especially since some of the same folks who are spreading these tall tales have fought against Medicare in the past and just this year supported a budget that would essentially have turned Medicare into a privatized voucher program. That will not happen on my watch. I will protect Medicare.

Now, because Medicare is such a big part of the health care system, making the program more efficient can help usher in changes in the way we deliver health care that can reduce costs for everybody. We have long known that some places; like the Intermountain Healthcare in Utah or the Geisinger Health System in rural Pennsylvania; offer high-quality care at costs below average. So the commission can help encourage the adoption of these common-sense best practices by doctors and medical professionals throughout the system; everything from reducing hospital infection rates to encouraging better coordination between teams of doctors.

Reducing the waste and inefficiency in Medicare and Medicaid will pay for most of this plan. Now, much of the rest would be paid for with revenues from the very same drug and insurance companies that stand to benefit from tens of millions of new customers. And this reform will charge insurance companies a fee for their most expensive policies, which will encourage them to provide greater value for the money; an idea which has the support of Democratic and Republican experts. And according to these same experts, this modest change could help hold down the cost of health care for all of us in the long run.

Now, finally, many in this chamber; particularly on the Republican side of the aisle; have long insisted that reforming our medical malpractice laws can help bring down the cost of health care. Now there you go. There you go. Now, I don't believe malpractice reform is a silver bullet, but I've talked to enough doctors to know that defensive medicine may be contributing to unnecessary costs. So I'm proposing that we move forward on a range of ideas about how to put patient safety first and let doctors focus on practicing medicine. I know that the Bush administration considered authorizing demonstration projects in individual states to test these ideas. I think it's a good idea, and I'm directing my Secretary of Health and Human Services to move forward on this initiative today.

Now, add it all up, and the plan I'm proposing will cost around $900 billion over 10 years; less than we have spent on the Iraq and Afghanistan wars, and less than the tax cuts for the wealthiest few Americans that Congress passed at the beginning of the previous administration. Now, most of these costs will be paid for with money already being spent; but spent badly; in the existing health care system. The plan will not add to our deficit. The middle class will realize greater security, not higher taxes. And if we are able to slow the growth of health care costs by just one-tenth of 1 percent each year; one-tenth of 1 percent; it will actually reduce the deficit by $4 trillion over the long term.

Now, this is the plan I'm proposing. It's a plan that incorporates ideas from many of the people in this room tonight; Democrats and Republicans. And I will continue to seek common ground in the weeks ahead. If you come to me with a serious set of proposals, I will be there to listen. My door is always open.

But know this: I will not waste time with those who have made the calculation that it's better politics to kill this plan than to improve it. I won't stand by while the special interests use the same old tactics to keep things exactly the way they are. If you misrepresent what's in this plan, we will call you out. And I will not; and I will not accept the status quo as a solution. Not this time. Not now.

Everyone in this room knows what will happen if we do nothing. Our deficit will grow. More families will go bankrupt. More businesses will close. More Americans will lose their coverage when they are sick and need it the most. And more will die as a result. We know these things to be true.

That is why we cannot fail. Because there are too many Americans counting on us to succeed; the ones who suffer silently, and the ones who shared their stories with us at town halls, in e-mails, and in letters.

I received one of those letters a few days ago. It was from our beloved friend and colleague, Ted Kennedy. He had written it back in May, shortly after he was told that his illness was terminal. He asked that it be delivered upon his death.

In it, he spoke about what a happy time his last months were, thanks to the love and support of family and friends, his wife, Vicki, his amazing children, who are all here tonight. And he expressed confidence that this would be the year that health care reform; that great unfinished business of our society, he called it; would finally pass. He repeated the truth that health care is decisive for our future prosperity, but he also reminded me that it concerns more than material things. "What we face," he wrote, "is above all a moral issue; at stake are not just the details of policy, but fundamental principles of social justice and the character of our country."

I've thought about that phrase quite a bit in recent days; the character of our country. One of the unique and wonderful things about America has always been our self-reliance, our rugged individualism, our fierce defense of freedom and our healthy skepticism of government. And figuring out the appropriate size and role of government has always been a source of rigorous and, yes, sometimes angry debate. That's our history.

For some of Ted Kennedy's critics, his brand of liberalism represented an affront to American liberty. In their minds, his passion for universal health care was nothing more than a passion for big government.

But those of us who knew Teddy and worked with him here; people of both parties; know that what drove him was something more. His friend Orrin Hatch; he knows that. They worked together to provide children with health insurance. His friend John McCain knows that. They worked together on a Patient's Bill of Rights. His friend Chuck Grassley knows that. They worked together to provide health care to children with disabilities.

On issues like these, Ted Kennedy's passion was born not of some rigid ideology, but

of his own experience. It was the experience of having two children stricken with cancer. He never forgot the sheer terror and helplessness that any parent feels when a child is badly sick. And he was able to imagine what it must be like for those without insurance, what it would be like to have to say to a wife or a child or an aging parent, there is something that could make you better, but I just can't afford it.

That large-heartedness; that concern and regard for the plight of others; is not a partisan feeling. It's not a Republican or a Democratic feeling. It, too, is part of the American character; our ability to stand in other people's shoes; a recognition that we are all in this together, and when fortune turns against one of us, others are there to lend a helping hand; a belief that in this country, hard work and responsibility should be rewarded by some measure of security and fair play; and an acknowledgment that sometimes government has to step in to help deliver on that promise.

This has always been the history of our progress. In 1935, when over half of our seniors could not support themselves and millions had seen their savings wiped away, there were those who argued that Social Security would lead to socialism, but the men and women of Congress stood fast, and we are all the better for it. In 1965, when some argued that Medicare represented a government takeover of health care, members of Congress; Democrats and Republicans; did not back down. They joined together so that all of us could enter our golden years with some basic peace of mind.

You see, our predecessors understood that government could not, and should not, solve every problem. They understood that there are instances when the gains in security from government action are not worth the added constraints on our freedom. But they also understood that the danger of too much government is matched by the perils of too little; that without the leavening hand of wise policy, markets can crash, monopolies can stifle competition, the vulnerable can be exploited. And they knew that when any government measure, no matter how carefully crafted or beneficial, is subject to scorn; when any efforts to help people in need are attacked as un-American; when facts and reason are thrown overboard and only timidity passes for wisdom, and we can no longer even engage in a civil conversation with each other over the things that truly matter; that at that point we don't merely lose our capacity to solve big challenges. We lose something essential about ourselves.

That was true then. It remains true today. I understand how difficult this health care debate has been. I know that many in this country are deeply skeptical that government is looking out for them. I understand that the politically safe move would be to kick the can further down the road; to defer reform one more year, or one more election, or one more term.

But that is not what the moment calls for. That's not what we came here to do. We did not come to fear the future. We came here to shape it. I still believe we can act even when it's hard. I still believe; I still believe that we can act when it's hard. I still believe we can replace acrimony with civility, and gridlock with progress. I still believe we can do great things and that here and now we will meet history's test.

Because that's who we are. That is our calling. That is our character. Thank you, God bless you, and may God bless the United States of America.

First State of the Union Address

January 27, 2010

Washington, D.C.

PRESIDENT BARACK Obama delivered his first State of the Union Address on January 27, 2010. His speech before both houses of Congress lasted more than an hour and touched on many of the most pressing issues facing the nation.

Obama acknowledges the many challenges that confronted his administration when he took office a year earlier, including wars in Iraq and Afghanistan and a severe economic recession. He points out that neither of the two wars was funded and that those wars, combined with the crashing economy, helped turn an economic surplus of $800 billion into a deficit of more than $1 trillion. In a more normal time, he says, such a situation would require cuts in governmental spending, but that because of the weakened economy, more spending was required. He also expresses empathy for the concerns of ordinary Americans struggling with the effects of unemployment, inadequate health care coverage, and the housing crisis, and he pledges to work on addressing those problems. The president recognizes that although the nation has passed through tough times, more struggle lies ahead. Obama appeals to members of both political parties to put an end to partisan bickering and to work together to solve important problems, and especially to restore public confidence in government.

Our Constitution declares that from time to time, the president shall give to Congress information about the state of our union. For 220 years, our leaders have fulfilled this duty. They've done so during periods of prosperity and tranquility. And they've done so in the midst of war and depression, at moments of great strife and great struggle.

It's tempting to look back on these moments and assume that our progress was inevitable—that America was always destined to succeed. But when the Union was turned back at Bull Run, and the Allies first landed at Omaha Beach, victory was very much in doubt. When the market crashed on Black Tuesday, and civil rights marchers were beaten on Bloody Sunday, the future was anything but certain. These were the times that tested the courage of our convictions and the strength of our union. And despite all our divisions and disagreements, our hesitations and our fears, America prevailed because we chose to move forward as one nation, as one people.

Again, we are tested. And again, we must answer history's call.

One year ago, I took office amid two wars, an economy rocked by a severe recession, a financial system on the verge of collapse and a government deeply in debt. Experts from across the political spectrum warned that if we did not act, we might face a second depression. So we acted—immediately and aggressively. And one year later, the worst of the storm has passed.

But the devastation remains. One in 10 Americans still cannot find work. Many businesses have shuttered. Home values have declined. Small towns and rural communities have been hit especially hard. And for those who'd already known poverty, life has become that much harder.

This recession has also compounded the burdens that America's families have been dealing with for decades—the burden of working harder and longer for less, of being unable to save enough to retire or help kids with college.

So I know the anxieties that are out there right now. They're not new. These struggles are the reason I ran for president. These struggles are what I've witnessed for years in places like Elkhart, Ind., Galesburg, Ill. I hear about them in the letters that I read each night. The toughest to read are those written by children—asking why they have to move from their home, asking when their mom or dad will be able to go back to work.

For these Americans and so many others, change has not come fast enough. Some are frustrated; some are angry. They don't understand why it seems like bad behavior on Wall

Street is rewarded, but hard work on Main Street isn't; or why Washington has been unable or unwilling to solve any of our problems. They're tired of the partisanship and the shouting and the pettiness. They know we can't afford it. Not now.

So we face big and difficult challenges. And what the American people hope—what they deserve—is for all of us, Democrats and Republicans, to work through our differences, to overcome the numbing weight of our politics. For while the people who sent us here have different backgrounds, different stories, different beliefs, the anxieties they face are the same. The aspirations they hold are shared: a job that pays the bills, a chance to get ahead, most of all, the ability to give their children a better life.

You know what else they share? They share a stubborn resilience in the face of adversity. After one of the most difficult years in our history, they remain busy building cars and teaching kids, starting businesses and going back to school. They're coaching Little League and helping their neighbors. One woman wrote to me and said, "We are strained but hopeful, struggling but encouraged."

It's because of this spirit—this great decency and great strength—that I have never been more hopeful about America's future than I am tonight. Despite our hardships, our union is strong. We do not give up. We do not quit. We do not allow fear or division to break our spirit. In this new decade, it's time the American people get a government that matches their decency, that embodies their strength.

And tonight, tonight I'd like to talk about how together we can deliver on that promise.

It begins with our economy.

Our most urgent task upon taking office was to shore up the same banks that helped cause this crisis. It was not easy to do. And if there's one thing that has unified Democrats and Republicans, and everybody in between, it's that we all hated the bank bailout. I hated it. I hated it. You hated it. It was about as popular as a root canal.

But when I ran for president, I promised I wouldn't just do what was popular—I would do what was necessary. And if we had allowed the meltdown of the financial system, unemployment might be double what it is today. More businesses would certainly have closed. More homes would have surely been lost.

So I supported the last administration's efforts to create the financial rescue program. And when we took that program over, we made it more transparent and more accountable. And as a result, the markets are now stabilized, and we've recovered most of the money we spent on the banks. Most but not all.

To recover the rest, I've proposed a fee on the biggest banks. Now, I know Wall Street isn't keen on this idea. But if these firms can afford to hand out big bonuses again, they can afford a modest fee to pay back the taxpayers who rescued them in their time of need.

Now, as we stabilized the financial system, we also took steps to get our economy growing again, save as many jobs as possible and help Americans who had become unemployed.

That's why we extended or increased unemployment benefits for more than 18 million Americans, made health insurance 65 percent cheaper for families who get their coverage through COBRA and passed 25 different tax cuts.

Now, let me repeat: We cut taxes. We cut taxes for 95 percent of working families. We cut taxes for small businesses. We cut taxes for first-time homebuyers. We cut taxes for parents trying to care for their children. We cut taxes for 8 million Americans paying for college.

I thought I'd get some applause on that one.

As a result, millions of Americans had more to spend on gas and food and other necessities, all of which helped businesses keep more workers. And we haven't raised income taxes by a single dime on a single person. Not a single dime.

Because of the steps we took, there are about 2 million Americans working right now who would otherwise be unemployed. Two hundred thousand work in construction and clean energy, 300,000 are teachers and other education workers. Tens of thousands are cops, firefighters, correctional officers, first responders. And we're on track to add another one-and-a-half-million jobs to this total by the end of the year.

The plan that has made all of this possible, from the tax cuts to the jobs, is the Recovery Act. That's right—the Recovery Act, also known as the stimulus bill. Economists on the left and the right say this bill has helped save jobs and avert disaster. But you don't have to take their word for it. Talk to the small business in Phoenix that will triple its work force because of the Recovery Act. Talk to the window manufacturer in Philadelphia who said he used to be skeptical about the Recovery Act, until he had to add two more work shifts just because of the business it created. Talk to the single teacher raising two kids who was told by her principal in the last week of school that because of the Recovery Act, she wouldn't be laid off after all.

There are stories like this all across America. And after two years of recession, the economy is growing again. Retirement funds have started to gain back some of their value. Businesses are beginning to invest again, and slowly some are starting to hire again.

But I realize that for every success story, there are other stories, of men and women who wake up with the anguish of not knowing where their next paycheck will come from, who send out resumes week after week and hear nothing in response. That is why jobs must be our No. 1 focus in 2010, and that's why I'm calling for a new jobs bill tonight.

Now, the true engine of job creation in this country will always be America's businesses. But government can create the conditions necessary for businesses to expand and hire more workers.

We should start where most new jobs do—in small businesses, companies that begin when—companies that begin when an entrepreneur—when an entrepreneur takes a chance on a dream, or a worker decides it's time she became her own boss. Through sheer grit and determination, these companies have weathered the recession, and they're ready to grow. But when you talk to small business owners in places like Allentown, Pa., or Elyria, Ohio, you find out that even though banks on Wall Street are lending again, they're mostly lending to bigger companies. Financing remains difficult for small business owners across the country, even those that are making a profit.

So tonight, I'm proposing that we take $30 billion of the money Wall Street banks have repaid and use it to help community banks give small businesses the credit they need to stay afloat. I'm also proposing a new small business tax credit—one that will go to over 1 million small businesses who hire new workers or raise wages. While we're at it, let's also eliminate all capital gains taxes on small business investment, and provide a tax incentive for all large businesses and all small businesses to invest in new plants and equipment.

Next, we can put Americans to work today building the infrastructure of tomorrow. From the first railroads to the interstate highway system, our nation has always been built to compete. There's no reason Europe or China should have the fastest trains, or the new factories that manufacture clean energy products.

Tomorrow, I'll visit Tampa, Fla., where workers will soon break ground on a new high-speed railroad funded by the Recovery Act. There are projects like that all across this country that will create jobs and help move our nation's goods, services and information.

We should put more Americans to work building clean energy facilities—and give rebates to Americans who make their homes more energy-efficient, which supports clean energy jobs. And to encourage these and other businesses to stay within our borders, it is time to finally slash the tax breaks for companies that ship our jobs overseas, and give those tax breaks to companies that create jobs right here in the United States of America.

Now, the House has passed a jobs bill that includes some of these steps. As the first order of business this year, I urge the Senate to do the same, and I know they will. They will. People are out of work. They're hurting. They need our help. And I want a jobs bill on my desk without delay.

But the truth is, these steps won't make up for the seven million jobs that we've lost over the last two years. The only way to move to full employment is to lay a new foundation for long-term economic growth, and finally address the problems that America's families have confronted for years.

We can't afford another so-called economic "expansion" like the one from the last decade—what some call the "lost decade"—where jobs grew more slowly than during any prior expansion, where the income of the average American household declined while the cost of health care and tuition reached record highs, where prosperity was built on a housing bubble and financial speculation.

From the day I took office, I've been told that addressing our larger challenges is too ambitious, such an effort would be too contentious. I've been told that our political system is too gridlocked, and that we should just put things on hold for a while.

For those who make these claims, I have one simple question: How long should we wait? How long should America put its future on hold?

You see, Washington has been telling us to wait for decades, even as the problems have grown worse. Meanwhile, China is not waiting to revamp its economy. Germany is not waiting. India is not waiting. These nations—they're not standing still. These nations aren't playing for second place. They're putting more emphasis on math and science. They're rebuilding their infrastructure. They're making serious investments in clean energy because they want those jobs. Well, I do not accept second place for the United States of America.

As hard as it may be, as uncomfortable and contentious as the debates may become, it's time to get serious about fixing the problems that are hampering our growth.

Now, one place to start is serious financial reform. Look, I am not interested in punishing banks. I'm interested in protecting our economy. A strong, healthy financial market makes it possible for businesses to access credit and create new jobs. It channels the savings of families into investments that raise incomes. But that can only happen if we guard against the same recklessness that nearly brought down our entire economy.

We need to make sure consumers and middle-class families have the information they need to make financial decisions. We can't allow financial institutions, including those that take your deposits, to take risks that threaten the whole economy.

Now, the House has already passed financial reform with many of these changes. And the lobbyists are trying to kill it. But we cannot let them win this fight. And if the bill that ends up on my desk does not meet the test of real reform, I will send it back until we get it right. We've got to get it right.

Next, we need to encourage American innovation. Last year, we made the largest investment in basic research funding in history—an investment that could lead to the world's cheapest solar cells or treatment that kills cancer cells but leaves healthy ones untouched. And no area is more ripe for such innovation than energy. You can see the results of last year's investments in clean energy—in the North Carolina company that will create 1,200 jobs nationwide helping to make advanced batteries, or in the California business that will put a thousand people to work making solar panels.

But to create more of these clean energy jobs, we need more production, more efficiency, more incentives. And that means building a new generation of safe, clean nuclear power plants in this country. It means making tough decisions about opening new offshore areas for oil and gas development. It means continued investment in advanced biofuels and clean coal technologies. And, yes, it means passing a comprehensive energy and climate bill with incentives that will finally make clean energy the profitable kind of energy in America.

I am grateful to the House for passing such a bill last year. And this year I'm eager to help advance the bipartisan effort in the Senate.

I know there have been questions about whether we can afford such changes in a tough economy. I know that there are those who disagree with the overwhelming scientific evidence on climate change. But here's the thing—even if you doubt the evidence, providing incentives for energy-efficiency and clean energy are the right thing to do for our future—because the nation that leads the clean energy economy will be the nation that leads the global economy. And America must be that nation.

Third, we need to export more of our goods. Because the more products we make and sell to other countries, the more jobs we support right here in America. So tonight, we set a new goal: We will double our exports over the next five years, an increase that will support 2 million jobs in America. To help meet this goal, we're launching a national export initiative that will help farmers and small businesses increase their exports, and reform export controls consistent with national security.

We have to seek new markets aggressively, just as our competitors are. If America sits on the sidelines while other nations sign trade deals, we will lose the chance to create jobs on our shores. But realizing those benefits also means enforcing those agreements so our trading partners play by the rules. And that's why we'll continue to shape a Doha trade agreement that opens global markets, and why we will strengthen our trade relations in Asia and with key partners like South Korea and Panama and Colombia.

Fourth, we need to invest in the skills and education of our people.

Now, this year, we've broken through the stalemate between left and right by launching a national competition to improve our schools. And the idea here is simple: Instead of rewarding failure, we only reward success. Instead of funding the status quo, we only invest in reform—reform that raises student achievement, inspires students to excel in math and science, and turns around failing schools that steal the future of too many young Americans, from rural communities to the inner city. In the 21st century, the best anti-poverty program around is a world-class education. And in this country, the success of our children cannot depend more on where they live than on their potential.

When we renew the Elementary and Secondary Education Act, we will work with Congress to expand these reforms to all 50 states. Still, in this economy, a high school diploma no longer guarantees a good job. That's why I urge the Senate to follow the House and pass a bill that will revitalize our community colleges, which are a career pathway to the children of so many working families.

To make college more affordable, this bill will finally end the unwarranted taxpayer subsidies that go to banks for student loans. Instead, let's take that money and give families a $10,000 tax credit for four years of college and increase Pell Grants. And let's tell another 1 million students that when they graduate, they will be required to pay only 10 percent of their income on student loans, and all of their debt will be forgiven after 20 years—and forgiven after 10 years if they choose a career in public service, because in the United States of America, no one should go broke because they chose to go to college.

And by the way, it's time for colleges and universities to get serious about cutting their own costs—because they, too, have a responsibility to help solve this problem.

Now, the price of college tuition is just one of the burdens facing the middle class. That's why last year I asked Vice President Biden to chair a task force on middle-class families. That's why we're nearly doubling the child-care tax credit, and making it easier to save for retirement by giving access to every worker a retirement account and expanding the tax credit for those who start a nest egg. That's why we're working to lift the value of

a family's single largest investment—their home. The steps we took last year to shore up the housing market have allowed millions of Americans to take out new loans and save an average of $1,500 on mortgage payments.

This year, we will step up refinancing so that homeowners can move into more affordable mortgages. And it is precisely to relieve the burden on middle-class families that we still need health insurance reform. Yes, we do.

Now, let's clear a few things up. I didn't choose to tackle this issue to get some legislative victory under my belt. And by now it should be fairly obvious that I didn't take on health care because it was good politics. I took on health care because of the stories I've heard from Americans with pre-existing conditions whose lives depend on getting coverage, patients who've been denied coverage, families—even those with insurance—who are just one illness away from financial ruin.

After nearly a century of trying—Democratic administrations, Republican administrations—we are closer than ever to bringing more security to the lives of so many Americans. The approach we've taken would protect every American from the worst practices of the insurance industry. It would give small businesses and uninsured Americans a chance to choose an affordable health care plan in a competitive market. It would require every insurance plan to cover preventive care.

And by the way, I want to acknowledge our first lady, Michelle Obama, who this year is creating a national movement to tackle the epidemic of childhood obesity and make kids healthier. Thank you. She gets embarrassed.

Our approach would preserve the right of Americans who have insurance to keep their doctor and their plan. It would reduce costs and premiums for millions of families and businesses. And according to the Congressional Budget Office—the independent organization that both parties have cited as the official scorekeeper for Congress—our approach would bring down the deficit by as much as $1 trillion over the next two decades.

Still, this is a complex issue, and the longer it was debated, the more skeptical people became. I take my share of the blame for not explaining it more clearly to the American people. And I know that with all the lobbying and horse-trading, the process left most Americans wondering, "What's in it for me?"

But I also know this problem is not going away. By the time I'm finished speaking tonight, more Americans will have lost their health insurance. Millions will lose it this year. Our deficit will grow. Premiums will go up. Patients will be denied the care they need. Small business owners will continue to drop coverage altogether. I will not walk away from these Americans and neither should the people in this chamber.

So, as temperatures cool, I want everyone to take another look at the plan we've proposed. There's a reason why many doctors, nurses and health care experts who know our system best consider this approach a vast improvement over the status quo. But if anyone from either party has a better approach that will bring down premiums, bring down the deficit, cover the uninsured, strengthen Medicare for seniors and stop insurance company abuses, let me know. Let me know. Let me know. I'm eager to see it.

Here's what I ask Congress, though: Don't walk away from reform. Not now. Not when we are so close. Let us find a way to come together and finish the job for the American people. Let's get it done. Let's get it done.

Now, even as health care reform would reduce our deficit, it's not enough to dig us out of a massive fiscal hole in which we find ourselves. It's a challenge that makes all others that much harder to solve, and one that's been subject to a lot of political posturing. So let me start the discussion of government spending by setting the record straight.

At the beginning of the last decade, the year 2000, America had a budget surplus of over $200 billion. By the time I took office, we had a one-year deficit of over $1 trillion and projected deficits of $8 trillion over the next decade. Most of this was the result of not paying for two wars, two tax cuts and an expensive prescription drug program. On top of that, the effects of the recession put a $3 trillion hole in our budget. All this was before I walked in the door.

Now—just stating the facts. Now, if we had taken office in ordinary times, I would have liked nothing more than to start bringing down the deficit. But we took office amid a crisis. And our efforts to prevent a second depression have added another $1 trillion to our national debt. That, too, is a fact.

I'm absolutely convinced that was the right thing to do. But families across the country are tightening their belts and making tough decisions. The federal government should do the same. So tonight, I'm proposing specific steps to pay for the trillion dollars that it took to rescue the economy last year.

Starting in 2011, we are prepared to freeze government spending for three years. Spending related to our national security, Medicare, Medicaid and Social Security will not be affected. But all other discretionary government programs will. Like any cash-strapped family, we will work within a budget to invest in what we need and sacrifice what we don't. And if I have to enforce this discipline by veto, I will.

We will continue to go through the budget, line by line, page by page, to eliminate programs that we can't afford and don't work. We've already identified $20 billion in savings for next year. To help working families, we'll extend our middle-class tax cuts. But at a time of record deficits, we will not continue tax cuts for oil companies, for investment fund managers and for those making over $250,000 a year. We just can't afford it.

Now, even after paying for what we spent on my watch, we'll still face the massive deficit we had when I took office. More importantly, the cost of Medicare, Medicaid and Social Security will continue to skyrocket. That's why I've called for a bipartisan fiscal commission, modeled on a proposal by Republican Judd Gregg and Democrat Kent Conrad. This can't be one of those Washington gimmicks that lets us pretend we solved a problem. The commission will have to provide a specific set of solutions by a certain deadline.

Now, yesterday, the Senate blocked a bill that would have created this commission. So I'll issue an executive order that will allow us to go forward, because I refuse to pass this problem on to another generation of Americans. And when the vote comes tomorrow, the Senate should restore the pay-as-you-go law that was a big reason for why we had record surpluses in the 1990s.

Now, I know that some in my own party will argue that we can't address the deficit or freeze government spending when so many are still hurting. And I agree—which is why this freeze won't take effect until next year—when the economy is stronger. That's how budgeting works. But understand—understand if we don't take meaningful steps to rein in our debt, it could damage our markets, increase the cost of borrowing and jeopardize our recovery—all of which would have an even worse effect on our job growth and family incomes.

From some on the right, I expect we'll hear a different argument—that if we just make fewer investments in our people, extend tax cuts including those for the wealthier Americans, eliminate more regulations, maintain the status quo on health care, our deficits will go away. The problem is that's what we did for eight years. That's what helped us into this crisis. It's what helped lead to these deficits. We can't do it again.

Rather than fight the same tired battles that have dominated Washington for decades, it's time to try something new. Let's invest in our people without leaving them a mountain of debt. Let's meet our responsibility to the citizens who sent us here. Let's try common sense. A novel concept.

To do that, we have to recognize that we face more than a deficit of dollars right now. We face a deficit of trust—deep and corrosive doubts about how Washington works that have been growing for years. To close that credibility gap we have to take action on both ends of Pennsylvania Avenue—to end the outsized influence of lobbyists, to do our work openly, to give our people the government they deserve.

That's what I came to Washington to do. That's why—for the first time in history—my administration posts on our White House visitors online. That's why we've excluded lobbyists from policymaking jobs, or seats on federal boards and commissions.

But we can't stop there. It's time to require lobbyists to disclose each contact they make on behalf of a client with my administration or with Congress. It's time to put strict limits on the contributions that lobbyists give to candidates for federal office.

With all due deference to separation of powers, last week the Supreme Court reversed a century of law that I believe will open the floodgates for special interests—including foreign corporations—to spend without limit in our elections. I don't think American elections should be bankrolled by America's most powerful interests, or worse, by foreign entities.

They should be decided by the American people. And I'd urge Democrats and Republicans to pass a bill that helps to correct some of these problems.

I'm also calling on Congress to continue down the path of earmark reform. Democrats and Republicans. Democrats and Republicans. You've trimmed some of this spending, you've embraced some meaningful change. But restoring the public trust demands more. For example, some members of Congress post some earmark requests online. Tonight, I'm calling on Congress to publish all earmark requests on a single Web site before there's a vote, so that the American people can see how their money is being spent.

Of course, none of these reforms will even happen if we don't also reform how we work with one another. Now, I'm not naive. I never thought that the mere fact of my election would usher in peace and harmony—and some post-partisan era. I knew that both parties have fed divisions that are deeply entrenched. And on some issues, there are simply philosophical differences that will always cause us to part ways. These disagreements, about the role of government in our lives, about our national priorities and our national security, they've been taking place for over 200 years. They're the very essence of our democracy.

But what frustrates the American people is a Washington where every day is Election Day. We can't wage a perpetual campaign where the only goal is to see who can get the most embarrassing headlines about the other side—a belief that if you lose, I win. Neither party should delay or obstruct every single bill just because they can. The confirmation of—I'm speaking to both parties now. The confirmation of well-qualified public servants shouldn't be held hostage to the pet projects or grudges of a few individual senators.

Washington may think that saying anything about the other side, no matter how false, no matter how malicious, is just part of the game. But it's precisely such politics that has stopped either party from helping the American people. Worse yet, it's sowing further division among our citizens, further distrust in our government.

So, no, I will not give up on trying to change the tone of our politics. I know it's an election year. And after last week, it's clear that campaign fever has come even earlier than usual. But we still need to govern.

To Democrats, I would remind you that we still have the largest majority in decades, and the people expect us to solve problems, not run for the hills. And if the Republican leadership is going to insist that 60 votes in the Senate are required to do any business at all in this town—a supermajority—then the responsibility to govern is now yours as well. Just saying no to everything may be good short-term politics, but it's not leadership. We were sent here to serve our citizens, not our ambitions. So let's show the American people that we can do it together.

This week, I'll be addressing a meeting of the House Republicans. I'd like to begin monthly meetings with both Democratic and Republican leadership. I know you can't wait.

Throughout our history, no issue has united this country more than our security. Sadly, some of the unity we felt after 9/11 has dissipated. We can argue all we want about who's to blame for this, but I'm not interested in relitigating the past. I know that all of us love this country. All of us are committed to its defense. So let's put aside the schoolyard taunts about who's tough. Let's reject the false choice between protecting our people and upholding our values. Let's leave behind the fear and division, and do what it takes to defend our nation and forge a more hopeful future—for America and for the world.

That's the work we began last year. Since the day I took office, we've renewed our focus on the terrorists who threaten our nation. We've made substantial investments in our homeland security and disrupted plots that threatened to take American lives. We are filling unacceptable gaps revealed by the failed Christmas attack, with better airline security and swifter action on our intelligence. We've prohibited torture and strengthened partnerships from the Pacific to South Asia to the Arabian Peninsula. And in the last year, hundreds of al-Qaida's fighters and affiliates, including many senior leaders, have been captured or killed—far more than in 2008.

And in Afghanistan, we're increasing our troops and training Afghan security forces so they can begin to take the lead in July of 2011, and our troops can begin to come home. We will reward good governance, work to reduce corruption and support the rights of all Afghans—men and women alike. We're joined by allies and partners who have increased their own commitments, and who will come together tomorrow in London to reaffirm our common purpose. There will be difficult days ahead. But I am absolutely confident we will succeed.

As we take the fight to al-Qaida, we are responsibly leaving Iraq to its people. As a candidate, I promised that I would end this war, and that is what I am doing as president. We will have all of our combat troops out of Iraq by the end of this August. We will support the Iraqi government—we will support the Iraqi government as they hold elections, and we will continue to partner with the Iraqi people to promote regional peace and prosperity. But make no mistake: This war is ending, and all of our troops are coming home.

Tonight, all of our men and women in uniform—in Iraq, in Afghanistan and around the world—they have to know that we—that they have our respect, our gratitude, our full support. And just as they must have the resources they need in war, we all have a responsibility to support them when they come home. That's why we made the largest increase in investments for veterans in decades—last year. That's why we're building a 21st century VA. And that's why Michelle has joined with Jill Biden to forge a national commitment to support military families.

Now, even as we prosecute two wars, we're also confronting perhaps the greatest danger to the American people—the threat of nuclear weapons. I've embraced the vision of John F. Kennedy and Ronald Reagan through a strategy that reverses the spread of these weapons and seeks a world without them. To reduce our stockpiles and launchers, while ensuring our deterrent, the United States and Russia are completing negotiations on the farthest-reaching arms control treaty in nearly two decades. And at April's nuclear security summit, we will bring 44 nations together here in Washington, D.C., behind a clear goal: securing all vulnerable nuclear materials around the world in four years, so that they never fall into the hands of terrorists.

Now, these diplomatic efforts have also strengthened our hand in dealing with those nations that insist on violating international agreements in pursuit of nuclear weapons. That's why North Korea now faces increased isolation and stronger sanctions—sanctions that are being vigorously enforced. That's why the international community is more united, and the Islamic Republic of Iran is more isolated. And as Iran's leaders continue to ignore their obligations, there should be no doubt: They, too, will face growing consequences. That is a promise.

That's the leadership that we are providing—engagement that advances the common security and prosperity of all people. We're working through the G-20 to sustain a lasting global recovery. We're working with Muslim communities around the world to promote science and education and innovation. We have gone from a bystander to a leader in the fight against climate change. We're helping developing countries to feed themselves and continuing the fight against HIV/AIDS. And we are launching a new initiative that will give us the capacity to respond faster and more effectively to bioterrorism or an infectious disease—a plan that will counter threats at home and strengthen public health abroad.

As we have for over 60 years, America takes these actions because our destiny is connected to those beyond our shores. But we also do it because it is right. That's why, as we meet here tonight, over 10,000 Americans are working with many nations to help the people of Haiti recover and rebuild. That's why we stand with the girl who yearns to go to school in Afghanistan, why we support the human rights of the women marching through the streets of Iran, why we advocate for the young man denied a job by corruption in Guinea. For America must always stand on the side of freedom and human dignity. Always.

Abroad, America's greatest source of strength has always been our ideals. The same is true at home. We find unity in our incredible diversity, drawing on the promise enshrined in our Constitution: the notion that we're all created equal, that no matter who you are or what you look like, if you abide by the law you should be protected by it, if you adhere to our common values you should be treated no different than anyone else.

We must continually renew this promise. My administration has a civil rights division that is once again prosecuting civil rights violations and employment discrimination. We finally strengthened our laws to protect against crimes driven by hate. This year, I will work with Congress and our military to finally repeal the law that denies gay Americans the right to serve the country they love because of who they are. It's the right thing to do.

We're going to crack down on violations of equal pay laws—so that women get equal pay for an equal day's work. And we should continue the work of fixing our broken immigration system—to secure our borders and enforce our laws and ensure that everyone who plays by the rules can contribute to our economy and enrich our nation.

In the end, it's our ideals, our values that built America—values that allowed us to forge a nation made up of immigrants from every corner of the globe, values that drive our citizens still. Every day, Americans meet their responsibilities to their families and their employers. Time and again, they lend a hand to their neighbors and give back to their country. They take pride in their labor and are generous in spirit. These aren't Republican values or Democratic values that they're living by, business values or labor values. They're American values.

Unfortunately, too many of our citizens have lost faith that our biggest institutions—our corporations, our media, and, yes, our government—still reflect these same values. Each of these institutions are full of honorable men and women doing important work that helps our country prosper. But each time a CEO rewards himself for failure, or a banker puts the rest of us at risk for his own selfish gain, people's doubts grow. Each time lobbyists game the system or politicians tear each other down instead of lifting this country up, we lose faith. The more that TV pundits reduce serious debates to silly arguments, big issues into sound bites, our citizens turn away.

No wonder there's so much cynicism out there. No wonder there's so much disappointment.

I campaigned on the promise of change—change we can believe in, the slogan went. And right now, I know there are many Americans who aren't sure if they still believe we can change—or that I can deliver it.

But remember this—I never suggested that change would be easy, or that I could do it alone. Democracy in a nation of 300 million people can be noisy and messy and complicated. And when you try to do big things and make big changes, it stirs passions and controversy. That's just how it is.

Those of us in public office can respond to this reality by playing it safe and avoid telling hard truths and pointing fingers. We can do what's necessary to keep our poll numbers high and get through the next election instead of doing what's best for the next generation.

But I also know this: If people had made that decision 50 years ago or 100 years ago or 200 years ago, we wouldn't be here tonight. The only reason we are here is because generations of Americans were unafraid to do what was hard, to do what was needed even when success was uncertain, to do what it took to keep the dream of this nation alive for their children and their grandchildren.

Our administration has had some political setbacks this year and some of them were deserved. But I wake up every day knowing that they are nothing compared to the setbacks that families all across this country have faced this year. And what keeps me going—what keeps me fighting—is that despite all these setbacks, that spirit of determination and optimism, that fundamental decency that has always been at the core of the American people, that lives on.

It lives on in the struggling small business owner who wrote to me of his company, "None of us," he said, ". . . are willing to consider, even slightly, that we might fail."

It lives on in the woman who said that even though she and her neighbors have felt the pain of recession, "We are strong. We are resilient. We are American."

It lives on in the 8-year-old boy in Louisiana, who just sent me his allowance and asked if I would give it to the people of Haiti.

And it lives on in all the Americans who've dropped everything to go someplace they've never been and pull people they've never known from the rubble, prompting chants of "USA! USA! USA!" when another life was saved.

The spirit that has sustained this nation for more than two centuries lives on in you, its people. We have finished a difficult year. We have come through a difficult decade. But a new year has come. A new decade stretches before us. We don't quit. I don't quit. Let's seize this moment—to start anew, to carry the dream forward and to strengthen our union once more.

Thank you. God bless you. And God bless the United States of America.

Remarks on Signing the Patient Protection and Affordable Care Act

March 23, 2010

Washington, D.C.

On March 23, 2010, President Barack Obama achieved one of his administration's top policy goals when he signed a historic health care reform bill into law. The Patient Protection and Affordable Care Act became one of the widest-reaching pieces of social legislation signed in decades. This law, the president says, places new restrictions on health insurance companies that limit their ability to increase rates, drop patients who become sick, and deny coverage to people with preexisting conditions. It also establishes government-run health insurance exchanges to increase competition and reduce premiums and provides tax breaks to middle-class families and small-business owners to help offset the cost of coverage.

In his remarks, the president cites examples of the kinds of people the act was designed to help. The president also alludes to the fierce political struggle surrounding the law. Republicans had opposed the legislation from the first, rejecting it on the ideological basis that it represented an unwarranted intrusion by government into citizens' lives. Some also thought that the law put too great a financial burden on government, especially when the United States was still struggling with the aftermath of the recession of 2008. Although these fears proved to be ungrounded, strong partisan opposition (colloquially calling the law Obamacare) helped energize a libertarian-conservative opposition to Obama's liberal politics.

Today, after almost a century of trying; today, after over a year of debate; today, after all the votes have been tallied, health insurance reform becomes law in the United States of America—today.

You know, it is fitting that Congress passed this historic legislation this week, for as we mark the turning of spring, we also mark a new season in America.

In a few moments, when I sign this bill, all of the overheated rhetoric over reform will finally confront the reality of reform. And while the Senate still has the last round of improvements to make on this historic legislation—and these are improvements I'm confident they will make swiftly—the bill I'm signing will set in motion reforms that generations of Americans have fought for and marched for and hungered to see.

It will take four years to implement fully many of these reforms, because we need to implement them responsibly. We need to get this right. But a host of desperately needed reforms will take effect right away, this year.

This year, we'll start offering tax credits to about 4 million small-business men and women, to help them cover the cost of insurance for their employees. That happens this year.

This year, tens of thousands of uninsured Americans with pre-existing conditions, the parents of children who have a pre-existing condition, will finally be able to purchase the coverage they need. That happens this year.

This year—this year, insurance companies will no longer be able to drop people's coverage, when they get sick—or they won't be able to place lifetime limits or restrictive annual limits on the amount of care they can receive.

This year—this year, all new insurance plans will be required to offer free preventive care. And this year, young adults will be able to stay on their parents' policies until they are 26 years old.

That happens this year.

And this year seniors who fall in the coverage gap known as the doughnut hole—will start getting some help. They'll receive $250 to help pay for prescriptions, and that will over time fill in the doughnut hole.

And I want seniors to know, despite what some have said, these reforms will not cut your guaranteed benefits. In fact, under this law, Americans on Medicare will receive preventive care without co-payments or deductibles. That begins this year.

Once this reform is implemented, health insurance exchanges will be created, a competitive marketplace, where uninsured people and small businesses will finally be able to purchase affordable quality insurance. They will be able to be part of a big pool and get the same good deal that members of Congress get. That's what's going to happen under this reform.

And when this exchange is up and running, millions of people will get tax breaks to help them afford coverage, which represents the largest middle-class tax cut for health care in history. That's what this reform's about.

This legislation will also lower costs for families and for businesses and for the federal government, reducing our deficit by over $1 trillion in the next two decades.

It is paid for, it is fiscally responsible. And it will help lift a decades-long drag on our economy. That's part of what all of you together worked on and made happen.

You know, that our generation is able to succeed in passing this reform is a testament to the persistence and the character of the American people, who championed this cause, who mobilized, who organized, who believed that people who love this country can change it.

It's also a testament to the historic leadership and uncommon courage of the men and women of the United States Congress, who have taken their lumps during this difficult debate.

You know, there are few tougher jobs in politics or government than leading one of our legislative chambers.

In each chamber, there are men and women who come from different places and face different pressures or reach different conclusions about the same things and feel deeply concerned about different things. And by necessity, leaders have to speak to those different concerns. It isn't always tidy. It is almost never easy.

But perhaps the greatest and most difficult challenge is to cobble together, out of these differences, the sense of common interest and common purpose that's required, to advance the dreams of all people, especially in a country as large and diverse as ours.

And we are blessed by leaders in each chamber who not only do their jobs very well, but who never lost sight of that larger mission. They didn't play for the short term, they didn't play to the polls or to politics:

One of the best speakers the House of Representatives has ever had—Speaker Nancy Pelosi.

One of the best majority leaders the Senate has ever had, Mr. Harry Reid.

To all of the terrific committee chairs, all the members of Congress who did what was difficult but did what was right—passed health-care reform—not just this generation of Americans will thank you, but the next generation of Americans will thank you.

And of course, this victory was also made possible by the painstaking work of members of this administration, including our outstanding Secretary of Health and Human Services, Kathleen Sebelius—and one of the unsung heroes of this effort, an extraordinary woman who led the reform effort from the White House, Nancy-Ann DeParle.

Today, I'm signing this reform bill into law on behalf of my mother, who argued with insurance companies even as she battled cancer in her final days.

I'm signing it for Ryan Smith, who's here today. He runs a small business with five employees. He's trying to do the right thing, paying half the cost of coverage for his workers. This bill will help him afford that coverage.

I'm signing it for 11-year-old Marcelas Owens, who's also here. Marcelas lost his mom to an illness, and she didn't have insurance and couldn't afford the care that she needed. So in her memory, he has told her story across America so that no other children have to go through what his family's experienced.

I'm signing it for Natoma Canfield. Natoma had to give up her health coverage after her rates were jacked up by more than 40 percent. She was terrified that an illness would mean she'd lose the house that her parents built. So she gave up her insurance, and now she's lying in a hospital bed as we speak, faced with just such an illness, praying that she can somehow afford to get well without insurance.

Natoma's family is here today because Natoma can't be. And her sister Connie's here. Connie, stand up.

I'm signing this bill for all the leaders who took up this cause through the generations, from Teddy Roosevelt to Franklin Roosevelt, from Harry Truman to Lyndon Johnson, from

Bill and Hillary Clinton to one of the deans who's been fighting this long, John Dingell, to Senator Ted Kennedy.

And it's fitting that Ted's widow, Vicki, is here. It's fitting that Teddy's widow, Vicki, is here, and his niece Caroline, his son Patrick, whose vote helped make this reform a reality. I remember seeing Ted walk through that door in a summit in this room a year ago—one of his last public appearances—and it was hard for him to make it. But he was confident that we would do the right thing.

Our presence here today is remarkable, and improbable. With all the punditry, all of the lobbying, all of the game-playing that passes for governing in Washington, it's been easy at times to doubt our ability to do such a big thing, such a complicated thing; to wonder if there are limits to what we as a people can still achieve. It's easy to succumb to the sense of cynicism about what's possible in this country. But today, we are affirming that essential truth, a truth every generation is called to rediscover for itself, that we are not a nation that scales back its aspirations. We are not a nation that falls prey to doubt or mistrust. We don't fall prey to fear. We are not a nation that does what's easy. That's not who we are. That's not how we got here.

We are a nation that faces its challenges and accepts its responsibilities. We are a nation that does what is hard, what is necessary, what is right. Here in this country, we shape our own destiny. That is what we do. That is who we are. That is what makes us the United States of America.

And we have now just enshrined—as soon as I sign this bill—the core principle that everybody should have some basic security when it comes to their health care.

And it is an extraordinary achievement that has happened because of all of you, and all the advocates all across the country.

So thank you. Thank you. Thank you, God bless you, and may God bless the United States of America.

Remarks Announcing Death
of Osama bin Laden

May 1, 2011
Washington, D.C.

ON MAY 2, 2011, President Barack Obama appeared on national news to announce that American forces had raided a compound in Abbottabad, Pakistan, and killed Osama bin Laden, head of the international terrorist organization known as al-Qaeda. Bin Laden was responsible for the attacks of September 11, 2001, which killed approximately three thousand people, and for numerous other incidents worldwide. The president used the occasion to remind the American people of their combined efforts to fight terrorism worldwide.

Obama begins his speech by announcing bin Laden's death. He follows with a brief description of the events of 9/11 and points out that Americans were unified in their efforts to help the victims and to take steps to prevent another attack. The president then outlines American actions during the war on terror, including the war in Afghanistan that drove the Taliban from power. He reminds Americans that the war on terror was never a war against Islam, pointing out that bin Laden himself was responsible for many Muslim deaths; praises the American and Pakistani intelligence efforts that located bin Laden's hideaway; and notes that the attack was approved by the Pakistani government. He concludes by declaring that for survivors and the families of the victims of 9/11 "justice has been done."

Good evening. Tonight I can report to the American people and to the world that the United States has conducted an operation that killed Osama bin Laden, the leader of Al Qaida and a terrorist who's responsible for the murder of thousands of innocent men, women, and children.

It was nearly 10 years ago that a bright September day was darkened by the worst attack on the American people in our history. The images of 9/11 are seared into our national memory: hijacked planes cutting through a cloudless September sky; the Twin Towers collapsing to the ground; black smoke billowing up from the Pentagon; the wreckage of Flight 93 in Shanksville, Pennsylvania, where the actions of heroic citizens saved even more heartbreak and destruction.

And yet we know that the worst images are those that were unseen to the world: the empty seat at the dinner table; children who were forced to grow up without their mother or their father; parents who would never know the feeling of their child's embrace; nearly 3,000 citizens taken from us, leaving a gaping hole in our hearts.

On September 11, 2001, in our time of grief, the American people came together. We offered our neighbors a hand, and we offered the wounded our blood. We reaffirmed our ties to each other and our love of community and country. On that day, no matter where we came from, what God we prayed to, or what race or ethnicity we were, we were united as one American family.

We were also united in our resolve to protect our Nation and to bring those who committed this vicious attack to justice. We quickly learned that the 9/11 attacks were carried out by Al Qaida, an organization headed by Osama bin Laden, which had openly declared war on the United States and was committed to killing innocents in our country and around the globe. And so we went to war against Al Qaida to protect our citizens, our friends, and our allies.

Over the last 10 years, thanks to the tireless and heroic work of our military and our counterterrorism professionals, we've made great strides in that effort. We've disrupted terrorist attacks and strengthened our homeland defense. In Afghanistan, we removed the Taliban Government, which had given bin Laden and Al Qaida safe haven and support. And around the globe, we worked with our friends and allies to capture or kill scores of Al

Qaida terrorists, including several who were a part of the 9/11 plot.

Yet Osama bin Laden avoided capture and escaped across the Afghan border into Pakistan. Meanwhile, Al Qaida continued to operate from along that border and operate through its affiliates across the world.

And so shortly after taking office, I directed Leon Panetta, the Director of the CIA, to make the killing or capture of bin Laden the top priority of our war against Al Qaida, even as we continued our broader efforts to disrupt, dismantle, and defeat his network.

Then, last August, after years of painstaking work by our intelligence community, I was briefed on a possible lead to bin Laden. It was far from certain, and it took many months to run this thread to ground. I met repeatedly with my national security team as we developed more information about the possibility that we had located bin Laden hiding within a compound deep inside Pakistan. And finally, last week, I determined that we had enough intelligence to take action and authorized an operation to get Osama bin Laden and bring him to justice.

Today, at my direction, the United States launched a targeted operation against that compound in Abbottabad, Pakistan. A small team of Americans carried out the operation with extraordinary courage and capability. No Americans were harmed. They took care to avoid civilian casualties. After a firefight, they killed Usama bin Laden and took custody of his body.

For over two decades, bin Laden has been Al Qaida's leader and symbol and has continued to plot attacks against our country and our friends and allies. The death of bin Laden marks the most significant achievement to date in our Nation's effort to defeat Al Qaida.

Yet his death does not mark the end of our effort. There's no doubt that Al Qaida will continue to pursue attacks against us. We must—and we will—remain vigilant at home and abroad.

As we do, we must also reaffirm that the United States is not and never will be at war with Islam. I've made clear, just as President Bush did shortly after 9/11, that our war is not against Islam. Bin Laden was not a Muslim leader, he was a mass murderer of Muslims. Indeed, Al Qaida has slaughtered scores of Muslims in many countries, including our own. So his demise should be welcomed by all who believe in peace and human dignity.

Over the years, I've repeatedly made clear that we would take action within Pakistan if we knew where bin Laden was. That is what we've done. But it's important to note that our counterterrorism cooperation with Pakistan helped lead us to bin Laden and the compound where he was hiding. Indeed, bin Laden had declared war against Pakistan as well and ordered attacks against the Pakistani people.

Tonight I called President Zardari, and my team has also spoken with their Pakistani counterparts. They agree that this is a good and historic day for both of our nations. And going forward, it is essential that Pakistan continue to join us in the fight against Al Qaida and its affiliates.

The American people did not choose this fight. It came to our shores and started with the senseless slaughter of our citizens. After nearly 10 years of service, struggle, and sacrifice, we know well the costs of war. These efforts weigh on me every time I, as Commander in Chief, have to sign a letter to a family that has lost a loved one or look into the eyes of a service member who's been gravely wounded.

So Americans understand the costs of war. Yet as a country, we will never tolerate our security being threatened nor stand idly by when our people have been killed. We will be relentless in defense of our citizens and our friends and allies. We will be true to the values that make us who we are. And on nights like this one, we can say to those families who have lost loved ones to Al Qaida's terror: Justice has been done.

Tonight we give thanks to the countless intelligence and counterterrorism professionals who've worked tirelessly to achieve this outcome. The American people do not see their work nor know their names, but tonight they feel the satisfaction of their work and the result of their pursuit of justice.

We give thanks for the men who carried out this operation, for they exemplify the professionalism, patriotism, and unparalleled courage of those who serve our country. And they are part of a generation that has borne the heaviest share of the burden since that September day.

Finally, let me say to the families who lost loved ones on 9/11 that we have never forgotten your loss nor wavered in our commitment to see that we do whatever it takes to prevent another attack on our shores.

And tonight let us think back to the sense of unity that prevailed on 9/11. I know that it has, at times, frayed. Yet today's achievement is a testament to the greatness of our country and the determination of the American people.

The cause of securing our country is not complete. But tonight we are once again reminded that America can do whatever we set our mind to. That is the story of our history, whether it's the pursuit of prosperity for our people or the struggle for equality for all our citizens, our commitment to stand up for our values abroad, and our sacrifices to make the world a safer place.

Let us remember that we can do these things not just because of wealth or power, but because of who we are: one Nation under God, indivisible, with liberty and justice for all.

Thank you. May God bless you, and may God bless the United States of America.

Gun Control Speech 1-15-16

January 15, 2016

Washington, D.C.

On January 5, 2016, President Barack Obama announced a series of executive actions meant to curb the increased gun violence that plagued his years in office. The measures the president proposed included encouragement of new technologies to prevent firearms accidents, increased support for enforcement of existing gun laws, and better access to mental health care to limit disturbed individuals' access to firearms. He focused most clearly on the enforcement of background checks for gun buyers. The speech on gun control came at the beginning of Obama's last year in office. He declared that he had no political motive in introducing the measures but simply hoped to prevent further mass shootings. In doing so, he helped shape the debate on gun control—and on the use of executive actions—for the 2016 presidential election.

Obama begins his speech by acknowledging the man who introduced him—Mark Barden, who in 2012 lost his seven-year-old son Daniel in the mass shooting at Sandy Hook Elementary School. Obama acknowledges the presence and the influence of the survivors of shootings— including former U.S. Representative Gabrielle Giffords (shot in the head at point-blank range during an attack in 2011)—and the families of victims. He criticizes the Republican-led Congress for its failure to enact meaningful reforms that might help limit gun violence.

The President. Thank you. Thank you, everybody. Please have a seat. Thank you. Thank you so much.

Mark, I want to thank you for your introduction. I still remember the first time we met and the time we spent together and the conversation we had about Daniel. And that changed me that day. And my hope, earnestly, has been that it would change the country.

Five years ago this week, a sitting Member of Congress and 18 others were shot at, at a supermarket in Tucson, Arizona. It wasn't the first time I had to talk to the Nation in response to a mass shooting, nor would it be the last. Fort Hood. Binghamton. Aurora. Oak Creek. Newtown. The Navy Yard. Santa Barbara. Charleston. San Bernardino. Too many.

Audience member. Too many.

Audience member. Too many.

Audience member. Too many.

The President. Now, thanks to a great medical team and the love of her husband Mark, my dear friend and colleague, Gabby Giffords, survived. She's here with us today with her wonderful mom. Thanks to a great medical team, her wonderful husband Mark, who, by the way, the last time I met with Mark—this is just a small aside—you may know Mark's twin brother is in outer space. He came to the office, and I said, "How often are you talking to him?" And he says, "Well, I usually talk to him every day, but the call was coming in right before the meeting so I think I may have not answered his call"—which made me feel kind of bad. That's a long-distance call. So I told him if his brother Scott is calling today, that he should take it. Turn the ringer on.

I was there with Gabby when she was still in the hospital, and we didn't think necessarily at that point that she was going to survive. And that visit right before a memorial—about an hour later Gabby first opened her eyes. And I remember talking to mom about that. But I know the pain that she and her family have endured these past 5 years and the rehabilitation and the work and the effort to recover from shattering injuries.

And then, I think of all the Americans who aren't as fortunate. Every single year, more than 30,000 Americans have their lives cut short by guns—30,000. Suicides. Domestic violence. Gang shootouts. Accidents. Hundreds of thousands of Americans have lost brothers and sisters, or buried their own children. Many have had to learn to live with a disability or learned to live without the love of their life.

A number of those people are here today. They can tell you some stories. In this room right here, there are a lot of stories. There's a lot of heartache. There's a lot of resilience, there's a lot of strength, but there's also a lot of pain. And this is just a small sampling.

The United States of America is not the only country on Earth with violent or dangerous people. We are not inherently more prone to violence. But we are the only advanced country on Earth that sees this kind of mass violence erupt with this kind of frequency. It doesn't happen in other advanced countries. It's not even close. And as I've said before, somehow, we become numb to it, and we start thinking that this is normal.

And instead of thinking about how to solve the problem, this has become one of our most polarized, partisan debates, despite the fact that there's a general consensus in America about what needs to be done. And that's part of the reason why, on Thursday, I'm going to hold a town hall meeting in Virginia on gun violence. Because my goal here is to bring good people on both sides of this issue together for an open discussion.

I'm not on the ballot again. I'm not looking to score some points. I think we can disagree without impugning other people's motives or without being disagreeable. We don't need to be talking past one another. But we do have to feel a sense of urgency about it. In Dr. King's words, we need to feel the "fierce urgency of now." Because people are dying. And the constant excuses for inaction no longer do, no longer suffice.

That's why we're here today. Not to debate the last mass shooting, but to do something to try to prevent the next one. To prove that the vast majority of Americans, even if our voices aren't always the loudest or most extreme, care enough about a little boy like Daniel to come together and take commonsense steps to save lives and protect more of our children.

Now, I want to be absolutely clear at the start—I've said this over and over again; this also becomes routine; there is a ritual about this whole thing that I have to do—I believe in the Second Amendment. And it's there written on the paper. It guarantees a right to bear arms. No matter how many times people try to twist my words around, I taught constitutional law, I know a little about this—I get it. But I also believe that we can find ways to reduce gun violence consistent with the Second Amendment.

I mean, think about it. We all believe in the First Amendment, the guarantee of free speech, but we accept that you can't yell "fire" in a theater. We understand there are some constraints on our freedom in order to protect innocent people. We cherish our right to privacy, but we accept that you have to go through metal detectors before being allowed to board a plane. It's not because people like doing that, but we understand that that's part of the price of living in a civilized society.

And what's often ignored in this debate is that a majority of gun owners actually agree. A majority of gun owners agree that we can respect the Second Amendment while keeping an irresponsible, law-breaking few from inflicting harm on a massive scale.

Today, background checks are required at gun stores. If a father wants to teach his daughter how to hunt, he can walk into a gun store, get a background check, purchase his weapon safely and responsibly. This is not seen as an infringement on the Second Amendment. Contrary to the claims of what some gun rights proponents have suggested, this hasn't been the first step in some slippery slope to mass confiscation. Contrary to claims of some Presidential candidates, apparently, before this meeting—this is not a plot to take away everybody's guns. You pass a background check, you purchase a firearm.

The problem is, some gun sellers have been operating under a different set of rules. A violent felon can buy the exact same weapon over the Internet with no background check, no questions asked. A recent study found that about 1 in 30 people looking to buy guns on one website had criminal records. One out of 30 had a criminal record. We're talking about individuals convicted of serious crimes: aggravated assault, domestic violence, robbery, illegal gun possession. People with lengthy criminal histories buying deadly weapons all too easily. And this was just one website within the span of a few months. So we've created a system in which dangerous people are allowed to play by a different set of rules than a responsible gun owner who buys his or her gun the right way and subjects themselves to a background check. That doesn't make sense. Everybody should have to abide by the same rules. Most Americans and gun owners agree. And that's what we tried to change 3 years ago, after 26 Americans—including

20 children—were murdered at Sandy Hook Elementary.

Two United States Senators, Joe Manchin, a Democrat from West Virginia, and Pat Toomey, a Republican from Pennsylvania, both gun owners, both strong defenders of our Second Amendment rights, both with "A" grades from the NRA—that's hard to get—worked together in good faith, consulting with folks like our Vice President, who has been a champion on this for a long time, to write a commonsense, compromise bill that would have required virtually everyone who buys a gun to get a background check. That was it. Pretty commonsense stuff. Ninety percent of Americans supported that idea. Ninety percent of Democrats in the Senate voted for that idea. But it failed because 90 percent of Republicans in the Senate voted against that idea.

How did this become such a partisan issue? Republican President George W. Bush once said, "I believe in background checks at gun shows or anywhere to make sure that guns don't get into the hands of people that shouldn't have them." Senator John McCain introduced a bipartisan measure to address the gun show loophole, saying, "We need this amendment because criminals and terrorists have exploited and are exploiting this very obvious loophole in our gun safety laws." Even the NRA used to support expanded background checks. And by the way, most of its members still do. Most Republican voters still do.

How did we get here? How did we get to the place where people think requiring a comprehensive background check means taking away people's guns?

Each time this comes up, we are fed the excuse that commonsense reforms like background checks might not have stopped the last massacre or the one before that or the one before that, so why bother trying. I reject that thinking. We know we can't stop every act of violence, every act of evil in the world. But maybe we could try to stop one act of evil, one act of violence.

Some of you may recall, at the same time that Sandy Hook happened, a disturbed person in China took a knife and tried to kill—with a knife—a bunch of children in China. But most of them survived because he didn't have access to a powerful weapon. We maybe can't save everybody, but we could save some.

Just as we don't prevent all traffic accidents, but we take steps to try to reduce traffic accidents.

As Ronald Reagan once said, if mandatory background checks could save more lives, "it would be well worth making it the law of the land." The bill before Congress 3 years ago met that test. Unfortunately, too many Senators failed theirs.

In fact, we know that background checks make a difference. After Connecticut passed a law requiring background checks and gun safety courses, gun deaths decreased by 40 percent—40 percent. Meanwhile, since Missouri repealed a law requiring comprehensive background checks and purchase permits, gun deaths have increased to almost 50 percent higher than the national average. One study found, unsurprisingly, that criminals in Missouri now have easier access to guns. And the evidence tells us that in States that require background checks, law-abiding Americans don't find it any harder to purchase guns whatsoever. Their guns have not been confiscated. Their rights have not been infringed.

And that's just the information we have access to. With more research, we could further improve gun safety, just as with more research, we've reduced traffic fatalities enormously over the last 30 years. We do research when cars, food, medicine, even toys harm people so that we make them safer. And you know what? Research, science, those are good things. They work. They do.

But think about this. When it comes to an inherently deadly weapon—nobody argues that guns are potentially deadly—weapons that kill tens of thousands of Americans every year, Congress actually voted to make it harder for public health experts to conduct research into gun violence, made it harder to collect data and facts and develop strategies to reduce gun violence. Even after San Bernardino, they've refused to make it harder for terror suspects who can't get on a plane to buy semiautomatic weapons. That's not right. That can't be right.

So the gun lobby may be holding Congress hostage right now, but they cannot hold America hostage. We do not have to accept this carnage as the price of freedom.

Now, I want to be clear. Congress still needs to act. The folks in this room will not rest until Congress does. Because once Congress gets on board with commonsense gun safety measures, we can reduce gun violence a whole lot more. But we also can't wait. Until we have a Congress that's in line with the majority of Americans, there are actions within my legal authority that we can take to help reduce gun violence and save more lives, actions that protect our rights and our kids.

After Sandy Hook, Joe and I worked together with our teams, and we put forward a whole series of executive actions to try to tighten up the existing rules and systems that we had in place. But today we want to take it a step further. So let me outline what we're going to be doing.

Number one, anybody in the business of selling firearms must get a license and conduct background checks or be subject to criminal prosecutions. It doesn't matter whether you're doing it over the Internet or at a gun show. It's not where you do it, but what you do.

We're also expanding background checks to cover violent criminals who try to buy some of the most dangerous firearms by hiding behind trusts and corporations and various cutouts.

We're also taking steps to make the background check system more efficient. Under the guidance of Jim Comey and the FBI and our Deputy Director Tom Brandon at AF—ATF, we're going to hire more folks to process applications faster, and we're going to bring an outdated background check system into the 21st century.

And these steps will actually lead to a smoother process for law-abiding gun owners, a smoother process for responsible gun dealers, a stronger process for protecting the people from—the public from dangerous people. So that's number one.

Number two, we're going to do everything we can to ensure the smart and effective enforcement of gun safety laws that are already on the books, which means we're going to add 200 more ATF agents and investigators. We're going to require firearms dealers to report more or lost—more lost or stolen guns on a timely basis. We're working with advocates to protect victims of domestic abuse from gun violence, where too often, people are not getting the protection that they need.

Number three, we're going to do more to help those suffering from mental illness get the help that they need. So high-profile mass shootings tend to shine a light on those few

mentally unstable people who inflict harm on others. But the truth is, is that nearly two in three gun deaths are from suicides. So a lot of our work is to prevent people from hurting themselves.

That's why we made sure that the Affordable Care Act, also known as Obamacare—finally, under—that law made sure that treatment for mental health was covered the same as treatment for any other illness. And that's why we're going to invest $500 million to expand access to treatment across the country.

It's also why we're going to ensure that Federal mental health records are submitted to the background check system and remove barriers that prevent States from reporting relevant information. If we can continue to destigmatize mental health issues, get folks proper care, and fill gaps in the background check system, then we can spare more families the pain of losing a loved one to suicide.

And for those in Congress who so often rush to blame mental illness for mass shootings as a way of avoiding action on guns, here's your chance to support these efforts. Put your money where your mouth is.

Number four, we're going to boost gun safety technology. Today, many gun injuries and deaths are the result of legal guns that were stolen or misused or discharged accidentally. In 2013 alone, more than 500 people lost their lives to gun accidents, and that includes 30 children younger than 5 years old. Now, in the greatest, most technologically advanced nation on Earth, there is no reason for this. We need to develop new technologies that make guns safer. If we can set it up so you can't unlock your phone unless you've got the right fingerprint, why can't we do the same thing for our guns? If there's an app that can help us find a missing tablet—which happens to me often the older I get—if we can do it for your iPad, there's no reason we can't do it with a stolen gun. If a child can't open a bottle of aspirin, we should make sure that they can't pull a trigger on a gun. Right? So we're going to advance research. We're going to work with the private sector to update firearms technology.

And some gun retailers are already stepping up by refusing to finalize a purchase without a complete background check or by refraining from selling semiautomatic weapons or high-capacity magazines. And I hope that more retailers and more manufacturers join them, because they should care as much as anybody about a product that now kills almost as many Americans as car accidents.

I make this point because none of us can do this alone. I think Mark made that point earlier. All of us should be able to work together to find a balance that declares the rest of our rights are also important. Second Amendment rights are important, but there are other rights that we care about as well. And we have to be able to balance them. Because our right to worship freely and safely, that right was denied to Christians in Charleston, South Carolina. And that was denied Jews in Kansas City. And that was denied Muslims in Chapel Hill and Sikhs in Oak Creek. They had rights too.

Our right to peaceful assembly, that right was robbed from moviegoers in Aurora and Lafayette. Our unalienable right to life and liberty and the pursuit of happiness, those rights were stripped from college students in Blacksburg and Santa Barbara and from high schoolers at Columbine and from first-graders in Newtown. First-graders. And from every family who never imagined that their loved one would be taken from our lives by a bullet from a gun.

Every time I think about those kids, it gets me mad. And by the way, it happens on the streets of Chicago every day.

So all of us need to demand a Congress brave enough to stand up to the gun lobby's lies. All of us need to stand up and protect its citizens. All of us need to demand Governors and legislatures and businesses do their part to make our communities safer. We need the wide majority of responsible gun owners who grieve with us every time this happens and feel like your views are not being properly represented to join with us to demand something better. And we need voters who want safer gun laws, and who are disappointed in leaders who stand in their way, to remember come election time.

I mean, some of this is just simple math. Yes, the gun lobby is loud and it is organized in defense of making it effortless for guns to be available for anybody, any time. Well, you know what, the rest of us, you—we all have to be just as passionate. We have to be just as organized in defense of our kids. This is not that complicated. The reason Congress blocks laws is because they want to win elections.

And if you make it hard for them to win an election if they block those laws, they'll change course, I promise you.

And yes, it will be hard, and it won't happen overnight. It won't happen during this Congress. It won't happen during my Presidency. But a lot of things don't happen overnight. A woman's right to vote didn't happen overnight. The liberation of African Americans didn't happen overnight. LGBT rights, that was decades' worth of work. So just because it's hard, that's no excuse not to try.

And if you ever have any doubt as to why you should feel that "fierce urgency of now," think about what happened 3 weeks ago. Zaevion Dobson was a sophomore at Fulton High School in Knoxville, Tennessee. He played football; beloved by his classmates and his teachers. His own mayor called him one of their city's success stories. The week before Christmas, he headed to a friend's house to play video games. He wasn't in the wrong place at the wrong time. He hadn't made a bad decision. He was exactly where any other kid would be. Your kid. My kids. And then, gunmen started firing. And Zaevion—who was in high school, hadn't even gotten started in life—dove on top of three girls to shield them from the bullets. And he was shot in the head. And the girls were spared. And he gave his life to save theirs, an act of heroism a lot bigger than anything we should ever expect from a 15-year-old. "Greater love hath no man than this, that a man lay down his life for his friends."

We are not asked to do what Zaevion Dobson did. We're not asked to have shoulders that big, a heart that strong, reactions that quick. I'm not asking people to have that same level of courage or sacrifice or love. But if we love our kids and care about their prospects, and if we love this country and care about its future, then we can find the courage to vote. We can find the courage to get mobilized and organized. We can find the courage to cut through all the noise and do what a sensible country would do.

That's what we're doing today. And tomorrow, we should do more. And we should do more the day after that. And if we do, we'll leave behind a nation that's stronger than the one we inherited and worthy of the sacrifice of a young man like Zaevion.

Thank you very much, everybody. God bless you. Thank you. God bless America.

Farewell Address

January 10, 2017

Chicago, Illinois

ON JANUARY 10, 2017, Barack Obama delivered the final official speech of his presidential career in his home town of Chicago, Illinois. In some ways the speech fell into the pattern set by other presidential farewell addresses from George Washington's onward. It summarized the country's accomplishments under Obama's leadership and set out a vision for the future. In other ways, however, the speech broke from tradition. Obama delivered it in Chicago rather than in Washington, and he directed many of his final remarks at ordinary citizens—the people, he said, who make change happen when they "get involved and they get engaged, and they come together to demand it."

Obama begins his speech by recognizing the influence of Chicago—the city where he began his political career—on his life and work. He states that America's strength has always lain in the ability of its citizens to enjoy life and liberty through the exercise of democracy and in their desire and ability to make that democracy more inclusive. Obama declares that although the country has a long way to go before it achieves its goals, he nonetheless is optimistic about its future. He concludes by calling for Americans to have faith in their own ability to shape the future.

THE PRESIDENT: Hello, Chicago! It's good to be home! Thank you, everybody. Thank you. Thank you so much. Thank you. All right, everybody sit down. We're on live TV here. I've got to move. You can tell that I'm a lame duck because nobody is following instructions. Everybody have a seat.

My fellow Americans—Michelle and I have been so touched by all the well wishes that we've received over the past few weeks. But tonight, it's my turn to say thanks. Whether we have seen eye-to-eye or rarely agreed at all, my conversations with you, the American people, in living rooms and in schools, at farms, on factory floors, at diners and on distant military outposts—those conversations are what have kept me honest, and kept me inspired, and kept me going. And every day, I have learned from you. You made me a better President, and you made me a better man.

So I first came to Chicago when I was in my early 20s. And I was still trying to figure out who I was, still searching for a purpose in my life. And it was a neighborhood not far from here where I began working with church groups in the shadows of closed steel mills. It was on these streets where I witnessed the power of faith, and the quiet dignity of working people in the face of struggle and loss.

AUDIENCE: Four more years! Four more years! Four more years!

THE PRESIDENT: I can't do that.

AUDIENCE: Four more years! Four more years! Four more years!

THE PRESIDENT: This is where I learned that change only happens when ordinary people get involved and they get engaged, and they come together to demand it.

After eight years as your President, I still believe that. And it's not just my belief. It's the beating heart of our American idea—our bold experiment in self-government. It's the conviction that we are all created equal, endowed by our Creator with certain unalienable rights, among them life, liberty, and the pursuit of happiness. It's the insistence that these rights, while self-evident, have never been self-executing; that We, the People, through the instrument of our democracy, can form a more perfect union.

What a radical idea. A great gift that our Founders gave to us: The freedom to chase our individual dreams through our sweat and toil and imagination, and the imperative to strive together, as well, to achieve a common good, a greater good.

For 240 years, our nation's call to citizenship has given work and purpose to each new generation. It's what led patriots to choose republic over tyranny, pioneers to trek west, slaves to brave that makeshift railroad to freedom. It's what pulled immigrants and refugees across oceans and the Rio Grande. It's what pushed women to reach for the ballot. It's what powered workers to organize. It's why GIs gave their lives at Omaha Beach and Iwo Jima, Iraq and Afghanistan. And why men and women from Selma to Stonewall were prepared to give theirs, as well.

So that's what we mean when we say America is exceptional—not that our nation has been flawless from the start, but that we have shown the capacity to change and make life better for those who follow. Yes, our progress has been uneven. The work of democracy has always been hard. It's always been contentious. Sometimes it's been bloody. For every two steps forward, it often feels we take one step back. But the long sweep of America has been defined by forward motion, a constant widening of our founding creed to embrace all and not just some.

If I had told you eight years ago that America would reverse a great recession, reboot our auto industry, and unleash the longest stretch of job creation in our history—if I had told you that we would open up a new chapter with the Cuban people, shut down Iran's nuclear weapons program without firing a shot, take out the mastermind of 9/11—if I had told you that we would win marriage equality, and secure the right to health insurance for another 20 million of our fellow citizens—if I had told you all that, you might have said our sights were set a little too high. But that's what we did. That's what you did.

You were the change. You answered people's hopes, and because of you, by almost every measure, America is a better, stronger place than it was when we started.

In 10 days, the world will witness a hallmark of our democracy.

AUDIENCE: Nooo—

THE PRESIDENT: No, no, no, no, no—the peaceful transfer of power from one freely elected President to the next. I committed to President-elect Trump that my administration would ensure the smoothest possible transition, just as President Bush did for me. Because it's up to all of us to make sure our government can help us meet the many challenges we still face.

We have what we need to do so. We have everything we need to meet those challenges.

After all, we remain the wealthiest, most powerful, and most respected nation on Earth. Our youth, our drive, our diversity and openness, our boundless capacity for risk and reinvention means that the future should be ours. But that potential will only be realized if our democracy works. Only if our politics better reflects the decency of our people. Only if all of us, regardless of party affiliation or particular interests, help restore the sense of common purpose that we so badly need right now.

That's what I want to focus on tonight: The state of our democracy. Understand, democracy does not require uniformity. Our founders argued. They quarreled. Eventually they compromised. They expected us to do the same. But they knew that democracy does require a basic sense of solidarity—the idea that for all our outward differences, we're all in this together; that we rise or fall as one.

There have been moments throughout our history that threatens that solidarity. And the beginning of this century has been one of those times. A shrinking world, growing inequality; demographic change and the specter of terrorism—these forces haven't just tested our security and our prosperity, but are testing our democracy, as well. And how we meet these challenges to our democracy will determine our ability to educate our kids, and create good jobs, and protect our homeland. In other words, it will determine our future.

To begin with, our democracy won't work without a sense that everyone has economic opportunity. And the good news is that today the economy is growing again. Wages, incomes, home values, and retirement accounts are all rising again. Poverty is falling again. The wealthy are paying a fairer share of taxes even as the stock market shatters records. The unemployment rate is near a 10-year low. The uninsured rate has never, ever been lower. Health care costs are rising at the slowest rate in 50 years. And I've said and I mean it—if anyone can put together a plan that is demonstrably better than the improvements we've made to our health care system and that covers as many people at less cost, I will publicly support it.

Because that, after all, is why we serve. Not to score points or take credit, but to make people's lives better.

But for all the real progress that we've made, we know it's not enough. Our economy doesn't work as well or grow as fast when a few prosper at the expense of a growing middle class and ladders for folks who want to get into the middle class. That's the economic argument. But stark inequality is also corrosive to our democratic ideal. While the top one percent has amassed a bigger share of wealth and income, too many families, in inner cities and in rural counties, have been left behind— the laid-off factory worker; the waitress or health care worker who's just barely getting by and struggling to pay the bills—convinced that the game is fixed against them, that their government only serves the interests of the powerful—that's a recipe for more cynicism and polarization in our politics.

But there are no quick fixes to this long-term trend. I agree, our trade should be fair and not just free. But the next wave of economic dislocations won't come from overseas. It will come from the relentless pace of automation that makes a lot of good, middle-class jobs obsolete.

And so we're going to have to forge a new social compact to guarantee all our kids the education they need—to give workers the power to unionize for better wages; to update the social safety net to reflect the way we live now, and make more reforms to the tax code so corporations and individuals who reap the most from this new economy don't avoid their obligations to the country that's made their very success possible.

We can argue about how to best achieve these goals. But we can't be complacent about the goals themselves. For if we don't create opportunity for all people, the disaffection and division that has stalled our progress will only sharpen in years to come.

There's a second threat to our democracy— and this one is as old as our nation itself. After my election, there was talk of a post-racial America. And such a vision, however well-intended, was never realistic. Race remains a potent and often divisive force in our society. Now, I've lived long enough to know that race relations are better than they were 10, or 20, or 30 years ago, no matter what some folks say. You can see it not just in statistics, you see it in the attitudes of young Americans across the political spectrum.

But we're not where we need to be. And all of us have more work to do. If every economic issue is framed as a struggle between a hard-working white middle class and an undeserving minority, then workers of all shades are going to be left fighting for scraps while the wealthy withdraw further into their private enclaves. If we're unwilling to invest in the children of immigrants, just because they don't look like us, we will diminish the prospects of our own children—because those brown kids will represent a larger and larger share of America's workforce. And we have shown that our economy doesn't have to be a zero-sum game. Last year, incomes rose for all races, all age groups, for men and for women.

So if we're going to be serious about race going forward, we need to uphold laws against discrimination—in hiring, and in housing, and in education, and in the criminal justice system. That is what our Constitution and our highest ideals require.

But laws alone won't be enough. Hearts must change. It won't change overnight. Social attitudes oftentimes take generations to change. But if our democracy is to work in this increasingly diverse nation, then each one of us need to try to heed the advice of a great character in American fiction—Atticus Finch—who said "You never really understand a person until you consider things from his point of view . . . until you climb into his skin and walk around in it."

For blacks and other minority groups, it means tying our own very real struggles for justice to the challenges that a lot of people in this country face—not only the refugee, or the immigrant, or the rural poor, or the transgender American, but also the middle-aged white guy who, from the outside, may seem like he's got advantages, but has seen his world upended by economic and cultural and technological change. We have to pay attention, and listen.

For white Americans, it means acknowledging that the effects of slavery and Jim Crow didn't suddenly vanish in the '60s—that when minority groups voice discontent, they're not just engaging in reverse racism or practicing political correctness. When they wage peaceful protest, they're not demanding special treatment but the equal treatment that our Founders promised.

For native-born Americans, it means reminding ourselves that the stereotypes about immigrants today were said, almost word for word, about the Irish, and Italians, and Poles—who it was said we're going to destroy the fundamental character of America. And as it turned out, America wasn't weakened by the presence of these newcomers; these newcomers embraced this nation's creed, and this nation was strengthened.

So regardless of the station that we occupy, we all have to try harder. We all have to start with the premise that each of our fellow citizens loves this country just as much as we do; that they value hard work and family just like we do; that their children are just as curious and hopeful and worthy of love as our own.

And that's not easy to do. For too many of us, it's become safer to retreat into our own bubbles, whether in our neighborhoods or on college campuses, or places of worship, or especially our social media feeds, surrounded by people who look like us and share the same political outlook and never challenge our assumptions. The rise of naked partisanship, and increasing economic and regional stratification, the splintering of our media into a channel for every taste—all this makes this great sorting seem natural, even inevitable. And increasingly, we become so secure in our bubbles that we start accepting only information, whether it's true or not, that fits our opinions, instead of basing our opinions on the evidence that is out there.

And this trend represents a third threat to our democracy. But politics is a battle of ideas. That's how our democracy was designed. In the course of a healthy debate, we prioritize different goals, and the different means of reaching them. But without some common baseline of facts, without a willingness to admit new information, and concede that your opponent might be making a fair point, and that science and reason matter—then we're going to keep talking past each other, and we'll make common ground and compromise impossible.

And isn't that part of what so often makes politics dispiriting? How can elected officials rage about deficits when we propose to spend money on preschool for kids, but not when we're cutting taxes for corporations? How do we excuse ethical lapses in our own party, but pounce when the other party does the same thing? It's not just dishonest, this selective sorting of the facts; it's self-defeating. Because,

as my mother used to tell me, reality has a way of catching up with you.

Take the challenge of climate change. In just eight years, we've halved our dependence on foreign oil; we've doubled our renewable energy; we've led the world to an agreement that has the promise to save this planet. But without bolder action, our children won't have time to debate the existence of climate change. They'll be busy dealing with its effects: more environmental disasters, more economic disruptions, waves of climate refugees seeking sanctuary.

Now, we can and should argue about the best approach to solve the problem. But to simply deny the problem not only betrays future generations, it betrays the essential spirit of this country—the essential spirit of innovation and practical problem-solving that guided our Founders.

It is that spirit, born of the Enlightenment, that made us an economic powerhouse—the spirit that took flight at Kitty Hawk and Cape Canaveral; the spirit that cures disease and put a computer in every pocket.

It's that spirit—a faith in reason, and enterprise, and the primacy of right over might—that allowed us to resist the lure of fascism and tyranny during the Great Depression; that allowed us to build a post-World War II order with other democracies, an order based not just on military power or national affiliations but built on principles—the rule of law, human rights, freedom of religion, and speech, and assembly, and an independent press.

That order is now being challenged—first by violent fanatics who claim to speak for Islam; more recently by autocrats in foreign capitals who see free markets and open democracies and and civil society itself as a threat to their power. The peril each poses to our democracy is more far-reaching than a car bomb or a missile. It represents the fear of change; the fear of people who look or speak or pray differently; a contempt for the rule of law that holds leaders accountable; an intolerance of dissent and free thought; a belief that the sword or the gun or the bomb or the propaganda machine is the ultimate arbiter of what's true and what's right.

Because of the extraordinary courage of our men and women in uniform, because of our intelligence officers, and law enforcement, and diplomats who support our troops—no foreign terrorist organization has successfully planned and executed an attack on our homeland these past eight years. And although Boston and Orlando and San Bernardino and Fort Hood remind us of how dangerous radicalization can be, our law enforcement agencies are more effective and vigilant than ever. We have taken out tens of thousands of terrorists—including bin Laden. The global coalition we're leading against ISIL has taken out their leaders, and taken away about half their territory. ISIL will be destroyed, and no one who threatens America will ever be safe.

And to all who serve or have served, it has been the honor of my lifetime to be your Commander-in-Chief. And we all owe you a deep debt of gratitude.

But protecting our way of life, that's not just the job of our military. Democracy can buckle when we give in to fear. So, just as we, as citizens, must remain vigilant against external aggression, we must guard against a weakening of the values that make us who we are.

And that's why, for the past eight years, I've worked to put the fight against terrorism on a firmer legal footing. That's why we've ended torture, worked to close Gitmo, reformed our laws governing surveillance to protect privacy and civil liberties. That's why I reject discrimination against Muslim Americans, who are just as patriotic as we are.

That's why we cannot withdraw from big global fights—to expand democracy, and human rights, and women's rights, and LGBT rights. No matter how imperfect our efforts, no matter how expedient ignoring such values may seem, that's part of defending America. For the fight against extremism and intolerance and sectarianism and chauvinism are of a piece with the fight against authoritarianism and nationalist aggression. If the scope of freedom and respect for the rule of law shrinks around the world, the likelihood of war within and between nations increases, and our own freedoms will eventually be threatened.

So let's be vigilant, but not afraid. ISIL will try to kill innocent people. But they cannot defeat America unless we betray our Constitution and our principles in the fight. Rivals like Russia or China cannot match our influence around the world—unless we give up what we stand for—and turn ourselves into just another big country that bullies smaller neighbors.

Which brings me to my final point: Our democracy is threatened whenever we take it for granted. All of us, regardless of party, should be throwing ourselves into the task of rebuilding our democratic institutions. When voting rates in America are some of the lowest among advanced democracies, we should be making it easier, not harder, to vote. When trust in our institutions is low, we should reduce the corrosive influence of money in our politics, and insist on the principles of transparency and ethics in public service. When Congress is dysfunctional, we should draw our congressional districts to encourage politicians to cater to common sense and not rigid extremes.

But remember, none of this happens on its own. All of this depends on our participation; on each of us accepting the responsibility of citizenship, regardless of which way the pendulum of power happens to be swinging.

Our Constitution is a remarkable, beautiful gift. But it's really just a piece of parchment. It has no power on its own. We, the people, give it power. We, the people, give it meaning. With our participation, and with the choices that we make, and the alliances that we forge. Whether or not we stand up for our freedoms. Whether or not we respect and enforce the rule of law. That's up to us. America is no fragile thing. But the gains of our long journey to freedom are not assured.

In his own farewell address, George Washington wrote that self-government is the underpinning of our safety, prosperity, and liberty, but "from different causes and from different quarters much pains will be taken . . . to weaken in your minds the conviction of this truth." And so we have to preserve this truth with "jealous anxiety;" that we should reject "the first dawning of every attempt to alienate any portion of our country from the rest or to enfeeble the sacred ties" that make us one.

America, we weaken those ties when we allow our political dialogue to become so corrosive that people of good character aren't even willing to enter into public service; so coarse with rancor that Americans with whom we disagree are seen not just as misguided but as malevolent. We weaken those ties when we define some of us as more American than others; when we write off the whole system as inevitably corrupt, and when we sit back and blame the leaders we elect without examining our own role in electing them.

It falls to each of us to be those those anxious, jealous guardians of our democracy; to embrace the joyous task we've been given to continually try to improve this great nation of ours. Because for all our outward differences, we, in fact, all share the same proud title, the most important office in a democracy: Citizen. Citizen.

So, you see, that's what our democracy demands. It needs you. Not just when there's an election, not just when your own narrow interest is at stake, but over the full span of a lifetime. If you're tired of arguing with strangers on the Internet, try talking with one of them in real life. If something needs fixing, then lace up your shoes and do some organizing. If you're disappointed by your elected officials, grab a clipboard, get some signatures, and run for office yourself. Show up. Dive in. Stay at it.

Sometimes you'll win. Sometimes you'll lose. Presuming a reservoir of goodness in other people, that can be a risk, and there will be times when the process will disappoint you. But for those of us fortunate enough to have been a part of this work, and to see it up close, let me tell you, it can energize and inspire. And more often than not, your faith in America—and in Americans—will be confirmed.

Mine sure has been. Over the course of these eight years, I've seen the hopeful faces of young graduates and our newest military officers. I have mourned with grieving families searching for answers, and found grace in a Charleston church. I've seen our scientists help a paralyzed man regain his sense of touch. I've seen wounded warriors who at points were given up for dead walk again. I've seen our doctors and volunteers rebuild after earthquakes and stop pandemics in their tracks. I've seen the youngest of children remind us through their actions and through their generosity of our obligations to care for

refugees, or work for peace, and, above all, to look out for each other.

So that faith that I placed all those years ago, not far from here, in the power of ordinary Americans to bring about change—that faith has been rewarded in ways I could not have possibly imagined. And I hope your faith has, too. Some of you here tonight or watching at home, you were there with us in 2004, in 2008, 2012—maybe you still can't believe we pulled this whole thing off. Let me tell you, you're not the only ones.

Michelle—Michelle LaVaughn Robinson, girl of the South Side—for the past 25 years, you have not only been my wife and mother of my children, you have been my best friend. You took on a role you didn't ask for and you made it your own, with grace and with grit and with style and good humor. You made the White House a place that belongs to everybody. And the new generation sets its sights higher because it has you as a role model. So you have made me proud. And you have made the country proud.

Malia and Sasha, under the strangest of circumstances, you have become two amazing young women. You are smart and you are beautiful, but more importantly, you are kind and you are thoughtful and you are full of passion. You wore the burden of years in the spotlight so easily. Of all that I've done in my life, I am most proud to be your dad.

To Joe Biden—the scrappy kid from Scranton who became Delaware's favorite son—you were the first decision I made as a nominee, and it was the best. Not just because you have been a great Vice President, but because in the bargain, I gained a brother. And we love you and Jill like family, and your friendship has been one of the great joys of our lives.

To my remarkable staff: For eight years—and for some of you, a whole lot more—I have drawn from your energy, and every day I tried to reflect back what you displayed—heart, and character, and idealism. I've watched you grow up, get married, have kids, start incredible new journeys of your own. Even when times got tough and frustrating, you never let Washington get the better of you. You guarded against cynicism. And the only thing that makes me prouder than all the good that we've done is the thought of all the amazing things that you're going to achieve from here.

And to all of you out there—every organizer who moved to an unfamiliar town, every kind family who welcomed them in, every volunteer who knocked on doors, every young person who cast a ballot for the first time, every American who lived and breathed the hard work of change—you are the best supporters and organizers anybody could ever hope for, and I will be forever grateful. Because you did change the world. You did.

And that's why I leave this stage tonight even more optimistic about this country than when we started. Because I know our work has not only helped so many Americans, it has inspired so many Americans—especially so many young people out there—to believe that you can make a difference—to hitch your wagon to something bigger than yourselves.

Let me tell you, this generation coming up— unselfish, altruistic, creative, patriotic—I've seen you in every corner of the country. You believe in a fair, and just, and inclusive America. You know that constant change has been America's hallmark; that it's not something to fear but something to embrace. You are willing to carry this hard work of democracy forward. You'll soon outnumber all of us, and I believe as a result the future is in good hands.

My fellow Americans, it has been the honor of my life to serve you. I won't stop. In fact, I will be right there with you, as a citizen, for all my remaining days. But for now, whether you are young or whether you're young at heart, I do have one final ask of you as your President—the same thing I asked when you took a chance on me eight years ago. I'm asking you to believe. Not in my ability to bring about change—but in yours.

I am asking you to hold fast to that faith written into our founding documents; that idea whispered by slaves and abolitionists; that spirit sung by immigrants and homesteaders and those who marched for justice; that creed reaffirmed by those who planted flags from foreign battlefields to the surface of the moon; a creed at the core of every American whose story is not yet written: Yes, we can.

Yes, we did. Yes, we can.

Thank you. God bless you. May God continue to bless the United States of America.

As prepared for delivery

It's good to be home. My fellow Americans, Michelle and I have been so touched by all the well-wishes we've received over the past few weeks. But tonight it's my turn to say thanks. Whether we've seen eye-to-eye or rarely agreed at all, my conversations with you, the American people—in living rooms and schools; at farms and on factory floors; at diners and on distant outposts—are what have kept me honest, kept me inspired, and kept me going. Every day, I learned from you. You made me a better President, and you made me a better man.

I first came to Chicago when I was in my early twenties, still trying to figure out who I was; still searching for a purpose to my life. It was in neighborhoods not far from here where I began working with church groups in the shadows of closed steel mills. It was on these streets where I witnessed the power of faith, and the quiet dignity of working people in the face of struggle and loss. This is where I learned that change only happens when ordinary people get involved, get engaged, and come together to demand it.

After eight years as your President, I still believe that. And it's not just my belief. It's the beating heart of our American idea—our bold experiment in self-government.

It's the conviction that we are all created equal, endowed by our Creator with certain unalienable rights, among them life, liberty, and the pursuit of happiness.

It's the insistence that these rights, while self-evident, have never been self-executing; that We, the People, through the instrument of our democracy, can form a more perfect union.

This is the great gift our Founders gave us. The freedom to chase our individual dreams through our sweat, toil, and imagination—and the imperative to strive together as well, to achieve a greater good.

For 240 years, our nation's call to citizenship has given work and purpose to each new generation. It's what led patriots to choose republic over tyranny, pioneers to trek west, slaves to brave that makeshift railroad to freedom. It's what pulled immigrants and refugees across oceans and the Rio Grande, pushed women to reach for the ballot, powered workers to organize. It's why GIs gave their lives at Omaha Beach and Iwo Jima; Iraq and Afghanistan—and why men and women from

Selma to Stonewall were prepared to give theirs as well.

So that's what we mean when we say America is exceptional. Not that our nation has been flawless from the start, but that we have shown the capacity to change, and make life better for those who follow.

Yes, our progress has been uneven. The work of democracy has always been hard, contentious and sometimes bloody. For every two steps forward, it often feels we take one step back. But the long sweep of America has been defined by forward motion, a constant widening of our founding creed to embrace all, and not just some.

If I had told you eight years ago that America would reverse a great recession, reboot our auto industry, and unleash the longest stretch of job creation in our history . . . if I had told you that we would open up a new chapter with the Cuban people, shut down Iran's nuclear weapons program without firing a shot, and take out the mastermind of 9/11 . . . if I had told you that we would win marriage equality, and secure the right to health insurance for another 20 million of our fellow citizens—you might have said our sights were set a little too high.

But that's what we did. That's what you did. You were the change. You answered people's hopes, and because of you, by almost every measure, America is a better, stronger place than it was when we started.

In ten days, the world will witness a hallmark of our democracy: the peaceful transfer of power from one freely-elected president to the next. I committed to President-Elect Trump that my administration would ensure the smoothest possible transition, just as President Bush did for me. Because it's up to all of us to make sure our government can help us meet the many challenges we still face.

We have what we need to do so. After all, we remain the wealthiest, most powerful, and most respected nation on Earth. Our youth and drive, our diversity and openness, our boundless capacity for risk and reinvention mean that the future should be ours.

But that potential will be realized only if our democracy works. Only if our politics reflects the decency of the our people. Only if all of us, regardless of our party affiliation or particular interest, help restore the sense of

common purpose that we so badly need right now.

That's what I want to focus on tonight—the state of our democracy.

Understand, democracy does not require uniformity. Our founders quarreled and compromised, and expected us to do the same. But they knew that democracy does require a basic sense of solidarity—the idea that for all our outward differences, we are all in this together; that we rise or fall as one.

There have been moments throughout our history that threatened to rupture that solidarity. The beginning of this century has been one of those times. A shrinking world, growing inequality; demographic change and the specter of terrorism—these forces haven't just tested our security and prosperity, but our democracy as well. And how we meet these challenges to our democracy will determine our ability to educate our kids, and create good jobs, and protect our homeland.

In other words, it will determine our future.

Our democracy won't work without a sense that everyone has economic opportunity. Today, the economy is growing again; wages, incomes, home values, and retirement accounts are rising again; poverty is falling again. The wealthy are paying a fairer share of taxes even as the stock market shatters records. The unemployment rate is near a ten-year low. The uninsured rate has never, ever been lower. Health care costs are rising at the slowest rate in fifty years. And if anyone can put together a plan that is demonstrably better than the improvements we've made to our health care system—that covers as many people at less cost—I will publicly support it.

That, after all, is why we serve—to make people's lives better, not worse.

But for all the real progress we've made, we know it's not enough. Our economy doesn't work as well or grow as fast when a few prosper at the expense of a growing middle class. But stark inequality is also corrosive to our democratic principles. While the top one percent has amassed a bigger share of wealth and income, too many families, in inner cities and rural counties, have been left behind— the laid-off factory worker; the waitress and health care worker who struggle to pay the bills—convinced that the game is fixed against them, that their government only serves the interests of the powerful—a recipe for more cynicism and polarization in our politics.

There are no quick fixes to this long-term trend. I agree that our trade should be fair and not just free. But the next wave of economic dislocation won't come from overseas. It will come from the relentless pace of automation that makes many good, middle-class jobs obsolete.

And so we must forge a new social compact—to guarantee all our kids the education they need; to give workers the power to unionize for better wages; to update the social safety net to reflect the way we live now and make more reforms to the tax code so corporations and individuals who reap the most from the new economy don't avoid their obligations to the country that's made their success possible. We can argue about how to best achieve these goals. But we can't be complacent about the goals themselves. For if we don't create opportunity for all people, the disaffection and division that has stalled our progress will only sharpen in years to come.

There's a second threat to our democracy—one as old as our nation itself. After my election, there was talk of a post-racial America. Such a vision, however well-intended, was never realistic. For race remains a potent and often divisive force in our society. I've lived long enough to know that race relations are better than they were ten, or twenty, or thirty years ago—you can see it not just in statistics, but in the attitudes of young Americans across the political spectrum.

But we're not where we need to be. All of us have more work to do. After all, if every economic issue is framed as a struggle between a hardworking white middle class and undeserving minorities, then workers of all shades will be left fighting for scraps while the wealthy withdraw further into their private enclaves. If we decline to invest in the children of immigrants, just because they don't look like us, we diminish the prospects of our own children—because those brown kids will represent a larger share of America's workforce. And our economy doesn't have to be a zero-sum game. Last year, incomes rose for all races, all age groups, for men and for women.

Going forward, we must uphold laws against discrimination—in hiring, in housing, in education and the criminal justice system.

That's what our Constitution and highest ideals require. But laws alone won't be enough. Hearts must change. If our democracy is to work in this increasingly diverse nation, each one of us must try to heed the advice of one of the great characters in American fiction, Atticus Finch, who said "You never really understand a person until you consider things from his point of view . . . until you climb into his skin and walk around in it."

For blacks and other minorities, it means tying our own struggles for justice to the challenges that a lot of people in this country face—the refugee, the immigrant, the rural poor, the transgender American, and also the middle-aged white man who from the outside may seem like he's got all the advantages, but who's seen his world upended by economic, cultural, and technological change.

For white Americans, it means acknowledging that the effects of slavery and Jim Crow didn't suddenly vanish in the '60s; that when minority groups voice discontent, they're not just engaging in reverse racism or practicing political correctness; that when they wage peaceful protest, they're not demanding special treatment, but the equal treatment our Founders promised.

For native-born Americans, it means reminding ourselves that the stereotypes about immigrants today were said, almost word for word, about the Irish, Italians, and Poles. America wasn't weakened by the presence of these newcomers; they embraced this nation's creed, and it was strengthened.

So regardless of the station we occupy; we have to try harder; to start with the premise that each of our fellow citizens loves this country just as much as we do; that they value hard work and family like we do; that their children are just as curious and hopeful and worthy of love as our own.

None of this is easy. For too many of us, it's become safer to retreat into our own bubbles, whether in our neighborhoods or college campuses or places of worship or our social media feeds, surrounded by people who look like us and share the same political outlook and never challenge our assumptions. The rise of naked partisanship, increasing economic and regional stratification, the splintering of our media into a channel for every taste—all this makes this great sorting seem natural, even inevitable. And increasingly, we become so secure in our bubbles that we accept only information, whether true or not, that fits our opinions, instead of basing our opinions on the evidence that's out there.

This trend represents a third threat to our democracy. Politics is a battle of ideas; in the course of a healthy debate, we'll prioritize different goals, and the different means of reaching them. But without some common baseline of facts; without a willingness to admit new information, and concede that your opponent is making a fair point, and that science and reason matter, we'll keep talking past each other, making common ground and compromise impossible.

Isn't that part of what makes politics so dispiriting? How can elected officials rage about deficits when we propose to spend money on preschool for kids, but not when we're cutting taxes for corporations? How do we excuse ethical lapses in our own party, but pounce when the other party does the same thing? It's not just dishonest, this selective sorting of the facts; it's self-defeating. Because as my mother used to tell me, reality has a way of catching up with you.

Take the challenge of climate change. In just eight years, we've halved our dependence on foreign oil, doubled our renewable energy, and led the world to an agreement that has the promise to save this planet. But without bolder action, our children won't have time to debate the existence of climate change; they'll be busy dealing with its effects: environmental disasters, economic disruptions, and waves of climate refugees seeking sanctuary.

Now, we can and should argue about the best approach to the problem. But to simply deny the problem not only betrays future generations; it betrays the essential spirit of innovation and practical problem-solving that guided our Founders.

It's that spirit, born of the Enlightenment, that made us an economic powerhouse—the spirit that took flight at Kitty Hawk and Cape Canaveral; the spirit that that cures disease and put a computer in every pocket.

It's that spirit—a faith in reason, and enterprise, and the primacy of right over might, that allowed us to resist the lure of fascism and tyranny during the Great Depression, and build a post-World War II order with other democracies, an order based not just on military power or national affiliations but on principles—the rule of law, human rights, freedoms of religion, speech, assembly, and an independent press.

That order is now being challenged—first by violent fanatics who claim to speak for Islam; more recently by autocrats in foreign capitals who see free markets, open democracies, and civil society itself as a threat to their power. The peril each poses to our democracy is more far-reaching than a car bomb or a missile. It represents the fear of change; the fear of people who look or speak or pray differently; a contempt for the rule of law that holds leaders accountable; an intolerance of dissent and free thought; a belief that the sword or the gun or the bomb or propaganda machine is the ultimate arbiter of what's true and what's right.

Because of the extraordinary courage of our men and women in uniform, and the intelligence officers, law enforcement, and diplomats who support them, no foreign terrorist organization has successfully planned and executed an attack on our homeland these past eight years; and although Boston and Orlando remind us of how dangerous radicalization can be, our law enforcement agencies are more effective and vigilant than ever. We've taken out tens of thousands of terrorists—including Osama bin Laden. The global coalition we're leading against ISIL has taken out their leaders, and taken away about half their territory. ISIL will be destroyed, and no one who threatens America will ever be safe. To all who serve, it has been the honor of my lifetime to be your Commander-in-Chief.

But protecting our way of life requires more than our military. Democracy can buckle when we give in to fear. So just as we, as citizens, must remain vigilant against external aggression, we must guard against a weakening of the values that make us who we are. That's why, for the past eight years, I've worked to put the fight against terrorism on a firm legal footing. That's why we've ended torture, worked to close Gitmo, and reform our laws governing surveillance to protect privacy and civil liberties. That's why I reject discrimination against Muslim Americans. That's why we cannot withdraw from global fights—to expand democracy, and human rights, women's rights, and LGBT rights—no matter how imperfect our efforts, no matter how expedient ignoring such values may seem. For the fight against extremism and intolerance and sectarianism are of a piece with the fight against authoritarianism and nationalist aggression. If the scope of freedom and respect for the rule of law shrinks around the world, the likelihood of war within and between nations increases, and our own freedoms will eventually be threatened.

So let's be vigilant, but not afraid. ISIL will try to kill innocent people. But they cannot defeat America unless we betray our Constitution and our principles in the fight. Rivals like Russia or China cannot match our influence around the world—unless we give up what we stand for, and turn ourselves into just another big country that bullies smaller neighbors.

Which brings me to my final point—our democracy is threatened whenever we take it for granted. All of us, regardless of party, should throw ourselves into the task of rebuilding our democratic institutions. When voting rates are some of the lowest among advanced democracies, we should make it easier, not harder, to vote. When trust in our institutions is low, we should reduce the corrosive influence of money in our politics, and insist on the principles of transparency and ethics in public service. When Congress is dysfunctional, we should draw our districts to encourage politicians to cater to common sense and not rigid extremes.

And all of this depends on our participation; on each of us accepting the responsibility of citizenship, regardless of which way the pendulum of power swings.

Our Constitution is a remarkable, beautiful gift. But it's really just a piece of parchment. It has no power on its own. We, the people, give it power—with our participation, and the choices we make. Whether or not we stand up for our freedoms. Whether or not we respect and enforce the rule of law. America is no fragile thing. But the gains of our long journey to freedom are not assured.

In his own farewell address, George Washington wrote that self-government is the underpinning of our safety, prosperity, and liberty, but "from different causes and from different quarters much pains will be taken . . . to weaken in your minds the conviction of this truth;" that we should preserve it with "jealous anxiety;" that we should reject "the first dawning of every attempt to alienate any portion of our country from the rest or to enfeeble the sacred ties" that make us one.

We weaken those ties when we allow our political dialogue to become so corrosive that people of good character are turned off from public service; so coarse with rancor that Americans with whom we disagree are not just misguided, but somehow malevolent. We weaken those ties when we define some of us as more American than others; when we write off the whole system as inevitably corrupt, and blame the leaders we elect without examining our own role in electing them.

It falls to each of us to be those anxious, jealous guardians of our democracy; to embrace the joyous task we've been given to continually try to improve this great nation of ours. Because for all our outward differences, we all share the same proud title: Citizen.

Ultimately, that's what our democracy demands. It needs you. Not just when there's an election, not just when your own narrow interest is at stake, but over the full span of a lifetime. If you're tired of arguing with strangers on the internet, try to talk with one in real life. If something needs fixing, lace up your shoes and do some organizing. If you're disappointed by your elected officials, grab a clipboard, get some signatures, and run for office yourself. Show up. Dive in. Persevere. Sometimes you'll win. Sometimes you'll lose. Presuming a reservoir of goodness in others can be a risk, and there will be times when the process disappoints you. But for those of us fortunate enough to have been a part of this work, to see it up close, let me tell you, it can energize and inspire. And more often than not, your faith in America—and in Americans—will be confirmed.

Mine sure has been. Over the course of these eight years, I've seen the hopeful faces of young graduates and our newest military officers. I've mourned with grieving families searching for answers, and found grace in Charleston church. I've seen our scientists help a paralyzed man regain his sense of touch, and our wounded warriors walk again. I've seen our doctors and volunteers rebuild after earthquakes and stop pandemics in their tracks. I've seen the youngest of children remind us of our obligations to care for refugees, to work in peace, and above all to look out for each other.

That faith I placed all those years ago, not far from here, in the power of ordinary Americans to bring about change—that faith has been rewarded in ways I couldn't possibly have imagined. I hope yours has, too. Some of you here tonight or watching at home were there with us in 2004, in 2008, in 2012—and maybe you still can't believe we pulled this whole thing off.

You're not the only ones. Michelle—for the past twenty-five years, you've been not only my wife and mother of my children, but my best friend. You took on a role you didn't ask for and made it your own with grace and grit and style and good humor. You made the White House a place that belongs to everybody. And a new generation sets its sights higher because it has you as a role model. You've made me proud. You've made the country proud.

Malia and Sasha, under the strangest of circumstances, you have become two amazing young women, smart and beautiful, but more importantly, kind and thoughtful and full of passion. You wore the burden of years in the spotlight so easily. Of all that I've done in my life, I'm most proud to be your dad.

To Joe Biden, the scrappy kid from Scranton who became Delaware's favorite son: you were the first choice I made as a nominee, and the best. Not just because you have been a great Vice President, but because in the bargain, I gained a brother. We love you and Jill like family, and your friendship has been one of the great joys of our life.

To my remarkable staff: For eight years—and for some of you, a whole lot more—I've drawn from your energy, and tried to reflect back what you displayed every day: heart, and character, and idealism. I've watched you grow up, get married, have kids, and start incredible new journeys of your own. Even when times got tough and frustrating, you never let Washington get the better of you. The only thing that makes me prouder than all the good we've done is the thought of all the remarkable things you'll achieve from here.

And to all of you out there—every organizer who moved to an unfamiliar town and kind family who welcomed them in, every volunteer who knocked on doors, every young person who cast a ballot for the first time, every American who lived and breathed the hard work of change—you are the best supporters and organizers anyone could hope for, and I will forever be grateful. Because yes, you changed the world.

That's why I leave this stage tonight even more optimistic about this country than I was when we started. Because I know our work has not only helped so many Americans; it has inspired so many Americans—especially so many young people out there—to believe you can make a difference; to hitch your wagon to something bigger than yourselves. This generation coming up—unselfish, altruistic, creative, patriotic—I've seen you in every corner of the country. You believe in a fair, just, inclusive America; you know that constant change has been America's hallmark, something not to fear but to embrace, and you are willing to carry this hard work of democracy forward. You'll soon outnumber any of us, and I believe as a result that the future is in good hands.

My fellow Americans, it has been the honor of my life to serve you. I won't stop; in fact, I will be right there with you, as a citizen, for all my days that remain. For now, whether you're young or young at heart, I do have one final ask of you as your President—the same thing I asked when you took a chance on me eight years ago.

I am asking you to believe. Not in my ability to bring about change—but in yours.

I am asking you to hold fast to that faith written into our founding documents; that idea whispered by slaves and abolitionists; that spirit sung by immigrants and homesteaders and those who marched for justice; that creed reaffirmed by those who planted flags from foreign battlefields to the surface of the moon; a creed at the core of every American whose story is not yet written:

Yes We Can.

Yes We Did.

Yes We Can.

Thank you. God bless you. And may God continue to bless the United States of America.

Donald John Trump

Donald John Trump

2017–

ONE OF the greatest upsets in American electoral history occurred in November 2016, when Donald J. Trump, a real estate businessman and television personality, won enough votes in the electoral college to become the forty-fifth president of the United States. Scarcely anyone had foreseen Trump's rise to political power. He had no political experience before the election and no practical military experience (he attended a military boarding school as a teenager). He won the election despite losing the popular vote to the Democratic candidate, Hillary Rodham Clinton, by approximately three million votes.

Trump came from a wealthy family. His grandfather had arrived from Germany in 1885 and laid the foundation of the family fortune by opening a restaurant in Seattle and a boarding house in Yukon territory, Canada, during the gold rush of the 1890s. Trump's father, Fred, ran the real estate company Elizabeth Trump & Son in New York City for half a century, until Donald Trump took over the company in 1971 and rebranded it as the Trump Organization. He later expanded the scope of the company's interests to include casinos in Atlantic City, New Jersey; golf courses in Aberdeenshire and Ayrshire, Scotland; and hotels throughout the world. He first wrote about his business interests and his approach to them in *The Art of the Deal* (1987), which he authored with the journalist Tony Schwartz.

For about two decades Trump owned and operated two of the most famous beauty pageants in the world: Miss Universe and Miss USA. However, because of widely publicized statements that Trump made about race and immigration, the broadcaster NBC refused to air the pageants as long as Trump was connected with them.

Trump's personal life was as varied as his business interests. He married Ivana Zelnickova, a model, in 1977 and had three children—Donald Jr., Ivanka, and Eric—with her before the couple divorced in 1992. The event that precipitated the divorce was Trump's much-publicized affair with Marla Maples, an actress who had been a participant in one of the Miss USA pageants. The couple married in 1993, after Maples had given birth to their daughter, Tiffany, and they divorced in 1999. In 2005, Trump married the Slovenian model Melania Knauss. She gave birth to their son, Barron, the following year. Trump himself had a small acting career, appearing in the 1994 film *The Little Rascals* and as a special guest on several television programs.

Trump's most visible role was his position as the host of the reality television series *The Apprentice* from 2003 to 2015. The program, which featured individuals contending for jobs with various Trump businesses, proved to be enormously successful and spawned several spinoffs, most famously *Celebrity Apprentice* (2008–2017), which Trump also hosted until beginning his presidential run in 2015. He was also credited as a producer or executive producer on both programs and on several spinoffs. Once again, however, his outspoken views on race and immigration led NBC Universal to terminate its relationship with him. Trump's role as host of *The Apprentice* was taken by the former California governor Arnold Schwarzenegger for the program's fifteenth season.

Trump's visibility on television gave him an advantage over other candidates in the Republican primaries leading up to the 2016 presidential election. In speeches he embraced a populist attitude, calling for deregulation and lower taxes in order to promote job growth while calling for increased investment in infrastructure. At the same time, he publicly eschewed so-called political correctness in his speech, voicing highly controversial (and sometimes inflammatory) views, especially about race, multiculturalism, and immigration. This tendency became even more pronounced after candidate Trump seemingly embraced the white nationalist alt-right by appointing the *Breitbart News* executive chairman Steve Bannon as the chief executive of his campaign. After the election, Bannon became Trump's chief strategist for the opening months of the president's administration.

Although he had no experience in politics before winning the presidency, Trump had voiced public opinions on politics as early as 1987, calling for a reduction in the federal deficit. After 2010 he became a leading figure in the so-called birther conspiracy, which alleged falsely that President Barack Obama had been born in Kenya and was therefore not eligible to be president. Trump also called for President Obama to release his student records to show that he was qualified to attend Harvard Law School. Shortly before the 2016 election, Trump finally acknowledged that Obama had been born in the United States, but he also stated that the birther rumors had been originally spread by Hillary Rodham Clinton during the 2008 presidential campaign.

Trump's former role as a media personality gave him a huge amount of free publicity during the campaign. It also focused attention on his frequent public misstatements. Major media outlets like the *Washington Post* and the *New York Times* pointed out numerous lies and falsehoods in Trump's statements and speeches. For his part, Trump claimed that the mainstream media misrepresented his views and asserted a media bias against his campaign and his presidency. Perhaps for this reason, much of his public communication has been done through a series of tweets on the social media platform Twitter. Although the tweets increase his populist credibility—they originate from his private account—they also confuse and occasionally contradict policies that he or his administration has stated in public.

In speeches, Trump's tendency to speak spontaneously has also proven to be problematic. Although the official transcript of a given speech may show what was written for the president, what Trump actually said while delivering the speech may be markedly different. In addition, the president's delivery—not just what he says but how he says it—can flavor interpretations of his intended meaning. His elliptical forms of address and his extensive use of social media mark President Trump as an innovator in presidential communication.

Inaugural Address

January 20, 2017

Washington, D.C.

On January 20, 2017, Donald Trump was sworn in as the forty-fifth president of the United States. His inaugural address echoed the tone Trump had set during the 2016 presidential campaign. Using the populist rhetoric he honed during the campaign season, the president declares that his election represented a victory for ordinary Americans who had been left behind by the upper classes, who were co-opting economic gains for their own benefit. In the speech he states, "The forgotten men and women of our country will be forgotten no longer."

Analysts noted that the address was unusually dark. Trump depicts the United States as a land of "rusted-out factories scattered like tombstones" and cities plagued by "crime and gangs and drugs that have stolen too many lives." He blames poor trade agreements and U.S. involvement in world affairs for the decline of the American worker, and he calls for new investment in infrastructure to create jobs and rebuild the economy. At the end, Trump evokes traditional images of patriotism: "a new national pride," he says, will overcome differences between Americans. He concludes with the same words that stirred his supporters during the campaign, declaring that united in patriotism, Americans will make America great again.

Chief Justice Roberts, President Carter, President Clinton, President Bush, President Obama, fellow Americans, and people of the world: thank you.

We, the citizens of America, are now joined in a great national effort to rebuild our country and to restore its promise for all of our people.

Together, we will determine the course of America and the world for years to come.

We will face challenges. We will confront hardships. But we will get the job done.

Every four years, we gather on these steps to carry out the orderly and peaceful transfer of power, and we are grateful to President Obama and First Lady Michelle Obama for their gracious aid throughout this transition. They have been magnificent.

Today's ceremony, however, has very special meaning. Because today we are not merely transferring power from one Administration to another, or from one party to another—but we are transferring power from Washington, D.C. and giving it back to you, the American People.

For too long, a small group in our nation's Capital has reaped the rewards of government while the people have borne the cost.

Washington flourished—but the people did not share in its wealth.

Politicians prospered—but the jobs left, and the factories closed.

The establishment protected itself, but not the citizens of our country.

Their victories have not been your victories; their triumphs have not been your triumphs; and while they celebrated in our nation's Capital, there was little to celebrate for struggling families all across our land.

That all changes—starting right here, and right now, because this moment is your moment: it belongs to you.

It belongs to everyone gathered here today and everyone watching all across America.

This is your day. This is your celebration.

And this, the United States of America, is your country.

What truly matters is not which party controls our government, but whether our government is controlled by the people.

January 20th 2017, will be remembered as the day the people became the rulers of this nation again.

The forgotten men and women of our country will be forgotten no longer.

Everyone is listening to you now.

You came by the tens of millions to become part of a historic movement the likes of which the world has never seen before.

At the center of this movement is a crucial conviction: that a nation exists to serve its citizens.

Americans want great schools for their children, safe neighborhoods for their families, and good jobs for themselves.

These are the just and reasonable demands of a righteous public.

But for too many of our citizens, a different reality exists: Mothers and children trapped in poverty in our inner cities; rusted-out factories scattered like tombstones across the landscape of our nation; an education system, flush with cash, but which leaves our young and beautiful students deprived of knowledge; and the crime and gangs and drugs that have stolen too many lives and robbed our country of so much unrealized potential.

This American carnage stops right here and stops right now.

We are one nation—and their pain is our pain. Their dreams are our dreams; and their success will be our success. We share one heart, one home, and one glorious destiny.

The oath of office I take today is an oath of allegiance to all Americans.

For many decades, we've enriched foreign industry at the expense of American industry;

Subsidized the armies of other countries while allowing for the very sad depletion of our military;

We've defended other nation's borders while refusing to defend our own;

And spent trillions of dollars overseas while America's infrastructure has fallen into disrepair and decay.

We've made other countries rich while the wealth, strength, and confidence of our country has disappeared over the horizon.

One by one, the factories shuttered and left our shores, with not even a thought about the millions upon millions of American workers left behind.

The wealth of our middle class has been ripped from their homes and then redistributed across the entire world.

But that is the past. And now we are looking only to the future.

We assembled here today are issuing a new decree to be heard in every city, in every foreign capital, and in every hall of power.

From this day forward, a new vision will govern our land.

From this moment on, it's going to be America First.

Every decision on trade, on taxes, on immigration, on foreign affairs, will be made to benefit American workers and American families.

We must protect our borders from the ravages of other countries making our products, stealing our companies, and destroying our jobs. Protection will lead to great prosperity and strength.

I will fight for you with every breath in my body—and I will never, ever let you down.

America will start winning again, winning like never before.

We will bring back our jobs. We will bring back our borders. We will bring back our wealth. And we will bring back our dreams.

We will build new roads, and highways, and bridges, and airports, and tunnels, and railways all across our wonderful nation.

We will get our people off of welfare and back to work—rebuilding our country with American hands and American labor.

We will follow two simple rules: Buy American and Hire American.

We will seek friendship and goodwill with the nations of the world—but we do so with the understanding that it is the right of all nations to put their own interests first.

We do not seek to impose our way of life on anyone, but rather to let it shine as an example for everyone to follow.

We will reinforce old alliances and form new ones—and unite the civilized world against Radical Islamic Terrorism, which we will eradicate completely from the face of the Earth.

At the bedrock of our politics will be a total allegiance to the United States of America, and through our loyalty to our country, we will rediscover our loyalty to each other.

When you open your heart to patriotism, there is no room for prejudice.

The Bible tells us, "how good and pleasant it is when God's people live together in unity."

We must speak our minds openly, debate our disagreements honestly, but always pursue solidarity.

When America is united, America is totally unstoppable.

There should be no fear—we are protected, and we will always be protected.

We will be protected by the great men and women of our military and law enforcement and, most importantly, we are protected by God.

Finally, we must think big and dream even bigger.

In America, we understand that a nation is only living as long as it is striving.

We will no longer accept politicians who are all talk and no action—constantly complaining but never doing anything about it.

The time for empty talk is over.

Now arrives the hour of action.

Do not let anyone tell you it cannot be done. No challenge can match the heart and fight and spirit of America.

We will not fail. Our country will thrive and prosper again.

We stand at the birth of a new millennium, ready to unlock the mysteries of space, to free the Earth from the miseries of disease, and to harness the energies, industries and technologies of tomorrow.

A new national pride will stir our souls, lift our sights, and heal our divisions.

It is time to remember that old wisdom our soldiers will never forget: that whether we are black or brown or white, we all bleed the same red blood of patriots, we all enjoy the same glorious freedoms, and we all salute the same great American Flag.

And whether a child is born in the urban sprawl of Detroit or the windswept plains of Nebraska, they look up at the same night sky, they fill their heart with the same dreams, and they are infused with the breath of life by the same almighty Creator.

So to all Americans, in every city near and far, small and large, from mountain to mountain, and from ocean to ocean, hear these words:

You will never be ignored again.

Your voice, your hopes, and your dreams, will define our American destiny. And your courage and goodness and love will forever guide us along the way.

Together, We Will Make America Strong Again.

We Will Make America Wealthy Again.

We Will Make America Proud Again.

We Will Make America Safe Again.

And, Yes, Together, We Will Make America Great Again. Thank you, God Bless You, And God Bless America.

Boy Scout Jamboree Speech

July 24, 2017
Glen Jean, West Virginia

ON JULY 24, 2017, President Donald Trump delivered a speech to the Boy Scouts of America at their National Jamboree in Glen Jean, West Virginia. In doing so, President Trump was participating in a long tradition of American presidents' addressing the organization, dating to Franklin Delano Roosevelt. Most presidential speeches to the Boy Scouts focused on the role of scouting in promoting citizenship. Trump's speech, however, more closely resembled a political rally speech meant to rouse enthusiasm in an audience.

Trump begins his speech by thanking the Boy Scouts and remarking on the size of his audience. He goes on to call out members of his administration who had been scouts themselves. He praises the "values, traditions, and skills" scouting teaches its members. His central theme in the address is about the value of hard work, and he uses the example of the real estate developer William Levitt to make the point that it is easy to work hard at something you love to do. Then, however, Trump moves off script to talk about politics in Washington, including his electoral college victory over Hillary Rodham Clinton. So unusual was Trump's speech that the following day a Boy Scouts spokesperson issued a statement declaring that the organization was resolutely nonpartisan and that Trump's remarks did not necessarily reflect the values of the organization.

Audience members. U.S.A.! U.S.A.! U.S.A.!

The President. Thank you, everybody. Thank you very much. I am thrilled to be here. Thrilled. And if you think that was an easy trip, you're wrong, but I am thrilled—19th Boy Scout Jamboree—wow—and to address such a tremendous group. Boy, you have a lot of people here. The press will say it's about 200 people. It looks like about 45,000 people. You set a record today. You set a record. That's a great honor, believe me.

Tonight we put aside all of the policy fights in Washington, DC, you've been hearing about with the fake news and all of that. We're going to put that—we're going to put that aside. And instead, we're going to talk about success, about how all of you amazing young Scouts can achieve your dreams. What to think of—what I've been thinking about—you want to achieve your dreams. I said, who the hell wants to speak about politics when I'm in front of the Boy Scouts? Right?

There are many great honors that come with the job of being President of the United States, but looking out at this incredible gathering of mostly young patriots—mostly young—I'm especially proud to speak to you as the honorary president of the Boy Scouts of America.

Audience members. U.S.A.! U.S.A.! U.S.A.!

The President. You are the young people of character and integrity who will serve as leaders in our communities and uphold the sacred values of our Nation.

I want to thank Boy Scouts President Randall Stephenson, Chief Scout Executive Michael Surbaugh, Jamboree Chairman Ralph de la Vega, and the thousands of volunteers who have made this a life-changing experience for all of you. And when they asked me to be here I said absolutely, yes.

Finally—and we can't forget these people—I especially want to salute the moms and the dads and troop leaders who are here tonight. Thank you for making scouting possible. Thank you, mom and dad troop leaders. When you volunteer for the Boy Scouts, you are not only shaping young lives, you are shaping the future of America.

The United States has no better citizens than its Boy Scouts. No better. The values, traditions, and skills you learn here will serve you throughout your lives, and just as importantly, they will serve your families, your cities, and in the future and in the present, will serve your country. The Scouts believe in putting America first.

You know, I go to Washington, and I see all these politicians, and I see the swamp. And it's not a good place. In fact, today I said we ought to change it from the word swamp to the word cesspool or perhaps to the word sewer. But it's not good. Not good. And I see what's going on, and believe me, I'd much rather be with you. That I can tell you.

I'll tell you the reason that I love this and the reason that I really wanted to be here is because as President, I rely on former Boy Scouts every single day, and so do the American people. It's amazing how many Boy Scouts we have at the highest level of our great Government. Many of my top advisers in the White House were Scouts. Ten members of my Cabinet were Scouts. Can you believe that? Ten.

Secretary of State Rex Tillerson is not only a Boy Scout, he's your former national president. The Vice President of the United States, Mike Pence—good guy—was a Scout, and it meant so much to him. Some of you here tonight might even have camped out in this yard when Mike was the Governor of Indiana, but the scouting was very, very important. And by the way, where are our Indiana Scouts tonight? I wonder if the television cameras will follow you. They don't like doing that when they see these massive crowds. They don't like doing that. Hi, folks. A lot of love in this big, beautiful place. Lot of love and a lot of love for our country. There's a lot of love for our country.

Secretary of the Interior Ryan Zinke is here tonight. Come here, Ryan. Ryan is an Eagle Scout from Big Sky country in Montana. Pretty good. And by the way, he is doing a fantastic job. He makes sure that we leave our national parks and Federal lands better than we found them, in the best scouting tradition. So thank you very much, Ryan.

Secretary of Energy Rick Perry, of Texas, an Eagle Scout from the great State. The first time he came to the national jamboree was in 1964. He was very young then. And Rick told me just a little while ago, it totally changed his life. So, Rick, thank you very much for being here. And we're doing a lot with energy.

And very soon, Rick, we will be an energy exporter. Isn't that nice, an energy exporter? In other words, we'll be selling our energy instead of buying it from everybody all over the globe. So that's good.

Secretary of Energy J. Richard Perry. Yes, sir. Energy dominant.

The President. We will be energy dominant. And I'll tell you what, the folks in West Virginia who were so nice to me, boy, have we kept our promise. We are going on and on. So we love West Virginia. We want to thank you.

Where's West Virginia, by the way? This—. Thank you.

Secretary Tom Price is also here. Today, Dr. Price still lives the Scout oath, helping to keep millions of Americans strong and healthy as our Secretary of Health and Human Services. And he's doing a great job. And hopefully, he's going to get the votes tomorrow to start our path toward killing this horrible thing known as Obamacare that's really hurting us, folks.

Audience members. U.S.A.! U.S.A.! U.S.A.!

The President. By the way, you going to get the votes?

Secretary of Health and Human Services Thomas E. Price. Hope so.

The President. He'd better get them. He'd better get them. Oh, he'd better—otherwise, I'll say, Tom, you're fired. I'll get somebody.

You'd better get Senator Capito to vote for it. You've got to get the other Senators to vote for it. It's time. After 7 years of saying repeal and replace Obamacare, we have a chance to now do it. They'd better do it. Hopefully, they'll do it.

As we can see just by looking at our Government, in America, Scouts lead the way. And another thing I've noticed—and I've noticed it all my life—there is a tremendous spirit with being a Scout, more so than almost anything I can think of. So whatever is going on, keep doing it. It's incredible to watch. Believe me. Each of these leaders will tell you that their road to American success—and you have to understand, their American success, and they are a great, great story, was paved with the patriotic American values and traditions they learned in the Boy Scouts. And some day, many years from now, when you look back on all of the adventures in your lives, you will be able to say the same: I got my start as a Scout just like these incredibly great people that are doing such a good job for our country. So that's going to happen.

Boy Scout values are American values, and great Boy Scouts become great, great Americans. As the Scout law says: "A Scout is trustworthy, loyal"—we could use some more loyalty, I will tell you that.

Audience members. ——"helpful, friendly, courteous, kind, obedient, cheerful, thrifty, brave, clean, and reverent."

The President. Very good. Very good. That was very impressive. You've heard that before.

But here you learn the rewards of hard work and perseverance. Never, ever give up, never quit. Persevere. Never, ever quit.

You learn the satisfaction of building a roaring campfire, reaching a mountain summit, or earning a merit badge after mastering a certain skill. There's no better feeling than an achievement that you've earned with your own sweat, tears, resolve, hard work. There's nothing like it. Do you agree with that?

Audience members. Yes!

The President. I'm waving to people back there so small I can't even see them. Man, this is—this is a lot of people. Turn those cameras back there, please. That is so incredible. By the way, what do you think the chances are that this incredible, massive crowd, record-setting, is going to be shown on television tonight? One percent or zero? The fake media will say: President Trump spoke—and you know what this is—President Trump spoke before a small crowd of Boy Scouts today. That's some—that is some crowd.

Fake media. Fake news. Thank you. And I'm honored by that, by the way, all of you people, they can't even see you. So thank you. I hope you can hear.

Through scouting you also learn to believe in yourself—so important—to have confidence in your ability and to take responsibility for your own life. When you face down new challenges, and you will have plenty of them, develop talents you never thought possible, and lead your teammates through daring trials, you discover that you can handle anything. And you learn it by being a Scout. It's great.

You can do anything. You can be anything you want to be. But in order to succeed, you must find out what you love to do. You have to find your passion. No what—no matter what they tell you—if you don't—I love you too. I don't know. It's a nice guy. Hey, what am I going to do? He sounds like a nice person. He, he, he, he. Thank you. I do. I do love you.

Audience members. We love Trump! We love Trump! We love Trump!

The President. By the way, just a question, did President Obama ever come to a jamboree?

Audience members. No!

The President. And we'll be back. We'll be back. The answer is no, and—but we'll be back. In life, in order to be successful—and you people are well on the road to success—you have to find out what makes you excited. What makes you want to get up each morning and go to work? You have to find it.

If you love what you do and dedicate yourself to your work, then you will gain momentum, and look—you have to, you need—the word momentum—you will gain that momentum, and each success will create another success. The word momentum.

I'll tell you a story that's very interesting for me when I was young. There was a man named William Levitt—Levittowns, you have some here, you have some in different States. Anybody ever hear of Levittown? And he was a very successful man. Became unbelievably—he was a homebuilder—became an unbelievable success and got more and more successful. And he built homes, and at night, he'd go to these major sites with teams of people, and he'd scour the sites for nails and sawdust and small pieces of wood. And they'd clean the site so when the workers came in the next morning, the sites would be spotless and clean, and he did it properly. And he did this for 20 years, and then, he was offered a lot of money for his company.

And he sold his company for a tremendous amount of money—at the time especially, this was a long time ago—sold his company for a tremendous amount of money. And he went out and bought a big yacht, and he had a very interesting life. I won't go any more than that because you're Boy Scouts, so I'm not going to tell you what he did.

Audience members. Boo!

The President. Should I tell you? Should I tell you?

Audience members. Yes!

The President. Oh, you're Boy Scouts, but you know life. You know life. So—look at you. Who would think this is the Boy Scouts, right?

So he had a very, very interesting life, and the company that bought his company was a big conglomerate. And they didn't know anything about building homes, and they didn't know anything about picking up the nails and the sawdust and selling it—and the scraps of wood. This was a big conglomerate based in New York City, and after about a 10-year period, they were losing a lot with it. It didn't mean anything to them, and they couldn't sell it.

So they called William Levitt up, and they said, would you like to buy back your company, and he said yes, I would. He so badly wanted it; he got bored with this life of yachts and sailing and all of the things he did in the South of France and other places. You won't get bored, right? You know, truthfully, you're workers. You'll get bored too, believe me. Of course, having a good few years like that isn't so bad. But what happened is, he bought back his company, and he bought back a lot of empty land. And he worked hard in getting in zoning, and he worked hard on starting to develop.

And in the end he failed, and he failed badly. Lost all of his money. He went personally bankrupt, and he was now much older. And I saw him at a cocktail party, and it was very sad, because the hottest people in New York were at this party. It was the party of Steve Ross—Steve Ross who was one of the great people—he came up and discovered, really founded Time Warner, and he was a great guy. He had a lot of successful people at the party.

And I was doing well so I got invited to the party. I was very young, and I go in—but I'm in the real estate business—and I see a hundred people, some of whom I recognize and they're big in the entertainment business. And I see, sitting in the corner, was a little old man who was all by himself. Nobody was talking to him. I immediately recognized that that man was the once-great William Levitt of Levittown, and I immediately went over; I wanted to talk to him more than the Hollywood show business communications people.

So I went over and talked to him, and I said, Mr. Levitt, "I'm Donald Trump." He said, "I know." I said, "Mr. Levitt, how are you doing?" He goes, "not well, not well at all." And I knew that, but he said "not well at all." And he explained what was happening and how bad it has been and how hard it has been. And I said what exactly happened? Why did this happen to you? You're one of the greats ever in our industry. Why did this happen to you? And he said, Donald, "I lost my momentum." I lost my momentum. A word you never hear when you're talking about success. When some of these guys that never made 10 cents, they're on television giving you things about how you're going to be successful, and the only thing they ever did was a book and a tape.

But I'll tell you, I'll tell you, it was very sad, and I never forgot that moment. And I thought about it, and it's exactly true. He lost his momentum. Meaning, he took this period of time off long—years—and then, when he got back, he didn't have that same momentum. In life, I always tell this to people, you have to know whether or not you continue to have the momentum, and if you don't have it, that's okay. Because you're going to go on, and you're going to learn, and you're going to do things that are great. But you have to know about the word momentum.

But the big thing: never quit. Never give up. Do something you love. When you do something you love—as a Scout I see that you love it. But when you do something that you love, you'll never fail. What you're going to do is give it a shot again and again and again. You're ultimately going to be successful, and remember this, you're not working. Because when you're doing something that you love like I do—of course, I love my business, but this is a little bit different. Who thought this was going to happen? We're having a good time. We're doing a good job. Doing a good job. But when you do something that you love, remember this, it's not work.

So you'll work 24/7, you're going to work all the time, and at the end of a year, you're not really working. You don't think of it as work. When you're not doing something that you like or when you're forced in to do something that you really don't like, that's called work. And it's hard work and tedious work.

So as much as you can, do something that you love, work hard, and never ever give up. And you're going to be tremendously successful. Tremendously successful.

Now, with that, I have to tell you our economy is doing great. Our stock market has picked up—since the election, November 8. Do we remember that date? Was that a beautiful date?

Audience members. Yes!

The President. What a date. Do you remember that famous night on television, November 8, where they said—these dishonest people—where they said there is no path to victory for Donald Trump? They forgot about the forgotten people. By the way, they're not forgetting about the forgotten people anymore. They're going crazy trying to figure it out. But I told them, far too late. It's far too late.

But do you remember that incredible night with the maps—and the Republicans are red, and the Democrats are blue—and that map was so red, it was unbelievable, and they didn't know what to say? And you know we have a tremendous disadvantage in the electoral college—popular vote is much easier. We have—because New York, California, Illinois—you have to practically run the East Coast. And we did. We won Florida. We won South Carolina. We won North Carolina. We won Pennsylvania.

We won and won. So when they said, there is no way to victory, there is no way to 270. I went to Maine four times because it's one vote, and we won. But we won—one vote. I went there because I kept hearing we're at 269. But then, Wisconsin came in. Many, many years— Michigan came in.

So—and we worked hard there. My opponent didn't work hard there, because she was told——

Audience members. Boo!

The President. She was told she was going to win Michigan, and I said, well, wait a minute, the car industry is moving to Mexico. Why is she going to move—she's there. Why are they allowing it to move? And by the way, do you see those car industry—do you see what's happening, how they're coming back to Michigan? They're coming back to Ohio. They're starting to peel back in.

And we go to Wisconsin—now, Wisconsin hadn't been won in many, many years by a Republican. But we go to Wisconsin, and we had tremendous crowds. And I'd leave these massive crowds. I'd say, why are we going to lose this State?

The polls, that's also fake news. They're fake polls. But the polls are saying—but we won Wisconsin. So I have to tell you what we did, in all fairness, is an unbelievable tribute to you and all of the other millions and millions of people that came out and voted for "Make America Great Again."

Audience members. U.S.A.! U.S.A.! U.S.A.!

The President. And I'll tell you what, we are, indeed, making America great again. What's going on is incredible.

We had the best jobs report in 16 years. The stock market on a daily basis is hitting an all time high. We're going to be bringing back very soon trillions of dollars from companies that can't get their money back into this country, and that money is going to be used to help rebuild America. We're doing things that nobody ever thought was possible.

And we've just started. It's just the beginning, believe me.

In the Boy Scouts, you learn right from wrong, correct?

Audience members. Yes!

The President. You learn to contribute to your communities, to take pride in your nation, and to seek out opportunities to serve. You pledge to help other people at all times. In the Scout oath, you pledge on your honor to do your best and to do your duty to God and your country.

And by the way, under the Trump administration, you'll be saying "Merry Christmas" again when you go shopping, believe me. Merry Christmas. They've been downplaying that little, beautiful phrase. You're going to be saying "Merry Christmas" again, folks.

But the words duty, country, and God are beautiful words. In other words, basically, what you're doing is, you're pledging to be a great American patriot. For more than a century that is exactly what our Boy Scouts have been. Last year, you gave more than 15 million hours of service to helping people in your communities. Incredible. That's an incredible stat. All of you here tonight will contribute more than 100,000 hours of service by the end of this jamboree—100,000.

When natural disaster strikes, when people face hardship, when the beauty and glory of our outdoor spaces must be restored and taken care of, America turns to the Boy Scouts because we know that the Boy Scouts never, ever, ever let us down.

Just like you know you can count on me, we know we can count on you because we know the values that you live by. Your values are the same values that have always kept America strong, proud, and free. And by the way, do you see the billions and billions and billions of additional money that we're putting back into our military? Billions of dollars. New planes, new ships, great equipment for our people that are so great to us. We love our vets. We love our soldiers. And we love our police, by the way. Firemen, police—we love our police. Those are all special people. Uniformed services.

Two days ago, I traveled to Norfolk, Virginia to commission an American aircraft carrier into the fleet of the United States Navy.

It's the newest, largest, and most advanced aircraft carrier anywhere in the world, and it's named for an Eagle Scout, the USS Gerald R. Ford. Everywhere it sails, that great Scout's name will be feared and revered, because that ship will be a symbol of American power, prestige, and strength.

Our Nation honors President Gerald R. Ford today because he lived his life the scouting way. Boy Scouts celebrate American patriots, especially the brave members of our Armed Forces. Thank you very much. Thank you. Thank you.

American hearts are warmed every year when we read about Boy Scouts placing thousands and thousands of flags next to veterans' gravesites all across the country. By honoring our heroes, you help to ensure that their memory never, ever dies. You should take great pride in the example you set for every citizen of our country to follow.

Generations of American Boy Scouts have sworn the same oath and lived according to same law. You inherit a noble American tradition, and as you embark on your lives, never cease to be proud of who you are and the principles you hold dear and stand by. Wear your values as your badge of honor. What you've done, few have done before you. What you've done is incredible. What you've done is admired by all. So I want to congratulate you, Boy Scouts.

Let your scouting oath guide your path from this day forward. Remember your duty. Honor your history. Take care of the people God put into your life. And love and cherish your great country.

You are very special people. You're special in the lives of America. You're special to me. But if you do what we say, I promise you that you will live scouting's adventure every single day of your life, and you will win, win, win and help people in doing so.

Your lives will have meaning and purpose and joy. You will become leaders, and you will inspire others to achieve the dreams they once thought were totally impossible, things that you said could never, ever happen are already happening for you. And if you do these things—and if you refuse to give in to doubt or to fear—then you will help to make America great again. You will be proud of yourself, be proud of the uniform you wear, and be proud of the country you love.

Audience members. U.S.A.! U.S.A.! U.S.A.!

The President. And never, ever forget, America is proud of you.

This is a very, very special occasion for me. I've known so many Scouts over the years. Winners. I've known so many great people. They've been taught so well, and they love their heritage. But this is very special for me. And I just want to end by saying very importantly: God bless you, God bless the Boy Scouts, God bless the United States of America.

Go out, have a great time in life, compete, and go out and show me that there is nobody—nobody—like a Boy Scout. Thank you very much, everybody. Thank you very much. Thank you. Thank you very much.

Arizona Rally Speech

August 22, 2017
Phoenix, Arizona

ON AUGUST 22, 2017, President Donald Trump delivered a speech before a crowd of supporters in Phoenix, Arizona. Ten days earlier, protests against a white nationalist and neo-Nazi rally in Charlottesville, Virginia, had ended in violence and the death of one protestor. Trump's response, according to Republicans and Democrats alike, was lackluster. In accordance with the talks given by the four people who preceded Trump at the Phoenix podium, Trump's speech was meant to give the president the chance to disavow the Charlottesville racists. Instead, he threatened to shut down the federal government if funding for his proposed border wall was denied and gave a lengthy defense of his response to the Charlottesville incident.

At the beginning of his speech, Trump praises the size of the audience, even requesting that cameras show the crowd. He moves on to criticize the news media for their response to his remarks about the Charlottesville violence, and he spends some time defending his comments. He continues by criticizing his fellow Republicans from Arizona and joking about a pardon for former sheriff Joe Arpaio, who had been convicted of contempt of court for racial profiling. Trump concludes by calling for unity among all Americans—although most of his speech emphasizes issues that divide them.

The President. Wow. What a crowd. What a crowd.

Audience members. Trump! Trump! Trump!

The President. And just so you know, from the Secret Service, there aren't too many people outside protesting, okay? That I can tell you. A lot of people in here. A lot of people pouring in right now, if they can get them in. Whatever you can do, fire marshal, we'll appreciate it.

And I want to thank our great Vice President, Mike Pence, for the introduction, as well as my friend, Dr. Ben Carson. And thank you to a very, very special man, Franklin Graham—Reverend Franklin Graham—for leading us in prayer. And thank you to Alveda King, the niece of the great Dr. Martin Luther King. It really shows you that America is indeed a nation of faith. We know that.

Well, I'm thrilled to be back in Phoenix, in the great State of Arizona, with so many thousands of hard-working American patriots. You know, I'd love if the cameras could show this crowd, because it is rather incredible. It is incredible. It is incredible.

As everybody here remembers, this was the scene of my first rally speech, right? The crowds were so big—almost as big as tonight—that the people said, right at the beginning, you know, there's something special happening here. And we went to center stage, almost

from day one, in the debates. We loved those debates. But we went to center stage, and we never left, right? It's all of us. We did it together. You were there at the start. You've been there every single day since. And I will never forget. Believe me, Arizona, I will never forget.

And I'm here tonight to send a message: We are fully and totally committed to fighting for our agenda, and we will not stop until the job is done. This evening, joined together with friends, we reaffirm our shared customs, traditions, and values. We love our country. We celebrate our troops. We embrace our freedom. We respect our flag. We are proud of our history. We cherish our Constitution, including, by the way, the Second Amendment.

Audience members. U.S.A.! U.S.A.! U.S.A.!

The President. We fully protect religious liberty. We believe in law and order, and we support the incredible men and women of law enforcement. And we pledge our allegiance to one Nation under God.

You always understood what Washington, DC, did not. Our movement is a movement built on love. It's love for fellow citizens; it's love for struggling Americans who have been left behind and love for every American child who deserves a chance to have all of their dreams come true. From the inner cities to the rural outposts, from the Sun Belt to the Rust

Belt, from East to West and North to South, our movement is built on the conviction that every American, from every background, is entitled to a government that puts their needs first.

It is finally time to rebuild our country, to take care of our people, and to fight for the jobs our great American workers deserve, and that's what we're doing.

Audience members. U.S.A.! U.S.A.! U.S.A.!

The President. After our amazing election victory, the forgotten men and women—remember we used to talk about the forgotten men and women before the election? Guess what? They're not forgotten—anyone, right? Anymore. No, they're not forgotten anymore, folks. In fact, they're trying to figure you out. They're saying, the obstructionists, "How do we get them to vote for us?" I don't think that's going to happen anytime soon.

Audience members. No!

The President. We believe that every American has the right to live with dignity. Respect for America demands respect for all of its people. Loyalty to our Nation requires loyalty to each other. We all share the same home, the same dreams, and the same hopes for a better future. A wound inflicted upon one member of our community is a wound inflicted upon us all. You saw last night. You saw last night.

Did anybody watch last night?

Audience members. Yes!

The President. Yes. When one part of America hurts, we all hurt. And when one American suffers an injustice, all of America suffers together. We're all together.

It's time for us to follow the example of our brave American soldiers—and I was with a lot of them last night. Fort Myers. No matter where they come from, no matter what faith they practice, they form a single unbreakable team. That's what we are: We're a team. As a nation, we're a team.

They're all united by their devotion to our country and to their mission. It's time for all of us to remember that we are all on the same team. We are all Americans, and we all believe, right now, in America first. And it's happening, and it's happening fast. I see all those red hats and white hats. It's all happening very fast. It's called "Make America Great Again." You see what's going on. It's coming back very fast.

We want every child to succeed, every community to prosper, and every struggling American to have a chance for a better life. What happened in Charlottesville strikes at the core of America. And tonight this entire arena stands united in forceful condemnation of the thugs who perpetrate hatred and violence.

But the very dishonest media, those people right up there with all the cameras——

Audience members. Boo!

Audience members. Trump! Trump! Trump!

Audience members. CNN sucks! CNN sucks! CNN sucks!

The President. So the—and I mean truly dishonest people in the media and the fake media—they make up stories, they have no sources, in many cases. They say "a source says"—there is no such thing. But they don't report the facts, just like they don't want to report that I spoke out forcefully against hatred, bigotry, and violence, and strongly condemned the neo-Nazis, the White supremacists, and the KKK.

I openly called for unity, healing, and love. And they know it because they were all there. So what I did——

[At this point, the President removed a sheet of paper from his breast pocket.]

The President. So what I did is—I thought I'd take just a second. And I'm really doing this, more than anything else—because you know where my heart is, okay? I'm really doing this to show you how damn dishonest these people are. So here is my first statement, when I heard about Charlottesville. And I have a home in Charlottesville; a lot of people don't know. Here's the first—I can't believe they haven't figured that one out yet. Now they know. Now they finally know.

But I just—I don't want to bore you with this, but I—it shows you how dishonest they are. And most of you know this anyway. So here's what I said, really fast—here's what I said on Saturday.

[The President read from the sheet of paper.]

"We're closely following the terrible events unfolding in Charlottesville, Virginia." This is me speaking. "We condemn in the strongest possible terms this egregious display of hatred, bigotry, and violence." That's me speaking on Saturday. Right after the event.

So I'm condemning—the strongest possible terms—egregious display, hatred, bigotry, and violence. Okay, I think you can't do much better, right? Okay. But they didn't want to put this on. They had it on initially, but then when they talk: "He didn't say it fast enough. He didn't do it on time. Why did it take a day? He must be a racist. It took a day."

Audience members. Boo!

The President. Dishonest people. So here is me—I hope they're showing how many people are in this room, but they won't. They don't even do that. The only time they show the crowds is when there's a disrupter or an anarchist in the room. I call them anarchists. Because believe me, we have plenty of anarchists. They don't want to talk about the anarchists.

So this is me.

[The President continued reading from the sheet of paper.]

"It has no place in America.

"I'm talking about hatred, bigotry, and violence.

"It has no place in America. What is vital now is a swift restoration of law and order and the protection of innocent lives. No citizen should ever fear for their safety, security in our society, and no child should ever be afraid to go outside and play or be with their parents and have a good time." This is me speaking.

Here's further. This is on Saturday, the first one. I did this three times. "We have to come together as Americans with love for the Nation and true affection. Really—and I say this so strongly—true affection for each other." I didn't say true affection for you and you. I said for each other, all of us. All of us. All of us. But they don't report it. They don't—they just let it go. "Above all else, we must remember this truth, no matter our color, creed, religion, or political party: We are all Americans first, we love our country, we love our God, and we love our flag."

Audience members. U.S.A.! U.S.A.! U.S.A.!

The President. Then, I went on. This is my first statement, and they said—remember, they said, "Well, he wasn't specific enough." "Why wasn't he more specific?" So in my second statement, I got really specific. And they said, "Why didn't he do it faster?" The—I'm telling you, folks—look, look, I know these people probably better than anybody. And a lot of people have a problem with it. Because look, what happens with them—if they're doing a story about me, I know if it's honest or false.

If you're reading a story about somebody, you don't know—you assume it's honest—because it's, like, the failing New York Times, which is, like, so bad. It's so bad. Or the Washington Post, which I call a lobbying tool for Amazon, okay? That's a lobbying tool for Amazon. Or CNN, which is so bad and so pathetic, and their ratings are going down.

Audience members. Boo!

Audience members. CNN sucks! CNN sucks! CNN sucks!

The President. Right?

Audience members. CNN sucks! CNN sucks! CNN sucks!

The President. But all the networks. I mean, CNN is really bad, but ABC this morning—I don't watch it much, but I'm watching in the morning, and they have little George Stephanopoulos talking to Nikki Haley, right? Little George. And he talks about the speech I made last night, which, believe it or not, got great reviews, right? They had a hard time. They were having a hard time, because it was with soldiers. We were somber; we were truthful. We were doing—we were saying things. And it really did. So he talked about it for, like, that much. And then, he goes, let's get back to Charlottesville. Charlottesville. And Nikki was great. She's doing a great job, by the way.

So now I say, we have to heal our wounds and the wounds of our country. I love the people of our country: the people, all of the people. It says, I love all of the people of our country. I didn't say I love you because you're Black, or I love you because you're White, or I love you because you're from Japan, or you're from China, or you're from Kenya, or you're from Scotland or Sweden. I love all the people of our country.

So I said, here's my—this is, by the way, folks, this is my exact words: I love all the people of our country. We're going to make America great again, but we're going to make it great for all of the people of the United States of America. And then, they say: "Is he a racist? Is he a racist?" Then, I did a second one.

[There was a disruption in the audience.]

So then, I did second one. Don't bother, it's only a single voice and not a very powerful voice.

Audience members. U.S.A.! U.S.A.! U.S.A.!

The President. How did he get in here? He's supposed to be with the few people outside.

How about all week they're talking about the massive crowds that are going to be outside? Where are they? Well, it's hot out. It is hot. I think it's too warm. You know, they show up in the helmets and the black masks, and they've got clubs, and they've got everything. Antifa!

Audience members. Boo!

The President. So on August the 14th—so that was it. And I said "all people"—I love all people, everything, right? Now I figure, I'm going to do it again; I'll be even more specific.

[The President continued reading from the sheet of paper.]

So I said: "Based on the events that took place over the last weekend in Charlottesville, I'd like to provide the Nation with an update." Because that was right after the event, the first one, right? "An update on ongoing Federal response to the horrific attack and violence that was witnessed by everybody. To anyone who acted criminally in this weekend's racist violence, you will be held fully accountable. Justice will be delivered." That's what I said. Listen to that. I said that. But they don't show that. They don't show it. They talk—they'll take one thing—like, seriously, "He was late" was the best thing. "He was late."

So I said, "To anyone who acted criminally in this weekend's racist violence." Okay, then, I go, "We must love each other, show affection for each other, and unite together in condemnation of hatred, bigotry, and violence. We must rediscover the bonds of love and loyalty that bring us together as Americans," right? Then I said, "racism is evil." Did they report that I said that racism is evil?

Audience members. No!

The President. You know why? Because they are very dishonest people.

So I said, "racism is evil." Now, they only choose, like, a half a sentence here or there, and then they just go on to this long rampage, or they put on these real lightweights all around the table that nobody ever heard of, and they all say what a bad guy I am.

But, I mean, did you ever see anything—and then you wonder why CNN is doing relatively poorly in the ratings. Because they're putting, like, seven people, all negative on Trump, and they fired Jeffrey Lord. Poor Jeffrey.

Audience members. Boo!

The President. Jeffrey Lord. I guess he was getting a little bit fed up, and he was probably fighting back a little too hard. They said, we'd better get out of here. We'll get him out.

[The President continued reading from the sheet of paper.]

"And those who caused violence in its name are criminals and thugs, including the KKK, neo-Nazis, White supremacists, and other hate groups that are repugnant to everything we hold true as Americans." Now, let me ask you, can it be any better than that? In all fairness.

Audience members. No!

The President. And you know, I mention that, but to the best of my knowledge, when there was a big problem, Barack Obama never said it took place because of radical Islamic terrorists. He never said that, right? He doesn't have to say.

Audience members. Boo!

The President. You know why? Because they have a double standard. Because the media is totally dishonest, and they have a double standard. You've never heard them say that. And in fact, if you use the term, you get criticized. But with me, they wanted me to say it. I said it, and I said it very clearly, but they refused to put it on.

[The President continued reading from the sheet of paper.]

"Those who spread violence in the name of bigotry strike the very core of America." These are my words. This was on Monday, August the 14th. So you had Saturday; you had Monday. I mean I was going to do one of these every week, but you would never get it right.

"In times such as these, America has always shown its true character, responding to hate with love, division with unity, and violence with an unwavering resolve for justice." Then, I finished, I said, "We will defend and protect the sacred rights of all Americans." "All" is capitalized, times five. Not just you. "And we will work together so that every citizen—every citizen—in this blessed land is free to follow their dreams and their hearts and to express the love and joy in their souls."

Okay, now—I mean—so, so they were having a hard time with that one, because I said everything. I hit them with neo-Nazi. I hit them with everything. I got the White supremacists, the neo-Nazi. I got them all in there. Let's see, yes, KKK—we have KKK. I got them all. So they're having a hard time.

So what did they say, right? "It should have been sooner. He's a racist." It should have been sooner. Okay. So it should have been—so then, the last one, on Tuesday. Tuesday, I did another one.

[The President continued reading from the sheet of paper.]

"We condemn in the strongest possible terms this egregious display of hatred, bigotry, and violence. It has no place in America." But they also said that he must be a racist because he never mentioned the driver of the car, who is a terrible person, drove the car, and he killed Heather, and it's a terrible thing. But they said I didn't mention—so these are my words: "The driver of the car is a murderer, and what he did was a horrible, inexcusable thing." They said I didn't mention.

And then, they asked me—just to finish it—they asked me, what about race relations in the United States? Now, I have to say they were pretty bad under Barack Obama. That I can tell you. But they asked me the question, and I said, "Well, I think jobs can have a very big and positive impact. I think if we continue to create jobs, like I've done—over 1 million since I've been in office"—way over one—"I think if we continue to create jobs at the levels that I'm creating jobs, I think that's going to have a tremendously positive impact on race relations." I do. I do.

And the other thing—very important—I believe wages will start going up, because we now have the lowest unemployment rate we've had in 17 years. So you're going to see wages go up, right? They haven't gone up for a long time. I believe wages now, because the economy is doing so well with respect to employment and unemployment, I believe wages will start to go up, and I think that will have a tremendously positive impact on race relations. You want it? Yes. Give that.

[The President gave the sheet of paper to an audience member.]

So that was my words. Now, you know, I was a good student. I always hear about the elite. You know, the elite—they're elite? I went to better schools than they did. I was a better student than they were. I live in a bigger, more beautiful apartment. And I live in the White House too, which is really great. I think—you know what? I think we're the elites; they're not the elites.

So the point is—and I didn't want to bore you, because you understand where I'm coming from. You people understand. But the point is that those were three different—there were two statements and one news conference. The words were perfect. They only take out anything they can think of. And for the most part, all they do is complain. But they don't put on those words, and they don't put on me saying those words. The media can attack me. But where I draw the line is when they attack you—which is what they do—when they attack the decency of our supporters.

You are honest, hard-working, tax-paying—and by the way, you're overtaxed, but we're going to get your taxes down. You're taxpaying Americans who love our Nation, obey our laws, and care for our people. It's time to expose the crooked media deceptions and to challenge the media for their role in fomenting divisions. And yes, by the way, they are trying to take away our history and our heritage. You see that.

Audience members. Boo!

The President. And I say it, and you know, we're all pros. We're all, like—we have a certain sense. We're smart people. These are truly dishonest people. And not all of them. Not all of them. You have some very good reporters. You have some very fair journalists. But for the most part, honestly, these are really, really dishonest people. And they're bad people. And I really think they don't like our country. I really believe that. And I don't believe they're going to change, and that's why I do this. If they would change, I would never say it.

The only people giving a platform to these hate groups is the media itself and the fake news. Oh, that's so funny—look back there, the live red lights, they're turning those suckers off fast, I'll tell you. They're turning those lights off fast.

Audience members. Boo!

The President. Like, CNN does not want its falling viewership to watch what I'm saying tonight, I can tell you. I mean, the advantage I have is that we do have a big voice. And you know, they're always saying, like, Twitter or social media—if I didn't have social media, I wouldn't be able to get the word out. I probably wouldn't be standing here, right? I probably wouldn't be standing here right now. If I don't have social media, I probably would not be standing. And do you ever notice when I go on and I'll put, like, out a tweet or a couple of tweets: "He's in a Twitter storm again." I don't do Twitter storms. You know, you'll put on a little tweet, "I'm going to be with the veterans today." They'll say, "Donald Trump is in a Twitter storm." These are sick people.

You know the thing I don't understand? You would think they'd want to make our country great again, and I honestly believe they don't. I honestly believe it. If you want to discover the source of the division in our country, look no further than the fake news and the crooked media, which would rather get ratings and clicks than tell the truth.

I mean, the New York Times has written some stories. How about this: The New York Times essentially apologized after I won the election, because their coverage was so bad, and it was so wrong, and they were losing so many subscribers that they practically apologized. I would say they did. They say, well, it wasn't really that much of an apology, because they were losing so many people, because they were misled. And I figured, this is great. And for about 2 weeks, I got good coverage. Then, they reverted back, and they're worse than ever before. You know, it's, like, one of those things. The Washington Post is terrible. But these are dishonest.

But let me tell you, you have some great honest papers. You have some great networks. I must tell you, Fox has treated me fairly. Fox treated me fairly. They've treated me fairly. Hey, I'll let you know—you know what, someday they might not treat me fairly, and I'll tell you about it, okay? But they've treated me fairly. And I don't mean all good. I get plenty of bad on Fox too. But at least it's within reason. And Hannity, how good is Hannity? He's saying. How good is Hannity? And he's a great guy, and he's an honest guy. And "Fox & Friends" in the morning is the best show, and it's the absolute most honest show. And it's the show I watch.

Not only does—oh, boy, those cameras are going off. Oh, wow. Why don't you just fold them up and take them home? Oh, those cameras are going off. Wow. That's the one thing: They're very nervous to have me on live television, because this can't happen. No, you know what? I'm a person that wants to tell the truth. I'm an honest person, and what I'm saying you know is exactly right.

Not only does the media give a platform to hate groups, but the media turns a blind eye to the gang violence on our streets, the failures of our public school, the destruction of our wealth at the hands of the terrible, terrible trade deals made by politicians that should have never been allowed to be politicians, and the unaccountable hostility against our incredible police, who work so hard at such a dangerous job.

My administration is committed to the idea that all Americans have the right to live in safety, security, and peace. We believe in the rule of law, because we know that freedom cannot exist if our people are not safe. And how safe are you at a Trump rally?

Remember at the beginning? Remember when this already started? When this started at the beginning, they used to send in thugs. They'd swing—our people are tougher than them, so it wasn't always very good for them. But they'd send in thugs, and our people would protect themselves, and then you'd go home, and you'd watch—there's violence. Let me tell you: You see this room? You've got people outside, but not very many. But see this room? You're safe in this room. You're very safe in this room. A big room.

The most sacred duty of government is to protect the lives of its citizens, and that includes securing our borders and enforcing our immigration laws.

Audience members. Build the wall! Build the wall! Build the wall!

The President. By the way, I'm just curious: Do the people in this room like Sheriff Joe? So was Sheriff Joe convicted for doing his job? That's what——

Audience members. Yes!

The President. He should have had a jury. But you know what? I'll make a prediction: I think he's going to be just fine, okay? But, but I won't do it tonight, because I don't want to cause any controversy. Is that okay? All right? But Sheriff Joe can feel good.

The people of Arizona know the deadly and heartbreaking consequences of illegal immigration: the lost lives, the drugs, the gangs, the cartels, the crisis of smuggling and trafficking. MS-13—we're throwing them out so fast, they never got thrown out of anything like this. We are liberating towns out on Long Island. We're liberating. Can you imagine, in this day and age—in this day and age, in this country—we are liberating towns? This is like from a different age. We are taking these people. They don't shoot people, because it's too fast and not painful. They cut them up into little pieces. These are animals. We are getting them out of here. We're throwing them in jails, and we're throwing them out of the country. We're liberating our towns. You've seen it. You've lived it. And you elected me to put a stop to it. And we are doing a phenomenal job of putting a stop to it. That I can tell you.

After years of defending other countries' borders—can you believe we fight for other countries? We want to defend their borders—we're finally defending our own borders, and we're showing compassion for the struggling American workers who are now starting to see the light, because plants are coming pouring back into our country. And by the way, we're doing a lot of good work on that. But a lot of people are coming back in. We have Foxconn; they make the iPhones, as you know, for Apple. And so many companies are building now in our country, including the auto companies who are coming back. Years of uncontrolled immigration have placed enormous pressure on the jobs and wages of working families, and they've put great burdens on local schools and hospitals. While this may be good for a handful of special interests, it's unfair to working people of all backgrounds, all throughout our country. We want every American community to succeed, including our immigrant communities, but they can't do that if we don't control our borders.

Earlier today I visited with the incredible men and women of ICE and the Border Patrol during a visit to Yuma Sector. I was over at the Yuma Sector. It was hot. It's, like, 115 degrees, I'm out signing autographs for an hour. I was there. That was a hot—you learn if you're in shape if you can do that, believe me. And they actually told me, "Actually, sir, it's relatively cool today." Can you believe that? But it was great.

And I met with the Border Patrol, and I met with ICE, and these are incredible people, the job they do. In fact, General Kelly, who was in charge of Homeland Security—where people coming in down 78 and almost 80 percent. He did so good, I made him my Chief of Staff. Right? That made sense. John—where's John? Where is he? Where is General Kelly? Get him out here. He's great. He's doing a great job.

But we did a lot. Before anything happened, we did a lot. We respect and cherish our ICE officers and our Border Patrol agents, and we respect and cherish our police officers and our firemen and all of our uniformed services.

But during that visit, I heard firsthand from the frontline agents about the security threats they confront each and every day, and I pledge my continued resolve to them—and all of you—to keep our country safe. All around the Nation, I have spent time with the wonderful Americans whose children were killed for the simple reason that our Government failed to enforce our immigration laws, already existing laws. And I promised these families, the deaths of their loved ones will not have been in vain. I promised them. I know so many of them.

One by one, we are finding the gang members, the drug dealers, and the criminals who prey on our people. We are throwing them out of the country, or we're putting them the hell, fast, in jail. We are cracking down on these sanctuary cities that shield criminal aliens, finally. And we are building a wall on the southern border, which is absolutely necessary.

Audience members. Build that wall! Build that wall! Build that wall!

The President. Build that wall. Now, the obstructionist Democrats would like us not to do it. But believe me, if we have to close down our Government, we're building that wall. Let me be very clear to Democrats in Congress who oppose a border wall and stand in the way of border security: You are putting all of America's safety at risk. You're doing that. You're doing that.

Again, the Border Patrol today—I said, "How important is the wall?" to some of the folks. I met with a lot of them. And they looked at me, they said, it's vital. It's vital. It's so vital. And you know, we have walls. I don't know if you know, we're already starting to fix a lot of the walls we already have, because we don't have to rebuild them. And we want walls that you can see through, in a sense. You want to see what's on the other side. But we're starting to fix a lot of the walls. We've done a lot of work. But I said to them, how are we doing and how important are the walls? And they said, Mr. President, you have no idea: It is desperately needed. We're going to have our wall. We're going to get our wall.

And that wall is also going to help us, very importantly, with the drug problem and the massive amounts of drugs that are pouring across the southern border. My administration will never back down in demanding immigration control. The American people voted for immigration control. That's one of the reasons I'm here. And that is what the American people deserve, and they're going to get it. So you put pressure. But believe me, one way or the other, we're going to get that wall.

Immigration security is also a matter—remember this—of national security. That's why we're implementing tough new vetting and screening protocols to keep radical Islamic terrorists out of our country. You look at what just happened in Spain and so many other places. Nope. We're really vetting. We're tough. Does anybody want me to be soft on the vetting, or would you like me——

Audience members. No!

The President. Extreme vetting. I came up with that term. That's what it has to be.

So I have a message for Congress tonight: Your job is to represent American families, American people, American workers. It's your job. You need to represent them on the border, on taxes, on health care—one vote—and on every other issue that affects their lives. And for our friends in the Senate—oh, boy—the Senate, remember this. Look, the Senate, we have to get rid of what's called the filibuster rule. We have to. And if we don't, the Republicans will never get anything passed. You're wasting your time. We have to get rid of the filibuster rule. Right now we need 60 votes, and we have 52 Republicans. That means that eight Democrats are controlling all of this legislation. We have over 200 bills.

Audience members. Boo!

The President. And we have to speak to Mitch, and we have to speak to everybody. And I want to tell you, we have some great, great Republican Senators. We really do. And they fought like hell to get that thing approved. They fought. They really did. They really fought.

Now, even on health care, because of reconciliation—which you don't know, it doesn't matter; it's a trick—we needed 51 votes. But when you need 51 and you have 52, and we include the Vice President, who always votes with us; he's the greatest. But you have no margin. But some of the best things in health care require 60 votes. So even when you say, we're voting on health care, like, across State lines—purchase across State lines. One of the most important things; I've been talking about it for 2 years during debates. It gives competition. Insurance companies come in; your prices go way down. Arizona is a disaster in terms of the price increase of your insurance, 116 percent increase.

You've got to get rid of the filibuster rule, you've got to go to a majority, you've got to go to 51 votes. And if they don't do that, they're playing—they're just wasting time.

All of the Democrats in Congress, that's the only thing they do well; they do one thing well. You know what it's called? They have no ideas; they have no policies. They obstruct. That's all they do. Their word is, we "resist." They don't resist. They obstruct. It's all they're good at it. It's all they're good at. That's all they do. On health care, they have 48 Democrats; we got no votes. We got no votes. And it would have been great health care. And by the way—would have been great health care for Arizona. Would have been great. So the Democrats have no ideas, no policy, no vision for the country, other than total socialism and maybe, frankly, a step beyond socialism from what I'm seeing.

Audience members. Boo!

The President. Under their plan for America, your taxes will double or triple, your services will diminish, and your borders will be left wide open for everybody to come in and enjoy our country.

Audience members. Boo!

The President. Obamacare is a disaster. And think—think—we were just one vote away from victory after 7 years of everybody proclaiming repeal and replace. One vote away. One—one vote. One vote away. We were one vote away. Think of it—7 years. The Republicans—and again, you have some great Senators. But we had—one vote away from repeal and replace.

Audience members. Drain the swamp! Drain the swamp! Drain the swamp!

The President. But you know, they all said, Mr. President, your speech was so good last night, please, please, Mr. President, don't mention any names. So I won't. I won't. No, I won't vote—one vote away. I will not mention any names. Very Presidential, isn't it? Very Presidential. And nobody wants me to talk about your other Senator, who's weak on borders, weak on crime. So I won't talk about him.

Audience members. Boo!

The President. Nobody wants me to talk about him. Nobody knows who the hell he is.

And now—see, I haven't mentioned any names—so now everybody is happy. But we are going to get rid of Obamacare. I will never stop. One vote. I will never stop. We're going to get rid of Obamacare.

Every day, we're keeping our promises, and that includes our promises to our great, great veterans. Who's a veteran here? It's getting better. Getting really good. Nobody has fixed it. Nobody has been able to do. And remember, I'm only here for less than 8 months. You know, when they talk about Obamacare, it was years. When they talk about—Hillary Clinton spent 8 years trying to get——

Audience members. Boo!

The President. Eight years trying to get health care.

Audience members. Lock her up! Lock her up! Lock her up!

The President. Well, it's obvious that we won the State of Arizona. Do you agree with that? It's pretty obvious. And we won it by a lot. And I hear we're winning it by even more right now.

But if you think about it—Clinton—they spent 8 years, and they weren't able to get health care. Other administrations spent all of their time, they weren't able to get it. Obama, what he did to get it, what he did to get it—including the guy—Gruber. Did you see Gruber got fired yesterday? He got fired, because he defrauded somebody or something. Something very bad happened. Check it out. Something happened. Gruber, who lied about Obamacare; who called everybody fools for believing it. Obamacare is gone. It's a disaster. It's gone. Premiums in other States are going up at numbers that are even higher than the State of Arizona. Insurance companies are fleeing, and it's gone.

So we're going to—I really believe that the Republicans, and maybe we'll get a couple of Senators that think they're going to lose their race on the Democratic side. Maybe. But we'll get it fixed. One vote. Speak to your Senator, please. Speak to your Senator.

We're reforming the VA to ensure our veterans have the care they so richly deserve, including choice, choice, choice. In other words, if you've got to wait for 7 days, and you're not feeling well, you go see a doctor, and we pay for your doctor. Isn't that good? And we got legislation approved that everybody said was impossible. It's called VA accountability. If somebody treats our veterans badly, we can fire them. We say, "You're fired, get out of here."

Everybody said you couldn't get that. They've been trying to get that passed for 40 years. We got great legislation. You ever hear these liars back there, where they say, "But Trump hasn't gotten legislation." I think we've gotten more in a short period of time, in this 7 months—I think we've gotten more than anybody, including Harry Truman, who was number one. But they will tell you we got none.

So we got VA accountability so that you can fire people that are treating our veterans badly or aren't doing their job. Isn't that great?

We've also obtained historic increase in defense spending to prevent and deter conflict. We believe in peace through strength. We're building up our military like never before. Thousands and thousands of brave Americans have paid the ultimate price for our freedom. Now it's up to us to preserve and protect their legacy.

Last night, as you know, I laid out my vision for an honorable and enduring outcome in a very tough place, a place where our country has failed: Afghanistan. This is a place where terrorists are trained, where you have people that are not exactly United States fans. Can I say that? And I will tell you that what we're going to do with our incredible military, they're going to make unbelievable sacrifices, and they've already made, in some cases, the ultimate sacrifice. But we're fighting for them. Our war fighters deserve the tools they need and the trust they've earned to fight and to win. Fight and to win.

And you see what's going on in North Korea. All of a sudden—I don't know, who knows. But I can tell you, what I said, that's not strong enough. Some people said it was too strong. It's not strong enough. But Kim Jong Un, I respect the fact that I believe he is starting to respect us. I respect that fact very much. Respect that fact. And maybe—probably not—but maybe something positive can come about. They won't tell you that, but maybe something positive can come about.

Every American deserves a Government that protects them, honors them, defends them, and fights for them. And by the way, speaking of that, you have three Congressmen in the audience—and your Governor, who met me at the plane, and he's now inside, but he said, I want to spend my time outside on security. I said, I think that's a great idea, Governor. But not that many people showed up, so I don't think it should be much of a problem. But you have a hell of a Governor—Governor Ducey. You have a great Governor.

And we have three Congressmen—a friend of mine who has been so great to me, Trent Franks. Where's Congressman Franks? Where is he? Get over here. Paul Gosar, Congressman. Congressman Andy Biggs. Get up here, fellas.

[The President greeted Reps. H. Trent Franks and Andrew S. Biggs.]

Thank you, fellas. Thank you, Congressmen. Never let them go, folks. Never let them go. Don't ever lose them. Thank you, fellas.

So, in Washington, we're taking power out of the hands of donors and special interests and putting that power back into the hands of the people that voted for us, okay? For us. The same failed voices in Washington who oppose our movement are the same people who gave us one terrible trade deal after another; who gave us one foreign policy disaster after another; who sacrificed our sovereignty, our wealth, and our jobs. We don't need advice from the Washington, DC, swamp.

We need right now to drain the swamp. That's what's happening too, believe me. Washington is full of people who are only looking out for themselves. But I don't come to Washington for me. You know, I've had a great life. I've had great success. I've enjoyed my life. Most people think I'm crazy to have done this. And I think they're right. But I enjoy it, because we've made so much—I don't believe that any President—I don't believe that any President has accomplished as much as this President in the first 6 or 7 months. I really don't believe it, including—including—a great Supreme Court Justice, Justice Gorsuch. Big thing.

I came to Washington for you. Your dreams are my dreams. Your hopes are my hopes. And your future is what I'm fighting for each and every day. It's so important. Our agenda is the pro-worker agenda. We've accomplished historic amounts in a short period of time. We've signed more than 50 pieces of legislation. They said we've signed none. None. We've signed 50. Appointed Justice Gorsuch, nominated 31 new Federal judges, with many more on the way. So importantly, we have aggressively cancelled job-killing regulations, and we're unleashing job-creating American energy like we've never unleashed before.

We've ended the war on beautiful, clean coal. And it's just been announced that a second brand new coal mine, where they're going to take out clean coal—meaning they're taking out coal, they're going to clean it—is opening in the State of Pennsylvania. The second one. And the State of West Virginia, which was way behind and lagging, was now, in terms of GDP increase, second last quarter to the State of Texas. How about that? West Virginia. And they have a great Governor in West Virginia, Governor Jim Justice, who just quit the Democrats and joined the Republican Party.

In the proud tradition of America's great leaders, from George Washington—please don't take his statue down, please. Please. Does anybody want George Washington's statue?

Audience members. No!

The President. No. Is that sad? Is that whole sad? To Lincoln, to Teddy Roosevelt—I see they want to take Teddy Roosevelt's down too. They're trying to figure out why. They don't know. They're trying to take away our culture. They're trying to take away our history. And our weak leaders, they do it overnight. These things have been there for 150 years, for 100 years. You go back to a university, and it's gone. Weak, weak people.

We are going to protect American industry. We are going to protect the American worker. No longer will we allow other countries to close our factories, steal our jobs, and drain our wealth. We are building our future with American hands, American labor, American iron, aluminum, and steel. We will buy American, and we will hire American.

I immediately withdrew the United States from the disastrous Trans-Pacific Partnership, would have been a disaster. And you know that one of the worst deals that anybody in history has ever entered into, we have begun formal renegotiation with Mexico and Canada on NAFTA. And I must be honest—and I've been talking about NAFTA for a long time—and I'm sorry it's taken 6 months—but we have to give notice. You have to see this. We have to give notice. And after the notice is given, you have to wait a long time. Then, you have to give another, no—then you have to wait a long time. Anyway, we started 2 days ago—Bob Lighthizer. Personally, I don't think we can make a deal, because we have been so badly taken advantage of. They have made such great deals—both of the countries, but in particular Mexico—that I don't think we can make a deal. So I think we'll end up probably terminating NAFTA at some point. Okay? Probably. But, but, I told you from the first day, we will renegotiate NAFTA, or we will terminate NAFTA. I personally don't think you can make a deal without a termination, but we're going to see what happens, okay? You're in good hands, I can tell you.

We are unleashing American energy. And I withdrew the United States from the job-killing Paris climate accord. People have no idea how bad that was for this country. Great for other countries. We were like the lapdog. Great for other countries. Our country was so behind.

Since I took the oath of office, we've added far more than 1 million jobs in the private sector. Unemployment is right now at almost a 17-year low. Wages are rising. The stock market is at its all time high in history. And economic growth has surged to 2.6 percent. Remember everybody said, you won't bring it up to 1 percent? You bring it up to 1.2 percent. And we've just started. Those regulations that we've gotten rid of, which—and we're going to have some regulation, but it's going to be sensible regulation. Those regulations are unleashing our economy.

So we have a GDP—it was shocking—about 2 weeks ago, it was announced for the quarter—2.6 percent. Remember I said we're going to try and hit 3 percent? We're already at 2.6. Maybe I'll have to increase my offer.

And so many of those people—you know, the economic council, when it got a little heat with the lies from the media, they sort of said, oh, we'll take a pass. Well, not all of them, but some of them did. But I remember the ones that did. But they'll say, we take—oh, we'll take. But people are now calling me, people that have been, like, we'll take a pass. "Don, can we get together for lunch? Let's do it privately instead of through a council." These people just don't get it. They are calling, and they're saying, how about getting together privately? They like it better—why should they

be on a council? You know, that's the way it is, folks. That's the way it is.

To bring more jobs and industry to our shores, we are committed to passing the first major tax reform in over 30 years. Now, we need the help of Congress, please. Okay? We need the help of Congress. And we really could use some Democrat help. We're giving you the biggest tax cut in the history of our country. The Democrats are going to find a way to obstruct. If they do, remember they are stopping you from getting a massive tax cut. Just remember that, okay?

Audience members. Boo!

The President. America's crushing business tax is a massive self-inflicted economic wound. We have one of the highest business tax rates anywhere in the world, pushing jobs and wealth out of our country. That is why we are going to lower the tax on American business to bring back those companies, bring them back to America. We want more products stamped with the letters "Made in the U.S.A."

We also want everyday Americans to be able to keep more of their own money. So for the Democratic Senators, especially the ones where I won their States by 20 and 30 points, I really hope you're going to come over to our side. Because again, when you have 52 Republicans, if you lose like 2, that's the end. You know what, as good as something is, it's hard to get 51 out of 52. So I hope some of the Democrats that are going to lose their election will come over and give everybody a big, beautiful tax cut, which is going to be great for the economy. It's time to pass a tax cut for the middle class families. We will make America the best place in the world to hire, grow, and start a business again. We want to lift our people from welfare to work, from dependence to independence, and from poverty to prosperity.

We're going to do an infrastructure bill. We will build gleaming new roads, bridges, highways, railways, waterways all across our beautiful land. Our greatest creations, our most incredible buildings, our most beautiful works of art are just waiting to be brought to life.

American hands will build this future. American energy will power this future. We have become an energy exporter for the first time ever just recently. And American workers will bring this future to life. We are the nation that dug out the Panama Canal, won wo world wars, put a man on the Moon, and defeated communism. We can do anything, we can build anything, and we can dream anything. It's time to remember what our brave soldiers never forgot: Americans share one flag, one home, and one glorious destiny. We live according to the same law, raise our children by the same values, and we are all made by the same almighty God.

As long as we remember these truths, as long as we have enough strength and courage in our souls, then there is no challenge too great, no task too large, no dream beyond our reach. We are Americans, and the future belongs to us. The future belongs to all of you. This is our moment. This is our chance. This is our opportunity to recapture our dynasty like never before, to rebuild our future, to deliver justice for every forgotten man and woman and child in America. Freedom will prevail. Our values will endure. Our citizens will prosper. Arizona will thrive. And our beloved Nation will succeed like never, ever before.

So to Americans young and old, near and far, in cities small and large, we say these words again tonight: We will make America strong again. We will make America wealthy again. We will make America proud again. We will make America safe again. And we will make America great again.

Thank you, Arizona! God bless you. Thank you. Thank you.

Statement to the United Nations

September 19, 2017

New York City, New York

ON SEPTEMBER 19, 2017, President Donald Trump addressed the United Nations in New York. His speech—much like his inaugural address eight months earlier—struck a distinctive tone. Combative and accusative, Trump singled out nations he regarded as threats to world peace in general and to American interests in particular, including Iran, North Korea, and Venezuela. In strong language the president, labeling the North Korean leader Kim Jong-un "Rocket Man," warns that provocations by the North Korean government might leave the United States no choice but to "totally destroy" the country. He singles out Iran as "a corrupt dictatorship" and a "murderous regime" that is working to undermine the nuclear deal worked out between the United States and other nations (a deal that Trump regarded as seriously flawed). According to Trump, the leftist regime in Venezuela squandered the wealth of the oil-rich nation and posed a danger to its own people.

Trump also denounces the internationalism that had characterized American involvement in the United Nations for the past half-century. He declares that nations are best served by pursuing their own interests. He asserts his intention to lead the United States in pursuing its own self-interest and calls on other nations to do the same. Only this way, he concludes, will the nations of the world achieve their goals of strength, independence, and patriotism.

Mr. Secretary-General, Mr. President, world leaders, and distinguished delegates: Welcome to New York. It is a profound honor to stand here in my home city, as a representative of the American people, to address the people of the world.

As millions of our citizens continue to suffer the effects of the devastating hurricanes that have struck our country, I want to begin by expressing my appreciation to every leader in this room who has offered assistance and aid. The American people are strong and resilient, and they will emerge from these hardships more determined than ever before.

Fortunately, the United States has done very well since Election Day last November 8. The stock market is at an all time high, a record. Unemployment is at its lowest level in 16 years, and because of our regulatory and other reforms, we have more people working in the United States today than ever before. Companies are moving back, creating job growth the likes of which our country has not seen in a very long time. And it has just been announced that we will be spending almost $700 billion on our military and defense. Our military will soon be the strongest it has ever been.

For more than 70 years, in times of war and peace, the leaders of nations, movements, and religions have stood before this assembly. Like them, I intend to address some of the very serious threats before us today, but also the enormous potential waiting to be unleashed.

We live in a time of extraordinary opportunity. Breakthroughs in science, technology, and medicine are curing illnesses and solving problems that prior generations thought impossible to solve. But each day also brings news of growing dangers that threaten everything we cherish and value. Terrorists and extremists have gathered strength and spread to every region of the planet. Rogue regimes represented in this body not only support terrorists, but threaten other nations and their own people with the most destructive weapons known to humanity.

Authority—and authoritarian powers seek to collapse the values, the systems, and alliances that prevented conflict and tilted the world toward freedom since World War II. International criminal networks traffic drugs, weapons, people; force dislocation and mass migration; threaten our borders; and new forms of aggression exploit technology to menace our citizens. To put it simply, we meet at a time of both immense promise and great peril. It is entirely up to us whether we lift the world to new heights or let it fall into a valley of disrepair.

We have it in our power, should we so choose, to lift millions from poverty, to help our citizens realize their dreams, and to ensure that new generations of children are raised free from violence, hatred, and fear. This institution was founded in the aftermath of two world wars to help shape this better future. It was based on the vision that diverse nations could cooperate to protect their sovereignty, preserve their security, and promote their prosperity.

It was in the same period, exactly 70 years ago, that the United States developed the Marshall Plan to help restore Europe. Those three beautiful pillars—they're pillars of peace, sovereignty, security, and prosperity. The Marshall Plan was built on the noble idea that the whole world is safer when nations are strong, independent, and free. As President Truman said in his message to Congress at that time: "Our support of European recovery is in full accord with our support of the United Nations. The success of the United Nations depends upon the independent strength of its members."

To overcome the perils of the present and to achieve the promise of the future, we must begin with the wisdom of the past. Our success depends on a coalition of strong and independent nations that embrace their sovereignty to promote security, prosperity, and peace for themselves and for the world.

We do not expect diverse countries to share the same cultures, traditions, or even systems of government. But we do expect all nations to uphold these two core sovereign duties: to respect the interests of their own people and the rights of every other sovereign nation. This is the beautiful vision of this institution, and this is the foundation for cooperation and success.

Strong, sovereign nations let diverse countries with different values, different cultures, and different dreams not just coexist, but work side by side on the basis of mutual respect. Strong, sovereign nations let their people take ownership of the future and control their own destiny. And strong, sovereign nations allow individuals to flourish in the fullness of the life intended by God.

In America, we do not seek to impose our way of life on anyone, but rather to let it shine as an example for everyone to watch. This week gives our country a special reason to take pride in that example. We are celebrating the 230th anniversary of our beloved Constitution, the oldest constitution still in use in the world today. This timeless document has been the foundation of peace, prosperity, and freedom for the Americans and for countless millions around the globe whose own countries have found inspiration in its respect for human nature, human dignity, and the rule of law. The greatest in the United States Constitution is its first three beautiful words. They are: "We the people."

Generations of Americans have sacrificed to maintain the promise of those words, the promise of our country, and of our great history. In America, the people govern, the people rule, and the people are sovereign. I was elected not to take power, but to give power to the American people, where it belongs. In foreign affairs, we are renewing this founding principle of sovereignty. Our Government's first duty is to its people, to our citizens: to serve their needs, to ensure their safety, to preserve their rights, and to defend their values.

As President of the United States, I will always put America first, just like you, as the leaders of your countries, will always, and should always, put your countries first. All responsible leaders have an obligation to serve their own citizens, and the nation-state remains the best vehicle for elevating the human condition. But making a better life for our people also requires us to work together in close harmony and unity to create a more safe and peaceful future for all people.

The United States will forever be a great friend to the world and especially to its allies. But we can no longer be taken advantage of or enter into a one-sided deal where the United States gets nothing in return. As long as I hold this office, I will defend America's interests above all else.

But in fulfilling our obligations to our own nations, we also realize that it's in everyone's interest to seek a future where all nations can be sovereign, prosperous, and secure. America does more than speak for the values expressed in the United Nations Charter. Our citizens have paid the ultimate price to defend our freedom and the freedom of many nations represented in this great hall. America's devotion is measured on the battlefields where our young men and women have fought and sacrificed alongside of our allies, from the beaches of Europe to the deserts of the Middle East to the jungles of Asia.

It is an eternal credit to the American character that even after we and our allies emerged victorious from the bloodiest war in history, we did not seek territorial expansion or attempt to oppose—and impose our way of life on others. Instead, we helped build institutions such as this one to defend the sovereignty, security, and prosperity for all.

For the diverse nations of the world, this is our hope. We want harmony and friendship, not conflict and strife. We are guided by outcomes, not ideology. We have a policy of principled realism, rooted in shared goals, interests, and values. That realism forces us to confront a question facing every leader and nation in this room. It is a question we cannot escape or avoid. We will slide down the path of complacency, numb to the challenges, threats, and even wars that we face. Or do we have enough strength and pride to confront those dangers today so that our citizens can enjoy peace and prosperity tomorrow?

If we desire to lift up our citizens, if we aspire to the approval of history, then we must fulfill our sovereign duties to the people we faithfully represent. We must protect our nations, their interests, and their futures. We must reject threats to sovereignty, from the Ukraine to the South China Sea. We must uphold respect for law, respect for borders, and respect for culture, and the peaceful engagement these allow. And just as the founders of this body intended, we must work together and confront together those who threaten us with chaos, turmoil, and terror.

The scourge of our planet today is a small group of rogue regimes that violate every principle on which the United Nations is based. They respect neither their own citizens nor the sovereign rights of their countries. If the righteous many do not confront the wicked few, then evil will triumph. When decent people and nations become bystanders to history, the forces of destruction only gather power and strength.

No one has shown more contempt for other nations and for the well-being of their own people than the depraved regime in North Korea. It is responsible for the starvation deaths of millions of North Koreans, and for the imprisonment, torture, killing, and oppression of countless more. We were all witness to the regime's deadly abuse when an innocent American college student, Otto Warmbier, was returned to America only to die a few days later. We saw it in the assassination of the dictator's brother using banned nerve agents in an international airport. We know it kidnapped a sweet 13-year-old Japanese girl from a beach in her own country to enslave her as a language tutor for North Korea's spies.

If this is not twisted enough, now North Korea's reckless pursuit of nuclear weapons and ballistic missiles threatens the entire world with unthinkable loss of human life. It is an outrage that some nations would not only trade with such a regime, but would arm, supply, and financially support a country that imperils the world with nuclear conflict. No nation on Earth has an interest in seeing this band of criminals arm itself with nuclear weapons and missiles.

The United States has great strength and patience, but if it is forced to defend itself or its allies, we will have no choice but to totally destroy North Korea. Rocket Man is on a suicide mission for himself and for his regime. The United States is ready, willing and able, but hopefully, this will not be necessary. That's what the United Nations is all about; that's what the United Nations is for. Let's see how they do.

It is time for North Korea to realize that the denuclearization is its only acceptable future. The United Nations Security Council recently held two unanimous 15-to-nothing votes adopting hard-hitting resolutions against North Korea, and I want to thank China and Russia for joining the vote to impose sanctions, along with all of the other members of the Security Council. Thank you to all involved. But we must do much more. It is time for all nations to work together to isolate the Kim regime until it ceases its hostile behavior.

We face this decision not only in North Korea. It is far past time for the nations of the world to confront another reckless regime, one that speaks openly of mass murder, vowing death to America, destruction to Israel, and ruin for many leaders and nations in this room. The Iranian Government masks a corrupt dictatorship behind the false guise of a democracy. It has turned a wealthy country with a rich history and culture into an economically depleted rogue state whose chief exports are violence, bloodshed, and chaos. The longest suffering victims of Iran's leaders are, in fact, its own people.

Rather than use its resources to improve Iranian lives, its oil profits go to fund Hizballah and other terrorists that kill innocent Muslims and attack their peaceful Arab and Israeli neighbors. This wealth, which rightly belongs to Iran's people, also goes to shore up Bashar al-Asad's dictatorship, fuel Yemen's civil war, and undermine peace throughout the entire Middle East.

We cannot let a murderous regime continue these destabilizing activities while building dangerous missiles, and we cannot abide by an agreement if it provides cover for the eventual construction of a nuclear program. The Iran deal was one of the worst and most one-sided transactions the United States has ever entered into. Frankly, that deal is an embarrassment to the United States, and I don't think you've heard the last of it, believe me.

It is time for the entire world to join us in demanding that Iran's Government end its pursuit of death and destruction. It is time for the regime to free all Americans and citizens of other nations that they have unjustly detained. And above all, Iran's Government must stop supporting terrorists, begin serving its own people, and respect the sovereign rights of its neighbors.

The entire world understands that the good people of Iran want change, and, other than the vast military power of the United States, that Iran's people are what their leaders fear the most. This is what causes the regime to restrict internet access, tear down satellite dishes, shoot unarmed student protestors, and imprison political reformers.

Oppressive regimes cannot endure forever, and the day will come when the people will face a choice. Will they continue down the path of poverty, bloodshed, and terror? Or will the Iranian people return to the nation's proud roots as a center of civilization, culture, and wealth where their people can be happy and prosperous once again?

The Iranian regime's support for terror is in stark contrast to the recent commitments of many of its neighbors to fight terrorism and halt its financing. In Saudi Arabia early last year, I was greatly honored to address the leaders of more than 50 Arab and Muslim nations. We agreed that all responsible nations must work together to confront terrorists and the Islamic extremism that inspires them. We will stop radical Islamic terrorism because we cannot allow it to tear up our Nation and, indeed, to tear up the entire world.

We must deny the terrorists safe haven, transit, funding, and any form of support for their vile and sinister ideology. We must drive them out of our nations. It is time to expose and hold responsible those countries who support and finance terror groups like Al Qaida, Hizballah, the Taliban, and others that slaughter innocent people. The United States and our allies are working together throughout the Middle East to crush the loser terrorists and stop the reemergence of safe havens they use to launch attacks on all of our people. Last month, I announced a new strategy for victory in the fight against this evil in Afghanistan. From now on, our security interests will dictate the length and scope of military operations, not arbitrary benchmarks and timetables set up by politicians. I have also totally changed the rules of engagement in our fight against the Taliban and other terrorist groups. In Syria and Iraq, we have made big gains toward lasting defeat of ISIS. In fact, our country has achieved more against ISIS in the last 8 months than it has in many, many years combined.

We seek the de-escalation of the Syrian conflict and a political solution that honors the will of the Syrian people. The actions of the criminal regime of Bashar al-Asad—including the use of chemical weapons against his own citizens, even innocent children—shock the conscience of every decent person. No society can be safe if banned chemical weapons are allowed to spread. That is why the United States carried out a missile strike on the airbase that launched the attack. We appreciate the efforts of United Nations agencies that are providing vital humanitarian assistance in areas liberated from ISIS, and we especially thank Jordan, Turkey, and Lebanon for their role in hosting refugees from the Syrian conflict.

The United States is a compassionate nation and has spent billions and billions of dollars in helping to support this effort. We seek an approach to refugee resettlement that is designed to help these horribly treated people, and which enables their eventual return to their home countries, to be part of the rebuilding process.

For the cost of resettling one refugee in the United States, we can assist more than 10 in their home region. Out of the goodness of our hearts, we offer financial assistance to hosting countries in the region, and we support recent agreements of the G-20 nations that will seek to host refugees as close to their home countries as possible. This is the safe, responsible, and humanitarian approach.

For decades, the United States has dealt with migration challenges here in the Western Hemisphere. We have learned that, over the long term, uncontrolled migration is deeply unfair to both the sending and the receiving countries. For the sending countries, it reduces domestic pressure to pursue needed political and economic reform and drains them of the human capital necessary to motivate and implement those reforms. For the receiving countries, the substantial costs of uncontrolled migration are borne overwhelmingly by low-income citizens whose concerns are often ignored by both media and government.

I want to salute the work of the United Nations in seeking to address the problems that cause people to flee from their homes. The United Nations and African Union led peacekeeping missions to have invaluable contributions in stabilizing conflicts in Africa. The United States continues to lead the world in humanitarian assistance, including famine prevention and relief in South Sudan, Somalia, and northern Nigeria and Yemen.

We have invested in better health and opportunity all over the world through programs like PEPFAR, which funds AIDS relief; the President's Malaria Initiative; the Global Health Security Agenda; the Global Fund To End Modern Slavery; and the Woman Entrepreneurs Finance Initiative, part of our commitment to empowering women all across the globe.

We also thank—. Thank you. We also thank the Secretary-General for recognizing that the United Nations must reform if it is to be an effective partner in confronting threats to sovereignty, security, and prosperity. Too often, the focus of this organization has not been on results, but on bureaucracy and process. In some cases, states that seek to subvert this institution's noble aims have hijacked the very systems that are supposed to advance them. For example, it is a massive source of embarrassment to the United Nations that some

governments with egregious human rights records sit on the U.N. Human Rights Council.

The United States is one out of 193 countries in the United Nations, and yet we pay 22 percent of the entire budget and more. In fact, we pay far more than anybody realizes. The United States bears an unfair cost burden, but to be fair, if it could actually accomplish all of its stated goals, especially the goal of peace, this investment would easily be well worth it.

Major portions of the world are in conflict and some, in fact, are going to hell. But the powerful people in this room, under the guidance and auspices of the United Nations, can solve many of these vicious and complex problems. The American people hope that one day soon the United Nations can be a much more accountable and effective advocate for human dignity and freedom around the world. In the meantime, we believe that no nation should have to bear a disproportionate share of the burden, militarily or financially. Nations of the world must take a greater role in promoting secure and prosperous societies in their own regions.

That is why in the Western Hemisphere, the United States has stood against the corrupt, destabilizing regime in Cuba and embraced the enduring dream of the Cuban people to live in freedom. My administration recently announced that we will not lift sanctions on the Cuban Government until it makes fundamental reforms.

We have also imposed tough, calibrated sanctions on the socialist Maduro regime in Venezuela, which has brought a once thriving nation to the brink of total collapse. The socialist dictatorship of Nicolas Maduro has inflicted terrible pain and suffering on the good people of that country. This corrupt regime destroyed a prosperous nation by imposing a failed ideology that has produced poverty and misery everywhere it has been tried. To make matters worse, Maduro has defied his own people, stealing power from their elected representatives to preserve his disastrous rule.

The Venezuelan people are starving, and their country is collapsing. Their democratic institutions are being destroyed. This situation is completely unacceptable, and we cannot stand by and watch. As a responsible neighbor and friend, we and all others have a goal. That goal is to help them regain their freedom, recover their country, and restore their democracy. I would like to thank leaders in this room for condemning the regime and providing vital support to the Venezuelan people.

The United States has taken important steps to hold the regime accountable. We are prepared to take further action if the Government of Venezuela persists on its path to impose authoritarian rule on the Venezuelan people. We are fortunate to have incredibly strong and healthy trade relationships with many of the Latin American countries gathered here today. Our economic bond forms a critical foundation for advancing peace and prosperity for all of our people and all of our neighbors. I ask every country represented here today to be prepared to do more to address this very real crisis. We call for the full restoration of democracy and political freedoms in Venezuela.

The problem in Venezuela is not that socialism has been poorly implemented, but that socialism has been faithfully implemented. From the Soviet Union to Cuba to Venezuela, wherever true socialism or communism has been adopted, it has delivered anguish and devastation and failure. Those who preach the tenets of these discredited ideologies only contribute to the continued suffering of the people who live under these cruel systems.

America stands with every person living under a brutal regime. Our respect for sovereignty is also a call for action. All people deserve a government that cares for their safety, their interests, and their well-being, including their prosperity.

In America, we seek stronger ties of business and trade with all nations of good will, but this trade must be fair and it must be reciprocal. For too long, the American people were told that mammoth multinational trade deals, unaccountable international tribunals, and powerful global bureaucracies were the best way to promote their success. But as those promises flowed, millions of jobs vanished and thousands of factories disappeared. Others gamed the system and broke the rules. And our great middle class, once the bedrock of American prosperity, was forgotten and left behind, but they are forgotten no more, and they will never be forgotten again.

While America will pursue cooperation and commerce with other nations, we are renewing our commitment to the first duty of every government: the duty of our citizens. This bond is the source of America's strength and that of every responsible nation represented here today.

If this organization is to have any hope of successfully confronting the challenges before us, it will depend, as President Truman said some 70 years ago, on the "independent strength of its members." If we are to embrace the opportunities of the future and overcome the present dangers together, there can be no substitute for strong, sovereign, and independent nations: nations that are rooted in their histories and invested in their destinies; nations that seek allies to befriend, not enemies to conquer; and most important of all, nations that are home to patriots, to men and women who are willing to sacrifice for their countries, their fellow citizens, and for all that is best in the human spirit.

In remembering the great victory that led to this body's founding, we must never forget that those heroes who fought against evil also fought for the nations that they loved. Patriotism led the Poles to die to save Poland, the French to fight for a free France, and the Brits to stand strong for Britain. Today, if we do not invest ourselves, our hearts, and our minds in our nations, if we will not build strong families, safe communities, and healthy societies for ourselves, no one can do it for us. We cannot wait for someone else, for faraway countries or far-off bureaucrats—we can't do it. We must solve our problems, to build our prosperity, to secure our futures, or we will build vulnerable to decay, domination, and defeat.

The true question for the United Nations today, for people all over the world who hope for better lives for themselves and their children, is a basic one: Are we still patriots? Do we love our nations enough to protect their sovereignty and to take ownership of their futures? Do we revere them enough to defend their interests, preserve their cultures, and ensure a peaceful world for their citizens?

One of the greatest American patriots, John Adams, wrote that the American Revolution was "effected before the war commenced. The Revolution was in the minds and hearts of the people." That was the moment when America awoke, when we looked around and understood that we were a nation. We realized who we were, what we valued, and what we would give our lives to defend. From its very first moments, the American story is the story of what is possible when people take ownership of their future. The United States of America has been among the greatest forces for good in the history of the world and the greatest defenders of sovereignty, security, and prosperity for all. Now we are calling for a great reawakening of nations, for the revival of their spirits, their pride, their people, and their patriotism. History is asking us whether we are up to the task. Our answer will be a renewal of will, a rediscovery of resolve, and a rebirth of devotion. We need to defeat the enemies of humanity and unlock the potential of life itself.

Our hope is a word—and world of proud, independent nations that embrace their duties, seek friendship, respect others, and make common cause in the greatest shared interest of all: a future of dignity and peace for the people of this wonderful Earth. This is the true vision of the United Nations, the ancient wish of every people, and the deepest yearning that lives inside every sacred soul.

So let this be our mission, and let this be our message to the world: We will fight together, sacrifice together, and stand together for peace, for freedom, for justice, for family, for humanity, and for the almighty God who made us all.

Thank you. God bless you, God bless the nations of the world, and God bless the United States of America. Thank you very much. Thank you.

INDEX